ECONOMIES OF
THE WORLD

ECONOMIES OF THE WORLD

Routledge
Taylor & Francis Group

LONDON AND NEW YORK

First Edition 2005

Routledge

Haines House, 21 John Street, London WC1N 2BP, United Kingdom
(a member of the Taylor & Francis Group)

ISBN 1 85743 263 0

Technical Editor: Kristina Wischenkämper
Cartographer: Tim Aspden
Editorial Director: Paul Kelly

Typeset in Palatino 9/11 and Stone Sans

Typeset by AJS Solutions, Huddersfield ● Dundee
Printed and bound by Gutenberg Press, Tarxien, Malta

Foreword

The first edition of *Economies of the World* provides a compact but fact-filled guide to the economies of 224 countries and major territories, from Afghanistan to Zimbabwe and from Greenland to the Falkland Islands.

Each chapter consists of:

- a brief introduction setting the political and institutional background to the country's or territory's economy;
- a colour map indicating the country's location in relation to its neighbours, as well as the position of its capital and other major towns and cities;
- a set of key demographic and financial indicators;
- and an economic overview of the country or territory, divided into about 10 sections, addressing the various sectors (for example, Agriculture, Industry, Mining, Manufacturing, Energy, Services, External Trade, Government Finance, and International Economic Co-operation), and concluding with a Survey and Prospects account of recent economic performance and likely future developments.

The coverage of each economic sector presents its contribution to the country's gross domestic product (GDP) and the proportion of the labour force working in it, the principal commodities produced and traded, and recent growth trends. In all, over 25,000 well-chosen economic facts provide concise and reliable introductions to every country and major territory in the world.

Economies of the World will be of great use in all libraries, educational institutions and companies, both to students and to those who are interested in and need ready access to global economic information.

Acknowledgements

The editors gratefully acknowledge particular indebtedness for permission to reproduce material from the following publications: the United Nations' *Demographic Yearbook, Statistical Yearbook, Monthly Bulletin of Statistics, Industrial Commodity Statistics Yearbook* and *International Trade Statistics Yearbook*; the Food and Agriculture Organization of the United Nations' Statistical Database and *Yearbook of Fishery Statistics*; the International Labour Office's Statistical Database and *Yearbook of Labour Statistics*; the World Bank's *World Bank Atlas, Global Development Finance, World Development Report* and *World Development Indicators*; the International Monetary Fund's Statistical Database and *International Financial Statistics* and *Government Finance Statistics Yearbook*; and the World Tourism Organization's *Yearbook of Tourism Statistics*.

In addition, we are grateful to Tim Aspden, who prepared the maps which appear in this volume.

Contents

Contents

Afghanistan

In 1978 the communist People's Democratic Party of Afghanistan achieved political supremacy in Afghanistan, until its defeat in 1992 by Islamist rebels, who declared an Islamic State. From 1996 the uncompromisingly militant Islamist Taliban prevailed. It was ousted in 2001 in a US-led military operation that also targeted the al-Qa'ida organization. An interim administration was established, under UN auspices. In mid-2002 an Emergency Loya Jirga (Grand National Council) elected a new head of state and approved a Transitional Authority cabinet. In 2004, at the country's first direct presidential election, Karzai was elected President. Afghanistan is located in south-western Asia, its capital at Kabul. The principal languages are Pashto and Dari.

Area and population
Area: 652,225 sq km
Population (mid-2002): 27,962,840
Population density (mid-2002): 42.9 per sq km
Life expectancy (years at birth, 2002): 42.6 (males 41.9; females 43.4)

Finance
Currency: afghani

1

Economy

In 2002/03, according to official estimates, Afghanistan's gross domestic product (GDP), excluding the illegal cultivation of poppies and production of drugs, was US $4,048m. Using a population estimate of 21.8m., this implied a per head GDP of $186. According to IMF estimates, GDP increased by 28.6% in 2002/03 and was expected to rise by about 20% in 2003/04.

AGRICULTURE

Agriculture (including hunting, forestry and fishing), according to Asian Development Bank (ADB) estimates, contributed 52% of GDP in 2002/03. According to FAO, 66.6% of the economically active population were employed in the agricultural sector in 2001. Livestock plays an important role in the traditional Afghan economy and is normally a major source of income for the country's numerous nomadic groups. However, the total livestock population has been seriously depleted, owing to the many years of conflict and prolonged drought. In 2002/03 the sector benefited from greater rainfall and the increased availability and better quality of seeds and fertilizers. Cereal production was estimated to have increased by 83%, compared with the previous year, to 3.6m. metric tons. Wheat production was estimated at 2.7m. tons. The production of fruits, vegetables and livestock products, such as dairy items, meat, wool and hides also increased in 2002/03. In that year dried fruit accounted for 40.5% of total exports. Agriculture was expected to grow considerably in 2003/04; cereal production was projected to increase by 50% to 5.4m. tons, the level Afghanistan required to be self-sufficient. Not every Afghan would have access yet to foodgrains, however, and the country would continue to be dependent on food assistance.

INDUSTRY

According to ADB estimates, the industrial sector (including mining, manufacturing, construction and power) contributed an estimated 24.1% of GDP in 2002/03, while the value of industrial output in that year increased by 21.1%, according to official estimates, compared with the previous year.

Mining

Mining and quarrying employed about 1.5% of the settled labour force in 1979. Natural gas was the major mineral export (accounting for about 23.6% of total export earnings, according to the IMF, in 1988/89). Salt, hard coal, copper, lapis lazuli, emeralds, barytes and talc are also mined. In addition, Afghanistan has small reserves of petroleum and iron ore. In 1998 the Taliban had claimed that monthly revenue from the allegedly renascent mining sector in Afghanistan totalled US $3.5m. (including revenue from the recently revived steel-smelting plant in Baghlan province). In 2003/04 the Transitional Administration planned to rehabilitate the mining industry.

Manufacturing

Manufacturing employed about 10.9% of the settled labour force in 1979. Afghanistan's major manufacturing industries included food products, cotton textiles, chemical fertilizers, cement, leather and plastic goods. In 1999 only one of the four existing cement plants in Afghanistan and about 10% of the textile mills remained in operation (prior to the Soviet invasion in 1979 there were about 220 state-owned factories operating in Afghanistan). The traditional handicraft sector has better survived the devastating effects of war, however, and carpets, leather, embroidery and fur products continued to be produced.

Energy

Energy is derived principally from petroleum (which is imported from Iran and republics of the former USSR, notably Turkmenistan) and coal. Afghanistan was estimated to have some 73m. metric tons of coal reserves. In 2003 the ADB undertook a feasibility study into the possibility of constructing a pipeline to transport natural gas from the Dauletabad gas fields in Turkmenistan to markets in Afghanistan, Pakistan and, potentially, India. The project had been proposed in 1996, but was postponed owing to political and security concerns; the plan was revived in 2001 following the establishment of the Interim Authority.

SERVICES

Services, according to ADB estimates, contributed 23.9% of GDP in 2002/03, while the value of the service sector's output increased by 39.5% compared with the previous year, according to official estimates.

EXTERNAL TRADE

In 2002/03 there was a deficit of an estimated US $132m. on the current account of the balance of payments. In the same year a trade deficit of $1,315m. was recorded. In 2002/03 total exports (excluding opium-related exports) reached an estimated $2,290m., of which $2,190m. accounted for re-exports. Total imports, meanwhile, increased to an estimated $3,605m. in 2002/03, of which official recorded imports amounted to $2,322m. Exports were expected to reach $2,870m. in 2003/04, of which $2,720m. was projected to be in the form of re-exports; imports were forecast to increase to $4,706m. In 2002/03 the principal exports were carpets and dried fruit; the principal imports were machinery and equipment, and household items and medicine. In 2002/03 the principal market for exports was India (which purchased an estimated 27.4% of the total) and the principal source of imports was Japan (an estimated 43.0%). Another major trading partner was Pakistan. These official statistics do not, however, include illegal trade and smuggling. If the illegal revenue from the export of opium were included, a large trade surplus would be recorded for 2002/03. In 2000 a UN Development Programme/World Bank study estimated that out of total exports of $1,200m., about $1,000m. was unofficially exported. In March 2003 Afghanistan signed a new preferential trade agreement with India. Two months earlier India and Iran had agreed to improve the road network linking Afghanistan with the Chabahar port in Iran. Afghanistan began to open trade routes with Central Asia in late 2002; in August 2003 a memorandum of understanding was signed with Uzbekistan. Trade relations with Pakistan, the USA and the European Union also improved.

GOVERNMENT FINANCE

In the financial year ending 19 March 2004 there was a projected budgetary deficit of US $350m., which was expected to be covered by financial assistance. In 2000, according to UN figures, Afghanistan received $88.2m. in bilateral official development assistance and $52.7m. in multilateral official development assistance. In 2002/03 Afghanistan received $26.4m. in bilateral grants and $157.1m. in multilateral assistance (this did not include grants of $51.24m.). Consumer prices in Kabul rose by an estimated average of 5.2% in 2002/03, compared with the previous year. They were projected to increase by 24.7% in 2003/04.

INTERNATIONAL ECONOMIC RELATIONS

Afghanistan is a member of the Colombo Plan, which seeks to promote economic and social development in Asia and the Pacific, and the Economic Co-operation Organization (ECO). In April 2003 Afghanistan applied for membership to the World Trade Organization.

SURVEY AND PROSPECTS

It is difficult to provide an accurate economic profile of Afghanistan, after more than 20 years of conflict, intermittent droughts and earthquakes and constant population movements. However, a data collection process has begun and more reliable statistics are becoming available, facilitated by the Afghan Transitional Administration's success since June 2002 in rebuilding government and financial institutions and restoring macroeconomic stability. In 2002 the Interim, and later Transitional, Administration began to address such problems as the severe food and fuel shortages, the lack of infrastructure and the difficulties posed by the return of millions of refugees to their ravaged farms and fields, often studded with mines or devastated by air-strikes. In early 2002 the Interim Authority devised a National Development Framework for the reconstruction programme, which focused on these challenges. It placed emphasis on allowing the private sector to lead Afghanistan's recovery and streamlining the public administration. In January international donors pledged US $4,500m. worth of aid over five years towards the reconstruction of Afghanistan, of which some $1,800m. had been disbursed by March 2003. The bulk of these funds, however, was dedicated to humanitarian assistance, and only a small proportion was invested in the country's reconstruction programmes. Nevertheless, by the end of 2003 a number of infrastructure projects, funded by international financial institutions and individual countries, were under way or had reached completion. A development budget of $1,780.4m. was set for 2003/04, to be financed fully by external assistance.

In 2003 the economy showed strong signs of recovery, largely owing to the end of major conflict and prolonged drought, international financial assistance and the Transitional Administration's economic policies. A new currency was launched in late 2002 and a sound monetary policy has since been in place; consequently, the exchange rate has been largely stable. Efforts to develop a modern banking sector commenced in 2003; the central bank was granted autonomy in mid-2003 and in September the Government approved a law allowing foreign banks to open branches in Afghanistan. Reconstruction of the education system was also under way; women were given equal employment rights, as well as access to education. The economy was expected to continue to grow in 2003/04; however, several serious risks remained. First, while the formal economy was recovering, so too was the criminal economy. Despite the introduction of a ban in January 2002 on poppy cultivation and the processing, trafficking and abuse of opiates, the large-scale planting of poppies during the collapse of law and order in late 2001 had allowed Afghanistan to resume its place as the largest supplier of opium in the world. The opium trade, and the associated violence and corruption, posed a serious threat to the Afghan economy. The lack of security and limited rule of law also hampered Afghanistan's successful reconstruction, especially in the provinces. Furthermore, there were concerns that international financial assistance might decrease prematurely.

Albania

The Republic of Albania lies in south-eastern Europe. In 1945 the Albanian Communist Party (ACP), led by Enver Hoxha, took power, and in 1946 the People's Republic of Albania was declared. The ACP, renamed the Party of Labour of Albania (PLA) in 1948, dominated Albanian politics until the electoral victory of the Democratic Party of Albania (DPA) in 1992. However, the DPA's second electoral success, in 1996, provoked violent opposition. At fresh elections in mid-1997 the Socialist Party of Albania (SPA, formerly the PLA) defeated the DPA, retaining its majority in mid-2001. The capital is Tirana. The language is Albanian.

Area and population

Area: 28,748 sq km
Population (mid-2002): 3,195,100
Population density (mid-2002): 111.1 per sq km
Life expectancy (years at birth, 2002): 70.4 (males 74.1; females 67.3)

Finance

GDP in current prices: 2002): US $4,695m. ($1,470 per head)
Real GDP growth (2002): 4.7%
Inflation (annual average, 2002): 7.8%
Currency: lek

Economy

In 2002, according to World Bank estimates, Albania's gross national income (GNI), measured at average 200002 prices, was US $4,410m., equivalent to $1,380 per head (or $4,040 on an international purchasing-power parity basis). During 1990–2002, it was estimated, the population declined at an average annual rate of 0.2%, while gross domestic product (GDP) per head increased, in real terms, by an average of 2.0% per year. Overall GDP increased, in real terms, at an average annual rate of 1.8% in 1990–2002; growth was officially estimated at 6.5% in 2001 and 4.7% in 2002.

AGRICULTURE

Agriculture (including forestry and fishing) contributed an estimated 32.4% of GDP in 2002. Some 72.2% of the labour force were engaged in the sector in 2001. An increasing degree of private enterprise was permitted from 1990, and agricultural land was subsequently redistributed to private ownership. The principal crops are wheat, sugar beet, maize, potatoes, barley and sorghum, and watermelons. Agricultural GDP increased at an average annual rate of 4.2%, in real terms, in 1990–2002; growth in the sector was 1.4% in 2001 and was officially estimated at 2.1% in 2002.

INDUSTRY

Industry (comprising mining, manufacturing, construction and utilities) accounted for an estimated 22.7% of GDP in 2002 and employed 6.5% of the labour force in 2001. Principal contributors to industrial output include mining, energy generation and food-processing. Construction has been the fastest-growing sector in recent years, contributing 10.8% of GDP in 2002. Industrial GDP declined at an average rate of 2.4% per year, in real terms, during 1990–2002; the GDP of the sector declined by 0.3% in 2001, but, according to official estimates, it increased by 2.0% in 2002.

Mining

Albania is one of the world's largest producers of chromite (chromium ore), possessing Europe's only significant reserves (an estimated 37m. metric tons of recoverable ore, constituting about 5% of total world deposits). The mining sector was centred on chromite and copper, following the closure of nickel and iron ore operations, together with more than one-half of the country's coal mines, in 1990. By 2001, however, chromite production had declined to 17,000 metric tons (compared with 587,000 tons in 1991), while output of copper also decreased significantly. Albania has petroleum resources and its own refining facilities, and there has been considerable foreign interest in the exploration of both onshore and offshore reserves since 1991. Proven reserves of petroleum were estimated at 165m. barrels in 2002.

Manufacturing

The manufacturing sector contributed an estimated 12.8% of GDP in 2002. The sector is based largely on the processing of building materials, agricultural products, minerals and chemicals. Manufacturing GDP declined, in real terms, at an average annual rate of 7.9% during 1990–2002; however, the GDP of the sector increased by 6.5% in 2001 and by 6.0% in 2002, according to World Bank estimates.

Energy

Hydroelectric generation accounted for some 98.7% of total electricity production in 2000. In 2001 imports of mineral fuels accounted for 9.9% of the value of total merchandise imports. An Albania–Macedonia–Bulgaria Oil Pipeline (AMBO) project, approved by the Albanian Government in December 2003, envisaged a 920-km pipeline, capable of transporting 750,000 barrels of petroleum per day, to connect the Bulgarian Black Sea port of Burgas with Vloreuml; and carry petroleum exports from Russia and the Caspian Sea region; construction work was scheduled to commence in 2005 and be completed by 2008. The construction of a major thermal installation in Vloreuml; was expected to begin in mid-2004.

SERVICES

Services employed 21.4% of the labour force in 2001 and provided an estimated 44.9% of GDP in 2002. The combined GDP of the services sector increased, in real terms, by an average of 4.8% per year during 1990–2002; growth in the sector was 13.6% in 2001 and was officially estimated at 5.5% in 2002.

EXTERNAL TRADE

In 2002 Albania recorded a visible trade deficit of US $1,155.1m., and there was a deficit of $407.5m. on the current account of the balance of payments. In 2001 the principal source of imports (accounting for an estimated 33.3%) was Italy; other major suppliers were Greece and Turkey. Italy was also the principal market for exports (taking an estimated 71.1% of the total); Greece and Germany were also important purchasers. The principal exports in 2001 were textiles, miscellaneous manufactured articles (particularly footwear) and base metals. The main imports in that year were machinery and mechanical appliances, mineral products, textiles, base metals, prepared foodstuffs and vegetable products.

GOVERNMENT FINANCE

Albania's overall budget deficit in 2002 was 42,943m. lekeuml; (some 7.0% of GDP). At the end of 2001 Albania's total external debt was US $1,094m., of which $970m. was long-term public debt. In that year the cost of servicing the debt was equivalent to 2.2% of the value of exports of goods and services. In 1991–2002 the average annual rate of inflation was 29.0%; consumer prices increased by an estimated 5.1% in 2002. The rate of unemployment was estimated at 15.0% in late 2003. Some 25.1% of the Albanian labour force were working abroad in 1996.

INTERNATIONAL ECONOMIC RELATIONS

Having reversed its long-standing policy of economic self-sufficiency, in 1991 Albania became a member of the World Bank, the IMF and the newly established European Bank for Reconstruction and Development (EBRD). In 1992 Albania became a founder member of the Black Sea Economic Co-operation group (known as the Organization of the Black Sea Economic Co-operation from May 1999).

SURVEY AND PROSPECTS

In 1992, in response to a serious economic crisis, a newly elected Government introduced an extensive programme of reforms, providing for the transfer to private ownership of farmland, state-owned companies and housing, and the abolition of price controls. A strict programme of high interest rates, reduced subsidies, banking reforms and trade liberalization was successful in reducing the budget deficit and stabilizing the currency. Nevertheless, illicit trade continued to account for a high proportion of revenue, and the country remained dependent on remittances from Albanian emigrants and foreign aid. Funding under the IMF's Poverty Reduction and Growth Facility (PRGF), which expired in July 2001, contributed to the restoration of high rates of growth, but poverty remained severe, particularly in rural areas.

Albania's rapid accession to the European Union (EU) was a priority for the Government. The installation of a new President and the appointment of a new Council of Ministers in July 2002 eased political tension, and negotiations on the signature of an initial Stabilization and Association Agreement with the EU commenced in January 2003. However, the Government had to address corruption and organized crime, and reform the security forces and judiciary, as a precondition to consideration for membership.

The rate of GDP growth in 2002 was the lowest for five years (principally owing to a decline in public and private investment, together with energy shortages and severe flooding at the end of September). Government strategy for 2003, supported by a new three-year credit arrangement under the IMF's PRGF, laid emphasis on the liberalization of the energy sector and improvement in tax-collection methods, and a moderate recovery in GDP growth was projected. With the aim of improving regional economic co-operation and furthering conformity with EU norms, during 2002–03 Albania ratified free-trade agreements with Bosnia and Herzegovina, Bulgaria, Croatia, the former Yugoslav republic of Macedonia, Romania and Serbia and Montenegro.

However, divisions within the ruling party and an accompanying lack of parliamentary consensus impeded administrative decisions and in the second half of 2003 resulted in the effective suspension of negotiations on the signature of the Stabilization and Association Agreement, despite government plans for their successful completion by the end of the year. In November EU officials declared that the Government had made inadequate progress in the implementation of the reforms required for admission, and urged immediate remedial measures. At the end of December, following the establishment by Prime Minister Fatos Nano of a coalition supporting rapid integration into the EU and the North Atlantic Treaty Organization (NATO), a reorganized administration was finally approved by the legislature, partially resolving the protracted political impasse. Nano made further pledges to combat organized crime. Also in December a significant advancement in the privatization programme was achieved with the sale of the country's Savings Bank, and further major divestments, notably of the principal state-owned telecommunications enterprise, were anticipated. In January 2004 the IMF approved a further disbursement of funds under the PRGF arrangement, following a review of Albania's overall economic and financial performance, which was declared, despite the delays in structural reforms, to be satisfactory. Government policy for that year emphasized the need to introduce significant tax-administration measures further to improve revenue collection.

Algeria

The Democratic and People's Republic of Algeria lies in north Africa. In 1963, having gained independence from French administration, Algeria was constituted as a presidential regime with the Front de Libération National as sole party. From 1989 the formation of competing political associations was permitted. The cancellation, in 1992, of the second round of voting in Algeria's first multi-party legislative elections precipitated a civil conflict between the forces of the State and the Islamist opposition that remained unresolved in mid-2004. Berber activists in the Kabyle region also violently oppose the State. Algeria's capital is Algiers. Arabic is the official language.

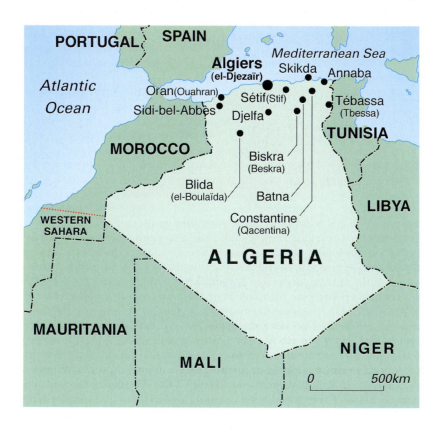

Area and population
Area: 2,381,741 sq km
Population (mid-2002): 31,320,430
Population density (mid-2002): 13.2 per sq km
Life expectancy (years at birth, 2002): 69.4 (males 67.5; females 71.2)

Finance
GDP in current prices: 2002): US $55,666m. ($1,777 per head)
Real GDP growth (2002): 4.1%
Inflation (annual average, 2002): 1.4%
Currency: dinar

Economy

In 2002, according to estimates by the World Bank, Algeria's gross national income (GNI), measured at average 2000–2002 prices, was US $53,814m., equivalent to $1,720 per head (or $5,330 on an international purchasing-power parity basis). During 1990–2002, it was estimated, the population increased at an average annual rate of 1.9%, while gross domestic product (GDP) per head, in real terms, showed a negligible increase. Overall GDP increased, in real terms, at an average annual rate of 1.9% in 1990–2002; it grew by 2.1% in 2001 and by 4.1% in 2002.

AGRICULTURE
Agriculture (including forestry and fishing) contributed 12.4% of GDP in 2002, and employed an estimated 24.1% of the labour force in 2001. Domestic production of food crops is insufficient to meet the country's requirements. The principal crops are wheat, potatoes and tomatoes. Dates are Algeria's principal non-hydrocarbon export; olives, citrus fruits and grapes are also grown, and wine has been an important export since the French colonial era. During 1990–2002 agricultural GDP increased at an average annual rate of 4.4%. Agricultural GDP increased by 13.2% in 2001 and by 4.8% in 2002.

INDUSTRY
Industry (including mining, manufacturing, construction and power) contributed 62.2% of GDP in 2002, and engaged 24.3% of the employed population in 2000. During 1990–2002 industrial GDP increased at an average annual rate of 1.6%. Industrial GDP declined by 0.3% in 2001, but increased by 2.0% in 2002.

Mining
The mining sector provides almost all of Algeria's export earnings, although it engaged only 1.6% of the employed population in 1987. Petroleum and natural gas, which together contributed an estimated 38.0% of GDP in 2001, are overwhelmingly Algeria's principal exports, providing 98.1% of total export earnings in 2000. Algeria's proven reserves of petroleum were 9,200m. barrels at the end of 2002, sufficient to maintain output at that year's levels—which averaged 1.66m. barrels per day (b/d)—for 17 years. With effect from April 2004 Algeria's production quota within the Organization of the Petroleum Exporting Countries (OPEC) was 750,000 b/d. Proven reserves of natural gas at the end of 2002 totalled 4,520,000m. cu m, sustainable at that year's production level (totalling 80,400m. cu m) for more than 56 years. Algeria currently transports natural gas through two pipelines to Spain and Italy, and feasibility studies were undertaken in 2001 regarding the possible construction of a further pipeline to supply other parts of Europe via Spain. Substantial reserves of iron ore, phosphates, barite (barytes), lead, zinc, mercury, salt, marble and

industrial minerals are also mined, and the exploitation of gold reserves commenced in 2001. The GDP of the hydrocarbons sector increased by 6.1% in 1999 and by an estimated 4.9% in 2000, while that of other mining activities declined by 3.0% in 1999 but expanded by an estimated 6.5% in 2000.

Manufacturing

Manufacturing engaged 12.2% of the employed population in 1987, and provided 9.5% of GDP in 2002. Measured by gross value of output, the principal branches of manufacturing in 1996 were food products, beverages and tobacco (which accounted for 52.3% of the total), metals, metal products, machinery and transport and scientific equipment (14.7%), non-metallic mineral products (10.2%), chemical, petroleum, coal, rubber and plastic products (8.6%), wood, paper and products (6.4%) and textiles and clothing (5.9%). During 1990–2002 the GDP of the manufacturing sector declined at an average annual rate of 0.1%. However, manufacturing GDP increased by 2.0% in 2001 and by 2.5% in 2002.

Energy

Energy is derived principally from natural gas (which contributed 96.7% of total electricity output in 2000). Algeria is a net exporter of fuels, with imports of energy products comprising only an estimated 1.4% of the value of merchandise imports in 2000.

SERVICES

Services engaged 60.0% of the employed labour force in 2000, and provided 25.4% of GDP in 2002. During 1990–2002 the combined GDP of the service sectors increased at an average annual rate of 1.9%. Services GDP increased by 2.3% in 2001 and by 4.6% in 2002.

EXTERNAL TRADE

In 2001 Algeria recorded a visible trade surplus of US $9,610m., while there was a surplus of $7,060m. on the current account of the balance of payments. France was the principal source of imports in 2000 (providing 23.6% of the total); other important suppliers were the USA, Italy and Germany. Italy was the principal market for exports (20.1%) in that year; other major purchasers were the USA, France, Spain, the Netherlands, Brazil and Turkey. The principal exports in 2000 were, overwhelmingly, mineral fuels, lubricants, etc.; other exports included vegetables, tobacco, hides and dates. The principal imports in that year were machinery and transport equipment, food and live animals, and basic manufactures.

GOVERNMENT FINANCE

In 2001 Algeria recorded an overall budget surplus of AD 131,000m., equivalent to 3.1% of GDP. Algeria's total external debt at the end of 2001 amounted to US $22,503m., of which $20,786m. was long-term public debt. In that year the cost of debt-servicing was equivalent to 19.5% of the value of exports of goods and services. The annual rate of inflation averaged 14.2% in 1990–2002. Consumer prices increased by an average of 3.5% in 2001 and by 2.2% in 2002. Some 29.8% of the labour force were unemployed in 2000.

INTERNATIONAL ECONOMIC RELATIONS

Algeria is a member of the Union of the Arab Maghreb (UMA), which aims to promote economic integration of member states, and also of OPEC.

SURVEY AND PROSPECTS

Despite the continued high levels of unemployment and poverty in the country, Algeria's economy showed a number of encouraging signs during 2003. The indefinite postponement of the controversial draft hydrocarbons law—which would have fully liberalized the sector and facilitated investment procedures for foreign companies seeking to operate in it—did not adversely affect hydrocarbon production, nor did it deter increased foreign participation in the sector; the export of hydrocarbons provided revenues valued at some US $24,000m. in that year. The Algerian Government had, in 2002, announced its intention further to develop natural gas production facilities and to more than double the export levels of that commodity to 85,000m. cu m per year by 2010, while plans to increase Algeria's oil production capacity from some 1.1m. b/d in early 2003—already substantially in excess of agreed OPEC quotas—to 1.5m b/d by late 2004 were apparently on target. Progress was also evident in the banking, energy, transport and telecommunications sectors; the latter, in particular, benefited from the acquisition of the third Global Standard for Mobiles licence by Kuwait's National Mobile Telecommunications Co at a cost of $421m. Furthermore, it was anticipated that Algeria's membership of the World Trade Organization would be confirmed during 2004. Algeria's macroeconomic position remained strong in 2003 as the country recorded a trade surplus of some $10,000m. and, according to official figures, overall GDP growth of 6.8%. However, the budget deficit was expected to widen in 2004, primarily owing to the increased expenditure required on social and reconstruction projects following a devastating earthquake in mid-2003, which left tens of thousands of people in the region surrounding the capital homeless, and job creation remained one of the Government's most pressing priorities.

American Samoa

American Samoa comprises the seven islands of Tutuila, Ta'u, Olosega, Ofu, Aunu'u, Rose and Swains, lying in the southern central Pacific Ocean. The chiefs of the eastern Samoan islands ceded their lands to the USA in 1904, and they became an Unincorporated Territory of the USA in 1922. The first direct gubernatorial elections were held in 1977. The present Governor took office following the death of Governor Tauese Sunia in March 2003. In 2001 the Governor affirmed American Samoa's wish to remain a US territory. The capital is Pago Pago, on Tutuila, and the officially designated seat of government is the village of Fagatogo. English and Samoan are spoken.

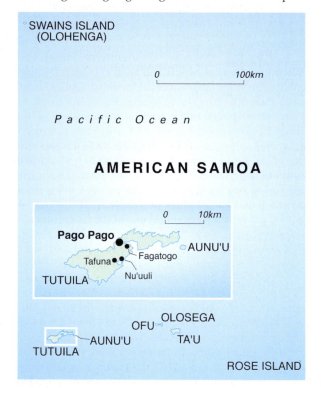

Area and population
Area: 201 sq km
Population (mid-2001): 70,000
Population density (mid-2001): 348.3 per sq km
Life expectancy (years at birth, 1995): Males 68.0; females 76.0

Finance
Inflation (annual average, 2001): 1.4%
Currency: US dollar

Economy

In 1985, according to estimates by the World Bank, American Samoa's gross national income (GNI), measured at average 1983–85 prices, was about US $190m., equivalent to $5,410 per head. GNI per head was estimated at some $8,000 in 1992. Between 1973 and 1985, it was estimated, GNI increased, in real terms, at an average rate of 1.7% per year, with real GNI per head rising by only 0.1% per year. In 1990–2000 the population increased by an average of 3.3% per year. An estimated 91,000 American Samoans live on the US mainland or Hawaii.

AGRICULTURE

Agriculture, hunting, forestry, fishing and mining engaged only 3.1% of the employed labour force in 2000. Agricultural production provides little surplus for export. Major crops are coconuts, bananas, taro, pineapples, yams and breadfruit. Local fisheries are at subsistence level, but tuna-canning plants at Pago Pago process fish from US, Taiwanese and South Korean vessels. Canned tuna constituted some 86.3% of export revenue in 2001, when earnings reached US $273.7m. Other fish products contributed a further $43.4m.

INDUSTRY

Within the industrial sector, manufacturing activities engaged 35.3% of the employed labour force in 2000. Fish-canning is the dominant industry, and in 2001 some 70% of those employed in these factories were guest workers from Samoa (formerly Western Samoa). Other manufacturing activities include meat-canning, handicrafts, dairy farming, orchid farming and the production of soap, perfume, paper products and alcoholic beverages. A garment factory began operations at Tafuna in 1995 and in the following year employed more than 700 people (although almost one-half of these employees were foreign workers). However, the island's garment manufacturing industry was adversely affected following a riot between local workers and Vietnamese employees at a clothing factory, during which a number of people were injured. The incident was widely condemned, and Governor Tauese Sunia stated that the future of the garment industry in American Samoa would require consideration. Exports of finished garments declined from US $15.4m. in 1997/98 to $4.6m. in 1998/99. In 2002 the management of the Daewoosa clothing manufacturer was ordered by the authorities to pay compensation to its employees owing to the poor working conditions at the factory, and in early 2003 the factory's South Korean owner was convicted of human trafficking. The construction sector engaged 6.4% of the employed labour force in 2000.

SERVICES

Service industries engage a majority of the employed labour force in American Samoa (55.2% in 2000). The Government alone employs almost one-third of workers, although in the mid-1990s a series of reductions in the number of public-sector employees were introduced. The tourist industry is developing slowly, and earned some US $10m. in 1998. The number of tourist arrivals rose from 41,050 in 1998 to 49,060 in 1999.

EXTERNAL TRADE

The visible trade deficit rose from US $83.4m. in the year ending September 1998 to $107.5m. in 1999, when imports (including items imported by the Government and goods by the fish-canning sector) totalled $452.6m. and exports reached $345.1m. Most of American Samoa's trade is conducted with the USA. Other trading partners in 1998/99 included New Zealand, which supplied 9.2% of total imports, Australia (8.6%) and Fiji (5.6%). The UN estimated that during 1990–2000 the Territory's exports increased at an average annual rate of 2.4%, while imports increased at a rate of 3.2% per year. Imports decreased by 1.0% in 2000 compared with the previous year. In 2000 the trade deficit was equivalent to the value of 22.9% of imports. However, in 2001 there was a reported trade surplus of $86.0m., equivalent to 37.0% of the value of imports.

GOVERNMENT FINANCE

In 2001 a fiscal surplus of US $200,000 was recorded, the Territory's first budgetary surplus in more than 20 years. Government revenues in 2001 surpassed budgeted expectations by more than $4.2m. The Government reported further surpluses for 2002 and 2003. Annual inflation averaged 2.8% in 1990–96. Consumer prices rose by 1.7% in 1998 and by 0.9% in 1999. An annual inflation rate of 5.2% was recorded in the third quarter of 2003. An estimated 5.2% of the total labour force were unemployed in 2000.

INTERNATIONAL ECONOMIC RELATIONS

American Samoa is a member of the Pacific Community, and is an associate member of the UN Economic and Social Commission for Asia and the Pacific (ESCAP).

SURVEY AND PROSPECTS

The issue of American Samoa's minimum wage structure has caused considerable controversy. The situation (in which American Samoa has a lower minimum wage than the rest of the USA) has been largely attributed to the presence of the two tuna-canning plants on the islands, which employ almost half of the labour force, and consequently exert substantial influence over the setting of wage levels. In 1991, while the minimum wage on the US mainland increased by some 12%, the rate in American Samoa remained unchanged (leaving the Territory's minimum wage level some 50% below that of the mainland). A US recommendation for modest increases in wage levels, implemented in mid-1996, was strongly opposed by the American Samoan Government, which argued that, with higher costs, the Territory's tuna-canning industry would be unable to compete with other parts of the world.

American Samoa's continued financial problems have been compounded by the high demand for government services from an increasing population, the limited economic and tax base and natural disasters. Attempts to reduce the persistent budget deficit and achieve a greater measure of financial security for the islands have included severe reductions in the number of public-sector employees, increased fees for government services and plans to diversify the economy by encouraging tourism and expanding manufacturing activity. Economic development, however, is hindered by the islands' remote location, the limited infrastructure and lack of skilled workers.

In February 1998 the American Samoa Economic Advisory Commission was established, to help the Territory attain self-sufficiency and reduce its budget deficit. Its task was facilitated in November of that year, when the so-called 'tobacco settlement' was reached. In late 1999 the Government opted to negotiate a loan of US $18.6m. from the US Department of the Interior, which was to be repaid from the proceeds of the 'tobacco settlement'. The money allowed the Government to pay outstanding debts—settlement of health care and utility bills were a condition stipulated by the USA—and to launch a programme of fiscal reforms. This was bolstered by an insurance settlement for damages sustained during Hurricane Val, in 1991, worth $47.9m.

In May 2001, meanwhile, the Government waived the provision requiring foreign employees to perform domestic duties for a year prior to progressing to other work. The move was welcomed by the tuna canneries, which were experiencing difficulties in recruiting sufficient workers. In 2002 the tuna-canning companies expressed concern that an impending US free trade agreement with Central American countries, which included the removal of tariffs on canned tuna, would threaten their exports to the USA. Nevertheless, in March 2003 the Senate approved a bill to levy tax on foreign tuna meat sold to the Territory's canneries. In December 2003 the USA declared American Samoa eligible for financing from a $30m. regional fund to offset the economic impact of Marshallese and Micronesian migrants. Total US federal expenditure in American Samoa was estimated at $154m. in 2002.

Andorra

A General Council and the Co-Princes (now the President of France and the Spanish Bishop of Urgel) have ruled the Principality of Andorra, in the eastern Pyrenees, since 1278. In 1993, at the first election to the General Council held under a new Constitution, the Agrupament Nacional Democràtic (AND) obtained the most seats. In 1997 the Unió Liberal (UL) won an overall majority in the Council. This success was matched by that of the Partit Liberal d'Andorra (PLA), as the UL had been renamed, at elections held in 2001. Andorra's capital is Andorra la Vella. The official language is Catalan.

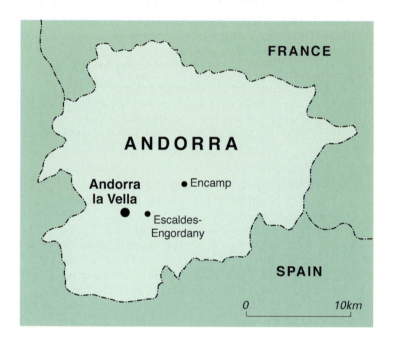

Area and population
Area: 468 sq km
Population (mid-2001): 70,000
Population density (mid-2001): 149.6 per sq km
Life expectancy (years at birth, 2002): 80.3 (males 76.8; females 83.7)

Finance
GDP in current prices: 1999): US $1,229m. ($14,939 per head)
Real GDP growth (1999): 3.7%
Currency: euro

Economy

In 2000 Andorra's national revenue totalled an estimated US $1,275m., equivalent to $19,368 per head. Traditionally an agricultural country, Andorra's principal crops are tobacco and potatoes; livestock-rearing is also of importance. However, the agricultural sector (including forestry and fishing) accounted for only 0.4% of total employment in 2002, and Andorra is dependent on imports of foodstuffs to satisfy domestic requirements.

INDUSTRY

Industry in Andorra includes the manufacture of cigars and cigarettes, together with the production of textiles, leather goods, wood products and processed foodstuffs. In addition to forested timber, natural resources include iron, lead, alum and stone. Including manufacturing and construction, industry provided 21.0% of total employment in 2002.

Energy

The country's hydroelectric power plant supplies only about one-quarter of domestic needs, and Andorra is dependent on imports of electricity and other fuels from France and Spain—in early 2003 the Spanish electricity group Endesa reached an agreement with the Andorran authorities to supply one-half of Andorra's electricity requirements until 2008. Andorra's total electricity consumption in 2002 amounted to 463.2m. kWh.

SERVICES

After 1945 Andorra's economy expanded rapidly, as a result of the co-principality's development as a retail centre for numerous European and overseas consumer goods, owing to favourable excise conditions. The development of facilities for winter sports also helped to make tourism an important feature of the modern Andorran economy. The services sector engaged 73.0% of the employed labour force in 2002. The trade in low-duty consumer items and tourism are Andorra's most important sources of revenue. An estimated 3.4m. tourists and 8.1m. excursionists (mostly from Spain and France) visited Andorra in 2002; tourism (including hotels) engaged 36.8% of the employed labour force in that year. The absence of income tax and other forms of direct taxation, in addition to the laws on secrecy governing the country's banks, favoured the development of Andorra as a 'tax haven'. The banking sector makes a significant contribution to the economy.

EXTERNAL TRADE

Andorra's external trade is dominated by the import of consumer goods destined for sale, with low rates of duty, to visitors. In 2002 imports were valued at €1,269.2m. and exports at €66.9m. Spain and France are Andorra's principal trading partners, respectively providing 50.0% and 24.5% of imports and taking 53.2% and 29.4% of exports in 2002.

GOVERNMENT FINANCE

In 2002 Andorra recorded a budgetary deficit of €20,000. For 2003 a balanced budget was forecast, with expenditure and revenue both totalling €270.4m. In the absence of direct taxation, the Government derives its revenue from levies on imports and on financial institutions, indirect taxes on petrol and other items, stamp duty and the sale of postage stamps. There is no recorded unemployment in Andorra: the restricted size of the indigenous labour force necessitates high levels of immigration.

INTERNATIONAL ECONOMIC RELATIONS

In March 1990 Andorra approved a trade agreement with the European Community (EC—now European Union—EU) which was effective from July 1991, allowing for the establishment of a customs union with the EC and enabling Andorran companies to sell non-agricultural goods to the EU market without being subject to the external tariffs levied on third countries. Andorra benefits from duty-free transit for goods imported via EU countries. In October 1997 Andorra's request to commence negotiations for membership of the World Trade Organization (WTO) was approved by the WTO General Council.

SURVEY AND PROSPECTS

Notable impediments to growth in Andorra include the narrow economic base and the inability of the agricultural, energy and manufacturing sectors to fulfil domestic needs. As part of a series of initiatives to establish Andorra as a major financial centre, a law regulating financial services was approved in 1993. In the following year legislation was approved requiring banks to invest as much as 4% of their clients' deposits in a fund intended to alleviate the public debt (there had been a succession of annual budgetary deficits in the 1980s and early 1990s).

Controversial legislation was adopted in 1996 to allow certain foreign nationals to become 'nominal residents' (individuals who, for the purposes of avoiding taxation, establish their financial base in Andorra), on condition that they pay an annual levy of some 1m. pesetas, in addition to a deposit. The practice of granting this status (without the levy) had been suspended in 1992; however, in the mid-1990s those already accorded nominal residency were estimated to contribute 90% of Andorra's bank deposits. Concerns were expressed regarding the Andorran banking sector, following the publication in January 1993 of a report by the French Government, which stated that Andorra was being used for money 'laundering' (the passage of profits from criminal activities through the banking system in order to legitimize them). These concerns increased as the impending conversion to the euro in 2002 led to substantial amounts of French and Spanish currency, which had been hoarded for tax purposes, being laundered in Andorra. In mid-2000, under its initiative to abolish 'harmful tax practices', the Organisation for Economic Co-operation and Development (OECD) identified a number of jurisdictions as 'tax havens' lacking financial transparency, and urged these to amend their national financial legislation. Many of the countries and territories identified agreed to follow a timetable for reform, with the aim of eliminating such practices by the end of 2005. Others at least entered into dialogue with OECD. A few did neither and were designated by OECD as 'uncooperative tax havens'.

In April 2002 OECD listed Andorra as one of seven states that remained 'uncooperative tax havens', which could be subject to financial sanctions by member states if non-compliance continued for a further year. The Government refuted OECD's allegations, claiming that the country's tax system was not designed to attract foreign capital. In mid-July, however, the prosecutor's office ordered a bank account to be 'frozen', following allegations that its contents, of €2m., were linked to a terrorist organization. In 2003 the International Monetary Fund (IMF) recommended that the Andorran Government afford more power to local financial regulatory bodies to inspect banking activities, and that the Institut Nacional Andorrà de Finances co-operate more closely with the Bank of Spain.

Angola

The Republic of Angola lies on the west coast of Africa. The Portuguese Government proclaimed Angola independent in 1975. Independence has been defined by armed conflict between the governing Movimento Popular de Libertação de Angola (MPLA) and the União Nacional para a Independência Total de Angola (UNITA). In 1992 UNITA participated in legislative elections. However, UNITA's leader, Dr Jonas Savimbi, denounced the MPLA's victory as fraudulent and hostilities resumed. In 2002, after Savimbi had been killed, the Government and UNITA signed a memorandum of understanding aimed at ending the civil war. Angola's capital is Luanda. The official language is Portuguese.

Area and population
Area: 1,246,700 sq km
Population (mid-2002): 13,895,700
Population density (mid-2002): 11.1 per sq km
Life expectancy (years at birth, 2002): 39.9 (males 37.9; females 42.0)

Finance
GDP in current prices: 2002): US $11,380m. ($819 per head)
Real GDP growth (2002): 17.1%
Inflation (annual average, 2002): 118.8%
Currency: kwanza

Economy

In 2002, according to estimates by the World Bank, Angola's gross national income (GNI), measured at average 2000–02 prices, was US $9,187m., equivalent to $660 per head (or $1,730 per head on an international purchasing-power parity basis). During 1990–2002, it was estimated, Angola's population increased at an average annual rate of 3.2%, while gross domestic product (GDP) per head declined, in real terms, by an average of 0.9% per year. Overall GDP increased, in real terms, at an average annual rate of 2.2% in 1990–2002; growth in 2002 was 17.1%.

AGRICULTURE

Agriculture, forestry and fishing contributed an estimated 7.9% of GDP in 2003. An estimated 71.6% of the total working population were employed in the agricultural sector in 2001. Coffee is the principal cash crop. The main subsistence crops are cassava, maize, sugar cane, bananas and sweet potatoes. Severe food shortages following a period of drought in late 2000 worsened in 2001, owing to continued low levels of agricultural productivity. During 1990–2002, according to the World Bank, agricultural GDP declined at an average annual rate of 0.2%. However, agricultural GDP increased by 10.0% in 2002.

INDUSTRY

Industry (including mining, manufacturing, construction and power) provided an estimated 61.4% of GDP in 2003, and employed an estimated 10.5% of the labour force in 1991. According to the World Bank, industrial GDP increased, in real terms, at an average annual rate of 3.1% in 1990–2001; growth in industrial GDP was 4.1% in 2001.

Mining

Mining contributed an estimated 54.3% of GDP in 2003. Petroleum production (including liquefied petroleum gas) accounted for an estimated 49.6% of GDP in that year. Angola's principal mineral exports are petroleum and diamonds. In addition, there are reserves of iron ore, copper, lead, zinc, gold, manganese, phosphates, salt and uranium.

Manufacturing

The manufacturing sector provided an estimated 3.7% of GDP in 2002. The principal branch of manufacturing is petroleum refining. Other manufacturing activities include food-processing, brewing, textiles and construction materials. According to the World Bank, the GDP of the manufacturing sector increased at an average annual rate of 0.5% in 1990–2001; growth in manufacturing GDP was 10.1% in 2001.

Energy

Energy is derived mainly from hydroelectric power, which provided 63.1% of Angola's electricity production in 2000, while petroleum accounted for 36.9%. Angola's power potential exceeds its requirements.

SERVICES

Services accounted for an estimated 30.7% of GDP in 2003, and engaged an estimated 20.1% of the labour force in 1991. In real terms, the GDP of the services sector declined at an average annual rate of 2.4% in 1990–2001, according to the World Bank. Services GDP declined by 4.4% in 2001.

EXTERNAL TRADE

In 2001 Angola recorded an estimated visible trade surplus of US $3,355m., while there was an estimated deficit of $1,431m. on the current account of the balance of payments. In 2002, according to estimates, the principal source of imports (15.4%) was Portugal; other major suppliers were the USA (11.2%) and South Africa (9.9%). In that year the principal market for exports, according to estimates, was the USA (42.0%); the People's Republic of China and Taiwan are also significant purchasers of Angola's exports. The principal exports in 2002 were crude petroleum, accounting for 90.5% of total export earnings, and diamonds (7.6%). The principal imports in 1985 were foodstuffs, transport equipment, electrical equipment and base metals.

GOVERNMENT FINANCE

In 2002 Angola recorded a budget surplus, including changes in payment arrears, of 2,108m. kwanza (equivalent to 0.5% of GDP). Angola's total external debt at the end of 2001 was US $9,600m., of which $7,443m. was long-term public debt. In that year the cost of debt-servicing was equivalent to 26.5% of the value of exports of goods and services. The average annual rate of inflation was 445.4% in 1990–2002. Consumer prices increased by an average of 105.6% in 2002 and of 76.6% in 2003.

INTERNATIONAL ECONOMIC RELATIONS

Angola is a member of both the Common Market for Eastern and Southern Africa and the Southern African Development Community, which was formed with the aim of reducing the economic dependence of southern African states on South Africa.

SURVEY AND PROSPECTS

From independence, exploitation of Angola's extensive mineral reserves, hydro-electric potential and abundant fertile land was severely impaired by internal conflict, as well as an acute shortage of skilled personnel. Following the ratification of a cease-fire agreement between the Government and UNITA in April 2002, Angola's prospects depended greatly on a definitive resolution of the civil strife, the successful reintegration of the displaced population and the rehabilitation of the country's devastated infrastructure. Despite civil conflict, the development of the petroleum sector continued apace in the late 1990s and early 2000s, although much petroleum revenue was used to finance the Government's military expenditure. In late 2003 operations commenced at two new deep-water oilfields, increasing total national output of crude petroleum to more than 1m. barrels per day (b/d); production was projected to reach some 2m. b/d by 2008. Foreign direct investment in petroleum-related projects remained high in 2002–03, but official external arrears continued to accumulate.

The IMF emphasized the importance of enhancing governance and transparency, particularly in the petroleum sector, in order to normalize relations with donors and creditors. In January 2004 a report published by US-based Human Rights Watch claimed that, according to IMF figures, the Angolan Government had failed to account for some US $4,220m. of total petroleum revenues of $17,800m. betweeen 1997 and 2002, equivalent to some 9% of GDP annually. The Minister of Finance, José Pedro de Morais, denounced the report, estimating the financial discrepancy in

1997–2002 at $674m., which he attributed to known deficiencies in the budgetary system and the financial management of the public sector. It was hoped that Angola's participation in the IMF's general data dissemination system, from February 2004, would improve the accuracy of its national statistics system. Meanwhile, poverty remained widespread; in the budget for 2004, the Government allocated 33% of expenditure to the social sector, an increase from 24% in 2003. The UN appealed for some $263m. from international donors for Angola in 2004, to be used for emergency assistance and development projects.

Anguilla

Anguilla, the most northerly of the Leeward Islands, in the Caribbean Sea, was a British colony from 1650 until 1967. In 1967 Saint Christopher-Nevis-Anguilla assumed the status of a State in Association with the United Kingdom. In May, however, the Anguillans repudiated government from Saint Christopher. In 1969 British security forces were deployed in Anguilla to install a British Commissioner. Anguilla formally separated from Saint Christopher-Nevis-Anguilla in 1980, under the terms of the Anguilla Act of 1971, assuming the status of British Dependent Territory (United Kingdom Overseas Territory from 1999). The capital is The Valley. English is the official language.

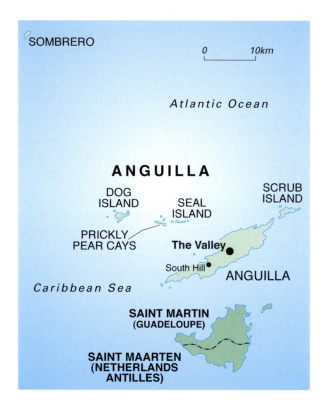

Area and population
Area: 96 sq km
Population (May 2001): 11,430
Population density (May 2001): 119.1 per sq km
Life expectancy (years at birth, 2001): 77.9 (males 77.9; females 78.0)

Finance

GDP in current prices: 2000): EC $290.5m. (EC $25,416 per head)
Real GDP growth (2001): 1.3%
Inflation (2002): 0.6%
Currency: Eastern Caribbean dollar

Economy

In 2001, according to estimates, the gross national income (GNI) of Anguilla, measured at current prices, was EC $295.38m., equivalent to EC $25,552 per head. During 1990–2001, it was estimated, the population increased at an average annual rate of 2.6%, while gross domestic product (GDP) per head increased, in real terms, by an average of 1.6% per year. Overall GDP increased, in real terms, at an average annual rate of 3.1% in 1990–2002; real GDP declined by 3.2% in 2002.

AGRICULTURE

Agriculture (including fishing) contributed 2.7% to GDP in 2002 and agriculture, fishing and mining engaged 3.3% of the employed labour force in the same year. Smallholders grow vegetables and fruit for domestic consumption; the principal crops are pigeon peas, sweet potatoes and maize. Livestock-rearing traditionally supplies significant export earnings, but the principal productive sector is the fishing industry (which is also a major employer). Real agricultural GDP decreased by an annual average of 1.0% during 1990–2002; growth was 15.1% in 2002.

INDUSTRY

Industry (including mining, manufacturing, construction, and power), which accounted for 17.1% of GDP in 2002 and (not including the small mining sector) engaged 18.8% of the employed labour force in 2001, is traditionally based on salt production and shipbuilding. Real industrial GDP increased by an annual average of 0.4% in 1990–2002, but decreased by 7.9% in 2002, primarily owing to a reversal, from 1999, in the hitherto sharp expansion of construction activity.

Mining

The mining and quarrying sector, contributed only 0.8% of GDP in 2002 and engaged only 0.2% of the working population in 1992. Anguilla's principal mineral product is salt. Mining GDP increased by an annual average of 7.8% during 1990–2002, in real terms, but decreased by 3.6% in 2002.

Manufacturing

The manufacturing sector, accounting for 2.4% of employment and for 1.3% of GDP in 2002, consists almost entirely of boat-building and fisheries processing. Real manufacturing GDP increased by an annual average of 8.7% in 1990–2002. GDP in the sector increased by 1.2% in 2002, in real terms.

The construction industry, which engaged 14.9% of the employed labour force in 2001, accounted for 8.5% of GDP in 2002. Until a slowdown in the late 1990s, growth in the construction industry was very high, owing to reconstruction work necessitated by the effects of 'Hurricane Luis'. However, GDP in the construction sector decreased at an annual average of 2.2% during 1990–2002, in real terms, and by 14.2% in 2002. Imported hydrocarbon fuels meet most energy needs.

SERVICES

The services sector accounted for 80.3% of GDP in 2002 and engaged 77.9% of the employed labour force in 2001. Tourism is increasingly the dominant industry of the economy, and is a catalyst for growth in other areas. The hotel and restaurant sector is the largest contributor to GDP, accounting for 25.1% of GDP in 2002. The contribution to GDP from the hotel and restaurant sector increased by 9.5% in 2001, but decreased by 8.3% in 2002. In 2003 tourist expenditure totalled US $61.7m. The USA provided 52.5% of visitors in the same year. The scheduled opening of Anguilla's first championship-standard golf course in 2005 was expected further to contribute to tourism revenues. The offshore financial institutions are also important contributors to the GDP of the service industry, with the banking and insurance sector contributing 13.1% of GDP in 2002. The real GDP of the services sector increased at an annual average of 4.6% in 1990–2002, although the sector declined by 3.9% in 2002, in real terms.

EXTERNAL TRADE

In 2001 Anguilla recorded a merchandise trade deficit of EC $154.6m., and a deficit on the current account of the balance of payments of EC $95.6m. The trade deficit was partly offset by receipts from the 'invisibles' sector: tourism, financial services, remittances from Anguillans abroad and official assistance. The principal sources of imports are the USA, Puerto Rico and the US Virgin Islands, the Netherlands Antilles, Trinidad and Tobago and the European Union (EU), mainly the United Kingdom. The principal markets for exports are the USA and St Maarten/St Martin. The main commodity exports are lobsters, fish, livestock and salt. Imports, upon which Anguilla is highly dependent, consist of foodstuffs, construction materials, manufactures, machinery and transport equipment.

GOVERNMENT FINANCE

In 2001, according to preliminary figures from the Eastern Caribbean Central Bank (ECCB), a budgetary surplus of EC $1.6m. was recorded. Anguilla's external public debt totalled an estimated US $9.8m. in 2002. Development assistance was estimated to total US $3.1m. in 1998. Consumer prices increased by an annual average of 3.1% in 1990–2003; the average annual rate of inflation increased by 2.9% in 2001, decreased by 1.4% in 2002 and increased by 6.9% in 2003. Some 7.8% of the labour force were unemployed in July 2002 (compared with 26% in 1985).

INTERNATIONAL ECONOMIC RELATIONS

In April 1987 Anguilla became the eighth member of the ECCB and in 2001 joined the regional stock exchange, the Eastern Caribbean Securities Exchange (based in Saint Christopher and Nevis), established in the same year. The Territory is also a member of the Organisation of Eastern Caribbean States (OECS), an associate member of the Association of Caribbean States (ACS) and the Economic Community for Latin America and the Caribbean (ECLAC). As a dependency of the United Kingdom, Anguilla has the status of Overseas Territory in association with the EU. In 1999 Anguilla was granted associate membership of the Caribbean Community and Common Market (CARICOM).

SURVEY AND PROSPECTS

Since its reversion to dependency on the United Kingdom, as a separate unit, the island has developed its limited resources. Both tourism, which has become the dominant industry, resulting in a high level of tourism-related activity in the construction industry during the 1990s, and the international financial sector have apparently benefited from the perceived stability of dependent status. However, Anguilla remains particularly vulnerable to adverse climatic conditions, as was demonstrated in October 1995, when Hurricane Luis devastated the island, and again in November 1999, when damage caused by Hurricane Lenny forced the temporary closure of the island's two largest tourist resorts. Real GDP decreased by 0.3% in 2000, compared with an increase of 8.7% in 1999; a decline, in part, attributed to the effects of Hurricane Lenny.

The economy recovered in 2001 to record growth of 2.1%, despite the decline in the tourist sector following the September 2001 terrorist attacks in the USA. However, a further decline in stop-over tourism contributed to a contraction of 3.2% of the economy in 2002. The new Government in 2000 committed itself to increased expenditure and increased state investment in tourism, financial services and fisheries. The Government also hoped to establish the island as a centre for information technology and electronic commerce, and to raise revenue from the sale and leasing of internet domain names. In June the Government launched an internet service which would facilitate the incorporation of offshore companies into the Anguilla tax system; the system is quick and cost-effective, and a total of 2,792 new International Business Companies had been registered by early 2003. In June 2003 the ECCB predicted an expansion in economic activity for the year as a whole of around 3.6%, led by a recovery in the construction sector. Given the importance of tourists to the island, the performance of Anguilla's economy in 2003 and 2004 depended on the reaction of the global economy to the US-led military campaign in Iraq; however, increases in the number of stop-over tourists (6.7%) and tourism receipts (11.6%) in 2003 boded well for overall economic recovery. The implementation in the 2003 budget of a range of measures to increase government revenues, including the introduction of an environmental levy and a customs service charge, was likely further to benefit the territory's healthy fiscal position.

Antigua and Barbuda

Comprising three islands (Antigua, Barbuda and Redonda) lying along the outer edge of the Leeward Islands chain, Antigua and Barbuda is a constitutional monarchy whose Head of State is the British sovereign. The territory became independent in 1981. Until the UPP triumphed in the 2003 general election, the Antigua Labour Party had been the dominant political force almost uninterruptedly since 1946. Efforts to counter Antigua and Barbuda's reputation as a centre for drugs-trafficking and money-laundering resulted, in 2001, in the recognition of the territory as a 'fully co-operative jurisdiction against money laundering' by the Financial Action Task Force. St John's is the capital. English is the official language.

Area and population
Area: 442 sq km
Population (mid-2002): 68,890
Population density (mid-2002): 155.9 per sq km
Life expectancy (years at birth, 2002): 71.4 (males 69.0; females 73.9)

Finance
GDP in current prices: 2002): US $710m. ($10,304 per head)
Real GDP growth (2002): 2.7%
Inflation (annual average, 2001): 1.4%
Currency: Eastern Caribbean dollar

Economy

In 2002, according to estimates by the World Bank, Antigua and Barbuda's gross national income (GNI), measured at average 2000–2002 prices, was US $647m., equivalent to $9,390 per head (or $9,960 per head on an international purchasing-power parity basis). During 1990–2002, it was estimated, the population increased at an average rate of 0.6% per year, while gross domestic product (GDP) per head increased, in real terms, by an average of 2.4% per year. Overall GDP increased, in real terms, at an average annual rate of 3.0% in 1990–2002. According to the Eastern Caribbean Central Bank (ECCB), real GDP increased by an estimated 2.1% in 2002.

AGRICULTURE

Agriculture (including forestry and fishing) engaged 23.3% of the active labour force in 2001, according to estimates by the UN's Food and Agriculture Organization. The sector contributed an estimated 3.5% of GDP in 2002. According to the ECCB, agricultural GDP increased, in real terms, between 1990 and 2002 at an average rate of 1.3% per year. The agricultural sector increased, in real terms, by 3.3% in 2000, decreased by 0.1% in 2001, before increasing by 1.0% in 2002. The principal crops are cucumbers, pumpkins, sweet potatoes, mangoes, coconuts, limes, melons and the speciality 'Antigua Black' pineapple. In 2000 the Ministry of Agriculture, Lands and Fisheries announced a programme to encourage farmers to increase production. Lobster, shrimp and crab farms are in operation, and further projects to develop the fishing industry were undertaken in the 1990s.

INDUSTRY

Industry (comprising mining, manufacturing, construction and utilities) employed 18.9% of the active labour force in 1991 and provided an estimated 20.2% of GDP in 2002. The principal industrial activity is construction, accounting for 11.6% of total employment in 1991. Industrial GDP increased, in real terms, at an average rate of 4.0% per year during 1990–2002. It rose by 6.5% in 2000, by 3.2% in 2001 and by 3.4% in 2002.

Mining

Mining and quarrying employed only 0.2% of the active labour force in 1991 and contributed an estimated 1.6% of GDP in 2002. The real GDP of the mining sector increased at an average rate of 2.8% per year during 1990–2002. It rose by 4.0% in 2000, by 2.0% in 2001 and by 2.0% in 2002.

Manufacturing

The manufacturing sector consists of some light industries producing garments, paper, paint, furniture, food and beverage products, and the assembly of household appliances and electrical components for export. Manufacturing contributed an estimated 2.1% of GDP in 2002, when construction provided 12.9%. In real terms, the GDP of the manufacturing sector increased at an average rate of 0.6% per year during 1990–2002. Manufacturing GDP increased by 3.0% in 2000, by 2.5% in 2001 and by 2.7% in 2002. Over the same period construction growth was 6.5%, 4.0% and 3.5%, respectively.

Energy

Most of the country's energy production is derived from imported fuel. Imports of mineral fuels, lubricants and related materials accounted for 10.5% of total imports in 1999.

SERVICES

Services provided 70.2% of employment in 1991 and an estimated 76.2% of GDP in 2002. The combined GDP of the service sectors increased, in real terms, at an average rate of 3.4% per year during 1990–2002. It rose by 2.2% in 2000, decreased by 0.9% in 2001 and increased by 2.5% in 2002. Tourism is the main economic activity, providing approximately 35% of employment in 1991, and accounting (directly and indirectly) for some 60% of GDP in the mid-1990s. By 1998 the industry showed significant signs of recovery, following the severe effects of 'Hurricane Luis' (despite suffering a minor set-back in September 1998, when 'Hurricane Georges' resulted in the closure of several hotels). Visitor arrivals increased from 470,975 in 1995 to 675,517 in 2000; expenditure by tourists reached $784.5m. in 2000, before decreasing to $734.6m. in 2001 and to $725.6m. in 2002 (according to preliminary figures). The real GDP of the hotels and restaurants sector decreased by 7.8% in 2001, but increased slightly in 2002, by 2.1%. Most stop-over tourists are from the United Kingdom (35% in 1998), the USA (31%), Canada (7%) and other Caribbean countries (16%). The decrease in US tourists following the terrorist attacks in the USA in September 2001 had an adverse affect on the sector; in 2001 tourist arrivals decreased to 193,176, compared with 206,871 in 2000. The sector recovered slightly in 2002 when 198,085 tourist arrivals were recorded, although there was an estimated decrease of 23.6% in the number of cruise-ship passengers.

EXTERNAL TRADE

Antigua and Barbuda recorded a visible trade deficit in 2002 of EC $785.3m. and a deficit of EC $276.8m. on the current account of the balance of payments. The country's principal trading partners are the other members of the Caribbean Community and Common Market (CARICOM), the USA, the United Kingdom and Canada. In 1999 the USA provided 49.4% of total imports and was also the most important market for exports (mainly re-exports).

GOVERNMENT FINANCE

In 2001 there was an estimated budgetary deficit of EC $117.5m. In 2002 debt-servicing costs accounted for some 2.1% of GDP. By the end of 2002 total external debt amounted to US $470.8m. The annual average rate of inflation was 2.3% in 1993–2001. Consumer prices rose by 0.8% in 2000 and by 1.4% in 2001. The annual rate of inflation was reported to have increased by 1.3% in 2002 and by 1.5% in 2003. The rate of unemployment at the end of 2000 was reported to be 8.1% of the labour force.

INTERNATIONAL ECONOMIC RELATIONS

Antigua and Barbuda is a member of CARICOM, the Organisation of Eastern Caribbean States (OECS), the Organization of American States, and is a signatory of the Cotonou Agreement (the successor agreement to Lomé Conventions) with the European Union (EU). Antigua and Barbuda is also a member of the Eastern Caribbean Securities Exchange (based in Saint Christopher and Nevis), established in 2001.

SURVEY AND PROSPECTS

In the late 20th century the Government sought to diversify the economy, which is dominated by tourism. Despite a deceleration in economic growth in 1998 (largely as a result of infrastructural damage caused by 'Hurricane Georges'), the economy grew by 4.9% in 1999. In October of that year it was reported that all but two of the country's external debts had been rescheduled and in August 2000 the United Kingdom agreed to cancel US $9m. in debt and to reschedule a further $6m. over 10 years. In the late 1990s the Government's attempts to develop the 'offshore' financial sector were restricted, following several cases of money-laundering; however, following the implementation of legislation to encourage transparency, restrictions on the sector were lifted in 2001. At the beginning of 2003 there were 21 licensed offshore banks, of which 11 were 'shell' banks with no physical presence on the islands.

Economic expansion continued in 2001 (1.5%), although at a slower rate than in the previous decade. This was primarily owing to the weak performance of the tourism sector and a slowdown in the growth of industrial sector. In November 2001, in anticipation of the economic downturn that was expected following the terrorist attacks in the USA in September, the Government unveiled a five-point adjustment plan. The plan's aims included: a reduction in government expenditure through improved tax collection; the introduction of a two-year public-sector wage freeze in order to contain inflation; and stimulation of the tourism and financial-services sectors. Growth in 2002 and 2003 was estimated at 2.1% and 3.2%, respectively; this recovery was owing, in part, to the resilience of the tourism revenue to the regional downturn in the sector. The economy also gained momentum from a buoyant construction industry in 2003, which expanded by 4.0%. According to reports, growth in 2004 was forecast at 2.5%, bolstered, in part, by an improved fiscal regime and by the robust construction sector. The improving economic situation was likely to result in a steady reduction of the country's large external debt.

Argentina

The Argentine Republic occupies almost the whole of South America south of the Tropic of Capricorn and east of the Andes. Throughout the 20th century government generally alternated between military and civilian rule. The so-called 'dirty war' between the military regime and its opponents in 1976–83 remained politically sensitive in the early 21st century. The election of Fernando de la Rúa of the Unión Cívica Radical as President in 1999 ended 10 years of Peronist rule under Carlos Menem. In 2001, however, economic disaster forced de la Rúa to resign. He was replaced by a succession of Presidents prior to the election of Néstor Kirchner in April 2003. Argentina's capital is Buenos Aires. The language is Spanish.

Area and population
Area: 2,780,400 sq km
Population (mid-2002): 37,928,280
Population density (mid-2002): 13.6 per sq km
Life expectancy (years at birth, 2002): 74.4 (males 70.8; females 78.1)

Finance
GDP in current prices: 2002): US $102,191m. ($2,694 per head)
Real GDP growth (2002): –10.9%
Inflation (annual average, 2002): 25.9%
Currency: new peso

Economy

In 2002, according to estimates by the World Bank, Argentina's gross national income (GNI), measured at average 2000–2002 prices, was US $154,145m., equivalent to $4,060 per head (or $9,930 on an international purchasing-power parity basis). During 1990–2002, it was estimated, Argentina's population increased at an average rate of 1.3% per year, while gross domestic product (GDP) per head increased, in real terms, by an average of 1.1% per year. Overall GDP increased, in real terms, at an average annual rate of 2.4% in 1990–2002. Real GDP decreased by 10.9% in 2002.

AGRICULTURE

Agriculture (including forestry and fishing) contributed an estimated 4.8% of GDP in 2001, and, in mid-2001, employed an estimated 9.5% of the labour force. The principal cash crops are wheat, maize, sorghum and soybeans. Beef production is also important. During 1990–2001 agricultural GDP increased at an average annual rate of 3.0%. The GDP of the sector declined by 1.8% in 2000, but increased by 1.0% in 2001.

INDUSTRY

Industry (including mining, manufacturing, construction and power) engaged 25.3% of the employed labour force in 1991 and provided an estimated 26.6% of GDP in 2001. During 1990–2001 industrial GDP increased, in real terms, at an estimated average annual rate of 2.8%. In 1990–2001 industrial GDP increased at an average annual rate of 2.8%; sectoral GDP decreased by 3.4% in 2000, and by a further 6.7% in 2001.

Mining

Mining contributed an estimated 2.6% of GDP in 2001, and employed 0.4% of the working population in 1991. Argentina has substantial deposits of petroleum and natural gas, as well as steam coal and lignite. The GDP of the mining sector increased, in real terms, at an average rate of 7.3% per year during 1993–98; growth of 2.3% was recorded in 1998.

Manufacturing

Manufacturing contributed an estimated 16.9% of GDP in 2001, and employed 17.3% of the working population in 1991. In 1997 the most important branches of manufacturing, measured by gross value of output, were food products and beverages (accounting for 21.2% of the total), paint products (12.2%), d petroleum refineries (4.4%) and iron and steel (4.0%). During 1990–2001 manufacturing GDP increased, in real terms, at an estimated average annual rate of 1.0%. However, manufacturing GDP decreased by 3.8% in 2000, and by a further 7.5% in 2001.

Energy

Energy is derived principally from natural gas (responsible for the production of 55.1% of total primary energy consumption in 2000) and hydroelectricity (32.4% in 2000). In 2000 6.9% of Argentina's total energy requirements were produced by its two nuclear power-stations. In 2001 imports of mineral fuels comprised 3.9% of the country's total imports.

SERVICES

Services engaged 62.7% of the employed labour force in 1991 and accounted for an estimated 68.6% of GDP in 2001. The combined GDP of the service sectors increased, in real terms, at an estimated average rate of 3.8% per year during 1990–2001; sectoral GDP decreased by 0.5% in 2000, and by a further 4.0% in 2001.

EXTERNAL TRADE

In 2002 Argentina recorded a visible trade surplus of US $17,239m., and there was a surplus of $9,592m. on the current account of the balance of payments. In 2001 (according to provisional figures) the principal source of imports (26%) was Brazil, followed by the USA (18%). Brazil was also the principal recipient of exports, accounting for 24% of total exports in that year. Other major trading partners in 2001 were the People's Republic of China, Chile and Spain. The principal exports in that year were food and live animals, machinery and transport equipment, mineral products and animal and vegetable oils and fats. The principal imports were machinery and transport equipment, chemical and mineral products, and basic manufactures.

GOVERNMENT FINANCE

In 2001 there was a budget deficit of 8,919.7m. new Argentine pesos, equivalent to 3.3% of GDP. Argentina's total external debt was US $136,709m. at the end of 2001, of which $85,337m. was long-term public debt. In that year, the total cost of debt-servicing was equivalent to 66.3% of revenue from exports of goods and services. The annual rate of inflation averaged 15.8% in 1990–2002; following deflation of 0.9% in 2000 and 1.1% in 2001, consumer prices once again increased in 2002, by 25.8%. According to the 2001 census, the national unemployment rate was 28.5%, equivalent to some 4.4m. people. In 2002 the unemployment rate stood at 19.7%.

INTERNATIONAL ECONOMIC RELATIONS

During 1986–90 Argentina signed a series of integration treaties with neighbouring Latin American countries, aimed at increasing bilateral trade and establishing the basis for a Latin American economic community. Argentina is a member of ALADI and of Mercosur.

SURVEY AND PROSPECTS

Economic growth in Argentina in the 1980s was hampered primarily by massive external debt obligations, limited access to financial aid and a scarcity of raw materials. The success of new economic measures introduced by the Government in the early 1990s (including a programme of privatization), drastically reduced inflation and helped to secure agreements to reschedule debt repayments and the disbursement of loans from international financial organizations. From mid-1998, however, the economy began to contract, with both trade and budget deficits widening, as international prices for certain commodities fell, adversely affecting exports. Exports declined further in 1999 following the devaluation of the Brazilian currency in January, and the economy entered recession; annual GDP declined by 3.4% in 1999. Further decreases in the price of commodity exports, as well as an uncompetitive US dollar (to which the peso was tied) and higher international interest rates, increased the debt burden, leading GDP to contract by 0.5% in 2000. In spite of a US $40,000m. loan from the IMF and an effective devaluation of the peso for foreign trade, throughout 2001 the economic situation worsened. A series of austerity measures, culminating in a freeze on bank deposits in December, met with sustained popular opposition. Faced with declining tax revenues, the Government failed to secure any further IMF funding, and in January 2002 a major default on the country's sovereign debt (estimated at $155,000m.) and a 30% devaluation of the peso inevitably ensued. The de la Rúa administration collapsed, initiating a period of political, civil and economic turmoil. In November 2002 the Government of Eduardo Duhalde announced its intention to default on payment obligations to the World Bank and the Inter-American Development Bank (IDB), in the absence of a new agreement with the IMF. Both institutions ceased to disburse funds with immediate effect. However, in January 2003 a new $6,700m. bridging agreement with the IMF was reached, following the Government's decision to authorize repayments to creditor institutions from its international reserves. The deal also established economic performance targets upon which disbursement would be conditional in mid-2003. In the same month the Central Bank announced the relaxation of exchange controls, the ending of which had also been an IMF condition. This followed the announcement, in November 2002, of the ending of the 'corralito' (the restrictions imposed on bank withdrawals), in force since December 2001. There had been fears that the end of the restrictions would result in a massive withdrawal of funds from the banking system. However, bank deposits had been increasing since the middle of the year and such fears were not realized.

In 2002 GDP contracted by 10.9%. However, in early 2003, despite domestic inflationary pressures and a slowdown in world trade, the economy gradually returned to growth; an increase in GDP of 6.5% was forecast for the year, with further economic growth of 5.0% predicted for 2004. Much of this improvement was owing to record agricultural production, and the devalued currency's positive impact on export levels. Nevertheless, concerns remained that such a level of economic growth was unsustainable without increased foreign investment, which would largely depend on reducing the country's enormous debt burden. In August 2003 the stand-by agreement reached at the beginning of the year expired and in the following month Argentina failed to repay US $2,900m. owed to the IMF. However, the day after what was effectively the largest default in the Fund's history the Kirchner Government announced that it had secured a new, three-year deal with the IMF, on extremely favourable terms. These included a primary fiscal surplus target of 3% in 2004, with no target agreed for the following two years, and an extension of $21,000m. in multilateral debt. Nevertheless, the Government did make certain concessions to the IMF; these included a 'freeze' on public-sector salaries, tax reforms, and a commitment to amend the so-called 'co-participation' law, under which provincial finances were allocated from central government revenues. This last measure was interpreted as essential in preventing another debt crisis. In November the World Bank offered $4,500m. in financing for social programmes. However, the Kirchner administration failed to replicate its success in negotiations with the multilateral organizations in its dealings with the country's private creditors, who rejected government proposals to reduce by 75% Argentina's defaulted sovereign debt. Moreover, attempts by foreign investors to obtain compensation for devalued assets, and to secure increases in public utility tariffs, remained a matter for urgent consideration in early 2004. In March the IMF agreed to release a further $3,100m. in loans, after the Argentine Government agreed to begin negotiations with private-sector creditors. None the less, President Kirchner remained reluctant to honour international obligations at the expense of Argentina's social stability.

Armenia

The Republic of Armenia lies in south-west Transcaucasia, on Turkey's north-eastern border. For much of its history Armenia has been under foreign rule. In the early 20th century some 1.5m. Armenians were estimated to have perished as a result of Turkish persecution. In 1920 a Soviet Republic of Armenia was founded that subsequently became a full union republic of the USSR. In 1991 Armenia seceded from the USSR. After independence hostilities with Azerbaijan over the disputed enclave of Nagornyi Karabakh escalated, and this conflict remained unresolved in the early 21st century. Armenia's capital is Yerevan. The official language is Armenian.

Area and population
Area: 29,743 sq km
Population (mid-2002): 3,072,000
Population density (mid-2002): 103.3 per sq km
Life expectancy (years at birth, 2002): 70.0 (males 67.0; females 73.0)

Finance
GDP in current prices: 2002): US $2,367m. ($771 per head)
Real GDP growth (2002): 12.9%
Inflation (annual average, 2002): 1.1%
Currency: dram

Economy

In 2002, according to estimates by the World Bank, Armenia's gross national income (GNI), measured at average 2000–02 prices, was US $2,427m., equivalent to $790 per head (or $3,060 on an international purchasing-power parity basis). During 1990–2002, it was estimated, the population decreased at an average rate of 1.2% per year, while gross domestic product (GDP) per head decreased, in real terms, by an annual average of 0.3%. Over the same period, Armenia's overall GDP decreased, in real terms, by an average of 1.4% annually. However, real GDP increased by 12.9% in 2002 and, according to official figures, GDP increased by 13.9% in 2003.

AGRICULTURE

According to the World Bank, agriculture and forestry contributed 25.9% of GDP in 2002 and, according to official figures, employed 45.1% of the working population in 2001. (However, FAO estimated the proportion of the working population employed in agriculture at just 12.4% in that year.) The principal crops are potatoes and other vegetables, cereals and fruit. Private farms accounted for some 98% of agricultural production by 1998. During 1990–2002, according to estimates by the World Bank, agricultural GDP increased, in real terms, at an average annual rate of 1.1%. The GDP of the sector increased by 11.6% in 2001 and by 4.4% in 2002.

INDUSTRY

According to the World Bank, in 2002 industry (including mining, manufacturing, construction and power) contributed 33.2% of GDP. The sector employed 16.7% of the working population in 2001, according to official figures. World Bank estimates indicated that during 1990–2001 real industrial GDP declined by an average of 9.5% annually. However, the GDP of the sector increased by 8.1% in 2000 and by 6.8% in 2001.

Mining

The mining sector has not yet been extensively developed. Copper, molybdenum, gold, silver and iron are extracted on a small scale, and there are reserves of lead and zinc. There are also substantial, but largely unexploited, reserves of mineral salt, calcium oxide and carbon. Production of gold decreased significantly in the 1990s, but the Government hoped to encourage a recovery in the industry, following the conclusion of an agreement with a Canadian company to develop new extraction facilities, the first of which went into production in 1998. In December 2003 the Government approved a three-year programme for the stimulation of diamond production in Armenia.

Manufacturing

In 2002, according to the World Bank, the manufacturing sector provided 21.6% of Armenia's GDP. According to IMF figures, in 2001 the principal branches of manufacturing, measured by gross value of output, were food-processing and beverages (accounting for 55.0% of the total), base metals and fabricated metal (12.4%), and jewellery and related articles (8.4%). According to the World Bank, during 1990–2002 the GDP of the manufacturing sector declined, in real terms, at an average annual rate of 3.8%. However, real sectoral GDP increased by 3.8% in 2001 and by 14.2% in 2002.

Energy

Armenia is heavily dependent on imported energy, much of which is supplied by Russia (petroleum and derivatives) and Turkmenistan (natural gas); there are also plans to build a natural gas pipeline to Armenia from Iran. It is, however, thought probable that Armenia has significant reserves of petroleum and natural gas. The country's sole nuclear power station, at Medzamor, was closed following the earthquake of 1988. However, in late 1995, in view of Armenia's worsening energy crisis, the station's second generating unit resumed operations, following restoration work. By July 1999 Armenia had a surplus of electricity, some of which was exported to Georgia; a new high-voltage electricity line opened between the two countries in December 2000. In September 1999 Armenia signed an initial agreement with the European Union (EU), providing for the closure of the Armenian Nuclear Power Plant at Medzamor by 2004. However, the Government subsequently claimed that the station could be operated safely for a longer period of time, following extensive renovation, and it sought international resources for the development of adequate alternative energy facilities; in the mean time both the EU and the USA were funding enhanced safety measures to permit the continuing use of the station. Meanwhile, in September 2003 Armenia transferred responsibility for the financial management of the Medzamor plant to Russia, in return for the settlement of its fuel arrears. In 2001 nuclear power contributed 35.6% of the country's electricity supply, thermoelectric power produced 47.3% and hydroelectric power provided 17.1% of the total (compared with 63.1% in 1994). Imports of mineral fuels comprised 21.4% of the value of merchandise imports in 2001.

SERVICES

The services sector contributed 40.9% of GDP in 2002, according to the World Bank, and official figures indicated that the sector (including utilities) engaged 38.3% of the employed labour force in 2001. According to the World Bank, during 1990–2001 the GDP of the sector declined by an average of 6.6% annually, in real terms. However, real services GDP increased by 4.2% in 2000 and by 9.3% in 2001.

EXTERNAL TRADE

In 2002 Armenia recorded a visible trade deficit of US $368.8m., while the deficit on the current account of the balance of payments was $148.0m. In 2001 the principal source of imports, according to official statistics, was Russia, which provided 19.8% of the total; other main sources were the United Kingdom (10.4%), the USA (9.6%), Iran (8.9%) and the United Arab Emirates (5.4%). In the same year Russia was also the main market for exports, accounting for 17.7% of the total. Other important purchasers were the USA (15.3%), Belgium (13.6%), Israel (9.8%), Iran (9.3%) and the United Kingdom (5.9%). The principal exports in 2001 were precious and semi-precious stones (in particular, diamonds), precious metals, imitation jewellery and coins; prepared foodstuffs, beverages and tobacco; base metals; mineral products; machinery and electrical equipment; and textiles. The principal imports in that year were mineral products; pearls, precious and semi-precious stones, precious metals, imitation jewellery and coins; machinery and electrical equipment; vegetable products; prepared foodstuffs, beverages and tobacco; and chemicals.

GOVERNMENT FINANCE

In 2002, according to IMF figures, there was a budgetary deficit of 7,700m. drams (equivalent to 0.6% of GDP). At the end of 2001 Armenia's total external debt was US $1,001m. (equivalent to 45.9% of GNI), of which $766m. was long-term public debt. In that year the cost of debt-servicing was equivalent to 8.4% of the value of exports of goods and services. Inflation increased at an average annual rate of 81.2% in 1993–2002. Consumer prices increased by 1.1% in 2002 and, according to official figures, by 4.7% in 2003. At the end of November 2002 an estimated 155,500 people were officially registered as unemployed, giving an unemployment rate of 9.2%.

INTERNATIONAL ECONOMIC RELATIONS

Armenia is a member of the IMF, the World Bank and the European Bank for Reconstruction and Development (EBRD), and it is also a member of the Organization of the Black Sea Economic Co-operation (BSEC). In February 2003 Armenia became a member of the World Trade Organization (WTO).

SURVEY AND PROSPECTS

The collapse of the Soviet central planning system, together with the effects of the earthquake in 1988 and of the conflict in Nagornyi Karabakh, exacerbated an already critical economic situation in Armenia. The economic blockade by Azerbaijan and, subsequently, Turkey, together with civil war in Georgia, resulted in widespread shortages and a decline in industrial production. A wide-ranging programme of reforms, including price liberalization and the promotion of privatization, was initiated in the early 1990s, and the first signs of economic recovery were observed by 1994. Although the economy was adversely affected by the economic crisis in Russia in 1998, as well as the political upheaval that followed the assassination in October 1999 of the Armenian Prime Minister and seven other government officials, by 2001 Armenia had recorded a significant improvement in economic performance. In 2002 economic growth of more than 12% was recorded (the highest level of GDP growth in more than a decade), and GDP increased further in 2003, according to official figures. A significant reduction in the fiscal deficit was also recorded in 2002. However, one-half of the population continued to subsist below the World Bank's national poverty level and the unemployment rate remained high. Moreover, export trade remained severely hampered by the lack of transport links with Azerbaijan and Turkey. It was anticipated, however, that the country's membership of the WTO from February 2003 would be of substantial benefit to the economy in the long term; an increase in trade volumes could already be observed by the end of the year. However, Armenia risked over-reliance on the market for diamonds, its primary source of export revenue.

Reform was implemented in the energy sector in 2003, with the privatization of two electricity-production plants and the transfer to Russian management of the power plant at Medzamor. In August the Government adopted a 12-year poverty reduction plan, supported by the World Bank, which aimed to reduce the percentage of the population living in poverty to 19% by 2015. In November 2003 the IMF approved the disbursement of further funding under its Poverty Reduction and Growth Facility (PRGF), approved in May 2001, following a review of Armenia's macroeconomic and financial situation. Although the overall performance of the economy was commended, the IMF emphasized the need to reform tax-collection methods to enable increased social spending and relieve the country's dependence on external financing to support the budgetary deficit; to increase fiscal transparency; to strengthen the banking system; and to improve the business environment by combating widespread corruption.

Aruba

Aruba, one of the 'Leeward Islands', lies in the southern Caribbean Sea. It was colonized by the Dutch in 1636 and became part of the Dutch possessions in the West Indies. In 1954 Aruba became part of the autonomous federation of the Netherlands Antilles. In 1983 it was agreed that Aruba should achieve full independence in 1996. In 1994, however, plans for Aruba's transition to independence were cancelled. Future independence would require the approval of the Aruban people, by referendum, and the support of a two-thirds' majority in the legislature. Oranjestad is the capital. Dutch is the official language.

Area and population
Area: 193 sq km
Population (mid-2001): 90,000
Population density (mid-2001): 466.3 per sq km
Life expectancy (years at birth, 2000): Males 70.0; females 76.0

Finance
GDP in current prices: 2001): US $1,889m. ($20,400 per head)
Real GDP growth (2001): −1.2%
Inflation (annual average, 2002): 3.4%
Currency: guilder

Economy

In 1997, according to the World Bank, Aruba's gross national income (GNI), measured at average 1995–97 prices, was estimated to be US $1,181m. During 1995–2002 the population increased at an average annual rate of 2.2% per year, while gross domestic product (GDP) per head increased, in real terms, by an average of 3.1% per year. Overall GDP increased, in real terms, at an average annual rate of 2.4% during 1995–2002. In 2002 real GDP decreased by 2.5%.

AGRICULTURE

Owing to the poor quality of the soil and the prohibitive cost of desalinated water, the only significant agricultural activity is the cultivation of aloes (used in the manufacture of cosmetics and pharmaceuticals); aloe-based products are exported. Some livestock is raised, and there is a small fishing industry (although in the mid-1990s fishing production contributed only some 12.5% of Aruba's annual consumption of fish and fish products). In 2000 the agricultural sector engaged 0.6% of the employed labour force.

INDUSTRY

The industrial sector, and the island's economy, was formerly based on the refining and transhipment of imported petroleum and petroleum products. In the early 1980s this sector accounted for one-quarter of GDP and provided almost all Aruba's exports. The San Nicolaas petroleum refinery ceased operations in 1985; however, in 1990 the plant partially reopened, following renovation; following further construction and revision works, production reached an estimated 202,000 b/d in 1999, an increase of 26% on the previous year's total. Following a further US $250m. renovation in 2000, production increased to 280,000 b/d. However, in April 2001 the refinery closed temporarily following an explosion; as a result, output fell by some 42% in the final quarter of 2001, compared with the corresponding period in 2000. There is a large petroleum transhipment terminal on Aruba, and a small petrochemicals industry. An advanced-technology coker plant opened in 1995 to supply liquefied petroleum gas, largely for export to the USA. There are believed to be exploitable reserves of hydrocarbons within Aruban territory, and Aruba also has reserves of salt.

Light industry is limited to the production of beverages, building materials, paints and solvents, paper and plastic products, candles, detergents, disinfectants, soaps and aloe-based cosmetics. There is a 'free zone', and the ports of Oranjestad and Barcadera provide bunkering and repair facilities for ships. In 1996 the Ports of Aruba Masterplan was presented, proposing the relocation (over a 20-year period) of all cargo operations to Barcadera, leaving Oranjestad's port to accommodate commercial, recreation and resort activities. The construction sector, which grew steadily in the 1980s, declined in importance following a moratorium on the construction of new hotels in 1992. Industry (including mining, manufacturing, construction and power) engaged 16.4% of the employed labour force in 2000.

SERVICES

The service industries are Aruba's principal economic activity, employing 83.0% of the active labour force in 2000. Financial services are well established in Aruba, particularly the data-processing sector, an important service to US companies in particular. Aruba's principal source of income is tourism; the hotels and restaurants sector alone was estimated to provide 10.5% of Aruba's GDP in 2002. However, in 2001 there was a slight decrease in the number of visitor arrivals, attributed mainly to the global economic slowdown and to the effects on tourism of the terrorist attacks on the USA in September of that year. The number of stop-over visitors decreased by 4.3%, to 691,420 while the number of cruise-ship passengers contracted by 0.6%, to 487,296. In 2002 the overall number of visitor arrivals increased, by 3.9%; however, this disguised a further 7.1% decrease in the number of stop-over visitors, to 642,627. The number of cruise-ship passengers increased by 19.5%, to 582,195. Strong growth in the first two months of 2003 was undermined by the repercussions of the US-led military campaign in Iraq; as a result, an overall decline in the tourism sector was recorded in that year. The number of stop-over visitors decreased slightly, to 641,906, and the number of cruise-ship passengers fell by 6.8%, to 542,327. In 2002 receipts from tourism totalled US $903.3m.

EXTERNAL TRADE

Aruba is obliged to import most of its requirements, particularly machinery and electrical equipment, chemical products and foodstuffs; in 2002 the island recorded a visible trade deficit of A Fl. 965.4m., and there was a deficit on the current account of the balance of payments of A Fl. 514.6m. In 2002 the principal source of imports, excluding the petroleum sector and the 'free zone', was the USA (60.4% of the total); other major sources were the Netherlands, the Netherlands Antilles and Venezuela. The principal markets for exports in 2002 was also the USA (accounting for 40.4% of the total), followed by Venezuela, the Netherlands Antilles and the Netherlands.

GOVERNMENT FINANCE

In 2002 the budget deficit was A Fl. 27.8m. In 1994 the level of Dutch development assistance was approximately US $35.5m. In 1998 Aruba received $10.7m. in bilateral aid and $0.6m. in multilateral aid. At the end of 2001 total government debt was A Fl. 1,243.1m. (equivalent to 36.3% of GDP), of which 42.1% was owed to external creditors, primarily the Government of the Netherlands. The average annual rate of inflation was 3.0% in 1995–2003. Consumer prices increased by 4.2% in 2002 and by 2.2% in 2003. 6.9% of the labour force were unemployed in 2000.

INTERNATIONAL ECONOMIC RELATIONS

As part of the Kingdom of the Netherlands, Aruba is classed as an Overseas Territory in association with the European Union. It forms a co-operative union with the Antilles of the Five in monetary and economic affairs. Aruba also has observer status with the Caribbean Community and Common Market (CARICOM).

SURVEY AND PROSPECTS

The closure of the San Nicolaas petroleum refinery in 1985 and Aruba's separation from the rest of the Netherlands Antilles in 1986 prompted the Aruban administration to institute a policy of retrenchment and austerity, except for investment in tourism development. By the beginning of the 1990s, however, the economy was performing strongly, stimulated by rapid growth in the construction and tourism sectors, and the reopening of the refinery in 1990.

In 1992, following six consecutive years of rapid economic growth, during which period there was a threefold increase in hotel capacity, a moratorium was imposed on

construction in the tourism industry, partly in recognition of the adverse environmental impact on the island and also to preserve the island's reputation as an
exclusive holiday destination for the wealthy. Economic growth subsequently slowed to a more sustainable level during the remainder of the decade, with real GDP
growth rates at an average of between 3%–4% annually.

During the the past decade Aruba has maintained low levels of inflation and of
unemployment, and in the early 21st century was considered to be one of the most
prosperous islands in the Caribbean. Concern has, however, been expressed that
Aruba's high public-sector wage bill and the generous nature of Aruba's social
welfare system, combined with the island's ageing population, will threaten the
future stability of public finance, which has already been hindered by a narrow
taxation base and poor revenue collection. Reports in early 2002 claimed that Aruba's
economic problems were worse than previously expected, with the repercussions of
the terrorist attacks on the USA in September 2001 badly affecting the tourism and
construction sectors, and real GDP duly declined by 0.7% in that year and by a further
2.5% in 2002. Despite this, in early 2003 the IMF predicted growth of 4% in 2003,
owing to a sharp increase in private and public investment (including a series of
government programmes worth some US $200m.), and a modest revival in tourism.
However, following the negative effect on tourism of the US-led military campaign in
Iraq from March 2003 and the weak performance of the Venezeulan economy,
projected growth for the year was reduced to 1%.

Australia

The Commonwealth of Australia occupies the island continent of Australia and its offshore islands. Australia's prominence in Asian affairs is reflected in its strong ties with the countries of South-East Asia. Executive power is vested in the British monarch, and in 1999 the electorate rejected the establishment of Australia as a republic. In 1993 Parliament approved the Native Title Act, granting Aboriginal people the right to claim title to their traditional lands. However, numerous unresolved issues, including Aboriginal access to land ownership, have delayed a full reconciliation between White and Aboriginal Australia. Australia's capital is Canberra. English is the official language.

Area and population
Area: 7,692,030 sq km
Population (mid-2002): 19,581,080
Population density (mid-2002): 2.5 per sq km
Life expectancy (years at birth, 2002): 80.4 (males 77.9; females 83.0)

Finance
GDP in current prices: 2002): US $410,590m. ($20,969 per head)
Real GDP growth (2002): 3.5%
Inflation (annual average, 2002): 3.0%
Currency: Australian dollar

Economy

In 2002, according to estimates by the World Bank, Australia's gross national income (GNI), measured at average 2000–02 prices, was US $386,623m., equivalent to US $19,740 per head (or US $26,960 per head on an international purchasing-power parity basis). During 1990–2002, it was estimated, the population increased at an average annual rate of 1.2%, while gross domestic product (GDP) per head increased, in real terms, by an average of 2.4%. Overall GDP increased, in real terms, at an average annual rate of 3.6% in 1990–2002. GDP expanded by 3.9% in 2001 and by 3.5% in 2002. GDP was forecast to increase by 3% in 2003.

AGRICULTURE

Agriculture (including forestry, hunting and fishing) contributed 3% of GDP in 2002, and engaged 4.3% of the employed labour force in the same year. The principal crops are wheat, fruit, sugar and cotton. Australia is the world's leading producer of wool. Export earnings from greasy wool rose from $A2,304m. in 2001 to $A2,482m. in 2002. The export of wine is of increasing importance, rising from 10m. litres in 1986 to 471m. litres in 2002. The value of wine exports increased by 30% in 2002 to $A2,287m. Australia had thus become the world's fourth largest wine exporter. Beef production is also important, beef being Australia's leading meat export and contributing an estimated 15% of the value of gross farm output in the year to March 2003. Between 1990 and 2000 agricultural GDP increased at an average annual rate of 1.9%, although it increased by 6.9%, compared with the previous year, in 1999, before declining by 4.3% in 2000. In 2002 agricultural production was severely affected by one of Australia's worst droughts in 100 years. According to FAO, total agricultural output declined by 16.4% and the production of crops decreased by 55.9% in this year. By late October some 40,000 employees of the agricultural sector had lost their jobs, and in January 2003 Australia was forced to import grain for the first time since 1995. Water shortages also adversely affected the dairy industry. The recurrent problem of bush fires was exacerbated from late 2001 by the prolonged drought. The drought came to an end in mid-2003.

INDUSTRY

Industry (comprising mining, manufacturing, construction and utilities) employed 21.1% of the working population in 2002, and provided 25.7% of GDP in 1999/2000. Industrial GDP increased at an average rate of 2.3% per year between 1990 and 2000, growing by 4.7% in 1999, before declining by 2.7% in 2000.

Mining

The mining sector employed 0.8% of the working population in 2002, and contributed 4.8% of GDP in the year to March 2003. Australia is one of the world's leading exporters of coal. Earnings from coal and related products in 2001/02 reached $A13,422m., accounting for 11.1% of total export receipts in that year. The other principal minerals extracted are iron ore, gold, silver, magnesite, petroleum and natural gas. Bauxite, zinc, copper, titanium, nickel, tin, lead, zirconium and diamonds are also mined. Between 1989/90 and 1996/97 the GDP of the mining sector increased at an average annual rate of 2.9%. Compared with the previous year, mining GDP rose by 9.8% in 1999/2000.

Manufacturing

Manufacturing contributed 10.9% of GDP in 2002. The sector employed 12.0% of the working population in the same year. Measured by the value of sales, the principal branches of manufacturing in 2000/01 were food, beverages and tobacco (22.1%), equipment and machinery (20.2%), petroleum, coal and chemical products (17.3%), metal products (16.6%), printing, publishing and recording (6.2%) and wood and paper products (6.2%). The manufacturing sector's GDP grew at an average annual rate of 2.0% between 1990 and 2000, increasing by 2.8% in 1999 and by 0.5% in 2000. Compared with the previous year, in 2002 the manufacturing sector's GDP grew by 4.2%.

Energy

Energy is derived principally from petroleum, natural gas and coal. Production of petroleum declined from 33,931m. litres in 1997/98 to 30,306m. litres in 1998/99, before increasing to 43,264m. litres in 2000/01. The production of black coal increased from 226.8m. tons in 1997/98 to 322m. tons in 2000/01.

SERVICES

The services sector provided 71.0% of GDP in 1999/2000, and engaged 74.4% of the employed labour force in 2002. The tourism industry has become Australia's second largest source of foreign-exchange earnings. The number of visitor arrivals increased from 4.5m. in 1999 to 4.8m. in 2002. Tourist receipts, however, declined from $A19,800m. in 2000 to an estimated $A15,344m. in 2001. It was estimated that in 2002 the tourism sector contributed 4.3% of GDP and accounted for 6.0% of total employment. The GDP of the services sector increased at an average annual rate of 4.1% between 1990 and 2000, rising by 3.9% in 1999 and by 4.5% in 2000.

EXTERNAL TRADE

In 2002 Australia recorded a visible trade deficit of US $5,404m., and there was a deficit of US $17,882m. on the current account of the balance of payments. In the year ending 30 June 2002 the principal source of imports was the USA (18.0%), followed by Japan (12.9%). Japan was the principal market for exports in that year (18.8%), followed by the USA (9.9%) and the Republic of Korea (8.1%). Other major trading partners are the People's Republic of China, New Zealand, the United Kingdom, Singapore and Taiwan. The principal exports in 2000/01 were metalliferous ores (sales of gold being of increasing significance), coal, machinery, non-ferrous metals, textile fibres (mainly wool) and meat (mainly beef). The principal imports were machinery (mainly road vehicles and transport equipment), basic manufactures, and chemicals and related products.

GOVERNMENT FINANCE

In the 2003/04 financial year a budgetary surplus of about $A2,200m. was forecast. In mid-2002 Australia's net external debt stood at $A329,763m. (equivalent to 46.1% of annual GDP). An estimated average of 5.6% of the labour force were unemployed in December 2003. The annual rate of inflation averaged 2.5% in 1990–2002. Consumer prices rose by 2.9% in 2001/02 and by 3.1% in 2002/03.

INTERNATIONAL ECONOMIC RELATIONS

Australia is a member of the UN Economic and Social Commission for Asia and the Pacific (ESCAP), the Asian Development Bank (ADB), the Pacific Islands Forum, the

Pacific Community and the Colombo Plan. In 1989 Australia played a major role in the creation of the Asia-Pacific Economic Co-operation group (APEC), which aimed to stimulate economic development in the region. Australia is also a member of the Organisation for Economic Co-operation and Development (OECD), of the Cairns Group and of the International Grains Council.

SURVEY AND PROSPECTS

Upon taking office in March 1996, the Howard Government confirmed its determination to achieve fiscal balance. One of the principal aims of the administration's programme was the transfer to the private sector of Telstra, the state-owned telecommunications company. The sale of one-third of the company's assets took place in November 1997, raising revenue of $A14,300m. and representing the most successful Australian flotation to date. In late 1999 a further 16.6% of Telstra's assets were sold. The Government also remained committed to the deregulation of the labour market. The 1999/2000 budget allocated additional funding (of $A800m.) to the biotechnology industry, the sector being regarded as a significant source of future economic growth. The 2000/01 budget provided for additional funding for rural communities. A total of $A1,800m. (of which $A562m. was to be allocated to regional health programmes) was to be released over the next four years. In the same month the Government introduced the controversial 10% goods-and-services tax (GST). For the first time in six years, the Government announced a budget deficit in 2001/02, largely owing to the global economic slowdown, lower tax revenues and spending on the housing and deportation of 'illegal immigrants'. Despite the weak global economy and poor performance of the agricultural sector, as a result of drought, the Australian economy continued to expand. By the end of 2001 the Reserve Bank of Australia's rate of interest had been reduced to its lowest level for 28 years, standing at 4.25%. Employment experienced positive growth, and the rate of unemployment declined in 2002. The trend in employment growth continued in 2003, with the rate of unemployment declining to a 22-year low of 5.6% in December.

The 2002/03 budget introduced further tax relief schemes for families, as well as increased expenditure on defence, protecting Australia's borders, domestic security, health, aged care and welfare reform. The economy performed well in 2002/03, despite the severe drought and stagnation in international growth, but the repercussions of the terrorist attacks on Bali in October 2002, the outbreak of Severe Acute Respiratory Syndrome (SARS) in East Asia in early 2003 and the military campaign in Iraq adversely affected the tourism industry. The increase in domestic spending in this year led to a rise in imports. The 2003/04 budget introduced further personal income tax reductions, increased spending on defence, education, health, and research and development in the industrial sector, and allocated drought relief for rural Australia. The economy was forecast to grow by an average 3.25% in 2003/04. Farm production and exports were expected to increase in this year, owing to the breaking of the drought and the strengthening of the global economy, although livestock production was forecast to decline again. The tourism industry was showing signs of recovery in late 2003. Interest rates were increased in November 2003 to 5.0% and again in December to 5.25%, in an attempt to control the burgeoning property prices and consumer debt. After a period of weakness in 2000–01, the value of the Australian currency increased by more than 30% against the US dollar between January 2003 and January 2004.

Austria

The Republic of Austria lies in central Europe. Since the Second World War the Sozialdemokratische Partei Österreichs (SPÖ) and the Österreichische Volkspartei (ÖVP) have dominated Austrian politics. Twelve years of SPÖ-ÖVP coalition government ended in 2000 when an ÖVP-Freiheitliche Partei Österreichs (FPÖ) coalition was formed. FPÖ participation in government damaged relations with fellow EU member states: in 1999 the FPÖ's leader, Dr Jörg Haider, had allegedly employed terminology previously associated with the German Nazi regime. The World Jewish Congress subsequently alleged that anti-Semitism had increased in Austria since the entry of the FPÖ into government. Austria's capital is Vienna. The population is 99% German-speaking.

Area and population
Area: 83,871 sq km
Population (mid-2002): 8,140,930
Population density (mid-2002): 97.1 per sq km
Life expectancy (years at birth, 2002): 79.4 (males 76.4; females 82.2)

Finance
GDP in current prices: 2002): US $202,954m. ($24,930 per head)
Real GDP growth (2002): 1.0%
Inflation (annual average, 2002): 1.8%
Currency: euro

Economy

In 2002, according to estimates by the World Bank, Austria's gross national income (GNI), measured at average 2000–02 prices, was US $190,340m., equivalent to $23,390 per head (or $28,240 per head on an international purchasing-power parity basis). During 1991–2002 the population grew at an estimated average rate of only 0.4% per year, while gross domestic product (GDP) per head increased, in real terms, at an average annual rate of 1.6%. Overall GDP grew, in real terms, at an average annual rate of 2.0% in 1991–2002; growth was 1.0% in both 2001 and 2002.

AGRICULTURE

The contribution of agriculture (including hunting, forestry and fishing) to GDP was 2.3% in 2002. In that year, according to the ILO, some 5.6% of the employed labour force were engaged in the agricultural sector. Austrian farms produce more than 90% of the country's food requirements, and surplus dairy products are exported. The principal crops are wheat, barley, maize and sugar beet. The GDP of the agricultural sector increased, in real terms, at an average annual rate of 2.7% in 1990–2001; it increased by 4.3% in 2000 and by 1.1% in 2001.

INDUSTRY

Industry (including mining and quarrying, manufacturing, construction and power) contributed 30.4% of GDP in 2002; according to the ILO, the sector engaged 29.4% of the employed labour force in that year. Industrial GDP increased, in real terms, at an average annual rate of 2.6% in 1990–2001; it increased by 5.2% in 2000 and by 0.3% in 2001.

Mining

In 2002 mining and quarrying contributed 0.4% of GDP; according to the ILO, the sector employed 0.2% of the employed labour force in that year. The most important indigenous mineral resource is iron ore (1.9m. metric tons, with an iron content of 31%, were mined in 2002). Austria also has deposits of petroleum, lignite, magnesite, lead and some copper. The GDP of the mining sector declined, in real terms, at an average rate of 2.6% per year during 1990–99; it declined by 2.7% in 1998, but increased by 4.4% in 1999.

Manufacturing

Manufacturing contributed 20.5% of GDP in 2002; according to the ILO, the sector engaged 19.5% of the employed labour force in that year. Measured by the value of output, the principal branches of manufacturing in 1998 were metals and metal products (accounting for 13.9% of the total), electrical machinery and telecommunications equipment (13.0%), food products (10.2%), wood and paper products (9.4%), and non-electrical machinery (9.2%). The production of non-metallic mineral products, beverages, chemicals and road vehicles are also important activities. The GDP of the manufacturing sector increased, in real terms, at an average annual rate of 2.8% during 1990–2000; it grew by 3.4% in 1999 and by 7.2% in 2000.

Energy

Hydroelectric power resources provide the major domestic source of energy, accounting for 69.6% of total electricity production in 2000, followed by gas (13.0%), coal (11.1%) and petroleum (3.3%). Austria is heavily dependent on imports of energy, mainly from eastern Europe. Net imports of energy for commercial use were equivalent to 71% of the total in 1997. Imports of mineral fuels and lubricants (including electrical current) accounted for 7.4% of the total cost of imports in 2002.

SERVICES

The services sector contributed 67.3% of GDP in 2002; according to the ILO, the sector engaged 65.0% of the employed labour force in that year. Tourism has traditionally been a leading source of revenue, providing receipts of €11,297m. in 2001. The GDP of the services sector increased, in real terms, at an average annual rate of 2.1% in 1990–2001; it grew by 2.8% in 2000 and by 1.5% in 2001.

EXTERNAL TRADE

In 2002, according to the IMF, Austria recorded a visible trade surplus of US $3,572m., and the current account of the balance of payments showed a surplus of $575m. Much of Austria's trade is conducted with other member countries of the European Union (EU), which accounted for 65.7% of Austria's imports and 60.1% of exports in 2002. In that year the principal source of imports (40.3%) was Germany; other major suppliers were Italy (7.2%), the USA (4.8%) and France (3.9%). Germany was also the principal market for exports (32.0%); other significant purchasers were Italy (8.5%), Switzerland (5.3%) and the USA (5.2%). The principal exports in 2002 were machinery and transport equipment (accounting for 42.7% of total export revenue) and basic manufactures (22.4%). The principal imports were also machinery and transport equipment (particularly road vehicles and electrical machinery) and basic manufactures (accounting, respectively, for 38.9% and 16.2% of total import costs).

GOVERNMENT FINANCE

The federal budget for 2002 produced a deficit of €828m., equivalent to 0.4% of GDP. The central Government's debt was 1,623,361m. Schilling at 31 December 1999, equivalent to 59.9% of annual GDP; this ratio had risen to 68% by 2003. The average annual rate of inflation was 2.3% in 1990–2002. According to the IMF, consumer prices increased by 2.4% in 2000, by 2.7% in 2001 and by 1.8% in 2002. In 2002 some 2.9% of the labour force were unemployed.

INTERNATIONAL ECONOMIC RELATIONS

Austria joined the EU in January 1995. The country is also a member of the Organisation for Economic Co-operation and Development (OECD).

SURVEY AND PROSPECTS

In 2003 Austria's main trading partners, Germany and Switzerland, experienced (respectively) low growth and economic stagnation. Yet, despite this, Austria achieved a rate of economic growth equivalent to the average EU rate of around 1.0%, owing largely to the country's proximity to the central and eastern European EU accession states, and to the wider eastern European markets, which were growing at double the rate of the EU. Austria's trade with eastern Europe had been increasing since the mid-1990s, and by 2002 accounted for 13.2% of total imports and 17.6% of total exports. Austria's economy gathered even more momentum in late 2003, driven mainly by industry and construction, although private demand remained subdued. Continued economic growth was projected for 2004, with GDP forecast to increase by 1.5%–2.0%, led by a general international economic recovery, particularly in the USA. Exports were projected to provide some stimulus, but the main engine for growth was expected to be capital spending and private consumption. In early 2004 Europe remained somewhat overshadowed by the weak state of the economy in Germany, but even there some signs of an upturn were emerging. This greater optimism was expected to revive Austrian domestic consumption. In the second half of 2003 Austria's economy was also buttressed by the measured stimulation of domestic demand: public-sector infrastructure spending boosted construction in particular, and tax incentives for direct investment led to increased capital expenditure. The gradual improvement of Austria's domestic competitiveness was another factor behind that country's relative success.

In 2003 Austria's manufacturing base enjoyed an estimated 10%–15% cost advantage over its closest competitors (Germany and Switzerland), owing to a combination of higher productivity and lower wage increases. Austria's labour costs were close to the EU average, while labour costs in Germany and Switzerland were significantly higher. That Austria had a more flexible labour market, in industry if not in services, than either Germany or Switzerland was also an advantage, although scope for improvements remained. However, the downturn in 2002 highlighted longer-term structural challenges facing the economy. Progress had been made on pensions reform, but more needed to be done. Moreover, the Government's recent successes in balancing the federal budget were mainly as a result of an increase in revenues; public expenditure, on the other hand, remained high, and had even risen in terms of its share of GDP. One of Austria's biggest economic challenges in the early 2000s was to reduce its ratio of public debt to GDP, which stood at 68% in 2003. In order to achieve this Austria needed to achieve budgetary surpluses, but continued low deficits were forecast. Short-term steps taken in an attempt to balance the budget had also endangered long-term priorities, such as research and development spending. More stringent restraints on expenditure were required in order to allow for the tax reforms to which the authorities were committed. Achieving balanced budgets by raising revenue in periods of relative growth was one thing, but the real test would be to make savings while not implementing wide-ranging reductions in expenditure.

Azerbaijan

The Azerbaijan Republic is situated in eastern Transcaucasia, on the Caspian Sea. In 1920 Azerbaijan was established as a Soviet Republic, and in 1936 became a full union republic of the USSR. In 1991 the Azerbaijan Supreme Soviet voted to restore the country's independence, and in December Azerbaijan joined the Commonwealth of Independent States. The first post-Soviet legislative election, held in 1995, demonstrated widespread support for President Heydar Aliyev and his New Azerbaijan Party. Azerbaijan's conflict with Armenia over the disputed enclave of Nagornyi Karabakh remained unresolved in the early 21st century. Baku is Azerbaijan's capital. The official language is Azerbaijani.

Area and population
Area: 86,600 sq km
Population (mid-2002): 8,184,340
Population density (mid-2002): 94.5 per sq km
Life expectancy (years at birth, 2002): 65.8 (males 63.0; females 68.6)

Finance
GDP in current prices: 2002: US $6,090m. ($744 per head)
Real GDP growth (2002): 10.6%
Inflation (annual average, 2002): 2.8%
Currency: manat

Economy

In 2002, according to World Bank estimates, Azerbaijan's gross national income (GNI), measured at average 2000–02 prices, was US $5,809m., equivalent to $710 per head (or $2,920 per head on an international purchasing-power parity basis). During 1992–2002, it was estimated, the population increased at an average rate of 1.0% per year, while gross domestic product (GDP) per head decreased, in real terms, at an average annual rate of 1.7%. Overall GDP decreased, in real terms, at an average annual rate of 0.7% in 1992–2002. Real GDP increased by 9.9% in 2001 and by 10.6% in 2002.

AGRICULTURE

Agriculture (including fishing) contributed 15.2% of GDP in 2002, when some 40.2% of the working population were employed in the sector. The principal crops are grain, apples, watermelons and other fruit, vegetables and cotton. By mid-1999 some 80% of state-owned agriculture had passed into private ownership, and by the end of 2001 all collective farms had been privatized. During 1992–2002, according to World Bank estimates, agricultural GDP decreased, in real terms, at an average annual rate of 0.1%. Real agricultural GDP increased by 9.1% in 2001 and by 9.0% in 2002.

INDUSTRY

Industry (including mining, manufacturing, construction and power) contributed 49.5% of GDP in 2002. In that year, according to official sources, 11.5% of the working population were employed in the sector. According to the World Bank, during 1992–2002 industrial GDP declined, in real terms, by an annual average of 4.1%, although real sectoral GDP increased by an estimated 12.1% in 2001 and by 5.1% in 2002. Those sectors associated with the petroleum industry, such as construction, have tended to experience steady growth, whereas non-petroleum-based industries have demonstrated a significant decline.

Mining

Mining accounted for 29.7% of GDP in 2002, when the sector employed 1.1% of the working population. Azerbaijan is richly endowed with mineral resources, the most important of which is petroleum. The country's known reserves of petroleum were estimated to total 1,000m. metric tons at the end of 2001, mainly located in offshore fields in the Caspian Sea. In September 1994 the Azerbaijani Government and a consortium of international petroleum companies, the Azerbaijan International Operating Company (AIOC), concluded an agreement to develop the offshore oilfields. By 2000 the State Oil Company of the Azerbaijan Republic (SOCAR) had signed more than 20 production-sharing agreements with international partners, largely for the exploration of new fields. Production of 'early' oil began in October 1997 and accounted for a 50% increase in overall petroleum extraction over the following two years. The petroleum was transported to the Russian Black Sea port of Novorossiisk, via Chechnya, although technical problems with the pipeline and the conflict in Chechnya caused regular closures; a new section of the pipeline, avoiding Chechnya, was completed in March 2000. A further pipeline, transporting petroleum from Baku to the Georgian port of Supsa, opened in April 1999. In October 2000 the Government of Azerbaijan signed an agreement with SOCAR and a consortium of petroleum companies on the construction of a pipeline from Baku, via Tbilisi (Georgia), to Ceyhan in Turkey. Construction work on what became known as the BTC pipeline commenced in April 2003 and was expected to conclude by the end of 2004. Azerbaijan also has substantial reserves of natural gas, most of which are located offshore. In July 1999 a massive gasfield was discovered at Shah Deniz in the Caspian Sea, with reserves estimated at more than 400,000m. cu m, and there were plans to construct a gas pipeline to transport natural gas to Erzurum (Turkey), via Tbilisi. The new gas pipeline was scheduled for completion in 2005, with an initial anticipated capacity of 2,000m. cu m per year. Other minerals extracted include gold, silver, iron ore, copper concentrates, alunite (alum-stone), iron pyrites, barytes, cobalt and molybdenum.

Manufacturing

Manufacturing accounted for some 6.7% of GDP in 2002, when it employed 4.5% of the population. In 2002 the principal branches of manufacturing, measured by gross value of output, were food products, beverages and tobacco (50.3%), refined petroleum products (accounting for 30.2% of the total), and chemicals and fibres (7.0%). The GDP of the sector declined, in real terms, at an annual average rate of 8.1% in 1993–2001. However, sectoral GDP increased by 8.5% in 2001 and by 5.0% in 2002.

Energy

In 1992 only around 6% of Azerbaijan's supply of primary energy was provided by petroleum and petroleum products, but by 2000 72.6% of electricity generation was derived from petroleum, while natural gas accounted for 19.2% of production, and the remainder was provided by hydroelectric stations. Fuels accounted for 15.1% of merchandise imports in 2001.

SERVICES

In 2002 the services sector provided an estimated 35.3% of GDP and accounted for 48.3% of employment. During 1992–2002 the GDP of the services sector increased, in real terms, at an average annual rate of 7.7%. Real sectoral GDP increased by an estimated 1.3% in 2001 and by 9.0% in 2002.

EXTERNAL TRADE

In 2002 Azerbaijan recorded a visible trade surplus of US $481.6m., but there was a deficit of $768.4m. on the current account of the balance of payments. In that year the principal source of imports was Russia (16.9%). Other major sources of imports were Turkey (9.4%), Kazakhstan (9.0%), Turkmenistan (7.2%) and France (7.1%). The USA, the United Kingdom and Germany were also important purchasers. The main market for exports was Italy (50.0%). Other important purchasers were France (7.7%) and Israel (7.1%). The principal exports in 2002 were mineral products (accounting for 88.9% of the total). The principal imports were machinery and electrical equipment (23.8%), mineral products (19.5%), base metals (16.9%), vehicles and transport equipment (7.4%), vegetable products (6.4%) and prepared foodstuffs, beverages and tobacco (5.0%).

GOVERNMENT FINANCE

Azerbaijan's budget deficit for 2001 was some 117,000m. manats (equivalent to some 0.4% of GDP). At the end of 2001 the country's total external debt was estimated to be

US $1,219m., of which $726m. was long-term public debt. The cost of debt-servicing in that year was equivalent to 5.3% of the value of exports of goods and services. Inflation increased by an average of 137.4% per year during 1991–2002. Consumer prices increased by an average of 1,664.5% in 1994, but the rate of inflation declined to 19.8% in 1996, and deflation was recorded in 1998–99. The average annual rate of inflation was 1.5% in 2001 and 2.8% in 2002. Some 50,963 people were registered as unemployed in 2002, although the actual rate of unemployment was thought to be much higher.

INTERNATIONAL ECONOMIC RELATIONS

Azerbaijan is a member of the IMF and the World Bank. It has also joined the Islamic Development Bank, the European Bank for Reconstruction and Development (EBRD), the Economic Co-operation Organization (ECO) and the Black Sea Economic Co-operation group (now known as the Organization of the Black Sea Economic Co-operation). In February 2000 Azerbaijan became a member of the Asian Development Bank.

SURVEY AND PROSPECTS

The dissolution of the USSR in 1991, the conflict in Nagornyi Karabakh and the disruption of trade routes through Georgia and Chechnya all caused significant economic problems in Azerbaijan. However, owing to its enormous mineral wealth, Azerbaijan's prospects for eventual economic prosperity were considered to be favourable. Agreements were concluded with international consortiums from the mid-1990s, and the development of export routes for the country's petroleum and natural gas reserves was expected greatly to improve Azerbaijan's economic situation. The Government's stabilization and reform programme, adopted in early 1995, had achieved considerable success by 1998, and confidence in the manat was rapidly restored after the adverse impact of the Russian financial crisis of 1998. A new Ministry of Fuel and Energy was established in 2001, to assume some regulatory responsibility for the petroleum sector.

Although foreign direct investment increased from US$227m. in 2001 to some $1,400m. in 2002, in August of that year the international organization Transparency International identified Azerbaijan as having one of the highest levels of perceived corruption world-wide (of a total of 102 countries, it was rated 95th). Moreover, the disbursement of funding under the IMF's Poverty Reduction and Growth Facility (approved in July 2001) was suspended in September 2002, owing to the Government's failure to comply with IMF recommendations. However, lending resumed in May 2003, and in November the International Finance Corporation and the EBRD each announced that they were to disburse $125m. in support of the construction of the BTC pipeline (see above). A number of agreements were signed in early February 2004, confirming financial arrangements for the pipeline's construction. Although GDP growth was expected to remain strong, with growth projected at 9.3% in 2003 and 8.1% in 2004, a major concern was the economy's vulnerability to a potential decline in world petroleum prices, together with the need to alleviate security risks associated with the BTC pipeline, which was expected to be inaugurated in early 2005. Meanwhile, Azerbaijan had to implement a strategy to enable its petroleum revenues to be managed in such a way as to stimulate sustained growth and reduce poverty and underemployment in the non-petroleum sector.

Bahamas

The Commonwealth of the Bahamas consists of islands, cays and rocks extending from east of the USA's Florida coast to the West Indies. The Bahamas became independent, within the British Commonwealth, in 1973. The Progressive Liberal Party was the dominant political force in 1967–92. In 1992 it ceded power to the Free National Movement, returning to government in 2002. Trading in illicit drugs has been a major problem. In 1995 new legislation aimed to prevent the abuse of Bahamian banks by drugs-traffickers. The Financial Action Task Force removed the Bahamas from their blacklist in 2001. The capital is Nassau. English is the official language.

Area and population
Area: 13,939 sq km
Population (mid-2002): 313,990
Population density (mid-2002): 22.5 per sq km
Life expectancy (years at birth, 2002): 72.1 (males 69.0; females 75.2)

Finance
GDP in current prices: 2000): US $4,818m. ($15,797 per head)
Real GDP growth (2000): 4.5%
Inflation (annual average, 2002): 2.2%
Currency: Bahamas dollar

Economy

In 2000, according to estimates by the World Bank, the Bahamas' gross national income (GNI), measured at average 1998–2000 prices, was US $4,533m., equivalent to US $14,960 per head (or US $16,400 per head on an international purchasing-power parity basis). During 1990–2002, it was estimated, the population increased at an average annual rate of 1.7%. In 1990–2000 gross domestic product (GDP) per head increased, in real terms, by an annual average of 0.1%. Overall GDP increased, in real terms, at an average rate of 1.8% per year in 1990–2000; according to the IMF, real GDP increased by 4.9% in 2000, decreased by 2.0% in 2001 and rose by an estimated 0.7% in 2002.

AGRICULTURE

Agriculture, hunting, forestry and fishing, which together accounted for only 3.4% of GDP in 1992 and engaged an estimated 4.0% of the employed labour force in 1999, were developed by the Government in the 1990s in an attempt to reduce dependence on imports (80% of food supplies were imported in the 1980s). In 1998, however, agricultural production accounted for only 1.0% of total land area. By the late 1990s, according to official estimates, agriculture contributed less than 3% of GDP. An increase in some areas of agricultural output has, none the less, resulted in the export of certain crops, particularly of cucumbers, tomatoes, pineapples, papayas, avocados, mangoes, limes and other citrus fruits. The development of commercial fishing has concentrated on conchs and crustaceans. In 2000 exports of Caribbean spiny lobster (crawfish) provided 26.5% of domestic export earnings, and accounted for 97.6% of the fishing total. There is also some exploitation of pine forests in the northern Bahamas.

INDUSTRY

Industry (comprising mining, manufacturing, construction and utilities) employed an estimated 16.6% of the working population in 1999 (construction accounted for 11.4%) and provided 10.8% of GDP in 1992.

Mining

Mining and manufacturing together contributed only 4.0% of GDP in 1992. Mining provided an estimated 1.2% of employment, and manufacturing 4.1%, in 1999. The islands' principal mineral resources are aragonite (which provided 8.1% of domestic export earnings in 2000) and salt. In late 2002 the Government granted a licence to an international oil company to explore for petroleum in Bahamian waters.

Manufacturing

The manufacturing sector contributed some 10% of GDP in 1982, since when it has declined, owing to the closure, in 1985, of the country's petroleum refinery. In 1992 the sector contributed 4.0% of GDP. In 1998 the principal branches of manufacturing, based on the value of output, were beverages, chemicals and printing and publishing. Exports of rum accounted for 5.9% of domestic export earnings in 2000. The construction sector experienced much activity in the latter part of the 20th century, owing to construction of hotels and tourist complexes and harbour developments.

Energy

Most of the energy requirements of the Bahamas are fulfilled by the petroleum that Venezuela and, particularly, Mexico provide under the San José Agreement (originally negotiated in 1980), which commits both the petroleum producers to selling subsidized supplies, on favourable terms, to the developing countries of the region. Excluding transhipments of petroleum, imports of mineral fuels accounted for 12.7% of total imports in 2001.

SERVICES

Service industries constitute the principal sectors of the economy, providing 85.3% of GDP in 1992 and about 78.9% of total employment in 1999. The Bahamas established its own shipping registry in 1976, and by 1983 had one of the largest 'open-registry' fleets in the world. In 1999 an international container transhipment facility was completed at Freeport, Grand Bahama; it was to act as an intercontinental hub port serving North America, the Caribbean and South America. Petroleum transhipment on Grand Bahama remains an important activity. At the end of 2002 a total of 1,348 vessels were registered under the Bahamian flag. With a combined displacement of 35.8m. grt, the fleet was the third largest in the world. Banking is the second most important economic activity in the Bahamas and there is a large 'offshore' financial sector. In May 2000 a stock exchange, where it was planned to develop trading in global depository receipts for overseas companies, began trading; by 2004 it was trading the shares of 17 local companies. Despite increasing competition, the Bahamas continues to be the principal tourist destination of the Caribbean. Tourism is the predominant sector of the economy, directly accounting for 15% of GDP in 1998 and employing some 30% of the working population. In 2001 travel receipts covered 75% of the cost of goods imported. In 2001 85.1% of stop-over visitors were from the USA, although attempts are being made to attract visitors from other countries and improve air access to resorts. Tourist arrivals increased from 4.18m. in 2001 to 4.40m. in 2002. Receipts from tourism declined from B $1,719m. in 2000 to B $1,636m. in 2001. The Bahamas receives more cruise-ship arrivals annually than any other Caribbean destination.

EXTERNAL TRADE

In 2002 the Bahamas recorded a visible trade deficit of US $1,019.3m., and there was a deficit of US $299.7m. on the current account of the balance of payments. The USA is the principal trading partner of the Bahamas, providing 85.8% total imports and taking 77.5% of exports in 2001. The principal exports in 2001 were basic manufactures (23.3% of total imports), machinery and transport equipment (22.6%) and mineral fuels and lubricants (12.7%). In that year the principal imports were chemicals (25.9% of total imports), food and live animals (21.4%), and mineral fuels and lubricants (18.2%).

GOVERNMENT FINANCE

In 2002 there was a budgetary deficit of B $140.6m. At 31 December 2002 the external debt of the central Government was some B $96.0m.; the cost of servicing foreign-currency debt in that year was US $74.1m., equivalent to 8.3% of current revenue. The debt-service ratio in 2002 was equivalent to 5.2% of the value of goods and services. The annual rate of inflation averaged 1.5% in 1995–2002; consumer prices increased by 2.2% in 2002. The rate of unemployment stood at some 8% of the labour force in 2001.

INTERNATIONAL ECONOMIC RELATIONS

The Bahamas is a member of the Caribbean Community and Common Market (CARICOM) and the Organization of American States (OAS), the Association of Caribbean States and is a signatory of the Cotonou Agreement with the European Union. In early 2004 the Government indicated it would present an official request for accession to the World Trade Organization at its next ministerial meeting.

SURVEY AND PROSPECTS

Economic expansion through foreign investment continued to be restricted in the latter part of the 20th century by fears of widespread corruption and instability, caused by the activities of illegal drugs-trafficking networks in the islands, although investor confidence was reported to have increased in the late 1990s. In spite of measures, taken from 1989, to combat corruption in the financial sector and thus improve the reputation of the country's economic institutions, in 2000 the Bahamas was listed by the Financial Action Task Force (FATF) as a non-co-operative jurisdiction and by the Organisation for Economic Co-operation and Development (OECD) as a tax 'haven'. Following the introduction of further legislation in late 2000, in 2001 the FATF removed the country from its 'blacklist', and OECD followed suit in March 2002. However, legal challenges were initiated against various aspects of the new financial legislation in late 2001 and early 2002, and the incoming Progressive Liberal Party (PLP) Government, elected in May 2002, pledged to review the recent financial legislation. By 2000 all but one of the state-owned hotels had been transferred to private ownership, under a privatization programme begun in 1993, with a number of foreign companies investing in large-scale projects. The divestment of the state electricity company, though delayed, was expected during the PLP administration. In addition, the loss-making Bahamasair Holdings was scheduled for privatization from September 2002, although plans remained at a preliminary stage in early 2004.

In August 2003 three consortia submitted bids for a 49% stake in the state telecommunications company. A reduction in revenues in the tourism sector (in large part attributable to the consequences for the sector of the commencement of the US-led military campaign to oust the regime of Saddam Hussein in Iraq) led the Prime Minister in July 2003 to abandon an agreed wage increase for 24,000 public servants in order to protect the fiscal position; in 2002 recruitment to the public sector had similarly been suspended. In late 2003 the Government announced its intention to reform the fiscal regime: in particular, the country's dependence on customs and excise taxes and stamp duties, incompatible with future regional and international trade agreements, was to be reduced; the loss was expected to be offset by the introduction of value-added tax. Economic growth, negative in 2001 and negligible in 2002, was expected to remain subdued in 2003, at around 1%, although there was optimism that an increase in tourism revenue would provide a boost for the economy in 2004.

Bahrain

The Kingdom of Bahrain consists of some 36 islands, situated midway along the Persian (Arabian) Gulf. Formerly a British Protected State, Bahrain seceded from the Federation of Arab Emirates to become a separate independent state in 1971. After the dissolution of the National Assembly in 1975 the ruling al-Khalifa family exercised near-absolute power. In 2001 voters approved reforms contained in a National Action Charter, and in 2002 the Amir of Bahrain announced the establishment of a constitutional monarchy, proclaiming himself King. Bahrain's first legislative elections for 27 years took place in October of that year. The capital is Manama. Arabic is the official language.

Area and population
Area: 712 sq km
Population (mid-2002): 671,970
Population density (mid-2002): 943.9 per sq km
Life expectancy (years at birth, 2002): 73.2 (males 72.1; females 74.5)

Finance
GDP in current prices: 2001): US $7,935m. ($12,189 per head)
Real GDP growth (2001): 0.0%
Inflation (annual average, 2002): 1.2%
Currency: dinar

Economy

In 2001, according to estimates by the World Bank, Bahrain's gross national income (GNI), measured at average 1999–2001 prices, was US $7,246m., equivalent to $11,130 per head (or $15,900 per head on an international purchasing-power parity basis). During 1990–2002, it was estimated, the population increased at an average annual rate of 2.4%, while gross domestic product (GDP) per head increased, in real terms, by an average of 2.6% per year during 1990–2001. Overall GDP increased, in real terms, at an average annual rate of 5.0% per year in 1990–2001; growth in 2002 was an estimated 5.1%.

AGRICULTURE

Agriculture (including hunting, forestry and fishing) engaged 0.9% of the labour force in 2001, and contributed an estimated 0.6% of GDP in 2002. The principal crops are dates, tomatoes, onions and cabbages. Livestock production is also important. Agricultural GDP increased at an average annual rate of 2.2% in 1993–2002. However, the GDP of the sector decreased by an estimated 7.4% in 2001 and by some 4.7% in 2002.

INDUSTRY

Industry (comprising mining, manufacturing, construction and utilities) engaged 54.5% of the employed labour force in 2001, and provided some 38.9% of GDP in 2002. During 1993–2002 industrial GDP increased by an average of 4.4% per year; growth of the sector was an estimated 4.1% in 2001 and about 4.4% in 2002.

Mining

Mining and quarrying engaged 0.2% of the employed labour force in 2001, and contributed an estimated 22.7% of GDP in 2002. The major mining activities are the exploitation of petroleum and natural gas, which in 2002 accounted for 16.3% of GDP. At the beginning of 2002 Bahrain's proven published reserves of crude petroleum were estimated to be only 100m. barrels. Including production from the Abu Saafa oilfield, situated between Bahrain and Saudi Arabia, all revenues from which have since 1996 been allocated to Bahrain, production for the whole of 2000 averaged 102,000 b/d. Bahrain's reserves of natural gas at the end of 2002 were put at 90,000m. cu m, sufficient to maintain production (at 2002 levels) for 10 years. Mining GDP increased by an annual average of 4.6% in 1993–2002. The sector's GDP increased by an estimated 0.9% in 2001 and by some 1.4% in 2002.

Manufacturing

In 2001 manufacturing engaged 25.6% of the employed labour force, and the sector provided an estimated 10.9% of GDP in 2002. Important industries include the petroleum refinery at Sitra, aluminium (Bahrain is the region's largest producer) and aluminium-related enterprises, shipbuilding, iron and steel, and chemicals. Since the mid-1980s the Government has encouraged the development of light industry. During 1993–2002 manufacturing GDP increased at an average annual rate of 4.4%; the sector's GDP increased by an estimated 6.7% in 2001 and by about 5.6% in 2002.

Energy

Industrial expansion has resulted in energy demand that threatens to exceed the country's 1,359-MW total installed generating capacity, particularly as not all of the installed capacity is operational, owing to the advanced age of a number of stations. (It was reported in 2000 that energy demands were increasing by more than 5% per year.) A programme of refurbishment and expansion, which included private-sector funding, had begun by 1999. Despite these improvements, and an agreement with Aluminium Bahrain to provide an additional 275 MW annually until 2004, it was estimated that a further 560 MW would be required by 2006.

SERVICES

The services sector engaged 44.6% of the employed labour force in 2001, and contributed some 60.5% of GDP in 2002. The financial services industry, notably the operation of 'offshore' banking units (OBUs), is a major source of Bahrain's prosperity. In early 2004 there were 51 registered OBUs. Bahrain has developed as a principal centre for Islamic banking and other financial services. In January 2002 Bahrain became the first country to publish a full set of regulations, including requirements in terms of capital adequacy, risk management, asset quality, liquidity management and corporate governance, for its Islamic banking sector. The first International Islamic Financial Market, with a liquidity management centre and Islamic ratings agency based in Bahrain, was inaugurated in August. In October the Government launched the Bahrain Financial Harbour project, at a cost of some US $1,300m., whereby the Manama port area was to be redeveloped in order to provide a home for the offshore financial sector and to protect Bahrain's status as the leading financial centre in the Gulf. Completion of the project was anticipated by 2009. During 1993–2002 the services sector showed an average GDP increase of 3.4% per year. The GDP of the sector increased by an estimated 2.0% in 2001 and by some 6.6% in 2002.

EXTERNAL TRADE

In 2002 Bahrain recorded a visible trade surplus of US $1,112.8m., but there was a deficit of $516.1m. on the current account of the balance of payments. In 2001 the principal sources of non-petroleum imports were Australia (accounting for 10.0% of the total), Saudi Arabia (9.0%), Japan, the USA, the United Kingdom and Germany. Saudi Arabia also provided most of Bahrain's petroleum imports (and accounted for 50.8% of all imports in 1990). The USA was the principal customer for Bahrain's non-petroleum exports (24.8% of the total) in 2001; other important markets were Saudi Arabia (14.8%) and Taiwan (10.2%). The principal exports are petroleum, petroleum products and aluminium. Sales of petroleum and petroleum products provided 67.8% of total export earnings in 2001. The principal import is crude petroleum (for domestic refining), accounting for 36.6% of total imports in 2001. The main category of non-petroleum imports (18.6% in 2001) is machinery and mechanical appliances, electrical, sound and television equipment.

GOVERNMENT FINANCE

In 2001 there was a budgetary deficit of BD 180.3m. (equivalent to 6.0% of GDP). Consumer prices decreased by an average annual rate of 0.2% in 1997–2002; however, inflation of 0.2% was recorded in 2001 and of 1.2% in 2002. Almost 59% of the labour force were expatriates in 2001. The official rate of unemployment was 5.6% in late 2001, but unofficial sources estimated unemployment to be in excess of 15% in 2003.

INTERNATIONAL ECONOMIC RELATIONS

Bahrain is a member of the Co-operation Council for the Arab States of the Gulf (Gulf Co-operation Council—GCC). The GCC's six members established a unified regional customs tariff in January 2003, and agreed to create a single market and currency no later than January 2010. The country is also a member of the Organization of Arab Petroleum Exporting Countries (OAPEC), the Arab Monetary Fund and the Islamic Development Bank.

SURVEY AND PROSPECTS

In recognition of the fact that Bahrain's reserves of petroleum and natural gas are nearing exhaustion, the Government has introduced measures both to diversify the country's industrial base and to attract wider foreign investment: non-petroleum exports reportedly increased by 125% between 1992 and 2001, although petroleum and related products still accounted for some two-thirds of total export earnings in the latter year. During the past decade the Government has continued to encourage greater participation of the private sector in economic development, and indicated that it would adopt a gradual approach to the privatization of state enterprises (excluding the petroleum sector), and would prioritize employment opportunities for Bahraini nationals. In late 2001 five committees were established by the Ministry of Labour and Social Affairs in order to tighten the regulations governing non-Bahraini employees and to create about 24,000 jobs for Bahrainis. By late 2000 only 14 state enterprises had been part-privatized, and the World Trade Organization, of which Bahrain is a member, urged the Government to accelerate economic liberalization by increasing private investment in the petroleum and telecommunications sectors. Following the foundation of the Telecommunications Regulatory Authority in 2002, in April 2003 the Government ended the monopoly of the state-owned Bahrain Telecommunications Company over the rapidly expanding mobile phone services market by granting, to MTC Vodafone Bahrain, a second GSM (Global System for Mobile Communications) licence. In January 2004 the Government announced plans to further liberalize the telecommunications sector by inviting applications for new licences in four areas of the industry, including public access mobile radio and paging. In addition, the Cabinet approved the privatization of electricity production in December 2003.

Several important construction projects made progress in the early years of the 21st century, as Bahrain's economy remained buoyant. Among several large-scale tourism projects initiated was a scheme to develop infrastructure on the Hawar islands, following the settlement of Bahrain's long-standing territorial dispute with Qatar. Furthermore, in 2002 the Government signed a six-year agreement with the Formula One authorities to enable Bahrain to be included in the international Grand Prix circuit from 2004. The racing track, with associated facilities, was completed in early March 2004 and the first Grand Prix was held there at the beginning of April. Meanwhile, despite a decline in oil prices and fears of a global economic recession in late 2001, growth of around 5% was sustained in that year and 2002, and investor confidence was enhanced by moves towards political liberalization in Bahrain. Despite the fear of regional instability that was a side-effect of the US-led military action in Iraq in early 2003, GDP growth was reported to be in the region of 4% in that year; stimulated by an increase in government spending, it was expected to rise to about 5% in 2004. Bahrain hoped to conclude negotiations for a free trade agreement with the USA by mid-2004; the deal was expected to provide a further boost to economic growth.

Bangladesh

The People's Republic of Bangladesh lies in southern Asia. Bangladesh was formerly East Pakistan, one of five provinces into which Pakistan was divided when Britain's former Indian Empire was partitioned in 1947. The secession of East Pakistan from Pakistan in 1971 prompted a civil war that resulted in the establishment of the independent People's Republic of Bangladesh. Bangladesh subsequently experienced lengthy periods of martial rule. Extreme instability has characterized civilian rule: in 2001 Sheikh Hasina Wajed of the Awami League became the first Prime Minister to complete a five-year term of office. The capital is Dhaka. Bengali is the state language.

Area and population
Area: 147,570 sq km
Population (mid-2002): 135,683,664
Population density (mid-2002): 919.5 per sq km
Life expectancy (years at birth, 2002): 62.6 (males 62.6; females 62.6)

Finance
GDP in current prices: 2002): US $47,328m. ($349 per head)
Real GDP growth (2002): 4.4%
Inflation (annual average, 2002): 3.4%
Currency: taka

Economy

In 2002, according to estimates by the World Bank, Bangladesh's gross national income (GNI), measured at average 2000–02 prices, was US $48,462m., equivalent to $360 per head (or $1,720 per head on an international purchasing-power parity basis). During 1990–2002, it was estimated, the population increased at an average annual rate of 1.8%, while gross domestic product (GDP) per head increased, in real terms, by an average of 3.0% per year. Overall GDP increased at an average annual rate of 4.8% in 1990–2002. GDP grew by 5.3% in 2001, and by 4.4% in 2002. GDP was projected to increase by 5.3% in 2003.

AGRICULTURE

Agriculture (including hunting, forestry and fishing) contributed an estimated 21.7% of total GDP in 2002/03. In 1999/2000 64.8% of the employed labour force were engaged in that sector. The principal sources of revenue in the agricultural sector are jute, tea, shrimps and fish. Raw jute and jute goods accounted for 5.2% of total export earnings in 2002/03. Despite severe flooding in 2000, Bangladesh achieved self-sufficiency in basic foods for the first time in 2000/01, mainly owing to increased rice production. The output of foodgrains declined in 2001/02; nevertheless, self-sufficiency in foodgrains was maintained. Agricultural production grew by 3.3% in 2002/03, largely owing to the expansion of the area under high-yielding variety crops. Agricultural GDP expanded at an average annual rate of 2.9% in 1990–2002.

INDUSTRY

Industry (including mining, manufacturing, power and construction) employed 10.7% of the working population in 1999/2000. The industrial sector contributed an estimated 26.6% of total GDP in 2002/03. During 1990–2002 industrial GDP increased at an average annual rate of 6.9%. According to official figures, growth in the industrial sector declined to 6.5% in 2001/02, owing to the global economic slowdown; in 2002/03, however, the rate of growth reached 7.3%.

Mining

Bangladesh's proven reserves of natural gas totalled 300,000m. cu m at the end of 2002. Production of natural gas increased from 10,700m. cu m in 2001 to 11,200m. cu m in 2002. It is envisaged that an exportable surplus of natural gas may eventually be produced. Bangladesh possesses substantial deposits of coal (estimated at more than 1,000m. metric tons), although difficulties of exploitation continue to make coal imports necessary, and petroleum.

Manufacturing

Manufacturing contributed an estimated 15.9% of GDP in 2002/03. The sector employed 7.6% of the working population in 1999/2000. The principal branches of the manufacturing sector include textiles, food products, garments and chemicals. During 1990–2002 manufacturing GDP increased at an average annual rate of 6.7%. According to official figures, the GDP of the manufacturing sector grew by an estimated 6.6% in 2002/03.

Energy

Energy is derived principally from natural gas (which contributed 85.0% of total electricity output in 1999). Imports of petroleum products and crude petroleum comprised 9.2% of the cost of total imports in 2002/03.

SERVICES

The services sector accounted for 51.7% of total GDP in 2002/03. In 1999/2000 24.5% of the employed labour force were engaged in the sector. The GDP of the services sector increased at an average annual rate of 4.8% during 1990–2002. According to official figures, the sector's GDP expanded by an estimated 5.8% in 2002/03.

EXTERNAL TRADE

In 2002, according to the IMF, Bangladesh recorded a visible trade deficit of US $1,635.6m., and there was a surplus of $741.5m. on the current account of the balance of payments. In 2002 the principal source of imports was India (which contributed 13.4% of the total), while the USA was the principal market for exports (accounting for 27.9% of the total). Other major trading partners were the People's Republic of China, Singapore, Germany and the United Kingdom. The principal exports in 2002/03 were ready-made garments (accounting for an estimated 49.8% of export revenue), knitwear and hosiery products, raw jute and jute goods, and frozen shrimp and fish. The principal imports were capital goods (an estimated 27.5% of the total), textiles, petroleum products, and iron and steel.

GOVERNMENT FINANCE

In 2003/04 the overall budgetary deficit was projected to amount to the equivalent of 4.2% of GDP. Bangladesh's total external debt was US $15,215m. at the end of 2001, of which $14,773m. was long-term public debt. In that year the cost of debt-servicing was equivalent to 7.3% of total revenue from exports of goods and services. The annual rate of inflation averaged 4.8% in 1990–2000. The annual inflation rate slowed to an average of 3.9% in 2000, before declining again, to 1.7%, in 2001. Consumer prices increased by an average of 2.4% in 2002. About 3.3% of the total labour force were unemployed in 1999/2000.

INTERNATIONAL ECONOMIC RELATIONS

Bangladesh is a member of the UN Economic and Social Commission for Asia and the Pacific (ESCAP), of the Asian Development Bank (ADB), of the South Asian Association for Regional Co-operation (SAARC) and of the Colombo Plan. Bangladesh is also a member of the International Jute Organization, which is based in Dhaka.

SURVEY AND PROSPECTS

The problems of developing Bangladesh include widespread poverty, malnutrition and underemployment, combined with an increasing population and a poor resource base—this last meaning that the country is particularly vulnerable to adverse climatic conditions and to fluctuations in international prices for its export commodities. Despite the frequency of natural disasters, food security has improved somewhat in recent years, as have efforts to enhance production methods (notably through subsidies and the increased use of high-yielding variety crops), storage and distribution facilities. The birth rate has decreased considerably, owing to a successful nation-wide birth-control campaign. In the 1990s high rates of growth were achieved in exports of non-traditional items, particularly ready-made garments and knitwear. Furthermore, recent discoveries of huge reserves of natural gas appear to offer opportunities both in terms of domestic fuel self-sufficiency and, in the longer term, export potential. Nevertheless, the increasing fiscal deficit, exacerbated by the heavy losses incurred by state-owned enterprises, continues to cause concern, as does Bangladesh's heavy dependence on foreign aid: total disbursed aid in 2001/02 amounted to US $1,442m.

In 2001/02 real GDP growth slowed to the lowest rate in six years, owing to a deceleration in all sectors of the economy. In particular, the global economic slow-down had led to a decline in textile exports; more than 1,000 textile factories closed down, resulting in almost 500,000 workers losing their jobs. In 2002/03 the economy regained momentum: exports and imports rose, the textile industry was showing signs of recovery and the wider trade deficit was more than offset by the increased level of remittances from Bangladeshis working abroad. Growth was experienced in all the sub-sectors of the industrial and service sectors. The economy was expected to continue to expand in this way in 2003/04. The predicted GDP growth rate of 5.3% for this year, however, was short of the 8% growth rate required for the country to meet its poverty-reduction target of 50% by 2010. Bangladesh needed to address the deteriorating law and order situation, the problem of corruption and inadequate infrastructure in order to attract greater foreign investment. In 2003 the Government agreed to follow a three-year IMF poverty-reduction programme in exchange for a loan of $500m. The Government also revealed a set of measures to curb corruption and improve tax collection; the fiscal deficit, however, was expected to grow as a result of costly economic reforms. In August it was announced that almost 60% of state-owned firms would be sold or liquidated by 2005. In the mean time, Prime Minister Begum Khaleda Zia declined to export natural gas to India, even though better trade relations would reduce Bangladesh's large trade deficit with India and provide funds for development. The expiry of the World Trade Organization's Multi-fibre Arrangement (MFA) at the end of 2004 was expected to have a severe impact on Bangladesh's garment industry (Bangladesh has been a beneficiary of the MFA quotas limiting garments exports to developed countries). The rapid establishment of domestic yarn and fabric industries thus became increasingly important in 2003/04 if Bangladesh was to compete with more advanced developing countries, such as China and India. Diversification of Bangladesh's export base was also necessary, in order to reduce the dependency on garment exports.

Barbados

Barbados, formerly a British colony, is the most easterly of the Caribbean islands. The Barbados Labour Party (BLP) won a general election in 1951, when universal suffrage was introduced, and held office until 1961. Barbados achieved independence in 1966, when the Democratic Labour Party (DLP) was in government. Executive power is vested in the British monarch, represented by a Governor-General. In 2000 the Prime Minister, Owen Arthur of the BLP, announced that there would be a referendum on the replacement of the monarchy with a republic. Bridgetown is the capital. English is the official language.

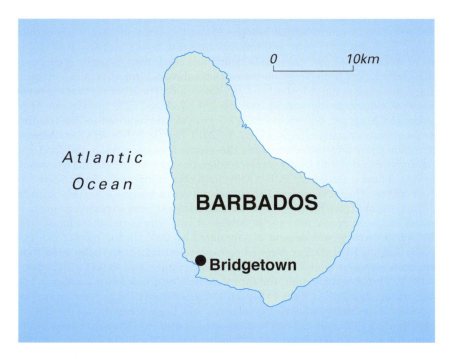

Area and population
Area: 430 sq km
Population (mid-2002): 269,380
Population density (mid-2002): 626.5 per sq km
Life expectancy (years at birth, 2002): 74.3 (males 70.5; females 77.9)

Finance
GDP in current prices: 2001): US $2,757m. ($10,281 per head)
Real GDP growth (2001): 1.5%
Inflation (annual average, 2002): 0.1%
Currency: Barbados dollar

Economy

In 2001, according to estimates by the World Bank, the island's gross national income (GNI), measured at average 1999–2001 prices, was US $2,614m., equivalent to US $9,750 per head (or US $15,560 on an international purchasing-power parity basis). Between 1990 and 2002 the population increased at an average rate of 0.4% per year. Barbados' gross domestic product (GDP) per head, increased, in real terms, at an average rate of 1.5% per year during 1990–2001. Overall GDP increased, in real terms, at an average annual rate of 1.8% in 1990–2001. According to the Central Bank, real GDP decreased by 0.4% in 2002; the economy expanded by an estimated 2.2% in 2003.

AGRICULTURE

Agriculture (including hunting, forestry and fishing) contributed an estimated 4.7% of GDP and engaged an estimated 4.2% of the employed labour force in 2001. Sugar remains the main commodity export, earning US $22.1m. in 2001, when output was an estimated 50,000 tons (compared with $26.7m. and 55,000 tons in 2000). Output in 2002 was reported to have fallen to 44,818 tons. In 2001, according to the UN, sugar accounted for 8.5% of total exports, compared with 10.1% in 2000. Sea-island cotton, once the island's main export crop, was revived in the mid-1980s. The other principal crops, primarily for local consumption, are sweet potatoes, carrots, yams and other vegetables and fruit. Fishing was also developed in the late 20th century. The GDP of the agricultural sector declined, in real terms, at an average rate of 1.2% per year during 1990–2001. Agricultural GDP was estimated to have increased by 6.9% in 2000, before decreasing by 8.1% in 2001.

INDUSTRY

In 2001 industry accounted for an estimated 15.9% of GDP, and an estimated 19.8% of the working population were employed in all industrial activities (manufacturing, construction, quarrying and utilities) in the same year. In real terms, industrial GDP increased at an average rate of 1.8% annually in 1990–2001. Real industrial GDP rose by 0.6% in 2000 and by 1.2% in 2001.

Mining

Owing to fluctuations in international prices, the production of crude petroleum declined substantially from its peak in 1985, to 328,000 barrels in 1997. In late 1996 the Barbados National Oil Company signed a five-year agreement with a US company to intensify exploration activity, with the aim of increasing petroleum production from 1,000 barrels per day (b/d) to 10,000 b/d by 2001. As a result of an onshore drilling programme begun in 1997, production increased markedly, reaching 708,500 barrels in 1999; however, production fell thereafter and stood at 463,699 barrels in 2001. After a temporary suspension in drilling as a result of low international oil prices, drilling was again resumed in October 2000. Production of natural gas decreased from 46.9m. cu m in 1998 to 38m. cu m in 1999 and 2000, and to 35m. cu m in 2001. Imports of mineral fuels accounted for 11.6% of total imports in 2001. Mining and construction contributed 0.7% of GDP in 2001 and employed an estimated 11.0% of the working population in 2001.

Manufacturing

Manufacturing contributed an estimated 6.1% of GDP and employed an estimated 7.2% of the working population in 2001. Excluding sugar factories and refineries, the principal branches of manufacturing were chemical, petroleum, rubber and plastic products, food products and beverages and tobacco. Manufacturing GDP decreased, in real terms, at an average rate of 0.1% per year during 1990–2001; it fell by 0.5% in 2000 and by 1.1% in 2001.

SERVICES

Service industries are the main sector of the economy, accounting for an estimated 79.3% of GDP and 76.0% of employment in 2001. The combined GDP of the service sectors increased, in real terms, at an average rate of 1.7% per year during 1990–2001. In 2000 the sector grew by 7.8% and, in 2001, by 2.6%. Business and general services contributed an estimated 18.9% of GDP in 2001. The Government has encouraged the growth of 'offshore' financial facilities, particularly through the negotiation of double taxation agreements with other countries. At the end of 2002 there were 4,206 international business companies and there were 2,981 foreign sales corporations operating in the country at the end of 2001. Barbados has an active anti-money-laundering regime, which was further strengthened by new legislation in 1998, although the island remained classified by the USA as a 'country of concern' with regard to money-laundering. Moreover, in May 2000 the Organisation for Economic Co-operation and Development (OECD) placed Barbados on a list of tax 'havens' that were likely to incur counter-measures from February 2002 if they failed to modify tax regimes in line with OECD requirements. However, Barbados avoided inclusion on a list of non-co-operating jurisdictions drawn up by the Financial Action Task Force on Money Laundering in September 2001, and was removed from the OECD list in January 2002. Tourism made a direct contribution of an estimated 10.3% to GDP in 2002, and it employed some 10.7% of the working population in 2001. Receipts from the tourist industry almost doubled between 1980 and 1988, and in 2000 totalled US $711.3m., falling to $686.8m. in 2001. Partly because of the reduction in the number of US tourists following the terrorist attacks in the USA of September 2001, stop-over tourist arrivals decreased from 545,027 in 2000 to 497,899 in 2002, while cruise-ship passenger arrivals also decreased over the same period, by 0.9%, to 523,253. In 2001 some 42.9% of stop-over arrivals were from the United Kingdom.

EXTERNAL TRADE

In 2001 Barbados recorded a visible trade deficit of US $681.1m., while there was a deficit of $94.4m. on the current account of the balance of payments. In 2001 the USA was both the principal source of imports (42.1%) and the largest single recipient of exports (15.0%). The United Kingdom accounted for 8.1% of imports and 11.7% of exports. Other major trading partners included the CARICOM (see below) countries, especially Trinidad and Tobago. The principal commodity exports in 2001 were food and live animals (21.0% of total exports), petroleum products (19.9%) chemicals (13.8%). The principal imports were machinery and transport equipment and basic manufactures.

GOVERNMENT FINANCE

For the financial year ending 31 March 2003 there was an estimated total budgetary deficit of Bds $269.1m. At December 2001 the total external debt of Barbados was

US $700.7m. In 2000 the cost of foreign debt-servicing was equivalent to 4.1% of the value of exports of goods and services. The average annual rate of inflation was 2.2% in 1995–2002. Consumer prices rose by an average of 2.6% in 2001 and by 0.2% in 2002. By the end of September 2003 the official unemployment rate was 10.3%, compared with 9.9% at the end of 2001.

INTERNATIONAL ECONOMIC RELATIONS

Barbados is a member of the Caribbean Community and Common Market (CAR-ICOM), of the Inter-American Development Bank (IDB), of the Latin American Economic System (SELA) and of the Association of Caribbean States.

SURVEY AND PROSPECTS

Political stability and consensus have contributed to the economic strengths of Barbados. Tourism dominates the economy but 'offshore' banking and sugar production are also important. The sugar industry came under increased pressure to reform from the 1990s, particularly as further liberalization of international trade was likely to make the island's principal export less competitive. The closure of major hotels for refurbishment in 1999 (until 2003) brought about a marginal temporary decline in tourism earnings. Furthermore, following the terrorist attacks of 11 September 2001 in the USA, the Barbados tourist industry suffered a significant decrease in bookings. A US $20m.–$25m. government plan to subsidize the industry and other affected sectors was proposed in the same month. Following a further contraction in 2002, reports indicated that the sector would record improved results in 2003. A phased liberalization of the telecommunications market commenced at the end of 2000 and was completed in August 2003. The proposed privatization of the Barbados National Bank and the Insurance Company of Barbados were also announced (the latter was transferred to the private sector in December 2000), and plans to partially privatize Grantley Adams International Airport were in progress in 2004. Following eight successive years of economic expansion, in 2001 a decrease in real GDP of 2.8% was recorded, and there was an estimated further decrease of 0.4% in 2002. The economy emerged from recession in 2003, however, when growth of some 2.2% was recorded; the Central Bank predicted growth for 2004 to be 3.0%–3.5%.

Belarus

The Republic of Belarus is situated in north-eastern Europe. In 1922 the Belarusian Soviet Socialist Republic (BSSR) joining with Russia as part of the USSR. In 1991 the BSSR declared its independence and subsequently became the Republic of Belarus. In 1991 Belarus signed the Minsk Agreement establishing the Commonwealth of Independent States. In 1997 Belarus signed a Treaty of Union with Russia. Constitutional amendments introduced in 1996 provoked widespread criticism within Belarus and abroad. Legislative elections held in 2000, and the re-election of Alyaksandr Lukashenka as President in 2001, were regarded as flawed by the international community. The capital is Minsk. The official languages are Belarusian and Russian.

Area and population
Area: 207,595 sq km
Population (mid-2002): 9,930,830
Population density (mid-2002): 47.8 per sq km
Life expectancy (years at birth, 2002): 68.3 (males 62.6; females 74.3)

Finance
GDP in current prices: 2002): US $14,304m. ($1,440 per head)
Real GDP growth (2002): 4.7%
Inflation (annual average, 2002): 42.5%
Currency: rouble

Economy

In 2002, according to estimates by the World Bank, Belarus's gross national income (GNI), measured at average 2000–02 prices, was US $13,533m., equivalent to $1,360 per head. In terms of purchasing-power parity, GNI in that year was equivalent to $5,330 per head. During 1990–2002 the population declined at an average annual rate of 0.2%, while gross domestic product (GDP) per head remained constant, in real terms. Over the same period, overall GDP declined, in real terms, by an average of 0.2% annually. However, real GDP increased by 4.7% in both 2001 and 2002.

AGRICULTURE

Agriculture contributed 11.7% of GDP in 2001, when 12.6% of the employed labour force were engaged in the sector, according to FAO estimates. The principal crops are potatoes, grain and sugar beet. Large areas of arable land (some 1.6m. ha) are still unused after being contaminated in 1986, following the accident at the Chornobyl nuclear power station in Ukraine. The Belarusian authorities have largely opposed private farming, and by 1999 collective and state farms still accounted for some 83% of agricultural land. However, private farms produced the majority of Belarus's potatoes, fruit and vegetables, as well as a significant proportion of total livestock-product output. In 1998, according to the IMF, 49.8% of total crop output was produced by the private sector. During 1990–2002, according to World Bank estimates, real agricultural GDP decreased at an average annual rate of 2.6%. Agricultural output increased, in real terms, by 1.4% in 2001 and by 1.5% in 2002.

INDUSTRY

Industry (comprising mining, manufacturing, construction and power) provided 38.1% of GDP in 2001, and engaged 34.7% of the employed labour force in 2000. According to the World Bank, industrial GDP decreased, in real terms, at an average annual rate of 0.3% during 1990–2002. However, industrial output increased by 5.9% in 2001 and by 4.3% in 2002, according to official figures.

Mining

Belarus has relatively few mineral resources, although there are small deposits of petroleum and natural gas, and important peat reserves. Peat extraction, however, was severely affected by the disaster at Chornobyl, since contaminated peat could not be burned. Belarus produced 50% of the former USSR's output of potash. However, production of potash declined in the 1990s. In 1994 only 0.6% of the labour force were engaged in mining and quarrying.

Manufacturing

According to the World Bank, the manufacturing sector contributed an estimated 32.1% of GDP in 2001, and it employed 26.5% of the labour force in 1994. Machine-building, power generation and chemicals are the principal branches of the sector. During 1990–2002 manufacturing GDP increased, in real terms, at an average annual rate of 0.6%, according to World Bank estimates. Overall sectoral GDP increased, in real terms, by 6.2% in 2001 and by 1.5% in 2002.

Energy

In 2000 much of Belarus's supply of energy was provided by natural gas (94.0%), with petroleum and petroleum products accounting for almost all of the remainder. In 2001, according to IMF figures, the country imported 89.5% of its crude-oil consumption, 99.2% of its natural gas consumption and 32.9% of its electricity consumption. Energy products comprised 27.4% of the total value of imports in 2001. There are two large petroleum refineries, at Novopolotsk and Mozyr. In 2000 Belarus's principal gas supplier, the Russian company Gazprom, announced plans to construct two new natural gas pipelines across Belarus, in order to halt the alleged misappropriation of supplies from existing pipelines in Ukraine. However, from the latter half of the 1990s Gazprom repeatedly threatened to reduce gas supplies to Belarus, owing to that country's energy arrears, which continued to rise, despite subsidized gas prices (a concession viewed to result from the signature of the Russia-Belarus Union Treaty). In late 2002 the Belarusian Government agreed to authorize the partial privatization of the domestic natural gas importer, Beltransgaz, enabling Gazprom to acquire a stake in the company, in return for the partial settlement of Belarus's arrears. However, negotiations over the valuation of the company subsequently stalled. In September 2003 President Alyaksandr Lukashenka and President Vladimir Putin of Russia held inconclusive talks over Russian plans to introduce market prices for gas exports to Belarus. The failure to reach agreement on either issue eventually led Gazprom temporarily to suspend gas supplies to Belarus in early 2004.

SERVICES

The services sector provided 50.2% of GDP in 2001, and accounted for 50.5% of total employment in 2000. The sector is led by transport and communications and trade and catering, which accounted for 13.0% and 11.3% of GDP, respectively, in 2001. According to World Bank estimates, during 1990–2002 the GDP of the services sector increased, in real terms, at an average annual rate of 0.6%. Sectoral GDP increased, in real terms, by 9.0% in 2001 and by 2.5% in 2002.

EXTERNAL TRADE

In 2002 Belarus recorded a visible trade deficit of US $914.3m., and there was a deficit of $377.5m. on the current account of the balance of payments. Trading partners outside the Commonwealth of Independent States (CIS) accounted for 30.8% of Belarus's imports and 45.3% of its exports in 2002. However, the accession to the European Union of a number of neighbouring countries in May 2004 was expected to have a negative impact on Belarusian foreign trade, as they imposed additional border and trade controls. In 2002 Belarus's principal trading partner was Russia (which accounted for 65.1% of total imports and 49.6% of exports). Germany was also an important source of imports (accounting for 7.6% of the total), and Latvia and the United Kingdom were significant purchasers of exports (accounting for 6.5% and 6.2% of the total, respectively). In 2000 the principal exports were machinery and metalworking, petroleum and gas, chemical and petroleum products, and light manufactures. The principal imports were petroleum and gas, machinery and metalworking, chemical and petroleum products, and metallurgy.

GOVERNMENT FINANCE

The 2001 state budget registered a deficit of 235,680m. readjusted roubles (equivalent to 2.5% of GDP). Belarus's total external debt was US $868.9m. at the end of 2001, of which $640.9m. was long-term public debt. In that year the cost of debt-servicing was equivalent to 2.8% of the value of exports of goods and services. During 1991–2002 consumer prices increased at an average rate of 286.0% per year. The average annual rate of inflation was 61.1% in 2001 and 65.0% in 2002. At the end of 2003 3.1% of the economically active population were registered as unemployed. However, the true rate of unemployment was believed to be far higher, as many people were unwilling to register, owing to the low level of official benefits.

INTERNATIONAL ECONOMIC RELATIONS

Belarus joined the IMF and the World Bank in 1992. It also became a member of the European Bank for Reconstruction and Development (EBRD). Belarus is pursuing membership of the World Trade Organization (WTO), at which it holds observer status, although its failure to introduce market economic principles made the prospect of early accession unlikely; in 2003 the WTO suggested that Belarus synchronize its accession negotiations with those of Russia.

SURVEY AND PROSPECTS

Following the dissolution of the USSR, Belarus experienced serious economic problems and a severe contraction in output in all sectors. Belarus was slow to adopt economic reforms, in an attempt to avoid the social costs associated with transition to a market economy, and economic policy was influenced by the country's aim of integration with Russia, as envisaged in a number of treaties and agreements signed from the mid-1990s. At the beginning of 2000 a redenominated rouble, equivalent to 1,000 new roubles, was introduced, and in September a single rouble exchange rate replaced the previous multiple exchange-rate system. In 2001 both the IMF and the World Bank resumed relations with Belarus, suspended since the mid-1990s (although the IMF resumed relations at an evaluative level only). Meanwhile, in April 2001 the legislature ratified a currency agreement with Russia, according to which the Russian rouble was to be adopted as the Belarusian currency from 2005, and a new single currency was to be introduced in 2008. The Government's reliance on Russia for favourably priced energy resources and bilateral barter trade had ensured that the economy was protected from serious decline. However, some observers thought it likely that Belarus's reluctance, in 2003, to finalize arrangements for the introduction of the single currency prompted the decision by Russia to remove subsidies on the gas supplied to Belarus, a measure that was likely severely to affect the economy. None the less, President Lukashenka set ambitious economic targets for 2004, which envisaged economic growth of 10% and a 71% increase in the minimum wage. In early 2004 the IMF praised the maintenance of economic growth in 2003 (when GDP increased by some 6.8%, in real terms, according to official figures), but warned that the Government's projections for 2004 were unrealistic. The annual rate of inflation was the highest in the region and there were problems within the industrial sector, where approximately 30% of enterprises were loss-making. The agricultural sector, in which some 60% of enterprises recorded a loss in 2003, was also in need of urgent reform. The IMF emphasized the fact that foreign and private-sector investment was likely to remain limited while the so-called golden share regulation, which permitted any company in which the Government retained as little as one share to come under renewed state control (even if this had not been anticipated when the firm was initially privatized), remained in place.

Belgium

The Kingdom of Belgium lies in north-western Europe. Belgium is a founder member of many important international organizations, including the European Union. Flemish and French are the main official languages. In the latter half of the 20th century political and economic polarization of Flemish-speaking Flanders and francophone Wallonia exacerbated linguistic divisions. In 1993 a federal state of Belgium was created. The coalition administration formed in 1999 was the first Belgian Government in 40 years not to include the Christian Democrats, and the first to be headed by a Liberal Prime Minister since 1884. Belgium's capital is Brussels.

Area and population
Area: 30,528 sq km
Population (mid-2002): 10,320,000
Population density (mid-2002): 338.1 per sq km
Life expectancy (years at birth, 2002): 78.4 (males 75.2; females 81.5)

Finance
GDP in current prices: 2002): US $247,634m. ($23,996 per head)
Real GDP growth (2002): 0.7%
Inflation (annual average, 2002): 1.6%
Currency: euro

Economy

In 2002, according to estimates by the World Bank, Belgium's gross national income (GNI), measured at average 2000–02 prices, was US $239,949m., equivalent to $23,250 per head (or $27,350 per head on an international purchasing-power parity basis). During 1990–2002, it was estimated, the population increased at an average annual rate of 0.3% per year, while gross domestic product (GDP) per head increased, in real terms, by an average of 1.7% per year. Overall GDP increased, in real terms, at an average annual rate of 2.0% during 1990–2002; it rose by 1.0% in 2001 and by 0.7% in 2002.

AGRICULTURE

Agriculture (including hunting, forestry and fishing) contributed 1.5% of GDP in 2001 and engaged 0.8% of the employed labour force. The principal agricultural products are sugar beet, cereals and potatoes. Pig meat, beef and dairy products are also important. Exports of live animals and animal and vegetable products accounted for 7.6% of Belgium's total export revenue in 2002. The agricultural sector was adversely affected by the dioxin contamination scandal in the late 1990s. According to World Bank estimates, agricultural GDP increased, in real terms, at an average annual rate of 2.7% in 1990–2001; it decreased by 2.2% in 2000 and by a further 4.0% the following year.

INDUSTRY

Industry (including mining and quarrying, manufacturing, power and construction) contributed 27.2% of GDP and engaged 24.3% of the employed labour force in 2001. According to World Bank estimates, real industrial GDP increased at an average rate of 1.8% per year in 1990–2001; it rose by 4.2% in 2000, before slowing to 0.4% in 2001.

Mining

Belgium has few mineral resources, and the country's last coal mine closed in 1992. In 2001 extractive activities accounted for only 0.1% of GDP and engaged only 0.1% of the employed labour force. Belgium is, however, an important producer of copper, zinc and aluminium, smelted from imported ores. The sector's GDP declined at an average rate of 2.5% per year during 1995–99, although it increased by 0.7% in 1999.

Manufacturing

Manufacturing contributed 18.9% of GDP in 2000 and engaged 17.9% of the employed labour force in 2001. In 2001 the main branches of manufacturing, in terms of value added, were chemicals, chemical products and man-made fibres (accounting for 20.0% of the total), basic metals and fabricated metal products (13.6%) and food products (13.1%). According to World Bank estimates, during 1995–2000 manufacturing GDP increased at an average annual rate of 3.3%; it rose by 1.3% in 1999 and by 3.6% in 2000.

Energy

Belgium's seven nuclear reactors accounted for 57.8% of total electricity generation in 2001 (one of the highest levels in the world). A further 40% was produced by coal-fired and natural gas power stations. The country's dependence on imported petroleum and natural gas has increased since 1988, following the announcement by the

Government in that year of the indefinite suspension of its nuclear programme and of the construction of a gas-powered generator. In December 2002 a bill was approved by the Chamber of Representatives to phase out the use of nuclear power by 2025, with the first nuclear power station scheduled to be closed in 2015. Imports of mineral fuels comprised an estimated 7.9% of the value of Belgium's total imports in 2002.

SERVICES

The services sector contributed 71.3% of GDP and engaged 74.9% of the employed labour force in 2001. The presence in Belgium of the offices of many international organizations and businesses is a significant source of revenue. In September 2000 Euronext was formed from the merger of the stock exchanges of Brussels (Brussels Exchanges), Amsterdam (Amsterdam Exchanges) and Paris (Paris Bourse). Tourism is an expanding industry in Belgium, and in 2001 an estimated 6.5m. foreign tourists visited the country. Tourism receipts totalled US $6,917m. in 2001 (including receipts from Luxembourg). According to World Bank estimates, the GDP of the services sector increased at an average annual rate of 2.1% in 1990–2001; it increased by 4.0% in 2000 and by 2.4% in 2001.

EXTERNAL TRADE

In 2002 Belgium recorded a visible trade surplus of US $7,395m., and there was a surplus of $8,371m. on the current account of the balance of payments. Belgium's principal source of imports in 2002 was Germany (providing 17.3% of the total); other major suppliers were the Netherlands (15.8%), France (12.6%), the United Kingdom (7.5%) and Ireland (7.0%). The principal market for exports in that year was Germany (accounting for 18.6% of the total); other major purchasers were France (16.3%), the Netherlands (11.7%) and the United Kingdom (9.6%). The principal exports in 2002 were road vehicles, medicinal and pharmaceutical products, non-metallic mineral manufactures, and organic chemicals. The principal imports in that year were road vehicles, medicinal and pharmaceutical products, non-metallic mineral manufactures, and petroleum and related products.

GOVERNMENT FINANCE

In 2001 there was budgetary surplus equivalent to 0.2% of GDP. The country's total external debt was equivalent to 107.5% of GDP in 2001. The annual rate of inflation averaged 2.1% in 1990–2002. Consumer prices increased by an annual average of 2.5% in 2001 and by 1.6% in 2002. In 2002 7.3% of the labour force were unemployed.

INTERNATIONAL ECONOMIC RELATIONS

Belgium is a member of the European Union (EU), including the European Monetary System (EMS), and of the Benelux Economic Union. Belgium is also a member of the European System of Central Banks (ESCB), which was inaugurated in 1998 under the auspices of the European Central Bank.

SURVEY AND PROSPECTS

In the late 1990s Belgium successfully reduced its large budget deficit and chronic public-sector debt in order to qualify for the final stage of economic and monetary union (EMU) within the EU. The reduction of the budget deficit to the equivalent of 0.9% of GDP and the level of public debt to 116.1% of GDP by 1999 (from 7% and 135%, respectively, in 1993) enabled Belgium to participate in the introduction of the

European single currency, the euro, which came into effect on 1 January 1999 (in 11 participating countries). On 1 January 2002 euro notes and coins were introduced and on 28 February the Belgian franc ceased to be legal tender. The first Verhofstadt administration, which presided over a period of growth in the economy, continued to reduce the budget deficit and public indebtedness, achieving the first budget surplus for 50 years (of 0.2%) in 2001. In September 2002 the Minister of Finance, Didier Reynders, criticized the decision of the European Commission (EC) to extend by two years to 2006 the deadline for France, Germany, Italy and Portugal to reduce their budget deficits to the amount permitted for members of the EMU. Supported by Austria, the Netherlands and Finland, Belgium accused the EC of treating the larger countries in the EMU more favourably than the smaller ones. In June 2001 the Government attempted to address the imbalances in the performances of the regional economies in Belgium, granting greater fiscal control to the regions (long a demand of the more affluent Flanders), with the discretion to raise or lower local taxes. In 2002, in an attempt to encourage investment, corporate income tax was reduced from 40% to 34% for large businesses and from 28% to 25% for small and medium-sized enterprises.

Following its re-election in 2003 the Verhofstadt Government presented a balanced budget plan for the fifth consecutive year for 2004. Belgium was one of only three countries in the eurozone without a budget deficit, along with Spain and Finland. There were accusations from opponents that the balanced budget plan had only been achieved for 2004 through the timely assumption of Belgacom's pension liabilities (the deal included a payment from Belgacom to the Government of €1,400m.) without which a deficit of 0.9% would have been presented. The Belgacom agreement formed part of the preparations for the partial divestment of Belgacom's shares, continuing the privatization programme that had partly financed Belgium's progress towards EMU membership, representing the largest European initial public offering in telecommunications in three years, in which Belgacom was expected to be valued at €10,000m.

The new administration pledged to reduce personal taxation, to create 200,000 jobs and to make Belgium a more attractive investment destination by further reducing the fiscal burden on the corporate sector. To partially finance the proposed €3,200m. reduction in personal income tax over four years, Didier, who had retained the finance portfolio, planned to raise additional funds by sponsoring a partial fiscal amnesty for the estimated €160,000m. of savings that Belgians held abroad to encourage them to repatriate the money. The employment target was particularly ambitious in view of the loss of 70,000 jobs in the previous three years and the fact that it was predicated on an average annual level of GDP growth of more than 2% over the following four years. The Government was relying on the private sector to create 35,000 additional jobs each year and for the remaining 60,000 to result from specific government measures, including tax breaks and subsidies and new job schemes. The health sector was expected to account for many new jobs, owing to the increasing requirements of Belgium's ageing population. Progress in job creation was considered essential for the long-term prospects of the economy, as social security and pension payments remained a serious burden on public finances, although at 7.3% in 2002, the rate of unemployment was lower than the EU average of 7.7%. The Government predicted that in 2004 the economy would grow by 1.8% and that national debt would fall below 100% of GDP for the first time in 20 years, although this was still far above the 60% limit set by the EU Stability and Growth Pact.

Belize

Belize lies on the Caribbean coast of Central America. Recognized as a British colony in 1862, Belize was known as British Honduras until 1973. The territory's first general election, in 1954, was won by the People's United Party (PUP). The PUP won all subsequent elections until 1984, when it was defeated by the United Democratic Party. Belize became independent, within the Commonwealth, in 1981. Much of the recent history of Belize has been dominated by a territorial dispute with Guatemala that still awaited a definitive resolution in the early 21st century. The capital is Belmopan. English is the official language.

Area and population
Area: 22,965 sq km
Population (mid-2002): 253,330
Population density (mid-2002): 11.0 per sq km
Life expectancy (years at birth, 2002): 69.7 (males 67.4; females 72.4)

Finance
GDP in current prices: 2002): US $843m. ($3,328 per head)
Real GDP growth (2002): 3.7%
Inflation (annual average, 2002): 2.2%
Currency: Belize dollar

Economy

In 2002, according to estimates by the World Bank, Belize's gross national income (GNI), measured at average 2000–02 prices, was US $750.3m., equivalent to US $2,960 per head (or $5,430 per head on an international purchasing-power parity basis). During 1990–2002 Belize's population grew at an average annual rate of 2.5%, while gross domestic product (GDP) per head increased, in real terms, at an average rate of 2.5% . Overall GDP increased, in real terms, at an average rate of 4.5% per year in 1990–2002; growth was 5.1% in 2001, slowing to 3.7% in 2002.

AGRICULTURE

Although 38% of the country is considered suitable for agriculture, only an estimated 6.7% of total area was used for agricultural purposes in 2001. Nevertheless, in 2001 agriculture, hunting, forestry and fishing employed an estimated 30.5 of the working population and contributed an estimated 15.5% of GDP. The principal cash crops are citrus fruits (citrus concentrates accounted for an estimated 20% of total domestic exports in 2001), sugar cane (sugar accounted for 18.8%) and bananas (an estimated 10.8%). Maize, red kidney beans and rice are the principal domestic food crops, and the development of other crops, such as cocoa, coconuts and soybeans (soya beans), is being encouraged. The country is largely self-sufficient in fresh meat and eggs. Belize has considerable timber reserves, particularly of tropical hardwoods, and the forestry sector is being developed. In 2001 fishing provided export earnings of an estimated US $31.9m. (16.1% of total domestic export revenue). The real GDP of the agricultural sector increased at an average annual rate of 6.7% during 1990–2001; real agricultural GDP increased by 4.2% in 2000 and by 12.3% in 2001.

INDUSTRY

Industry (including mining, manufacturing, construction, water and electricity) employed 17.0% of the working population in 1999 and contributed 23.6% of GDP in 2001.

Mining

Mining and quarrying accounted for an estimated 0.7% of GDP in 2001 and for only 0.4% of employment in 1999. Industrial GDP increased at an average annual rate of 4.0% during 1990–2001; real industrial GDP increased by an estimated 17.9% in 2000 and by 3.6% in 2001.

Manufacturing

Manufacturing accounted for an estimated 13.0% of GDP in 2001 and employed 9.4% of the working population in 1999. Dominant activities are the manufacture of clothing and the processing of agricultural products, particularly sugar cane (for sugar and rum). Manufacturing GDP increased at an average rate of 4.1% per year during 1990–2001; the sector increased by 19.6% in 2000 and by 1.9% in 2001.

Energy

Imports of mineral fuels accounted for 8.2% of the total cost of retained imports in 2001. Hydroelectric power was developed in the 1990s; in the late 1990s the Mollejón hydroelectric station, on the Macal River, began operations. Financed by the International Finance Corporation and the Caribbean Development Bank, the project attracted criticism over its cost and efficiency. In 2001 construction began of a controversial second hydroelectric dam at Chalillo on the Macal River; upon completion, the dam would be operated by its Canadian contractor before transfer to state ownership in 2031. The dam was expected to provide 5.3 MW of electricity annually and, according to the Government, would provide Belize's energy needs for 50 years. Environmentalist groups contended that the dam would destroy the habitat of some 40 species of rare animals and birds, including the endangered scarlet macaw. Following a protracted appeals process initiated in early 2002 by the Belize Alliance of Conservation Non-Government Organizations, in January 2004 the Privy Council in the United Kingdom ruled in favour of the Belizean Government's decision that construction of the dam should proceed.

SERVICES

The services sector employed 55.5% of the working population in 1999 and contributed 60.9% of GDP in 2001. Tourist development is concentrated on promoting 'eco-tourism', based on the attraction of Belize's natural environment, particularly its rain forests and the barrier reef, the second largest in the world. Tourist arrivals totalled 244,072 in 2001, a 3.9% increase compared with the previous year. However, according to provisional figures, tourist arrivals more than doubled, to 519,212, in 2002. The increase was mainly in the cruise-ship sector, where a cut in the passenger tax rate and the opening of new facilities had prompted a significant rise in numbers. The inauguration of a new air service to Montego Bay, Jamaica, operated by Air Jamaica, also contributed to the increase in the number of tourist arrivals in that year. According to UN estimates, the GDP of the services sector increased, in real terms, at an average rate of 3.6% per year during 1990–2001; real sectoral GDP increased by 10.5% in 2000 and by 2.0% in 2001. Belize's 'offshore' financial centre opened in 1996 and by 2003 there were more than 25,000 registered 'offshore' companies.

EXTERNAL TRADE

In 2001 Belize recorded a trade deficit of US $189.9m. and a deficit of US $162.7m. on the current account of the balance of payments. In that year the principal source of imports was the USA (accounting for 48.0% of the total). The USA was also the principal export market, accounting for 53.8% of total exports, followed by the United Kingdom (23.0%). Mexico is another important trading partner. The principal exports in 2001 were food and live animals (89.0%). The principal imports in that year were basic manufactures, machinery and transport equipment and food and live animals.

GOVERNMENT FINANCE

For the financial year 2001/02 there was a budgetary deficit of BZ $174.8m, equivalent to 10.9% of GDP. Belize's total external debt was US $708.4m. in 2001, of which US $657.6m. was long-term public debt In 2001 the cost of debt-servicing was equivalent to 25.1% of the value of exports of goods and services. The annual rate of inflation averaged 2.0% in 1990–2002. Consumer prices increased by 1.2% in 2001 and by 2.1% in 2002. In 2002 some 9.0% of the economically active population were unemployed. Many Belizeans, however, work abroad, and remittances to the country from such workers are an important source of income. Emigration, mainly to the USA, is offset by the number of immigrants and refugees from other Central American countries, particularly El Salvador.

INTERNATIONAL ECONOMIC RELATIONS

Belize is a member of the Caribbean Community and Common Market (CARICOM), and in 1991 acceded to the Organization of American States (OAS). In September 1992 Belize was granted membership of the Inter-American Development Bank (IDB). Belize is also a member of the Central American Integration System (SICA). In 2001 Central American countries, including Belize, reached agreement with Mexico on regional integration through the 'Plan Puebla-Panamá', a series of joint projects intended to integrate the transport, industry and tourism of the countries involved. As a member of the Commonwealth, Belize enjoys low tariffs on its exports to the European Union (EU) under the Cotonou Agreement, and tariff-free access to the USA under the Caribbean Basin Initiative.

SURVEY AND PROSPECTS

On taking office in September 1998 the Musa administration inherited an extremely weak fiscal position, including a public-sector deficit of some BZ $51m. (equivalent to 4.0% of GDP). The new Government undertook a restructuring of the tax system: in April 1999 value-added tax was replaced with a broad-based 8% sales tax. The Musa administration also began a large-scale public investment programme, expanded market opportunities for bananas (despite the phasing out of the EU preferential market for Caribbean bananas) and increased investment in the tourism sector. As a result, GDP increased by 11.1% in 2000. The country was adversely affected by both 'Hurricane Keith', which struck in October 2000, causing an estimated BZ $523m.-worth of damage, and by 'Hurricane Iris', which struck in October 2001, causing an estimated US $250m.-worth of damage. As a result, growth in the economy slowed in 2001, to 5.1%. In April 2001, following an EU–USA agreement regarding banana imports, the EU preferential market for Caribbean bananas ended. From 1 July a transitional system, issuing licences according to historical trade patterns, was implemented, while the definitive tariff-only system was to be in place by 1 January 2006. This was expected to adversely affect banana revenue.

Also in 2001 the Government approved a Sugar Industry Bill, intended to reform the sector, reducing the state's role while encouraging outside investment. In September the Government announced that the 15-year exclusive licence held by Belize Telecommunications Ltd (BTL) would not be renewed, and that the telecommunications sector would be liberalized. In 2002 BTL was unsuccessful in judicial attempts to have contracts awarded to a rival company, INTELCO, declared null and void. Growth of 3.7% in 2002 mainly reflected expansion in the tourism sector. In November of that year the IMF expressed concern at the country's current-account deficit, which was equivalent to an estimated 20% of GDP in 2001. It urged the Government to reduce the fiscal deficit to 5.0% of GDP in the 2002/03 financial year and advised against proposals for a government-subsidized national health service and affordable housing scheme. Nevertheless, in the months preceding the general election of March 2003, the ruling PUP pledged to build a further 5,000 affordable houses, as well as to increase public-sector pay. Following its re-election, the PUP Government faced the challenge of maintaining the popularity it enjoyed in its first term in office, while curbing public expenditure in an attempt to reduce the fiscal deficit. The economy grew by an estimated 3.0% in 2003.

Benin

The Republic of Benin is situated in West Africa. Benin (Dahomey until 1975) gained independence from France in 1960. From 1973 the regime of Maj. (later Gen.) Mathieu Kérékou pursued Marxist-based policies. After multi-party elections in 1991, the largest grouping in the Assemblée nationale comprised three parties allied in support of Nicéphore Soglo, who was subsequently elected President. Kérékou was re-elected President in 1996 and 2001, and supporters of Kérékou gained a majority in the Assemblée nationale elected in March 2003. Benin's administrative capital is Porto-Novo, although most government offices are in the economic capital, Cotonou. French is the official language.

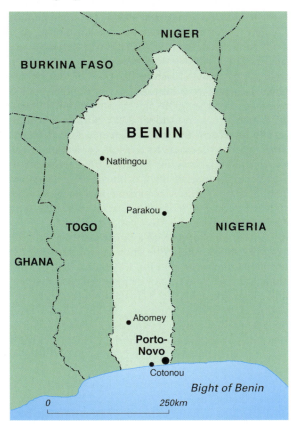

Area and population
Area: 112,622 sq km
Population (mid-2002): 6,603,440
Population density (mid-2002): 58.6 per sq km
Life expectancy (years at birth, 2002): 51.2 (males 50.1; females 52.4)

Finance
GDP in current prices: 2002): US $2,690m. ($407 per head)
Real GDP growth (2002): 5.3%
Inflation (annual average, 2002): 2.5%
Currency: CFA franc

Economy

In 2002, according to estimates by the World Bank, Benin's gross national income (GNI), measured at average 2000–02 prices, was US $2,503m., equivalent to $380 per head (or $1,020 on an international purchasing-power parity basis). During 1990–2002, it was estimated, the population increased at an average annual rate of 2.9%, while gross domestic product (GDP) per head increased, in real terms, by an average of 1.9% per year. Overall GDP increased, in real terms, at an average annual rate of 4.8% in 1990–2002; growth in 2002 was 6.0%, according to the IMF.

AGRICULTURE
Agriculture (including forestry and fishing) contributed 36.9% of GDP in 2002. In 2001 an estimated 53.0% of the labour force were employed in the sector. The principal cash crops are cotton (exports of which accounted for an estimated 65.0% of total exports in 2001), cashew nuts and oil palm. Benin is normally self-sufficient in basic foods; the main subsistence crops are yams, cassava and maize. The World Bank estimated that agricultural GDP increased at an average annual rate of 5.6% in 1990–2002; growth in 2002 was 5.6%.

INDUSTRY
Industry (including mining, manufacturing, construction and power) contributed 14.9% of GDP in 2002, and engaged 10.4% of the employed labour force at the time of the 1992 census. According to the World Bank, industrial GDP increased at an average annual rate of 5.0% in 1990–2002; growth in 2002 was 6.5%.

Mining
Mining contributed only 0.2% of GDP in 2002, and engaged less than 0.1% of the employed labour force in 1992. Petroleum extraction at Sémé was terminated on the grounds of unprofitability in 1998, contributing to a 82.2% decline in mining GDP in the following year. However, a contract signed between Benin and the multinational Zetah Oil Company in October 1999 envisaged the exploitation of Sémé's remaining petroleum reserves, estimated at some 22m. barrels, and operations recommenced in 2000. Marble and limestone are also exploited commercially. There are also deposits of gold, phosphates, natural gas, iron ore, silica sand, peat and chromium. The GDP of the mining sector declined at an average annual rate of 28.6% in 1994–2001; growth in mining GDP was negligible in 2001.

Manufacturing
The manufacturing sector, which contributed 9.3% of GDP in 2002, engaged 7.8% of the employed labour force in 1992. The sector is based largely on the processing of primary products (principally cotton-ginning and oil-palm processing). Construction materials and some simple consumer goods are also produced for the domestic

market. According to the World Bank, manufacturing GDP increased at an average annual rate of 6.3% in 1990–2002; growth in 2002 was 6.4%.

Energy

Benin is at present highly dependent on imports of electricity from Ghana (which supplied some 85% of total available production in 1996). It is envisaged that a hydroelectric installation on the Mono river, constructed and operated jointly with Togo, will reduce Benin's dependence on imported electricity, and a second such installation is under construction downstream. In 2000 100% of Benin's electricity production was derived from petroleum. In that year the construction of a further electricity line, to run from Lagos, Nigeria, to Togo, through Benin, was proposed by the Governments of the three countries. A pipeline to supply natural gas from Nigeria to Benin, Togo and Ghana was expected to come on stream in 2005, three years later than initially planned. Imports of mineral fuels and lubricants accounted for 17.3% of the value of total imports in 2001.

SERVICES

The services sector contributed 48.3% of GDP in 2002, and engaged 31.8% of the employed labour force in 1992. The port of Cotonou is of considerable importance as an entrepôt for regional trade: re-exports comprised an estimated 38.5% of the value of total exports in 1997. According to the World Bank, the GDP of the services sector increased at an average annual rate of 4.1% in 1990–2002; growth in 2002 was 4.6%.

EXTERNAL TRADE

In 2002 Benin recorded a visible trade deficit of an estimated US $276.7m., while there was a deficit of $217.1m. on the current account of the balance of payments. In 2001 the principal source of imports (23.0%) was France; other major sources were the People's Republic of China, Côte d'Ivoire, Ghana and Nigeria. The principal market for exports in that year was India (30.6%); other important purchasers were Ghana, Brazil, Indonesia and Nigeria. The principal exports in 2001 were raw cotton, cashew nuts and gold. The main imports in that year were refined petroleum products, textile yarn and fabrics, non-metallic mineral manufactures (principally cement), meat and meat preparations, road vehicles and parts, medicinal and pharmaceutical products, and cereals and cereal preparations.

GOVERNMENT FINANCE

In 2002 Benin recorded an overall budget deficit of an estimated 44,900m. francs CFA (equivalent to 2.4% of GDP). The country's total external debt at the end of 2001 was US $1,665m., of which $1,503m. was long-term public debt. In that year the cost of debt-servicing was equivalent to 7.9% of the value of exports of goods and services. The annual rate of inflation, which had been negligible prior to the 50% devaluation of the CFA franc in January 1994, increased to 38.5% in 1994, but slowed to an average of 3.5% per year in 1995–2002. Consumer prices increased by 2.4% in 2002. About one-quarter of the urban labour force was estimated to be unemployed in 1997.

INTERNATIONAL ECONOMIC RELATIONS

Benin is a member of the Economic Community of West African States (ECOWAS), of the West African organs of the Franc Zone, of the African Petroleum Producers' Association (APPA), of the Conseil de l'Entente and of the Niger Basin Authority.

SURVEY AND PROSPECTS

Benin has experienced considerable economic growth since the early 1990s. A three-year Enhanced Structural Adjustment Facility (ESAF) was agreed with the IMF in August 1996. The renewal of co-operation with the IMF ensured debt-relief measures, notably along concessionary terms by the 'Paris Club' of official creditors.The IMF suspended disbursements for several months in 1998, following delays in the privatization of several major state enterprises. In July 2000, as part of their initiative for heavily indebted poor countries (HIPCs), the IMF and the World Bank cancelled some US $460m. of Benin's debt and announced a further three-year enhanced HIPC programme for 2000–03. Also in that month the IMF approved funding of some $35.7m., under its Poverty Reduction and Growth Facility (PRGF, the successor to ESAF), in support of the Government's economic programme for 2000–03. (In July 2002 the IMF announced that the PRGF arrangement was to be extended until 2004, and additional debt relief, amounting to $5m., was also granted under the HIPC initiative.) However, proposed restructuring and divestiture programmes continued to be implemented only sporadically.

Although the primary marketing of the important crop of seed cotton was transferred, in January 2001, from the parastatal Société Nationale pour la Promotion Agricole (SONAPRA) to the private sector, the privatization of SONAPRA itself was postponed, and was expected to take place in 2004. None the less, by the early 2000s the country's cotton sector was one of the most liberalized in western or central Africa. A considerable increase in cotton production in 2002 contributed significantly to the strong GDP growth recorded in that year, partly compensating for a sharp decline in international prices for that commodity. In the early 2000s programmes to open the water and electricity sectors to private-sector involvement were being developed; moreover, it was also intended that the telecommunications and postal operations of the Office des Postes et des Télécommunications be separated, with the former to be transferred to private management by late 2004. The Government also implemented a series of measures to improve the regulation of state expenditure, including a number of civil service reforms, the first stages of which took effect from early 2003. GDP growth of 5.6% was projected for 2003, and the Government aimed to increase growth to 7.0% by 2005.

Bermuda

The Bermudas, or Somers Islands, are an isolated archipelago in the Atlantic Ocean, some 917 km off the coast of South Carolina, USA. Bermuda was first settled by the British in 1609. It has had a representative assembly since 1620, and became a British crown colony in 1684. Bermuda was granted internal self-government by the Constitution that was introduced in 1968. The majority of participants in a referendum held in 1995 registered their opposition to independence from the United Kingdom. Bermuda is a United Kingdom Overseas Territory. Hamilton is the capital. The official language is English.

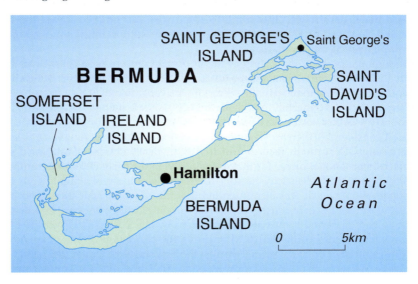

Area and population
Area: 53 sq km
Population (mid-2001): 60,000
Population density (mid-2001): 1,125.7 per sq km
Life expectancy (years at birth, 2000): Males 71.1; females 77.8

Finance
GDP in current prices: year ending 31 March 2000): US $2,624m. ($41,651 per head)
Inflation (annual average, 2002): 2.3%
Currency: Bermuda dollar

Economy

In 1997, according to estimates by the World Bank, Bermuda's gross national income (GNI), measured at average 1995–97 prices, was US $2,128m. During 1991–2001, it was estimated, the population increased at an average annual rate of 0.6%, while overall gross domestic product (GDP) increased, in real terms, at an average annual rate of 2.0% in 1990–98 and of 4.2% in 1996/97–1999/2000; growth was estimated at 1% in 2002 and 2003. In 2000 GDP per head was estimated to be equivalent to some US $34,600, one of the highest levels in the world.

AGRICULTURE

Agriculture (including fishing and quarrying) engaged only an estimated 1.5% of the employed labour force in 2000, and the sector makes a minimal contribution to GDP. The principal crops were potatoes, tomatoes, carrots, bananas, citrus fruits and cabbage. Flowers (notably lilies) are grown for export. Other vegetables and fruit are also grown, but Bermuda remains very dependent upon food imports, which, with beverages and tobacco, accounted for 19.0% of total imports in 1999. Livestock-rearing includes cattle and goats (both mainly for dairy purposes), pigs and poultry. There is a small fishing industry, mainly for domestic consumption.

INDUSTRY

Industry (including mining, manufacturing, construction and public utilities) contributed about 10.2% of GDP in 1993 and engaged an estimated 11.4% of the employed labour force in 2000. The main activities include ship repairs, boat-building and the manufacture of paints and pharmaceuticals. The principal industrial sector is construction (in which an estimated 6.9% of the total labour force were engaged in 2000). Most of Bermuda's water is provided by privately-collected rainfall. Energy requirements are met mainly by the import of mineral fuels (fuels accounted for 3.8% of total imports in 1999).

SERVICES

Bermuda is overwhelmingly a service economy, with service industries engaging 87.1% of the employed labour force in 2000. In 1995, despite the growth of financial services, it was estimated that tourism still accounted for almost one-half of foreign exchange earnings. Visitor expenditure accounted for 19.1% of GDP in 1999/2000. In 2000 an estimated 13.8% of the employed labour force worked in restaurants and hotels, but tourism is estimated to account for some 60% of all employment, directly and indirectly. The sector earned an estimated B $349.7m. in 2001. The total number of tourists, particularly of cruise-ship passengers, is strictly controlled, in order to maintain Bermuda's environment and its market for wealthier visitors. Most tourists come from the USA (some 46.4% of total arrivals in 2001). In 2001 454,444 tourists visited Bermuda, a decrease of 15.5% on the 2000 figure. In September 2003 the impact of 'Hurricane Fabian' led to the cancellation of several cruise-ship visits and the temporary closure of the international airport to commercial aircraft. In addition, two leading hotels suffered extensive damage. That year's tourism revenue was expected to suffer as a result.

There is a significant commercial and 'offshore' financial sector, and in 2000 Bermuda was the world's third-largest insurance market, having doubled in size during the 1990s. In late 2001 the industry was under huge pressure from claims made in connection to the September terrorist attacks in the USA, although increased demand for insurance and reinsurance services led to a number of new companies being formed at the same time. According to Fitch, a US ratings agency, nearly 100 insurers started up in Bermuda in 2001–02. In March 2002 the US Department of the Treasury began an investigation into the reasons why many formerly US-based firms had relocated to the island. It was estimated that, in 1995, the entire financial sector contributed more than one-third of foreign exchange earnings. An estimated 18.7% of the employed labour force were engaged directly in the finance, insurance, real estate and business sectors in 2000. International business was estimated to account for 15.3% of GDP in 2002, when the number of companies registered in Bermuda totalled 13,318 (compared with 13,286 in 2001). The sector's real GDP was reported to have increased by some 0.9% in 2002. Another important source of income is the 'free-flag' registration of shipping, giving Bermuda the fifth largest such fleet in the world in 1995. In 1999 Bermuda passed the Electronic Transactions Act, designed to create an infrastructure to support the country's burgeoning 'e-commerce' sector, which was intended to become Bermuda's third major service industry, alongside financial services and tourism.

EXTERNAL TRADE

Bermuda is almost entirely dependent upon imports, has very few commodity exports and, therefore, consistently records a large visible trade deficit (B $668m. in 2000), which was reported to have increased to some $700m. in 2002. Receipts from the service industries normally ensure a surplus on the current account of the balance of payments ($197m. in 2000, reported to have decreased to around $70m. in 2002). The USA is the principal source of imports (72.8% of total imports in 1999) and the principal market for exports. Other important trading partners include the United Kingdom, Canada and France. The main exports are rum, flowers, medicinal and pharmaceutical products and the re-export of petroleum products. The principal imports are machinery and food, beverages and tobacco.

GOVERNMENT FINANCE

In 2000 Bermuda recorded a provisional budgetary surplus of some B $21.7m. A deficit of some $78.9m. was forecast for the 2003/04 financial year. The average annual rate of inflation was 2.6% in 1990–2001. The rate was estimated at 2.3% in 2002 and 3.6% in 2003. Some 1.5% of the labour force were registered unemployed in 1995, although unofficial sources estimated that the rate might be as high as 15%. In February 2001 the government figures indicated that unemployment had fallen for the first time since 1993. In 2000 foreign workers comprised some 19.5% of those employed in the Territory.

INTERNATIONAL ECONOMIC RELATIONS

Bermuda, the oldest colony of the United Kingdom, has the status of Overseas Territory in association with the European Union and has also been granted Designated Territory status by the British Government (this allows Bermudian-based funds and unit trusts access to the British market). Bermuda's financial services also benefit from a special tax treaty with the USA. In 2000 Bermuda joined the Caribbean Tourism Organization. In July 2003 Bermuda became an associate member of the Caribbean Community and Common Market (CARICOM).

SURVEY AND PROSPECTS

Bermudians enjoy a high standard of living, although addressing the inequality of the distribution of wealth is a key objective of the PLP Government that took office in mid-2003, as is local disquiet at the cost of property. The Government borrowed B $85m. to underpin the 2004/05 budget, which was mostly intended for expenditure on social projects, such as housing for the homeless and health services. Proximity to the USA and the parity of the US and Bermuda dollars help both tourist and financial industries, and Bermuda's status as a United Kingdom Overseas Territory remains a perceived contributor to political stability and financial integrity.

The Territory's insurance industry has experienced a period of rapid expansion and remains the most important component of the financial sector. Another rapidly growing sector in Bermuda are trust funds. Measures to assist the under-performing tourist industry (including a reduction in customs duties on certain goods) were introduced in budgets during the late 1990s. The ongoing decline in the sector, the island's biggest employer, was likely to also affect the retail sector, and to lead to an overall increase in unemployment. Although the number of cruise-ship passengers increased in 1998, 1999 and 2000, there was a large decrease (14.4%) in 2001, partly owing to the repercussions of the terrorist attacks on the USA in September. The number of air arrivals fell consistently during 1998–2001. In late 2002, in an effort to halt the consequent decline in tourist receipts, the Bermuda Alliance for Tourism launched a rebranding of Bermuda as a luxury destination, in order to attract higher-spending visitors. In August 2002 it was reported that visitor arrivals increased by 2.7% in the first half of the year. Bermuda received some 215,618 visitors during January–June, compared with 209,927 in the corresponding period of 2001. Air arrivals, however, regarded as a more accurate measure of the state of the tourist sector, decreased by 6.4%.

Despite the damage caused to the sector by Hurricane Fabian in September 2003, the 2004/05 budget projections included reduced expenditure on tourism; an indication that funding provided by the Government had been spent unwisely in the past. In the long term, the Government will need to address the differences between the requirements of the international businesses domiciled on Bermuda and the needs of Bermudians employed in other sectors. Concerns were also raised over how much further the international business sector could expand without putting excessive strain on the local infrastructure. Furthermore, commentators regarded the island's continuing heavy dependence on the tourism and 'offshore' finance sectors as potentially risky; in particular, discussion of changes to Bermuda's tax exemption laws resulted in several international business companies indicating their intentions to move to other regimes if financial conditions were to deteriorate, an eventuality which the island's high inflation rate made more likely. Repair costs for the infra-structural damage caused to the island by Hurricane Fabian were likely to total several million Bermudan dollars. The restoration of the Causeway, the main road to the international airport, was regarded as the priority of the Scott administration in order to keep the disruption caused to the tourism industry to a minimum. During her February budget address, the Minister of Finance, Paula Cox, predicted the economy would expand by between 2% and 2.5% in 2004.

Bhutan

The Kingdom of Bhutan lies in the Himalaya mountains. In 1949 an Indo-Bhutan Treaty of Friendship was concluded, whereby Bhutan agrees to seek the (non-binding) advice of the Indian Government regarding its foreign relations. A campaign of intimidation and violence directed by militant Nepalese against the Bhutanese Government in 1990 precipitated a complex refugee crisis that has remained intractable to the efforts of Bhutan and Nepal to resolve it. In 1998 King Jigme relinquished his role as Head of Government to the Council of Ministers. A committee to draft a written constitution was inaugurated in 2001. Bhutan's capital is Thimphu. Dzongkha is the official language.

Area and population
Area: 38,364 sq km
Population (mid-2002): 850,820
Population density (mid-2002): 21.9 per sq km
Life expectancy (years at birth, 2002): 61.3 (males 60.2; females 62.4)

Finance
GDP in current prices: 2002): US $594m. ($698 per head)
Real GDP growth (2002): 7.7%
Inflation (annual average, 2002): 2.5%
Currency: ngultrum

Economy

In 2002, according to estimates by the World Bank, Bhutan's gross national income (GNI), measured at average 2000–02 prices, was US \$505m., equivalent to \$590 per head. During 1990–2002, it was estimated, the population increased at an average annual rate of 3.0%, while gross domestic product (GDP) per head increased, in real terms, by an average of 3.4%. Overall GDP increased, in real terms, at an average annual rate of 6.5% in 1990–2002. Real GDP growth was estimated at 7.0% in 2001 and at 7.7% in 2002.

AGRICULTURE

Agriculture (including livestock and forestry) contributed an estimated 32.9% of GDP in 2002. About 94% of the economically active population were employed in the sector in the early 2000s. The principal sources of revenue in the agricultural sector are apples, oranges and cardamom. Timber production is also important; about 60% of the total land area is covered by forest. Agricultural GDP increased, in real terms, at an average annual rate of 3.4% in 1990–2002; it increased by an estimated 3.2% in 2001 and 2.5% in 2002.

INDUSTRY

Industry (including mining, manufacturing, utilities and construction) employed only about 0.9% of the labour force in 1990, but contributed an estimated 36.4% of GDP in 2002. Industrial GDP increased at an average annual rate of 9.3% in 1990–2002; growth in the sector was estimated at 13.4% in 2001, and at 12.0% in 2002.

Mining

Mining and quarrying contributed an estimated 1.7% of GDP in 2002. Calcium carbide is the principal mineral export (contributing 13.1% of total export revenue in 1998). Gypsum, coal, limestone, slate and dolomite are also mined. Mining GDP increased by an average rate of an estimated 9.9% per year in 1990–99.

Manufacturing

Manufacturing contributed an estimated 7.9% of GDP in 2002. The most important sector is cement production, and there is a calcium carbide plant and a ferro-alloy plant. Small-scale manufacturers produce, *inter alia*, textiles, soap, matches, candles and carpets. Manufacturing GDP increased at an average annual rate of an estimated 6.2% in 1990–2002; it declined by an estimated 6.2% in 2000, before increasing by 7.2% in 2001 and by 4.9% in 2002.

Energy

Energy is derived principally from hydroelectric power. The Chhukha hydroelectric power (HEP) project, with a generating capacity of about 336 MW, provides electricity for domestic consumption and also for export to India. The Indian-financed Tala HEP project, scheduled for completion in 2005, is to have an installed capacity of 1,020 MW. Expenditure on the project (including the cost of repairing damage by floods in 2000) was expected to reach some Nu 36,000m. The Kurichhu power project, completed in 2003, exported 90% of its electricity to India in the same year. In 2002/03 exports of electricity provided 43.7% of total export revenue, while in 1999 the cost of imports of diesel oil and petroleum was equivalent to 10.4% of total import costs.

SERVICES

The services sector, which employed only about 3.4% of the labour force in 1981/82, contributed an estimated 30.7% of GDP in 2002. The tourism sector has become increasingly significant. In 2003 the total number of foreign visitors was 6,093, and in that year receipts from tourism totalled US $8.4m. The GDP of the services sector increased at an average annual rate of an estimated 6.8% in 1990–2002; growth was estimated at 4.2% in 2001 and at 8.7% in 2002.

EXTERNAL TRADE

In the financial year ending 30 June 2002, according to the Asian Development Bank (ADB), Bhutan recorded a visible trade deficit of US $90.7m., and there was a deficit of $8.5m. on the current account of the balance of payments. In 2002 the principal source of imports (an estimated 75.0%) was India, which was also the principal market for exports (an estimated 93.5%). The principal exports in 1999 were electricity, calcium carbide, cement and particle board. The principal imports in 1997 were telecommunications equipment, rice and diesel oil.

GOVERNMENT FINANCE

The 2003/04 budget envisaged a deficit of Nu 383.2m. (revenue Nu 11,154.5m., expenditure Nu 11,537.7m.). Bhutan's total external debt amounted to US $265.2m. at the end of 2001, all of which was long-term public debt. In that year the cost of debt-servicing was equivalent to 3.3% of the value of exports of goods and services. The average annual rate of inflation was 8.1% in 1990–2002. Consumer prices increased by an annual average of 3.4% in 2001 and 2.5% in 2002. By 2000 the rising level of unemployment was beginning to cause concern; an estimated 50,000 school-leavers were expected to join the labour force over the next five years.

INTERNATIONAL ECONOMIC RELATIONS

Bhutan is a member of the UN Economic and Social Commission for Asia and the Pacific (ESCAP), of the Asian Development Bank (ADB), of the Colombo Plan and of the South Asian Association for Regional Co-operation (SAARC), all of which seek to improve regional co-operation, particularly in economic development.

SURVEY AND PROSPECTS

The Seventh Plan (1992–97) asserted seven main objectives: self-reliance, with emphasis on internal resource mobilization; sustainability, with emphasis on environmental protection; private-sector development; decentralization and popular participation; human resources' development; balanced development in all districts; and national security. The Eighth Plan (1997–2002) further refined the seven objectives of the Seventh Plan and explicitly added another: 'the preservation and promotion of cultural and traditional values'. The guiding goal was declared as the establishment of sustainability in development, while balancing achievements with the popular sense of contentment. Core areas were to be the further development of HEP, further industrialization, development of the infrastructure and social services, human resource development, and renewable natural resources. In June 2002 the Minister of Finance reported that actual expenditure on the Eighth Plan had reached around

Nu 40,000m., some 33% more than the original planned outlay. Nevertheless, the overall resource deficit was limited to Nu 307.8m., owing to a substantial increase of Nu 7,580m. in domestic revenues to Nu 20,580m. The Ninth Plan, effective from July, consisted, unlike previous plans, of separate programmes and budget allocations for individual sectors and dzongkhags (local districts). The dzongkhag plans became geog-based through the devolution of powers to GYT members, under new rules approved by the National Assembly at its 80th session. The central Government, however, maintained financial control in order to ensure budgetary discipline. Expenditure during these five years was expected to reach Nu 70,000m. Domestic revenue, which was forecast to reach Nu 30,000m., and external resources, amounting to an estimated Nu 35,000m. (of which Nu 20,000m. was requested as assistance from India) were expected to cover the proposed outlay. GDP was forecast to grow at an average annual rate of 6%–7% in 2002–07.

The production of low-cost electricity by the Chhukha HEP project helped to stimulate growth in the industrial sector in the 1990s. It was hoped that, on completion, Bhutan's Kurichhu and Tala schemes would earn sufficient revenue for Bhutan to achieve economic self-reliance. In mid-2001 new legislation was enacted to reform the electricity supply industry and to develop and regulate the country's HEP resources; a Bhutan Electricity Authority was established. Multilateral investment in Bhutan's financial sector was agreed by the Government for the first time in September 1998, when the ADB and the US Citibank purchased shares in the Bhutan National Bank. Two important measures were implemented in 1999: a formal personal income tax (to be levied only on wealthier Bhutanese) was introduced, and the country was opened up to foreign investment (foreign investors were to be permitted up to 51% ownership in a joint venture), although the stock exchange remained closed to external investors.

Bolivia

The Republic of Bolivia is situated in South America. Independence from Spanish rule was achieved in 1825. In 1969 the armed forces seized power and, until 1982, Bolivia remained, virtually uninterruptedly, under actual or quasi-military rule. (A coup staged in 1980 was the 189th in Bolivia's 154 years of independence.) Since the late 1980s civilian Governments have frequently been destabilized by severe economic problems; by unrest arising from coca-eradication programmes; by the prevalence of (often drugs-related) corruption; and by popular opposition to agrarian and free-market reforms. Bolivia's administrative capital is La Paz; its judicial capital is Sucre. The official languages are Aymará, Quechua and Spanish.

Area and population
Area: 1,098,581 sq km
Population (mid-2002): 8,697,080
Population density (mid-2002): 7.9 per sq km
Life expectancy (years at birth, 2002): 63.2 (males 61.8; females 64.7)

Finance
GDP in current prices: 2002): US $7,678m. ($883 per head)
Real GDP growth (2002): 2.5%
Inflation (annual average, 2002): 0.9%
Currency: boliviano

Economy

In 2002, according to World Bank estimates, Bolivia's gross national income (GNI), measured at average 2000–2002 prices, totalled US $7,857.7m., equivalent to about $900 per head (or $2,300 per head on an international purchasing-power parity basis). During 1990–2002, it was estimated, the population increased at an average annual rate of 2.4%, while gross domestic product (GDP) per head increased, in real terms, by an average of 1.0% per year. Bolivia's overall GDP increased, in real terms, at an average annual rate of 3.4% in 1990–2002; GDP increased by an estimated 2.8% in 2002.

AGRICULTURE

Agriculture (including forestry and fishing) contributed an estimated 15.4% of GDP, measured at constant prices, in 2002. In 2000 4.9% of the working population was employed in agriculture. Wood accounted for 1.8% of export earnings in 2002. The principal cash crops are soybeans (which accounted for 13.7% of export earnings in 2002), sugar, edible oils and coffee. Beef and hides are also important exports. In the period 1992–2001 agricultural GDP increased at an average annual rate of 2.8%; it rose by 3.8% in 2001 and by 0.6% in 2002.

INDUSTRY

Industry (including mining, manufacturing, construction and power) provided some 32.1% of GDP, measured at constant prices, in 2002. In 2000 28.2% of the working population was employed in industry. In 1992–2001 industrial GDP increased at an average annual rate of 3.5%; it decreased by 0.2% in 2001, before increasing by 0.9% in 2002.

Mining

Mining (including petroleum exploration) contributed an estimated 10.3% of GDP, measured at constant prices, in 2002 and employed about 1.7% of the working population in 2000. Investment in mineral exploitation increased 10-fold between 1991 and 1996. Funding for gold-exploration projects, however, decreased from US $45m. in 1996 to $20m. in 1997, while investment in polymetallic projects increased from $8m. in 1996 to $15m. in the following year. Investment in petroleum exploration totalled an estimated US $1m. in 2002, compared with $374m. in 1998. In 2002 nine foreign companies were involved in petroleum exploration in the country. Zinc, tin, silver, gold, lead and antimony are the major mineral exports. Tungsten and copper continue to be mined. Exports of zinc and tin earned an estimated $111.3m. and $48.5m., respectively, in 2002. In 1992–2001 the GDP of the mining sector increased at an average annual rate of 3.4%; mining GDP decreased by 1.4% in 2001, but increased by 4.0% in 2002.

Manufacturing

In 2002 manufacturing accounted for an estimated 18.0% of GDP, measured at constant prices, and in 2000 some 15.3% of the working population was employed in the sector. The GDP of this sector increased during 1992–2001 at an average annual rate of 3.5%; it rose by 1.8% in 2001 and by 2.2% in 2002. Measured by the value of output, the principal branches of manufacturing in 1998 were petroleum refining

(36.4%), food products (34.2%—including beverages 12.6% and meat preparations 8.0%) and cement (5.0%).

Energy

Energy is derived principally from hydroelectricity and natural gas. In 2002 electricity generation totalled 3,695m. kWh, of which 59% was provided by hydroelectric plants. In 2001 production of crude petroleum increased by 13.0%, to 11.4m. barrels; however, in 2002 this figure decreased by 0.8%, to 11.3m. barrels. In 2002 imports of fuels comprised an estimated 4.7% of total merchandise imports, compared with 6.2% in the previous year. Earnings from exports of petroleum accounted for 5.7% of the total in 2002. Exports of natural gas accounted for 20.1% of total export earnings in the same year. Reserves of natural gas were estimated at 18,300,000m. cu ft at the end of 2000. During the late 1990s several major new natural gas deposits were discovered, which significantly increased the country's total known reserves. In October 2003 a plan to export natural gas to the USA via the Chilean port of Patillos was suspended following public opposition.

SERVICES

The services sector accounted for some 52.4% of GDP, measured at constant prices, in 2002 and engaged 67.0% of the employed population in 2000. During the period 1992–2001 the GDP of this sector increased at an average annual rate of 4.2%; services GDP increased by 1.9% in 2001 and by 2.7% in 2002.

EXTERNAL TRADE

In 2002 Bolivia recorded a visible trade deficit of US $233.4m., and there was a deficit of $346.8m. on the current account of the balance of payments. In 2001 the main sources of imports were the USA (16.6%), Argentina (16.9%), Brazil (16.2%) and Chile (8.4%). Brazil, the USA, Colombia and the United Kingdom were the major recipients of Bolivian exports in 2001 (22.1%, 13.9%, 14.1% and 5.4%, respectively). The principal imports in that year included industrial materials and machinery, transport equipment and consumer goods. The principal legal exports were metallic minerals, natural gas, soybeans and wood. In 1997 the UN claimed that more than 50% of Bolivia's export earnings came from the illegal trade in coca and its derivatives (mainly cocaine).

GOVERNMENT FINANCE

In 2001 Bolivia's overall budget deficit amounted to 3,561.7m. bolivianos (equivalent to 6.7% of GDP). Bolivia's total external debt at the end of 2001 was US $4,682m., of which $3,116m. was long-term public debt. The cost of debt-servicing in that year was equivalent to 31.1% of the total value of exports of goods and services. In 1990–2002 the average annual rate of inflation was 7.7%. Consumer prices increased by an average of 1.6% in 2001 and 0.9% in 2002. In October 2002 an estimated 12.9% of the labour force in urban areas was unemployed.

INTERNATIONAL ECONOMIC RELATIONS

In May 1991 Bolivia was one of five Andean Pact countries to sign the Caracas Declaration providing the foundation for a common market. In October 1992 Bolivia officially joined the Andean free-trade area, removing tariff barriers to imports from Colombia, Ecuador and Venezuela. Bolivia also agreed to sign a free-trade accord with Mexico in September 1994. In January 1997 a free-trade agreement with

Mercosur, equivalent to associate membership of the organization, came into effect. In mid-1999 an agreement on the rationalization of their respective customs systems (thus moving closer to the formation of a regional free-trade area) was reached between Mercosur and the Andean Community; the two-year accord came into effect in August. Bolivia is a member of the Andean Community, and in 1989 the Andean Social Development Fund was established. The country is also a member of the Organization of American States (OAS), and of the Latin American Integration Association (ALADI). Bolivia became the 97th contracting party to GATT (which was superseded by the World Trade Organization, WTO, in 1995) in 1989.

SURVEY AND PROSPECTS

The development of Bolivia's fossil fuels export sector was seen as crucial to economic growth in the early 21st century; a series of concessions for oil and natural gas projects were awarded in the late 1990s. A major new gas deposit near Santa Cruz, with total reserves estimated at 1,700,000m. cu ft, was discovered in 1998. In July 2001 an international consortium was formed in order to construct a pipeline, some 640 km in length, from the Margarita gasfield to the Chilean port of Patillos, for export to the USA. However, public opposition led to the project being suspended October 2003. The future of the pipeline, which had been forecast to increase Bolivia's GDP by an additional 1% per year, appeared uncertain in early 2004, particularly in view of a competitive gas export project elsewhere.

Official development assistance was equivalent to an estimated 9.0% of GNP in 2003. The country's severe debt burden was widely acknowledged to be a major factor inhibiting economic growth in the late 1990s, and in recognition of this the World Bank and the IMF approved a debt-relief package worth US $760m. under the Heavily Indebted Poor Countries' Initiative, which was released in October 1998. A further disbursement was allocated under the scheme in 2001. However, economic growth in the early 21st century was adversely affected by social unrest, low commodity prices and coca eradication policies, which reduced incomes in the informal sector. Despite demands for increased public spending to alleviate social ills, successive Governments committed themselves to the maintenance of IMF-sponsored fiscal economic policies. The economy grew by 1.5% in 2001 and by a further 2.8% in 2002. Upon taking office in August 2002, President Sánchez de Lozada announced a five-year economic recovery plan that aimed to reduce unemployment and increase internal demand. The plan was to receive US $1,800m. in funding from the Corporación Andina de Formento—CAF (Andean Development Corporation) and $1,000m. in funding from both the Inter-American Development Bank (IDB) and the World Bank. However, plans to increase tax revenues to a sustainable level were abandoned in February 2003 following civil unrest. Despite this, in early April the Government reached a stand-by agreement with the IMF, worth US $118m., and in early July some $15m. in loans was disbursed. The new Government of Carlos Mesa Gisbert projected to reduce the fiscal deficit, in order to qualify for further IMF funding. In order to achieve this, in April 2004 the administration proposed imposing a 50% tax on future oil and gas production. However, despite a declaration by the new President to seek new agreements with the multilateral lenders in early 2004, the Government was likely to be constrained by the lack of progress on gas export projects. Further aid from the USA was likely to be dependent on the success of the coca-eradication programme, which the new Mesa Government declared it planned to reduce in size. GDP growth of 2.5% was forecast for 2003.

Bosnia and Herzegovina

Bosnia and Herzegovina is situated in south-eastern Europe. The state emerged in its present form from the conflict that, from 1991, engulfed the republics hitherto constituting Yugoslavia. In accordance with the General Framework Agreement for Peace in Bosnia and Herzegovina, signed in 1995, Bosnia and Herzegovina is a single state, which consists of two independent political entities: the Federation of Bosnia and Herzegovina, comprising the Bosniak (Muslim)- and Croat-majority areas, and the Serb Republic, comprising the Serb-majority area. The central Government of Bosnia and Herzegovina has a three-member collective presidency of one Bosniak, one Croat and one Serb. The capital is Sarajevo. The principal languages are Bosnian, Croatian and Serbian.

Area and population
Area: 51,129 sq km
Population (mid-2002): 4,120,642
Population density (mid-2002): 80.6 per sq km
Life expectancy (years at birth, 2002): 72.8 (males 69.3; females 76.4)

Finance
GDP in current prices: 2002): US $5,249m. ($1,274 per head)
Real GDP growth (2002): 3.9%
Inflation (2002): –0.2% in Federation of Bosnia and Herzegovina; 1.7% in the Serb Republic of Bosnia and Herzegovina
Currency: convertible marka

Economy

In 2002, according to World Bank estimates, Bosnia and Herzegovina's gross national income (GNI), measured at average 2000–02 prices, was US $5,233m., equivalent to $1,270 per head (or $5,800 on an international purchasing-power parity basis). During 1994–2002, it was estimated, the population of Bosnia and Herzegovina increased at an average annual rate of 1.6%, while gross domestic product (GDP) per head increased, in real terms, by an average of 18.7% per year. Overall GDP increased, in real terms, at an average annual rate of 20.5% in 1994–2002; real growth was 4.5% in 2001 and, according to IMF estimates, was 3.8% in 2002.

AGRICULTURE

Agriculture (including forestry and fishing) contributed an estimated 12.1% of GDP in 2002. In 2001 about 4.8% of the labour force were employed in the agricultural sector. The major agricultural products are tobacco and fruit, and the livestock sector is also significant. Imports of foodstuffs comprised 4.1% of total imports in 1997. According to World Bank estimates, the GDP of the agricultural sector increased, in real terms, by an annual average of 5.0% in 1994–2000. Total agricultural GDP, at current prices, increased from 1,114.2m. konvertibilna marka (KM or convertible marka) in 2001 to KM 1,143.6m. in 2002.

INDUSTRY

Industry (mining, manufacturing, utilities and construction) contributed an estimated 26.0% of GDP in Bosnia and Herzegovina in 2002. Some 47.5% of the labour force were employed in the industrial sector in 1990. According to World Bank estimates, industrial GDP increased, in real terms, by an annual average of 26.0% in 1994–2000. Total industrial GDP, at current prices, increased from KM 2,395.7m. in 2001 to KM 2,457.6m. in 2002.

Mining

The mining sector contributed 2.3% of GDP in 2002. Bosnia and Herzegovina possesses extensive mineral resources, including iron ore, lignite, copper, lead, zinc and gold. Total mining GDP, at current prices, increased from KM 208.6m. in 2001 to KM 221.0m. in 2002.

Manufacturing

Manufacturing contributed 12.3% of GDP in 2002. The manufacturing sector is based largely on the processing of iron ore, non-ferrous metals, coal, and wood and paper products. Manufacturing GDP increased, in real terms, by an annual average of 17.2% in 1994–2000. Total manufacturing GDP, at current prices, increased from KM 1,073.5m. in 2001 to KM 1,162.0m. in 2002.

Energy

The civil conflict resulted in the destruction of much of the electric power system in Bosnia and Herzegovina. Prior to the conflict, the system comprised 13 hydroelectric installations and 12 coal- and lignite-fuelled thermal power installations. In 2000 50.7% of electricity production was derived from coal and 48.8% from hydroelectric power. Electric power accounted for 3.2% of total imports in 1997.

SERVICES

The services sector contributed an estimated 61.9% of GDP in 2002. According to World Bank estimates, the GDP of the services sector increased, in real terms, by an annual average of 35.9% in 1994–2000. Total services GDP, at current prices, increased from KM 5,092.1m. in 2001 to KM 5,840.6m. in 2002.

EXTERNAL TRADE

In 2002 Bosnia and Herzegovina recorded a visible trade deficit of US $3,403.7m., and there was a deficit of $2,138.5m. on the current account of the balance of payments. In 2002 the principal source of imports was Croatia (which accounted for 16.3% of total imports); other important suppliers were Germany, Slovenia, Italy, Yugoslavia (now Serbia and Montenegro), Hungary and Austria. In that year the main market for exports was Yugoslavia (which accounted for 20.1% of total exports); other significant purchasers were Croatia, Germany, Italy, Switzerland and Slovenia. The principal exports in 1997 were wood and paper products, iron and steel, electric power and fabricated metal products. The main imports in that year were foodstuffs and electric power.

GOVERNMENT FINANCE

Bosnia and Herzegovina's overall budget deficit for 2002 was estimated at KM 489.0m., equivalent to 4.5% of GDP. The country's total external debt was estimated at US $2,226m. at the end of 2001 (of which $2,045m. was public debt), and the cost of debt-servicing was equivalent to about 19.1% of the value of exports of goods and services. Consumer prices, according to the IMF, declined by an average of 0.3% in 1998, and increased by 3.4% in 1999, by 5.1% in 2000 and by an estimated 3.1% in 2001; the inflation rate was estimated at only 0.3% in 2002. The rate of unemployment was estimated at 20% in 2003.

INTERNATIONAL ECONOMIC RELATIONS

Bosnia and Herzegovina became a member of the IMF in December 1995 and was admitted to the World Bank in April 1996. In July 1999 the first summit meeting of the Stability Pact for South-Eastern Europe took place in Bosnia and Herzegovina, with the aim of adopting a common strategy for regional stability.

SURVEY AND PROSPECTS

The civil conflict in 1992–95 resulted in extensive damage to the economy. Following the signature of the Dayton peace agreement in December 1995, economic reconstruction commenced, and Bosnia and Herzegovina was admitted to the IMF. An early priority of the reconstruction programme was the resolution of the considerable foreign debt that Bosnia and Herzegovina had inherited from the former Yugoslavia. The new national currency, fixed at par with the German Deutsche Mark, was officially introduced in June 1998. In October agreement was reached with the 'Paris

Club' of creditor governments on the reduction of external debt. Following large inflows of foreign assistance, the economy rapidly recovered from the effects of the civil conflict under the IMF-supported economic reconstruction and development programme, although unemployment remained high, and corruption and poor customs controls continued to contribute to a major loss of revenue (and consequently to the increasing current-account deficit and public debt). In addition, performance varied widely in each of the two entities, with a high level of inflation and declining industrial production recorded in the Serb Republic. A further stand-by arrangement was approved by the IMF in August 2002 (and subsequently extended until the end of February 2004).

Despite the replacement of the reformist-led coalitions in both entities at elections in October 2002, the implementation of measures urged by the international community continued, under pressure from the High Representative. During 2002 the High Representative imposed a series of economic regulations, with the ultimate aim of unifying principal sectors, such as telecommunications, banking, and tax and customs administration, throughout the country, as a prerequisite for membership of the European Union (EU). At the end of 2003 an IMF mission concluded that real GDP had increased three-fold since 1995, while the rate of inflation had declined steadily. The most significant progress was demonstrated by the return of large numbers of refugees and internally displaced civilians, which was supported by foreign remittances. Nine regional free-trade agreements were concluded in 2002–03, and the country's admission to the World Trade Organization was envisaged for 2004. However, the continuing restrictive bureaucracy was widely perceived as a impediment to rapid structural reforms and stimulation of private investment was necessary to compensate for an anticipated sharp decline in international assistance, following the sustained recovery. Principal reforms to be implemented in co-operation with the IMF included the introduction of value-added tax by mid-2005 to improve revenue levels, the continuation of regulatory measures in the banking sector (initiated in 2003) and further privatization. Negotiations with the EU on the signature of a Stabilization and Association Agreement were scheduled to commence in 2004, subject to a favourable review of progress made in undertaking stipulated reforms, particularly essential restructuring of the intelligence services and armed forces, and also to the Government's co-operation with the International Criminal Tribunal for the former Yugoslavia.

Botswana

The Republic of Botswana is situated in southern Africa. Botswana was formerly Bechuanaland, which became a British protectorate in 1885. Bechuanaland was made independent of British High Commission rule in 1963. In 1966 Bechuanaland became the independent Republic of Botswana, within the Commonwealth, with Sir Seretse Khama, the leader of the Bechuanaland Democratic Party (BDP) as the country's first President. The BDP, restyled the Botswana Democratic Party at independence, won the largest number of seats in the territory's first legislative elections, held in 1965, and in all subsequent elections. Botswana's capital is Gaborone. English is the official language, and Setswana the national language.

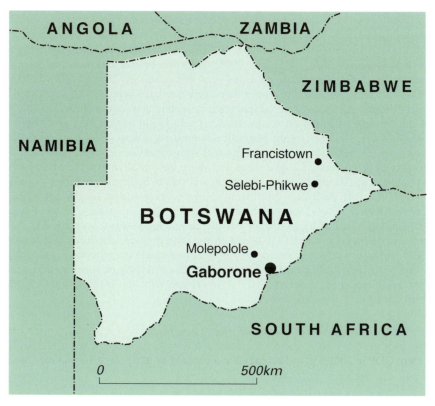

Area and population
Area: 581,730 sq km
Population (mid-2002): 1,711,770
Population density (mid-2002): 2.9 per sq km
Life expectancy (years at birth, 2002): 40.4 (males 40.2; females 40.6)

Finance

GDP in current prices: 2002): US $5,188m. ($3,031 per head)
Real GDP growth (2002): 3.5%
Inflation (annual average, 2002): 8.1%
Currency: pula

Economy

In 2002, according to estimates by the World Bank, Botswana's gross national income (GNI), measured at average 2000–02 prices, was US $5,103m., equivalent to $2,980 per head (or $7,770 on an international purchasing-power parity basis). During 1990–2002, it was estimated, the population increased by an average of 2.5% per year, while gross domestic product (GDP) per head increased, in real terms, by an average of 2.7% per year. Overall GDP increased, in real terms, at an average annual rate of 5.3% in 1990–2002; growth in 2002 was 3.5%.

AGRICULTURE

Agriculture (including hunting, forestry and fishing) contributed 2.6% of GDP in 2001/02, according to provisional figures, and engaged 15.6% of the employed labour force in 1996. The principal agricultural activity is cattle-raising (principally beef production), which supports about one-half of the population and contributes more than 80% of agricultural GDP. As a member of the African, Caribbean and Pacific (ACP) group of states and a signatory to successive Lomé Conventions, Botswana has traditionally enjoyed preferential trade relations with the European Union (EU), including a quota to supply 18,910 metric tons of beef per year; however, under the Cotonou Agreement, which was concluded in mid-2000, the quota was to be phased out by 2007, when Botswana and the other ACP states were to establish reciprocal trade arrangements with the EU in order to achieve compatibility with the rules of the World Trade Organization. The main subsistence crops are vegetables, pulses and roots and tubers, although Botswana is not self-sufficient in basic foods. Agricultural GDP decreased at an average annual rate of 0.6% in 1990–2002; however, growth of 3.4% was recorded in 2002.

INDUSTRY

Industry (including mining, manufacturing, construction and power) engaged 25.6% of the employed labour force in 1996 and, according to provisional figures, provided 48.9% of GDP in 2001/02. Industrial GDP increased at an average annual rate of 4.6% in 1990–2002; growth in 2002 was 6.0%.

Mining

Mining contributed 36.3% of GDP in 2001/02, according to provisional figures, although the sector engaged only 4.3% of the employed labour force in 1996. In terms of value, Botswana is the world's largest producer of diamonds (which accounted for 84.5% of export earnings in 2001, according to provisional figures); copper-nickel matte and soda ash are also exported. In addition, coal, gold, cobalt and salt are mined, and there are known reserves of plutonium, asbestos, chromite, fluorspar, iron, manganese, potash, silver, talc and uranium. In 1998 a new minerals code included measures to encourage non-diamond mining projects. According to provisional official figures, the GDP of the mining sector increased, in real terms, at an average annual rate of 4.0% in 1991/92–2001/02; mining GDP increased by 17.2% in 2000/01, but declined by 3.1% in 2001/02.

Manufacturing

Manufacturing engaged 8.5% of the employed labour force in 1996 and provided 4.5% of GDP in 2001/02, according to provisional figures. The GDP of the manufacturing sector increased at an average annual rate of 4.1% in 1990–2002; growth in 2002 was 3.6%.

Energy

Energy is derived principally from fuel wood and coal; the use of solar power is currently being promoted as an alternative source of energy. According to provisional figures, imports of fuels accounted for 6.7% of the value of total imports in 2001.

SERVICES

The services sector contributed 48.6% of GDP in 2001/02, according to provisional figures, and engaged 58.7% of the employed labour force in 1996. Within the sector, tourism is of considerable importance, being the third largest source of total foreign exchange. The GDP of the services sector increased at an average annual rate of 7.6% in 1990–2002; growth in 2002 was 4.5%.

EXTERNAL TRADE

In 1999 Botswana recorded a visible trade surplus of US $674.5m., and there was a surplus of $516.8m. on the current account of the balance of payments. In 2001 countries of the Southern African Customs Union (SACU—see below) provided 77.6% of imports. European countries (principally the United Kingdom) took 89.0% of exports in 2001; other important purchasers were the countries of SACU. The principal exports in that year were diamonds and copper-nickel matte. The principal imports were machinery and electrical equipment, food, beverages and tobacco, vehicles and transport equipment, and chemicals and rubber products.

GOVERNMENT FINANCE

In the financial year to 31 March 2003 the central Government recorded a budgetary deficit of an estimated P2,169.1m. Botswana's external debt totalled US $369.9m. at the end of 2001, of which $349.2m. was long-term public debt. In that year the cost of debt-servicing was equivalent to 1.7% of the value of exports of goods and services. The average annual rate of inflation was 9.9% in 1990–2002; consumer prices increased by an annual average of 8.1% in 2002. Some 15.8% of the labour force were unemployed in 2000.

INTERNATIONAL ECONOMIC RELATIONS

Botswana is a member of the Southern African Development Community (SADC) and (with Lesotho, Namibia, South Africa and Swaziland) of SACU. In September 2000 SADC commenced the implementation phase of its Protocol on Trade, which provided for the establishment of a regional free-trade area; all trade tariffs between member countries were to be eliminated gradually over a 12-year period.

SURVEY AND PROSPECTS

Botswana's high rate of growth during the 1980s was based predominantly on the successful exploitation of diamonds and other minerals. However, domestic factors, such as a vulnerability to drought, in conjunction with the world-wide economic recession of the early 1990s, depressed Botswana's economy and exemplified the need to reduce dependence on diamond-mining, to diversify agricultural production and to broaden the manufacturing base. The encouragement of private-sector growth was a key element of Botswana's eighth National Development Plan (1997/98–2002/03); privatizations were planned in the telecommunications, utilities and aviation sectors. However, there were considerable delays in the divestment of state-owned enterprises, and in early February 2004 the Government suspended its search for a strategic partner for Air Botswana, which was to be the country's first parastatal to undergo privatization, after the only two qualified bidders withdrew from negotiations. The ninth National Development Plan (2003/04–2008/09) was presented in 2002; the Government's main priority was to effect economic diversification by embracing recent technological developments. Diamond exports declined in 1998, but recovered in 1999, and increased again in 2000, when the expansion of the Orapa diamond mine was completed. However, Botswana's persistent dependence on the diamond sector has remained a source of potential weakness, and in 2001 demand fell, as global economic growth slowed, particularly in the USA; none the less, revenue increased, largely as a result of the pula losing value against the dollar.

In 2002 government revenues from diamond sales declined, despite an increase in production. A new diamond mine commenced operations in north-eastern Botswana in October of that year, and in late 2003 a large kimberlite deposit was discovered in the north-west of the country. Furthermore, a new gold mine at Mupane in north-eastern Botswana was expected to begin production in late 2004, with projected output of 100,000 troy oz per year. In 2000, as part of efforts to diversify the economic base and create sustainable employment, the Government established an International Financial Services Centre (IFSC). Botswana's proximity to South Africa, substantial tax incentives, and the stability of a well-established democratic system of government were all expected to attract international financial companies to the country, and by November 2002 11 projects had been approved for operation under the IFSC. In 2003 the Government issued bonds for the first time in order to raise additional revenue and encourage the development of the financial services sector. Meanwhile, the HIV/AIDS pandemic represented a significant threat to continued economic growth, diminishing the work-force and depleting government resources through expenditure on projects to counter the disease. With more than one-third of the population estimated to be infected with HIV, estimated average life expectancy had declined from around 60 years in the early 1990s to 40 years by 2002, and was expected to fall to about 36 years by 2005.

Brazil

The Federative Republic of Brazil lies in South America. Brazil achieved independence from Portugal in 1822. From 1964 until 1985, when Tancredo Neves was elected President, Brazil was under military rule. Neves died before taking office. His replacement, José Sarney, was succeeded in 1990 by Fernando Collor de Mello, who resigned in 1992 and was replaced by Itamar Franco. In 1993 voters endorsed the retention of the presidential system. In 1998 Fernando Henrique Cardoso was re-elected for a second consecutive presidential term. He was succeeded in 2002 by Luiz Inácio (Lula) da Silva of the Partido dos Trabalhadores. Brasília is the capital. The official language is Portuguese.

Area and population
Area: 8,547,404 sq km
Population (mid-2002): 174,485,408
Population density (mid-2002): 20.4 per sq km
Life expectancy (years at birth, 2002): 68.9 (males 65.7 females 72.3)

Finance

GDP in current prices: 2002): US $452,387m. ($2,593 per head)
Real GDP growth (2002): 1.5%
Inflation (annual average, 2002): 8.4%
Currency: real

Economy

In 2002, according to estimates by the World Bank, Brazil's gross national income (GNI), measured at average 2000–02 prices, was US $497,393m., equivalent to US $2,850 per head (or $7,250 per head on an international purchasing-power parity basis). During 1990–2002, it was estimated, the population increased at an average annual rate of 1.4%, while gross domestic product (GDP) per head increased, in real terms, by an average of 1.1% per year. Overall GDP increased, in real terms, at an average annual rate of 2.5% in 1990–2002; real GDP grew by 1.5% in 2002.

AGRICULTURE

Agriculture (including hunting, forestry and fishing) engaged 18.7% of the economically active population, according to census figures, in 2000, and, according to the World Bank, contributed 9.2% of GDP in 2001. The principal cash crops are soya beans, coffee, tobacco, sugar cane and cocoa beans. Subsistence crops include wheat, maize, rice, potatoes, beans, cassava and sorghum. Beef and poultry production are also important, as is fishing (particularly tuna, crab and shrimp). In September 2003 a temporary decree permitted the planting of transgenic soy for the 2004 harvest; it is anticipated that permanent legislation will follow. During 1990–2001, according to the World Bank, agricultural GDP increased at an average annual rate of 3.4%. Agricultural GDP increased by 9.3% in 2000 and by an estimated 10.0% in 2001.

INDUSTRY

Industry (including mining, manufacturing, construction and power) employed 21.4% of the working population in 2000 and, according to the World Bank, provided 33.4% of GDP in 2001. During 1990–2001 industrial GDP increased at an average annual rate of 1.9%. Industrial GDP grew by 4.9% in 2000; however, a decline of 0.4% was recorded in the sector in 2001.

Mining

Mining contributed 1.6% of GDP in 1999. Mining GDP grew by 3.9% in 2001 and by 10.4% in 2002. The major mineral exports are iron ore (haematite—in terms of iron content, Brazil is the largest producer in the world), manganese, tin and aluminium. Gold, phosphates, platinum, uranium, copper and coal are also mined. In 1990 deposits of niobium, thought to be the world's largest, were discovered in the state of Amazonas. Brazil's reserves of petroleum were estimated at 9m. 42-gallon barrels in 2000.

Manufacturing

Manufacturing contributed 20.7% of GDP in 2001. In 2000 the sector engaged 13.5% of the total employed population. There is considerable state involvement in a broad range of manufacturing activity. While traditionally-dominant areas, including textiles and clothing, footwear and food- and beverage-processing, continue to contribute a large share to the sector, more recent developments in the sector have resulted in the emergence of machinery and transport equipment (including road vehicles and components, passenger jet aircraft and specialist machinery for the petroleum industry), construction materials (especially iron and steel), wood and sugar cane derivatives, and chemicals and petrochemicals as significant new manufacturing activities. According to the World Bank, manufacturing GDP declined at an average rate of 0.1% per year in 1990–2001; however, the sector's GDP grew by 6.1% in 2000 and by 0.6% in 2001.

Energy

In 2000 87.3% of total electricity production was provided by hydroelectric power. Other energy sources, including petroleum, coal and nuclear power, accounted for the remaining 12.7%. Attempts to exploit further the country's vast hydroelectric potential (estimated at 213,000 MW) were encouraged by the completion of ambitious dam projects at Itaipú, on the border with Paraguay (expected to produce as much as 35% of Brazil's total electricity requirements when fully operational), and at Tucuruí, on the Tocantins river. In late 2000 it was announced that plans were under way further to expand the hydroelectric power-station at Itaipú, increasing its generating capacity to 14,000 MW. By 1999 electricity production by hydroelectric sources was more than 50 times that of 1989. Following energy shortages caused by a drought in 2001, there were plans for the construction of thermal power-stations; however, by early 2004 the new plants had yet to be built and the country was still vulnerable to shortages. The Angra I nuclear power plant, inaugurated in 1985, has subsequently operated only intermittently, while financial constraints hindered the completion of the Angra II plant, which became operational in mid-2000, preventing further development of the country's nuclear programme. However, in August 2003 it was announced that Brazil would begin to produce enriched uranium in 2004. In the same month the Government made public its plan to construct a natural gas pipeline connecting the Urucu natural gas reserve in Amazonia to neighbouring cities. The pipeline is expected to carry 2.2m. cu m per day when it becomes operational in 2006. Fuel imports comprised 14.4% of the value of total merchandise imports in 2001.

SERVICES

The services sector contributed an estimated 57.4% of GDP in 2001 and engaged 59.9% of the employed labour force in 2000. According to the World Bank, the GDP of the services sector increased at an average rate of 2.6% per year in 1990–2001. The GDP of the services sector was estimated to have increased by 1.5% in 2001.

EXTERNAL TRADE

In 2002 Brazil recorded a trade surplus of US $13,143m. There was a deficit of US $7,696m. on the current account of the balance of payments. In 2002 the principal source of imports (21.8%) was the USA, which was also the principal market for exports (25.4%). Other major trading partners were Germany, Argentina, Japan, the Netherlands, Mexico and the People's Republic of China. The principal exports in 2001 were machinery and transport equipment, food and live animals and basic manufactures. The principal imports in the same year were machinery and transport equipment, chemical products and mineral fuels (notably petroleum).

GOVERNMENT FINANCE

The 2002 federal budget recorded expenditure of R $289,596m. and revenue of R $321,855m. Brazil's external debt was R $226,362m. in 2001, of which US $189,748m. was long-term debt. In that year the cost of debt-servicing was equivalent to 75.4% of the value of exports of goods and services. The annual rate of inflation averaged 57.4% in 1993–2002. Consumer prices increased by an average of 6.8% in 2001 and by 8.4% in 2002. Official figures indicated an average unemployment rate of 7.1% of the labour force in 2003. (Unemployment in São Paulo rose sharply from 6.4% in 2001 to 8.4% in 2002.)

INTERNATIONAL ECONOMIC RELATIONS

Brazil is a member of ALADI, Mercosul/Mercosur, the Association of Tin Producing Countries (ATPC) and the Cairns Group. Brazil also joined the Comunidade dos Países de Língua Portuguesa (CPLP), founded in 1996.

SURVEY AND PROSPECTS

In October 1998, following his re-election, President Cardoso announced details of a three-year programme of fiscal adjustment, including drastic cuts in budgetary expenditure. In January 1999, however, the devaluation of the Brazilian currency (thus abandoning the exchange-rate policy agreed with the IMF) precipitated a period of renewed capital flight, seriously depleting the country's reserves and leading to turmoil on international financial markets. Brazil and the IMF subsequently reached agreement on a revised programme for 1999–2001, thus permitting lending to resume. However, by November 2000 the level of public debt had reached 48.5% of GDP, above the target set by the IMF. Moreover, the recovery that followed the 1999 crisis was adversely affected in 2001 by the effects of the terrorist attacks in the USA in September and by the financial crisis in Argentina, as well as by high petroleum prices and by the need to ration electricity. Inflationary pressure increased throughout the year, leading to high interest rates, which reached 19% in July 2001. In an attempt to increase confidence in the country's economy, and also partly because of Brazil's strong overall economic performance, in August a US $15,000m. loan was approved by the IMF. In exchange, Cardoso's Government was required to reduce expenditure by some US $4,120m. in 2001–02.

The predicted success of the left-wing candidate Lula da Silva in the months preceding the presidential elections of October 2002 resulted in anxiety in international financial circles about the possibility of increased government expenditure should he come to power. This, coupled with a first-quarter decrease in GDP, led President Cardoso in June to draw US $10,000m. of the previously-negotiated IMF loan, in order to replenish reserves and buy back foreign debt. In mid-July the Central Bank unexpectedly cut interest rates, in an attempt to stimulate growth before the elections, while the Government further reduced budgetary expenditure. Nevertheless, the economy continued to flounder, and in August the IMF announced a rescue package of US $30,400m., part of a 15-month stand-by agreement until December 2003. The loan was the largest ever disbursed by the Fund. The deal was dependent on the agreement of all presidential candidates to maintain current fiscal policy and commit to a primary budget surplus of 3.75% of GDP in 2003. Although the IMF loan settled financial markets temporarily, the real continued to depreciate.

During the first year of his Government President da Silva continued the economic policies of the previous administration, maintaining high interest rates and keeping to strict inflation targets in an attempt to stabilize Brazil's economy. Many of the new President's traditional supporters were dismayed at his decision to make economic, not social, policy a priority in his first year in office; however, the international community and the IMF were impressed by the new Government's economic orthodoxy. In early 2003 the Central Bank raised the base interest rate from 20% to 26.5%, although by the beginning of 2004 the rate had fallen to 16.5%. Foreign investment decreased in the first six months of 2003. Between January and June of that year there was only US $3,500m. of direct foreign investment, compared with US $9,600m. in the same period in 2002; however, investments recovered in the second half of the year. In late 2003 a new loan, worth US $14,800m., was negotiated with the IMF, although Minister of Finance Antônio Palôcci insisted that the loan was only a precautionary measure and not intended for use. In return, Brazil agreed to maintain a primary budget surplus equivalent to 4.25% of GDP. In December the Congresso approved the 2004 budget, which sought to increase government spending and reduce inflation. The budget anticipated revenue of R $402,200m. and expenditure of R $299,600m.

Moves towards a proposed Free Trade Area of the Americas (FTAA), first broached at the First Summit of the Americas held in Miami, USA, in 1994 and to be concluded by 2005, faltered in 2002 and 2003 with Brazil's resistance to open its markets further without receiving greater access to US markets in return; specifically targeted were agricultural products such as orange juice, sugar, cotton and soya, which enjoyed protection in the USA. Soya was a cause of specific complaint, with the Brazilian Government claiming that though farm subsidies were not open to renegotiation until 2004, they should be maintained at 1994 levels (soya was unsubsidized in the USA in 1994 and by 2002 received some US $4,000m. in support). The protected US steel industry was another source of contention. Following the failure of the fifth WTO Ministerial Conference, in Cancún, Mexico, in September 2003, progress between Brazil and the USA on the FTAA seemed increasingly unlikely; however, in November the two countries reached an accord whereby countries would be able to opt out of individual clauses. The agreement allowed negotiations to proceed in 2004.

British Virgin Islands

The British Virgin Islands comprise more than 60 islands and cays at the northern end of the Leeward Islands. They were annexed by the British in 1672, and in 1872 became part of the British colony of the Leeward Islands. The Governor of the Leeward Islands administered the British Virgin Islands until 1960, when an appointed Administrator assumed direct responsibility. A new Constitution was introduced in 1967. In 1977 an amended Constitution gave more extensive internal self-government. The islands are a United Kingdom Overseas Territory. Road Town is the capital. The official language is English.

Area and population
Area: 153 sq km
Population (1999): 19,864
Population density (1999): 129.8 per sq km
Life expectancy (years at birth, 2001): 75.6 (males 74.6; females 76.6)

Finance
GDP in current prices: 2000): US $683m. ($33,640 per head)
Inflation (annual average, 2001): 3.1%
Currency: US dollar

Economy

In 2002, according to estimates by the Caribbean Development Bank (CDB), the British Virgin Islands' gross domestic product (GDP) was US $780.49m., equivalent to some $37,162 per head. The population doubled during 1984–94 to 17,903, primarily owing to a large influx of immigrants from other Caribbean Islands, the United Kingdom and the USA. During 1991–2002, it was estimated, the population increased at an average annual rate at 2.1%, while GDP increased, in real terms, by some 4% per year during 1995–99, according to reports. Growth was reported to be 5.1% in 2002.

AGRICULTURE

Agriculture (including forestry and fishing) contributed 1.6% of GDP in 2002, and engaged 1.9% of those in paid employment in 1996. The Territory produces fruit and vegetables for domestic consumption or export to the US Virgin Islands, and some sugar cane (for the production of rum). Food imports accounted for 18.9% of total import costs in 1997. The fishing industry caters for local consumption and export, and provides a sporting activity for tourists, although the Government was looking to develop deep-sea fishing commercially for domestic and export markets.

INDUSTRY

Industry (including mining, manufacturing, construction and public utilities) accounted for 5.2% of GDP in 2002 and engaged 21.3% of the employed labour force in 1996. The mining sector is small (0.3% of GDP in 2002), consisting of the extraction of materials for the construction industry and of some salt. Manufacturing, which provided 0.8% of GDP in 2002, consists mainly of light industry; there is one rum distillery, two factories for the production of ice, some plants producing concrete blocks and other construction materials, small boat manufacture and various cottage industries. Construction activity accounted for 2.4% of GDP in 2002. Most energy requirements must be imported (mineral fuels accounted for an estimated 8.5% of total imports in 1997).

SERVICES

Services, primarily tourism and financial services, constitute the principal economic sector of the British Virgin Islands, contributing 93.3% of GDP in 2001. The tourist industry earned some US $313.9m. in 2002, and employed one-third of the working population, directly or indirectly, in 1995. The British Virgin Islands is the largest 'bareboat' chartering centre in the Caribbean, and approximately 60% of stop-over visitors stay aboard yachts. Nevertheless, in 2002 the restaurants and hotels sector contributed 13.5% of GDP. The number of stop-over visitors increased by an average of 13.6% per year in 1992–99, reaching 295,600 in 2001 (most of whom were from the USA); the ratio of tourists to local population is therefore higher than at any other Caribbean destination. The 2001 budget included $53m. to be spent on renovations to the Beef Island airport, in addition to further investment to the country's infrastructure, which was expected to provide a boost to tourism revenue in the second half of the decade.

Financial services expanded rapidly as a result of legislative measures adopted in 1984, and in 2000 the 'offshore' sector contributed over half of direct government revenue (some US $100m.). There were a cumulative total of 360,000 International Business Company (IBC) registrations in the islands 1984–2002. The islands have also recorded significant growth in the establishment of mutual funds and of insurance companies. In January 2002 the Government created the Financial Services Commission, an independent regulatory authority for the sector, in order to meet international demands for a clear separation between the Government and financial services regulation.

EXTERNAL TRADE

In 1999 the British Virgin Islands recorded a trade deficit of US $206.3m. (exports were worth some 1.0% of imports); the deficit was estimated to have increased to $224.7m. in 2001, remaining at around that level in 2002–03. The trade deficit is normally offset by receipts from tourism, development aid, remittances from islanders working abroad (many in the US Virgin Islands) and, increasingly, from the offshore financial sector. The principal sources of imports (most of the islands' requirements must be imported) are the USA (which provided 56.9% of imports in 1997), Trinidad and Tobago, Antigua and Barbuda, and also the United Kingdom. The principal markets for the limited amount of exports are the US Virgin Islands and the USA and Puerto Rico; rum is exported to the USA. Machinery and transport equipment are the main import (accounting for 28.3% of total imports in 1997), and fruit and vegetables, rum, sand and gravel the main exports.

GOVERNMENT FINANCE

The budget for the 2001/02 financial year projected revenue of US $191.5m. against recurrent expenditure of $142.2m., amounting to a projected surplus of $49.3m. The surplus was to be allocated to capital expenditure and the national relief fund. In 1995/96 there was a deficit of $22m. on the current account of the balance of payments. British budgetary support ceased in 1977, but the United Kingdom grants assistance for capital development. At the end of 2001 total external debt was estimated to be $49.0m., a decrease of 32.1% from 2001. In 1998 the territory received $1.2m. in development assistance. Central Government debt to GDP ratio was estimated at 10.0% in the same year. The average annual rate of inflation was 4.1% in 1990–2001; consumer prices increased by an average of 3.1% in 2001 and by an estimated 0.4% in 2002. The rate of unemployment stood at around 3.6% in 2002, according to the Caribbean Development Bank.

INTERNATIONAL ECONOMIC RELATIONS

The British Virgin Islands became an associate member of the Caribbean Community and Common Market (CARICOM) in 1991; it is a member of CARICOM's Caribbean Development Bank (CDB) and an associate member of the Organisation of Eastern Caribbean States (OECS). In economic affairs the Territory has close affiliations with the neighbouring US Virgin Islands, and uses US currency. As a dependency of the United Kingdom, the islands have the status of Overseas Territory in association with the European Union (EU).

SURVEY AND PROSPECTS

The economy of the British Virgin Islands is largely dominated by tourism and by the provision of international financial services. The 'offshore' financial sector, which developed rapidly in the last two decades of the 20th century, is an important source of employment and provided 51% of direct government revenue in 1998. Despite ongoing efforts to attract insurance and trust companies to the islands, it was estimated that in early 2000 IBCs still accounted for around 90% of government revenues from financial services. International attempts, notably by the Organisation for Economic Co-operation and Development, to encourage the reform of 'offshore' financial centres are therefore of great concern to the British Virgin Islands, particularly as IBCs, which are not taxed and which are not obliged to disclose their directors or shareholders, have been singled out for particular criticism. Nevertheless, revenue from annual licence fees paid by 'offshore' companies remained strong in the early 20th century.

Despite the rise of the financial sector, tourism remains the most important sector of the economy, as the construction and retail sectors, amongst others, are to a certain extent dependent on its performance. In the long term, however, the Government hoped to encourage greater diversification of the economy, in order to reduce reliance on tourism and financial services, both of which remained vulnerable to external pressures. Although the aftermath of the September 2001 terrorist attacks in the USA adversely affected tourism revenues in 2002, which was only partially offset by increased activity in the 'offshore' banking sector, the economy performed strongly in 2003. In March 2004, in his 2004/05 budget address, the Minister of Finance, Health and Welfare, announced the introduction of an emergency reserve fund to protect the vulnerable economy. The surplus for the financial year was projected at US $11.9m., while the economy was estimated to have grown by 3.2% in 2003. Growth of 2.7% was forecast for 2004.

Brunei

The Sultanate of Brunei lies in South-East Asia. Brunei, a traditional Islamic monarchy, formerly included most of the coastal regions of North Borneo and Sarawak. During the 19th century large areas of territory were ceded to the United Kingdom, reducing the sultanate to its present size. In 1888 Brunei became a British Protected State. The United Kingdom remained responsible for Brunei's defence and external affairs until the Sultanate's declaration of independence in 1984. In 1967 Sir Omar Ali Saifuddin III, who had been Sultan since 1950, abdicated in favour of his son, Hassanal Bolkiah. The capital is Bandar Seri Begawan. The principal language is Malay.

Area and population
Area: 5,765 sq km
Population (mid-2002): 350,630
Population density (mid-2002): 60.8 per sq km
Life expectancy (years at birth, 2002): 76.1 (males 74.8; females 77.4)

Finance
GDP in current prices: 2001): B$7,619.2m. (B$22,062 per head)
Real GDP growth (2001): 1.5%
Inflation (annual average, 2001): 0.6%
Currency: Brunei dollar

121

Economy

In 1998, according to estimates by the World Bank, Brunei's gross national income (GNI), measured at average 1996–98 prices, was US $7,754m., equivalent to US $24,100 per head (or US $24,910 on an international purchasing-power parity basis). In 1990–2002, it was estimated, the population increased by an annual average of 2.6%, while gross domestic product (GDP) per head decreased, in real terms, by an average of 0.7% per year during 1990–98. Brunei's overall GDP increased at an estimated average annual rate of 1.5% during 1990–2000. Real GDP grew by an estimated 1.5% in 2001 and by an estimated 4.1% in 2002.

AGRICULTURE

Agriculture (including forestry and fishing) employed less than an estimated 0.7% of the working population and provided 2.7% of GDP in 2001. In 2000 an estimated 1.3% of the total land area was cultivated; the principal crops include rice, cassava, bananas and pineapples. In the 1990s Brunei imported about 80% of its total food requirements. During 1990–98 agricultural GDP increased, in real terms, at an average annual rate of 2.7%. Agricultural GDP increased by an estimated 1.8% in 2000 and by an estimated 2.3% in 2001.

INDUSTRY

Industry (comprising mining, manufacturing, construction and utilities) employed 24.1% of the working population in 1991 and contributed an estimated 46.4% of GDP in 2001. Total industrial GDP increased at an average annual rate of 1.2% in 1990–98. Industrial GDP, including oil and gas services, increased by an average of 6.6% per year in 1993–97. Industrial GDP increased by an estimated 2.1% in 1997, and declined by 1.0% in 1998.

Mining

Brunei's economy depends almost entirely on its petroleum and natural gas resources. Mining and quarrying employed only 5.0% of the working population in 1991, but the petroleum sector provided an estimated 36.3% of GDP in 2001. Proven reserves of petroleum at the end of 2002 amounted to 1,400m. barrels, sufficient to sustain production at that year's levels (averaging 210,000 barrels per day) for approximately 18 years. Output of natural gas in 2002 totalled 11,500m. cu m, from proven reserves at the end of that year of some 390,000m. cu m (sustainable for less than 35 years). Crude petroleum, natural gas and petroleum products together accounted for an estimated 89.7% of total export earnings in 2000. The GDP of the petroleum and gas sector declined by an annual average of 0.3% in 1990–97 and by an estimated 1.6% in 1998. However, in 2000 it recovered by an estimated 3.2%.

Manufacturing

Manufacturing is dominated by petroleum refining. The sector employed 3.8% of the working population in 1991 (increasing to 5.4% in 1995) and, together with mining and quarrying, contributed an estimated 40.2% of GDP in 2001. Since the mid-1980s Brunei has attempted to expand its manufacturing base. In the mid-1990s the textile industry provided the largest non-oil and -gas revenue; other industries included cement, mineral water, canned food, dairy products, silica sands products, footwear and leather products, the design and manufacture of printed circuits, publishing and printing. Manufacturing GDP (including mining and quarrying) increased by an estimated 3.5% in 2000 and by an estimated 1.0% in 2001.

SERVICES

Services employed 73.7% of the working population in 1991 and provided 50.9% of GDP in 2001. In that year the sector comprising wholesale and retail trade, restaurants and hotels contributed 9.0% of GDP, and the finance sector also 9.0%. Plans are under way to develop Brunei as a regional centre for finance and banking. The GDP of the banking and finance sector increased by an annual average of 7.7% in 1993–97 and by an estimated 3.8% in 1998. The tourism sector is also being actively promoted as an important part of Brunei's policy of diversification away from its reliance on petroleum and natural gas; 2001 was designated 'Visit Brunei Year'. In 2000 1.3m. people visited Brunei, and in 1998 receipts from tourism totalled US $37m. During 1990–98 the combined GDP of the service sectors increased, in real terms, at an average rate of 3.5% per year. GDP of the services sector increased by an estimated 7.1% in 1997 and by 3.9% in 1998.

EXTERNAL TRADE

In 2001 Brunei recorded a visible trade surplus of B $4,553.6m. and, as a result of high investment income from abroad, in the same year there was a surplus of $6,789.1m. on the current account of the balance of payments. In 2001 the principal source of imports (23.4%) was Singapore; other major suppliers were Malaysia, the USA, the United Kingdom and Japan. The principal market for exports in that year was Japan, which accounted for 46.0% of total exports (mainly natural gas on a long-term contract); other significant purchasers were the Republic of Korea (also a purchaser of natural gas), Thailand and Singapore. Principal imports comprised basic manufactures, machinery and transport equipment, food and live animals and miscellaneous manufactured articles; principal exports were mineral fuels and lubricants.

GOVERNMENT FINANCE

In 1997 there was a budgetary deficit of B $27m. (equivalent to 0.3% of GDP). Brunei has no external public debt. International reserves were unofficially estimated at US $38,000m. in 1997 but were estimated to have declined to US $20,000m. in late 1998. Annual inflation averaged 1.9% in 1992–2001; consumer prices increased by 1.2% in 2000 and by 0.6% in 2001. Foreign workers, principally from Malaysia and the Philippines, have helped to ease the labour shortage resulting from the small size of the population, and comprised about 41% of the labour force in 2000, compared with 30% in 1998 (owing to an exodus of foreign workers in that year). However, the rate of unemployment was estimated at 4.7% in 2001, reflecting a shortage of non-manual jobs for the well-educated Bruneians.

INTERNATIONAL ECONOMIC RELATIONS

Brunei is a member of the Association of South East Asian Nations (ASEAN). In October 1991 the member states formally announced the establishment of the ASEAN Free Trade Area (AFTA), which was to be implemented over 15 years (later reduced to 10), and, as a member of ASEAN, Brunei endorsed Malaysia's plan for an East Asia Economic Caucus. AFTA was formally established in 2002. Brunei was a founder member of the Asia-Pacific Economic Co-operation (APEC) forum, initiated in

November 1989, and is also a member of the UN Economic and Social Commission for Asia and the Pacific (ESCAP), which aims to accelerate economic progress in the region. In 1994 the East ASEAN Growth Area (EAGA) was established, encompassing Mindanao, in the Philippines, Sarawak and Sabah, in Malaysia, Kalimantan and Sulawesi, in Indonesia, and Brunei.

SURVEY AND PROSPECTS

The eighth (2001–05) National Development Plan continued the emphasis of the sixth (1991–95) and seventh (1996–2000) Plans on diversification of the economy to reduce the country's dependence on income from petroleum and natural gas. In 1996 the Government announced proposals to develop Brunei as a Service Hub for Trade and Tourism (SHuTT) by 2003, following earlier plans for the development of the private sector and the conversion of Brunei into a regional centre for banking and finance. Various measures were taken to accelerate the broadening of Brunei's economic base, which had been impeded by high labour costs, a limited internal market and lack of a domestic entrepreneurial culture. However, the regional financial crisis, which began in 1997, resulted in the depreciation of the Brunei dollar, a decrease in income from the stock market and a sharp reduction in tourist arrivals, owing to the recession in other Asian countries. The situation was compounded by a significant decline in the international price of petroleum from mid-1997, by the huge financial losses arising from alleged mismanagement of the Brunei Investment Agency (BIA), and by the collapse of the Amedeo Development Corporation, which was responsible for many building projects in Brunei.

In an attempt to address the economic situation, budgetary allocations were drastically reduced, halting much government investment (although complaints from the business community caused the Government to reverse some decisions). Service industries were then also adversely affected by the exodus of thousands of unemployed foreign workers. Concerns over the future of the Sultanate's economy increased; a report released by the Brunei Darussalam Economic Council (BDEC) in February 2000 warned of its unsustainable nature. In December 2000, however, the discovery of significant new oil and gas reserves by Brunei Shell Petroleum provided a stimulus for renewed activity in the petroleum sector, although a further downturn in world oil prices in the latter part of 2001 compounded losses in other sectors of the economy, which continued to suffer the effects of the regional economic deceleration. While the disputes arising from the collapse of the Amedeo Corporation were largely resolved by the Sultan's formation of Global Evergreen in 2001, foreign investors continued to be deterred by the repercussions of the scandal. In early 2003 the Brunei Economic Development Board announced plans to attract foreign investment in the country through the solicitation of proposals for the development of a gas pipeline, power plant and jetty at Sungai Liang, as well as the development of an additional port facility at Pulau Muara Besar; it was hoped that the projects would create an estimated 6,000 jobs and attract US $4,500m. of investment over the next five years. Meanwhile, a report issued by the Asia-Pacific Economic forum focused on the need for Brunei's Government to improve levels of co-ordination among government agencies and thus overcome the challenges to increasing foreign investment posed by the slow bureaucratic procedures and a lack of transparency.

Bulgaria

The Republic of Bulgaria lies in in south-eastern Europe. In 1946 the Bulgarian monarchy was abolished and a republic proclaimed. A Soviet-style Constitution was adopted in 1947, when Bulgaria was designated a People's Republic. In 1989 the removal from the presidency of Todor Zhivkov, leader of the Bulgarian Communist Party, initiated a process of political reform that culminated, in 1990, in multi-party legislative elections. The country was renamed the Republic of Bulgaria in 1990. In 2001 the former monarch, Simeon Saxe-Coburg Gotha, became Prime Minister following the electoral success of an alliance including his National Movement. The capital is Sofia. The official language is Bulgarian.

Area and population
Area: 110,994 sq km
Population (mid-2002): 7,868,000
Population density (mid-2002): 70.9 per sq km
Life expectancy (years at birth, 2002): 71.9 (males 68.7; females 75.3)

Finance
GDP in current prices: 2002): US $15,608m. ($1,984 per head)
Real GDP growth (2002): 4.3%
Inflation (annual average, 2002): 5.8%
Currency: new lev

Economy

In 2002, according to estimates by the World Bank, Bulgaria's gross national income (GNI), measured at average 2000–02 prices, was US $14,116m., equivalent to $1,790 per head (or $6,840 per head on an international purchasing-power parity basis). During 1990–2002, it was estimated, the population decreased at an average rate of 0.9% per year, while gross domestic product (GDP) per head increased, in real terms, at an average annual rate of 0.1%. According to the World Bank, Bulgaria's overall GDP declined, in real terms, by an average of 0.8% annually during 1990–2002. However, real GDP increased by 4.0% in 2001 and by 4.3% in 2002.

AGRICULTURE

Agriculture contributed some 12.5% of GDP in 2002, when the sector (including hunting, forestry and fishing) engaged 25.6% of the employed labour force. In 1990 private farming was legalized, and farmland was restituted, in its former physical boundaries, to former owners and their heirs; by the end of 1999 96% of land restitution had been completed. In 1996 privately owned farms supplied 75.4% of total agricultural production. The principal crops are wheat, maize, barley, sunflower seeds, potatoes, tomatoes and melons. Bulgaria is also a major exporter of wine, and there is a large exportable surplus of processed agricultural products. During 1990–2002, according to the World Bank, the average annual GDP of the agricultural sector increased, in real terms, by 1.1%. Real agricultural GDP increased by 0.5% in 2001 and by 1.1% in 2002.

INDUSTRY

Industry provided some 27.8% of GDP in 2002, when the sector (including mining, manufacturing, construction and utilities) engaged 27.9% of the employed labour force. According to the World Bank, industrial GDP declined, in real terms, at an average annual rate of 3.5% in 1990–2002. However, real industrial GDP increased by 4.2% in 2001 and by 3.1%.

Mining

In 2002 mining accounted for some 1.4% of GDP and mining and quarrying engaged 1.2% of the employed labour force. Coal, iron ore, copper, manganese, lead and zinc are mined, and petroleum is extracted on the Black Sea coast.

Manufacturing

The manufacturing sector accounted for 17.1% of GDP in 2002, when it engaged 20.5% of the employed labour force. Based on the value of output, in 1999 the main branches of manufacturing were food products, beverages and tobacco products, machinery, refined petroleum products, basic metals, chemicals and chemical products, and clothing. The GDP of the manufacturing sector increased by 6.5% in 1998, but declined by 5.9% in 1999.

Energy

Bulgaria's production of primary energy in 2001 was equivalent to 54.0% of gross consumption. Coal and nuclear power, produced by the country's sole nuclear power station, at Kozloduy, are the main domestic sources of energy. (In 2003 plans were announced for the construction of a second nuclear power plant, at Belene.) In 2001 nuclear power provided 50.2% of electric energy, while coal accounted for 42.8% of electricity production. Bulgaria has established itself as a major regional electricity exporter. Imports of mineral fuels and lubricants comprised 22.2% of the value of merchandise imports in 2001, according to provisional figures.

SERVICES

The services sector contributed some 59.7% of GDP in 2002, and engaged 46.4% of the employed labour force. Tourism revenues increased significantly in 2002–03. The World Bank estimated that the real GDP of the services sector decreased at an average rate of 2.5% per year in 1990–2002. However, the real GDP of the sector increased by 4.2% in 2001 and by 4.9% in 2002.

EXTERNAL TRADE

In 2002 Bulgaria recorded a visible trade deficit of US $1,594.4m., and there was a deficit of $679.3m. on the current account of the balance of payments. In that year the principal sources of imports were Russia, which provided 14.5% of the total and Germany, which provided 14.3%. Italy (11.3%), Greece (6.0%) and France (5.6%) were also major suppliers. The main market for exports in 2002 was Italy (taking 15.4% of the total); Germany (9.5%), Turkey (9.3%), Greece (9.2%) and France (5.3%) were also significant purchasers. The principal exports in 2001 were base metals, mineral products, chemicals, and clothing and accessories. The principal imports in that year were mineral fuels and lubricants (particularly petroleum and petroleum products), chemicals and related products, nuclear machinery and mechanical appliances, vehicles and transport equipment, electrical equipment and machinery, and base metals.

GOVERNMENT FINANCE

In 2002 Bulgaria recorded a budgetary deficit of an estimated 876m. new leva (equivalent to 2.7% of GDP). Bulgaria's total external debt at the end of 2001 was US $9,615m., of which $7,378m. was long-term public debt. In that year the cost of debt-servicing was equivalent to 17.4% of revenue from exports of goods and services. The annual rate of inflation averaged 61.4% in 1996–2002. Consumer prices increased by 1,058.4% in 1997, but by only 22.3% in 1998 and by 2.6% in 1999, before increasing by 10.3% in 2000, by 7.4% in 2001 and by 5.8% in 2002. Some 12.7% of the labour force were registered as unemployed at November 2003.

INTERNATIONAL ECONOMIC RELATIONS

In 1990 Bulgaria became a member of the IMF and the World Bank, and it was a founding member of the European Bank for Reconstruction and Development (EBRD), established in the same year. Bulgaria is a member of the Organization of the Black Sea Economic Co-operation. The country made a formal application for membership of the European Union (EU) in 1996.

SURVEY AND PROSPECTS

At the beginning of the 1990s, in an effort to prevent economic collapse, the Government introduced an extensive programme of privatization and restructuring of the banking system, and adopted austerity measures in 1991. In May 1996 there was a dramatic reduction in the value of the lev, and in September the IMF suspended the disbursement of funds. Following the resumption of negotiations between a new, interim administration and the IMF, agreement was reached in March 1997 on the adoption of structural reforms. The Government established a currency control board in July, which fixed the exchange rate of the lev to that of the German Deutsche Mark. Bulgaria began accession talks with the EU in March 2000 and was expected to accede to the organization in 2007. In order to comply with conditions for EU membership, two of the Kozloduy nuclear power installation's six reactors were closed at the end of 2002; an agreement had been reached with the EU in November on the closure of two additional reactors by 2006, but in early 2003 the Supreme Administrative Court ruled the Government's decision on the early closure of the third and fourth reactors to be illegal.

In 2003 progress continued to be made in reducing the unemployment rate (which, none the less, remained high), maintaining a low rate of consumer-price inflation and increasing growth, although the external current-account deficit was significant, equivalent to more than 8% of GDP. The governing coalition lost both cohesion and popularity in 2003, and the results of the local elections of October–November prompted the governing party's junior coalition partner, the Movement for Rights and Freedoms, to make increased economic demands. None the less, an unforecast budgetary surplus was recorded in 2003, for the first time in five years, based on strong revenue increases. Although investor confidence had been undermined in late 2002, when long-delayed progress towards the privatization of the state tobacco company, Bulgartabac, and the Bulgarian Telecommunications Company (BTC) was halted owing to claims that legislation on privatization had been violated, a 65% stake in BTC was eventually divested in February 2004. Bulgartabac was to be divided into a number of smaller units prior to its sale, and plans for the partial privatization of seven electricity distribution companies were also launched in 2003. The budget for 2004 envisaged continued growth, of some 5.3%, and an annual rate of inflation of 4%–5%, while further restructuring of the railway and energy sectors was a priority for the Government.

Burkina Faso

Burkina Faso (formerly the Republic of Upper Volta) is situated in West Africa. It achieved full independence from France in 1960. From 1966 until 1987 Upper Volta (renamed Burkina Faso—'Land of Incorruptible Men'—in 1984) underwent intermittent periods of military rule. In 1983 Capt Thomas Sankara seized power and implemented radical, 'revolutionary' policies. In 1987 Capt Blaise Compaoré led a further armed coup, subsequently becoming Head of State. In 1991 Compaoré was elected, as a civilian, to the presidency, to which position he was re-elected in 1998. The capital is Ouagadougou. French is the official language.

Area and population
Area: 274,200 sq km
Population (mid-2002): 11,831,090
Population density (mid-2002): 43.1 per sq km
Life expectancy (years at birth, 2002): 41.7 (males 40.6; females 42.6)

Finance
GDP in current prices: 2002): US $2,839m. ($240 per head)
Real GDP growth (2002): 5.6%
Inflation (annual average, 2002): 2.2%
Currency: CFA franc

Economy

In 2002, according to estimates by the World Bank, Burkina Faso's gross national income (GNI), measured at average 2000–02 prices, was US $2,642m., equivalent to $220 per head (or $1,010 on an international purchasing-power parity basis). During 1990–2002, it was estimated, the population increased at an average annual rate of 2.4%, while gross domestic product (GDP) per head increased, in real terms, by an average of 2.3% per year. Overall GDP increased, in real terms, at an average annual rate of 4.8% in 1990–2002; growth in 2002 was 5.6%.

AGRICULTURE

According to the Banque centrale des états de l'Afrique de l'ouest, agriculture (including livestock-rearing, forestry and fishing) contributed 34.9% of GDP in 2002. About 92.2% of the labour force were employed in agriculture in 2001. The principal cash crop is cotton (exports of which accounted for an estimated 54.1% of the value of total exports in 2002). Smaller amounts of other crops, including karité nuts (sheanuts) and sesame seed, are also exported. The main subsistence crops are millet, sorghum, maize and rice. Burkina is almost self-sufficient in basic foodstuffs in non-drought years. Livestock-rearing is of considerable significance, contributing 9.7% of GDP and 21.0% of export revenue in 2002, according to IMF estimates. During 1990–2002 agricultural GDP increased at an average annual rate of 4.5%. Agricultural GDP increased by 4.6% in 2002.

INDUSTRY

Industry (including mining, manufacturing, construction and power) contributed 19.3% of GDP in 2002, but engaged only 2.0% of the employed labour force in 1996. During 1990–2002 industrial GDP increased at an average annual rate of 4.4%; growth in 2002 was 7.6%.

Mining

Although Burkina has considerable mineral resources, extractive activities accounted for 0.4% of GDP in 2002, and engaged only 0.1% of the employed labour force in 1996. However, the development of reserves of gold (exports of which contributed an estimated 2.4% of the value of total exports in 2002) has since brought about an increase in the sector's economic importance, while there is considerable potential, subject to the development of an adequate infrastructure, for the exploitation of manganese, zinc and limestone. The country's other known mineral reserves include phosphates, silver, lead and nickel.

Manufacturing

The manufacturing sector engaged only 1.4% of the employed labour force in 1996, and (together with electricity, gas and water) contributed 15.3% of GDP in 2002. The sector is dominated by the processing of primary products: major activities are cotton-ginning, the production of textiles, food-processing (including milling and sugar-refining), brewing and the processing of tobacco and of hides and skins. Motorcycles and bicycles are also assembled. According to the World Bank, manufacturing GDP increased at an average annual rate of 5.0% in 1990–2002; growth was 7.7% in 2002.

Energy

Two hydroelectric stations supplied about one-third of Burkina's electricity output in 1998; the remainder was derived from thermal power stations (using imported fuel). The country's hydropower capacity is being expanded, and in 2000 the interconnection of the south of Burkina Faso with the electricity network of Côte d'Ivoire was finalized; a link with Ghana's electricity grid is also planned. Imports of petroleum products comprised an estimated 18.6% of the value of total imports in 2002.

SERVICES

The services sector contributed 45.8% of GDP in 2002, and engaged 7.8% of the employed labour force in 1996. The GDP of the services sector increased at an average annual rate of 4.9% in 1990–2002; growth was 5.9% in 2002.

EXTERNAL TRADE

In 2002 Burkina recorded an estimated visible trade deficit of 217,500m. francs CFA, while there was a deficit of an estimated 224,800m. francs CFA on the current account of the balance of payments. In 2002 the principal sources of imports were France (which provided 19.6% of the total) and Côte d'Ivoire (18.8%); Japan and Germany were also major suppliers. The principal markets for exports in that year were France (45.3%), Côte d'Ivoire and Singapore. The principal exports in 2002 were cotton, and livestock and livestock products (including hides and skins). In the same year the principal imports were capital equipment, petroleum products, food products and raw materials.

GOVERNMENT FINANCE

In 2002 Burkina recorded an overall budget deficit of an estimated 108,400m. francs CFA, equivalent to an estimated 5.4% of GDP. Burkina's total external debt was US $1,490m. at the end of 2001, of which $1,310m. was long-term public debt. In that year the cost of debt-servicing was equivalent to 11.5% of the value of exports of goods and services. The annual rate of inflation, which was negligible prior to the 50% devaluation of the CFA franc in January 1994, increased to 25.1% in 1994, but slowed thereafter, to 7.4% in 1995 and an average of 2.3% per year in 1996–2002. Consumer prices increased by 2.3% in 2002. Some 71,280 people were unemployed in 1996, according to the national census, equivalent to only 1.4% of the total labour force.

INTERNATIONAL ECONOMIC RELATIONS

Burkina is a member of numerous regional organizations, including the Economic Community of West African States (ECOWAS), the West African organs of the Franc Zone, the Conseil de l'Entente, the Liptako–Gourma Integrated Development Authority, and the Permanent Inter-State Committee on Drought Control in the Sahel (CILSS).

SURVEY AND PROSPECTS

Burkina Faso has experienced strong growth since the devaluation of the CFA franc in 1994, as the competitiveness of its principal exports has been enhanced. In September 1999 the IMF approved funding under an Enhanced Structural Adjustment Facility (later replaced by the Poverty Reduction and Growth Facility—PRGF), equivalent to some US $49m., in support of the Government's economic programme for 1999–2002. During this period considerable success was achieved in reducing inflation, from more than 5.0% in 1998 to 2.3% in 2002, and in lowering the external current-account deficit. However, the fiscal deficit increased during this period, as efforts to improve the collection of taxes met with only limited success. In July 2000 the IMF and the World Bank announced that Burkina Faso was to receive some $400m. in debt-service relief under their original initiative for heavily indebted poor countries and a further $300m. under an enhanced framework.

A record cotton crop was recorded in 2001, contributing to solid growth in that year, despite concerns about a decline in the international price of cotton and an increase in international petroleum prices. However, unrest in Côte d'Ivoire (a significant trade route to and from Burkina) from late 2002 had a detrimental impact on the Burkinabè economy, which was reflected in the lower rate of GDP growth projected for 2003, at 2.6%. In June 2003 the IMF approved a PRGF, equivalent to some $34m., in support of the Government's economic programme for 2003–06, which aimed to contain inflation at less than 3% and achieve real GDP growth of 5.2% by 2005. Meanwhile, the Government was to advance its programme of structural reform, although the proposed privatizations of the telecommunications company, the Office National des Télécommunications, and of the electricity company, the Société Nationale Burkinabè d'Electricité, were delayed. The economy of Burkina Faso continued to be dependent on a narrow resource base, particularly on cotton, and therefore vulnerable to external exigencies, while poverty remained widespread, particularly in rural areas.

Burundi

The Republic of Burundi is located in central Africa. Since Burundi achieved independence from Belgium in 1962 tensions between the Tutsi and the Hutu, the two main ethnic groups, have persistently compromised stability. In 1996, amid widespread inter-ethnic violence, the army seized power. Little substantive progress towards resolving the resultant political crisis was achieved until 2000, when an agreement providing for power-sharing between the Tutsi and the Hutu was endorsed by national institutions, Hutu and Tutsi political associations. Transitional organs of government were installed on 1 November 2001 for a three-year transitional period. The capital is Bujumbura. The official languages are French and Kirundi.

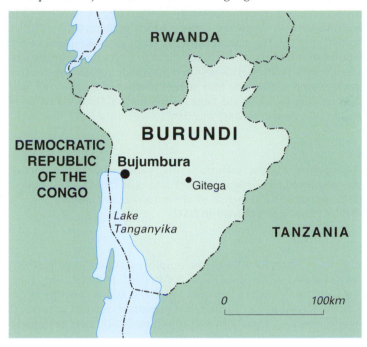

Area and population
Area: 27,834 sq km
Population (mid-2002): 7,071,000
Population density (mid-2002): 254.0 per sq km
Life expectancy (years at birth, 2002): 40.8 (males 38.7; females 43.0)

Finance
GDP in current prices: 2002): US $719m. ($102 per head)
Real GDP growth (2002): 3.6%
Inflation (annual average, 2002): −1.4%
Currency: Burundian franc

Economy

In 2002, according to estimates by the World Bank, Burundi's gross national income (GNI), measured at average 2000–02 prices, was US $704m., equivalent to $100 per head (or $610 per head on an international purchasing-power parity basis). During 1990–2002, it was estimated, the population increased at an average annual rate of 2.2%, while gross domestic product (GDP) per head declined, in real terms, by an average of 3.0% per year. Overall GDP declined, in real terms, at an average annual rate of 0.9% in 1990–2002; growth in 2002 was 3.6%.

AGRICULTURE

Agriculture (including forestry and fishing) contributed an estimated 49.3% of GDP in 2002. An estimated 90.2% of the labour force were employed in the sector at mid-2001. The principal cash crops are coffee (which accounted for 50.0% of export earnings in 2001) and tea. The main subsistence crops are cassava and sweet potatoes. Although Burundi is traditionally self-sufficient in food crops, population displacement as a result of the political crisis resulted in considerable disruption in the sector. The livestock-rearing sector was also severely affected by the civil war. During 1990–2002, according to the World Bank, agricultural GDP declined at an average annual rate of 0.1%; growth in 2002 was 3.9%.

INDUSTRY

Industry (comprising mining, manufacturing, construction and utilities) engaged 21.8% of the employed labour force in 1991 and contributed an estimated 19.4% of GDP in 2002. Industrial GDP increased at an average annual rate of 0.3% in 1990–2002; growth of 25.4% was recorded in 2002.

Mining

Mining and power engaged 0.1% of the employed labour force in 1990 and contributed an estimated 1.1% of GDP in 2001. Gold (alluvial), tin, tungsten and columbo-tantalite are mined in small quantities, although much activity has hitherto been outside the formal sector. Burundi has important deposits of nickel (estimated at 5% of world reserves), vanadium and uranium. In addition, petroleum deposits have been discovered. The GDP of the mining sector increased at an average annual rate of 3.4% in 1997–2001, according to IMF estimates; growth in 2001 was an estimated 14.3%.

Manufacturing

Manufacturing engaged 1.2% of the employed labour force in 1990 and contributed an estimated 8.8% of GDP in 2001. The sector consists largely of the processing of agricultural products (coffee, cotton, tea and the extraction of vegetable oils). A number of small enterprises also produce beer, flour, cement, footwear and textiles. Manufacturing GDP increased at an average annual rate of 2.5% in 1997–2001, according to IMF estimates. Manufacturing GDP increased by 3.2% in 2000 and remained constant in 2001.

Energy

Energy is derived principally from hydroelectric power (an estimated 38.6% of electricity consumed in 2001 was imported). Peat is also exploited as an additional source of energy. Imports of refined petroleum products comprised 12.4% of the value of imports in 2001.

SERVICES

The services sector contributed an estimated 31.3% of GDP in 2002, but engaged only 4.4% of the employed labour force in 1990. According to the World Bank, the GDP of the services sector declined at an average annual rate of 0.2% in 1990–2002, but increased by 3.5% in 2002.

EXTERNAL TRADE

In 2002 Burundi recorded an estimated trade deficit of US $72.9m., and there was a deficit of $2.8m. on the current account of the balance of payments. In 2001 the principal source of imports (15.5%) was Belgium; other important suppliers in that year were Saudi Arabia, France and Kenya. The principal market for exports in 2001 (31.0%) was the United Kingdom; other important markets were Belgium, Germany, Kenya and Rwanda. The main imports in 2001 were refined petroleum products, road vehicles and parts, medicinal and pharmaceutical products, and cereals and cereal preparations. The principal exports in that year were coffee, tea and gold.

GOVERNMENT FINANCE

In 2002 the budget deficit was 178.2m. Burundian francs, equivalent to less than 0.1% of GDP. Burundi's external debt at the end of 2001 was US $1,065m., of which $974m. was long-term public debt. In that year the cost of debt-servicing was equivalent to 39.8% of revenue from the export of goods and services. Total outstanding debt at the end of 2002 was estimated at $1,112m. (including $149m. of arrears). The annual rate of inflation averaged 12.9% in 1990–2002. Consumer prices declined by 1.4% in 2002.

INTERNATIONAL ECONOMIC RELATIONS

Burundi, with its neighbours Rwanda and the Democratic Republic of the Congo, is a member of the Economic Community of the Great Lakes Countries (CEPGL). Burundi is also a member of the Common Market for Eastern and Southern Africa (COMESA), and of the International Coffee Organization.

SURVEY AND PROSPECTS

Burundi's acute economic decline after 1993, owing to the severe political upheaval and accompanying population displacement, was further exacerbated by the regional economic sanctions imposed following the coup of July 1996. In addition, the decline in the international price of coffee (the principal export crop) resulted in substantial losses in the sector from 1997. By early 1999, when sanctions were revoked, a sustained decline in government revenue had resulted in the depletion of official reserves, and the Government was obliged to borrow heavily in order to meet its financing requirements. As a result, domestic and foreign debts had accumulated at an unsustainable level, and Burundi was defaulting on its debt-servicing obligations, while smuggling and tax evasion were largely unchecked. In May 2000 the IMF and the World Bank announced the resumption of international credit to Burundi. Following the signing of a peace agreement in August of that year, a transitional power-sharing Government was installed in November 2001. Although hostilities continued in part of the country, further agreements improved prospects for reaching a permanent peace settlement.

Following a strong economic recovery in 2001–02, real GDP contracted slightly in 2003, owing to the adverse effects of poor weather conditions on the agricultural sector. In January 2004 the IMF commended the Government's economic programme for 2002–03, which was declared to have made considerable progress in improving social and economic conditions, controlling inflation, and mobilizing financial assistance. The Fund approved a three-year Poverty Reduction and Growth Facility (PRGF) to support the country's economic reform programme. Reduction of the high external debt-servicing burden was to be a priority for the Government, and the country was expected to qualify for debt relief under the enhanced initiative of the IMF and World Bank for heavily indebted poor countries. Considerable funds pledged at an international donor conference, convened in Belgium earlier in January, under the auspices of the UN Development Programme and the Belgian Government, were to support a number of reconstruction programmes, including the resettlement of refugees and internally displaced persons. The Government's main short-term objective under the PRGF-supported programme was to increase productivity in the agricultural sector (thereby also developing the rural economy), and, in particular, implementing reforms of the coffee sector. Continued progress in the peace process was expected to establish favourable conditions for sustained economic growth.

Cambodia

The Kingdom of Cambodia is situated in South-East Asia. In 1953 Cambodia gained independence from French rule. From 1964 the Government was confronted by a Marxist insurgency movement, the Khmers Rouges. In 1975 the Khmers Rouges gained power and Cambodia (renamed Democratic Kampuchea) underwent a pre-arranged programme of radical social deconstruction during which an estimated 1.7m. people died. In 1977 the Communist Party of Kampuchea (CPK), with Pol Pot as the Secretary of the Central Committee, was revealed as the ruling organization. The CPK was ousted following the capture of Phnom-Penh by Vietnamese forces in 1979. The capital is Phnom-Penh. Khmer is the official language.

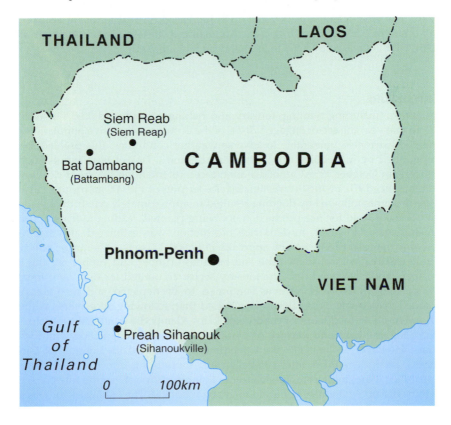

Area and population

Area: 181,035 sq km
Population (mid-2002): 12,487,190
Population density (mid-2002): 69.0 per sq km
Life expectancy (years at birth, 2002): 54.6 (males 51.9; females 57.1)

Finance

GDP in current prices: 2002): US $3,677m. ($294 per head)
Real GDP growth (2002): 4.5%
Inflation (annual average, 2002): 3.2%
Currency: riel

Economy

In 2002, according to the World Bank, Cambodia's gross national income (GNI), measured at average 2000–02 prices, was US $3,483m., equivalent to $280 per head (or $1,590 per head on an international purchasing-power parity basis). During 1990–2002, it was estimated, the population increased at an average annual rate of 2.6%. while gross domestic product (GDP) per head increased, in real terms, by an average of 2.6% per year. Cambodia's overall GDP increased, in real terms, at an average annual rate of 5.3% during 1990–2002. According to the Asian Development Bank (ADB), GDP increased by 5.5% in 2001 and by 5.0% in 2002.

AGRICULTURE

Agriculture (including hunting, forestry and fishing) contributed 35.6% of GDP in 2002. In that year the sector engaged 70.2% of the economically active population, but remained extremely vulnerable to adverse weather conditions, this problem being compounded by inadequate rural infrastructure and a lack of farm inputs such as fertilizers. In October 1999 Cambodia announced its intention to export rice for the first time since 1970, owing to an estimated rice surplus of 140,000 metric tons. In 2002 severe droughts followed by flooding resulted in approximately one-fifth of the land area normally used for rice production not being planted, leading to fears of future rice shortages. However, in 2003 rice production was estimated at 4.3m. tons, exceeding planned production by approximately 600,000 tons. Other principal crops include cassava, maize, sugar cane and bananas. Timber and rubber are the two principal export commodities. The forestry sector accounted for only an estimated 2.3% of GDP in 2002, as reserves continued to be depleted and reafforestation remained inadequate. From 1999 it was hoped that, following agreements with the IMF and multilateral donors for conditional loans, Cambodia would take measures to enforce logging bans and forestry regulations imposed in conjunction with the aid donors. However, in late 2002 the Government terminated the contract of Global Witness, an independent international group monitoring efforts being made to combat illegal logging, prompting concerns that efforts to reform the forestry sector might be disrupted and that some aid might be withheld. The fishing sector was also adversely affected by deforestation, which caused reductions in freshwater fishing catches, owing to the silting up of lakes and rivers. According to official estimates, however, the GDP of the fishing sector increased at an average annual rate of 3.8% in 1995–2002, following a period of decline in the early 1990s, and contributed an estimated 12.2% of GDP in 2002. According to the ADB, agricultural GDP increased, in real terms, at an average annual rate of 2.0% during 1995–2002. The GDP of the agricultural sector expanded by 2.2% in 2001 but contracted by 2.7% in 2002.

INDUSTRY

Industry (including mining, manufacturing, construction and power) contributed 28.0% of GDP in 2002, and employed 10.5% of the labour force in that year. According to the ADB, in real terms, industrial GDP increased at an average annual rate of 14.3% during 1995–2002. Growth in industrial GDP was 12.9% in 2001 and 17.7% in 2002.

Mining

In 2002 mining and quarrying contributed only 0.3% of GDP. Cambodia has limited mineral resources, including phosphates, gem stones, iron ore, bauxite, silicon and manganese ore, of which only phosphates and gem stones are, at present, being exploited. In the 1990s several agreements on petroleum exploration were signed with foreign enterprises. Cambodia's resources of natural gas were unofficially estimated to be 1,500,000m.–3,500,000m. cu m in 1992, and petroleum reserves were estimated to be between 50m. and 100m. barrels. According to the ADB, the GDP of the mining sector increased, in real terms, at an average annual rate of 7.2% during 1995–2002; growth in mining GDP was 13.4% in 2001 and 18.9% in 2002.

Manufacturing

The manufacturing sector contributed 20.2% of GDP in 2002 and employed 8.7% of the labour force in the same year. The sector is dominated by rice milling and the production of ready-made garments, household goods, textiles, tyres and pharmaceutical products. The manufacture of garments, mostly for export, grew rapidly during the 1990s, and by the end of 2000 160,000 workers were engaged in garment manufacture. Exports of clothing rose in value by 13.2% in 2001, compared with the previous year, to reach US $1,147m. However, the abandonment by the USA of its textile import quota at the end of 2004 would, it was feared, have a serious impact upon the performance of the Cambodian garment sector; many textile factories based in Cambodia were expected to relocate to China in order to take advantage of that country's lower labour costs and more secure business environment. The Government was also attempting to promote the establishment of agro-industrial enterprises (sugar and vegetable oil refineries and factories producing paper pulp) and to encourage the production of fertilizers, petroleum and heavy construction and mechanical equipment. According to the ADB, the GDP of the manufacturing sector increased, in real terms, at an average annual rate of 17.2% during 1995–2002. Growth in manufacturing GDP was 14.2% in 2001 and 15.1% in 2002.

Energy

Energy is derived principally from timber. All commercial energy used in Cambodia is imported. In the late 1990s the country had an installed capacity of 28.7 MW, of which 15 MW was accounted for by an oil-fired thermal power plant and the rest by diesel generating units. Owing to a lack of spare parts and a shortage of fuel, only a small percentage of the generating capacity can be utilized. Cambodia has considerable hydropower potential, and two hydropower plants were under construction in the late 1990s. In late 2002 Cambodia signed an agreement with the Governments of China, Thailand, Laos, Myanmar and Viet Nam to form a regional power distribution system, which would enable hydropower development in the Mekong River area.

SERVICES

The services sector contributed 36.4% of GDP in 2002 and engaged 19.5% of the economically active population in that year. The tourism sector has become increasingly significant. In 2000 greater political stability led to an increase in tourist arrivals to 466,365. Receipts from tourism in that year were estimated at US $228m. In 2001, despite the effects of the terrorist attacks on the USA in September, arrivals increased to 604,919. It was feared that the bombing in Bali, Indonesia, in October 2002 would affect the growth of Cambodia's tourism sector by deterring visitors to the region. In that year 786,546 tourists visited Cambodia. However, in 2003, designated 'Visit Cambodia Year' by the Government, tourist arrivals declined to 701,014. In real terms, according to the ADB, the GDP of the services sector increased at an average annual rate of 5.9% during 1995–2002. Growth in the sector was 4.2% in 2001 and 4.5% in 2002.

EXTERNAL TRADE

In 2002 Cambodia recorded a visible trade deficit of US $563.5m., while there was a deficit of $64.0m. on the current account of the balance of payments. In 2002 the principal sources of imports were Thailand (30.2%) and Singapore (21.5%); other major sources were Hong Kong, the People's Republic of China and Viet Nam. In the same year the principal market for exports was the USA (61.4%); other important purchasers were Germany, the United Kingdom and Singapore. The principal exports in 2001 were garments (accounting for 77.8% of the total), sawn timber, logs and rubber. The principal imports were petroleum products (accounting for 8.2% of the total), cigarettes and motorcycles. Re-exports (which were a result of the differences in tariffs on goods imported by Cambodia and its neighbours) remained important, although they declined from 53% of total exports in 1993 to an estimated 21.2% in 2000.

GOVERNMENT FINANCE

Cambodia's overall budget deficit in 2002 was 577,040m. riels. Cambodia's external debt at the end of 2001 totalled US $2,704m., of which $2,401m. was long-term public debt. In that year the cost of debt-servicing was equivalent to 1.3% of revenue from exports of goods and services. The annual rate of inflation averaged 5.1% during 1995–2002; consumer prices increased by 3.3 % in 2002 and by an estimated 3.0% in 2003.

INTERNATIONAL ECONOMIC RELATIONS

Cambodia is a member of the UN Economic and Social Commission for Asia and the Pacific (ESCAP), of the Asian Development Bank, of the Mekong River Commission and of the Colombo Plan. Cambodia was formally admitted to the Association of South East Asian Nations (ASEAN) in April 1999. Following the implementation of the ASEAN Free Trade Area (AFTA) in January 2002, Cambodia was granted until 2007 to comply with the 0%–5% tariff agreement.

SURVEY AND PROSPECTS

In February 2000 the Government announced a three-year US $1,400m. economic development programme intended to promote growth and to reduce poverty. At the annual meeting of bilateral and multilateral donors in Paris in May, $548m. of fresh aid was pledged to Cambodia in response to the Government's appeals. At the next annual meeting, held in Tokyo in June 2001, the country received a further $615m. and, in June 2002, at a meeting held in Phnom-Penh, it was awarded a further $635m. (Aid, however, was partly dependent upon the fulfilment of government pledges to reduce military spending, to address the problem of illegal logging and to decrease expenditure on the civil service payroll.) From 2000 there was considerable progress in the structural reform of several key areas, particularly the financial sector. In 2001 the Government initiated its second Socioeconomic Development Plan, to be implemented in 2001–05, as part of its ongoing effort to combat poverty. The Plan aimed to expand opportunities for the poor through the promotion of stable and sustained economic growth.

In August a $42m. demobilization programme was endorsed by the World Bank and other bodies, enabling Cambodia to continue the reduction of its armed forces and permit higher levels of expenditure on the social sector. In 2002, however, the programme attracted controversy after the Government admitted that many of those allegedly demobilized had never undertaken military service and were thus receiving payments from the programme fraudulently. In November the Chinese Government announced that it had cancelled Cambodia's foreign debt, significantly improving the country's situation. However, it was widely recognized that the Government needed to continue to implement key reforms, particularly in the public sector, if Cambodia was eventually to be able to compete with its regional neighbours. In September 2003 the World Trade Organization (WTO) approved Cambodia's membership application, greatly enhancing the country's economic prospects. However, the political uncertainty that ensued in the aftermath of the July 2003 general election was thought likely to act as a deterrent to foreign investment and tourism in the short term. In addition, it was feared that, if the country was unable to form a new Government by March 2004, it would fail to meet the deadline imposed by the WTO for the ratification of its membership of the organization. The ADB estimated that the economy expanded by 5.0% in 2003.

Cameroon

The Republic of Cameroon lies on the west coast of Africa. A Federal Republic of Cameroon came into existence in 1961, comprising the French and British zones into which the territory had been divided. Ahmadou Ahidjo, leader of the Union camerounaise (Union nationale camerounaise from 1966; Rassemblement démocratique du peuple camerounais from 1985), served as President (initially of French Cameroons) from 1960 until 1982, when he resigned and was replaced by Paul Biya. Biya has been re-elected in every presidential election since 1984, most recently in 1997. The capital is Yaoundé. French and English are the official languages.

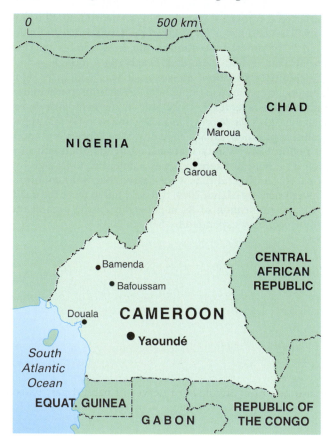

Area and population

Area: 475,442 sq km
Population (mid-2002): 15,522,760
Population density (mid-2002): 32.6 per sq km
Life expectancy (years at birth, 2002): 48.1 (males 47.2; females 49.0)

Finance
GDP in current prices: 2002): US $9,060m. ($584 per head)
Real GDP growth (2002): 4.4%
Inflation (annual average, 2002): 2.8%
Currency: CFA franc

Economy

In 2002, according to estimates by the World Bank, Cameroon's gross national income (GNI), measured at average 2000–02 prices, was US $8,746m., equivalent to $560 per head (or $1,640 per head on an international purchasing-power parity basis). During 1990–2002, it was estimated, the population increased at an average annual rate of 2.4%, while gross domestic product (GDP) per head declined, in real terms, by an average of 0.5% per year. Overall GDP increased, in real terms, at an average annual rate of 1.9% in 1990–2002; growth in 2002 was 4.4%.

AGRICULTURE
Agriculture (including hunting, forestry and fishing) contributed 42.6% of GDP in 2002. An estimated 58.2% of the labour force were employed in agriculture in 2001. The principal cash crops are cocoa beans (which accounted for 6.5% of export earnings in 2001), cotton and coffee. The principal subsistence crops are roots and tubers (mainly cassava), maize and sorghum; Cameroon is not, however, self-sufficient in cereals. In 1995 an estimated 42% of the country's land area was covered by forest, but an inadequate transport infrastructure has impeded the development of the forestry sector. None the less, illegal logging and poaching in the country's forests remains a significant problem. Livestock-rearing makes an important contribution to the food supply. During 1990–2002, according to the World Bank, the real GDP of the agricultural sector increased at an average annual rate of 4.9%; growth in 2002 was 6.3%.

INDUSTRY
Industry (including mining, manufacturing, construction and power) employed 8.9% of the labour force in 1990, and contributed 19.6% of GDP in 2002. During 1990–2002, according to the World Bank, industrial GDP increased at an average annual rate of 0.2%; growth of 6.8% was recorded in 2002.

Mining
Mining contributed 4.0% of GDP in 2000/01, but employed only 0.1% of Cameroon's working population in 1985. Receipts from the exploitation of the country's petroleum reserves constitute a principal source of government revenue. Deposits of limestone are also quarried. Significant reserves of natural gas, bauxite, iron ore, uranium and tin remain largely undeveloped. According to the IMF, the GDP of the mining sector increased by an average of 2.5% per year in 1995/96–2000/01; growth in 2000/01 was 0.6%.

Manufacturing
Manufacturing contributed an estimated 11.3% of GDP in 2002, and employed an estimated 7% of the working population in 1995. The sector is based on the processing of both indigenous primary products (petroleum-refining, agro-industrial activities) and of imported raw materials (an aluminium smelter uses alumina imported from

Guinea). According to the World Bank, manufacturing GDP increased at an average annual rate of 2.8% in 1990–2002; growth in 2002 was 8.4%.

Energy

In 2000 hydroelectric power installations supplied 98.9% of Cameroon's energy. In 2001 imports of mineral fuels accounted for 18.4% of the value of total imports.

SERVICES

Services contributed 37.8% of GDP in 2002. During 1990–2002, according to the World Bank, the GDP of the services sector increased at an average annual rate of 0.2%; growth in 2002 was 1.6%.

EXTERNAL TRADE

In 2000/01 Cameroon recorded a visible trade surplus of an estimated 380,500m. francs CFA, but there was a deficit of 109,900m. francs CFA on the current account of the balance of payments. In 2001 the principal source of imports (24.1%) was France; other major suppliers were Nigeria, the USA and Germany. The principal market for exports in that year (27.1%) was Italy; other significant purchasers were Spain, France, the Netherlands and the People's Republic of China. The principal exports in 2001 were crude petroleum and oils, timber and timber products, coffee, cocoa beans, raw cotton and aluminium. The principal imports in that year were machinery and transport equipment, semi-finished materials, mineral fuels and lubricants, and food and live animals.

GOVERNMENT FINANCE

In 2002, according to preliminary estimates, there was a budget deficit of 227,000m. francs CFA (equivalent to 3.3% of GDP). Cameroon's total external debt at the end of 2001 was US $8,338m., of which $6,913m. was long-term public debt. In that year the cost of debt-servicing was equivalent to 12.6% of revenue from exports of goods and services. The annual rate of inflation averaged 4.6% in 1990–2002; consumer prices increased by 2.8% in 2002. An estimated 5.8% of the labour force were unemployed in mid-1985.

INTERNATIONAL ECONOMIC RELATIONS

Cameroon is a member of the Central African organs of the Franc Zone), of the Communauté économique des états de l'Afrique centrale (CEEAC), of the International Cocoa Organization and of the International Coffee Organization.

SURVEY AND PROSPECTS

In 1997 the IMF approved a three-year loan for Cameroon, equivalent to about US $221m., under the Enhanced Structural Adjustment Facility. In October 2000 the IMF and the World Bank's International Development Association agreed to support a debt-reduction package for Cameroon, worth an estimated $2,000m., under the enhanced initiative for heavily indebted poor countries, thus substantially reducing Cameroon's debt-service obligations and allowing increased expenditure on social and welfare services. In December the IMF approved another three-year loan, equivalent to about $144m., under the Poverty Reduction and Growth Facility, in support of efforts to improve social services, reduce poverty and maintain a stable macroeconomic environment. In December 2003 the IMF approved the Government's request for a one-year extension of the programme, in view of unexpectedly slow progress on structural reforms to the economy and Cameroon's continued failure to repay its commercial creditors.

A 1,070-km pipeline to transport crude petroleum from southern Chad to the southern Cameroonian port of Kribi was inaugurated in October 2003. It was hoped that royalties from the pipeline, projected to reach some $500m. over a 25-year production period, would partially offset the decline in direct revenue from petroleum, daily production of which decreased from a peak of 164,000 barrels in the mid-1980s to some 85,000 barrels in 2002. Real GDP growth was estimated at 4.2% in 2003, as a result of the expanding non-petroleum sector. None the less, the appreciation of the CFA franc against the US dollar threatened the competitiveness of Cameroon's agricultural exports in 2004, and fraud and corruption remained a hindrance to economic development, as did the country's generally poor physical infrastructure.

Canada

Canada occupies most of the northern part of North America. The Liberals and the Conservative Party (formerly the Progressive Conservative Party, which merged with the Canadian Alliance in 2003) have dominated federal-level politics since 1968. In 1993, however, the Bloc Québécois (BQ) formed the official opposition and declared that it would pursue sovereignty for Québec, where political self-determination remains a sensitive issue. (Four-fifths of the Québec population speak French as a first language.) In 1995, in a provincial referendum, the Québec electorate narrowly rejected sovereignty proposals. In 1998 the Supreme Court ruled that no province could leave the federation without prior negotiations with the federal and provincial governments. The capital is Ottawa. English and French are the official languages.

Area and population
Area: 9,984,670 sq km
Population (mid-2002): 31,414,000
Population density (mid-2002): 3.1 per sq km
Life expectancy (years at birth, 2002): 79.8 (males 77.2; females 82.3)

Finance
GDP in current prices: 2002): US $715,692m. ($22,783 per head)
Real GDP growth (2002): 3.3%
Inflation (annual average, 2002): 2.2%
Currency: Canadian dollar

Economy

In 2002, according to estimates by the World Bank, Canada's gross national income (GNI), measured at average 2000–2002 prices, was US $700,454m., equivalent to US $22,300 per head (or $28,070 on an international purchasing-power parity basis). The country's population increased at an average annual rate of 1.0% in 1990–2002, while gross domestic product (GDP) per head increased, in real terms, by an average of 1.7% per year. Overall GDP increased, in real terms, at an average rate of 2.8% per year in 1990–2002; GDP increased by 3.3% in 2002.

AGRICULTURE

Agriculture (including forestry and fishing) contributed 2.0% of GDP (in constant 1997 prices) in 2002 and the sector (excluding forestry and fishing) engaged 2.1% of the economically active population in the same year. The principal crops are wheat, barley and other cereals, which, together with livestock production (chiefly cattle and pigs) and timber, provide an important source of export earnings. In 2003 the cattle industry was affected by a minor outbreak of bovine spongiform encephalopathy (BSE—commonly known as 'mad cow disease') in Alberta; the USA, Japan and Australia subsequently suspended the import of Canadian beef. Canada is a leading world exporter of forest products and of fish and seafood. The production of furs is also important. In real terms, the GDP of the agricultural sector decreased at an average annual rate of 0.3% in 1997–2002. Agricultural GDP decreased by 7.6% in 2001 and by a further 5.2% in 2002.

INDUSTRY

Industry (including mining, manufacturing, construction and power) provided 29.3% of GDP (in constant 1997 prices) in 2002, and the sector (including forestry and fishing) employed 23.4% of the economically active population in the same year. Industrial GDP increased, in real terms, at an average annual rate of 3.4% in 1997–2002. Industrial GDP decreased by 1.3% in 2001, but increased by 1.9% in 2002.

Mining

Mining provided 3.4% of GDP (in constant 1997 prices) in 2002, but employed only 1.8% of the economically active population in the same year (together with forestry, fishing, petroleum and gas). Canada is a major world producer of zinc, asbestos, nickel, potash and uranium. Gold, silver, iron, copper, cobalt and lead are also exploited. There are considerable reserves of petroleum and natural gas in Alberta, off the Atlantic coast and in the Canadian Arctic islands. The GDP of the mining sector increased, in real terms, at an average rate of 0.1% in 1997–2002. Mining GDP rose by 1.6% in 2001, but decreased by 1.7% in 2002.

Manufacturing

Manufacturing contributed 17.9% of GDP (in constant 1997 prices), and employed 15.1% of the economically active population, in 2002. The principal branches of manufacturing in 2002, measured by the value of shipments, were transport equipment (accounting for 23.1% of the total), food products (12.1%), chemical products (7.3%), paper and allied products (6.3%), primary metal industries (6.2%) and wood industries (5.7%). The GDP of the sector increased, in real terms, at an average rate of 4.5% per year in 1997–2002. Manufacturing GDP decreased by 3.8% in 2001, but increased by 2.6% in 2002.

Energy

Energy is derived principally from hydroelectric power (which provided 59% of the electricity supply in 2000) and from geo-thermal and nuclear power-stations. In 2002 Canada's total energy production (including nuclear energy) totalled an estimated 577,280 GWh. In 2002 energy products accounted for 12.0% of Canada's exports and 4.6% of imports.

SERVICES

Services provided 68.7% of GDP (in constant 1997 prices), and engaged 74.4% of the economically active population, in 2002. The combined GDP of the service sectors increased, in real terms, at an average rate of 5.4% per year in 1997–2002. Services GDP increased by 3.4% in 2001 and by 4.0% in 2002.

EXTERNAL TRADE

In 2002 Canada recorded a visible trade surplus of US $36,838m., and there was a surplus of US $14,908m. on the current account of the balance of payments. In 2002 the USA accounted for 83.8% of Canada's total exports and 71.5% of total imports; the countries of the European Union (EU) and Japan were also important trading partners. The principal exports in that year were machinery and equipment, motor vehicles and parts and industrial goods. The principal imports were machinery and equipment, motor vehicles and parts and industrial goods. In January 1989 a free-trade agreement with the USA entered into force, whereby virtually all remaining trade tariffs imposed between the two countries were to be eliminated over a 10-year period. Negotiations with the USA and Mexico, aimed at the eventual creation of a full North American free-trade area, concluded in December 1992 with the signing of an agreement. The North American Free Trade Agreement (NAFTA) entered into operation on 1 January 1994. Since the implementation of NAFTA, however, disagreements have persisted between Canada and the USA over alleged violations of the Agreement by the US Government in relation to bilateral trade in softwood lumber, wheat and other commodities. At a third Summit of the Americas, held in Québec in April 2001, a timetable for a proposed Free Trade Area of the Americas, to take effect by 2005, was agreed upon. Negotiations commenced in late 2002 and were to conclude by January 2005. Since the mid-1990s the Canadian Government has implemented measures aimed at expanding trade in the Far East, notably with the People's Republic of China, the Republic of Korea, Indonesia and Viet Nam. In November 1996 Canada finalized a trade agreement with Chile, which, from June 1997, phased out most customs duties by 2002. In October 1998 negotiations began with the members of the European Free Trade Association (EFTA) for the creation of a free-trade area, while Canada has also pursued efforts to develop similar arrangements with the EU. Bilateral agreements on trade, communications and the prevention of financial crime were signed with Mexico in 2003.

GOVERNMENT FINANCE

For the financial year 2002/03, there was a consolidated budget surplus of C $8,333m. The annual rate of inflation averaged 2.1% in 1990–2002. Consumer prices increased by an average of 2.6% in 2001 and by 2.2% in 2002. The rate of unemployment averaged 7.2% in 2001 and 7.7% in 2002.

SURVEY AND PROSPECTS

Many sectors of Canadian industry rely heavily on foreign investment. Following the international recession of the mid-1970s, Canada's average annual rate of inflation remained above 4% throughout the 1980s. A series of budgetary deficits were attributable largely to high interest rates, which continued into the early 1990s, to the detriment of a sustained economic recovery. Government spending and foreign borrowing were reduced in the mid-1990s, as part of a series of deflationary measures. This emphasis on fiscal stringency led, in part, in August 1996, to the country's first current-account surplus in the balance of payments since 1984. The recovery was further aided by low rates of domestic inflation and by the beneficial effects of NAFTA on Canadian export sales to the USA and continued strongly throughout the late 1990s and early 2000s. In 2001 Canada and Mexico agreed to eliminate tariffs on goods worth an annual US $1,950m. Proposals for the 2003/04 budget included provisions for increased expenditure on health care and for reductions in corporate and personal rates of taxation, while achieving a budgetary surplus for the third successive year.

In late 2001 the rate of inflation fell below 1%; although by the end of 2002 it had risen to 2.8%, it fell again, to 1.6%, by the end of 2003. In 2001 the Bank of Canada cut interest rates to 2.75%, the lowest level in 40 years, in an effort to reverse a weakening trend in economic activity. GDP growth in 2002 was 3.3%, the highest of any G-7 member state. Growth was estimated at 1.7% in 2003 and was forecast to increase by 2.7% in 2004. The Government projected a combined budgetary surplus of C $95,000m. for the period 2000–05. Nine of the 13 provinces and territories reported a budgetary deficit in 2002/03. The predominance of trade with the USA (in which Canada, assisted by currency fluctuations favourable to its exports, maintained a substantial surplus in the early 2000s) compensated for deficits with other major trading partners, including the EU and Japan, and allowed Canada to record substantial trade surpluses in the early 2000s. However, in spite of its strong recovery, the Canadian economy remains vulnerable to adverse movements in world prices for its major exports of raw materials. In 2003 the strength of the Canadian dollar also had a negative effect on exports. The Canadian airline industry was particularly badly affected by the terrorist attacks on the USA in September 2001; in November of that year Canada 3000, the country's second largest airline, ceased operations, and the national carrier Air Canada reported heavy losses and made 9,000 staff redundant. The ban on the import of Canadian beef in several countries in 2003 following the outbreak of BSE in Alberta also had an adverse affect on the cattle industry.

Cape Verde

An archipelago in the North Atlantic Ocean forms the Republic of Cape Verde. Independence from Portugal was granted to Cape Verde in 1975, Aristides Pereira of the Partido Africano da Independência do Guiné e Cabo Verde (PAIGC) becoming the country's first President. In 1981 the Cape Verde wing of the PAIGC was renamed the Partido Africano da Independência de Cabo Verde (PAICV), which abandoned the pursuit of unification with Guinea-Bissau. At multi-party elections in 1991 the Movimento para a Democracia was victorious. In 2001 the PAICV returned to power. Cidade de Praia is the capital. Portuguese is the official language.

Area and population
Area: 4,036 sq km
Population (mid-2002): 458,030
Population density (mid-2002): 113.5 per sq km
Life expectancy (years at birth, 2002): 70.1 (males 66.6; females 72.9)

Finance
GDP in current prices: 2002): US $631m. ($1,378 per head)
Real GDP growth (2002): 4.0%
Inflation (annual average, 2002): 1.9%
Currency: escudo

Economy

In 2002, according to estimates from the World Bank, Cape Verde's gross national income (GNI), measured at average 2000–02 prices, was US $590m., equivalent to $1,290 per head (or $4,720 per head on an international purchasing-power parity basis). During 1990–2002, it was estimated, the population increased at an average annual rate of 2.5%, while gross domestic product (GDP) per head increased, in real terms, by an average of 2.9% per year. Overall GDP increased, in real terms, at an average annual rate of 5.5% in 1990–2002; growth in 2002 was 4.0%.

AGRICULTURE

Agriculture (including forestry and fishing) contributed 11.2% of GDP in 2001, and employed an estimated 22.3% of the economically active population in that year. The staple crop is maize; potatoes, sweet potatoes, cassava, coconuts, sugar cane, mangoes, bananas and vegetables are also cultivated. Export earnings from fish and crustaceans declined from 262.0m. escudos (20.2% of the total value of exports, excluding fuel) in 1997 to 37.7m. escudos (1.9%) in 2001. Lobster and tuna are among the most important exports. Moreover, the total fish catch declined from 14,730 metric tons in 1981 to 6,573 tons in 1992. In 1994 a five-year project was announced for the redevelopment of the fishing industry, with investment of US $28m. By 2000 the annual catch had recovered somewhat to 10,821 tons, although it declined again in 2001, to 9,653 tons. During 1990–2002 the GDP of the agricultural sector increased, in real terms, at an average annual rate of 3.6%; growth in 2002 was 1.4%.

INDUSTRY

Industry (including construction and power) contributed 18.3% of GDP in 2001, and employed 30.6% of the labour force in 1990. During 1990–2001 industrial GDP increased, in real terms, at an average annual rate of 5.3%; growth in 2001 was 4.8%.

Mining

Mining employed 0.4% of the labour force in 1990 and contributed less than 1% of GDP in 1998. Salt and pozzolana, a volcanic ash used in cement manufacture, are the main non-fuel minerals produced.

Manufacturing

Manufacturing contributed 8.1% of GDP in 2001 and employed about 6% of the labour force in 1995. The most important branches, other than fish-processing, are clothing, footwear, rum distilling and bottling. Legislation enacted in 1999 provided for the transformation of industrial parks at Mindelo and Praia into free-trade zones, and for the establishment of a further free-trade zone on Sal island. During 1990–2001 the GDP of the manufacturing sector increased, in real terms, at an average annual rate of 3.9%; an increase of 4.7% was recorded in 2001.

Energy

Energy is derived principally from hydroelectric power and gas. Imports of mineral fuels comprised 5.6% of the value of total estimated imports in 2001.

SERVICES

Services accounted for 70.6% of GDP in 2001. Tourism has been identified as the area with the most potential for economic development. A new international airport on Santiago, due to open in 2004, was expected to give considerable impetus to the development of the tourism sector. The airport on São Vicente island was upgraded to international capacity in 2000. Plans were also under way for the construction of two further international airports, on São Vicente and Boa Vista. In 2003 the Government allocated 120m. escudos to upgrade the road network. Tourist arrivals increased from 52,000 in 1998 to 115,282 in 2001. During 1990–2001 the combined GDP of the service sectors increased, in real terms, at an average annual rate of 6.0%; growth in 2001 was 3.3%.

EXTERNAL TRADE

In 2002 Cape Verde recorded a trade deficit of US $236.1m., and there was a deficit of $71.5m. on the current account of the balance of payments. In 2002 the principal source of imports was Portugal (55.3%); another major supplier was the Netherlands. Portugal was also the principal market for exports (88.4%) in that year. The principal exports in 2001 were clothing (49.0%) and footwear (39.8%). The principal imports in that year were cereals and cereal preparations, refined petroleum and passenger vehicles.

GOVERNMENT FINANCE

In 2002 there was an estimated budgetary deficit of 8,226m. escudos (equivalent to 11.2% of GDP). Cape Verde's total external debt at the end of 2001 was US $359.6m., of which $340.2m. was long-term public debt. In that year the cost of debt-servicing was equivalent to 5.2% of the value of exports of goods and services. The annual rate of inflation averaged 4.0% in 1992–2003. Consumer prices increased by an average of 1.3% in 2003. In 2003 unemployment affected some 21% of the labour force, according to official figures.

INTERNATIONAL ECONOMIC RELATIONS

Cape Verde is a member of the Economic Community of West African States (ECOWAS), which promotes trade and co-operation in West Africa, and is a signatory to the Lomé Convention and subsequent Cotonou Agreement.

SURVEY AND PROSPECTS

Cape Verde's agricultural economy is highly vulnerable to severe periodic drought, making self-sufficiency in food production impossible; approximately 85% of the country's total food requirements are imported. The country benefits from considerable external assistance (which totalled 3,632m. escudos in 2000) and substantial remittances from emigrants. There are about 700,000 Cape Verdeans living outside the country, principally in the USA, the Netherlands, Portugal, Italy and Angola. In 2002, according to the central bank, private remittances from emigrants provided an estimated 9,701.9m. escudos, equivalent to 13.2% of GDP. The Government has attempted to attract emigrants' capital into the light-industry and fishing sectors by offering favourable tax conditions to investors.

In March 1998 Cape Verde and Portugal signed an agreement providing for their respective currencies to become linked through a fixed exchange rate, thus transforming the Cape Verde escudo into a convertible currency. In 2001 two financial co-operation agreements were signed by Portugal and Cape Verde, in an attempt to strengthen the Cape Verdean economy. In April 2002 the IMF approved a Poverty Reduction and Growth Facility worth some US $12.7m. in support of Cape Verde's economic programme for 2002–05 (as outlined in a new National Development Plan). In September the African Development Bank granted Cape Verde a $3.3m. loan to finance further economic reforms, and the Government and the UN signed an assistance framework plan, valid until 2005, aimed at aiding Cape Verde's development and reducing poverty. In November 2003 the Instituto Nacional de Estatística published a report estimating that the number of people living in poverty in Cape Verde had risen from 30% in 1989 to 36% in 2002. In December 2003 the IMF commended the country's recent economic performance, noting that GDP growth remained strong and inflation low, but emphasized the need to implement measures to accumulate increased levels of international reserves. The Government implemented a number of fiscal reforms in early 2004, including the introduction of value-added tax, and estimated GDP growth in 2003 at 7%. Economic objectives for 2004 were to control public spending, reduce debt, encourage foreign investment and continue with the privatization of state-owned companies.

Cayman Islands

The Cayman Islands lie west-north-west of Jamaica, in the Caribbean Sea, and comprise three main islands: Grand Cayman, Little Cayman and Cayman Brac. They came under acknowledged British rule in 1670, but until 1877 there was no administrative connection between Grand Cayman and the islands of Little Cayman and Cayman Brac. The islands formed a dependency of Jamaica until 1959. The islands are a United Kingdom Overseas Territory. The 1959 Constitution was revised in 1972, 1992 and 1994. George Town is the capital. The official language is English.

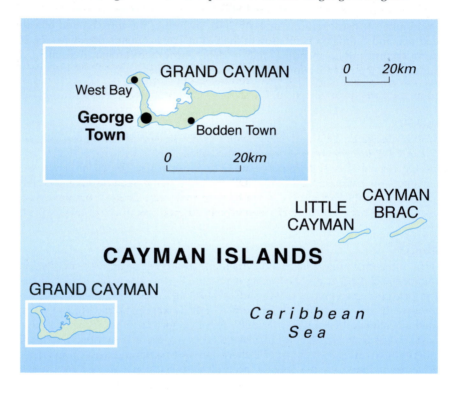

Area and population
Area: 262 sq km
Population (mid-2000): 35,000
Population density (mid-2000): 133.6 per sq km

Finance
Inflation (annual average, 2002): 2.4%
Currency: Cayman Islands dollar

Economy

In 2001, according to estimates by the Caribbean Development Bank (CDB), the Cayman Islands' gross domestic product (GDP) was US $1,845.2m., equivalent to some $44,571 per head. During 1991–2001, according to estimates, the population increased at an average annual rate of 3.8%, while GDP increased, in real terms, by 4.1% per year during 1991–2002; growth in 2002 was estimated at 1.7%.

AGRICULTURE

Agriculture (which engaged only 1.4% of the employed labour force in 1995 and provided some 0.5% of GDP in 1997) is limited by infertile soil, low rainfall and high labour costs. The principal crops are citrus fruits and bananas, and some other produce for local consumption. Flowers (particularly orchids) are produced for export. Livestock-rearing consists of beef cattle, poultry (mainly for eggs) and pigs. The traditional activity of turtle-hunting has virtually disappeared; the turtle farm (the only commercial one in the world) now produces mainly for domestic consumption (and serves as a research centre), following the imposition of US restrictions on the trade in turtle products in 1979. Fishing is mainly for lobster and shrimp.

INDUSTRY

Industry, engaging 12.6% of the employed labour force in 1995 and providing some 15.5% of GDP in 1997, consists mainly of construction and related manufacturing, some food-processing and tourist-related light industries. The construction sector contributed an estimated 9.3% of GDP in 1999, while manufacturing activities accounted for only about 2.3% of the total in that year. Energy requirements are satisfied by the import of mineral fuels and related products (10.9% of total imports in 1996).

SERVICES

Service industries dominate the Caymanian economy, accounting for 86.0% of employment in 1995 and contributing 83.9% of GDP in 1999. The tourist industry is the principal economic activity, and in 1991 accounted for 22.9% of GDP and employed, directly and indirectly, some 50% of the working population. The industry earned an estimated US $585.1m. in 2001. Most visitors are from the USA (71.0% of tourist arrivals in 1999). The Cayman Islands is one of the largest 'offshore' financial centres in the world; at the end of 2002 there were 388 banks and trust companies and 4,285 mutual funds on the islands, according to the Cayman Islands Monetary Authority. In 1995 the financial services sector engaged 18.9% of the working population, and in 1999 contributed about 36.0% of GDP.

EXTERNAL TRADE

In 2001 the Cayman Islands recorded an estimated trade deficit of US $645.1m. (commodity exports represented less than 1% of the value of total imports). Receipts from tourism and the financial sector, remittances and capital inflows normally offset the trade deficit. The principal source of imports is the USA (which provided some 76.7% of total imports in 1996), which is also one of the principal markets for exports (34.6% in 1994). Other major trading partners in 1996 included the United Kingdom, Japan and the Netherlands Antilles (which received 10.6% of total exports in that year). The principal exports in the 1980s were meat (mainly turtle meat, the export of which was subsequently banned under international treaty) and chemical products (in the late 1980s and early 1990s second-hand cars were a significant export). Principal exports in the 1990s were fish and cut flowers. The principal imports are machinery and transport equipment (26.0% of total imports in 1996), foodstuffs (18.6%), manufactured articles (18.5%) and basic manufactures (13.6%).

GOVERNMENT FINANCE

An estimated government surplus in its recurrent operations of US $0.5m. was recorded in 2001. Capital development aid from the United Kingdom ceased in 1982. In 1998 official development assistance totalled US $0.2m. At the end of 1999 the public debt stood at US $114.8m. The average annual rate of inflation was 3.4% in 1990–2001 and stood at an estimated 1.7% in 2002. According to official census figures, only 63% of the resident population of the islands were Caymanian in 1994 (compared with 79% in 1980). At the census of October 1999 some 5.3% of the labour force were unemployed. According to a report by the Economics and Statistics Office, the unemployment rate stood at 3.6% in October 2003. In the same month, some 48.5% of the working population were Caymanian.

INTERNATIONAL ECONOMIC RELATIONS

The United Kingdom is responsible for the external affairs of the Cayman Islands, and the dependency has the status of Overseas Territory in association with the European Union (EU). The Cayman Islands gained associate-member status in Caribbean Community and Common Market (CARICOM) in 2002; the territory is also a member of CARICOM's Caribbean Development Bank.

SURVEY AND PROSPECTS

Both the principal economic sectors, 'offshore' finance and tourism, benefit from the Cayman Islands' political stability, good infrastructure and extensive development. Tourism continued to expand in the 1990s, although the Government attempted to limit tourist numbers in order to minimize damage to the environment, particularly the coral reef, and to preserve the islands' reputation as a destination for visitors of above-average wealth. The financial sector, which benefits from an absence of taxation and of foreign exchange regulations, recorded consistently high levels of growth during the 1990s, and provided an estimated 30% of GDP in 1998. The banking sector was reckoned to be the world's fifth largest in 2000, owing to the absence of direct taxation, lenient regulation and strict confidentiality laws.

The Cayman Islands have a policy of openly confronting the issues of financial transparency and of money-laundering, and an information exchange treaty with the USA was ratified in 1990. However, despite the efforts of the authorities, the vulnerability of the islands' financial services sector to exploitation by criminal organizations continued to cause concern, and it was feared that if the Government did not impose further controls, then the British Government would be obliged to impose more stringent regulatory measures in response to international pressure. In June 2000 the Cayman Islands were included on a list of harmful tax regimes compiled by an agency of the Organisation for Economic Co-operation and Development (OECD) and were urged to make legislative changes, introducing greater legal and administrative transparency. The Government said that it would seek to be removed from the list as swiftly as possible and pledged to adopt international standards of legal and administrative transparency by 2005. In 2001, following stricter regulation of the private banking sector, the Cayman Islands were removed from the blacklist. In November, in a further move to increase international confidence in its financial regulation, the Government signed a tax information exchange agreement with the USA, designed to reduce the potential for abuse of the tax system.

Although the economy continued to grow in the late 1990s, consultant economic advisers warned the Government that increases in public spending, and the increased subsidization of Cayman Airways, were unsustainable, while fears remained that reforms to the financial services sector would reduce the islands' ability to attract international business. Indeed, in October 2001 the Chamber of Commerce linked an economic downturn to the negative impact of OECD pressure on the financial services sector, although the global economic slowdown and the adverse affects on the tourism industry of the September 2001 terrorist attacks in the USA were also regarded as factors in the economic decline. Moreover, the Government's decision to increase the annual licensing fee charged to 'offshore' financial institutions in the 2002 budget was widely criticized as being potentially damaging to the industry.

In late 2002 the financial sector faced further disruption when the United Kingdom, under pressure from an EU investigation into tax evasion, demanded that the Cayman Islands disclose the identities and account details of Europeans holding private savings accounts on the islands. The Cayman Islands, along with some other British Overseas Territories facing similar demands, claimed it was being treated unfairly compared with more powerful European countries, such as Switzerland and Luxembourg, and refused to make any concessions. The British Paymaster-General demanded that the Cayman Islands enact the necessary legislation to implement the EU's Savings Tax Directive by 30 June 2004; the Legislative Assembly, after the British Government pledged to safeguard the territory's interests, voted to accept British/EU demands by 1 January 2005. Meanwhile, the investigation into Parmalat in 2003–04 placed the 'offshore' financial sector under further scrutiny. Despite these set-backs, the sector performed strongly in 2002, and was expected to remain buoyant in 2003, offsetting the decline in tourism, which had failed to recover from the post-2001 slowdown. Economic growth was expected to remain stable at around 1.9% in 2003 and 2.1% in 2004, compared with an estimated 1.7% in 2002.

Central African Republic

The Central African Republic (CAR) is located in the heart of equatorial Africa. The CAR achieved independence from France in 1960. In 1965 Col Jean-Bédel Bokassa seized power in a military coup. In 1979 Bokassa was himself deposed in a coup. In 1981 Gen. André Kolingba established military rule. In elections held in 1993 the Mouvement pour la libération du peuple centrafricain emerged as the victorious party; its leader, Ange-Félix Patassé, was elected President (and re-elected in 1999). Since an attempted military insurrection in 1996 the CAR has experienced severe political and social instability. Patassé was overthrown in March 2003, and Gen. François Bozizé assumed power. The capital is Bangui. The national language is Sango, but French is the official language.

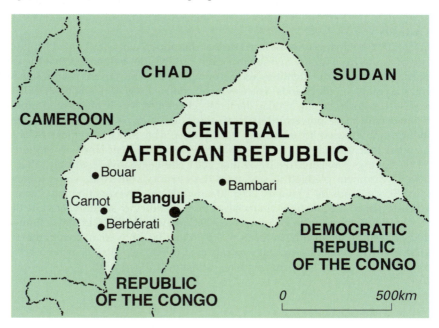

Area and population
Area: 622,984 sq km
Population (mid-2002): 3,828,000
Population density (mid-2002): 6.1 per sq km
Life expectancy (years at birth, 2002): 42.9 (males 42.1; females 43.7)

Finance
GDP in current prices: 2002): US $1,075m. ($281 per head)
Real GDP growth (2002): 4.2%
Inflation (annual average, 2002): 3.4%
Currency: CFA franc

Economy

In 2002, according to estimates by the World Bank, the CAR's gross national income (GNI), measured at average 2000–02 prices, was US $1,011m., equivalent to $260 per head (or $1,190 per head on an international purchasing-power parity basis). During 1990–2002, it was estimated, the population increased at an average annual rate of 2.0%, while gross domestic product (GDP) per head declined, in real terms, by an average of 0.4% per year. Overall GDP increased, in real terms, at an average annual rate of 1.8% in 1990–2002; growth in 2002 was 4.2%, according to the World Bank.

AGRICULTURE

Agriculture (including hunting, forestry and fishing) contributed 54.8% of GDP in 2002. About 71.8% of the economically active population were employed in the sector in 2001. The principal cash crops have traditionally been cotton (which accounted for an estimated 6.5% of export earnings in 2002) and coffee (only an estimated 1.0% of total exports in 2002, compared with 9.4% in 1999). In mid-2003 FAO warned that, although improved security would allow the 2003 cotton harvest to be sent to ginning complexes in Chad, there remained a severe shortage of seeds for the April–May 2004 planting season. Livestock and tobacco are also exported. The major subsistence crops are cassava (manioc) and yams. The Government is encouraging the cultivation of horticultural produce for export. The exploitation of the country's large forest resources represents a significant source of export revenue (exports of wood accounted for an estimated 50.1% of the total in 2002, increasing from 31.0% in 1999). Rare butterflies are also exported. Agricultural GDP increased at an average annual rate of 3.8% during 1990–2002; growth in 2002 was 4.0%.

INDUSTRY

Industry (including mining, manufacturing, construction and power) engaged 3.5% of the employed labour force in 1990 and provided 21.6% of GDP in 2002. Industrial GDP increased at an average annual rate of 1.5% in 1990–2002; growth in 2002 was 4.0%.

Mining

Mining and quarrying engaged a labour force estimated at between 40,000 and 80,000 in the late 1990s, and contributed 4.3% of GDP in 1999. The principal activity is the extraction of predominantly gem diamonds (exports of diamonds provided an estimated 36.6% of total export revenue in 2002). The introduction of gem-cutting facilities and the eradication of widespread 'black market' smuggling operations would substantially increase revenue from diamond mining. The reopening in 1997 of the Bangui diamond bourse, which had been established in 1996, was intended to increase revenue by levying a 10% sales tax on transactions. In July 2003 the CAR became a participant in the Kimberley Process, an international certification scheme aimed at excluding diamonds from the world market that have been traded for arms by rebel movements in conflict zones. Deposits of gold are also exploited. The development of uranium resources may proceed, and reserves of iron ore, copper, tin and zinc have also been located. Mining activity was largely suspended following Gen. François Bozizé's seizure of power in March 2003, pending an audit of companies involved in the sector. It was hoped that the adoption of a new mining code in December would revive the sector and increase transparency in licensing procedures. According to IMF estimates, the GDP of the mining sector increased by an average of 7.0% per year during 1992–94, but declined by an average of 4.6% per year in 1994–97, before increasing by 0.8% in 1998 and by 3.5% in 1999.

Manufacturing

The manufacturing sector engaged 1.6% of the employed labour force in 1988. Manufacturing, which contributed 9.4% of GDP in 2000, is based on the processing of primary products. In real terms, the GDP of the manufacturing sector increased at an average annual rate of 0.8% in 1990–2002; growth in 2002 was 4.0%.

Energy

In 1999, according to preliminary figures, 97.7% of electrical energy generated within the CAR was derived from the country's two hydroelectric power installations. Imports of petroleum products comprised an estimated 9.7% of the cost of merchandise imports in 2002.

SERVICES

Services engaged 15.5% of the employed labour force in 1988 and provided 23.6% of GDP in 2001. In real terms, the GDP of the services sector decreased at an average rate of 1.5% per year during 1990–2002; it declined by 5.2% in 2001, but increased by 4.8% in 2002.

EXTERNAL TRADE

In 2002 the CAR recorded a visible trade surplus of an estimated 23,100m. francs CFA, and there was a deficit of an estimated 18,900m. francs CFA on the current account of the balance of payments. In 1996 the principal source of imports was France (providing 39.5% of the total), while the principal markets for exports were Belgium-Luxembourg (accounting for 60.1% of the total) and France (30.9%). Other major trading partners in that year were Cameroon, Japan and the United Kingdom. The principal exports in 2002 were wood products, diamonds and cotton. The principal imports in 1996 were road vehicles, machinery, basic manufactures, cotton, mineral fuels and lubricants, chemical products and food.

GOVERNMENT FINANCE

In 2002 there was an estimated budget surplus of 27,600m. francs CFA (equivalent to 3.9% of GDP). At the end of 2001 the CAR's external debt was US $821.9m., of which $756.9m. was long-term public debt. In that year the cost of debt-servicing was equivalent to 11.9% of revenue from exports of goods and services. Consumer prices rose by 24.5% in 1994, following the devaluation of the currency, and by 19.2% in 1995. The annual rate of inflation averaged 3.7% in 1990–2002; consumer prices increased by an average of 2.7% in 2002. In 1995 7.6% of the labour force were unemployed.

INTERNATIONAL ECONOMIC RELATIONS

The CAR is a member of the Central African organs of the Franc Zone and of the Communauté economique des états de l'Afrique centrale (CEEAC).

SURVEY AND PROSPECTS

The CAR's land-locked position, the inadequacy of the transport infrastructure and the country's vulnerability to adverse climatic conditions and to fluctuations in international prices for its main agricultural exports have impeded sustained economic growth. Periodic political instability has also severely disrupted economic activity. In mid-1998 the IMF approved a three-year Enhanced Structural Adjustment Facility, valued at US $66m., to support the CAR's economic programme for 1998–2000. The accumulation of external and domestic payments arrears aggravated social tensions and led to mass protests by public-sector workers from late 2000. Further unrest, following the attempted coups in May 2001 and October 2002, and the consequent disruption to road links with Cameroon, destabilized the domestic economy and adversely affected international trade. The corruption scandal of July 2002 also undermined creditor confidence in the CAR. The Government was unable to complete its IMF-approved programme of structural and fiscal reforms, and the IMF and the World Bank suspended operations in the CAR; discussions with the IMF failed to reach agreement in early 2003, following the refusal of the USA to support further lending to the Patassé Government. Between October 2002 and March 2003 economic activity was disrupted by civil conflict.

Following his assumption of power in March, Bozizé and his new transitional Government began diplomatic efforts to secure financial assistance from international donors. In May the UN appealed for $9.5m. in emergency aid for the CAR, estimating that some 2.2m. people were 'in a situation of humanitarian distress'. One of the first actions of the new administration was to commence payment of salary arrears owed to public servants, as industrial action over non-payment had paralysed many sectors of the economy, but by late 2003 the Government was again having difficulty in paying wages. Anti-corruption measures were implemented, and in mid-2003 the new regime suspended mining and timber licences awarded under the previous administration, pending a review of the sectors. It was estimated that 50% of potential revenue from taxes on diamond exports were lost to smuggling and corruption under the Patassé administration. Meanwhile, insecurity persisted in much of the country, particularly in rural areas, adversely affecting agricultural production. Despite the Bozizé administration's reforms, and substantial assistance from the Communauté économique et monétaire de l'Afrique centrale, France and the People's Republic of China, the country's fiscal and economic position remained precarious in 2003, and real GDP declined by an estimated 7% in that year. The normalization of relations with international donors remained a priority, but largely depended on improved stability and continued progress towards a return to civilian rule.

Chad

The Republic of Chad is located in north central Africa. Chad achieved independence from France in 1960. The independent republic has experienced several ethnic and regional conflicts, particularly in northern regions. In 1990 the Mouvement patriotique du salut (MPS) overthrew President Hissène Habré, and Idriss Deby was installed as Head of State. In 1993 an interim legislature was established. Deby was elected as President in 1996. The MPS secured victory at legislative elections in 1997, consolidating its position further in 2002. Deby was re-elected as President in 2001. The capital is N'Djamena. French and Arabic are the official languages.

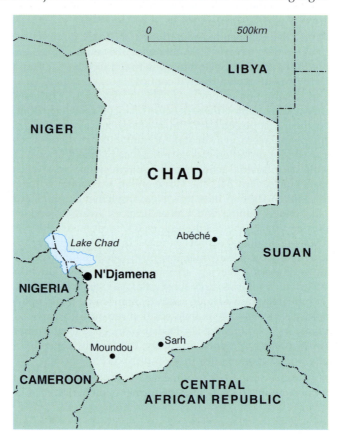

Area and population
Area: 1,284,000 sq km
Population (mid-2002): 8,144,430
Population density (mid-2002): 6.3 per sq km
Life expectancy (years at birth, 2002): 47.7 (males 46.1; females 49.3)

Finance
GDP in current prices: 2002): US $1,935m. ($238 per head)
Real GDP growth (2002): 10.9%
Inflation (annual average, 2002): 5.2%
Currency: CFA franc

Economy

In 2002, according to estimates by the World Bank, Chad's gross national income (GNI), measured at average 2000–02 prices, was US $1,758m., equivalent to $220 per head (or $1,000 on an international purchasing-power parity basis). During 1990–2002, it was estimated, the population increased at an average annual rate of 2.9%, while gross domestic product (GDP) per head increased, in real terms, by an average of 0.7% per year. Overall GDP increased, in real terms, at an average annual rate of 3.7% in 1990–2002, according to the World Bank; growth in 2002 was 10.9%.

AGRICULTURE
Agriculture contributed 36.8% of GDP in 2002, according to the World Bank; some 74.3% of the labour force were employed in the sector in 2001. The principal cash crop is cotton (exports of which contributed an estimated 28.1% of total export revenue in 2002, a decline from 41.1% in 2001). The principal subsistence crops are sorghum, millet and groundnuts. Livestock-rearing, which contributed an estimated 44.1% of exports in 2002 (overtaking cotton as the country's principal export), also makes an important contribution to the domestic food supply. During 1990–2002 agricultural GDP increased at an average annual rate of 5.2%; growth in 2002 was also 5.2%.

INDUSTRY
Industry contributed 13.8% of GDP in 2002. About 4.2% of the population were employed in the sector in 1990. During 1990–2002 industrial GDP increased at an average annual rate of 2.4%; the sector's GDP increased by 10.7% in 2002.

Mining
The mining sector (including fishing) contributed 3.2% of GDP in 2000, according to the IMF. For many years the only minerals exploited were natron (sodium carbonate), salt, alluvial gold and materials for the construction industry. However, long-delayed plans to develop sizeable petroleum reserves in the Doba Basin and at Sedigi, in the south of the country, were being pursued in the early 2000s, and production of petroleum at Doba commenced in mid-2003 (see below). There is believed to be considerable potential for the further exploitation of gold, bauxite and uranium. During 1994–2000 the GDP of the mining sector (including fishing) declined at an average annual rate of 0.2%, according to the IMF; growth of 0.8% was recorded in 2000.

Manufacturing
The manufacturing sector, which contributed 9.9% of GDP in 2002, operates mainly in the south of the country, and is dominated by agro-industrial activities, notably the processing of the cotton crop by the state-controlled Société Cotonnière du Tchad (COTONTCHAD). During 1994–2000 manufacturing GDP increased at an average

annual rate of 14.0%, according to the IMF; however, the GDP of the sector declined by 1.9% in 2000.

Energy

Chad is heavily dependent on imports of mineral fuels (principally from Cameroon and Nigeria) for the generation of electricity. Imports of mineral fuels comprised an estimated 17.9% of the total value of merchandise imports in 1995. The use of wood-based fuel products by most households has contributed to the severe depletion of Chad's forest resources. In November 2000 the Cameroonian Prime Minister announced the creation of a technical committee to instigate the export of electricity to Chad. None the less, by 2002 only 2% of households in Chad had access to electricity.

SERVICES

Services contributed 49.4% of GDP in 2002. The GDP of the sector increased at an average annual rate of 3.6% in 1990–2002; growth in 2002 was 15.2%.

EXTERNAL TRADE

In 2002 Chad recorded an estimated visible trade deficit of 400,100m. francs CFA, and there was a deficit of 674,000m. francs CFA on the current account of the balance of payments. In 1995 Chad's principal source of imports (41.3%) was France; other major suppliers were Cameroon, Nigeria and the USA. The principal markets for exports include Cameroon and France. The principal exports in 2002 were livestock and cotton. The principal imports in 1995 were petroleum products, road vehicles and parts, sugar and cereals.

GOVERNMENT FINANCE

In 2001 Chad recorded an overall budgetary surplus of 3,653m. francs CFA (equivalent to 0.3% of GDP). Chad's external debt at the end of 2001 totalled US $1,104m., of which $992m. was long-term public debt. In that year the cost of debt-servicing was equivalent to 7.9% of earnings from exports of goods and services. Consumer prices declined by an annual average of 2.1% in 1990–93. There was a sharp increase in the rate of inflation in 1994, to an average of 40.4%, following the 50% devaluation of the currency. Thereafter, the rate of inflation slowed to an average of 6.2% in 1995–2002; consumer prices increased by 5.2% in 2002.

INTERNATIONAL ECONOMIC RELATIONS

Chad is a member of the Central African organs of the Franc Zone and of the Communauté économique des états de l'Afrique centrale (CEEAC); the Lake Chad Basin Commission is based in N'Djamena.

SURVEY AND PROSPECTS

Economic growth in Chad has traditionally been inhibited by a number of factors: conflict has deterred investment in the development of considerable mineral wealth and other resources, leaving the economy over-dependent on cotton, while the country's land-locked position has been compounded by infrastructural deficiencies. Chad thus remains among the world's least developed countries, although the extraction of petroleum, which commenced in mid-2003, was expected to result in significant economic growth from the mid-2000s.

In January 2000 the IMF approved funding under its Poverty Reduction and Growth Facility (PRGF) in support of the Government's economic programme for 1999–2002. Furthermore, in May 2001 the Bretton Woods institutions declared Chad eligible for debt-service relief under their enhanced initiative for heavily indebted poor countries. The IMF increased Chad's PRGF by some US $6.8m. in January 2002, in order to alleviate the adverse effects of declining world prices for cotton, and in October the IMF agreed to a request by the Chadian authorities to extend the facility to December 2003. Meanwhile, in late 2000 a consortium led by the US ExxonMobil Corporation, and supported by Petronas of Malaysia and the US ChevronTexaco Corporation, began work to develop substantial petroleum resources in three fields in the Doba Basin. Operations commenced in July 2003, and the 1,070-km pipeline to transport petroleum from Doba to the port of Kribi in Cameroon was officially inaugurated in October. Initial output was estimated at 50,000 barrels per day (b/d), but was expected to increase to its peak level, of some 225,000 b/d, by the end of 2003; production was expected to continue for 25–30 years. The completion of the project was expected to double Chad's GDP, compared with that recorded in the early 2000s, in addition to alleviating the country's dependence on fuel imports. The Assemblée nationale adopted legislation whereby 72% of state revenue from the petroleum sector would be dedicated to the development of health, education, agriculture and infrastructure, while a further 10% would be held in trust for future generations.

In February 2001 the World Bank appointed an international advisory group to monitor the implementation of the project, and in September 2002, following the publication of a report by the group, which was critical of several aspects of the management of the project, the World Bank announced that it would intensify its monitoring of the development. Moreover, an independent committee was to give consent to all proposals for government expenditure from funds generated by the export of petroleum. Meanwhile, work commenced in 2000 on the construction of a pipeline from petroleum reserves at Sedigi to a new refinery in Farcha, near N'Djamena. The refinery would supply a new 16-MW power station in the capital, and provide fuel for local transportation requirements. However, although the construction of the pipeline had reportedly been completed by 2002, work on the refinery had been suspended in 2001, while the assassination, in September 2003, of the chief executive of the company responsible for overseeing the project was expected to lead to further delays. The successful pursuit of this and other efforts to develop the Chadian economy will largely depend on the Government's ability to maintain domestic peace and to satisfy the international community of its commitment to transparent governance and respect for human rights.

Chile

The Republic of Chile mainly lies along the Pacific Coast of South America. Chile gained independence from Spain in 1818. In 1989 President Aylwin replaced President Pinochet, who had assumed power following a coup in 1973. In 1991 the findings of a Comisión Nacional de Verdad y Reconciliación (established to investigate human rights abuses allegedly committed under Pinochet) caused popular outrage. In 2001, however, the Santiago Appeal Court ruled that Pinochet was mentally unfit to stand trial on any charges. Eduardo Frei Ruiz-Tagle was elected as President in 1993. He was succeeded by Ricardo Lagos Escobar in 2000. Santiago is the capital. The language is Spanish.

Area and population

Area: 756,096 sq km
Population (mid-2002): 15,578,820
Population density (mid-2002): 20.6 per sq km
Life expectancy (years at birth, 2002): 76.7 (males 73.4; females 80.0)

Finance

GDP in current prices: 2002): US $64,154m. ($4,118 per head)
Real GDP growth (2002): 2.1%
Inflation (annual average, 2002): 2.5%
Currency: peso

Economy

In 2002, according to estimates by the World Bank, Chile's gross national product (GNI), measured at average 2000–02 prices, was US $66,318m., equivalent to $4,260 per head (or $9,180 per head on an international purchasing-power parity basis). During 1990–2002, it was estimated, the population increased by an average of 1.5% per year, while gross domestic product (GDP) per head increased, in real terms, at an average annual rate of 4.3%. Overall GDP increased, in real terms, at an average annual rate of 5.6% in 1991–2002; real GDP increased by 2.2% in 2002.

AGRICULTURE

Agriculture (including forestry and fishing) contributed an estimated 6.0% of GDP, at constant prices, in 2001. About 13.5% of the employed labour force were engaged in this sector in 2002. Important subsistence crops include wheat, oats, barley, rice, beans, lentils, maize and chick-peas. Industrial crops include sugar beet, sunflower seed and rapeseed. Fruit and vegetables are also important export commodities (together contributing 8.6% of total export revenues in 2001), particularly, beans, asparagus, onions, garlic, grapes, citrus fruits, avocados, pears, peaches, plums and nuts. The production and export of wine has increased significantly in recent years. Forestry and fishing, and derivatives from both activities, also make important contributions to the sector. During 1990–2001 agricultural GDP increased, in real terms, by an average of 2.4% per year; agricultural GDP increased by 6.7% in 2000 and by 6.5% in 2001.

INDUSTRY

Industry (including mining, manufacturing, construction and power) contributed an estimated 37.8% of GDP, at constant prices, in 2001 and accounted for 23.9% of the employed labour force in 2002. During 1990–2001 industrial GDP increased by an average of 5.6% per year. GDP growth in all industrial sectors was 4.2% in 2000 and 2.2% in 2001.

Mining

Mining contributed an estimated 8.9% of GDP, at constant prices, in 2001 and engaged 1.3% of the employed labour force in 2002. Chile, with some 22% of the world's known reserves, is the world's largest producer and exporter of copper. Copper accounted for 87.5% of Chile's total export earnings in 1970, but the proportion had decreased to about 25.7% by 2001. Gold, silver, iron ore, nitrates, molybdenum, manganese, lead and coal are also mined, and the whole sector contributed 40.1% of total export earnings in 2001. In real terms, the sector's GDP increased by an estimated 5.2% in 2000 and by 3.6% in 2001. Petroleum and natural gas deposits have been located in the south, and plans to exploit significant reserves of lithium are under consideration.

Manufacturing

Manufacturing contributed an estimated 16.7% of GDP, at constant prices, in 2001, and engaged 14.1% of the employed labour force in 2002. The most important branches of manufacturing, measured by gross value of output, are food and non-ferrous metals. Manufacturing GDP increased by an average of 4.1% per year in 1990–2001. The sector's GDP increased by 4.0% in 2000, but declined by 0.3% in 2001.

Energy

In 2000 electric energy was derived mainly from hydroelectric power (46.2%), coal (27.0%) and natural gas (21.9%). Chile produces some 40% of its national energy requirements. Plans are under consideration to develop Chile's vast hydroelectric potential (estimated at 18,700 MW—the largest in the world). Meanwhile, Chile imported fuel and energy products equivalent to some 17.0% of the value of total merchandise imports in 2001.

SERVICES

The services sector contributed an estimated 56.1% of GDP, in constant prices, in 2001 and engaged some 62.6% of the employed labour force in 2002. The financial sector continued to expand in the early 21st century, fuelled, in part, by the success of private pension funds. During 1990–2001 services GDP increased by an average of 5.2% per year. The sector's GDP increased, in real terms, by 3.8% in 2000 and by 2.5% in 2001.

EXTERNAL TRADE

In 2002 Chile recorded a visible trade surplus of US $2,513m., but there was a deficit of $553m. on the current account of the balance of payments. In 2001 Argentina was the principal source of imports (17.8%), while the USA was the principal market for exports (19.4%). Other major trading partners were Japan, the United Kingdom, Brazil and the People's Republic of China. In 2001 the principal exports were copper and copper manufactures (25.7% of total export revenue), fish (8.7%), fruit (6.5%) and chemical products (6.2%). The principal imports in that year were machinery and transport equipment, and mineral and chemical products.

GOVERNMENT FINANCE

In 2001 there was a budgetary deficit of some 101,580m. pesos (equivalent to 0.2% of GDP). Chile's external debt totalled some US $38,360m. at the end of 2001, of which $5,544m. was long-term public debt. Debt-servicing costs in that year were equivalent to some 28.1% of the value of exports of goods and services. The annual rate of inflation averaged 8.3% in 1990–2002, and stood at 2.5% in 2002. An estimated 9.0% of the labour force were unemployed in 2002.

INTERNATIONAL ECONOMIC RELATIONS

Chile is a member of the Latin American Integration Association (ALADI) and was admitted to the Rio Group in 1990 and to the Asia-Pacific Economic Co-operation group (APEC) in 1994. Chile is also among the founding members of the World Trade Organization (WTO).

SURVEY AND PROSPECTS

Owing to the relaxation of import duties in the early 1980s, Chile's potential in the agricultural and manufacturing sectors was stifled by cheaper imported goods.

Exports of fruit, seafoods and wines, however, have expanded considerably, yet Chile remains heavily dependent on exports of copper and on the stability of the world copper market. Chile entered a period of recession during 1999, largely as a result of depressed world prices for copper; the economy contracted by 1.1% in that year. In an attempt to stimulate exports, in September the Central Bank abandoned its strict regulation of the peso, allowing the currency to float against the US dollar. Confidence returned to the economy in 2000 with GDP growth of 4.4%.

In an attempt to stimulate recovery, the new Government of President Lagos initiated a public works programme, designed to increase the incomes of skilled and semi-skilled workers, and introduced tax rebates of up to US $400 for about 1m. people. Other government initiatives included encouraging foreign investment in growth areas such as tourism and new technology and promoting investment in Chile's disparate regions. Tax and financial sector reforms were introduced to encourage inward investment and improve tax collection in 2001, but high unemployment and low investment levels continued to stifle consumer demand. Although high imported petroleum prices and declining prices for copper contributed to lower growth rates in 2001 and 2002 (3.1% and 2.2%, respectively), Chile's trade balance none the less remained stable, as market confidence increased.

By 2003 unemployment remained high (at an estimated 8.5%) and the Lagos Government faced increasing public hostility for its failure to implement significant economic reform. Nevertheless, in that year, as international prices for Chile's principal commodities improved, annual growth estimates were revised upwards, to 3.5%. A free trade agreement with the USA, Chile's largest trading partner, was concluded in October and came into effect in January 2004 and was expected significantly to enhance Chile's prospects for future growth.

China, People's Republic

The People's Republic of China, proclaimed in 1949, covers a vast area of eastern Asia. Until his death in 1976, Mao Zedong was the leading political figure. From the late 1970s Deng Xiaoping introduced a programme of economic reform. In 1989 demonstrations in favour of limited political reform were ruthlessly suppressed. Since the death of Deng Xiaoping in 1997 economic reform has continued to be pursued without significant political concessions. A new generation of leadership under President Hu Jintao was installed in March 2003. Beijing is the capital. The principal language is Northern Chinese (Mandarin).

Area and population
Area: 9,572,900 sq km
Population (mid-2002): 1,280,974,848
Population density (mid-2002): 133.8 per sq km
Life expectancy (years at birth, 2002): 71.1 (males 69.6; females 72.7)

Finance
GDP in current prices: 2002): US $1,237,145m. ($966 per head)
Real GDP growth (2002): 8.0%
Inflation (annual average, 2002): −0.8%
Currency: yuan

170

Economy

In 2002, according to estimates by the World Bank, China's gross national income (GNI), measured at average 2000–02 prices, was US $1,209,528m., equivalent to some $940 per head (or $4,390 on an international purchasing-power parity basis). During 1990–2002, it was estimated, the population increased at an average annual rate of 1.0%, while gross domestic product (GDP) per head increased, in real terms, by an average annual rate of 8.6%, one of the highest growth rates in the world. Overall GDP increased, in real terms, at an average annual rate of 9.7% in 1990–2002; growth in 2002 was 8.0%, compared with the previous year.

AGRICULTURE

Agriculture (including forestry and fishing) contributed 15.4% of GDP in 2002, and employed 44.1% of the working population in that year. China's principal crops are rice (production of which accounted formore than 30% of the total world harvest in 2002), sweet potatoes, wheat, maize, soybeans, sugar cane, tobacco, cotton and jute. According to the World Bank, agricultural GDP increased at an average annual rate of 3.7%, in real terms, in 1990–2002. Growth in agricultural GDP was 2.8% in 2002, compared with the previous year.

INDUSTRY

Industry (including mining, manufacturing, construction and power) contributed 51.1% of GDP in 2002 and engaged 21.4% of the employed labour force in that year. According to the World Bank, industrial GDP increased at an average annual rate of 12.7%, in real terms, in 1990–2002. Growth in industrial GDP was 7.9% in 2002, compared with the previous year.

Mining

The mining sector accounted for less than 0.8% of total employment in 2002. Output in the sector accounted for some 5.3% of total industrial production in 2002. China has enormous mineral reserves and is the world's largest producer of natural graphite, antimony, tungsten and zinc. Other important minerals include coal, iron ore, molybdenum, tin, lead, mercury, bauxite, phosphate rock, diamonds, gold, manganese, crude petroleum and natural gas.

Manufacturing

The manufacturing sector contributed an estimated 44.5% of GDP in 2002, and the sector accounted for 11.3% of total employment in that year. China is a leading world producer of chemical fertilizers, cement and steel. The GDP of the manufacturing sector increased at an average annual rate of 11.8%, in real terms, during 1990–2002, according to the World Bank. Growth in the GDP of the manufacturing sector was 8.1% in 2002 compared with the previous year.

Energy

Energy is derived principally from coal (66.1% in 2002); other sources are petroleum (23.4%), hydroelectric power (7.8%) and natural gas (2.7%). China became a net importer of crude petroleum in 1993. By December 1999 the People's Republic's largest hydroelectric power station, at Ertan, was fully functioning. The 18,200-MW

Three Gorges hydropower scheme on the Changjiang (River Yangtze), the world's largest civil engineering project, is scheduled for completion in 2009 and will have a potential annual output of 84,700m. kWh. China's national grid was also scheduled for completion in that year. The Three Gorges hydropower scheme began supplying power to eastern and central provinces in July 2003. Imports of mineral fuels comprised 7.2% of the cost of total imports in 2002. From the late 1990s China was increasingly seeking to develop and transport petroleum and gas reserves from Central Asia, and work on a 4,200-km pipeline from Xinjiang to Shanghai was under way in late 2002, with a view to completion in 2004. Discussions also took place in 2003 between the Chinese and Russian Governments on a proposal to build a pipeline from the Siberian petroleum fields in Argarsk to the Chinese centre of Daqing. It was unclear in late 2003 whether this plan would be carried out, with a possibility that the Siberian petroleum might be exported to Japan instead.

SERVICES

Services contributed 33.5% of GDP in 2002 and engaged 28.6% of the employed labour force in that year. Tourism, along with retail and wholesale trade, is expanding rapidly. Receipts from tourism increased by 14.6% in 2002 to reach US $20,385m. During 1990–2002, according to the World Bank, the GDP of the services sector increased at an average annual rate of 8.9% in real terms. Growth in the GDP of the services sector was 9.4% in 2002 compared with the previous year.

EXTERNAL TRADE

In 2002 China recorded a trade surplus of US $44,167m., and there was a surplus of $35,422m. on the current account of the balance of payments. In 2002 the principal source of imports was Japan (which provided 18.1% of total imports). Other important suppliers were Taiwan (12.9%), the Republic of Korea (9.7%) and the USA (9.2%). The principal markets for exports in 2002 were the USA (21.5% of total exports), Hong Kong (18.0%) and Japan (14.9%). Most of the goods exported to Hong Kong are subsequently re-exported. The principal imports in 2001 were machinery and transport equipment, chemicals and related products, and basic manufactures such as textiles. The principal exports in that year were machinery and transport equipment, textiles and clothing, and footwear.

GOVERNMENT FINANCE

In 2002 China's overall budget deficit was 314,951m. yuan, equivalent to 2.9% of GDP. China's total external debt at the end of 2001 stood at US $170,110m., of which $126,190m. was long-term public debt. In 2001 the cost of debt-servicing was equivalent to 7.8% of the value of exports of goods and services. The annual rate of inflation averaged 6.0% in 1990–2002. Consumer prices rose by 0.7% in 2001 but declined by 0.8% in 2002. The rate of inflation was unofficially estimated at 0.9% in 2003. According to official figures, the number of unemployed persons in 2002 was estimated at 25.6m. (7.3% of the total labour force). In 2002, according to the Asian Development Bank, the total number of registered unemployed in urban areas was some 7,700,000 (4.0% of the urban labour force). Meanwhile, the number of rural unemployed was unofficially estimated at 150m. in 2001.

INTERNATIONAL ECONOMIC RELATIONS

China joined the Asian Development Bank (ADB) in 1986 and the Asia-Pacific Economic Co-operation forum (APEC) in 1991. In 1994 China became a member of the Association of Tin Producing Countries (ATPC). In July 1995 China was granted observer status at the World Trade Organization (WTO), which had succeeded the General Agreement on Tariffs and Trade (GATT) in January of that year. China was finally admitted as a full member in December 2001. China joined the Bank for International Settlements (BIS) in 1996. In the same year the secretariat of the Tumen River Economic Development Area (TREDA) was established in Beijing by the Governments of China, North and South Korea, Mongolia and Russia. China is also a member of the UN Economic and Social Commission for Asia and the Pacific (ESCAP).

SURVEY AND PROSPECTS

In 1978 Deng Xiaoping introduced the 'open door' reform policy, which aimed to decentralize the economic system and to attract overseas investment to China. The state monopoly on foreign trade was gradually relinquished, commercial links with foreign countries were diversified and several Special Economic Zones were established. China subsequently experienced many years of rapid economic expansion, becoming one of the fastest-growing economies in the world. However, critics warned that much of this growth was uneven, being concentrated mainly in the southern and eastern urban coastal regions, while leaving the rural interior of the country relatively underdeveloped. In response, the Government initiated a number of massive infrastructural projects to open up the western parts of the country.

By the late 1990s the revitalization of the loss-making state-owned enterprises (SOEs) and the reform of the weak banking sector had become increasingly urgent issues. The process of SOE reform, however, was constrained by the necessity to minimize the number of workers being made redundant, amid concerns about possible social unrest. It was hoped that the restructuring of the SOEs would lead them away from traditional heavy industries in favour of more knowledge-based and consumer-orientated industries, with the assistance of private entrepreneurship. The CCP's decision in 2001 to admit private business people to its ranks for the first time indicated a new emphasis on private enterprise as the impetus for economic growth. In October 2001, in an effort to curb the pace of redundancies, the legislation regulating SOE bankruptcies was suspended. The creation of new employment opportunities and the improvement of social welfare provision were identified as official priorities.

The objectives of the Tenth Five-Year Plan, for the period 2001–06, included a growth rate of 7% per annum, greater scientific and technological advancement, the intensification of infrastructure projects and improved environmental protection, as well as the completion of the transition to a socialist market economy. Meanwhile, concerns about the validity of official figures continued: in 2001 officials from the National Bureau of Statistics admitted to widespread inaccuracies in the organization's reporting. In August 2001, in preparation for WTO membership, the Government removed price controls on 128 items, but retained controls of prices of some strategic commodities, such as natural gas, electricity supplies and basic telecommunication services. It was anticipated that China's accession to the WTO, which finally took place in December 2001, would help to overcome the political obstacles to the restructuring of the SOEs and banks, as these institutions would henceforth be obliged to become competitive in external markets. In the short term, accession to the WTO was likely to cause a consolidation of domestic industries, which would exert negative pressures on the economy. Some analysts predicted that as many as 40m. jobs in the state sector would be lost in the five years following China's accession to the WTO. In the longer term, however, WTO entry was expected to generate increased investment in China. Foreign direct investment reached a record US $52,700m. in 2002, but declined to an estimated $51,000m. in 2003. The deceleration in the economy of the USA, one of the People's Republic's major trading partners, adversely affected China's trade balance in 2001, but the surplus increased substantially in 2002, before declining in 2003.

Despite strong growth overall in 2002–03, China's economy faced several serious problems in the medium term. Much of the impressive economic growth had been state-generated, in the form of expensive major public-works projects, and this had resulted in an increasing budget deficit. There were fears that the growing public debt would eventually lead to a major failure of state banks. In order to avoid this, the Government therefore needed to reduce public spending, at a time when social security provisions were coming under increasing pressure from newly redundant workers. Private consumption growth was weaker in 2002 than in 2001, but recovered in 2003. Fears that the repercussions of the recent outbreak of Severe Acute Respiratory Syndrome (SARS) would affect the economy were confirmed in July when it was revealed that GDP growth had decreased to 6.7% in the second quarter of 2003, with growth in the services sector slowing to a mere 0.8%. However, from mid-2003 the economy made a rapid recovery. The official growth rate of 9.1% for 2003 as a whole represented the highest level of annual GDP growth since 1996, and concerns were raised that the Chinese economy might be 'overheating'. In 2003 there was also growing international pressure on China to liberalize its exchange-rate policy, amid concerns that the yuan was undervalued, at the fixed rate of 8.3 to the US dollar. The ADB forecast a GDP growth rate of 7.9% in 2004. A major challenge for the Chinese Government in the early 21st century, meanwhile, remained the balancing of economic reform with political stability and with environmental concerns.

China (Taiwan)

The Republic of China has, since 1949, been confined mainly to the province of Taiwan, located off the south-east coast of the Chinese mainland. After his defeat by the communist revolution in China, Gen. Chiang Kai-shek (President of the Chinese Republic since 1928) established a Kuomintang (KMT, Nationalist Party) regime on Taiwan. This regime continued to represent China at the UN until 1971, when it was replaced by the People's Republic. The KMT lost its majority in the legislature in December 2001. Taipei is the capital. The official language is Northern Chinese (Mandarin).

Area and population
Area: 36,188 sq km
Population (mid-2001): 22,463,172
Population density (mid-2001): 620.7 per sq km
Life expectancy (years at birth, 2002): Males 73.3; females 78.8

Finance
GDP in current prices: 2001): US $281,178m. ($12,586 per head)
Real GDP growth (2001): -2.18%
Inflation (annual average, 2002): -0.2%
Currency: new Taiwan dollar

Economy

In 2002, according to official figures, Taiwan's gross national income (GNI), at current prices, totalled US $289,272m., equivalent to US $12,916 per head. During 1990–2002, it was estimated, the population increased at an average annual rate of 0.8%, while in terms of US dollars real gross domestic product (GDP) per head increased by an average of 3.9% per year. Overall GDP increased, in terms of New Taiwan dollars, at an average annual rate of 5.4% in 1990–2002. Having contracted by 2.2% in 2001, GDP increased by 3.6% in 2002.

AGRICULTURE

Agriculture (including hunting, forestry and fishing) contributed 1.8% of GDP in 2002, and employed 7.5% of the working population. The principal crops are rice, sugar cane, maize, sweet potatoes and pineapples. Agricultural GDP increased by 0.1%, in real terms, during 1990–2002. Compared with the previous year, agricultural GDP increased by 4.7% in 2002.

INDUSTRY

Industry (comprising mining, manufacturing, construction and utilities) employed 35.2% of the working population, and provided 29.6% of GDP in 2002. Industrial GDP increased, in real terms, at an average rate of 4.2% per year between 1990 and 2002. Compared with the previous year, industrial GDP increased by 5.0% in 2002.

Mining

Mining contributed 0.4% of GDP in 2002, and employed less than 0.1% of the working population. Coal, marble and dolomite are the principal minerals extracted. Taiwan also has substantial reserves of natural gas. The GDP of the mining sector decreased at an average rate of 1.0% per year between 1990 and 2002. Mining GDP increased by 2.1% in 2002.

Manufacturing

Manufacturing contributed 24.5% of GDP in 2002, and employed 27.1% of the working population. The most important branches, measured by gross value of output, are electronics (particularly personal computers), plastic goods, synthetic yarns and the motor vehicle industry. The sector's GDP grew at an average annual rate of 4.5%, in real terms, in 1990–2002. Manufacturing GDP increased by 6.3% in 2002, compared with the previous year.

Energy

In 2002 49.2% of Taiwan's energy supply was derived from imported petroleum. Imports of crude petroleum accounted for 6.0% of total import expenditure in 2002. In that year nuclear power supplied 8.7% of Taiwan's energy requirements.

SERVICES

The services sector contributed 68.6% of GDP in 2002, while engaging 50.2% of the employed labour force. In 1990–2002 the GDP of this sector increased at an average annual rate of 6.6%. In 2002 services GDP increased by 3.3%, compared with the previous year.

EXTERNAL TRADE

In 2002 Taiwan recorded a visible trade surplus of US $24,770m., and there was a surplus of US $25,710m. on the current account of the balance of payments. In 2002 the principal sources of imports were Japan (accounting for 24.2%) and the USA (16.1%). The principal markets for exports in that year were Hong Kong (23.6%), the USA (20.5%) and Japan (9.2%). Trade with the People's Republic of China (mainly via Hong Kong) is of increasing significance. Taiwan's principal imports in 2002 were electronic products, machinery, mineral products and chemical and related products. The principal exports in that year were electronic products, machinery and electrical and mechanical appliances, textiles, and base metals.

GOVERNMENT FINANCE

The 2003 budget proposals envisaged revenue of NT $1,357,848m. and expenditure of NT $1,627,970m., the deficit thus being projected at NT $270,122m. Expenditure was projected at NT $1,591,600m. in 2004. At the end of June 2003 Taiwan's long-term external public debt was US $62m. The cost of debt-servicing remained equivalent to a negligible percentage of the value of exports of goods and services. The annual rate of inflation averaged 2.1% during the period 1990–2002. Consumer prices remained virtually unchanged in 2001, and declined by 0.2% in 2002, with a similar trend being observed in the first half of 2003. Some 4.9% of the labour force were unemployed in October 2003 (compared with 5.3% a year earlier); the rate of unemployment stood at 4.5% in January 2004. There is a shortage of labour in certain sectors.

INTERNATIONAL ECONOMIC RELATIONS

Taiwan became a member of the Asian Development Bank (ADB) in 1966, and of the Asia-Pacific Economic Co-operation forum (APEC) in late 1991. In September 1992 Taiwan was granted observer status at the General Agreement on Tariffs and Trade (GATT), and was finally granted membership of the successor World Trade Organization (WTO) in November 2001, effective from 1 January 2002.

SURVEY AND PROSPECTS

Taiwan's economic growth since 1949 has been substantial, with its economy usually proving to be very resilient to world recession, owing to the versatility of its manufacturing base and its large reserves of foreign exchange (estimated at US $196,609m. in October 2003). In 2001, however, the economic deceleration in the USA (Taiwan's major export market) adversely affected the island's growth. Exports, normally accounting for approximately 50% of GDP, decreased sharply, with the electronics industry being particularly badly affected, and by late 2001 Taiwan was experiencing its worst recession in 40 years. The level of unemployment rose steadily, despite an extensive government-initiated employment-creation programme. From late 2002, as economic growth resumed, the rate of unemployment began to decline.

In May 2002 the Government announced a new six-year national development plan, Challenge 2008, consisting of US $75,000m. of spending on infrastructure and public construction projects, as well as US $1,440m. in low-interest loans for research and development, and enhanced English-language education to take into account the growth of 'e-commerce' and the internet. One of the largest infrastructure projects in recent years, a US $12,800m. high-speed railway linking Taipei and Kaohsiung, when completed in 2005, was expected to integrate the island's western seaboard into a single commercial zone, as well as provide technology transfers from its Japanese developers. The national development plan also aimed to create 700,000 new jobs, with a view to keeping average unemployment below 4%, and maintaining GDP growth at above 5%. The Government also hoped that the plan would double the number of tourist visits. Despite such plans, compared with the previous year direct investment from abroad declined by 64.8% in 2002, partly owing to increasing competition from China. (Foreign investment decreased by 21.5% year-on-year during January–September 2003.) The Government feared that the increasing cross-Straits links it had been promoting were causing an excessive outflow of funds to China.

Also during 2002 moves toward a consolidation of the banking and financial sector gathered momentum, as regulatory barriers separating banks, insurance companies and securities firms were removed, following the introduction of a new law in late 2001. In May 2002 the Government also announced plans to privatize several state-owned banks by 2006, and sell all its stakes in commercial banks by 2010. Meanwhile, Taiwan's privatization programme (first introduced in 1989) continued, with Chinese Petroleum, China Shipbuilding, and Chunghwa Telecom scheduled for sale by the end of 2003, Taiwan Tobacco and Liquor, and Tang Eng Iron Works by the end of 2004 and Taiwan Power by the end of 2005. The privatization process had been delayed in recent years by opposition from labour unions and vested interest groups. Estimates for GDP growth were lowered following the outbreak of Severe Acute Respiratory Syndrome (SARS) in Taiwan in early 2003. From mid-2003, however, the Taiwanese economy recovered rapidly from the effects of SARS, with record growth in exports in the second half of the year. GDP thus expanded by 3.2% in 2003. A GDP growth rate of 4.7% was projected for 2004.

Colombia

The Republic of Colombia lies in the north-west of South America. In 1819 Colombia achieved independence from Spain as part of Gran Colombia, which included Ecuador, Panama and Venezuela. For more than a century ruling power in Colombia has been shared between the Partido Conservador Colombiano (PCC) and the Partido Liberal Colombiano (PL). According to official estimates, lawlessness during 1949–58, known as 'La Violencia', caused the deaths of some 280,000 people. Since the 1960s Colombia has been destabilized by anti-government guerrilla insurgencies and by the activities of illegal drugs cartels. The capital is Santafé de Bogotá. The language is Spanish.

Area and population
Area: 1,141,748 sq km
Population (mid-2002): 43,744,848
Population density (mid-2002): 38.3 per sq km
Life expectancy (years at birth, 2002): 71.8 (males 67.5; females 76.3)

Finance
GDP in current prices: 2002): US $82,194m. ($1,879 per head)
Real GDP growth (2002): 1.5%
Inflation (annual average, 2002): 6.3%
Currency: peso

Economy

In 2002, according to estimates by the World Bank, Colombia's gross national income (GNI), measured at average 2000–02 prices, was US $80,100.9m., equivalent to $1,830 per head (or $5,870 per head on an international purchasing-power parity basis). During 1990–2002, it was estimated, the population increased at an average annual rate of 1.9%, while gross domestic product (GDP) per head increased, in real terms, by an average of 0.6% per year. Colombia's overall GDP increased, in real terms, by an average of 2.5% per year in 1990–2002; GDP grew by 1.5% in 2002.

AGRICULTURE

Agriculture (including hunting, forestry and fishing) contributed an estimated 13.0% of GDP in 2001, and employed some 21.0% of the labour force in 2002. The principal cash crops are coffee (which accounted for 6.2% of official export earnings in 2001), cocoa, sugar cane, bananas, tobacco, cotton and cut flowers. Rice, cassava, plantains and potatoes are the principal food crops. Timber and beef production are also important. During 1990–2001 agricultural GDP decreased at an average annual rate of 1.1%. Agricultural GDP increased by 4.7% in 2000, but decreased by 0.1% in 2002.

INDUSTRY

Industry (including mining, manufacturing, construction and power) employed 19.3% of the labour force in 2002, and contributed an estimated 29.9% of GDP in 2001. During 1990–2001 real industrial GDP increased at an average annual rate of 1.4%. Industrial GDP increased by 4.4% in 2000, but decreased by 0.1% in 2001.

Mining

Mining contributed an estimated 6.4% of GDP in 2000 and employed 1.5% of the labour force in 2002. Petroleum, natural gas, coal, nickel, emeralds and gold are the principal minerals exploited. Silver, platinum, iron, lead, zinc, copper, mercury, limestone and phosphates are also mined. According to the UN, growth in mining GDP was 7.4% in 1998 and 16.2% in 1999.

Manufacturing

Manufacturing contributed an estimated 16.3% of GDP in 2001, and employed 13.2% of the labour force in 2002. During 1990–2001 manufacturing GDP declined at an average annual rate of 1.3%. Manufacturing GDP increased by 10.5% in 2000, but decreased by 0.1% in 2001. Based on the value of output, the most important branches of manufacturing were food products, beverages, chemical products, textiles and transport equipment.

Energy

Hydroelectricity provided 73.0% of Colombia's electricity requirements in 2000. In the early 1990s a rapid expansion programme of thermal power-stations was undertaken in order to increase electricity output in line with demand, which increased by 4.5% per year in the 1990s, and to reduce reliance on hydroelectric power. Natural gas provided some 18.8% of electricity requirements in 2000. The country is self-sufficient in petroleum and coal, and these minerals accounted for 34.5% of export revenues in 2001.

SERVICES

The services sector contributed an estimated 57.1% of GDP in 2001, and engaged 59.5% of the labour force in 2002. During 1990–2001 the combined GDP of the service sectors increased, in real terms, at an estimated average rate of 3.6% per year. The GDP of the services sector increased by 1.2% in 2000 and by 2.1% in 2001.

EXTERNAL TRADE

In 2001 Colombia recorded a visible trade surplus of US $508m. and there was a deficit of $1,789m. on the current account of the balance of payments. The country's principal trading partner in 2001 was the USA, which provided 34.7% of imports and took 43.4% of exports. Other important trading partners in that year were Venezuela and Ecuador. The principal exports in 2001 were minerals (particularly petroleum and its derivatives and coal), chemicals, vegetables and vegetable products, textiles and leather products, and foodstuffs, beverages and tobacco. The principal imports in 2001 were machinery and transport equipment, chemicals, foodstuffs, beverages and tobacco, textiles and leather products, and vegetables and vegetable products. A significant amount of foreign exchange is believed to be obtained from illegal trade in gold, emeralds and, particularly, the drug cocaine.

GOVERNMENT FINANCE

In 1998 there was a budgetary deficit of 6,940,600m. pesos in central government spending, equivalent to 5.3% of GDP. Colombia's external debt amounted to US $36,399m. at the end of 2001, of which $21,777m. was long-term public debt. Debt-servicing was equivalent to 36.1% of the value of exports of goods and services. In 1990–2002 the average annual rate of inflation was 18.1%; consumer prices increased by an annual average of 8.6% in 2001 and by 7.2% in 2002. According to provisional estimates, annual inflation totalled 6.5% in 2003. Some 14.8% of the labour force were unemployed in August 2003.

INTERNATIONAL ECONOMIC RELATIONS

Colombia is a member of ALADI and of the Andean Community. Both organizations attempt to increase trade and economic co-operation within the region.

SURVEY AND PROSPECTS

A programme of structural reform was adopted in 1990–94, resulting in the liberal-ization of trade and the reorganization of the public sector. Strong economic growth was recorded during this period, not least because of the discovery of significant petroleum reserves. However, during 1994–98 GDP slowed, unemployment soared and the fiscal deficit widened. In the late 1990s economic problems in Colombia were compounded by a fall in the international price of the country's principal export commodities, petroleum and coffee, and by high interest rates, which had led to a rise in the cost of debt-servicing. In September 1999 the central bank allowed the flotation of the peso, the value of which had depreciated by 23% since the beginning of the year. In the same month, the Government secured some US $6,900m. in financial assistance from international donors, including an IMF credit worth some $2,700m. (which was approved in December) in support of its economic programme for 1999–2002, which emphasized further fiscal reform, the restructuring of the financial sector and a reduction in public spending, as well as the introduction of new social welfare programmes to alleviate the effects of austerity measures.

The privatization programme planned for 2000 failed to get under way, with the sale of electrical companies delayed as a result of guerrilla attacks on power installations and low investor interest in the public banks. Furthermore, Colombia was unable to take full advantage of the high price of petroleum in 2000 and 2001 because of guerrilla attacks on pipelines. In February 2002 the US Administration announced plans to donate $98m. to the Colombian Government in order to establish a military unit to protect the Caño Limón pipeline. One of the Uribe Government's priorities on assuming office in August 2002 was the reform of the tax, pensions and labour sectors. In support of these proposed reforms, in January 2003 the IMF and the World Bank announced new loans to Colombia of $2,200m. and $3,300m., respectively. Although the government proposals were defeated in a referendum in October 2003, and the Congreso approved only limited fiscal measures in December, in January 2004 the IMF nevertheless endorsed Colombia's economic performance, and made available a further $145m. in loans.

Meanwhile, the heavy debt burden, the absence of significant new petroleum discoveries and political uncertainty in neighbouring Venezuela (Colombia's second largest trading partner) continued to threaten the economic recovery. Such negative aspects were, however, offset by the significant impact on investor confidence of the Government's progress in its campaign against rebel groups. The business community was also encouraged in 2003 by President Uribe's decisive measures to restructure the state telecommunications and petroleum companies, as well as by continued low inflation, a decline in unemployment and a decrease in the fiscal deficit (which was reduced to the equivalent of 2.9% of GDP in 2003, compared with 3.6% in 2002). Growth was estimated at 3.2% in 2003 and was forecast at 3.5% in 2004.

Comoros

The Union of the Comoros is an archipelago situated between the island of Mada-gascar and the African mainland. The Comoros declared their independence from France in 1975, although France maintained control of the island of Mayotte. In 1999, as a secessionist crisis dating from 1997 remained unresolved, Col Assoumani Azali seized power. In 2001 a new Constitution provided for the partial autonomy of each island in a new Union of the Comoros. In 2002 Azali was elected as Federal President. Nation-wide elections to a new federal legislature, the Assemblée de l'Union, took place in April 2004. The capital, which is situated on the island of Ngazidja, is Moroni. The official languages are Comorian, French and Arabic.

Area and population

Area: 1,862 sq km
Population (mid-2002): 585,940
Population density (mid-2002): 314.7 per sq km
Life expectancy (years at birth, 2002): 63.3 (males 61.6; females 64.9)

Finance

GDP in current prices: 2002: US $256m. ($437 per head)
Real GDP growth (2002): 3.0%
Inflation (annual average, 2001): 3.5%
Currency: Comoros franc

Economy

In 2002, according to estimates from the World Bank, the gross national income (GNI) of the Comoros (excluding Mayotte), measured at average 2000–02 prices, was US $228m., equivalent to $390 per head (or $1,640 per head on an international purchasing-power parity basis). During 1990–2002, it was estimated, the population increased at an average annual rate of 2.6%, while gross domestic product (GDP) per head declined, in real terms, by an average of 1.4% per year. Overall GDP increased, in real terms, at an average annual rate of 1.1% in 1990–2002; growth in 2002 was 3.0%.

AGRICULTURE

Agriculture (including hunting, forestry and fishing) contributed 35.4% of GDP in 2002. Approximately 73.3% of the labour force were employed in the agricultural sector in 2001. In 2000 the sector accounted for some 88.4% of export earnings. The principal cash crops are vanilla, cloves and ylang-ylang. Cassava, taro, rice, maize, pulses, coconuts and bananas are also cultivated. According to the World Bank, the real GDP of the agricultural sector increased at an average annual rate of 3.5% in 1990–2002; growth in 2001 was 3.0%.

INDUSTRY

Industry (including manufacturing, construction and power) contributed 10.6% of GDP in 2002. Some 9.4% of the labour force were employed in the industrial sector in 1990. According to the World Bank, the Comoros' industrial GDP increased at an average annual rate of 7.5% in 1990–2002; industrial GDP increased by 2.0% in 2002.

Manufacturing

The manufacturing sector contributed 3.6% of GDP in 2002. The sector consists primarily of the processing of agricultural produce, particularly of vanilla and essential oils. According to the World Bank, manufacturing GDP increased at an average annual rate of 4.1% in 1990–2002; manufacturing GDP increased by 2.3% in 2002.

Energy

Electrical energy is derived from wood (some 80%), and from thermal installations. Imports of petroleum products comprised 18.2% of the total cost of imports in 2002.

SERVICES

The services sector contributed 54.0% of GDP in 2002. Strong growth in tourism from 1991 led to a significant expansion in trade, restaurant and hotel activities, although political instability inhibited subsequent growth. According to the World Bank, the GDP of the services sector decreased at an average rate of 3.2% per year in 1990–2002; however, it increased by 3.5% in 2002.

EXTERNAL TRADE

In 2001, according to estimates, the Comoros recorded a visible trade deficit of 18,632m. Comoros francs, but there was a surplus of 7,357m. Comoros francs on the current account of the balance of payments. In 2000 the principal source of imports was South Africa (accounting for some 54.2% of the total); other major sources were France, Pakistan and Kenya. France was the principal market for exports (43.5%); other important purchasers were Singapore, the USA and the United Kingdom. The leading exports in 2002 were vanilla (providing 66.5% of the total), cloves and ylang-ylang. The principal imports in that year were petroleum products (18.2%), rice, vehicles and parts, and meat and fish.

GOVERNMENT FINANCE

The Comoran budget deficit was estimated at 3,085m. Comoros francs in 2002 (equivalent to 2.4% of GDP). The Comoros' external public debt at the end of 2001 totalled US $245.9m., of which $220.8m. was long-term public debt. In that year the cost of debt-servicing was equivalent to 3.7% of the value of exports of goods and services. According to the IMF, the annual rate of inflation averaged 1.5% during 1995–99. The rate rose to 25.3% in 1994, following a 33.3% devaluation of the Comoros franc in January 1994, but slowed thereafter, reaching 1.1% in 1999. An estimated 20% of the labour force were unemployed in 2000.

INTERNATIONAL ECONOMIC RELATIONS

In 1985 the Comoros joined the Indian Ocean Commission (IOC). The country is also a member of the Common Market for Eastern and Southern Africa (COMESA) and of the Franc Zone.

SURVEY AND PROSPECTS

The Comoros has a relatively undeveloped economy, with high unemployment, a limited transport system, a severe shortage of natural resources and heavy dependence on foreign aid, particularly from France. An intensification of political instability on the islands, following the seizure of power by the army in April 1999, had a particularly adverse effect on maritime trade and tourism. Following the conclusion of an agreement on national reconciliation in February 2001, in July a group of 'Friends of the Comoros', co-ordinated by the World Bank (and also including the European Union (EU), the Organisation internationale de la francophonie, France, Mauritius and Morocco), pledged some US $11.5m. in aid to assist with constitutional developments towards the establishment of a new Comoran entity, as well as to alleviate poverty and improve the economy. Furthermore, it was hoped that a number of agreements reached later that year, worth an estimated €5.9m., would encourage the further development of the production of vanilla, ylang-ylang and cloves, and increase international demand for those crops.

After partial devolution in 2002, conflicts over the distribution of political power led to the prolonged closure of ports on Ngazidja, which adversely affected local government finances on the island. Following a mission to the Comoros in July, the IMF rejected the possibility of granting a loan to the islands, owing to ongoing political instability, despite recent improvements in economic performance, which were partly attributed to the suspension of sanctions against Nzwani by the Organization of African Unity (now the African Union) in May 2001. The IMF warned that the islands had experienced a significant decline in income, with a concurrent increase in consumer prices.

In November 2002 the federal Government and the EU signed a National Indicator Programme on co-operation during 2002–07; the Comoros was to receive €27.3m. under the Programme, mostly for education. During much of 2003 considerable economic disruption was caused, particularly on Ngazidja, by disputes over the distribution of political power and revenues following partial devolution. Meanwhile, the value of Comoran vanilla exports increased substantially, as international prices for the commodity escalated, owing to a severe decline in output in Madagascar, the world's principal producer. However, prices for cloves remained low throughout the year, and widespread poverty in the Comoros was exacerbated by steep rises in prices for essential foodstuffs. In February 2004 President Azali approved a six-month transitional budget aimed at creating conditions for economic recovery and the resumption of negotiations with international donors.

Congo, Democratic Republic

The Democratic Republic of the Congo (DRC) lies in central Africa. Having gained independence from Belgium as the Republic of the Congo, in 1964 the country was renamed the DRC. In 1965 Joseph-Désiré Mobuto (elected President in 1970) seized power. The DRC became the Republic of Zaire in 1971. However, in 1997 the leader of rebel forces, Laurent-Désiré Kabila, declared himself President of the DRC. In 1999 the DRC signed an agreement with five regional states to end civil war in the country, and UN peace-keeping troops were deployed. After his assassination in 2001, Kabila was succeeded by his son, Maj.-Gen. Joseph Kabila. Transitional executive and legislative institutions were inaugurated in 2003, in accordance with a power-sharing agreement. Kinshasa is the capital. French is the official language.

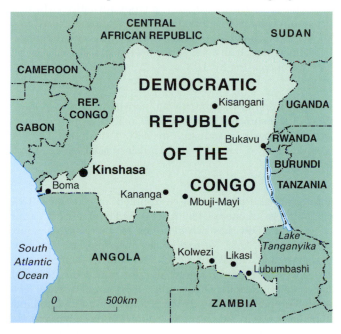

Area and population
Area: 2,344,885 sq km
Population (mid-2002): 53,797,020
Population density (mid-2002): 22.9 per sq km
Life expectancy (years at birth, 2002): 43.5 (males 41.0; females 46.1)

Finance
GDP in current prices: 2002: US $5,704m. ($106 per head)
Real GDP growth (2002): 3.0%
Inflation (annual average, 2002): 31.5%
Currency: new Congolese franc

Economy

In 2002, according to estimates by the World Bank, the gross national income (GNI) of the DRC, measured at average 2000–02 prices, was US $5,045m., equivalent to $90 per head (or $580 per head on an international purchasing-power parity basis). During 1990–2002, it was estimated, the population increased at an average annual rate of 3.2%, while gross domestic product (GDP) per head declined, in real terms, by an average of 7.5% per year. Overall GDP decreased, in real terms, at an average annual rate of 4.6% in 1990–2002; GDP declined by an estimated 2.0% in 2001, but increased by an estimated 3.0% in 2002.

AGRICULTURE
Agriculture (including forestry, livestock, hunting and fishing) contributed an estimated 56.3% of GDP in 2002. About 59.4% of the working population were employed in agriculture at mid-2001. The principal cash crops are coffee (which accounted for 8.8% of export earnings in 1999, although its contribution declined to an estimated 0.8% in 2000), palm oil and palm kernels, sugar, tea, cocoa, rubber and cotton. Agricultural GDP increased at an average annual rate of 0.4% in 1990–2002, declining by 5.4% in 2001, but increasing by 3.0% in 2002.

INDUSTRY
Industry (including mining, manufacturing, construction and public works, and power) contributed an estimated 18.8% of GDP in 2002. Some 15.9% of the working population were employed in industry in 1991. Industrial GDP declined at an average annual rate of 7.5% in 1990–2002, but increased by 3.8% in 2001 and by 3.0% in 2002.

Mining
Mining (including mineral processing) contributed an estimated 9.8% of GDP in 2001. Mineral products accounted for at least 89.1% of export earnings in 2000. Diamonds, of which the DRC has rich deposits, are the principal source of foreign exchange, accounting for 49.8% of export earnings in 2000. The most important minerals are copper and cobalt (of which the country has 65% of the world's reserves). Manganese, zinc, tin and gold are also mined. In 1998–2002 there was extensive illicit exploitation of the DRC's mineral resources by rebel factions. In 2001 illicit mining of the country's abundant resources of columbite-tantalite (coltan) exceeded that of diamonds in the east of the country (although international demand subsequently declined). In early 2004 a British-based enterprise, America Mineral Fields, announced a major investment in the Kolwezi Tailings retreatment project (a major resource of copper and cobalt), and also in the redevelopment of a copper and zinc mine in the south of the country. There are extensive offshore reserves of petroleum (revenue from petroleum accounted for 23.2% of export earnings in 2000). The sector's GDP (including the processing of minerals) decreased at an average annual rate of 22.5% in 1990–95, but increased by an average of 2.1% per year in 1996–2001; growth in 2001 was estimated at 7.5%.

Manufacturing
Manufacturing contributed an estimated 3.9% of GDP in 2002. The most important sectors are textiles, cement, engineering and agro-industries producing consumer

goods. Manufacturing GDP declined at an average annual rate of 12.4% in 1990–95 and of 8.0% in 1996–2001; an estimated decline of 12.5% was recorded in 2001.

Energy

Energy is derived principally from hydroelectric power. In 2000 an estimated 99.7% of electricity production was generated by hydroelectric plants. In 2000 imports of petroleum comprised 7.2% of the value of total merchandise imports.

SERVICES

The services sector contributed an estimated 24.9% of GDP in 2002, and employed some 19.0% of the working population in 1991. The GDP of the services sector decreased at an average annual rate of 10.2% in 1990–2002, declining by 8.7% in 2001, but increasing by 3.0% in 2002.

EXTERNAL TRADE

In 2002 the DRC recorded an estimated trade surplus of US $27m., but there was a deficit of $159m. on the current account of the balance of payments. In 1995 the principal source of imports (an estimated 16.6%) was Belgium-Luxembourg; other major suppliers were South Africa, Nigeria, Ecuador, the United Kingdom and Germany. In that year South Africa was the principal market for exports (taking an estimated 29.6% of the total); the USA, Belgium-Luxembourg and Angola were also important markets for exports. In 2000 the principal exports were mineral products (mainly industrial diamonds, crude petroleum, cobalt and copper) and agricultural products (primarily coffee). The principal import was petroleum.

GOVERNMENT FINANCE

In 2002 the overall budget deficit (before interest rescheduling) was estimated at 34,242m. new Congolese francs, equivalent to 1.8% of GDP. At the end of 2001 external debt totalled US $11,392m., of which $7,584m. was long-term public debt. In that year the cost of debt-servicing was equivalent to 1.7% of the value of exports of goods and services. At the end of 2002 external public debt was estimated at $10,434m. Annual inflation averaged 450.8% in 1993–2002. Consumer prices increased by 359.9% in 2001 and by 31.5% in 2002.

INTERNATIONAL ECONOMIC RELATIONS

The DRC maintains economic co-operation agreements with its neighbours, Burundi and Rwanda, through the Economic Community of the Great Lakes Countries. The DRC is also a member of the International Coffee Organization and of the Common Market for Eastern and Southern Africa (COMESA). In September 1997 the DRC became a member of the Southern African Development Community (SADC).

SURVEY AND PROSPECTS

Potentially one of Africa's richest states, the DRC has extensive agricultural, mineral and energy resources. During the early 1990s, however, most foreign investment in the country was withdrawn, and by June 1994 government revenues had declined to such an extent that it was suspended from the IMF. The administration of Laurent-Désiré Kabila, which came to power in May 1997, secured foreign investment to revive the highly lucrative mining sector and subsequently succeeded in restoring some financial stability. A new currency, the Congolese franc, replaced the new zaire from June 1998. However, the outbreak of civil war in August resulted in a further deterioration in the financial situation, with repeated depreciation of the new currency, the resumption of hyperinflation and an increase in the budget deficit. Rebel factions gained control of much of the east of the country, where they systematically exploited mineral resources (thereby financing the continuing civil conflict). Ugandan and Rwandan forces supporting the rebels benefited significantly from gaining control of mineral concessions in the east, while Zimbabwe became involved in the conflict on behalf of the DRC Government, in return for significant control of the mining industry.

Following the succession to the presidency of Joseph Kabila in January 2001, significant progress in peace negotiations was achieved, and a UN embargo on trade in unlicensed diamonds was imposed in May. In the same month the new Government implemented an IMF-monitored plan for the rehabilitation of public finances, which included the introduction of an official 'floating' exchange rate. After commending the authorities' commitment to market reforms, the IMF approved a three-year rehabilitation and reconstruction programme, supported by a Poverty Reduction and Growth Facility (PRGF) arrangement (officially commencing in April 2002). In January 2002, in response to Kabila's urgent appeals for aid, international donors pledged to release considerable development assistance to support the continuation of the peace process; in September the Paris Club of creditor Governments approved a large-scale rescheduling of the DRC's external debt. The first year of the PRGF-supported programme resulted in considerable progress in post-conflict recovery, with a resumption in economic growth. The IMF announced that overall fiscal performance at the end of 2002 had exceeded targets, while consumer prices had declined sharply from hyperinflation levels. The authorities had also begun to implement structural reforms, including restructuring of the banking sector, and the introduction of new mining regulations. Following considerable advancement in the peace process, most foreign troops supporting the combatant groups were withdrawn from the DRC by October 2002. An extensive power-sharing accord, which incorporated the principal rebel factions, was reached in December, and, after the adoption of a new Constitution in April 2003, a new transitional Government of national unity was installed in July. (However, the resumption of intensive fighting in the north-east of the country necessitated a reinforcement of the peace-keeping contingent.)

After a further IMF review in July, it was decided that economic progress had been sufficient for the country to qualify for an 80% reduction in external debt under the enhanced initiative for heavily indebted poor countries. Government priorities were to reduce corruption, rehabilitate infrastructure and introduce further reform of government institutions and state-owned enterprises. At the end of 2003 a meeting of bilateral and multilateral donors, convened under the auspices of the World Bank, pledged further aid to support the recovery programme, but urged greater state accountability, following condemnation by the UN Security Council of illicit exploitation of the country's natural resources during the civil conflict. The announcement of major mining projects in early 2004 (see above) demonstrated a significant improvement in the private-investor confidence, despite continued fighting in the east of the country.

Congo, Republic

The Republic of the Congo is located in central Africa. In 1960 the Congo became fully independent of France. After a military coup in 1968, the Government adopted Marxist ideology. In 1979 President Col Jacques-Joachim Yhombi-Opango surrendered his powers to a Provisional Committee, and Col (later Gen.) Denis Sassou-Nguesso became President. In 1992 multi-party elections were held, and Pascal Lissouba was elected President. Lissouba was re-elected in 1997, but civil conflict ensued, and military forces led by Sassou-Nguesso seized power later that year. Sassou-Nguesso was elected as President in 2002. Brazzaville is the capital. The official language is French.

Area and population
Area: 342,000 sq km
Population (mid-2002): 3,189,770
Population density (mid-2002): 9.3 per sq km
Life expectancy (years at birth, 2002): 53.1 (males 51.6; females 54.5)

Finance
GDP in current prices: 2002): US $ 3,014m. ($945 per head)
Real GDP growth (2002): 3.5%
Inflation (annual average, 2002): 4.6%
Currency: CFA franc

Economy

In 2002, according to estimates by the World Bank, the Congo's gross national income (GNI), measured at average 2000–02 prices, was US $2,232m., equivalent to $700 per head (and $700 on an international purchasing-power parity basis). During 1990–2002, it was estimated, the population increased at an average annual rate of 3.0%, while gross domestic product (GDP) per head declined, in real terms, by an average of 1.1% per year. Overall GDP increased, in real terms, at an average annual rate of 1.9% in 1990–2002; growth in 2002 was 3.5%.

AGRICULTURE

Agriculture (including forestry and fishing) contributed 6.1% of GDP in 2002, and employed about 39.9% of the total labour force in 2001. The staple crops are cassava and plantains, while the major cash crops are sugar cane, oil palm, cocoa and coffee. Forests cover about 57% of the country's total land area, and forestry is a major economic activity. Sales of timber provided an estimated 8.4% of export earnings in 1995, but in February 1998, to encourage local processing of wood, forestry companies were prohibited from exporting rough timber. Following the implementation of liberalization measures in the sector, output of timber was expected to increase significantly in the early 2000s. In 2002 exports of cork and wood provided 7.7% of export earnings. During 1990–2002 agricultural GDP increased at an average annual rate of 1.4%; growth in 2002 was 4.4%.

INDUSTRY

Industry (including mining, manufacturing, construction and power) contributed 65.6% of GDP in 2002, and employed an estimated 14.7% of the labour force in 1990. During 1990–2002 industrial GDP increased at an average annual rate of 2.4%; growth in 2002 was 1.4%.

Mining

Mining and manufacturing contributed an estimated 63.5% of GDP in 2001. The hydrocarbons sector is the only significant mining activity. In 2002 sales of petroleum and petroleum products provided an estimated 88.1% of export earnings. Annual petroleum production (an estimated 103m. barrels in 2001, according to the US Geological Survey) was expected to continue to grow, as a result of major exploration and development planned at various offshore deposits, in particular near to the maritime border with Angola. Deposits of natural gas are also exploited. Lead, zinc, gold and copper are produced in small quantities, and the large-scale mining of magnesium was expected to commence in 2004. There are also exploitable reserves of diamonds, phosphate, iron ore, bauxite and potash. In October 2001 the Government issued the Portuguese company Escom a licence to prospect for diamonds in the far north of the country. The real GDP of the petroleum sector (extraction and refining) increased at an average annual rate of 4.9% in 1995–2001, but declined by an estimated 7.5% in 2001.

Manufacturing

Manufacturing contributed 5.2% of GDP in 2002. The most important industries, the processing of agricultural and forest products, were adversely affected by the civil conflict in the late 1990s, but began to recover in the early 2000s, as political stability was restored. The textile, chemical and construction materials industries are also significant. During 1990–2002 manufacturing GDP increased at an average annual rate of 0.5%; growth of 9.0% was recorded in 2002.

Energy

In 2000 some 99.7% of total electricity production was generated by hydroelectric plants. Imports of fuel and energy comprised an estimated 23.7% of the value of total imports in 2000. The construction of a new hydroelectric dam at Imboulou, some 200 km north of Brazzaville, commenced in late 2003, with an anticipated completion date of 2009.

SERVICES

The services sector contributed 28.4% of GDP in 2002. During 1990–2002, it was estimated, the GDP of the services sector increased at an average annual rate of 1.5%; growth of 5.3% was recorded in 2002.

EXTERNAL TRADE

In 2002 the Congo recorded a visible trade surplus of an estimated 1,597,700m. francs CFA, but there was an estimated deficit of 34,500m. francs CFA on the current account of the balance of payments. In 1995 the principal source of imports (32.0%) was France, while the USA was the principal market for exports (22.6%). Italy and the Netherlands are also important trading partners. The principal exports in 2002 were petroleum and petroleum products, and cork and wood. The principal imports in 1996 were machinery, chemical products, iron and steel and transport equipment.

GOVERNMENT FINANCE

The budget surplus for 2002, according to provisional figures, was 12,700m. francs CFA (equivalent to 0.6% of GDP). The country's external debt totalled US $4,896m. at the end of 2001, of which $3,631m. was long-term public debt. In that year the cost of debt-servicing was equivalent to 3.7% of the value of exports of goods and services. The annual rate of inflation averaged 6.3% in 1990–2002. Consumer prices increased by an average of 4.3% in 2002.

INTERNATIONAL ECONOMIC RELATIONS

The Republic of the Congo is a member of the Central African organs of the Franc Zone and of the Communauté économique des états de l'Afrique centrale (CEEAC).

SURVEY AND PROSPECTS

Economic performance in the late 1990s was adversely affected by civil conflict and ensuing instability. In November 1997 the World Bank suspended relations with the Congo in response to the non-payment of debt arrears, while the outbreak of further hostilities in December 1998 led to the suspension of all donor activity. In recent years the high relative level of debt (which in 2001 was equivalent to 234.5% of GNI) has remained a major impediment to the resumption of aid, and weaknesses in the implementation of reforms and a lack of strict budget control have prevented the Congo from qualifying for relief under the Bretton Woods institutions' initiative for heavily indebted poor countries. None the less, in November 2000 the IMF approved a credit of some US $14m. for the Congo in emergency post-conflict assistance, and in August 2001 the World Bank declared that the Congo had cleared all of its overdue service payments and was again eligible for credit.

Major reforms, involving restructuring and privatization, were introduced in a number of important sectors in the early 2000s, including banking and petroleum. A new mining code, aimed at encouraging foreign investment, was introduced in late 2003, while the implementation of reforms in the forestry sector resulted in the opening, in early 2004, of the first eucalyptus forest in the Congo to be operated within the private sector. Meanwhile, a new cement-producing company, the Nouvelle Société des Ciments du Congo, commenced operations in 2002, as a joint enterprise between the Congolese Government and a Chinese company, to replace a state-owned company that had closed during the civil conflict.

A programme of post-conflict reconstruction emphasized major infrastructural improvements, including the construction of a year-round river port at Lékéti and a new international airport in the north of the country. The restoration of peace in the Pool region, following the signing of a cease-fire agreement in March 2003, was expected to facilitate the eventual return to pre-conflict levels of international trade through the port at Pointe-Noire and the Congo-Océan railway line (which was to be transferred to private-sector management in 2004). In the longer term, however, the Congo's economic development was likely to depend on the successful implementation of credible privatization programmes, tighter budget control, greater economic transparency and the maintenance of political stability.

Cook Islands

The Cook Islands are located in the southern Pacific Ocean, lying between American Samoa, to the west, and French Polynesia, to the east. They were proclaimed a British protectorate in 1888, and a part of New Zealand in 1901. In 1965 the Cook Islands became a self-governing Territory in free association with New Zealand. The capital is Avarua. English and Cook Islands Maori are the official languages.

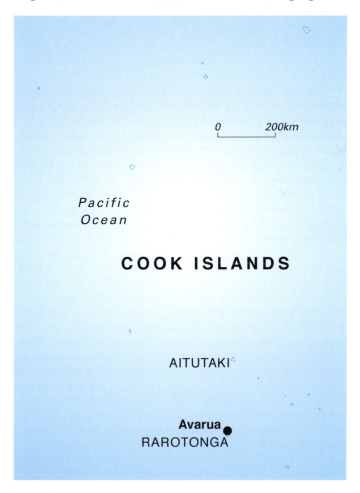

Area and population
Area: 237 sq km
Population (December 2001): 18,027
Population density (December 2001): 76.1 per sq km
Life expectancy (years at birth, 2002): 71.6 (males 69.2; females 74.2)

Finance
GDP in current prices: 2000): $NZ 171.6m. ($NZ 9,587 per head)
Real GDP growth (2000): 9.8%
Inflation (2002): 3.4%
Currency: New Zealand dollar

Economy

In 2001, according to the Asian Development Bank (ADB), the Cook Islands' gross domestic product (GDP), measured at current prices, totalled an estimated $NZ183.8m. GDP increased, in real terms, at an average annual rate of 1.9% in 1990–2001. According to official figures, GDP rose by 2.2% in 2002 and by an estimated 1.8% in 2003. A growth rate of 0.2% was forecast for 2004.

AGRICULTURE

According to estimates by the ADB, agriculture (including hunting, forestry and fishing) contributed 12.0% of GDP in 2001. In that year the sector engaged some 38% of the economically active population, according to FAO estimates. In 2000 only 35% of Rarotonga households were classified as being agriculturally active, compared with 74% in the southern outer islands. According to ADB estimates, the real GDP of the agricultural sector contracted by 3.3% per year in 1990–2001. Compared with the previous year, the sector's GDP decreased by 27.5% in 1999 , but increased by an estimated 32.4% in 2000, before decreasing again by 24.0% in 2001. In 2002 the sector provided 32.6% of export earnings (compared with 5.3% in the previous year). Papaya is the Cook Islands' most important export crop. Papaya exports were worth some $NZ250,000 in 1998. Other important cash crops are coconuts and tropical fruits such as mangoes, pineapples and bananas. Cassava, sweet potatoes and vegetables are cultivated as food crops. Pigs and poultry are kept. The sale of fishing licences to foreign fleets provides an important source of income. However, illegal fishing in the islands' exclusive economic zone increased during the 1990s, and in March 2003 the Government announced harsher penalties in an attempt to deal with this problem. Aquaculture, in the form of giant clam farming and pearl oyster farming, was developed during the 1980s. The pearl industry expanded considerably during the 1990s. Pearl oyster farming at Manihiki and Penrhyn Island was the islands' most important industry, and pearls were the most important export commodity by 2000, when they contributed 92.1% of total export earnings. The industry was adversely affected, however, by Cyclone Martin which devastated Manihiki Atoll in late 1997 and by a bacterial pearl shell disease in 2000. In response to the infection, the pearl industry agreed to a number of measures designed to protect the environment and reduce overfarming. In 2002 pearl exports earned $NZ6.4m., equivalent to 58.6% of total earnings.

INDUSTRY

According to ADB estimates, industry (comprising mining and quarrying, manufacturing, construction and power) provided 7.4% of GDP in 2001. The sector engaged 12.1% of employees in 1993. Industrial GDP increased, in real terms, at an average rate of 2.4% per year during 1990–2001. Compared with the previous year, the industrial sector's GDP increased by some 6.8% in 2000 but decreased by 0.8% in 2001.

Manufacturing

Manufacturing contributed 4.1% of GDP in 1995, and engaged 4.5% of employees in 1993. The manufacturing and mining sectors together accounted for an estimated 2.8% of GDP in 2001, according to ADB estimates. The real GDP of manufacturing and mining declined at an average rate of 0.2% per year during 1990–2001. Compared with the previous year, however, the two sectors' GDP increased by 3.5% in 2001. The most important industrial activities are fruit-processing, brewing, the manufacture of garments and handicrafts. Construction contributed an estimated 2.9% of GDP in 2001 and engaged 3.4% of the employed labour force in 1993.

Energy

The islands depend on imports for their energy requirements. Mineral fuels accounted for 26.7% of total imports in 2002. In September 1997 the Government signed an agreement with a consortium of Norwegian companies to mine cobalt, nickel, manganese and copper by extracting mineral-rich nodules found in the islands' exclusive economic zone (EEZ) between Aitutaki and Penrhyn. It was estimated that the deep-sea mining project, which was expected to begin in 2003/04, could earn the islands up to US $15m. per year and US $600m. in total. Trial operations began in 1999.

SERVICES

Service industries contributed an estimated 80.5% to GDP in 2001 and engaged 80.8% of the employed labour force in 1993. Tourism expanded considerably in the late 1980s and early 1990s, and earned an estimated $NZ93.9m. in 2000/01. Visitor arrivals rose from 72,781 in 2002 to 78,328 in the following year. The trade, restaurants and hotels sector contributed 32.0% of GDP in 2001 and engaged 20.9% of the employed labour force in 1993. 'Offshore' banking, introduced to the islands in 1982, expanded rapidly, with more than 2,000 international companies registered by 1987. In 1992 the islands were established as an alternative domicile for companies listed on the Hong Kong Stock Exchange. The financial and business services sector provided 10.7% of GDP in 2001 and engaged 3.6% of the employed labour force in 1993. A significant proportion of the islands' revenue is provided by remittances from migrants (who outnumber the residents of the islands).

EXTERNAL TRADE

In 2002 the Cook Islands recorded a trade deficit of $NZ91.2m. In the same year there was a surplus on the current account of the balance of payments equivalent to 6.3% of GDP. This figure declined slightly to an estimated 5.9% in 2003. The principal exports in 2002 were basic manufactures (which accounted for 58.8% of total exports). The principal imports were machinery and transport equipment (which cost 27.2% of total imports), food and live animals (23.3%) and basic manufactures (17.7%). The principal sources of imports in 2002 were New Zealand (79.1% of the total). Japan and Australia were the principal markets for exports (44.1% and 22.1%).

GOVERNMENT FINANCE

According to official estimates, in the financial year ending June 2002 there was an overall budgetary surplus of $NZ0.5m., and a similar surplus was forecast for 2002/03. In mid-2003 the Government announced a budget that emphasized reduced spending, as well as the establishment of a reserve trust fund with US $185,000.

Development assistance from New Zealand totalled $NZ6.2m. in 1999/2000, and was to remain at this level for the following three financial years. (New Zealand is the guarantor of the Cook Islands' borrowing from the ADB, which had reached a total of $NZ25m. at 31 October 2001.) Aid from New Zealand totalled $NZ6.24m. in 2003/04. Development assistance from Australia totalled $A10.4m. in 2002/03. It was estimated at the end of 2002 that the islands' external debt amounted to some US $54m. The annual rate of inflation averaged 3.1% in 1990–2001. Average consumer prices rose by 3.9% in 2002 and by 2.4% in 2003. The ADB estimated the unemployment rate to be 12.7% in 1998. By 2001, however, the employment situation had improved significantly, owing to increased demand for workers in the tourism and retail sectors.

INTERNATIONAL ECONOMIC RELATIONS

The Cook Islands is a member of the Pacific Community and the Pacific Islands Forum and an associate member of the UN Economic and Social Commission for Asia and the Pacific (ESCAP). In late 1999 the Cook Islands were granted observer status at the Lomé Conventions with the European Union (superseded by the Cotonou Agreement).

SURVEY AND PROSPECTS

During the 1990s and early 2000s development plans sought to expand the economy by stimulating investment in the private sector and developing the islands' infrastructure. In 1995 it was announced that the New Zealand dollar was to become the sole legal currency of the islands, following a financial crisis that led the Government to withdraw the Cook Islands dollar from circulation and to introduce a retrenchment programme. Between 1996 and 1998 the number of public-sector workers was reduced from 3,350 to 1,340, and the number of ministries from 52 to 22. (By early 2004, however, there were renewed concerns for the islands' financial welfare when it was reported that the number of public-sector employees had increased to some 1,800 and public payroll expenditure had risen by 30% in only two years.) In addition, a radical economic restructuring programme was announced in 1996, in response to a deepening financial crisis, which had led the Government to default on a debt of US $100m. to an Italian bank. Negotiations took place between the Cook Islands Government and its major creditors, the Governments of Italy and Nauru and the New Zealand Government Superannuation Fund, in late 1998, at which an agreement to reschedule the islands' external debt was concluded. The Government of France (also a major creditor) refused to participate in the arrangement. The Government subsequently adopted a policy of accumulating reserves for the purposes of debt-servicing as an annual budgetary allocation.

Plans to restructure the 'offshore' sector, announced in 1998, were expected to increase revenue. However, the islands' financial regulations were severely criticized by the Financial Action Task Force (FATF), which in early 2004 continued to include the Cook Islands on a list of countries and territories of which the banking systems were allegedly being used for the purposes of 'money-laundering'. Large-scale emigration remained a serious and deepening concern for the Cook Islands' economy in the late 1990s and early 2000s, and in August 2002 the Government announced that it would allocate US $23,350 to the campaign to encourage islanders resident abroad to return. Meanwhile, the success of the tourist industry and the dramatic increase in arrivals to the islands led to expressions of concern that

Rarotonga, in particular, was unable to sustain the growth. Reports indicated that waste disposal and energy provision were inadequate in relation to the demands of large numbers of visitors and that pollution of the lagoon was occurring as a result. In January 2003 the Cook Islands Tourism Corporation appealed for a moratorium on all new tourism projects following an independent report into the environmental and social impact of the industry on the islands. However, a project to expand the runway at Rarotonga airport, allowing for the arrival of larger aircraft, was expected to be completed by 2005.

Costa Rica

The Republic of Costa Rica lies in the Central American isthmus. In 1821 Costa Rica declared its independence from Spain. Under José Figueres Ferrer, founder of the Partido de Liberación Nacional (PLN), Costa Rica became one of the most democratic countries in Latin America. In 1978 Rodrigo Carazo Odio of the Partido Unidad Opositora coalition became President. PLN candidates regained presidential office in 1982 and 1986. In 1990 Rafael Angel Calderón Fournier of the Partido Unidad Social Cristiana (PUSC) was elected. All presidential elections since 1994 have been won by candidates of the PUSC. San José is the capital. The language spoken is Spanish.

Area and population
Area: 51,100 sq km
Population (mid-2002): 3,941,750
Population density (mid-2002): 77.1 per sq km
Life expectancy (years at birth, 2002): 77.1 (males 74.8; females 79.5)

Finance
GDP in current prices: 2002): US $16,887m. ($4,284 per head)
Real GDP growth (2002): 2.8%
Inflation (annual average, 2002): 9.2%
Currency: colón

Economy

In 2002, according to estimates by the World Bank, Costa Rica's gross national income (GNI), measured at average 2000–02 prices, was US $16,168.9m., equivalent to $4,100 per head (or $8,260 per head on an international purchasing-power parity basis). During 1990–2002, it was estimated, the population increased by an average of 2.2% per year, while gross domestic product (GDP) per head increased, in real terms, by an average of 2.4% per year. Overall GDP increased, in real terms, by an average annual rate of 4.6% in 1990–2002; GDP increased by 3.0% in 2002.

AGRICULTURE

Agriculture (including hunting, forestry and fishing) contributed an estimated 8.1% of GDP in 2002 and employed 15.9% of the economically active population. In 2000 banana production employed some 40,000 people directly and a further 100,000 indirectly. The principal cash crops are bananas (which accounted for 8.9% of general export earnings in 2002), coffee (3.1% of general export earnings), flowers and tropical fruit. Seafood exports were also significant. Sugar cane, rice, maize and beans are also cultivated. According to the World Bank, the real GDP of the agricultural sector increased at an average annual rate of 3.6% during 1990–2001. Real agricultural GDP increased by an estimated 0.4% in 2000, but declined by 1.0% in 2001.

INDUSTRY

Industry (including mining, manufacturing, construction and power) employed 22.5% of the economically active population in 2002 and provided an estimated 27.9% of GDP. According to the World Bank, real industrial GDP increased at an average annual rate of 5.5% during 1990–2001. However, the GDP of the sector decreased by 2.0% in 2000 and grew by only 0.1% in 2001. Mining employed only 0.1% of the economically active population in 2002 and contributed an estimated 0.2% of GDP. In June 2002 open-cast mining was banned by presidential decree in order to preserve the environment and the future of eco-tourism in Costa Rica.

Manufacturing

The manufacturing sector employed 14.3% of the employed work-force in 2002 and contributed an estimated 20.1% of GDP. In terms of the value of output, the principal branches of manufacturing in 1999 were food products (37.4%), chemical products (11.4%), beverages (8.4%) and paper and paper products (4.8%). Production of computer components by the US manufacturer Intel began in 1998. According to the World Bank, real GDP of the manufacturing sector increased at an average annual rate of 6.0% during 1990–2001. However, the sector's GDP remained stagnant in 2000 and increased by just 0.1% in 2001.

Energy

Energy is derived principally from petroleum and hydroelectric power. The Arenal hydroelectricity project was inaugurated in 1979; however, its full generating capacity of 1,974 MW did not fulfil Costa Rica's electricity requirements, and in late 1993 the state electricity company, Instituto Costarricense de Electricidad (ICE) began its third electricity development programme. The programme included a US $300m. hydroelectric power project on the Río Reventazón, completed in 2000, and the country's first wind-generated power plant. In 2000 the ICE announced plans to build a 1,250 MW hydroelectric plant at Boruca by 2011. In 2000 hydroelectric power accounted for 82.1% of total electrical energy generation. Imports of fuels and lubricants accounted for an estimated 7.4% of the total value of imports in 2001.

SERVICES

The services sector employed 61.3% of the economically active population in 2002, and provided an estimated 64.0% of GDP. According to the World Bank, the real GDP of this sector increased at an average annual rate of 4.3% during 1990–2001. Real GDP increased by 4.3% in 2000 and by 1.6% in 2001. Tourism is the country's most important source of foreign-exchange earnings and in 2000 the sector employed some 152,000 people. Receipts from tourism totalled an estimated US $1,078m. in 2002 and tourist arrivals numbered 1,113,359. Of these, approximately 38% originated from the USA. In 2002 the Costa Rican Tourism Institute requested assistance from the Government to aid future expansion of the sector, including exemption from land and import taxes.

EXTERNAL TRADE

In 2002 Costa Rica recorded a visible trade deficit of US $1,263.4m. and there was a deficit of $1,682.8m. on the current account of the balance of payments. In 2002 the principal source of imports (53.1%) was the USA; other major suppliers were Mexico, Venezuela and Japan. The USA was also the principal market for exports (50.2%) in 2001; other significant purchasers were the Netherlands, Guatemala and Germany. The principal exports in 2002 were electrical components for microprocessors, textiles and bananas. The principal imports in that year were machinery and transport equipment and basic manufactures.

GOVERNMENT FINANCE

In 2001 there was an estimated budgetary deficit of 259,311.5m. colones (equivalent to some 4.8% of GDP). Costa Rica's estimated total external debt at the end of 2001 was US $4,586m., of which $3,424m. was long-term public debt. The cost of debt-servicing in that year was $695m., equivalent to 9.0% of exports of goods and services. The annual rate of inflation averaged 14.9% in 1990–2002. Consumer prices increased by 11.3% in 2001 and by 9.2% in 2002. Some 6.4% of the labour force were unemployed in 2002.

INTERNATIONAL ECONOMIC RELATIONS

Costa Rica is a member of the Central American Common Market (CACM) and the Inter-American Development Bank (IDB). In May 2000 legislation was passed enhancing the Caribbean Basin Initiative, first introduced in 1983, granting North American Free Trade Agreement (NAFTA) parity to products from 24 states, including Costa Rica. In April 2001 the Government concluded a free trade agreement with Canada, which was promulgated in November 2002. In late January 2003 the first round of talks on the establishment of a Central American Free Trade Agreement (CAFTA) with the USA were held in San José between representatives of the Governments of Costa Rica, El Salvador, Guatemala, Honduras, Nicaragua and the USA. Further negotiations took place throughout 2003. In October, during a round of talks in Houston, Texas, USA, disagreement emerged over US demands that Costa Rica liberalize its telecommunications industry, over which the ICE enjoyed a monopoly.

The Costa Rican Government strongly resisted such a move; however, in December, at a final round of negotiations in the US capital, it agreed to open up certain parts of the industry. The USA countered these concessions with demands that Costa Rica also end the state monopoly of the insurance sector, prompting the Costa trade delegation to withdraw from the negotiations in protest. In January 2004, nevertheless, the two countries reached an agreement whereby the Costa Rican Government would partially privatize telecommunications and insurance sectors in return for agricultural subsidies. Costa Rica was more successful in finalizing the terms of a free trade agreement with the Caribbean Community and Common Market (CARICOM). The agreement, reached in March 2003 and scheduled to take effect in January 2004, excluded just 58 of 6,000 locally produced products from free trade terms.

SURVEY AND PROSPECTS

During the 1990s successive Governments adopted austerity measures aimed at addressing the country's high public-sector deficit. Measures promoting increased foreign investment and enabling private-sector participation in activities formerly confined to the state sector, including the deregulation of the banking system, were implemented in 1996. The IMF urged the incoming Rodríguez administration in 1998 to expedite the divestment of public assets, initiated by the previous Government, and to use the proceeds to reduce the country's public domestic debt, which was equivalent to 27.6% of GDP in 1997. However, the Government's efforts to end the state's monopoly in the telecommunications, energy and insurance sectors proved unsuccessful in 1999, owing to legislative opposition. A similar attempt in 2000 resulted in public protests. In October 2003 the President of the IDB, Enrique Iglesias, recommended liberalization of several state monopolies in Costa Rica. Following the agreement reached with the USA in January 2004, as part of the ongoing CAFTA negotiations, partial and gradual liberalization of the telecommunications and insurance sectors were expected by 2006.

In March 1998 the US microprocessor manufacturer Intel began production at the first of four plants under construction in Costa Rica. Exports from the Intel plants, situated in a free-trade zone close to the capital, contributed some 3%–4% of GDP in 1999, superseding the traditional exports of bananas and coffee. However, despite expectations that it would remain the country's principal source of exports, in 2000 there was a significant decrease in microchip exports, owing to plant restructuring. In May 2001, following a brief closure for modernization, the Intel plant re-opened; however, sales of microchips fell by 60% in 2001. By June 2002 the company reported a 5% increase in sales in the first half of the year. Sales continued to increase and contributed more than US $1,000m. to export revenues in 2002.

The agricultural sector was affected by fluctuations in the prices of coffee and bananas. International coffee prices reached a 30-year low in early 2001 and production suffered. In 2000 the Government channelled US $23m. from the national coffee stabilization fund to aid small farmers. Central American producers, as well as Mexico, Colombia and Brazil, agreed to retain up to 10% of their stocks in 2001, in order to allow the price of coffee to rise; however, the arrangement proved difficult to enforce. Furthermore, the 2001 and 2002 coffee crops were threatened by a plague. In 2001 coffee exports totalled $163.4m., compared with $274.0m. in the previous year. There was a slight improvement in 2002, when exports stood at $165.3m. Costa Rican coffee producers announced in 2001 that the production of 'gourmet' beans was to be expanded, as demand for fine coffee was rapidly increasing. Subsequently, in July 2002 farmers destroyed 120,000 bags of low-quality coffee beans as part of a regional strategy to improve the quality of coffee on the world market.

In late 2000 the situation in the banana industry became critical, with the three principal exporters, Chiquita Brands, Banana Development Corporation and Standard Fruits Company, cancelling contracts. Exports of bananas fell by US $100m. in 2000, to $553.2m. (10.1% of total exports). Production in 2000 was an estimated 2.3m. metric tons. In April 2001, despite resistance from the multinationals, the Government fixed the price of a 40 lb box at $5.25. In July 2001 more than 1,000 ha of banana plantations were destroyed in an attempt to prevent the further spread of the 'sigatoka negra' blight. In early 1999, following the European Union's (EU) failure to satisfy the World Trade Organization that its banana-import regime complied with international trade regulations, the USA was permitted to impose compensatory tariffs on specific imports from the EU. These tariffs were removed, following an EU-USA accord in April 2001, under which the EU preferential market ended. From 1 July a transitional system, issuing licences according to historical trade patterns, was implemented, while the definitive tariff-only system was to enter into force on 1 January 2006. In May 2002 heavy rains destroyed banana crops worth some US $30m. on the country's Atlantic coast, causing revenue from banana exports to fall from $509m. in 2001 to an estimated $468m. in 2002.

In May 2001 the Central American countries, including Costa Rica, agreed to establish, with Mexico, the 'Plan Puebla–Panamá'. This was a series of joint transport, industry and tourism projects intended to integrate the region.

In 2002 the new Pacheco Government pledged to reform the tax system and to seek ways to curb public-sector expenditure in order to reduce the budget deficit. Following the recommendations of an all-party commission earlier in the year, in December the Congreso approved further tax reforms aimed at reducing the fiscal deficit to 3% of GDP by the end of 2003 and eradicating it completely by 2006. These included changes to the tax code and the levying of VAT on a wider range of goods and services. The reforms were to be accompanied by a 5.9% limit on any increases in government spending and the reduction of the budgets of the national electricity institution, social security departments and the state petroleum refinery. However, following the slow progress of the reforms through the legislature, in July the Government was forced to introduce a US $75m. spending cut, and in September the fiscal deficit target for 2003 was increased to 3.9% of GDP. The reforms were finally approved by the Asamblea in January 2004.

An IMF report in March 2003 highlighted concerns about the increasing dollarization of savings accounts and the lack of state control over 'offshore' financial institutions. The Fund also advocated increased participation of the private sector as a way to alleviate the strain on the state's finances. In October the IDB granted a loan of US $350m. to fund improvements to the nation's infrastructure and health and transport systems. GDP increased by an estimated 2.2% in 2003 and was forecast to increase by 3.5% in 2004.

Côte d'Ivoire

Ivory Coast

The Republic of Côte d'Ivoire lies on the west coast of Africa. Côte d'Ivoire became independent of France in 1960. Dr Félix Houphouët-Boigny, leader of the Parti démocratique de la Côte d'Ivoire—Rassemblement démocratique africain, was the country's first President. Henri Konan Bédié, elected as President in 1995, was overthrown in 1999 by Brig.-Gen. Robert Gueï. In 2000 Laurent Gbagbo was elected as President. Following severe unrest in the north and west, a new Government of National Reconciliation was formed in early 2003. The administrative capital is Yamoussoukro, although most government offices remain in Abidjan, the economic capital. French is the official language.

Area and population
Area: 322,462 sq km
Population (mid-2002): 16,774,870
Population density (mid-2002): 52.0 per sq km
Life expectancy (years at birth, 2002): 45.3 (males 43.1; females 48.0)

Finance
GDP in current prices: 2002): US $11,717m. ($699 per head)
Real GDP growth (2002): −0.9%
Inflation (annual average, 2002): 3.1%
Currency: CFA franc

Economy

In 2002, according to estimates by the World Bank, Côte d'Ivoire's gross national income (GNI), measured at average 2000–02 prices, was US $10,264m., equivalent to $610 per head (or $1,430 on an international purchasing-power parity basis). During 1990–2002, it was estimated, the population increased at an average annual rate of 3.0%, while gross domestic product (GDP) per head declined, in real terms, by an average of 0.7% per year. Overall GDP increased, in real terms, at an average annual rate of 2.2% in 1990–2002; real GDP remained constant in 2001 and declined by 0.9% in 2002.

AGRICULTURE

Agriculture (including forestry and fishing) contributed 27.0% of GDP in 2002, and employed about 48.1% of the labour force in 2001. Côte d'Ivoire is the world's foremost producer of cocoa, and the contribution of exports of cocoa and related products to total export earnings was 28.1% in 2000, increasing to an estimated 44.6% in 2002. Côte d'Ivoire is also among the world's largest producers and exporters of coffee. Other major cash crops include cotton, rubber, bananas and pineapples. The principal subsistence crops are maize, yams, cassava, plantains and, increasingly, rice (although large quantities of the last are still imported). Excessive exploitation of the country's forest resources has led to a decline in the importance of this sector, although measures have now been instigated to preserve remaining forests. Abidjan is among sub-Saharan Africa's principal fishing ports; however, the participation of Ivorian fishing fleets is minimal. During 1990–2002 agricultural GDP increased at an average annual rate of 2.9%. Agricultural GDP declined by 1.6% in 2001, but increased by 0.3% in 2002.

INDUSTRY

Industry (including mining, manufacturing, construction and power) contributed 24.3% of GDP in 2002. According to UN estimates, 11.5% of the labour force were employed in the sector in 1994. During 1990–2002 industrial GDP increased at an average annual rate of 2.7%. Industrial GDP declined by 2.4% in 2001, but increased by 3.5% in 2002.

Mining

Mining and quarrying contributed only 0.6% of GDP in 2002. Commercial exploitation of important offshore reserves of petroleum and natural gas commenced in the mid-1990s. Gold and diamonds are also mined, although illicit production of the latter has greatly exceeded commercial output. There is believed to be significant potential for the development of nickel deposits, and there are also notable reserves of manganese, iron ore and bauxite.

Manufacturing

The manufacturing sector, which contributed 18.6% of GDP in 2002, is dominated by agro-industrial activities (such as the processing of cocoa, coffee, cotton, palm kernels, pineapples and fish). Crude petroleum is refined at Abidjan, while the tobacco industry uses mostly imported tobacco. During 1990–2002 manufacturing GDP increased by an average of 1.9% per year. The GDP of the sector declined by 1.7% in 2001, but increased by 3.0% in 2002.

Energy

Some 52.4% of Côte d'Ivoire's electricity generation in 2000 was derived from thermal sources, while 36.6% was derived from hydroelectric installations, and 11.0% from petroleum. Since 1995 the country has exploited indigenous reserves of natural gas, with the intention of becoming not only self-sufficient in energy, but also a regional exporter; the first stage of a major gas-powered turbine and power station in Abidjan commenced operations in 1999. Imports of fuel products accounted for some 33.8% of the value of total merchandise imports in 2000.

SERVICES

The services sector contributed 48.7% of GDP in 2002, and (according to UN estimates) employed 37.4% of the labour force in 1994. The transformation of Abidjan's stock market into a regional exchange for the member states of the Union économique et monétaire ouest-africaine (UEMOA) was expected to enhance the city's status as a centre for financial services. Abidjan's position as a major hub of regional communications and trade has been threatened by political unrest since the late 1990s, particularly following the rebel uprising of 2002–03. The GDP of the services sector increased by an average of 1.5% per year in 1990–2002. The GDP of the sector increased by 2.3% in 2001, but declined by 5.2% in 2002.

EXTERNAL TRADE

In 2002 Côte d'Ivoire recorded a visible trade surplus of US $2,734.5m., and there was a surplus of $767.2m. on the current account of the balance of payments. In 2000 the principal source of imports was Nigeria (which supplied 26.6% of total imports); France (20.3%) was also a notable supplier. France was the principal market for exports in 2000 (taking 14.9% of total exports), followed by the Netherlands, the USA and Mali. The principal exports in 2000 were cocoa and related products, petroleum and related products, coffee and coffee substitutes, and cork and wood. The principal imports in the same year were petroleum products, machinery and transport equipment, food and live animals (notably cereals and cereal preparations, and frozen fish), chemicals and related products, and basic manufactures.

GOVERNMENT FINANCE

Côte d'Ivoire recorded an overall budget deficit of 83,500m. francs CFA in 2002 (equivalent to 1.0% of GDP). The country's total external debt was US $11,582m. at the end of 2001, of which $9,963m. was long-term public debt. In that year the cost of debt-servicing was equivalent to 13.5% of the value of exports of goods and services. The annual rate of inflation averaged 2.7% in 1990–93. Consumer prices increased by an average of 26.1% in 1994 (following the devaluation of the currency at the beginning of the year); the inflation rate slowed to an annual average of 14.3% in

1995, and averaged 3.2% in 1996–2002. Consumer prices increased by 3.2% in 2002. Some 114,880 persons were registered as unemployed at the end of 1992.

INTERNATIONAL ECONOMIC RELATIONS

Côte d'Ivoire is a member of numerous regional and international organizations, including the Economic Community of West African States (ECOWAS), the West African organs of the Franc Zone, the African Petroleum Producers' Association (APPA), the International Cocoa Organization (ICCO), the International Coffee Organization and the Conseil de l'Entente. The African Development Bank has its headquarters in Abidjan; however, in February 2003 contingency measures for a relocation to Tunisia for a period of at least two years were announced, as a result of heightened instability in Côte d'Ivoire.

SURVEY AND PROSPECTS

In the late 1990s and early 2000s the economy of Côte d'Ivoire was adversely affected by international economic and domestic political developments, including a sharp fall in international prices for cocoa. By the time of the *coup d'état* of December 1999 Côte d'Ivoire's financial situation was precarious. In October 2000 the World Bank suspended assistance to Côte d'Ivoire, following a failure to repay debt totalling US $39.8m, and continuing political instability resulted in a decline in GDP in 2000. However, in September the IMF restored co-operation with Côte d'Ivoire, which had been suspended since late 1998. The World Bank resumed full co-operation in February 2002, after all outstanding debt had been paid, as did the European Union (EU), which had suspended assistance in mid-1999, following revelations of the misappropriation of aid.

An expected return to economic growth was largely inhibited by the consequences of the rebellion that commenced in September 2002 and the loss of government control over northern cotton-growing regions, although cocoa-growing regions remained largely under government control. A good cocoa crop and a sharp increase in international prices for the commodity at the end of 2002 were among the principal factors that prevented a dramatic economic decline in that year, despite heightened political instability from September. None the less, the international trade of the country was severely disrupted, particularly as a result of the closure of the border with Burkina Faso for a period of 12 months. Abidjan's status as an *entrepôt* for trade with land-locked neighbouring countries was challenged by the effects of this closure, and that of the Abidjan–Ouagadougou railway line, and consequently much trade was lost to Accra, Ghana; Cotonou, Benin; and Lomé, Togo.

Concerns were also expressed, in late 2003, that earnings from that year's cocoa crop were likely to be considerably lower than the previous year's, partially owing to disruption caused by the conflict. Although some progress towards the restoration of political stability had been made by early 2004, inter-ethnic tensions persisted in many regions of the country, and the potential for a renewal of conflict remained. An improvement in the economic position of Côte d'Ivoire remained largely dependent on the long-term restoration of political order, while further assistance from the IMF would be conditional on the effective implementation of structural reforms.

Croatia

The Republic of Croatia is situated in south-eastern Europe. In 1918 a Kingdom was proclaimed that united Serbia with Montenegro and the Habsburg lands (modern Croatia, Slovenia and Vojvodina). In 1929 the country's name was changed to Yugoslavia, which was invaded by Axis forces in 1941. In 1944 Croatia became part of the federal, Communist Yugoslav republic. In 1991 Croatia issued a declaration of dissociation from the Socialist Federal Republic of Yugoslavia, and proclaimed its independence. In 1997 constitutional amendments included a prohibition on the re-establishment of a union of Yugoslav states. Zagreb is the capital. The principal language in Croatian, although the Serb minority speak Serbian.

Area and population
Area: 56,542 sq km
Population (mid-2002): 4,376,860
Population density (mid-2002): 77.4 per sq km
Life expectancy (years at birth, 2002): 74.8 (males 71.0; females 78.6)

Finance

GDP in current prices: 2002): US $22,421m. ($5,123 per head)
Real GDP growth (2002): 5.2%
Inflation (annual average, 2002): 2.0%
Currency: kuna

Economy

In 2002, according to estimates by the World Bank, Croatia's gross national income (GNI), measured at average 2000–02 prices, was US $20,314m., equivalent to $4,640 per head (or $9,760 per head on an international purchasing-power parity basis). During 1990–2002, it was estimated, the population declined at an average annual rate of 0.7%, while gross domestic product (GDP) per head increased, in real terms, by an average of 0.2% per year. Overall GDP declined, in real terms, at an average annual rate of 0.6% in 1990–2002; however, real GDP increased by 3.8% in 2001 and by 5.2% in 2002.

AGRICULTURE

Agriculture (including hunting, forestry and fishing) contributed 9.0% of GDP in 2001. About 7.8% of the employed labour force were engaged in the sector in 2002. The principal crops are maize, wheat, potatoes and sugar beet. In late 2003 the Croatian authorities declared a fishery and ecological zone in the Adriatic Sea, in an attempt to protect fish resources. The GDP of the agricultural sector declined, in real terms, at an average annual rate of 2.2% in 1990–2001; however, agricultural GDP increased by 1.3% in 2000 and by 6.7% in 2001.

INDUSTRY

Industry (including mining, manufacturing, construction and power) contributed 29.3% of GDP in 2001, and engaged 30.7% of the employed labour force in 2002. Industrial GDP declined, in real terms, at an average annual rate of 4.4% during 1990–2001; however, GDP in the industrial sector increased by 1.5% in 2000 and by 4.3% in 2001.

Mining

The mining sector contributed 5.5% of GDP in 1998, and engaged just 0.5% of the employed labour force in 2002. Croatia has many exploitable mineral resources, including petroleum, coal and natural gas. The GDP of the mining sector declined by 2.4% in 1998; mining production increased by 1.9% in 1999.

Manufacturing

The manufacturing sector contributed 20.7% of GDP in 2001, and engaged 21.0% of the employed labour force in 2002. The GDP of the manufacturing sector declined, in real terms, at an average annual rate of 4.3% per year during 1990–2001; however, manufacturing GDP increased by 4.1% in 2000 and by 6.0% in 2001.

Energy

Of total electricity production in 2000, 55.1% was provided by hydroelectric power, 15.8% by petroleum, 14.7% by natural gas and 14.5% by coal. However, the country remains dependent on imported fuel, which accounted for some 12.2% of total imports in 2002.

SERVICES

Services provided 61.8% of GDP and engaged 61.5% of the employed labour force in 2002. The virtual elimination of tourism in Croatia (which in the late 1980s accounted for some 82% of Yugoslavia's total tourism trade) represented the largest war-related economic loss. There was a significant recovery in the tourism sector in the 1990s; by 2002 tourist arrivals had increased to 6,944,000 (compared with 3,805,000 in 1999). The GDP of the services sector increased, in real terms, at an average annual rate of 0.9% in 1990–2001; however, the GDP of the sector increased by 5.0% in 2000 and by 4.8% in 2001.

EXTERNAL TRADE

In 2002 Croatia recorded a visible trade deficit of US $5,273.9m., while there was a deficit of $1,586.9m. on the current account of the balance of payments. In 2002 the principal source of imports was Italy (17.3%); other major sources were Germany, Slovenia, Russia, Austria and France. The principal market for exports in that year was Italy (22.7%); other important purchasers were Bosnia and Herzegovina, Germany, Slovenia and Austria. The principal exports in 2002 were machinery and transport equipment, miscellaneous manufactured articles (particularly clothing and accessories), basic manufactures, chemical products, mineral fuels and food and live animals. The main imports in that year were machinery and transport equipment (most notably road vehicles), basic manufactures, mineral fuels (particularly petroleum and petroleum products), miscellaneous manufactured articles, chemical products and foodstuffs.

GOVERNMENT FINANCE

Croatia's overall budgetary deficit for 2002 was 3,872.0m. kuna (equivalent to 2.2% of GDP). The country's total external debt was US $10,742m. at the end of 2001, of which $6,400m. was long-term public debt. In that year the cost of debt-servicing was equivalent to 27.9% of the value of exports of goods and services. Consumer prices increased at an average annual rate of 73.6% in 1990–2002. However, the average rate of inflation was only 4.8% in 2001, and declined further in 2002, to 2.0%. The average annual rate of unemployment at January 2004 was estimated at 19.5%.

INTERNATIONAL ECONOMIC RELATIONS

Croatia was admitted to the IMF in January 1993, and became a member of the European Bank for Reconstruction and Development (EBRD) in April of that year. In November 2000 Croatia was admitted to the World Trade Organization (WTO). In February 2003 Croatia made a formal application for membership of the European Union (EU). In early 2003 Croatia also joined the Central European Free Trade Association (CEFTA).

SURVEY AND PROSPECTS

The outbreak of civil conflict in Croatia in the early 1990s resulted in a rapid deterioration of the economy. A new national currency, the kuna, was introduced in May 1994. In October of that year the IMF extended its first stand-by loan to Croatia, in support of an economic reform programme. The Government subsequently received reconstruction loans from other official creditors and concluded a rescheduling agreement with the 'Paris Club' of donor nations. In April 1996 an agreement was reached with the 'London Club' of commercial creditor banks, establishing Croatia's share of the foreign commercial bank debt incurred by the former Yugoslavia. In March 1997 the IMF approved a further three-year credit arrangement. Following the election of a new coalition Government in early 2000, relations with the USA and with western European Governments improved (resulting in increased financial aid). In early 2002 the IMF declared itself satisfied with Croatia's implementation of a further stand-by arrangement (agreed in March 2001).

Significant progress had also been achieved in the privatization of state-owned enterprises, particularly in the financial sector. In early 2003 the IMF approved a 14-month stand-by credit for Croatia (which, however, the Government viewed as precautionary), to support continued fiscal consolidation and structural reform, with emphasis on stabilizing the public-debt ratio and accelerating progress in privatization. A further IMF review in November commended progress made in fiscal discipline under the stand-by arrangement, concluding that real GDP growth had been higher and inflation lower than expected, while the current-account deficit had benefited from a strong increase in tourism revenue. Nevertheless, external debt also increased in that year, and was viewed as a potential threat to stability.

The new Government, elected in the same month, planned to continue the existing programme of reforms, particularly the rehabilitation of infrastructure and the privatization of public enterprises and remaining state-owned banks, with the ultimate aim of joining the EU. (However, the administration's lack of an outright parliamentary majority was viewed as a potential impediment to the adoption of further legislation on reform.) Following Croatia's application for membership of the EU (formally submitted in early 2003), early admission to the organization, by 2007, was regarded as being conditional on sustained reforms and the Government's co-operation with the UN International Criminal Tribunal for the Former Yugoslavia.

Cuba

The Republic of Cuba comprises two main islands and numerous keys and islets in the Caribbean Sea, south of Florida, USA. In 1898 Spain ceded Cuba to the USA. In 1902 it became an independent republic. Cuba was ruled by Fulgencio Batista Zaldivar from 1933 until 1944, and again, from 1952 until his defeat, in 1959, by guerrilla forces led by Dr Fidel Castro Ruz. In 1961 Cuba became a communist state, against which, since 1962, the USA has maintained an economic and political blockade. Castro has occupied the office of President of the Council of State since 1976. The capital is Havana. The language spoken is Spanish.

Area and population
Area: 110,860 sq km
Population (mid-2002): 11,263,330
Population density (mid-2002): 101.6 per sq km
Life expectancy (years at birth, 2002): 77.1 (males 75.0; females 79.3)

Finance
GDP in current prices: 2000): 27,635m. pesos (2,470 pesos per head)
Real GDP growth (2000): 5.6%
Inflation (1999): 0.3%
Currency: peso

Economy

In 2002 Cuba's gross domestic product (GDP), measured at constant 1997 prices, was an estimated 27,574m. pesos. During 1991–2000, it was estimated, GDP declined, in real terms, at an average annual rate of 1.4%. However, GDP increased by 6.1% in 2000 and by 3.0% in 2001. In 2002, according to official figures, GDP grew by 1.1%. During 1990–2002 the population increased by an average of 0.5% per year.

AGRICULTURE

Agriculture (including hunting, forestry and fishing) contributed 6.3% of GDP, measured at constant 1997 prices, in 2002 and employed 24.4% of the labour force in 2000. The principal cash crop has traditionally been sugar cane, with sugar and its derivatives accounting for 27.4% of export earnings in 2000. The sugar crop in 1998 was the worst in 50 years, reaching only some 3.3m. metric tons. It recovered slightly by 2000, amounting to 3.6m. tons, but fell short of expectations in 2001, to an estimated 3.5m. tons, owing to a drought and the destruction caused by 'Hurricane Michelle'. In 2002 sugar production reached only 3.6m. tons and it was estimated that production declined further in 2003, to only 2.2m. tons. In 2002, as a result of the damage caused by the hurricane, together with the ongoing poor harvests, the Government announced that it would have to import sugar to meet domestic demand. In June the Government announced that, following recent production decreases, it intended to rationalize the sugar industry through a programme of restructuring—this would involve the closure of several sugar refineries and the loss of approximately 100,000 jobs in the sector. Approximately 60% of plantation area would be reallocated to other crops in an attempt to produce enough sugar to satisfy domestic needs, while sugar would only be exported while revenues continued to exceed production costs. In that year 70 of Cuba's sugar mills were closed down as the industry became increasingly unprofitable; 71 mills remained active. In 2000 Cuba produced some 30,600 tons of tobacco and in 2002 it produced 327.2m. cigars. Other important crops are rice, citrus fruits (487,700 tons in 2002), plantains and bananas. Fishing exports in 2000 reached 87.8m. pesos. Cuba's principal seafood export markets were Japan, France, Spain, Italy and Canada. In real terms, the GDP of the agricultural sector declined at an average rate of 0.5% per year during 1996–2002. Agricultural GDP decreased by 7.3% in 2001 and by 2.2% in 2002.

INDUSTRY

Industry (including mining, manufacturing, construction and power) contributed 27.0% of GDP, measured at constant 1997 prices, in 2002. The sector employed 24.0% of the labour force in 2000. Industrial GDP decreased, in real terms, at an average rate of 5.7% per year in 1996–2002. The sector's GDP declined by 0.5% in 2001 and by 2.1% in 2002.

Mining

Mining contributed 1.5% of GDP, measured at constant 1997 prices, in 2002 and employed 1.3% of the labour force in 2000. Nickel is the principal mineral export. In 2002 nickel and cobalt output reached 75,200 metric tons, a decrease of some 1.7% compared with the previous year. Cuba also produces considerable amounts of chromium and copper, some iron and manganese, and there are workable deposits of gold and silver. The GDP of the mining sector increased by an average of 3.3% per year in 1996–2002; sectoral GDP declined by 2.3% in 2001 and increased by only 0.4% in 2002.

Manufacturing

Manufacturing contributed 17.2% of GDP, measured at constant 1997 prices, in 2002. The sector employed 16.0% of the labour force in 2000. The principal branches of manufacturing were food products, beverages and tobacco, machinery and industrial chemicals. In 2000 50% of the state citrus marketing company was purchased by a French-Spanish company, Altadis. During 1996–2002 manufacturing GDP increased, in real terms, at an average annual rate of 1.2%. The sector's GDP declined by 1.2% in 2001 and by 1.1% in 2002. The biomedical industry continued to expand in the 1990s, and in 1999 a joint venture was agreed with the pharmaceutical manufacturer SmithKline Beecham to market the Cuban meningitis vaccine.

Energy

Energy is derived principally from petroleum and natural gas. In 2003 total crude petroleum production was 4.3m. metric tons; production was expected to expand by up to 8% in 2004. In 2002 Cuba produced approximately 3.5m. metric tons of crude petroleum and 584.7m. cu m of natural gas. Imports of mineral fuels accounted for 24.0% of the total cost of imports in 2000. Formerly, some 13m. tons of petroleum were imported annually from the USSR, with 2m. tons being re-exported, but from 1990 imports were dramatically reduced. In 2003 the country generated its entire electricity requirement from domestically-produced petroleum and natural gas. Cuba expected to be self-sufficient in oil production by 2005. To this end, in 2001 Cuba began talks with Mexico on a possible bilateral agreement on energy efficiency, and in November Venezuela agreed to meet one-third of Cuba's petroleum requirements, on preferential terms, in exchange for medical and sports services. Despite some disruption to petroleum shipments from Venezuela in 2002, owing to domestic unrest in that country, in 2003 Venezuela exported an average of 53,000 b/d to Cuba. In 1999 Cuba opened up 112,000 sq km of its waters to foreign exploration, dividing the area into 51 blocks. Various foreign companies subsequently signed contracts to explore several of the blocks and in late 2003 the Spanish company Repsol YPF announced plans to install one of the world's largest deep-sea drilling rigs in the area in the following year. In 2000 two oil-processing plants were planned for Santiago de Cuba and Cienfuegos and two power-generation plants were being built by Sherritt Power of Canada. In December Cuba announced that construction of the Juragua nuclear power plant, which had never been completed, was to be abandoned. However, in February 2001 the Slovakian engineering company, SES Tlmace, won a contract to reconstruct the oil-burning power-station in Santa Cruz. In June the construction of a 25-km petroleum pipeline between Matanzas province and Puerto Escondido was being finalized. When complete, it was to be operated by the state petroleum company.

SERVICES

Services accounted for 66.6% of GDP, measured at constant 1997 prices, in 2002. The sector employed 51.6% of the labour force in 2000. Tourism is one of the country's principal sources of foreign exchange, earning an estimated US $1,850m. in 2001, and development of the sector remains a priority of the Government. In 2001 1.8m. tourists visited the country. Following a downturn in tourist arrivals in late 2001 and 2002, attributable largely to the impact of the September 2001 terrorist attacks on the USA, the sector recovered in 2003, when arrivals reached an estimated 1.9m. The country's 21 airports were modernized and expanded through state and foreign investment during the late 1990s. In real terms, the GDP of the service sector increased at an average rate of 4.4% per year during 1996–2002. The GDP of services increased by 5.9% in 2001 and by 3.0% in 2002.

EXTERNAL TRADE

In 1999 Cuba recorded a trade deficit of US $600m., and a deficit of $350m. on the current account of the balance of payments. In 2000 the principal source of imports was Venezuela (18.6%). In 2000 Russia was the principal market for exports, accounting for 19.4% of the total. Other major trading partners were Spain and Canada. The principal imports in 2000 were mineral fuels, machinery and transport equipment. The principal exports in that year were food and live animals, and crude materials (excluding fuels).

GOVERNMENT FINANCE

In 2002 Cuba recorded an estimated budget deficit of 1,000m. pesos. According to the Central Bank, the country's external debt totalled 10,893.3m. pesos in 2001. Cuba's debt to the former USSR was estimated to be $20,000m. in 2000. In December of that year the Russian Government proposed writing off 70% of this debt and renegotiating the remainder through the 'Paris Club' of Western government creditors. However, the Cuban Government refused to negotiate with the Paris Club and disputed the size of the debt owed to Russia. Bilateral discussions with Russia took place in 2000–01 and included the possible conversion of debt to equity through joint-venture contracts. According to official figures, some 5.8% of the labour force were unemployed at the end of 2000. Although no index of consumer prices is published, official estimates put inflation at 2.9% in 1998 and at 0.3% in 1999.

INTERNATIONAL ECONOMIC RELATIONS

Cuba is a member of the Latin American Economic System and of the Group of Latin American and Caribbean Sugar Exporting Countries.

SURVEY AND PROSPECTS

In the early 1990s Cuba suffered severe economic decline, prompted by the collapse of the USSR and by the consequent termination of the favourable aid and trade arrangements that had supported the Cuban economy. Resultant shortages, particularly of petroleum and basic raw materials, seriously affected production in all sectors and necessitated wide-ranging austerity measures. In 1994, in a significant departure from the country's traditional command economy, a series of adjustment measures was introduced. The measures included the introduction of new taxes and the drastic reduction (by some 40%) of subsidies to loss-making state enterprises. In December 1994 a new 'convertible peso' was introduced to regulate the circulation of foreign currency. A new investment law, approved in September 1995, opened all sectors of the economy, with the exception of defence, health and education, to foreign participation and introduced the possibility of 100% foreign ownership.

In 1996 the USA intensified its sanctions against Cuba with the introduction of the Cuban Liberty and Solidarity (Helms-Burton) Act. Denied access to medium- and long-term loans, Cuba's indebtedness increased substantially as high-interest short-term loans were contracted in order to finance production, most notably in the sugar industry. In 1997 three free-trade zones were opened to attract foreign investment. During 1999 the Central Bank made known its intention henceforth to prefer to conduct international transactions in euros, hoping thus to weaken the stranglehold of the US dollar on the Cuban economy. In October 2001 the Government announced that, thenceforth, only US paper currency would be accepted, owing to the high cost of handling and exporting US coin currency. In July 2003 the Government announced that state-owned companies would be prohibited from using US dollars for transactions made within Cuba; these would have to be made in convertible pesos, as would import and debt payments and purchases from joint-venture companies, although the latter were exempted from the new regulations.

In 1999 the largest investments were in the mining (specifically nickel), tourism and telecommunications sectors. In December a 50% stake in Habanos, the state-owned cigar distributor, was sold for US $500m. In mid-2000 the EU called for a WTO disputes panel to rule on Section 211 of the 1998 US Omnibus Appropriations Act, under which trademarks used in connection with assets confiscated by the Cuban Government could not be registered without permission from the original owner. This followed a 1999 US court ruling against Havana Club International, a joint venture between Pernod Ricard of France and Cuba's Havana Rum and Liquors, concerning the use of the Havana Club rum brand name in the USA (the ruling was upheld by the US Supreme Court in October 2000). In response to the ruling, Cuba announced a new Bacardí brand, initiating a further dispute, this time with the Bacardí company in Bermuda. In January 2002 the WTO ruled that, in part, Section 211 violated the pact on protection of intellectual property and recommended that the USA bring its measures into conformity with the pact. In 2003 the US-Cuba Trademark Protection Act was passed by the US Congress, establishing procedures through which the Cuban Government's trademark registration and renewal process could be monitored, in order to ensure further protection for US trademarks in Cuba.

In October 2000, following an acrimonious passage through the US Congress, legislation was approved that allowed US food and medicine sales to Cuba. However, the potential for such trade was restricted by the conditions attached, such as a ban on financing by US banks or official credits. Imports of most Cuban goods remained illegal. Other sanctions legislation, such as the Torricelli and Helms-Burton Acts and the 'Trading with the Enemy' Act, remained operational, including a clause of the Torricelli Act that forbade ships to enter US ports within six months of entering a Cuban port for the purpose of trade. However, in February 2001 the USA granted the first licence to run a scheduled route to Cuba to the shipping company, Crowley Liner Services. In July further regulations regarding US sales to Cuba were introduced. The Cuban Government responded by refusing to trade with the USA under what it considered 'discriminatory and humiliating terms'. However, in November, in the wake of Hurricane Michelle, both Cuba and the USA allowed temporary trade in products necessary to the reconstruction and aid effort. In September 2002, although the trade and travel restrictions remained in operation, the first US food fair since 1959 was held in Havana as the business sector chose to take advantage of the easing of the embargo. According to the Government, by November 2003 Cuban businesses had signed food contracts worth US $510m. with US companies since the end of 2001. In 2003 economic growth exceeded official predictions, reaching an estimated 2.6%, compared with 1.1% in the previous year. The recovery was believed to have been driven by a revival in the tourism industry, as well as by rising international nickel prices and an increase in the level of remittances sent by Cubans abroad. In late 2003 a report issued by the UN Economic Commission for Latin America and the Caribbean (ECLAC) identified Cuba's international isolation, bureaucratic inefficiency, shortage of foreign exchange and the ongoing US sanctions against the country as the main factors in the island's economic problems. The report stated that if Cuba was to effect a long-term economic recovery it would have to reduce state control over the economy and lift the restrictions on small businesses, essentially adopting a policy of greater liberalization. However, the Government seemed unlikely to implement such reforms.

Cyprus

The Republic of Cyprus is an island in the eastern Mediterranean Sea. In 1974, after Greek officers of the Cypriot National Guard had staged a coup, the Turkish army occupied the northern third of the island, where Turkish Cypriots subsequently established a *de facto* Government and, in 1975, declared a 'Turkish Federated State of Cyprus' (TFSC). In 1983 the 'TFSC' unilaterally declared an independent 'Turkish Republic of Northern Cyprus' (TRNC). The Greek Cypriot administration, meanwhile, claims to be the Government of all Cyprus, and is generally recognized as such. Nicosia is the capital. About 75% of the population speak Greek and almost all of the remainder Turkish. Following the rejection of a UN-proposed reunification plan for Cyprus by Greek Cypriot voters at the referendums held on both sides of the island in April 2004, only the internationally recognized, Greek Cypriot administered part of Cyprus acceded to the European Union on 1 May.

Area and population
Area: 9,251 sq km (including 'TRNC' 3,355 sq km)
Population (mid-2002): 764,970 (excluding Turkish settlers in TRNC)
Population density (mid-2002): 82.7 per sq km
Life expectancy (years at birth, 2002): 77.3 (males 75.5; females 79.1)

Finance
GDP in current prices: 2001): US $9,131m. ($12,004 per head, excluding population of 'TRNC')
Real GDP growth (2002): 2.0%
Inflation (annual average, Government-controlled area, 2002): 2.8%
Currency: Cyprus pound, Turkish lira

Economy

In 2001, according to estimates by the World Bank, Cyprus's gross national income (GNI), measured at average 1999–2001 prices, was US $9,372m., equivalent to $12,320 per head (or $17,660 per head on an international purchasing-power parity basis). During 1990–2002, it was estimated, the population increased at an average annual rate of 1.0%, while gross domestic product (GDP) per head increased, in real terms, by an average of 3.0% per year. Overall GDP increased, in real terms, by an estimated annual average of 4.0% in 1990–2002; growth was 4.0% in 2001 and some 2.0% in both 2002 and 2003. In the 'TRNC' GNI was officially estimated at $941.4m., or $4,409 per head, in 2002. GNI increased, in real terms, at an average annual rate of 2.9% in 1995–2002, while real GDP increased at an average annual rate of 4.8% in 1994–99. GDP declined by 5.4% in 2001, but increased by 6.2% in 2002 and by an estimated 5.1% in 2003. However, GDP per head in the 'TRNC' remains only about one-third of that of the remainder of the island.

AGRICULTURE

According to provisional figures, agriculture (including hunting, forestry and fishing) contributed some 4.1% of GDP in 2002. In the government-controlled area an estimated 8.0% of the employed labour force were engaged in the sector in 2001. The principal export crops of the government-controlled area are citrus fruit (which accounted for 6.3% of domestic export earnings in 2001), potatoes (7.5% in the same year) and vegetables; grapes are cultivated notably for the wine industry, and barley is the principal cereal crop. In an effort to offset the island's vulnerability to drought, during the 1990s the Greek Cypriot authorities granted concessions for the construction and operation of several desalination plants. The GDP of the area's agricultural sector increased by an average of 0.9% per year in 1995–2002. Agricultural GDP increased by 3.8% in 2001 and by an estimated 5.4% in 2002. In the 'TRNC' an estimated 15.8% of the working population were employed in agriculture, forestry and fishing in 2002, and the sector contributed some 9.5% of GDP in 2003. The principal crops of the 'TRNC' are citrus fruit, vegetables, potatoes, barley and wheat. The 'TRNC' imports water from Turkey in order to address the problem of drought. In early 2002 the Government of Turkey announced that it was to proceed with long-standing plans for the construction of a pipeline to transport fresh water to the 'TRNC'. The GDP of the agricultural sector increased by an average of 1.0% per year in 1994–99. Agricultural GDP decreased by 13.2% in 2000, but increased by 16.1% in 2001 and by 18.9% in 2002.

INDUSTRY

Industry (comprising mining, manufacturing, construction and utilities) engaged an estimated 21.5% of the employed labour force in the government-controlled area in 2001, and accounted for around 20.3% of GDP in 2002. Industrial GDP increased by an average of 0.9% per year in 1995–2002. The GDP of the sector increased by 1.2% in 2001 and by about 1.9% in 2002. In the 'TRNC' the industrial sector contributed about 16.4% of GDP in 2003, and engaged an estimated 24.9% of the working labour force in 2002. Industrial GDP in the 'TRNC' increased at an annual average rate of 2.0% in 1994–99.

Mining

In the government-controlled area mining, principally the extraction of material for the construction industry, provided only 0.3% of GDP in 2002, and engaged just 0.2% of the employed labour force in 2001. Minerals accounted for 5.5% of domestic exports (by value) from the government-controlled sector in 2000. In early 2001 it was announced that 25 foreign oil companies had expressed interest in acquiring exploration rights for potential petroleum and gas deposits in the eastern Mediterranean within Cyprus's economic zone. The GDP of the mining sector increased at an average annual rate of 7.3% in 1995–2002. Mining GDP rose by 0.6% in 2001 and by some 7.0% in 2002. In the 'TRNC' mining and quarrying contributed an estimated 0.6% of GDP in 2003. The GDP of the 'TRNC' mining sector increased by an average of 1.3% per year in 1994–99. The sector's GDP increased by 11.8% in 2000, but decreased by 13.5% in 2001; however, mining GDP again increased, by 7.4%, in 2002.

Manufacturing

Manufacturing accounted for an estimated 9.9% of GDP in the government-controlled area in 2002, and engaged about 12.1% of the employed labour force in 2001. Clothing represents the southern sector's main export commodity, providing 8.4% of domestic export earnings in 2001. The GDP of the manufacturing sector increased by an average of less that 0.1% per year in 1995–2002. Manufacturing GDP declined by 2.1% in 2001 and by an estimated 2.2% in 2002. In the 'TRNC' the manufacturing sector provided an estimated 5.8% of GDP in 2003. The GDP of the 'TRNC' manufacturing sector increased at an average annual rate of 1.4% in 1994–99. Manufacturing GDP rose by 3.6% in 2000, declined by 6.9% in 2001, but increased by 5.7% in 2002.

Energy

Energy is derived almost entirely from imported petroleum, and mineral fuels and lubricants comprised 12.0% of total imports (including goods for re-export) in the government-controlled area in 2001. The Greek Cypriot Government is encouraging the development of renewable energy sources, including solar, wind and hydro-electric power. Mineral fuels, lubricants, etc. comprised about 8.4% of total imports in the 'TRNC' in 2003.

SERVICES

The services sector in the government-controlled area contributed an estimated 75.6% of GDP in 2002, and engaged around 70.5% of the employed labour force in 2001. Within the sector, financial and business services provided an estimated 21.2% of overall GDP in 2002 and generated some 10.1% of employment in 2001. In 2003 there were 29 'offshore' banking units in the government-controlled area, and the number of registered 'offshore' enterprises was estimated to total more than 40,000. In the 'TRNC' the services sector contributed an estimated 74.1% of GDP in 2003, and engaged about 59.3% of the employed labour force in 2002. Both Cypriot communities have undertaken measures to expand their tourism industries, which are important generators of revenue and employment. Tourist arrivals to the government-controlled area increased from 2,686,205 in 2000 to 2,696,700 in 2001, but declined to 2,418,200 in 2002. Receipts from tourism in 2002 amounted to an estimated C£1,200m., compared with C£1,277 in 2001. In 2002 a total of around

425,556 tourists (316,193 of whom were from Turkey) visited the 'TRNC'. Net tourism receipts in the 'TRNC' were estimated at US $117.1m. in 2003. The Greek Cypriot authorities have also attempted to enhance the island's status as an entrepôt for shipping and trade throughout the Eastern Mediterranean, while Cyprus's shipping registry has developed rapidly, to become the world's sixth largest by the end of 2000. In the government-controlled area the GDP of the services sector increased at an average annual rate of 4.5% in 1995–2002. Services GDP increased by 4.8% in 2001 and by 1.8% in 2002. Services GDP in the 'TRNC' increased by an average of 5.8% per year in 1994–99.

EXTERNAL TRADE

In 2002 the government-controlled area recorded a visible trade deficit of US $2,859.2m. and a deficit of $517.1m. on the current account of the balance of payments. The 'TRNC' recorded a visible trade deficit in 2002 of $365.9m., while there was a deficit of $24.0m. on the current account of the balance of payments. In 2001 the principal sources of imports to the government-controlled area were the USA (which supplied 9.4% of merchandise imports) and Greece (8.9%); Italy, the United Kingdom, Germany and Japan were also important suppliers. The United Kingdom was the principal purchaser of Greek Cypriot exports in 2001, taking 20.6% of the total; Russia, Greece and Syria were also important markets. The principal domestic exports from the government-controlled area in 2001 were pharmaceutical products, clothing, cigarettes, potatoes and citrus fruit. The principal imports in that year were road vehicles, fuels and lubricants, manufactured goods, food and beverages. In 2003 the principal imports to the 'TRNC' were machinery and transport equipment, basic manufactures, food and live animals, mineral fuels and lubricants, and beverages and tobacco; the principal exports were industrial products, and food and live animals, and minerals. Turkey is by far the principal trading partner of the 'TRNC', supplying an estimated 62.1% of imports and taking 41.6% of exports in 2003, although the United Kingdom purchased 25.4% of exports in that year.

GOVERNMENT FINANCE

In 2002 the government-controlled area recorded a budget deficit of an estimated C£215.1m., equivalent to 3.5% of GDP. External debt totalled C£1,796.0m. at the end of 1999, of which C£1,142.3m. was medium- and long-term public debt. In that year the cost of debt-servicing was equivalent to 5.8% of the value of exports of goods and services. The annual rate of inflation averaged 3.6% in 1990–2002. Consumer prices increased by an average of 2.0% in 2001 and by 2.8% in 2002. The rate of unemployment in the government-controlled area was 4.7% of the labour force in January 2004. The 2003 budget of the 'TRNC' envisioned a balance of revenue and expenditure. In the 'TRNC' the average increase in prices for the 12 months to December averaged 72.3% in 1994–99; the rate of inflation in the 'TRNC' was 53.2% in the year to December 2000, 76.8% in the year to December 2001, 24.5% in the year to December 2002, and 12.6% in the year to December 2003. According to official figures, 1.6% of the 'TRNC' labour force were unemployed in 2003.

INTERNATIONAL ECONOMIC RELATIONS

An application to become a full member of the European Union (EU), with which Cyprus has an association agreement, was submitted by the Greek Cypriot Government in July 1990; accession negotiations commenced in March 1998 and in December

2002 Cyprus was formally invited to join the EU from 1 May 2004. A Treaty of Accession was signed in April 2003 and ratified in July. The 'TRNC' has guest status at the Economic Co-operation Organization (ECO).

SURVEY AND PROSPECTS

At the beginning of the 21st century the Greek Cypriot economy was enjoying strong growth, owing in large part to continued advances in the services sector, notably in tourism. Other particular areas of investment promotion were in information technology, and in financial and medical services. Although the economy initially proved more resilient than had been anticipated following the terrorist attacks on the USA in September 2001, with growth in that year almost attaining the targeted 4.5%, growth in 2002 was only 2.0%, with losses in the tourism sector in particular. Prospects for the property and construction sectors were improved, however, by the easing of restrictions on property purchases by foreigners in anticipation of Cyprus's accession to the EU. The European Commission predicted that growth in 2003 would again be around 2.0%, and that the economy would grow by some 3.4% in 2004. The steady decline in the rate of inflation in the 1990s was reversed in 2000, as a period of enhanced consumer demand, together with sustained increases in world petroleum prices, coincided with the depreciation in the value of the euro (to which the Cyprus pound has been linked since January 1999) in relation to the US dollar.

Recent economic policy has been shaped principally with a view to achieving the criteria required for EU membership. In July 2002 the Government raised the rate of value-added tax from 10% to 13%, and in 2003 the rate was raised further, to 15%—the lowest permissible rate for an EU member. As a result, inflation was expected to rise to 3.9% in that year. Furthermore, the budget deficit was progressively reduced in 1998–2000 (owing to tighter fiscal policies, postponement of defence-related outlays, and more efficient tax collection), and remained constant in 2001. However, the budget deficit increased to some 3.5% of GDP in 2002 (above the EU 'ceiling' of 3%). Meanwhile, the Government undertook a reform of tax arrangements for 'offshore' banks and other enterprises in order to comply with EU accession procedures: the EU is opposed to Cyprus's practice of charging 'offshore' companies less tax (4.5%) than domestic companies (25%). A new uniform tax rate of 10% was reportedly favourable enough to deter the more prestigious 'offshore' businesses from leaving, while also being attractive to new investors. Moreover, the Government pledged full compliance with efforts by the Organisation for Economic Co-operation and Development (of which Cyprus is not a member) to combat tax evasion and money-laundering. Despite the prospect of tighter regulation, the 'offshore' sector was continuing to expand. In May 2003 the Government published a Strategic Development Plan for 2004–06, which identified as its principal aims sustainable economic development and the maximization of the benefits of Cyprus's membership of the EU from 1 May 2004.

The economy of the 'TRNC', although substantially less prosperous and affected by diplomatic isolation, has also achieved significant growth since the 1980s, with considerable assistance from Turkey. By 2002/03 higher education had become one of the territory's most significant economic sectors, with 27,748 students, many from Turkey, attending private universities in the 'TRNC'. The tourism sector was also expanding, although the development of the north as an international tourist destination remained hampered by the embargo on direct flights to the 'TRNC' (visitors must first land in Turkey). The holiday property sector in the 'TRNC' was also adversely affected by uncertainty over the legal status of property owned by Greek Cypriots prior to the 1974 invasion. The close linkage with the Turkish economy, including the use of the Turkish lira as currency in the 'TRNC', has resulted in persistently high levels of inflation, and has rendered northern Cyprus particularly vulnerable to adverse economic developments in Turkey. The new 'TRNC' coalition administration that took office in mid-2001 undertook to pursue free-market policies and to accelerate privatization. However, during 2001–02 13 banks and numerous businesses collapsed. The crisis further emphasized the economic divergence of the Turkish and Greek Cypriot communities, notably clear disparities in wealth between north and south, and also exacerbated long-term weaknesses in the 'TRNC' such as the comparative lack of diversification of the manufacturing sector and a high rate of emigration. Meanwhile, the loss of income in the form of essential grants and subsidies from Turkey (which suffered a severe financial crisis from early 2001) adversely affected the public sector, which remains the largest employer in the 'TRNC', employing more than 20% of the working population.

There was considerable evidence that the economic crisis in Turkey was encouraging Turkish Cypriot elements that favoured participation in Cyprus's accession negotiations with the EU and broader Cypriot reunification. The unexpected easing of restrictions on movement across the internal border from late April brought considerable benefits to the Turkish Cypriot economy, in particular the tourist sector, as large numbers of Greek Cypriots and foreign tourists undertook crossings to the north. In June the European Commission pledged to provide financial assistance to the 'TRNC' worth €12m., of which €9m. was intended to promote economic development in the 'TRNC' and €3m. was for projects aimed at bringing the Turkish Cypriot community closer to the EU. Anecdotal evidence suggested that many Turkish Cypriots were seeking to obtain Republic of Cyprus passports in order to acquire EU residency rights after 2004. Following Turkish Cypriot endorsement of the proposed reunification plan on 24 April, the EU announced measures to alleviate the trade embargo in force against the 'TRNC' (whereby commodities produced in the 'TRNC' were to be exported via Greek-administered Cyprus to EU member states without tariffs).

Czech Republic

The Czech Republic lies in central Europe. The Republic of Czechoslovakia was established in 1918. Communist control of the country became complete in 1948. In 1968, in order to suppress the reformist regime of Alexander Dubcek, Warsaw Pact forces invaded Czechoslovakia. In 1989 a process of dramatic, peaceful political change (the 'velvet revolution') culminated in the installation of Václav Havel, a dissident leader, as President. In 1990 Czechoslovakia was renamed the Czech and Slovak Federative Republic (CzSFR) and free legislative elections were held. On 1 January 1993 the CzSFR was dissolved into separate Czech and Slovak Republics. The capital is Prague. Czech is the official language.

Area and population
Area: 78,866 sq km
Population (mid-2002): 10,209,830
Population density (mid-2002): 129.5 per sq km
Life expectancy (years at birth, 2002): 75.8 (males 72.4; females 79.0)

Finance
GDP in current prices: 2002: US $69,590m. ($6,816 per head)
Real GDP growth (2002): 2.0%
Inflation (annual average, 2002): 1.8%
Currency: koruna

Economy

In 2002, according to estimates by the World Bank, the Czech Republic's gross national income (GNI), measured at average 2000–02 prices, was US $56,717m., equivalent to $5,560 per head (or $14,500 per head on an international purchasing-power parity basis). During 1990–2002, it was estimated, the population decreased at an annual average rate of 0.1%, while gross domestic product (GDP) per head increased, in real terms, by an average of 0.6% per year. Overall GDP increased, in real terms, at an average annual rate of 0.5% in 1990–2002; annual growth was 3.1% in 2001 and 2.0% in 2002.

AGRICULTURE

In 2002 agriculture (including hunting, forestry and fishing) contributed 3.7% of GDP and engaged an estimated 4.4% of the employed labour force. The principal crops are wheat, sugar beet, barley, potatoes and hops (the Czech Republic is a major beer producer and exporter). According to estimates by the World Bank, the GDP of the agricultural sector increased, in real terms, at an average annual rate of 4.5% in 1990–2001. However, agricultural GDP declined by 1.5% in 2000 and by 5.3% in 2001.

INDUSTRY

Industry (including manufacturing, mining, construction and power) contributed 38.4% of GDP and engaged an estimated 38.7% of the employed labour force in 2002. According to estimates by the World Bank, the GDP of the industrial sector declined, in real terms, at an average annual rate of 2.0% in 1990–2001. However, real industrial GDP increased by 1.5% in 2001 and, according to IMF estimates, by 4.8% in 2002.

Mining

In 2002 the mining sector contributed 1.2% of GDP and engaged an estimated 1.1% of the employed labour force. The principal minerals extracted are coal and lignite. According to the IMF, production of mining and quarrying increased, in real terms, by 1.4% in 1996, but declined by 2.9% in 1997, by 5.3% in 1998 and by 12.1% in 1999; however, growth in the sector was 9.2% in 2000, slowing to 1.9% in 2001 and 0.3% in 2002.

Manufacturing

The manufacturing sector contributed 26.7% of GDP and engaged an estimated 29.6% of the employed labour force in 2002. Based on the value of output, the most important branches of manufacturing in 1999 were food products and beverages (accounting for 13.6% of the total), non-electric machinery and domestic appliances (8.5%), metal products (8.3%) and basic metals (7.8%). According to the IMF, manufacturing production increased, in real terms, by 3.0% in 1998, but declined by 2.6% in 1999; however, manufacturing output was estimated to have increased by 5.0% in 2000, by 7.5% in 2001 and by 5.4% in 2002.

Energy

In 2000 coal provided 73.3% of total electricity production and nuclear power 18.6%. Imports of mineral fuels comprised 7.6% of the value of total imports in 2002.

SERVICES

The services sector contributed 57.9% of GDP and engaged an estimated 56.9% of the employed labour force in 2002. Tourism is an important source of revenue, providing receipts of an estimated US $2,900m. in 2002. According to the World Bank, the GDP of the services sector increased, in real terms, at an average annual rate of 2.2% in 1990–2001. Real GDP in the services sector increased by 1.1% in 2000 and by 6.2% in 2001.

EXTERNAL TRADE

In 2002 the Czech Republic recorded a visible trade deficit of US $2,240m., and there was a deficit of $4,485m. on the current account of the balance of payments. In 2002 the principal source of imports (32.5%) was Germany; other major sources were Italy and Slovakia. Germany was also the principal market for exports (36.5%) in that year; other important purchasers were Slovakia, the United Kingdom and Austria. The principal exports in 2002 were machinery and transport equipment, basic manufactures, miscellaneous manufactured articles and chemical products. The principal imports in that year were machinery and transport equipment, basic manufactures, chemicals and related products, miscellaneous manufactured articles and mineral fuels.

GOVERNMENT FINANCE

In 2002 there was a budgetary deficit of 45,700m. koruny (equivalent to 2.0% of GDP). The Czech Republic's total external debt was US $21,691m. at the end of 2001, of which $5,915m. was long-term public debt. In that year the cost of debt-servicing was equivalent to 11.2% of the value of exports of goods and services. The annual rate of inflation averaged 6.0% in 1990–2002; consumer prices increased by 4.7% in 2001 and by 1.8% in 2002. In 2003 the average annual rate of unemployment was estimated at 9.4%.

INTERNATIONAL ECONOMIC RELATIONS

The Czech Republic is a member of the IMF and the World Bank. It is also a member of the European Bank for Reconstruction and Development (EBRD), and in late 1995 became the first post-communist state in Eastern Europe to be admitted to the Organisation for Economic Co-operation and Development (OECD). In December 2002 the Czech Republic was formally invited to become a full member of the European Union (EU) from May 2004.

SURVEY AND PROSPECTS

The Czech Republic was considered to have successfully undertaken the transition to a market economic system. In 1992–95 the country's programme of rapid privatization, price and currency stabilization and the establishment of a new banking system attracted widespread foreign investment. In 1996, however, economic growth decelerated and a budgetary deficit was recorded for the first time. Several banks ceased operations, and investor confidence was weakened by cases of embezzlement. In early 1999 the economy began to recover, following the Government's relaxation of monetary policies in late 1998 and significant progress in the restructuring of banks and state enterprises. The country subsequently benefited from strong export performance, and from a dramatic increase in foreign direct investment. Growth in GDP was recorded from 2000, although the restructuring process resulted in a rapidly increasing overall fiscal deficit and also contributed to a significant rise in the rate of unemployment.

Following severe flooding in 2002, the Government's plans for monetary restraint were thwarted. The total cost of funding damage reparation was estimated at US $3,600m.; moreover, the flooding adversely affected tourism (the number of tourist arrivals was 4.6m. in 2002, compared with 5.2m. in 2001), and was likely to cause long-term damage to private industry. The wider fiscal deficit (including regional budgets) was estimated to have reached some 4% of GDP in 2002, and preliminary figures indicated that it increased further in 2003, to represent as much as 7.6% of GDP. Moreover, the rate of unemployment continued to increase dramatically, although moderate growth, of an estimated 1.7%, was maintained in 2003.

In September 2003 a proposal for fiscal reform, involving tax increases and reductions in welfare expenditure, with the aim of reducing the overall budgetary deficit to some 4% of GDP by 2006, was approved by the Chamber of Deputies, despite opposition from President Václav Klaus to planned increases in value-added tax. Although the Czech Republic acceded to the EU at the beginning of May 2004, the country's fiscal position was likely to delay the Government's adoption of the common European currency, the euro, until after 2007, owing to the EU's requirement that the public-finance deficit be restrained to below 3% of GDP.

Denmark

The Kingdom of Denmark is situated in northern Europe. Denmark's Constitution was radically revised in 1953, to allow, among other things, for female succession to the throne. In 1972, Margrethe, the eldest daughter of the late King, Frederik IX, became the first queen to rule Denmark for nearly 600 years. In 1973, following a referendum, Denmark entered the European Community (now European Union). In 2000, in a referendum held by the Venstre (Liberals)-led Government, Danish voters rejected the adoption of the single European currency, the euro. The capital is Copenhagen. The language is Danish.

Area and population
Area: 43,098 sq km
Population (mid-2002): 5,373,250
Population density (mid-2002): 124.7 per sq km
Life expectancy (years at birth, 2002): 77.2 (males 74.8; females 79.5)

Finance
GDP in current prices: 2002): US $174,798m. ($32,5313 per head)
Real GDP growth (2002): 1.6%
Inflation (annual average, 2002): 2.4%
Currency: krone

Economy

In 2002, according to estimates by the World Bank, Denmark's gross national income (GNI), measured at average 2000–02 prices, was US $162,743m., equivalent to $30,290 per head (or $29,450 per head on an international purchasing-power parity basis). During 1990–2002 Denmark's population grew at an average annual rate of 0.4%, while gross domestic product (GDP) per head increased, in real terms, at an average rate of 2.0% per year. Overall GDP increased, in real terms, at an average annual rate of 2.1% in 1990–2002; growth was 1.0% in 2001 and 1.6% in 2002.

AGRICULTURE

Agriculture (including forestry and fishing) employed 3.2% of the economically active population in 2002, and contributed an estimated 2.5% of GDP, measured at current prices, in the same year. The principal activities are pig-farming and dairy farming; Denmark is a major exporter of pork products, and exports of live pigs and of pig meat accounted for an estimated 4.8% of total export revenue in 2002. Most of Denmark's agricultural production is exported, and the sector accounted for 15.5% of total exports in 2002. The fishing industry accounted for 3.1% of total export earnings in that year. Agricultural GDP increased, in real terms, at an average annual rate of 2.4% in 1990–2001; the GDP of the sector grew by 0.8% in 2000 and by 1.3% in 2001.

INDUSTRY

Industry (including mining, manufacturing, construction, power and water) employed 24.3% of the working population and provided an estimated 25.4% of GDP in 2002. Industrial GDP increased, in real terms, at an average annual rate of 1.8% in 1990–2001; it grew by 5.4% in 2000 and by 0.4% in 2001.

Mining

Mining accounted for only 0.2% of employment and provided 2.5% of GDP in 2002. Denmark has few natural resources, but exploration for petroleum reserves in the Danish sector of the North Sea in the 1970s proved successful. Natural gas has also been extensively exploited. In 1989, in north-western Jutland, it was established that there was a significant reserve of sand which could be exploited for rich yields of titanium, zirconium and yttrium. The GDP of the mining sector increased, in real terms, at an average annual rate of 8.2% in 1990–99; the sector's GDP declined by 2.7% in 1998, but grew by 10.8% in 1999 and by 12.1% in 2000.

Manufacturing

Manufacturing employed 16.9% of the working population and contributed 16.0% of GDP in 2002. Measured by value of output, in 1998 the most important manufacturing industries were food products (accounting for 22.0% of the total), non-electric machinery and domestic appliances (12.8%), chemicals and pharmaceuticals (8.1%), metal products (7.0%), and furniture (4.1%). Manufacturing GDP increased, in real terms, at an average annual rate of 1.9% in 1990–2001; it grew by 6.7% in 2000 and by 2.3% in 2001.

Energy

Energy is derived principally from petroleum and natural gas. Since 1996 Denmark has produced enough energy to satisfy its domestic consumption, and the degree of self-sufficiency in petroleum and natural gas production amounted to 203% and 160%, respectively, in 2000. In that year total petroleum production amounted to 21m. cu m and total gas output was 11,300m. cu m. In 2002 imports of mineral fuels accounted for 4.5% of the total cost of imports, while exports of mineral fuels contributed 7.4% of total export revenue. In 2000 46.0% of electricity was produced from coal, 24.3% from natural gas and 12.2% from petroleum. The use of renewable sources of energy (including wind power) has been encouraged. In 2000 Denmark derived 15% of its energy from wind-turbines, and planned to increase the share to 50% by 2030.

SERVICES

Services engaged 72.5% of the employed population and provided 72.1% of GDP, measured at current prices, in 2002. In real terms, the combined GDP of the service sectors increased at an average rate of 2.4% per year in 1990–2001; it rose by 3.1% in 2000 and by 1.5% in 2001.

EXTERNAL TRADE

In 2002, according to the IMF, Denmark recorded a visible trade surplus of US $8,308m. and a surplus of $4,991m. on the current account of the balance of payments. Most Danish trade is with the other member states of the European Union (EU), which accounted for 71.8% of imports and 65.0% of exports in 2002. The principal source of imports in 2002 was Germany (contributing 22.3% of the total); other major suppliers were Sweden (12.1%), the United Kingdom (9.0%), the Netherlands (6.9%) and France (6.1%). Germany was also the principal market for exports (accounting for 19.4% of the total); other major purchasers included Sweden (11.8%), the United Kingdom (9.7%), the USA (6.4%) and Norway (6.0%). The principal exports in 2002 were machinery and transport equipment (accounting for 29.2% of total export revenue), food and food products (18.0%), miscellaneous manufactured articles (16.4%) and chemicals and related products (12.9%). The principal imports in 2002 were machinery and transport equipment (accounting for 37.2% of total import costs), basic manufactures (15.8%), miscellaneous manufactured articles (14.8%), and chemicals and related products (10.9%).

GOVERNMENT FINANCE

In 2000 there was a budget surplus of 20,804m. kroner, equivalent to 1.6% of GDP, compared with a budgetary deficit equal to almost 4% of GDP in 1993. Public-sector debt was equivalent to 42% of GDP in 2002. The average annual rate of inflation was 2.2% in 1990–2002. Consumer prices increased by 2.3% in 2001 and by 2.4% in 2002. The rate of unemployment was 4.9% in 2002.

INTERNATIONAL ECONOMIC RELATIONS

Denmark is a member of the EU, the Nordic Council and the Nordic Council of Ministers.

SURVEY AND PROSPECTS

Denmark is a small open economy, which is highly dependent on trade with other countries. Foreign trade accounts for about two-thirds of GDP and about two-thirds of foreign trade is with other EU members. Large surpluses on the trade and current-account balances have been used to reduce indebtedness; in 2002 public-sector debt was equivalent to 42% of GDP, one of the lowest debt ratios in the EU. (The Government aimed to reduce it to 26% by 2010.) Owing to its reliance on trade, a principal objective of the country's foreign policy has been to maintain a stable exchange rate. Denmark did not, however, participate in the EU's programme of economic and monetary union (EMU). Despite government support for entry into EMU, it was rejected in a referendum in 1993 and this was confirmed by a second plebiscite in September 2000. Denmark has, however, maintained a stable rate of exchange with the new common European currency, the euro.

Like many EU countries, Denmark was facing a serious challenge to the long-term prospects of the economy as a result of demographic changes, resulting in a smaller labour force and a larger elderly population, which would affect the sustainability of public finances. The Government aimed to address this problem largely through the increased involvement of immigrants and refugees in the labour market, setting a target of 87,000 more people in employment by 2010. Denmark, which is attractive to foreign investors owing to its well-educated labour force and its stable economic conditions, was geographically well placed to benefit from the enlargement of the EU in May 2004. It was also possible that enlargement would contribute to the growth of Denmark's work-force. To avoid abuse of the benefit system, however, for the first seven years following accession Denmark has imposed conditions on potential workers from central and Eastern European countries, limiting residence permits to those with full-time employment and excluding them from child-care leave and unemployment benefit.

Denmark's economy was characterized in the 1990s by high economic growth but this slowed in 2001–03, as exports were adversely affected by the international recession. Investment activity also decelerated owing to market uncertainty following the terrorist attacks on the USA in September 2001. However, private consumption remained high, fuelled by increased spending power, partly due to capital gains in the housing market and low rates of interest. The deceleration in growth began to have an impact on unemployment in 2002 and 2003. Wage increases slowed but were still higher than those in neighbouring countries, leading to a loss of competitiveness that was compounded by the appreciation of the krone against the US dollar (owing to its tie to the euro). However, above average increases in productivity maintained an increasing market share for Danish exports, and the forecast international recovery and a reduction in the level of income tax (tax cuts of 9,500m. kroner were to be implemented over four years from 2004) were expected to prompt a return to more rapid growth in 2004.

Djibouti

The French Territory of the Afars and the Issas, situated in the Horn of Africa, became independent as the Republic of Djibouti in 1977. In 1991, discontented with the status of the Rassemblement pour le progrès as Djibouti's sole legal party, the Front pour la restauration de l'unité et de la démocratie (FRUD) launched an anti-Government insurrection. In 1994 a peace agreement was signed between the Government and one faction of the now divided FRUD, and in 2000 hostilities were concluded between the Government and another FRUD faction that had continued to oppose it. The capital is Djibouti. Arabic and French are the official languages.

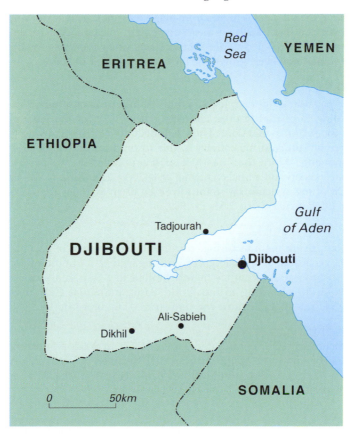

Area and population
Area: 23,200 sq km
Population (mid-2002): 656,510
Population density (mid-2002): 28.3 per sq km
Life expectancy (years at birth, 2002): 49.6 (males 48.6; females 50.7)

233

Finance
GDP in current prices: 2002): US $597m. ($909 per head)
Real GDP growth (2002): 1.6%
Inflation (2001): 1.4%
Currency: Djibouti franc

Economy

In 2002, according to estimates by the World Bank, Djibouti's gross national income (GNI), measured at average 2000–02 prices, was US $590m., equivalent to $900 per head (or $2,070 on an international purchasing-power parity basis). During 1990–2002, it was estimated, the population increased at an average annual rate of 2.8%, owing partly to the influx of refugees from neighbouring Ethiopia and Somalia, while gross domestic product (GDP) per head decreased, in real terms, by an average of 3.3% per year. Overall GDP declined, in real terms, at an average annual rate of 0.6% during 1990–2002; however, growth of 1.6% was recorded in 2002.

AGRICULTURE

Agriculture (including hunting, forestry and fishing) provided only 3.5% of GDP in 2002, according to official figures, although some 78.7% of the labour force were engaged in the sector in mid-2001. There is little arable farming, owing to Djibouti's unproductive terrain, and the country is able to produce only about 3% of its total food requirements. More than one-half of the population are pastoral nomads, herding goats, sheep and camels. During 1990–2000, according to the World Bank, the real GDP of the agricultural sector increased at an average annual rate of 0.4%; agricultural GDP increased by 2.5% in 2000.

INDUSTRY

Industry (comprising manufacturing, construction and utilities) provided 16.0% of GDP in 2002, according to official figures, and engaged 11.0% of the employed labour force in 1991. Industrial activity is mainly limited to a few small-scale enterprises. During 1990–2000, according to the World Bank, industrial GDP declined at an average annual rate of 4.2%; however, industrial GDP increased by 1.1% in 2000.

Manufacturing

The manufacturing sector contributed 3.4% of GDP in 2002. Almost all consumer goods have to be imported. Manufacturing GDP declined by an average of 7.5% per year in 1990–2000, according to the World Bank. However, the GDP of the sector increased by 0.9% in 2000.

Energy

In 1986 work commenced on a major geothermal exploration project, funded by the World Bank and foreign aid. In that year Saudi Arabia granted Djibouti US $21.4m. for the purchase and installation of three electricity generators, with a combined capacity of 15 MW. Total electricity generating capacity rose from 40 MW to 80 MW in 1988, when the second part of the Boulaos power station became operative. This figure continued to rise during the 1990s, and in 2002 Djibouti produced 246.7m. kWh of electricity. Nevertheless, imported fuels continued to satisfy a large proportion of

Djibouti's energy requirements. Imports of petroleum products accounted for 18.5% of the value of total imports in 1999.

SERVICES

Djibouti's economic viability is based on trade through the international port of Djibouti, and on the developing service sector, which accounted for 80.5% of GDP in 2002, according to official figures, and engaged 13.8% of the employed labour force in 1991. In May 2000 the Government and Dubai Ports International (DPI) signed an agreement providing DPI with a 20-year contract to manage the port of Djibouti. During 1990–2000, according to the World Bank, the GDP of the services sector declined at an average annual rate of 0.2%. Services GDP increased by 1.6% in 2000.

EXTERNAL TRADE

In 2002, according to official figures, Djibouti recorded a visible trade deficit of 36,270m. Djibouti francs, and there was a deficit of 2,744m. Djibouti francs on the current account of the balance of payments. According to the IMF, the principal sources of imports in 1999 were France (26.2%), Ethiopia and Saudi Arabia. The principal markets for exports in 1998 were Somalia (53.0%) and Yemen. The principal imports in 1999 were food and beverages, machinery and electrical appliances, qat (a narcotic leaf), petroleum products and vehicles and transport equipment. Most exports are unclassified.

GOVERNMENT FINANCE

Djibouti recorded a budget deficit of 839m. Djibouti francs in 2000 (equivalent to 0.9% of GDP). The country's total external debt was US $262.0m. at the end of 2001, of which $234.9m. was long-term public debt. In 2000 the cost of debt-servicing was equivalent to an estimated 5.5% of revenue from exports of goods and services. The annual rate of inflation averaged 4.8% during 1989–97. Consumer prices increased by an estimated 2.4% in 2000. In 1996 unemployment was estimated to affect some 58% of the labour force.

INTERNATIONAL ECONOMIC RELATIONS

Djibouti is a member of the Intergovernmental Authority on Development and numerous other international organizations, including the African Development Bank, the Arab Fund for Economic and Social Development and the Islamic Development Bank. In 1995 Djibouti became a member of the World Trade Organization.

SURVEY AND PROSPECTS

Djibouti is heavily dependent on foreign assistance, and the decline in foreign aid since 1986 has led to financial problems. Attempts by aid donors, notably France, to insist on structural reforms to the economy were initially resisted by the Government, but in mid-1995 considerable reductions in government spending were announced, and in April 1996 the IMF approved Djibouti's first stand-by credit, equivalent to US $6.7m. In October 1999 the IMF agreed a $26.5m. loan to support the Government's three-year economic reform programme, and an initial payment of $3.8m. was released immediately. However, the payment of the balance was conditional on Djibouti implementing its 1999–2002 programme of economic and financial reform, which included reforms to tax, revenue administration and budget management; the completion of the army demobilization programme by the end of 2000; the reform of the civil service, thus lowering the wage bill; and the publication of a privatization programme for the six principal state-owned enterprises. Despite continued delays in the army demobilization programme and the reform of the civil service, in November 2001 the IMF disbursed a further $5.0m., and in December 2002, following the completion of the third policy review, the IMF released funds totalling $6.0m.

In 2003 economic growth continued to be driven predominantly by activity in the expanding services sector, which benefited from the sizeable foreign military contingents stationed in Djibouti as part of the fight against international terrorism, as well as increased activity at the port of Djibouti. In May France agreed to contribute €30m. per year over a 10-year period in order to maintain its military presence in the country, while the USA was to pay Djibouti $31m. for hosting its military base; when combined, these payments would cover more than 80% of the annual wage bill for the civil service. Moreover, in late 2003 the USA also announced that Djibouti would receive aid worth some $90m. during 2004, making Djibouti the largest recipient of US assistance in Africa. Meanwhile, according to the central bank, inflation remained at historically low levels, with price rises of just 1.4% and 1.5% recorded in 2001 and 2002, respectively.

Dominica

The Commonwealth of Dominica is situated in the Windward Islands group of the West Indies. Dominica became an independent republic within the Commonwealth in 1978. Post-independence politics were dominated, from 1980 until 1995, by the Dominica Freedom Party (DFP). Following the DFP's electoral success in 1980, Eugenia Charles, the party's leader, became the Caribbean's first female Prime Minister. At the general election held in 1995 the Dominica United Workers' Party gained the largest number of seats in the House of Assembly. In 2000 the Labour Party of Dominica was returned to power after two decades in opposition. Roseau is the capital. English is the official language.

Area and population
Area: 751 sq km
Population (mid-2002): 71,800
Population density (mid-2002): 95.6 per sq km
Life expectancy (years at birth, 2002): 73.3 (males 71.0; females 75.8)

Finance
GDP in current prices: 2002): US $254m. ($3,543 per head)
Real GDP growth (2002): −2.8%
Inflation (annual average, 2002): 0.2%
Currency: Eastern Caribbean dollar

Economy

In 2002, according to estimates by the World Bank, Dominica's gross national income (GNI), measured at average 2000–2002 prices, was US $228.3m., equivalent to $3,180 per head (or $4,840 per head on an international purchasing-power parity basis). Between 1990 and 2001 the population decreased by an average annual rate of 0.1%, while gross domestic product (GDP) per head increased, in real terms, by an average of 0.8% per year. Overall GDP increased, in real terms, by an average of 0.7% per year in 1990–2002; GDP decreased by 4.9% in 2001 and by 2.7% in 2002.

AGRICULTURE

Agriculture (including forestry and fishing) is the principal economic activity, accounting for an estimated 17.1% of GDP in 2002. In 1997 the sector engaged 23.7% of the employed labour force. The principal cash crop is bananas. The banana industry, which was already experiencing difficulties (owing to a decline in prices), was adversely affected by a September 1997 ruling of the World Trade Organization (WTO) against Dominica's preferential access to the European (particularly the British) market. In 1998 banana production decreased by some 27%, to some 30,000 metric tons, while receipts from banana exports fell by 8.9% to EC $42.2m. (some 24.8% of total domestic exports). After remaining at the same level in 1999, banana output was estimated to have increased slightly in 2000 and 2001 (to 31,000 tons and 33,000 tons, respectively). In 2001 receipts from banana exports totalled US $9.5m. (some 21.8% of total domestic exports). Banana output was estimated to have decreased to 29,000 tons in 2002. Other important crops include coconuts (which provide copra for export as well as edible oil and soap), mangoes, avocados, papayas, ginger, citrus fruits and, mainly for domestic consumption, vegetables. Non-banana crops have grown in significance during recent years, from one-half of total crop production to about two-thirds in 2002. Livestock-rearing and fishing are also practised for local purposes. In August 2002 a US $10m., Japanese-funded renovation of the Roseau Fisheries Complex was completed. In addition, 12 smaller, Japanese-funded, fisheries projects were also due to get under way later in the year, and research into the construction of another multi-purpose fisheries complex in Ports-mouth was expected to commence in March. Dominica has extensive timber reserves (more than 40% of the island's total land area is forest and woodland), and international aid agencies are encouraging the development of a balanced timber industry. The GDP of the agricultural sector decreased at an average annual rate of 1.6% in 1990–2002. In real terms, agricultural GDP declined by 6.6% in 2001 and by an estimated 0.6% in 2002.

INDUSTRY

Industry (comprising mining, manufacturing, construction and utilities) provided 19.3% of GDP in 2002, and employed 18.2% of the employed labour force in 1997. Real industrial GDP increased at an average rate of 1.1% per year during 1990–2002; the sector decreased by 5.1% in 2001 and by an estimated 10.4% in 2002. Manufacturing activity is mainly small-scale and dependent upon agriculture.

Mining

The mining sector contributed only 0.7% of GDP in 2002. There is some quarrying of pumice, and there are extensive reserves of limestone and clay. Pumice is useful to the construction industry, which accounted for 6.5% of GDP in 2002, and employed 8.4% of the employed labour force in 1997.

Manufacturing

Extensive infrastructure development by the Government has maintained high levels of activity in the construction sector in recent years. The GDP of the construction sector decreased at an average annual rate of 0.1%, in real terms, during 1990–2002; the sector's GDP declined by 2.2% in 2001 and by an estimated 22.9% in 2002. The Government has also encouraged the manufacturing sector in an attempt to diversify the economy. In 2002 manufacturing contributed 7.2% of GDP and, in 1997, employed 8.8% of the employed work-force. Real manufacturing GDP increased at an average rate of 0.2% per year during 1990–2002; in 2000 the manufacturing sector increased strongly, by 8.5%, but the sector's GDP decreased by 8.6% in 2001 and by an estimated 0.3% in 2002. There is a banana-packaging plant, a brewery and factories for the manufacturing and refining of crude and edible vegetable oils and for the production of soap, canned juices and cigarettes. Furniture, paint, cardboard boxes and candles are also significant manufactures.

Energy

In 2000 70% of Dominica's energy requirements were supplied by hydroelectric power. Investment in a hydroelectric development scheme and in the water supply system has been partially financed by the export of water, from Dominica's extensive reserves, to drier Caribbean islands such as Aruba. A hydroelectric power-station, with a generating capacity of 1.24 MW, began operation at Laudat in 1990. In 2001 Dominica's imports of mineral fuels totalled 9.9% of the cost of total imports. In 1998 a geothermal energy project in Soufrière began producing electricity, following investment of EC $25m. from a US company. In December 1996 the state-owned Dominica Electricity Services (Domlec) was privatized, with the British Government's overseas private finance institution, the Commonwealth Development Corporation (CDC), buying 72% of the company. The CDC outlined planned to increase electricity generation by 80% by 2000. Construction of a new 20-MW electric power plant, at an estimated cost of EC $80m., was scheduled for completion by early 2001.

SERVICES

Services engaged 53.8% of the employed labour force in 1997, and provided 63.6% of GDP in 2002. The combined GDP of the service sectors increased at an average rate of 2.6% per year during 1990–2002; in 2001 the sector declined by 1.5% and by an estimated further 2.9% in 2002. The tourist industry is of increasing importance to the economy and exploits Dominica's natural history and scenery. Since 1998 the Government has placed considerable emphasis on the country's potential as an 'eco-tourism' destination, pursuing a development programme funded by the European Union (EU). The majority of tourists are cruise-ship passengers. Arrivals from cruise ships increased dramatically in the 1990s, from 6,777 in 1990 to 244,603 in 1998. Following a decline in 1999, to 202,003, cruise-ship arrivals recovered strongly in 2000, to 239,544. However, this figure decreased again in 2001, to an estimated

207,627. In 2002 tourism receipts totalled an estimated EC $119.2m. In early 2004 the Government signed a three-year agreement with a cruise-ship operator, which, it was hoped, would increase revenue to the sector. In 1990 the Government decided to proceed with the construction of an international airport. However, in 2003 proposals for the project were still under review, although the Republic of China (Taiwan) had pledged US $35m.

EXTERNAL TRADE

In 2002 Dominica recorded a visible trade deficit of US $160.55m. and a deficit of US $123.55m. on the current account of the balance of payments. The principal source of imports in 2001 was the USA, which accounted for 36.4% of total imports, followed by Trinidad and Tobago (17.5%) and the United Kingdom (10.2%). The principal market for exports in 2001 was Jamaica, which received 23.2% of total exports; the United Kingdom, which receives a large proportion of Dominica's banana production, took 21.1% of total domestic exports. The principal imports in 2001 were machinery and transport equipment, basic manufactures (such as paper) and food and live animals. The principal exports in the same year were soap and bananas.

GOVERNMENT FINANCE

In 2002, according to preliminary ECCB figures, there was an estimated budget deficit of EC $34m. At the end of 2001 Dominica's total external debt was US $206.5m., of which US $184.5m. was long-term public debt. In the same year the cost of debt-servicing was equivalent to 12.7% of the value of exports of goods and services. The annual rate of inflation averaged 1.2% in 1995–2002; consumer prices increased by an average of 1.5% in 2001 and by 0.2% in 2002. An estimated 23.1% of the labour force were unemployed in 1997.

INTERNATIONAL ECONOMIC RELATIONS

Dominica is a member of the Organization of American States (OAS), the Caribbean Community and Common Market (CARICOM), the OECS, and is a signatory of the Cotonou Agreement, the successor arrangement to the Lomé Conventions between the African, Caribbean and Pacific (ACP) countries and the European Union. Dominica is also a member of the Eastern Caribbean Securities Exchange (based in Saint Christopher and Nevis). Under the Charles administration, the island received considerable overseas aid.

SURVEY AND PROSPECTS

The Dominican economy is heavily dependent on the production of coconut-based products and bananas, and their export to a limited market, and is thus vulnerable to adverse weather conditions, price fluctuations and economic conditions in its principal markets. The slowdown, and then contraction, in economic growth in 1999–2002 was largely attributable to the weak performance of the major productive sectors. In the 1990s growth in the economy slowed, owing to the uncertainty surrounding Dominica's preferential access to the European market and the devastation of the 1995 banana crop by a hurricane.

Efforts to expand the country's economic base have been impeded by poor infrastructure and, in terms of tourism, a paucity of desirable beaches. During the 1990s the Government succeeded in expanding the tourist sector, aided by an 'eco-tourism' development programme with EU funding. None the less, there was a decrease in both visitor arrivals and gross visitor expenditure in 2001 and 2002, although the sector recovered slightly in 2003 and was expected to continue to improve in 2004.

Banana exports decreased from the end of the 1990s, owing to drought, a fall in producer prices and uncertainties caused by the continuing dispute over the EU's banana import regime. Many marginal farmers were unable to attain the new stringent quality standards of the industry, another contributing factor in the decline in banana output. The end to the banana trade dispute in April 2001 was expected to have further adverse effects on the sector in the early years of the 21st century (from 2006 the EU's import regime was to be replaced by a universal tariff system). In 2002 the Government announced the proposed privatization of the Banana Marketing Corporation.

In the late 1990s and early 2000s the island's public finances weakened considerably, owing to an increase in expenditure caused by a rising wage bill and debt-servicing obligations, as well as to a concurrent decrease in savings and foreign grants. In spite of the introduction in 1998 of value-added tax (VAT), Dominica's tax system remained inefficient, with its narrow base, collection difficulties and substantial exemptions contributing to stagnating revenues. In 2002 structural reforms were planned in the areas of taxation policy and public administration, privatization and agricultural diversification. Austerity measures announced in July and contained in the 2002/03 budget included a reduction in the number of cabinet ministers, increases in fuel, sales and telephone-service taxes, and higher fees for passports and postage stamps. In addition, parliament approved an extra, reportedly temporary, 4% (reduced to 1% in July 2003) income tax, known as the 'Stabilization Levy', to be paid by virtually every earner.

In August 2003, in support of the reforms, the IMF agreed to provide a one-year US $4.3m. stand-by credit for Dominica; significant funds were also provided by CARICOM and the EU. Although the budget did not heed all of the recommendations made by the IMF, proposed expenditure in 2002/03 was reduced by 15%, in an attempt to decrease the island's crippling fiscal deficit (estimated to be total some EC $30m. in 2002) and large external debt. Further austerity measures, including tax increases and public-sector salary cuts, were included in the 2003/04 budget; furthermore, in February 2004 the Government announced that the public-sector wage bill would be reduced by 10%. In December 2003 the IMF approved a further US $11.4m. credit for Dominica under its Poverty Reduction and Growth Facility. The Fund also endorsed the Government's efforts in complying with the 2002 stand-by agreement. In a reflection of the Government's adherence to the IMF programme, in December 2003 the Government announced the sale of its controlling stake in the National Commercial Bank of Dominica, which henceforth became known as the National Bank of Dominica. Plans were also announced for the consolidation of the country's financial supervisory bodies into a single regulatory authority, the Financial Services Unit. In January 2004 the World Bank approved a US $3m. structural-adjustment loan to aid the rationalization of the public sector. According to official estimates, 2003 was likely to see a further, but less severe, contraction in real GDP of 0.7%, with the possibility of a return to growth in 2004.

Dominican Republic

The Dominican Republic occupies part of the island of Hispaniola in the Caribbean Sea. Gen. Rafael Leónidas Trujillo Molin dominated the country from 1930 until 1961. In 1962 Dr Juan Bosch Gaviño became President. Bosch's overthrow in a coup in 1963 led to civil war in 1965. Dr Joaquín Balaguer Ricardo Balaguer of the Partido Reformista Social Cristiano was elected as President in 1966. He regained the presidency in 1970, 1974, 1986 and 1990. Balaguer's re-election in 1994 was vitiated by allegations of electoral fraud. A Pact for Democracy ended the ensuing political crisis. The capital is Santo Domingo. Spanish is the official language.

Area and population
Area: 48,422 sq km
Population (mid-2002): 8,634,690
Population density (mid-2002): 178.3 per sq km
Life expectancy (years at birth, 2002): 68.0 (males 64.9; females 71.5)

Finance
GDP in current prices: 2002): US $21,285m. ($2,465 per head)
Real GDP growth (2002): 4.1%
Inflation (annual average, 2002): 5.2%
Currency: peso

Economy

In 2002, according to estimates by the World Bank, the Dominican Republic's gross national income (GNI), measured at average 2000–02 prices, was US $20,049m., equivalent to $2,320 per head (or $5,870 per head on an international purchasing-power parity basis). During 1990–2002, it was estimated, the population increased by an average of 1.7% per year, while gross domestic product (GDP) per head increased, in real terms, by an average of 3.7% per year. Overall GDP increased, in real terms, by an average of 5.5% per year in 1990–2002. Real GDP increased by 3.2% in 2001 and by 4.1% in 2002.

AGRICULTURE

Agriculture, including hunting, forestry and fishing, contributed an estimated 11.8% of GDP, at constant 1970 prices, in 2002, and employed 15.1% of the employed labour force in the same year. The principal cash crops are sugar cane (sugar and sugar derivatives accounted for an estimated 12.0% of total export earnings in 1999), coffee and cocoa beans and tobacco. Agricultural GDP increased, in real terms, by an average of 4.4% per year during 1990–2002. Real agricultural GDP increased by an estimated 8.1% in 2001 and by an estimated 2.5% in 2002. In 2001 the Government intended to implement a US $400m. development plan for fruit cultivation. In November 2002 it was reported that Japan was considering funding $400m. of agricultural and environmental projects in the country, including: a $70m. project to encourage the production of rice; a $10m. river basin reforestation project; and a $48m. loan intended to fund the sewer system in Santiago.

INDUSTRY

Industry (including mining, manufacturing, construction and power) employed 20.8% of the economically active population in 2002, and contributed an estimated 32.7% of GDP, at constant 1970 prices, in that year. Industrial GDP increased, in real terms, by an average of 5.9% per year during 1990–2002. Real industrial GDP decreased by an estimated 0.2% in 2001, but increased by an estimated 3.6% in 2002.

Mining

Mining contributed an estimated 1.4% of GDP, at constant 1970 prices, in 2002, but employed only 0.3% of the economically active population in the same year. The major mineral export is ferronickel (providing approximately 24.6% of total export earnings in 2000). Gold and silver are also exploited, and there are workable deposits of gypsum, limestone and mercury. The slump in world prices forced the ferro-nickel mine at Bonao to close in late 1998. Following an increase in prices in early 2000, the mine was reopened; however, it was closed again in October 2001 for three months, owing to a decrease in demand and prices. In February 2002 the Government reached agreement with Placer Dome of Canada on a 25-year concession to operate the Sulfuros de Pueblo Viejo mine. There were plans to develop other mines throughout the country. Real mining GDP decreased by an annual average of 1.5% during 1990–2002. The GDP of the mining sector decreased, in real terms, by an estimated 15.6% in 2001 and by an estimated 2.7% in 2002.

Manufacturing

Manufacturing contributed an estimated 16.0% of GDP, at constant 1970 prices, in 2002, and employed 14.1% of the economically active population in that year. Important branches of manufacturing included beer and cigarettes. The most dynamic sector in 1999 was construction, in particular cement production. In mid-2001 there were 490 companies operating in 46 free-trade zones in the Dominican Republic, employing some 194,000 people. In 2001 a new free-trade zone was planned for San Pedro de Macorís. The passage of USA-Africa-Caribbean trade legislation in May 2000 gave Dominican apparel exports to the USA tariff-free status. The GDP of the manufacturing sector increased, in real terms, at an average rate of 4.5% per year during 1990–2002. Real manufacturing GDP decreased by an estimated 1.3% in 2001, but increased by an estimated 4.0% in 2002.

Energy

Energy is derived principally from petroleum; however, there is no domestic petroleum production. Imports of mineral fuels accounted for an estimated 13.2% of the total cost of imports in 1996. In the early 2000s construction was under way on a variety of energy projects, including: a 300 MW oil-fired power-station and a 300 MW gas-fired power-station, including a liquefied natural gas terminal; a regasification plant and a 500 MW gas-fired power-station; a hydroelectric dam in Altagracia, to supply drinking water and electricity to the province; and four mini-hydroelectric plants, together generating 16 MW. The Monción dam in Santiago Rodríguez, which included a 54 MW hydroelectric plant, was inaugurated in September 2001. York Caribbean Windpower, a subsidiary of York Research (USA), constructed a US $160m. wind park in Puerto Plata that became operational in mid-2002. In October 2000 the signing of the Caracas energy accord gave the Dominican Republic the option to buy petroleum from Venezuela under the preferential terms of the San José Agreement. However, in September 2003 Venezuela halted petroleum sales to the Dominican Republic, owing to a deterioration in diplomatic relations between the two countries.

SERVICES

The services sector contributed an estimated 55.5% of GDP, at constant 1970 prices, in 2002, and employed 64.0% of the economically active population in that year. The GDP of the services sector expanded at an average annual rate of 5.6% during 1990–2002. Real services GDP increased by an estimated 4.3% in 2001 and by an estimated 4.8% in 2002.

EXTERNAL TRADE

In 2002 the Dominican Republic recorded a visible trade deficit of US $3,699.1m., and there was a deficit of $875.2m. on the current account of the balance of payments. In 2000 the principal source of imports was the USA (49.8%); other major suppliers were Venezuela, Mexico and Japan. In the same year the USA was the principal market for exports (43.1% of the total); other significant purchasers were Belgium-Luxembourg and Puerto Rico. The principal exports in 1999 were iron and steel and sugar and sugar derivatives. In 1999 exports from the free-trade zones amounted to an estimated $3,200.4m. The principal imports in 1999 were petroleum and petroleum products, and food products. In 2001 banana exports totalled $35m., compared with $23m. in 2000.

GOVERNMENT FINANCE

In 2002 there was an estimated budgetary deficit of RD $216.0m. (equivalent to 0.1% of GDP). The Dominican Republic's total external debt at the end of 2001 was US $5,093m., of which $3,749m. was long term public debt. In that year the cost of debt-servicing was equivalent to 6.0% of total revenue from exports of goods and services. In 1990–2002 the average annual rate of inflation was 9.9%. Consumer prices increased by an average of 8.9% in 2001 and by 5.2% in 2002. An estimated 16.1% of the total labour force was unemployed in 1998.

INTERNATIONAL ECONOMIC RELATIONS

In July 1984 the Dominican Republic was granted observer status in CARICOM. In December 1989 the country was accepted as a member of the ACP nations covered by the Lomé Convention (which expired in February 2000 and was replaced by the Cotonou Agreement in June). In 1990 the Dominican Republic's application for full membership of CARICOM was threatened when ACP nations accused the Dominican Republic of breaking an agreement made under the Lomé Convention concerning the export of bananas to countries of the European Community (now the European Union). An agreement, originally signed in August 1998, establishing a free-trade area between CARICOM countries and the Dominican Republic, came into effect on 1 December 2001. In March 2004 the Dominican Republic reached a free-trade agreement with the USA; the agreement had to be approved by the legislature.

SURVEY AND PROSPECTS

From the 1990s onwards the economy of the Dominican Republic was severely affected by the unstable nature of the country's electricity supply. Interruptions in the supply of electricity lasted up to 20 hours per day. The restructuring of the state electricity company (Corporación Dominicana de Electricidad—CDE) was repeatedly delayed, although in May 1999 the generating and distribution operations of the CDE were partially privatized. In July 2001 President Rafael Hipólito Mejía Domínguez approved legislation that provided a framework for the electricity industry. However, widespread protests became a regular occurrence from 2001, owing to continuing power cuts and the Government's failure to resolve the ongoing energy crisis. Trade unions called for the annulment of the privatization contracts that had been awarded to two electricity distribution companies—the US-owned company AES and the Spanish-owned Unión Fenosa—owing to allegations that since privatization the country's electricity service had become both more unreliable and more expensive. However, in October 2002 it was reported that the Government had instructed the power companies to raise their tariffs as it was no longer willing to subsidize electricity costs for any but the poorest areas of the country.

On 1 January 2001 a programme of fiscal measures, including an increase in consumer taxes, a rise in tariffs on imported luxury goods, a tax increase on cars, insurance, advertising, flights, security, commercial rents, gambling, cigarettes and beer, and a corporation tax of 1.5%, came into effect. In 2002, despite several attempts by the Central Bank to stabilize the currency, the peso experienced significant devaluation. Meanwhile, the Government signed a 'Stability and Economic Development Pact' with members of the business sector, revising taxation measures and aiming to encourage economic growth and the stabilization of the currency.

In mid-2003 the dissolution of the country's second-largest commercial bank, Banco Intercontinental, SA (Baninter), forced the Government to seek financial assistance from the IMF in order to overcome the economic crisis that had resulted from massive misappropriation of funds at the bank. The IMF subsequently agreed a US $618m. loan, the release of which was subject to the implementation of certain fiscal policies and structural measures. Further assistance from the World Bank and the Inter-American Development Bank brought the total of agreed loans to the country to approximately $1,200m., to be disbursed over a period of two years. However, the IMF agreement was suspended in October, following the Government's announcement that it planned to buy back Unión Fenosa's stake in two of the country's power distribution companies, at an estimated cost of $700m. The IMF stated that it intended to withhold the funds while it assessed the impact of the renationalization of the power companies.

In August 2003 the Government announced the temporary imposition of a 5% tax on imports, a measure condemned by the business community. Meanwhile, the value of the Dominican currency continued to depreciate sharply throughout 2003. In response, in December the Government created a council, dominated by the military, to monitor what it described as 'politically motivated' currency speculation and to attempt to bring about an increase in the value of the peso. However, it was generally believed that the weak currency was attributable to the climate of economic uncertainty in the country and, in the following month, the Government indicated that it had abandoned attempts forcibly to strengthen the peso. The Central Bank subsequently raised interest rates in an attempt to halt rising inflation and the peso's continuing depreciation. The 2004 budget, approved by the Congreso Nacional in January of that year, put revenue at 120,000m. pesos, comprising 100,000m. pesos of regular income with the remainder in the form of international aid and donations. Following the approval of the budget, the IMF agreed to resume disbursement of funds, on condition that the Government implement tax reform. The economy was expected to contract by an estimated 3% in 2003.

Ecuador

The Republic of Ecuador lies on the west coast of South America. In 1822 Ecuador achieved independence from Spain as part of Gran Colombia, from which it seceded in 1830. Until 1948 Ecuador's political life was characterized by a rapid succession of presidents, dictators and juntas. Thereafter, military interventions in politics and government occurred frequently. The junta that assumed power in 1976 announced its intention to lead the country to a truly representative democracy and in 1978 a newly-drafted Constitution was approved. In 2000 the army was instrumental in the replacement of President Mahuad by Vice-President Noboa. Quito is the capital. Spanish is the official language.

Area and population

Area: 272,045 sq km
Population (mid-2002): 13,112,100
Population density (mid-2002): 48.2 per sq km
Life expectancy (years at birth, 2002): 70.6 (males 67.9; females 73.5)

Finance
GDP in current prices: 2002): US $24,347m. ($1,857 per head)
Real GDP growth (2002): 3.0%
Inflation (annual average, 2002): 12.5
Currency: US dollar

Economy

In 2002, according to estimates by the World Bank, Ecuador's gross national income (GNI), measured at average 2000–2002 prices, was US $19,048m., equivalent to $1,450 per head (or $3,222 per head on an international purchasing-power parity basis). During 1990–2002, it was estimated, the population increased at an average annual rate of 2.1%, while gross domestic product (GDP) per head decreased, in real terms, at an average annual rate of 0.1% in 1990–2001. Overall GDP increased, in real terms, at an average annual rate of 7.4% in 1990–2002; GDP increased by 3.0% in 2002.

AGRICULTURE

Agriculture (including hunting, forestry and fishing) contributed 9.9% of GDP in 2002. According to census figures, some 27.3% of the labour force were employed in the agricultural sector in 2001. Ecuador is the world's leading exporter of bananas, and coffee and cocoa are also important cash crops. The seafood sector, particularly the shrimp industry, expanded rapidly in the 1980s, and by the 1990s Ecuador was the second largest producer of shrimps in the world. Ecuador's extensive forests yield valuable hardwoods, and the country is a leading producer of balsawood. Exports of cut flowers increased from US $0.5m. in 1985 to $283m. in 2002 (equivalent to 5.7% of the total value of exports). During 1990–2001 agricultural GDP increased at an average annual rate of 2.6%. According to the IMF, sectoral GDP grew by 0.4% in 2001 and by 3.7% in 2002.

INDUSTRY

Industry (including mining, manufacturing, construction and power) employed 21.4% of the urban labour force in 1998, and provided 37.5% of GDP in 2002. During 1990–2001 industrial GDP increased at an average annual rate of 3.0%. According to the IMF, the sector grew by 5.1% in 2001 and by 1.6% in 2002.

Mining

Mining contributed 14.5% of GDP in 2002, although the mining sector employed only 0.3% of the urban labour force in 1998. Petroleum and its derivatives remained the major exports in the early 21st century. In 2002 some 143.5m. barrels of crude petroleum were produced, of which about 60% was exported. In 2002 proven petroleum reserves were estimated at 4,574m. barrels. Earnings from petroleum exports amounted to some US $2,033m. in 2002, equivalent to 41.0% of the total value of exports. Natural gas is extracted, but only a small proportion is retained. Gold, silver, copper, antimony and zinc are also mined. In real terms, the GDP of the mining sector increased at an average rate of 4.1% per year during 1990–2001. According to the IMF, mining GDP increased by 1.7% in 2001, but decreased by 3.5% in 2002.

Manufacturing

Manufacturing contributed 15.0% of GDP in 2002, and employed 14.7% of the labour force in urban areas in 1998. The most important branches of manufacturing were food, beverages and tobacco, textiles, clothing and leather and mineral and basic metallic products. Petroleum refining was also important. During 1990–2001 manufacturing GDP increased at an average annual rate of 2.3%. It increased by 2.9% in 2001 and by a further 2.6% in 2002, according to the IMF.

Energy

Energy is derived principally from thermoelectric and hydroelectric plants. The country has an installed capacity of 3.2m. MW, one-half of which is produced domestically. Most domestic output comes from the Paute hydroelectricity plant. In 2003 plans were under way to build a hydroelectricity station at Mazar, south of Paute, to alleviate the effects of the frequent power shortages. The new plant was expected to produce a further 180 MW of electricity. Imports of fuels and lubricants comprised 3.9% of the value of total imports in 2002.

SERVICES

The services sector contributed 52.6% of GDP in 2002. Some 71.2% of the urban labour force were employed in services in 1998. The sector's GDP increased at an average annual rate of 1.6% during 1991–2000. It increased by 5.0% in 2001 and by a further 3.5% in 2002, according to the IMF.

EXTERNAL TRADE

In 2002 Ecuador recorded a visible trade deficit of US $1,004m., and a deficit of $1,222m. on the current account of the balance of payments. In 2002 the principal source of imports was the USA (accounting for 23.0% of the total), which was also the principal market for exports (39.9%). Other major trading partners were the People's Republic of China, Colombia, Germany, Italy, Japan, the Republic of Korea, Panama and Peru. The principal exports in 2002 were petroleum and petroleum derivatives (41.0%), bananas (19.8%) and seafood products (7.0%). The principal imports in 2002 were consumer goods (33.6%), industrial raw materials (25.9%) and capital goods for industry (23.2%).

GOVERNMENT FINANCE

In 2002 there was a budgetary deficit of about US $185m. In 2002 some 28.7% of government expenditure was financed by revenue from petroleum. Ecuador's total external debt was US $13,910m. at the end of 2001, of which $11,149m. was long-term public debt. In that year the cost of debt-servicing was equivalent to 21.4% of the total value of exports of goods and services. The average annual rate of inflation in 1990–2002 was 39.3%; the rate averaged 37.7% in 2001 and 12.5% in 2002. The rate of unemployment decreased from an average of 14.0% in 1999 to 9.3% in 2002.

INTERNATIONAL ECONOMIC RELATIONS

Ecuador is a member of the Andean Community, the Organization of American States (OAS) and of the Asociación Latinoamericana de Integración (ALADI). In 1992 Ecuador withdrew from the Organization of the Petroleum Exporting Countries (OPEC) and announced its intention of seeking associate status. In 1995 Ecuador joined the World Trade Organization (WTO).

SURVEY AND PROSPECTS

In the mid-1990s Ecuador's proven petroleum reserves almost tripled, following discoveries in the Amazon region, and the Government signed contracts with numerous companies for further exploration and drilling. In late 1997 work to expand the capacity of the trans-Ecuadorean pipeline from 330,000 b/d to 410,000 b/d began. Construction of a new pipeline for heavy crudes (Oleoducto para Crudos Pesados—OCP), financed by a consortium of private companies at a cost of US $594m., also began in 2002, despite concerted protests from indigenous groups and environmental activists. However, construction of the new pipeline, the completion of which was expected to double Ecuador's petroleum production, was delayed, owing to worries about its environmental impact; it was completed in late 2003.

From 2000 attempts to privatize a number of state-owned industries were repeatedly impeded by political turmoil and trade union opposition. The programme suffered a major setback in May 2002 with the suspension of the sale of EMELEC, the state electricity utility, owing to a lack of interested investors.

In the wake of Ecuador's default on its sovereign debt in August 1999, the country's relationship with the IMF continued to be of critical importance; in April 2000 a 12-month stand-by credit of US $304m. was approved to support the costly dollarization process, which was implemented in a bid to reduce inflation and to rebuild the country's fragile banking system. The loan was conditional on fiscal reforms; however, opposition from the Congreso Nacional, as well as from indigenous organizations and trade unions, stalled the implementation of these reforms, which also included a proposed increase in value-added tax (VAT). Upon congressional approval of a 2% VAT increase in April 2001, the IMF disbursed a further $48m. In January 2003 the new President, Lucio Gutiérrez, secured a further $500m. in IMF loans, following government pledges of fiscal reform. In August the IMF disbursed a further $42m., in spite of the lack of progress in the Government's reform programme. The IMF arrangement was conditional on the administration allocating a greater proportion of oil revenues towards debt repayment, which was projected at some 40% of the national budget in 2003. However, reports of a significant fall in petroleum production in 2003 led to fears that government revenues would not improve, despite high international oil prices and the completion of the new pipeline in September. Furthermore, by late 2003 little progress had been made on IMF-mandated proposals to place the state telecommunications companies Andinatel and Pacifictel under private management. In early 2004 the non-petroleum economy remained stagnant; unemployment was estimated to have increased to some 11.7%, and some 60% of the population continued to live in poverty.

Egypt

The Arab Republic of Egypt occupies the north-eastern corner of Africa, extending into the Sinai Peninsula. In 1952 army officers led by Lt-Col Gamal Abd an-Nasir (Nasser) seized power, and in 1956 Nasser was elected President. Egypt was defeated by Israel in the Six-Day War of 1967. After Nasser's death in 1970, Col Anwar Sadat became President. In 1973 Egypt was again defeated in war with Israel, concluding a peace treaty in 1979. After Sadat's assassination in 1981, Lt-Gen. Hosni Mubarak assumed the presidency. Mubarak was re-elected and confirmed by referendum in 1987, 1993 and 1999. The capital is Cairo. Arabic is the official language.

Area and population
Area: 1,002,000 sq km
Population (mid-2002): 66,371,672
Population density (mid-2002): 66.2 per sq km
Life expectancy (years at birth, 2002): 67.1 (males 65.3; females 69.0)

Finance
GDP in current prices: 2002): US $89,845m. ($1,354 per head)
Real GDP growth (2002): 3.0%
Inflation (annual average, 2002): 2.7%
Currency: Egyptian pound

Economy

In 2002, according to estimates by the World Bank, Egypt's gross national income (GNI), measured at average 2000–02 prices, was US $97,607m., equivalent to $1,470 per head (or $3,710 per head on an international purchasing-power parity basis). During 1990–2002, it was estimated, the population increased at an average annual rate of 2.0%, while gross domestic product (GDP) per head increased, in real terms, by 2.1% per year. Overall GDP increased, in real terms, at an annual average rate of 4.2% in 1990–2002. At factor cost, real GDP increased by 7.1% in the year ending 30 June 2003.

AGRICULTURE

Agriculture (including forestry and fishing) contributed 16.5% of GDP in 2002/03, and employed an estimated 32.6% of the economically active population in 2001. The principal crops include sugar cane, maize, tomatoes and wheat. Exports of food and live animals accounted for 9.4% of total exports in 2001. During 1990–2002 agricultural GDP increased at an average annual rate of 3.5%. Agricultural GDP grew by 2.8% in 2002/03.

INDUSTRY

Industry (including mining, manufacturing, construction and power) engaged 22.6% of the employed labour force in 1999, and provided 34.7% of GDP in 2002/03. During 1990–2002 industrial GDP expanded at an average annual rate of 5.4%. Industrial GDP increased by 1.9% in 2002/03.

Mining

Mining contributed 8.9% of GDP in 2002/03. Egypt's mineral resources include petroleum, natural gas, phosphates, manganese, uranium, coal, iron ore and gold. Although the mining sector employed only 0.3% of the working population in 1999, petroleum and petroleum products accounted for 37.6% of total export earnings in 2001. Petroleum production averaged an estimated 751,000 barrels per day in 2002, and at the end of that year Egypt's oil reserves were estimated to total 3,700m. barrels (sufficient to sustain production at 2002 levels for a little over 14 years). At the end of 2002 Egypt's proven natural gas reserves totalled 1,660,000m. cu m, sustainable for more than 73 years at constant production levels (totalling 22,700m. cu m in 2002). Until the early part of this century all the natural gas produced was consumed domestically, but the Government began exporting in 2003. In mid-2003 BP Egypt announced the largest petroleum discovery in the country for 14 years, and there were also major discoveries of natural gas and condensate in that year. Mining GDP increased by 2.8% in 2002/03.

Manufacturing

Manufacturing engaged 13.2% of the employed labour force in 1999 and contributed 19.3% of GDP in 2002/03. Based on the value of output, the main branches of manufacturing in 1997 were food products (accounting for 19.6% of the total), petroleum refining (15.4%), chemicals (12.4%), textiles (12.2%), metals and metal products (9.3%) and non-metallic mineral manufactures (7.6%). In 2003 the Government announced major plans to develop the petrochemicals industry. During 1990–2002 the real GDP of the manufacturing sector increased by an average of 6.2% per year. Manufacturing GDP expanded by 2.6% in 2002/03.

Energy

Energy is derived principally from natural gas (which provided 65.2% of total electricity output in 2000), petroleum (16.1%) and hydroelectric power (18.7%). In 2001 fuel imports accounted for about an estimated 4.9% of the value of merchandise imports.

SERVICES

Services contributed 48.8% of GDP in 2002/03, and employed 48.7% of the working population in 1999. By the late 1980s tourism had become one of the most dynamic sectors of the Egyptian economy. For much of the 1990s, however, the sector was severely undermined by the campaign of violence aimed by fundamentalist Islamists at tourist targets, and visitor numbers and tourism revenues declined significantly. By 1999 there were signs of a recovery in the sector, although this was reversed as a result of the regional insecurity arising from the Israeli–Palestinian violence from late 2000, the terrorist attacks against the USA in September 2001 and, temporarily, by the US-led intervention in Iraq in early 2003. In 1990–2002 the real GDP of the services sector increased by an average of 3.2% per year. Services GDP increased by 4.2% in 2002/03.

EXTERNAL TRADE

In 2002 Egypt recorded a visible trade deficit of US $5,747m., although there was a surplus of $470m. on the current account of the balance of payments. In 2001 the principal source of imports (14.4%) was the USA; other major suppliers were Germany, Saudi Arabia and Italy. The principal market for exports was Italy (9.1%), followed by the USA (8.3%), the Netherlands and India. Egypt's principal exports in 2001 were petroleum and petroleum products, basic manufactures, food and live animals, chemicals and clothing. The principal imports were machinery and transport equipment, food and live animals, basic manufactures and chemicals.

GOVERNMENT FINANCE

For the financial year 2003/04 there was a projected deficit of £E28,700m. in the state public budget (equivalent to an estimated 7.0% of GDP). Egypt's external debt totalled US $29,234m. at the end of 2001, of which $25,243m. was long-term public debt. In that year the cost of servicing the foreign debt was equivalent to 8.9% of the value of exports of goods and services. The annual rate of inflation averaged 7.4% in 1990–2002. Consumer prices increased by an average of 2.2% in 2001, and by 2.7% in 2002. An estimated 9.0% of the total labour force were unemployed in mid-2002.

INTERNATIONAL ECONOMIC RELATIONS

Egypt is a member of the Common Market for Eastern and Southern Africa (COMESA), the Council of Arab Economic Unity, the Organization of Arab Petroleum Exporting Countries (OAPEC), the African Petroleum Producers' Association, and the Co-operation Council for the Arab States of the Gulf (Arab Co-operation Council).

SURVEY AND PROSPECTS

Following an impressive macro-economic performance during much of the 1990s, which resulted in strong GDP growth and low inflation, Egypt's economy suffered a series of major reverses from the late 1990s and a serious liquidity crisis, resulting primarily from a depletion in the main sources of hard currency, prompted intervention by the Government and the Central Bank in mid-2000. The Egyptian pound's fixed exchange rate against the US dollar was informally abandoned, and in January 2001, under a series of fiscal reforms, control over the exchange rate was transferred to the Central Bank, which introduced a 'managed peg' system. Nevertheless, in 2001 the pound was devalued on a further three occasions and in January 2003, in anticipation of further economic difficulties resulting from a likely US-led military campaign against the regime of Saddam Hussain in Iraq, the Government abandoned the pound's peg to the US dollar and allowed the currency to float freely.

The USA agreed to provide US $2,300m. worth of loan guarantees and economic grants to offset the expected economic repercussions of the conflict in Iraq, namely significantly decreased revenues from tourism and the Suez Canal. However, the tourism industry experienced a resurgence in 2003 and this was expected to continue in the coming years. Furthermore, the discovery of major gas reserves and the commencement of gas exports was predicted to improve the country's trade balance as well as attract further overseas investment in development projects. Nevertheless, Egypt's external debt continued to rise during the year; the cost of servicing this debt, combined with the devaluation of the pound, increased inflationary pressures on the economy, resulting in a rapid rise in wholesale prices. Although the economy was projected to grow by 3.0% in 2004, this remained insufficient to provide employment for the growing number of Egyptians entering the job market each year, and both the high level of unemployment and the widening budget deficit remained major causes for concern.

El Salvador

The Republic of El Salvador lies on the Pacific coast of Central America. Since independence (from Spain) was achieved in 1839, El Salvador has been characterized by political violence. From 1980 a civil war was fought between government forces and those mobilized by the Frente Democrático Revolucionario and the Frente Farabundo Martí para la Liberación Nacional (FMLN). The conflict was formally concluded in 1992, when the FMLN was legitimized. At presidential elections in 1994, 1999 and 2004 the candidate of the Alianza Republicana Nacionalista (ARENA) was successful. ARENA became the largest single party in the legislature following elections in 2003. San Salvador is the capital. The language is Spanish.

Area and population
Area: 21,041 sq km
Population (mid-2002): 6,523,910
Population density (mid-2002): 310.1 per sq km
Life expectancy (years at birth, 2002): 69.7 (males 66.5; females 72.8)

Finance
GDP in current prices, 2002): US $14,287m. ($2,190 per head)
Real GDP growth (2002): 2.3%
Inflation (annual average, 2002): 1.9%
Currency: colón

Economy

In 2002, according to estimates by the World Bank, El Salvador's gross national product (GNI), measured at average 2000–02 prices, was US $13,538m., equivalent to $2,080 per head (or $4,570 per head on an international purchasing-power parity basis). In 1990–2002, the population increased at an average annual rate of 2.1%, while gross domestic product (GDP) per head increased, in real terms, by an average of 2.1% per year. Overall GDP increased, in real terms, at an average annual rate of 4.2% in 1990–2002. GDP grew by 2.1% in 2002.

AGRICULTURE

Agriculture (including hunting, forestry and fishing) contributed an estimated 8.9% of GDP and employed some 19.7% of the employed labour force in 2002. The principal cash crops are coffee and sugar cane. Maize, beans, rice and millet are the major subsistence crops. During 1990–2001 agricultural GDP increased at an average annual rate of 0.9%. The sector's GDP decreased by an estimated 3.1% in 2000, and by further estimated 2.1% in 2001. The agricultural sector was badly affected by the 2001 earthquakes that struck the country in early 2001. In March the Inter-American Development Bank (IDB) pledged some US $1,278.5m. in emergency assistance, of which US $132.6m. was intended for rehabilitation and development of agriculture; a further US $101.0m. was made available for redevelopment of the coffee industry, which had been particularly badly affected. During May–August a serious drought in Central America destroyed crops, affecting some 150,000 Salvadoreans alone. Output of coffee, affected by the earthquakes and the drought, was reduced to 2.3m. 46 kg sacks in 2001/02, compared to 3.6m. sacks in 2000/01, and the sector decreased by an estimated 13% in 2001. In 2000 coffee accounted for 22.4% of export earnings, excluding *maquila* zones; this fell to a preliminary 5.2% in 2003. In October 2002 the Government announced that it would loan some US $192m. to the coffee industry over the next three years. Despite this, many producers dismissed their workers or began to cultivate other crops. El Salvador's fishing catch was relatively small; however, in mid-2003 a Spanish firm, Grupo Calvo, opened a tuna-processing plant at Punta Gorda, which aimed to export 25,000 metric tons of tuna per year.

INDUSTRY

Industry (including mining, manufacturing, construction and power) contributed an estimated 29.4% of GDP in 2002, when the sector engaged 19.3% of the employed labour force. During 1990–2001 industrial GDP increased at an average annual rate of 5.1%. The sector's GDP increased by an estimated 2.8% in 2000 and by an estimated 5.0% in 2001.

Mining

El Salvador has no significant mineral resources, and the mining sector employed less than 0.1% of the economically active population in 2002, and contributed only an estimated 0.5% of GDP in 2001. Small quantities of gold, silver, sea-salt and limestone are mined or quarried. The mining sector increased by 0.4% in 1999 and by 3.0% in 2000.

Manufacturing

Manufacturing contributed an estimated 24.6% of GDP and employed 18.1% of the active labour force in 2002. The most important branches of manufacturing (excluding the in-bond industry) were food products, chemical products, petroleum products, textiles, apparel (excl. footwear) and beverages. During 1990–2001 manufacturing GDP increased at an average annual rate of 5.3%. The sector's GDP increased by an estimated 4.1% in 2000 and by an estimated 4.2% in 2001. By the late 1990s manufacturing had become the highest-earning export sector, generating the equivalent of 58% of total exports in 2001. There is a thriving offshore (*maquila*) manufacturing sector, which in 2003 generated more than one-half (an estimated 60%) of the country's total exports. In 1995–2000 *maquila* exports increased at an average annual rate of 20%. However, as a consequence of the natural disasters in El Salvador and the faltering US economy, growth decreased substantially after 2000; the sector expanded by 2.5% in 2001, rising slightly to 6.5% in 2002. Following the earthquakes in early 2001, the IDB pledged some US $62.2m. to the industry and commerce sector and a further $574.7m. to the housing sector to fund a renovation and reconstruction programme. In September the IDB announced a loan of $70m. and in December the World Bank pledged $270m. over three years, to help reconstruction efforts.

Energy

Energy is derived principally from imported fuel. Mineral products accounted for an estimated 13.5% of the cost of merchandise imports in 2001. In 2003 El Salvador derived almost one-half (48.1%) of its electricity from petroleum, compared with just 6.8% in 1990. An estimated further 28.5% of total electricity production in 2003 was contributed by hydroelectric installations. In 2001 construction began on an electricity interconnection between El Salvador and Honduras, part of a planned Central American regional power network.

SERVICES

The services sector contributed an estimated 61.6% of GDP and employed 55.9% of the economically active population in 2002. The GDP of the services sector increased by an average of 4.9% per year in 1990–2001. The sector grew by an estimated at 3.0% in 2000 and by an estimated 1.2% in 2001. The promising tourism sector was severely damaged by the civil war, but recovered in the late 1990s. In 2001 receipts from tourism totalled US $235m.

EXTERNAL TRADE

In 2002 El Salvador recorded a visible trade deficit of US $1,905.5m., while there was a deficit of $383.8m. on the current account of the balance of payments. Following the earthquakes in 2001, remittances from workers abroad increased, with payments from the USA alone totalling some US $1,935m. in that year. Remittances in 2003 were equivalent to about 14% of annual GDP and totalled about $2,100m. In 2003 almost one-half of total imports (an estimated 49.8%) was provided by the USA; other major suppliers were Guatemala, Costa Rica and Honduras. The USA was also the principal market for exports (taking an estimated 67.6% of exports, mostly from the *maquila* sector, in 2003); other significant purchasers were the Guatemala, Honduras and Costa Rica. In 2001 the main exports were prepared foodstuffs, beverages, spirits and vinegar, tobacco and manufactures substitutes, chemicals and related products, vegetable products (76.3% of which was coffee) and mineral products. In the same year the principal imports were machinery and electrical equipment, mineral products and chemicals and related products.

GOVERNMENT FINANCE

In 2001 there was an estimated budgetary deficit of 426.4m. colones, equivalent to some 3.1% of GDP. El Salvador's external debt totalled US $4,683m. at the end of 2001, of which $3,257m. was long-term public debt. In that year the cost of debt-servicing was $384m., equivalent to 6.3% of exports of goods and services. The average annual rate of inflation was 7.4% in 1990–2002; consumer prices increased by an average of 3.7% in 2001 and by 1.9% in 2002. Some 6.2% of the labour force were unemployed in 2002.

INTERNATIONAL ECONOMIC RELATIONS

El Salvador is a member of the Central American Common Market (CACM), which aims to increase trade within the region and to encourage monetary and industrial co-operation.

SURVEY AND PROSPECTS

The Government of Calderón Sol (1994–99) achieved considerable progress in reducing financial imbalances and in addressing the problem of widespread poverty. The administration also made advances in the divestment of state assets in the sectors of electricity distribution and telecommunications. A private pensions system also began operating in 1998, intended to replace gradually the existing state system. The Flores administration, inaugurated in June 1999, announced a plan for economic reactivation designed to galvanize agricultural and industrial production. In particular, the introduction of value-added tax on imported consumer goods and the prospect of more easily available credit were expected to improve the competitiveness of the agricultural sector. A revision of the tax system was expected to produce a significant increase in revenue. Economic expansion of some 2.1% was recorded in both 2000 and 2001.

The introduction, in January 2001, of the US dollar as an official currency alongside the colón, anchored to the colón at a fixed rate of exchange, was intended to stabilize the economy, to lower interest rates, and to stimulate domestic and foreign investment. In late 2002 the Central Bank estimated that US dollars accounted for 99% of money in El Salvador, including both currency in circulation and bank deposits. In February 2002 the Government announced plans to increase public investment by 23% in that year. The extra funds were intended to rebuild schools and roads damaged by the earthquakes of 2001 and were expected to generate some 30,000 jobs. The establishment of a special unit in 2002 increased tax collection efficiency. In January–May 2003 tax revenue rose by 7.2%, compared with the same period in the previous year.

In March 2001 the free-trade agreement with Mexico was implemented. In May the Central American countries, including El Salvador, reached the basis of a deal with Mexico, the 'Plan Puebla–Panamá', to integrate the region through joint transport, industry and tourism projects. In November El Salvador, Guatemala, Honduras and Nicaragua (known as the CA-4 group of countries) began negotiations with Canada on a free-trade agreement.

Negotiations towards a further free-trade agreement, to be known as the Central American Free Trade Agreement (CAFTA), was concluded between the CA-4 group of countries and the USA in December 2003. The agreement entailed the gradual elimination of tariffs on most industrial and agricultural products over the next 10 and 20 years, respectively. However, the World Bank warned that El Salvador would lose a substantial proportion of its customs revenue when the tariff barriers were removed, leading to an increase in the fiscal deficit by as much as 1.0% in 2004. The economy was forecast to grow by 1.6% in 2003 and by 2.6% in 2004.

Equatorial Guinea

The Republic of Equatorial Guinea comprises the islands of Bioko, Corisco, Great Elobey, Little Elobey and Annobón, and Río Muni on the west coast of mainland Africa. In 1979 President Francisco Macías Nguema was overthrown by Lt-Col (later Gen.) Teodoro Obiang Nguema Mbasogo. In 1993 the ruling Partido Democrático de Guinea Ecuatorial (PDGE) won multi-party legislative elections, which were boycotted by most opposition parties. The PDGE officially obtained more than 90% of the votes in the legislative elections of 1999, and, with its allies, won an overwhelming majority at parliamentary elections in April 2004. Opposition parties withdrew from the presidential election held in December 2002. Malabo is the capital. The official languages are Spanish and French.

Area and population
Area: 28,051 sq km
Population (mid-2002): 481,420
Population density (mid-2002): 17.2 per sq km
Life expectancy (years at birth, 2002): 53.4 (males 51.9; females 54.8)

Finance

GDP in current prices: 2002): US $2,173m. ($4,515 per head)
Real GDP growth (2002): 0.2%
Inflation (2001): 8.8%
Currency: CFA franc

Economy

In 2001, according to estimates by the World Bank, Equatorial Guinea's gross national income (GNI), measured at average 1999–2001 prices, was US $327m., equivalent to $700 per head (or $5,680 per head on an international purchasing-power parity basis). During 1990–2002, it was estimated, the population increased at an average annual rate of 2.6%, while gross domestic product (GDP) per head increased, in real terms, by an average of 13.6% per year. Overall GDP increased, in real terms, at an average annual rate of 16.6% in 1990–2002, according to the World Bank. According to the IMF, real GDP increased by 17.6% in 2002.

AGRICULTURE

Agriculture (including hunting, forestry and fishing) contributed 5.0% of GDP in 2002 (compared with 51.6% of GDP in 1995). The sector employed an estimated 70.1% of the labour force in 2001. The principal cash crop is cocoa. The Government is encouraging the production of bananas, spices (vanilla, black pepper and coriander) and medicinal plants for export. The main subsistence crops are cassava and sweet potatoes. Exploitation of the country's vast forest resources (principally of okoumé and akoga timber) provided 4.3% of export revenue in 2002. Almost all industrial fishing activity is practised by foreign fleets, notably by those of countries of the European Union. During 1990–2002, according to the World Bank, the real GDP of the agricultural sector increased at an average annual rate of 5.6%. According to the IMF, agricultural GDP declined by 7.8% in 2001, but increased by 2.5% in 2002.

INDUSTRY

Industry (including mining, manufacturing, construction and power) contributed 89.9% of GDP in 2002 (compared with 27.3% of GDP in 1995). During 1990–2001, according to the World Bank, industrial GDP increased at an average annual rate of 37.1%. According to the IMF, industrial GDP rose by 21.1% in 2002.

Mining

Extractive activities were minimal during the 1980s, and the mining sector employed less than 0.2% of the working population in 1983. However, the development of onshore and offshore reserves of petroleum and of offshore deposits of natural gas led to unprecedented economic growth during the 1990s. Exports of petroleum commenced in 1992 and provided 94.9% of total export earnings by 2002. The petroleum sector contributed 87.2% of GDP in 2002 (compared with 18.2% of GDP in 1995). Petroleum production increased from 56,601 barrels per day (b/d) in 1997 to an estimated 246,969 b/d in 2002. The existence of deposits of gold, uranium, iron ore, titanium, tantalum and manganese has also been confirmed. During 1997–2002 the GDP of the petroleum sector increased at an average annual rate of 32.9%, according to the IMF; growth in 2002 was 21.4%.

Manufacturing

The manufacturing sector contributed only 0.1% of GDP in 2002. Wood-processing constitutes the main commercial manufacturing activity. During 1997–2002 manufacturing GDP increased at an average annual rate of 7.4%, according to the IMF; growth in 2002 was 12.4%.

Energy

An estimated total of 23m. kWh of electric energy was generated in 2000. Bioko is supplied by a 3.6-MW hydroelectric installation, on the Riaba river, and the 10.4-MW Punta Europa gas-fired plant located at the northern end of the island. There is a further 3.6-MW installation on the mainland. Imports of fuel products comprised 7.7% of the value of total imports in 1990, prior to the discovery of large reserves of petroleum in Equato-Guinean territory.

SERVICES

The services sector contributed 5.2% of GDP in 2002. The dominant services are trade, restaurants and hotels, and government services. During 1990–2001, according to the World Bank, the GDP of the services sector increased at an average annual rate of 9.5%. According to the IMF, growth in 2002 was 14.3%.

EXTERNAL TRADE

In 2002 there was a visible trade surplus of 778,100m. francs CFA, while the deficit on the current account of the balance of payments was 127,400m. francs CFA. In 2002 the Federal Republic of Yugoslavia (now Serbia and Montenegro) was the principal source of imports (29.1%), while the USA was the principal destination of exports (28.3%). Other major trading partners were Spain, the People's Republic of China, the United Kingdom and France. In 2002 petroleum and timber constituted the principal sources of export revenue, while in 1990 the principal imports were ships and boats, petroleum and related products and food and live animals.

GOVERNMENT FINANCE

In 2002 the budget surplus was estimated at 185,128m. francs CFA (equivalent to 12.5% of GDP). Equatorial Guinea's external debt was US $238.9m. at the end of 2001, of which $192.1m. was long-term public debt. In that year the cost of debt-servicing was equivalent to 0.1% of the value of exports of goods and services. The rate of inflation averaged 7.5% per year in 1990–98. Following the devaluation of the CFA franc in January 1994, consumer prices rose by an estimated 38.9% in that year. The annual average rate of inflation was 8.8% in 2001 and 7.6% in 2002.

INTERNATIONAL ECONOMIC RELATIONS

Equatorial Guinea is a member of the Central African organs of the Franc Zone, including the Communauté économique et monétaire de l'Afrique centrale (CEMAC).

SURVEY AND PROSPECTS

Equatorial Guinea suffered a severe economic decline under the Macías regime. The Obiang Nguema administration has achieved some success in rehabilitating and diversifying the primary sector, although the significance of the country's traditional industries has declined substantially since the commencement of petroleum exports in 1992. Petroleum production led to exceptional economic growth from the late

1990s; GNI per head nearly trebled in 1996–98. In 1996, however, the IMF suspended its activities in Equatorial Guinea, following the largely unsuccessful implementation of an economic development programme, and the Fund subsequently urged the Government to increase transparency in the management of petroleum contracts and revenue. Despite a largely favourable IMF assessment released in December 2003, concerns remained that an inefficient taxation system and insufficient budgetary discipline were undermining revenue from the profitable petroleum and timber sectors.

Equatorial Guinea is burdened by a large external debt, although a protocol on debt conversion was signed with Spain, the country's largest creditor, in November 2003. Economic relations with the USA have also strengthened in recent years as a result of major investments in the development of Equato-Guinean oilfields by US energy companies and the approval by the US Overseas Private Investment Corporation, in June 2000, of financing, worth US $173m., for the construction and operation of a methanol plant on Bioko. Construction of an extensive new port facility at Luba began in September 2002, and a new condensate plant, with an annual capacity of 3.4m. metric tons, was scheduled to open in 2007. However, although construction and infrastructure projects proliferated from the 1990s, the levels of extreme poverty have not been addressed. The absence of any visible improvement in living standards among the general population since the early 1990s has been variously attributed to corruption, the disadvantageous terms of many contracts negotiated by the state petroleum company, Guinea Ecuatorial de Petróleo (GEPetrol), and reduced international aid. Equatorial Guinea's petroleum output was projected to increase to approximately 315,300 b/d in 2004, with GDP growth of 14.7% forecast for 2003.

Eritrea

The State of Eritrea is bounded to the north-west by Sudan, to the south and west by Ethiopia, and to the south-east by Djibouti. The State's borders were first defined in 1889 by a treaty concluded between Italy and the Ethiopian Emperor, Menelik. By 1962 Eritrea's status had been effectively transformed into that of an Ethiopian province. Armed struggle against the Ethiopian Government, waged principally, from the mid-1970s, by the Eritrean People's Liberation Front (EPLF), became full-scale war after 1977. Following the EPLF's victory, a UN-supervised referendum was held in 1993, at which national independence was endorsed. Asmara is the capital. The major language groups include Afar, Tigre and Tigrinya.

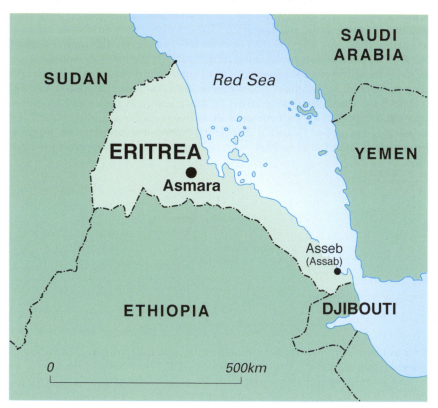

Area and population
Area: 121,144 sq km
Population (mid-2002): 4,308,840
Population density (mid-2002): 35.6 per sq km
Life expectancy (years at birth, 2002): 57.6 (males 55.8; females 59.3)

Finance
GDP in current prices: 2002: US $582m. ($135 per head)
Real GDP growth (2002): 9.2%
Inflation (2001): 18.1%
Currency: nakfa

Economy

In 2002, according to estimates by the World Bank, Eritrea's gross national income (GNI), measured at average 2000–02 prices, was US $670m., equivalent to $160 per head (or $950 per head on an international purchasing-power parity basis). During 1992–2002, it was estimated, the population increased at an average annual rate of 2.7%, while gross domestic product (GDP) per head increased, in real terms, by an average of 3.3% per year. Overall GDP increased, in real terms, at an average annual rate of 6.1% in 1992–2002; growth in 2002 was 9.2%.

AGRICULTURE

By far the most important sector of the economy is agriculture, which, despite a reduction in food production of roughly 40% between 1980 and 1990, still sustains 90% of the population. In 2002 agriculture (including forestry and fishing) accounted for an estimated 11.7% of GDP. In 2001 the sector employed an estimated 77.2% of the economically active population. Most sedentary agriculture is practised in the highlands, where rainfall is sufficient to cultivate the main crops: teff (an indigenous grain), potatoes, sorghum, barley, millet and wheat. As a result of serious environmental degradation (caused directly and indirectly by the war of independence), water scarcity and unreliable rainfall, projects have been undertaken to build water reservoirs and small dams, while badly eroded hillsides have been terraced and new trees planted in order to prevent soil erosion. Although fishing activity is on a very small scale, the total catch increased considerably in the first half of the 1990s, reaching 3,267 metric tons in 1996. The total catch subsequently declined, but rose to 12,612 tons in 2000, before falling again, to 8,820 tons, in 2001. According to the UN, sustainable yields of as much as 70,000 tons per year may be possible. In real terms, the GDP of the agricultural sector increased at an average annual rate of 2.2% in 1992–2002. Agricultural GDP increased by 20.0% in 2002.

INDUSTRY

In 2002 industrial production (comprising mining, manufacturing, construction and utilities) accounted for an estimated 24.8% of GDP. Some 5.0% of the labour force were employed in the industrial sector in 1990. Eritrea's industrial base traditionally centred on the production of glass, cement, footwear and canned goods, but most industrial enterprises were badly damaged during the war of independence. Although some of the 42 public-sector factories—producing textiles, footwear, beverages and other light industrial goods—were operating in 1991, they were doing so at only one-third of capacity. By 1995 production had increased considerably, mostly as a result of substantial government aid. Industrial GDP increased, in real terms, at an average annual rate of 12.8% in 1992–2002. Industrial GDP increased by 7.0% in 2002.

Mining

Eritrea's mineral resources are believed to be of significant potential value, although in 2002 mining and quarrying accounted for less than 0.1% of GDP. Of particular importance, in view of Eritrea's acute energy shortage, is the possibility of large reserves of petroleum and natural gas beneath the Red Sea. Production-sharing agreements for the exploration of petroleum and gas were signed with the Anadarko Petroleum Corpn of the USA in 1995 and 1997. However, Anadarko's first three deep drills were dry, and in May 1999 the company began reducing operations by removing most of its operational staff. Other mineral resources include potash, zinc, magnesium, copper, iron ore, marble and gold. New legislation on mining, adopted in 1995, declared all mineral resources to be state assets, but recognized an extensive role for private investors in their exploitation.

Manufacturing

The manufacturing sector provided an estimated 11.7% of GDP in 2002. Until mid-1997 imported petroleum was processed at the Assab refinery, whose entire output of petroleum products was delivered to Ethiopia. The authorities announced that they would import refined petroleum for the immediate future. Eritrea purchases its own petroleum requirements from Ethiopia under a quota arrangement; however, trade between the two countries was disrupted by the outbreak of hostilities in May 1998. The GDP of the sector increased, in real terms, at an average annual rate of 8.9% in 1992–2002. It increased by 7.1% in 2002.

Energy

Most electric energy is provided by four thermal power stations, largely dependent on imported fuel. Imports of fuel and energy comprised an estimated 8.9% of the total cost of imports in 2000. However, electricity is provided to only some 10% of the population, the remainder relying on fuelwood and animal products. In mid-1999 the discovery of geothermal potential at the Alid volcanic centre raised hopes that Eritrea's energy problems could be alleviated.

SERVICES

The services sector contributed an estimated 63.5% of GDP in 2002. The dominant services are trade, public administration and transport. The GDP of the services sector increased, in real terms, at an average annual rate of 6.3% in 1992–2002. Services GDP increased by 6.6% in 2002.

EXTERNAL TRADE

In 2002, according to estimates by the IMF, Eritrea recorded a trade deficit of US $481.7m., and there was a deficit of $99.6m. on the current account of the balance of payments. In 2001 the principal sources of non-petroleum imports were Italy (accounting for an estimated 18.7% of the total), Saudi Arabia and the United Arab Emirates. Exports in that year were mostly to Sudan (48.9%) and Italy. Eritrea's principal exports in 2002 were food and live animals (73.2% of the total), crude materials and basic manufactures. The main non-petroleum imports in that year were machinery and transport equipment (29.6% of the total), food and live animals, and basic manufactures.

GOVERNMENT FINANCE

In 2002 it was estimated that Eritrea's budget deficit reached 2,728.5m. nakfa, equivalent to 30.2% of GDP. Eritrea's external debt at the end of 2001 totalled US $409.6m., of which $397.6m. was long-term public debt. The cost of debt-servicing represented 2.0% of the value of exports of goods and services in that year. The annual rate of inflation averaged 8.9% in 1996–2002. Consumer prices increased by an estimated average of 14.6% in 2001 and by 16.9% in 2002. Unemployment and underemployment are estimated to affect as many as 50% of the labour force.

INTERNATIONAL ECONOMIC RELATIONS

In 1993 Eritrea was admitted to the group of African, Caribbean and Pacific (ACP) countries party to the Lomé Convention; in September 2001 Eritrea ratified the Cotonou Agreement, the successor of the Lomé Convention. Eritrea became a member of the IMF in 1994.

SURVEY AND PROSPECTS

Since Eritrea achieved independence, the establishment of a strong market-based economy has been a government priority. Under a Recovery and Rehabilitation Programme, commenced in 1993, emphasis was placed on improving agricultural productivity, promoting export-orientated industries, developing financial and tourism services, and restructuring the public administration. In November 1997 the Government introduced the nakfa as the national currency (Eritrea had retained the Ethiopian birr as its monetary unit since independence), initially at par with the birr. However, the adoption of the new currency led to tensions with Ethiopia, adversely affecting cross-border trade, and, following the outbreak of hostilities in May 1998, Ethiopia re-routed its maritime commerce via Djibouti. The conflict, which ended in December 2000, had a devastating effect on the Eritrean economy. Trade with Ethiopia, which previously accounted for two-thirds of Eritrean exports, virtually ceased, and Eritrea was estimated to have spent at least US $1m. per day on the war. This expenditure, coupled with the failure of successive harvests, increased Eritrea's already considerable reliance on donations from aid organizations, and the need to feed, clothe and shelter the vast numbers of people displaced during the war has placed a further strain on government finances.

The planned demobilization of large numbers of the Eritrean armed forces has proceeded only slowly, and President Afewerki's increasingly repressive tendencies during the early 2000s resulted in the cancellation and suspension of some $400m. of development funding, on which the country remains heavily dependent. Eritrea suffered severe drought and food shortages during 2003, with crop production at approximately one-quarter of its average levels at mid-year, and by early 2004 it was estimated that some 1.9m. Eritreans were in need of humanitarian assistance. Despite these difficulties, the IMF forecast GDP growth of some 5% in 2003, although a number of serious economic challenges remained for Eritrea, including the reduction of its large budget and trade deficits.

Estonia

The Republic of Estonia is situated in north-eastern Europe. In 1940 the Estonian Soviet Socialist Republic was incorporated into the USSR. In 1990 the Estonian Supreme Soviet proclaimed the beginning of a transition towards independence and restored articles of the 1938 Constitution describing Estonia's independence. After the State Committee for the State of Emergency seized power in the USSR in August 1991, Soviet military units entered Tallinn but did not prevent deputies to the Estonian Supreme Council from declaring the full and immediate independence of Estonia. In September the Soviet State Council recognized Estonian independence. Tallinn is the capital. Estonian is the official language.

Area and population
Area: 45,227 sq km
Population (mid-2002): 1,358,000
Population density (mid-2002): 30.0 per sq km
Life expectancy (years at birth, 2002): 71.1 (males 65.1; females 77.1)

Finance
GDP in current prices: 2002): US $6,413m. ($4,722 per head)
Real GDP growth (2002): 5.8%
Inflation (annual average, 2002): 3.6%
Currency: kroon

Economy

In 2002, according to World Bank estimates, Estonia's gross national income (GNI), measured at average 2000–02 prices, was US $5,605m., equivalent to $4,130 per head (or $11,120 per head on an international purchasing-power parity basis). During 1990–2002, it was estimated, the population declined at an average annual rate of 1.2%, while gross domestic product (GDP) per head increased, in real terms, by an average of 0.9% per year. Overall GDP decreased, in real terms, at an average annual rate of 0.4% during 1990–2002. However, according to official figures, real GDP increased by 6.5% in 2001 and by 6.0% in 2002.

AGRICULTURE

Agriculture (including hunting, forestry and fishing) contributed 5.4% of GDP in 2002. In that year the sector provided 7.0% of employment. Animal husbandry is the main activity in the agricultural sector. Some 27.4% of Estonia's land is cultivable. The principal crops are grains, potatoes and fruits and vegetables. Forestry products are also important. During 1990–2002, according to the World Bank, agricultural GDP declined, in real terms, at an average annual rate of 3.5%. The GDP of the sector decreased by 6.7% in 2001, but increased by 2.5% in 2002.

INDUSTRY

Industry (including mining and quarrying, manufacturing, construction and power) contributed 29.3% of GDP in 2002. In that year the sector provided 31.3% of employment. The sector is dominated by machine-building, electronics and electrical engineering. During 1990–2002, according to the World Bank, industrial GDP declined, in real terms, at an average annual rate of 2.6%. However, industrial GDP increased by 5.8% in 2001 and by 5.0% in 2002.

Mining

Mining and quarrying contributed 1.1% of GDP in 2002, when it provided 1.0% of employment. Estonia's principal mineral resource is oil-shale, and there are also deposits of peat and phosphorite ore. There are total estimated reserves of oil-shale of some 4,000 metric tons. However, annual extraction of oil-shale had declined to some 11.7m. tons by 2000, compared with some 31m. tons in 1980. Phosphorite ore is processed to produce phosphates for use in agriculture, but development of the industry has been accompanied by increasing environmental problems. According to official figures, the GDP of the mining and quarrying sector increased by 10.0% in 2001 and by 10.6% in 2002.

Manufacturing

In 2002 the manufacturing sector accounted for 18.6% of GDP and engaged an estimated 21.9% of the employed labour force. The sector is based on products of food- and beverage-processing (especially dairy products), textiles and clothing, fertilizers and other chemical products, and wood and timber products (particularly furniture). The World Bank estimated that in 1992–2002 the GDP of the manufacturing sector increased, in real terms, at an average annual rate of 1.2%. Real manufacturing GDP increased by 8.2% in 2001 and by 5.0% in 2002.

Energy

The country relies on oil-shale for over 90% of its energy requirements. In 2002 imports of mineral fuels accounted for 7.3% of total imports.

SERVICES

The services sector accounted for 65.3% of GDP in 2002, and engaged 61.7% of the employed population. During 1990–2002, according to the World Bank, the GDP of the services sector increased, in real terms, by an annual average of 1.4%. The GDP of the sector increased by 5.5% in 2001 and by 2.1% in 2002.

EXTERNAL TRADE

In 2002 Estonia recorded a visible trade deficit of US $1,103.5m., while there was a deficit of $801.6m. on the current account of the balance of payments. After 1991 trade with the West, particularly Scandinavia, increased considerably, while trade with former Soviet republics declined from about 90% of the pre-1991 total to some 30% by 1995. In 2002 Finland was Estonia's principal trading partner, accounting for 15.5% of imports and 20.3% of exports. Other important sources of imports were Russia, Germany and Sweden, and Sweden, Russia, Germany and Latvia were important purchasers of exports. In 2002 the principal exports were machinery and electrical goods (22.0% of total export revenue), wood and wood products (12.1%), textiles (10.0%), base metals (8.8%), miscellaneous manufactured articles (7.7%), foodstuffs, beverages and tobacco (6.8%), mineral products (5.7%), transport vehicles (5.4%) and chemicals (5.2%). The principal imports were machinery and electrical goods (27.7%), transport vehicles (10.6%), base metals (9.6%), chemical products (7.8%), mineral products (7.7%), foodstuffs, beverages and tobacco (7.2%), and textiles (7.1%).

GOVERNMENT FINANCE

In 2002, according to preliminary figures, there was a general consolidated budgetary surplus of 1,283.8m. kroons (equivalent to 1.2% of GDP). Estonia's external debt totalled US $2,852m. at the end of 2001, of which $187m. was long-term public debt. In the same year the cost of debt-servicing was equivalent to 7.4% of the value of exports of goods and services. The annual rate of inflation reached 1,069% in 1992. However, in 1993, following a programme of radical monetary reform, the average annual rate of inflation was reduced to 89%. During 1992–2002 the annual rate of inflation averaged 20.1%. Consumer prices increased by 3.5% in 2002 and by 1.3% in 2003. Some 40,519 people (approximately 4.9% of the labour force) were officially registered as unemployed at December 2003.

INTERNATIONAL ECONOMIC RELATIONS

In 1992 Estonia became a member of the IMF and the World Bank. It also joined the European Bank for Reconstruction and Development. In November 1999 Estonia became a member of the World Trade Organization (WTO). Estonia signed a free-trade agreement with the European Union (EU) in 1994. It became an associate member of the EU in June 1995, and applied for full membership in December. Estonia acceded to the EU on 1 May 2004.

SURVEY AND PROSPECTS

Even before it regained independence in mid-1991, Estonia had begun a transition to a market economy, and far-reaching economic reforms were continued thereafter.

However, despite Estonia's relative prosperity during the Soviet period, the collapse of the USSR and its internal economic system resulted in serious economic difficulties.

In June 1992 Estonia introduced a new currency, the kroon, pegged at a rate of 8:1 against the German Deutsche Mark, enhancing international financial confidence in the country. The economy was adversely affected by the Russian financial crisis of 1998, but it recovered in 2000, and Estonia's final stand-by arrangement with the IMF expired in 2001.

Strong growth was recorded in 2002, and preliminary figures indicated that this was maintained in 2003, with domestic investment and consumption stimulated by Estonia's anticipated membership of the EU from May 2004. The budget remained in surplus in 2003, unemployment declined and the rate of consumer-price inflation was the lowest to be recorded since independence. The Government elected in early 2003 had adopted a preliminary programme for the gradual diminution, by 2% per year, of the rate of personal income tax in 2004–06 (the income-tax rate was 26% in 2003). However, divisions within the governing coalition resulted in the adoption of a modified programme in November 2003, according to which the rate of income tax was to decline by 1% in 2004 and 2007, and by 2% in the intervening years.

Economic growth of 5.6% was predicted in 2004, and consumer prices were expected to rise by 3.8%. However, the large deficit on the current account of the balance of payments (which had increased by more than two-fold in 2002, and was projected to reach the equivalent of 12.8% of GDP in 2003), together with a concurrent decline in foreign direct investment, meant that the economy remained vulnerable to adverse external influences. In October 2003 the IMF recommended that the Government implement structural and fiscal reforms to address the country's remaining macroeconomic problems, in order to permit the early adoption of the common European currency, the euro.

Ethiopia

The Federal Democratic Republic of Ethiopia is situated in eastern Africa. Ethiopia was dominated almost uninterruptedly by Haile Selassie from 1916 until 1974, when he was deposed in a military-led revolution. In 1977 Lt-Col Mengistu Haile Mariam assumed power. He was ousted by insurgent forces in 1991. In elections to a Constituent Assembly in 1994, the Ethiopian People's Revolutionary Democratic Front (EPRDF) gained the most seats. In 1995 legislative power was transferred from a transitional Council of Representatives to a bicameral Federal Parliamentary Assembly. The EPRDF (and allies) won legislative elections in that year and in 2000. Addis Ababa is the capital. Amharic is the official language.

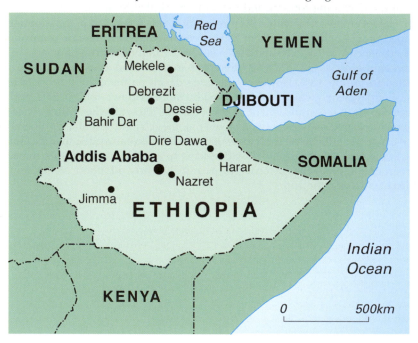

Area and population
Area: 1,133,380 sq km
Population (mid-2002): 67,334,600
Population density (mid-2002): 59.4 per sq km
Life expectancy (years at birth, 2002): 48.0 (males 46.8; females 49.4)

Finance
GDP in current prices: 2002): US $5,989m. ($89 per head)
Real GDP growth (2002): 5.0%
Inflation (annual average, 2002): 1.6%
Currency: birr

Economy

In 2002, according to estimates by the World Bank, Ethiopia's gross national income (GNI), measured at average 2000–02 prices, was US $6,420m., equivalent to $100 per head (or $720 per head on an international purchasing-power parity basis): one of the lowest recorded levels of GNI per head for any country in the world. During 1990–2002, it was estimated, the population increased at an average annual rate of 2.3%, while gross domestic product (GDP) per head increased, in real terms, by an average of 1.8% per year. Overall GDP increased, in real terms, at an average annual rate of 4.1% during 1990–2002; growth in 2002 was 5.0%.

AGRICULTURE

Agriculture (including forestry and fishing) contributed 52.3% of GDP in 2002, and employed an estimated 82.0% of the economically active population in 2001. The principal cash crop is coffee (which accounted for 53.0% of export earnings in 2000). The principal subsistence crops are cereals (maize, sorghum, wheat, barley, and teff) and sugar cane. During 1990–2002 agricultural GDP increased at an average annual rate of 2.9%; growth in 2002 was 4.5%.

INDUSTRY

Industry (including mining, manufacturing, construction and power) employed 2.0% of the labour force in 1995, and provided 11.1% of GDP in 2002. During 1990–2002 industrial GDP increased by an average of 3.6% per year. It rose by 5.4% in 2002.

Mining

Mining contributed only an estimated 0.5% of GDP (at constant 1980/81 prices) in 2000/01, and employed less than 0.1% of the labour force in 1995. Ethiopia has reserves of petroleum, although these have not been exploited, and there are also deposits of copper and potash. Gold, tantalite, soda ash, kaolin, dimension stones, precious metals and gemstones, salt, and industrial and construction materials are mined. In April 2000 a US company discovered large petroleum deposits in the west of the country, and in June 2003 the Ethiopian Government granted an exploration licence to Petronas of Malaysia. During 1996/97–2000/01 mining GDP increased by an estimated average of 7.4% per year; growth in 2000/01 was an estimated 8.4%.

Manufacturing

Manufacturing employed only 1.6% of the labour force in 1995, and contributed 7.0% of GDP in 2002. During 1990–2001 manufacturing GDP increased at an average annual rate of 2.6%. It increased by 7.9% in 2001.

Energy

In years of normal rainfall, energy is derived principally from Ethiopia's massive hydroelectric power resources. In 2000 97.5% of Ethiopia's electricity was produced by hydroelectric power schemes. Imports of mineral fuels accounted for an estimated 20.1% of the cost of total imports in 2000. In 1993 agreement was reached with the World Bank on the financing of a project to construct a liquefied gas unit to exploit gas reserves in the Ogaden. In late 1995 the Government announced plans to develop

273

geothermal energy sources at 15 sites in various regions of the country. Ethiopia's electricity generating capacity is expected to reach 713 MW by 2005.

SERVICES

Services, which consisted mainly of wholesale and retail trade, public administration and defence, and transport and communications, employed 9.5% of the labour force in 1995, and contributed 36.5% of GDP in 2002. The combined GDP of the service sectors increased, in real terms, at an average rate of 5.5% per year during 1990–2002. It rose by 5.5% in 2002.

EXTERNAL TRADE

In 2002 Ethiopia recorded a visible trade deficit of US $974.8m., and there was a deficit of $149.5m. on the current account of the balance of payments. In 2000 the principal source of imports (19.1%) was Yemen; other major suppliers were Italy, Japan, the People's Republic of China and India. The principal market for exports in that year were Germany (19.6%), Japan, Djibouti, Saudi Arabia, Italy, Somalia and Switzerland. The principal exports in 2000 were food and live animals, coffee, and leather and leather products. The principal imports in that year were machinery and transport equipment, mineral fuels and related products, and basic manufactures.

GOVERNMENT FINANCE

In the fiscal year 2002/03 it was estimated that Ethiopia's budgetary deficit reached 4,776m. birr. Ethiopia is the principal African recipient of concessionary funding, and the largest recipient of EU aid. At the end of 2001 Ethiopia's total external debt was $5,697m., of which $5,532m. was long-term public debt. In that year the cost of debt-servicing was equivalent to an estimated 18.7% of total earnings from the export of goods and services. The annual rate of inflation averaged 10.1% in 1990–96, but slowed to average 0.2% in 1997–2001. Consumer prices increased by 1.9% in 2000, but declined by 5.4% in 2001. There were 28,350 persons registered as applicants for work in the 12 months to June 1996.

INTERNATIONAL ECONOMIC RELATIONS

Ethiopia is a member of the African Development Bank and the Common Market for Eastern and Southern Africa. In July 2001 Ethiopia ratified the Cotonou Agreement, the successor of the Lomé Convention of the EU.

SURVEY AND PROSPECTS

Ethiopia remains one of the poorest countries in the world, and the country's economy continues to suffer from the effects of recurrent, catastrophic drought, which severely disrupts agricultural production (the country's economic base). The rapidly expanding population has further highlighted structural deficiencies in this sector, which, coupled with the scarcity of land and the lack of agricultural development, have resulted in massive environmental degradation and, in turn, widespread poverty and famine. The Ethiopian economy is also heavily dependent on assistance and grants from abroad, particularly in times of drought. Many donors suspended aid for the duration of the war with Eritrea, which was estimated to have cost Ethiopia some US $2,900m., and the country's economic difficulties were further exacerbated by the renewed failure of crop harvests in 1999 and 2000. Following the cessation of fighting between Ethiopia and Eritrea in mid-2000, the World Bank agreed to resume development assistance to Ethiopia.

From early 2001 Ethiopia also benefited from significant IMF assistance under the Poverty Reduction and Growth Facility and qualified for additional debt relief from the initiative for heavily indebted poor countries; in 2003 aid granted under these two programmes totalled $17.2m. Nevertheless, following a severe lack of rainfall during 2002–03, it was estimated that some 13m. Ethiopians were in need of emergency food assistance. The Government introduced value-added tax on certain goods at a rate of 10% in January 2003, which was expected to increase government revenues, thus enabling greater expenditure on health, education and infrastructural projects. However, while the Government pledged to limit expenditure on defence to just 2% of GDP in 2003/04, and projected GDP growth of 6.7% for that financial year, its most urgent priorities remained to secure and make effective use of greater amounts of development assistance and to improve its distribution system for food aid.

Falkland Islands

The Falkland Islands are in the south-western Atlantic Ocean, north-east of Cape Horn, South America. British sovereignty was established in 1833 and the islands became a Crown Colony of the United Kingdom. However, Argentina did not relinquish a claim to sovereignty over the islands, and negotiations to resolve the dispute began in 1966 at the instigation of the UN. In April 1982 Argentina invaded the Falkland Islands, establishing a military governorship. British forces recaptured the islands in June. The Falkland Islands are a United Kingdom Overseas Territory. Argentina and the United Kingdom continued to dispute the sovereignty of the Falkland Islands. Stanley is the capital. The language is English.

Area and population
Area: 12,173 sq km
Population (8 April 2001): 2,913
Population density (8 April 2001): 0.24 per sq km

Finance
Inflation (annual average, 2002): 0.6%
Currency: Falkland Islands pound

Economy

Most of the agricultural land on the Falkland Islands is devoted to the rearing of sheep. However, the land is poor and more than four acres are required to support one animal. In the late 1990s annual exports of wool were valued at some £3.5m.

Some vegetables are produced (notably in a hydroponic market garden), and there are small dairy herds. From 1987, when a licensing system was introduced for foreign vessels fishing within a 150-nautical-mile conservation and management zone, the economy was diversified and the islands' annual income increased considerably. Revenue from the sale of licences totalled £25m. in 1991, but subsequently declined (following the Argentine Government's commencement of the sale of fishing licences in 1993), and totalled some £21.6m. in 1998/99. The revenues, estimated at £23m. for the financial year 2000/01, fund social provisions and economic development programmes. In the late 1980s about one-third of the world's total catch of *Illex* and *Loligo* squid was derived from this fishing zone. However, over-fishing in the area surrounding the conservation zone had a detrimental effect on stocks of fish in the islands' waters, and frequently the Government has been obliged to call an early halt to the exploitation of both squid types.

INDUSTRY

Manufacturing

Manufacturing activity on the islands reflects the predominance of the agricultural sector: a wool mill on West Falkland produces yarns for machine knitting, hand knitting and weaving. Several small companies in the Falklands produce garments for local and export sales. Some fish-processing also takes place on East Falkland.

Energy

The Falkland Islands are heavily dependent on imports of all fuels, except peat. Wind power is used in many remote locations to offset this dependence and reduce pollution of the atmosphere. The Falkland Islands Government licensed five con-sortia to explore for hydrocarbons in waters north of the islands in October 1996. These companies, including Shell, Amerada Hess and LASMO, drilled six explora-tion wells in 1998. Five of the six wells had minor traces of hydrocarbons present, but no commercial quantities of petroleum were found in the initial phase of drilling. A British prospecting company has been granted an exploration licence to search for minerals on the islands. Mineral sands including garnet and rutile were being appraised, while more valuable minerals such as gold were being sought. In July 2002 the Falkland Islands Government granted 10 petroleum exploration licences to the Falklands Hydrocarbon Consortium (comprising Global Petroleum Ltd, Hard-man Resources Ltd and Falkland Islands Holdings) for an area covering 57,700 sq km to the south of the islands.

SERVICES

The Falkland Islands Development Corporation oversees the islands' economic development on behalf of the Government. Since the 1980s the Government has sought to promote the development of the tourism sector. Tourism, and in parti-cular eco-tourism, was developing rapidly in this century, and the number of visitors staying on the Falklands Islands had grown to some 3,000 a year, while around 40,000 tourists per year sail through Stanley harbour on their way to Antarctica and sub-antarctic islands such as South Georgia. The sale of postage stamps and coins represents a significant source of income; the value of sales of the former was £296,229 in 1996/97, while the value of sales of the latter totalled £49,351 in 1995/96.

EXTERNAL TRADE

In 2000 the islands recorded an estimated trade surplus of £28,041,897. Fish, most of which is purchased by the United Kingdom, Spain and Chile, is the islands' most significant export. The principal imports are fuel, provisions, alcoholic beverages, building materials and clothing. In early 2001 the Government brought 100 reindeer from the South Georgia Islands (with the aim of increasing the number to 10,000 over the next 20 years) in order to export venison to Scandinavia and Chile.

GOVERNMENT FINANCE

Ordinary budget estimates for the financial year 1999/2000 envisaged revenue of £52,339,241 and expenditure of £40,449,156. The annual rate of inflation averaged 4.5% in 1990–98; consumer prices increased by 6.2% in 2000, and by 0.8% in 2001. There is a significant shortage of local labour on the islands.

SURVEY AND PROSPECTS

Since 1982 the economy of the Falkland Islands has enjoyed a period of strong and sustained growth, partly owing to substantial investment by the British Government during the 1980s, but primarily as a result of the introduction of the fisheries licensing scheme in 1987. It was anticipated that royalties derived from the sale of licences for the exploration and exploitation of hydrocarbons would strengthen the economy further; however, the Falkland Islands Government was expected to utilize such revenue to finance the islands' defence expenditure, and possibly to reimburse the British Government for part of the cost of the 1982 conflict. The services sector expanded rapidly during the late 1990s, while the importance of the agricultural sector has decreased, not least because of its reliance on direct and indirect subsidies. The revenues from the sale of fishing licences, fund social provisions and economic development programmes, including subsidies to the wool industry, which is in long-term decline, owing to the oversupply of that commodity on the international market. The Government's development plan emphasized agricultural diversification and the promotion of tourism as its main economic aims. Following the early closure, for conservation reasons, of the *illex* fishery and a consquential reduction in licensing fees, the Falkland Islands Government was in April 2004 preparing an austere budget for the 2004/05 fiscal year; an approximate 5% decrease in expenditure was widely anticipated to account for the anticipated £10m. shortfall in income.

Faroe Islands

The Faroe Islands are a group of 18 islands (of which 17 are inhabited) in the Atlantic Ocean, between Scotland and Iceland. They have been under Danish administration since Queen Margrethe I of Denmark inherited Norway in 1380. The Home Rule Act of 1948 gave the Faroese control over their internal affairs and the Islands chose not to join the European Community (now European Union) with Denmark in 1973. In 2004, following legislative elections, a coalition Government was formed by members of the People's Party, the Union Party and the Social Democratic Party. The capital is Tórshavn. Faroese is the principal language.

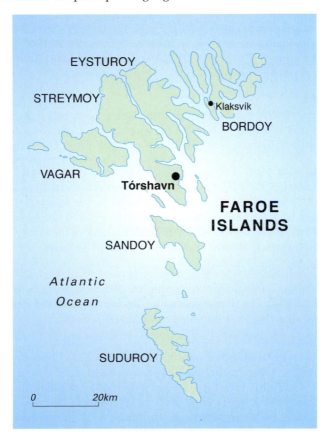

Area and population
Area: 1,399 sq km
Population (mid-2001): 50,000
Population density (mid-2001): 35.7 per sq km
Life expectancy (years at birth, 1996–2000): 78.3 (males 75.2; females 81.4)

Finance
GDP in current prices: 2001): 9,357m. kroner (200,800 kroner per head)
Real GDP growth (2001): 12.6%
Inflation (annual average, 2002): –0.2%
Currency: krone

Economy

In 1995 gross national product (GNP), estimated at 1990 prices, was US $829m., equivalent to $19,000 per head. Between 1973 and 1988, it was estimated, GNP increased, in real terms, at an average rate of 4.5% per year, with real GNP per head rising by 3.3% annually. Between 1989 and 1993, however, real GNP decreased dramatically, at an average rate of 9.4% per year. During 1994–95 real GNP increased by 4.2%. The population declined at an average annual rate of 1.6% in 1989–95, but increased by 1.1% per year in 1995–1999. Gross domestic product (GDP) increased, in real terms, by about 9.6% in 2002.

AGRICULTURE

Agriculture (principally sheep-farming) and fishing contributed 20.5% of GDP in 2000. Potatoes and other vegetables are the main crops. Only about 6% of the land surface is cultivated. Fishing is the dominant industry. In 1999 fishing, aquaculture and fish-processing accounted for 25.1% of GDP; the sector employed 23% of the labour force in 1994. Fishing accounted for 93.1% of exports in 2000. Most fishing takes place within the 200-nautical-mile (370-km) fisheries zone imposed around the Faroes in 1977. In the 1980s fish farming began to be encouraged. The traditional hunting of pilot whales continues to provide an important source of meat for the Faroese. The Faroe Islands resumed commercial hunting of the minke whale in 1993 and began trading in whale meat in 2002 after a halt of 14 years.

INDUSTRY

Industry (including mining, manufacturing, construction and power) contributed 19.0% of GDP in 2000. The dominant sectors are fishing-related industries, such as fish-drying and -freezing, and ship maintenance and repairs.

Mining

Mining and quarrying contributed only 0.3% of GDP in 2000. 'Brown coal' (lignite) is mined on Suðuroy. The potential for petroleum production around the islands is believed to be significant. Following the resolution of a boundary dispute with the United Kingdom in May 1999, in mid-2000 the Ministry of Petroleum issued seven exploration licences (of six to nine years' duration) to 12 oil companies, organized into five groups, in the 'golden corner' (formerly the White Zone), an area south-east of the Faroe Islands; exploratory drilling commenced in mid-2001. In November the US company Amerada Hess announced that it had discovered petroleum in considerable quantities. It was expected, however, that, owing to Faroese tax laws, the islands would not derive any substantial income from the reserves for 12 years. The Danish authorities also stated that they intended to renegotiate Denmark's subsidy agreement with the Faroe Islands should the latter start to make a profit from the petroleum reserves. In January 2002 the Faroes Oil and Gas Company (FOGC—Føroya Kolvetni) became the first Faroese company to be listed on the London Stock Exchange.

Manufacturing

Manufacturing contributed 11.4% of GDP in 2000. The dominant sector is fish-processing, which accounted for 5.7% of GDP in 1999. Technical repairs and ship-yards contributed 2.1% of GDP in 1999, while exports of vessels accounted for 6.9% of exports in 2000. A small textile industry exports traditional Faroese woollens.

Energy

The energy sector contributed 2.1% of GDP in 2000. About 48% of the islands' energy requirements are provided by a hydroelectric power plant. In July 2003 Elfelagið SEV, the state electricity company, announced that it was to construct a power station in conjunction with a Scottish firm, Wavegen. The power station was to use tunnels built into cliffs on the shoreline to exploit energy from the sea. Imports of fuels and related products accounted for 12.1% of imports in 2000.

SERVICES

The services sector accounted for 60.6% of GDP in 2000. In November 2003 an independent Faroese securities market was launched in co-operation with the Icelandic stock market.

EXTERNAL TRADE

In 2000 the Faroe Islands recorded a trade deficit of 404m. kroner, while there was a surplus of 317m. kroner on the current account of the balance of payments. Denmark was the Faroes' principal source of imports (31.4%) in 2002; other major suppliers were Norway (18.7%), Germany (7.6%) and Sweden (6.5%). The United Kingdom was the principal market for exports (24.4%) in that year; other major purchasers were Denmark (20.5%), Spain (11.6%) and France (including Monaco) (8.2%). In 2002 the European Union (EU) as a whole took 80.1% of exports and supplied 63.5% of imports. The principal imports in 2000 were products for household consumption (accounting for 28.3% of the total cost of imports), intermediate goods for industries other than agriculture or construction (19.0%) and machinery and other capital equipment (10.5%). Principal exports in that year were chilled or frozen fish fillets (contributing 27.9% of total export revenue), chilled or frozen fish (22.5%), and chilled of frozen salmon and trout (18.0%).

GOVERNMENT FINANCE

Danish subsidies are an important source of income to the islands, and accounted for 27.9% of total government revenue in 2000. In that year, including the central government grant of 973m. kroner as revenue, the Faroese Government recorded a budget surplus of 605m. kroner; the surplus for 2001 was estimated at 710m. kroner. At the end of 1999 the net foreign debt was estimated at 447m. kroner. The annual rate of inflation was 4.3% in 2000 and 7.7% in 2001. In the 1980s there was an acute labour shortage in the Faroes, but by mid-1995 unemployment had increased to some 16% of the labour force. By mid-2003, however, unemployment had declined to 3% of the labour force.

INTERNATIONAL ECONOMIC RELATIONS

The Faroe Islands did not join the European Community (now EU) with Denmark in 1973, but did secure favourable terms of trade with Community members and special concessions in Denmark and the United Kingdom. Agreements on free trade were concluded between the Faroe Islands and Iceland, Norway, Sweden, Finland and Austria in 1992–93 and between the Faroe Islands and the EU in January 2004. In international fisheries organizations, where Denmark is represented by the EU, the Kingdom maintains separate membership in respect of the Faroe Islands (and Greenland). The Faroe Islands is also a member of the Nordic Council.

SURVEY AND PROSPECTS

During the 1980s the Faroes' principal source of income, the fishing industry, was expanded with the help of substantial investment and official subsidies, financed by external borrowing. However, depletion of stocks and the resulting decline in catches, together with a fall in export prices, led to a reduction in export earnings and a financial crisis in the early 1990s (GDP was estimated to have declined by some 20% in 1993). The Danish Government attempted to stabilize the economy by restructuring the banking sector and by extending significant loans (by the end of 1997 it was estimated that the Faroes owed some 5,500m. kroner to the Danish Government, equivalent to 140,000 kroner per head).

The report of an independent commission of inquiry into Denmark's response to the crisis in the Faroes, which had been established by the islanders in 1995, was published in early 1998 and levelled accusations of serious mismanagement at Danish government officials, and at the Danish Den Danske Bank. In June 1998 an agreement was reached by the Faroese and Danish Governments regarding a reduction of Faroese debt to Denmark as a form of compensation. Denmark's annual subsidy (of 1,000m. kroner) provides nearly one-third of the Faroes' budget. However, a number of oil companies commenced exploratory offshore drilling in Faroese waters during 2001, and initial results proved promising. The discovery of substantial and commercially-viable reserves of natural gas and petroleum would enable the Faroese economy to diversify, thereby reducing its overwhelming dependence on Danish subsidies as well as on the fisheries sector.

From the end of the 1990s the Faroe Islands experienced a period of economic prosperity with high levels of growth and low unemployment. In May 2003 a nationwide strike began after the Government rejected a pay agreement reached between workers and management at the state-owned electricity company, Elfelagið SEV. About 12,000 members from five trade unions went on strike in sympathy with the electricity workers, closing schools, nurseries and shops and causing severe disruption to the docks, the postal service and public transport. The dispute was finally settled after 28 days. The strike, together with a sharp decline in fish prices, lower economic activity and tax reductions, contributed to a decline in GDP growth to an estimated 3.6% in 2003, compared with 9.5% in 2002.

Fiji

The Republic of Fiji comprises more than 300 islands situated south of the equator in the Pacific Ocean. Since 1970, tensions between Fijians of Melanesian and Fijians of Indian origin have frequently destabilized the country. In 1999 Mahendra Chaudhry, leader of the Indian-dominated Fiji Labour Party, became Fiji's first ethnic Indian premier. Chaudhry's Government was overthrown in 2000 by rebels who declared that they were seeking to reclaim Fiji for indigenous Fijians. Chaudhry's campaign to reinstate his People's Coalition Government was unsuccessful. A general election held in 2001 was won by the newly formed Fiji United Party. Suva is the capital. Fijian and Hindi are the principal languages.

Area and population
Area: 18,376 sq km
Population (mid-2002): 823,300
Population density (mid-2002): 44.8 per sq km
Life expectancy (years at birth, 2002): 67.3 (males 64.6; females 70.3)

Finance

GDP in current prices: 2002): US $1,878m. ($2,281 per head)
Real GDP growth (2002): 4.4%
Inflation (annual average, 2002): 0.8%
Currency: Fiji dollar

Economy

In 2002, according to estimates by the World Bank, Fiji's gross national income (GNI), measured at average 2000–2002 prices, was US $1,775m, equivalent to $2,160 per head (or $5,310 on an international purchasing-power parity basis). During 1990–2002, it was estimated, the population increased at an average annual rate of 0.9%, while gross domestic product (GDP) per head increased, in real terms by an average of 1.8%. According to figures from the Asian Development Bank (ADB), overall GDP increased, in real terms, at an average annual rate of 2.6% in 1990–2002. Following a contraction of 3.2% in 2000, the ADB estimated that Fiji's GDP had increased by 4.0% in 2001, by 3.8% in 2002 and by 5.0% in 2003. The organization predicted an increase of 4.1% in 2004.

AGRICULTURE

In 2002 agriculture (including forestry and fishing) contributed an estimated 15.2% of GDP. In 2001, according to FAO, the sector engaged 39.6% of the economically active population. The principal cash crop is sugar cane, which normally accounts for about 80% of total agricultural production and 30% of the country's GDP. Following the successful implementation of a crop rehabilitation programme in the late 1990s, the sugar industry subsequently experienced a sharp decline in output owing to problems arising from the coup in May 2000 and from the issue of expiring land leases. In 2002 sugar accounted for 19.7% of total export earnings. Sugar production declined by 25.9% in 2001 but increased by 41.7% in 2002. Other important export crops are coconuts and ginger, while the most significant subsistence crop is paddy rice. Fishing became an increasingly important activity from the mid-1990s. In 2002 fish products earned some $F89.9m in export revenue (7.5% of domestic export receipts). During 1990–2002, according to ADB estimates, agricultural GDP rose by an average annual rate of just 0.6%. The sector's GDP was estimated to have increased by 1.7% in 2001 and by 1.1% in 2002.

INDUSTRY

Industry (including mining, manufacturing, construction and power) engaged 33.8% of the total number of paid employees in 1998, and provided an estimated 25.4% of GDP in 2002. The GDP of the industrial sector, according to the ADB, increased at an average rate of 3.6% per year during 1990–2002. The industrial sector's GDP was estimated to have increased by 7.4% in 2001 and by 5.1% in 2002.

Mining

Mining contributed an estimated 2.4% of GDP in 2002, and engaged 1.8% of those in paid employment in 1999. Gold and silver are the major mineral exports. Production of gold increased from 2,823 kg in 2001 to 3,829 kg in 2002, when exports earned

$F78.1m, equivalent to 6.5% of total export earnings. A copper-mining project in Namosi, central Viti Levu, began operations in 1997. The mining sector's GDP, however, remained almost constant in real terms (increasing at an average annual rate of less than 0.05%) between 1990 and 2002, a particularly sharp decrease of 14.1% being recorded in 2000.

Manufacturing

Manufacturing contributed an estimated 14.8% of GDP in 2002 and engaged 26.0% of paid employees in 1999. The sector's GDP increased at an estimated average annual rate of 3.8% during 1990–2002. Compared with the previous year, manufacturing GDP rose by 11.6% in 2001 and by 3.9% in 2002. The most important branch of the sector is food-processing, in particular sugar, molasses and coconut oil. The ready-made garment industry is also important and has particularly benefited from the tax-exemption scheme implemented by the Government in 1987. Garments represented 20.5% of export earnings in 2002.

Energy

Energy is derived principally from hydroelectric power, which provided some 90% of Fiji's electricity in the late 1990s. The electricity, gas and water sector accounted for 4.4% of GDP in 2002. Imports of mineral fuels represented 17.2% of the total cost of imports in 2002.

SERVICES

The services sector contributed an estimated 58.6% of GDP in 2002. During 1990–2002 the sector's GDP rose by an average annual rate of 2.6%, according to ADB estimates. The GDP of the services sector contracted by an estimated 1.8% in 2000 before rising by 3.6% in 2001 and by 4.9% in 2002. Tourism is Fiji's largest source of foreign exchange. In 2000, however, arrivals fell to 294,070 and earnings to $413.5m., as a result of the events surrounding the coup of May of that year. In 2001 the industry earned $F495.5m. By 2002 tourist numbers had recovered to 397,859. Arrivals were reported to have totalled an estimated 430,800 in 2003, providing revenue of $F615.4m. in that year. An increase in tourist arrivals was expected in 2004 with the introduction of budget airline services from Australia and New Zealand. Most visitors are from Australia (31.1% of total arrivals in 2002), followed by New Zealand (17.2%), the USA (14.8%), the United Kingdom (10.9%) and Japan (6.6%).

EXTERNAL TRADE

In 1999 Fiji recorded a visible trade deficit of US $115.6m., but a surplus of US $12.7m. on the current account of the balance of payments. In 2003 the deficit on the current account of the balance of payments was equivalent to 3.7% of GDP. According to the ADB, export earnings decreased from $F1,223.9m. in 2001 to $F1,194.8m. in 2002, while the cost of imports increased from $F1,807.9m. to $F1,953.2m. in the same period. In 2002 the principal sources of imports were Australia (37.3%), New Zealand (16.9%) and Singapore (16.0%). The principal markets for exports were Australia (19.8%), the USA (25.6%) and the United Kingdom (10.8%). The principal imports in that year were machinery and transport equipment (22.9% of total costs in that year). The principal exports were sugar, gold, fish, re-exported petroleum products and ready-made garments.

GOVERNMENT FINANCE

In 2003 there was a projected budgetary deficit equivalent to 4.0% of GDP. In 2003/04 Fiji received financial assistance from Australia totalling an estimated $A20.0m. and in the same period New Zealand contributed $NZ4.1m. in development aid. In late 2003 the European Union announced its decision to release development aid withheld since the coup of 2000. Assistance was resumed with a payment of US $27m. for education. Fiji's total external debt was US $188.1m. at the end of 2001, of which US $159.2m. was long-term public debt. In that year the cost of debt-servicing was equivalent to 2.0% of the revenue from goods and services. The average annual rate of inflation was 3.4% in 1990–2000. According to the ADB, the inflation rate increased to 4.3% in 2001, but declined to 0.7% in the following year, before rising to a projected 3.8% in 2003. An estimated 12.1% of the total labour force were unemployed in 2000. Since 1987 Fiji has suffered a very high rate of emigration, particularly of skilled and professional personnel. Although the rate of emigration of professional and technical workers decreased by 2.8% in 2001, the number of emigrants from the services sector increased by 28.2%.

INTERNATIONAL ECONOMIC RELATIONS

Fiji is a member of the UN Economic and Social Commission for Asia and the Pacific (ESCAP), the Pacific Islands Forum, the Pacific Community, the Colombo Plan and the International Sugar Organization. Fiji is also a signatory of the South Pacific Regional Trade and Economic Co-operation Agreement—SPARTECA and the Lomé Conventions and successor Cotonou Agreement with the European Union (EU). In 1996 Fiji was admitted to the Melanesian Spearhead Group.

SURVEY AND PROSPECTS

The overthrow of the Government during a coup in May 2000 and the subsequent installation of an unelected authority had a severe impact on Fiji's economy. A significant amount of that year's excellent sugar crop was not harvested, and a large proportion of tourist bookings was cancelled. In addition, the islands lost a considerable sum of revenue owing to cancellation of foreign aid and investment, and the Government was unable to collect taxes worth more than $F90m. Moreover, the country faced further hardship through the imposition of economic sanctions and trade union boycotts from abroad (which particularly affected the mining sector and garment manufacture). It was estimated that 6,700 people lost their jobs in the second half of 2000, the overwhelming majority of these having been engaged either in tourist-related activities or in manufacturing. In response to the economic difficulties following the coup, the Government introduced an emergency interim budget in July 2000, including austerity measures which were successful in keeping government debt at a manageable level.

The 2001 budget, announced in November 2000, reduced business taxes, as a way of stimulating investment in the economy. The Government signalled a yet more interventionist policy in the 2002 budget, with all income derived from exports in the 2001/02 financial year to be tax-exempt, with the percentage of export income taxed to rise gradually to 100% during 2003–09. Budgeted expenditure for 2002 was F$1,255m. This included $F283m. in capital expenditure for investment, and the Government established the Fiji Investment Corporation to manage and promote investment in tourism, forestry, fisheries and inter-island shipping services. The budget projected an increase in economic growth to 3.5% in 2002, which the Reserve Bank later revised to 4.4%.

The 2003 budget, announced in November 2002, was widely criticized for its proposal to increase value-added tax from 10% to 12.5%. Opponents claimed that the higher tax would increase inflationary pressures and contribute towards the continued emigration of skilled workers from Fiji. In April 2003 the Government announced that the restructuring of Fiji's important sugar industry would be postponed for at least a further year because of disagreement among stakeholders. It was hoped that sugar farmers would be given assistance to diversify their activities before 2007 when the European Union (EU) protocol governing sugar prices (under which Fiji had been guaranteed the sale of its sugar at preferential rates) was due to expire.

Finland

The Republic of Finland lies in northern Europe. In 1809 Finland became an autonomous Grand Duchy under the Russian Empire. During the Russian revolution of 1917 Finland declared its independence. The country's politics have subsequently been characterized by coalition governments and consensus between the parties. The Finnish Social Democratic Party and the Finnish Centre Party have usually been the dominant participants in government. At a general election held in 1987, the combined non-socialist parties gained a majority in the Eduskunta (parliament) for the first time since 1945. Finland joined the European Union in 1995. The capital is Helsinki. Finnish and Swedish are the official languages.

Area and population

Area: 338,145 sq km
Population (mid-2002): 5,199,000 (including Åland Islands)
Population density (mid-2002): 15.4 per sq km
Life expectancy (years at birth, 2002): 78.2 (males 74.8; females 81.5)

Finance
GDP in current prices: 2002: US $130,797m. ($25,158 per head)
Real GDP growth (2002): 1.6%
Inflation (annual average, 2002): 1.7%
Currency: euro

Economy

In 2002, according to estimates by the World Bank, Finland's gross national income (GNI), measured at average 2000–02 prices, was US $122,231m., equivalent to $23,510 per head (or $25,440 per head on an international purchasing-power parity basis). During 1991–2002, it was estimated, the population increased at an average annual rate of 0.3%, while gross domestic product (GDP) per head increased, in real terms, by an average of 2.4% per year. Overall GDP increased, in real terms, at an average annual rate of 2.8% per year in 1991–2002; growth was 0.7% in 2001 and 1.6% in 2002.

AGRICULTURE
Agriculture (including hunting, forestry and fishing) contributed an estimated 3.5% of GDP in 2002 and employed 5.4% of the working population in that year. Forestry is the most important branch of the sector, with products of the wood and paper industries providing about 21.5% of export earnings in 2002. Animal husbandry is the predominant form of farming. The major crops are barley, oats and sugar beet. During 1990–2001 agricultural GDP increased, in real terms, by an average of 0.3% per year; agricultural GDP increased by 6.1% in 2000, but declined by 2.9% in 2001.

INDUSTRY
Industry (including mining, manufacturing, construction and power), provided 31.1% of GDP in 2002 and employed 27.0% of the working population in that year. Industrial GDP increased, in real terms, by an average of 3.4% per year during 1990–2001; industrial GDP grew by 10.1% in 2000, but declined by 0.6% in 2001.

Mining
Mining and quarrying contributed 0.2% of GDP in 2002 and employed 0.3% of the working population in the same year. The GDP of the mining sector increased, in real terms, at an average rate of 3.4% per year during 1995–99; mining GDP declined by 17.8% in 1998, but increased by 18.0% in 1999. Gold is the major mineral export, and zinc ore, copper ore and lead ore are also mined in small quantities.

Manufacturing
Manufacturing provided 23.4% of GDP in 2002, and in the same year employed 19.7% of the working population. The most important branches of manufacturing are the electronics industry (particularly mobile telephones), transport equipment, metal products and food and beverages. The GDP of the manufacturing sector increased, in real terms, at an average rate of 5.4% per year during 1990–2000; the sector's GDP increased by 7.1% in 1999 and by 12.5% in 2000.

Energy
Of total energy generated in 2000 32.1% was derived from nuclear energy, 18.9% from coal, 20.9% from hydroelectric power, 14.4% from natural gas and 0.9% from

petroleum. At the end of 2000 there were four nuclear reactors in operation; plans for the construction of a fifth reactor were approved by the Eduskunta in May 2002. In mid-December 2003 a contract was signed with a consortium of French and German companies to construct a new 1,600-MW nuclear reactor in Olkiluoto in south-west Finland (two reactors were already in operation there); the reactor was scheduled for completion in 2009. Imports of mineral fuels comprised 11.4% of the total cost of imports in 2002.

SERVICES

Services provided 65.4% of GDP in 2002 and engaged 67.7% of the employed labour force in the same year. In real terms, the combined GDP of the services sector increased at an average rate of 1.7% per year during 1990–2001; growth in the sector's GDP was recorded at 3.9% in 2000 and 1.8% in 2001.

EXTERNAL TRADE

In 2002 Finland recorded a visible trade surplus of US $13,143m., and there was a surplus of $10,205m. on the current account of the balance of payments. In 2002 the principal source of imports was Germany (providing 15.2% of total imports); other major sources were Sweden (11.4%), Russia (10.0%) and the USA (6.7%). Germany was also the principal market for exports in the same year (accounting for 11.9% of total exports); other major purchasers were the United Kingdom (9.7%), the USA (8.9%) and Sweden (8.7%). The EU accounted for 54.0% of exports and 55.7% of imports in 2002. The principal exports in that year were machinery and transport equipment (mainly electronic products, notably mobile telephones), basic manufactures (mainly paper, paperboard and manufactures) and chemicals and related products. The principal imports were machinery and transport equipment, basic manufactures, chemicals and related products, and mineral fuels and lubricants.

GOVERNMENT FINANCE

In 2002 Finland recorded an overall budget surplus of €842m. (equivalent to 0.6% of GDP). In the same year Finland's gross public debt amounted to some €4,634m. The average annual rate of inflation was 1.2% during 1990–2002. Consumer prices increased by 2.8% in 2001, and by 1.6% in 2002. The rate of unemployment declined from 15.4% in 1995 to 9.1% in 2002.

INTERNATIONAL ECONOMIC RELATIONS

Finland is a member of the Nordic Council and the Organisation for Economic Co-operation and Development. In January 1995 it left the European Free Trade Association and joined the European Union (EU).

SURVEY AND PROSPECTS

Early 2003 was marked by weak economic growth in Finland, owing to a sluggish global economy and the resultant depressed levels in exports and investment. However, there were signs of a general worldwide recovery by the middle of the year, particularly in the USA, which was expected to stimulate growth in the euro area in the latter half of the year. Nevertheless, the Bank of Finland forecast annual GDP growth of 1.3%, slightly lower than the previous year's rate of increase. Annual GDP growth, however, was expected to reach 3.0% in 2004 and 2005, and was projected to be broadly based, with an improvement in exports, an upturn in investment and a continued and stable rise in household consumption. None the less, Finland's growth prospects remained linked to developments in the world economy and to short-term fluctuations in the information and communications technology sector (the country's most important industrial sector in terms of export revenue).

Despite accelerating growth, unemployment was forecast to fall only slightly in the short term; a larger than projected rise in real wages in the private sector was expected to limit demand for labour. Finland suffers from a high and persistent level of structural unemployment, and as yet no steps have been taken to rectify this.

The rate of inflation slowed more quickly than forecast in 2003, owing to the appreciation of the euro, the moderate trend in import prices and to specific domestic factors, such as the reduction in car tax. Inflation was expected to be dominated by temporary factors in 2004: the reduction in excise duties and resulting lower retail prices for alcoholic beverages, and, to some extent also, lower prices for restaurant services. However, inflation was forecast to rise again in 2005.

Government finances remained relatively stable in 2003, despite the deceleration in the rate of GDP growth and the lack of exceptional tax revenues resulting from rising share prices. This fiscal stability was supported by the restrained growth in central government expenditure, compared with the rest of the economy. However, central government surpluses were expected to contract, and possibly even go into deficit, during 2004; at the same time, local government was projected to give cause for concern, as its structural funding deficit appeared to be increasing even before the expected growth in expenditure on health care and other forms of care towards the end of the decade. Despite these concerns, public finances as a whole were expected to remain in surplus, owing to the surplus in employment pension funds.

France

The French Republic is situated in western Europe. The Fifth Republic was established in 1958, under wartime leader Gen. Charles de Gaulle. Georges Pompidou succeeded to the presidency in 1969, and was followed, in 1974, by the centrist Valéry Giscard d'Estaing. François Mitterrand, the leader of the Parti Socialiste, was elected as President in 1981 and 1988, ceding office, in 1995, to the Gaullist Jacques Chirac. Chirac was re-elected in 2002, in which year parties of the centre-right obtained a majority of deputies at legislative elections, ending a period of 'cohabitation'. Paris is the capital. French is the principal language.

Area and population
Area: 543,965 sq km
Population (mid-2002): 59,441,600
Population density (mid-2002): 109.3 per sq km
Life expectancy (years at birth, 2002): 79.7 (males 75.9; females 83.5)

Finance
GDP in current prices: 2002: US $1,409,604m. ($23,714 per head)
Real GDP growth (2002): 1.0%
Inflation (annual average, 2002): 1.9%
Currency: euro

Economy

In 2002, according to estimates by the World Bank, France's gross national income (GNI), measured at average 2000–02 prices, was US $1,342,735m., equivalent to $22,010 per head (or $26,180 on an international purchasing-power parity basis). During 1990–2002, it was estimated, the population increased by an average of 0.4% per year, while gross domestic product (GDP) per head increased, in real terms, by an average of 1.4% per year. Overall GDP increased, in real terms, at an average rate of 1.8% per year in 1990–2002. Real GDP increased by 1.8% in 2001 and by 1.0% in 2002, the lowest annual growth since 1996.

AGRICULTURE

Agriculture (including forestry and fishing) contributed 2.9% of GDP in 2001, and engaged 3.2% of the economically active population in that year. The principal crops are wheat, sugar beet, maize and barley. Livestock, dairy products and wine are also important. Agricultural GDP increased, in real terms, by an average of 1.4% per year in 1990–2001; it declined by 0.8% in 2000 and by 1.1% in 2001. The sector was adversely affected in 2000–01 by the outbreak of Bovine Spongiform Encephalopathy (BSE—'Mad Cow Disease') and its human variant, Creutzfeldt-Jakob Disease, v-CJD); by the end of 2000 a number of the country's major export markets for beef had placed restrictions on the export of meat from France.

INDUSTRY

Industry (including mining, manufacturing, construction and power) provided 25.6% of GDP in 2001, and employed 26.6% of the working population in 1994. Industrial GDP increased, in real terms, by an average of 1.5% per year during 1990–2001; it increased by 4.4% in 2000 and by 1.7% in 2001.

Mining

Mining and quarrying contributed 0.4% of GDP in 1997, and employed 0.3% of the working population in 1994. Coal is the principal mineral produced, while petroleum and natural gas are also extracted. In addition, metallic minerals, including iron ore, copper and zinc, are mined. In real terms, the GDP of the mining sector increased by 3.8% in 1996, but declined by 8.6% in 1997.

Manufacturing

Manufacturing provided 18.4% of GDP in 2000, and employed 18.8% of the working population in 1994. Measured by the value of output, the most important branches of manufacturing in 1995 were machinery and transport equipment (accounting for 31% of the total), food, beverages and tobacco (17%), chemicals (10%) and fabricated metal products (6%). According to the World Bank, manufacturing GDP increased, in real terms, at an average annual rate of 2.0% in 1990–1999.

Energy

France has only limited fossil fuel resources, and in the early 2000s was the world's largest producer of nuclear power per head of population. In 2000 nuclear power provided 77.5% of total electricity production and hydroelectric power 12.5%. Imports of fuel products comprised 9.5% of the value of total merchandise imports in 2001; in the early 2000s the major sources of petroleum imported to France were Saudi Arabia and Norway. In late 1998 the NorFra pipeline, which connected Norway's Troll gas field in the North Sea to the French national gas grid, opened, becoming the first pipeline to link a foreign production field to France. By 2005 it was anticipated that this pipeline would supply one-third of France's total national gas requirements The GDP of the energy sector increased, in real terms, at an average rate of 1.5% per year in 1990–99.

SERVICES

Services accounted for 71.5% of GDP in 2001, and employed 68.7% of the working population in 1994. In the late 1990s and early 2000s France was consistently the country with the largest quantity of tourist visitors in the world; there were an estimated 77,012,000 tourist arrivals in 2002, and in 2000 tourism receipts totalled US $29,900m. The combined GDP of all service sectors increased, in real terms, at an average rate of 2.1% per year in 1990–2001; it increased by 3.7% in 2000 and by 2.1% in 2001.

EXTERNAL TRADE

In 2002 France recorded a trade surplus of US $9,000m. and there was a surplus of $25,700m. on the current account of the balance of payments. In 2001 the principal source of imports (providing 16.7% of the total) was Germany; other major sources were Italy (8.9%), the USA (8.9%), and the United Kingdom (7.5%). Germany was also the principal market for exports (accounting for 14.3% of the total); other major trading partners were the United Kingdom (9.8%), Spain (9.6%), the USA (8.8%) and Italy (8.8%). The EU as a whole provided 59.2% of imports in 1998 and took 62.6% of exports. The principal exports in 2001 were machinery and transport equipment, chemicals, basic manufactures, and miscellaneous manufactured articles. The principal imports were machinery and transport equipment, basic manufactures and miscellaneous manufactured articles.

GOVERNMENT FINANCE

The budget deficit for 2002 amounted to €47,446m., equivalent to 3.1% of GDP. In 2002 gross state debt was equivalent to 59.1% of annual GDP. The average annual rate of inflation in 1990–2002 was 1.7%. Consumer prices increased by 1.6% in 2001 and by 1.9% in 2002. The rate of unemployment declined from 12.3% in 1997 to 8.8% in 2001, but had risen again, to 9.6%, by July 2003.

INTERNATIONAL ECONOMIC RELATIONS

France is a member of the European Union (EU), and of the Organisation for Economic Co-operation and Development, and presides over the Franc Zone.

SURVEY AND PROSPECTS

France adopted the euro in January 1999 as a single currency unit for transactions throughout the eurozone and as an internationally traded currency, and as legal tender in cash from 1 January 2002. The French economy exhibited vigorous expansion from 1997 to 2000, although growth slowed in 2001 and negative growth was recorded in the final quarter of 2002.

The implementation, by the Jospin administration, from January 2000 of legislation reducing the duration of the working week from 39 to 35 hours, was initially regarded as contributing to an appreciable reduction in unemployment. However, in response to concerns that this system inhibited flexibility for enterprises and necessitated additional costs, the Raffarin administration, in January 2003, approved legislation that introduced further flexibility to the system.

A number of major state-owned corporations have been wholly or partially privatized since 1993, although France remained the eurozone country with the highest general government expenditure and revenue (in both cases in excess of 50%) as a share of GDP in 2001. France has, moreover, been slow to implement European Commission requirements on opening markets to competition and on restricting state subsidies, particularly in the energy sector. In June 2000 the European Commission commenced legal proceedings against France for failing to ensure that competition in electricity markets, permitted since February of that year, would be fair, and in May 2001 legal proceedings against France began with regard to its failure to create competition in gas markets. In October 2002 the European Commission ruled that the state electricity company, Electricité de France (EdF), was obliged to repay €900m. that it had received as a subsidy from the State. However, in November 2002 France approved a directive of the Council of the European Union, to the effect that the electricity and gas markets were to be fully liberalized by July 2004 for enterprises, and by July 2007, for individual customers. In July 2002 Raffarin announced that the capital of both EdF and Gaz de France was progressively to be opened to private investors, although both companies would remain within the public sector; in July 2003 the Government also announced proposals for the state-controlled telecommunications company, France Télécom, to be transferred to majority private ownership.

The announcement, in March 2003 that the anticipated budget deficit for that year had increased to be in excess of the 3.0% limit permitted by the eurozone Stability and Growth Pact, as a result of lower than expected growth, led to France being issued with a formal warning by the European Commission for failing to fulfil its obligations with regard to fiscal consolidation. (The budget deficit for 2002, at 3.1% of GDP, had also breached the terms of the Pact.) The Commission subsequently launched its excessive deficit procedure, in accordance with which France could be fined by an amount equivalent to up to 0.5% of GDP. The French Government subsequently announced that the anticipated budget deficit for 2003 had increased further, to the equivalent of 4.0% of GDP, and that the anticipated budget deficit for 2004 would also be in excess of 3.0%, partially because of a government pledge to reduce income tax. None the less, in late November 2003 the European Commission decided to suspend the excessive deficit procedure against France (and a similar procedure that had been launched against Germany), although the French Government was to be expected to implement various structural reforms in order that the budget deficit for 2005 meet the requirements of the Pact.

In mid-2003 the French Government announced proposals to implement reforms to the public-sector pension system; although these proposals, which obliged public-sector employees to work for additional years before they would be eligible for a full state pension, initially precipitated widespread demonstrations and protests, later in the year both houses of Parlement approved the reform proposals of Prime Minister Raffarin. This development appeared to mark a significant step towards economic reform in France, for both economic and political reasons: although the need for such reforms had been apparent for several years, because of an ageing population, widespread public opposition towards similar plans proposed by the centre-right Government of Alain Juppé in the mid-1990s had widely been regarded as a principal contributory factor in the defeat of the centre-right parties in the 1997 general election.

French Guiana

French Guiana lies on the north coast of South America. The territory was confirmed as French in 1817, and in 1946 it became a Department of France. In 1974 French Guiana was granted regional status, as part of France's governmental reorganization, acquiring greater economic autonomy. Industrial and political unrest in the late 1970s prompted demands for greater autonomy, and in 1982–83 some power over local affairs was devolved to the new Conseil Régional. In 2001 the French Government approved proposals on greater autonomy presented to it by the Conseil Général and the Conseil Régional. The capital is Cayenne. French is the official language.

Area and population
Area: 83,534 sq km
Population (March 1999): 156,790
Population density (March 1999): 1.9 per sq km
Life expectancy (years at birth, 1999): Males 71.7; females 79.2

Finance
GDP in current prices, 1999): US $1,488m. ($9,342 per head)
Real GDP growth (1999): 1.6%
Inflation (annual average, 2002): 1.5%
Currency: euro

Economy

In 2001 French Guiana's gross domestic product (GDP), measured at current prices, was US $1,308m., equivalent to $7,737 per head. Between 1990 and 2001, according to UN estimates, GDP increased, in real terms, at an average rate of 3.1% per year; growth in 2001 was 1.6%. Between the censuses of 1990 and 1999, according to provisional figures, the population increased at an average annual rate of 3.5%.

AGRICULTURE

According to FAO estimates, agriculture (including fishing) engaged 18.1% of the economically active population in mid2001. In 1999 the sector contributed 5.2% of GDP. The dominant activities are fisheries and forestry, although the contribution of the latter to export earnings has declined in recent years. In 1998 exports of shrimps provided some 22.4% of total export earnings. The principal crops for local consumption are cassava, vegetables and rice, and sugar cane is grown for making rum. Rice, pineapples and citrus fruit are cultivated for export. According to UN estimates, agricultural GDP decreased at an average annual rate of 0.8% in 1990–98; in 1998 agricultural GDP increased by an estimated 0.3%.

INDUSTRY

Industry, including construction, engaged about 15.6% of the employed labour force in 1999 and, according to official sources, contributed 18.7% of GDP.

Mining

The mining sector is dominated by the extraction of gold, which involves small-scale alluvial operations as well as larger local and multinational mining concerns. Exploration activity intensified in the mid-1990s, and the proposed construction of a major new road into the interior of the Department was expected to encourage further development. Officially-recorded gold exports were estimated at 4,857 kg in 1999 (actual production levels and sales are believed to be higher than published levels). In 2002 about 3 metric tons (96,450 troy oz) of gold were mined. Crushed rock for the construction industry is the only other mineral extracted in significant quantities, although exploratory drilling of known diamond deposits began in 1995. Deposits of bauxite, columbo-tantalite and kaolin are also present.

Manufacturing

There is little manufacturing activity, except for the processing of fisheries products (mainly shrimp-freezing) and the distillation of rum. In 1990–98 industrial GDP (excluding construction) increased at an average annual rate of 7.8%. The construction sector expanded at an average of 2.0% per year in the same period.

Energy

French Guiana was heavily dependent on imported fuels for the generation of energy prior to the flooding of the Petit-Saut hydroelectric dam on the River Sinnamary, in 1994. Together with existing generating plants, the 116-MW dam was expected to satisfy the territory's electrical energy requirements for about 30 years. Fuel imports accounted for 11.3% of total imports in 2000.

SERVICES

The services sector engaged 77.7% of the employed labour force in 1999 and, according to official sources, contributed 76.1% of GDP. The European Space Agency's satellite-launching centre at Kourou (established in 1964 and expanded during the 1990s) has provided a considerable stimulus to the economy, most notably the construction sector (which engaged 7.5% of the employed labour force in 1999). The tourist sector expanded in the last two decades of the 20th century, although its potential is limited by the lack of infrastructure away from the coast. In 2002 some 65,000 visitor arrivals were recorded. In early 2003 the French Minister of Overseas Departments announced plans to stimulate the economies of French Guiana, Guadeloupe and Martinique that included the introduction of tax incentives for the hotel sector.

EXTERNAL TRADE

In 2000 French Guiana recorded a trade deficit of 499m. euros. In that year the principal source of imports was metropolitan France (which supplied 55.8% of total imports in 2000); the Department's other major suppliers were Trinidad and Tobago, Italy and Japan. Metropolitan France was also the principal market for exports in 2000 (63.6%); other important purchasers were Switzerland, Guadeloupe and the USA. The principal imports in 2000 were food and agricultural products and road vehicles and parts. The principal exports were metals and metal products and food and agricultural products.

GOVERNMENT FINANCE

Under the 1998 regional budget it was envisaged that expenditure would total €67m., while revenue was €63m. By September 1988 French Guiana's external debt had reached US $1,200m. The annual rate of inflation averaged 1.5% in 1990–2003; consumer prices increased by an average of 1.5% in 2002 and by 2% in 2003. Unemployment in mid-2002 was estimated at 23% of the total labour force. However, there is a shortage of skilled labour, offset partly by immigration.

INTERNATIONAL ECONOMIC RELATIONS

As an integral part of France, French Guiana is a member of the European Union (EU).

SURVEY AND PROSPECTS

Economic development in French Guiana has been hindered by the Department's location, poor infrastructure away from the coast and lack of a skilled indigenous labour force, although there is considerable potential for further growth in the fishing, forestry and tourism (notably 'eco-tourism') sectors. A particular concern throughout the 1990s was the rapid rise in the rate of unemployment; youth unemployment and related social problems were widely interpreted as having contributed to the violence in Cayenne in late 1996.

French Guiana's geographical characteristics—large parts of the territory are accessible only by river—have resulted in difficulties in regulating key areas of the economy, such as gold-mining and forestry. Considerable concern has been expressed regarding the ecological consequences of such a lack of controls; moreover, the flooding of a large area of forest (some 340 sq km), as part of the Petit-Saut barrage project, prompted disquiet among environmental groups, as did uncertainty regarding the ecological implications of the satellite-launching programme at Kourou.

Proposals for the creation of a national park, covering 2.5m. ha of the south of French Guiana, with the aim of protecting an expanse of equatorial forest, were hindered in the early 2000s by the need to reconcile ecological concerns with economic priorities and the needs of the resident communities, notably the demands of gold prospectors.

The budget deficit represents a significant obstacle to growth, while high demand for imported consumer goods (much of which is generated by relatively well-remunerated civil servants, who constitute about two-thirds of the working population) undermines progress in reducing the trade deficit.

In mid-2001 the decision by the French Government to abandon a sugar cane plantation project was met with disappointment by local politicians. The plantation of some 8,000 ha of sugar cane, with an estimated annual output of 65,000 tons of raw sugar, had been expected to generate significant employment opportunities. However, the project was considered to be too costly by the Government, which subsequently pledged to undertake a plan for the development of the agricultural sector in French Guiana.

French Polynesia

French Polynesia consists of the following island groups in the South Pacific Ocean: the Windward Islands (including Tahiti and Moorea) and the Leeward Islands which, together, constitute the Society Archipelago; the Tuamotu Archipelago, comprising some 80 atolls east of the Society Archipelago; the Austral Islands, south of Tahiti; and the Marquesas Archipelago, north-east of Tahiti. Tahiti became a French colony in 1880. The other island groups were annexed in the late 19th century. In 1946 French Polynesia became an Overseas Territory. The Territory became an Overseas Country of France in 2004. Papeete is the capital. French and Tahitian are the official languages.

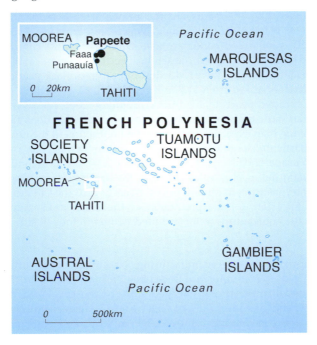

Area and population
Area: 4,167 sq km
Population (mid-2002): 240,000
Population density (mid-2002): 57.5 per sq km
Life expectancy (years at birth): n.a.

Finance
GDP in current prices: 2000): US $3,448m. ($14,670 per head)
Real GDP growth (2000): 4.0%
Inflation (annual average, 2002): 2.9%
Currency: CFP franc

Economy

In 2000, according to World Bank estimates, French Polynesia's gross national income (GNI), measured at average 1998–2000 prices, was US $3,794m., equivalent to $16,150 per head (or $24,360m. per head on an international purchasing-power parity basis). During 1990–2000, it was estimated, the population increased at an average annual rate of 1.8%, while GDP per head increased at an average annual rate of 0.5%. Overall gross domestic product (GDP) increased, in real terms, at an average annual rate of 2.3% in 1990–2000. Real GDP increased by 4.0% in both 1999 and 2000.

AGRICULTURE

Agriculture, forestry and fishing contributed only 4.7% of GDP in 2000, but provided most of French Polynesia's exports. The sector engaged 4.0% of the employed labour force at December 2002. Coconuts are the principal cash crop, and in 2002 the estimated harvest was 88,000 metric tons. Vegetables, fruit (especially pineapples and citrus fruit), vanilla and coffee are also cultivated. Most commercial fishing, principally for tuna, is conducted, under licence, by Japanese and Korean fleets. Another important activity is the production of cultured black pearls, of which the quantity exported increased from 112 kg in 1984 to 8,182 kg in 1999. In 2000 export earnings from cultured pearls totalled US $175.9m. By 2001, however, development of the black pearl industry appeared to have decelerated. Auctions early in the year raised less revenue than expected, with a marked reduction in the number of buyers from Japan in particular, largely owing to the downturn in that country's economy, as well as from Europe and the USA. In December 2001 the pearl industry lowered prices to maintain the level of sales, while at the same time forming a centralized buying syndicate, ensuring minimum prices. In early 2003 the Government allocated some francs CFP 150m. for the promotion of the black pearl industry overseas. Production by the aquaculture sector included 44 metric tons of shrimps in 2001.

INDUSTRY

Industry (comprising mining, manufacturing, construction and utilities) engaged 17.1% of the employed labour force at December 2002, and provided 15.5% of GDP in 1997. Mining and manufacturing engaged 7.5% of the employed labour force at December 2002, and provided 7.0% of GDP in 1997. Construction is an important industrial activity, contributing 5.3% of GDP in 1997, and engaging 8.8% of the employed labour force at December 2002.

Manufacturing

There is a small manufacturing sector, which is heavily dependent on agriculture. Coconut oil and copra are produced, as are beer, dairy products and vanilla essence. Important deposits of phosphates and cobalt were discovered during the 1980s.

Energy

Hydrocarbon fuels are the main source of energy in the Territory, with the Papeete thermal power station providing about three-quarters of the electricity produced. Hydroelectric and solar energy also make a significant contribution to French Polynesia's domestic requirements. Hydroelectric power dams, with the capacity to generate the electricity requirements of 36% of Tahiti's population, have been constructed. Solar energy is also increasingly important, especially on the less-populated islands.

SERVICES

Tourism is the Territory's major industry. In 1990 the trade, restaurants and hotels sector contributed 22.7% of GDP. In 2002 some 189,000 tourists visited French Polynesia, compared with about 227,660 in the previous year. Receipts from tourism totalled an estimated 49,900m. francs CFP in 2000. French Polynesia's hotel capacity amounted to 3,357 rooms in 2000. The services sector engaged 78.9% of the employed labour force at December 2002, and provided 80.4% of GDP in 1997.

EXTERNAL TRADE

In 2000, according to the Institut d'Émission d'Outre-Mer (IEOM—the French over-seas reserve bank), French Polynesia recorded a visible trade deficit of 81,052m. francs CFP. On the current account of the balance-of payments there was a surplus of 45,660m. francs CFP, equivalent to 11% of GDP and an increase of 75.8% compared with the previous year. In 2002 the value of imports reached 160,156.3m. francs CFP, while that of exports amounted to 21,074.5m. francs CFP. In 2002 the principal sources of imports were France (which provided 46.3% of total imports), the USA (9.2%) and New Zealand (7.5%). The principal markets for exports in that year were Japan (accounting for 31.1% of the total), Hong Kong (30.4%) and the USA (15.0%). The principal imports in 2002 included aircraft and aeronautical craft (16.8% of the total) and road vehicles (9.2%). In 2001 the principal commodity exports were cultured black pearls (providing some 58.8% of total export revenue).

GOVERNMENT FINANCE

A budgetary deficit of 38,314m. francs CFP was projected in 2001. In 2002 expenditure by the French State in the Territory totalled 131,626m. francs CFP, 25.8% of which was on the military budget. The budget for 2003 envisaged expenditure of 170,000m. francs CFP. The total external debt was estimated at US $390m. in 1992. The annual rate of inflation averaged 1.3% in 1990–2002. In 2001 inflation increased by an average of 1.0%, and in 2002 it rose by an average of 2.9%. A high unemployment rate (recorded at 13.2% of the labour force in 1996) is exacerbated by the predominance of young people in the population (in 1996 some 43% of the population were under the age of 20 years).

INTERNATIONAL ECONOMIC RELATIONS

French Polynesia forms part of the Franc Zone, and is an associate member of the UN Economic and Social Commission for Asia and the Pacific (ESCAP). Although France is also a member of the organization, French Polynesia has membership in its own right of the Pacific Community, which is based in New Caledonia and provides technical advice, training and assistance in economic, cultural and social develop-ment to the region.

SURVEY AND PROSPECTS

French Polynesia's traditional agriculture-based economy was distorted by the pre-sence of large numbers of French military personnel (in connection with the nuclear-testing programme which began in 1966), stimulating employment in the construction industry and services at the expense of agriculture, and encouraging migration from the outer islands to Tahiti. These dramatic changes effectively transformed French Polynesia from a state of self-sufficiency to one of import dependency in less than a generation. The development of tourism had a similar effect.

The Contract for Development, an agreement for metropolitan France to provide the Territory with 28,300m. francs CFP annually between 1996 and 2006, was concluded in 1995 and took effect upon completion of the last series of nuclear tests in early 1996. It was hoped that the arrangement would enable French Polynesia to establish an economy that was more reliant upon local resources and would consequently create greater employment. During a visit to French Polynesia in mid-2003, President Chirac of France confirmed that the annual grant of €151m. would be continued indefinitely.

French Polynesia's steady economic growth has partly been as a result of the development of the services sector, notably in hotel construction and other tourism-related services, which has led to significant employment creation. Other sectors of the economy, such as pearl farming, however, have not expanded as rapidly, principally because of regional economic conditions (notably the recession in Japan, one of the largest importers of black pearls).

The continued expansion of GDP throughout the late 1990s was principally due to the financial support provided by France, but also to a significant rise in the number of tourists visiting the Territory (a 16.8% increase between 1997 and 1999). It was hoped that revenue from tourism would eventually replace the grants provided by the French State. In 2001 customs duties were decreased, while VAT rates were maintained at similar levels, as the Government continued the anti-inflationary policy that it had instigated in 1996. The principal aim of the 2002 budget, however, was to avoid recession and to counter the repercussions of the deteriorating global economic situation. VAT rates were increased by an average of 3.3%, and total VAT receipts for the year were expected to reach 36,600m. francs CFP. The 2002 budget also introduced new taxes on alcohol, soft drinks, sugar and new road vehicles. The Government defended the introduction of these new taxes by citing the 'economic uncertainties' faced by French Polynesia. The 2003 budget allocated more than 5% of expenditure to social housing programmes.

The tourism sector proved vulnerable in the wake of the terrorist attacks on the USA on 11 September 2001. The number of visitor arrivals declined sharply in late 2001, and by early 2002 many of French Polynesia's hotels were reporting occupancy rates as low as 35%. In 2002 the total number of visitors declined by 17.0% compared with the previous year. In mid-2003 the National Assembly approved the Overseas Territories Development Bill, which would provide support for economic and social development in French Polynesia (together with New Caledonia and Wallis and Futuna) by attracting foreign investment, and among other benefits allow for overseas French residents to travel to mainland France to take advantage of free education.

Gabon

The Gabonese Republic is an equatorial country on the west coast of Africa. Gabon achieved independence from France in 1960. Léon M'Ba, the new Republic's President, established a one-party state. His successor, Albert-Bernard (later Omar) Bongo, instituted the Parti démocratique gabonais (PDG) as the ruling party. Multi-party legislative elections held in 1990 were won by the PDG, as were polls in 1996 and 2001. The PDG was also the dominant party in indirect elections to the Sénat held in 1997 and 2003. In 1993, in Gabon's first multi-party presidential election, Bongo was re-elected. He was returned to office again in 1998. Libreville is the capital. The official language is French.

Area and population
Area: 267,667 sq km
Population (mid-2002): 1,290,600
Population density (mid-2002): 4.8 per sq km
Life expectancy (years at birth, 2002): 59.2 (males 57.3; females 61.4)

Finance
GDP in current prices: 2002): US $4,971m. ($3,852 per head)
Real GDP growth (2002): 3.0%
Inflation (annual average, 2002): 0.2%
Currency: CFA franc

Economy

In 2002, according to estimates by the World Bank, Gabon's gross national product (GNI), measured at average 2000–02 prices, was US $4,027m., equivalent to $3,120 per head (or $5,320 per head on an international purchasing-power parity basis). During 1990–2002, it was estimated, the population increased at an average annual rate of 2.7%, while gross domestic product (GDP) per head declined, in real terms, by an average of 0.3% per year. Overall GDP increased, in real terms, at an average annual rate of 2.4% in 1990–2002; growth in 2002 was 3.0%.

AGRICULTURE
Agriculture (including forestry and fishing) contributed an estimated 6.5% of GDP in 2002. About 36.6% of the labour force were employed in the agricultural sector in 2001. Cocoa, coffee, oil palm and rubber are cultivated for export. Gabon has yet to achieve self-sufficiency in staple crops: imports of food and live animals accounted for 15.1% of the value of total imports in 2000. The principal subsistence crops are plantains, cassava and maize. The exploitation of Gabon's forests (which cover about 75% of the land area) is a principal economic activity. In 2002 okoumé timber accounted for an estimated 69% of all timber production. Although Gabon's territorial waters contain important fishing resources, their commercial exploitation is minimal. Agricultural GDP declined at an average annual rate of 0.1% in 1990–2002; however, growth in 2002 was 4.9%.

INDUSTRY
Industry (including mining, manufacturing, construction and power) contributed an estimated 55.8% of GDP in 2002. About 14.1% of the working population were employed in the sector in 1991. Industrial GDP increased at an average annual rate of 1.6% in 1990–2002; growth in 2002 was 2.7%.

Mining
Mining accounted for an estimated 44.7% of GDP in 2002 (with 43.1% contributed by the petroleum sector alone). In 2002 sales of petroleum and petroleum products provided an estimated 79.0% of export revenue. Gabon is among the world's foremost producers and exporters of manganese (which contributed an estimated 4.6% of export earnings in 2002). Major reserves of iron ore remain undeveloped, owing to the lack of appropriate transport facilities, and there are also substantial niobium (columbium) reserves at Mabounie. Small amounts of gold are extracted, and the existence of many mineral deposits, including talc, barytes, phosphates, rare earths, titanium and cadmium, has also been confirmed. In 1996–2002, according to the IMF, mining GDP declined at an estimated average annual rate of 6.5%. The IMF estimated a decline of 2.1% in mining GDP in 2002.

Manufacturing

The manufacturing sector contributed an estimated 7.1% of GDP in 2002. The principal activities are the refining of petroleum and the processing of other minerals, the preparation of timber and other agro-industrial processes. The chemicals industry is also significant. According to IMF estimates, manufacturing GDP increased at an average annual rate of 6.8% in 1996–2002; growth in 2002 was an estimated 3.9%.

Energy

In 2000 71.3% of electrical energy was provided by hydroelectric power, 18.1% by petroleum and 10.7% by natural gas. Imports of fuel and energy comprised an estimated 4.2% of the total value of merchandise imports in 2000.

SERVICES

Services engaged 18.8% of the economically active population in 1991 and provided an estimated 37.7% of GDP in 2002. The GDP of the services sector increased at an average annual rate of 3.7% in 1990–2002; growth in 2002 was 3.1%.

EXTERNAL TRADE

In 2002 Gabon recorded a visible trade surplus of US $1,722.0m., and there was a surplus of $32.8m. on the current account of the balance of payments. In 2000 the principal source of imports (44.1%) was France; other major sources were the USA and the Netherlands. The principal market for exports in that year was the USA (62.6%); Australia and the People's Republic of China were also important purchasers. The principal exports in 2002 were petroleum and petroleum products, timber and manganese. The principal imports in 2000 were machinery and transport equipment, food and live animals, and chemicals and related products.

GOVERNMENT FINANCE

In 2002 there was an estimated budgetary surplus of 121,900m. francs CFA (equivalent to 3.5% of GDP). Gabon's external debt totalled US $3,409m. at the end of 2001, of which $3,030m. was long-term public debt. In that year the cost of debt-servicing was equivalent to 13.9% of the value of exports of goods and services. In 1996–2002 the average annual rate of inflation was 1.2%. Consumer prices increased by 0.5% in 2002. The Government estimated about 20% of the labour force to be unemployed in 1996.

INTERNATIONAL ECONOMIC RELATIONS

Gabon is a member of the Central African organs of the Franc Zone, and of the Communauté économique des états de l'Afrique centrale (CEEAC). In 1996 Gabon, which had been a member of the Organization of the Petroleum Exporting Countries (OPEC) since 1973, withdrew from the organization.

SURVEY AND PROSPECTS

Gabon's potential for economic growth is based on its considerable mineral and forestry resources. Petroleum provides the country's principal source of income, but production is estimated to be in long-term decline. Gabon's economic situation deteriorated substantially in 1998–99 as a result of falling petroleum prices and the negative impact of the Asian economic crisis on timber exports. Further strain was placed on the economy by the suspension of loans from the Agence française de développement, and from March 1999 Gabon had no IMF programme. The economy began to recover in 2000, and in October the IMF approved a new 18-month stand-by agreement, worth some US $119m. However, the Government largely failed to implement a sufficiently strict austerity policy in accordance with the IMF's recommendations.

As petroleum prices declined in 2001, arrears of foreign debt continued to accumulate, despite the rescheduling of some $532m. owed to the 'Paris Club' of international creditors. In mid-2002 the Government concurred with predictions by the World Bank that petroleum production in Gabon would decline by some 50%, in relation to 1996 levels, during the following five years. None the less, revenue from petroleum exports was estimated to have increased in 2003, following improvements in extractive technologies and a rise in international prices. Efforts to lower the level of public debt remained a key priority for 2004, particularly as this was expected to reach 40% of government revenue within the following five years. It was also hoped that measures to diversify the economy, and thus reduce reliance on mineral exports, could be achieved through further development of the forestry, agriculture, fisheries and services sectors, notably with the promotion of Gabon as a tourist destination. It was hoped that a new stand-by arrangement with the IMF would be agreed by mid-2004. However, levels of government corruption were reported to be increasing in the early 2000s, and allegations of nepotism and misappropriation continued to threaten Gabon's financial credibility.

Gambia

The Republic of The Gambia is situated around the River Gambia on the west coast of Africa. The Gambia became an independent country, within the Commonwealth, in 1965. In 1994 Dr Dawda Kairaba Jawara, President since 1970, was deposed by a self-styled Armed Forces Provisional Ruling Council, led by Lt (later Col) Yahya Jammeh. In 1996 Jammeh contested and won a presidential election as a civilian. Legislative elections held in 1997 and 2002 were won by the Alliance for Patriotic Reorientation and Construction. In 2001 Jammeh was re-elected to the presidency. Banjul is the capital. The official language is English.

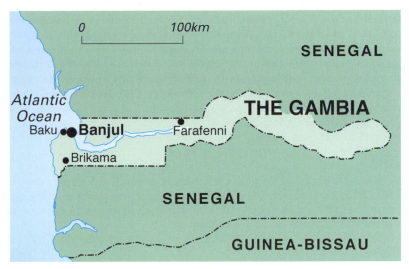

Area and population
Area: 11,295 sq km
Population (mid-2002): 1,375,710
Population density (mid-2002): 121.8 per sq km
Life expectancy (years at birth, 2002): 57.1 (males 55.4; females 58.9)

Finance
GDP in current prices: 2002): US $388m. ($282 per head)
Real GDP growth (2002): −0.6%
Inflation (annual average, 2001): 4.5%
Currency: dalasi

Economy

In 2002, according to estimates by the World Bank, The Gambia's gross national income (GNI), measured at average 2000–02 prices, was US $392m., equivalent to

$280 per head (or $1,680 on an international purchasing-power parity basis). During 1990–2002, it was estimated, the population increased at an average annual rate of 3.3%, while gross domestic product (GDP) per head remained constant. Overall GDP increased, in real terms, at an average annual rate of 3.3% in 1990–2002; GDP increased by 6.1% in 2001, but declined by 0.6% in 2002.

AGRICULTURE

Agriculture (including forestry and fishing) contributed 40.5% of GDP in 2002. About 78.6% of the labour force were employed in the sector in 2001. The dominant agricultural activity is the cultivation of groundnuts. Exports of groundnuts and related products accounted for an estimated 68.2% of domestic export earnings in 1999; however, a significant proportion of the crop is frequently smuggled for sale in Senegal, and the industry is also vulnerable to drought, which destroyed over 50% of the 2001/02 harvest. Cotton, citrus fruits, mangoes, avocados and sesame seed are also cultivated for export. The principal staple crops are rice, millet, sorghum and maize, although The Gambia remains heavily dependent on imports of rice and other basic foodstuffs. Fishing makes an important contribution both to the domestic food supply and to export earnings: exports of fish and fish products contributed an estimated 12.6% of the value of domestic exports in 1999. In 2001 the Government announced the construction of a major new fishing port in Banjul, at a cost of US $10m. Agricultural GDP increased at an average annual rate of 5.9% in 1990–2002; growth in 2002 was 10.0%.

INDUSTRY

Industry (including manufacturing, construction, mining and power) contributed 15.0% of GDP in 2002. About 9.7% of the labour force were employed in the sector at the time of the 1993 census. Industrial GDP increased at an average annual rate of 3.8% in 1990–2002; growth in 2002 was 13.0%.

Mining

The Gambia has no economically viable mineral resources, although seismic surveys have indicated the existence of petroleum deposits off shore, and there were plans to drill an exploratory well by the end of 2004. Deposits of kaolin and salt are currently unexploited.

Manufacturing

Manufacturing contributed an estimated 5.2% of GDP in 2002, and employed about 6.3% of the labour force in 1993. The sector is dominated by agro-industrial activities, most importantly the processing of groundnuts and fish. Beverages and construction materials are also produced for the domestic market. Manufacturing GDP increased at an average annual rate of 2.1% in 1990–2002; growth in 2002 was 6.0%.

Energy

The Gambia is highly reliant on imported energy. Imports of fuel and energy comprised an estimated 11.9% of the value of total merchandise imports in 2000.

SERVICES

The services sector contributed 44.6% of GDP in 2002. The tourism industry is of particular significance as a generator of foreign exchange. Tourism contributed about

10% of annual GDP in the early 1990s, and employed about one-third of workers in the formal sector at that time. The international response to the 1994 coup and its aftermath had a severe impact on tourism to The Gambia, although the industry recovered strongly from 1996 onwards. The Jammeh administration has expressed its intention further to exploit the country's potential as a transit point for regional trade and also as a centre for regional finance and telecommunications. The GDP of the services sector increased at an average annual rate of 3.1% in 1990–2002; growth in 2002 was 0.8%.

EXTERNAL TRADE

In 2001 The Gambia recorded a visible trade deficit of US $60.2m., while there was a deficit of $9.3m. on the current account of the balance of payments. In 1999 the principal source of imports was Germany, which supplied an estimated 13.8% of total imports; other major sources were the United Kingdom, France, the People's Republic of China and Belgium. The two largest markets for exports in that year were Belgium (an estimated 7.7% of total exports) and the United Kingdom. The Gambia's principal domestic exports in 1999 were groundnuts and related products, fish and fish products, and fruit and vegetables. The principal imports in that year were food and live animals, machinery and transport equipment, basic manufactures and mineral fuels and lubricants.

GOVERNMENT FINANCE

In 2001, according to preliminary figures, there was an overall budget deficit of D499.2m. The Gambia's total external debt was US $489.2m. at the end of 2001, of which $437.5m. was long-term public debt. In that year the cost of debt-servicing was equivalent to 3.8% of the value of exports of goods and services. The average annual rate of inflation was 4.6% in 1990–2002; consumer prices increased by an average of 4.9% in 2002. The rate of unemployment was estimated at some 26% of the labour force in mid-1994.

INTERNATIONAL ECONOMIC RELATIONS

The Gambia is a member of the Economic Community of West African States (ECOWAS), of the Gambia River Basin Development Organization (OMVG), of the African Groundnut Council, of the West Africa Rice Development Association (WARDA), and of the Permanent Inter-State Committee on Drought Control in the Sahel (CILSS).

SURVEY AND PROSPECTS

The military coup of July 1994 caused considerable economic disruption to The Gambia. A return to growth from 1995 was, in large part, underpinned by the recovery in the tourism sector. The installation of elected civilian institutions in early 1997 prompted the international economic community to recommence full support, which had been partially suspended following the coup, and in mid-1998 the IMF approved an Enhanced Structural Adjustment Facility (subsequently renamed the Poverty Reduction and Growth Facility, PRGF) in support of the Government's economic programme for 1998–2001.

In December 2000 it was announced that The Gambia was to receive US $91m. in debt-service relief over 15 years under the IMF/World Bank initiative for heavily indebted poor countries. The Gambia's overriding dependence on the largely unmodernized groundnut sector remains an obstacle to sustained growth, although the gradual introduction of reforms, which sought to improve relations between public- and private-sector interests, and between production and marketing interests, in the sector, commenced in 2000. Concern has also been expressed at the level of borrowing incurred by the Jammeh Government to finance its extensive infrastructural programme; the level of The Gambia's international indebtedness has risen sharply since 1995.

In March 2002 the USA finally lifted economic sanctions imposed on the Gambia following the 1994 coup, and on 1 January 2003 The Gambia became eligible for funding under the US African Growth and Opportunity Act. In July the IMF approved a further PRGF, in support of the economic programme for 2002–05, equivalent to some $27m. However, economic performance in 2003 was poor, with high inflation, weak growth and an increasing fiscal deficit recorded. Moreover, between September and December the Gambian currency, the dalasi, depreciated by 43% against the US dollar. In December the IMF suspended PRGF assistance to The Gambia and issued a statement expressing concern at the deteriorating economic situation and alleged inaccuracies in economic data provided by the Gambian authorities. In March 2004 the IMF requested that The Gambia repay two non-complying disbursements (equivalent to a total of some $10.1m.) that had been made following PRGF reviews in 2001.

Georgia

Georgia is situated in west and central Transcaucasia. In 1921, following an invasion by Bolshevik troops, a Georgian Soviet Socialist Republic (SSR) was proclaimed. In 1922 the SSR was absorbed into the Transcaucasian Soviet Federative Socialist Republic, a founder member of the USSR. In 1991 Georgia became the first republic to secede from the USSR. In 1992 a State Council was formed, with Eduard Shevardnadze as Chairman. He was subsequently elected to what was effectively a presidential role, and was directly elected to the restored post of President in 1995 and 2000. Shevardnadze relinquished power in November 2003, after allegations of electoral malpractice in that month's legislative elections prompted widespread, non-violent protests. Tbilisi is the capital. Georgian is the official language.

Area and population
Area: 69,700 sq km
Population (mid-2002): 5,177,000
Population density (mid-2002): 74.3 per sq km
Life expectancy (years at birth, 2002): 71.7 (males 68.4; females 75.0)

Finance
GDP in current prices: 2002: US $3,324m. ($642 per head)
Real GDP growth (2002): 5.4%
Inflation (annual average, 2002): 5.6%
Currency: lari

Economy

In 2002, according to estimates by the World Bank, Georgia's gross national income (GNI), measured at average 2000–02 prices, was US $3,346m., equivalent to $650 per head (or $2,210 per head on an international purchasing-power parity basis). During

1990–2002, it was estimated, the population decreased by an average of 0.4% per year, while gross domestic product (GDP) per head decreased, in real terms, by an annual average of 6.7%. Overall GDP decreased, in real terms, by an average of 7.1% annually during 1990–2002. Real GDP increased by 4.7% in 2001 and by 5.4% in 2002.

AGRICULTURE

Agriculture contributed an estimated 19.6% of GDP in 2002, and the sector (including hunting, forestry and fishing) provided 52.7% of employment in 2001. Georgia's exceedingly favourable climate allows the cultivation of subtropical crops, such as tea and oranges. Other fruit (including wine grapes), flowers, tobacco and grain are also cultivated. The mountain pastures are used for sheep- and goat-farming. In 1996 private agricultural production provided more than 85% of total output. Although the GDP of the agricultural sector declined dramatically from 1990, growth was recorded from 1995. During 1995–2000, according to the World Bank, agricultural GDP increased, in real terms, by an average of 1.4% per year. According to IMF figures, agricultural GDP increased by 8.2% in 2001, but declined by 1.4% in 2002.

INDUSTRY

Industry contributed 23.1% of GDP in 2002, and the sector (comprising mining, manufacturing, utilities and construction) provided 9.3% of employment in 2001. The most significant parts of the sector are the agro-processing and energy industries. According to the World Bank, industrial GDP decreased, in real terms, by an annual average of 5.4% in 1995–2000. According to IMF figures, industrial GDP declined by 4.5% in 2001, but increased by 7.8% in 2002.

Mining

Mining and quarrying accounted for just 0.4% of employment in 2001. The principal minerals extracted are coal, petroleum and manganese ore, but reserves of high-grade manganese ore are largely depleted. There are also deposits of coal, copper, gold and silver. Substantial natural gas deposits were discovered in 1994–96.

Manufacturing

According to the World Bank, the manufacturing sector contributed 7.5% of GDP in 2000, and it provided 5.5% of employment in 2001. Although the machinery and metal-working industries, traditionally the most important parts of the sector, were in decline in the late 1990s, manufacturing GDP increased, in real terms, by an average of 7.6% per year in 1991–2000. Real manufacturing GDP increased by 3.0% each year in 1999 and 2000.

Energy

From 1993, when the prices of imported energy were raised to international market prices, there was a significant reduction in the amount of fuel imported, leading to widespread energy shortages. In 2000 hydroelectric power accounted for 79.2% of total electricity production and natural gas for 17.0% of production. However, the country's largest hydroelectric power station was located in the secessionist region of Abkhazia, and the IMF estimated that more than one-third of the power it produced was consumed without payment. Imports of fuel and energy comprised an estimated 18.5% of total imports in 2002. In April 1999 a pipeline transporting petroleum to Supsa, on Georgia's Black Sea coast, from Baku, Azerbaijan, officially entered into service. There were also plans for the construction of a natural gas pipeline from Baku to Erzurum, Turkey, via Georgia, by 2005; in October 2003 an agreement was signed, according to which Georgia was to receive 5% of the gas transported by the pipeline, as a transit fee. In the mean time, Georgia obtained natural gas from Russia, via Armenia. However, Georgia hoped to become less dependent on Russia for its energy requirements, by developing its own energy resources. Construction work on a pipeline to carry petroleum from Baku to Ceyhan, Turkey, via Tbilisi (known as the BTC pipeline) commenced in April 2003, and was to expected to conclude by the end of 2004; some 248 km of the 1,767-km pipeline were to traverse Georgia.

SERVICES

The services sector contributed an estimated 57.3% of GDP in 2002, and engaged 38.0% of the employed labour force in 2001. Trade and transport and communications are the sector's most significant areas of activity. According to the World Bank, the GDP of the services sector decreased, in real terms, by an annual average of 8.6% in 1995–2000. However, real sectoral GDP increased by 1.7% in 1999 and by 5.5% in 2000.

EXTERNAL TRADE

In 2002 Georgia recorded a visible trade deficit of US $458.2m., and there was a deficit of $250.5m. on the current account of the balance of payments. In 2001 Turkey was the principal source of imports (accounting for 21.1% of the total), followed by Russia (18.3%); other major sources were Azerbaijan, Germany and Ukraine. The principal market for exports in that year was Russia (accounting for 28.5% of the total), while Turkey purchased 26.6% of exports; other important purchasers were Turkmenistan, the United Kingdom and Switzerland. The principal exports in 2002 were aircraft, iron and steel scrap, unwrought or semi-manufactured gold, and wine and related products. The principal imports in that year were petroleum products, crude petroleum and natural gas, medicines and sugar.

GOVERNMENT FINANCE

In 2002 there was a budgetary deficit of 147.1m. lari (equivalent to 2.0% of GDP). At the end of 2001 Georgia's total external debt was US $1,714m., of which $1,314m. was long-term public debt. The cost of debt-servicing in that year was equivalent to 9.0% of the value of exports of goods and services. The annual rate of inflation averaged 23.9% during 1994–2002. Consumer prices increased by 4.7% in 2001 and by 5.6% in 2002. In 2002 the rate of unemployment was 12.3%, according to the IMF.

INTERNATIONAL ECONOMIC RELATIONS

In 1992 Georgia became a member of the IMF and the World Bank, as well as joining the European Bank for Reconstruction and Development (EBRD). Georgia is also a member of the Organization of the Black Sea Economic Co-operation. In June 2000 Georgia became a full member of the World Trade Organization (WTO).

SURVEY AND PROSPECTS

The collapse of the USSR in 1991 and the outbreak of three armed conflicts in Georgia adversely affected the country's economy. Although the Government embarked on a programme of comprehensive stabilization from 1994, the *de facto* secession of Abkhazia and South Ossetia eroded government control, while declining tax revenues weakened the Government's ability to provide basic services and resulted in accumulating wages and pensions arrears.

Economic progress was severely disrupted by the Russian financial crisis of 1998, but growth had recovered by 2001, when the IMF resumed lending to Georgia, which had been suspended since July 1999. However, the release of funds was disrupted in 2002–03, as the Government failed to comply with the IMF's recommendations, which included the need for budgetary reductions, improved tax-collection methods and the payment of wages and pensions arrears. None the less, a new tax code was adopted in 2003, and Georgia was estimated to have recorded average annual GDP growth of at least 7%. Agreement was also reached on the construction of the planned Baku–Tbilisi–Erzurum natural gas pipeline, and construction work commenced on the BTC export pipeline. However, although the economy was likely to be stimulated in the short term by increased activity in the construction sector and transit fees, in the longer term the country would benefit from greater access to regional markets and, in particular, improved relations with Russia, which in recent years had imposed a visa regime and strict border controls.

There were hopes that the new regime that took office after the removal from power of President Eduard Shevardnadze in November 2003, following flawed parliamentary elections, would implement wide-ranging institutional reforms and undertake measures to eliminate pervasive corruption. To this end, the Government was negotiating international assistance, and the lending programmes of the IMF and the World Bank were expected to resume by mid-2004. Meanwhile, it was important that the Government worked to reduce tensions with the authorities in Ajaria (where a major port, Batumi, was situated), while the energy sector required major reform to counter wide-scale power shortages and the privatization of many large enterprises had still to be implemented.

Germany

The Federal Republic of Germany, established in 1990 upon the unification of the Federal Republic of Germany (FRG, West Germany) and the German Democratic Republic (GDR, East Germany), lies in the heart of Europe. The FRG had been established in 1949 in the US, British and French occupation zones into which Germany had been divided in 1945, while Soviet-occupied Eastern Germany had declared itself the GDR. In 1990, following the first all-German elections since 1933, a coalition Government dominated by the Christlich-Demokratische Union Deutschlands, the Christlich-Soziale Union and the Freie Demokratische Partei was formed. Berlin is the capital. The language is German.

Area and population
Area: 357,027 sq km
Population (mid-2002): 82,495,000
Population density (mid-2002): 231.1 per sq km
Life expectancy (years at birth, 2002): 78.7 (males 75.6; females 81.6)

Finance
GDP in current prices: 2002): US $1,976,240m. ($23,956 per head)
Real GDP growth (2002): 0.2%
Inflation (annual average, 2002): 1.3%
Currency: euro

Economy

In 2002, according to estimates by the World Bank, Germany's gross national income (GNI), measured at average 2000–2002 prices, was US $1,870,383m., equivalent to $22,670 per head (or $26,220 per head on an international purchasing-power parity basis). During 1991–2002, it was estimated, the population increased by an average of 0.3% per year, while Germany's gross domestic product (GDP) per head grew, in real terms, by an average of 1.2% annually. Overall GDP expanded, in real terms, at an average annual rate of 1.5% in 1991–2002; growth was 0.6% in 2001 and 0.2% in 2002.

AGRICULTURE

Agriculture (including hunting, forestry and fishing) engaged 2.5% of the employed labour force in 2002, and provided 1.1% of Germany's GDP in that year. The principal crops are sugar beet, wheat, potatoes and barley. Wine production is also important in western Germany. Agricultural GDP increased, in real terms, at an average annual rate of 1.3% in 1990–2001; it declined by 0.4% in 2000 and expanded by 1.2% in 2001.

INDUSTRY

Industry (including mining, power, manufacturing and construction) engaged 31.9% of the employed labour force and contributed 28.6% of GDP in 2002. Industrial GDP increased at an average annual rate of just 0.1% in 1990–2001; it expanded by 3.8% in 2000 and declined by 1.3% in 2001.

Mining

The mining sector engaged 0.4% of the employed labour force and contributed 2.2% of GDP in 2002. The principal mining activities are the extraction of lignite (low-grade brown coal), hard coal and salts.

Manufacturing

The manufacturing sector employed 23.2% of the employed labour force and provided 22.1% of GDP in 2002. Measured by value of output, the principal branches of manufacturing in 1999 were transport equipment (accounting for 18.3% of the total), non-electric machinery (11.8%), chemical products (10.0%) and food products (9.7%). Passenger motor cars remain an important export. During the 1990s companies specializing in microelectronics and biotechnology performed well in both eastern and western Germany. Real manufacturing GDP remained largely unchanged in 1991–2000; it declined by 1.4% in 1999 and increased by 6.1% in 2001.

Energy

Of the total energy produced in 2001, coal accounted for 51.5% (24.3% was hard coal and 27.2% was lignite, or brown coal, which is primarily used in the eastern Länder), nuclear power accounted for 30.1%, natural gas for 11.7% and petroleum for 0.8%. In

2000 the Government announced plans to abandon the use of nuclear power by 2021; the closure of nuclear reactors began in 2003. In 2002 imports of mineral fuels accounted for 8.1% of Germany's total imports.

SERVICES

Services engaged 65.6% of the employed labour force and contributed 70.2% of GDP in 2002. The GDP of the services sector increased, in real terms, at an average annual rate of 2.4% in 1990–2001: it grew by 3.3% in 2000 and by 1.7% in 2001.

EXTERNAL TRADE

In 2002 Germany recorded a visible trade surplus of US $122,180m., and there was a surplus of $46,590m. on the current account of the balance of payments. More than one-half of Germany's total trade in 2002 was conducted with other countries of the European Union (EU). France is the most significant individual trading partner, supplying 9.5% of imports and purchasing 10.8% of exports in 2002. Other principal sources of imports in that year were the Netherlands (8.3%), the USA (7.7%) and the United Kingdom (6.4%); the other major purchasers of exports were the USA (10.3%), the United Kingdom (8.4%) and Italy (7.3%). The principal imports in 2002 were machinery and transport equipment (accounting for 37.8% of the total, with road vehicles and parts comprising 9.5%), basic manufactures (12.6%), miscellaneous manufactured articles (12.4%), and chemicals and related products (10.5%). The principal exports were machinery and transport equipment (accounting for 52.0% of the total, with road vehicles and parts comprising 18.8%), basic manufactures (13.5%), chemicals and related products (12.3%), and miscellaneous manufactured articles (9.7%).

GOVERNMENT FINANCE

The budgetary deficit for 2001 totalled €49,612m. (equivalent to 2.4% of GDP). Annual inflation averaged 2.2% during 1991–2002. Consumer prices rose by an annual average of 2.4% in 2001 and 1.3% in 2002. Some 8.7% of the labour force were unemployed in April 2002.

INTERNATIONAL ECONOMIC RELATIONS

Germany is a member of the EU and of the Organisation for Economic Co-operation and Development (OECD).

SURVEY AND PROSPECTS

In the opening years of the 21st century Germany's economy stagnated, while the budgetary deficit, which had persisted since unification a decade earlier, continued to cause problems. In both 2002 and 2003 Germany's annual budgetary deficit was greater than the ceiling of 3% of GDP permitted under the terms of the EU's Stability and Growth Pact (SGP). Together with France, which had also exceeded the limit, Germany persuaded other EU member states to allow a suspension of the SGP to allow for economic recovery. However, in January 2004 lawyers acting on behalf of the European Commission announced that they were to launch punitive legal action against Germany and France for breaching the terms of the SGP.

Analysts predicted that Germany would exceed the 3% limit yet again in 2004. According to the Deutsches Institut für Wirtschaftsforschung (DIW—German Institute for Economic Research), Germany's output decreased slightly in the first half of 2003, largely owing to adverse international conditions, including the continued appreciation of the euro, which suppressed external demand and precipitated a decrease in exports, and the uncertainty generated by the conflict in Iraq. Germany's domestic economy was also weak, with the rate of employment continuing to fall and disposable income registering only a slight increase. Moreover, the propensity of households to save remained high, not least because of widespread uncertainty regarding the consequences of the 'Agenda 2010' reforms. This was accompanied by gloomy prospects for businesses and a further decline in capital investment.

Some signs of improvement emerged in mid-2003, however, as the global economic recovery, initially predicted to take place in the first half of the year, gradually began to materialize (particularly in the USA). An economic upturn was also predicted to take place during 2004 in Germany, which was expected to benefit from expansionary monetary policy in the euro zone. Moreover, by early 2004 a rise in share prices and improved earnings in the banking sector had resulted in better financial conditions for businesses. The uncertainty caused by the Iraq crisis, which had paralyzed the economy for the first half of 2003, had abated, and business confidence was returning. The recovery was, however, still hampered by several factors. The appreciation of the euro continued to curb exports and favour imports, fiscal policy was to remain restrictive in 2004, and tax cuts in 2004 were to be counterbalanced by reductions in government spending and by the requisite diminution in tax concessions. As a result, the increase in the real income of private households was to be modest. As long as the propensity to save remained strong, private consumption was expected to increase only very gradually. Accordingly, the DIW predicted that GDP would stagnate in 2003 and would rise only moderately in 2004.

Ghana

The Republic of Ghana lies on the west coast of Africa. Ghana was granted independence, within the Commonwealth, in 1957. From 1966 government alternated between civilian and military regimes. In 1981 Flight-Lt Jerry Rawlings seized power for a second time. In 1992 Rawlings was elected President as a civilian, while the National Democratic Coalition (NDC) secured the majority of seats in multi-party legislative elections. Both President Rawlings and the NDC were successful at elections held in 1996. In 2000 the New Patriotic Party became the largest parliamentary party, while John Kufuor was elected as President. The capital is Accra. English is the official language.

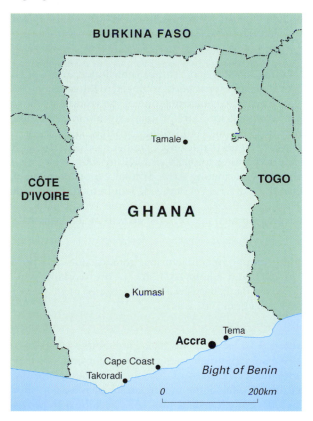

Area and population
Area: 238,537 sq km
Population (mid-2002): 20,070,910
Population density (mid-2002): 84.1 per sq km
Life expectancy (years at birth, 2002): 57.6 (males 56.3; females 58.8)

Finance
GDP in current prices: 2002): US $6,021m. ($300 per head)
Real GDP growth (2002): 4.5%
Inflation (annual average, 2002): 14.8%
Currency: new cedi

Economy

In 2002, according to estimates by the World Bank, Ghana's gross national income (GNI), measured at average 2000–02 prices, was US $6,489m., equivalent to $270 per head (or $2,000 on an international purchasing-power parity basis). During 1990–2002, it was estimated, the population increased at an average annual rate of 2.4%, while gross domestic product (GDP) per head increased, in real terms, by an average of 1.9% per year. Overall GDP increased at an average annual rate of 4.3% in 1990–2002; growth in 2002 was 4.6%.

AGRICULTURE
Agriculture (including forestry and fishing) contributed 39.2% of GDP in 2002. An estimated 56.6% of the labour force were employed in the sector in 2001. The principal cash crops are cocoa beans (Ghana being one of the world's leading producers, and exports of which accounted for 31.6% of total exports in 1999, although their contribution declined to 15.8% in 2000), coffee, bananas, cassava, oil palm, coconuts, limes, kola nuts and shea-nuts (karité nuts). Timber production is also important, with the forestry sector accounting for 4.4% of GDP in 2002, and cork and wood, and manufactures thereof, contributing 9.0% of total export earnings in 2000. Fishing satisfies more than three-quarters of domestic requirements, and contributed 4.9% of GDP in 2002. During 1990–2002, according to the World Bank, agricultural GDP increased at an average annual rate of 3.4%; growth in 2002 was 4.1%.

INDUSTRY
Industry (including mining, manufacturing, construction and power) contributed 28.2% of GDP in 2002, and employed 12.8% of the working population in 1984. According to the World Bank, industrial GDP increased at an average annual rate of 3.1% in 1990–2002; growth in 2002 was 6.3%.

Mining
Mining contributed 5.3% of GDP in 2002, and employed 0.5% of the working population in 1984. Gold and diamonds are the major minerals exported, although Ghana also exploits large reserves of bauxite and manganese ore. According to central bank figures, the GDP of the mining sector increased by an average of 3.7% per year in 1993–2002; growth in 2002 was 4.5%, according to provisional figures.

Manufacturing
Manufacturing contributed 10.1% of GDP in 2002, and employed 10.9% of the working population in 1984. The most important sectors are food processing, textiles, vehicles, cement, paper, chemicals and petroleum. According to the World Bank, manufacturing GDP declined at an average annual rate of 1.8% in 1990–2002; the GDP of the sector remained constant in 2002.

Energy

According to figures published by the World Bank, some 91.7% of Ghana's production of electricity was from hydroelectric power in 2000, with the Akosombo and Kpong plants being the major sources. Low rainfall resulted in a severe energy crisis in 1998, prompting the Government to accelerate plans for the further development of thermal power. In August 1999 the Governments of Ghana, Benin, Togo and Nigeria agreed jointly to finance the West African Gas Pipeline, which was to supply natural gas from Nigeria to the three recipient countries. The project was scheduled to be completed in 2005. Imports of fuel comprised 22.7% of the total value of merchandise imports in 2001. Electricity is exported to Benin and Togo.

SERVICES

The services sector contributed 32.6% of GDP in 2002, and engaged 26.1% of the working population in 1984. According to the World Bank, the GDP of the services sector increased at an average annual rate of 5.5% in 1990–2002; growth in 2002 was 4.4%.

EXTERNAL TRADE

In 2002 Ghana recorded a visible trade deficit of US $689.9m., and there was a deficit of $30.6m. on the current account of the balance of payments. In 2000 the principal source of imports was Nigeria (10.9%); other major sources were the United Kingdom, the USA and Germany. Switzerland was the principal market for exports (taking 23.5% of the total) in that year; other important purchasers were the United Kingdom, the Netherlands and the USA. The principal exports in 2000 were gold (which accounted for 36.7% of total export earnings), cocoa beans and timber and timber products. The principal imports in 2000 were machinery and transport equipment, petroleum products, basic manufactures, and food and live animals.

GOVERNMENT FINANCE

Ghana's overall budget deficit for 2002 was 3,310,900m. cedis (equivalent to 6.8% of GDP). Ghana's external debt totalled US $6,759m. at the end of 2001, of which $5,921m. was long-term public debt. In the same year the cost of debt-servicing was equivalent to 12.7% of exports of goods and services. In 1990–2002 the average annual rate of inflation was 25.3%. Consumer prices increased by 14.8% in 2002. In 1995 some 41,000 people were registered as unemployed in Ghana.

INTERNATIONAL ECONOMIC RELATIONS

Ghana is a member of the Economic Community of West African States (ECOWAS), of the International Cocoa Organization (ICCO), and of the International Coffee Organization (ICO).

SURVEY AND PROSPECTS

Although Ghana's economy has made steady progress since the transfer to civilian rule in 1992, it remains vulnerable to unfavourable weather conditions and to fluctuations in international commodity prices. In May 1999 the IMF approved a three-year Enhanced Structural Adjustment Facility (subsequently renamed the Poverty Reduction and Growth Facility—PRGF), equivalent to US $209.4m., in support of the Government's economic reform programme.

Economic concerns, following a sustained fall in prices of gold and cocoa during 1999–2000, were widely regarded as being a major factor in ensuring the election to the presidency, in December 2000, of John Kufuor, who was perceived to be a proponent of greater economic reform, particularly closer monitoring of public expenditure. The price of petroleum and electricity and water tariffs were significantly increased during 2001, and by the end of the year the state-owned water and electricity companies were reportedly able to cover their operating costs.

In February 2002 it was announced that Ghana was to receive a total of some $3,700m. in debt-service relief from its creditors over a period of 20 years, under the initiative of the IMF and the World Bank for heavily indebted poor countries (HIPCs). It was forecast that this would allowe Ghana to reduce debt-servicing payments from an annual average of $350m. in 1997–2000 to an annual average of $230m. in 2002–2004.

In May 2003 the IMF approved a new three-year arrangement under the PRGF, amounting to some $258m., and also agreed to provide Ghana with additional assistance of some $22m. under the enhanced HIPC initiative. Following the first review of economic performance under the PRGF in December, the IMF commended Ghana's progress, noting particularly the restoration of fiscal discipline and improved levels of official reserves.

In 2003 the Government adopted a policy of price adjustment for petroleum, electricity and water in an attempt to halt losses in the public enterprises responsible for these sectors, and the liberalization of petroleum prices, under a deregulation programme, was planned for mid-2004. The value of exports of gold and cocoa increased signicantly in 2003, to an estimated $770m. and $772m. (compared with $380m. in 2001), respectively, as a result of a strong recovery in international prices for these commodities in 2002–03. The quantity of goods being shipped through Ghana's ports also increased dramatically in 2003, largely owing to continuing instability in Côte d'Ivoire.

In January 2004 it was announced that Ghana had achieved three of the four convergence criteria required for participation in a proposed West African Monetary Zone, which was scheduled to be inaugurated in July 2005 with the launch of a common currency, to be known as the 'eco'. GDP growth of 4.9% was estimated for 2003, and inflation of 13.8% was forecast for 2004.

Gibraltar

The City of Gibraltar lies in southern Europe. Spain claims Gibraltar as a part of its territory, while the United Kingdom maintains that the Treaty of Utrecht (1713) granted sovereignty over Gibraltar to the United Kingdom in perpetuity (with the stipulation that, if the United Kingdom relinquished the colony, it would be returned to Spain). The 1969 Constitution contained a provision that the British Government would never enter into arrangements whereby the people of Gibraltar would pass under the sovereignty of another state against their freely and democratically expressed wishes. Gibraltar has the status of a United Kingdom Overseas Territory. English is the official language.

Area and population
Area: 6 sq km
Population (1998): 27,025
Population density (1998): 4,158 per sq km

Finance
Inflation (annual average, 2002): 0.7%
Currency: Gibraltar pound

Economy

In 1999/2000 Gibraltar's gross domestic product (GDP), measured at current prices, was £411m., equivalent to £15,120 per head. Gibraltar's population totalled some 28,231 at the census of May 2001.

AGRICULTURE

Gibraltar lacks agricultural land and natural resources, and the territory is dependent on imports of foodstuffs and fuels. Foodstuffs were estimated to account for 12% of total imports (excluding petroleum products) in 1997.

INDUSTRY

The industrial sector (including manufacturing, construction and power) employed 16.6% of the working population in 1997.

Manufacturing

Manufacturing employed 3.3% of the working population in 1997. The most important sectors are shipbuilding and ship-repairs, and small-scale domestic manufacturing (mainly bottling, coffee-processing, pottery and handicrafts).

Energy

Gibraltar is dependent on imported petroleum for its energy supplies. Mineral fuels (excluding petroleum products) accounted for about 41.0% of the value of total imports in 1997.

SERVICES

Tourism and banking make a significant contribution to the economy. In 1997 revenue from tourism was estimated at US $300m. Visitor arrivals by air in 2003 totalled some 133,000, according to official figures, around double the yearly figures recorded in the mid-1990s. The number of visitor arrivals via the land frontier also reached a record high in 2003; 7,205,815 people crossed into Gibraltar during that year. In 1997 the financial sector employed about 12% of the working population. Several Spanish banks have established offices in Gibraltar, encouraging the growth of the territory as an 'offshore' banking centre, while the absence of taxes for non-residents has also encouraged the use of Gibraltar as a financial centre. The value of bank deposits increased by more than 480% in the period 1987–95. By March 2003 there were 18 banks and 31 licensed insurance companies operating in Gibraltar. In November 2002, however, the European Commission (EC) ruled that Gibraltar's tax-free status was illegal and ordered Gibraltar to close its tax 'haven', which was unique in the European Union (EU). Tax reforms subsequently negotiated with the Organisation for Economic Co-operation and Development (OECD) were awaiting approval by the EC in 2004. In April 2004 it appeared likely that the new tax regime would be rejected by the EC; it was reported that Peter Caruana, Gibraltar's Chief Minister, had written to the British Government suggesting that the territory might leave the EU in order to maintain its tax privileges.

EXTERNAL TRADE

In 1997 Gibraltar recorded a visible trade deficit of £173m. In that year the principal source of imports was the United Kingdom (accounting for 57% of the total). Other major trading partners included Spain, Japan and the Netherlands. The principal imports in 1997 were mineral fuels and manufactured goods. The principal re-exports in that year were petroleum products, manufactured goods and wines, spirits, malt and tobacco.

GOVERNMENT FINANCE

In the year ending 31 March 1999 there was a budgetary deficit of £30.7m. The annual rate of inflation averaged 2.7% during 1990–2001. The average annual rate was 1.1% in 2000 and 1.8% in 2001. According to the British Foreign and Commonwealth Office, the average annual rate of inflation stood at 1.7% in 2002. An estimated 4.0% of the labour force were unemployed in 1998.

INTERNATIONAL ECONOMIC RELATIONS

Gibraltar joined the European Community (EC—now EU) with the United Kingdom in 1973.

SURVEY AND PROSPECTS

The Gibraltar economy is based on revenue from the British defence forces, tourism, shipping, and banking and finance. In 1988 the Gibraltar Government declared its aim to develop the territory as an 'offshore' financial centre, to stimulate private investment, and to promote the tourism sector. A project to build a new financial and administrative centre on land reclaimed from the sea commenced in 1990, and in the same year a Financial Services Commission was appointed to regulate financial activities in Gibraltar. In 1994, following the reduction in British military personnel in Gibraltar, revenue from the British defence forces (which had accounted for some 60% of the economy in 1985) contributed only 10% to total government revenue. In 1999 there was a sudden increase in gambling outlets in Gibraltar, as leading operations transferred from the United Kingdom. By mid-2000 the Government had issued seven new licences.

Greece

The Hellenic Republic lies in south-eastern Europe. In 1967 Greece's constitutional monarchy was overthrown by army officers. Col Georgios Papadopoulos dominated the new regime, which banned all political activity. In 1973 Papadopoulos became President of a newly declared republic, but was then himself overthrown in a coup. Civilian rule resumed in 1974. From 1981 until 1989 the Panhellenic Socialist Movement (PASOK) governed. It was succeeded, in 1989, by a coalition administration formed by the Left Coalition and the New Democracy Party (ND), which was succeeded, in turn, by an ND Government. PASOK was returned to office in 1993, 1996 and 2000, but was removed from power by ND at elections held in March 2004. Athens is the capital. The language is Greek.

Area and population

Area: 131,957 sq km
Population (mid-2002): 10,630,700
Population density (mid-2002): 80.6 per sq km
Life expectancy (years at birth, 2002): 78.4 (males 75.8; females 81.1)

Finance
GDP in current prices: 2002): US $132,834m. ($12,495 per head)
Real GDP growth (2002): 4.0%
Inflation (annual average, 2002): 3.6%
Currency: euro

Economy

In 2002, according to estimates by the World Bank, Greece's gross national income (GNI), measured at average 2000–02 prices, was US $123,906m., equivalent to $11,660 per head (or $18,240 per head on an international purchasing-power parity basis). During 1990–2002, it was estimated, the population increased at an average annual rate of 0.4%, while gross domestic product (GDP) per head increased, in real terms, at an average annual rate of 2.2%. Overall GDP increased, in real terms, at an average annual rate of 2.6% in 1990–2002. Real GDP increased by 4.1% in 2001 and by 3.8% in 2002.

AGRICULTURE
Agriculture (including hunting, forestry and fishing) contributed some 7.1% of GDP in 2001, and engaged 15.8% of the employed labour force in 2002. The principal cash crops are fruit and vegetables (which, together, accounted for 10.4% of total export earnings in 2001), cereals, sugar beet and tobacco. Real agricultural GDP increased at an average annual rate of 1.7% in 1990–2000; the GDP of the agricultural sector increased by 3.8% in 1999 and by 0.4% in 2000.

INDUSTRY
Industry (including mining, manufacturing, utilities and construction) provided 21.6% of GDP in 2001, and engaged 22.5% of the employed labour force in 2002. During 1990–2000 industrial GDP increased at an average annual rate of 1.1%, in real terms; sectoral GDP increased by 2.3% in 1999 and by 4.6% in 2000. Following the International Olympic Committee's—IOC announcement, in 1997, that the 2004 Olympic Games would be held in Athens, public expenditure on infrastructure projects stimulated growth in the construction industry. Construction accounted for 7.8% of GDP in 2001.

Mining
Mining and quarrying contributed 0.7% of GDP in 2001, and engaged 0.5% of the employed labour force in 2002. Mineral fuels and lubricants, iron and steel, and aluminium and aluminium alloys are the major mineral and metal exports. Lignite, magnesite, silver ore and marble are also mined. In addition, Greece has small reserves of uranium and natural gas.

Manufacturing
Manufacturing provided 13.4% of GDP in 2001, and engaged 13.7% of the employed labour force in 2002. The GDP of the manufacturing sector increased, in real terms, by an annual average of 0.6% in 1990–98; manufacturing production increased by an annual average of 1.6% in 1998–2002.

Energy

Energy is derived principally from lignite, which accounted for 64.2% of production in 2000, followed by petroleum (16.6%) and natural gas (11.1%). Greece is exploiting an offshore petroleum deposit in the north-eastern Aegean Sea. Solar power resources are also being developed. Mineral fuels represented 15.2% of the total value of imports in 2001.

SERVICES

The services sector contributed 71.3% of GDP in 2001, and engaged 61.7% of the employed labour force in 2002. Tourism is an important source of foreign exchange. In 2002 visitor arrivals totalled 14.2m., while receipts from the tourist sector reached US $9,741m. (an increase of 5.6%, compared with the previous year). During 1990–2000 the GDP of the services sector increased, in real terms, at an average annual rate of 2.8%; sectoral GDP increased by 3.5% in 1999 and by 4.4% in 2000.

EXTERNAL TRADE

In 2002 Greece recorded a visible trade deficit of US $21,452m., and there was a deficit of $10,405m. on the current account of the balance of payments. In 2001 the principal source of imports was Germany (13.9%), closely followed by Italy (12.2%); other major sources were France (including Monaco), the Netherlands and the United Kingdom. The principal market for exports in that year was also Germany (11.3%); other major purchasers were Italy, the United Kingdom, the USA, Bulgaria and Cyprus. The principal exports in 2001 were basic manufactures (in particular, non-ferrous metals), miscellaneous manufactured articles (especially clothing and accessories), food and live animals, machinery and transport equipment, mineral fuels and lubricants, chemicals and crude materials. The principal imports were machinery and transport equipment (most notably road vehicles and parts), mineral fuels and lubricants (mainly petroleum and petroleum products), basic manufactures, chemicals, miscellaneous manufactured articles, and food and live animals.

GOVERNMENT FINANCE

In 2002 there was a budgetary deficit of €1,743m. (equivalent to 1.2% of GDP), according to provisional figures. Greece's total public external debt was estimated at €148,023m. at the end of 2002. In 1999 the cost of debt-servicing was equivalent to 9% of GDP. In 1990–2002 the average annual rate of inflation was 8.3%; consumer prices increased by 3.4% in 2001 and by 3.6% in 2002. The official rate of unemployment was 9.6% in 2002.

INTERNATIONAL ECONOMIC RELATIONS

Greece is a member of the European Union (EU), the Organisation for Economic Co-operation and Development (OECD) and the Organization of the Black Sea Economic Co-operation.

SURVEY AND PROSPECTS

From the second half of the 1990s the Government's priority was to ensure the admittance of Greece to EU economic and monetary union (EMU) by 2001. The projected budgetary deficit for 1999 met the target for EMU entry and in February–March 2000 a rate of inflation of 2% was recorded, thereby qualifying Greece for full EMU membership from 1 January 2001. Greece thus became the 12th member country in the so-called 'euro-zone', and the common European currency, the euro, duly replaced the drachma as the country's legal tender from 1 January 2002. Although Greece did not satisfy the requirement stipulated in the Maastricht Treaty that the ratio of government debt to GDP be less than 60% (it was estimated at 104.9% in 2002), the Government aimed to achieve this objective by the end of the decade.

A programme of privatization to generate revenue, with the aim of reducing the level of public debt, demonstrated some progress in 2003. The average rate of inflation remained at about 3.4% in 2003 (much higher than the EU average), but was projected to decline slightly in 2004–05, while the rate of unemployment had declined steadily from 1999. Although the Government's policy of fiscal discipline was largely successful, it was made more difficult by requirements for increased spending on social security. Estimated growth in GDP of 4.7% in 2003 (higher than the anticipated level) was stimulated by construction activity relating to Greece's hosting of the Olympic Games in August 2004 and by EU structural aid. Meanwhile, improved relations with Turkey resulted in a project for the construction of an Ankara (Turkey)–Kotomini (Greece) pipeline (agreed in March 2002).

The stabilization of the countries of the former Yugoslavia and the Balkans also provided Greece with an opportunity to expand its commercial influence in the region. However, the admission to the EU of several central and eastern European countries in May 2004 was to result in a reduction in EU transfers to Greece, as funds were to be diverted to new members.

With the staging of the Olympic Games in August 2004, investment growth was expected to continue in that year, while tourist arrivals were projected to increase sharply (after the adverse effect on tourism of US-led military action in Iraq in early 2003 and fears of possible terrorist attacks in the region).

At legislative elections on 7 March 2004 the socialist Government was removed from office by the centre-right New Democracy Party of Konstantinos Karamanlis. Priorities for the new administration included the completion of infrastructure projects, the promotion of energy-market liberalization and measures to address public-sector corruption. At that time it was widely reported that progress on around one-half of the construction projects under way in Athens (including the roof of the main Olympic stadium) was inadequate, prompting concern that they would not be completed on schedule. Closer integration with the EU and a continued improve-ment in relations with neighbouring countries was regarded as essential, with a resolution of the issue of Cyprus critical to Turkey's prospects of accession to the EU and, consequently, long-term good relations with Greece.

Greenland

Greenland, the world's largest island, lies in the North Atlantic Ocean, east of Canada. Greenland came under Danish rule in 1380. In 1953 it became part of the Kingdom of Denmark. In 1972 Greenlanders were opposed to joining the European Community (EC, now European Union), but were bound by Denmark's decision to join. From 1979 the island assumed full administration of its internal affairs. In 1982 Greenland's voters opted to withdraw from the EC; Greenland was subsequently accorded the status of an overseas territory in association with the Community. Nuuk (Gothåb) is the capital. Greenlandic and Danish are the official languages.

Area and population
Area: 2,166,086 sq km
Population (mid-2001): 60,000
Population density (mid-2001): 0.03 per sq km
Life expectancy (years at birth, 1996–2000): 65.4 (males 62.8; females 68.0)

Finance
GDP in current prices: 1998): 7,706m. kroner (137,421 kroner per head)
Real GDP growth (1998): 7.8%
Inflation (annual average, 2002): 4.1%
Currency: krone

Economy

In 1994, according to preliminary official estimates, Greenland's gross national product (GNP) was 6,381m. kroner, equivalent to some 114,800 kroner per head. The population increased at an average annual rate of 0.1% in 1990–2000. The economy enjoyed overall growth during the 1970s and 1980s, but gross domestic product (GDP) declined by 9%, in real terms, in 1990, and continued to decline significantly (owing to depleted fish stocks and the discontinuation of lead and zinc mining) until 1994 and 1995, when real growth rates of 5% and 3%, respectively, were recorded. GDP increased, in real terms, by 1.5% in 1996, 1.4% in 1997 and by 7.8% in 1998.

AGRICULTURE

Agriculture (including animal husbandry, fishing and hunting) employed 7.9% of the working population in 2000. Fishing dominates the commercial economy, as well as being important to the traditional way of life. In 2000 the fishing industry accounted for 95.6% of Greenland's total export revenue. The industry, including the processing of the catch, employed 25.3% of the paid labour force in 1996. The cod catch has declined substantially, however, since 1989. The traditional occupation of the Greenlanders is seal-hunting, which remains important in the north. The only feasible agricultural activity in the harsh climate is livestock-rearing, and only sheep-farming has proved to be of any commercial significance. There are also herds of domesticated reindeer.

INDUSTRY

Industry (including mining, manufacturing, construction and public works) employed some 18.6% of those in paid employment in 2000.

Mining

Mining earned 13.0% of total export revenue in 1990, but in 2000 employed less than 0.1% of the working population. A Swedish company extracted lead, zinc and some silver at the important mine at Marmorilik in the north-west. The mine was closed, however, in 1990. In November 2001 an Australian company announced that it was to establish a mine to extract niobium (a metal used in the manufacture of electronic components) in Greenland. In recent years there have been several discoveries of petroleum, natural gas and other mineral deposits (including gold). In May 2003 the Bureau of Minerals and Petroleum announced that it would open a new licensing round in 2004 for petroleum exploration off the coast of Greenland; 10-year licences were to be offered from April for four selected offshore areas. Previously, however, only three companies had taken licences in the area, as drilling off Greenland was expensive, owing to the depth of the water and the climate.

Manufacturing

Manufacturing is mainly dependent upon the fishing industry. Manufacturing employed 9.7% of the working population in 2000; 8.0% of the working population were employed in the fishing industries.

Energy

Water power (melt water from the ice-cap and glaciers) is an important potential source of electricity. All mineral fuels are imported. Mineral fuels accounted for 18.7% of total imports in 2000.

SERVICES

The services sector employed 73.6% of the working population in 2000; it is dominated by public administration, which alone employed 48.7% of the working population in that year.

EXTERNAL TRADE

In 2001 Greenland recorded a trade deficit of 459.8m. kroner. The principal trading partner remains Denmark, although its monopoly on trade ceased in 1950. Denmark supplied 66.0% of imports and received 84.4% of exports in 2001. Trade is still dominated by companies owned by the Landsstyre. The principal exports are fish and fish products, and the principal imports are machinery and transport equipment.

GOVERNMENT FINANCE

Greenland is dependent upon large grants from the central Danish Government. In 2000 central government expenditure on Greenland included some 2,725m. kroner in the form of a direct grant to the Landsstyre. Greenland has few debts, and also receives valuable revenue from the European Union (EU), for fishing licences. The annual rate of inflation averaged 0.9% in 1995–99, and stood at 0.7% in 1999, 1.7% in 2000 and 2.8% in 2001. In 2002 an estimated 6.5% of the labour force were unemployed.

INTERNATIONAL ECONOMIC RELATIONS

Greenland, although a part of the Kingdom of Denmark, withdrew from the European Community (now EU) in 1985. It remains a territory in association with the EU, however, and has preferential access to European markets. The loss of EU development aid has been offset by the annual payment for member countries to retain fishing rights in Greenlandic waters.

SURVEY AND PROSPECTS

Greenland's economy is dominated by the fishing industry, but remains a subsistence, barter economy for a large part of the population. Migration to the towns and the rejection of a traditional life-style by many young people have, however, created new social and economic problems. Dependence on a single commodity leaves the economy vulnerable to the effects of depletion of fish stocks and fluctuating international prices. Any development or progress is possible only with Danish aid, which is already fundamental to Greenlandic finances. In an effort to generate revenue from the tourism industry, the Landsstyre undertook, in 1990, to achieve a target of 35,000 tourist arrivals (equivalent to 500m. kroner) annually by 2005; by 1994 the campaign was showing positive results and tourist arrivals had doubled compared with levels in previous years.

Grenada

Grenada is the most southerly of the Windward Islands, in the West Indies. The country also includes some of the islands known as the Grenadines. In 1979 the Prime Minister, Eric Gairy was replaced in a coup by the leader of the New Jewel Movement, Maurice Bishop. Bishop's execution in 1983 by forces of the People's Revolutionary Army prompted an invasion by (mainly) US forces. General elections held since 1984 have been won on four occasions by the New National Party, most recently in 2003. St George's is the capital. The majority of the population speak English.

Area and population
Area: 344 sq km
Population (mid-2002): 101,710
Population density (mid-2002): 295.2 per sq km
Life expectancy (years at birth, 2002): 67.4 (males 65.9; females 68.8)

Finance

GDP in current prices: 2002: US $414m. ($4,070 per head)
Real GDP growth (2002): –0.5%
Inflation (annual average, 2002): 1.6%
Currency: Eastern Caribbean dollar

Economy

In 2002, according to estimates by the World Bank, Grenada's gross national income (GNI), measured at average 2000–02 prices, was US $356.4m., equivalent to US $3,500 per head (or US $6,330 per head on an international purchasing-power parity basis). In 1990–2002 Grenada's population increased at an average rate of 0.7% per year, while gross domestic product (GDP) per head increased, in real terms, by an average of 1.8% per year. Overall GDP increased, in real terms, at an average annual rate of 2.8% in 1990–2002. Real GDP decreased by 3.8% in 2001 and by a further 1.1% in 2002.

AGRICULTURE

According to preliminary figures, agriculture (including hunting, forestry and fishing) contributed 9.6% of GDP in 2002. The sector engaged 13.8% of the employed labour force in 1998. Grenada, known as the Spice Island of the Caribbean, is one of the world's largest producers of nutmeg (Indonesia produces some 75% of the world's total). In 2002, according to preliminary IMF data, sales of nutmeg and mace (the pungent red membrane around the nut) accounted for 23.1% of Grenada's domestic export earnings. The other principal cash crops are cocoa and bananas. Exports of bananas were suspended in early 1997 by the Windward Islands Banana Development and Exporting Company (WIBDECO) because of poor quality, but were permitted to resume in late 1998, following a rehabilitation programme. Nevertheless, exports of bananas were still greatly reduced in 1999–2002. Livestock production, for domestic consumption, is important on Carriacou. There are extensive timber reserves on the island of Grenada; forestry development is strictly controlled and involves a programme of reafforestation. Exports of fish contributed an estimated 7.4% of domestic export earnings in 2002. Agricultural GDP increased at an average annual rate of 0.2% in 1990–2002. The sector decreased by 2.8% in 2001, but expanded by 19.0% in 2002.

INDUSTRY

Industry (mining, manufacturing, construction and utilities) provided 21.1% of GDP in 2002 and engaged 23.9% of the employed labour force in 1998.

Mining

The mining sector accounted for only 0.2% of employment in 1998 and 0.4% of GDP in 2002.

Manufacturing

Manufacturing, which contributed 6.3% of GDP in 2002 and employed 7.4% of the working population in 1998, consists mainly of the processing of agricultural products and of cottage industries producing garments and spice-based items. A nutmeg oil distillation plant commenced production in 1995, and exports of the oil earned some EC $2m. in that year. From the late 1990s the electronic component sector gained in significance. Exports from this sector accounted for nearly two-fifths (39.2%) of domestic merchandise exports in 2002. Rum, soft drinks, paints and varnishes, household paper products and the tyre-retreading industries are also important. Manufacturing GDP increased by an average of 4.6% per year in 1990–2002. The sector's GDP decreased by 7.6% in 2001 and by 4.0% in 2002. Overall, industrial GDP increased by an annual average of 4.8% in 1990–2002. The GDP of the industrial sector decreased by 9.5% in 2001, but increased by 0.3% in 2002.

Energy

Grenada is dependent upon imports for its energy requirements, and in 2002 fuel accounted for an estimated 9.9% of the total cost of imports.

SERVICES

The services sector contributed 69.2% of GDP in 2002, when hotels and restaurants accounted for some 7.6% of GDP. Tourism receipts totalled around EC $240.1m. in 2002. From the mid-1980s until the late 1990s Grenada's tourist industry experienced a rapid expansion. However, total visitor arrivals declined dramatically in the early 21st century. The decrease was mainly owing to a massive fall in cruise-ship arrivals (26.6% in 2000, 18.2% in 2001 and 8.0% in 2002). Stop-over arrivals, however, remained relatively stable in all three years. Of total stop-over visitors (excluding non-resident Grenadians) in 2001, 29.7% were from the USA, 26.3% from the United Kingdom and 25.4% from Caribbean countries. The GDP of the services sector increased at an average annual rate of 3.1% in 1990–2002; however, the sector contracted by 1.0% in 2001 and by a further 2.8% in 2002.

EXTERNAL TRADE

In 2002 Grenada recorded a visible trade deficit of EC $385.97m. and there was a deficit of $319.10m. on the current account of the balance of payments. In 2002 the principal source of imports was the USA, accounting for 45.8% of the total, according to preliminary figures. The USA is also the principal market for exports, taking 38.9% of the total in the same year. The principal exports are electronic components and nutmeg. The principal imports in 2002 were machinery and transport equipment, basic manufactures and foodstuffs. The trade deficit is partly offset by earnings from tourism, capital receipts and remittances from Grenadians working abroad.

GOVERNMENT FINANCE

In 2002 there was an overall budgetary deficit of EC $210.2m. (equivalent to 19.3% of GDP). Grenada's total external debt was US $215.0m. at the end of 2001, of which US $160.7m. was long-term public debt. In 2001 the cost of debt-servicing was equivalent to 5.8% of the value of exports of goods and services. The average annual rate of inflation was 2.2% in 1990–2002; consumer prices increased by 3.2% in 2001 and by an estimated 3.0% in 2002. According to IMF estimates, 12.2% of the labour force were unemployed at the end of 2002, although some opposition politicians claimed the real rate was in excess of 20%. Grenada receives some EC $21m. per year in remittances from more than 100,000 Grenadians living abroad, especially in Canada, the USA and the United Kingdom.

INTERNATIONAL ECONOMIC RELATIONS

Grenada is a member of CARICOM. It is also a member of the Economic Commission for Latin America and the Caribbean (ECLAC), the Organization of American States (OAS), the Organisation of Eastern Caribbean States (OECS) and is a signatory of the Cotonou Agreement, the successor arrangement to the Lomé Conventions between the African, Caribbean and Pacific (ACP) countries and the European Union. Grenada is a member of the Eastern Caribbean Securities Exchange (based in Saint Christopher and Nevis).

SURVEY AND PROSPECTS

Grenada's economy remains fairly dependent upon agriculture, which is vulnerable to adverse weather conditions and infestation by pests. In 1990 the economy's susceptibility to the fluctuations in international commodity prices was demonstrated following the breakdown of Grenada's cartel agreement with Indonesia (signed in 1987). The two countries subsequently concluded several informal agreements in an attempt to stabilize the world nutmeg market through closer co-operation. From 1997 a decline in production of nutmeg in Indonesia resulted in higher prices on the external market, stimulating a significant increase in Grenada's output. In 1999 export earnings from nutmeg increased to US $14.9m. (compared with US $8.7m. in 1998). However, this figure had decreased to US $12.8m. by 2002, according to preliminary figures. The need for further economic diversification has recently been underscored by the loss, from 2006, of preferential access to European markets for banana producers of the ACP countries.

In the late 1990s the Government attempted to diversify the economy partly through the expansion of the 'offshore' financial sector. Since the introduction of legislation in 1997, some 900 'offshore' financial companies (including 21 banks) have been registered in Grenada; in September 1999 the creation of a regulatory body, the International Business and Finance Corporation, was announced. In January 2000, moreover, the Government established the Grenada International Financial Services Authority (GIFSA) to regulate the international financial services sector. In the same year, following Grenada's inclusion on international money-laundering and tax 'havens' blacklists and the collapse (and subsequent government takeover) of an 'offshore' bank, the Government introduced measures to strengthen the GIFSA. These included: redoubling efforts to combat money-laundering and drugs-trafficking; the establishment of a bank supervision department to ensure that all financial institutions operated within the norms of the sector; and a review of all existing legislation governing the financial services sector to comply with the requirements of the Organisation for Economic Co-operation and Development (OECD) by March 2001. As part of this effort, the Government has revoked the licences of over 40 'offshore' banks and trusts, and, after making a commitment to move towards the exchange of information in tax investigations by 2005, in March 2002 Grenada was removed from the OECD list. The country was also removed from the FATF list in February 2003 following improvements to the supervisory capacity of the Financial Intelligence Unit, the police force and GIFSA. By May 2003 there were just five 'offshore' banks operating in Grenada; the 'offshore' sector also included 2,775 international business companies at the end of 2002.

The most promising sector of the economy was tourism, from which revenue more than doubled between 1990 and 2000. However, revenue from the sector fell in 2001 as a result of repercussions of the terrorist attacks in the USA in September of that year. Revenues and tourist arrivals recovered in 2002, and in the latter part of that year the Government announced plans to invest EC $15m. in tourism in 2003, in an attempt to further stimulate the sector. Growth in tourism during the 1990s, in turn, stimulated the construction sector, the GDP of which expanded by an annual average of 6.4% in 1990–2000; however, the sector registered a contraction of 19.3% in 2001 and expanded by only 1.0% in 2002. Some 95% of taxpayers were effectively exempted from personal income tax obligations after April 1996, when the Government raised significantly the income threshold for liability for this tax. In 2001 the IMF again urged the Grenadian Government to tighten fiscal policy in order to improve the state of public finances (which continued to suffer from sizeable internal and external debts), warning that otherwise the high economic growth of recent years would become unsustainable. In particular, the IMF called for the removal of discretionary tax concessions. Reduced government revenue and increased salary costs resulted in an increase in the fiscal deficit from 3.2% in 2000 to 8.4% of GDP in 2001, financed mainly through local commercial borrowing and an accumulation of arrears. The deficit was estimated to have widened further, to the equivalent of 19.4% of GDP in 2002, financed mainly through local commercial borrowing and an accumulation of arrears. The economic contraction of 3.8% in 2001 was a result of an international downturn in tourism, lower international prices for nutmeg, reduced production of some other crops, and production cutbacks in a local electronics plant. A further contraction in GDP of 1.1% was recorded in 2002, although a return to positive growth (of around 1%), boosted by a recovering tourism industry and a buoyant construction sector, was anticipated in 2003.

Guadeloupe

Guadeloupe is the most northerly of the Windward Islands group in the West Indies. It was first occupied by the French in 1635, and gained departmental status in 1946. In 1974 Guadeloupe was granted the status of a Region, and an indirectly elected Conseil Régional was formed. As a result of decentralization reforms, direct elections to a new Conseil Régional were held in 1983. In 2001 the French Government declared itself in favour of proposals on greater autonomy presented to it by the Conseil Général and the Conseil Régional. The capital is the town of Basse-Terre. French is the official language.

Area and population
Area: 1,705 sq km
Population (March 1999): 422,496
Population density (March 1999): 247.8 per sq km
Life expectancy (years at birth, 1995–2000): 77.3 (males 73.6; females 80.9)

Finance
GDP in current prices: 1999): US $4,645m. ($10,953 per head)
Real GDP growth (1999): 0.6%
Inflation (annual average, 2002): 2.3%
Currency: euro

Economy

In 2001, according to UN estimates, Guadeloupe's gross domestic product (GDP), measured at current prices, was US $4,460m., equivalent to $10,323 per head. During 1990–2001 GDP increased, in real terms, at an average annual rate of 2.2%; growth in 2001 was 4.6%. Between the censuses of 1990 and 1999, according to provisional figures, the population increased at an average annual rate of 1.0%.

AGRICULTURE
Agriculture, hunting, forestry and fishing contributed an estimated 4.1% of GDP in 1999 and, according to FAO estimates, engaged 2.9% of the economically active population in mid-2001. The principal cash crops are bananas and sugar cane; exports of the former provided 21.9% of total export earnings in 1997, while exports of raw sugar accounted for 23.7% of the total in that year. Yams, sweet potatoes and plantains are the chief subsistence crops. Fishing, mostly at an artisanal level, fulfilled about two-thirds of domestic requirements in the 1990s; shrimp-farming was developed during the 1980s. According to UN estimates, agricultural GDP decreased at an average annual rate of 0.3% in 1990–98; the sector increased by 4.1% in 1998.

INDUSTRY
The industrial sector (including mining, manufacturing, construction and power) contributed an estimated 15.9% of GDP in 1999 and engaged 11.5% of the total labour force in 1998. Manufacturing, mining and power provided some 6.8% of GDP in 1998, while construction contributed 9.1%.

Manufacturing
The main manufacturing activity is food processing, particularly sugar production, rum distillation, and flour-milling. The sugar industry was in decline in the 1990s, owing to deteriorating equipment and a reduction in the area planted with sugar cane (from 20,000 ha in 1980 to 9,600 ha in 1999). Industrial GDP (excluding construction) increased at an average annual rate of 5.2% in 1990–98. Construction expanded at an average rate of 2.2% per year in the same period.

Energy
Of some 700,000 tons of petroleum imported annually, about one-third is used for the production of electricity. Efforts are currently being concentrated on the use of renewable energy resources—notably solar, geothermal and wind power—for energy production; there is also thought to be considerable potential for the use of sugar cane as a means of generating energy in Guadeloupe. Imports of mineral fuels accounted for 5.8% of total expenditure on imports in 1995.

SERVICES

The services sector engaged 52.8% of the total labour force in 1998 and provided an estimated 80% of GDP in 1999. Tourism superseded sugar production in 1988 as the Department's principal source of income, and there is significant potential for the further development of the sector, particularly 'eco-tourism'. In 2000 tourist arrivals totalled 623,134, and receipts from tourism amounted to US $418m. In 2000 more than 70% of arrivals came from metropolitan France or dependent territories.

EXTERNAL TRADE

In 1998 Guadeloupe recorded a trade deficit of 9,999.7m. French francs. In 1997 the principal source of imports (62.9%) was metropolitan France, which was also the principal market for exports (60.7%). Martinique, the USA and Germany are also important trading partners. The principal exports in 1997 were sugar, bananas, boats and rum. The principal imports in 1995 were machinery and transport equipment (mainly road vehicles), food and live animals, miscellaneous manufactured articles, basic manufactures and chemicals.

GOVERNMENT FINANCE

Guadeloupe's budget deficit was estimated by the metropolitan authorities to amount to some 800m. French francs (including arrears) in 1993. Under the 1997 regional budget it was envisaged that expenditure would total 1,700m. French francs. The annual rate of inflation averaged 1.8% in 1990–2002; consumer prices increased by 2.6% in 2001 and by 2.3% in 2002. Some 25.7% of the labour force were unemployed in mid-2002.

INTERNATIONAL ECONOMIC RELATIONS

As an integral part of France, Guadeloupe belongs to the European Union (EU).

SURVEY AND PROSPECTS

Economic growth in Guadeloupe has been restricted by certain inherent problems: its location; the fact that the domestic market is too narrow to stimulate the expansion of the manufacturing base; the lack of primary materials; and the inflated labour and service costs compared with those of neighbouring countries. Economic activity was severely disrupted in 1989, when 'Hurricane Hugo' struck the islands. The French Government undertook to provide more than 2,000m. French francs for reconstruction, and additional aid for the modernization of the sugar industry. The banana-growing sector and the tourist industry, both of which were particularly adversely affected, recovered well. However, Hurricanes Luis and Marilyn, which struck in September 1995, caused severe infrastructural damage.

In the late 1990s Guadeloupe's banana sector was adversely affected by declining prices on the European market, while a dispute between the USA and four major Latin American producers and the EU over the latter's banana import regime also threatened the sector. This dispute was resolved in April 2001 when it was agreed that the quota system currently employed by the EU was to be replaced by a universal tariff system from 2006.

Concern was expressed that tourism in the Guadeloupean dependency of Saint-Martin (an island shared with the Dutch territory of St Maarten) would be adversely affected by the decision of AOM Compagnie Aérienne Française (now Air Liberté) to cease flights to St Maarten in March 2001. Moreover, it was thought that a renewed monopoly on flights by Air France would further affect the tourism sector (the deregulation of air transport in 1986, ending Air France's monopoly on flights to Guadeloupe, was a major factor in attracting more visitors to the main island). In November 2002 the French hotel group Accor announced that it would close its five hotels in Martinque and Guadeloupe, citing high operating costs, poor industrial relations and decreasing tourist arrivals. In early 2003 the French Minister of Overseas Departments announced plans to stimulate the economies of Guadeloupe, Martinique and French Guiana that included the introduction of tax incentives for the hotel sector. Furthermore, in late 2003 it was announced that a subsidiary of Air Caraïbe was to begin an additional air service between Paris and Pointe-à-Pitre.

Guam

Guam is the southernmost and largest of the Mariana Islands, situated some 2,170 km south of Tokyo (Japan) and 5,300 km west of Honolulu (Hawaii). The island was ceded to the USA by Spain in 1898, and in 1950 became an Unincorporated US Territory. In 1970 Guam elected its first Governor, and in 1972 was granted one Delegate to the US House of Representatives. In 1982 voters expressed their support for Commonwealth status. In late 2003 a draft Guam Commonwealth Act still awaited a hearing in the US Congress. English is the official language.

Area and population
Area: 549 sq km
Population (mid-2002): 159,350
Population density (mid-2002): 290.3 per sq km
Life expectancy (years at birth, 2002): 77.8 (males 75.5; females 80.3)

Finance
Inflation (annual average, 2001): −1.3%
Currency: US dollar

Economy

In 2000, according to estimates by the Bank of Hawaii (BOH), Guam's gross national income (GNI), at current prices, was US $2,772.8m., equivalent to $16,575 per head. Between 1988 and 1993, it was estimated, GNI increased, in real terms, at an average rate of some 10% per year, and by 3.9% in 1994. In 1990–2002, according to World Bank figures, the population increased at an average annual rate of 1.5%.

AGRICULTURE

Agriculture (including forestry, fishing and mining) engaged only 0.5% of the employed labour force in 2000. The principal crops cultivated on the island include watermelons, cucumbers, bananas, runner beans, aubergines, squash, tomatoes and papaya. Livestock reared includes pigs, cattle, goats and poultry.

INDUSTRY

The industrial sector accounted for some 15% of gross domestic product (GDP) in 1993. Construction and manufacturing engaged an estimated 8.9% of the employed labour force in 2002. Construction is the dominant industrial activity and is closely related to the tourist industry, which declined significantly in the early 21st century. Construction engaged 6.1% of the employed labour force in 2002. Manufacturing industries, including textile and garment production and boat-building, engaged an estimated 2.8% of the employed labour force in 2002. Guam is a low-duty port and an important distribution point for goods destined for Micronesia. Re-exports constitute a high proportion of Guam's exports, major commodities being petroleum and petroleum products, iron and steel scrap, and eggs.

SERVICES

Service industries dominate the economy, engaging 90.1% of the employed labour force in 2002. The federal and territorial Governments alone employed 27.9% of workers in that year. Tourism is Guam's most important industry, providing 18% of GDP in 1994. In 2002 some 1,058,700 tourists (of whom 74% were Japanese) visited the island, a decrease of 8.7% compared with the previous year. In 1999 tourism earned an estimated US $1,908m.; the sector engaged an estimated 21.4% of the employed labour force in 1994.

EXTERNAL TRADE

The Territory consistently records a visible trade deficit. Total exports were valued at US $75.7m. in 1999, compared with $47.9m. in 1994, in which year imports of petroleum and petroleum products alone cost $163.7m. In 1999 total imports (excluding petroleum and petroleum products) were valued at $38.7m. Japan provided an estimated 53.9% of total imports in 1999.

GOVERNMENT FINANCE

In 2001 total budgetary operational expenditure stood at US $335.6m. and revenue at $446.8m. In 2002 federal expenditure on the territory totalled $1,215.8m., comprising military spending of $561.7m., non-defence expenditure of $552.2m. and other federal assistance of $101.9m. Guam's unemployment rate stood at 11.4% in 2002.

The annual average rate of inflation was 10.1% in 1990–95 and stood at 5.3% in 1995. Consumer prices decreased by 0.5% in 1998 and by 0.3% in 1999.

INTERNATIONAL ECONOMIC RELATIONS

Guam is a member of the Pacific Community and an associate member of the UN's Economic and Social Commission for Asia and the Pacific (ESCAP). In early 1996 Guam joined representatives of the other countries and territories of Micronesia at a meeting in Hawaii, at which a new regional organization, the Council of Micronesian Government Executives, was established. The body aimed to facilitate discussion of economic developments in the region and to examine possibilities for reducing the considerable cost of shipping essential goods between the islands.

SURVEY AND PROSPECTS

In the 1990s Guam's economy benefited from increased foreign investment, notably from Japan and the Republic of Korea. Much of this investment resulted in the rapid expansion of the tourist industry. The island continues to receive considerable financial support from the USA. In 2002 federal government expenditure on Guam reached some US $1,114m., of which $562m. was allocated to US military installations. Considerable interest in establishing an 'offshore' financial centre on Guam has been expressed; the development of such a centre, however, was dependent upon the achievement of Commonwealth status, which would allow the introduction of new tax laws.

In the early 2000s a series of natural disasters, notably Typhoon Pongsona in December 2002, severely damaged the island's infrastructure. Moreover, the tourism sector was badly affected by the repercussions of the suicide attacks on the USA in September 2001, compounded by the continued economic difficulties in Japan (the principal source of the island's visitors). In 2003 the industry continued to stagnate as a result of the war in Iraq and the outbreak of Severe Acute Respiratory Syndrome (SARS) in China and then elsewhere. Meanwhile, the Government faced a growing fiscal shortfall due to declining private sector employment and accelerated rates of emigration (GDP was reported to have contracted by some 25% since the late 1990s). Moreover, the island's new Republican administration was unable to reduce its own employment costs, despite a substantial decline in US federal employment on the island. A series of measures intended to stimulate economic activity and improve public finances, including exemptions in business taxes and increased import duties, were reported to have effected only a limited improvement. In April 2003 the Legislature approved the issuance of some $246m. in new debt aimed at refinancing the Government's pensions and public service provision system. Nevertheless, in early 2004 it was hoped that measures to rehabilitate and diversify the island's attractions would coincide with a recovery in the region's major tourist markets.

Guatemala

The Republic of Guatemala lies in the Central American isthmus. From 1960 civil war was waged in Guatemala between successive (mainly) military regimes and guerrilla insurgencies. In 1986 power was transferred from the military to a civilian Government. Elections held in 1995 were notable for the participation, for the first time in more than 40 years, of the left wing. In 1996 the Government and the main guerrilla grouping, the Unidad Revolucionaria Nacional Guatemalteca, signed a peace treaty, concluding the civil war. The capital is Guatemala City. The official language is Spanish.

Area and population
Area: 108,889 sq km
Population (mid-2002): 11,991,950
Population density (mid-2002): 110.1 per sq km
Life expectancy (years at birth, 2002): 65.9 (males 63.1; females 69.0)

Finance
GDP in current prices: 2002): US $23,252m. ($1,939 per head)
Real GDP growth (2002): 2.0%
Inflation (annual average, 2002): 8.0%
Currency: quetzal

Economy

In 2002, according to estimates by the World Bank, Guatemala's gross national income (GNI), measured at average 2000–02 prices, was US $20,929m., equivalent to $1,750 per head (or $3,880 per head on an international purchasing-power parity basis). During 1990–2002, it was estimated, the population increased by an average of 2.7% per year, while gross domestic product (GDP) per head increased, in real terms, by an average of 1.1% per year. Overall GDP increased, in real terms, at an average annual rate of 3.7% in 1990–2002; GDP grew by an estimated 2.2% in 2002.

AGRICULTURE

Agriculture, including hunting, forestry and fishing, contributed an estimated 22.5% of GDP, measured in constant prices, in 2002. In 2002 an estimated 38.7% of the active labour force were employed in this sector. The principal cash crops are coffee (which accounted for 12.7% of export earnings in 2001), sugar cane and bananas. Exports of shrimps are also significant. In recent years the country has successfully expanded production of less traditional crops, such as mangoes, berries and green beans. The drought and subsequent food crisis of May–August 2001 resulted in the destruction of crops in many areas of the country. In September 2001 the Government announced an aid programme of 'soft' loans and refinancing credits for the coffee sector; the programme was to include an advertising campaign to encourage domestic coffee sales. None the less, owing to a regional crisis in the coffee industry, coffee exports fell by an estimated 38% in 2002, compared with the harvest of 2001. During 1990–2002 agricultural GDP increased, in real terms, by an estimated average of 2.6% per year. Growth in agricultural GDP was 1.2% in 2001 and an estimated 1.8% in 2002.

INDUSTRY

Industry, including mining, manufacturing, construction and power, contributed an estimated 19.3% of GDP, measured in constant prices, in 2002. This sector employed an estimated 20.0% of the working population in 2002. Industrial GDP increased by an estimated average of 3.6% per year in 1990–2002. Growth in industrial GDP was 1.3% in 2001 and an estimated 1.0% in 2002.

Mining

Mining contributed an estimated 0.6% of GDP, measured in constant prices, in 2002 and employed an estimated 0.2% of the working population in 2002. The most important mineral export is petroleum, which accounted for only 4.5% of total export earnings in 2001. In addition, copper, antimony, lead, zinc and tungsten are mined on a small scale. There are also deposits of nickel, gold and silver. Mining GDP increased by 0.8% in 2001 and by estimated 9.8% in 2002.

Manufacturing

Guatemala's industrial sector is the largest in Central America. Manufacturing contributed an estimated 12.8% of GDP, measured in constant prices, in 2002 and employed an estimated 13.6% of the working population in 2000. The main branches of manufacturing, measured by gross value of output, are food-processing, textiles, plastic products, paper and paper products, pharmaceuticals and industrial chemicals. Manufacturing GDP increased by an average of 2.4% per year in 1990–2002.

Growth in manufacturing GDP was 1.1% in 2001 and an estimated 0.8% in 2002. Guatemala's clothing assembly, or *maquila*, manufacturing sector expanded in the late 1990s and employed some 80,000 workers in 1998. However, in 2001, owing to the introduction of a business tax and the economic slowdown in the USA towards the end of the year, the sector contracted; 38 *maquila* factories closed, while a further 229 were threatened with closure.

Energy

Energy is derived principally from mineral fuels and hydroelectric power. Petroleum provided 39.9% of electric energy in 2000 while hydroelectric power was responsible for 37.8% of total electricity production in the same year. Guatemala is a marginal producer of petroleum and, in 2001, produced an estimated 8.9m. barrels. Petroleum reserves were estimated at 526m. barrels in January 2000. Reserves of natural gas were put at some 109,000m. cu ft in the same year. Imports of petroleum and petroleum products comprised 12.0% of the value of total imports in 2001. In late 1998 80% of the capital of the state-owned Empresa Eléctrica de Guatemala was sold to foreign investors for US $520m. At the same time, the Instituto Nacional de Electrificación was sold for $100m. In late 2001 Guatemala and Mexico reached agreement, under the 'Plan Puebla–Panamá', on a project to link their electricity grids. It was hoped that the project would improve regional power infrastructure and attract investment in the sector.

SERVICES

In 2002 the services sector contributed an estimated 58.2% of GDP, measured in constant prices, and, in the same year, the sector employed an estimated 37.5% of the working population. The GDP of the services sector increased by an average of 4.4% per year in 1990–2002; growth in the sector was 3.2% in 2001 and an estimated 2.9% in 2002.

EXTERNAL TRADE

In 2002 Guatemala recorded a visible trade deficit of US $2,950.0m., and there was a deficit of $1,193.0m. on the current account of the balance of payments. In 2002 the principal source of imports (36.1%) was the USA; other major suppliers were Mexico, Japan and El Salvador. The USA was also the principal market for exports (taking 30.2% of exports in that year); other significant purchasers were El Salvador, Honduras, Costa Rica and Nicaragua. The main exports in 2001 were chemical products, coffee, vegetables and fruits. The principal imports were machinery and transport equipment, chemicals and mineral fuels and lubricants, particularly petroleum products.

GOVERNMENT FINANCE

In 2001 there was a budgetary deficit of 638.7m. quetzales, equivalent to some 0.4% of GDP. At the end of 2001 Guatemala's total external debt stood at US $4,526m. of which US $3,179m. was long-term public debt, in that year equivalent to 17.5% of GDP. In that year the cost of debt-servicing totalled $435m. In 1990–2002 the average annual rate of inflation was 10.7%. Consumer prices increased by an average of 7.3% in 2001 and by 8.1% in 2002. An estimated 1.8% of the labour force were unemployed in 2002.

INTERNATIONAL ECONOMIC RELATIONS

Guatemala is a member of the Central American Common Market (CACM). In 2000 Guatemala, El Salvador and Honduras signed a free-trade agreement with Mexico, which promised greater market access and increased bilateral trade. As a consequence of the implementation of the agreement, trade with Mexico increased by 22% in 2002, in spite of a fall in the overall value of exports in that year. In May 2001 the Central American countries, including Guatemala, reached an agreement with Mexico to establish a series of joint transport, industry and tourism projects intended to integrate the region, called the 'Plan Puebla–Panamá'. Negotiations towards a free-trade agreement, to be known as the Central American Free Trade Agreement (CAFTA), took place throughout 2003 between the Guatemala, Costa Rica, El Salvador, Honduras, Nicaragua and the USA. The agreement, which was expected to be ratified in early 2004, entailed the gradual elimination of tariffs on most industrial and agricultural products over the next 10 and 20 years, respectively, and was expected to lead to an increase in exports.

SURVEY AND PROSPECTS

In 1991 the Government adopted a structural adjustment programme in order to address the serious fiscal imbalances and external debt problems that had characterized the previous decade. The resultant economic recovery enabled the Government to resume relations with international credit agencies and to clear debt arrears. However, low tax revenue was a major problem, forcing the Government to borrow heavily, keeping interest rates high, discouraging investment and impeding growth. In 1995 the implementation of a series of tax reforms facilitated a new stand-by agreement with the IMF. The signing of the peace accord in December 1996, which signalled the end of the civil conflict, improved Guatemala's economic prospects significantly. It was envisaged that expenditure of US $2,500m. would be required to implement the accord. In January 1997 international donors pledged $1,900m. in loans and donations towards the Government's reconstruction programme. However, the funding was contingent upon the Government significantly increasing tax revenues. Significant increases were expected following the creation of an independent tax superintendency in 1998. However, as a result of the destruction caused by 'Hurricane Mitch' in November 1998, the curtailment of external credit from banks owing to instability in the international financial markets, and declining international prices for Guatemala's principal agricultural exports, economic growth slowed significantly in 1999. The incoming Government of Alfonso Portillo introduced a Fiscal Pact, which comprised eight distinct areas: fiscal balance of payments, state revenue, tax administration, public spending, public debt, public property, supervision and control mechanisms, and fiscal decentralization. One of the Pact's principal aims was to increase tax revenue to 12% of GDP by 2002, either through an increased rate of VAT or more effective collection of VAT. In August 2001 a 12% increase in VAT was introduced.

In December 2000 legislation was approved to allow the circulation of the US dollar and other convertible currencies, for use in a wide range of transactions, from 1 May 2001. However, in May a constitutional challenge to the law was made, which argued that it violated the constitutional requirement that the Central Bank remain in exclusive control of foreign exchange. In June the Financial Action Task Force on Money Laundering (FATF) added Guatemala to their 'blacklist' of countries targeted for international scrutiny regarding potential money-laundering activities within the banking sector. The country remained on the list in February 2004. In February 2002, at a meeting in Washington, DC, international donors pledged a further US $1,300m. in loans and grants to aid Guatemala's post-war reconstruction programmes, less than the Government had been hoping for. The Portillo administration's lack of progress in implementing the peace accords was considered the main reason for the shortfall in funding. The funding was also contingent on the Government improving public finances and accelerating the implementation of the peace accords. The aid was to be directed towards the judicial, health and education sectors.

In June 2002 the Government formulated the 2002–04 Economic Action Plan, which aimed to develop the private sector and attract foreign investment. A state-funded agency was established to encourage foreign investment and a series of privatization and public works programmes were created. Tax incentives were also introduced for private sector companies who invested in infrastructure projects. In September the Congreso approved a budget which envisaged increased government spending in 2003. Opposition parties claimed that the budget was overly ambitious and suspected that surplus funds would be diverted to the campaign for the November 2003 elections. The following month the approval, by a narrow congressional majority, for the issue of US $700m. of bonds on the European markets caused further concern that the Government would spend the money on expensive voter-pleasing initiatives. The IMF similarly criticized the sale and suggested any further government expenditure should be funded by an increase in taxation. In January 2003 President Portillo introduced, by decree, tax rises on numerous goods, including fuel and wheat.

Remittances from citizens working abroad represented the second largest hard currency inflow into the country after non-traditional exports. Remittances increased by approximately 30% in 2003, when they totalled US $2,070m. The incoming administration of President Oscar Berger Perdomo was expected to restore business-sector confidence; the new Government pledged to foster economic growth and create jobs through austere economic policies and the encouragement of domestic and foreign investment. Tax revenue fell in 2003 to less than 10% of GDP. It was likely in 2004 that the IMF would bring pressure to bear on the Berger administration to meet the 12% target agreed in the 1996 peace accords. The economy was estimated to have grown by 2.1% in 2003 and was forecast to expand by 3.0% in 2004.

Guinea

The Republic of Guinea lies on the west coast of Africa. After gaining full independence from France in 1958, the regime of Ahmed Sekou Touré pursued policies of socialist revolution. In 1984, following Sekou Touré's death, the army seized power. Col (later Gen.) Lansana Conté became President, to which office he was elected in 1994. Legislative elections held in 1995 and 2002 were won by the pro-Conté Parti pour l'unité et le progrès (PUP). Conté was re-elected as President in 1998 and again in 2003, in an election boycotted by the principal opposition parties. Conakry is the capital. The official language is French.

Area and population
Area: 245,857 sq km
Population (mid-2002): 7,744,350
Population density (mid-2002): 31.5 per sq km
Life expectancy (years at birth, 2002): 52.3 (males 50.9; females 53.7)

Finance
GDP in current prices: 2002): US $3,174m. ($410 per head)
Real GDP growth (2002): 4.3%
Inflation (annual average, 2002): 2.9%
Currency: Guinean franc

Economy

In 2002, according to estimates by the World Bank, Guinea's gross national income (GNI), measured at average 2000–02 prices, was US $3,137m., equivalent to $410 per head (or $1,990 on an international purchasing-power parity basis). During 1990–2002, it was estimated, the population increased at an average annual rate of 2.5%, while gross domestic product (GDP) per head increased, in real terms, by an average of 1.4% per year. Overall GDP increased, in real terms, at an average annual rate of 3.9% in 1990–2002. The IMF estimated real GDP growth at 4.2% in 2002.

AGRICULTURE

Measured at constant 1996 prices, agriculture (including hunting, forestry and fishing) contributed an estimated 19.1% of GDP in 2002. About 83.5% of the labour force were employed in the agricultural sector in 2001. The principal cash crops are fruits, oil palm, groundnuts and coffee. Important staple crops include cassava, rice and other cereals and vegetables. The attainment of self-sufficiency in rice and other basic foodstuffs remains a priority. The food supply is supplemented by the rearing of cattle and other livestock. The Government has made efforts towards the commercial exploitation of Guinea's forest resources (forests cover about two-thirds of the country's land area) and substantial fishing stocks. According to the World Bank, during 1990–2002 agricultural GDP increased at an average annual rate of 3.9%. The IMF estimated growth in agricultural GDP at 5.1% in 2002.

INDUSTRY

Industry (including mining, manufacturing, construction and power) contributed an estimated 32.5% of GDP (at 1996 prices) in 2002. An estimated 1.9% of the employed labour force were engaged in the industrial sector in 1990. According to the World Bank, industrial GDP increased at an average annual rate of 4.4% in 1990–2002. The IMF estimated growth in industrial GDP at 4.6% in 2002.

Mining

Mining contributed an estimated 17.0% of GDP (at 1996 prices) in 2002. Only 0.7% of the employed labour force were engaged in the sector at the time of the 1983 census. Guinea is the world's foremost exporter of bauxite and the second largest producer of bauxite ore, possessing between one-quarter and one-third of known reserves of the mineral. In 2001 exports of aluminium ore and concentrates and aluminium hydroxide together provided 71.0% of export earnings. Despite the importance to the national economy of the extraction of bauxite, only a small proportion of output is processed into alumina in Guinea; various plans to increase the production of alumina have been proposed. Production of alumina increased by an average of 7.6% per year in 1998–2002, according to the US Geological Survey, although the mining of bauxite declined slightly during the same period. Gold and diamonds are also mined: in 2001 gold contributed 20.6% of export earnings; in 2002 diamonds contributed some 4.9% of export revenue. Exploitation of valuable reserves of high-grade iron ore at Mt Nimba, near the border with Liberia, has been impeded by political instability in the region. The expansion of the gold mine at Siguiri by the Société Ashanti Goldfields de Guinée, the country's principal gold-mine operator, was expected to be completed by mid-2004. Of Guinea's other known mineral deposits, only granite is exploitable on a commercial scale. The GDP of the mining sector increased at an average annual rate of 2.8% in 1997–2002, according to the IMF; growth in 2002 was 2.9%.

Manufacturing

The manufacturing sector remains largely undeveloped, contributing only an estimated 4.3% of GDP (at 1996 prices) in 2002. In 1983 only 0.6% of the employed labour force were engaged in the manufacturing sector. Other than the country's one alumina smelter, most industrial companies are involved in import-substitution, including the processing of agricultural products and the manufacture of construction materials. According to the World Bank, manufacturing GDP increased at an average annual rate of 4.6% in 1990–2001. The IMF estimated growth in manufacturing GDP at 6.1% in 2002.

Energy

Electricity generation is, at present, insufficient to meet demand, and power failures outside the mining and industrial sectors (in which the largest operators generate their own power supplies) have been frequent. However, Guinea possesses considerable hydroelectric potential. The 75-MW Garafiri dam project was inaugurated in 1999, and a further major scheme, at Kaléta, was scheduled for completion in the mid-2000s. In the mean time, some 600,000 metric tons of hydrocarbons are imported annually, and in 2001 imports of fuel accounted for 18.6% of the value of total merchandise imports. In October 2001 it was announced that the Nigerian National Petroleum Corpn was to begin supplying petroleum products to Guinea

SERVICES

The services sector contributed an estimated 48.4% of GDP (at 1996 prices) in 2002. During 1990–2002, according to the World Bank, the sector's GDP increased at an average annual rate of 2.5%. The IMF estimated growth in services GDP at 1.9% in 2002.

EXTERNAL TRADE

In 2002 Guinea recorded a visible trade surplus of US $217.7m., while there was a deficit of $46.0m. on the current account of the balance of payments. The principal suppliers of imports in 2001 were France (which supplied 17.4% of the total), Belgium, Côte d'Ivoire and the USA. The principal markets for exports in that year were France (which took 26.0% of exports), the USA, Ireland and Spain. Ukraine and Russia are notable markets for Guinean bauxite. The principal exports in 2001 were aluminium ore and concentrate, gold and aluminium hydroxide. The principal imports included machinery and transport equipment, refined petroleum products, food and live animals, and basic manufactures.

GOVERNMENT FINANCE

In 2002 Guinea's overall budget deficit was estimated at 451,200m. FG, equivalent to 7.1% of GDP. The country's total external debt was US $3,254m. at the end of 2001, of which $2,844m. was long-term public debt. In that year the cost of debt-servicing was equivalent to 12.3% of the value of exports of goods and services. Annual inflation averaged 5.2% in 1991–2002; consumer prices increased by an average of 3.0% in 2002.

INTERNATIONAL ECONOMIC RELATIONS

Guinea is a member of the Economic Community of West African States (ECOWAS), of the Gambia River Basin Development Organization (OMVG), of the International Coffee Organization, of the West Africa Rice Development Association (WARDA) and of the Mano River Union.

SURVEY AND PROSPECTS

Guinea's potential for the attainment of wealth is substantial, owing to its valuable mineral deposits, water resources and generally favourable climate; however, the economy remains over-dependent on revenue from bauxite reserves and on external assistance, the country's infrastructure is inadequate and its manufacturing base narrow.

Since 1985 economic liberalization measures have been undertaken, and by the late 1990s success had been achieved in reducing the rate of inflation, foreign-exchange reserves had increased, as had private investment in the economy, while considerable GDP growth had been achieved. However, insecurity in neighbouring Liberia and Sierra Leone during the 1990s had a detrimental effect on Guinea's economy, and instability in the southern regions of Guinea in 2000–01 adversely affected agricultural output. Conversely, the rebellion that commenced in Côte d'Ivoire in September 2002 resulted in a marked increase in international trade routed through the port of Conakry, as access to the larger Ivorian port at Abidjan became increasingly uncertain, although another consequence of the unrest was the loss of economically significant remittances from Guinean citizens, principally cocoa farmers, ordinarily resident in Côte d'Ivoire.

In December 2000 the IMF and the World Bank announced that Guinea would be a recipient of some \$880m. in debt relief as part of their initiative for heavily indebted poor countries. In May 2001 the IMF approved a three-year arrangement under its Poverty Reduction and Growth Facility for Guinea, worth US \$82m. over three years. Measures adopted as part of a Poverty Reduction Strategy Paper in 2001 sought to reduce poverty, and to improve levels of health care and education. A decline in international prices for bauxite in 2002 was counterbalanced by a good harvest and an increase in industrial output, and the target for GDP growth agreed with the IMF was attained in that year. However, in 2003 political instability, both within Guinea and in neighbouring countries, and frequent interruptions to water and electricity supplies contributed to much lower GDP growth than anticipated, at an estimated 3.6%. In the longer term sustained growth remains dependent on the maintenance of political stability, continued economic reform and a diversification and expansion of the manufacturing sector.

Guinea-Bissau

The Republic of Guinea-Bissau lies on the west coast of Africa. After 1974 the Partido Africano da Independência da Guiné e Cabo Verde (PAIGC) established a single-party socialist state. In 1980 President Luís Cabral was deposed in a coup led by João Vieira, and in 1991 the PAIGC's political monopoly was terminated. Multi-party legislative elections held in 1994 were won by the PAIGC, while Vieira was elected as President. In 1999 Vieira was overthrown. Kumba Yalá of the Partido para a Renovação Social was elected President in 2000. In September 2003 senior army officers deposed Yalá and installed Henrique Rosa, a business executive, as interim President. The PAIGC emerged as the largest party in the legislature following elections in March 2004, and subsequently formed a minority Government. Bissau is the capital. The official language is Portuguese.

Area and population
Area: 36,125 sq km
Population (mid-2002): 1,252,670
Population density (mid-2002): 34.7 per sq km
Life expectancy (years at birth, 2002): 47.2 (males 45.7; females 48.7)

Finance
GDP in current prices: 2002: US $216m. ($172 per head)
Real GDP growth (2002): –4.2%
Inflation (annual average, 2002): 0.9%
Currency: CFA franc

Economy

In 2002, according to estimates by the World Bank, Guinea-Bissau's gross national income (GNI), measured at average 2000–02 prices, was US $193m., equivalent to $150 per head (or $750 on an international purchasing-power parity basis). During 1990–2002, it was estimated, the population increased at an average annual rate of 2.4%, while gross domestic product (GDP) per head decreased, in real terms, by an average of 1.5% per year. Overall GDP decreased, in real terms, at an average annual rate of 0.9% in 1990–2002; real GDP increased by 0.2% in 2001, but declined by 4.2% in 2002.

AGRICULTURE

Agriculture (including forestry and fishing) contributed 57.3% of GDP in 2002, and employed an estimated 82.5% of the labour force in 2001. The main cash crops are cashew nuts (which contributed 95.6% of total export earnings in 2001) and cotton. Other crops produced include rice, roots and tubers, groundnuts, maize, millet and sorghum. Livestock and timber production are also important. The fishing industry developed rapidly during the 1990s, and earnings from fishing exports and the sale of fishing licences are a significant source of government revenue (revenue from fishing licences was 7,430m. francs CFA in 2001, equivalent to 26.0% of total revenue). According to the World Bank, agricultural GDP increased, in real terms, by an average of 3.8% per year in 1990–2002; growth in 2002 was 8.1%.

INDUSTRY

Industry (including mining, manufacturing, construction and power) employed an estimated 4.1% of the economically active population at mid-1994 and provided 13.0% of GDP in 2002. According to the World Bank, industrial GDP decreased, in real terms, by an average of 1.9% per year in 1990–2001; however, growth of 6.6% was recorded in 2001.

Mining

The mining sector is underdeveloped, although Guinea-Bissau possesses reserves of bauxite, phosphates, diamonds and gold. A Canadian company was attempting to develop phosphate mining at Farim, in the north of the country, in the early 2000s, while exploration for commercially viable petroleum reserves was also taking place off shore.

Manufacturing

The sole branches of the manufacturing sector are food-processing, brewing and timber- and cotton-processing, while there are plans to develop fish-processing. Manufacturing, mining and power contributed 10.5% of GDP in 2002. According to the World Bank, manufacturing GDP decreased, in real terms, by an average of 1.6% per year in 1990–2001; however, growth of 5.6% was recorded in 2001.

Energy

Energy is derived principally from thermal and hydroelectric power. Imports of petroleum and petroleum products comprised 6.2% of the value of total imports in 2001. Energy production since 1999 has been insufficient to supply demand in Bissau,

357

mainly owing to fuel shortages caused by government-set low prices, and to equipment failures caused by poor maintenance. As a result, most energy is currently supplied by private generators.

SERVICES

Services employed an estimated 19.4% of the economically active population at mid-1994, and provided 29.6% of GDP in 2002. According to the World Bank, the combined GDP of the service sectors increased, in real terms, at an average rate of 1.1% per year in 1990–2001; growth in 2001 was 9.2%.

EXTERNAL TRADE

In 2001 Guinea-Bissau recorded a trade deficit of US $32.6m., and there was a deficit of $37.8m. on the current account of the balance of payments. In 2001 the principal source of imports was Portugal (29.9%); other major suppliers were Senegal and the People's Republic of China. In that year India was the principal market for exports (85.6%). The principal export in 2001 was cashew nuts. The principal imports in that year were food and live animals, transport equipment, electrical equipment and machinery, and passenger vehicles.

GOVERNMENT FINANCE

In 2002 there was an estimated budgetary deficit of 5,900m. francs CFA, equivalent to 3.9% of GDP. Guinea-Bissau's total external debt was US $668.3m. at the end of 2001, of which $627.2m. was long-term public debt. In that year the cost of debt-servicing was equivalent to 41.1% of the total value of exports of goods and services. In 1990–2002 the average annual rate of inflation was 27.0%. Consumer prices increased by an average of 0.9% in 2002.

INTERNATIONAL ECONOMIC RELATIONS

Guinea-Bissau is a member of the Economic Community of West African States (ECOWAS) and of the West African organs of the Franc Zone.

SURVEY AND PROSPECTS

Guinea-Bissau is one of the world's poorest countries. Its economy is largely dependent on the traditional rural sector, which employs the vast majority of the labour force and produces primarily for subsistence. The economy remains very dependent on foreign financing, which accounts for a significant part of budget revenue, and on exports of cashew nuts.

The extensive destruction of public buildings and private business premises during the military uprising of June 1998 imposed a heavy burden on the country's underdeveloped infrastructure, necessitating appeals for humanitarian aid. Following the overthrow of President Vieira in May 1999, the Government urged the international community to continue providing economic aid. In December 2000 the IMF and the World Bank awarded some US $790m. in debt-service relief as part of their enhanced initiative for heavily indebted poor countries. Moreover, a three-year Poverty Reduction and Growth Facility, worth some $18m., was awarded by the IMF in support of the Government's 2000–03 programme of economic reform. However, in May 2001, as the Government appeared to be struggling to achieve its objectives, the IMF and the World Bank suspended the aid programme, pending an investigation into the disappearance of $15m. in donor assistance. Although Guinea-Bissau was still able to resort to bilateral aid, the suspension represented a significant set-back, as 80% of the 2001 budget was to be financed by foreign aid. The results of the investigation, published in November, indicated the presence of non-justifiable government expenditure, valued at some 10,500m. francs CFA.

Meanwhile, a programme of privatization, which had been interrupted by the military conflict, resumed in May. With support from the World Bank, more than 24 public and parastatal companies in the sectors of telecommunications, tourism, fishing, and port and airport management were to be divested by 2006. An IMF/World Bank mission in November, at the end of a three-month short-term macroeco-nomic programme, found some signs of economic improvement, but a final assess-ment, in March 2002, indicated that the Government had failed to meet fiscal targets, and IMF aid was not resumed. Furthermore, the 2002 budget was not approved until July of that year, with government spending hitherto effected by decree. The banking sector had been seriously threatened by the political upheavals since 1998, and during early 2002 several banks ceased operations. The economy continued to deteriorate during 2003, and army and public-sector workers were unpaid for several months, leading to social tension and a series of strikes that paralysed public services. Following the coup in September, interim President Rosa appealed to the interna-tional community for $35m. in immediate aid, notably for the payment of salary arrears. In December the UN Development Programme agreed to oversee an emer-gency aid fund, and in January 2004 the World Bank donated $13m. to be used primarily to settle internal debts, demobilize former combatants and organize the legislative elections. In February an IMF mission noted an improvement in the financial management of the country.

Guyana

The Co-operative Republic of Guyana lies on the north coast of South America. Guyana, formerly British Guiana, a colony of the United Kingdom, achieved independence in 1966. All legislative elections held between 1968 and 1992 were won by the People's National Congress. In 1992 the left-wing People's Progressive Party (PPP), in alliance with the CIVIC movement, gained a narrow victory. Dr Cheddi Bharat Jagan, the leader of the PPP, accordingly succeeded Desmond Hoyte as President. The PPP/CIVIC alliance retained power following elections held in 1997 and 2001. Georgetown is the capital. English is the official language.

Area and population

Area: 214,969 sq km
Population (mid-2002): 771,970
Population density (mid-2002): 3.6 per sq km
Life expectancy (years at birth, 2002): 64.3 (males 61.5; females 66.9)

Finance

GDP in current prices: 2002): US $710m. ($919 per head)
Real GDP growth (2002): 0.3%
Inflation (annual average, 2002): 5.3%
Currency: Guyana dollar

Economy

In 2002, according to estimates by the World Bank, Guyana's gross national income (GNI), measured at average 2000–02 prices, was US $651m., equivalent to US $840 per head (or US $3,780 per head on an international purchasing-power parity basis). During 1990–2002, it was estimated, the population increased at an average annual rate of 0.5%, while gross domestic product (GDP) per head increased, in real terms, by an average of 2.7% per year. Overall GDP increased, in real terms, at an average annual rate of 3.1% in 1990–2002; growth in 2002 was 1.1%.

AGRICULTURE

Agriculture (including forestry and fishing) provided an estimated 36.3% of GDP in 2002 and employed an estimated 17.3% of the total labour force in mid-2001. The principal cash crops are sugar cane (sugar providing an estimated 24.3% of the value of total domestic exports in 2002) and rice (9.2% in 2002). The sugar industry alone accounted for an estimated 13.1% of GDP in 2002, and, it was estimated, employed about 24,000 people at peak season in 2000. At the beginning of the 21st century the sugar industry was threatened by the disappearing preferential markets and the increasing cost of employment. Despite this, sugar exports increased by 9.4% in 2002. In June the Government announced a major restructuring of the state sugar company, Guysuco (Guyana Sugar Corpn Inc), including the construction of a new refinery at Berbice. Vegetables and fruit are cultivated for the local market, and livestock-rearing is being developed. Fishing is also important, particularly shrimp fishing, which accounted for an estimated 6.6% of GDP in 2002. Agricultural production increased at an average annual rate of 5.2% during 1990–2001. Agricultural GDP increased by 3.4% in 2001 and by a further 3.4% in 2002.

Timber resources in Guyana are extensive and underdeveloped. In 2002 the forestry sector contributed an estimated 1.9% of GDP. About three-quarters of the country's total land area consists of forest and woodland. In 2002 timber shipments provided an estimated 7.3% of total domestic exports, compared with 6.7% in the previous year. Although foreign investment in Guyana's largely undeveloped interior continues to be encouraged by the Government, there is much popular concern at the extent of the exploitation of the rainforest. The forestry sector increased at an average annual rate of 7.4% in 1992–2002. In 2001 the sector increased by 3.1%, but in 2002 it declined by 7.7%.

INDUSTRY

Industry (including mining, manufacturing and construction) provided an estimated 36.2% of GDP in 2002 and engaged 20.4% of the employed labour force in 1992. Industrial GDP increased at an average annual rate of 6.6% in 1990–2001. Industrial GDP increased, in real terms, by 3.0% in 2001, but remained stagnant in 2002.

Mining

Mining contributed an estimated 15.0% of GDP in 2002, and employed 4.8% of the total working population in 1980. Bauxite, which is used for the manufacture of aluminium, is one of Guyana's most valuable exports, and accounted for an estimated 7.2% of total domestic exports in 2001, a significant decrease on the previous year. This fall in the value of bauxite exports followed the withdrawal, in January 2002, of the US-based aluminium company Alcoa from the Aroaima bauxite and aluminium mine, owing to high production costs and unfavourable investment conditions. Alcoa sold its share to the Guyana Government. Figures for 2002 indicated that bauxite production subsequently decreased by 18.5% and exports by 42.1%, compared with 2001. In September 2002 the Government merged the Bermine and Aroaima bauxite companies, in an effort to improve the performance of the sector. The registered production of gold (which accounted for 27.8% of domestic exports in 2002) increased considerably during the late 1980s and 1990s. After reaching a peak in 1998, productivity declined in 1999, owing to high production costs and poor ore quality. Production recovered in 2000 and in 2001 gold output increased by 26.4%. However, a decline of 4.2% was registered in 2002, although the value of gold exports increased by 7.3% in the same year. In 2000 the gold industry was estimated to directly employ some 32,000 people. There are also significant diamond resources and some petroleum reserves. In 2000 Mazaruni Granite Products Ltd initiated a US $34m. development and modernization programme of granite production. The GDP of the mining sector was estimated to have increased by an average of 6.1% per year in 1992–2002. The sector's GDP increased, in real terms, by 4.2% in 2001, but decreased by 6.9% in 2002. In 2000 a seven-year programme was initiated to develop and regenerate one of the principal bauxite mining towns, Linden, through the promotion of non-bauxite enterprises.

Manufacturing

Manufacturing (including power) accounted for an estimated 3.4% of GDP in 2002 and, according to the 1980 census, employed 14.4% of the total working population. The main activities are the processing of bauxite, sugar, rice and timber. Manufacturing GDP increased at an average annual rate of 7.7% in 1990–2001. Manufacturing GDP increased by 2.5% in 2001 and by 10.9% in 2002.

Energy

Energy requirements are almost entirely met by imported hydrocarbon fuels. In 2002 fuels and lubricants constituted 22.3% of the total value of imports (mainly from Venezuela and Trinidad and Tobago). Despite the border dispute, in early 2001 Venezuela granted Guyana, along with a number of other Caribbean nations, entry to the Caracas energy accord for special petroleum concessions. In November 2002 Venezuela agreed to supply oil at a discount of 25%, providing that the price on world markets remained above US $30 per barrel. Construction began in mid-2002 on the 100 MW Amaila Falls hydroelectric power project, while further hydroelectric projects were in the planning stage. However, the project failed to gain the support of the state power company, Guyana Power and Light Inc, and construction was halted in early 2003. In June 2002 the Inter-American Development Bank (IDB) approved a loan for US $27.4m. to fund the extension of electricity lines to the coastal regions.

SERVICES

The services sector contributed an estimated 27.5% of GDP in 2002 and engaged 43.2% of the employed labour force in 1980. The GDP of the services sector increased by an average of 3.0% per year in 1990–2001. Services GDP increased, in real terms, by an estimated 0.9% in 2001 and by 0.4% in 2002.

EXTERNAL TRADE

In 2002 Guyana recorded a visible trade deficit of US $68.2m. and a deficit of US $106.7m. on the current account of the balance of payments. In 1998 the principal source of imports was the USA (26.6%). Trinidad and Tobago and the United Kingdom are other important suppliers of imports. In 1998 Canada was the principal market for exports (26.9% of total exports); the United Kingdom, Trinidad and Tobago and the Netherlands are also significant recipients. The principal exports are gold, sugar, bauxite and rice, and the principal imports are consumer goods and fuel and lubricants.

GOVERNMENT FINANCE

In 2002 the overall budget deficit was an estimated G $13,098.1m. (equivalent to 7.8% of GDP). According to World Bank estimates, by the end of 2001 Guyana's external debt totalled US $1,406m. of which US $1,180m. was long-term public debt. The cost of debt-servicing in 2001 was US $44m; equivalent to 6.6% of exports of goods and services. The annual rate of inflation averaged 5.6% in 1995–2002. Consumer prices increased by 1.5% in 2001 and by 6.0% in 2002. An estimated 11.7% of the labour force were unemployed in 1992.

INTERNATIONAL ECONOMIC RELATIONS

Guyana is a founder member of CARICOM. It is also a member of the UN Economic Commission for Latin America and the Caribbean (ECLAC) and of the International Sugar Organization.

SURVEY AND PROSPECTS

In 1988, in response to serious economic decline, the Government introduced an extensive recovery programme of adjustment measures and structural reforms. Funds were made available under two Enhanced Structural Adjustment Facilities (ESAF), approved by the IMF in 1990 and in 1994. In 1996 negotiations with the 'Paris Club' of creditor nations and Trinidad and Tobago resulted in the cancellation of 67% of Guyana's bilateral debt with five creditor nations (a total reduction of US $395m.). In 1998, following a substantial period of drought that adversely affected economic growth, the Government secured a new three-year ESAF with the IMF, and in May 1999 the IMF and the World Bank declared that Guyana had become eligible for some US $410m. in nominal debt-service relief under the Heavily Indebted Poor Countries (HIPC) initiative. It was hoped that the estimated 24% reduction in the external debt burden would permit increased budgetary spending on education and social welfare. However, following industrial action by public-sector workers in mid-1999, the Government was obliged to grant salary increases of 26.6%, thereby reducing the funds available for development expenditure; the decision was criticized by the IMF.

In November 2000 Guyana became eligible for additional debt relief under the enhanced HIPC initiative. Upon successful completion of a series of pre-arranged conditions, including economic growth and attacking poverty, Guyana was to qualify for additional debt relief totalling US $590m. In August 2001 Guyana and Brazil signed the Partial Scope Agreement, whereby import duties on a range of products and the 25% levy on ocean freight imports would be waived. In late 2001 the Bank of Guyana initiated discussions with the Caribbean Financial Action Task Force (based in Trinidad and Tobago) on the creation of a special unit to ensure that Guyana's financial system was clean and transparent.

The political impasse between the Government and PNC/Reform and the high crime rate hindered efforts to attract foreign investment to Guyana in 2002–03. Nevertheless, in the 2002 budget, the Jagdeo administration reiterated its aims to reduce poverty and further to industrialize the economy. In September the IMF made a US $73m. three-year credit available to the Government for a poverty reduction scheme. In recognition of Guyana's success in making progress towards structural reform and maintaining economic stability, in November the IMF also approved a US $64m. debt-relief programme under the HIPC initiative. In January 2004 the IMF, the World Bank's International Development Association and the Paris Club announced that Guyana had met the criteria for the additional debt relief agreed in November 2000 and would receive the remaining US $334.5m. in credit. This was in addition to US $20m. in loans that had been cancelled by the People's Republic of China in August 2003. Despite reform efforts by the Jagdeo Government, in October 2003 the World Trade Organization criticized Guyana's slow economic growth and its continued economic dependence on gold, sugar, bauxite and rice. It emphasized the importance of pursuing economic reform and trade liberalization and of diversifying the country's production and export base in order to reduce economic vulnerability.

Haiti

The Republic of Haiti mainly comprises the western part of the Caribbean island of Hispaniola. After his election as President in 1957, Dr François Duvalier established a dictatorship. Duvalier was succeeded by his son, who was ousted in 1986. Leslie Manigat's elected Government was overthrown by the army in 1988. In 1990 Fr Jean-Bertrand Aristide was elected President. Aristide was overthrown in 1991 by a military junta, but was reinstated in 1994, following US intervention. Aristide was succeeded in 1995 by René Préval, whose presidency was marked by instability. Aristide was returned to the office of President in 2000 but resigned in early 2004, following a rebellion against his Government. The capital is Port-au-Prince. French and Creole are the official languages.

Area and population
Area: 27,750 sq km
Population (mid-2002): 8,286,490
Population density (mid-2002): 298.6 per sq km
Life expectancy (years at birth, 2002): 50.1 (males 49.1; females 51.1)

Finance
GDP in current prices: 2002): US $3,590m. ($433 per head)
Real GDP growth (2002): −0.9%
Inflation (annual average, 2002): 9.9%
Currency: gourde

Economy

In 2002, according to estimates by the World Bank, Haiti's gross national income (GNI), measured at average 2000–02 prices, was US $3,678m., equivalent to $440 per head (or $1,580 per head on an international purchasing-power parity basis). In 1990–2002 the population increased at an average annual rate of 2.1%, while gross domestic product (GDP) per head decreased, in real terms, by an average of 2.8% per year. Haiti's overall GDP decreased, in real terms, at an average annual rate of 0.7% in 1990–2002; real GDP decreased by 0.9% in 2001/02.

AGRICULTURE

Agriculture (including hunting, forestry and fishing) contributed an estimated 27.4% of GDP in 2000/01, measured at constant 1986/87 prices. About 61.7% of the total labour force were engaged in agricultural activities in mid-2001. The principal cash crop is coffee (which accounted for 4.1% of export earnings in 1999/2000). However, from 1998 coffee production decreased significantly, prompting the Government to announce plans for its revival in 2003. The export of oils for cosmetics and pharmaceuticals is also important. The main food crops are sugar, bananas, maize, sweet potatoes and rice. Falling quality and cheaper imports of sugar cane forced closure of all the country's major sugar factories in recent years, although one of them, at Darbonne, near Léogane, reopened in January 2001. During 1990–2000, according to the World Bank, the real GDP of the agricultural sector decreased at an average annual rate of 1.8%; agricultural GDP decreased by an estimated 3.6% in 1999/2000, but increased by an estimated 0.6% in 2000/01.

INDUSTRY

Industry (including mining, manufacturing, construction and power) contributed 15.9% of GDP at constant prices in 2000/01. About 8.8% of the employed labour force were engaged in the sector in 1990. According to the World Bank, industrial GDP declined at an average annual rate of 0.9% in 1990–2000; it increased by 3.3% in 1999/2000, but decreased by an estimated 1.3% in 2000/01.

Mining

Mining contributed 0.1% of GDP at constant prices in 2000/01. About 1% of the employed labour force were engaged in extractive activities in 1990. Marble, limestone and calcareous clay are mined. There are also unexploited copper, silver and gold deposits.

Manufacturing

Manufacturing contributed 7.9% of GDP at constant prices in 2000/01. Some 35,000 people were engaged in the sector in mid-2000. The most important branches of manufacturing were food products, textiles (including apparel, leather and fur products and footwear), chemicals (including rubber and plastic products) and tobacco. Manufacturing GDP decreased by an average of 11.8% per year in 1989–99; manufacturing GDP decreased by 0.1% in 1999/2000, but increased by an estimated 0.2% in 2000/01.

Energy

Energy is derived principally from local timber and charcoal. In 1999 38.4% of the country's public electricity came from hydroelectric power, while 61.6% of electricity came from petroleum. Severe shortfalls of electricity in 2000–01 led the Government to contract a Dominican and a US-Haitian company to add 70 MW to the national supply, increasing it by one-third. Imports of fuel products accounted for 17.1% of the value of imports in 1999/2000.

SERVICES

The services sector contributed 56.6% of GDP at constant prices in 2000/01 and engaged 22.8% of the employed labour force in 1990. According to the World Bank, the GDP of the services sector increased by an average of 0.1% per year in 1990–2000. It increased by 3.9% in 1999/2000, but decreased by an estimated 0.2% in 2000/01.

EXTERNAL TRADE

In 2000/01 Haiti recorded a visible trade deficit of US $399.3m., and there was a deficit of $53.5m. on the current account of the balance of payments. In 1998 the principal source of imports (60%) was the USA; the USA was also the principal market for exports (87%) in that year. Other significant trading partners were France, Canada, Japan and the Dominican Republic. The principal exports in 1999/2000 were manufactured articles (30.7%) and coffee (4.1%). The principal imports in that year were food and live animals (22.7%), manufactured goods and mineral fuels. In 2000 smuggling was estimated to have accounted for two-thirds of Haiti's imports.

GOVERNMENT FINANCE

In the financial year ending 30 September 2002 there was a budgetary deficit of 2,541.8m. gourdes (equivalent to 2.8% of GDP). At the end of 2001 Haiti's total external debt was US $1,250m., of which $1,028m. was long-term public debt. In that year the cost of debt-servicing was equivalent to 5.2% of the total value of exports of goods and services. The annual rate of inflation averaged 13.9% in 1995–2002. Consumer prices increased by an average of 14.0% in 2001 and by 9.9% in 2002. Some 60% of the labour force were estimated to be unemployed in 2001. Remittances from Haitians living abroad were equivalent to 17% of GDP in 2000.

INTERNATIONAL ECONOMIC RELATIONS

Haiti is a member of the International Coffee Organization and the Latin American Economic System (SELA). In July 2002 Haiti became a full member of the Caribbean Community and Common Market (CARICOM). Haiti is also a signatory of the European Union's (EU) Cotonou Agreement, which replaced the Lomé Convention from June 2000, although from 2000 the disbursement of funds under this accord were suspended while the political crisis continued.

SURVEY AND PROSPECTS

In terms of average income, Haiti is the poorest country in the Western hemisphere, and there is extreme inequality of wealth. The suspension of all non-humanitarian aid and the imposition of successive, and increasingly severe, economic sanctions by the international community, following the military coup of September 1991, had devastating effects on the Haitian economy, serving to exacerbate the extreme poverty endured by the majority of the population. Following the return to civilian rule in late 1994, sanctions were ended and preparations made for the release of aid and new loans. At a meeting of donor nations in Paris in January 1995 measures were agreed for the implementation of an Emergency Economic Recovery Programme, subject to the conclusion of a stand-by agreement with the IMF. However, structural adjustment measures stipulated by the IMF, notably the divestment of public enterprises and the rationalization of the civil service, were not approved by the legislature until late 1996.

The IMF subsequently approved a three-year credit of US $131m. under an Enhanced Structural Adjustment Facility (ESAF), which, in turn, facilitated access to further multilateral development aid totalling in excess of $1,000m. However, owing to a parliamentary crisis the majority of the reforms were not implemented, thus obstructing the disbursement of development aid. By the time of the expiry of the ESAF in October 1999 the bulk of the IMF financing had not been drawn. Furthermore, in November the Alexis administration, which was inaugurated in March of that year, revealed that international agencies had almost entirely failed to honour promises to finance its $311m. short-term economic action plan, initiated in May.

Economic growth slowed further from 2000 onwards, exacerbated by the ongoing political impasse, which continued to impede investment and private-sector confidence, as well as the implementation of the necessary structural adjustments that would allow economic development. The main source of growth was the continued expansion of exports, principally from the textile sector. However, it was the continuing suspension of international aid to Haiti that was the main reason for the deteriorating economy. Although humanitarian funds (estimated at $55m. in 2002) continued to be disbursed, the international community made it clear that confidence in Haiti's democratic process had to be restored before financial aid could be resumed. In September 2002 the Permanent Council of the OAS approved a resolution formally requesting that the international community resume financial aid to Haiti in order to avert a humanitarian crisis; it was hoped that up to $500m. of suspended aid and loans would be released upon the Government's fulfilment of certain conditions.

From October 2002 the currency experienced significant devaluation, in part owing to rumours (which were subsequently denied) that the Government intended to convert balances held in dollar bank accounts into gourdes at rates lower than market prices. In an attempt to encourage foreign investment the Government approved a new law offering several incentives, including a 15-year 'tax holiday', to foreign businesses prepared to invest in the country. In early 2003 the Government attempted to stabilize the country's fiscal situation: a revised budget for 2002/03 was adopted, monetary policy was made stricter, and a flexible system for the pricing of domestic fuel, which had previously been heavily subsidized, was introduced.

In mid-2003 prospects for the resumption of international aid improved when the Government reached an agreement with the IMF. Under the terms of the accord, the Government promised to implement various currency stabilization and cost-cutting measures over the course of the fiscal year in return for loans totalling between $100m. and $150m. Shortly afterwards, in an attempt to secure further aid, the Government paid $32m. in arrears to the Inter-American Development Bank (IDB), enabling the release of $146m. of 'frozen' loans from the IDB. In early 2004 the World Bank announced that it would provide the country with some economic assistance, despite its failure to clear $35m. of debt arrears. However, the ongoing political instability continued to threaten Haiti's economic prospects.

Honduras

The Republic of Honduras lies in the Central American isthmus. Military rule was officially ended in 1980, when elections to a Constituent Assembly were held. Although the Partido Liberal secured an absolute majority in the legislature in 1981, real power remained with Col Gustavo Alvarez Martínez until his removal by a group of army officers in 1984. In 1993–97, during the presidency of Carlos Roberto Reina Idiaquez, the influence of the military was reduced and past human rights violations were investigated. Reina was succeeded by Carlos Roberto Flores Facussé. In 2001 Ricardo Maduro Joest became President. Tegucigalpa is the capital. The national language is Spanish.

Area and population
Area: 112,492 sq km
Population (mid-2002): 6,755,060
Population density (mid-2002): 60.0 per sq km
Life expectancy (years at birth, 2002): 67.2 (males 64.2; females 70.4)

Finance
GDP in current prices: 2002): US $6,594m. ($976 per head)
Real GDP growth (2002): 2.0%
Inflation (annual average, 2002): 7.7%
Currency: lempira

Economy

In 2002, according to estimates by the World Bank, Honduras' gross national income (GNI), measured at average 2000–02 prices, was US $6,213.6m., equivalent to $920 per head (or $2,450 per head on an international purchasing-power parity basis). During 1990–2002, it was estimated, the population increased at an average annual rate of 2.8%, while gross domestic product (GDP) per head increased, in real terms, by an average of 0.3% per year. Overall GDP increased, in real terms, at an average annual rate of 3.1% in 1990–2002; growth was 2.5% in 2002.

AGRICULTURE

Agriculture (including hunting, forestry and fishing) contributed an estimated 13.5% of GDP and employed 39.6% of the economically active population in 2002. The principal cash crop is traditionally coffee, although owing to high production costs and low prices on the world markets, coffee exports contributed only 13.7% of all export earnings in 2002, compared with 24.8% in 2000. Banana production decreased during the 1990s and in 1998 more than 70% of the total crop was destroyed as a result of 'Hurricane Mitch'. Furthermore, in June 2000 one of the principal banana corporations, Chiquita Brands, announced a substantial reduction in its operations in the country following hurricane damage and a downturn in the market. In spite of these set-backs, by 2002 earnings from banana exports had risen to 13.0% of total export earnings, compared with just 3.0% in 1999. The main subsistence crops include maize, plantains, beans, rice, sugar cane and citrus fruit. Exports of shellfish make a significant contribution to foreign earnings (supplying 13.9% of total export earnings in 2002). Agricultural GDP increased at an average annual rate of 2.0% during 1990–2001; the sector increased by 9.5% in 2001, but decreased by 0.9% in 2002.

INDUSTRY

Industry (including mining, manufacturing, construction and power) contributed an estimated 30.8% of GDP and employed 20.1% of the economically active population in 2002. Industrial GDP increased at an average annual rate of 3.7% during 1990–2001; it increased by 5.2% in 2000 and by 1.6% in 2001.

Mining

Mining contributed an estimated 1.9% of GDP and employed 0.2% of the economically active population in 2002. In that year gold was the major mineral export, contributing an estimated 6.0% of total export earnings. Lead, zinc, silver, copper and low-grade iron ore are also mined. In addition, small quantities of petroleum derivatives are exported. Until the end of the 1990s, when new funding was announced, the gold, silver and other mineral deposits had remained unexplored. The GDP of the mining sector increased by an average of 5.4% per year in 1991–2000; it increased by 1.7% in 2000, but decreased by 3.3% in 2001.

Manufacturing

Manufacturing contributed an estimated 20.4% of GDP and employed 14.3% of the economically active population in 2002. The most important branches, measured by gross value of output, were food products, beverages (including beer), cigarettes, apparel and wood products. In 2000 the successful *maquiladora* (assembly plant) sector employed some 100,000 local workers. Manufacturing GDP increased at an average annual rate of 4.1% during 1990–2001; the sector by 5.6% in 2000 and by 5.2% in 2001.

Energy

Energy is derived principally from hydroelectric power, which accounted for some 61.9% of electricity production in 2000. Petroleum accounted for the remaining 38.1% of electrical energy output. Imports of mineral fuels and lubricants accounted for an estimated 14.1% of the value of total imports in 2002. Fuel wood remains a prime source of domestic energy. In 2001 the US company, AES Corporation, announced plans to construct a US $650m. natural gas plant that would supply some 800 MW of electricity to Honduras and other countries in the region. In September 2003 the Government cancelled an agreement with the US concern's Honduran subsidiary, AES Honduras, to supply 200 MW of electricity per year. In May 2002 a cable connecting the electricity distribution networks of Honduras and El Salvador was activated; the connection process was completed in September. Nevertheless, in 2003 there were frequent power shortages throughout the country. The state-run energy company, ENEE (Empresa Nacional de Energía Eléctrica), began cutting power to certain parts of the country, in an attempt to ensure that large cities were not without electricity. Furthermore, in June it reached an agreement to import electricity from Costa Rica.

SERVICES

The services sector contributed an estimated 55.8% of GDP and engaged 40.3% of the working population in 2002. The GDP of the services sector increased by an average of 3.7% per year in 1990–2001; the sector increased by 4.4% in 2000 and by 4.5% in 2001.

EXTERNAL TRADE

In 2002 Honduras recorded a visible trade deficit of US $874m., while there was a deficit of $266.2m. on the current account of the balance of payments. Workers' remittances from abroad were a vital source of income; remittances totalled about $409m. in 2000 and were forecast to reach $1,250m. in 2004. The majority of remittances came from the USA, home to an estimated 500,000 Hondurans. In 2002 the principal source of imports (40.8%) was the USA; other major suppliers were El Salvador, Guatemala and Mexico. The USA was also the principal market for exports (50%) in that year; other significant purchasers were El Salvador, Guatemala and Germany. The principal exports in 2002 were shellfish and bananas. The principal imports in 2002 were machinery and electrical equipment, chemicals and related products, and mineral products.

GOVERNMENT FINANCE

In 1999 there was a budgetary deficit of 3,576m. lempiras (equivalent to 4.7% of GDP in that year). Honduras' external debt totalled US $5,051m. at the end of 2001, of which $4,501m. was long-term public debt. In that year the cost of debt-servicing represented 11.2% of the value of exports of goods and services. The annual rate of inflation averaged 16.1% in 1990–2002. Consumer prices increased by an annual average of 8.8% in 2001 and 8.1% in 2002. Some 4.2% of the labour force were unemployed in 2001; however, it was estimated that more than 35% of the work-force were underemployed.

INTERNATIONAL ECONOMIC RELATIONS

Honduras is a member of the Central American Common Market (CACM). In December 2003 negotiations towards a Central American Free Trade Agreement (CAFTA) between Honduras, El Salvador, Guatemala, Nicaragua and the USA were concluded. The Agreement, which was due to be ratified in 2004, entailed the gradual elimination of tariffs on most industrial and agricultural products over the next 10 and 20 years, respectively. It was hoped that the advent of CAFTA would encourage export-oriented growth in Honduras and in the region.

SURVEY AND PROSPECTS

In terms of average income, Honduras is among the poorest nations in the Western hemisphere, with some 79% of the population living below the poverty line. In October 1998 the Honduran economy was devastated by the effects of 'Hurricane Mitch'. Much of the country's infrastructure was destroyed, and as many as 2.13m. people left homeless. The total cost to the economy of the hurricane damage was estimated at $5,000m. In May 1999 the Consultative Group for Honduras of international financial agencies and donor countries agreed to provide $2,800m. for the reconstruction process. In March the IMF approved a three-year Enhanced Structural Adjustment Facility (ESAF) totalling $215m., and in the following month the 'Paris Club' of creditor governments agreed to suspend Honduras' bilateral debt-service payments for a period of three years, and offered a 67% reduction in its debt of $1,170m. on the condition that it complied with the terms of the ESAF. These included commitments by the Government to reduce public expenditure, rationalize state bureaucracy, and sustain its privatization programme. The successful implementation of these measures also facilitated further debt relief under the 'Heavily Indebted Poor Countries' (HIPC) initiative of the World Bank, to which Honduras was admitted in December 1999. However, in December 2000 the IMF suspended a $22m. disbursement to the Honduran Government owing to the lack of progress in its privatization programme.

In 2000 the economy grew by 5.2%, in part owing to the continuing growth in the *maquiladora* sector and investment in the post-hurricane reconstruction programme. Growth slowed to 2.6% in 2001, however, mainly owing to low international prices for bananas and coffee exports and the effects of the drought. The rising crime rate and tax incentives offered by Nicaragua were also reported to be responsible for the closure of several *maquiladora* plants and branches of international firms in Honduras in 2001.

The Government of Ricardo Maduro Joest, which took office in January 2002, pledged to maintain an austere economic policy and to reduce violent crime in an attempt to attract foreign investment and qualify for further IMF funding. Honduras was scheduled to resume debt-rescheduling payments to the Paris Club of creditors at the end of 2002, although the new Government was successful in its request that payments be suspended for a further year. However, in order to secure further financial assistance, including qualification for a new HIPC initiative worth some $960m. over the next 15 years, the Government had to convince the IMF of its intention to reduce the fiscal deficit. To this end, in early 2002 President Maduro declared his intention to proceed with the much-delayed privatization of the state telecommunications company, Hondutel, and of ENEE. The first stage of the privatization of ENEE was completed by the end of 2002; however, the sale of Hondutel was further delayed and in November the Government announced plans to sell a 25% stake in the telecommunications company by 2005. The first private telecommunications contract, to supply 50,000 fixed telephone lines, was awarded in late 2003.

The Government also introduced a number of new taxes, principally on government services, introduced measures to eliminate tax evasion, and announced a series of reforms intended to reduce public-sector expenditure, prompting discontent among public workers throughout 2002. In December 2002 the IMF announced that a new funding agreement would be delayed until March 2003. Under pressure to reduce the high fiscal deficit sufficiently to satisfy the IMF, in February 2003 Maduro announced that the rate of taxation on high incomes would be increased and that public-sector salaries would be 'frozen'. The measures were met with further opposition from workers, culminating in a mass demonstration in late August. A proposal to link public-sector wages to GDP growth met with further hostility in October. Finally, in February 2004, the IMF announced that Honduras had met the criteria to qualify for debt relief. Some US $15.4m. was immediately released under the HIPC initiative, with a further $110m. available under a three-year Poverty Reduction and Growth Facility programme. However, the Fund stipulated continuing stringent legislative reforms and set the ambitious fiscal targets of a reduction in the budget deficit to 1.8% of GDP by 2006 (it was equivalent to 4.5% of GDP in 2003) and a fall in the annual inflation rate to 5% by 2007.

The 2004 budget, approved in December 2003, forecast a fiscal deficit of 3% and GDP growth of 4% in 2004. Although the budget met IMF criteria, the Maduro Government faced a formidable task in fulfilling economic targets, not only owing to continued low agricultural prices and weak exports, but also because it lacked the necessary political consensus to implement reform.

Hong Kong

A Special Administrative Region (SAR) of the People's Republic of China, Hong Kong lies in eastern Asia, mainly off the south coast of China. Hong Kong Island was ceded to the United Kingdom under the Treaty of Nanking (Nanjing) in 1842. The Kowloon Peninsula was acquired by the Convention of Peking (Beijing) in 1860. The New Territories were leased from China in 1898 for a period of 99 years. Chinese sovereignty resumed in 1997. Since then Hong Kong has been administered by a Chief Executive, accountable to the State Council of China. Victoria is the capital. The official languages are Chinese and English.

Area and population

Area: 1,098 sq km
Population (mid-2002): 6,773,000
Population density (mid-2002): 6,168.3 per sq km
Life expectancy (years at birth, 2002): 80.0 (males 77.5; females 82.6)

Finance

GDP in current prices: 2002): US $161,532m. ($23,849 per head)
Real GDP growth (2002): 2.3%
Inflation (annual average, 2002): –3.0%
Currency: HK dollar

Economy

In 2002, according to estimates by the World Bank, Hong Kong's gross national income (GNI), measured at average 2000–02 prices, was US $167,600m., equivalent to US $24,750 per head (or US $26,810 on an international purchasing-power parity basis). During 1990–2002, it was estimated, the population increased by an average of 1.4% per year, while gross domestic product (GDP) per head increased, in real terms, at an average annual rate of 2.5% per year. Overall GDP increased, in real terms, at an average rate of 4.0% in 1990–2002; growth in 2002 was 2.3%, compared with the previous year.

AGRICULTURE

Agriculture and fishing together employed only 0.3% of the working population in 2002, and contributed less than 0.1% of GDP in 2001. Crop production is largely restricted to flowers, vegetables and some fruit and nuts, while pigs and poultry are the principal livestock. An outbreak of avian influenza led to the slaughter of some 1.25m. poultry in May 2001. In early 2004 a new outbreak in neighbouring countries prompted the Government to implement stringent preventative measures. Hong Kong relies heavily on imports for its food supplies.

INDUSTRY

Industry (including mining, manufacturing, construction and power) provided an estimated 13.4% of GDP in 2001 and employed 18.3% of the working population in 2002.

Manufacturing

Manufacturing employed 9.0% of the working population in 2002, and contributed an estimated 5.2% of GDP in 2001. Measured by the value of output, the principal branches of manufacturing are textiles and clothing, plastic products, metal products and electrical machinery (particularly radio and television sets).

SERVICES

The services sector plays the most important role in the economy, accounting for an estimated 86.5% of GDP in 2001 and employing 81.4% of the working population in 2002. The value of Hong Kong's invisible exports (financial services, tourism, shipping, etc.) was US $45,159m. in 2002. Revenue from tourism totalled an esti-mated US $10,117m. in 2002. The number of visitors to the territory rose from 13.7m. in 2001 to 16.6m. in 2002. A new Disney theme park, to be opened in 2005/06, was expected further to increase the number of visitors to Hong Kong. The repercussions of the terrorist attacks on the USA in September 2001, however, adversely affected the tourism industry, as did the outbreak of Severe Acute Respiratory Syndrome (SARS) in April 2003. The territory's banking and mercantile houses have branches throughout the region, and Hong Kong is regarded as a major financial centre, owing partly to the existence of an excellent international telecommunications network and to the absence of restrictions on capital inflows.

EXTERNAL TRADE

In 2002 Hong Kong recorded a visible trade deficit of US $5,131m. and there was a surplus of US $17,483m. on the current account of the balance of payments. Re-exports constituted 91.6% of total exports in 2002. The principal sources of Hong Kong's imports in 2002 were the People's Republic of China (44.3%) and Japan (11.3%); the principal markets for exports (including re-exports) were the People's Republic of China (39.3%) and the USA (21.3%). Other major trading partners included Taiwan, Germany and the United Kingdom. In 2001 the principal domestic exports were clothing, textiles, electrical machinery, data-processing equipment, and photographic apparatus. The principal imports in that year were foodstuffs, chemicals, textiles, machinery, transport equipment, and other manufactured articles.

GOVERNMENT FINANCE

In 2003/04 the budget deficit was an estimated HK $49,000m. (equivalent to 4.0% of GDP), the shortfall being considerably lower than the previous projection of HK $78,000m. A further improvement was anticipated for 2004/05, a deficit of HK $42,600m. (3.4% of GDP) being projected. The annual rate of inflation averaged 3.9% in 1990–2002. The consumer price index declined by 1.6% in 2001, and by 3.1% in 2002. Consumer prices continued to decrease in 2003 and were expected to decline for the sixth consecutive year during at least the first half of 2004. As a result of the SARS crisis, the rate of unemployment increased dramatically in mid-2003, to reach a record 8.7% of the labour force, before declining to 7.3% towards the end of the year. The shortage of skilled labour continued.

INTERNATIONAL ECONOMIC RELATIONS

Hong Kong is a member of the Asian Development Bank (ADB) and an associate member of the UN Economic and Social Commission for Asia and the Pacific (ESCAP). The territory became a member of Asia-Pacific Economic Co-operation (APEC) in 1991. Hong Kong joined the Bank for International Settlements (BIS) in 1996, and in early 1997 announced its participation in the IMF's New Arrangements to Borrow (NAB) scheme. After mid-1997 Hong Kong remained a separate customs territory, within the World Trade Organization (WTO).

SURVEY AND PROSPECTS

Under the terms of the Basic Law, Hong Kong's financial system remained unchanged following the transfer to Chinese sovereignty in mid-1997. The territory continued as a free port, and the Hong Kong dollar was retained, remaining freely convertible and linked to the US currency. In 2001 the deceleration in the economy of the USA resulted in the weakening of one of Hong Kong's major export markets, which was compounded by the events of 11 September of that year. Despite Hong Kong's general recovery from the recessionary conditions of the late 1990s, consumer prices continued to fall in 2001–03. Domestic retail sales declined by 1.2% in 2001 and by 2.7% in 2002.

The property market remained depressed in 2002. The Government had, in September 2001, declared a moratorium on the sale of subsidized public housing, which was removed in July 2002. In November 2002, however, the Government imposed a moratorium on property sales and land auctions until the end of 2003, in an attempt to halt the decline in property prices, which had decreased by 65% since 1997. The Hong Kong Monetary Authority stated in June 2002 that some 150,000 middle-class homeowners were experiencing negative equity. By late 2003, however, the property market appeared to be recovering. The Hong Kong stock market, as measured by the Hang Seng Index, remained subdued during 2002, closing at 9,300 points at the end of December, but recovered during 2003 and had exceeded 13,000 points by early 2004.

Meanwhile, unemployment increased sharply, as companies downsized operations and new graduates entered the labour market, these developments being compounded by the effects of the SARS outbreak in 2003. The number of bankruptcy orders rose from 9,151 in 2001 to 25,238 in 2002. As the budget deficit continued to place pressure on the economy, in early 2004 the Government declared its aim to raise HK $112,000m. over the next five years, in an effort to balance the budget. By late 2002 there was increasing debate about delinking (and therefore devaluing) the Hong Kong dollar from its US counterpart, in order to allow Hong Kong prices to adjust more easily to those of mainland China, and granting Hong Kong more flexibility in monetary policy. In the longer term, Hong Kong faced rising competition from Shanghai as China's leading financial centre. An increasing number of foreign investors were conducting business directly with the mainland and transferring regional offices there, where in the past Hong Kong had acted as an intermediary. Furthermore, Shanghai was expected to overtake Hong Kong as the world's largest container port by 2015.

In April 2003, following the outbreak of SARS, the warning by the World Health Organization (WHO) against travel to Hong Kong had a serious impact on the territory's economy. In the same month the Government announced a range of measures to assist those in the most vulnerable sectors of the economy, such as tourism, catering and retailing. This programme of financial aid, which incorporated tax rebates and a reduction in rents and utility charges for businesses, envisaged expenditure of HK $11,800m. Visitor arrivals in Hong Kong decreased by 67.9% in May 2003 compared with the corresponding month of the previous year. However, following the removal of the WHO travel warning in late May and the apparent end of the SARS epidemic in June, from mid-2003 the economy began to show signs of a quick recovery.

The tourism sector benefited especially from a sharp increase in tourist arrivals from the Chinese mainland, following the launch in late July of a new policy to allow Guangdong residents to visit Hong Kong individually rather than as part of a tour group. Despite political tensions, economic relations with the Chinese mainland were expected to develop following the signing of the Closer Economic Partnership Agreement (CEPA) in June 2003. Under this agreement, various taxes levied by China on Hong Kong's products were to be removed or substantially reduced. From the beginning of 2004 Hong Kong banks were also to be permitted to conduct personal banking services in Chinese yuan. Despite the contraction in GDP recorded in the second quarter of the year, the growth rate for 2003 as a whole reached 3.3%, with an increase of as much as 6% predicted for 2004.

Hungary

The Republic of Hungary lies in eastern Europe. At elections held in 1947 the Communists became the largest single political party, and in 1949 a People's Republic was established. Soviet troops suppressed an uprising against Communist domination in 1956. Popular demands for democracy from 1989 culminated, in 1990, in Hungary's first free multi-party elections since 1945. The Hungarian Democratic Forum was victorious. Legislative elections held in 1994, 1998 and 2001 were won, respectively, by the Hungarian Socialist Party (HSP), the Federation of Young Democrats-Hungarian Civic Party, and a coalition of the HSP and the Alliance of Free Democrats. Budapest is the capital. The language is Hungarian.

Area and population
Area: 93,030 sq km
Population (mid-2002): 10,166,000
Population density (mid-2002): 109.3 per sq km
Life expectancy (years at birth, 2002): 72.6 (males 68.4; females 76.8)

Finance
GDP in current prices: 2002): US $65,843m. ($6,477 per head)
Real GDP growth (2002): 3.3%
Inflation (annual average, 2002): 5.3%
Currency: forint

Economy

In 2002, according to estimates by the World Bank, Hungary's gross national income (GNI), measured at average 2000–02 prices, was US $53,702m., equivalent to $5,280 per head (or $12,810 per head on an international purchasing-power parity basis). During 1990–2002, it was estimated, the population decreased at an average annual rate of 0.2%, while gross domestic product (GDP) per head increased, in real terms, by an average of 1.4% per year. Hungary's overall GDP increased, in real terms, at an average annual rate of 1.2% during 1990–2002; real GDP increased by 3.8% in 2001 and by 3.3% in 2002.

AGRICULTURE

Agriculture (including hunting, forestry and fishing) contributed 4.3% of GDP in 2001, and 6.2% of the employed labour force were engaged in the sector in 2002. The principal crops are wheat, maize, sugar beet, barley and potatoes. Viticulture is also important. During 1990–2000, according to the World Bank, real agricultural GDP declined at an average annual rate of 3.3%. The GDP of the sector increased by 0.9% in 1999, but declined by 3.5% in 2000.

INDUSTRY

Industry (including mining, manufacturing, construction and power) contributed 31.3% of GDP in 2001, and engaged 34.1% of the employed labour force in 2002. According to preliminary government figures, 52% of total industrial production was exported in 2002; industrial exports increased by 8.7% in 2001 and by 5.7% in 2002. In 2002 the output of the construction sector increased by 20% compared with the previous year, owing to state-financed infrastructural investment. The World Bank estimated that real industrial GDP increased at an average annual rate of 2.5% in 1990–2000. Industrial GDP increased by 7.2% in 1999 and by 9.2% in 2000.

Mining

Mining and quarrying accounted for just 0.2% of GDP in 2001, and engaged 0.4% of the employed labour force in 2002. Hungary's most important mineral resources are lignite (brown coal) and natural gas. Petroleum, bauxite and hard coal are also exploited. During 1990–98 the output of the mining sector declined at an average annual rate of 11.1%. Production fell by 8.4% in 1997 and by 20.4% in 1998.

Manufacturing

The manufacturing sector contributed 22.7% of GDP in 2001, and engaged 24.8% of the employed labour force in 2002. In 1999 the principal branches of the sector, in terms of their contribution to gross production, were food products (accounting for 16.6% of the total), motor vehicles (14.4%), office, accounting and computing machinery (8.9%) and chemicals (7.5%). Manufacturing GDP increased, in real terms, at an average annual rate of 7.6% in 1991–2000. Manufacturing GDP increased by 8.0% in 1999 and by 11.0% in 2000.

Energy

In 2000 40.0% of Hungary's electricity production was generated by nuclear power, 27.7% was generated by coal, 18.9% by natural gas and 12.6% by petroleum. Fuel imports represented 5.4% of the value of total merchandise imports in 2001.

SERVICES

The services sector has a significant role in the Hungarian economy, contributing 64.4% of GDP in 2001, and engaging 59.7% of the employed labour force in 2002.

According to the World Bank, the GDP of the services sector increased, in real terms, at an average rate of 1.0% per year in 1990–2000. The GDP of the services sector increased by 3.2% in 1999 and by 2.9% in 2000.

EXTERNAL TRADE

In 2002 Hungary recorded a visible trade deficit of US $2,119m., and there was a deficit of $2,644m. on the current account of the balance of payments. In 2001 the principal source of imports was Germany (accounting for 24.9% of the total); other major sources were Italy, Austria and Russia. Germany was also the principal market for exports in that year (35.6%); other important purchasers were Austria, Italy and France. The principal exports in 2000 were machinery and transport equipment, miscellaneous manufactured articles (most notably clothing and accessories), basic manufactures, chemical products, and food and live animals. The main imports in that year were machinery and transport equipment (most notably electrical machinery and apparatus), basic manufactures, miscellaneous manufactured articles, chemical products and mineral fuels.

GOVERNMENT FINANCE

Hungary's overall budgetary deficit in 2000 was an estimated 464,700m. forint (equivalent to 4.1% of GDP). The country's total external debt at the end of 2001 was estimated to be US $30,289m., of which $12,681m. was long-term public debt. In that year the cost of debt-servicing was equivalent to 37.2% of the value of exports of goods and services. The annual rate of inflation averaged 17.9% in 1990–2002; consumer prices increased by 9.2% in 2001 and by 5.3% in 2002. The average rate of unemployment was 5.8% in 2002.

INTERNATIONAL ECONOMIC RELATIONS

Hungary is a member of the European Bank for Reconstruction and Development (EBRD), and was admitted to the Organisation for Economic Co-operation and Development (OECD) in March 1996. Hungary became an associate member of the European Union (EU) in February 1994, and subsequently applied for full EU membership. Hungary acceded to the EU on 1 May 2004.

SURVEY AND PROSPECTS

In 1990 the Hungarian Government pledged to effect a full transition to a Western-style market economy, and by the late 1990s the Government's fiscal policy had resulted in a decline in both the public-sector deficit and the annual rate of inflation. In December 1999 it was announced that, as a result of the country's success in achieving economic stabilization, Hungary would be one of the first applicant nations to be admitted to the EU; in December 2002 it was invited to become a full member from May 2004. None the less, in early 2003 the IMF warned that Hungary should reduce fiscal spending or anticipate the introduction of economic austerity measures if it was to fulfil the economic criteria for EU accession.

In mid-2003 the Government and the central bank took action to reduce expenditure and the forint was devalued. Later that month the central bank was compelled to increase the base rate of interest on two occasions, in an effort to control inflation. There was a further, dramatic increase in the base rate in late November. As a result, although GDP growth remained positive in 2003, the rate of inflation increased, and the deficit on the current account of the balance of payments widened significantly.

The budgetary deficit for 2003 was high, and was estimated to represent some 5.6% of GDP. The Government aimed to reduce the fiscal deficit to 4.6% of GDP in 2004, and a new Minister of Finance duly took office in February. (However, the National Bank of Hungary anticipated a deficit equivalent to some 5.3% of GDP in that year.) The EU stipulated that countries intending to adopt the common European currency, the euro, should record a budgetary deficit of no more than 3% of GDP in the two preceding years. Thus, Hungary's adoption of the euro, originally envisaged for 2008, appeared likely to be deferred until 2010.

Iceland

The Republic of Iceland is situated near the Arctic Circle in the North Atlantic Ocean. From 1959 until 1971 the country was governed by a coalition of the Independence Party and the Social Democratic Party. Following elections in 1971 a coalition was formed in which the Progressive Party and the People's Alliance were the main partners. In various combinations the above-mentioned parties have been the principal partners in coalition administrations formed after all subsequent elections up to and including that of 1999. In 1980, following her election as President, Vigdís Finnbogadóttir became the world's first popularly elected female Head of State. Reykjavík is the capital. Icelandic is the official language.

Area and population
Area: 103,000 sq km
Population (mid-2002): 283,990
Population density (mid-2002): 2.8 per sq km
Life expectancy (years at birth, 2002): 80.1 (males 78.4; females 82.8)

Finance
GDP in current prices: 2002): US $8,608m. ($30,311 per head)
Real GDP growth (2002): 0.0%
Inflation (annual average, 2002): 5.2%
Currency: króna

Economy

In 2002, according to estimates by the World Bank, Iceland's gross national income (GNI), measured at 2000–02 prices, was US $7,944m., equivalent to $27,970 per head (or $28,590 per head on an international purchasing-power parity basis). During 1991–2002, it was estimated, the population increased at an average annual rate of 0.9%, while gross domestic product (GDP) per head increased, in real terms, by an average of 1.8% per year. Iceland's overall GDP increased, in real terms, at an average annual rate of 2.6% during 1991–2002; GDP increased by 3.0% in 2001 but negligible growth was achieved in 2002.

AGRICULTURE

Agriculture (including fishing and fish processing) contributed some 13.9% of GDP in 2002 (agriculture alone accounted for only 1.5%); 7.3% of the employed labour force were engaged in the agricultural and fishing sectors in the same year. The principal agricultural products are dairy produce and lamb, although these provided less than 1% of export earnings in 2002. Marine products accounted for 53.0% of total export earnings in 2002. A cod quota system is in place to avoid the depletion of fish stocks through over-fishing as happened in previous years. During 1990–99 agricultural GDP (including fishing) declined at an average annual rate of 1.6%; agricultural GDP (excluding fishing) increased at an average annual rate of 1.1% over the same period, while the GDP of the fishing sector declined by 2.3% per year. Agricultural GDP (excluding fishing) increased, in real terms, by 3.2% in 1998 and by 3.9% in 1999; the GDP of the fishing sector declined by 8.0% in 1998 and by 1.6% in 1999.

INDUSTRY

Industry (including mining, manufacturing, construction and power) contributed 21.1% of GDP in 2002 and engaged 23.0% of the employed labour force. Mining activity is negligible. During 1990–2001 industrial GDP increased at an average annual rate of 3.1%; industrial GDP increased by 7.7% in 2000 and by 3.6% in 2001.

Manufacturing

Manufacturing contributed 16.7% of GDP in 1997, and employed 14.3% of the labour force in 2002. The most important sectors, measured by gross value of output (excluding fish processing, which dominates the sector), are the production of aluminium, diatomite, fertilizer, cement and ferro-silicon. In March 2003 the Althingi approved proposals to construct a new aluminium smelter in the Eastern Highlands, despite considerable popular opposition on environmental grounds. The proposals included the damming of two rivers to create a reservoir of 22 sq km above Vatnajökull (Europe's biggest glacier), in order to produce hydroelectric power for the smelter. Fish processing contributed 4.9% of GDP in 1997; however, the GDP of the fish-processing sector declined by 5.3% in 1998 and by 1.1% in 1999. Manufacturing GDP (including fish processing) increased, in real terms, at an average annual rate of 2.4% in 1990–99; it grew by 4.1% in 1998 and by 4.9% in 1999.

Energy

Iceland is potentially rich in hydroelectric and geothermal power, but both energy sources are significantly underexploited. Hydroelectric power has promoted the development of the aluminium industry, while geothermal energy provides nearly all the country's heating and hot water. In 2000 hydroelectric power provided 82.7% of the country's electricity; petroleum provided only 0.1% in the same year. Fuel imports comprised 8.6% of the value of merchandise imports in 2002. In 2001 Iceland announced its intention to develop the world's first economy free of carbon dioxide emissions by using hydrogen or methanol-powered fuel cells. Hydrogen-fuelled buses began operating in Reykjavík in 2003. In December 2001 the Government approved plans for the construction of a new hydroelectric power plant in Kárahnjúkar, in the east of the country.

SERVICES

Services contributed 62.4% of GDP in 1997 and employed 69.7% of the labour force in 2002. GDP from services increased, in real terms, at an average annual rate of 3.4% during 1990–2001; it grew by 6.3% in 2000 and by 0.9% in 2001. The tourism sector is becoming an increasingly significant source of revenue; the number of foreign visitors totalled 302,913 in 2000; receipts from tourism totalled 37,148m. krónur in 2002.

EXTERNAL TRADE

In 2002 Iceland recorded a visible trade surplus of US $145m., while there was a deficit of $24m. on the current account of the balance of payments. In 2002 the principal sources of imports were the USA (providing 11.1% of the total), Germany (10.7%), Denmark (8.5%) and Norway (8.0%); the principal market for exports was Germany (accounting for 18.5% of the total), followed by the United Kingdom (17.5%) the Netherlands (10.8%) and the USA (also 10.8%). In 1999 EU member countries provided 60.0% of Iceland's merchandise imports and took 64.2% of its exports. The principal imports in 2002 were machinery and transport equipment (which accounted for 32.3% of the total value of imports), basic manufactures (14.6%), chemicals and related products (11.2%), and food and live animals (9.5%). The principal exports in the same year were food and live animals (accounting for 62.5% of the total value of exports—fish, crustaceans, molluscs and fish preparations provided 53.0% of the total), and basic manufactures (22.9%—aluminium provided 18.9% of the total).

GOVERNMENT FINANCE

In 2002 there was a budgetary deficit of 4,133m. krónur, equivalent to 0.5% of GDP. Iceland's net external debt was equivalent to 56.3% of GDP at the end of 1998; the cost of debt-servicing was equivalent to an estimated 21.0% of export earnings in the same year. The annual rate of inflation averaged 3.6% in 1990–2002; consumer prices increased by 6.4% in 2001 and by 5.2% in 2002. The unemployment rate averaged 3.3% in 2002.

INTERNATIONAL ECONOMIC RELATIONS

Iceland is a member of the Nordic Council, the Nordic Council of Ministers, the European Free Trade Association (EFTA) and the Organisation for Economic Co-operation and Development (OECD). Although Iceland is not a member of the European Union (EU), it joined the EU's Schengen Agreement along with Denmark, Finland and Sweden (all EU members) by virtue of its membership in the Nordic passport union (Norway also joined).

SURVEY AND PROSPECTS

During the late 1990s the Icelandic economy expanded rapidly, partly as a result of the recovery of the fishing industry but largely owing to the diversification of the economy through extensive deregulation and restructuring (begun in the early 1990s). The tourism sector has expanded rapidly, while significant biotechnology and information technology industries have also been developed. The financial sector has benefited from the liberalization of capital flows and a series of privatizations.

The year 2003 was marked by a sharp rise in national expenditure. Consumption and investment together rose by 6.8% in real terms, compared with a 3.0% decline in 2002. This increase was mirrored by a rapid rise in the current-account deficit to an estimated 35,000m. krónur, equivalent to 4.3% of GDP. In 2003 economic growth was estimated at 2.5%, the rate of inflation close to 2% and unemployment at 3.3%.

Controversial proposals to build a large aluminium smelting plant and associated hydroelectric power plants in Kárahnjúkar in the Eastern Highlands were approved by the Althingi in March 2003; the smelting plant (which was scheduled to be completed in 2007) was expected to double Iceland's annual exports of aluminium. The construction of the Kárahnjúkar dam began in late 2003, and was expected to accelerate in 2004, when building work on the aluminium plant and harbour facility at Reyðarfjörður was to commence.

Iceland's total fish catch was expected to increase by 6.5% during 2004, on the assumption that the capelin catch would be comparable to that in previous years. Economic growth was forecast to reach 3% in 2004, primarily through private-sector activity (growth in the public sector, on the other hand, was expected to be less than 1%). However, owing to the heightened level of construction activity at Kárahnjúkar and rising national expenditure, the current-account deficit was projected to increase to 45,000m. krónur in 2004, equivalent to 5.3% of GDP. Inflation was expected to reach 2.5% in 2004. The conclusion of wage agreements and the development of the króna exchange rate were to be influential determinants on price developments in 2004–05. Disposable income per head was expected to rise by 2%, in real terms, in 2004. Demand for labour was forecast to grow, while unemployment was expected to fall to around 3% in the course of the year.

Iceland has benefited greatly from its membership of the European Economic Area, but is reluctant to join the EU, owing to the potentially adverse effects of the Common Fisheries Policy on the Icelandic fishing industry. However, the Government is likely to come under increased pressure in the future to establish some form of link with the European single currency, the euro, to protect certain industries, notably tourism, from the effects of currency fluctuations.

India

The Republic of India forms a natural sub-continent, with the Himalaya mountain range to the north. Two sections of the Indian Ocean—the Arabian Sea and the Bay of Bengal—lie to the west and east, respectively. After a prolonged struggle against British colonial rule, India became independent, within the Commonwealth, in 1947. The United Kingdom's Indian Empire was partitioned between India and Pakistan. In 1950 India became a republic. In 2004 the Congress Party and its allies won an unexpected victory at a general election, defeating the National Democratic Alliance led by the Bharatiya Janata Party. New Delhi is the capital. Hindi is the official language.

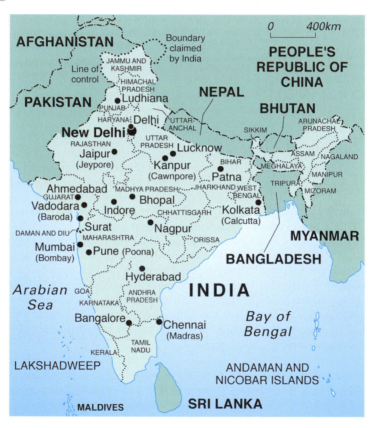

Area and population

Area: 3,166,414 sq km (including the Indian-controlled part of Jammu and Kashmir)
Population (mid-2002): 1,048,278,528
Population density (mid-2002): 331.1 per sq km
Life expectancy (years at birth, 2002): 61.0 (males 60.1; females 62.0)

Finance
GDP in current prices: 2002): US $515,012m. ($491 per head)
Real GDP growth (2002): 4.4%
Inflation (annual average, 2002): 4.4%
Currency: Indian rupee

Economy

In 2002, according to estimates by the World Bank, India's gross national income (GNI), measured at average 2000–02 prices, was US $501,532,323m., equivalent to $480 per head (or $2,570 per head on an international purchasing-power parity basis). During 1990–2002, it was estimated, the population increased at an average annual rate of 1.8%, while gross domestic product (GDP) per head increased, in real terms, by an average of 3.6% in 1990–2002. Overall GDP increased, in real terms, at an average annual rate of 5.4% in 1990–2002; the rate of growth reached 5.5% in 2001/02, but declined to 4.4% in 2002/03, owing to severe drought and, consequently, low agricultural output. In 2003/04 the economy was forecast to recover significantly; the growth rate was initially expected to reach 6.5%, but was later revised to a projected 7.5%–8.0%.

AGRICULTURE
Agriculture (including forestry and fishing) contributed an estimated 24.9% of GDP in 2001/02. About 59.2% of the economically active population were employed in agriculture in 2001. The principal cash crops are cotton (cotton accounted for 4.2% of total export earnings in 2002/03), tea, rice, spices, sugar cane and groundnuts. Coffee and jute production are also important. The average annual growth rate in the output of the agricultural sector was 2.3% in 1990–2002; agricultural GDP grew by 5.7% in 2001/02 and contracted by 3.1% in 2002/03. In 2003/04 agricultural GDP was expected to grow by 7.7%.

INDUSTRY
Industry (including mining, manufacturing, power and construction) contributed an estimated 25.9% of GDP in 2001/02. According to World Bank estimates, about 12.9% of the working population were employed in the industrial sector in 1995. Industrial GDP increased at an average annual rate of 5.5% in 1990–2002; the rate of growth of the GDP of the industrial sector reached 3.3% in 2001/02 and 6.1% in 2002/03.

Mining
Mining contributed an estimated 2.2% of GDP in 2001/02, and employed 0.6% of the working population in 1991. Iron ore and cut diamonds are the major mineral exports. Coal, limestone, zinc and lead are also mined. In 2002 India was the third largest coal producer in the world after the People's Republic of China and the USA. According to the Asian Development Bank (ADB), mining GDP increased at an average annual rate of 4.1% during 1994/95–2000/01.

Manufacturing
Manufacturing contributed an estimated 15.3% of GDP in 2001/02, and employed 10.0% of the working population in 1991. The GDP of the manufacturing sector

increased at an average annual rate of 5.8% during 1990–2002; manufacturing GDP rose by 3.4% in 2001/02 and by 6.1% in 2002/03. In 1998 the most important branches, measured by gross value of output, were food products (accounting for 16.8% of the total), iron and steel (11.1%), textiles (9.6%) and industrial chemicals (8.5%).

Energy

In late 1998 India had a total generating capacity of 81,000 MW. In 2001/02 thermal plants accounted for an estimated 81.9% of total power generation and hydroelectric plants (often dependent on monsoons) for 14.3%; the remaining 3.7% was contributed by nuclear power. Imports of mineral fuels, lubricants, etc. comprised 36.7% of the cost of total imports in 2000.

SERVICES

The services sector, which is dominated by the rapidly expanding data-processing business, the growing number of business call centres and the tourism industry, contributed an estimated 49.2% of GDP in 2001/02, and engaged 20.5% of the economically active population in 1991. The GDP of the services sector increased by an average of 7.5% per year in 1990–2002; the rate of growth reached 6.8% in 2001/02 and 7.1% in 2002/03. The sector was expected to expand by 8.4% in 2003/04.

EXTERNAL TRADE

In 2002 India recorded a trade deficit of US $12,416m., and there was a surplus of $4,656m. on the current account of the balance of payments. In 2002/03 the principal source of imports (7.2%) and the principal market for exports (20.7%) was the USA. Other major trading partners were Japan, the United Kingdom, Belgium, Hong Kong, the United Arab Emirates and Germany. The principal exports in 2002/03 were ready-made garments, pearls, precious and semi-precious stones and mineral fuels and lubricants. The principal imports were mineral fuels and lubricants, pearls, precious and semi-precious stones and machinery and mechanical appliances.

GOVERNMENT FINANCE

In the financial year ending 31 March 2004 there was a projected budgetary deficit of Rs 1,536,370m., equivalent to 5.6% of GDP. In 2000, according to the UN, India's total official development assistance stood at US $1,487.2m. (of which $775.3m. was in the form of grants and $711.9m. was in the form of loans). India's total external debt was $97,320m. at the end of 2001, of which $82,695m. was long-term public debt. In that year the cost of debt-servicing was equivalent to 11.7% of earnings from the exports of goods and services. The average annual rate of inflation was an estimated 8.2% in 1990–2002; consumer prices rose by 3.8% in 2001 and by 4.2% in 2002. In rural India the number of people wholly unemployed comprised about 6% of the potential labour force for adult males in the early 2000s, but the proportion was around 23% when account was taken of underemployment.

INTERNATIONAL ECONOMIC RELATIONS

India is a member of the ADB, of the UN Economic and Social Commission for Asia and the Pacific (ESCAP), of the South Asian Association for Regional Co-operation (SAARC) and of the Colombo Plan.

SURVEY AND PROSPECTS

The process of wide-ranging economic reform initiated in 1991, including trade and investment liberalization, industrial deregulation, disinvestment by the Government in public enterprises and their gradual privatization, financial and tax reforms, etc., has continued despite several changes in government. By 2003 a variety of sectors—including power, coal, telecommunications, postal services, tourism, car manufacturing, transport (with the exception of the railways) and insurance—had been opened up to private (domestic and foreign) investment. Restrictions on foreign participation in a number of sectors (including the pharmaceuticals industry) were eased or removed in 2001/02 to encourage greater foreign investment, although confidence in the initiative was somewhat undermined, later in the year, by the collapse of the US energy corporation, Enron, the largest foreign investor in India. In late 2002 ministers finally reached a compromise to sell a stake in Hindustan Petroleum Corpn Ltd to a strategic investor and a portion of Bharat Petroleum Corpn Ltd to the public through a share offering; however, in September 2003 the Supreme Court ruled that parliamentary approval was needed before the sales could proceed, delaying the process even further. In January 2004 the Government agreed to raise limits on foreign investment in the petroleum and banking sectors.

Despite the global economic slowdown and an unexpected monsoon failure, the economy in 2002/03 improved in the areas of exports, industrial production, foreign-exchange reserves, foreign investment and inflation. In 2001/02 India recorded a current-account surplus for the first time in 23 years. The surplus increased in 2002/03, but declined in 2003/04. The substantial recovery in the agricultural sector (assisted by a good monsoon), along with an increase in foreign-exchange reserves, continued growth in industrial production and the services sector, and a rising stock market, contributed to strong growth in the economy in 2003/04. The high GDP growth rate (projected at 7.5%–8.0%, according to revised forecasts) was also attributed to interest-rate reductions, infrastructure improvements and demographic changes. However, attempts to address India's unwieldy fiscal deficit (traditionally fuelled by the country's modest tax base and cumbersome local government apparatus) have been largely frustrated by the repeated stalling of the divestment programme and the costs associated with natural disasters and volatile foreign relations and internal security concerns; the deficit remains a major cause of concern to potential foreign investors and international donors. The 2003/04 Union budget envisaged a fiscal deficit equivalent to 5.6% of GDP. Furthermore, although GDP growth was expected to reach the annual average target of 8% contained in the Tenth Five-Year Plan (2002–07), analysts warned that the success was largely due to the agricultural sector, where the year's expansion was exaggerated by the contraction in 2002/03. Further economic reforms were needed to ensure a high level of economic performance in 2004/05 and beyond. Value-added tax was scheduled to be introduced at state level from the beginning of 2003/04, eventually to replace the central sales tax, but by early 2004 the states had yet to agree on its implementation.

It was hoped that attempts to restore normal relations between India and Pakistan in early 2004 and the planned implementation of a South Asia Free Trade Area by 1 January 2006 would lead to an increase in trade between the two neighbours.

The late 1990s witnessed India's rapid emergence as a 'software superpower'; in 2000 software exports constituted the country's single largest export item, earning, according to the National Association of Software and Service Companies (Nasscom), an estimated US \$3,900m. in 1999/2000. The rapidly expanding industry presented increasing employment opportunities. Nevertheless, concern grew over the high number of qualified information technology professionals leaving the country for better-paid work elsewhere. In the early 2000s business call centres had become the fastest growing industry in India, expanding by 70% in 2002. An increasing number of multinational companies were transferring their call centre operations to India, largely owing to cheaper labour costs and low long-distance telephone charges. More than 170,000 people were employed in the outsourcing industry in mid-2003. In 2002/03 software exports expanded to reach \$9,500m., despite the global economic slowdown; of the total, exports of information technology services, products and technology raised \$7,200m., while the outsourcing industry provided \$2,300m. Nasscom forecast that the revenue from call centres would reach \$24,000m. annually by 2008.

Indonesia

The Republic of Indonesia consists of a group of about 17,500 islands, lying between mainland South-East Asia and Australia. In 1966 independent Indonesia's first President, Dr Sukarno, transferred emergency executive powers to military commanders, led by Gen. Suharto, who became President in 1968 and remained in power until 1998, when violent unrest precipitated his resignation. In 1999 Abdurrahman Wahid was elected as President, but was deposed in 2001, and replaced by the Vice-President, Megawati Sukarnoputri. In 2004 Sukarnoputri was defeated by Susilo Bambang Yudhoyono in the country's first direct presidential election. The capital is Jakarta. Bahasa Indonesia is the official language.

Area and population

Area: 1,922,570 sq km
Population (mid-2002): 211,716,400
Population density (mid-2002): 110.1 per sq km
Life expectancy (years at birth, 2002): 66.4 (males 64.9; females 67.9)

Finance
GDP in current prices: 2002): US $172,911m. ($817 per head)
Real GDP growth (2002): 3.7%
Inflation (annual average, 2002): 11.5%
Currency: rupiah

Economy

In 2002, according to estimates by the World Bank, Indonesia's gross national income (GNI), measured at average 2000–02 prices, was US $149,879m., equivalent to $710 per head (or $2,990 per head on an international purchasing-power parity basis). During 1990–2002, it was estimated, the population increased at an average annual rate of 1.4%, while gross domestic product (GDP) per head increased, in real terms, by an average of 2.6% per year. Overall GDP increased, in real terms, by an average of 4.1% per year in 1990–2002. According to official figures, GDP increased by 3.7% in 2002 and by 4.1% in 2003.

AGRICULTURE
Agriculture, forestry and fishing contributed 17.5% of GDP in 2002, and engaged 43.8% of the employed labour force in 2001. Principal crops for domestic consumption were rice, cassava and maize. Once self-sufficient in rice, Indonesia was obliged to import supplies from the 1990s onwards, owing to increasing domestic demand. In the late 1990s Indonesia remained a major exporter of rubber and palm oil. Other principal cash crops were coffee, spices, tea, cocoa, tobacco, bananas, coconuts and sugar cane. In 2000 an estimated 58% of Indonesia's land area was covered by tropical rain forests. In 2001 there were demands for a tightening of controls on the exploitation of the country's natural resources owing to the prevalence of illegal and unsustainable practices, particularly in the forestry sector. In January 2003 a report published by the Environmental Investigation Agency (EIA) blamed the corruption endemic in Indonesia for the obstruction of efforts to prevent the widespread environmental damage caused by illegal logging practices. In late 2003 a devastating flash flood in a tourist resort on the island of Sumatra was attributed to massive illegal logging in the area. During 1990–2002, according to the Asian Development Bank (ADB), agricultural GDP increased by an estimated average of 2.1% per year. The GDP of the sector expanded by 1.0% in 2001 and by 1.7% in 2002.

INDUSTRY
Industry (including mining, manufacturing, construction and power) engaged 18.7% of the employed labour force in 2001 (including activities not adequately defined), and provided 44.5% of GDP in 2002. During 1990–2002, according to the ADB, industrial GDP increased by an average of 5.4% per year. The GDP of the sector increased by 3.3% in 2001 and by 3.7% in 2002.

Mining
Mining engaged only 0.5% of the employed labour force in 2000, but contributed 11.9% of GDP in 2002. Indonesia's principal mineral resource is petroleum, and the country is a leading exporter of liquefied natural gas. At the end of 2002 proven

reserves of petroleum amounted to 5,000m. barrels, enough to sustain production at that year's level (averaging 1.28m. barrels per day) for approximately 11 years. In 2002 natural gas production was 70,600m. cu m, from proven reserves amounting to 262,000m. cu m, enough to sustain production at that year's level for approximately 37 years. In the same year coal production was 63.3m. metric tons, from proven reserves of 5,370m. metric tons, sufficient to sustain production at that year's level for a further 52 years. With effect from 1 April 2004 Indonesia's petroleum production quota was set by the Organization of the Petroleum Exporting Countries (OPEC) at 1.218m. barrels per day. In 1992 Indonesia became the world's second largest producer of tin. Bauxite, nickel, copper, gold, silver and coal are also mined. During 1990–2002, according to the ADB, mining GDP increased by an average of 3.4% per year. The GDP of the sector remained constant in 2001, but increased by 2.2% in 2002.

Manufacturing

Manufacturing contributed 25.0% of GDP in 2002, and engaged 13.3% of the employed labour force in 2001. Apart from petroleum refineries, the main branches of the sector include food products, textiles, clothing and footwear, transport equipment, electrical machinery and electronic equipment. According to the ADB, manufacturing GDP increased by an estimated average of 6.4% per year in 1990–2002. Manufacturing GDP increased by 4.1% in 2001 and by 4.0% in 2002.

Energy

During the 1980s Indonesia broadened the base of its energy supplies to include gas, coal, hydroelectricity and geothermal energy, in addition to the traditional dependence on petroleum. In 2000, of the total 92,821m. kWh of electricity produced, natural gas accounted for 34.3%, coal for 31.1%, petroleum for 21.9% and hydroelectricity for 9.8%. In 2001 imports of petroleum and its products comprised 17.9% of the value of merchandise imports.

SERVICES

Services (including trade, transport and communications, finance and tourism) provided an estimated 38.1% of GDP in 2002, and engaged 37.5% of the employed labour force in 2001. Tourism is normally one of the principal sources of foreign exchange, although following the terrorist attack on the tourist destination of Bali in October 2002 it was feared that revenues from tourism might suffer significantly in subsequent years. The number of tourists increased to 5.2m. in 2001 but decreased to 5.0m. in 2002. In 2001 revenue from tourism totalled US $5,411m., having decreased from a total of $5,749m. in 2000. According to the ADB, the GDP of the services sector expanded by an estimated average of 3.7% per year in 1990–2002. The sector's GDP increased by 4.6% in 2001 and by 4.4% in 2002.

EXTERNAL TRADE

In 2002 Indonesia recorded a visible trade surplus of US $23,121m. In the same year a surplus of $7,450m. was recorded on the current account of the balance of payments. In 2002 the principal source of imports (14.1%) and principal market for exports (21.1%) was Japan. Other major suppliers were Singapore, the USA, the People's Republic of China, the Republic of Korea and Australia; other major purchasers were the USA, Singapore, the Republic of Korea, the People's Republic of China and Taiwan. The principal exports in 2001 were petroleum and its products, clothing, textiles, electronic equipment and plywood. In the same year the principal imports were machinery, mechanical appliances and electrical equipment, mineral and chemical products and textiles.

GOVERNMENT FINANCE

The budget for 2001/02 projected a deficit of Rp. 17,340,000m. In 2003 the budget deficit was expected to reach the equivalent of 1.9% of GDP. Indonesia's total external debt stood at US $135,704m. at the end of 2001, of which $68,378m. was long-term public debt. In that year the cost of debt-servicing was equivalent to 23.6% of revenue from exports of goods and services. The annual rate of inflation averaged 16.0% in 1995–2002. Consumer prices rose by an average of 11.9% in 2002 and by an estimated 6.6% in 2003. In 2002, according to the ADB, 9.1% of the labour force were unemployed. The level of underemployment remained very high.

INTERNATIONAL ECONOMIC RELATIONS

Indonesia is a member of the UN Economic and Social Commission for Asia and the Pacific (ESCAP), the Association of South East Asian Nations (ASEAN), the Asian Development Bank (ADB), the Asia-Pacific Economic Co-operation (APEC) forum, the Colombo Plan and OPEC. As a member of ASEAN, Indonesia signed an accord in January 1992, pledging to establish a free trade zone, to be known as the ASEAN Free Trade Area (AFTA), within 15 years (subsequently reduced to 10 years), beginning in January 1993. AFTA was formally established on 1 January 2002.

SURVEY AND PROSPECTS

The Indonesian economy was particularly badly affected by the repercussions of the regional financial crisis from mid-1997 and by political instability. In 2001 the impeachment of President Wahid, combined with the IMF's continued refusal to release funds in support of the Government's economic reforms, led to a rapid downturn in the capital and currency markets. The accession of Megawati Sukarnoputri to the presidency in July 2001, however, seemed to restore a measure of political stability, which it was hoped would engender an economic revival. In September the IMF finally released a US $395m. loan to Indonesia.

In the following month, in an effort to reduce the Government's energy subsidies in line with IMF requirements, the House of Representatives approved legislation to liberalize the oil and gas sector by terminating the 30-year monopoly held by Pertamina, the state oil and gas company. At the annual meeting of the Consultative Group for Indonesia (CGI—a donor grouping chaired by the World Bank and incorporating IMF representatives) held in November 2001, donors pledged $3,140m. for 2002. However, $1,300m. of this aid was conditional upon the Government increasing its efforts to privatize state-owned assets, improve the legal system and revive the troubled banking sector.

In October 2002 the economy was placed under severe strain by the terrorist attack on the island of Bali. As well as severely affecting the tourism sector, the bombing served to exacerbate further the problem of declining foreign investment in the country; in 2002 foreign direct investment (FDI) was estimated at $9,740m., a decrease of 35% compared with the previous year. Exports also continued to slow, affected by economic deceleration in the country's principal export markets—Japan, the USA and Singapore.

In January 2003 the Government implemented price rises on several fuel and utility tariffs in accordance with the reform programme recommended by the IMF and other international donors. However, in the face of widespread protests, the increases were rescinded shortly afterwards. Meanwhile, the IMF announced that it had reached a new agreement with the Government concerning its ongoing reform programme; the arrangement would allow Indonesia to draw $450m. of the $1,800m. that remained available to it under the terms of the $5,000m. extended fund facility. In 2003 high levels of consumer spending continued to underpin economic growth. However, there was no significant increase in FDI over the course of the year, in part owing to the security concerns prompted by domestic unrest, particularly in the provinces of Aceh and Papua, and to the continued terrorist activity in the country, highlighted by the bombing of the Marriott Hotel in Jakarta in August. Despite the effects of the attack, an overall improvement in the country's economic performance in 2003, largely as a result of the ongoing implementation of reforms, prompted the Government to announce the termination of its involvement with the IMF at the end of the year. In order to ensure that it retained investor confidence, however, in September 2003 the Government released a plan outlining its intention to continue to implement reforms and to encourage the expansion of investment, employment and exports once it had emerged from the supervision of the IMF.

In early 2004 the closure of the agency established in 1998 to supervise the revival of the banking sector—the Indonesian Bank Restructuring Agency (IBRA)—signified further progress in the rehabilitation of the country's banking sector. It was feared, however, that the discovery of a corruption scandal at Bank Negara Indonesia (BNI) in late 2003 might undermine investor confidence in the progress of reforms in the financial sector.

At the CGI meeting held in December 2003 donors pledged $2,800m. of budgetary support for 2004. In March 2004, furthermore, partly as a means of financing the budget deficit, Indonesia released its first global bond since 1996; the issue attracted strong demand from overseas investors and raised a total of $1,000m. in 10-year bonds. GDP growth of between 4% and 5% was anticipated in 2004. In the long term, Indonesia's economic performance continued to depend upon improving conditions for investment, in large part through the continued implementation of reforms in the legal and judicial sector.

Iran

The Islamic Republic of Iran lies in western Asia. In 1979 opposition to his regime forced the Shah (Emperor) of Iran, Muhammad Reza Pahlavi, to leave the country. Ayatollah Ruhollah Khomeini, a fundamentalist Shi'ite Muslim leader, assumed power and Iran became an Islamic republic. For most of the 1980s domestic and foreign policy was dominated by war with Iraq. Following Khomeini's death in 1989, President Khamenei was elected as Iran's spiritual leader. In that year Hashemi Rafsanjani was elected as President. After a second term, Rafsanjani was succeeded, in 1997, by Sayed Muhammad Khatami. President Khatami was re-elected in 2001. Tehran is the capital. The principal language is Farsi.

Area and population

Area: 1,648,043 sq km
Population (mid-2002): 65,540,224
Population density (mid-2002): 39.8 per sq km
Life expectancy (years at birth, 2002): 68.9 (males 66.5; females 71.7)

Finance

GDP in current prices: 2002): US $107,522m. ($1,641 per head)
Real GDP growth (2002): 5.9%
Inflation (annual average, 2002): 14.3%
Currency: rial

Economy

In 2002, according to estimates by the World Bank, Iran's gross national income (GNI), measured at average 2000–02 prices, was US $112,098m., equivalent to $1,710 per head (or \$6,340 per head on an international purchasing-power parity basis). During 1990–2002, it was estimated, the population increased at an average annual rate of 1.6%, while gross domestic product (GDP) per head increased, in real terms, by an average of 2.7% per year. Overall GDP increased, in real terms, at an average annual rate of 4.4% in 1990–2002; growth was an estimated 3.3% in 2001/02 (Iranian year to March) and some 7.4% in 2002/03.

AGRICULTURE

Agriculture (including forestry and fishing) contributed an estimated 13.2% of GDP in 2001/02. About 23.5% of the employed labour force were engaged in agriculture at the time of the 1996 census. The principal cash crops are fresh and dried fruit and nuts, which accounted for some 15.8% of non-petroleum export earnings in 2001/02. The principal subsistence crops are wheat, barley, sugar beet and sugar cane. Imports of cereals comprised some 8.4% of the value of total imports in 2001/02. Agricultural GDP increased by an average of 4.2% per year in 1990–2002; the sector's GDP increased by an estimated 2.8% in 2000/01 and by about 4.7% in 2001/02.

INDUSTRY

Industry (including mining, manufacturing, construction and power) contributed an estimated 34.6% of GDP in 2001/02, and engaged 31.2% of the employed labour force at the 1996 census. During 1990–2002 industrial GDP increased by an average of 0.3% per year; growth was estimated at 7.5% in 2000/01 and at 5.0% in 2001/02.

Mining

Mining (including petroleum refining) contributed an estimated 15.8% of GDP in 2001/02, although the sector engaged only 0.8% of the working population in 1996. Metal ores are the major non-hydrocarbon mineral exports, and coal, magnesite and gypsum are also mined. The sector is dominated by the hydrocarbons sector, which contributed an estimated 14.9% of GDP in 2001/02. At the end of 2002 Iran's proven reserves of petroleum were estimated at 89,700m. barrels, sufficient to maintain the 2002/03 level of production—averaging 3.31m. barrels per day (b/d)—for almost 74 years. However, since 1999 several important discoveries of petroleum have been made, leading to estimates that reserves might be closer to 130,000m. barrels. With effect from April 2004, Iran's production quota within the Organization of the Petroleum Exporting Countries (OPEC) was 3.45m. b/d. Iran's reserves of natural gas (23,000,000m. cu m at the end of 2002) are the second largest in the world, after those of Russia. The GDP of the mining sector increased by an average of 0.8% per year in 1991/92–2000/01; mining GDP was estimated to have increased by 4.8% in 2000/01 and by 9.6% in 2001/02.

Manufacturing

Manufacturing (excluding petroleum refining) contributed about 14.0% of GDP in 2001/02, and engaged 17.8% of the employed labour force in 1996. The most important sectors, in terms of value added, are textiles, food processing and transport equipment. The sector's GDP increased by an average of 5.8% per year in 1990–2002, with growth estimated at 8.0% in 2000/01 and at 10.0% in 2001/02.

Energy

Principal sources of energy are natural gas (providing around 76.6% of total electricity production in 2000) and petroleum (some 20.4% in the same year). Imports of mineral fuels and lubricants comprised just 3.5% of the value of total imports in 2001/02. The first phase of Iran's South Pars offshore gasfield (an extension of Qatar's North Field) was brought on stream in January 2003.

SERVICES

The services sector contributed an estimated 52.2% of GDP in 2001/02, and engaged 45.3% of the employed labour force in 1996. During 1990–2002 the GDP of the services sector increased by an average of 7.7% per year; the sector's GDP increased by an estimated 4.6% in both 2000/01 and 2001/02.

EXTERNAL TRADE

According to provisional figures, in the year ending March 2003 Iran recorded a visible trade surplus of US $4,400m., and there was a surplus of $3,731m. on the current account of the balance of payments. In 2001/02 the principal source of imports was Germany (which supplied 10.3% of total imports); other major suppliers included the United Arab Emirates (UAE), France and Italy. The principal markets for exports in 1999/2000 were Japan and the United Kingdom (which took, respectively, 16.5% and 15.4% of total exports); the UAE, Italy and the Republic of Korea were also important markets for Iranian exports. Other than petroleum and natural gas, Iran's principal exports in 2001/02 were chemical products, pistachios and other nuts and fruits, and carpets. Exports of petroleum and gas comprised 84.4% of the value of total exports in 2001/02. The principal imports in 2000/01 were machinery and transport equipment, basic manufactures, chemicals, and food and live animals.

GOVERNMENT FINANCE

For the financial year ending 20 March 2002 Iran recorded a budget deficit estimated at IR 3,380,100m., equivalent to 0.5% of GDP. Iran's total external debt was US $7,483m. at the end of 2001, of which $5,295m. was long-term public debt. In that year the cost of debt-servicing was equivalent to 4.9% of the value of exports of goods and services. The annual rate of inflation averaged 24.0% in 1990/91–2000/01. Consumer prices increased by an average of 11.4% in 2001/02 and 15.8% in 2002/03. Almost 16% of the total labour force were estimated to be unemployed in 2002/03.

INTERNATIONAL ECONOMIC RELATIONS

Iran is a member of OPEC, of the Economic Co-operation Organization (ECO), of the Developing Eight (D-8) group of Islamic countries, and was admitted to the Group of 15 developing countries (G-15) in mid-2000.

SURVEY AND PROSPECTS

Notable weaknesses in the Iranian economy include the Government's dependence on revenue from the petroleum sector, high rates of unemployment and inflation, and disparities in the distribution of income. Additional strain has, moreover, been placed on domestic resources by the presence in Iran of large numbers of refugees from Afghanistan and Iraq.

A major emphasis of the Third Five Year Development Plan (TFYDP), which took effect in March 2000, was to be the reduction of Iran's dependence on the oil sector as the principal generator of wealth. President Khatami advocated as fundamental to the Plan the restructuring of the state portfolio and the elimination of monopolies, together with wide-ranging tax reforms. A priority was to be job creation, with a target of some 765,000 new posts annually. Growth under the plan was forecast at some 6% annually, and major new oil and gas discoveries from 1999 enhanced confidence that the Plan's ambitious objectives might be realized. Moreover, the installation in mid-2000 of a new Majlis with a 'reformist' majority was expected to expedite Khatami's economic liberalization measures, although despite being elected to a second presidential term in June 2001, Khatami continued to encounter strong opposition to reform from 'conservatives' within the Islamic regime.

Despite strong growth in 2000/01, largely reflecting the high level of petroleum export earnings, and while inflation and unemployment were reported to be at their lowest levels for some years, the implementation of vital structural reforms proceeded slowly. The TFYDP allowed for the private ownership of banks for the first time since the Revolution; by early 2003 four private banks had been authorized to commence operations and the Government declared its intention to privatize all banks except Bank Melli Iran. The country's first private insurance firm was established in February 2003. In addition, a return to international capital markets was achieved, with two Eurobond issues totalling €1,000m. being issued during 2002, while the introduction of a unified exchange rate for the rial was announced in March of that year.

Meanwhile, a stabilization fund was established in March 2000, into which were paid petroleum revenues exceeding budgeted income; one-half of its value was to be reserved for use in the event of a future decline in international oil prices below budgeted levels, while the remainder was intended for private sector development and export promotion. In addition to the high petroleum prices, the Khatami administration's economic programme was further strengthened in May 2000 by a decision by the World Bank (despite US objections) to resume lending for the first time since 1994. Iran received a further World Bank loan in December 2002. A new foreign investment law passed by the Expediency Council in May 2002 resulted in government approval for the first foreign take-over of an Iranian company. Assisted by buoyant oil revenues, real GDP showed sustained growth in 2001/02 and 2002/03.

The budget for 2003/04 allocated increased spending on defence and infrastructural investment, as well as a further injection of funds into job creation schemes. Moreover, in August 2003 the Vice-President and Head of the Management and Planning Organization, Muhammad Sattarifar, announced that there would be no budget deficit in 2003/04, based largely on the expectation of surplus oil revenues of US $6,000m. The USA's ongoing efforts to hinder foreign investment in the Iranian economy were encapsulated in 2003 by an attempt to prevent the signing of an agreement between Iran and a Japanese consortium to develop the Azadegan oilfield (discovered in 1999 and believed to contain 5,000m.–6,000m. barrels of recoverable reserves). Later in the year, the US Administration of George W. Bush lifted some economic sanctions against Iran in order to ease the transfer of financial and material aid in the aftermath of the earthquake at Bam.

Although vital economic reforms have taken place under President Khatami, Iran remains heavily dependent on revenue from the oil sector, and there is a need to accelerate the privatization of state-owned enterprises and to attract higher levels of foreign investment in order to provide employment for a rapidly expanding population.

Iraq

The Republic of Iraq lies in western Asia. In 1921 Amir Faisal ibn Hussain, a member of the Hashimi dynasty of Arabia, was proclaimed King of Iraq. The monarchy was overthrown in 1958 in a military revolution that brought to power a left-wing nationalist regime. In 1968 members of the Arab Renaissance (Baath) Socialist Party seized power, vesting supreme authority in a Revolutionary Command Council (RCC). Saddam Hussain was RCC Chairman and President of Iraq from 1979 until April 2003, when a US-led coalition removed the Baath Party from power. An Iraqi Interim Government took office on 1 June 2004. Baghdad is the capital. The official language is Arabic.

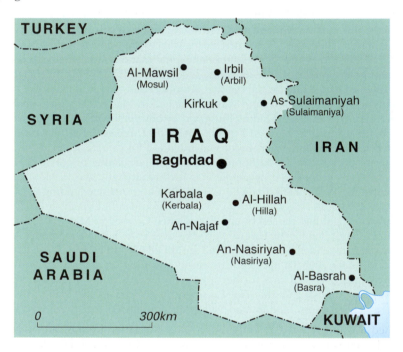

Area and population
Area: 438,317 sq km
Population (mid-2002): 24,256,320
Population density (mid-2002): 55.3 per sq km
Life expectancy (years at birth, 2002): 61.0 (males 59.1; females 63.1)

Finance
GDP in current prices: 1999): US $70,215m. ($3,144 per head)
Real GDP growth (1999): 8.0%
Currency: Iraqi dinar

Economy

In 2002, according to estimates by the UN's Economic and Social Commission for Western Asia (ESCWA), Iraq's gross domestic product (GDP), measured in current prices, was ID 5,924,542m. In terms of US dollars, GDP was $5,265.9m. ($212 per head) in 2002. Real GDP growth was estimated at 9% in 2001 and 7% in 2002. Over the period 1990–2002 the population increased by an average of 2.5% per year, according to estimates by the World Bank.

AGRICULTURE

Agriculture (including forestry and fishing) contributed 30.0% of GDP in 2002, compared with 15.3% in 1989—i.e. prior to the invasion of Kuwait. An estimated 9.6% of the labour force were employed in agriculture in 2001. Dates are the principal cash crop. Other crops include wheat, barley, potatoes, tomatoes, melons and oranges. Production of eggs, milk and poultry meat is also important. During 1990–2001, according to FAO data, agricultural production declined by an average of 3.8% per year; however, output increased by 8.0% in 2001. Output of cereals fell from 3.45m. metric tons in 1990 to an estimated 1.45m. metric tons in 2002.

INDUSTRY

Industry (including mining, manufacturing, construction and power) employed 19.1% of the labour force in 1987; the sector provided 16.2% of GDP in 2002 (compared with 37.9% in 1989).

Mining

Mining (including production of crude petroleum and gas) employed 1.3% of the labour force in 1987. The sector contributed less than 0.1% of GDP in 1994 (compared with 17.9% in 1989), and by 1995 its contribution was negative. Iraq had proven reserves of 112,500m. barrels of petroleum at the end of 2002, as well as 3,110,000m. cu m of natural gas. Reserves of phosphates, sulphur, gypsum and salt are also exploited.

Manufacturing

Manufacturing employed 7.4% of the labour force in 1987, and contributed 0.7% of GDP in 1995 (compared with 12.3% in 1989). The mining and manufacturing sectors combined accounted for 10.6% of GDP in 2002. Measured by the value of output, chemical, petroleum, coal, rubber and plastic products accounted for 35.2% of manufacturing activity in 1986. Other important branches of the sector in that year were food products (providing 15.8% of manufacturing output), non-metallic mineral products (12.6%) and textiles (6.1%).

Energy

Energy is derived principally from petroleum, which accounted for an estimated 98.2% of total electricity generation in 2000.

SERVICES

The services sector employed 67.2% of the labour force in 1987, and contributed 53.8% of GDP in 2002 (compared with 46.7% in 1989).

EXTERNAL TRADE

In 1996, according to the *Middle East Economic Digest* of London, Iraq recorded a trade surplus of US $300m. In that year, according to the same source, the current account of the balance of payments was estimated to be in balance. Crude petroleum was by far the most important export before the imposition of economic sanctions. According to the IMF, the value of Iraq's imports in 2002 was ID 1,810.7m.

GOVERNMENT FINANCE

Budget proposals for 2004, published in late 2003, forecast expenditure of NID 20,145,100m. and revenue of NID 19,258,800m. The Iraqi Government estimated that, at 1 January 1991, its total external debt stood at ID 13,118m. (US $42,320m.); and that the servicing of the debt over the period 1991–95 would cost ID 23,388m. ($75,450m.). These estimates did not, however, take into account loans made to Iraq during the Iran–Iraq War by Saudi Arabia and Kuwait. The *Middle East Economic Digest* estimated that in 1996 the average rate of inflation was 450%, compared with inflation averaging 24.4% per year in 1985–89.

INTERNATIONAL ECONOMIC RELATIONS

Iraq is a member of the Arab Fund for Economic and Social Development, the Council of Arab Economic Unity, the Organization of Arab Petroleum Exporting Countries, the Organization of the Petroleum Exporting Countries and the Arab Co-operation Council. Iraq was granted observer status at the World Trade Organization in February 2004.

SURVEY AND PROSPECTS

Under the terms of UN Resolution 986, instituting the so-called oil-for-food programme whereby supply and distribution of humanitarian and consumer goods to Iraq and the sale of Iraqi petroleum were monitored by the UN, Iraq was initially permitted to sell petroleum to the value of US $2,000m. over a six-month period (subsequently extended), commencing in December 1996. The oil-for-food programme eventually spanned 13 phases between this date and March 2003, with exports of crude petroleum totalling US $64,231m. The lengths of the phases and the export quotas were altered to take into account the varying needs of the Iraqi economy; moreover, production was often hindered by the ailing infrastructure of the oil industry. However, by 2001 Iraq was estimated to be gaining an additional $1,000m. annually through smuggling. The US-led coalition's military campaign to oust Saddam Hussein took place during the 13th phase of the oil-for-food programme, and the removal from power of the Baathist regime effectively brought to an end the programme and its attendant system of sanctions. In early 2003 industry sources estimated Iraq's oil production capacity to be around 2.8m. b/d; capacity prior to the Gulf crisis of 1990–91 was in the region of 3.5m. b/d. The hiatus in production caused by the recent conflict in Iraq came to an end on 22 April 2003, and the first post-war sales of oil were achieved in mid-June. At the beginning of August the Ministry of Oil announced plans to achieve production levels of 2.8m. b/d by April 2004. US company Kellogg Brown & Root (part of the Halliburton Group) was awarded one of the first contracts for the reconstruction and redevelopment of Iraq's infrastructure, namely that of repairing, maintaining and operating the apparatus of the oil industry, in the immediate aftermath of the conflict.

According to an official UN report compiled in March 1991, Iraq's war with the multinational force 'wrought near apocalyptic results on the economic infrastructure', relegating Iraq to a 'pre-industrial age but with all the disabilities of post-industrial dependency on an intensive use of energy and technology'. The damage to the infrastructure was reflected in every sector, with recovery undoubtedly obstructed by more than a decade of international sanctions. The failure of irrigation and drainage systems, compounded by the inability of farmers to obtain pesticides and fertilizers, resulted in very poor harvests, while reduced production of animal feed resulted in a significant decrease in livestock and livestock products. The consequences for the Iraqi population of the resultant food shortages were particularly severe. Upon his resignation in September 1998, the first co-ordinator of the UN oil-for-food programme estimated that 4,000–5,000 Iraqi children were dying each month as a result of contaminated water supplies, poor sanitation, malnutrition and inadequate health facilities. His successor resigned in February 2000, as did the head of World Food Programme operations, in protest at what they considered to be the consequences of the sanctions regime and the inadequacy of the humanitarian programme to meet the basic requirements of the Iraqi people. A report issued by the International Committee of the Red Cross in February 2000 stated that infant mortality had risen threefold since the imposition of economic sanctions in 1990. In late February 2003, as a US-led military campaign to oust the regime of Saddam Hussain appeared to be imminent, a leaked UN document reportedly warned that such a conflict could lead to 'a humanitarian emergency of proportions well beyond the capacity of UN agencies and other aid organizations' (a prediction which, in the event, proved somewhat alarmist). Following the US-led coalition's success in ousting the regime of Saddam Hussain in April, attention focused on the cost of rebuilding Iraq and the considerable commercial and government debts accrued by the former regime. The CPA established the Development Fund for Iraq (DFI), to be administered by the Central Bank of Iraq, to fund reconstruction efforts. An initial deposit of US $1,000m. was placed in the fund, comprising receipts from the oil-for-food programme (the remainder of which—approximately $5,600m.—the UN transferred to the DFI by the end of the year), and was to be further supplemented by 95% of future proceeds from oil exports. The US Agency for International Development (USAID) was responsible for awarding contracts for reconstruction work totalling $900m. in eight key areas: seaport administration; personnel support; capital construction; theatre logistics support; public health; primary and secondary education; local government; and airport administration. The USA's Bechtel Group was awarded large contracts, worth $680m. and $1,800m., for the restoration of basic services such as water, sewerage and electricity. Estimates for the total cost of the reconstruction of Iraq ranged between $26,000m. and $140,000m. However, Iraq's outstanding debts were estimated at $100,000m.–$200,000m., thus precluding the possibility of future proceeds from Iraq's oil exports financing both reconstruction and debt-servicing.

International efforts were made to reduce Iraq's external debt from October 2003. The World Bank pledged US $3,000m.–$5,000m. for reconstruction over the next five years following similar offers from the EU ($231m.), Japan ($1,500m.), Spain ($300m.) and the United Kingdom ($835m.). Furthermore, at a conference of international donors convened to discuss Iraqi debt reduction in Madrid, Spain, Japan offered a further $3,500m. in low-interest loans, and Saudi Arabia announced an aid package worth $1,000m. At the beginning of November the US Senate approved an $87,500m. emergency funding package for aid and military operations in Iraq and Afghanistan, of which $20,000m. was earmarked as a non-repayable grant for reconstruction in Iraq. In late December President Putin of Russia proposed that Iraq be absolved of at least 65% of its estimated $8,000m. debt to Russia; moreover, the Russian Government supported the view that agreements signed by Russian oil companies and the former Baathist regime were still legally binding. The UAE and Qatar announced in January 2004 that they were prepared to waive most of the $7,000m. they were owed by Iraq following talks with US envoy James Baker, who had been tasked by President Bush with leading efforts to reduce Iraq's debt burden. In February the Iraqi Ministry of Finance issued a request for proposals to establish officially the level of Iraq's indebtedness.

Ireland

The Republic of Ireland consists of 26 of the 32 counties that comprise the island of Ireland. In 1920 the island was partitioned, the six north-eastern counties remaining part of the United Kingdom. In 1922 the southern counties achieved dominion status, under the British Crown, as the Irish Free State. After 1937 the Irish Free State enjoyed full sovereignty within the Commonwealth. Ties with the Commonwealth were ended in 1949, when the 26 southern counties became a republic. At a general election held in 2002 Fiana Fáil narrowly failed to achieve an overall majority in the legislature. Dublin is the capital. Irish is the official first language.

Area and population
Area: 70,182 sq km
Population (mid-2002): 3,877,550
Population density (mid-2002): 55.2 per sq km
Life expectancy (years at birth, 2002): 77.1 (males 74.4; females 79.8)

Finance

GDP in current prices: 2002): US $119,916m. ($30,926 per head)
Real GDP growth (2002): 3.6%
Inflation (annual average, 2002): 4.7%
Currency: euro

Economy

In 2002, according to estimates by the World Bank, Ireland's gross national income (GNI), measured at average 2000–2002 prices, was US $92,552m., equivalent to $23,870 per head (or $28,040 on an international purchasing-power parity basis). During 1990–2002, it was estimated, the population increased at an average annual rate of 0.8%, while gross domestic product (GDP) per head increased, in real terms, by an average of 5.9% per year. Overall GDP increased, in real terms, at an average annual rate of 6.8% in 1990–2002; it grew by 5.8% in 2001 and by 3.6% in 2002.

AGRICULTURE

Agriculture (including forestry and fishing) contributed an estimated 3.2% of GDP in 2002. An estimated 6.4% of the working population were employed in the sector in 2003. Beef and dairy production dominate Irish agriculture (in 2001 meat and meat preparations accounted for 18% of total exports while dairy products and birds' eggs accounted for 1.0%). Principal crops include sugar beet, barley, wheat and potatoes. Agricultural GDP declined by an average of 0.3% per year during 1996–2002; it increased by 1.1% in 2001, but declined by 2.4% in 2002.

INDUSTRY

Industry (comprising mining, manufacturing, construction and utilities) provided 39.7% of GDP in 2002, and employed an estimated 27.7% of the working population in 2003. Industrial GDP increased by an average of 16.3% per year during 1996–2002; it grew by 12.7% in 2002.

Mining

Mining (including quarrying and turf production) provided employment to 0.4% of the working population in 1997. Ireland possesses substantial deposits of lead-zinc ore and recoverable peat, both of which are exploited. Natural gas, mainly from the Kinsale field, and small quantities of coal are also extracted. A significant natural gas deposit discovered in 1999 was expected to yield sufficient gas to meet more than one-half of the country's current average demand. Offshore reserves of petroleum have also been located and several licences awarded to foreign-owned enterprises to undertake further exploration. During 1980–90 mining production decreased by an average of 1.7% per year.

Manufacturing

Manufacturing was estimated to employ 20.3% of the working population in 1997. The manufacturing sector comprises many high-technology, largely foreign-owned, capital-intensive enterprises. The electronics industry accounted for 32.6% of the value of exports in 1996. During 1992–96 manufacturing production increased by an average of 10.1% per year.

Energy

Electricity is derived principally from natural gas, which provided 39.1% of total requirements in 2000, while coal provided 36.3% and petroleum 19.6%. In 2001 imports of mineral fuels were 3.9% (by value) of total merchandise imports.

SERVICES

Service industries (including commerce, finance, transport and communications, and public administration) contributed 57.1% of GDP in 2002, and employed an estimated 65.9% of the working population in 2003. The financial sector is of increasing importance to Ireland. An International Financial Services Centre in Dublin was opened in 1990; by mid-2003 more than 430 companies were participating in the Centre, many of which were foreign concerns attracted by tax concessions offered by the Irish Government. Tourism is one of the principal sources of foreign exchange. Revenue from the tourism and travel sector amounted to an estimated US $3,069m. in 2002. The GDP of the services sector increased by an average of 7.0% per year during 1996–2002, and by an estimated 4.7% in 2002.

EXTERNAL TRADE

In 2002, according to IMF statistics, Ireland recorded a visible trade surplus of US $34,898m. while there was a deficit of $925m. on the current account of the balance of payments. In 2002 the principal source of imports (35.9%) was the United Kingdom; other major sources were the USA (15.4%) and Germany (6.4%). The United Kingdom was also the principal market for exports (23.9%); other major purchasers were the USA (17.5%), Belgium (14.4%), Germany (7.2%) and France (5.0%). In 2002 principal imports included office equipment and other electrical machinery, chemical products, road vehicles and parts, and other manufactured items. Principal exports included electronic goods, chemicals, and food and live animals.

GOVERNMENT FINANCE

In 2002 there was a budgetary surplus of €94.9m. (equivalent to 1.7% of GDP). At the end of 2001 Ireland's total national debt was estimated to be IR£28,499m. The annual rate of inflation averaged 3.3% in 1996–2002. The rate decreased from 5.2% in 2000 to 4.0% in 2001, but increased to 4.7% in 2002. An estimated 4.4% of the labour force were unemployed in 2003, compared with 10.3% in 1997.

INTERNATIONAL ECONOMIC RELATIONS

Ireland is a member of the European Union (EU), and of the EU Exchange Rate Mechanism (ERM).

SURVEY AND PROSPECTS

In the late 1990s the Irish economy enjoyed an unprecedentedly high rate of growth, which was attributed to prudent fiscal and monetary management, an expanding, well-qualified labour force and social partnership agreements between the Government, businesses and trade unions, providing for guaranteed pay rises in return for productivity and 'no strike' agreements. In addition government policies offering financial incentives to foreign-owned enterprises resulted in a substantial increase in direct foreign investment and expansion in the financial services and electronic manufacturing industries. However, the Irish economy suffered a number of reverses in the early 2000s, experiencing reduced growth and a sharp increase in the rate of inflation as the outbreak of foot-and-mouth disease adversely affected the agriculture and tourism industries and the world-wide economic slowdown reduced levels of foreign investment. GDP growth of just 4% was forecast in 2003, compared with the 11.5% increase recorded in 2000, and by mid-2003 unemployment had risen to its highest level since 1999.

The competitiveness of the economy was greatly hampered by the continued strength of the euro as well as by the Government's imprudent fiscal policy during 2000–02, and the Economic and Social Research Institute urged the Government to increase investment in infrastructural projects in order to prevent the economy from further stagnation. The 2004 budget duly envisaged a significant rise in expenditure on infrastructural projects; however, much of the 5% rise in total government spending was allocated to cover the increases in public-sector pay, which had been agreed under the new social partnership programme, 'Sustaining Progress'. There were tentative signs of an economic recovery during late 2003 and early 2004 as inflation continued to fall (it was expected to average just 2% in 2003 as a whole), and, while growth rates comparable with the 'Celtic Tiger' period during the 1990s were highly unlikely, it appeared that Ireland could look forward to a sustained period of growth (of around 5% per year) from 2005 onwards.

Israel

The State of Israel lies in western Asia. In 1948, following the termination of the United Kingdom's Palestine mandate, the State of Israel was proclaimed. Cease-fire agreements with Arab neighbours in 1949 left Israel in control of 75% of Palestine, including West Jerusalem. In 1967 the Six-Day War left Israel in possession of all Jerusalem, the West Bank area, the Sinai Peninsula, the Gaza Strip and the Golan Heights. In 1991 negotiations commenced between the parties to the Arab–Israeli conflict on the basis of UN Security Council Resolutions 242 and 338. The Israeli Government's designated capital is Jerusalem. Hebrew is the official language.

Area and population
Area: 22,145 sq km (including Golan and East Jerusalem)
Population (mid-2002): 6,494,220
Population density (mid-2002): 293.3 per sq km
Life expectancy (years at birth, 2002): 79.4 (males 77.3; females 81.4)

Finance
GDP in current prices: 2000): US $110,386m. ($17,709 per head)
Real GDP growth (2000): 6.0%
Inflation (annual average, 2002): 5.6%
Currency: new shekel

Economy

In 2000, according to estimates by the World Bank, Israel's gross national income (GNI), measured at average 1998–2000 prices, was US $104,128m., equivalent to $16,710 per head (or $19,260 per head on an international purchasing-power parity basis). During 1990–2002, it was estimated, the population increased at an average annual rate of 2.8%, while during 1990–2000 gross domestic product (GDP) per head increased, in real terms, by an average of 2.2% per year. Overall GDP increased, in real terms, at an average annual rate of 5.2% in 1990–2000; growth was 2.2% in 1999 and 6.0% in 2000. However, negative growth was recorded in both 2001 and 2002.

AGRICULTURE

Agriculture (including hunting, forestry and fishing) contributed 1.7% of GDP in 2001, and in 2002 engaged 2.0% of the employed labour force. Most agricultural workers live in large co-operatives (*kibbutzim*), of which there were 268 at December 1999, or co-operative smallholder villages (*moshavim*), of which there were 411. Israel is largely self-sufficient in foodstuffs. Citrus fruits constitute the main export crop. Other important crops are vegetables (particularly tomatoes and potatoes), wheat, melons and grapes. The export of exotic fruits, winter vegetables and flowers has increased significantly in recent years. Poultry, livestock and fish production are also important. According to FAO data, agricultural output increased at an average annual rate of 1.1% in 1990–2002; production increased by 2.5% in 2001, but declined by 2.7% in 2002.

INDUSTRY

Industry (comprising mining, manufacturing, construction and power) contributed 23.3% of GDP in 2001, and engaged 22.5% of the employed labour force in 2002. The State plays a major role in all sectors of industry, and there is a significant co-operative sector. Industrial production increased by an average of 5.9% annually in 1988–95.

Mining

The mining and manufacturing sectors together contributed 16.6% of GDP in 2001, and engaged 16.5% of the employed labour force in 2002; mining and quarrying employed about 0.2% of the working population in 1997. Israel has small proven reserves of petroleum (of some 3.9m. barrels), from which less than 500 barrels per day are currently produced; however, in 1999 potential new reserves were discovered in central Israel and off the southern coast. Some natural gas is also produced, and significant offshore gas discoveries were made in the south in 1999 and 2000. Phosphates, potash, bromides, magnesium and other salts are mined, and Israel is the world's largest exporter of bromine. Gold, in potentially commercial quantities, was discovered in 1988.

Manufacturing

Manufacturing employed 19.3% of the working population in 1997. The principal branches of manufacturing, measured by gross revenue, in 1996 were food products, beverages and tobacco (accounting for 17.4% of the total), chemical, petroleum and coal products (15.0%), electrical machinery (12.1%), metal products (11.1%), scientific, photographic, optical equipment, etc. (8.0%), paper, publishing and printing (6.5%), textiles and clothing (5.6%), non-metallic mineral manufactures (5.4%), rubber and plastic products (5.1%) and non-electrical machinery (5.0%).

Energy

Energy is derived principally from coal (accounting for 69.0% of total electricity output in 2000) and imported petroleum (30.9% in 1999); however, it is intended that natural gas should eventually become Israel's principal energy source. Imports of mineral fuels comprised 8.0% of the total value of imports in 2002.

SERVICES

Services contributed 75.0% of GDP in 2001, and engaged 74.6% of the employed labour force in 2002. Tourism is an important source of revenue, although the sector has been severely damaged by regional instability and a series of bomb attacks carried out by militant Islamist groups in recent years. In 2000 some 2.4m. tourists visited Israel and receipts from tourism totalled US $3,859m. However, the significant upsurge in violence from September 2000 has once again deterred many foreign visitors, resulting in hotel closures, redundancies and a reduction in air travel. Tourist arrivals decreased to some 1.2m. in 2001, and to about 0.9m. in 2002. Receipts from tourism in 2001 were US $2,460m. Financial services are also important: banking, insurance, real estate and business services together contributed 30.4% of GDP in 2001, and employed 15.4% of the working population in 2002.

EXTERNAL TRADE

In 2002 Israel recorded a visible trade deficit of US $3,757m., and there was a deficit of $2,135m. on the current account of the balance of payments. Excluding trade with the West Bank and Gaza Strip, in 2002 the principal source of imports was the USA, which supplied 18.5% of imports to Israel; other major suppliers were the Belgo-Luxembourg Economic Union (BLEU), Germany, the United Kingdom and Switzerland. The USA was also the principal market for exports, taking 40.3% of Israeli exports in that year; other important purchasers were the BLEU, Hong Kong, the United Kingdom and Germany. Israel is the world's largest supplier of polished diamonds. The principal exports in 2002 were basic manufactures (chiefly non-metallic mineral manufactures), machinery and transport equipment, chemicals and related products, and miscellaneous manufactured articles. The principal imports in that year were basic manufactures (mainly non-metallic mineral manufactures), machinery and transport equipment, chemicals and related products, and miscellaneous manufactured articles.

GOVERNMENT FINANCE

In 2001 the overall budgetary deficit (excluding net allocation of credit) rose from the planned NIS 8,400m. (equivalent to some 1.7% of GDP) to NIS 21,300m. (equivalent to about 4.6% of GDP). This was mainly due to increased spending on security provisions prompted by the al-Aqsa *intifada*. Government revenue each year normally includes some US $3,000m. in economic and military aid from the USA. At 31 December 2000 Israel's gross foreign debt amounted to $64,877m., of which $27,762m. was government debt. During 1990–2002 consumer prices rose at an average annual rate of 8.5%. Annual inflation averaged 1.1% in 2001 and 5.6% in 2002. The unemployment rate was reported to be in excess of 10% in 2002.

SURVEY AND PROSPECTS

The most significant factor affecting the Israeli economy in the 1990s was the mass influx of Jews from the former USSR, which led to a substantial increase in the population, additional flexibility in the labour market and growth in construction. In 1996, however, a period of economic slowdown began, reflecting an end to the demand boom and reduced tourism revenues following an increase in Islamist violence.

In May 1998 foreign-exchange restrictions were ended, allowing the shekel to become fully convertible. After the Government of Ehud Barak was elected in mid-1999 and the Middle East peace process was revived, the economy entered a period of recovery, with a significant improvement in business activity and increased foreign investment. Moreover, inflation declined to its lowest level since 1967. The strong rate of economic growth in 2000 was led by the success of Israel's high-technology sector. However, in the fourth quarter of 2000 the economic boom ended as a new *intifada* by Palestinians in the West Bank and Gaza dramatically reduced foreign investment and tourism revenues, while the global economic downturn had a particularly detrimental effect on high-tech companies. The negative growth in the Israeli economy in 2001 was reported to have been the first contraction since 1953; negative growth was also recorded in 2002, and in March 2003 the IMF described the Israeli economy as being 'in the midst of a deep recession'.

Following the deregulation of the domestic telecommunications market and the privatization of Bank Hapoalim—Israel's largest bank—in 2000, the Government of Ariel Sharon defined its own privatization programme in May 2001, although structural reforms have generally proceeded slowly. In mid-September 2003 the Cabinet approved an austerity budget for 2004, which included reductions in public expenditure of NIS 10,000m. The budget proposed making reductions in welfare and education spending, but Minister of Finance Binyamin Netanyahu was forced to reduce cuts in defence spending following protests by the Prime Minister and the Minister of Defence. The cuts in public spending outlined in the budget prompted a general strike to be organized by the Histadrut labour organization in early November. The Knesset approved the austerity budget in January 2004. In February official statistics revealed that the Israeli economy had grown by 1.3% in 2003—the first such rise for three years—but this was considered insufficient to keep pace with the expanding population and the ongoing financial effects of the al-Aqsa *intifada*. The potential for Israeli economic growth in the long term will be dependent upon progress towards a comprehensive and enduring regional peace settlement.

Italy

The Italian Republic mainly comprises a peninsula, extending from southern Europe into the Mediterranean Sea. The Kingdom of Italy was proclaimed in 1861 and the country was unified in 1870. From 1940 Italy supported Nazi Germany in the Second World War. In 1946 Italy became a republic. Until 1963 the Partito della Democrazia Cristiana (DC) held power unchallenged. The remainder of the century was marked by the rapid succession of mainly coalition governments. Carlo Azeglio Ciampi was elected President in 1999. In 2001 the Casa delle Libertà coalition won a majority in both houses of Parliament. Rome is the capital. Italian is the principal language.

Area and population
Area: 301,338 sq km
Population (mid-2002): 57,919,232
Population density (mid-2002): 192.2 per sq km
Life expectancy (years at birth, 2002): 79.7 (males 76.8; females 82.5)

Finance
GDP in current prices; 2002): US $1,180,921m. ($20,389 per head)
Real GDP growth (2002): 0.4%
Inflation (annual average, 2002): 2.5%
Currency: euro

413

Economy

In 2002, according to estimates by the World Bank, Italy's gross national income (GNI), measured at average 2000–02 prices, was US $1,097,943m., equivalent to $18,960 per head (or $25,320 per head on an international purchasing-power parity basis). During 1990–2002, it was estimated, the population increased at an average rate of 0.2% per year, while Italy's gross domestic product (GDP) per head increased, in real terms, by an average of 1.3% per year. Overall GDP increased, in real terms, at an average annual rate of 1.4% in 1990–2002; growth in 2002 was 0.4%.

AGRICULTURE

Agriculture (including forestry and fishing) contributed 2.8% of GDP in 2002 and engaged 5.0% of the employed labour force. The principal crops are sugar beet, maize, grapes, wheat and tomatoes. Italy is a leading producer and exporter of wine. According to the World Bank, during 1990–2001 the real GDP of the agricultural sector increased at an average rate of 1.6% per year. Real agricultural GDP declined by 2.9% in 2000, and by 1.0% in 2001.

INDUSTRY

Industry (including mining, manufacturing, construction and power) contributed 27.7% of GDP in 2001; 31.6% of the employed labour force were engaged in industrial activities in 2002. In 1990–2001 industrial GDP increased, in real terms, at an average annual rate of 1.1% per year. Real industrial GDP increased by 2.6% in 2000 and by 1.2% in 2001.

Mining

The mining sector contributed just 0.5% of GDP in 2000, and engaged only 0.3% of the employed labour force in 2002. The major product of the mining sector is petroleum (reserves of which were estimated at 620m. barrels in 2002), followed by rock salt, talc, fluorspar and barytes. Italy also has reserves of lignite, lead and zinc. Reserves of epithermal gold in Sardinia were discovered in 1996. In 2001 mining contributed 0.9% to total industrial output, measured by production value at factor cost. Average annual growth in the GDP of the mining sector was negligible in 1990–2000; mining GDP declined by 1.1% in 1999 and by 4.6% in 2000.

Manufacturing

Manufacturing contributed 20.1% of GDP in 2001; 22.6% of the employed labour force were engaged in the sector in 2002. In 2001 the most important branches of manufacturing, measured by production value at factor cost, were metals and metal products (12.1% of total industrial output), non-electric machinery (10.7%), food (9.1%), electric machinery (7.7%), and chemical products (7.2%). In 1990–2001 the GDP of the manufacturing sector increased, in real terms, at an average annual rate of 1.3%, according to the World Bank. Manufacturing GDP increased by 3.1% in 2000 and by 0.7% in 2001.

Energy

More than 80% of energy requirements are imported. In 2000 natural gas-fired stations provided 37.5% of electricity production, petroleum provided 31.8%, coal-fired electricity generating stations provided 11.3%, and hydroelectric power stations provided 16.4%. In 1987 Italy's four nuclear power stations ceased production following a referendum on the use of nuclear power. In September 2003 a power failure, caused by an outage in supply lines from France and Switzerland, affected almost the entire peninsula and highlighted the vulnerability of Italy's energy sector, which imports an estimated 17% of its electricity. In 2001 fuel imports accounted for 9.4% of the value of total merchandise imports.

SERVICES

Services engaged 63.4% of the employed labour force in 2002 and accounted for 69.5% of GDP in 2001. Tourism is an important source of income, and in 2002 a total of 39,799,000m. foreigners visited Italy, an increase of some 11.3% compared with 2001. Tourism receipts totalled €26,915m. in 2002. The combined GDP of the services sector increased, in real terms, at an estimated average rate of 1.8% per year in 1990–2001. Services GDP increased by 3.3% in 2000 and by 2.1% in 2001.

EXTERNAL TRADE

In 2002 Italy recorded a visible trade surplus of US $16,693m., and a deficit of $7,117m. on the current account of the balance of payments. In 2002 the principal source of imports (17.8%) was Germany; other major suppliers were France (11.3%), the Netherlands (5.9%) and the United Kingdom (5.0%). Germany was also the principal market for exports (13.7%); other major purchasers in that year were France (12.2%), the USA (9.7%), the United Kingdom (6.9%) and Spain (6.3%). In 2002 Italy's fellow members of the European Union (EU) purchased 38.6% of its exports. The principal exports in 2002 were machinery and transport equipment, basic manufactures, chemicals and related products, and clothing and footwear. The principal imports were machinery and transport equipment, basic manufactures, chemicals and related products, and food and live animals.

GOVERNMENT FINANCE

The budgetary deficit for 2001 was equivalent to 1.4% of annual GDP. At the end of 2001 Italy's total accumulated government debt was equivalent to 109.4% of annual GDP. The annual rate of inflation averaged 3.5% in 1990–2002; consumer prices increased by an annual average of 2.8% in 2001 and 2.5% in 2002. As a percentage of the total labour force, unemployment was 9.0% in 2002.

INTERNATIONAL ECONOMIC RELATIONS

Italy is a member of the EU, the Organisation for Economic Co-operation and Development (OECD), and the Central European Initiative.

SURVEY AND PROSPECTS

Italy has long-term structural problems, principally the underdevelopment of the southern part of the country, a low level of agricultural productivity, and heavy dependence on imported energy supplies.

Despite a continuing high level of public debt, Italy was among the first countries to adopt the single European currency, the euro, in January 1999. In February 2000 it was announced that the gas market was to be liberalized by January 2003 to comply with EU regulations, ending the monopoly held by the principal producer and distributor of gas and petroleum, Eni. The privatization programme proceeded with the partial sale of government stakes in Eni and Enel (electricity), although in early 2002 Enel still owned some 80% of the generating capacity. In October 2003 the Government sold a further 6.6% stake in Enel to Morgan Stanley for €2,200m. and Ente Tabacchi Italiano, the state tobacco monopoly, was sold in the same year for €2,300m. These, together with other sales of government stakes (in Eni and the postal service, Poste Italiane, earned an estimated €16,600m. This sum helped reduce public debt, which remained the highest in the EU, to the equivalent of 106.2% of GDP by the end of 2003.

In 2003 Italy suffered a number of financial scandals; in August Cirio, one of its largest food producers was declared bankrupt after defaulting on bonds worth more than €2,000m. and in December it was revealed that Parmalat, the country's eighth largest company, had an unacknowledged deficit of €14,300m. The CEOs of both companies and other family members and executives were subsequently arrested in connection with alleged diversion of funds. In February 2004 the Government unveiled plans for the creation of a new financial regulatory authority.

In 2003 Italy officially lapsed into recession with negative growth in the first two quarters but then recovered in the final two quarters to achieve estimated real GDP growth over the year of 0.5%. This recovery was expected to continue and strengthen in 2004 owing to the impact of income and corporate tax reductions introduced in the 2003 budget, together with continued low interest rates and a reduction in inflation. Inflation during 2003, however, remained higher in Italy than the prevailing rates in the rest of the euro area. The current account deficit expanded in 2003 as exports were adversely affected by the appreciation of the euro against the US dollar. This was compounded by increased petroleum prices, owing to the situation in Iraq, and lower receipts from tourism.

The draft budget for 2004 aimed to raise revenue and reduce the budget deficit from the equivalent of an estimated 2.5% in 2003 to 2.2% in 2004. It envisaged spending cuts of €16,000m. and introduced one-off measures including a controversial plan for an amnesty for illegal construction work, which it was hoped would raise €3,200m. through the imposition of fines for previously undertaken illegal building. Italy's reliance on the implementation of one-off measures to reduce the deficit without the introduction of the necessary structural reforms to lower expenditure on health, pensions and administration has previously been the subject of criticism. However, in early 2004 the Government was attempting (against significant opposition from the three largest trade unions and the opposition) to pass legislation to reform the pensions system, which would come into effect in 2008 and would save the Government the equivalent of 0.7% of GDP annually. Failure to reduce expenditure on pensions was likely to cause a decline in the country's long-term credit rating, which would increase the cost of repaying the public debt.

The economic disparity between the north and the south persists, with unemployment levels in southern regions at 21% in 2000, compared with less than 5% in the north. Furthermore, the forthcoming enlargement of the EU to include countries of central and eastern Europe is likely to be to the detriment of those regions in Italy benefiting from special regional development status within the Union, since income per head in much of the southern parts of the country will exceed 75% of the EU average, the key criterion.

Japan

Japan lies in eastern Asia. Four large islands, named Hokkaido, Honshu, Shikoku and Kyushu, account for about 98% of the country's land area. Following its defeat in the Second World War, Japan was placed under US military occupation. A new democratic constitution, which took effect in 1947, renounced war and abandoned the doctrine of the Emperor's divinity. Japan regained its independence in 1952. Since its formation in 1955, the Liberal-Democratic Party (LDP) has dominated Japanese politics. The LDP remained the largest single party following elections to the lower and upper houses of the legislature held, respectively, in 2003 and 2004. Tokyo is the capital. The language is Japanese.

Area and population
Area: 377,864 sq km
Population (mid-2002): 127,144,432
Population density (mid-2002): 336.5 per sq km
Life expectancy (years at birth, 2002): 81.9 (males 78.4; females 85.3)

Finance
GDP in current prices: 2002): US $3,978,782m. ($31,293 per head)
Real GDP growth (2002): −0.7%
Inflation (annual average, 2002): −0.9%
Currency: yen

Economy

In 2002, according to estimates by the World Bank, Japan's gross national income (GNI), measured at average 2000–02 prices, was US $4,265,616m., equivalent to $33,550 per head (or $26,070 per head on an international purchasing-power parity basis). During 1990–2002, it was estimated, the population increased by an average annual of 0.2%, while gross domestic product (GDP) per head increased, in real terms, by an average of 0.8% per year. According to World Bank figures, overall GDP increased, in real terms, by an average annual rate of 1.1% in 1990–2002. According to official sources, compared with the previous year GDP contracted by more than 0.2% in 2001 but increased by 0.3% in 2002.

AGRICULTURE
Agriculture (including forestry and fishing) contributed 1.3% of GDP, and engaged 4.7% of the employed labour force, in 2002. The principal crops are rice, potatoes, cabbages, sugar beets, and citrus fruits. During 1990–2002 according to official sources, agricultural GDP declined, in real terms, at an average rate of 2.9% annually. Compared with the previous year, the sector's GDP increased by 2.4% in 2002.

INDUSTRY
Industry (including mining, manufacturing, construction and utilities) contributed 29.1% of GDP, and engaged 29.7% of the employed labour force, in 2002. During 1990–2002, according to official sources, industrial GDP decreased at an average annual rate of 0.1%. In 2002 the industrial sector's GDP declined by 2.1%.

Mining
Mining and quarrying contributed 0.1% of GDP and engaged less than 0.1% of the employed labour force in 2002. While the domestic output of limestone and sulphur is sufficient to meet domestic demand, all of Japan's requirements of bauxite, crude petroleum and iron ore, and a high percentage of its requirements of copper ore and coking coal are met by imports.

Manufacturing
In 2002 manufacturing contributed 19.7% of GDP, and in that year 19.3% of the employed labour force were engaged in the sector. Manufacturing GDP decreased by an average of 0.5% per year in 1990–2002. Manufacturing GDP declined for the second successive year in 2002, when it contracted by almost 2.0%. The most important branches of manufacturing are machinery and transport equipment, electrical and electronic equipment, and iron and steel.

Energy
Japan imports most of its energy requirements, with imports of crude and partly refined petroleum comprising 10.8% of the value of total imports in 2002. Thermal

energy accounted for 61% of electricity output in 2001, nuclear power for 30% and hydropower for 9%. There are proposals to construct a further 20 nuclear reactors by 2010. There were fears of energy shortages after Tokyo Electric Power was forced to close a number of nuclear reactors owing to safety concerns in 2002. In October 2000 Japan secured negotiation rights over the world's largest undeveloped oilfield, in Iran. In February 2004 a deal worth US $2,000m. was signed granting Japan rights to exploit Iran's Azadegan oil field. In 2003, meanwhile, Japan also held negotiations with Russia on proposals to import petroleum from Siberia via pipelines to Sakhalin, on the Pacific coast, and to Nakodka, Russia's closest port to Japan.

SERVICES

The services sector contributed 69.6% of GDP, and engaged 65.6% of the employed labour force, in 2002. The GDP of the services sector increased by an average of 2.3% annually in 1990–2002, expanding by 1.2% in 2002 compared with the previous year. Tourist receipts, totalling US $3,499m. in 2002, are an important source of revenue.

EXTERNAL TRADE

In 2002 Japan recorded a trade surplus of US $93,830m., and there was a surplus of $112,450m. on the current account of the balance of payments. In 2002 the principal market for exports was the USA (28.5%), which was also a major source of imports (17.1%). The principal source of imports in that year was the People's Republic of China (18.3%), which was also a major major market for exports (9.6%). Other major suppliers in 2002 were Australia, Indonesia, the Republic of Korea and Taiwan, and other leading purchasers of Japanese exports were the Republic of Korea, Taiwan and Hong Kong. The principal imports in 2002 were machinery and transport equipment, textiles, petroleum, and food and live animals. The principal exports in that year were machinery and transport equipment.

GOVERNMENT FINANCE

The budget for the financial year ending March 2004 projected expenditure of 81,790,000m. yen, an increase of 0.7% compared with the previous year. The budget for 2004/05 envisaged expenditure of 82,110,900m. yen; the Government was to issue new bonds totalling a record 36,590,000m. yen, which were to account for 44.6% of total revenue. Despite reductions in spending on defence, public works and overseas aid in 2004/05, a fiscal deficit of 19,000,000m. yen was anticipated. According to World Bank figures, the annual rate of inflation averaged 0.6% in 1990–2002. Consumer prices declined by 0.9% in 2002. According to official figures, the rate of deflation was 0.3% in 2003, when consumer prices declined for the fifth consecutive year. Having decreased to 4.9% in December 2003 (its lowest level for two years), the rate of unemployment rose to 5.0% of the labour force in January 2004.

INTERNATIONAL ECONOMIC RELATIONS

Japan is a member of the UN Economic and Social Commission for Asia and the Pacific (ESCAP), the Asia-Pacific Economic Co-operation (APEC) forum, the Asian Development Bank (ADB), the Organisation for Economic Co-operation and Development (OECD), the Colombo Plan and the World Trade Organization (WTO).

SURVEY AND PROSPECTS

Following a period of rapid economic expansion in the 1980s, Japan underwent a period of prolonged economic stagnation, including several recessions, during the

1990s and re-entered recession in 2001. On becoming Prime Minister in April 2001, Junichiro Koizumi pledged to introduce major structural reforms, to address the problem of the country's debt burden, to compel the closure of businesses with excessive bad debts and to transfer the state-managed postal savings system to the private sector. However, he faced immense opposition to such plans from elements within his own party, which had strong ties with vested interest groups.

The yen declined to its lowest point against the US dollar for three years in December 2001, having lost almost 13% of its value since January. Consumer demand remained depressed, partly because declining prices encouraged consumers to wait for further price reductions. By December 2001, furthermore, the unemployment rate had reached its highest level since the Second World War. Meanwhile, the economic deceleration in the USA from 2001 limited Japan's ability to implement an export-led recovery, and also had an indirect adverse effect on Japan's regional trade, as other Asian countries reliant on extensive export revenue from the USA found their purchasing power for Japanese goods reduced.

In the financial sector, the process of consolidation was widespread from 2000, and bankruptcies of high-profile organizations continued. The banking system remained troubled by bad loans, with an estimated 81,540,000m. yen of such loans having been cancelled between 1992 and March 2002. In September 2002 the Government announced plans to buy back shares in Japanese banks that had been sold by the institutions in order to cover losses from bad loans, and in late 2002 plans to reform the banking sector, including the possible nationalization of several major banks, were blocked by anti-reformist elements within the LDP. None the less, the Government committed itself to halving the ratio of non-performing loans by 2005.

By 2002 Japan's public debt had risen to the equivalent of almost 140% of GDP, in part owing to the series of massive economic stimulus 'packages' that the Government had introduced in its attempts to revitalize the economy. In August 2002 Koizumi revealed plans for only limited tax cuts, greatly disappointing the business community. A modified reform plan was announced in October , but was criticized for its lack of boldness and a specific timeframe. The Government announced a supplementary budget of 3,000m. yen in November, half of which would be spent on public works and the remainder on social security.

Political instability and a lack of confidence in the Government's commitment to reform contributed to the Japanese stock market's decline, and in early March 2003 the benchmark Nikkei 225 index declined to its lowest level for more than 20 years, falling to below 8,000 points—a decrease of 80% compared with its peak of December 1989. Stronger economic performance was evident in 2003, following increases in the export sector in particular (Japanese exports to China reached a record US $5,000m. in July 2003 alone). The unemployment rate began to stabilize. The stock market also showed signs of recovery, and by March 2004 the Nikkei 225 index had exceeded 11,500 points. Overall GDP growth in 2003 was initially estimated at 2.7%. Growth in the fourth quarter of 2003 reached 6.4% compared with the corresponding period of the previous year, representing the highest growth rate for 13 years. Preliminary forecasts for GDP growth in 2004 and 2005 were 1.8% for both years; however, in early 2004 the IMF revised the forecast for growth in 2004 to as much as 3%.

Meanwhile, Japan faced renewed international pressure to combat continuing deflation, which remained a potential threat to the economy. The yen appreciated by around 10% against the US dollar during 2003, owing primarily to the weakening of the US currency, thus raising some concerns over the competitiveness of Japanese exports. However, the appreciation of the yen against the dollar was curbed by the Japanese Government's intervention in the currency market, with a record 20,057,000m. yen being spent on supporting the yen in 2003. In December of that year plans were announced for large increases in spending on currency intervention in 2004. In the banking sector, the failure of two major banks (Resona Bank and Ashikaga Bank) in 2003 prompted the Government to draft a proposal to make public funds available, on certain conditions, to institutions facing insolvency.

Jordan

The Hashemite Kingdom of Jordan lies in western Asia. In 1920 Palestine and Transjordan were placed under British administration by a League of Nations mandate. In 1921 Abdullah ibn Hussein, a member of the Hashimi dynasty of Arabia, was proclaimed Amir of Transjordan. The British mandate was terminated in 1946, when Transjordan attained full independence and Abdullah was proclaimed King. In 1952 the crown passed to Hussein ibn Talal. During the Six-Day War of 1967 Israeli military gains included possession of the whole of Jerusalem and the West Bank. King Hussein was succeeded by his son, Abdullah ibn al-Hussein, in 1999. The capital is Amman. The official language is Arabic.

Area and population
Area: 89,342 sq km
Population (mid-2002): 5,171,340
Population density (mid-2002): 57.9 per sq km
Life expectancy (years at birth, 2002): 70.8 (males 68.6; females 73.3)

Finance
GDP in current prices: 2002): US $9,296m. ($1,798 per head)
Real GDP growth (2002): 4.9%
Inflation (annual average, 2002): 1.8%
Currency: dinar

Economy

In 2002, according to estimates by the World Bank, the East Bank of Jordan's gross national income (GNI), measured at average 2000–02 prices, was US $9,084m., equivalent to $1,760 per head (or $4,070 per head on an international purchasing-power parity basis). During 1990–2002, it was estimated, the population increased at an average annual rate of 4.2%, while the East Bank's gross domestic product (GDP) per head increased, in real terms, by an average of 0.7% per year. Overall GDP increased, in real terms, by an average annual rate of 4.9% in 1990–2002; official reported growth was 4.3% in 2001 and 5.3% in 2002.

AGRICULTURE
Agriculture (including hunting, forestry and fishing) contributed about 2.3% of Jordan's GDP in 2002. The sector accounted for an estimated 3.9% of the country's employed labour force in that year. The principal cash crops are vegetables, fruit and nuts, which accounted for about 6.7% of export earnings in 2003. Wheat production is also important. During 1990–2001 the sector's GDP decreased at an average annual rate of 0.2%. Agricultural GDP declined by 20.4% in 1999, owing to severe drought in that year, but increased by 6.3% in 2000.

INDUSTRY
Industry (including mining, manufacturing, construction and power) provided an estimated 25.5% of GDP in 2002, when about 21.5% of the country's active labour force were employed in the sector. During 1990–2001 industrial GDP increased by an average of 4.8% per year. The sector's GDP increased by 4.8% in 1999 and by 4.7% in 2000.

Mining
Mining and quarrying contributed an estimated 3.2% of GDP in 2002. The sector accounted for about 1.1% of the employed labour force in that year. Phosphates and potash are the principal mineral exports, together accounting for around 14.4% of total export earnings in 2003. Jordan also has reserves of oil-bearing shale, but exploitation of this resource is at present undeveloped. The GDP of the mining sector declined by an estimated 5.9% in 1998.

Manufacturing
Manufacturing provided an estimated 15.6% of GDP in 2002, and engaged some 12.6% of the employed labour force in that year. In 1997 the most important branches of manufacturing, measured by gross value of output, were food, beverages and tobacco (accounting for 25.3% of the total), refined petroleum products (17.4%), chemicals (11.0%), non-metallic mineral products (9.1%) and metal products (7.2%). Manufacturing GDP increased by an average of 5.3% per year in 1990–2001; the sector recorded growth of 5.8% in 1999 and 5.7% in 2000.

Energy

Energy is derived principally from imported petroleum, but attempts are being made to develop alternative sources of power, including wind and solar power. In 2000 petroleum provided 89.4% of total electricity production, while natural gas accounted for 10.1%. Imports of mineral fuels comprised some 16.1% of the total value of imports in 2003. Following an agreement signed in mid-2001, Egyptian gas was to be supplied to Jordan via a proposed high-capacity pipeline from mid-2003.

SERVICES

Services accounted for some 72.1% of Jordan's GDP in 2002. In that year an estimated 74.7% of the total employed labour force were engaged in the service sector. During 1990–2001 the GDP of the service sector increased by an average of 4.7% per year. Services GDP increased by 3.2% in 1999 and by 2.2% in 2000.

EXTERNAL TRADE

In 2002 Jordan recorded a visible trade deficit of US $1,680.4m., and there was a surplus of $467.9m. on the current account of the balance of payments. In 2003 the People's Republic of China was the main source of imports (with 8.1% of the total), while the USA was the principal market for exports (with 28.5% of the total). Other major trading partners in that year were Germany, Saudi Arabia and Iraq. The principal exports in 2003 were miscellaneous manufactured articles, chemicals and minerals, while the principal imports were machinery and transport equipment, basic manufactures, and mineral fuels and lubricants.

GOVERNMENT FINANCE

In 2003 there was an estimated budget deficit of JD 844m. Jordan's external debt totalled US $7,480m. at the end of 2001, of which US $6,600m. was long-term public debt. In that year the cost of debt-servicing was equivalent to 10.7% of the value of exports of goods and services. The annual rate of inflation averaged 3.2% in 1990–2002. Consumer prices increased by an annual average of 1.8% in 2002 and 2.3% in 2003. Unemployment was officially put at 15.3% of the labour force in 2002, but unofficially estimated to be 20%–30%.

INTERNATIONAL ECONOMIC RELATIONS

Jordan is a member of the Council of Arab Economic Unity, the Arab Co-operation Council, the Arab Monetary Fund and the World Trade Organization (WTO). In September 1999 the Jordanian parliament ratified the Jordanian-European Partnership Agreement (signed with the EU in November 1997), which provides for the creation of a duty-free zone and the abolition of import duties by 2010.

SURVEY AND PROSPECTS

Since the early 1990s the Jordanian economy has been constrained by a heavy burden of foreign debt and by the loss, owing to the imposition of UN sanctions, of its vital Iraqi market. Nevertheless, the conclusion of a peace treaty with Israel in 1994, as well as the recent improvement in relations with other Arab states, has created new opportunities in tourism, transport, banking and trade. Exports from Jordan to the USA rose considerably following the conclusion of a bilateral free-trade agreement which took effect in late 2001 (from JD 164.6m. in that year to JD 467.9m. in 2003).

Jordan has implemented an IMF-supported adjustment and reform programme with the aim of reducing state intervention in industry and, through privatization, raising funds to support the repayment of foreign debt. In order to encourage foreign investment, all foreign-exchange restrictions were revoked in June 1997. By early 2001 the restructuring of a number of state enterprises was under way, notably in the utilities, transport and telecommunications sectors. Jordan is deemed to have brought its external debt under control, a process facilitated by a series of debt-relief measures by Western creditors in the late 1990s and early part of this century; however, the IMF has recommended a faster pace of structural reform and the introduction of new banking legislation. In November 2001 the Government announced a two-year social and economic programme involving a new programme of large-scale industrial privatization, the receipts from which are to be used to fund vital education, health and development projects. It was reported in early 2003 that the programme had achieved considerable success thus far.

Meanwhile, a value-added tax was introduced in 2001, while in January 2002 a new income tax law reduced the tax burden on private companies in an effort to encourage competition. In December of that year the WTO agreed to exempt Jordanian exports from income tax for a five-year period. In January 2001 the Aqaba region was accorded the status of a Special Economic Zone, which was officially inaugurated in May; the Government hoped that the zone would attract investment worth US $6,000m. and create as many as 70,000 new jobs by 2020. Meanwhile, the economic growth rate was deemed to be insufficient to reduce unemployment and raise living standards. The 1999–2003 Plan forecast GDP growth reaching 6% by 2003.

Since the outbreak of the al-Aqsa *intifada* in September 2000, the impact on regional security of the Israeli–Palestinian conflict has hampered efforts by the Jordanian Government to attract foreign investment, and has had a particularly detrimental effect on Jordan's tourist and banking sectors. Moreover, the conflict in Iraq during March–April 2003 was especially damaging to the Jordanian economy; official figures showed a significant decline in Jordan's trade with its vital trading partner during that year.

Kazakhstan

The Republic of Kazakhstan extends from the Volga river in the west to the Altai mountains in the east, from the Siberian plain in the north to the Central Asian deserts in the south. In 1936 the Kazakh Autonomous Soviet Socialist Republic became a full Union Republic of the USSR. In 1991 Kazakhstan became the last of the republics to declare independence from the USSR, and was redesignated the Republic of Kazakhstan. In that year the country was formally recognized as a co-founder of the Commonwealth of Independent States. Astana is the capital. The official language is Kazakh.

Area and population
Area: 2,717,300 sq km
Population (mid-2002): 14,794,830
Population density (mid-2002): 5.4 per sq km
Life expectancy (years at birth, 2002): 63.6 (males 58.7; females 68.9)

Finance
GDP in current prices: 2002: US $24,205m. ($1,636 per head)
Real GDP growth (2002): 9.5%
Inflation (annual average, 2002): 5.8%
Currency: tenge

Economy

In 2002, according to estimates by the World Bank, Kazakhstan's gross national income (GNI), measured at average 2000–02 prices, was US $22,268m., equivalent to

$1,510 per head (or $5,480 per head on an international purchasing-power parity basis). During 1990–2002, it was estimated, the population decreased at an average annual rate of 0.8%, while gross domestic product (GDP) per head decreased, in real terms, by an average of 0.4% per year. Overall GDP declined, in real terms, at an average annual rate of 1.2% in 1990–2002. However, real GDP increased by 13.5% in 2001 and by 9.6% in 2002.

AGRICULTURE

Agriculture (including forestry and fishing) contributed an estimated 7.9% of GDP in 2002, when the sector provided 35.5% of total employment. There are large areas of land suitable for agriculture, and Kazakhstan is a major producer and exporter of agricultural products. The principal crops include fruit, sugar beet, vegetables, potatoes, cotton and, most importantly, cereals. Livestock-breeding is also important, and Kazakhstan is a significant producer of karakul and astrakhan wools. The GDP of the agricultural sector decreased, in real terms, by an average of 4.9% per year in 1990–2002. Agricultural GDP increased by 16.9% in 2001, but declined by 6.0% in 2002.

INDUSTRY

Industry (including mining, manufacturing, construction, and power) contributed an estimated 35.5% of GDP in 2002, when the sector provided 16.3% of total employment. Measured by the gross value of output, the principal branches of industry in 1997 were the fuel industry (accounting for 27.7% of the total), metal-processing (23.9%), food-processing (15.4%) and electrical power generation (14.1%). Industrial GDP declined, in real terms, at an average annual rate of 4.3% in 1990–2002. However, the GDP of the sector increased by 15.1% in 2001, and there was growth of 10.7% in 2002.

Mining

Mining and quarrying provided 2.0% of employment in 1998. Kazakhstan possesses immense mineral wealth, and large-scale mining and processing industries have been developed. There are major coalfields (in the Karaganda, Turgai, Ekibastuz and Maikuben basins), as well as substantial deposits of iron ore, lead, zinc ore, titanium, magnesium, chromium, tungsten, molybdenum, gold, silver, copper and manganese. Petroleum is extracted, and Kazakhstan possesses what are believed to be among the world's largest unexploited oilfields (in the Caspian depression) and substantial reserves of natural gas. The discovery of major petroleum reserves at the offshore Kashagan oilfield was announced in mid-2000. At the end of 2002 Kazakhstan's proven total reserves (onshore and offshore) of petroleum and natural gas were estimated at 1,200m. metric tons and 1,840,000m. cu m, respectively.

Manufacturing

Manufacturing provided 10.2% of employment in 1998, and an estimated 17.4% of GDP in 2002. The GDP of the manufacturing sector declined at an average annual rate of 23.2% in 1990–95.

Energy

In 2000 coal-fired thermal power stations provided about 69.9% of annual domestic electricity production, while hydroelectric power stations accounted for 14.6% of production and natural gas for 10.6%. In 2002 mineral fuels accounted for approximately 12.7% of total imports.

SERVICES

In 2002 the services sector contributed some 56.6% of GDP, and provided 48.2% of employment. During 1990–2002 the GDP of the services sector increased, in real terms, at an average annual rate of 3.2%. Services GDP increased by 10.8% in 2001 and by 8.6% in 2002.

EXTERNAL TRADE

In 2001 Kazakhstan recorded a visible trade surplus of US $2,301.2m., and there was a deficit of $695.8m. on the current account of the balance of payments. In 2002 the principal source of imports was Russia (accounting for 39.1% of total imports). Other major suppliers were the USA and Germany. The principal market for exports in that year was Bermuda (accounting for 20.7% of total exports). Other important purchasers of exports were Russia, the People's Republic of China, Italy and Switzerland. The main exports in 2002 were petroleum and gas condensate and base metals. The principal imports in that year were machinery and electrical equipment, mineral products, vehicles, base metals and chemicals.

GOVERNMENT FINANCE

In 2002 Kazakhstan recorded a budgetary deficit of some 13,000m. tenge (equivalent to approximately 0.3% of GDP). At the end of 2001 Kazakhstan's external debt amounted to US $14,372m. of which $3,446m. was long-term public debt. In that year the cost of debt-servicing was equivalent to 31.4% of the value of exports of goods and services. The annual rate of inflation averaged 79.9% during 1992–2002. Inflation slowed in the latter half of the 1990s, and consumer prices increased by 8.4% in 2001 and by 5.8% in 2002. In 2002 9.3% of the labour force were unemployed.

INTERNATIONAL ECONOMIC RELATIONS

In addition to its membership of the economic bodies of the Commonwealth of Independent States (CIS), Kazakhstan has joined the Asian Development Bank (ADB), is a 'Country of Operations' of the European Bank for Reconstruction and Development (EBRD) and is a member of the Economic Co-operation Organization (ECO).

SURVEY AND PROSPECTS

After independence in 1991, contraction in all sectors was recorded annually until 1995, when signs of an economic recovery emerged, following the initiation in 1993 of a comprehensive stabilization and reform programme, with support from the international financial community. A large-scale programme of privatization was extended in 1996 to include the strategic hydrocarbons and metallurgical sectors, thereby increasing foreign direct investment (already the highest per head among the CIS countries).

In 1998 the economy was severely affected by the economic crises in Russia and Asia, and the subsequent decline in world prices of Kazakhstan's principal exports. However, by mid-2000 Kazakhstan announced that it had been able to repay fully all debts owed to the IMF, seven years ahead of schedule, as the result of improved regional demand, increased world petroleum prices and prudent macroeconomic policies. Strong economic growth was recorded in 2001–02, and Kazakhstan's long-term economic prospects were considered to be highly favourable, owing to the country's immense, and largely unexploited, hydrocarbons and other mineral resources.

The discovery, announced in July 2000, of substantial petroleum deposits at the offshore Kashagan oilfield (thought to be the world's second largest) was expected to be of enormous benefit to the economy, although delays in the development of the field were announced in 2003, and the commercial extraction of petroleum was not expected to commence before 2007. However, petroleum exports had increased significantly following the official opening, in November 2001, of a new, 1,500-km petroleum pipeline, connecting the onshore Tengiz field in western Kazakhstan with Novorossiisk, on the Russian Black Sea coast. In addition, the extraction of petroleum and natural gas was expected to expand significantly as a result of a trilateral agreement, signed with Azerbaijan and Russia in May 2003, on the division of mineral resources in the Caspian seabed, and work was expected to commence in 2004 on the construction of a long-delayed, 3,000-km petroleum export pipeline between Kazakhstan and the People's Republic of China. Meanwhile, the Government hoped to use its mineral wealth to implement a programme for the diversification of the economy. To this end, a National Fund had been established in 2001, although its management was criticized for a lack of transparency. Moreover, growth in the non-petroleum sector remained highly dependent on the implementation of further structural reforms, the liberalization of trade and an improved business environment.

Kenya

The Republic of Kenya lies on the east coast of Africa. The country became independent, within the Commonwealth, in 1963, and a republic in 1964. Jomo Kenyatta was Kenya's first President. Following Kenyatta's death in 1978, Daniel arap Moi was elected President in 1979. In 1982 Kenya officially became a one-party state. In 1992 and 1997, in multi-party elections, Moi was re-elected, while the Kenya African National Union (KANU) was the most successful political party. In 2002 Moi stepped down, and Mwai Kibaki of the National Rainbow Coalition (NARC) was elected President. Nairobi is the capital. Kiswahili is the official language.

Area and population
Area: 580,367 sq km
Population (mid-2002): 31,344,580
Population density (mid-2002): 54.0 per sq km
Life expectancy (years at birth, 2002): 50.9 (males 49.8; females 51.9)

Finance
GDP in current prices: 2002): US $12,140m. ($387 per head)
Real GDP growth (2002): 1.8%
Inflation (annual average, 2002): 2.0%
Currency: Kenya shilling

Economy

In 2002, according to estimates by the World Bank, Kenya's gross national income (GNI), measured at average 2000–02 prices, was US $11,296m., equivalent to $360 per head (or $990 per head on an international purchasing-power parity basis). During 1990–2002, it was estimated, the population increased at an average annual rate of 2.5%, while gross domestic product (GDP) per head declined, in real terms, by an average of 0.8% per year. Overall GDP increased, in real terms, at an average annual rate of 1.6% in 1990–2002. Real GDP increased by 1.8% in 2002.

AGRICULTURE

Agriculture (including forestry and fishing) contributed 19.1% of GDP and employed about 74.6% of the labour force in 2002. The principal cash crops are tea (which contributed 29.3% of total export earnings in 2000) and coffee (accounting for 9.8% of export earnings in 2000). Horticultural produce (Kenya is the world's fourth largest exporter of cut flowers), pyrethrum, sisal, sugar cane and cotton are also important. Maize is the principal subsistence crop. There is a significant dairy industry for domestic consumption and export. During 1990–2002, according to the World Bank, agricultural GDP increased at an average annual rate of 0.7%. Agricultural GDP increased by 1.0% in 2002.

INDUSTRY

Industry (including mining, manufacturing, construction and power) contributed 18.3% of GDP in 2002, and employed an estimated 19.8% of the total labour force in 1995. During 1990–2002, according to the World Bank, industrial GDP increased at an average annual rate of 1.4%. Industrial GDP increased by 1.4% in 2002.

Mining

Mining contributed 0.2% of GDP (at factor cost) in 2001. Soda ash is the principal mineral export. Fluorspar, iron ore, salt, limestone, gold, gemstones (including rubies and sapphires), vermiculite and lead are also mined. Kenya has substantial reserves of titanium.

Manufacturing

Manufacturing contributed 12.7% of GDP in 2002. During 1990–2002, according to the World Bank, manufacturing GDP increased at an average annual rate of 1.9%. Manufacturing GDP increased by 3.5% in 2002.

Energy

Owing to severe drought, hydroelectric power accounted for only 34.1% of total electricity generated in 2000 (compared with 56.6% in 1999 and 72.8% in 1998), while a further 54.8% was derived from petroleum (34.5% in 1999 and 18.5% in 1998).

Energy for domestic use is derived principally from fuel wood and charcoal. The prolonged drought led to severe power shortages in 2000. In February 2004 it was announced that the Kenyan and Tanzanian national grids were to be connected to that of Zambia under a cross-border energy project; the first phase of the project, which was to cost some US $300m., was to be commissioned in 2007, followed by a second phase in 2012. In 2000 imports of mineral fuels and lubricants (including crude petroleum intended for refining) comprised 26.2% of the value of total imports.

SERVICES

The services sector contributed 62.6% of GDP in 2002, and engaged 15.5% of the total labour force in 1991. Tourism makes an important contribution to Kenya's economy, and has been the country's principal source of foreign exchange since 1987. In 1998, however, a decline of 10.6% in tourist arrivals, to 894,300, was attributed partly to the effects of civil unrest in coastal areas during 1997. In 1999–2000 there was some recovery in tourism, with arrivals increasing to 1,036,628 in 2000. The GDP of the services sector increased at an average annual rate of 2.9% in 1990–2002, according to the World Bank. Services GDP increased by 3.6% in 2002.

EXTERNAL TRADE

In 2001 Kenya recorded a visible trade deficit of US $1,282.1m., and there was a deficit of $317.8m. on the current account of the balance of payments. In 2000 the principal source of imports was the United Arab Emirates (which supplied 19.5% of total imports in that year); other major suppliers were the United Kingdom, South Africa, Saudi Arabia and Japan. Uganda was the principal market for Kenya's exports (purchasing 18.0%) in that year; other important purchasers were the United Kingdom, Tanzania, Pakistan and the Netherlands. The principal exports in 2000 were tea, vegetables and fruit, coffee and refined petroleum products. The principal imports in that year were petroleum and petroleum products, aircraft and parts, cereals and cereal preparations, and road vehicles and parts.

GOVERNMENT FINANCE

In the financial year ending 30 June 2003 there was a budgetary deficit of Ks. 32,814m., equivalent to 3.2% of GDP. The country's external debt was US $5,833m. at the end of 2001, of which $4,930m. was long-term public debt. In that year the cost of debt-servicing was equivalent to 15.4% of the value of exports of goods and services. The annual rate of inflation averaged 13.8% in 1990–2002; consumer prices increased by an average of 4.3% in 2002. Some 23% of the labour force were estimated to be unemployed in late 2000, and the rate of unemployment was reported to be approaching 30% by October 2001.

INTERNATIONAL ECONOMIC RELATIONS

Kenya is a member of the Common Market for Eastern and Southern Africa and, with Tanzania and Uganda, of the East African Community. The International Tea Promotion Association is based in Kenya.

SURVEY AND PROSPECTS

Kenya's economy is reasonably diversified, although most employment is dependent on agriculture. Agricultural development has been intermittently hindered by adverse weather conditions (generally low rainfall, although severe flooding occurred in 1997–98), resulting in sporadic food shortages, and also by rural ethnic unrest. Moreover, the country is highly vulnerable to fluctuations in international prices for its cash crops, most notably tea and coffee. Poverty is widespread, with population growth considerably higher than growth in GNI per head, which actually declined every year between 1997 and 2002. Hopes that the change in Government in December 2002 would lead to a rapid recovery were disappointed to a large extent, and economic performance remained weak in 2003, as the expected resumption of IMF lending, which had been suspended in 2001, was delayed.

A new agreement with the IMF was eventually reached in November 2003, when a three-year Poverty Reduction and Growth Facility (PRGF) arrangement, worth some US $252.8m., was approved. In addition, at a meeting of the World Bank's Consultative Group held later that month, donors pledged some $4,100m. in grants and concessionary loans for Kenya, to be disbursed over a three-year period. The IMF and donor funding was to support the Government's ambitious Economic Recovery Strategy for Wealth and Employment Creation, which aimed to achieve a return to the higher growth rates of the 1980s, with an average annual increase in GDP of 4.7% forecast for 2003–07, and the fostering of an economic environment that could support the creation of some 500,000 jobs per year. The Government also planned to improve conditions for business by reducing bureaucracy and high energy and communications costs; however, although there were signs of increased investment in the first part of 2004, Kenya's record of attracting and retaining private-sector finance had been described by the World Bank as 'dismal' in the previous year.

There was some increase in private-sector borrowing, but this remained below expectations, despite low interest rates. Moreover, the competitiveness of Kenyan companies was hampered by the Government's decision to issue fewer work permits for foreign workers. Also of concern was the Government's reluctance to reduce the state's interest in strategic sectors; there was some movement towards restructuring and privatization (of companies involved in telecommunications, electricity generation and banking), but there appeared to be little real political impetus behind the divestiture programme. Public-sector salaries, which accounted for more than 9% of GDP, remained a source of contention with the IMF, which advocated a reduction in the wage bill, although the Government was also under pressure from elsewhere to raise low state pay, which was regarded by many as an incentive for the endemic corruption which the Government had promised to eradicate.

Kiribati

The Republic of Kiribati comprises 33 atolls scattered within an area of about 5m. sq km in the mid-Pacific Ocean. In 1979 the Gilbert Islands became an independent republic within the Commonwealth, under the name of Kiribati. Ieremia Tabai was the country's first President. In 1982, at Kiribati's first presidential election, President Tabai was confirmed in office. Tabai was succeeded as President in 1991 by Teatao Teannaki. Teburoro Tito was elected as President in 1994 and re-elected in 1998 and again in February 2003. He was replaced by Anote Tong in July 2003. The capital is the island of Bairiki, in Tarawa Atoll. The principal languages are I-Kiribati (Gilbertese) and English.

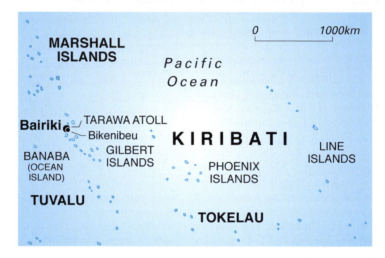

Area and population

Area: 811 sq km
Population (mid-2002): 94,700
Population density (mid-2002): 116.8 per sq km
Life expectancy (years at birth, 2002): 64.1 (males 61.8; females 66.7)

Finance

GDP in current prices: 2002): US $44m. ($468 per head)
Real GDP growth (2002): 2.8%
Inflation (2001): 5.9%
Currency: Australian dollar

Economy

In 2002, according to estimates by the World Bank, Kiribati's gross national income (GNI), measured at average 2000–2002 prices, was US $77m., equivalent to US $810 per head. During 1990–2002, it was estimated, the population increased by an average of 2.3% per year, while gross domestic product (GDP) per head increased, in real terms, by an estimated average of 0.3% per year. Overall GDP, according to revised estimates by the Asian Development Bank (ADB), expanded, in real terms, by 1.8% in 2001, by 1.0% in 2002 and by 2.5% in 2003. The ADB forecast an increase of 1.8% in real GDP for 2004.

AGRICULTURE

According to official figures, agriculture (including fishing), contributed an estimated 14.2% of monetary GDP in 2002. In 2002, according to FAO, agriculture engaged 26% of the economically active population. The principal cash crop is coconut, yielding copra—which accounted for an estimated 23.4% of domestic export earnings in 2000 (compared with 63.9% in the previous year). Construction of a new copra mill, near Betio port, began in March 2002. Bananas, screw-pine (*Pandanus*), breadfruit and papaya are cultivated as food crops. The cultivation of seaweed began on Tabuaeran in the mid-1980s: seaweed provided an estimated 15.9% of domestic export earnings in 2000. Pigs and chickens are kept. Fish provided only 1.8% of export earnings in 2000 (compared with 46.2% in 1990); however, pet fish are a significant export commodity, contributing 13.6% of export earnings in 1999 (although this figure declined to 1.9% in 2000). The sale of fishing licences to foreign fleets (notably from South Korea, Japan, the People's Republic of China, Taiwan and the USA) provides an important source of income: revenue from the sale of fishing licences reached a record $A52m. in 2001 but declined to $A32m. in 2002. The GDP of the agriculture, fishing and seaweed sectors increased at an average annual rate of 0.8% in 1991–2000. According to the ADB, agricultural GDP rose by 0.2% in 2001 but decreased by 4.5% in 2002.

INDUSTRY

Industry (including manufacturing, construction and power) contributed an estimated 10.9% of monetary GDP in 2002. Industrial GDP increased by an average of 0.5% per year in 1991–2000. Compared with the previous year, industrial GDP was estimated by the ADB to have expanded by 21.6% in 2001, but to have contracted by 7.8% in 2002.

Mining

Mining of phosphate rock on the island of Banaba, which ceased in 1979, formerly provided some 80% of export earnings. Interest from a phosphate reserve fund (the Revenue Equalization Reserve Fund—RERF), established in 1956, continues to be an important source of income. The production of solar-evaporated salt for export to other islands of the Pacific (for use on fishing vessels with brine refrigeration systems) began on Kiritimati in 1985.

Manufacturing

Manufacturing, which contributed an estimated 0.8% of monetary GDP in 2002, is confined to the small-scale production of coconut-based products, soap, foods, handicrafts, furniture, leather goods and garments. Manufacturing GDP increased by an annual average of 5.6% in 1991–2000. In 2002, compared with the previous year, the GDP of the manufacturing sector contracted by an estimated 3.0%, in contrast to the 18.6% increase recorded in 2001.

Energy

Production of electrical energy declined from 14.5m. kWh in 2000 to 12.5m. kWh in 2001. Mineral fuels accounted for an estimated 8.8% of total import costs in 2000. In August 2001 the European Union (EU) announced that it planned to fund the introduction of 1,500 new solar energy systems, valued at more than $A6m., to Kiribati. Moreover, in May 2003 the Government announced the completion of a Japanese-funded programme to construct a new power station, to install two new generating units and to upgrade 16 km of power lines. The project, which cost a total of US $11m. to implement, was expected to ensure a power supply sufficient to meet Kiribati's increasing demand.

SERVICES

Services provided 75.0% of monetary GDP in 2002. Tourism makes a significant contribution to the economy: the trade and hotels sector provided an estimated 16.6% of GDP in 2000. Tourist arrivals at Tarawa and Kiritimati rose from 3,112 in 1999 to 4,829 in 2000, in which year receipts from tourism reached $A2.2m. Arrivals for 2003 totalled 4,288. The GDP of the services sector increased at an annual average rate of 5.1% in 1991–2000. According to revised estimates from the ADB, the services sector's GDP decreased by 0.5% in 2001 but increased by 3.2% in 2002.

EXTERNAL TRADE

In 2001 Kiribati recorded a trade deficit of an estimated US $27.6m., and a surplus of US $1.7m. on the current account of the balance of payments. In that year Kiribati's trade deficit decreased to the equivalent of 58.5% of GDP, as a decline in income from copra exports was more than offset by a fall in imports. By 2003 the ADB estimated that the deficit on the current account was equivalent to 21.5% of GDP. In 2002 the principal sources of imports were France (29.1%), Australia (26.6%) and Fiji (12.7%). The principal recipients of exports in that year were Japan (55.9%) and Thailand (16.9%). The major imports in 2000 were food and live animals, machinery and transport equipment, manufactures, mineral fuels, beverages and tobacco, and chemicals. The major domestic exports were copra, seaweed and shark fins.

GOVERNMENT FINANCE

Budgetary expenditure for 2002, announced in December 2001, was projected at $A77.9m., 15% less than the revised estimates for 2001, and required a drawdown of $A16.7m. from the RERF. In 2002, according to the ADB, the government surplus increased to reach the equivalent of 21.4% of GDP, but a deficit of 12.9% of GDP was projected for 2003. In April 2003 the interim administration enacted a budget providing for expenditure of $A32m. over the next five months. Kiribati's total external debt was estimated by the ADB to have risen from US $8m. in 2001 to $14m. in 2002 In 2001 the cost of debt-servicing was equivalent to 7.9% of revenue from exports of goods and services. The annual rate of inflation averaged 3.1% in 1990–2000. Consumer prices increased by an annual average of 6.0% in 2001 and by 3.2% in 2002. About 2.8% of the labour force were unemployed in 1990. Only around 8,600 people, equivalent to less than 20% of the working-age population, were formally employed in 2001.

INTERNATIONAL ECONOMIC RELATIONS

Kiribati is a member of the Pacific Community, the Pacific Islands Forum and the Asian Development Bank (ADB); it is an associate member of the UN Economic and Social Commission for Asia and the Pacific (ESCAP), and is a signatory to the South Pacific Regional Trade and Economic Co-operation Agreement (SPARTECA) and to the Lomé Conventions and successor Cotonou Agreement with the EU. The Council of Micronesian Government Executives, of which Kiribati was a founder member in 1996, aims to facilitate discussion of economic developments in the region and to examine possibilities for reducing the considerable cost of shipping essential goods between the islands.

SURVEY AND PROSPECTS

According to UN criteria, Kiribati is one of the world's least-developed nations. The islands' vulnerability to adverse climatic conditions was illustrated in early 1999 when a state of national emergency was declared following a prolonged period of severe drought. Kiribati's extremely limited export base and dependence on imports of almost all essential commodities result in a permanent trade deficit, which in most years is only partially offset by revenue from fishing licence fees, interest earned on the RERF and remittances from I-Kiribati working overseas. The RERF usually provides the Government with investment income equivalent to around 33% of GDP per year. In 2001 the ADB estimated that the value of the RERF was such that Kiribati had sufficient foreign reserves to cover the costs of 10 years of imports. By the end of 2001 the value of the fund was put at US $329m. Although the value of the RERF had trebled within 10 years, the fund declined in value in 2001 as a result of the downturn in world stock markets (its assets being invested in offshore markets). By the end of 2003, however, international stocks had begun to recover.

   The country is reliant on foreign assistance for its development budget. Official development assistance declined from a total of US $20.9m. in 1999 to US $17.9m. in 2000. In 2003/04 Australia provided $A11.4m. in development assistance, with emphasis on the management of human resources, governance, health, education and improved customs procedures, within the framework of a new co-operation strategy. New Zealand provided $NZ3.14m. in bilateral aid for 2003/04. In early 2003 Kiribati established a non-government body to secure US $840,000 in EU funding under the Cotonou Agreement, which would be spent on projects over the next five years. Development finance was expected to be received from Taiwan following the establishment of diplomatic relations in late 2003. Dependence on external finance, however, is widely regarded as having left Kiribati vulnerable to foreign exploitation. Moreover, concern has been expressed that, although foreign companies specializing in advanced technology (particularly telecommunications and satellite systems) are seeking to establish operations in the islands, Kiribati will not benefit significantly from the major investment involved in such projects.

   In 2000 the Government generated some US $400,000 of revenue through the sale of I-Kiribati passports to investors in the islands. Further passport sales in 2001 were worth US $375,000 and, combined with sales of Kiribati Residential Permits, produced more than $A2.5m. in revenue. The Government's policy of subsidizing copra producers following a sharp fall in world prices of the commodity, however, had a negative impact on the economy; in 2001 these subsidies totalled $A2m. The economy recovered somewhat in 2001, largely as a result of a substantial increase in recurrent government expenditure, an improvement in copra production and the implementation of various development projects. Modest rates of economic growth were maintained in 2002–03. The Government's National Development Strategy for 2000–03 sought to reform the public sector and promote private-sector development.

Investors have in the past been deterred by the country's weak banking system and shortage of investment opportunities. It was estimated in 2001 that around 75% of capital belonging to Kiribati's companies and private citizens was invested abroad. The new proposals were intended to encourage greater investment in the country's private sector, which would allow the creation of jobs and the broadening of the islands' narrow base of exports.

Korea, Democratic People's Republic

The Democratic People's Republic of Korea (North Korea) occupies the northern part of the Korean peninsula, in eastern Asia. In 1945 Korea was divided at latitude 38°N into military occupation zones, with Soviet forces in the North and US forces in the South. A provisional People's Committee, led by Kim Il Sung of the Korean Communist Party, was established in the North in 1946 and accorded government status. In 1948 the Democratic People's Republic of Korea was proclaimed. The Korean Workers' Party has held power in North Korea since 1949. Pyongyang is the capital. The language is Korean.

Area and population
Area: 122,762 sq km
Population (mid-2002): 22,519,390
Population density (mid-2002): 183.4 per sq km
Life expectancy (years at birth, 2002): 65.8 (males 64.4; females 67.1)

Finance
GDP in current prices, 1999): US $10,369m. ($469 per head)
Real GDP growth (1999): 6.2%
Currency: won

Economy

In 2002, according to South Korean estimates, the DPRK's gross national income (GNI) was about US $17,045m., equivalent to some $762 per head. It was estimated that in 1998 the North Korean economy declined for the ninth successive year, contracting by 1.1%, in real terms. In 1999, however, it was estimated that the economy grew by 6.2%, and in 2000 by 1.3%. Growth was estimated at 3.7% in 2001 and at 1.2% in 2002. During 1990–2002, according to estimates by the World Bank, the population increased by an annual average of 1.0%.

AGRICULTURE

Agriculture (including forestry and fishing) contributed an estimated 30.2% of gross domestic product (GDP) in 2002, according to South Korean sources. In 2002, according to FAO estimates, 28.7% of the economically active population were employed in agriculture. The principal crops are rice, maize, potatoes, sweet potatoes and soybeans. The DPRK is not self-sufficient in food, and imports substantial amounts of wheat, rice and maize annually. Food shortages became a severe problem from the mid-1990s. By 1999 the food situation had improved to some extent, owing to fertilizer aid from international donors, agrarian reform and increased potato production, although shortages continued and were exacerbated by severe drought in 2000 and 2001, and subsequent typhoons and floods. According to the World Food Programme, cereal shortfalls of some 40,000 tons affected 2.2m. people in December 2003. In December 2000 the Government launched an intensive campaign for potato growing and double-crop farming, and in November 2001 construction began on a 7,000-ha goat farm near Pyongyang. According to South Korean estimates, grain production was 3.9m. tons in 2001 and 4.1m. tons in 2002. Potato production was 2.3m. tons in 2001 and 1.9m. tons in 2002, according to FAO. The raising of livestock (principally cattle and pigs), forestry and fishing are important. During 1991–2002, according to FAO, agricultural production decreased by an annual average of 1.8%. In 2002, according to South Korean estimates, agricultural GDP rose by 4.2%, following an increase of 6.8% in 2001 and a decline of 1.9% in 2000.

INDUSTRY

In 2002, according to South Korean estimates, industry (including mining, manufacturing, construction and power) contributed 38.2% of GDP. In 1990 the industrial sector employed 31.6% of the labour force. In 2002 the GDP of the mining and manufacturing sector declined by an estimated 2.5%, compared with 2001 (when an increase of 3.9% was estimated), but that of the construction sector increased by an estimated 10.4%, compared with a rise of 7.0% in 2001.

Mining

Mining contributed 7.8% of GDP in 2002, according to South Korean estimates. The DPRK possesses considerable mineral wealth, with large deposits of coal, iron, lead, copper, zinc, tin, silver and gold. The country was formerly the second largest producer of magnesia products in the world, but output is believed to have declined significantly. There are unexploited offshore deposits of petroleum and natural gas.

South Korean sources estimated that in 2002 output in the mining sector declined by 3.8%—compared with growth rates of 5.8% in 2000 and 4.8% in 2001.

Manufacturing

In 2002, according to South Korean estimates, the manufacturing sector contributed 18.0% of GDP (light industries 7.0% and heavy industries 11.0%). In the 1990s industrial development concentrated on heavy industry (metallurgy—notably steel production—machine-building, cement and chemicals). The textiles industry has provided significant exports. South Korean sources estimated that the GDP of the manufacturing sector declined by 2.0% in 2002, following an increase of 3.5% in 2001.

Energy

In 2000 it was estimated that 86% of the DPRK's energy supply was derived from coal, followed in importance by hydroelectricity and petroleum (6%). A 30-MW nuclear reactor was believed to have been inaugurated in 1987. Light-water nuclear reactors were being constructed, for the purpose of electricity generation, in accordance with an agreement concluded with the USA in 1994. However, in December 2003 construction of the reactors was suspended for one year, following North Korea's resumption of its nuclear weapons programme. In 2000, according to South Korean sources, some 67% of the DPRK's electricity was generated by hydro-electric power stations, with the remaining 33% of the country's requirements being provided by thermal power stations. During the 1990s the DPRK experienced increasing power shortages, as generation and transmission infrastructure deterio-rated. Although South Korean sources estimated that electricity production increased by some 30% between 1986 and 1994, output is insufficient for the DPRK's needs, and there have been frequent reports of rationing in an effort to conserve fuel and energy. The DPRK's total electricity consumption in 1998 was only 61% of that in 1991. Severe drought in the late 1990s and 2000 adversely affected the production of hydroelectric power. In early 2003 the DPRK was attempting to increase its electricity output through the construction of new hydroelectric power plants in various provinces. In May 2003 the DPRK also reportedly signed a memorandum concerning a high-voltage grid project with a Swiss company. Petroleum imports totalled only around 0.6m. metric tons in 2001 and 2002. The USA suspended fuel oil shipments in late 2002, following Pyongyang's alleged admission that it was pursuing a secret nuclear programme. From the 1990s, and especially in early 2002, the DPRK sought greater foreign assistance in developing its offshore oilfields, located to the west in the Bohai Sea, and also in the north-east, near Chongjin city. A limited number of joint ventures were established with foreign oil companies. In 1999 the DPRK succeeded in produ-cing 300,000 tons of petroleum from a well located off Sukchon County, equivalent to about half the amount of petroleum imported in that year, although falling far short of the amount needed to meet the country's acute energy needs. In 2001, according to South Korean sources, per caput energy consumption in North Korea in 2001 was 0.73 tons of oil equivalent, around six times less that the figure for South Korea.

SERVICES

The services sector employed an estimated 30.4% of the labour force in 1990. South Korean sources estimated that in 2002 the DPRK's services sector accounted for 31.6% of GDP. In 2002 output in the sector was estimated to have declined by 0.2%, having decreased by 0.3% in 2001, and increased by 1.2% in 2000.

EXTERNAL TRADE

The trade deficit, including exchanges with South Korea, totalled US $889.0m. in 2002. In 2002 total exports, excluding trade with South Korea, reached $735.0m. and imports totalled $1,525.4m., thus giving a trade deficit of $790.4m. (compared with a deficit of $970.1m. in the previous year). The DPRK's principal source of imports in 2002 was the People's Republic of China (accounting for 24.7% of total imports), followed by the Republic of Korea (19.5%) and Thailand (7.1%). The principal market for exports was the Republic of Korea, which purchased 27.0% of total exports, followed by China (26.9%), and then Japan (23.3%). China was a source of crude petroleum, food and vehicles, while Japan was a destination for industrial and agricultural goods. Inter-Korean trade increased by 28% in 2000, to reach US $425.2m., rising to $403.0m. in 2001. In 2002 inter-Korean trade increased by 59% to $641.7m. Total trade (excluding exchanges with the Republic of Korea) increased by 15.1% to reach $2,270m. in 2001, but decreased slightly, by 0.4%, to $2,260.4m. in 2002. The principal exports in that year were live animals (35.5% of the value of total exports, excluding trade with the Republic of Korea), textiles (16.7%) and machinery and electrical equipment (11.6%). Other export commodities in the late 1990s included tobacco and silk. The principal imports in 2002 were mineral products (15.5% of the value of total imports, excluding trade with the Republic of Korea), machinery and electrical equipment (15.4%), and textiles (10.4%). Other import items included road vehicles, chemicals and groceries. The 2002 budget envisaged revenue and expenditure balancing at 22,174m. won, compared with 21,571m. won in 2001. A budgetary deficit of 38.7m. won was recorded in 2001. The DPRK's total external debt was estimated to be US $12,460m. in 2000. The average annual rate of inflation in 1993 was estimated at 5%. However, following the introduction of market-orientated reforms in 2002, the inflation rate was said to have reached 4,000% in that year.

SURVEY AND PROSPECTS

It is difficult to present an accurate economic profile of the DPRK, owing to the lack of reliable statistical data. North Korea's economic situation deteriorated sharply in the early 1990s, following the abandonment, in 1991 and 1992, respectively, of the barter trading system between the DPRK and the USSR (then its major trading partner) and China in favour of trade conducted exclusively in convertible currencies. The USSR also substantially reduced deliveries of crude petroleum and cereals, resulting in a severe decline in industrial production.

The years 1994–97 were designated 'a period of adjustment in socialist economic construction', during which emphasis was to be transferred from traditional heavy industries to agriculture, light industry and trade. The Rajin-Sonbong Free Economic and Trade Zone was established in 1991 in the north-east of the country; however, attempts to attract foreign capital into the Zone were largely unsuccessful. The severe food shortages in the mid-1990s prompted Pyongyang to appeal for international food aid and humanitarian assistance.

From the late 1990s the DPRK slowly began to open up its economy, developing trading relations with various European and Asian countries and increasing the number of limited joint ventures with foreign firms. In October 2000 the DPRK reportedly established a research institute on capitalism, and it was believed that Kim Jong Il was seeking to introduce Chinese-style economic reforms following his visit to China in January 2001. The DPRK also began developing its information technology

(IT) industry, and by 2001 was operating six official websites. Joint IT ventures were established with institutes in the South, and in October the DPRK launched its first e-mail service provider in co-operation with a company based in China. In May the DPRK joined Intelsat (an international commercial satellite telecommunications organization), and in November the country agreed to adopt the global system for mobile communications (GSM) in the Rajin-Sonbong enterprise zone.

During 2002 there were signs of a significant change in economic policy. In July the Government abandoned rationing, allowing farmers to sell produce at market prices, and wages were raised by a factor of 10–17, to take into account the concomitant price rises caused by the reforms. State assistance was reduced, and the value of the won decreased to as little as one-fiftieth of its previous value in relation to the US dollar. (In 2003 academics at Kim Il Sung University in Pyongyang reportedly revised economics textbooks to reflect changes in the DPRK's economic system.) Also in 2002, a new 150-km waterway linking Pyongyang and Nampo was completed in October; and from December, in apparent displeasure with US policy towards the DPRK, the North Korean Government prohibited the use of the US dollar and adopted the euro as its official currency of foreign exchange.

A further major reform of 2002 was the creation in September of a 'Special Administrative Region' in the city of Sinuiju, followed later in the year by the establishment of a special industrial zone at Kaesong and a new tourist zone at Mount Kumgang. Whilst prospects for the special zone in Sinuiju were inauspicious following the arrest of its governor, Yang Bin, it was hoped that the special zone at Kaesong, on the border with South Korea, would attract investment from South Korean small- and medium-sized enterprises. In 2003 South Korean companies Hyundai and Korea Land were developing an international business park in Kaesong.

In March 2003 the Minister of Finance announced that the state budget's revenue would be 13.6% higher than in 2002, while expenditure would be 14.4% higher than in the previous year. Defence spending amounted to 15.4% of total projected expenditure, an increase of 0.5% in comparison with the previous year. The Government would also issue bonds for the first time in 50 years. However, analysts remained doubtful about Kim Jong Il's ability to restructure the economy without destabilizing the foundations of the ruling regime, and prospects for economic development remained uncertain in the context of international tension over the DPRK's nuclear weapons programme. Suspected state-sponsored trade in weapons and narcotics was believed to account for a significant proportion of government income. The economic reforms of 2002 seemed in 2003 to have improved availability of commodities to some extent; however, price increases as a result of the reforms were believed to have brought further hardship to some sectors of the population. The South Korean Ministry of Unification believed that the North Korean economy had shown modest growth in 2003. There were concerns in early 2004 that the introduction of new legislation in Japan in January allowing the Japanese Government to impose economic sanctions on countries considered to be a threat to national security might be damaging to the North Korean economy, were such measures to be taken against the DPRK.

Korea, Republic

The Republic of Korea (South Korea) occupies the southern part of the Korean peninsula, in eastern Asia. In 1945 Korea was divided at latitude 38°N into military occupation zones, with Soviet forces in the north and US forces in the south. In 1948 the US-administered south became the independent Republic of Korea, while the Democratic People's Republic of Korea was proclaimed in the Soviet-administered north. A three-year war between north and south ended in 1953, and the two countries remain divided at the cease-fire line, separated by a UN-supervised demilitarized zone. Seoul is the capital. The language is Korean.

Area and population
Area: 99,313 sq km
Population (mid-2002): 47,640,000
Population density (mid-2002): 479.7 per sq km
Life expectancy (years at birth, 2002): 75.5 (males 71.8; females 79.4)

Finance
GDP in current prices: 2002): $476,690m. ($10,006 per head)
Real GDP growth (2002): 6.3%
Inflation (annual average, 2002): 2.8%
Currency: won

Economy

In 2002, according to estimates by the World Bank, the Republic of Korea's gross national income (GNI), measured at average 2000–02 prices, was US $473,050m., equivalent to $9,930 per head (or $16,480 per head on an international purchasing-power parity basis). During 1990–2002, it was estimated, the population increased at an average annual rate of 0.9%, while gross domestic product (GDP) per head increased, in real terms, by an average of 5.0% per year. Overall GDP increased, in real terms, at an average annual rate of 5.9% in 1990–2002. GDP increased by 6.3% in 2002 compared with the previous year.

AGRICULTURE
Agriculture (including forestry and fishing) contributed 3.9% of GDP in 2002, and engaged 10.4% of the employed labour force in 2003. The principal crop is rice, but maize, barley, potatoes, sweet potatoes and fruit are also important, as is the raising of livestock (principally pigs and cattle). Fishing provides food for domestic consumption, as well as a surplus for export. In the late 1990s the Republic of Korea was one of the world's leading ocean-fishing nations. During 1990–2002, according to figures from the World Bank, agricultural GDP increased by an average of 1.7% per year. Agricultural GDP increased by 1.9% in 2001. There was a decrease in agricultural GDP of 4.1% in 2002.

INDUSTRY
Industry (including mining and quarrying, manufacturing, power and construction) contributed 40.3% of GDP in 2002, and engaged 28.1% of the employed labour force in 2000. Industry is dominated by large conglomerate companies (*chaebol*), with greatly diversified interests, especially in construction and manufacturing. According to figures from the World Bank, during 1990–2002 industrial GDP increased at an average annual rate of 6.5%. Industrial GDP increased by 2.9% in 2001 and by 6.1% in 2002.

Mining
South Korea is not richly endowed with natural resources, and mining and quarrying contributed only 0.3% of GDP in 2002. In 2001 less than 0.1% of the employed labour force were engaged in the sector. There are deposits of coal (mainly anthracite).Other minerals include iron ore, lead, zinc, silver, gold and limestone, and sizeable offshore reserves of natural gas have been discovered. According to figures from the Asian Development Bank (ADB), mining GDP declined at an average annual rate of 0.8% in 1990–2002.

Manufacturing
Manufacturing contributed 28.8% of GDP in 2002, and engaged 19.7% of the employed labour force in 2001. The most important branches of manufacturing

include electrical machinery, transport equipment—mainly road motor vehicles and ship-building, non-electrical machinery, chemicals, food products, iron and steel, and textiles. During 1990–2002, manufacturing GDP increased by an average of 7.6% per year. The sector's GDP increased by 2.1% in 2001. Manufacturing GDP expanded by an estimated 6.3% in 2002.

Energy

Energy is derived principally from nuclear power, coal and petroleum. In 2003 40.2% of total electricity output was generated by nuclear power, while thermal and hydroelectric power provided 57.6% and 2.1%, respectively. A total of 14 nuclear power plants were to be constructed between 1993 and 2006. The Republic of Korea also produces liquefied natural gas for domestic and industrial consumption. Imports of petroleum and its products comprised an estimated 15.8% of the value of merchandise imports in 2003.

SERVICES

The services sector contributed 55.8% of GDP in 2002, and engaged 61.0% of the employed labour force in 2000. An important source of 'invisible' export earnings has been overseas construction work, mostly in the Middle East. Receipts from tourism are also significant (totalling an estimated US $5,276.9m. in 2002). During 1990–2002, according to figures from the World Bank, the GDP of the services sector increased at an average annual rate of 6.0%. The GDP of the sector increased by 3.4% in 2001. Growth was estimated at 7.6% in 2002.

EXTERNAL TRADE

In 2002 the Republic of Korea recorded a visible trade surplus of US $14,180m., and there was a surplus of $6,092m. on the current account of the balance of payments. Japan and the USA were the principal sources of imports in 2003 (accounting for, respectively, 20.3% and 13.9% of total imports in that year); another important supplier was the People's Republic of China. The People's Republic of China emerged as the principal market for exports in 2003 (purchasing 18.1%), followed by the USA (17.7%). The main exports in 2003 were electrical machinery, miscellaneous manufactured articles, road vehicles, textiles and chemical products. The principal imports in that year were machinery and transport equipment (especially electrical machinery), petroleum and petroleum products, basic manufactures and chemical products.

GOVERNMENT FINANCE

The Republic of Korea's budget surplus for 2003 was projected at the equivalent of 2.7% of GDP—the third consecutive year of surplus. The budget for 2004 envisaged expenditure of 168,272,000m. won (including capital expenditure of 24,647,000m. won). At the end of 2001 the Republic of Korea's total external debt was US $117,652m., of which $33,742m. was long-term public debt. In that year the cost of debt-servicing was equivalent to 13.8% of the value of exports of goods and services. The average annual rate of inflation was 4.8% in 1990–2002. Consumer prices increased by an average of 2.7% in 2002 and by 3.6% in 2003. The rate of unemployment increased from 3.1% of the labour force in 2002 to 3.4% in 2003.

INTERNATIONAL ECONOMIC RELATIONS

The Republic of Korea is a member of the UN Economic and Social Commission for Asia and the Pacific (ESCAP), the ADB, Asia-Pacific Economic Co-operation (APEC), the Colombo Plan and the Organisation for Economic Co-operation and Development (OECD).

SURVEY AND PROSPECTS

In 1997 the Republic of Korea experienced its most serious economic crisis in 50 years. Several major *chaebol* collapsed, the won depreciated substantially against the US dollar and foreign-exchange reserves were almost depleted. The country was forced to seek extensive assistance from the IMF.

President Kim Dae-Jung assumed office in February 1998, promising widespread economic reform, and accepted a three-year programme formulated by the IMF, which stipulated the implementation of stringent economic and financial liberalization measures. By the end of 1999 the economy appeared to have made a remarkable recovery, and in December 2000 the IMF ended its rescue programme, which it declared to have been a success. Economic difficulties however, mainly resulting from incomplete reform of the banking sector and *chaebol*, persisted. Official intervention was much in evidence from 2001, reversing previous IMF-led policy, with many heavily-indebted companies receiving government aid. Vested interest groups with links to the *chaebol* continued to resist reform, and restructuring of the *chaebol* seemed to have stalled.

In early 2003 the Fair Trade Commission launched a large-scale investigation of *chaebol* business practices. In October the Commission imposed fines totalling 31,500m. won in connection with illegal transactions at six companies, which included Samsung, LG Group and Hyundai companies as well as SK Group. Economic difficulties in the banking sector continued in 2003, with an ongoing financial crisis at credit card lender LG Card. Meanwhile, organized labour movements continued to arrange industrial action by workers fearing unemployment and seeking better working conditions, and strikes were held during 2001 and 2002. There was further industrial unrest in 2003 in connection with railway privatization and lawsuits filed against union leaders.

Although the overall rate of average unemployment in 2003 was 3.4%, the rate of unemployment amongst young people was believed to be much higher. Decreased demand from the USA, the country's principal export market, and the deceleration in the world economy substantially reduced the Republic of Korea's trade surplus and rate of growth in 2001. Sales of semiconductors, computers and other such goods were particularly badly affected. Strong GDP resumed in 2002, however, in part aided by a recovery in exports. The corporate and financial sectors reported record profits in 2002, reflecting the success of reforms introduced during the preceding years. Although the Republic of Korea co-hosted the football World Cup with Japan in mid-2002, the overall economic benefits were limited, with much of the financing for infrastructure having been spent during the previous three years, and many businesses closing during major matches. Furthermore, far fewer foreign visitors attended the event than expected.

In 2003, according to the Bank of Korea, GDP growth decreased to around 3.1%, owing largely to weak domestic consumption and low corporate investment, with the economy having entered recession in the first half of the year, for the first time since

1998. In July 2003 the Government announced a supplementary budget of 4,500,000m. won, aimed at halting the economic decline. However, recovery was evident in the second half of the year, driven by strong growth in the export sector. Total exports increased by 19.3% in 2003, with exports to China having increased by 47.8%, compared with the previous year.

Also in 2003, the country experienced its worst typhoon for 100 years, which caused more than 100 deaths and damage to property estimated at US $3,600m. Another dramatic incident in 2003 was the suicide of a South Korean farmer in September during the course of a summit meeting of the World Trade Organization (WTO) in Cancún, Mexico, in protest at the Organization's policies. Meanwhile, continued uncertainty over the North Korean nuclear programme was likely to reduce business confidence, especially among foreign investors. Increased tension with North Korea was reflected in the draft budget for 2004, announced in August 2003, which outlined plans to increase spending on defence by 8%.

In February 2004 the Republic of Korea approved its first free-trade agreement, with Chile. The agreement prompted protests by South Korean farmers fearing the effect of increased competition in the agricultural sector. GDP growth in 2004 was forecast at 5.2% by the Bank of Korea in late 2003; however, the IMF stated a lower estimate, of 4.75%. Economic prospects were adversely affected by internal political instability in early 2004, with the impeachment of President Roh in March prompting a sharp decrease in the value of the South Korean currency and a decline in stock market prices.

Kuwait

The State of Kuwait lies at the north-west extreme of the Persian (Arabian) Gulf. Kuwait became part of Turkey's Ottoman Empire in the 16th century. Towards the end of Ottoman rule Kuwait became a semi-autonomous Arab monarchy, with local administration controlled by the as-Sabah family, which remains the ruling dynasty. In 1899 the ruler of Kuwait accepted British protection, surrendering control over external relations. Kuwait became fully independent in 1961, when the United Kingdom and Kuwait terminated the 1899 treaty. In 1990 Kuwait was invaded by Iraqi armed forces, remaining under occupation until February 1991. The capital is Kuwait City. Arabic is the official language.

Area and population
Area: 17,818 sq km
Population (mid-2002): 2,103,900
Population density (mid-2002): 118.1 per sq km
Life expectancy (years at birth, 2002): 76.2 (males 75.8; females 76.9)

Finance
GDP in current prices: 2001): US $32,791m. ($16,040 per head)
Real GDP growth (2001): −1.0%
Inflation (annual average, 2002): 1.4%
Currency: dinar

Economy

In 2001, according to estimates by the World Bank, Kuwait's gross national income (GNI), measured at average 1999–2001 prices, was US $37,352m., equivalent to $18,270 per head (or $18,800 on an international purchasing-power parity basis). During 1990–2002, it was estimated, the population decreased at an average annual rate of 0.1%, while gross domestic product (GDP) per head increased, in real terms, by an average of 0.8% per year during 1992–2001. Overall GDP was estimated to have declined, in real terms, by some 10% annually in 1990–92. Following reconstruction, the gradual increase in oil production contributed to a renewed period of economic advance after 1992, with average annual GDP growth, in real terms, for the period 1992–2001 estimated at 5.1%. However, real GDP declined by 1.0% in 2001.

AGRICULTURE
Agriculture (including hunting, forestry and fishing) contributed 0.4% of GDP in 2002. About 1.1% of the labour force were employed in the sector in mid-2002. The principal crops are tomatoes, cucumbers, potatoes, aubergines, cauliflower and dates. Owing to scarcity of water, little grain is produced, and the bulk of food requirements is imported. (Imports of food and live animals accounted for 14.0% of merchandise imports in 2002.) Livestock, poultry and fishing are also important. During 1992–97 agricultural GDP increased, in real terms, by an average of 30.3% per year. Agricultural production, which fell by some 84% in 1991, had recovered to pre-occupation levels by the mid-1990s; output increased at an average annual rate of 1.4% in 1995–2001.

INDUSTRY
Industry (including mining, manufacturing, construction and power) provided 51.0% of GDP in 2002, and employed 23.1% of the labour force in 1995. During 1993–2001 industrial GDP increased, in real terms, at an average annual rate of 0.9%.

Mining
Mining and quarrying contributed 39.5% of GDP in 2002, although the sector engaged only 2.1% of the labour force in 1995. The production of petroleum and its derivatives is the most important industry in Kuwait, providing 91.6% of export revenue in 2002. At the end of 2002 the country's proven recoverable reserves of petroleum were 96,500m. barrels, representing about 9.2% of world reserves. According to oil industry figures, Kuwait's petroleum production averaged 1.87m. barrels per day (b/d) in 2002. With effect from 1 April 2004, Kuwait's production quota, as agreed by Organization of the Petroleum Exporting Countries (OPEC), was 1.89m. b/d. Kuwait aimed to increase its production capacity from 2.5m. b/d in 2000 to 4.0m. b/d by 2020. There are significant reserves of natural gas (1,490,000m. cu m

at the end of 2002) associated with the petroleum deposits. During 1993–2001 the GDP of the mining sector increased, in real terms, at an average rate of 0.8% per year.

Manufacturing

Manufacturing provided 6.6% of GDP in 2002, and employed 5.4% of the labour force in 1995. Petroleum refineries accounted for 75.9% of manufacturing activity, measured by gross value of output, in 1997. Of the other branches of manufacturing, the most important are the production of building materials (and related activities such as aluminium extrusion), fertilizer production, food processing and the extraction of salt and chlorine. During 1993–2001 manufacturing GDP increased, in real terms, at an average annual rate of 1.5%.

Energy

Electrical energy is derived from Kuwait's own resources of petroleum (providing 75.6% of total electricity production in 2000) and both local and imported natural gas (24.4%). (The value of fuel imports in 2001 was equivalent to 0.5% of the value of total merchandise imports.) Total installed electricity-generating capacity increased from 6,898 MW in 1996 to 9,298 MW in 2000, following the completion of a 2,400-MW plant at Subiya; however, the proposed 2,500-MW az-Zour North plant was not scheduled for completion until 2006. Under the terms of an accord signed in early 2002, Qatar is to supply natural gas to the az-Zour plant from the end of 2005.

SERVICES

Services contributed 48.6% of GDP in 2002, and employed 74.8% of the labour force in 1995. Kuwait's second most important source of revenue is investment abroad (the total value of which was estimated to be in excess of US $45,000m. in the late 1990s), both in petroleum-related ventures and in other industries, chiefly in the USA, Western Europe and Japan; many such investments are held by the Reserve Fund for Future Generations (RFFG—to which 10% of petroleum revenues must by law be contributed each year, and which is intended to provide an income after hydrocarbon resources have been exhausted) and managed by the Kuwait Investment Authority. Prior to the Iraqi invasion the value of the RFFG was believed to have been some $100,000m. As part of its efforts to diversify the economy, the Government planned to develop the islands of Bubiyan and Failaka into major tourist resorts. In January 2004 a US company was selected as project manager for the Bubiyan island project, the first phase of which—the construction of a new port—was expected to cost about $800m. The combined GDP of the service sectors increased, in real terms, at an average rate of 2.9% per year during 1993–2001.

EXTERNAL TRADE

In 2002 Kuwait recorded a visible trade surplus of US $7,249m., and there was a surplus of $4,192m. on the current account of the balance of payments. In 2002 the principal sources of imports were the USA and Japan, which provided, respectively, 11.0% and 10.7% of total imports; other important suppliers in that year were Germany, Saudi Arabia, Italy and the People's Republic of China. Details concerning the destination of Kuwait's petroleum exports are not available for recent years; however, the major markets for non-petroleum exports in 2002 included Saudi Arabia (13.3%), the UAE, Indonesia and India. The principal exports are petroleum and petroleum products. The principal imports are machinery and transport equipment, which accounted for 39.8% of total imports in 2002, basic manufactures and other manufactured goods, food and live animals, and chemicals and related products.

GOVERNMENT FINANCE

A budget surplus of KD 791m. was recorded for the financial year ending 30 June 2004. Kuwait's total external debt in mid-1996 was estimated to be equivalent to 8.5% of GDP. The average annual rate of inflation in 1995–2002 was 1.7%; consumer prices increased by an annual average of 1.4% in 2002. National unemployment was estimated at only 1.4% in the mid-1990s and reported to be only 1% in 2001, the lowest rate in the region; however, underemployment was unofficially reported to be in excess of 50%.

INTERNATIONAL ECONOMIC RELATIONS

Kuwait is a member of the GCC; the six GCC states established a unified regional customs tariff in January 2003, and it has been agreed to create a single market and currency no later than January 2010. Kuwait also belongs to the Organization of Arab Petroleum Exporting Countries (OAPEC) and to OPEC. Kuwait is a major aid donor, disbursing loans to developing countries through the Kuwait Fund for Arab Economic Development (KFAED) and the Arab Fund for Economic and Social Development (AFESD).

SURVEY AND PROSPECTS

Despite its significant, oil-based wealth, Kuwait has a number of fundamental weaknesses in its economic structure: instability in its relations with Iraq have necessitated a high level of defence expenditure; reliance on oil revenues has impeded diversification into other industries; and its constitutional commitment to provide employment for all Kuwaitis has resulted in a heavy burden on government spending (an estimated 84% of the annual budget is allocated to salaries and subsidies). In 1999 the Government attempted to address this problem by proposing new taxes for companies and expatriate workers that would be used to create an employment fund to facilitate private-sector work for Kuwaitis. The value of shares quoted on the Kuwait Stock Exchange (KSE) declined during 1999–2001, apparently demonstrating a lack of investor confidence in the Government's economic reforms despite new legislation, enacted in May 2000, which allowed non-GCC investors to enter the market. However, since then shares have traded strongly and by February 2004 the KSE share value was reported to be at its highest recorded level.

During the early years of this century plans by the Kuwait Petroleum Corporation to allow foreign participation in a development project (known as 'Project Kuwait'), valued at US $7,000m., for the northern oilfields made slow progress; the project aimed to increase production from 400,000 b/d to 900,000 b/d by its completion date of 2005. Approval by the Majlis was still required in April 2004, and, despite assurances that all reserves would remain Kuwaiti-owned, many Kuwaitis remained opposed to any foreign involvement in the petroleum sector. Nevertheless, in 2001 the Kuwaiti Government pursued legislation that would increase foreign investment in the economy, including the limited participation of international oil companies in the petroleum sector and measures that would permit foreign banks to operate in Kuwait; the legislation was eventually passed by the Majlis in 2003. Moreover, in November 2003 the legislature approved plans to deregulate the aviation sector—a decision that brought to an end the monopoly of the state-owned Kuwait Airways Corporation and opened the industry to international competition.

The recovery in world petroleum prices from late 1999, despite being interrupted in the period following the September 2001 suicide attacks in the USA, was the principal factor contributing to budget surpluses during 1999/2000–2002/03. (An increase in expenditure in 2003/04 led to a deficit in that year.) Petroleum prices reached particularly high levels in early 2003, reflecting uncertainty regarding oil supplies in the event of a US-led military campaign against the Iraqi regime of Saddam Hussain. The removal of the threat from Saddam Hussain's Baathist regime provided a special impetus to construction in areas other than the hydrocarbons sector. In particular, huge infrastructure and tourism projects provided grounds for optimism that the economy could be successfully diversified. It was hoped that another increase in government expenditure in the 2004/05 budget, which was expected to lead to a 15% increase in the fiscal deficit, would further stimulate growth in the non-petroleum sector. On 1 January 2003 Kuwait pegged the dinar to the US dollar, as part of the GCC plan to create a single currency by 2010. Real GDP was estimated to have declined by 0.5% in the 2002/03 fiscal year, although non-oil GDP increased by some 5%. Economic growth was expected to benefit strongly from the reconstruction of Iraq.

Kyrgyzstan

The Kyrgyz Republic is situated in eastern Central Asia. In 1936 the Kyrgyz Soviet Socialist Republic (SSR) was established as a full union republic of the USSR. In 1990 the Kyrgyz Supreme Soviet voted to change the name of the republic from the Kyrgyz SSR to the Republic of Kyrgyzstan. The Supreme Soviet declared Kyrgyzstan's independence from the USSR in 1991. In that year Kyrgyzstan was among the 11 signatories to the Almaty (Alma-Ata) Declaration, which formally established the Commonwealth of Independent States. Bishkek is the capital. The state language is Kyrgyz, and Russian also has the status of an official language.

Area and population
Area: 199,900 sq km
Population (mid-2002): 5,003,890
Population density (mid-2002): 25.0 per sq km
Life expectancy (years at birth, 2002): 64.5 (males 60.4; females 68.9)

Finance
GDP in current prices: 2002): US $1,632m. ($326 per head)
Real GDP growth (2002): -0.5%
Inflation (annual average, 2002): 2.1%
Currency: som

Economy

In 2002, according to estimates by the World Bank, Kyrgyzstan's gross national product (GNI), measured at average 2000–02 prices, was US $1,454m., equivalent to $290 per head (or $1,520 per head on an international purchasing-power parity basis). During 1990–2002, it was estimated, the population increased by an annual average of 1.0%, while gross domestic product (GDP) per head declined, in real terms, at an average annual rate of 3.9%. Overall GDP declined, in real terms, at an estimated average annual rate of 2.9% in 1990–2002. Real GDP increased by 5.3% in 2001, but decreased by 0.5% in 2002.

AGRICULTURE

Agriculture (including forestry and fishing) contributed an estimated 38.7% of GDP in 2003, according to preliminary official figures. In 1999 52.4% of the labour force were employed in the sector. By tradition, the Kyrgyz are a pastoral nomadic people, and the majority of the population (some 65.2% in 1999) reside in rural areas. Livestock-rearing, once the mainstay of agricultural activity, is declining in importance. Only about 7% of the country's land area is arable; of this, some 70% depends on irrigation. The principal crops are grain, potatoes, vegetables and sugar beet. By 2002, according to government figures, collective farms accounted for only around 6% of agricultural production, while state farms accounted for just under 2%. The GDP of the agricultural sector increased, in real terms, by an average of 1.6% per year in 1990–2002; real agricultural GDP increased by 7.3% in 2001 and by 3.3% in 2002.

INDUSTRY

Industry (comprising manufacturing, mining, utilities and construction) contributed an estimated 22.9% of GDP in 2003, according to preliminary official data. The industrial sector provided 11.6% of employment in 1999. Real industrial GDP declined at an average annual rate of 8.5% in 1990–2002; the GDP of the sector increased, in real terms, by 5.2% in 2001, but contracted by 11.2% in 2002.

Mining

In 1999 the mining and quarrying sector employed just 0.5% of the work-force. Kyrgyzstan has considerable mineral deposits, including coal, gold, tin, mercury, antimony, zinc, tungsten and uranium. In May 2001 the Government announced the discovery of new deposits of petroleum, estimated to total 70m. barrels, in an oilfield in the west. Production of gold from the Kumtor mine, which is believed to contain the eighth largest deposit of gold in the world, began in January 1997. As a result, Kyrgyzstan had become the 10th largest extractor and seller of gold in the world by 2001.

Manufacturing

According to World Bank estimates, manufacturing contributed 10.5% of GDP in 2002. The manufacturing sector employed 7.2% of the work-force in 1999. In 2002 the principal branches of manufacturing, measured by gross value of output, were food products, beverages and tobacco (accounting for 34.0% of the total) and metallurgy (29.9%). Real manufacturing GDP declined by an average of 12.3% per year in 1990–2002; according to the World Bank, the GDP of the sector declined by 3.0% in 2001, but registered an increase of 3.1% in 2002.

Energy

Kyrgyzstan's principal source of domestic energy production (and also a major export) is hydroelectricity (generated by the country's mountain rivers), which provided 91.7% of the country's total energy requirements in 2000. Kyrgyzstan has insufficient petroleum and natural gas to meet its needs, and substantial imports of hydrocarbons are thus required; Kyrgyzstan exports electricity to Kazakhstan and Uzbekistan in return for coal and natural gas, respectively. Imports of mineral fuels comprised 27.8% of the value of total recorded imports in 2002. Exports of electricity contributed some 15.8% of the value of total exports in 2000.

SERVICES

In 2003, according to preliminary official figures, the services sector contributed an estimated 38.4% of GDP. Services provided 36.1% of employment in 1999. In 1990–2002 the GDP of the sector declined, in real terms, by an average of 2.9% per year; services GDP increased by 3.3% in 2001 and by 4.2% in 2002.

EXTERNAL TRADE

In 2002 Kyrgyzstan recorded a visible trade deficit of US $54.0m., and a deficit of $34.7m. on the current account of the balance of payments. In 2003 the principal source of recorded imports (24.6%) was Russia; other major suppliers were Kazakhstan, the People's Republic of China, the USA, Uzbekistan and Germany. The main market for exports in that year was the United Arab Emirates (24.8%). Other principal markets were Switzerland, Russia and Kazakhstan. The main exports in 2002 were precious and semi-precious stones and metals, mineral products, textiles, foodstuffs, beverages and tobacco, machinery and chemicals. The principal recorded imports in that year were mineral products (mostly petroleum and natural gas), machinery and electrical equipment, chemicals, foodstuffs, beverages and tobacco, textiles and metals.

GOVERNMENT FINANCE

In 2002 Kyrgyzstan recorded an overall budgetary deficit of 776.9m. soms (equivalent to 1.0% of GDP). Kyrgyzstan's total external debt was US $1,717m. at the end of 2001, of which $1,256m. was long-term public debt. In that year the cost of debt-servicing was equivalent to 29.8% of the value of exports of goods and services. Annual inflation averaged 65.7% in 1992–2002. Consumer prices increased by 18.7% in 2000, by 6.9% in 2001 and by 2.2% in 2002. The average rate of unemployment was 12.5% in 2002.

INTERNATIONAL ECONOMIC RELATIONS

Kyrgyzstan participates in the economic bodies of the Commonwealth of Independent States (CIS), and has also joined the European Bank for Reconstruction and Development (EBRD), as a 'Country of Operations', and the Economic Co-operation Organization (ECO). In addition, Kyrgyzstan is a member of the Asian Development Bank (ADB). In February 1995 Kyrgyzstan signed a 10-year 'partnership and co-operation' agreement with the European Union. In October 1998 Kyrgyzstan became the first CIS country to join the World Trade Organization (WTO).

SURVEY AND PROSPECTS

Following independence in 1991, the Kyrgyz Government embarked on an ambitious programme of economic reforms to establish a market-based economy and achieve macroeconomic stabilization. Although significant growth was registered in 1996–97, the economy slowed considerably from mid-1998, owing to reduced growth in gold and agricultural production and the financial crisis in Russia. The privatization programme was relaunched in 1998, and in 2000 the Government approved a further two-year privatization programme to facilitate the sale of strategic enterprises; by the end of 2003 official figures revealed that 7,060 state enterprises had been privatized since 1991. There was rapid growth in GDP in 2000–01, and in 2001 an annual rate of inflation of less than 10% was recorded for the first time since independence.

In November 2001 it was reported that the IMF had agreed to cancel or restructure a proportion of the country's external debt, and in March 2002 the 'Paris Club' of creditor countries agreed to reschedule, over a period of 20 years, the repayment of some US $95m., which had been due to be serviced in 2002–04. In October 2002 a conference was held in Bishkek, at which international donors pledged some $700m. for 2003–05, a significant proportion of which was to be used in support of the country's poverty reduction programme. However, in 2002 GDP registered its first decline since 1995, largely owing to reduced industrial output after a landslide at the Kumtor gold mine. Although growth resumed in 2003, reaching some 5.2%, in the medium term it was likely to be severely affected by the economy's reliance on the output of the mine, the closure of which was anticipated in 2010; new gold projects were not expected to be able to compensate for the consequent decline in production. The introduction of value-added tax on agricultural products and the adoption of a new property tax was expected to be of substantial benefit to the economy in 2004, and additional large-scale privatization commenced in 2003. In October of that year the Government announced plans to divest Kairat Bank, the country's fifth largest, and in February 2004 Gazprom of Russia agreed to acquire a majority stake in Kyrgyzneftegaz, the state-owned petroleum and natural gas company. Ultimately, however, sustained economic growth was dependent on the greater diversification of both exports (trade in which was already constrained by regional restrictions on commerce, as well as Kyrgyzstan's lack of access to the sea) and industry.

Laos

The Lao People's Democratic Republic is situated in South-East Asia. The sovereignty of the former Kingdom of Laos was recognized by France in 1953. In 1975 the insurgent Neo Lao Haksat (Lao Patriotic Front) gained control of the country, abolishing the monarchy and establishing the Lao People's Democratic Republic. Although the 20th anniversary of the beginning of communist rule was celebrated in 1995, the Government was gradually attempting to replace communist ideology with Lao nationalism. The results of elections at the congress of the Lao People's Revolutionary Party in 1996 consolidated apparent progress towards military-dominated, authoritarian government. Vientiane is the capital. The official language is Lao (Laotian).

Area and population
Area: 236,800 sq km
Population (mid-2002): 5,530,090
Population density (mid-2002): 23.4 per sq km
Life expectancy (years at birth, 2002): 55.1 (males 54.1; females 56.2)

Finance
GDP in current prices: 2002): US $1,680m. ($304 per head)
Real GDP growth (2002): 5.0%
Inflation (annual average, 2002): 10.6%
Currency: new kip

Economy

In 2002, according to estimates by the World Bank, Laos's gross national income (GNI), measured at average 2000–02 prices, was US $1,709m., equivalent to $310 per head (or $1,610 per head on an international purchasing-power parity basis). During 1990–2002, it was estimated, the population increased by an annual average of 2.5%, while gross domestic product (GDP) per head increased, in real terms, by an average of 3.6% per year. Overall GDP increased, in real terms, at an average annual rate of 6.1% in 1990–2002. According to the Asian Development Bank (ADB), GDP increased by 5.8% in 2001 and by 5.9% in 2002.

AGRICULTURE

Agriculture (including forestry and fishing) contributed an estimated 50.4% of GDP in 2002. An estimated 76.3% of the working population were employed in the sector in 2001. Rice is the staple crop. Other crops include sweet potatoes, maize, cassava and sugar cane; coffee is grown for export. In 2000 forest covered about 55.4% of the country's total land area. Wood products were the third largest export commodity in 2001, accounting for an estimated 23.2% of total export revenue. The cultivation and illicit export of narcotic drugs is believed to be widespread. Despite having been outlawed in 1997, opium production was estimated to total 120 metric tons in 2003. According to the UN Office on Drugs and Crime (formerly the UN Office of Drug Control and Crime Prevention), Laos was the third largest source of illicit opium in the world in that year, behind Afghanistan and Myanmar. However, the Government was achieving some success in its efforts to eliminate opium production; the area under cultivation was steadily decreasing. During 1990–2002, according to the ADB, agricultural GDP increased by an average of 4.5% per year. Compared with the previous year, the rate of growth was estimated at 3.8% in 2001 and at 4.0% in 2002.

INDUSTRY

Industry (including mining, manufacturing, construction and utilities) contributed an estimated 24.7% of GDP in 2002. The sector employed about 6.3% of the working population in 1990. During 1990–2002, according to the ADB, industrial GDP increased at an average annual rate of 11.0%. Growth in the sector was estimated at 10.1% in 2001 and at 10.3% in 2002.

Mining

Mining contributed only an estimated 0.5% of GDP in 2002. Laos has, however, considerable mineral resources: iron ore (the country's principal mineral resource), coal, tin and gypsum are among the minerals that are exploited. Other known mineral deposits include zinc, copper, nickel, potash, lead, limestone and small quantities of gold, silver and precious stones. During 1990–2002, according to the ADB, the GDP of the mining sector increased by an average of 17.4% per year. Growth was estimated at 1.2% in 2001 and at 10.1% in 2002.

Manufacturing

Manufacturing contributed an estimated 19.1% of GDP in 2002, although the sector employed less than 1% of the working population in the mid-1980s. It is mainly confined to the processing of raw materials (chiefly sawmilling) and agricultural produce, the production of textiles and garments (a principal export commodity), and the manufacture of handicrafts and basic consumer goods for the domestic market. According to the ADB, manufacturing GDP increased at an average annual rate of 12.1% in 1990–2002; manufacturing GDP increased by 12.1% in 2001 and by 13.0% in 2002.

Energy

Electrical energy is principally derived from hydroelectric power. Electricity is exported to Thailand and Viet Nam, and is one of Laos's principal sources of foreign exchange. In 2001 the country's total electricity generation reached an estimated 3,590m. kWh. Laos's total hydroelectric power potential was estimated at 25,000 MW in 2000. In 2002 the Government granted a concession to the Nam Theun 2 Power Company (NTPC), enabling it to assume control of the construction of a US $1,100m. hydroelectric dam—Nam Theun 2. In November 2003 the Electricity Generating Authority of Thailand signed an agreement with the NTPC to buy 995 MW of electricity over 25 years, at an estimated cost of US $5,000m. Nam Theun 2 was scheduled for completion in 2009. Also in 2002, Laos signed an agreement with Cambodia, China, Myanmar, Thailand and Viet Nam concerning the establishment of a regional power distribution system, which would form the basis for a pro-gramme of hydropower development in the Mekong region. Laos is totally dependent on imports, mainly from Thailand, for supplies of mineral fuels.

SERVICES

The services sector contributed an estimated 25.0% of GDP in 2002, and engaged 17.2% of the total labour force in 1980. Receipts from tourism increased from US $43.6m. in 1996 to $114m. in 2000, but decreased to $104m. in 2001. Tourist arrivals declined from 737,208 in 2000 to 673,823 in 2001. According to the ADB, the GDP of the services sector increased at an average annual rate of 6.5% in 1990–2002. Annual increases were estimated at 5.7% in 2001 and again at 5.7% in 2002.

EXTERNAL TRADE

In 2001 Laos recorded a visible trade deficit of US $216.8m., and there was a deficit of $82.4m. on the current account of the balance of payments. Remittances from relatives residing overseas are a significant source of income for many Lao. In 2002 Thailand was the principal source of imports, supplying an estimated 58.2% of the total. Viet Nam was also an important source of imports (12.2%) in that year, along with China, Singapore and Japan. The principal destination of exports from Laos in 2002 was Viet Nam, purchasing 25.9% of the total. Other significant purchasers in that year were Thailand (an estimated 19.2%), France (7.5%) and Germany (5.4%). It was estimated that the main exports in 2001 were electricity (32.6% of the total), garments (28.6%), wood products (23.2%) and motorcycles (6.7%). The principal imports in that year were consumer goods (49.4%), investment goods (29.3%), materials for the garments industry (11.8%) and motorcycle parts for assembly (5.3%).

GOVERNMENT FINANCE

In the financial year ending 30 September 2002 Laos projected an overall budget deficit of 1,133,000m. kips. At the end of 2001 the country's external debt totalled US $2,495m., of which $2,456m. was long-term public debt. In that year the cost of debt-servicing was equivalent to 9.0% of revenue from export of goods and services. Consumer prices increased by an annual average of 37.7% in 1995–2002. According to the ADB, the annual rate of inflation averaged 7.8% in 2001, before increasing to 10.6% in 2002 and to an estimated 14.0% in 2003. The unemployment rate totalled 2.4% in 1995, according to the census conducted in that year.

INTERNATIONAL ECONOMIC RELATIONS

Laos is a member of the UN Economic and Social Commission for Asia and the Pacific (ESCAP), of the Asian Development Bank (ADB), of the Association of South East Asian Nations (ASEAN), of the Colombo Plan, which promotes economic and social development in Asia and the Pacific, and of the Mekong River Commission.

SURVEY AND PROSPECTS

From 1986 the Government undertook a radical programme of economic liberalization, known as the New Economic Mechanism, with the aim of transforming the hitherto centrally planned economy into a market-orientated system. Various reforms were introduced, including the enactment of a liberal foreign investment law in 1988 and the implementation of a privatization programme. Laos has remained extremely underdeveloped, however, and, as one of the poorest countries in Asia, is heavily reliant on external aid. The regional economic crisis of 1997 resulted in a significant loss of foreign capital for Laos, as Thailand and other countries affected by the crisis had been among the most important investors in the country. Having reached US $159.8m. in 1996, according to the ADB, foreign direct investment subsequently declined to only $33.9m. in 2000, before rising to $83.3m. in 2001. By early 2001 the economy had begun to recover.

The Fifth Five-Year Plan (2001–05), announced at the Seventh Congress of the Lao People's Revolutionary Party (LPRP) in March 2001, envisaged an average annual GDP growth rate of between 7.0% and 7.5%. The Plan emphasized the eradication of poverty, the restriction of opium cultivation and integrated rural development through the strengthening of basic political units. Other targets included a reduction in the annual level of inflation to a single-digit rate, the maintenance of a stable exchange rate and the restriction of the budget deficit to the equivalent of 5% of GDP. International donors, however, were disappointed at the Plan's failure to incorporate development of the private sector, while corruption among Lao officials and the lack of skilled personnel to manage the financial sector remained causes for concern. Having declined sharply in value in 1997 and fluctuated thereafter, the national currency suffered another significant depreciation in mid-2002. This weakening of the kip was accompanied by a rise in inflation, which reached a high of 18% in May 2003 (according to the IMF).

In 2003 the country's increasing security problems, together with a decrease in the amount of foreign aid to the country, threatened economic stability. In that year, according to the ADB, GDP growth was an estimated 5.5%. In early 2004 it was feared that a regional epidemic of avian influenza would have a negative impact upon economic growth, owing to the enforced destruction of some of the country's poultry stock. None the less, GDP was expected to record strong growth in that year, benefiting from improvements in the global economy which, it was hoped, would lead to increasing inflows of foreign direct investment. However, further reforms remained essential if an environment were to be created in which sustained economic growth might be achieved. The reduction of state involvement in the country's commercial sector and increased access to the resources necessary to reduce the country's high level of poverty remained priorities.

Latvia

The Republic of Latvia is situated in north-eastern Europe. The Treaty of Non-Aggression signed by Germany and the USSR in 1939 provided for the incorporation of Latvia into the USSR. The Latvian Soviet Socialist Republic was duly absorbed into the USSR in 1940. After German occupation, Soviet Latvia was re-established in 1944–45. In 1990 the Latvian Supreme Council announced the beginning of a transitional period that was to lead to full political and economic independence. In 1991 the Supreme Council proclaimed the full independence of Latvia, and the independent Republic of Latvia was recognized by the USSR State Council. Riga is the capital. The official language is Latvian.

Area and population

Area: 64,589 sq km
Population (mid-2002): 2,335,000
Population density (mid-2002): 36.2 per sq km
Life expectancy (years at birth, 2002): 70.3 (males 64.6; females 75.8)

Finance

GDP in current prices: 2002): US $8,406m. ($3,600 per head)
Real GDP growth (2002): 6.1%
Inflation (annual average, 2002): 2.0%
Currency: lats

Economy

In 2002, according to estimates by the World Bank, Latvia's gross national income (GNI), measured at average 2000–02 prices, was US $8,134m., equivalent to $3,480 per head (or $8,940 per head on an international purchasing-power parity basis). During 1990–2002, it was estimated, the population decreased by an annual average of 1.1%, while gross domestic product (GDP) per head decreased at an average annual rate of 1.5%, in real terms. Overall GDP decreased, in real terms, by an annual average of 2.6% in 1990–2002; however, according to official figures, real GDP increased by 6.1% in 2002 and by 7.5% in 2003.

AGRICULTURE

Agriculture (including hunting, forestry and fishing) contributed 4.5% of GDP in 2003, and provided 15.5% of employment in 2002. The principal sectors are dairy farming and pig-breeding. Cereals, sugar beet, potatoes and fodder crops are the main crops grown. As part of the process of land reform and privatization, the liquidation of collective and state farms was undertaken in the early 1990s (some 38% of all arable land had been privatized by 1995). In 2003 Latvia approved a seven-year ban on the sale of rural land to foreign purchasers. Fishing makes an important contribution to the economy (an estimated 70% of the total annual catch is exported). There was considerable growth potential in the forestry industry (43.9% of Latvia's land area is classified as forest), and output increased rapidly from 1996. Agricultural GDP decreased, in real terms, by an average of 5.2% per year in 1990–2002; however, according to official figures, the real GDP of the sector (excluding fishing) increased by 4.2% in 2002 and by 2.6% in 2003.

INDUSTRY

Industry (comprising mining and quarrying, manufacturing, construction and utilities) contributed 24.5% of GDP in 2003, and provided 25.5% of employment in 2002. Industrial GDP declined, in real terms, at an average annual rate of 7.4% in 1990–2002. However, real sectoral GDP increased by 6.9% in 2001 and by 5.8% in 2002.

Mining

Mining and quarrying contributed just 0.2% of GDP in 2003, and employed only 0.3% of workers in 2002. Latvia has limited mineral resources, the most important being peat, dolomite, limestone, gypsum, amber, gravel and sand. Offshore and onshore petroleum reserves have been located. The GDP of the mining sector decreased at an average annual rate of 14.5% in 1990–98; however, real mining GDP increased by 5.7% in 1999, by 8.1% in 2000, by 16.7% in 2001, by 7.7% in 2002 and by 7.2% in 2003.

Manufacturing

The manufacturing sector contributed 14.9% of GDP in 2003, and provided 16.9% of employment in 2002. In 2001 the principal branches of manufacturing, measured by value of output, were food products (31.6%), wood products, light industry and machinery and equipment. Real manufacturing GDP decreased by an average of 6.4% per year in 1990–2002. However, according to official figures, the GDP of the sector increased, in real terms, by 7.2% in 2002 and by 9.1% in 2003.

Energy

Latvia is highly dependent on imported fuels to provide energy. In 2002 imports of mineral products represented 9.7% of the total value of Latvia's imports. Electric energy is supplied primarily by Estonia and Lithuania, and petroleum products are supplied by Russia and Lithuania. In 2000 hydroelectric plants provided some 68.2%

of annual domestic electricity production in Latvia; a further 27.3% was derived from natural gas, and the remainder from petroleum and coal.

SERVICES

The services sector has increased in importance, and in 2003 it contributed 70.9% of GDP; the sector accounted for 59.0% of employment in 2002. The sector's GDP increased, in real terms, by an average of 2.6% annually during 1990–2002; according to official figures, real services GDP increased by 5.9% in 2002 and by 7.0% in 2003.

EXTERNAL TRADE

In 2002 Latvia recorded a visible trade deficit of US $1,444m., and there was a deficit of $647m. on the current account of the balance of payments. The principal source of imports in 2002 was Germany, which accounted for 17.2% of total imports; other major sources were Lithuania, Russia, Finland, Sweden, Estonia and Poland. The main market for exports in that year was also Germany, accounting for 15.5% of total exports; other significant purchasers were the United Kingdom, Sweden, Lithuania, Estonia and Denmark. The principal exports in 2002 were wood and wood products, followed by base metals and manufactures, textiles, prepared foodstuffs, beverages and tobacco, machinery and electrical equipment, miscellaneous manufactured items, and chemicals. The principal imports in that year were machinery and electrical equipment, chemicals, vehicles and transport equipment, mineral products, base metals and manufactures, textiles, and foodstuffs, beverages and tobacco.

GOVERNMENT FINANCE

In 2001 the consolidated state budget recorded a deficit of 64.6m. LVL (equivalent to 1.4% of GDP). Latvia's total external debt at the end of 2001 was US $5,710m., of which $978m. was long-term public debt. In that year the cost of debt-servicing was equivalent to 13.7% of the value of exports of goods and services. Annual inflation averaged 43.9% in 1991–2002; the rate of increase in consumer prices had slowed to an average of 17.6% by 1996, and it continued to decline in subsequent years. Consumer prices increased by 1.9% in 2002 and by 2.9% in 2003. At 1 March 2004 some 94,900 people were registered as unemployed (representing 9.0% of the economically active population).

INTERNATIONAL ECONOMIC RELATIONS

Latvia is a member (as a 'country of operations') of the European Bank for Reconstruction and Development (EBRD). An agreement on a free-trade area between Latvia, Lithuania and Estonia entered into effect in April 1994, and in July of that year Latvia signed an agreement on free trade with the European Union (EU); Latvia became an associate member of the EU in June 1995, and a full member on 1 May 2004. Latvia became a member of the World Trade Organization (WTO) in February 1999.

SURVEY AND PROSPECTS

The Government's programme of stabilization, initiated in 1992, achieved considerable success. A crisis in the banking sector in 1995 undermined economic recovery, but following the introduction of new legal requirements and stricter bank licensing regulations the situation was stabilized by 1996. Growth slowed in 1999, largely as a consequence of the Russian economic crisis of 1998. However, there were signs of economic recovery in 2000, and in 2001 Latvia demonstrated one of the best economic performances of all the candidate countries for EU membership. The rate of inflation in 2002 was the lowest to be recorded since independence, and strong growth was recorded in both 2002 and 2003. However, there was concern at the sizeable budgetary deficit, particularly since the EU stipulated that the public-finance deficit of member states be restrained to less than 3% of GDP.

In anticipation of the increased financial commitments associated with membership of the EU and NATO from 2004 and in order to conform with EU practices, in December 2003 the Saeima adopted legislative amendments increasing the rate of value-added tax (VAT) from 9% to 18%, and imposing VAT of 5% on a number of previously untaxed goods from 1 May 2004 (the rate of corporate income tax, however, was to be reduced from 19% to 15%, in an effort to encourage increased foreign direct investment). None the less, international concerns focused on Latvia's role as a regional financial centre and the difficulties in eliminating the associated practice of money 'laundering' (the processing of illicitly obtained funds into legitimate holdings). Although Latvia was the poorest of the EU accession countries, its economy was expected to continue to expand rapidly. The budget for 2004 envisaged GDP growth of 6.1%, in real terms, and an annual rate of consumer-price inflation of around 3%, together with a budgetary deficit equivalent to some 2% of GDP.

Lebanon

The Republic of Lebanon lies in western Asia. Lebanon was administered by France from 1920 until independence was declared in 1941. After Israel's establishment in 1948, and during the Arab–Israeli wars, thousands of Palestinians fled to Lebanon. From 1975 conflict between the right-wing Maronite Christian Phalangist Party and Palestinians escalated into full-scale civil war. Lebanon's constitutional order subsequently became a major divisive issue and militias of various warring factions took control of most of the country. No enduring semblance of civil order was regained until 1990, when, in accordance with the Ta'if agreement, the Constitution was amended. Beirut is the capital. Arabic is the official language.

Area and population
Area: 10,452 sq km
Population (mid-2002): 4,441,240
Population density (mid-2002): 424.9 per sq km
Life expectancy (years at birth, 2002): 69.88 (males 67.6; females 72.0)

467

Finance
GDP in current prices: 2002): US $17,294m. ($3,894 per head)
Real GDP growth (2002): 1.0%
Inflation (2001): 1.3%
Currency: Lebanese pound

Economy

In 2002, according to estimates by the World Bank, Lebanon's gross national income (GNI), measured at average 2000–02 prices, was US $17,726m., equivalent to $3,990 per head (or $4,470 per head on an international purchasing-power parity basis). During 1990–2002, it was estimated, the population increased at an average annual rate of 1.7%, while gross domestic product (GDP) per head increased, in real terms, by an average of 4.3% per year. Overall GDP increased, in real terms, at an average annual rate of 6.1% in 1990–2002; although zero growth was registered in 2000, GDP growth of some 1.3% was recorded in 2001. According to the Ministry of Finance, GDP increased by 2% in 2002.

AGRICULTURE

According to the UN Economic and Social Commission for Western Asia (ESCWA), agriculture (including hunting, forestry and fishing) contributed an estimated 9.9% of GDP in 2002. According to FAO data, some 3.2% of the labour force were employed in the sector in that year. The principal crops are potatoes, citrus fruits, tomatoes, cucumbers and onions. Viticulture is also significant. Hashish is a notable, albeit illegal, export crop, although the Government is attempting to persuade growers to switch to other crops. The GDP of the agricultural sector was estimated to have increased by an average of 2.0% annually in 1994–2002, although agricultural GDP declined by an estimated 0.7% in 1999. According to FAO data, agricultural production increased by 6.1% in 2000, but declined by 5.8% in 2001; however, an increase of 6.4% was recorded in 2002.

INDUSTRY

The industrial sector (including manufacturing, construction and power) contributed 18.7% of GDP in 2002, according to estimates by ESCWA. Some 25.9% of the labour force were employed in industry in 1997. Lebanon's only mineral resources consist of small reserves of lignite and iron ore, and their contribution to GDP is insignificant. The GDP of the industrial sector decreased by an estimated average of 0.7% per year in 1994–2002; however, industrial GDP grew by an estimated 3.7% in 1998 and by 1.4% in 1999.

Manufacturing

ESCWA figures indicate that manufacturing contributed an estimated 9.7% of GDP in 2002. The sector employed about 10% of the labour force in 1985. The most important branches have traditionally been food-processing, petroleum refining, textiles and furniture and woodworking. Manufacturing GDP was estimated to have decreased at an average annual rate of 4.7% in 1994–2002.

Energy

Energy is derived principally from thermal power stations, using imported petroleum (which accounted for 94.3% of total electricity production in 2000). However, in order to meet Lebanon's growing energy requirements, plans for the construction of an offshore pipeline—capable of importing 6m.–9m. cu m of natural gas per day from Syria—were scheduled for completion in 2003. A second pipeline was planned that would enable Lebanon to import an estimated 9m. cu m of natural gas per day from Egypt and 3m. cu m per day from Syria by 2005.

SERVICES

The services sector contributed an estimated 71.4% of GDP in 2002, according to ESCWA data. In 1997 some 65.1% of the working population were employed in the sector, which has traditionally been dominated by trade and finance (accounting for an estimated 32.2% and 13.7% of GDP, respectively, in 2002). Financial services, in particular, withstood many of the disruptions inflicted on the economy by the civil conflict, although the Beirut Stock Exchange did not recommence trading until 1996. Lebanon is also becoming increasingly important as a centre for telecommunications. Recent efforts to revive the tourist industry have met with considerable success, and have been a major source of growth in the construction industry. Tourist arrivals increased by 13.1% in 1998, by 6.7% in 1999 and by 10.1% in 2000 (despite the regional impact of the Israeli–Palestinian crisis, which has partly undermined the revival of Lebanon's tourist industry). Numbers of tourist arrivals from Gulf and other Arab states were reported to be increasing in 2001 and 2002. The GDP of the services sector increased at an average annual rate of some 2.8% in 1994–2002; the sector's GDP was estimated to have increased by 5.9% in 1998 and by 2.0% in 1999.

EXTERNAL TRADE

In 2003 Lebanon recorded a trade deficit of US $5,644m. The principal markets for exports in 2002 were Switzerland (which took 12.6% of Lebanese exports in that year) and Saudi Arabia (9.2%); other significant purchasers included the United Arab Emirates and Syria. The principal supplier of imports in 2002 was Italy (10.8%); Germany, France and the USA were also important suppliers. The principal exports in 2003 were jewellery, machinery and electrical equipment, and food products. The principal imports in that year were mineral products, machinery and electrical equipment, chemical products, and vehicles.

GOVERNMENT FINANCE

In 2003 Lebanon recorded an overall budget deficit of £L2,591,000m., equivalent to 29.4% of recorded expenditure (compared with a forecast deficit of £L2,125,000m. in the Budget Law 2003). Budget forecasts for 2004 projected a deficit of £L2,850,000m., equivalent to 30.8% of budgeted expenditure. At the end of 2001 Lebanon's total external debt was US $12,450m., of which $8,957m. was long-term public debt. The cost of debt-servicing in that year was equivalent to 50.9% of the value of exports of goods and services. According to the Ministry of Finance, Lebanon's total domestic and external debt totalled L£50,193,000m. at the end of 2003. The annual rate of inflation averaged 23.9% in 1990–97. However, this reflected high rates of inflation in the aftermath of the civil war, consumer prices decreased by an average of 0.9% in 2000, but increased by 1.3% in 2001 and by 4.3% in 2002. In 1997, according to official figures, 8.5% of the labour force were unemployed (representing a significant decline from a level of 35% in 1990), although youth unemployment was reported to be much higher.

INTERNATIONAL ECONOMIC RELATIONS

Lebanon is a member of the Arab Fund for Economic and Social Development, the Arab Monetary Fund and the Islamic Development Bank. A customs union with Syria entered into effect in January 1999, and in 2002 the creation of a free-trade zone was under discussion. Lebanon is also involved in efforts to finalize establishment of a Greater Arab Free Trade Area. A Euro-Mediterranean Association Agreement was signed with the European Union (EU) in June 2002. Lebanon has observer status with the World Trade Organization, and was undergoing negotiations with a view to becoming a full member of the organization in 2004.

SURVEY AND PROSPECTS

By the end of the 1990s the Lebanese Government had achieved considerable success in rehabilitating and expanding basic infrastructure, as envisaged under the first phase of its Horizon 2000 investment programme, which covers the period 1995–2007. The second phase was to focus on development of social infrastructure, with investment of US $5,000m. envisaged on education, health and sanitation projects in 1998–2002. The reconstruction process was undertaken with the support of the international donor community, which in late 1996 pledged grants and concessionary loans totalling some $3,200m. However, GDP growth since 1996 has been considerably lower than the targeted annual average of 8% under Horizon 2000. The principal factors inhibiting growth have been identified as the failure to control both the budget deficit and the accumulated public debt (equivalent to 185% of GDP by the end of 2003). In early 1999 the World Bank agreed to disburse some $600m. in concessionary loans over a three-year period, and in April 2000 the EU granted its first aid programme to Lebanon (worth around $47.9m.). However, in 1999 the Lebanese economy was in recession, owing to the decline in domestic demand and inadequate levels of job creation; no overall growth was recorded in 2000.

The withdrawal of Israeli troops from southern Lebanon in May 2000 brought about an acceleration of the country's economic reconstruction, despite the high costs involved in rehabilitation projects for the south. The return of Rafik Hariri to the Lebanese premiership in October afforded further optimism, particularly in the construction sector. The new Government pledged to stimulate growth by reducing taxation and import duties, by encouraging the privatization of state-owned enterprises, and by controlling public expenditure in order to reduce the state debt. Liberalization of trade, both regionally and through association with the EU, was also identified as a priority.

In October 2001 the IMF recommended a devaluation of the Lebanese pound as a means of easing the Government's fiscal crisis. A value-added tax of 10% was introduced in February 2002. Although the National Assembly approved the Budget Law 2003 in January of that year, the Cabinet continued to debate the proposed economic reforms, which included tax increases, further privatization of state concerns and reductions in public spending, and a failure to reach a consensus led to the resignation of Hariri and his Cabinet in April (although a new Government was subsequently formed under Hariri). Furthermore, throughout 2003 and early 2004 the planned privatization of several vital state-owned interests, notably Electricité du Liban, Middle East Airlines and the mobile telephone network, was delayed as a result of ongoing political disagreements.

The Lebanese economy was expected to suffer from the effects of the temporary loss of trade with Iraq, as a result of the conflict there during early 2003 (see the chapter on Iraq), which also had an effect on the tourist industry in Lebanon. Meanwhile, in early 2001 international donors apparently agreed to provide the Lebanese authorities with $458m., in order to assist the economic reform programme. An aid package totalling an estimated $4,300m. was agreed by international donors in late November 2002, in order to provide further assistance with Lebanon's debt restructuring and to finance development projects. Such funding, in addition to the willingness of the Lebanese to tolerate economic austerity, as well as eventual progress towards a Middle East peace settlement, will be essential to the restoration of international competitiveness and enhanced investment.

Lesotho

The Kingdom of Lesotho is entirely surrounded by South Africa. Formerly the British protectorate of Basutoland, the country became independent in 1966, with King Moshoeshoe II as Head of State. In 1990 Maj.-Gen. Justin Lekhanya dethroned King Moshoeshoe, whose elder son succeeded him, as King Letsie III. After a 'royal coup' in 1994, an agreement was concluded that provided for the restoration of Moshoeshoe and of the elected organs of government. King Letsie III was restored to the throne in 1996, after Moshoeshoe's death. In 1998 the Lesotho Congress for Democracy (LCD) secured an overwhelming electoral victory. Subsequent instability caused power to be transferred to an Interim Political Authority. At elections held in 2002 the LCD was again victorious. Maseru is the capital. The official languages are English and Sesotho.

Area and population

Area: 30,355 sq km
Population (mid-2002): 2,086,700
Population density (mid-2002): 68.7 per sq km
Life expectancy (years at birth, 2002): 35.7 (males 32.9; females 38.2)

Finance

GDP in current prices: 2002): US $730m. ($350 per head)
Real GDP growth (2002): 3.8%
Inflation (annual average, 2002): 33.8%
Currency: loti

Economy

In 2002, according to estimates by the World Bank, Lesotho's gross national income (GNI), measured at average 2000–02 prices, was US $981m., equivalent to $470 per head (or $2,710 per head on an international purchasing-power parity basis). During 1990–2002, it was estimated, the population increased at an average annual rate of 1.8%, while gross domestic product (GDP) per head increased, in real terms, by an average of 2.0% per year. Overall GDP increased, in real terms, at an average annual rate of 3.9% in 1990–2002; growth in 2002 was 3.8%.

AGRICULTURE

Agriculture, forestry and fishing contributed 16.7% of GDP in 2002, and employed some 37.6% of the labour force in mid-2001. The principal agricultural exports are wool and mohair, cereals and live animals. The main subsistence crops are maize, sorghum and wheat. Lesotho remains a net importer of staple foodstuffs, largely owing to its vulnerability to adverse climatic conditions, especially drought; it was estimated that the country might be able to produce only 10% of its cereal requirements in 2004. During 1990–2002 agricultural GDP decreased at an average annual rate of 0.2%. Agricultural GDP decreased by 1.6% in 2002.

INDUSTRY

Industry (including mining, manufacturing, construction and power) provided 41.6% of GDP in 2002, and engaged 27.9% of the labour force in 1990. During 1990–2002 industrial GDP increased by an average of 9.0% per year. Industrial GDP increased by 9.0% in 2002.

Mining

Mining contributed 0.1% of GDP in 2002. Lesotho has reserves of diamonds, which during the late 1970s provided more than 50% of visible export earnings, but large-scale exploitation of these ceased in 1982; however, it is planned to reopen the Letseng-la Terai mine, and industrial mining at other sites is envisaged. Lesotho also possesses deposits of uranium, lead and iron ore, and is believed to have petroleum deposits. The GDP of the mining sector increased by an average of 3.0% per year in 1996/97–2002/03; growth in 2002/03 was 8.8%.

Manufacturing

Manufacturing contributed 19.2% of GDP in 2002. During 1990–2002 manufacturing GDP increased by an average of 6.5% per year; growth in 2002 was 8.0%.

Energy

The Lesotho Highlands Water Project (LHWP) provides hydroelectricity sufficient for all Lesotho's needs and for export to South Africa; phases 1A and 1B were inaugurated in 1998 and 2004, respectively. The scheme was expected to be completed by about 2030. Prior to the LHWP more than 90% of Lesotho's energy requirements were imported from South Africa. Imports of fuel and energy comprised an estimated 18.5% of the total value of imports in 1995.

SERVICES

The services sector contributed 41.7% of GDP in 2002. During 1990–2002 the GDP of the services sector increased at an average annual rate of 2.7%. Services GDP decreased by 0.7% in 2001, but increased by 3.6% in 2002.

EXTERNAL TRADE

In 2002 Lesotho recorded a visible trade deficit of US $381.2m. and a deficit of $118.8m. on the current account of the balance of payments. In 2000 the principal source of imports (85.3%) was the Southern African Customs Union (SACU—i.e. chiefly South Africa—see below), which was also the second largest market for exports (40.7%), behind the USA (57.5%). The principal exports in 2002 were clothing, foodstuffs and footwear. The principal imports in 2001 were manufactured goods, food and live animals, and machinery and transport equipment.

GOVERNMENT FINANCE

In the financial year ending 31 March 2003 there was an overall budgetary deficit of M328m. (equivalent to 4.2% of GDP in that year). Lesotho's external debt totalled US $592.5m. at the end of 2001, of which $573.3m. was long-term public debt. In that year the cost of debt-servicing was equivalent to 12.4% of revenue from exports of goods and services. The annual rate of inflation averaged 10.4% in 1990–2002; consumer prices declined by an average of 9.7% in 2001, but increased by 33.2% in 2002. It was estimated that 31.4% of the labour force were unemployed in July 2002. In 2002 an estimated 62,200 Basotho were employed as miners in South Africa (compared with some 95,900 in 1997).

INTERNATIONAL ECONOMIC RELATIONS

Lesotho is a member of the Common Monetary Area (with Namibia, South Africa and Swaziland), and a member of SACU (with Botswana, Namibia, South Africa and Swaziland). Lesotho also belongs to the Southern African Development Community (SADC).

SURVEY AND PROSPECTS

Impediments to economic development in Lesotho include vulnerability to drought and serious land shortages, combined with the country's dependence on South Africa (the Lesotho currency, the loti, is fixed at par with the South African rand, exposing Lesotho to fluctuations within the South African economy). From 1988 Lesotho undertook major economic reforms, supported by the IMF and other donors. However, by the late 1990s the strong growth that had prevailed for most of the decade was being eroded, while retrenchment in the South African gold-mining sector resulted in a marked decline in remittances from Basotho working abroad. The Government accelerated its programme of privatization in 2000, with, most notably, the sale of a 70% holding in the Lesotho Telecommunications Corporation. Under a utilities reform project, initiated in May 2001, the Lesotho Electricity Corporation began a restructuring process in preparation for transfer to private ownership. An agreement was reached with South Africa in January 2001 to restructure bilateral economic relations and to increase mutual co-operation for economic development. In March the IMF approved a three-year loan of some US $31m., under the Poverty Reduction and Growth Facility, on condition that Lesotho encouraged private economic activity, limited the role of the public sector and strengthened fiscal stability.

The Lesotho Revenue Authority, intended to improve the administration of taxation and other revenue, commenced operations in January 2003, and a value-added tax was introduced in July of that year. The textile industry has benefited considerably from the USA's African Growth and Opportunities Act (AGOA), for which Lesotho was first declared eligible in April 2001; under its terms, textiles and clothing made in Lesotho have unlimited access to the US market, and by early 2002 exports of these products to the USA had increased by nearly 40%. Lesotho's qualification for the benefits of the AGOA attracted interest from foreign investors in Lesotho, notably Taiwanese textile manufacturers. By mid-2003 an estimated 50,000 Basotho were employed in the textile industry, with further expansion planned. Strong textile exports, together with marked expansion in the GDP of the mining sector, were key factors contributing to favourable economic growth in 2001–03. However, adverse weather conditions led to severe food shortages during the same period, and substantial external assistance was required as agricultural productivity declined.

Liberia

The Republic of Liberia lies in West Africa. In 1990 the National Patriotic Front of Liberia (NPFL) staged an armed insurrection against the Government and rapidly gained territory. The conflict subsequently escalated into a multi-factional civil war that lasted, despite a series of peace agreements and the establishment of successive coalition governments, until 1996. In 1997 Charles Taylor, erstwhile leader of the recently dissolved NPFL, was elected as President. Following Taylor's departure into exile and the conclusion of a comprehensive peace agreement in August 2003, a UN mission was deployed in Liberia, and a transitional government of national unity was installed in October. Monrovia is the capital. The official language is English.

Area and population
Area: 97,754 sq km
Population (mid-2002): 3,295,050
Population density (mid-2002): 33.7 per sq km
Life expectancy (years at birth, 2002): 41.8 (males 40.1; females 43.7)

Finance
GDP in current prices: 2002): US $564m. ($171 per head)
Real GDP growth (2002): 4.2%
Inflation (annual average, 2002): 14.2%
Currency: Liberian dollar

Economy

In 2002, according to IMF estimates, Liberia's gross domestic product (GDP) was US $489m., equivalent to $150 per head. During 1990–2002, it was estimated, the population increased at an average annual rate of 2.6%, while there was no discernible increase in GDP per head. Overall GDP increased, in real terms, at an average annual rate of 2.6% in 1990–2002; growth was 4.2% in 2002.

AGRICULTURE

Agriculture (including forestry and fishing) contributed an estimated 76.9% of GDP in 2002. An estimated 66.6% of the labour force were employed in the sector in that year. The principal cash crops are rubber (which accounted for an estimated 39.0% of export earnings in 2002), cocoa and coffee. The principal food crops are rice, cassava, sweet potatoes, yams, plantains and bananas. Timber production has traditionally represented an important source of export revenue, providing an estimated 57.7% of export earnings in 2002. Agricultural GDP, according to the IMF, declined at an average annual rate of 5.5% in 1990–2002; the GDP of the agricultural sector increased by 21.5% in 2000, by 5.9% in 2001 and by an estimated 4.6% in 2002.

INDUSTRY

Industry (including mining, manufacturing, construction and power) contributed an estimated 7.4% of GDP in 2002, and employed 8% of the labour force in 1999. Industrial GDP, according to the IMF, declined at an average annual rate of 14.8% in 1988–2002; the GDP of the industrial sector increased by 61.6% in 2000, but declined by 2.8% in 2001 and by an estimated 24.4% in 2002.

Mining

Mining contributed less than 0.1% of GDP in 2002, and engaged 5.1% of the employed labour force in 1980. Gold and diamonds are mined, and Liberia possesses significant amounts of barytes and kyanite. The production and export of mineral products were severely disrupted from 1990, as a result of the civil conflict. In 1997 total mineral reserves were estimated to include more than 10m. carats of diamonds and 3m. troy oz of gold. In the late 1990s illicit mining and export of diamonds remained widespread, while official revenue from the mining sector (amounting to only about US $1m.) was mainly derived from local production of alluvial gold and diamonds. The GDP of the mining sector, according to the IMF, declined at an average annual rate of 40.1% in 1988–2002; mining GDP increased by 49.8% in 2000, but declined by 74.9% in 2001 and by an estimated 69.9% in 2002.

Manufacturing

Manufacturing provided an estimated 5.4% of GDP in 2002, and engaged about 1.2% of the employed labour force in 1980. Manufacturing GDP, according to the IMF, declined at an average annual rate of 5.6% in 1990–2002; the GDP of the manufacturing sector increased by 62.8% in 2000, but by only 0.9% in 2001, and declined by an estimated 23.7% in 2002.

Energy

Energy is derived from the consumption of fossil fuels (62.2%) and from hydro-electric power (37.8%). Imports of mineral fuels and lubricants comprised an estimated 20.0% of the value of total imports in 2002.

SERVICES

The services sector contributed an estimated 15.7% of GDP in 2002, and employed about 22% of the labour force in 1999. The GDP of the services sector, according to the IMF, declined at an average annual rate of 3.6% in 1990–2002; however, the GDP of the sector increased by 15.0% in 2000, by 3.2% in 2001 and by an estimated 7.0% in 2002. Liberia's large open-registry ('flag of convenience') merchant shipping fleet has become an increasingly significant source of foreign exchange. In 2002 revenue from Liberia's maritime programme accounted for an estimated 18.4% of total revenue.

EXTERNAL TRADE

In 2002 Liberia recorded an estimated visible trade deficit of US $25.6m., and there was a deficit of $28.7m. on the current account of the balance of payments. In 2002 the principal source of imports (25.5%) was the Republic of Korea; other major suppliers in that year were Japan, Germany and France. The principal market for exports in 2002 was Germany (55.8%); other important purchasers were Poland and France. The principal exports in 2002 were timber and rubber. The principal imports in that year were food (particularly rice) and live animals, mineral fuels (principally petroleum), machinery and transport equipment, and basic manufactures.

GOVERNMENT FINANCE

Liberia's overall budgetary deficit was US $7.4m. (equivalent to 1.3% of GDP) in 2002, according to IMF estimates. The country's external debt totalled $1,987m. at the end of 2001, of which $1,012m. was long-term public debt. In that year the cost of debt-servicing was equivalent to 0.6% of the value of exports of goods and services. Consumer prices increased by 12.2% in 2001 and by an estimated 14.2% in 2002. In early 2002 unemployment was estimated at about 87% of the labour force.

INTERNATIONAL ECONOMIC RELATIONS

Liberia is a member of the Economic Community of West African States (ECOWAS) and the Mano River Union, both of which aim to promote closer economic co-operation in the region.

SURVEY AND PROSPECTS

Prior to the 1989–96 civil conflict, exports of iron ore, rubber and forestry products accounted for a significant proportion of Liberia's gross national income. Following the occupation of significant regions by rebel forces, production of these commodities was severely disrupted, although some informal exports continued. After elections in July 1997, the new Government announced that national revenue had dwindled to a negligible amount, while debt arrears had increased dramatically, and introduced measures to regain control of public expenditure. Substantial levels of growth were recorded in subsequent years (although GDP remained at about one-third of the pre-conflict level), while domestic production, particularly of timber, rubber and rice, increased steadily.

In 2000 a new tax system was introduced, currency reforms were implemented, and the financial position of the central bank was strengthened. Most significantly, however, a progressive deterioration in Liberia's relations with donors and external creditors resulted in a suspension in the disbursement of post-conflict financial assistance. In May 2001 a UN ban on exports of diamonds from Liberia was imposed, and economic recovery began to slow considerably in that year, with rubber, logging and farming activity disrupted by continued rebel operations in parts of the country and failure to repair infrastructure damaged during the 1989–96 conflict.

In March 2003 the IMF suspended Liberia's voting and related rights in the Fund, owing to the country's continued arrears. In June a major rebel offensive against the capital, Monrovia, to oust President Charles Taylor resulted in a critical humanitarian situation, which attracted international attention. After Taylor relinquished power in early August, rebel forces ceded partial control of Monrovia to peace-keeping troops and commercial activity began to normalize. (However, a dramatic decline in foreign-exchange reserves, already at low levels, was partially attributed to looting by Taylor and his associates.) A comprehensive power-sharing agreement between the Government and rebels, signed on 18 August, provided for the the installation of a power-sharing administration, the National Transitional Government, on 14 October. The Chairman of the National Transitional Government immediately introduced measures to remove monopolies on the import of rice and fuel, resulting in a rapid reduction in prices. Major infrastructural projects, including the restoration of water and electricity to Monrovia, were initiated, while, for the first time since the 1989–96 conflict, the extensive rehabilitation of roads, with financial assistance from the People's Republic of China, was planned.

Following the deployment of the UN Mission in Liberia from 1 October 2003, significant progress was reported in the disarmament of former rebel combatants, and humanitarian conditions continued to improve, although sporadic hostilities continued in some parts of the country. The illegal production of diamonds continued in some regions, and at the end of the year the UN Security Council extended the embargoes in force against Liberia. In early February 2004, however, a UN-sponsored conference of international donors pledged some US $520m. (exceeding expectations) to support reconstruction and humanitarian efforts, and projects for infrastructural rehabilitation and employment creation. The resumption of relations with the IMF was expected to be a priority for the authorities, and emergency assistance from the Fund would be dependent on the security situation, and on the ability to operate of the National Transitional Government.

Libya

The Great Socialist People's Libyan Arab Jamahiriya extends along the Mediterranean coast of North Africa. The country attained independence as the United Kingdom of Libya in 1951. Muhammad Idris as-Sanusi, Amir of Cyrenaica, became King Idris of Libya, but was deposed in 1969 in a revolution led by nationalist army officers. A Revolution Command Council was established, with Col Muammar al-Qaddafi as Chairman, and a Libyan Arab Republic was proclaimed. In mid-2004 Qaddafi remained, effectively, Head of State, although he continued to reject that nomenclature. The administrative capital was formerly Tripoli, but in 1988 most government departments and the legislature were relocated to Sirte. Arabic is the official language.

Area and population
Area: 1,775,500 sq km
Population (mid-2002): 5,533,940
Population density (mid-2002): 3.1 per sq km
Life expectancy (years at birth, 2002): 72.6 (males 70.4; females 75.5)

Finance
GDP in current prices: 2000): US $34,137m. ($6,453 per head)
Real GDP growth (1999): 2.0%
Currency: dinar

Economy

In 1989, according to estimates by the World Bank, Libya's gross national income (GNI), measured at average 1987–89 prices, was US $23,333m., equivalent to $5,310 per head. (In 1994, according to unofficial estimates, GNI at current prices was $26,000m., equivalent to $5,650 per head.) During 1990–2002, it was estimated, the population increased at an average annual rate of 2.1%, while, according to the IMF, gross domestic product (GDP) per head declined, in real terms, by an average of 0.7% per year. Overall GDP increased, in real terms, at an average annual rate of 1.7% in 1990–2002. Real GDP increased by 0.5% in 2001, but declined by 0.2% in 2002.

AGRICULTURE

Agriculture (including forestry and fishing) contributed an estimated 8.6% of GDP in 2001, and engaged 17.9% of the employed labour force in 1996. The principal subsistence crops are wheat and barley; other crops include watermelons, potatoes, onions, olives, tomatoes, dates and citrus fruits. Output is limited by climatic conditions and irrigation problems, although cultivable land was being significantly increased by the Great Man-made River Project, whereby water was to be carried from the south of the country to the north and thence to the east and west. However, the highly ambitious nature of the scheme has provided engineers with serious difficulties and by early 2004, after 20 years of construction work, the project remained little more than half completed. Agriculture is based mainly on animal husbandry; sheep are the principal livestock, but goats, cattle, camels, horses and poultry are also kept. During 1994–2001 agricultural GDP increased at an average annual rate of 1.6%; the sector's GDP increased by 1.7% in 2000 and by 2.7% in 2001.

INDUSTRY

Industry (including mining, manufacturing, construction and power) contributed an estimated 50.5% of GDP in 2001, and engaged 29.9% of the employed labour force in 1996. Virtually all of the industrial sector is state-controlled. During 1994–2001 the GDP of the industrial sector increased at an average annual rate of 1.5%; industrial GDP increased by 3.5% in 2000 and by 3.9% in 2001.

Mining

Mining contributed 36.1% of GDP in 2001, but engaged only 2.5% of the employed labour force in 1996. The petroleum and natural gas sector contributed 34.1% of GDP in 2001, and engaged 1.7% of the employed labour force in 1996. Libya's economy depends almost entirely on its petroleum and natural gas resources. The National Oil Corporation of Libya (NOC) controls about three-quarters of the petroleum produced in Libya, largely through production-sharing agreements. At the end of 2002 proven recoverable reserves of petroleum were estimated at 29,500m. barrels, sufficient to enable production to be maintained—at that year's levels, averaging 1.38m. barrels per day (b/d)—until 2061. With effect from 1 April 2004 Libya's production quota within the Organization of the Petroleum Exporting Countries (OPEC) was 1,258,000 b/d. Libya's natural gas reserves are extensive (estimated at 1,310,000m. cu m at the end of 2002). Libya also has reserves of iron ore, salt, limestone, clay, sulphur and gypsum. The GDP of the mining sector decreased, in real terms, by an annual average of 0.4% in 1994–2001; mining GDP declined by 1.3% in 2000, but increased by 3.0% in 2001.

Manufacturing

Manufacturing contributed 5.9% of GDP in 2001, and engaged 10.5% of the employed labour force in 1996. The principal manufacturing activity is petroleum refining. There are three refineries, at Brega, Ras Lanouf and Az-Zawiyah. A petrochemicals site is located at Brega, and in the late 1990s there were plans to construct a new petrochemicals complex at Ras Lanouf. Other important manufacturing activities were the production of iron, steel and cement, and the processing of agricultural products. The GDP of the manufacturing sector increased at an average annual rate of 3.6% during 1994–2001; the sector's GDP increased by 2.2% in 2000 and by 2.5% in 2001.

Energy

Energy is derived almost exclusively from oil-fired power. Libya is a net exporter of fuels (less than 10% of petroleum production is used for domestic energy requirements), with imports of energy products comprising only an estimated 0.2% of the value of merchandise imports in 1998.

SERVICES

Services contributed 40.9% of GDP in 2001, and engaged 52.2% of the employed labour force in 1996. Visitor arrivals declined from 1.8m. in 1995 to 962,559 in 2000. Receipts from tourism in 1999 amounted to US $28m. In an attempt to stimulate growth in the tourism sector, the Government invested heavily in 1996–2001 to expand and rehabilitate tourism infrastructure. During 1994–2001 the GDP of the services sector increased at an annual average rate of 2.3%; services GDP increased by 3.3% in 2000 and by 2.8% in 2001.

EXTERNAL TRADE

In 1999 Libya recorded a visible trade surplus of US $2,762m., and there was a surplus of $1,984m. on the current account of the balance of payments. In 1999 the principal sources of imports were Italy (which provided 18.3% of total imports), Germany (14.5%), the Republic of Korea, the United Kingdom and France. The principal market for exports in that year was Italy (37.8%); Germany, Spain, France and Viet Nam were also important purchasers. The petroleum sector is overwhelmingly Libya's principal generator of exports revenue: exports of mineral fuels, lubricants, etc. accounted for 94.8% of Libya's export earnings in 1997. The principal imports were machinery and transport equipment, basic manufactures, and food and live animals.

GOVERNMENT FINANCE

There was a projected budgetary surplus of LD 3,128m. in 2003. In the previous year a surplus of LD 939m. had been recorded. Libya's total external debt was about

US $3,800m. at the end of 1999, according to estimates quoted by the *Middle East Economic Digest*. According to the same source, the rate of inflation averaged an estimated 24.0% in 1999, compared with 5.6% in 1997. The rate of unemployment was unofficially estimated to be about 30% in 2003.

INTERNATIONAL ECONOMIC RELATIONS

Libya is a member of the Arab Monetary Fund, the Council of Arab Economic Unity, the Islamic Development Bank, the Organization of Arab Petroleum Exporting Countries, OPEC and the Union du Maghreb arabe (Union of the Arab Maghreb).

SURVEY AND PROSPECTS

During 2003–04 prospects for the major improvement and modernization of the Libyan economy were bolstered by a number of extremely important political decisions. The appointment in mid-2003 of Shukri Muhammad Ghanem, a former Libyan representative to OPEC, as Secretary of the GPC precipitated a new phase of economic reform; Ghanem swiftly announced plans to divest more than 360 state-owned entities during 2004 and to establish a stock exchange, although he emphasized that the privatization scheme would not involve companies in the hydrocarbons or chemical sectors.

In September 2003 the decision to accept civil responsibility for the Lockerbie bombing facilitated the formal removal of UN sanctions, which had been imposed in 1992 and suspended in 1999. Although the USA initially remained unwilling to remove unilateral 'secondary' sanctions imposed on Libya in 1996, thus excluding US companies from signing potentially lucrative contracts, it was anticipated that large numbers of European and Asian petroleum companies would seek to take advantage of the opportunities to assume increased roles in the further development of the country's hydrocarbons industry. However, in April 2004 the USA lifted the sanctions which had outlawed commercial activities and financial transactions between Libyan and US companies.

Meanwhile, in late 2003 the Libyan Government pledged to increase petroleum production capacity to more than 2m. b/d by 2010. Libya also possesses considerable reserves of natural gas, with major potential for further discoveries. An underwater pipeline linking Libya with Italy, scheduled to be completed in late 2004, is expected to enable some 8,000m. cu m per year of natural gas to be exported to Europe.

Libya also elicited praise from the IMF following the country's first ever Article IV consultation in August 2003, although the Fund identified Libya's main challenge as the generation of sufficient growth and employment opportunities to absorb the rapidly growing labour force; indeed, unemployment remained at around 30%. The devaluation of the dinar by more than 50% in early 2002 and the exchange rate reform carried out in mid-2003 were expected to increase the flow of foreign direct investment into the country. Despite forecast GDP growth of 5.6% in 2003, Libya's reliance on petroleum revenues remained a major concern. Attempts are under way, however, to develop the country's largely untapped tourism potential after the enactment of a five-year investment plan, at a cost some US $7,000m., and the improvement in relations with many Western countries in the wake of Libya's decision to abandon its nuclear weapons programme, provided further optimism for economic development.

Liechtenstein

The Principality of Liechtenstein is in central Europe. Liechtenstein has been an independent state since 1719, except while under French domination briefly in the 19th century. Prince Franz Josef II succeeded as ruling Prince in 1938. In 1984 Prince Franz Josef transferred executive power to his son, Prince Hans-Adam, although he remained titular Head of State until his death in 1989, when he was succeeded by Hans-Adam II. In 1996 the Landtag (parliament) adopted a unanimous motion of loyalty in the hereditary monarchy, after Prince Hans-Adam II had threatened to resign. Constitutional amendments, approved in 2003, extended the powers of the monarch. Vaduz is the capital. The official language is German.

Area and population
Area: 160 sq km
Population (mid-2001): 30,000
Population density (mid-2001): 187.5 per sq km

Finance
GDP in current prices: 1999): US $1,141m. ($35,376 per head)
Real GDP growth (1999): 1.5%
Currency: Swiss franc

Economy

In 1997 Liechtenstein's gross national product (GNP) per head was estimated by the World Bank to be US $50,000, at average 1995–97 prices, ranking as the highest in the world at that time. During 1986–95 the population increased at an average annual rate of 1.4%. During 1990–99, it was estimated, GDP grew at an average annual rate of 1.6%; GDP increased by 4.5% in 1998 but declined by 0.9% in 1999.

AGRICULTURE

Following the Second World War, the importance of agriculture declined in favour of industry. Within the agricultural sector the emphasis is on cattle-breeding, dairy-farming and market gardening. The principal crops are maize and potatoes. In addition, wine is produced, and forestry is a significant activity. In 2002 1.3% of those employed in Liechtenstein worked in agriculture (including forestry).

INDUSTRY

In 2002 44.9% of those employed in Liechtenstein worked in industrial activity (including mining and quarrying, processing industries, energy and water supply and construction). The metal, machinery and precision instruments industry is by far the most prominent sector. Other important areas are the pharmaceutical, textiles and ceramics industries.

Energy

In 1999 some 92.9% of energy requirements were imported from other countries. In that year natural gas supplied 24.2% of energy requirements, electricity 23.6%, fuel oil 23.5%, motor fuel (petrol) 19.2%, diesel 8.2% and firewood 1.2%.

SERVICES

In 2002 53.9% of those employed in Liechtenstein worked in the services sector. Financial services are of great importance. Numerous foreign corporations, holding companies and foundations (estimated to number about 75,000) have nominal offices in Liechtenstein, benefiting from the Principality's stable political situation, tradition of bank secrecy (although stricter banking legislation was introduced in 1997 and in 2000–02, partly to increase the transparency of the sector) and low fiscal charges. Such enterprises pay no tax on profit or income, contributing instead an annual levy on capital or net worth. These levies account for about 20% of the Principality's annual direct revenue. In 1980 Liechtenstein adopted legislation to increase controls on foreign firms, many of which were thereafter subject to audit and entered in the public register. Following the Principality's accession to the European Economic Area (EEA) in 1995, the registration of foreign banks was permitted. New legislation governing insurance companies was approved in 1996, and during the late 1990s the insurance sector expanded rapidly. The building and hotel trades and other service industries are also highly developed.

EXTERNAL TRADE

With a very limited domestic market, Liechtenstein's industry is export-orientated. In 2002 total exports amounted to 2,813.5m. Swiss francs (with imports totalling 1,360.5m. Swiss francs). Switzerland is the principal trading partner, receiving

12.7% of exports in 1998. In that year members of the European Union (EU) accounted for 37.8% of total exports. Specialized machinery, artificial teeth and other materials for dentistry, and frozen food are important exports. The sale of postage stamps, mainly to tourists, provided about 3.0% of the national income in 1997.

GOVERNMENT FINANCE

The 2002 budget envisaged a deficit of 46.5m. Swiss francs. The annual average rate of inflation increased from 1.9% in 1988 to 5.9% in 1991, decreasing again, to 0.5%, in 1997. Traditionally the unemployment rate has been negligible; in 1999 the rate of unemployment (as a percentage of those employed) was 1.2%. More than one-third of Liechtenstein's population are resident foreigners, many of whom provide the labour for industry, while in December 1999 9,741 workers crossed the borders from Austria and Switzerland each day to work in the Principality.

INTERNATIONAL ECONOMIC RELATIONS

Liechtenstein has important economic links with neighbouring Switzerland. It is incorporated in a customs union with that country, and uses the Swiss franc as its currency. Liechtenstein became a member of the European Free Trade Association (EFTA) in May 1991, and the EEA in May 1995. The Principality is also a member of the European Bank for Reconstruction and Development (EBRD).

Lithuania

The Republic of Lithuania is situated in north-eastern Europe. According to the 'Secret Protocols' to the 1939 Treaty of Non-Aggression signed by the USSR and Nazi Germany, Lithuania was to come under German influence. However, the subsequent Nazi-Soviet Treaty on Friendship and Existing Borders granted the USSR control of Lithuania. In 1990 Lithuania was the first Soviet republic to declare independence, although this was not recognized by the USSR State Council until 1991. In April 2004 Valdas Adamkus (President in 1998–2002) was again elected as President, following the impeachment of Rolandas Paksas. Vilnius is the capital. The official language is Lithuanian.

Area and population
Area: 65,300 sq km
Population (mid-2002): 3,476,000
Population density (mid-2002): 53.2 per sq km
Life expectancy (years at birth, 2002): 71.9 (males 66.2; females 77.6)

Finance
GDP in current prices: 2002): US $13,796m. ($3,969 per head)
Real GDP growth (2002): 6.7%
Inflation (annual average, 2002): 0.3%
Currency: litas

Economy

In 2002, according to estimates by the World Bank, Lithuania's gross national income (GNI), measured at average 2000–02 prices, was US $12,715m., equivalent to $3,660 per head (or $9,880 per head on an international purchasing-power parity basis). During 1990–2002 the population decreased by an annual average of 0.5%, while gross domestic product (GDP) per head declined, in real terms, by an average of 1.0% per year. Overall GDP decreased, in real terms, by an average of 1.5% annually. However, real GDP increased by 6.3% in 2001 and by 6.8% in 2002.

AGRICULTURE

Agriculture (including hunting, forestry and fishing) contributed 7.2% of GDP in 2002, when it engaged 17.8% of the employed population. The principal crops are cereals, sugar beet, potatoes and vegetables. In 1991 legislation was adopted permitting the restitution of land to its former owners, and the privatization of state-owned farms and reorganization of collective farms was initiated. By the mid-1990s almost 40% of arable land was privately cultivated. Legislation approved in January 2003 authorized the sale of agricultural land to foreign owners, although its implementation was to be subject to a seven-year transition period. Real agricultural GDP decreased, in real terms, by an annual average of 1.5% during 1990–2001. The GDP of the sector decreased by 6.9% in 2001, but increased by 3.0% in 2002.

INDUSTRY

Industry (including mining, manufacturing, construction and power) contributed 34.7% of GDP in 2002, when the sector engaged 27.5% of the employed population. According to World Bank estimates, industrial GDP declined by an annual average of 7.0%, in real terms, during 1990–2001; however, the GDP of the sector increased by 16.4% in 2001 and by 4.0% in 2002.

Mining

In 2001 mining and quarrying contributed 0.7% of GDP, and it provided just 0.3% of employment in 2002. Lithuania has significant reserves of peat and materials used in construction (limestone, clay, dolomite, chalk, and sand and gravel), as well as small deposits of petroleum and natural gas. Real mining GDP increased by 18.9% in 2000 and by 30.6% in 2001. In terms of production, the GDP of the sector increased by 13.0% in 2003, according to preliminary official data.

Manufacturing

The manufacturing sector provided 23.1% of GDP in 2002, when it engaged 18.5% of the employed labour force. Based on the value of output, the principal branches of manufacturing in 1996 were food products (particularly dairy products—accounting for 9.5% of the total), refined petroleum products, textiles and clothing, and chemicals. The World Bank estimated that manufacturing GDP declined, in real terms, by an annual average of 7.6% during 1990–2001. However, sectoral GDP increased by 4.0% in 2002 and, according to preliminary official figures, manufacturing GDP increased by 14.1% in 2003, in terms of production.

Energy

In 2000 nuclear power accounted for 75.7% of gross electricity production, followed by natural gas, which accounted for 15.3%. Lithuania has substantial petroleum-refining and electricity-generating capacities, which enable it to export refined petroleum products and electricity. In 1999 Lithuania exported an estimated 55.9% of its gross electricity production. In 2003 imports of mineral products accounted for 18.2% of the total value of merchandise imports, according to provisional figures.

SERVICES

The services sector contributed 58.0% of GDP in 2002, when it provided 54.7% of total employment. The Baltic port of Klaipėda is a significant entrepôt for regional trade. The GDP of the services sector decreased, in real terms, by an annual average of 0.2% in 1990–2001. However, real services GDP increased by 2.6% in 2001 and by 5.9% in 2002.

EXTERNAL TRADE

In 2002 Lithuania recorded a visible trade deficit of US $1,314.9m., and there was a deficit of $720.7m. on the current account of the balance of payments. In 2003 the principal source of imports was Russia (accounting for 22.2% of the total, according to preliminary figures); other major sources were Germany and Poland. Switzerland was the main market for exports in that year (accounting for an estimated 11.7% of the total, according to preliminary figures). Other principal markets were Russia, Germany, Latvia, the United Kingdom and France. According to preliminary data, in 2003 the principal exports were mineral products (representing an estimated 19.7% of total exports), followed by vehicles and transportation equipment (15.2%), textiles (13.6%), machinery and electrical equipment (11.1%), chemical products (6.6%) and miscellaneous manufactured articles (6.1%). The principal imports were machinery and electrical equipment (representing an estimated 18.8% of total imports), mineral products (18.2%), vehicles and transportation equipment (15.7%), chemical products (8.6%), textiles (7.5%), base metals (6.0%), and plastics and rubber (5.3%).

GOVERNMENT FINANCE

In 2001, according to IMF estimates, there was a budgetary deficit of 171.8m. litai (equivalent to 0.4% of GDP). Lithuania's total external debt was US $5,248m. at the end of 2001, of which $2,359m. was long-term public debt. In that year the cost of debt-servicing was equivalent to 31.0% of the value of exports of goods and services. Annual inflation averaged 62.1% in 1991–2002. The average annual rate of inflation declined from 1,021% in 1991 to 24.6% by 1996. In 2002 the rate of inflation was 0.3%, and deflation of 1.4% was recorded in 2003. The average rate of unemployment was 12.4% in 2003, when 203,900 people were officially registered as unemployed.

INTERNATIONAL ECONOMIC RELATIONS

Lithuania is a member, as a 'Country of Operations', of the European Bank for Reconstruction and Development (EBRD), as well as of the IMF and the World Bank. An agreement on a free-trade area between Lithuania, Latvia and Estonia entered into force in April 1994. In December 2000 Lithuania became a member of the World Trade Organization (WTO). Lithuania became an associate member of the European Union (EU) in June 1995. In February 2000 Lithuania officially commenced the negotiation process towards full membership, and it acceded on 1 May 2004.

SURVEY AND PROSPECTS

By the mid-1990s the Government's stabilization programme had achieved modest success: the development of the private sector was well advanced, most prices had been liberalized and progress had been achieved in restructuring the financial sector. However, the economy contracted in 1999, largely owing to the economic crisis in Russia in 1998. Following the controversial sale of part of the Government's stake in the Mažeikiai NAFTA petroleum refinery in late 1999, other major privatizations were initiated from 2000, and much was achieved in the way of recovery in that year. The last remaining state-owned bank was privatized in 2002, and energy-sector privatization was under way. The initial phase of the privatization of the gas utility, Lietuvos Dujos, was completed in 2002, and further shares were divested in early 2004; the privatization of a major electricity-distribution company, Vakaru skirsto-mieji tinklai, had also been finalized by early 2004.

Meanwhile, in an effort to facilitate increased integration with EU economies and further reorientate foreign trade, from February 2002 the national currency's fixed rate of exchange was linked to the common European currency, the euro, instead of the US dollar, resulting in increased business confidence and investment and lower import costs. In June of that year formal agreement had been reached with the EU on the closure of the Ignalina nuclear power plant; the first of the plant's reactors was to be decommissioned in 2005 and the second in 2009, in return for substantial financing from the EU to compensate for the costs incurred. Reforms were implemented in 2002, and there were changes to taxation legislation and the pensions system, as well as new regulations to combat money 'laundering' (the processing of illicitly obtained funds into legitimate holdings), and the introduction of a new labour code at the beginning of 2003.

Macroeconomic performance was better than anticipated in 2002–03, stimulated by improved domestic demand, and came despite the deceleration in economic growth recorded throughout much of Europe. In 2003 GDP increased by 8.9%, according to preliminary official figures (Lithuania's highest rate of growth since independence), and gentle deflation was recorded (assisted by increased local competition and the depreciation of the dollar against the euro). The country's anticipated fiscal deficit for 2004, equivalent to some 3.3% of GDP (just over the 3% limit set by the EU), was based on the need for increased expenditure in order to meet EU accession require-ments. Lithuania planned to adopt the euro in 2007.

Luxembourg

The Grand Duchy of Luxembourg is a land-locked country in Western Europe. The Belgo-Luxembourg Economic Union has existed since 1921, except in 1940–44, when the Grand Duchy was occupied by Germany. In 1948 the Benelux Economic Union was inaugurated between Belgium, Luxembourg and the Netherlands. Luxembourg is a founder member of the European Community (now European Union). In 1964 Grand Duchess Charlotte abdicated, after a reign of 45 years, and was succeeded by her son, Prince Jean. In 2000 Grand Duke Jean was succeeded by his eldest son, Prince Henri. Luxembourg-Ville is the capital. Letzeburgish, a German-Moselle-Frankish dialect, is the official language.

Area and population
Area: 2,586 sq km
Population (mid-2002): 443,500
Population density (mid-2002): 171.5 per sq km
Life expectancy (years at birth, 2002): 78.8 (males 75.7; females 81.7)

Finance
GDP in current prices: 2002): US $20,062m. ($45,236 per head)
Real GDP growth (2002): 0.8%
Inflation (annual average, 2002): 2.1%
Currency: euro

Economy

In 2002, according to estimates by the World Bank, Luxembourg's gross national income (GNI), measured at average 2000–02 prices, was US $17,221m., equivalent to $38,830 per head (or $51,060 per head on an international purchasing-power parity basis). During 1990–2002, it was estimated, the population increased at an average rate of 1.3% per year, while gross domestic product (GDP) per head grew, in real terms, by an average of 3.7% per year. Overall GDP increased, in real terms, at an average annual rate of 5.1% in 1990–2002; growth in 2002 was 0.8%.

AGRICULTURE

Agriculture (including forestry and fishing) contributed 0.5% of GDP in 2002. In the same year an estimated 1.3% of the employed labour force were engaged in the agricultural sector. The principal crops are cereals, potatoes and wine grapes. Live-stock-rearing is also of some importance. According to the IMF, agricultural GDP declined at an average annual rate of 0.4% in 1990–95 and, according to the World Bank, it grew by 1.3% per year during 1995–2000. However, in 2000, real agricultural GDP fell by 0.5%.

INDUSTRY

Industry (including mining, manufacturing, construction and power) provided 16.6% of GDP and engaged an estimated 22.4% of the employed labour force in 2002. Industrial GDP increased, in real terms, at an average annual rate of 0.3% in 1990–95 and by 5.0% per year in 1995–2000; it rose by 9.3% in 1999 and by 5.2% in 2000.

Manufacturing

Manufacturing activities, excluding power and water, constitute the most important industrial sector, contributing 9.5% of GDP and engaging 11.9% of the employed work-force in 2002. Although the country's deposits of iron ore are no longer exploited, the iron and steel industry remains one of the most important sectors of the Luxembourg economy; metal manufactures accounted for an estimated 28.1% of total exports in 2001. The Luxembourg steel industry is dominated by Arcelor, which was formed in June 2001 by the merger of the Luxembourg-based Aciéries Réunies de Burbach-Eich-Dudelange SA—ARBED and the steel companies Usinor, of France, and Aceralia, of Spain, to form the world's largest steel group. In January 2003 Arcelor announced that no further investment would be made in the two smelting furnaces in the Val du Fensch and that hot-phase production would gradually cease. The steelworks, which employed around 1,500 workers and contributed 85% of the Val du Fensch's annual revenue, would eventually close in 2010. Machinery and equipment provided 24.0% of total exports in 2001. Other important branches of manufacturing are basic manufactures and chemicals and related products. According to the IMF, real manufacturing GDP increased by an average of 1.5% per year in 1990–95 and, according to the World Bank, by 4.7% per year in 1995–2000; it grew by 7.5% in 1999 and by 6.1% in 2000.

Energy

In 2000 53.1% of electricity was derived from natural gas and 27.7% from hydroelectric installations. Fuel imports comprised 7.1% of the value of total imports in 2000.

SERVICES

The services sector contributed 82.8% of GDP and engaged 76.4% of the employed labour force in 2002. Favourable laws governing banking secrecy and taxation have encouraged the development of Luxembourg as a major international financial centre. Financial services contributed 21.9% of GDP in 2001. In 2003 there were 178 banks in Luxembourg, and about 23,000 people were employed in banking activities. In 2002 there were 14,335 holding companies registered in Luxembourg. Stock exchange activities (notably the 'Eurobond' market and investment portfolio management) are also prominent; at April 2000 Luxembourg's investment fund sector was the biggest in Europe, with assets of €848,000m. At the end of 2000 there were 94 approved insurance companies in Luxembourg, as well as 264 reinsurance companies. According to the IMF, the GDP of the services sector increased, in real terms, at an average annual rate of 6.8% in 1990–95 and, according to World Bank figures, by 6.2% per year in 1995–2000; it rose by 3.6% in 1999 and by 8.2% in 2000.

EXTERNAL TRADE

In 2002, according to IMF figures, Luxembourg recorded a visible trade deficit of US $2,163m.; however, there was a surplus on the current account of the balance of payments of $1,636m. Other members of the European Union (EU) account for much of Luxembourg's foreign trade (supplying 89.9% of imports and purchasing 84.5% of exports, according to provisional figures for 2002). In 2002 the principal source of imports (34.8%) was Belgium; other major providers were Germany (26.3%), France (15.3%) and the Netherlands (5.1%). The principal market for exports in that year was Germany (25.1%); other major purchasers were France (19.8%), Belgium (11.9%), the United Kingdom (7.4%) and Italy (5.8%). The principal exports in 2002 were manufactured goods, particularly metal manufactures, and machinery and transport equipment. The principal imports were machinery, transport equipment, manufactured articles, notably metal manufactures, and chemical products.

GOVERNMENT FINANCE

In 2002 a small budgetary surplus, of €500,000, was recorded. Government debt was equivalent to 6.2% of GDP in 1999. The annual rate of inflation averaged 2.2% in 1990–2002; consumer prices rose by 2.7% in 2001 and by 2.1% in 2002. Unemployment averaged 3.8% in 2003. Cross-border commuters from neighbouring states totalled 94,500 in 2002, constituting more than one-third of the total employed in Luxembourg.

INTERNATIONAL ECONOMIC RELATIONS

Luxembourg was a founder member of the EU and of the Benelux Economic Union. Luxembourg is also a member of the European Bank for Reconstruction and Development, and the European System of Central Banks (ESCB), inaugurated in 1998.

SURVEY AND PROSPECTS

Luxembourg's economy expanded at an average annual rate of more than 5% during 1985–2000, recording increases in GDP even in the early 1990s when neighbouring countries were in recession. In January 1999 Luxembourg participated in the adoption of the euro as the single unit of currency for transactions throughout the eurozone and as an internationally traded currency in the 11 EU countries participating in economic and monetary union.

The country's economic success was based on its development as an international financial centre, following the decline in the importance of the country's previously dominant iron and steel industry. In order to promote the country's long-term prospects, the IMF recommended tax reform, the restructuring of the pension system, the introduction of measures to improve the flexibility of the labour market and continuing support to the financial sector through effective supervision. Government proposals to reduce corporate and personal taxes, and to promote private pension savings took effect from the budget of 2002. The IMF also warned that the rapid growth of the late 1990s was unlikely to be replicated in the future and that the sharp rise in expenditure at central government level might become unsustainable. This economic growth, which has ensured buoyant public finances, was achieved with virtually no inflationary effect, although an increase in petroleum prices provoked a steep rise in inflation, of 3%, in early 2003 (the annual average was estimated to be 2.1%). A strengthening euro was expected to help reduce inflation in early 2004, leading to a predicted annual average of 2%.

Rapid economic expansion in Luxembourg has attracted an increasing number of cross-border workers from neighbouring countries, who accounted for more than one-third of the work-force in 2002. These workers pay social security contributions in Luxembourg but retire to their native countries to spend their pensions, which are financed by Luxembourg. The solution advanced by the Government was to eschew further job creation in favour of the development of high-technology industries (with a substantial value added), which do not require a larger work-force. This plan was also expected to help to diversify the economy away from too great a dependence on the financial sector, the future profitability of which was likely to be eroded by the effects of EU integration, including the harmonization of taxation and regulatory structures.

The financial sector had anticipated with consternation the potential consequences of the removal of banking secrecy at the behest of the EU. Its apprehensions were allayed, at least temporarily, when the new EU taxation rules concerning overseas investments, which were highly favourable to Luxembourg, were agreed in early 2003. They allowed Luxembourg (as well as Austria and Belgium) to retain banking secrecy for at least the next six years, while other EU countries were to begin exchanging account details from 2005 in an attempt to eliminate tax fraud. Instead, in Luxembourg, Austria and Belgium a withholding tax would be levied on non-residents' savings. The tax would rise incrementally from 15% in 2005 to 35% in 2010. Crucially, Switzerland would have to apply the same rate of tax, thus avoiding 'capital flight' from Luxembourg. Luxembourg also secured an agreement that it would not be forced to exchange banking information in the future without parallel action from Switzerland (which was extremely unlikely). Luxembourg also hoped to diversify into the potentially lucrative cross-border pensions fund market, and had already installed a flexible regulatory regime in order to take full advantage of pending EU legislation (expected to be adopted in 2005) allowing pension-fund providers to offer services and products to customers across the EU. A comparatively modest increase in GDP, of 2.5%, was forecast for 2004. It was predicted that in the same year the fiscal deficit would exceed 3% of GDP.

Macao

A Special Administrative Region of the People's Republic of China, Macao lies in eastern Asia, opposite Hong Kong on the western side of the mouth of the Xijiang (Sikiang) River. Established by Portugal in 1557 as a permanent trading post with China, Macao became a Portuguese Overseas Province in 1951. In 1956 Macao was redefined as a 'Special Territory' under Portuguese jurisdiction. Sovereignty was transferred to China in 1999. Since then Macao has been governed by a Chief Executive, accountable to the State Council of China. The city of Macao is the capital. Chinese and Portuguese are the official languages.

Area and population
Area: 27.3 sq km
Population (end 2003): 448,495
Population density (end-2003): 16,428 per sq km
Life expectancy (years at birth, 2002): 79.2 (males 76.9; females 81.6)

Finance
GDP in current prices: 2001): US $6,199m. ($14,089 per head)
Real GDP growth (2001): 2.1%
Inflation (annual average, 2002): −2.6%
Currency: pataca

495

Economy

In 2001, according to estimates by the World Bank, Macao's gross national income (GNI), measured at average 1999–2001 prices, was US $6,329m., equivalent to $14,380 per head (or $18,970 per head on an international purchasing-power parity basis). During 1990–2001, it was estimated, the population increased at an average annual rate of 1.6%, while gross domestic product (GDP) per head increased, in real terms, at an average annual rate of 0.9%. Overall GDP increased, in real terms, at an average annual rate of 2.5% in 1990–2001. In 2001 GDP growth decelerated to 2.1%, reflecting the global economic slowdown. GDP increased by 10.1% in 2002.

AGRICULTURE

Agriculture is of minor importance. The main crops are rice and vegetables. Cattle, pigs and chickens are reared.

INDUSTRY

Industry (including mining, manufacturing, construction and public utilities) accounted for 12.9% of total GDP in 2001 and employed 28.5% of the economically active population in 2002. The mining sector is negligible.

Manufacturing

The manufacturing sector contributed 8.0% of total GDP in 2001 and engaged 20.4% of the economically active population in 2002. The most important manufacturing industry is the production of textiles and garments, which accounted for 61.0% of the value of total output in 2000. Exports of textiles and garments increased from 15,325.2m. patacas in 2001 to 15,616.8m. patacas in 2002. Other industries include footwear and furniture.

Energy

Macao possesses few natural resources. Energy is derived principally from imported petroleum. Imports of fuels and lubricants accounted for 7.2% of total import costs in 2002. The territory receives some electricity and water supplies from the People's Republic of China.

SERVICES

The services sector accounted for 87.1% of GDP in 2001 and employed 71.1% of the economically active population in 2002. Tourism makes a substantial contribution to the territory's economy. Receipts from gambling taxes accounted for 60% of the Government's recurrent revenue in 2000. In that year, according to official figures, the tourism and gambling industries contributed an estimated 38% of GDP, while the 10 licensed casinos employed 6% of the labour force. The number of tourist arrivals increased steadily during the 1990s, with visitors from the People's Republic of China rising particularly rapidly. Despite the outbreak of Severe Acute Respiratory Syndrome (SARS) in early 2003, the number of tourist arrivals increased from 11.53m. in 2002 to 11.88m. in 2003. Visitors from China and those from Hong Kong accounted for 36.8% and 44.2% respectively of the total of arrivals in 2002. Legislation regulating 'offshore' banking was introduced in 1987. It was hoped that the territory would develop as an international financial centre. The Financial System Act, which took effect in September 1993, aimed to improve the reputation of Macao's banks by curbing the unauthorized acceptance of deposits. A law enacted in April 1995 aimed to attract overseas investment by offering the right of abode in Macao to entrepreneurs with substantial funds (at least US $250,000) at their disposal. From December 1999, upon the territory's reversion to Chinese sovereignty, Macao administered its own finances and was exempt from taxes imposed by central government. The pataca was retained, remaining freely convertible.

EXTERNAL TRADE

In 2002 Macao recorded a trade deficit of 1,398.0m. patacas, following a deficit of 697.4m. patacas in 2001. These figures compared with a surplus of 2,282.8m. patacas in 2000. The principal sources of imports in 2002 were the People's Republic of China (which supplied 41.7% of the total) and Hong Kong (14.5%), followed by Japan (6.7%) and Taiwan (also 6.7%). The principal market for exports was the USA (which purchased 48.4%), followed by the People's Republic of China (15.6%) and Hong Kong (5.8%). The main exports were textiles and garments (which accounted for 82.5% of the total), machines and apparatus, and footwear. The principal imports were raw materials for industry, fuels, foodstuffs and other consumer goods. In December 1999 Macao retained its status as a free port and remained a separate customs territory.

GOVERNMENT FINANCE

In 2002 a budgetary surplus of 1,740m. patacas was recorded. In the following year the surplus was reported to have reached 3,900m. by November. The average annual rate of inflation (excluding rents) between 1990 and 1998 was 5.9%. A deflation rate of 3.2% was registered in 1999. Deflation rates of 1.6% in 2000, 2.0% in 2001 and 2.6% in 2002 were recorded. According to official figures, the level of unemployment decreased from a peak of 7.1% of the labour force in early 2000 to 6.3% in 2002, declining to an estimated 5.5% in the final quarter of 2003. There is a shortage of skilled labour in Macao.

INTERNATIONAL ECONOMIC RELATIONS

In 1991 Macao became a party to the General Agreement on Tariffs and Trade (GATT, subsequently superseded by the World Trade Organization—WTO) and an associate member of the UN Economic and Social Commission for Asia and the Pacific (ESCAP). In June 1992 Macao and the European Community (now the European Union) signed a five-year trade and economic co-operation agreement, granting mutual preferential treatment on tariffs and other commercial matters. The agreement was extended in December 1997. Macao remained a 'privileged partner' of the EU after December 1999. Macao also retained its membership of WTO after December 1999.

SURVEY AND PROSPECTS

After recording trade surpluses between 1998 and 2000, Macao's trade balance reverted to deficit in 2001 and increased sharply in 2002. Macao's trading position had been considerably weakened by the relative appreciation of the pataca against the currencies of its South-East Asian competitors. Attempts to diversify the economy in order to reduce dependence on tourism and the textile industry were made, although during the 1990s many non-textile operations were relocated to China and to South-East Asia, where labour costs were lower. Notably, Macao faced increasing competition from the nearby Zhuhai Special Economic Zone on the Chinese mainland. Nevertheless, foreign investment in Macao rose strongly during the first half of 2002, totalling 1,000m. patacas, an increase of 20% year-on-year. In late 2002 the Government announced a series of tax reduction initiatives aimed at assisting the development of small- and medium-sized enterprises, to promote future growth.

In 1993, meanwhile, the Macao Government announced a major land-reclamation programme, the 470,000-sq m Nam Van Lakes project, initially scheduled for completion in 2001, which was planned to enlarge the territory's peninsular area by 20%. The development was to incorporate residential and business accommodation for 60,000 people. The project was subsequently jeopardized by a sharp decline in the property market, which remained depressed in 1999 and 2000. In 2002, however, the property market showed signs of recovery, with transactions increasing by 56.1% on an annual basis during the first three quarters of that year. The Nam Van Lakes scheme was just one of several large projects being developed in the SAR. In October 2002 construction work began on a third bridge linking Macao and Taipa Island, due for completion in 2004. The Government hoped that such public-works projects would create the new jobs necessary to reduce the relatively high level of unemployment.

In December 2001 STDM lost its long-standing monopoly of the gambling industry, and the Government awarded casino-operating licences to three other companies. Gambling continued to be an important source of income for the SAR—the Government estimated that taxes from the casinos would amount to 6,930m. patacas in 2003, or nearly half the Government's fiscal budget of 14,120m. patacas for that year. In the event, revenue from taxes on gambling was even higher than expected in 2003, amounting to an estimated 9,100m. patacas in the first 11 months of the year alone. Further development of the hotel and tourism sector was envisaged, with a particular view to dispelling the territory's unsavoury reputation. A 12th casino opened in January 2004.

Macao's tourist industry was adversely affected by the travel restrictions imposed following the outbreak of Severe Acute Respiratory Syndrome (SARS) on the Chinese mainland in early 2003. In mid-2003, therefore, the Macao Government initiated a tourism promotion scheme, costing 30m. patacas. By the end of 2003 Macao's tourism industry appeared to have recovered completely from the effect of SARS, with tourist arrivals for the year reportedly reaching a new record.

The Chinese authorities planned greater integration of Macao within the Zhujiang (Pearl River) Delta region, particularly with regard to infrastructural development. In early 2003 the authorities of the Macao SAR and the mainland Zhuhai Special Economic Zone planned jointly to develop a new industrial zone later that year. The Macao-Zhuhai industrial project was officially inaugurated in December 2003, and in January 2004 the Macao Government opened bidding for a land-reclamation project in connection with the cross-border industrial park. Meanwhile, in October 2003 the Closer Economic Partnership Arrangement (CEPA), a free-trade agreement, was signed between Macao and mainland China. In addition, Macao's importance to China's trade relations with Portuguese-speaking countries was emphasized at the first Forum for Economic and Trade Co-operation between China and Portuguese-Speaking Countries, which was held in Macao in October 2003. Macao's economy grew strongly in 2002, the rate of 10.1% being considerably higher than that recorded in 2001. Prospects for 2003 also appeared very favourable, with record economic growth of 25% being recorded in the third quarter of the year.

Macedonia

The former Yugoslav republic of Macedonia (FYRM) is situated in south-eastern Europe. After the Second World War Macedonia became part of the new communist-led Federative People's Republic of Yugoslavia. In 1991 the Macedonian Sobranie (Assembly) declared the republic of Macedonia to be a sovereign territory. Macedonian secession was effectively acknowledged by the Federal Republic of Yugoslavia in 1992. Following an ethnic Albanian uprising in early 2001, international peace-keeping forces were deployed in the FYRM. The Constitution was amended in November to incorporate ethnic Albanian demands. President Boris Trajkovski died in February 2004, as the result of an aeroplane accident. Skopje is the capital. The principal language is Macedonian.

Area and population
Area: 25,713 sq km
Population (mid-2002): 2,038,000
Population density (mid-2002): 79.3 per sq km
Life expectancy (years at birth, 2002): 72.0 (males 69.0; females 75.1)

Finance
GDP in current prices: 2002): US $3,712m. ($1,821 per head)
Real GDP growth (2002): 0.3%
Inflation (annual average, 2002): 1.8%
Currency: new denar

Economy

In 2002, according to World Bank estimates, the FYRM's gross national income (GNI), measured at average 2000–02 prices, was US $3,456m., equivalent to $1,700 per head (or $6,210 per head on an international purchasing-power parity basis). During 1990–2002, it was estimated, the population increased by an average of 0.6% per year, while gross domestic product (GDP) per head declined, in real terms, at an average annual rate of 1.0%. Overall GDP declined, in real terms, at an average annual rate of 0.5% in 1990–2002; real GDP declined by 4.5% in 2001, but increased by 0.3% in 2002.

AGRICULTURE

Agriculture (including hunting, forestry and fishing) contributed an estimated 11.8% of GDP in 2002, when 23.9% of the employed labour force were engaged in the sector. Dairy farming is significant, and the principal agricultural exports are tobacco, vegetables and fruit. The wine industry is of considerable importance, and the FYRM is also a producer of wheat, maize and barley. During 1990–2002, according to the World Bank, the GDP of the agricultural sector increased, in real terms, at an average annual rate of 0.2%; real agricultural GDP declined by 10.8% in 2001, but increased by 2.1% in 2002.

INDUSTRY

In 2002 industry contributed an estimated 28.9% of GDP and engaged 33.3% of the employed labour force. During 1990–2002, according to the World Bank, the GDP of the industrial sector declined, in real terms, at an average annual rate of 3.8%; real industrial GDP declined by 6.5% in 2001 and by 5.6% in 2002.

Mining

Mining contributed an estimated 0.6% of GDP and engaged 1.2% of the employed labour force in 2002. The only major mining activity is the production of lignite (brown coal), although there are also deposits of iron, zinc, lead, copper, chromium, manganese, antimony, silver, gold and nickel. Production in the mining and quarrying sector increased at an average annual rate of 5.9% in 1996–2000.

Manufacturing

The manufacturing sector contributed an estimated 18.6% of GDP in 2002, and engaged 23.6% of the employed labour force. In 1996 the principal branches of the sector, measured by gross value of output, were food products (accounting for 19.1% of the total), textiles and clothing (11.9%), machinery (11.0%), chemicals, and iron and steel. The GDP of the manufacturing sector decreased, in real terms, at an average annual rate of 5.3% in 1990–2002; real manufacturing GDP declined by 3.9% in 2001 and by 5.4% in 2002.

Energy

Energy is derived principally from coal and lignite, which provided 79.8% of the electricity generated in 2000. The first stage of a pipeline from the Bulgarian border to carry natural gas to the FYRM from Russia became operational in late 1995. A 214-km pipeline, which was to transport petroleum from the Greek port of Thessaloníki to

Skopje, was inaugurated in July 2002. Imports of mineral fuels accounted for 13.2% of the value of total imports in 2002.

SERVICES

Services accounted for an estimated 59.3% of GDP and engaged 42.8% of the employed labour force in 2002. Regional instability, notably ethnic hostilities in the north of the FYRM in 2001, has had an adverse impact on tourist activity. During 1990–2002, according to the World Bank, the GDP of the services sector increased, in real terms, at an average annual rate of 0.9%; services GDP declined by 1.6% in 2001, but rose by 3.6% in 2002.

EXTERNAL TRADE

In 2002 the FYRM recorded a visible trade deficit of US $767.6m., while there was a deficit of $325.3m. on the current account of the balance of payments. In 2002 the principal source of imports was Germany (accounting for 14.3%); other major sources were Greece, the FRY, Slovenia, Bulgaria, Russia and Italy. The principal market for exports in that year was the FRY (22.1%); other important purchasers were Germany, Greece, the USA, Italy and Croatia. The principal exports in 2002 were miscellaneous manufactured articles (notably clothing and accessories), basic manufactures (particularly iron and steel), beverages and tobacco, food and live animals, machinery and transport equipment, and chemicals. The main imports in that year were machinery and transport equipment (particularly road vehicles and parts), basic manufactures, mineral fuels and lubricants (notably petroleum and petroleum products), food and live animals, chemical products and miscellaneous manufactured articles.

GOVERNMENT FINANCE

The FYRM recorded an overall budgetary deficit of 13,019m. new denars (equivalent to 5.4% of GDP) in 2002. The fiscal deficit was estimated to have declined to 3,412m. new denars (equivalent to 1.4% of GDP) in 2003. At the end of 2001 the FYRM's total external debt was estimated at US $1,423m., of which $1,136m. was long-term public debt. In that year the cost of debt-servicing was equivalent to 12.9% of the value of exports of goods and services. The annual rate of inflation averaged 67.6% in 1990–2002. Consumer prices increased by 1.8% in 2002. The rate of unemployment was estimated at some 31.9% in 2002.

INTERNATIONAL ECONOMIC RELATIONS

The FYRM is a member of the IMF and the European Bank for Reconstruction and Development (EBRD). It become a member of the World Trade Organization (WTO) in April 2003.

SURVEY AND PROSPECTS

The FYRM's economic prospects were significantly improved by the removal, in late 1995, of the Greek embargo on trade with the FYRM and the UN sanctions against the FRY, which had severely disrupted the FYRM's trading links. Progress was achieved through mass privatization, and a stock exchange was opened in Skopje in March 1996. The NATO aerial bombardment of the FRY in March–June 1999, resulting in a mass influx of refugees from Kosovo, strained the FYRM's resources. Following the end of the conflict, however, Macedonian enterprises profited from involvement in the reconstruction of infrastructural damage in Kosovo, and from Serbia's economic regeneration. A significant improvement in relations between Greece and the FYRM also provided for substantial Greek investment. The introduction of value-added tax in 2000 proved successful, and in November the IMF approved a new three-year loan to support the Government's economic reforms. However, ethnic hostilities in the north of the country in early 2001 prompted renewed fears of widespread civil conflict, and a substantial deterioration of the fiscal position ensued.

Following the negotiation of a peace agreement in August, the authorities requested considerable donor assistance to finance the reconstruction of damaged infrastructure and housing, and the relocation of displaced civilians. A Stabilization and Association Agreement was signed with the European Union (EU) in April. A major donor aid conference, sponsored by the EU and the World Bank, finally took place in March 2002; international donors pledged a total of US $515m. to support reconstruction. In September the Government, which had been widely regarded as responsible for mismanagement and widespread corruption, was replaced. Measures to investigate suspected embezzlement in public institutions and to combat further malpractice were immediately introduced.

In October the WTO formally approved the FYRM's accession, and it became a full member in April 2003. A further stand-by credit agreement with the IMF was signed in early 2003, and in October the Fund approved the disbursement of further funds. (An agreement providing for the continuance of IMF-recommended policies was expected to be negotiated on the expiry of the existing arrangement in June 2004.) The Government's success in adhering to IMF conditions of fiscal restraint and fulfilling targets for growth and low inflation was commended; however, reduced state expenditure (resulting in a lower than anticipated budgetary deficit) caused delays in implementing investment projects. The Government also proved slow to introduce measures to reform the pension system and privatize or close loss-making enter-prises, which would adversely affect unemployment. None the less, economic growth was projected to accelerate in 2004–05, as a result of increased external funding and private investment. The death of President Boris Trajkovski on 26 February 2004 produced conditions of political uncertainty in the country, prior to an election in April; the country's formal application for membership of the EU, due to take place on the same day, was finally submitted on 22 March. Furthermore, an outbreak of ethnic Albanian violence in Kosovo in March prompted fears of renewed destabilization in the FYRM.

Madagascar

The Republic of Madagascar mainly comprises the island of Madagascar in the western Indian Ocean. The country gained its independence from France in 1960. Multi-party politics were suspended in 1975–90. In 1991 political reforms provided for the suspension of the Constitution and the appointment of a transitional Government, pending elections. In 1993 Albert Zafy was elected President. Following Zafy's impeachment in 1996, Didier Ratsiraka (Head of State 1975–93) was elected President in 1997. The result of a presidential election held in 2001 remained disputed until 2002, when the High Constitutional Court declared Marc Ravalomanana the winner. Ratsiraka refused to accept the ruling, and civil conflict ensued for several months. The capital is Antananarivo. Malagasy is the official language.

Area and population

Area: 587,041 sq km
Population (mid-2002): 16,437,220
Population density (mid-2002): 28.0 per sq km
Life expectancy (years at birth, 2002): 56.3 (males 54.4; females 58.4)

Finance
GDP in current prices: 2002): US $4,514m. ($275 per head)
Real GDP growth (2002): −11.9%
Inflation (annual average, 2002): 15.9%
Currency: ariary

Economy

In 2002, according to estimates by the World Bank, Madagascar's gross national income (GNI), measured at average 2000–02 prices, was US $3,913m., equivalent to about $240 per head (or $720 per head on an international purchasing-power parity basis). During 1990–2002, it was estimated, the population increased at an average annual rate of 2.9%, while gross domestic product (GDP) per head decreased, in real terms, by an average of 2.0% per year. Overall GDP increased, in real terms, at an average annual rate of 0.9% in 1990–2002; GDP increased by 6.0% in 2001, but decreased by 11.9% in 2002.

AGRICULTURE

In 2002 the agricultural sector (including forestry and fishing) accounted for 31.5% of GDP and employed an estimated 73.4% of the labour force. Rice, the staple food crop, is produced on some 50% of cultivated land. Since 1972, however, imports of rice have been necessary to supplement domestic production. The most important cash crops are vanilla (which accounted for 24.1% of total export revenue in 2002), cloves and coffee. Following a long drought in 2003, vanilla production was estimated to have halved in that year, leading to a dramatic escalation in world prices. Sugar, coconuts, tropical fruits, cotton and sisal are also cultivated. Cattle-farming is important. Sea fishing by coastal fishermen (particularly for crustaceans) is being expanded, while vessels from the European Union fish for tuna and prawns in Madagascar's exclusive maritime zone, within 200 nautical miles (370 km) of the coast, in return for compensation. According to the World Bank, agricultural GDP increased by an average of 1.7% per year in 1990–2002; the sector's GDP increased by 4.0% in 2001, but declined by 1.4% in 2002.

INDUSTRY

Industry (including mining, manufacturing, construction and power) contributed 14.3% of Madagascar's GDP in 2002, and employed about 5.5% of the labour force in 1999. According to the World Bank, industrial GDP increased at an average annual rate of 0.2% in 1990–2002; the sector's GDP increased by 7.6% in 2001, but declined by 25.1% in 2002.

Mining

The mining sector contributed only 0.3% of GDP in 1991 and, together with manufacturing, engaged about 1.5% of the labour force in 1993. However, Madagascar has sizeable deposits of a wide range of minerals, principally chromite (chromium ore), which, with graphite and mica, is exported, together with small quantities of semi-precious stones. A proposed major project to resume the mining of ilmenite (titanium ore) in south-eastern Madagascar, which would generate US $550m. over a 30-year period but which had prompted considerable controversy on environmental grounds, received approval from the Government in 2001, pending the completion of further studies. Other potential mineral projects included the exploitation of an estimated 100m. metric tons of bauxite in the south-east of the country, and of nickel and cobalt deposits in central Madagascar. Following exploratory drilling for petroleum at three offshore areas in the early 1990s, it was announced that only non-commercial deposits of oil and gas had been discovered, although contracts for further exploration were granted in 1997 and 1999. The mining of sapphires commenced in southern Madagascar in 1998, but in March 1999 the Government ordered the suspension of sapphire mining pending the results of studies into the effects of exploitation on the environment; however, unauthorized mining continued on a wide scale.

Manufacturing

Manufacturing contributed 10.9% of GDP in 2002. The petroleum refinery at Toamasina, using imported petroleum, provides a significant share of export revenue. Other important branches of manufacturing are textiles and clothing, food products, beverages and chemical products. The introduction of a new investment code in 1990 and the creation of a number of export processing zones achieved some success in attracting foreign private investment, particularly in the manufacturing branches of textiles, cement, fertilizers and pharmaceuticals. According to the World Bank, manufacturing GDP remained constant in 1990–2002; the GDP of the sector increased by 10.7% in 2001, but decreased by 25.1% in 2002.

Energy

Energy generation depends on imports of crude petroleum (which accounted for 29.7% of the value of total imports in 2002) to fuel thermal installations, although hydroelectric resources have also been developed, and accounted for an estimated 67.6% of electricity production in 2001. In 2004 the Government was in the process of privatizing the national electricity and water utility, Jiro sy rano Malagasy (JIRAMA).

SERVICES

The services sector accounted for 54.2% of GDP in 2002, and engaged some 10.9% of the labour force in 1993. According to the World Bank, the GDP of the services sector increased by an average of 1.3% per year in 1990–2002; services GDP increased by 6.1% in 2001, but declined by 11.1% in 2002.

EXTERNAL TRADE

In 2002 Madagascar recorded a visible trade deficit of US $117m., and there was a deficit of $298m. on the current account of the balance of payments. The principal source of imports in 2001 was France (21.5%); other major suppliers were the People's Republic of China and South Africa. France was also the principal market for exports (accounting for 29.7% of exports in that year); the USA was also an important purchaser. The principal exports in 2002 were vanilla, crustaceans and cloves. The principal imports in that year included petroleum, raw materials and spare parts, consumer goods, equipment goods and food.

GOVERNMENT FINANCE

Madagascar's overall budget deficit for 2002 was estimated at 1,863,100m. francs MG (equivalent to 6.2% of GDP). Madagascar's external debt totalled US $4,160m. at the end of 2001, of which $3,793m. was long-term public debt. In the same year the cost of debt-servicing was estimated to be equivalent to 43.3% of the value of exports of goods and services. The annual rate of inflation averaged 15.7% in 1990–2001; consumer prices increased by 6.9% in 2001 and by 15.9% in 2002. About 6% of the labour force was estimated to be unemployed in 1995.

INTERNATIONAL ECONOMIC RELATIONS

Madagascar is a member of the Indian Ocean Commission and of the Common Market for Eastern and Southern Africa (COMESA). An application was made to join the Southern African Development Community (SADC) in 2003.

SURVEY AND PROSPECTS

Madagascar's dominant agricultural sector is vulnerable to adverse climatic conditions, including cyclones, and to fluctuations in the market prices of the country's principal exports. In December 2000 the IMF and the World Bank agreed to support a comprehensive debt reduction package under the enhanced initiative for heavily indebted poor countries (HIPCs). The IMF approved a loan, of US $103m., in March 2001 under the Poverty Reduction and Growth Facility (PRGF). Also in March Madagascar was declared eligible to benefit from the USA's African Growth and Opportunity Act, allowing duty free access to the US market, and both exports to the USA and foreign investment in Madagascar increased dramatically as a result. In December the IMF reported that economic performance had been favourable in 2001, but expressed concern at the persistently high level of poverty in the country.

Economic activity was paralysed from the beginning of 2002—amid political uncertainty caused by the disputed presidential election—by the strikes called by Marc Ravalomanana and the blockades ordered by Didier Ratsiraka. In February the World Bank estimated that the strike was costing Madagascar up to $14m. per day (the entire annual savings from debt-relief) and that 50,000 jobs were threatened. The closure of the central bank from the end of January also resulted in the freezing of the nation's assets, rendering Madagascar unable to service its debts and at risk of default; real GDP for the year declined by 11.9%.

Companies in the export processing zone (specializing in textiles for export) and in the agricultural sector were severely affected by the political crisis, being highly dependent on foreign purchasers and the transportation network; tourism also was drastically curtailed. In July international donors pledged some $2,300m. (one-half of which was to be supplied by the Bretton Woods institutions) over a period of four years towards the reconstruction and development of the country; this subsequently enabled the authorities to repay the arrears on all external payments. From August the foreign-exchange markets reopened and the currency remained broadly stable after an initial decline. In October the IMF fully disbursed a structural adjustment credit of $100m., and in November it approved an Emergency Economic Recovery Credit and other loans aimed at public-sector management and private-sector development; in December the Fund granted $15m. under the PRGF and extended the arrangement until November 2004, in addition to allotting $4m. in interim assistance under the HIPC initiative.

The economy recovered well in 2003, with growth estimated at some 9.6% and slower inflation, and a Poverty Reduction Strategy Paper was adopted in July. However, the country suffered from a particularly severe cyclone in March 2004, which adversely affected infrastructure of the aquaculture, rice and vanilla sectors, undermining the GDP growth rate of 6% and inflation rate of 5% forecast for that year. In response, the IMF immediately released $35m. in funds and extended the PRGF further, to March 2005. Meanwhile, Madagascar's new currency, the ariary (which had been introduced in July 2003 to replace the franc MG), depreciated considerably in early 2004, prompting significant increases in food and fuel prices, but optimism with regard to potential foreign investment.

Malawi

The Republic of Malawi is situated in southern central Africa. The former British protectorate of Nyasaland gained independence, as Malawi, in 1964. In 1966 Malawi became a republic and a one-party state, with Dr Hastings Kamuzu Banda as its first President. Malawi was the only African country to maintain full diplomatic relations with South Africa during the apartheid era. In 1994, in multi-party elections, Dr (Elson) Bakili Muluzi was elected as President, while the United Democratic Front (UDF) emerged as the leading party. Muluzi and the UDF were successful at elections in 1999. In May 2004 Dr Bingu wa Mutharika, of the UDF, was elected to the presidency, although the Malawi Congress Party, the sole legal party in 1966–93, secured the majority of seats in the National Assembly. Lilongwe is the capital. The official language is English.

Area and population

Area: 118,484 sq km
Population (mid-2002): 10,743,330
Population density (mid-2002): 90.7 per sq km
Life expectancy (years at birth, 2002): 40.2 (males 39.8; females 40.6)

Finance

GDP in current prices: 2002): US $1,880m. ($175 per head)
Real GDP growth (2002): 1.8%
Inflation (annual average, 2002): 14.7%
Currency: kwacha

Economy

In 2002, according to estimates by the World Bank, Malawi's gross national income (GNI), measured at average 2000–02 prices, was US $1,728m., equivalent to $160 per head (or $570 per head on an international purchasing-power parity basis). During 1990–2002, it was estimated, the population increased at an average annual rate of 2.0%, while gross domestic product (GDP) per head increased, in real terms, by an average of 0.9% per year. Overall GDP increased, in real terms, at an average annual rate of 2.9% in 1990–2002; real GDP increased by 1.8% in 2002 and by 4.4% in 2003.

AGRICULTURE
Measured at constant 1994 prices, agriculture (including forestry and fishing) contributed 38.1% of GDP in 2003, and engaged an estimated 82.1% of the labour force in 2002. The principal cash crops are tobacco (which accounted for 56.9% of total export earnings in 2002), tea and sugar cane. The principal food crops are maize, potatoes, cassava, plantains, groundnuts and pulses. Periods of severe drought and flooding have necessitated imports of basic foods in recent years. In March 2004 the Government forecast a 24% decline in maize production in that year, owing to late and erratic rainfall. During 1990–2002, according to the World Bank, agricultural GDP increased at an average annual rate of 5.4%. According to official figures, growth in agricultural GDP was 2.4% in 2002 and 6.8% in 2003.

INDUSTRY
Industry (including manufacturing, mining, construction and power) contributed 15.6% of GDP in 2003, and engaged 4.5% of the employed labour force in 1998. During 1990–2002, according to the World Bank, industrial GDP increased by an average of 1.4% per year. Industrial GDP decreased by 1.5% in 2002, but increased by 4.1% in 2003.

Mining
Mining and quarrying contributed 1.1% of GDP in 2003, and engaged less than 0.1% of the employed labour force in 1998. Limestone, coal and gemstones are mined, and there are plans to develop deposits of bauxite, high-calcium marble and graphite. There are also reserves of phosphates, uranium, glass sands, asbestos and vermiculite. In August 2000 an Australian company announced its intention to establish a uranium mine in northern Malawi, near the border with Tanzania; it was anticipated that production would commence in 2005. Environmental and financial concerns have delayed plans to exploit an estimated 30m. metric tons of bauxite deposits at Mount Mulanje. The GDP of the mining sector increased at an average annual rate of 15.1% in 1994–2003, according to official figures; mining GDP decreased by 38.6% in 2002, but increased by 23.4% in 2003.

Manufacturing

Manufacturing contributed 10.6% of GDP in 2003, and engaged 2.7% of the employed labour force in 1998. During 1990–2002, according to the World Bank, manufacturing GDP increased by an average of 0.1% per year. Manufacturing GDP decreased by 0.1% in 2002, but increased by 1.2% in 2003.

Energy

Production of electrical energy is by hydroelectric (principally) and thermal installations. Some 90% of energy for domestic use is derived from fuel wood. In October 1997 an agreement was signed to link Malawi's electricity system to the Cahora Bassa hydroelectric dam in Mozambique, but completion of the project was not expected until 2006. In October 2000 a hydroelectric power plant, with a generation capacity of 64 MW, was opened at Kapichira. In January 2001 the Government introduced a campaign to widen access to electricity, especially in rural areas; in 2001 only 4% of Malawians had access to electricity. In 2003 the Government was examing the possibility of establishing coal-fired power stations. Imports of fuel comprised an estimated 9.6% of the value of total imports in 1998.

SERVICES

The services sector contributed 46.3% of GDP in 2003, and engaged 11.0% of the employed labour force in 1998. The GDP of the services sector increased by an average of 2.0% per year in 1990–2002, according to the World Bank. Services GDP increased by 3.2% in 2002 and by 2.8% in 2003.

EXTERNAL TRADE

In 2002 Malawi recorded a visible trade deficit of US $150.8m., while there was a deficit of $200.7m. on the current account of the balance of payments. In 2001 the principal source of imports was South Africa (39.7%); Zimbabwe and Zambia were also notable suppliers. South Africa was also the principal market for exports (19.1%) in that year; other important markets were the USA, Germany, Japan and the Netherlands. The principal exports in 2002 were tobacco, tea and sugar. The principal imports in 1998 were machinery and transport equipment (particularly road vehicles and parts), basic manufactures, food and live animals (notably cereals and cereal preparations), chemicals and related products, and mineral fuels.

GOVERNMENT FINANCE

In the financial year ending 30 June 2002 Malawi's overall budget deficit was an estimated 10,959m. kwacha (equivalent to 8.1% of GDP). The country's external debt totalled US $2,602m. at the end of 2001, of which $2,483m. was long-term public debt. In that year the cost of debt-servicing was equivalent to 7.8% of exports of goods and services. The annual rate of inflation averaged 28.8% in 1990–2002; consumer prices increased by an average of 22.7% in 2001 and by 14.8% in 2002. Some 1.1% of the labour force were unemployed in 1998.

INTERNATIONAL ECONOMIC RELATIONS

Malawi is a member of the Southern African Development Community and also of the Common Market for Eastern and Southern Africa (COMESA). Nine members of COMESA, including Malawi, became inaugural members of the COMESA Free

Trade Area in October 2000. The country belongs to the International Tea Promotion Association and to the International Tobacco Growers' Association.

SURVEY AND PROSPECTS

Upon assuming office in May 1994, the Muluzi administration inherited an economy weakened not only by natural impediments to growth (including Malawi's land-locked position, the vulnerability of the dominant agricultural sector to drought, and a high rate of population growth), but also by the severe mismanagement of economic affairs by the Banda regime. The Muluzi Government continued policies of economic liberalization and diversification initiated in the last years under Banda. However, by 1997, as adherence to the programme slackened, the budget deficit widened and GDP growth slowed, leading to the suspension of IMF disbursements. In October 1999 the IMF approved a loan worth US $10.6m. in support of the Government's economic programme for 1999–2000. However, a significant decline in revenue from tobacco exports adversely affected the economy in 2000, and GDP growth failed to meet expected targets. The devaluation of the kwacha continued throughout 2000–03. (From May 2000 the central bank discontinued its policy of quoting an exchange rate for the kwacha and allowed the markets to determine the currency's relative value.) In November 2000 Malawi was granted debt relief equating to $1,000m. under the World Bank's initiative for heavily indebted poor countries (HIPCs), and in December the IMF approved a loan of some $65m. under its Poverty Reduction and Growth Facility (PRGF), disbursing $9m. immediately.

Structural reforms planned for 2001 included the continuing restructuring of the civil service and of the tax system, in addition to progress with the privatization of state-owned enterprises. However, unsatisfactory progress in the implementation of the IMF-supported economic programme repeatedly delayed the first review of performance under the PRGF arrangement, and thus further disbursements. More-over, in late 2001 and early 2002 the European Union (EU), the USA and other donors suspended aid to Malawi, in response to concerns regarding corruption and economic mismanagement. In April 2002 Malawi was suspended from the HIPC initiative over allegations of corruption concerning the sale of its grain reserves. Meanwhile, in February President Muluzi declared a state of national disaster and appealed for $21.6m. in international aid, as an estimated 70% of the population were seriously affected by food shortages, following severe flooding in 2001. In response, the USA provided some $29m. of aid in August; in the following months the IMF and the International Development Association provided emergency financial aid packages, and the World Bank approved grants and loans worth around $100m. to improve agricultural production and disaster management. In July 2003, in conjunction with the World Bank, the Government launched a financial management, transparency and accountability project, aimed at improving economic governance. In October the IMF finally completed the first review of Malawi's economic performance under the PRGF arrangement approved in December 2000, authorizing the disbursement of some $9m. The Fund extended the arrangement until December 2004, and agreed to resume interim assistance under the HIPC initiative. The EU and other donors also conditionally agreed to resume lending to Malawi, and in early 2004 the EU was preparing a three-year programme, worth €45m., to counter food insecurity in Malawi.

Malaysia

The Federation of Malaysia, situated in South-East Asia, consists of 13 states. The 11 states of Malaya, under British protection, were united as the Malayan Union in 1946 and became the Federation of Malaya in 1948. Malaya was granted independence, within the Commonwealth, in 1957. Malaysia was established in 1963, through the union of the independent Federation of Malaya (renamed the States of Malaya), Singapore, and the former British colonies of Sarawak and Sabah. Subsequently, Singapore left the federation and the States of Malaya were styled Peninsular Malaysia. The Supreme Head of State is an elected monarch. Kuala Lumpur is the capital, although Putrajaya has been developed as the administrative capital. The official language is Bahasa Malaysia.

Area and population
Area: 329,847 sq km
Population (mid-2002): 24,304,580
Population density (mid-2002): 73.7 per sq km
Life expectancy (years at birth, 2002): 72.0 (males 69.6; females 74.7)

Finance
GDP in current prices: 2002): US $95,157m. ($3,915 per head)
Real GDP growth (2002): 4.2%
Inflation (annual average, 2002): 1.8%
Currency: ringgit

Economy

In 2002, according to estimates by the World Bank, Malaysia's gross national income (GNI), measured at average 2000–02 prices, was US $85,956m., equivalent to $3,540 per head (or $8,280 per head on an international purchasing-power parity basis). During 1990–2002, it was estimated, the population increased at an annual average of 2.4%, while gross domestic product (GDP) per head increased, in real terms, by an average of 3.7% per year. Overall GDP increased, in real terms, at an average annual rate of 6.2% in 1990–2002. According to the Bank Negara Malaysia (BNM), GDP increased by 4.1% in 2002 and by 5.2% in 2003.

AGRICULTURE
Agriculture (including forestry and fishing) contributed 9.1% of GDP in 2003, according to the BNM. The sector engaged 15.2% of the employed labour force in 2000. The principal subsistence crop is rice. Malaysia is the world's leading producer of palm oil, exports of which contributed an estimated 6.5% of the value of total merchandise exports in 2003. Other important cash crops include rubber (which accounted for 1.2% of total exports in 2003), cocoa, coconuts, bananas, tea and pineapples. Sawlogs accounted for only an estimated 0.6% of total exports in 2003, owing to a government policy of sustainable management which led to the imposition of restrictions on exports of logs in 1993. During 1990–2002, according to the Asian Development Bank (ADB), agricultural GDP increased, in real terms, at an average annual rate of 0.5%. According to the BNM, agricultural GDP increased by 3.0% in 2002 and by 5.5% in 2003.

INDUSTRY
Industry (including mining, manufacturing, construction and utilities) contributed 47.0% of GDP in 2003. The sector engaged 37.0% of the employed labour force in 2000. During 1990–2002, according to the ADB, industrial GDP increased, in real terms, at an average annual rate of 7.3%. According to the BNM, industrial GDP grew by 3.9% in 2002 and by 7.0% in 2003.

Mining
Mining contributed 10.0% of GDP in 2003. However, it engaged only 0.4% of the employed labour force in 2000. At the end of 2002 estimated proven gas reserves stood at 2,120,000m. cu m, and petroleum reserves at 3,000m. barrels. Petroleum production in 2002 averaged 833,000 barrels per day from Malaysia's 33 oilfields, enough to sustain production for less than 11 years. At that year's level, natural gas production could be sustained for less than 43 years. Exports of crude petroleum provided an estimated 5.0% of total export earnings in 2003. Malaysia is one of the world's leading producers of tin, although in 2003 sales of this commodity accounted

for only 0.1% of total export revenue. Bauxite, copper, iron, gold and coal are also mined. The GDP of the mining sector increased at an average annual rate of 4.3% in 1990–2002, according to the ADB. Mining GDP increased by 3.7% in 2002 and by 4.8% in 2003, according to the BNM.

Manufacturing

Manufacturing (the largest export sector) contributed 30.2% of GDP in 2003. The manufacturing sector engaged 27.6% of the employed labour force in 2000. The most important branches of manufacturing include electrical machinery and appliances, food products, metals and metal products, non-electrical machinery, transport equipment, rubber and plastic products, chemical products, wood products and furniture. During 1990–2002 manufacturing GDP increased, in real terms, at an average annual rate of 8.1%. Manufacturing GDP increased by 4.0% in 2002 and by 8.2% in 2003.

Energy

Energy is derived principally from Malaysia's own reserves of hydrocarbons. The country's dependence on petroleum as a source of electric energy declined from 55.9% in 1990 to 8.8% in 2000. The share contributed by natural gas increased from 22.0% to 78.5% over the same period. In 2000 hydropower and coal accounted for 10.1% and 2.6%, respectively, of the country's electricity production, which reached 75,300m. kWh in 2002. Construction of a controversial 2,400-MW hydroelectric dam at Bakun, in Sarawak, was postponed in 1997, owing to the financial crisis. In early 2004 construction of the dam had yet to commence, as the Government was considering making further reductions to the scale of the project. Imports of mineral fuels comprised 4.7% of the value of merchandise imports in 2002.

SERVICES

The services sector contributed 43.9% of GDP in 2003. It engaged 47.8% of the employed labour force in 2000. Tourism makes a significant contribution to the economy. Tourist arrivals rose from almost 12.8m. in 2001 to 13.3m. in 2002; receipts from the sector reached RM 25,781.1m. in the latter year. However, it was feared that, in the aftermath of the terrorist attack in Bali in October 2002, Malaysia's tourism sector might be adversely affected; following the attack, warnings were issued by several foreign governments against travel to Malaysia. In 2003 these fears were borne out when tourist arrivals declined to 10.6m. In 2003 the financial and real estate sector, along with business services, contributed 10.9% of GDP. The banking system in Malaysia was severely damaged by the regional financial crisis in 1997; a series of mergers subsequently took place as part of plans to consolidate the sector. The GDP of the services sector increased by an average of 7.8% per year in 1990–2002. Services GDP grew by 4.2% in 2002 and by 3.9% in 2003.

EXTERNAL TRADE

In 2002 Malaysia recorded a visible trade surplus of US $18,135m., with a surplus of $7,190m. on the current account of the balance of payments. In 2003 the principal source of imports (providing 17.4% of the total) was Japan; other major suppliers were the USA (15.2%), Singapore (12.0%), the People's Republic of China and the Republic of Korea. The principal market for exports (18.0%) was the USA; other significant purchasers were Singapore (16.4%) and Japan (10.9%). The principal imports in 2002 were machinery and transport equipment, basic manufactures and chemicals. The principal exports in 2003 were electrical machinery and parts (particularly semiconductors and electronic equipment), chemicals, textiles, palm oil and products, crude petroleum and liquefied natural gas.

GOVERNMENT FINANCE

In 2002 there was a federal budgetary deficit of approximately RM 20,253m. The 2004 budget envisaged expenditure of RM 112,500m., resulting in a deficit equivalent to 3.3% of GDP. At the end of 2001 Malaysia's external debt totalled US $43,351m., of which $24,068m. was long-term public debt. The cost of debt-servicing in that year was equivalent to 6.0% of the value of exports of goods and services. The annual rate of inflation averaged 3.2% in 1990–2002. Consumer prices increased by an average of 1.4% in 2001 and by 1.8% in 2002. In 2002 3.5% of the labour force were unemployed.

INTERNATIONAL ECONOMIC RELATIONS

Malaysia is a member of the UN Economic and Social Commission for Asia and the Pacific (ESCAP), the Asian Development Bank (ADB), the Association of South East Asian Nations (ASEAN), the Colombo Plan and Asia-Pacific Economic Co-operation (APEC), all of which aim to accelerate economic progress in the region. In January 1992 the member states of ASEAN agreed to establish a free-trade zone, the ASEAN Free Trade Area (AFTA). The original target for the reduction of tariffs to between 0% and 5% was 2008, but this was subsequently advanced to 2003 and then 2002, when AFTA was formally established. Malaysia itself, however, was granted a three-year delay in January 2001 for the opening of its politically-sensitive automotive industry to the free-trade agreements, fearing competition from Thailand.

SURVEY AND PROSPECTS

In September 1998 the Malaysian Government introduced controversial capital controls to limit the repercussions of regional developments and ensure stability in domestic prices and exchange rates. The ringgit was fixed at 3.80 to the US dollar and from 1 October became non-convertible overseas. These and other measures enabled Malaysia to reduce interest rates and raise domestic demand without destabilizing the currency. The economy therefore made a rapid recovery from the regional economic crisis of 1997/98, and the last of the capital controls for non-residents were removed in May 2001, although the ringgit 'peg' remained in place.

In July 1999, meanwhile, the Government intensified its efforts towards the reform of the financial sector, announcing plans for the forcible restructuring of the country's numerous banks and finance companies. By August 2001 51 banks had merged under the plans, highlighting the substantial progress made in financial sector reforms. In April 2001 the Government announced the Eighth Malaysia Plan (EMP), which gave economic projections for 2001–05. According to the EMP, the economy was to grow at an average annual rate of 7.5% over the next five years. The Government also expected to achieve a substantial reduction in levels of poverty.

Despite the economic recovery of 1999–2000, however, foreign investment in Malaysia decreased in 2001, partly owing to the increasing attractiveness of the People's Republic of China as a destination for foreign investment, before rising in 2002. In 2002, while global demand for Malaysia's principal export commodities, such as electrical and electronic goods, remained slow, an increase in the prices of palm oil, crude petroleum and chemicals, amongst others, contributed to a recovery in exports.

Following the retirement of Prime Minister Mahathir Mohamad in October 2003, his successor, Abdullah Ahmad Badawi, deferred several large-scale infrastructure projects and launched an anti-corruption campaign in an attempt to reduce public spending. He also announced his intention to focus on developing the country's agricultural sector and to prioritize educational reforms.

A significant downturn in exports in the second half of 2003 was largely attributable to a contraction in the electronics sector; it was feared that the relocation of many electronics companies to China had affected sectoral expansion. GDP expanded by 5.2% in 2003 and, in the same year, the budget deficit was equivalent to 5.5% of GDP. Despite increasing pressure for a review of the viability of the currency 'peg', owing to a decline in the value of the US dollar from late 2003, the arrangement was expected to remain in place in 2004. The Government predicted GDP growth of between 5.5% and 6.0% for the year. However, reforms to the country's education and health sectors would continue to be necessary in the long term, in order to minimize Malaysia's reliance on foreign direct investment and on exports to drive economic growth.

Maldives

The Republic of Maldives is in southern Asia. The country comprises 1,190 small coral islands, grouped in 26 natural atolls, in the Indian Ocean. The Maldives became fully independent, outside the Commonwealth, in 1965. Formerly an elective sultanate, the country became a republic for a second time in 1968, following a referendum. After independence, Amir Ibrahim Nasir was the first President. Nasir was succeeded by Maumoon Abdul Gayoom in 1978. President Gayoom was re-elected in 1983, 1988, 1993 and 1998. Despite unprecedented anti-Government protests in September 2003, President Gayoom was re-elected for a sixth term a month later. Malé is the capital. Dhivehi is the national language.

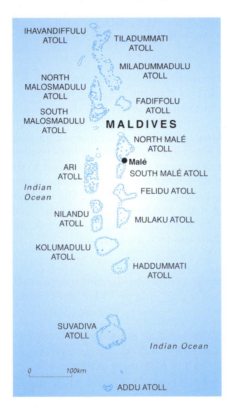

Area and population

Area: 298 sq km
Population (mid-2002): 286,680
Population density (mid-2002): 962.0 per sq km
Life expectancy (years at birth, 2002): 66.1 (males 66.5; females 65.6)

517

Finance

GDP in current prices: 2002): US $618m. ($2,155 per head)
Real GDP growth (2002): 2.3%
Inflation (annual average, 2002): 0.9%
Currency: rufiyaa

Economy

In 2002, according to estimates by the World Bank, the Maldives' gross national income (GNI), measured at average 2000–02 prices, was US $598m., equivalent to $2,090 per head. During 1990–2002, it was estimated, the population increased at an average annual rate of 2.5%, while gross domestic product (GDP) per head increased, in real terms, by an average of 4.6% per year during 1990–2001. Overall GDP increased, in real terms, at an average annual rate of 7.3% in 1990–2001. According to the Asian Development Bank (ADB), GDP growth increased to 6.0% in 2002, but slowed to 4.2% in 2003. An initial projection of GDP growth for 2004 was 2.8%.

AGRICULTURE

Agriculture and fishing contributed an estimated 9.4% of GDP (at constant 1995 prices) in 2002. About 14% of the total working population were employed in the sector (more than 10% in fishing) in 2000. In 2002 revenue from exports of marine products totalled 716.7m. rufiyaa, thus accounting for 61.7% of total export earnings. In February 1999 the Kooddoo Fisheries Complex in the South Huvadhu Atoll, the largest fisheries project ever implemented in the Maldives, was officially opened. In January 2001 the fresh fish export market was opened to the private sector. Small quantities of various fruits, vegetables and cereals are produced, but virtually all of the principal staple foods have to be imported. The dominant agricultural activity (not including fishing) in the Maldives is coconut production. Agricultural GDP increased, in real terms, by an annual average of 1.9% in 1990–2002. Real agricultural GDP grew by 1.7% in 2001 and by 1.4% in 2002.

INDUSTRY

Industry (including mining, manufacturing and construction) employed about 19% of the working population in 2000, and provided an estimated 15.5% of GDP in 2002.

Mining

Mining and quarrying contributed an estimated 0.6% of GDP in 2002, and employed 0.5% of the working population in 2000. No reserves of petroleum or natural gas have, as yet, been discovered in Maldivian waters.

Manufacturing

The manufacturing sector employed 13% of the working population in 2000. Including electricity, gas and water, the manufacturing sector contributed 11.7% of GDP in 2002. There are only a small number of 'modern' manufacturing enterprises in the Maldives, including fish-canning, garment-making and soft-drink bottling. Although cottage industries (such as the weaving of coir yarn and boat-building) employ nearly one-quarter of the total labour force, there is little scope for expansion, owing to the limited size of the domestic market. Because of its lack of manufacturing industries, the Maldives has to import most essential consumer and capital goods. In the late 1980s and 1990s traditional handicrafts, such as lacquer work and shell craft, revived as a result of the expansion of the tourism sector. Manufacturing GDP increased, in real terms, by an annual average of 5.8% in 1990–2002. Real manufacturing GDP grew by 2.7% in 2001 and by 1.5% in 2002.

Energy

Energy is derived principally from petroleum, imports of which comprised 11.8% of the cost of imports in 2001. Owing to a surge in commercial activities and a significant increase in construction projects in Malé, demand for electricity in the capital grew rapidly in the late 1980s and early 1990s. Accordingly, plans were formulated in late 1991 to augment the generating capacity of the power station in Malé and to improve the distribution network. By early 1998 20 islands had been provided with electricity (equivalent to about 60% of the total population). In early 2001 the third phase of the Malé power project, further to increase the capital's power supply, was under way. In December the ADB agreed to provide a loan to improve the supply of electricity to some 40 outer islands.

SERVICES

Following the decline of the shipping industry in the 1980s, tourism gained in importance as an economic sector, and by 1989 it had overtaken the fishing industry as the Maldives' largest source of foreign exchange. In 1999 the tourism sector provided 18.5% of GDP. In 2001 tourist arrivals decreased by 1.3%, compared with the previous year, to reach 460,984, owing to the global economic slowdown and concerns over travel safety and stability in the South Asian region after the terrorist attacks on the USA in September. By the end of 2002, however, tourist arrivals had increased by 5.1%; receipts from tourism in that year reached an estimated 892.1m. rufiyaa. In 2003 tourist arrivals increased by 16.3% to reach 563,593. In late 2001 a four-year plan was under way to convert 12 islands into holiday resorts and to increase the number of hotel beds by 4,000. The services sector contributed 75.1% of GDP in 2002. Compared with the previous year, the GDP of the services sector expanded by 4.3% in 2002.

EXTERNAL TRADE

In 2002 the Maldives recorded a visible trade deficit of US $211.1m., and there was a deficit of $44.0m. on the current account of the balance of payments. In 2002 the principal source of imports was Singapore (accounting for 25.8% of the total); other major sources were Sri Lanka, India and France. The principal market for exports was the USA (accounting for 38.4% of the total); other major purchasers were Sri Lanka, Thailand and Japan. The principal exports were marine products (tuna being the largest export commodity) and clothing. The principal imports were machinery and mechanical appliances and electrical equipment, mineral products and textile and textile articles.

GOVERNMENT FINANCE

Foreign grant aid in 2000 totalled an estimated US $17.7m.; Japan is the Maldives' largest aid donor (disbursing $11.9m. in 1997). The 2003 budget envisaged expenditure of 3,826.5m. rufiyaa and revenue of 2,987.8m., including grants of 113.4m. rufiyaa. The budgetary deficit increased significantly to the equivalent of 7.8% of

GDP in 2002 and was expected to reach about 8.5% of GDP in 2003. The Maldives' total external debt was US $234.9m. at the end of 2001, of which $180.7m. was long-term public debt. In that year the cost of debt-servicing was equivalent to 4.6% of revenue from exports of goods and services. During 1990–2002 the average annual rate of inflation was 6.1%. Consumer prices increased by only 0.7% in 2001, and by 0.9% in 2002 (despite a July 2001 8% devaluation of the rufiyaa). According to the ADB, 2.0% of the labour force were unemployed in 2001.

INTERNATIONAL ECONOMIC RELATIONS

The Maldives is a member of the UN Economic and Social Commission for Asia and the Pacific (ESCAP), the ADB, the Colombo Plan and the South Asian Association for Regional Co-operation (SAARC).

SURVEY AND PROSPECTS

One result of the rapid growth and increasing importance of the tourism sector in the Maldives in the late 1990s was the Government's efforts to improve the infrastructure (including development of communication systems, sanitation and water supply). By 1999 the Maldivian telecommunications company, DHIRAAGU, had provided telephone facilities to all of the inhabited islands. In mid-1999 DHIRAAGU signed a 47m.-rufiyaa contract with a French telecommunications company for the supply and implementation of a mobile cellular telephone system for the Maldives. By February 2004 more than 72,000 inhabitants had subscribed to mobile cellular telephones, with coverage reaching more than 70% of the population. In mid-2000 DHIRAAGU launched its 'Instant Internet Access'. However, despite a recovery in fish exports and buoyant tourism receipts in the latter half of the 1990s, the current-account deficit persisted and the trade deficit continued to grow.

In April 2000 Air Maldives, a joint venture between the Government and a Malaysian company, Naluri Bhd, permanently ceased operating international flights, owing to estimated losses of US $50m.–$70m. This outcome adversely affected the tourist industry and business confidence. The tourist industry suffered further in 2001, owing to the suicide attacks on the USA and the subsequent military action in Afghanistan. The fisheries sector, however, fared better. In early 2001 the Government opened up the export of fresh and canned fish to the private sector, and in that year the Maldives Industrial Fisheries Company recorded a 13% increase in sales of fish, compared with the previous year. In 2002 the fisheries sector continued to expand (earnings from fish exports increased by 35%, compared with the previous year) and tourism gradually began to recover. The current-account deficit, however, remained high and the fiscal deficit continued to grow, largely owing to an increase in government expenditure. Furthermore, the islands continued to experience a shortage of domestic labour: in 2003 about 33,765 expatriate workers (mainly from India, Sri Lanka and Bangladesh) were employed in the Maldives, and it was estimated that in 1999 almost 20% of the country's GDP went to non-Maldivians. Although the growth in overall GDP declined in 2003, the tourist industry improved substantially and the fishing industry continued to expand.

The Government pledged to continue to open up the public sector to private investment in 2004. In January President Gayoom announced that the 2004 budget would focus on accelerating social and economic progress. The Government had commenced the introduction of necessary reforms for the development of the financial market. In June 2000 the Maldives was one of more than 30 countries and territories named by the Organisation for Economic Co-operation and Development (OECD) as unfair tax havens, but was subsequently removed from the list. Meanwhile, public expenditure needs to be further curtailed for the Government to make any significant progress in strengthening the economy. The high average annual rate of population growth (estimated at 2.7% in 1990–95), which has placed a heavy burden on the economy in general and on the congested capital island of Malé in particular, is an issue that is effectively being addressed (according to the results of the March 2000 census, the rate of population increase had fallen to 1.9% in 1995–2000).

From 1997, in an attempt to solve the problem of overcrowding in Malé, the artificially constructed island of Hulhumalé was developed as a suburb to relieve congestion in the capital. The first group of people was appointed to move to the island in early 2004. The demand for local construction and transport generated by this project and other regional development programmes was expected to benefit the economy. In March 2002 the Maldives and the ADB signed a partnership agreement to reduce poverty. Some of the aims were to reduce absolute poverty from 43% in 1998 to 25% by 2015 and to promote involvement of local communities in public sector decision-making. Two other key issues that require prompt attention are: the protection of the fragile environment to ensure sustainable economic growth; and an improvement in Maldivian teaching standards in order to upgrade the national skills base.

Mali

The Republic of Mali is situated in West Africa. Mali, the former French colony of Soudan, became an independent state in 1960, following the secession of Senegal from the Federation of Mali, founded in 1959. In 1968 President Modibo Keita was overthrown in a military coup. Lt Moussa Traoré became Head of State. In 1991 Gen. Amadou Toumani Touré assumed power, leading a provisional Government. A multi-party system was introduced, and Alpha Oumar Konaré was elected President in 1992 and 1997. Touré was elected President, as a civilian, in 2002. Bamako is the capital. The official language is French.

Area and population
Area: 1,240,192 sq km
Population (mid-2002): 11,346,250
Population density (mid-2002): 9.1 per sq km
Life expectancy (years at birth, 2002): 44.8 (males 43.9; females 45.7)

Finance
GDP in current prices: 2002): US $3,163m. ($279 per head)
Real GDP growth (2002): 9.6%
Inflation (annual average, 2002): 5.0%
Currency: CFA franc

Economy

In 2002, according to estimates by the World Bank, Mali's gross national income (GNI), measured at average 2000–02 prices, was US $2,770m., equivalent to $240 per head (or $840 on an international purchasing-power parity basis). During 1990–2002, it was estimated, the population increased at an average annual rate of 2.5%, while gross domestic product (GDP) per head increased, in real terms, by an average of 1.8% per year. Overall GDP increased, in real terms, at an average annual rate of 4.3% in 1990–2002. Real GDP increased by 1.5% in 2001 and by 9.6% in 2002, according to the World Bank, largely as a result of a significant increase in the cotton crop. However, the IMF estimated real GDP growth in 2001 and 2002 at 13.3% and 4.4%, respectively, based on a revised methodology of compiling national accounts.

AGRICULTURE

Agriculture (including livestock-rearing, forestry and fishing) contributed 37.1% of GDP in 2002. An estimated 79.9% of the labour force were employed in the sector in that year. Mali is among Africa's foremost producers and exporters of cotton (exports of which contributed an estimated 22.4% of the value of merchandise exports in 2002). Cotton production increased significantly in 2001/02, to a record 570,900 metric tons, reflecting a marked expansion in the area of land cultivated for the crop in that year; output declined to 439,700 tons in 2002/03. Shea-nuts (karité nuts), groundnuts, vegetables and mangoes are also cultivated for export. The principal subsistence crops are millet, sorghum, fonio, rice and maize. Cereal imports remain necessary in most years, although a crop of 2,300m. tons was forecast for 2002/03, some 22% more than in the previous year. The livestock-rearing and fishing sectors make an important contribution to the domestic food supply and (in the case of the former) to export revenue, although both are highly vulnerable to drought. According to the World Bank, agricultural GDP increased by an average of 3.2% per year in 1990–2002, declining by 13.0% in 2001, but increasing by 19.5% in 2002. According to the IMF, however, agricultural GDP increased by 31.7% in 2001, but declined by an estimated 4.4% in 2002. (Figures for the agricultural sector were particularly affected by the revised methodology for calculating national accounts, principally owing to a change in the timing of recording agricultural output: for example, crops produced and marketed in the 2001/02 season would now be recorded in the data for 2001.)

INDUSTRY

Industry (including mining, manufacturing, construction and power) contributed 26.4% of GDP in 2002. According to the World Bank, industrial GDP increased at an average annual rate of 8.8% in 1990–2001. Industrial GDP increased by 26.1% in 2001 and by 20.0% in 2002, according to the IMF.

Mining

Mining contributed 11.7% of GDP in 2002. The importance of the sector has increased with the successful exploitation of the country's gold reserves: exports of gold contributed 65.2% of the value of total exports in 2002. Output of gold has increased significantly since the mid-1990s, as new mining facilities have commenced operations, and by 2002 exports of gold had increased to 66.1 metric tons, yielding 111,600m. francs CFA, compared with 6.6 tons (39,800m. francs CFA) in 1996. In 2001 Mali became the third largest gold producer in Africa, and further increases in production were anticipated. Salt, diamonds, marble and phosphate rock are also mined. The future exploitation of deposits of iron ore and uranium is envisaged. According to the IMF, the GDP of the mining sector increased at an average annual rate of 46.8% in 1996–2002; growth in mining GDP reached 181.3% in 1997, before slowing to an estimated 23.1% by 2002.

Manufacturing

The manufacturing sector, including electricity and water, contributed 7.5% of GDP in 2002. The main areas of activity are agro-industrial (chiefly the processing of cotton, sugar and rice). Brewing and tobacco industries are represented, and some construction materials are produced for the domestic market. According to the World Bank, manufacturing GDP increased at an average annual rate of 2.7% in 1990–2001. Manufacturing GDP declined by 14.1% in 2001, according to the IMF, but increased by an estimated 25.6% in 2002.

Energy

Of total electric energy generated in 1995, about 80% was derived from hydroelectric installations. Mali began to receive power supplies from the Manantali hydroelectric project (constructed and operated under the auspices of the Organisation pour la mise en valeur du fleuve Sénégal—OMVS) from December 2001, and there were also plans to link the Malian network with those of Côte d'Ivoire, Burkina Faso and Ghana. An agreement on energy supply was also reached with Algeria in February 1998. In July 2000 Belgium provided a loan of 2,600m. francs CFA for the construction of two high-voltage power stations in Bamako. Imports of petroleum products comprised 17.5% of the value of merchandise imports in 2002.

SERVICES

The services sector contributed 36.5% of GDP in 2002. In preparation for the African Nations Cup football tournament, which Mali hosted in early 2002, the Government began to implement a social development programme, 'Mali 2002', which was also intended to develop the tourism industry. Under the programme, the construction of two new international airports was envisaged, as well as other infrastructural improvements. According to the World Bank, the GDP of the services sector increased at an average annual rate of 2.9% in 1990–2001. Services GDP increased by 5.7% in 2001 and by an estimated 1.1% in 2002, according to the IMF.

EXTERNAL TRADE

In 2002 Mali recorded a visible trade surplus of an estimated 133,100m. francs CFA, while there was a deficit of 99,700m. francs CFA on the current account of the balance of payments. In 2002 the principal sources of imports were Côte d'Ivoire and France (which supplied, respectively, 17.0% and 13.5% of total imports). The largest market for exports were Thailand (which accounted for 14.7% of total exports), India (8.1%) and Germany (5.3%). The principal exports in 2002 were gold and cotton, together comprising 87.6% of total exports. The principal imports in that year were machines and vehicles, chemical products, petroleum products, foodstuffs and construction materials.

GOVERNMENT FINANCE

In 2002, according to IMF estimates, Mali recorded an overall budget deficit of 85,200m. francs CFA, equivalent to 3.6% of GDP. Mali's total external debt was US $2,890m. at the end of 2001, of which $2,616m. was long-term public debt. In that year the cost of debt-servicing was equivalent to 8.8% of the value of exports of goods and services. The annual rate of inflation averaged 4.0% in 1990–2002. Consumer prices increased by 5.1% in 2002.

INTERNATIONAL ECONOMIC RELATIONS

Mali is a member of numerous international and regional organizations, including the Economic Community of West African States (ECOWAS), the West African organs of the Franc Zone, the African Groundnut Council, the Liptako-Gourma Integrated Development Authority, the Niger Basin Authority and the OMVS.

SURVEY AND PROSPECTS

Mali's economic development is hindered by its vulnerability to drought, its dependence on imports and its narrow range of exports. The country also lacks facilities for the processing of its important cotton crop; it was reported in 2002 that only 1% of Mali's cotton crop was processed in the country.

In August 1999 the IMF approved a loan for Mali under the Enhanced Structural Adjustment Facility (ESAF), equivalent to about US $633m., in support of the Government's programme of economic reform for 1999–2002. (The facility was subsequently extended for a further year.) Mali's external debt remains at a high level, despite a rescheduling of commitments along concessionary lines by official creditors in 1996, the granting of some $870m. in debt-service relief under the initiative of the IMF and the World Bank for heavily indebted poor countries (HIPCs) in 2000, and the cancellation by France, in September 2002, of €80m. of bilateral debt; in March 2003 the Bretton Woods institutions announced that Mali had reached completion point under the terms of the HIPC initiative, thus becoming eligible for additional debt-relief. Mali's strong economic performance in 2001–02 was largely attributable to favourable climatic conditions, resulting in large cotton and cereal crops, and an increase in gold production. GDP growth was forecast to slow to 3.2% in 2003, largely owing to the effects of the political crisis in Côte d'Ivoire (through which more than 70% of Mali's external trade, excluding gold, was previously shipped, and where some 800,000 Malians reside), although agricultural output in Mali was projected to increase by around 11% as a result of good rainfall.

The Government of Prime Minister Ahmed Mohamed Ag Hamani, appointed in October 2002, announced its commitment to the IMF-supported programme of reforms, and to a Poverty Reduction Strategy Paper agreed by the previous administration and the Fund in May 2002. The Government announced various infrastructural projects, including proposals to improve access to water and electricity supplies in rural areas, and the construction of a highway to link Kita, west of Bamako, with Saraya in eastern Senegal. The Government also pursued a programme of privatization, notably transferring the railway from Bamako to Dakar, Senegal, to private management in 2003. In addition, the cotton sector was undergoing restructuring and a partial transfer to private ownership, having been adversely affected by a decline in international prices during the late 1990s, and the transfer of the state oilseed-processing plant to private ownership was scheduled to take place in 2004. None the less, in the absence of a more diversified economic base, Mali's economy remained vulnerable both to external shocks and to fluctuations in the terms of trade of its principal import and export commodities.

Malta

The Republic of Malta is in southern Europe. The country comprises an archipelago
in the central Mediterranean Sea. Malta, which had been a Crown Colony of the
United Kingdom since 1814, became an independent sovereign state, within the
Commonwealth, in 1964. Malta became a republic in 1974. The electoral victory of the
Partit Nazzjonalista in 1987 ended the 16-year tenure in office of the Malta Labour
Party. Malta acceded to the European Union on 1 May 2004. Valletta is the capital.
Maltese and English are the official languages.

Area and population
Area: 316 sq km
Population (mid-2002): 397,000
Population density (mid-2002): 1,256.3 per sq km
Life expectancy (years at birth, 2002): 78.1 (males 75.9; females 80.3)

Finance
GDP in current prices: 2001): US $3,614m. ($9,150 per head)
Real GDP growth (2001): −0.7%
Inflation (annual average, 2002): 2.2%
Currency: Maltese lira

Economy

In 2001, according to estimates by the World Bank, Malta's gross national income (GNI), measured at average 1999–2001 prices, was US $3,632m., equivalent to $9,200 per head (or $16,790 per head on an international purchasing-power parity basis). During 1990–2002, it was estimated, the population increased at an average annual rate of 0.8%, while during 1990–2001 gross domestic product (GDP) per head increased, in real terms, at an average annual rate of 3.5%. Overall GDP increased, in real terms, at an average annual rate of 4.4% in 1990–2001; GDP declined by 0.7% in 2001.

AGRICULTURE

Agriculture (including hunting, forestry and fishing) contributed an estimated 2.8% of GDP in 2002. Some 1.9% of the working population were employed in the sector in 2003. The principal export crop is potatoes. Tomatoes and other vegetables, cereals (principally wheat and barley) and fruit are also cultivated. Livestock and livestock products are also important, and efforts are being made to develop the fishing industry. Exports of food and live animals accounted for 6.9% of total exports in 2000. According to FAO figures, Malta's agricultural production increased at an average rate of 1.7% per year in 1990–2002. Output rose by 2.7% in 2001, but declined by 4.4% in 2002.

INDUSTRY

Industry (including mining, manufacturing and construction) provided an estimated 26.3% of GDP in 2002, and engaged 29.8% of the employed labour force in 2003. Industrial production (including electricity and water, but excluding construction) increased at an average rate of 12.2% per year in 1990–96. It rose by 11.0% in 1995, but declined by 4.7% in 1996.

Mining

Mining and quarrying, together with construction, contributed 3.4% of GDP in 2002, and engaged 7.8% of the employed labour force in 2003 (mining and quarrying alone engaged just 0.7% of the employed labour force). The mining sector's output expanded at an average annual rate of 18.3% in 1990–96. Production rose by 26.6% in 1995 and by 11.0% in 1996. The principal activities are stone and sand quarrying. There are reserves of petroleum in Maltese offshore waters, and petroleum and gas exploration is proceeding.

Manufacturing

Manufacturing (excluding government enterprises) contributed an estimated 22.9% of GDP in 2002. Some 19.2% of the working population were employed in the manufacturing sector in 2003. Based on the gross value of output, the principal branches of manufacturing, excluding ship-repairing, in 1999 were transport equipment and machinery (accounting for 54.7% of the total), food products and beverages (12.4%) and textiles, footwear and clothing (8.4%). Manufacturing production increased at an average rate of 7.6% per year in 1990–96. It advanced by 8.1% in 1995, but declined by 6.2% in 1996.

Energy

Energy is derived principally from imports of crude petroleum (the majority of which is purchased, at preferential rates, from Libya) and coal. Imports of mineral fuels comprised 8.2% of the value of total imports in 2001.

SERVICES

Services (including public utilities and other government enterprises) provided 70.9% of GDP in 2002, and engaged 68.3% of the employed labour force in 2003. Tourism is a major source of foreign exchange earnings. In 2003 Malta received 1,126,601 foreign visitors, and revenue from the sector reached LM 260.7m. in 2001. In 2003 some 8.7% of the employed labour force were engaged in hotels and catering establishments.

EXTERNAL TRADE

In 2002 Malta recorded a visible trade deficit of US $424.5m., and there was a deficit of $83.9m. on the current account of the balance of payments. More than two-thirds of Malta's trade is with the countries of the European Union (EU). In 2001 the principal source of imports (accounting for 19.9% of the total) was Italy (including San Marino); other major suppliers were France (15.0%), the USA (11.6%) and the United Kingdom (10.0%). The USA was the principal market for exports (taking 19.8% of the total); other significant purchasers of exports were Germany (13.1%), Singapore (11.8%) and France (9.3%). The principal domestic exports in 2003 were machinery and transport equipment, accounting for 67.2% of the total, and miscellaneous manufactured articles (20.8%). The principal imports were machinery and transport equipment, accounting for 48.4%, basic manufactures (11.4%), and miscellaneous manufactured articles (11.2%).

GOVERNMENT FINANCE

In 2002 Malta recorded a budgetary deficit of LM 48.3m. (equivalent to 2.9% of GDP in that year). At the end of 1997 Malta's external debt totalled US $1,034m., of which $125m. was long-term public debt. In that year the cost of debt-servicing was equivalent to 2.1% of the value of exports of goods and services. The annual rate of inflation averaged 2.9% in 1990–2001; consumer prices increased by 2.4% in 2000 and by 2.9% in 2001. In 2003 8.2% of the labour force were unemployed.

INTERNATIONAL ECONOMIC RELATIONS

Malta is a member of the World Trade Organization (WTO) and of the European Bank for Reconstruction and Development (EBRD).

SURVEY AND PROSPECTS

Malta signed an association agreement with the European Community (EC, now EU) in 1970, allowing favourable trading conditions for Malta, together with economic assistance from that organization. In July 1990 Malta formally applied for full membership of the EC, and in June 1993 the European Commission confirmed Malta's eligibility for eventual accession to the EU. However, following the transfer of power to the Malta Labour Party in October 1996, the new Government announced that EU membership would not be sought, although it was proposed eventually to replace the 1970 association agreement with the formation of a 'free-trade zone' affording Malta certain commercial and social links with the EU. On resuming office in September 1998, the Nationalist Party resumed negotiations for full membership of the EU. Accession talks formally ended on 13 December 2002 and in a non-binding referendum on 8 March 2003 53.6% voted in favour of membership of the EU compared with 46.3% against. The decision to proceed with accession to the EU was confirmed by the victory of the Nationalist Party (Partit Nazzjonalista) in a general election on the 12 April. On 16 April Malta signed the EU accession treaty in Athens, Greece, with nine other applicant countries, all of whom joined the EU on 1 May 2004.

Following the closure, in 1979, of the British military base and naval docks, on which Malta's economy had been largely dependent, successive governments have pursued a policy of restructuring and diversification. The domestic market is limited, owing to the small population. There are few natural resources, and almost all raw materials have to be imported. Malta's development has therefore been based on the promotion of the island as an international financial centre and on manufacturing for export (notably in non-traditional fields, such as electronics, information technology and pharmaceuticals), together with the continuing development of tourism.

Following its accession to power in 1998 the Nationalist Government attempted to address the budget deficit. A budget reduction programme, which included limits on public-sector expenditure (particularly wage increases), a privatization programme and more stringent efforts to combat the country's high level of tax evasion and the large 'parallel' economy, aimed to reduce the deficit to 3% of GDP by 2004. It was also hoped that privatization would increase investment in Malta's inadequate infrastructure. Malta's small-scale, open economy was particularly affected by the terrorist attacks on the USA in September 2001, the SARS (severe acute respiratory syndrome) health scare and the US-led military action in Iraq in early 2003, all of which adversely affected Malta's important tourism industry.

In late 2003, with accession to the EU imminent, structural reforms were also making their mark on the Maltese economy. During 2003 employment in manufacturing fell by some 1,150 jobs, although this was offset by a rise in employment in the service sector. In other respects, Malta faced the same challenges as the other EU member states whose ranks it joined on 1 May 2004: restraining government expenditure, modernizing the welfare state, removing labour market inflexibilities, boosting international competitiveness, and generating stronger economic growth. Likewise, pensions reform was a priority: expenditure on old-age pensions was expected to more than double during 2004–24, to about 11% of GDP, according to the IMF. Moreover, in line with present trends, the number of workers supporting one pensioner was forecast to decrease from four to two over the same period.

Marshall Islands

The Republic of the Marshall Islands lies within the area of the Pacific Ocean known as Micronesia. In 1947 the UN authorized the USA to administer the Islands within a Trust Territory of the Pacific Islands. Between 1946 and 1958 two remote atolls, Bikini and Enewetak, were extensively used in nuclear testing. The US military continues to test strategic missile systems on Kwajalein atoll. The 1986 Compact of Free Association between the Marshall Islands and the USA was renewed in May 2003. The capital is the Dalap-Uliga-Darrit Municipality. The indigenous population comprises various ethno-linguistic groups, but English is widely understood.

Area and population
Area: 181 sq km
Population (mid-2002): 53,200
Population density (mid-2002): 293.3 per sq km
Life expectancy (years at birth, 2002): 62.7 (males 61.1; females 64.6)

Finance
GDP in current prices: 2002): US $108m. ($2,026 per head)
Real GDP growth (2002): 4.0%
Inflation (2000): 1.6%
Currency: US dollar

Economy

In 2001, according to estimates by the World Bank, the Marshall Islands' gross national income (GNI), measured at average 1999–2001 prices, was US $115m., equivalent to $2,190 per head. During 1990–2001, it was estimated, the population increased at an average annual rate of 2.0%, while gross domestic product (GDP) declined, in real terms, at an average rate of 1.5% per year. According to the Asian Development Bank (ADB), GDP decreased by 3.1% in 2000, but increased by 1.6% in 2001 and by 3.8% in 2002.

AGRICULTURE

Agriculture is mainly on a subsistence level. The sector (including fishing and livestock-rearing) contributed an estimated 13.7% of GDP in 1999/2000. According to FAO, the sector engaged 6,000 people in 2001. The principal crops are coconuts, cassava and sweet potatoes. In 2000 some 2,706 short tons of copra were produced (a decrease of 19.2% compared with the previous year), and in that year exports of coconut oil and copra accounted for 31.0% of the total value of exports. Copra production suffered a severe decline in the late 1990s, following sustained low prices, an ageing tree stock and a reduction in the number of government-owned vessels used for transport purposes. The fishing sector incorporates a commercial tuna-fishing industry, including a tuna-canning factory and transhipment base on Majuro. The cultivation of seaweed was developed extensively in 1992, and in 1994 a project to cultivate blacklip pearl oysters on Arno Atoll was undertaken with US funding. The sale of fishing licences is an important source of revenue and earned the islands an estimated US $3m. in 2000/01. The Marshall Islands expected to receive annual revenues of some $21m. following the renewal of a treaty between the USA and the Forum Fisheries Agency (FFA) group of Pacific island nations in 2003. In 2001 the Japanese Government funded the construction of a commercial fishing base at Jaluit Atoll. According to initial estimates by the ADB, compared with the previous year the GDP of the agricultural sector declined by 13.9% in 1998, but increased by 1.7% in 1999 and by 3.7% in 2000.

INDUSTRY

Industrial activities (including mining, manufacturing, construction and power) contributed an estimated 15.1% of GDP in 1999/2000, and engaged 9.4% of the employed labour force in 1988. Between 1990 and 1999 industrial GDP declined at an average annual rate of 1.5%. According to provisional estimates by the ADB, compared with the previous year the GDP of the industrial sector rose by 1.3% in 1999 and by 3.7% in 2000. The islands have few mineral resources, although there are high-grade phosphate deposits on Ailinglaplap Atoll.

Manufacturing

Manufacturing activity, which provided 1.8% of GDP in 1999/2000, consists mainly of the processing of coconuts (to produce copra and coconut oil) and other agricultural products and of fish. According to the ADB, the manufacturing sector engaged a total of 800 workers in 2000.

SERVICES

The services sector provided an estimated 71.3% of GDP in 1999/2000. The international shipping registry experienced considerable expansion following the political troubles in Panama in 1989, and continued to expand in the mid-1990s (largely as a result of US ships' reflagging in the islands). The shipping industry also benefited from the construction of a floating dry-dock on Majuro in 1995. Tourist receipts reached US $4m. in 1999. The number of tourist arrivals rose from 5,246 in 2000 to 5,399 in 2001. According to initial estimates by the ADB, compared with the previous year the GDP of the services sector expanded by only 0.2% in 1998, before contracting by 0.5% in 1999 and by 0.8% in 2000.

EXTERNAL TRADE

In the financial year ending 30 September 2001 the Marshall Islands recorded an estimated trade deficit of US $52.2m., but a surplus of $14.4m. on the current account of the balance of payments. The only significant domestic exports in 2000 were coconut products and fish. The principal imports included mineral fuels and lubricants (which accounted for 43.6% of total expenditure on merchandise imports), food and live animals, and machinery and transport equipment. In that year the principal sources of imports were the USA (which provided 61.4% of total imports) and Japan (5.1%). The USA was also the principal export destination, receiving 71.2% of total exports.

GOVERNMENT FINANCE

A budgetary surplus equivalent to 9.1% of GDP was forecast for 2001/02. Financial assistance from the USA, in accordance with the terms stipulated in the Compact of Free Association, contributes a large part of the islands' revenue. Aided by an increase in this support, estimates for 2001/02 envisaged a rise in budgetary expenditure to US $74m. (compared with $66m. in the previous year). Recurrent expenditure was projected to increase from $55m. in 2000/01 to $59m. in 2001/02. The islands' external debt was estimated at $67.0m. in 2000/01. In that year the cost of debt-servicing (including repayments) was equivalent to 168.7% of the value of exports of goods and services. The Marshall Islands received $551 of aid per caput in 2003. In 2000/01 budgeted aid from the USA amounted to $20.7m. (35% of which was to be provided under the Compact agreement). The US aid budget for 2002 included a grant of $2.5m. to the Marshall Islands for an extension of the Military Use and Operating Rights Agreement (in addition to its mandatory annual payments of support for Enewetak Atoll and the Compact of Free Association). Aid is also provided by Japan and Taiwan. According to the ADB, annual inflation in Majuro averaged 5.7% in 1990–99. Consumer prices were estimated to have increased by an annual average of 1.6% in 2000 and by an estimated 0.8% in both 2001 and 2002. The unemployment rate stood at 30.0% of the economically active population in 2000.

INTERNATIONAL ECONOMIC RELATIONS

The Marshall Islands is a member of the Pacific Community, the Pacific Islands Forum, the South Pacific Regional Trade and Economic Co-operation Agreement (SPARTECA), the UN Economic and Social Commission for Asia and the Pacific (ESCAP) and the Asian Development Bank (ADB). In early 1996 the Marshall Islands and other countries and territories of Micronesia established the Council of Micronesian Government Executives. The new body aimed to facilitate discussion of economic developments in the region, and to examine possibilities for reducing the considerable cost of shipping essential goods between the islands.

SURVEY AND PROSPECTS

The introduction, from the mid-1990s, of retrenchment measures in the public sector was welcomed by several international financial organizations and supported by the ADB. However, it was subsequently observed that reform of the public sector, which until the recession of the mid-1990s had employed up to one-half of the economically-active population, had been accompanied by a decline in employment in the private sector, leading to a very high rate of unemployment (according to US assessments, the highest of any US-affiliated state in the Pacific) and emigration.

In 1999 the Kabua Government reduced import duties by more than 50% on many items, in an attempt to revitalize the local economy. Reforms to promote the private sector were also announced. During the 1990s the Marshall Islands sought to diversify its international economic relations. The Marshall Islands has since 1998 notably benefited from numerous economic agreements with Taiwan, worth an estimated US $20m., which have financed many projects including the construction of roads, the acquisition of boats, and the development of the agricultural sector. However, concern was expressed by the ADB in 1999 that reliance on external aid was hampering economic reform in the Marshall Islands (in 2000 bilateral and multilateral aid to the Marshall Islands totalled $57.2m.) In June 2001 the ADB approved a programme of low-interest loans totalling $12m., urging the Government to use it to improve budgeting and accounting practices. In December 2002 the ADB approved a further total of $7.25m. in loans and grants in order to improve the country's infrastructure. Nevertheless, it was considered that reforms of the public sector in the mid-1990s, combined with low world prices for Marshallese products, had contributed directly to the islands' economic decline.

The lack of internationally marketable natural resources and the remote location of the islands also present major difficulties for the Marshall Islands Government in its efforts to revitalize and expand the economy. Attempts to overcome these obstacles, including the introduction of passport sales and efforts to promote gambling and 'offshore' financial services have generated political controversy, both domestically and internationally. None the less, in October 2002 the Marshall Islands was removed from the Financial Action Task Force (FATF) list of Non Co-operative Countries and Territories following the successful implementation of a series of regulatory measures. The Government has also been able to obtain a further source of income by expanding ship registrations, to the effect that in 2002 the Marshallese merchant fleet was reportedly the sixth largest in the world. A notable feature of the amended Compact of Free Association, which was signed by the Governments of the Marshall Islands and the USA in May 2003, was the planned gradual decrement in grant assistance over the 20-year period of the renewed Compact. It was intended that this would represent less of a strain on the Marshall Islands' economy than had the five-yearly reductions in funding implemented under the original Compact, in compensation for which the Marshall Islands had implemented a number of projects such as the controversial sale of passports. The new terms also provided for the establishment of a trust fund, revenue from which would supersede US direct assistance from 2003.

Martinique

Martinique is one of the Windward Islands in the West Indies. It has been a French possession since 1635, and in 1946 became a Department of France. In 1974 Martinique was granted regional status. An indirectly elected Conseil Régional was created, with some control over the local economy. In 1982 and 1983 the French Government granted local councils greater control over taxation, policing and the economy. Direct elections to the Conseil Régional were held in 1983. In 2001 the French Government approved proposals on greater autonomy presented to it by the Conseil Général and the Conseil Régional. The capital is Fort-de-France. French is the official language.

Area and population
Area: 1,100 sq km
Population (March 1999): 381,427
Population density (March 1999): 346.8 per sq km
Life expectancy (years at birth, 1997):   males 75.2; females 81.7

Finance
GDP in current prices: 1999): US $4,566m. ($11,979 per head)
Real GDP growth (1999): 0.6%
Inflation (annual average, 2002): 2.2%
Currency: euro

Economy

In 2001 Martinique's gross domestic product (GDP), measured at current prices, was estimated at US $4,161m., equivalent to $10,723 per head. During 1990–2001, according to UN estimates, GDP increased, in real terms, at an average rate of 1.5% per year; growth in 2001 was 2.1%. Between the censuses of 1990 and 1999, according to provisional figures, the population increased at an average annual rate of 0.7%.

AGRICULTURE

Agriculture, hunting, forestry and fishing contributed an estimated 5% of GDP in 1998, and according to FAO figures, engaged an estimated 3.7% of the labour force in mid-2001. The principal cash crops are bananas (which accounted for some 36.6% of export earnings in 1997), sugar cane (primarily for the production of rum), limes, melons and pineapples. The cultivation of cut flowers is also of some significance. Roots and tubers and vegetables are grown for local consumption. Agricultural production increased at an average rate of 1.3% per year during 1990–98. It increased by 6.7% in 1997, but declined by 0.2% in 1999.

INDUSTRY

The industrial sector (including construction and public works) contributed an estimated 15% of GDP in 1998, and engaged 10.6% of the total labour force in the same year. Mining, manufacturing and power provided some 10% of GDP in 1998.

Manufacturing

The most important manufacturing activities are petroleum refining (exports of refined petroleum products accounted for some 16.0% of the value of total exports in 1997) and the processing of agricultural products—the production of rum being of particular significance. Exports of rum provided some 10.0% of export earnings in 1997. Martiniquais rum was accorded the designation of Appellation d'origine contrôlée (AOC) in 1996 (the first AOC to be designated outside metropolitan France). Other areas of activity include metals, cement, chemicals, plastics, wood, printing and textiles.

Energy

Energy is derived principally from mineral fuels. Imports of mineral fuels (including crude petroleum destined for the island's refinery) accounted for 7.5% of the value of total imports in 1995.

SERVICES

The services sector engaged 55.2% of the total labour force in 1998 and provided an estimated 80% of GDP in the same year. Tourism is a major activity on the island and one of the most important sources of foreign exchange. In 2001 506,104 tourists visited the island. In 2001 earnings from the tourism industry totalled an estimated €226.6m.

EXTERNAL TRADE

In 2000 Martinique recorded a trade deficit of 9,495.5m. French francs. In 2000 the principal source of imports (63.5%) was metropolitan France, which was also the principal market for exports (57.8%). Guadeloupe, Germany, Venezuela and

Belgium-Luxembourg were also significant trading partners. The principal exports in 1997 were bananas, refined petroleum products, rum, flavoured or sweetened water and boats. The principal imports in 1995 were machinery and transport equipment (especially road vehicles), food and live animals, miscellaneous manufactured articles, basic manufactures, chemicals and mineral fuels.

GOVERNMENT FINANCE

In 2001 the departmental budget was expected to balance. The annual rate of inflation averaged 2.0% in 1990–2002; consumer prices increased by 2.1% in 2001 and by 2.2% in 2002. Some 26.3% of the labour force were unemployed in 2002. In 1990 the level of emigration from the island was estimated at about 15,000 per year; most of the emigrants were under 25 years of age.

INTERNATIONAL ECONOMIC RELATIONS

As an integral part of France, Martinique belongs to the European Union (EU).

SURVEY AND PROSPECTS

Martinique's economic development has created a society that combines a relatively high standard of living with a weak economic base in agricultural and industrial production, as well as a chronic trade deficit. Levels of unemployment and emigration are high (in 1990 some 30% of Martiniquais nationals were resident in France), although the rate of growth of both these factors has slowed since the mid-1980s. The linking of wage levels to those of metropolitan France, despite the island's lower level of productivity, has increased labour costs and restricted development. In the late 1990s the value of banana exports declined owing to a significant fall in prices on the European market, while an ongoing dispute between the USA and four Latin American countries and the EU over the latter's banana import regime also threatened Martinique's banana-growing sector. This dispute was resolved in April 2001 when it was agreed that the quota system currently employed by the EU was to be replaced by a universal tariff system from 2006. Moreover, a succession of industrial disputes severely disrupted economic activity in 1999.

In November 2002 the French hotel group Accor announced that it would close its five hotels in Martinque and Guadeloupe, citing high operating costs, poor industrial relations and decreasing tourist arrivals. In early 2003 the French Minister of Overseas Departments announced plans to stimulate the economies of Martinique, Guadeloupe and French Guiana that included the introduction of tax incentives for the hotel sector. Furthermore, in late 2003 it was announced that a subsidiary of Air Caraïbe was to begin an additional air service between Paris and Fort-de-France.

Mauritania

The Islamic Republic of Mauritania lies in north-west Africa. Mauritania achieved independence from France in 1960. Moktar Ould Daddah was elected President in 1961. Ould Daddah was deposed in 1978, and a Military Committee for National Recovery (MCNR) established. The Military Committee for National Salvation, which succeeded the MCNR, renounced Mauritania's territorial claims in Western Sahara. A Constitution adopted in 1991 provided for multi-party politics. In 1992 Col Maawiya Ould Sid'Ahmed Taya, who had assumed the presidency in 1984, was elected to office. President Taya was re-elected in 1997 and 2003. Nouakchott is the capital. Arabic is the official language.

Area and population
Area: 1,030,700 sq km
Population (mid-2002): 2,828,010
Population density (mid-2002): 2.7 per sq km
Life expectancy (years at birth, 2002): 52.1 (males 49.8; females 54.5)

Finance
GDP in current prices: 2002): US $983m. ($348 per head)
Real GDP growth (2002): 5.1%
Inflation (annual average, 2002): 3.8%
Currency: ouguiya

Economy

In 2002, according to estimates by the World Bank, Mauritania's gross national income (GNI), measured at average 2000–02 prices, was US $1,163m., equivalent to $410 per head (or $1,740 on an international purchasing-power parity basis). During 1990–2002, it was estimated, the population increased at an average annual rate of 3.0%, while gross domestic product (GDP) per head increased, in real terms, by an average of 1.2% per year. According to the World Bank, overall GDP increased, in real terms, at an average annual rate of 4.2% in 1990–2002; GDP increased by 4.6% in 2001 and by 5.1% in 2002. (According to IMF figures, GDP growth in 2001 and 2002 was 4.0% and 3.3%, respectively.)

AGRICULTURE
Agriculture (including forestry and fishing) contributed 20.8% of GDP in 2002. In that year about 52.4% of the labour force were employed in the sector. Owing to the unsuitability of much of the land for crop cultivation, output of staple foods (millet, sorghum, rice and pulses) is insufficient for the country's needs. Livestock-rearing is the principal occupation of the rural population. Fishing, which in 2002 provided 43.4% of export earnings, supplies 5%–10% of annual GDP and up to 30% of budgetary revenue, and also makes a significant contribution to domestic food requirements. During 1990–2002, according to the World Bank, agricultural GDP increased by an average of 4.4% per year. Agricultural GDP declined by 0.2% in 2001, but increased by 2.0% in 2002.

INDUSTRY
Industry (including mining, manufacturing, construction and power) provided 29.4% of GDP in 2002. An estimated 11.6% of the labour force were employed in the industrial sector in 1994. During 1990–2002, according to the World Bank, industrial GDP increased at an average annual rate of 2.6%. Industrial GDP increased by 1.4% in 2001 and by 4.8% in 2002.

Mining
Mining contributed 12.2% of GDP in 2002. The principal activity in this sector is the extraction of iron ore, exports of which contributed 55.6% of total merchandise export earnings in 2002. Gypsum, salt, gold and copper are also mined. Other exploitable mineral resources include diamonds, phosphates, sulphur, peat, manganese and uranium. In October 1999 highly valuable blue granite deposits were discovered in the north of the country. Many international companies were involved in offshore petroleum exploration in Mauritania in the early 2000s, with reserves at the offshore Shafr el Khanjar and Chinguetti fields estimated at 450m.–1,000m. barrels; production was expected to commence in 2006. In September 2000 a five-year programme

intended to accelerate the growth of the mining sector commenced, with a US $16.5m. loan from the World Bank. The GDP of the mining sector declined by an average of 4.3% per year in 1998–2002, according to the IMF. Mining GDP declined by 9.2% in 2001 and by 7.3% in 2002.

Manufacturing

The manufacturing sector contributed 8.9% of GDP in 2002. Fish-processing (which contributed 3.9% of GDP in 2002) is the most important activity. The processing of minerals (including imported petroleum) is also of some significance. According to the World Bank, manufacturing GDP increased at an average annual rate of 1.6% in 1990–2002; it increased by 5.9% in 2001 and by 1.3% in 2002.

Energy

Mauritania began to utilize electricity generated at hydroelectric installations constructed under the austpices of the Organisation pour la mise en valeur du fleuve Sénégal (OMVS) in late 2002, thus reducing the country's dependence on power generated at thermal stations. Imports of petroleum products comprised 8.8% of the value of merchandise imports in 2001.

SERVICES

The services sector contributed 49.9% of GDP in 2002, and engaged an estimated 25.8% of the labour force in 1994. According to the World Bank, the combined GDP of the services sector increased by an average rate of 5.1% per year during 1990–2002. Services GDP increased by 8.5% in 2001 and by 7.0% in 2002.

EXTERNAL TRADE

In 2002 Mauritania recorded a visible trade deficit of an estimated US $87.7m. and a deficit of an estimated $51.2m. on the current account of the balance of payments. In 2002 the principal source of imports (20.8%) was France; other major suppliers were the Belgo-Luxembourg Economic Union, Spain and Germany. The principal markets for exports in that year were Italy (14.8%), France (14.4%), Spain and the Belgo-Luxembourg Economic Union. The principal exports in 2002 were iron ore and fish, crustaceans and molluscs. The principal imports in 2001 were capital goods, foodstuffs, vehicles and components, construction materials and petroleum products.

GOVERNMENT FINANCE

Mauritania's overall budget surplus for 2002 was UM 20,900m., equivalent to 7.8% of GDP. Mauritania's total external debt was US $2,164m. at the end of 2001, of which $1,865m. was long-term public debt. In that year the cost of debt-servicing was equivalent to 22.8% of the value of exports of goods and services. The annual rate of inflation averaged 5.7% in 1990–2002; consumer prices increased by an average of 4.7% in 2001 and by 3.9% in 2002. The overall rate of unemployment in 2000 was 28.9%

INTERNATIONAL ECONOMIC RELATIONS

Mauritania is a member of the Islamic Development Bank, of the OMVS and of the Union of the Arab Maghreb.

SURVEY AND PROSPECTS

Mauritania's economy is largely dependent on fishing and on the exploitation of iron ore, although the exploitation of petroleum reserves, principally at offshore locations, was expected to contribute significantly to GDP growth from the mid-2000s. Economic adjustment programmes have been undertaken since the late 1980s, including agreements with the IMF and the World Bank, resulting in the liberalization and restructuring of the economy. In July 1999 the IMF approved a three-year loan worth US $56.5m. under its Enhanced Structural Adjustment Facility (ESAF) to support the Government's 1999–2002 economic programme. In February 2000 Mauritania became one of the first countries to receive assistance under the joint IMF/World Bank initiative for heavily indebted poor countries, which would amount to a reduction of Mauritania's debt by $622m.; in June 2002 Mauritania became the sixth country to reach 'completion point' under the initiative. In July 2003 a further arrangement, worth some $8.8m., was agreed with the IMF for 2003–05, under the Poverty Reduction and Growth Facility (PRGF—the successor of the ESAF).

From the late 1980s government revenue has been bolstered by the sale of fishing licences to foreign fleets. In 2001 the European Union (EU) renewed its fishing agreement with Mauritania. In return for increased financial aid (of some €430m. during 2001–06), EU vessels were granted improved fishing rights in Mauritania's waters. In the early 2000s the services sector was a major source of economic growth, in particular in the areas of trade, transport and telecommunications, while considerable potential exists for the expansion of activities related to tourism. Significant improvements to the communications infrastructure, under way and planned in the mid-2000s, were expected to facilitate continued growth in the services sector; in particular, the construction of a new highway linking the two principal cities, Nouakchott and Nouadhibou, was expected to improve prospects for both tourism and external trade. Although a drought in late 2002, which resulted in a depleted cereals harvest and a lower than average fish catch, ensured that growth in that year, was lower than anticipated, economic indicators in the early 2000s were generally favourable. A substantial reorganization and simplification of the taxation system was implemented in 2003, and, following initial difficulties, the transfer to majority private ownership of the state electricity company was expected to be completed by mid-2004. Meanwhile, further economic progress remained largely dependent on the diversification of Mauritania's production base. GDP growth of 5.4% was projected for 2003.

Mauritius

The Republic of Mauritius lies in the Indian Ocean. Mauritius became independent, within the Commonwealth, in 1968. In 1992 the Republic of Mauritius was proclaimed. At the most recent general election, in 2000, an alliance of the Mouvement Socialiste Militant and the Mouvement Militant Mauricien won 54 of the 62 directly elective seats in the National Assembly. In 2002 Karl Offman was elected as President by an extraordinary session of the National Assembly, which was boycotted by opposition deputies. Although formally elected for five years, Offman relinquished office to Sir Anerood Jugnauth in October 2003. Port Louis is the capital. English is the official language.

Area and population
Area: 2,040 sq km
Population (mid-2002): 1,212,350
Population density (mid-2002): 594.3 per sq km
Life expectancy (years at birth, 2002): 71.9 (males 68.4; females 75.5)

Finance
GDP in current prices: 2002): US $4,532m. ($3,738 per head)
Real GDP growth (2002): 4.4%
Inflation (annual average, 2002): 6.7%
Currency: Mauritian rupee

Economy

In 2002, according to estimates by the World Bank, Mauritius' gross national income (GNI), measured at average 2000–02 prices, was US $4,669m., equivalent to $3,850 per head (or $10,530 per head on an international purchasing-power parity basis). During 1990–2002, it was estimated, the population increased at an average annual rate of 1.1%, while gross domestic product (GDP) per head increased, in real terms, by an average of 4.1% per year. Overall GDP increased, in real terms, at an average annual rate of 5.3% in 1990–2002; growth in 2002 was 4.4%.

AGRICULTURE

Agriculture (including hunting, forestry and fishing) contributed 5.9% of GDP in 2003, according to provisional estimates, and engaged 9.3% of the employed labour force in that year. The principal cash crops are sugar cane (sugar accounted for 19.8% of export earnings in 2003, according to provisional figures), tea and tobacco. Food crops include potatoes and vegetables. Poultry farming is also practised. During 1990–2002, according to the World Bank, the GDP of the agricultural sector increased, in real terms, at an average rate of 1.1% per year; growth in 2002 was 7.8%.

INDUSTRY

Industry (including mining, manufacturing, construction and utilities) contributed 28.5% of GDP in 2003, according to provisional estimates, and engaged 37.1% of the employed labour force in that year. During 1990–2002, according to the World Bank, industrial GDP increased, in real terms, at an average annual rate of 5.6%; growth in 2002 was 5.3%. Mining is negligible, accounting for only 0.3% of employment and 0.1% of GDP in 2003.

Manufacturing

Manufacturing contributed 20.3% of GDP in 2003, according to provisional estimates, and engaged 27.2% of the employed labour force in that year. The principal branches of manufacturing are textiles and clothing and food products, mainly sugar. Clothing (excluding footwear) provided 58.9% of export earnings in 2003. Factories in the Export Processing Zone (EPZ) process import raw materials to produce goods for the export market. Textile firms accounted for 88.4% of total EPZ employment in 1998 and 84.4% of EPZ exports (mainly in the form of clothing) in 1997. Other important products include fish preparations, watches and clocks, and precious stones. Export receipts from EPZ products represented almost 76.4% of total export earnings in 1999. During 1990–2002, according to the World Bank, the GDP of the manufacturing sector, increased, in real terms, at an average annual rate of 5.4%; growth in 2002 was 5.5%.

Energy

Electric energy is derived principally from thermal (oil-fired) and hydroelectric power stations. Bagasse (a by-product of sugar cane) is also used as fuel for generating electricity; in 1992 a programme was initiated to enable Mauritius eventually to derive 15% of its energy requirements from bagasse. Imports of refined petroleum products comprised 9.4% of the value of merchandise imports in 2003, according to provisional figures. Thermal energy accounted for 95.6% of electricity generated in 2002.

SERVICES

The services sector contributed 65.6% of GDP in 2003, according to provisional estimates, and engaged 53.5% of the employed labour force in that year. Tourism is the third most important source of revenue, after agriculture and manufacturing. The number of foreign tourist arrivals increased to 702,018 in 2003 from 422,000 in 1995. Receipts from tourism were estimated to total Rs 19,397m. in 2003. An 'offshore' banking sector and a stock exchange have operated since 1989. According to the World Bank, the real GDP of the services sector increased at an average annual rate of 6.3% in 1990–2001; growth in 2001 was 6.7%.

EXTERNAL TRADE

In 2002 Mauritius recorded a visible trade deficit of US $188.1m., and there was a surplus of $259.2m. on the current account of the balance of payments. In 2003 the principal source of imports (12.1%) was South Africa; other major suppliers were France (11.8%), India and the People's Republic of China. The principal market for exports (30.8%) was the United Kingdom; other significant purchasers were France and the USA. The principal exports in 2003 were clothing and sugar. The principal imports in that year were refined petroleum products and textile yarn and fabrics.

GOVERNMENT FINANCE

In 2001/02 there was an estimated budgetary deficit of Rs 8,144m. (equivalent to 5.9% of GDP). Mauritius' external debt totalled US $1,724m. at the end of 2001, of which $765m. was long-term public debt. In that year the cost of debt-servicing was equivalent to 6.9% of the value of exports of goods and services. The annual rate of inflation averaged 6.6% in 1990–2001. Consumer prices increased by an average of 4.2% in 2000 and 5.4% in 2001. About 9.9% of the labour force were unemployed in 2003.

INTERNATIONAL ECONOMIC RELATIONS

Mauritius is a member of the Common Market for Eastern and Southern Africa (COMESA), the Southern African Development Community (SADC) and the Indian Ocean Commission (IOC), which aims to promote regional economic co-operation. Mauritius was among the founder members of the Indian Ocean Rim Association for Regional Co-operation (IOR—ARC) in 1997.

SURVEY AND PROSPECTS

Mauritius' economy was traditionally dependent on sugar production, and economic growth was therefore vulnerable to adverse climatic conditions and changes in international prices for sugar. However, since the 1980s the Government has pursued a successful policy of diversification, encouraging labour-intensive manufacturing (particularly of clothing) in the EPZ, and extensive reforms have been implemented with IMF support. Port Louis has been established as a free port. Since the mid-1990s the Government has continued to promote further measures to achieve economic diversification and liberalization, aimed at encouraging foreign investment and increasing export revenue. The expansion of tourism has also been actively pro-moted. The geographical location of Mauritius, as well as a number of incentive measures implemented by the Government, has contributed to its successful estab-lishment as an international financial centre. By the late 1990s the island had become a significant provider of 'offshore' banking and investment services for a number of south Asian countries (particularly India), as well as for members of SADC and IOR—ARC groupings.

Since 1999 the Prime Minister has also promoted the country as a future hub of communications and information technology, as a means of encouraging the next stage of economic development and transferring the emphasis towards services. The construction of a free zone 'cybercity' was initiated, with an investment of US $110m. from India, and in 2000 a South Africa–Far East underwater fibre optic cable was laid, linking Port Louis to both regions. However, a number of issues remained of concern, including growing unemployment, high inflation, excessive public debt, inadequate labour-force skills and an ageing population. A record drought in 1998–2000 caused an estimated Rs 2,000m. of damage and reduced the sugar harvest by an estimated 40%. In August 2001 the Prime Minister announced a restructuring and centralization plan for the sugar industry, whereby 7,000 workers were to be invited to retire over three years and several factories were closed, in order to reduce costs and improve international competitiveness.

The textile industry, the country's second largest foreign-exchange earner, was eroded by the transfer, in 2000, of the operations of more than 20 major Mauritian manufacturers to Madagascar, owing to lower costs in that country. Furthermore, in January 2002 more than 1,000 textile workers in the EPZ were made redundant, owing to a decline in trade following the suicide attacks on the USA in September 2001; exports to the USA had previously been expected to increase, as a result of the USA's African Growth and Opportunity Act (AGOA), which granted duty-free access to the US market for textile products from Mauritius. The expiry of the preferential Multi-Fibre Agreement with the EU in December 2004 will pose a further threat to the textiles industry, exposing it to direct competition from countries with lower labour costs, particularly those in Asia. The budgetary deficit was somewhat reduced in 2003, but remained a concern, as did the high level of unemployment. The Government's focus on funding and developing education was an effort to match the skills of the work-force to the requirements of the the economy. Growth of some 5.1% and inflation of 4% were forecast by the Government for 2004.

Mayotte

Mayotte forms part of the Comoros archipelago lying between Madagascar and the African mainland. Since the Comoros unilaterally declared independence in 1975, Mayotte has been administered by France. The independent Comoran state claims sovereignty of Mayotte, and represents it in international organizations, including the UN. In 1976 France introduced the status of Collectivité Territoriale for the island. Until 1999 the island's main political party demanded full departmental status for Mayotte. In July 2001, however, Mayotte was granted the status of Collectivité Départementale for a period of 10 years. Dzaoudzi is the capital. The official language is French.

Area and population
Area: 374 sq km
Population (mid-2000): 143,000
Population density (mid-2000): 387.7 per sq km

Finance
Currency: euro

Economy

Mayotte's gross domestic product (GDP) per head in 1991 was estimated at 4,050 French francs. Between the censuses of 1991 and 2002 the population of Mayotte increased at an average annual rate of 10.1%.

AGRICULTURE

The economy is based mainly on agriculture. In 1997 18.6% of the employed labour force were engaged in this sector. The principal export crops are ylang-ylang and vanilla. Rice, cassava and maize are cultivated for domestic consumption. Livestock-rearing and fishing are also important activities. However, Mayotte imports large quantities of foodstuffs, which comprised 27.0% of the value of total imports in 2002.

INDUSTRY

Industry (which is dominated by the construction sector) engaged 21.5% of the employed population in 1997. There are no mineral resources on the island. Imports of mineral products comprised 5.0% of the value of total imports in 1997; in 2002 base metals and metal products comprised 7.4% of the value of total imports.

SERVICES

Services engaged 59.8% of the employed population in 1997. The annual total of tourist arrivals (excluding cruise-ship passengers) increased from 6,700 in 1995 to 21,000 in 1999, and was estimated at 35,000 in 2002. Receipts from tourism in 1999 totalled 50m. French francs.

EXTERNAL TRADE

In 2002 Mayotte recorded a trade deficit of €175.5m. The principal source of imports in 1997 was France (60%); the other major supplier was South Africa. France was also the principal market for exports (taking 68% of exports in that year); the other significant purchaser was Réunion. The principal exports in 2002 were ylang-ylang and vanilla. The principal imports in that year were foodstuffs, electrical machinery, apparatus and appliances, transport equipment, chemicals and related products, and base metals and metal products.

GOVERNMENT FINANCE

In 1997 Mayotte's total budgetary revenue was estimated at 1,022.4m. French francs, while total expenditure was estimated at 964.2m. French francs. Official debt was 435.7m. French francs at 31 December 1995. Mayotte recorded deflation of 2.0% in the year to December 2003. Some 29% of the labour force were unemployed in 2003.

SURVEY AND PROSPECTS

Mayotte suffers from a persistently high trade deficit, owing to its reliance on imports, and is largely dependent on French aid. From the late 1980s the French Government granted substantial aid to finance a number of construction projects, in an attempt to encourage the development of tourism on the island. Mayotte's remote location, however, continued to prove an impediment to the development of the tourist sector. A five-year Development Plan (1986–91) included measures to improve infrastructure and to increase investment in public works; the Plan was subsequently extended to the end of 1993. In 1995 Mayotte received credit from

France to finance further investment in infrastructure, particularly in the road network.

As Mayotte's labour force has continued to increase (mostly owing to a high birth rate and the continued arrival of illegal immigrants—estimated to number some 45,000 in mid-2002), youth unemployment has caused particular concern. In 1997 37.8% of the unemployed population were under 25 years of age. In December 2002 a development agreement was signed with the French Government for the period 2003–07; of the €115m. required for its implementation, the French State was to provide €104m. It was hoped that as well as improving regional transport links, the establishment of Air Mayotte International in 2002 would increase tourist arrivals to the island, although by early 2004 the airline had yet to receive the full authorization required to commence operations. Transfers from the French State to Mayotte increased from €243m. in 2001 to €337m. in 2004.

Mexico

The United Mexican States is bordered to the north by the USA, and to the south by Guatemala and Belize. From 1929 until 2000 the country was dominated by the Partido Revolucionario Institucional (PRI), for much of that time in an effective one-party system, although a democratic form of election was maintained. In 2000 Vicente Fox Quesada, representing the Alianza por el Cambio, an alliance of the Partido Acción Nacional and the Partido Verde Ecologista de México, was elected as President, ending the PRI's 71-year hegemony in Mexican government. Mexico City is the capital. Spanish is the principal language.

Area and population
Area: 1,964,375 sq km
Population (mid-2002): 100,921,480
Population density (mid-2002): 51.4 per sq km
Life expectancy (years at birth, 2002): 74.4 (males 71.7; females 77.0)

Finance
GDP in current prices: 2002): US $637,205m. ($6,314 per head)
Real GDP growth (2002): 0.7%
Inflation (annual average, 2002): 5.0%
Currency: peso

Economy

In 2002, according to estimates by the World Bank, Mexico's gross national income (GNI), measured at average 2000–02 prices, was US $596,703m., equivalent to $5,910 per head (or $8540 per head on an international purchasing-power parity basis). During 1990–2002, it was estimated, the population increased at an average annual rate of 1.6%, while gross domestic product (GDP) per head increased, in real terms, by an average of 1.3% per year. Overall GDP increased, in real terms, at an average annual rate of 2.9% in 1990–2002; GDP increased by 0.7% in 2002.

AGRICULTURE

Agriculture (including forestry and fishing) contributed an estimated 4.0% of GDP in 2002 and engaged about 18.1% of the employed labour force in 2001. The staple food crops are maize, wheat, sorghum, barley, rice, beans and potatoes. The principal cash crops are coffee, cotton, sugar cane, and fruit and vegetables (particularly tomatoes). Livestock-raising and fisheries are also important. During 1990–2001, according to World Bank estimates, agricultural GDP increased at an average annual rate of 1.6%; agricultural GDP rose by 0.6% in 2000 and by 1.9% in 2001. The reduction and eventual removal of import tariffs proposed under NAFTA was a significant blow to Mexico's agriculture sector, which had lower subsidies and higher overhead costs than in the USA; the elimination of tariffs on 21 products in January 2003 was offset by a US $10,000m. aid programme, announced in November 2002.

INDUSTRY

Industry (including mining, manufacturing, construction and power) engaged an estimated 25.9% of the employed labour force in 2001, and provided an estimated 26.1% of GDP in 2002. During 1990–2001 industrial GDP increased by an average of 3.3% per year; industrial GDP increased by 6.1% in 2000, but decreased by 3.5% in 2001.

Mining

Mining contributed an estimated 1.3% of GDP in 2002, and engaged an estimated 0.3% of the employed labour force in 2001. During 1990–2001 the GDP of the mining sector increased by an average of 1.9% per year; mining GDP increased by 3.8% in 2000 and by 0.8% in 2001. Mexico has large reserves of petroleum (which accounted for 7.9% of total export earnings in 2001) and natural gas. Zinc, salt, silver, copper, celestite and fluorite are also major mineral exports. In addition, mercury, bismuth, antimony, cadmium, manganese and phosphates are mined, and there are significant reserves of uranium.

Manufacturing

Manufacturing provided an estimated 20.4% of GDP in 2002, and engaged an estimated 18.9% of the employed labour force in 2001. Manufacturing GDP increased by an annual average of 3.6% in 1990–2001; the sector increased by 6.9% in 2000, but decreased by 3.0% in 2001. In 2001 the most important branches of manufacturing (based on value of output) were metals and machinery, food, beverages and tobacco, and chemicals. By December 2000 Mexico had 3,703 *maquiladora* export plants (where intermediate materials produced on US territory are processed or assembled on the

Mexican side of the border), providing an estimated 1.3m. jobs and making an increasingly significant contribution to the sector (accounting for an estimated 48.6% of total revenue from manufacturing exports in 2002).

Energy

Energy is derived principally from mineral fuels and lubricants and hydroelectric power. In 2000 some 47.5% of total output of electricity production was derived from petroleum, 19.8% came from natural gas, 16.2% was derived from hydroelectric plants and 9.3% came from coal-powered plants. During the late 1990s the Government initiated a programme to deregulate the energy sector; in 1997 private consortia were awarded concessions to build and lease power-stations in Mexico. In 2001 fuel imports accounted for 3.0% of total merchandise imports. In late 2001 the Governments of Mexico and Guatemala reached agreement, under the regional 'Plan Puebla-Panamá' (a series of joint transport, industry and tourism projects intended to integrate the Central American region), to link their electricity grids. In 2002 the Government's planned reform of the energy sector faced congressional opposition. In 2003, according to the state concern Petróleos Mexicanos (PEMEX), oil production was 3,371,000 barrels per day, while production of natural gas was 4,498m. cu ft per day.

SERVICES

The services sector contributed an estimated 69.9% of GDP in 2002, and engaged an estimated 55.6% of the employed labour force in 2001. According to government figures, the GDP of the sector increased by an average of 3.7% per year in 1990–2001; the sector experienced growth of 7.4% in 2000 and of 1.0% in 2001. Tourism is one of Mexico's principal sources of foreign exchange. In 2002 there were an estimated 19.7m. foreign visitors to Mexico (mostly from the USA and Canada), providing revenue of US $8,858m.

EXTERNAL TRADE

In 2002 Mexico recorded a visible trade deficit of an estimated US $7,995m., and there was a deficit of $14,069m. on the current account of the balance of payments. In 2002 the principal source of imports (63.4%) was the USA, which was also the principal market for exports (89.1%). The principal exports in that year were electric and electronic products, parts for road vehicles, and industrial machinery and the principal imports were electric and electronic products, industrial machineryand transport equipment. In 2002 imports from Mercosur (Mercado Común del Sur, or Southern Common Market) countries almost doubled, while exports decreased slightly.

GOVERNMENT FINANCE

In 2002 there was an estimated budgetary deficit of 135,098.0m. new pesos, equivalent to 2.2% of GDP. Mexico's external debt totalled an estimated US $158,290m. at the end of 2001, of which $86,199m. was long-term public debt. In that year the cost of debt-servicing was equivalent to 26.1% of the value of exports of goods and services. The average annual rate of inflation was 16.1% in 1990–2002. Consumer prices increased by an average of 5.0% in 2002. Some 1.9% of the total labour force were officially recorded as unemployed in 2002, according to ILO figures.

INTERNATIONAL ECONOMIC RELATIONS

Mexico is a member of the Inter-American Development Bank (IDB), and of the Latin American Integration Association. Mexico was admitted to the Asia-Pacific Economic Co-operation group (APEC) in 1993, and joined the Organisation for Economic Co-operation and Development (OECD) in 1994. Mexico is also a signatory nation to the North American Free Trade Agreement (NAFTA). In mid-March 2004 Mexico concluded a free trade agreement with Japan.

SURVEY AND PROSPECTS

Mexico's economic development, centred on the expansion of the petroleum industry, was impeded from the mid-1980s by the decrease in international petroleum prices, in addition to the persistent problems of the flight of capital, the depreciation of the peso, a shortage of foreign exchange and vast foreign debt. A programme of tax reform and economic liberalization was undertaken from the late 1980s, but in late 1994 and early 1995 a sharp devaluation of the peso provoked a financial crisis, necessitating a stringent policy of economic adjustment and the procurement of substantial international credit facilities. During 1995–97 a state agency, FOBAPROA, assumed some US $65,000m. in bank liabilities as a result of the crisis. In 1998, despite a dramatic decline in the price of petroleum and the adverse effects of a fall in the value of the peso against the US dollar, GDP growth of 5.0% was recorded, not least because of the strength of the manufacturing sector. A reform of the banking sector was undertaken in May 1999, creating the Instituto para la Protección al Ahorro Bancario to manage the assets previously assumed by FOBAPROA and removing all restrictions on foreign ownership of banks. In 1999 economic performance was again favourable and in 2000 GDP growth accelerated to 6.6%, reflecting continuing strong export growth, particularly in the *maquiladora* industries. However, there was an economic slowdown in 2001; GDP declined by 0.2%, with the *maquiladora* sector being particularly badly affected, contracting by 8.9% in that year. In 2003 the *maquiladora* sector continued to suffer from decreasing export revenues and decreasing employment. In 2002 remittances from Mexicans living in the USA were estimated to be $13,270m., or 2.2% of GDP.

The 2003 budget, passed in December 2002, set a strict fiscal deficit of 0.5% of GDP; finances were boosted in early 2003 by a massive increase in crude petroleum export prices, as a result of uncertain supplies from Venezuela and the US-led military campaign in Iraq, as well as by a weak new peso (oil revenues were paid in US dollars). Free trade became a prominent issue in the latter half of 2003; at the fifth Ministerial Conference of the World Trade Organization, held in Cancún in September, Mexico joined the so-called G-20 (subsequently renamed the G-19) group of developing nations opposed to the developed world's agricultural subsidies. Ongoing negotiations over the proposed Free Trade Area of the Americas also ran into difficulties in late 2003 over each country's level of participation. NAFTA, which reached its 10th anniversary on 1 January 2004, also faced criticism from various sectors. It was claimed that although Mexican agricultural exports had doubled during the 10 years that NAFTA had been in place, 1.3m. jobs had been lost in the agricultural sector.

In 2003 the Mexican economy was adversely affected by the sluggish economy of its largest trading partner, the USA. At the same time, the People's Republic of China, with its lower labour costs, threatened Mexico's position as the second largest exporter to the USA. In August 2003 unemployment reached a six-year high of 4.0%. Throughout the second half of 2003 the Government experienced problems in convincing a hostile Congreso to approve its reform agenda. In December President Fox was forced to abandon the Government's commitment to the privatization, closure or merger of several state-run companies in order that his proposed budget receive congressional approval. A revised and more moderate budget, which included increased expenditure on agriculture, education and anti-poverty programmes was eventually passed by the Congreso in late December. Economic growth in 2004 was predicted to be 3.1%, and the Banco Central forecast that the rate of inflation would be 3% in that year.

Micronesia

The Federated States of Micronesia forms (with Palau) the archipelago of the Caroline Islands, about 800 km east of the Philippines. The USA previously administered Micronesia within the Trust Territory of the Pacific Islands, established by the UN in 1947. In 1979 the districts of Yap, Truk, Ponape and Kosrae ratified a new Constitution to become the Federated States of Micronesia. US administration formally ended in 1986. Micronesia's Compact of Free Association with the USA, first signed in 1983, was renegotiated in November 2002 and signed in May 2003. Kolonia is the capital. The indigenous population comprises various ethno-linguistic groups, but English is widely understood.

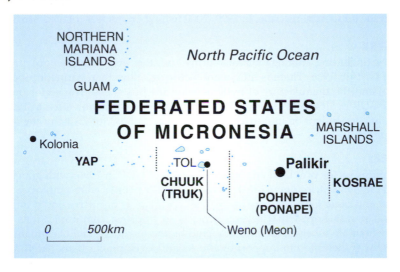

Area and population

Area: 700 sq km
Population (mid-2002): 122,380
Population density (mid-2002): 174.8
Life expectancy (years at birth, 2002): 66.5 (males 64.9; females 68.1)

Finance

GDP in current prices: 2002): US $232m. ($1,897 per head)
Real GDP growth (2002): 2.0%
Currency: US dollar

Economy

In 2002, according to estimates by the World Bank, gross national income (GNI) in the Federated States of Micronesia, measured at average 1999–2002 prices, was US $242m., equivalent to $1,980 per head. During 1990–2002, it was estimated, the population increased at an average annual rate of 2.0%, while gross domestic product (GDP) per head decreased, in real terms, by an average of 0.5% per year. Overall GDP increased, in real terms, an average annual rate of 1.6% in 1990–2002; growth in 2002 was 2.0%.

AGRICULTURE

Agriculture is mainly on a subsistence level, although its importance is diminishing. The principal crops are coconuts (from which some 500 short tons of copra were produced in 2001), bananas, betel-nuts, cassava and sweet potatoes. White pepper-corns are produced on Pohnpei. The sector (including forestry and fishing) contributed 19.1% to GDP in 1996 and engaged 55.3% of the employed labour force in 2000. Exports of bananas accounted for 1.2% of export earnings in 1999, while exports of marine products accounted for 91.9% of total export revenue in that year. Fees earned from fisheries licensing agreements, mainly with Japan, account for a substantial percentage of domestic budgetary revenue. In 1999/2000 fishing access fees totalled $16.8m.

INDUSTRY

Industry (including mining, manufacturing, utilities and construction) provided 3.9% of GDP in 1996. There is little manufacturing, other than garment production (in Yap) and the manufacture of buttons using trochus shells. The sector provided 1.4% of GDP in 1996 and engaged 3.5% of the employed labour force in 1994. The islands are dependent on imported fuels (which accounted for 20.3% of the value of total imports in 1999).

SERVICES

The services sector provided an estimated 77.0% of GDP in 1996 (with government services alone contributing 42.1%). A total of 6,015 people were employed by the national and state Governments in 1996/97. Tourism is an increasingly important industry; it was hoped that several projects to improve communications would further stimulate tourism, hitherto hindered by the territory's remote situation. The industry was identified in a report by the Asian Development Bank (ADB) in mid-1995 as having the greatest potential for development and thus contribution to the islands' economic growth. In 2001, however, the number of visitor arrivals declined to 15,265, compared with 20,051 in the previous year.

EXTERNAL TRADE

In the financial year ending September 2001 there was a visible trade deficit of an estimated US $130.8m., but an estimated surplus of $3.3m. on the current account of the balance of payments. The principal sources of imports in 1999 were the USA (which supplied 43.9% of the total) and Australia (19.8%). Japan was the principal market for exports in 1999, purchasing 83.9% of the total. In 1999 the main imports were food and live animals (24.8% of the total), mineral fuels and lubricants (20.3%), machines and transport equipment (19.5%) and basic manufactures (18.9%). The dominant exports were fish and fish products, mainly in the form of re-exports to Japan by foreign vessels (accounting for 91.9% of total export earnings in 1999).

GOVERNMENT FINANCE

In 1999/2000 there was an estimated budget surplus of US $0.4m. However, the fiscal surpluses reported for 2002 and 2003 were estimated to have been resulted primarily from increased US aid payments. The Federated States of Micronesia relies heavily on financial assistance, particularly from the USA, which according to the IMF provided an estimated $97.7m. (equivalent to 42.1% of GDP) in 2002. At the end of the 2000/01 financial year the islands' total external debt was estimated at US $58m., and in that year the cost of debt-servicing was forecast by the ADB to be equivalent to 22.0% of the value of exports of goods and services. However, by the end of 2002 the Government had successfully repaid its outstanding commercial debt; the public debt-service ratio, meanwhile, declined sharply to 6.0% of the value of exports. According to the ADB, the inflation rate steadily decreased from an estimated annual average of 6.0% in 1993 to 1.5% in 1998, before rising to 2.6% in 1999 and to 3.2% in 2000, then declining to 2.6% in 2001. According to the ADB, some 2.6% of the labour force were unemployed in 2000.

INTERNATIONAL ECONOMIC RELATIONS

The Federated States of Micronesia is a member of the Pacific Community, the Pacific Islands Forum, the South Pacific Regional Trade and Economic Co-operation Agreement (SPARTECA), the UN Economic and Social Commission for Asia and the Pacific (ESCAP) and the Asian Development Bank (ADB). In November 2002 the Federated States of Micronesia was announced as the location of the headquarters for the Tuna Commission, a new multilateral agency to manage migratory fish stocks in the central and western Pacific region. The organization's remit included the management of waters outside each nation's 200-mile exclusive economic zone, in accordance with the framework established under the 1995 UN Fish Stocks Agreement. The Council of Micronesian Government Executives, of which the Federated States of Micronesia was a founder member in 1996, aims to facilitate discussion of economic developments in the region and to examine possibilities for reducing the considerable cost of shipping essential goods between the islands.

SURVEY AND PROSPECTS

The islands are vulnerable to adverse climatic conditions, as was illustrated in late 1997 and early 1998, when a prolonged drought caused problems throughout the islands, and in 2002 following a series of tropical storms. The country's prospects for economic development are, furthermore, constrained by the islands' remote position and lack of marketable commodities. An extremely high rate of natural increase in the population has exacerbated certain economic problems, but is, however, partially offset by an annual emigration rate of more than 2%. With the renegotiation of several terms of the Compact of Free Association from late 1999, the USA emphasized its continued commitment to the economic development of the islands, including the promotion of greater self-sufficiency, in return for improved accountability regarding US funding by the Micronesia Government.

In December 2000 the ADB approved a US $8m. loan to fund a six-year reform programme of the health and education sectors, and followed this in December 2001 with a further loan of $13m., targeted at job creation, increasing production for both domestic and export markets, and the development of a competitive services sector. However, the private sector continued to be constrained by the disproportionately high cost of domestic labour, rates of pay in the public sector having risen substantially in recent years as a result of the large external inflows (although public sector salaries were 'frozen' under the 2004 budget). Moreover, an IMF report released in

February 2003 noted that infrastructure for the private sector remained underdeveloped, notwithstanding the authorities' largely positive oversight of the banking sector. Further criticism was attached to the private sector's role as an effective provider of services to the public sector, and the public sector's tendency to operate in unequal competition with private-sector interests. Concerns also continued as to the relative lack of progress in restructuring the economy in preparation for the potentially dramatic impact of the decline and eventual withdrawal of direct US aid in 2023 (upon the expiry of the Compact as amended in 2003): according to the UN, bilateral and multilateral aid to Micronesia totalled $101.6m. in 2000, the latter accounting for only $5.0m. of the total. The trust fund for Micronesia established to alleviate such pressures upon expiry of the Compact was expected to remain vulnerable to international economic performance, the majority of this capital being invested in US stock markets. Moreover, it was considered in some quarters that the amended Compact of Free Association represented a substantial real reduction in Micronesia's grant income.

Moldova

The Republic of Moldova is situated in south-eastern Europe. The Moldovan Soviet Socialist Republic (SSR) formally joined the USSR in 1940. Between July 1941 and August 1944 the Moldovan SSR was reunited with Romania. However, the Soviet Army reannexed the region in 1944, and the Moldovan SSR was re-established. In 1991 the Moldovan parliament and the 'Grand National Assembly' proclaimed Moldova's independence from the USSR. In that year Moldova was among the 11 signatories to the Alma-Ata (Almaty) declaration establishing the Commonwealth of Independent States. The capital is Chişinău. The official language is Moldovan.

Area and population

Area: 33,800 sq km
Population (mid-2002): 4,255,010
Population density (mid-2002): 125.9 per sq km
Life expectancy (years at birth, 2002): 67.8 (males 64.0; females 71.6)

Finance

GDP in current prices: 2002): US $1,621m. ($381 per head)
Real GDP growth (2002): 7.2%
Inflation (annual average, 2002): 5.1%
Currency: leu

Economy

In 2002, according to estimates by the World Bank, Moldova's gross national income (GNI), measured at average 2000–02 prices, was US $1,671m., equivalent to $460 per head (or $1,560 on an international purchasing-power parity basis). During 1990–2002, it was estimated, the population decreased by an annual average of 0.2%, while gross domestic product (GDP) per head declined, in real terms, at an average rate of 7.1% per year. Overall GDP declined, in real terms, at an average annual rate of 7.3% in 1990–2002; however, GDP increased by 6.1% in 2001 and by 7.2% in 2002.

AGRICULTURE

As a result of its extremely fertile land and temperate climate, Moldova's economy is dominated by agriculture and related industries. Some 85% of the country's terrain is cultivated. In 2002 agriculture contributed some 25.1% of GDP. In 2001 the sector (including hunting, forestry and fishing) provided 51.0% of employment. Principal crops include wine grapes and other fruit, tobacco, vegetables and grain. The wine industry has traditionally occupied a central role in the economy, and was revived after the Soviet Government's anti-alcohol campaign of the mid-1980s. The private ownership of land was legalized in 1991, although the sale of agricultural land was not to be permitted until 2001. Private farmers accounted for an estimated 67% of Moldova's agricultural output in 1999. According to the World Bank, the GDP of the agricultural sector declined, in real terms, at an average rate of 7.9% per year during 1990–2002. Agricultural GDP increased by 4.3% in 2001 and by 2.0% in 2002.

INDUSTRY

In 2002 industry (including mining, manufacturing, power and construction) contributed 24.2% of GDP; in 2001 the sector provided 13.9% of employment. Between 1990 and 2002, according to the World Bank, industrial GDP declined at an average rate of 11.0% per year. However, real industrial GDP increased by 17.4% in 2001 and by 6.0% in 2002.

Mining

Mining and quarrying employed just 0.1% of the working population in 2001. Moldova has extremely limited mineral resources, and there is no domestic production of fuel or non-ferrous metals. Activity is focused primarily on the extraction and processing of industrial minerals such as gypsum, limestone, sand and gravel. Deposits of petroleum and natural gas were discovered in southern Moldova in the early 1990s; total reserves of natural gas have been estimated at 22,000m. cu m.

Manufacturing

The manufacturing sector provided 9.1% of employment in 2001 and contributed 18.2% of GDP in 2002. The sector is dominated by food-processing, wine and tobacco production, machine-building and metalworking, and light industry. In 1994 the principal branches, measured by gross value of output, were food-processing and beverages (57.8%), tobacco (4.9%), non-metallic mineral products (4.6%) and textiles (4.0%). According to the World Bank, manufacturing GDP declined, in real terms, by an annual average of 0.4% in 1995–2002. Manufacturing GDP increased by 17.8% in 2001 and by 6.0% in 2002.

Energy

Moldova relies heavily on imported energy—primarily natural gas and petroleum products—from Russia, Romania and Ukraine. Moldova was seeking to become self-sufficient in natural gas, following the discovery of gas reserves in the south of the country. A large proportion of natural gas imports supply the Moldoveneasca power station, located in Transnistria, which contributed some 85% of the country's electrical generating capacity in 1996. In 2000 natural gas accounted for 92.3% of electricity production, and coal accounted for 5.0% (compared with 43.8% in 1994). Mineral products comprised an estimated 26.5% of the value of total imports in 2001.

SERVICES

Services accounted for 50.7% of GDP in 2002, and provided 35.1% of total employment in 2001. The GDP of the services sector declined, in real terms, by an annual average of 2.5% in 1991–2002. Services GDP decreased, in real terms, by 0.5% in 2001, but increased by 4.4% in 2002.

EXTERNAL TRADE

In 2002 Moldova recorded a visible trade deficit of US $378.2m., while there was a deficit of $97.3m. on the current account of the balance of payments. In 2002, according to the IMF, the principal source of imports was Ukraine (accounting for 19.6% of the value of total imports). Other major suppliers were Russia, Romania, Italy and Germany. The main market for exports in that year was Russia (37.1% of the value of total exports). Other important purchasers were Ukraine, Italy, Romania and Germany. In 2002 the principal imports were mineral products, machinery and mechanical appliances, chemicals and related products, and textiles. The main exports in that year were food products, beverages and tobacco (accounting for some 41.5% of the value of total exports), textiles and vegetable products.

GOVERNMENT FINANCE

In 2002 the state budget recorded a deficit of 447m. Moldovan lei (equivalent to 2.0% of GDP). Moldova's total external debt at the end of 2001 was US $1,214m., of which $779m. was long-term public debt. In that year the cost of debt-servicing was equivalent to 19.4% of the value of exports of goods and services. Consumer prices increased by an annual average of 118.8% during 1991–2002. The average rate of inflation was 9.7% in 2001 and 5.5% in 2002. The average rate of unemployment was 7.9% in 2003.

INTERNATIONAL ECONOMIC RELATIONS

Moldova became a member of the IMF and the World Bank in 1992. It also joined the European Bank for Reconstruction and Development (EBRD). Moldova subsequently became a member of the Organization of the Black Sea Economic Co-operation, and it became a full member of the World Trade Organization in July 2001.

SURVEY AND PROSPECTS

In common with other former Soviet republics following independence, Moldova's planned transition to a market economic system was hampered by the serious disruptions in inter-republican trade. Another factor that adversely affected economic performance was the armed conflict in Transnistria (the main industrial centre) in the first half of 1992 and the region's subsequent attempts to secede from

Moldova. Moldova introduced its own national currency, the Moldovan leu, in November 1993. Although the IMF initially declared itself satisfied with Moldova's accelerated structural reforms, after 1998 the reform process stalled, and lending was repeatedly suspended in 1999–2003.

The communist Government elected in 2001 cancelled several privatization agreements and concerns over the possible renationalization of the national airline and the electricity-distribution networks in 2002–03 resulted in reduced investment. The privatization programme, originally scheduled for completion by the end of 2002, had been extended until 2005. Meanwhile, in April 2002 an agreement was signed with the World Bank supporting Moldova's request for the restructuring of its external debt (equivalent to over 150% of GDP), but in August 2003 debt-service payments to bilateral creditors were suspended. The annual rate of consumer-price inflation increased in 2003, to some 18.0%, although inflation was expected to decline to between 4.5% and 8.0% in 2004, and economic growth, of 5%, was expected to be maintained. None the less, there was concern about the sustainability of growth and the country's endemic poverty, and the IMF recommended that the Government implement measures to combat corruption, reduce state interference in economic activity, accelerate privatization and maintain a liberal trade regime.

Monaco

The Principality of Monaco lies in western Europe. The country is an hereditary monarchy, which has been ruled by the Grimaldi dynasty since 1297. In 1861 Monaco became an independent state under the protection of France. Since 1911, when a Constitution was promulgated, legislative power has been vested jointly in the Prince and a Conseil National. Prince Rainier III, the reigning prince, succeeded his grandfather, Prince Louis II, in 1949, and a new Constitution was approved in 1962. Constitutional changes, approved in 2002, transferred certain powers of the Prince to the Conseil National. French is the official language.

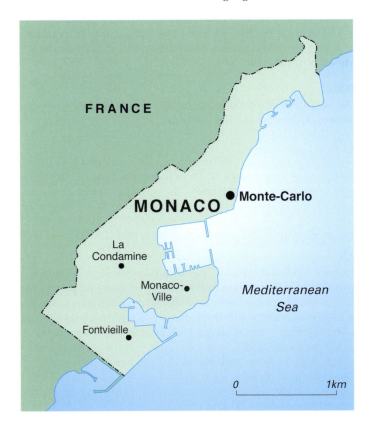

Area and population
Area: 2 sq km
Population (mid-2001): 30,000
Population density (mid-2001): 15,398.2 per sq km
Life expectancy (years at birth, 2002): 81.2 (males 77.8; females 84.5)

Finance
GDP in current prices: 1999): US $803m. ($24,267 per head)
Real GDP growth (1999): 2.9%
Currency: euro

Economy

In 2001, according to World Bank estimates, Monaco's gross national income (GNI), measured at average 1999–2001 prices, was equivalent to approximately US $24,700 per head. In 2000, according to World Bank estimates, GNI, measured at average 1998–2000 prices, was equivalent to approximately $25,200 per head, or approximately $25,700 on an international purchasing-power parity basis. According to UN estimates, Monaco's gross domestic product (GDP) was $847m. in 1995 (equivalent to $26,470 per head). During 1990–95 GDP increased, in real terms, at an average annual rate of 1.1%. GDP grew by 2.2% in 1995. The annual rate of population increase averaged 0.6% in 1990–2000. Monaco has the highest population density of all the independent states in the world.

AGRICULTURE
There is no agricultural land in Monaco. In 1990 a Belgian enterprise established an offshore fish farm for sea bass and sea bream.

INDUSTRY
Industry (excluding construction and public works) accounted for 11.6% of economic activity in 1993, and engaged some 17.0% of those employed in the private sector in 2002. Industry is mainly light in Monaco. The principal sectors, measured by gross value of output, are chemicals, pharmaceuticals and cosmetics (which together accounted for 46.5% of all industrial revenue in 2002), plastics, micro-electronics and electrical goods, paper and card manufacture, and clothing and textiles.

SERVICES
Service industries represent the most significant sector of the economy in Monaco, contributing 49.1% of total revenue in 1993, and providing employment to 83.0% of those working in the private sector in 2002. Banking and finance accounted for more than 38% of the services sector and employed some 1,400 people in the late 1990s. At the end of 2002 the total value of deposits in Monaco's private banking sector was estimated at €18,600m. By 2002 it was estimated that the share of national revenue provided by the casino had declined to around 5%, while trade accounted for 38.1% of revenue in that year, and banking and financial activities accounted for some 17.5%.

Tourism is also an important source of income, providing an estimated 25% of total government revenue in 1991 and engaging some 20% of the employed labour force in the late 1990s. In 2002 262,520 tourists (excluding excursionists) visited Monaco, representing a decrease of some 2.7%, compared with 2001. Including excursionists, some 4m. people visited the Principality in 1992, and in that year revenue from tourism totalled US $1,300m. The greatest number of visitors (excluding excursionists) in 2002 were from Italy (23.2%), France (15.8%), the United Kingdom (14.5%) and the USA (9.7%). In that year the conference industry accounted for 30.4% of the nights spent at Monaco's foreign hotels.

EXTERNAL TRADE

Monaco's external trade is included in the figures for France. Revenue is derived principally from real estate, light and medium industry, indirect taxation and tourism.

GOVERNMENT FINANCE

In 2003 there was a budgetary deficit of €23.2m.: expenditure amounted to €616.7m. In 2000 value-added tax (VAT) contributed 52.8% of total government revenue. In the late 1990s it was estimated that less than 3% of the population were unemployed in the Principality.

SURVEY AND PROSPECTS

Monaco is largely dependent on imports from France, owing to its lack of natural resources. There is a severe labour shortage in the Principality, and the economy is reliant on migrant workers (many of whom remain resident in France and Italy). Following the establishment of a casino in the 1860s, tourism became the dominant sector in the economy. In particular, the Principality has sought to establish itself as a major centre of the conference industry; about one-third of the visitors to Monaco in 1994 were connected with this sector, compared with one-10th in the early 1970s.

From the 1980s, however, the industry and real estate sectors expanded, as a series of land reclamation projects increased Monaco's area by 20%, and the Principality's railway station was relocated underground. A number of foreign companies and banks are registered in Monaco in order to take advantage of the low rates of taxation on company profits. Since the removal of French restrictions on foreign exchange in 1987, Monaco's banking industry (which includes an 'offshore' sector) has expanded. The opening of a new conference and cultural centre in mid-2000 was expected to result in the further expansion of Monaco's business conference industry.

The role of tourism in the economy was expected to grow further, following the construction of a new pier for luxury vessels, completed in August 2002. Further measures, which aimed to create an additional 350 berthing spaces for leisure yachts in Monaco (in addition to the 350 already extant), were announced in 2003, although the number of tourist visits recorded in 2002 was some 12.6% less than in 2000, reflecting weaknesses in the international economy. The shipping and telecommunications industries were also a focus of expansion in the Principality in the early 2000s.

Mongolia

Situated in central Asia, Mongolia was formerly the Manchu province of Outer Mongolia. In 1924 the Mongolian People's Republic was proclaimed. Until 1990 the Mongolian People's Revolutionary Party (MPRP) was the only legal political party. Constitutional amendments adopted in that year, however, included the deletion of references to the MPRP as the 'guiding force' in Mongolian society. In 1996 a coalition of opposition parties—the Democratic Alliance—achieved a resounding victory in legislative elections. At the subsequent general election, in 2000, the MPRP re-established itself as the leading party. At the 2004 election, however, the MPRP's position was greatly weakened. Ulan Bator is the capital. Khalkha Mongolian is the principal language.

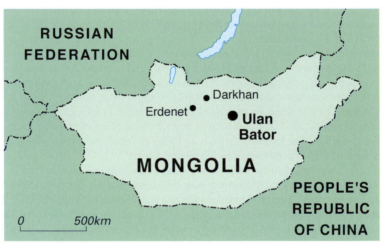

Area and population
Area: 1,564,116 sq km
Population (mid-2002): 2,448,510
Population density (mid-2002): 1.6 per sq km
Life expectancy (years at birth, 2002): 62.9 (males 60.1; females 65.9)

Finance
GDP in current prices: 2002): US $1,262m. ($515 per head)
Real GDP growth (2002): 3.7%
Inflation (annual average, 2001): 8.0%
Currency: tögrög (tugrik)

Economy

In 2002, according to estimates by the World Bank, Mongolia's gross national income (GNI), measured at average 2000–02 prices, was US $1,088m., equivalent to $440 per head (or $1,650 per head on an international purchasing-power parity basis). During 1990–2002, it was estimated, the population increased by an average annual rate of 1.3%, while gross domestic product (GDP) per head decreased, in real terms, by an average of 0.9% per year. Overall GDP increased, in real terms, by an average annual rate of 0.4% in 1990–2002. According to Mongolian sources, GDP increased by 4.0% in 2002 and by 5.5% in 2003.

AGRICULTURE

According to figures from the Asian Development Bank (ADB), agriculture (including forestry) contributed 20.7% of GDP in 2002. The sector engaged 44.9% of the employed labour force in 2002. Animal herding is the main economic activity and is practised throughout the country. By mid-1995 more than 90% of all livestock was privately owned. Livestock numbers (sheep, goats, horses, cattle and camels) reached a new record of 33.6m. at the end of 1999 but, following exceptionally severe weather, declined to fewer than 23.7m. in 2002, before recovering to almost 26.2m. in 2003. The principal crops are cereals, potatoes and vegetables. During 1990–2001, according to figures from the World Bank, the GDP of the agricultural sector increased, in real terms, at an average annual rate of 1.8%. According to the ADB, agricultural GDP decreased by 18.5% in 2001 and by 10.5% in 2002.

INDUSTRY

Industry (comprising manufacturing, mining, construction and utilities) provided 23.5% of GDP in 2002, according to the ADB, and engaged 11.4% of the employed labour force in 2002. According to the World Bank, during 1990–2001 industrial GDP declined, in real terms, at an average rate of 1.8% per year. According to the ADB, the industrial sector's GDP increased by 16.2% in 2001 and by 5.0% in 2002.

Mining

Mining contributed 8.6% of GDP in 2002, according to the ADB. Mongolia has significant, largely unexplored, mineral resources and is a leading producer and exporter of copper, gold, molybdenum and fluorspar concentrates. Export of copper concentrate in 2003 was worth an estimated US $159m. The copper-molybdenum works at Erdenet, a Mongolian-Russian joint venture, is the most important mining operation in the country. The value of copper concentrate in Mongolia's total exports, however, decreased from 53.0% in 1995 to 27.6% in 2002. During 2003 a Canadian company continued to upgrade the Oyuu Tolgoi (Turquoise Hill) mineral deposits at Khanbogd, South Gobi, not only raising its estimates of copper and gold content but also finding plentiful supplies of underground water. Copper production was provisionally scheduled to begin in 2006. Other mineral resources include coal, tungsten, tin, uranium and lead. In May 2000 Mongolia's coal reserves were estimated at 150,000m. metric tons. Gold production rose from 4.5 tons in 1995 to 13.7 tons in 2001, before declining to 12.1 tons in 2002. Petroleum reserves were discovered in 1994. Extraction of crude petroleum, from the Tamsag basin, commenced in 1997. According to the ADB, compared with the previous year the GDP of the mining sector expanded by 9.6% in 2001 but decreased by 6.8 % in 2002. In 2003, according to official sources, output of coal reportedly rose by 5%, extraction of petroleum and gas by 31.5% and other minerals by 18.1%.

Manufacturing

The manufacturing sector accounted for 9.5% of GDP in 2002, according to the ADB. Manufacturing industries are based largely on the products of the agricultural and animal husbandry sector. Mongolia is one of the world's foremost producers of cashmere, and also manufactures garments, leather goods and carpets. The principal branches of manufacturing include food products, textiles and non-metallic mineral products. According to figures from the ADB, manufacturing GDP increased by 31.8% in 2001 and by 12.2% in 2002.

Energy

Energy is derived principally from thermal power stations, fuelled by coal. Most provincial centres have thermal power stations or diesel generators, while smaller rural centres generally rely on small diesel generators. In more isolated areas wood, roots, bushes and dried animal dung are used for domestic fuel. The Ulan Bator No. 4 power station, the largest in the country, went into operation in 1985. Its capacity of 380 MW doubled Mongolia's generating capacity. In 2000, according to the World Bank, imports of energy products comprised 19.1% of the total value of merchandise imports. Mongolia imports electricity and petroleum products from Russia. Production of crude petroleum increased sharply from 73,700 barrels in 2001 to 139,200 barrels in 2002.

SERVICES

The services sector contributed an estimated 55.8% of GDP in 2002, according to the ADB, and engaged an estimated 43.7% of the employed labour force in 2000. During 1990–2001, according to figures from the ADB, the GDP of the sector decreased, in real terms, by an average of 0.4% annually. According to the ADB, the GDP of the services sector increased by 8.2% in 2001 and by 12.1% in 2002.

EXTERNAL TRADE

In 2002, according to the IMF, Mongolia recorded a visible trade deficit of US $156.2m., and there was a deficit of $158.0m. on the current account of the balance of payments. In 2003 the trade deficit reached $187.1m. In 2002 the principal source of imports was Russia, supplying 34.1% of the total. Other major suppliers were the People's Republic of China (24.4%), the Republic of Korea (12.2%) and Japan (6.1%). China was the principal market for exports in that year, purchasing 42.4% of the total. Other important purchasers were the USA (31.6%) and Russia (8.6%). The principal imports in 2003 were machinery (20.2%) and mineral products (19.2%). The principal exports in 2003 were minerals (33.3% of the total), textiles and textile products (25.5%) and precious metals and jewellery (23.3%).

GOVERNMENT FINANCE

The budget for 2004 envisaged a deficit of 85,994.9m. tögrög. Mongolia's total external debt was US $885.0m. at the end of 2001, of which $823.8m. was long-term public debt. In that year the cost of debt-servicing was equivalent to 7.7% of the value of exports of goods and services. The annual rate of inflation averaged 97.5% during 1991–97. According to IMF figures, during 1998–2001 the average annual inflation rate was 9.0%. However, the rate of annual inflation declined to 3.1% in 2002, according to an official source. Annual inflation in 2003 was 4.7%. The number of registered unemployed persons decreased to 38,600 (4.6% of the labour force) at the end of 2000, and to 30,900 by the end of 2002. The number of unregistered unemployed persons was believed to be far greater, with unemployment reaching some 17% of the labour force in 2002. The number of registered unemployed persons in 2003 was 33,300.

INTERNATIONAL ECONOMIC RELATIONS

In 1989 Mongolia joined the Group of 77 (an organization of developing countries, founded under the auspices of UNCTAD to promote economic co-operation). In February 1991 Mongolia became a member of the Asian Development Bank (ADB) as well as of the IMF and World Bank. In 1994 the European Union (EU) announced the inclusion of Mongolia in TACIS, the EU's programme of technical assistance to the Commonwealth of Independent States. In 1997 Mongolia became a member of the World Trade Organization (WTO). In July 1998 Mongolia was admitted to the ASEAN Regional Forum (ARF), and in May 2000 the country became a member of the European Bank for Reconstruction and Development (EBRD). Mongolia is also a member of the UN Economic and Social Commission for Asia and the Pacific (ESCAP).

SURVEY AND PROSPECTS

The Democratic Alliance coalition Government, elected in June 1996, initiated a wide-ranging programme of economic reforms. At the end of that year the Government announced a four-year economic programme and, with the help of external aid, a much-needed restructuring of Mongolia's financial system was instigated. Plans for the transfer of state assets to the private sector were also revealed. By 2000, however, the privatization programme had made little progress.

Severe drought in late 1999 was followed in early 2000 by several months of acutely cold weather. In consequence, by mid-2000 an estimated 3m. head of livestock had died. International donors offered financial aid, in response to government appeals, and Red Cross relief teams were mobilized to take food and medicine to isolated herding families suffering extreme hardship. In early 2001 weakened animals faced even more severe conditions, with deep snow and exceptionally low temperatures.

The annual livestock census in December 2001 revealed that numbers had decreased by more than 7m. head during the previous three years, and further losses were recorded in 2002. Prime Minister Enkhbayar had expressed concern about the state of the nomadic herding economy, declaring that it was important to improve the quality of stock and raise yields to meet the growing needs of large towns, especially Ulan Bator. He therefore advocated a gradual replacement of traditional nomadic family herding by livestock farming settlements, with adequate provision of winter care for animals and community facilities for herders. The national development plan announced in 2001 aimed to end Mongolia's traditional dependency on nomadic herding and envisaged the building of new towns and urbanizing 90% of the population during the next 30 years. These towns would be linked by a 2,400-km east–west highway, which would serve as a development corridor across the country as well as foster new trade zones on the Russian and Chinese borders.

The Great Khural also approved legislation allowing for the privatization of various state industries in the period to 2004. In May 2002 a stake of 76% in the Trade and Development Bank of Mongolia was purchased by Swiss and US interests. APU, the distillery and soft drinks manufacturer, was transferred to the private sector in the same year. The Agricultural Bank was sold to a Japanese-financed company in February 2003, and in December of that year the Mongol Daatgal insurance company was successfully privatized. The State's 80% share in NIC, the oil import company, was purchased by the Mongolian rival distribution company, Petrovis, in February 2004.

In June 2002, meanwhile, the Great Khural approved a land privatization law, which proved to be controversial. (The law came into force in May 2003). Mongolia remained dependent on external aid, with public debt having risen to the equivalent of 80% of GDP, the majority of which was owed to foreign institutions. Between 1991 and 2002 Mongolia received a total of US $2,500m. in aid: of this, 52.5% was in the form of grants (of which 46% was allocated for technical assistance) and 47.5% as loans. The Mongolia Consultative Group (formerly the Mongolia Assistance Group) convened in Tokyo, Japan, in November 2003 and promised an aid programme of $335m. in grants and loans for the coming year. Meanwhile, by 2002 there were signs of an improvement in the economy. Foreign investment increased to US $125m. in 2001 (from $91m. in 2000), mainly owing to renewed interest in Mongolia's copper and gold resources, especially from China (which had accounted for 37% of foreign investment during the preceding three years). The country's foreign-exchange reserves increased from $205.6m. in 2001 to $349.5m. in 2002. In 2002 GDP per head reached US $3,423 in urban areas but was only $1,245 in rural areas, illustrating a marked disparity. The ADB envisaged overall GDP growth of around 5% in 2004.

Montserrat

Montserrat is one of the Leeward Islands in the West Indies. It was first settled by the British in 1632. Montserrat formed part of the federal colony of the Leeward Islands from 1871 until 1956, when the federation was dissolved and the presidency of Montserrat became a separate colony. From 1960 Montserrat had its own adminis- trator, and in that year the Constitution came into force. The island is a United Kingdom Overseas Territory. In 1997 the eruption of the Soufrière Hills volcano left some two-thirds of the island uninhabitable and destroyed the capital, Plymouth. The official language is English.

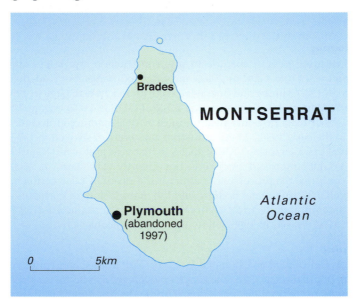

Area and population
Area: 102 sq km
Population (mid-2001): 3,000
Population density (mid-2001): 29.4 per sq km

Finance
Currency: Eastern Caribbean dollar

Economy

In 2002, according to figures from the Eastern Caribbean Central Bank (ECCB), Montserrat's gross domestic product (GDP) at market prices was an estimated EC $102.7m., equivalent to EC $19,542 per head. In 1990–2002 real GDP decreased by an annual average of 7.8%; real GDP expanded by 4.6% in 2002.

AGRICULTURE

Agriculture (including forestry and fishing) contributed an estimated 1.4% of GDP in 2002, and engaged 6.6% of the employed labour force in 1992. The sector was almost destroyed by the volcanic eruptions of 1997, which caused an 81.3% decline in agricultural production, and a return to subsistence farming. The sector's GDP contracted by a further 33.3% in 1998, in real terms, but increased by 7.6% in 1999 and by 36.6% in 2000. A contraction of 17.3% in agricultural GDP in 2001 was followed, in 2002, by a 40.7% recovery. Prior to the volcanic eruption the principal crops grown were white potatoes, onions, rice and sea-island cotton. Cattle, goats, sheep and poultry were also farmed. Montserrat's fisheries are under-exploited, owing to the absence of a sheltered harbour. A further eruption of the Soufrière Hills volcano in July 2003 destroyed some 95% of that year's food crop.

INDUSTRY

Manufacturing

Industry (including mining, manufacturing, construction and public utilities) contributed some 23.2% to GDP in 2002, and engaged some 30.9% of the employed labour force in 1987. Mining and quarrying contributed 1.1% of GDP in 1996, but only 0.1% in 2002. Manufacturing contributed 0.7% of GDP in 2002, engaged 5.6% of the employed labour force (together with mining) in 1992, and accounted for about 70% of exports in the early 1990s. Many industrial sites were destroyed in 1997, causing a decline in real manufacturing GDP of 45.2% in that year and of 85.0% in 1998. In 1999 the sector's GDP improved by 10.6%, but growth was static in 2000–02. Light industries comprise the processing of agricultural produce (also cotton and tropical fruits), as well as spring-water bottling and the manufacture of garments and plastic bags. The assembly of electrical components, which accounted for 69% of export earnings in 1993, ceased in 1998, following further volcanic activity.

Construction

Construction contributed an estimated 16.4% of GDP in 2002 and employed 17.5% of the working population in 1988. The sector enjoyed growth in the early 1990s, owing to reconstruction programmes in response to the devastation caused by 'Hurricane Hugo' in 1989. Activity in the sector declined in the mid-1990s, before increasing in the middle of the decade, owing to reconstruction work following the volcanic eruptions. In 1999, however, real construction GDP fell by 13.5%, and it decreased by a further 36.0% in 2000 and 7.7% in 2001. However, the construction industry expanded by some 39.4% in 2002, although a further contraction of 3% was expected in 2003.

Energy

Energy requirements are dependent upon the import of hydrocarbon fuels (7.3% of total imports in 1998).

SERVICES

It is hoped to re-establish Montserrat as a data-processing centre, and as a centre for financial services, which previously provided an important source of government revenue. The tourism sector, which in 2002 contributed some EC $22.2m. in gross visitor expenditure, remains important to the island, and it is hoped to establish

Montserrat as a centre for environmental tourism with the volcano itself as the premier attraction. Output from the hotel and restaurant sector decreased by an annual average of 19.1% between 1994–2002, but most dramatically in 1996 and 1997, when revenues declined by 78.2% and 42.9%, respectively, although increases of 8.3%, 7.7%, 4.3% and 27.4% were recorded in 1998, 1999, 2000 and 2001, respectively. The hotel and restaurant sector, however, declined by some 8.6% in 2002 and the tourism industry as a whole was estimated to have declined considerably in 2003. The real GDP of the services sector decreased by an annual average of 10.3% during 1994–2002, but increased by 4.4% in 2002. Services contributed some 75.3% of GDP in 2002.

EXTERNAL TRADE

In 2002 Montserrat recorded an estimated visible trade deficit of EC $56.5m. Earnings from the services sector, mainly tourist receipts and net transfers (in particular, the remittances from Montserratians abroad and the income of foreign retired people), generally offset persistent trade deficits. There was an estimated deficit on the current account of the balance of payments of EC $22.2m. in 2002. The principal trading partner is the USA (55.1% of imports in 2000 and 18.2% of exports in 2000). Other trading partners include the United Kingdom, Trinidad and Tobago and Saint Vincent and the Grenadines. The export of rice and of electrical components, previously the most important of the island's few exports, ceased in 1998 following further volcanic activity. Export receipts were, however, estimated to have increased to some EC $5m. by 2003. Food imports constituted 15.3% of total imports in 2000; the principal imports are machinery and transport equipment and basic manufactures.

GOVERNMENT FINANCE

In 2002, according to preliminary figures, there was a budgetary deficit of EC $33.5m. The capital budget is funded almost entirely by overseas aid, notably from the United Kingdom and Canada. The United Kingdom provided aid worth £14.5m. for 1995–98 (additional assistance for emergency housing and other services necessitated by continued volcanic activity had brought this total to £55m. by early 1998). In 1999 official development assistance totalled US $65.6m. Montserrat's total external public debt was estimated to be equivalent to around 10.9% of GDP in 2002. The average annual rate of inflation was static in 1999 and 0.9% in 2000. According to official data, the rate stood at 4.9% in 2001. The rate of inflation at the end of 2003 stood at 1.2%. The Caribbean Development Bank estimated the unemployment rate to stand at some 13% of the labour force in 2001, compared with around 8.3% in 1994.

INTERNATIONAL ECONOMIC RELATIONS

Montserrat is a member of the ECCB, the Caribbean Community and Common Market (CARICOM), the Organisation of Eastern Caribbean States (OECS) and, as a dependency of the United Kingdom, has the status of Overseas Territory in association with the European Union (EU). The territory is also a member of the regional stock exchange, the Eastern Caribbean Securities Exchange (based in Saint Christopher and Nevis), established in 2001.

SURVEY AND PROSPECTS

The eruption of the Soufrière Hills volcano in June 1997, and subsequent volcanic activity, rendered the southern two-thirds of Montserrat, including the capital,

Plymouth, uninhabitable. Much of the country's infrastructure, including the main port and airport, was destroyed, and the island's agricultural heartland devastated. The implications for the island's principal industry, tourism, were extremely severe. In August the British Government announced a five-year reconstruction programme for the development of the 'safe areas' in the north of the island. However, by mid-February 1998 the population of Montserrat had declined to just 2,850 (the population was an estimated 11,581 in 1994) owing to the lack of employment prospects and to poor living conditions. Of the remaining work-force, some 25% were employed by the Government or statutory bodies. The population was believed to total some 35,000 by mid-2001, and it was hoped that a reduction in volcanic activity would encourage Montserratians resident abroad to return home, thereby stimulating the economy. It was anticipated that the ongoing reconstruction efforts and the development of the island as a centre for environmental tourism would stimulate short-term economic growth, while in the long-term it was hoped to re-establish Montserrat as a centre for international financial services. However, the Territory's economic prospects depended entirely on the activity of the volcano, and although reconstruction work was in progress, other areas of the economy were likely to remain at extremely low levels of output for some years.

The repercussions of the September 2001 terrorist attacks in the USA and the subsequent US-led 'war on terror' in Afghanistan and Iraq adversely affected tourism on the island in 2001–02, providing a further blow to the economy. Moreover, the massive volcanic eruption in July 2003 ensured the island did not benefit from the growth in regional tourism in 2003 and early 2004. Nevertheless, real GDP grew by 4.6% in 2002 and an estimated 1.2% in 2003; further growth was expected in 2004. The Government set aside EC $7m. of the 2004 budget for a 'tourism repositioning strategy' aimed at capitalizing on Montserrat's considerable environmental assets; this amount was in addition to $9m. provided in October 2003 by the British Government for development of the local tourist industry. The major projects scheduled for completion in 2004 were a new port and an airstrip of at least 600 m, capable of taking small aircraft for flights to neighbouring islands, and funded by the EU and the United Kingdom.

Morocco

The Kingdom of Morocco is situated in north-west Africa. By 1958 the independent Sultanate of Morocco included the territory of France's former Moroccan protectorate, established in 1912, and most of its Spanish counterpart. The Sultan (Muhammad V) was restyled King of Morocco in 1957. In 1961 he was succeeded by his son, who took the title of Hassan II. In 1999 King Hassan was succeeded by his son, who took the title Muhammad VI. Morocco's sovereignty over the territory of Western Sahara (formerly Spanish Sahara) remained disputed in mid-2004. Rabat is the capital. Arabic is the official language.

Area and population
Area: 710,850 sq km (including the disputed territory of Western Sahara, 252,120 sq km)
Population (mid-2002): 29,640,540
Population density (mid-2002): 41.7 per sq km
Life expectancy (years at birth, 2002): 70.8 (males 68.8; females 72.8)

Finance
GDP in current prices: 2002): US $37,263m. ($1,257 per head)
Real GDP growth (2002): 4.5%
Inflation (annual average, 2002): 2.8%
Currency: dirham

Economy

In 2002, according to estimates by the World Bank, Morocco's gross national income (GNI), measured at average 2000–02 prices, was US $35,354m., equivalent to $1,190 per head (or $3,690 per head on an international purchasing-power parity basis). During 1990–2002, it was estimated, the population increased at an average annual rate of 1.8%, while gross domestic product (GDP) per head increased, in real terms, by an average of 1.0% per year. According to official figures, overall GDP increased, in real terms, at an average annual rate of 2.5% in 1990–2002; it increased by 7.2% in 2001 and by 3.2% in 2002.

AGRICULTURE

Agriculture (including forestry and fishing) contributed 16.5% of GDP in 2002, and engaged 43.6% of the employed labour force in 2001. The principal crops are cereals (mainly wheat and barley), sugar beet, potatoes, citrus fruit, tomatoes and sugar cane. Almost all of Morocco's meat requirements are produced within the country. The sale of licences to foreign fishing fleets is an important source of revenue. In 2001 seafoods and seafood products accounted for an estimated 9.3% of total exports. During 1990–2002 agricultural GDP increased at an average annual rate of 0.4%. Agricultural GDP declined by 15.7% in 2000, as a result of severe drought; however, it increased by 27.6% in 2001 and by 5.6% in 2002.

INDUSTRY

Industry (including mining, manufacturing, construction and power) engaged 19.7% of the employed labour force in 2001, and provided 31.1% of GDP in 2002. During 1990–2002 industrial GDP increased by an average of 3.0% per year. Industrial GDP rose by 5.0% in 2001 and by 2.7% in 2002.

Mining

Mining and quarrying contributed 1.9% of GDP in 2002; the sector engaged 0.6% of the labour force in 2000. The major mineral exports are phosphate rock and phosphoric acid, which together earned an estimated 12.5% of export revenues in 2001. Morocco is the world's largest exporter of phosphate rock. Petroleum exploration activity was revived at the end of the 1990s, and in August 2000 the discovery of major oil and natural gas reserves in the Talsinnt region of eastern Morocco was announced. Coal, salt, iron ore, barytes, lead, copper, zinc, silver, gold and manganese are mined. Deposits of nickel, cobalt and bauxite have been discovered. During 1990–2002 mining GDP increased at an average annual rate of 1.3%. Mining GDP increased by 3.0% in 2001 and by 3.2% in 2002.

Manufacturing

Manufacturing employed 12.3% of the labour force in 2000, and contributed 20.0% of GDP in 2002. The most important branches, measured by gross value of output, are food-processing, textiles, and chemicals. During 1990–2002 manufacturing GDP was estimated to have increased at an average annual rate of 2.8%. Manufacturing GDP rose by 4.2% in 2001 and by 2.8% in 2002.

Energy

Electric energy is derived principally from thermal power stations (which accounted for an estimated 94.5% of production in 2001) using coal and imported petroleum and gas. Facilities for generating hydroelectric and wind power have also been developed. Imports of fuel and energy products comprised an estimated 17.6% of the value of total merchandise imports in 2001.

SERVICES

The services sector contributed 52.4% of GDP in 2002, and engaged 36.7% of the employed labour force in 2001. The tourist industry is generally a major source of revenue, and tourist arrivals reached 2.2m. in 2002. The GDP of the services sector increased by an estimated average of 3.2% per year during 1990–2002. The GDP of the sector rose by 3.8% in 2001 and by 2.8% in 2002.

EXTERNAL TRADE

In 2002 Morocco recorded a visible trade deficit of US $3,036m., but there was a surplus of $1,488m. on the current account of the balance of payments. In 2001 the principal source of imports was France (which provided an estimated 24.1% of merchandise imports); other major suppliers in that year included Spain, the United Kingdom, and Germany. France was also the principal market for exports (32.8%) in 2001; Spain, the United Kingdom and Italy were also important purchasers of Moroccan exports. The principal exports in 2001 were manufactured garments, phosphates and phosphoric acid, hosiery, and seafoods and seafood products. The principal imports in that year were crude petroleum and textiles.

GOVERNMENT FINANCE

In the financial year ending 30 June 2000 there was a budget deficit of 2,261m. dirhams, equivalent to 0.7% of GDP. Morocco's total external debt in 2000 was US $16,962m., of which $14,325m. was long-term public debt. The cost of debt-servicing in that year was equivalent to 17.8% of exports of goods and services. The annual rate of inflation averaged 3.8% in 1989–2002. Annual inflation slowed to just 0.6% in 2001, but increased to 2.8% in 2002. Some 12.5% of the labour force were unemployed in 2001.

INTERNATIONAL ECONOMIC RELATIONS

Morocco is a member of the African Development Bank, the Islamic Development Bank and of the Arab Fund for Economic and Social Development. It is a founder member of the Union du Maghreb arabe (Union of the Arab Maghreb).

SURVEY AND PROSPECTS

Since 1980 the Moroccan authorities have undertaken a series of economic reforms (under the auspices of the IMF), including the reduction of taxes, tariffs and subsidies and the introduction of a more efficient tax system. Efforts to stimulate foreign investment have had considerable success, while a programme of privatization has bolstered government revenue.

In March 2000 a trade and co-operation agreement with the European Union (EU) came into effect, which provided for the establishment of a free-trade zone with the EU within 10 years. The Government was able to compensate for the loss of revenue from the fisheries accord with the EU, which expired in 2001, with the sale, for US $1,100m., of Morocco's second mobile cellular telephone operating licence and the partial privatization of Maroc Télécom—35% of which was sold to the French telecommunications company Vivendi for $2,330m.

The tourism sector, which contributes an estimated 8% of GDP per year, was adversely affected by the volatile situation in the Middle East from 2002 and the suicide bombings launched against Western targets in Casablanca in May 2003. Nevertheless, the Government continued with ambitious plans to raise the number of tourist visitors to Morocco to 10m. by 2010 and to significantly increase tourism revenues.

The 2004 budget forecast GDP growth of 3.0% for that year, although analysts maintained that much higher growth was needed in order to reduce endemic poverty in the country and to stimulate job creation. There were, however, a number of positive macroeconomic developments in 2003–04: the rate of inflation remained low; a balance of payments surplus was recorded; and foreign exchange reserves increased. Furthermore, Morocco and the USA signed a free-trade agreement in early March 2004, and a number of high-profile privatizations were also scheduled for that year.

Mozambique

The Republic of Mozambique lies on the east coast of Africa. Mozambique achieved full independence from Portuguese rule in 1975. International mediation in an armed conflict between the Frente de Libertação de Moçambique (Frelimo) Government and the guerrilla Resistência Nacional Moçambicana (Renamo), resulted, in 1994, in Renamo's participation in presidential and legislative elections. Frelimo's presidential candidate, Joaquim Alberto Chissano, was reconfirmed in office, and Frelimo also secured an overall majority in the legislature. In 1999 Chissano was re-elected President, while Frelimo secured an outright majority in the legislature. Maputo is the capital. The official language is Portuguese.

Area and population
Area: 799,380 sq km
Population (mid-2002): 18,438,330
Population density (mid-2002): 23.1 per sq km
Life expectancy (years at birth, 2002): 42.6 (males 41.2; females 43.9)

Finance
GDP in current prices: 2002): US $3,920m. ($213 per head)
Real GDP growth (2002): 9.9%
Inflation (annual average, 2002): 16.8%
Currency: metical

Economy

In 2002, according to estimates by the World Bank, Mozambique's gross national income (GNI), measured at average 2000–02 prices, was US $3,869m., equivalent to $210 per head. During 1990–2002, it was estimated, the population increased at an average annual rate of 2.2%, while gross domestic product (GDP) per head increased, in real terms, by an average of 4.2% per year. Overall GDP increased, in real terms, at an average annual rate of 6.6% in 1990–2002; growth in 2002 was 9.9%. According to official figures, growth in 2002 was 8.3%.

AGRICULTURE
Agriculture (including forestry and fishing) contributed 24.3% of GDP in 2002. In mid-2002 an estimated 80.8% of the economically active population were employed in the sector. Fishing is the principal export activity: fish, crustaceans and molluscs accounted for 14.2% of total export earnings in 2001. The principal cash crops are fruit and nuts, cotton, sugar cane and copra. The main subsistence crop is cassava. During 1990–2002, according to the World Bank, agricultural GDP increased by an average of 3.5% per year; growth in 2002 was 7.3%.

INDUSTRY
Industry (including mining, manufacturing, construction and power) employed 5.6% of the economically active population in 1997, and provided 25.2% of GDP in 2002. During 1990–2002, according to the World Bank, industrial GDP increased at an average annual rate of 14.3%; growth in 2002 was 21.9%.

Mining
Mining and quarrying contributed 0.3% of GDP in 2002, and employed 0.5% of the economically active population in 1997. Only coal, bauxite, marble, gold and salt are exploited in significant quantities, although gravel and crushed rocks are also mined. The exploitation of commercially viable levels of graphite began in 1994, but production ceased in 2000. Formal production of bentonite also ceased in 2002, although small amounts were still processed. There are reserves of other minerals, including high-grade iron ore, precious and semi-precious stones, and natural gas. Plans began in 1994 to exploit natural gas reserves at Pande, in the province of Inhambane, which were estimated at 55,000m. cu m. A South African company, SASOL Ltd, was granted a 25-year concession to develop gasfields at Pande and Temane (also in Inhambane province); it was anticipated that the Government would receive revenues of some US $900m. from the project, and the construction of a pipeline to transport the gas to South Africa was completed in 2003. A gas-processing centre was scheduled to open in Temane in early 2004. In 2003 the Government announced that it was to invest $20m. in gas prospecting in Sofala province. In 1999 the largest reserve of titanium in

the world (estimated at 100m. metric tons) was discovered in the district of Chibuto, in the province of Gaza; production from the Limpopo Corridor Sands Project in Chibuto was expected to begin in 2007 and last for some 35 years, providing up to 1m. tons of titanium per year. In 2003 plans were announced for the exploitation of further titanium reserves in Nampula province; it was hoped that production would commence in 2005, providing up to 2.5% of GDP. According to government targets, minerals were to account for 10% of exports and 6% of GDP by 2005. According to official figures, mining GDP increased at an average annual rate of 7.1% in 1991–02; growth in 2002 was 2.1%.

Manufacturing

Manufacturing contributed 13.2% of GDP in 2002, and employed 3.0% of the economically active population in 1997. A large aluminium smelter, Mozal, was opened in 2000 and expanded in 2003, with the completion of Mozal 2, which was expected to double capacity, to some 506,000 metric tons of aluminium ingots per year. It was estimated that Mozal contributed around 2.1% of GDP in 2002, and unwrought aluminium and alloys accounted for 54.5% of total export earnings in 2001. During 1994–2002, according to the World Bank, manufacturing GDP increased at an average annual rate of 14.0%; growth in 2002 was 6.2%.

Energy

Electrical energy is derived principally from hydroelectric power, which provided some 99.6% of total electricity production in 2000. Mozambique's important Cahora Bassa hydroelectric plant on the Zambezi River supplies electricity to South Africa and Zimbabwe. In late 2003 an extended power supply from Cahora Bassa to Zambézia province was opened. From 1999 a consortium involving Mozambican, French and German companies financed a feasibility study for the construction of a hydroelectric power plant at Mepanda Uncua, some 70 km downstream of Cahora Bassa, which would help to support the 900-MW energy requirement of the Mozal smelter. Construction of the plant, which would have a generating capacity of 2,500 MW, was projected to cost some US $1,500m. It was envisaged that power from the plant, which would not be completed before 2007, would also be exported to South Africa. Mozambique currently imports all of its petroleum requirements. Imports of mineral fuels and lubricants comprised 15.9% of the value of total imports in 2001.

SERVICES

The services sector engaged 12.3% of the economically active population in 1997, and contributed 50.5% of GDP in 2002. By the end of the 1990s tourism was the fastest growing sector of the economy, and was estimated to contribute some US $32m. annually to the budget. It was hoped that the formal opening, in April 2002, of the Great Limpopo Transfrontier Park, comprising South Africa's Kruger National Park, Zimbabwe's Gonarezhou National Park and Mozambique's Limpopo National Park, would attract additional tourists. The GDP of the services sector increased by an average of 2.2% per year in 1990–2002, according to the World Bank; services GDP increased by 1.1% in 2001, but declined by 6.2% in 2002.

EXTERNAL TRADE

In 2002 Mozambique recorded a trade deficit of US $581.1m., and there was a deficit of $420.6m. on the current account of the balance of payments. In 2001 the principal source of imports was South Africa (40.3%); Portugal was also a major supplier. In the same year South Africa was the principal market for exports (receiving 15.3%); Zimbabwe was another significant purchaser. The principal exports in 2002 were aluminium, electricity and prawns. The principal imports in 2001 were machinery and transport equipment, refined petroleum products, food and live animals (principally cereals and cereal preparations), basic manufactures and chemicals. Production from the Mozal aluminium smelter almost doubled the value of total exports in 2001, to some $703m.

GOVERNMENT FINANCE

In 2003 there was an overall budgetary deficit of 5,139,000m. meticais. Mozambique's total external debt was estimated at US $4,466m. at the end of 2001, of which $3,772m. was long-term public debt. In that year the cost of debt-servicing was equivalent to 3.4% of the total value of exports of goods and services. The average annual rate of inflation was 11.9% in 1998–2002; consumer prices increased by an average of 9.0% in 2002. According to official figures, the number of unemployed was 118,000 at the end of 1996.

INTERNATIONAL ECONOMIC RELATIONS

Mozambique is a member of the Southern African Development Community (SADC). In November 2000 Mozambique was invited by the Common Market for Eastern and Southern Africa (COMESA) to rejoin the organization (Mozambique left COMESA in 1993, when it joined SADC).

SURVEY AND PROSPECTS

In terms of average income, Mozambique is one of the poorest countries in the world. During the 1980s economic development was severely frustrated by the effects of the civil war. Since 1990 there has been considerable progress in liberalizing the economy. Increased production in rural areas, continued structural reform and the partial restoration of the infrastructure contributed to significant GDP growth from 1993, and in 1994–98 Mozambique's economy was one of the fastest growing in the world.

In June 1999 the Bretton Woods institutions reduced Mozambique's public debt by almost two-thirds, significantly decreasing the country's annual servicing obligations for the period 1999–2005, and the IMF approved a three-year loan for Mozambique, equivalent to some US $78.5m., under the Enhanced Structural Adjustment Facility (later renamed the Poverty Reduction and Growth Facility—PRGF). In March 2000 the 'Paris Club' of official creditors deferred all payments due on the country's external debt for one year, following severe flooding in southern and central Mozambique, and the IMF increased the PRGF arrangement to some $113m. In April the IMF agreed to grant Mozambique a further $600m. in debt relief under the enhanced terms of the initiative for heavily indebted poor countries.

A decline in prices for cashew nuts in 2000–01 (principally as a result of a collapse in demand in India, but also partly owing to the liberalization of Mozambique's cashew-processing industry, as requested by the World Bank) led to economic uncertainty and an increase in the country's trade deficit. None the less, strong economic growth was recorded in 2001, owing to the increased output of the Mozal smelter and a recovery in the agricultural sector, following the floods in 2000. During 2002 Mozambique's foreign debt was drastically reduced by the cancellation of its obligations to Russia, Italy, Germany and the United Kingdom. In June the IMF commended Mozambique's rapid post-flood recovery, extending the PRGF arrangement by one year.

In 2003 foreign investment and aid continued to contribute significantly to infrastructural developments. In October, at a meeting of the World Bank's Consultative Group, donors pledged some $790m. in assistance for 2004, mostly in the form of grants. GDP growth of some 7.0% and inflation of 10.8% were estimated in 2003. Meanwhile, the Government maintained its commitment to the country's Action Plan for the Reduction of Absolute Poverty; it was estimated that 54% of the population were living below the poverty line in 2003, compared with 69% in 1997. GDP growth of 8% was forecast for 2004, largely owing to the expansion of Mozal, and inflation was projected to decline to 9%.

Myanmar

The Union of Myanmar (formerly Burma) lies in the north-west region of South-East Asia. In 1988 the army seized power and established a State Law and Order Restoration Council (SLORC). In 1990 the National League for Democracy (NLD) won an outright majority of seats in a new assembly. However, the SLORC remained the de facto Government. In 1997 the SLORC was replaced by a State Peace and Development Council. Since 1988 NLD founder Aung San Suu Kyi has been at the forefront of democratic opposition to the ruling juntas. Yangon is the capital. The official language is Myanmar (Burmese).

Area and population
Area: 676,552 sq km
Population (mid-2002): 48,895,300
Population density (mid-2002): 72.3 per sq km
Life expectancy (years at birth, 2002): 58.9 (males 56.2; females 61.8)

Finance

GDP in current prices: year ending 31 March 2002): 3,523,515m. kyats (72,062 kyats per head)
Real GDP growth (2001): 9.7%
Inflation (annual average, 2002): 57.1%
Currency: kyat

Economy

In 1986, according to estimates by the World Bank, Myanmar's gross national income (GNI), measured at average 1984–86 prices, was US $7,450m., equivalent to $200 per head. In 1990–2002, it was estimated, the population increased at an annual average rate of 1.6%. According to the Asian Development Bank (ADB), Myanmar's gross domestic product (GDP) increased, in real terms, by an annual average of 7.2% between 1990/91 and 2000/01 (years ending 31 March). Real GDP growth was officially declared to be 13.7% in 2000/01 and 11.1% in 2001/02. However, according to the IMF, GDP increased by 6.2% in the former year.

AGRICULTURE
According to the ADB, agriculture (including forestry and fishing) contributed an estimated 57.2% of GDP in 2001/02. The sector engaged an estimated 69.9% of the employed labour force in the previous year. Rice is the staple crop, and has traditionally been among Myanmar's principal export commodities. Exports of rice and rice products provided 21.6% of total export earnings in 1994/95; however, the proportion had declined to 4.4% by 2001/02. In 2003 the Government announced plans intended to liberalize the rice trade. However, in January 2004 it banned the export of rice for six months, a ban that resulted in significant overproduction and a consequent decline in domestic rice prices. In 2001/02 pulses and beans accounted for 11.1% of total exports. Other crops include sugar cane, groundnuts, maize, sesame seed, tobacco and rubber. Myanmar is one of the largest sources of illicit opium in the world, and it has been speculated that the Government is involved in its export. In 2003, according to a survey conducted by the UN Office on Drugs and Crime, Myanmar was the world's second biggest producer of opium, behind Afghanistan. However, ongoing government efforts to eradicate illicit poppy cultivation were achieving some success, reflected by an overall decline in opium production in 2003. The fishing sector is also important. Sales of teak and other hardwood provided 11.0% of total export revenue in 2001/02. (Teak is frequently felled illegally and smuggled across the border into Thailand.) Between 1990/91 and 2000/01, according to the ADB, the real GDP of the agricultural sector increased by an annual average of 5.8%. Annual agricultural GDP growth measured 11.5% in 1999/2000 and 11.0% in 2000/01.

INDUSTRY
Industry (including mining, manufacturing, construction and utilities) provided an estimated 10.5% of GDP in 2001/02, according to the ADB. The industrial sector engaged 12.2% of the employed labour force (excluding activities not adequately defined) in 1997/98. Between 1990/91 and 2000/01, according to the ADB, industrial

GDP increased by an annual average of 10.7%. Industrial GDP growth measured 13.8% in 1999/2000 and 21.3% in 2000/01.

Mining

Mining and quarrying contributed an estimated 0.5% of GDP in 2001/02 and engaged 0.7% of the employed labour force in 1997/98. Production of crude petroleum decreased steadily from 1980, and from 1988 Myanmar was obliged to import petroleum. Significant onshore and offshore discoveries of natural gas and petroleum have resulted from exploration and production-sharing agreements with foreign companies, the first of which was signed in 1989. Other important minerals that are commercially exploited include tin, zinc, copper, tungsten, coal, lead, jade, gemstones, silver and gold; however, some of Myanmar's potentially lucrative mineral resources remain largely unexploited. According to the ADB, the GDP of the mining sector increased by an annual average of 18.3% between 1990/91 and 2000/01. Growth in the GDP of the mining sector measured 36.3% in 1999/2000 and 28.0% in 2000/01.

Manufacturing

Manufacturing contributed an estimated 7.8% of GDP in 2001/02 and engaged 9.2% of the employed labour force in 1997/98. The most important branches are food and beverage processing, the production of industrial raw materials (cement, plywood and fertilizers), petroleum refining and textiles. The sector is adversely affected by shortages of electricity and the high price of machinery and spare parts. From mid-2003 a US ban on imports from Myanmar had a serious impact upon the textile sector; textiles and garments had previously constituted the majority of Myanmar's exports to the USA. The real GDP of the manufacturing sector increased, according to the ADB, at an average rate of 8.4% per year between 1990/91 and 2000/01. Manufacturing GDP rose by 14.5% in 1999/2000 and by 23.0% in 2000/01.

Energy

Energy is derived principally from natural gas, which accounted for 57.0% of electricity production in 2000; petroleum contributed 6.1% and hydroelectric power 36.9%. In January 2002 the Government announced that its third Five-Year Plan would give priority to the construction of three hydropower plants, in order to accelerate the development of the country's industrial sector. Imports of mineral fuels, lubricants, etc. accounted for 20.9% of total imports in 2001/02.

SERVICES

The services sector contributed 32.4% of GDP in 2001/02 and engaged 20.8% of the employed labour force in 1997/98. Tourism revenue increased substantially over the period 1992–95, and became the country's second largest source of foreign exchange in 1995/96. In 2001 tourist arrivals reached 204,862, while revenue totalled approximately US $45m. in that year. Following the terrorist attack on the Indonesian island of Bali in October 2002, the number of tourists visiting Myanmar increased substantially; it was believed that the country was perceived to be a safer destination than others in the region. According to the ADB, the GDP of the services sector increased by an average of 7.3% per year between 1990/91 and 2000/01. GDP growth in the sector measured 9.2% in 1999/2000 and 13.4% in 2000/01.

EXTERNAL TRADE

In 2001 Myanmar recorded a visible trade deficit of US $271.1m., and there was a deficit of $308.5m. on the current account of the balance of payments. In 2002 the principal sources of imports were the People's Republic of China (which supplied 21.8% of the total) and Singapore (20.1%); other major suppliers were Thailand, the Republic of Korea and Malaysia. The principal market for exports (31.7%) was Thailand; other significant purchasers were the USA (13.2%), India and the People's Republic of China. Illegal trade is widespread, and was estimated to be equivalent to 50% of official trade in 1995/96. The principal imports in 2001/02 were machinery and transport equipment, basic manufactures and mineral fuels and lubricants. The principal exports in that year were pulses and beans, teak and other hardwood and rice and rice products.

GOVERNMENT FINANCE

In the financial year ending 31 March 2000 there was a budgetary deficit of 1,580m. kyats, equivalent to 0.07% of GDP (according to the IMF). Myanmar's external debt at the end of 2001 totalled US $5,670m., of which $5,007m. was long-term public debt; in that year the cost of servicing external debt was equivalent to 3.1% of exports of goods and services. The annual rate of inflation averaged 11.9% in 1998–2002. Prices declined by 0.2% in 2000, but increased by 21.2% in 2001 and by 57.0% in 2002, according to the ADB. The number of registered unemployed persons in 1997/98 was equivalent to 2.5% of the labour force.

INTERNATIONAL ECONOMIC RELATIONS

Myanmar is a member of the UN Economic and Social Commission for Asia and the Pacific (ESCAP), the Asian Development Bank and the Colombo Plan, which promote economic development in the region. In July 1997 Myanmar acceded to the Association of South East Asian Nations (ASEAN). Myanmar was granted a 10-year period from 1 January 1998 to comply with the tariff reductions (to between 0% and 5%) required under the ASEAN Free Trade Area (AFTA), which was formally established on 1 January 2002.

SURVEY AND PROSPECTS

Following the limited liberalization of Myanmar's centrally planned economy in 1988, the country began to attract foreign investment and to develop a small private sector. However, foreign investment was severely limited by international criticism of continued violations of human rights (culminating in the imposition of US sanctions in May 1997 and the decision of the European Union (EU) to revoke Myanmar's special trading privileges), inadequate infrastructure and widespread corruption. Consumer boycotts in the USA and Europe of companies investing in Myanmar led to the withdrawal from the country of several large investors. Myanmar was also affected by the regional economic crisis of 1997–98. The slow progress towards liberalization achieved since 1988 began to be reversed. Thus, from the late 1990s Myanmar was effectively sustained by a 'parallel' economy, mainly comprising unofficial border trade with the People's Republic of China, Thailand and India. The currency continued to depreciate sharply, and by September 2002 the kyat had declined to a low of 1,150 to the US dollar. The official exchange rate, meanwhile, remained at about six kyats to the dollar, having been fixed at the same level for nearly 40 years.

In 2001 the seemingly more liberal stance shown by the SPDC began to mitigate international attitudes towards Myanmar, especially in Asia. In April Japan agreed to offer US $28m. in bilateral aid to Myanmar, for the purpose of the rehabilitation of a hydroelectric dam. In March 2001 the Government implemented its third Five-Year Plan. The previous plan had, according to the SPDC, achieved an average annual growth rate of 8.4%. The plan beginning in 2001 projected average annual GDP growth rates in excess of 8% until 2005/06. The main aims of the plan were: to promote the establishment of agro-based industries; to develop the power and energy sectors; to expand the agriculture, meat and fish sectors in order to meet local demand and provide a surplus for export; to establish forest reserves; to extend the health and education sectors; and to develop the rural areas. In November 2001 a report released by the ADB stressed that the Government needed to implement a wide range of reforms if Myanmar's prospects for growth were to improve. It warned that the junta's policy of funding its annual budget deficit through an expansion of credit from the country's central bank was unsustainable in the long term.

In early 2003 the country's private banking sector experienced a crisis when the failure of several financial services groups to pay investors led to panic withdrawals from the country's 20 private banks. The Government was forced to intervene, imposing withdrawal limits and providing financial assistance to the banks that were most severely affected. In May 2003, following the rearrest of Suu Kyi, Myanmar's economic prospects deteriorated further. Japan, previously Myanmar's most important foreign donor, announced the suspension of economic aid, and the USA and the EU both strengthened their sanctions against the country, with the USA effectively banning all imports from Myanmar. The ongoing effect of the sanctions, combined with the junta's inconsistent agricultural policies and a dramatic increase in inflation, contributed to the continuing downturn in the economy in 2003. In March 2004 Japan announced that it intended to resume aid donations to the country, apparently owing to the release of several political prisoners earlier in the year. However, Myanmar's economic performance continued to depend in the long term upon an improvement in the country's political situation.

Namibia

The Republic of Namibia lies in south-western Africa. In 1950 the International Court of Justice issued a ruling that South West Africa, as Namibia was then known, should remain under international mandate and that South Africa should submit it to UN control. South Africa refused to comply with this judgment, however, and in 1966 extended its security and apartheid laws to the area. Namibia did not finally achieve independence until 1990. The South West African People's Organisation of Namibia has been the leading political party since independence, during which time Dr Samuel Nujoma has been President. Windhoek is the capital. The official language is English.

Area and population
Area: 824,292 sq km
Population (mid-2002): 1,823,200
Population density (mid-2002): 2.2 per sq km
Life expectancy (years at birth, 2002): 49.3 (males 48.1; females 50.5)

Finance
GDP in current prices: 2002): US $2,793m. ($1,532 per head)
Real GDP growth (2002): 3.0%
Inflation (annual average, 2002): 11.3%
Currency: Namibian dollar

Economy

In 2002, according to estimates by the World Bank, Namibia's gross national income (GNI), measured at average 2000–02 prices, was US $3,253m., equivalent to US $1,780 per head (or $6,650 per head on an international purchasing-power parity basis). During 1990–2002, it was estimated, the population increased at an average annual rate of 2.4% per year, while gross domestic product (GDP) per head increased, in real terms, by an average of 1.9% per year. Overall GDP increased, in real terms, at an average annual rate of 4.3% in 1990–2002. Real GDP increased by 2.7% in 2001 and by 3.0% in 2002.

AGRICULTURE

According to the Bank of Namibia, agriculture (including hunting, forestry and fishing) contributed 11.2% of GDP in 2002. About 39.7% of the labour force were employed in the sector in 2002. Namibia has potentially one of the richest fisheries in the world. Government revenue from sales of fishing concessions was projected at N $70m. in the financial year ending 31 March 1999, and exports of fish and fish products provided 28.5% of total export earnings in 1998. Legislation aimed at developing aquaculture was adopted in 2003, and a number of fish farms were established. The principal agricultural activity is beef production; the production of karakul sheepskins is also important. In addition, sealing and ostrich farming are practised on a commercial basis. The main subsistence crops are maize, millet and root crops, although Namibia remains highly dependent on imports of basic foods, especially in drought years. Plantations of seedless grapes were developed on the banks of the Orange river in the late 1990s, and projected growth in production was expected to make them the second largest agricultural export after beef. In 2002 the South African Government granted Namibia limited access to fish in its territorial waters. Agricultural GDP increased at an average annual rate of 4.1% in 1990–2002. Agricultural GDP decreased by 0.4% in 2001, but increased by 3.0% in 2002.

INDUSTRY

Industry (including mining, manufacturing, construction and power) contributed 30.4% of GDP in 2002, and engaged 15.0% of the employed labour force in 1991. During 1990–2002 industrial GDP increased by an average of 2.3% per year. Industrial GDP increased by 1.6% in 2001 and by 1.8% in 2002.

Mining

Mining and quarrying contributed 14.3% of GDP in 2002, and engaged 3.7% of the employed labour force in 1991. Namibia has rich deposits of many minerals, and is among the world's leading producers of gem diamonds (some 95% of diamonds mined in Namibia are of gem quality). Diamond-mining contributed 81.8% of the sector's GDP in 2001, and diamonds are the principal mineral export, accounting for an estimated 50.1% of export earnings in 2002; in 2000 Namibia produced 5% of world diamond output by value. The mining of offshore diamond deposits is of increasing importance, with offshore recoveries of gem-quality diamonds accounting for about 56% of the country's output in 1999. Some US $500,000m.-worth of diamonds were estimated to be lying on the continental shelf off the Namibian coast in 2001. A new Diamond Act, liberalizing exploration, came into force in 2000. Uranium is also an important mineral export. In addition, zinc, lead, gold, salt, fluorspar, marble and semi-precious stones are extracted, and there are also considerable deposits of hydrocarbons, lithium, manganese, tungsten, cadmium and vanadium. Namibia is also believed to have substantial reserves of coal, iron ore and platinum. Copper production, which ceased in 1998, following the liquidation of the Tsumeb Corporation, resumed at the former Tsumeb sites in September 2000. The Skorpion zinc mine and refinery near Rosh Pinah, opened in mid-2003 by Anglo American plc, was expected to contribute some 4% of GDP on reaching full production in the second half of 2004. Production of an estimated 150,000 metric tons of zinc per year was anticipated over a period of 15 years. In late 2001 development began on a mine and smelter complex for high-grade silicon metal at Omaruru. Mining GDP increased at an average annual rate of 2.7% in 1993–2001; the sector's GDP decreased by 1.7% in 2000 and by 6.1% in 2001.

Manufacturing
Manufacturing contributed 10.7% of GDP in 2002, and engaged 5.8% of the employed labour force in 1991. The sector has hitherto remained underdeveloped, largely owing to Namibia's economic dependence on South Africa. The principal manufacturing activities are the processing of fish (which contributed 19.4% of manufacturing GDP in 2001) and minerals for export; brewing, meat processing and the production of chemicals are also significant. Namibia's first diamond-cutting and -polishing factory was inaugurated in 1998. Manufacturing GDP increased by an average of 2.6% per year in 1990–2002. Manufacturing GDP increased by 0.8% in 2001 and by 3.5% in 2002.

Energy
In 2000 97.6% of Namibia's electricity production was derived from hydroelectric power. There is a hydroelectric station at Ruacana, on the Cunene river at the border with Angola, and a second hydroelectric power station was planned at Divundu on the Okavango river; a project to construct a power station at Epupa remained stalled in 2004, following a disagreement between the Namibian and Angolan Governments over the most appropriate site. Sizeable offshore deposits of natural gas are also to be exploited commercially: a planned 750-MW power plant would supply the domestic market, and it is anticipated that a surplus will be produced for export to South Africa. Domestic electricity generation increased significantly in 2000, enabling the proportion of electrical energy imported to be reduced to 34.8% in that year. A power transmission line, linking the Namibian and South African electricity grids, was inaugurated in southern Namibia in 1999. Imports of mineral fuels and lubricants accounted for 5.9% of the value of total merchandise imports in 1997.

SERVICES
The services sector contributed 58.4% of GDP in 2002. Tourism is expanding rapidly, and has been the focus of a major privatization initiative. The acquisition of Walvis Bay in March 1994, and subsequent establishment there of a free-trade zone, was expected to enhance Namibia's status as an entrepôt for regional trade. By March 2004 it was estimated that the free-trade zone had attracted some N $80m. of direct foreign investment. The GDP of the services sector increased at an average annual

rate of 4.4% in 1990–2002. Services GDP increased by 3.9% in 2001 and by 3.5% in 2002.

EXTERNAL TRADE

In 2002 Namibia recorded a visible trade deficit of US $178.9m., although there was a surplus of US $96.5m. on the current account of the balance of payments. South Africa is the dominant source of imports, providing 84.3% of the total in 1997. In 1993 the United Kingdom (34.4%) and South Africa (27.4%) were the principal markets for Namibian exports. The principal exports in 2002 were diamonds and other mineral products, food and live animals (notably fish and meat) and manufactured goods. The principal import groups in 1997 included food, live animals, beverages and tobacco; machinery and electrical goods; transport equipment; chemicals and chemical products; textiles, clothing and footwear; metals and metal products; and mineral fuels and lubricants.

GOVERNMENT FINANCE

In the financial year ending 31 March 2004 Namibia recorded an estimated overall budget deficit of N $1,408.5m. In 1997 South Africa officially cancelled the external public debt inherited by Namibia at independence. Namibia's external debt was estimated at US $716m. in 2003. The annual rate of inflation averaged 10.0% in 1990–2002; consumer prices increased by an average of 11.3% in 2002. Some 35% of the labour force were unemployed in 2001.

INTERNATIONAL ECONOMIC RELATIONS

Namibia is a member of the Common Market for Eastern and Southern Africa, of the Southern African Development Community, and of the Southern African Customs Union (with Botswana, Lesotho, South Africa and Swaziland).

SURVEY AND PROSPECTS

Despite a vulnerability to drought, Namibia's potential for economic prosperity is high, given its abundant mineral reserves and rich fisheries, as well as a well-developed infrastructure, all of which were enhanced by the acquisition, in 1994, of sovereignty over Walvis Bay and of important diamond-mining rights. However, Namibia's economic progress continues to be largely influenced by its dependence on South Africa. (The Namibian dollar, introduced in 1993, is at par with the rand.) Although the average level of income per head is among the highest in the region, there remain extreme disparities in the distribution of wealth; in 1994 land-reform legislation was enacted in an effort to redress this problem, but implementation has been very slow. In April 2001 the Government announced that it had allocated N $100m. to acquire land for redistribution on a voluntary basis over a five-year period. At this time approximately 4,000 (mainly white-owned) farms occupied 52% of the total land area, while the Government had acquired only some 6% of the land required for resettlement.

In October 2002 the Government announced that it was considering the seizure of white-owned farms for redistribution to the landless black population, and criticized white farmers for taking advantage of the voluntary basis for land redistribution by charging excessively high prices for their land. In March 2004 the Government estimated that it would cost more than US $150m. over a five-year period to redistribute some 9m. ha of land among an estimated 240,000 applicants. At that time some 700 farms had already been transferred. Meanwhile, a rural exodus in recent years has resulted in high rates of urban unemployment and attendant social problems such as crime.

The Nujoma Government's first National Development Plan, covering the period 1995–2000, aimed principally to reduce poverty and encourage sustainable economic growth (averaging 5% annually during the plan period) through policies of diversification, in an attempt to prevent potential over-dependence on the mining and fishing sectors. After a disappointing performance in 1998, the economy improved in 1999 and 2000. However, GDP growth slowed in 2001, to 2.7%, as a result of lower agricultural output, particularly in the fishing sector, before recovering slightly, to 3.0%, in 2002. The second National Development Plan, covering 2001–06, projected GDP growth of 4% per year over the period.

In January 2002 it was reported that, with assistance from the Brazilian Government, Namibia planned to conduct a geological survey of the offshore continental shelf, with the intention of extending its exclusive economic zone from 200 to 350 nautical miles. In November 2001 Namibia became eligible to export certain products to the USA free from tariffs, under the African Growth and Opportunity Act (AGOA); it was estimated that 90% of products made in Namibia would qualify for duty-free access to the US market until 2008. In December 2002 and 2003 Namibia's eligibility for tariff preferences under AGOA was renewed. The continued expansion of the mining sector, notably at the Skorpion zinc mine and refinery, was expected to contribute significantly to increased real GDP growth in 2004 and 2005, which was forecast at 4.3% and 5.0%, respectively.

Nauru

The Republic of Nauru is a small island in the central Pacific Ocean. In 1947 the island was placed under UN Trusteeship, with Australia as the administering power on behalf of Australia, New Zealand and the United Kingdom. Nauru became independent in 1968. In 1999 Nauru became a full member of the Commonwealth and of the UN. There is no official capital. Nauruan is the language of the Nauruan inhabitants of the island.

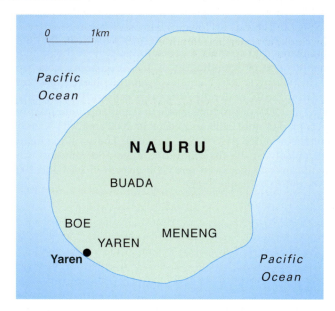

Area and population
Area: 21 sq km
Population (mid-2000): 11,845
Population density (mid-2000): 556 per sq km
Life expectancy (years at birth, 2002): 62.7 (males 59.7; females 66.5)

Finance
GDP in current prices: 1999): US $34m. ($2,830 per head)
Real GDP growth (1999): –1.9%
Currency: Australian dollar

Economy

In 1999, according to UN estimates, Nauru's gross domestic product (GDP), measured at current prices, was US $34m., equivalent to $2,830 per head. In 1991–99, it was estimated, GDP decreased, in real terms, at an average annual rate of 5.9%. The population increased by an annual average of 2.0% per year in 1990–2000. The UN estimated that GDP declined, in real terms, by 7.3% in 1997, by 1.9% in 1998 and again by 1.9% in 1999. According to official estimates, Nauru's GDP grew by 0.8% in 2000. Real GDP growth of around 3% was predicted for 2001.

AGRICULTURE

Agricultural activity comprises mainly the small-scale production of tropical fruit, vegetables and livestock, although the production of coffee and copra for export is increasingly significant. According to FAO, agriculture engaged some 20% of the economically active population in 2001. Coconuts are the principal crop. Bananas, pineapples and the screw-pine (*Pandanus*) are also cultivated as food crops, while the islanders keep pigs and chickens. However, almost all Nauru's requirements (including most of its drinking water) are imported. Increased exploitation of the island's marine resources was envisaged following the approval by Parliament of important fisheries legislation in 1997 and 1998. Funding for a new harbour for medium-sized vessels was secured from the Government of Japan in 1998, and in early 1999 the Marshall Islands Sea Patrol agreed to provide assistance in the surveillance of Nauru's exclusive economic zone. Revenue from fishing licence fees totalled $A8.5m. in 2000.

INDUSTRY

Mining

Until the early 1990s Nauru's economy was based on the mining of phosphate rock, which constituted four-fifths of the island's surface area. Phosphate extraction has been conducted largely by indentured labour, notably by I-Kiribati and Tuvaluan workers. Exports of phosphates declined to an average of 0.51m. tons annually in 1990–97 (compared with 1.58m. tons per year in the 1980s), mainly owing to the collapse of the Australian market. As a result of the Asian financial crisis, exports of phosphate declined by almost 18% in 1998 compared with the previous year. In 2001 phosphate exports were suspended in the second half of the year when a processing plant was blockaded by landowners seeking additional compensation for the use of their land by the plant. Mining production, meanwhile, decreased by 7.9% in 2000. Primary deposits of phosphate are expected to be exhausted by 2005. Feasibility studies have been conducted into the mining of secondary and residual deposits, although this activity would be less profitable. An Australian engineering company was expected to undertake a detailed survey of the island's potential for secondary phosphate mining in early 2004. Revenue from phosphate sales has been invested in a long-term trust fund (the Nauru Phosphate Royalties Trust (NPRT), the assets of which totalled about US $900m. in 1992), in the development of shipping and aviation services, and in property purchases in Australia and elsewhere.

Energy

Energy is derived principally from imported petroleum. Output of electrical energy totalled 30m. kWh in 2000.

EXTERNAL TRADE

The country's trade balance deteriorated significantly in 2001. Although imports decreased by 16.3%, exports declined by 61.5% compared with the previous year, resulting in a trade deficit of US $18.4m. The principal imports are food and live animals (which comprised 83.7% of total imports in 1993/94, while beverages accounted for a further 4.1%), machinery and transport equipment (2.8%) and non-metallic mineral manufactures (4.9%). Phosphates are the most important export, earning $A38.1m. in 1995; exports of crude fertilizers to Australia totalled $A8.5m. in 2001. The principal export markets in 2001 were New Zealand (which purchased 30.6% of the total), Australia (25.3%), Thailand (15.8%) and the Republic of Korea (12.3%).(The principal sources of imports were Australia (supplying 49.4%), the USA (16.9%) and Indonesia (7.9%).

GOVERNMENT FINANCE

The national budget for 1998/99 envisaged total revenue of $A38.7m. and expenditure of $A37.2m. (dramatically reduced from expenditure of $A61.8m. in the previous year). According to the Asian Development Bank (ADB), the budgetary deficit was projected at the equivalent of 6.1% of GDP in 1999/2000 and at 10.6% in 2000/01. A fiscal deficit of $A40m.–$A50m. was envisaged in 2001/02. Total public debt was equivalent to 60.8% of GDP in 2000, an apparent improvement on figures in previous years. In 2000 overseas development assistance was estimated at US $4.0m., of which $2.9m. was bilateral aid. Development assistance from Australia amounted to $A3.3m. in 1999/2000. Nauru's external debt was estimated at $A280m. in 2000. In that year the cost of debt-servicing was equivalent to an estimated 13% of total revenue from the exports of goods and services. Consumer prices increased by 4.0% in 1998, by 6.7% in 1999 and by 17.9% in 2000; the annual rate of inflation averaged 4.0% in 2001. The rate of unemployment among those aged 15–19 in the late 1990s was estimated by the ADB to be 33% of males and 52% of females.

INTERNATIONAL ECONOMIC RELATIONS

Nauru is a member of the Pacific Community, of the Pacific Islands Forum and of the UN Economic and Social Commission for Asia and the Pacific (ESCAP), all of which aim to promote regional development. Nauru is also a member of the Asian Development Bank (ADB).

SURVEY AND PROSPECTS

After gaining independence in 1968, Nauru benefited from sole control of phosphate earnings and, as a result, its income per head was among the highest in the world. This, however, had serious repercussions for the country, which became excessively dependent on imported labour, imports of consumer goods and convenience foods, causing health and social problems. Another effect of phosphate mining was to render 80% of the island both uninhabitable and uncultivable, leading to chronic overcrowding.

Nauru lost a significant amount from its Phosphate Royalties Trust during the 1990s through theft and fraud by accountants and other financial advisers. Measures to reform the financial sector, in response to allegations that Nauru's 'offshore' banking services were being abused for the purposes of 'money-laundering', were announced in early 2000. However, serious allegations of 'money-laundering' re-emerged in 2001, leading the Financial Action Task Force (FATF) to impose counter-measures, prescribing increased monitoring, surveillance and transparency in financial transactions. Despite these measures, in March 2003 the US Government of George W. Bush obliged Nauru's President to sign papers effectively ending the island's 'offshore' banking industry or face severe economic sanctions. The country remained on the FATF list in 2004, following the organization's annual review in February. However, Nauru was removed from the OECD's's list of unco-operative tax havens in December 2003.

Nauru received significant financial assistance in late 2001 in exchange for co-operating with Australia in its 'Pacific Solution' to the problem of asylum-seekers. By the end of 2001, in addition to meeting the costs of detaining the refugees in camps, the Australian Government had committed total aid exceeding $A30m. The aid was allocated to various programmes, including $A10m. towards fuel to power the island's electricity generators and $A3m. towards the purchase of new generators.

Nauru's GDP declined throughout the 1990s, and in the early 2000s the economic outlook remained poor. It was unclear how the substantial budgetary deficit envisaged for 2001/02 would be fully financed; the Government had hitherto relied upon loans from official bilateral sources, overseas corporations or funds from the NPRT, the assets of which had been seriously depleted by 2001. The Bank of Nauru, meanwhile, another source of budgetary support and financing of phosphate royalty payments to landowners, was believed to have become practically insolvent. During 2001, furthermore, the repeated suspensions of Air Nauru's operations, owing to lack of funds, had led to serious disruptions in the provision of food, fuel and other essential supplies to the island. By early 2002 government payrolls and payments to several creditors had been severely delayed. In January 2003 President Dowiyogo broadcast an appeal for emergency aid, claiming that the island was on the verge of bankruptcy. A report published by the ADB in April stated that Nauru's economic situation was very serious and deteriorating. Furthermore, the report claimed that development assistance given to the country in the past had had little impact because of a lack of political commitment to change and a shortage of skills among the working population.

In late 2003 the Australian Government announced that it was considering the possibility of offering Australian citizenship to Nauruans when revenue from the island's role as an immigration detention centre (which since 2001 had constituted Nauru's most important source of income) was no longer available. In April 2004 receivers acting on behalf of creditors in the USA seized Nauru's property portfolio, including five buildings in Sydney and Melbourne. The Nauruan Government had been given until early May to repay a debt of more than US $200m. to a US finance corporation.

Nepal

The Kingdom of Nepal is situated in the Himalaya mountains. A limited constitutional monarchy, established in 1951, was ended in 1962 by the reassertion of absolute
royal power. The 1990 Constitution provided for a return to constitutional monarchy
and for multi-party politics. In 2001 nine members of the royal family, including the
King and Queen, were shot dead by Crown Prince Dipendra. Since 1996 Maoist
insurgents have orchestrated an anti-Government 'people's war' in west Nepal.
Kathmandu is the capital. Nepali is the official language.

Area and population
Area: 147,181 sq km
Population (mid-2002): 24,122,310
Population density (mid-2002): 163.9 per sq km
Life expectancy (years at birth, 2002): 60.1 (males 59.9; females 60.2)

Finance
GDP in current prices: 2002): US $5,493m. ($228 per head)
Real GDP growth (2002): –0.6%
Inflation (annual average, 2002): 2.4%
Currency: Nepalese rupee

Economy

In 2002, according to estimates by the World Bank, Nepal's gross national income
(GNI), measured at average 2000–02 prices, was US $5,621m., equivalent to $230 per
head (or $1,350 per head on an international purchasing-power parity basis). During
1990–2002, it was estimated, the population increased at an average annual rate of
2.4%, while gross domestic product (GDP) per head increased, in real terms, by an
average of 2.1% per year. Overall GDP increased, in real terms, at an average annual

rate of 4.5% in 1990–2002. Real GDP grew by 4.7% in 2001, but decreased by 0.5% in 2002.

AGRICULTURE

Agriculture (including forestry and fishing) contributed an estimated 38.1% of GDP in the fiscal year ending 15 July 2002. The sector engaged 76.1% of the employed labour force in 1999. The principal crops are rice, maize, millet, wheat, sugar cane, potatoes and vegetables and melons. During 1990–2002 agricultural GDP increased by an average of 2.5% per year. The agricultural sector grew by 4.3% in 2001 and 1.7% in 2002.

INDUSTRY

Industry (comprising mining, manufacturing, construction and utilities) employed only 9.8% of the labour force in 1999, but provided an estimated 21.9% of GDP in 2001/02. About 60% of Nepal's industrial output comes from traditional cottage industries, and the remainder from modern industries. During 1990–2002 industrial GDP increased at an average annual rate of 6.8%. Industrial production grew by 8.7% in 2000, by 2.5% in 2001 and by 1% in 2002.

Mining

Mining employed only 0.08% of the labour force in 1999, and contributed an estimated 0.5% of GDP in 2001/02. Mica is mined east of Kathmandu, and there are also small deposits of lignite, copper, talc, limestone, cobalt and iron ore. Geophysical investigations have indicated that the Siwalik range and the Terai belt are potential prospective areas for petroleum.

Manufacturing

Manufacturing contributed an estimated 8.4% of GDP in 2001/02, and employed about 5.8% of the labour force in 1999. Manufacturing GDP increased by an average annual rate of 8.0% in 1990–2002. Manufacturing production grew by 3.6% in 2001, but declined by 5.9% in 2002. The principal branches of the sector include textiles—particularly carpets and rugs, food products, wearing apparel and tobacco products. Traditional cottage industries include basket-making and the production of cotton fabrics and edible oils.

Energy

Energy is derived principally from traditional sources (particularly fuelwood). Imports of mineral fuel and lubricants (mainly for the transport sector), however, comprised an estimated 14.3% of the cost of total imports in 2001/02. In addition, Nepal's rivers are exploited for hydroelectric power (HEP) production, but in July 2002 it was estimated that only about 1% of the country's huge potential generating capacity (83m. kW) was being utilized. In January 2004 the 144,000-kW Kali Gandaki A HEP plant was officially inaugurated. The project, the country's largest, began generating electricity in 2002. Nepal was hoping to export excess electricity to India. Several other HEP projects were under construction in the early 2000s.

SERVICES

The services sector employed 14.0% of the labour force in 1999. The sector contributed an estimated 40.0% of GDP in 2001/02. The GDP of the services sector increased at an average annual rate of 5.9% in 1990–2002. By 1996 tourism had emerged as Nepal's major source of foreign exchange; in 1999/2000 revenue from tourism amounted to 12.9% of total foreign-exchange earnings. In 2000 the number of foreign visitors declined to 463,646, compared with 491,504 in the previous year, owing to the suspension of Indian Airlines flights in the first five months of the year, regular strikes and security fears. In 2001 the number of tourists declined again, to 361,247, owing to the massacre of most of the royal family in June, intermittent strikes and the escalating Maoist insurgency. The reduction in the number of foreign visitors was also due to regional tension and the attacks on the USA in September. The worsening domestic security situation caused tourist arrivals to decline by 28% in 2002.

EXTERNAL TRADE

In 2001 Nepal recorded a visible trade deficit of US $765.2m., and there was a deficit of $339.3m. on the current account of the balance of payments. In 2002 India was the principal source of imports (supplying 20.4% of the total) and the principal market for exports (47.0%). Other major trading partners were the People's Republic of China, the United Arab Emirates and the USA. The principal exports in 2001/02 were basic manufactures, manufactured goods and articles and garments. The principal imports were basic manufactures, machinery and transport equipment, and mineral fuels and lubricants.

GOVERNMENT FINANCE

In 2002 there was an estimated overall budget deficit of NRs 16,749m. (equivalent to 3.8% of GDP). Foreign aid plays a vital role in the Nepalese economy. Nepal's total external debt was US $2,700m. at the end of 2001, of which $2,643m. was long-term public debt. In that year the cost of debt-servicing was equivalent to 4.9% of receipts from exports of goods and services. The annual rate of inflation averaged 8.6% in 1990–2001. The national urban consumer-price index rose by 2.5% in 2000 and by 2.7% in 2001. According to official figures, inflation increased by 2.9% in 2002. According to the Asian Development Bank (ADB), in 1999/2000 47% of Nepali workers were underemployed, while urban unemployment, a major problem, particularly among educated youths, stood at 7%.

INTERNATIONAL ECONOMIC RELATIONS

Nepal is a member of the UN Economic and Social Commission for Asia and the Pacific (ESCAP), the ADB, of the Colombo Plan and of the South Asian Association for Regional Co-operation (SAARC), all of which seek to encourage regional economic development. Nepal's entry into the World Trade Organization (WTO) was approved in September 2003, and membership was expected to take effect in 2004.

SURVEY AND PROSPECTS

With an inhospitable terrain, comprising isolated valleys and very high mountains, Nepal is among the least developed countries in the world. Successive administrations since 1991 have followed a policy of economic liberalization: many state enterprises have been privatized (although there have been numerous delays in the process), and there have been attempts to reduce the fiscal deficit, to increase revenue mobilization, to restructure and improve the financial sector, and to institute and operate open trade and investment policies.

In February 1993, as part of a series of economic reforms introduced in an attempt to develop industry further and to increase exports to countries other than India, the Nepalese rupee was made fully convertible for current-account transactions. Nepal's Ninth Five-Year Plan (1997–2002) was launched in July 1997, with projected expenditure of US $7,170m. The main goal of the Plan was to eliminate poverty and reduce unemployment by focusing on the vital agricultural sector. However, unemployment increased, and the rate of growth achieved during the period reached only 3.6%, compared with the targeted 6%. Despite protests by the business sector, value-added tax (VAT) was fully implemented by the Government in August 1999. The high VAT threshold was lowered in the budget for 2000/01. For the first time in 19 years, Nepal's GDP registered a negative growth rate in 2001/02: the economy contracted by 0.5%, according to official figures, largely owing to negative growth rates in the non-agricultural sector. Tourism and foreign trade fared particularly poorly, owing to a worsening internal security situation, regional tension and the suicide attacks on the USA.

Although the extension of the 1996 trade treaty with India was forecast to boost trade with India, the global economic slowdown adversely affected Nepal's export industry. However, the remittances of some 700,000 Nepalese working abroad provided a boost for the economy. A moderate recovery in 2002/03 was facilitated by the cease-fire agreement in January 2003. GDP growth rose to 2.4% in 2002/03, largely owing to a revival of the manufacturing sector, export trade and tourist industry. Preliminary estimates indicated that Nepal's exports and imports increased in that year by 3.3% and 15.2%, respectively. Tax collection also improved, and significant progress was made in the implementation of financial-sector reforms. The interim Government's 2003/04 budget (announced in July 2003) depended heavily on foreign aid to achieve the development expenditure target and projected an ambitious GDP growth rate of 4.5%. The collapse of the cease-fire in late August and the worsening political situation, however, made these targets unlikely to be met (although in February 2004 the ADB predicted that overall GDP growth would recover to about 4%). In the first half of the fiscal year remittances and tourism receipts grew; the trade deficit, however, widened owing to a higher growth of imports compared with exports. The price of major commodities (food and non-food) also increased in this period, resulting in a rise in inflation.

In 2002 the interim Government launched the Tenth Five-Year Plan, which aimed for a 4.3%–6.2% growth rate during 2002–07. One of the objectives of the plan was to reduce the level of poverty to 30% from 42%. The 2003/04 development budget gave priority to projects in areas such as education, drinking water and roads. The budget also introduced the theme of public-private partnerships. In November 2003 the IMF approved a three-year US $72m. Poverty Reduction and Growth Facility for Nepal, in support of the country's povery reduction strategies. In order to attract further foreign investment, however, the restoration of law and order was essential: the precarious security situation continued to pose the greatest risk to economic growth and poverty reduction.

Netherlands

The Kingdom of the Netherlands is situated in western Europe. After liberation from Nazi occupation in 1945, the Netherlands abandoned its traditional policy of neutrality, subsequently joining Western European Union and NATO. In 1960 economic union was established between the Netherlands, Belgium and Luxembourg. The Netherlands was a founder member of the European Community (now European Union). All post-war administrations have been formed by various coalitions between the several 'confessional' Catholic and Protestant and 'progressive' Socialist and Liberal parties. In 1980 Queen Juliana abdicated in favour of her eldest daughter, Beatrix. Amsterdam is the capital. The national language is Dutch.

Area and population
Area: 41,528 sq km (including coastal water)
Population (mid-2002): 16,144,000
Population density (mid-2002): 388.7 per sq km
Life expectancy (years at birth, 2002): 78.6 (males 76.0; females 81.1)

Finance

GDP in current prices: 2002): US $413,741m. ($25,628 per head)
Real GDP growth (2002): 0.1%
Inflation (annual average, 2002): 3.5%
Currency: euro

Economy

In 2002, according to estimates by the World Bank, the Netherlands' gross national income (GNI), measured at average 2000–02 prices, was US $386,774.4m., equivalent to $23,960 per head (or $27,470 per head on an international purchasing-power parity basis). During 1990–2002, it was estimated, the population grew at an average annual rate of 0.6% per year, while gross domestic product (GDP) per head increased, in real terms, at an average annual rate of 1.9% in 1990–2002. Overall GDP increased, in real terms, at an average annual rate of 2.5% in 1990–2001; growth in 2001 was an estimated 6.7%, but fell to 3.6% in 2002.

AGRICULTURE

Agriculture (including hunting, forestry and fishing) contributed 2.3% of GDP in 2000. Although only 3.1% of the employed labour force were engaged in the sector in 2002, the Netherlands is a net exporter of agricultural products: in 2003 exports of food and live animals provided 12.6% of total export earnings. The principal crops are potatoes, sugar beet, wheat and onions. The main agricultural activity is horti-culture; market gardening is highly developed, and the production of cut flowers and bulbs has traditionally been a significant industry, although its contribution to export earnings has declined in recent years. Livestock farming is also an important activity. During 1990–2000 agricultural GDP increased, in real terms, at an average annual rate of 2.3%; following an increase of 3.3% in 2001, it fell by 0.6% in 2002.

INDUSTRY

Industry (including mining, manufacturing, construction and power) contributed an estimated 26.1% of GDP in 2002. About 20.0% of the employed labour force were engaged in the sector in 2002. Industrial GDP increased, in real terms, at an average annual rate of 1.7% in 1990–99; it rose by 5.5% in 2001 and by 0.8% in 2002.

Mining

Extractive activities provided 2.6% of GDP in 2002. In that year about 0.1% of the employed labour force were engaged in mining and quarrying. The principal mineral resource is natural gas. Total extraction in 2002 was an estimated 75,000m. cu m. Reserves of petroleum and salts are also exploited. The GDP of the mining sector declined, in real terms, at an average annual rate of 1.2% in 1995–99; it increased by 19.2% in 2001, but subsequently decreased by 10.0% in 2002.

Manufacturing

Manufacturing contributed 16.1% of GDP in 2002. The sector accounted for 13.4% of the employed labour force in 2001. Measured by the value of output, the principal branches of manufacturing in 1999 were food products, beverages and tobacco (accounting for 22.4% of the total), electrical and optical equipment (9.8%) and basic chemicals and man-made fibres (9.8%). Several multinational companies are dom-iciled in the Netherlands. Manufacturing GDP increased at an average annual rate of 2.4% in 1995–99; it grew by an estimated 1.2% in 2001 and by an estimated 0.1% in 2002.

Energy

In 2000 natural gas provided 57.5% of total electricity production, coal 28.4%, petroleum 3.5%, nuclear energy 4.4% and hydroelectric power 0.2%. Imports of mineral fuels comprised 5.9% of the value of total imports in 2003; fuel exports accounted for 2.8% of total exports by value in that year. In recent years successive governments have sought to promote the utilization of 'renewable' energy resources.

SERVICES

The services sector contributed an estimated 71.6% of GDP in 2002, and engaged 73.4% of the employed labour force in 2001. Within the sector, financial services, tourism and transport are of considerable importance. The GDP of the services sector increased, in real terms, at an average annual rate of 3.1% in 1990–99; it rose by 4.1% in 1998 and by 3.8% in 1999.

EXTERNAL TRADE

In 2002 the Netherlands recorded a visible trade surplus of €26,995m. and there was a surplus of €9,457m. on the current account of the balance of payments. In 2003 the principal source of imports was Germany (contributing 20.0% of the total); other major suppliers were Belgium (11.3%), the USA (7.8%), the United Kingdom (7.2%) and France (5.5%). Germany was also the principal market for exports (accounting for 24.4% of the total); other major purchasers in 2003 were Belgium (11.9%), the United Kingdom (10.3%), France (10.0%) and Italy (6.0%). The principal exports in 2003 were office machines and automatic data-processing machines, petroleum, road vehicles and organic chemicals. The principal imports in that year were also office machines and automatic data-processing machines, followed by petroleum, road vehicles, and telecommunications and sound equipment.

GOVERNMENT FINANCE

In 2002 the Netherlands recorded an overall budgetary deficit of €6,902m., equivalent to 1.6% of GDP. In the same year government debt, according to IMF figures, was estimated to be equivalent to 51.0% of GDP. In 1990–2002 the annual rate of inflation averaged 2.7%. Consumer prices increased by 3.3% in 2002 and by 2.1% in 2003. The annual average rate of registered unemployment grew from 2.3% in 2002 to 3.4% in 2003.

INTERNATIONAL ECONOMIC RELATIONS

The Netherlands is a founder member of the European Union (EU), of the Benelux Economic Union, of the Organisation for Economic Co-operation and Development (OECD) and of the European Bank for Reconstruction and Development (EBRD).

SURVEY AND PROSPECTS

In the early 1990s the hitherto buoyant, export-led growth of the Dutch economy was undermined by a series of budget deficits, a high level of unemployment and fluctuations in international prices for natural gas. The administration of Wim Kok (1994–2002), pursuing a policy of economic consensus, which helped to limit industrial unrest, sought to reduce public expenditure, to restrain labour costs and to deregulate commercial activity, and shifted much of the burden of social-security contribution from the employer to the employee. This, together with the increasing importance of part-time work, contributed to a progressive reduction in the level of unemployment from 1992.

Between 1995 and 2000 the Netherlands recorded annual rates of economic growth above the EU average. In 1999 the Netherlands recorded its first budgetary surplus (equivalent to about 1% of GDP) for some 25 years. However, the state of the economy deteriorated sharply between 2001 and 2003, recording average annual GDP growth of just 0.5%. Registered unemployment rose from 2.0% of the total labour force in 2001 to 3.4% in 2003. The global economic downturn was particularly severely felt in the Netherlands as a result of the country's dependence on trade. This was further exacerbated by a decline in competitiveness owing to a combination of decreasing industrial production and increasing labour costs. (Labour costs in the Netherlands had risen 10% more than those of competing countries between 1997 and 2003.) Between 2001 and 2003 government revenue also decreased, while expenditure continued to mount. This trend was provoked by a drop in investment spending, and by the increasing demands for state-funded health care, welfare benefits and pensions, all of which stemmed from rising levels of unemployment and demographic ageing.

Balkenende's administration, which came to power in May 2002, proposed to stimulate the economy by enhancing competitiveness and commercial productivity. In order to achieve this, the Government pledged to simplify commuter travel regulations, to reduce administrative costs for businesses by one-quarter during its term in office, and to negotiate a two-year wage 'freeze' with the trade unions. The austerity budget announced in September 2003 for the following year proposed a €16,900m. reduction in government expenditure and a comprehensive reform of the health system. It aimed to encourage labour participation by restricting access to unemployment and disability benefits and by the planned abolition in 2005 of early retirement tax benefits. The Government maintained that these stringent measures were necessary in order to adhere to the EU Stability and Growth Pact (SGP). In October the trade unions agreed to a freeze in collectively agreed wages during 2004, with the possibility of a minimal pay increase in 2005, dependent on economic performance. In return, the Government agreed to postpone the abolition of early retirement tax relief until 2006. In 2004 unemployment was predicted to reach 7% and the planned budget deficit of 2.4% of GDP was based on an economic growth forecast of 1%. However, in February 2004 official sources forecast that, without increased revenue or spending cuts, the budget deficit would reach 3.3% of GDP in 2004, thus breaking the 3% ceiling laid down in the SGP.

Netherlands Antilles

The Netherlands Antilles comprises two groups of islands in the Caribbean Sea. The main group consists of Bonaire and Curaçao, which (together with Aruba) are known as the 'Leeward Islands'. To the north-east lie the small islands of St Eustatius, Saba and St Maarten (the northern half of the last island being a dependency of the French overseas department of Guadeloupe), known as the 'Windward Islands'. The capital is Willemstad, on the island of Curaçao. The official languages are Dutch and Papiamento, which is the dominant language of the 'Leeward Islands'. English is the official language of the 'Windward Islands'.

Area and population
Area: 800 sq km
Population (mid-2001): 220,000
Population density (mid-2001): 275.0 per sq km
Life expectancy (years at birth, 1995-2000): 75.5 (males 72.5; females 78.4)

Finance

GDP in current prices: 1999): US $2,515m. ($11,783 per head)
Real GDP growth (1999): −2.9%
Inflation (annual average, 2002): 0.4%
Currency: guilder

Economy

In 1994 the gross national income (GNI) of the Netherlands Antilles, measured at current prices, was an estimated US $1,550m., equivalent to some $8,800 per head. In 1990–2002 the population increased by an average of 1.3% per year, while gross domestic product (GDP) increased, in real terms, by an average of 0.4% per year during 1990–95, and stood at some $2,682m. in 2002 (equivalent to $12,247 per head). Real GDP declined by 2.3% in 2001, but increased by 0.4% in 2002.

AGRICULTURE

Agriculture, together with forestry, fishing and mining, contributed only 0.6% of GDP in 1997. Agriculture, forestry and fishing employed 1.1% of the working population on Curaçao in 2000. Some 8% of the total land area is cultivated. The chief products are aloes (Bonaire is a major exporter), sorghum, divi-divi, ground-nuts, beans, fresh vegetables and tropical fruit. A bitter variety of orange is used in the production of Curaçao liqueur. There is also some fishing.

INDUSTRY

Industry (comprising manufacturing, construction, power and water) contributed 16.7% of GDP in 1997. Industry (including mining, manufacturing, power and construction) employed 18.0% of the working population on Curaçao in 2000.

Mining

The mining and quarrying sector employed only 0.3% of the working population on Curaçao in 2000. Apart from some phosphates on Curaçao (exploited until the mid-1980s), and some limestone and salt on Bonaire, the islands have no other significant mineral reserves. Aggregate is quarried on St Maarten and consumed primarily by the local construction industry. In 2000 the Government sponsored a geologic review of offshore sediments that are located 5 km south-west of Saba; results indicated the potential of a resource of 500m. barrels of petroleum.

Manufacturing

Manufacturing contributed 5.7% of GDP in 1997, and employed 9.0% of the working population on Curaçao in 2000; activities include food-processing, production of Curaçao liqueur, and the manufacture of paint, paper, soap and cigarettes. Bonaire has a textile factory, and Curaçao's 'free zone' is of considerable importance in the economy, but the 'Windward Islands' have very few manufacturing activities. Petroleum-refining (using petroleum imported from Venezuela) is the islands' principal industrial activity, with the Curaçao refinery leased to the Venezuelan state petroleum company. Production capacity at the refinery was 116.8m. barrels per year in 2001, according to the US Geological Survey; however, industrial action in Venezeula led to the closure of the refinery during December 2002–March 2003, impacting heavily upon the islands' economy. Petroleum transhipment is also important, and ship repairs at the Curaçao dry dock make a significant contribution to the economy.

SERVICES

The services sector contributed 82.7% of GDP in 1997, and engaged 81.0% of the employed labour force on Curaçao in 2000. The Netherlands Antilles is a major 'offshore' financial centre. In June 2000 the Netherlands Antilles was urged by the Organisation for Economic Co-operation and Development (OECD) to improve the accountability and transparency of its financial services; in response, the Government announced that it was to review its taxation legislation to comply more closely with OECD's standards. In April 2002 the Netherlands Antilles was removed from the list of those countries deemed to be unco-operative tax 'havens' after OECD favourably assessed the Government's legislative amendments. In the same month an agreement was signed with the USA, pledging to share information on tax matters, with the aim of combating money-laundering and associated criminal activities. The financial and business services sector contributed 24.7% of GDP in 1997, and employed 14.4% of the Curaçao working population in 2000. Operational income from the offshore sector increased significantly in the early to mid-1990s, from NA Fl. 210.6m. in 1992 to NA Fl. 375.6m. in 1995. A major industry for all the islands (particularly St Maarten) is tourism, which is the largest employer after the public sector. In late 2001 and early 2002 the tourist industry suffered from the repercussions of the terrorist attacks on the USA in September 2001. However, the number of cruise-ship passenger arrivals rallied strongly in the second half of 2002 and, although the number of stop-over visitors declined, tourism receipts were reported to have increased by 7.6% in that year overall, compared with 2001. The outlook for 2003 was not so positive, however; the tourism sector was expected to contract as a result of the economic downturn in the USA and the repercussions of the US-led military campaign in Iraq. In addition to tourism, Curaçao, in particular, has sought to establish itself as a centre for regional trade, exploiting its excellent harbours. In 1998 a free-trade zone was established at the island's airport, which further enhanced Curaçao's entrepôt status.

EXTERNAL TRADE

In 2002 the Netherlands Antilles recorded a visible trade deficit (excluding most transactions in petroleum) of NA Fl. 1,026.8m., much of which was offset by revenue from services; there was a deficit of NA Fl. 32.3m. on the current account of the balance of payments. The petroleum industry dominates the trade figures of the Netherlands Antilles, particularly of the 'Leeward Islands'. In 1998 fuel imports comprised 54.4% of total merchandise imports. In the same year the principal source of imports (43.4%) was Venezuela (which provides crude petroleum), and the principal market for exports (15.3%) was the USA. The USA is an important trading partner for all the islands of the Netherlands Antilles, as are the Netherlands and other Caribbean countries. Petroleum is the principal commodity for both import and export, and accounted for 54.4% of imports and 86.0% of exports in 1998. The Netherlands Antilles also imports machinery and transport equipment, manufactured goods, and chemicals and related products, while it exports aloes, Curaçao liqueur and some light manufactures.

GOVERNMENT FINANCE

In 2002 the general Government (including island governments) recorded a budgetary deficit of NA Fl. 142.3m., which was equivalent to some 3.0% of GDP. In the same year the central Government recorded a deficit of NA Fl. 52.5m. on its budget. The administrations of the islands tend to operate with deficits. At the end of 2000 the combined public domestic debts of the central Government and the island Government of Curaçao were NA Fl. 3,236.2m. (67.4% of GDP). Total foreign debt stood at NA Fl. 559.8m. in 2000, owed chiefly to the Netherlands. The foreign debt in 2000 was estimated to be the equivalent of 12.7% of GDP. In 1998 the Netherlands Antilles received $125.7m. in bilateral aid and $3.4m. in multilateral aid. The average annual rate of inflation was 2.3% in 1995–2002. Consumer prices increased by an average of 15.8% in 2001 and by 0.4% in 2002. The rate of unemployment in the labour force was an estimated 14.2% for the Netherlands Antilles as a whole in 2002; 15.6% of the Curaçao work-force were unemployed in the same year. Figures from the 2001 census showed that the rate of unemployment in St Maarten stood at 12.2%, with the rate of youth unemployment at 24.1%.

INTERNATIONAL ECONOMIC RELATIONS

The Netherlands Antilles, as part of the Kingdom of the Netherlands, has the status of an Overseas Territory in association with the European Union. In 1988 the Netherlands Antilles was accorded observer status by the Caribbean Community and Common Market (CARICOM).

SURVEY AND PROSPECTS

The relative isolation of the individual islands has led to the development of semi-independent economies, and economic conditions vary considerably between them. Notwithstanding, the Netherlands Antilles experienced relatively strong economic growth in the 1980s and early 1990s, but the past decade witnessed a progressive weakening of the economy, leading to a prolonged recession, high unemployment and increasing rates of emigration. The direct causes of this decline were considered to be the decline in both the financial services and the petroleum-refining industries, combined with the damage to tourist infrastructure caused by Hurricanes Luis and Marilyn in September 1995.

Under the terms of the structural adjustment programme (SAP), undertaken from 1996 in consultation with the IMF, which aimed to eliminate the fiscal deficit over a period of four years, the civil service was to be rationalized, public sector wages were to be frozen and pension arrangements reviewed, while new indirect taxes were to be introduced. Successive administrations, however, recorded only limited success in implementing the terms of the SAP and its successor, the National Recovery Plan, which was adopted in late 1998, in part owing to the great unpopularity of many of the measures to be undertaken.

Following stringent measures announced by the Pourier Government in June 2001, the Dutch Government released NA Fl. 153m. (to be spent in 2002–06) to encourage sustained economic development and to support the Netherlands Antilles Government in improving the quality of its administration and education systems. The Netherlands was expected to approve the release of €125m. in additional funds in 2003, and the Dutch and Netherlands Antillean Governments agreed on a more prominent role for the Central Bank in the monitoring and implementation of the IMF targets.

During rounds of the Article IV consultation visits in March 2003, an IMF team concluded that although the Netherlands Antilles is experiencing a period of 'fragile growth', there was a continued need for financial reforms and savings, especially in the health-care sector, government institutions and limited companies. In 2002 the long formation period of the new Government and the consequent lack of a government programme, coupled with the slowing world economy and weak international tourism market, damaged confidence, leading to only a slight increase in real GDP, according to central bank figures. Continued low-level growth was anticipated in 2003–05.

New Caledonia

New Caledonia lies in the South Pacific Ocean, east of Queensland, Australia. It became a French possession in 1853, as a dependency of Tahiti. In 1860 a separate administration was established, and in 1885 a Conseil Général was elected. From 1887 separate administrations existed, for Melanesian Kanaks and expatriates, until New Caledonia became a French Overseas Territory in 1946. In 1998 the electorate approved the Nouméa Accord, which postponed any referendum on independence for 15–20 years, but provided for a gradual transfer of power to local institutions. The Territory became an Overseas Country of France in 1999. The capital is Nouméa. French is the official language.

Area and population
Area: 18,575 sq km
Population (mid-2002): 220,000
Population density (mid-2002): 11.8 per sq km
Life expectancy (years at birth): n.a.

Finance
GDP in current prices: 2000): US $2,682m. ($12,611 per head)
Real GDP growth (2000): 2.1%
Inflation (annual average, 2002): 1.9%
Currency: CFP franc

Economy

In 2000, according to World Bank estimates, New Caledonia's gross national income (GNI) at average 1998–2000 prices totalled US $2,989m., equivalent to $14,050 per head (or $21,960 per head on an international purchasing-power parity basis). During 1990–2000, it was estimated, the population rose at an average annual rate of 2.4%, while gross domestic product (GDP) per head decreased, in real terms, by an average of 0.7%. Overall GDP increased in real terms, at an average annual rate of 1.6% in 1990–2000, rising by 0.9% in 1999 and by 2.1% in 2000.

AGRICULTURE
Agriculture and fishing contributed only 1.9% of GDP in 1999, and 4.8% of the employed labour force were engaged in the sector in 2001. Maize, yams, sweet potatoes and coconuts have traditionally been the principal crops. However, pumpkins (squash) became an important export crop for the Japanese market during the 1990s, with 2,200 metric tons exported in 2000 (compared with 500 tons in 1993). Livestock consists mainly of cattle and pigs. The main fisheries products are tuna and shrimps (most of which are exported to Japan). An estimated total of 1,810 metric tons of farmed shrimps and prawns was produced in 2001 (compared with 632 tons in 1993). The value of prawn exports increased from 1,797m. francs CFP in 2000 to 1,958m. in 2001.

INDUSTRY
Industry (comprising mining, manufacturing, construction and utilities) provided 19.6% of GDP in 1997, and employed 28.0% of the working population in 2001.

Mining
Although mining employed only 3.4% of New Caledonia's working population in 2001, it constitutes the most important industrial sector. In 1999 mining and quarrying contributed an estimated 10% of GDP. New Caledonia possesses among the world's largest known nickel deposits and is a major producer of ferro-nickel. Sales of nickel ores and concentrates and nickel mattes accounted for 34.2% of export revenues in 2000. In 2001 a Canadian company announced that it would proceed with the construction of a fully integrated nickel-cobalt mining and processing facility at Goro, in the South Province, with an envisaged annual production capacity of 54,000 tons of nickel. The project, which was to cost an estimated US $1,460m., envisaged the construction of a deep-water port, international airport, power station and associated infrastructure, and was expected to provide 2,000 jobs. However, work was suspended in late 2002, while the Canadian company sought more capital; operations were not expected to begin until the second half of 2006 at the earliest. Compared with the previous year, metallurgical production increased by 3.9% in 2001. The introduction of the single European currency, effected in January 2002, provided a boost to the nickel industry. (Both the one and two-euro coins used New Caledonian nickel.) In November 2001, however, in response to a decline in world nickel prices, the Société Minière du Sud Pacifique (SMSP) announced plans to reduce its mining activity by 50%, entailing the redundancy of 600 workers. Nevertheless, this did not affect the SMSP's joint project with a Canadian company: the

construction of a new nickel-smelting plant in the North Province. Construction had yet to commence in late 2003; the plant was to employ 700 people and produce up to 54,000 tons of nickel a year.

Manufacturing

The manufacturing sector, which provided 4.0% of GDP in 1997 and (together with electricity, gas and water) engaged 11.0% of the employed labour force in 2001, consists mainly of small and medium-sized enterprises, most of which are situated around the capital, Nouméa, producing building materials, furniture, salted fish, fruit juices and perishable foods.

Energy

Electrical energy is provided mainly by thermal power stations (78.5% in 2001), by hydroelectric plants and, more recently, by wind power. Mineral fuels accounted for 14.8% of total imports in 2000. A plant producing wind-generated electricity near Nouméa provides some 4.5m. kWh of energy per year. In 2001 nine windmills were installed on Lifou, one of the Loyalty Islands, to deliver more than 800,000 kWh through the island's electricity network, as part of the Government's attempt to reduce expensive imports of diesel fuel. Plans were announced in early 2003 to install a further 31 windmills in the South Province.

SERVICES

Service industries together contributed 73.7% of GDP in 1999 and engaged 67.1% of the employed labour force in 2001. The tourism sector in New Caledonia, however, has failed to witness an expansion similar to that experienced in many other Pacific islands, and tourist arrivals have been intermittently affected by political unrest. The number of tourist arrivals declined to 100,515 in 2001; before rising to 103,933 in 2002. Receipts from tourism decreased from US $110m. in 2000 to $93m. in 2001.

EXTERNAL TRADE

In 2000 New Caledonia recorded a visible trade deficit of some 42,490m. francs CFP, and there was a surplus of 25,242m. francs CFP, equivalent to 7.2% of that year's GDP, on the current account of the balance of payments (a deficit of 3,000m. francs CFP was registered in 1999). In 2001, however, the trade deficit increased to an estimated 64,700m. francs CFP. The principal imports in 1999 were mineral fuels, foodstuffs and machinery and transport equipment. France is the main trading partner, providing some 40.3% of imports and purchasing 26.1% of exports in 2001; other major trading partners in that year were Japan (which purchased 23.1% of exports), Taiwan (17.6% of exports), Australia and Singapore.

GOVERNMENT FINANCE

The budget for 2001 envisaged revenue and expenditure balancing at 81,337m. francs CFP. Budgetary expenditure for 2002 was set at 86,400m. francs CFP. Budgetary aid from France totalled the equivalent of €755,317m. in 2001, increasing to €777,965 in 2002. The annual rate of inflation in Nouméa averaged 1.9% in 1990–2003. The rate of inflation rose by an average of 1.9% in 2002 and by 1.2% in 2003. Some 16.0% of the labour force were unemployed in 2001. A total of 10,325 were registered as unemployed in June 2002.

INTERNATIONAL ECONOMIC RELATIONS

New Caledonia forms part of the Franc Zone, is an associate member of the UN Economic and Social Commission for Asia and the Pacific (ESCAP) and is a member, in its own right, of the Pacific Community. Following the adoption of the Nouméa Accord in 1998, New Caledonia obtained observer status at the Pacific Islands Forum in September 1999.

SURVEY AND PROSPECTS

New Caledonia's economy is vulnerable to factors affecting the islands' important nickel industry, which included political unrest during the 1980s and fluctuations in international prices for the commodity. The Nouméa Accord, approved by referendum in November 1998, aimed to improve the economic conditions of the Kanak population and to increase their participation in the market economy and in public administration. Despite previous attempts to redress the balance of New Caledonian society (most importantly with the Matignon Accord of 1988), the indigenous population remained largely excluded from New Caledonia's economic and political administration, and a considerable proportion continued to experience economic hardship.

In mid-1999 the RPCR leader, Jacques Lafleur, revealed proposals for the creation of an inter-provincial committee for economic development, which would allow the comparatively wealthy South Province to assist the economic development of the other Provinces. Moreover, it was hoped that the development of those sectors generally considered not to have reached their full potential (notably tourism, aquaculture, fishing and farm agriculture) would alleviate the economic uncertainty created by the need to reduce dependency on France. In an effort to encourage investment in New Caledonia, legislation to replace the system of tax deductions with one of tax credits was expected to be adopted in 2002.

In the tourism sector, visitor arrivals declined by 8.3% in 2001 compared with the previous year, but rose by 3.4% in 2002. In March 2003, furthermore, Air France ceased its operations in New Caledonia. The route to Tokyo, where Air France would provide connections to Paris, was taken over by Air Calédonie International (Air-Calin), which was given a tax concession by the French Government on the cost of two new aircraft.

In late 1999 a joint French and Australian research mission made an offshore discovery of what was believed to be the world's largest gas deposit, measuring an estimated 18,000 sq km. It was hoped that this indicated the presence of considerable petroleum reserves. The effect of the decline in world nickel prices during 2001 was compounded by the downturn in the aviation industry that followed the terrorist attacks on the USA in September (aeronautical companies normally being significant consumers of special nickel alloys). Nickel prices, however, recovered in mid-2002 and rose strongly during 2003.

In mid-2003 the National Assembly approved the Overseas Territories Development Bill, which would provide support for economic and social development in New Caledonia (together with French Polynesia and Wallis and Futuna) by attracting foreign investment, and among other benefits allow for overseas French nationals to travel to mainland France to take advantage of free education.

New Zealand

The Dominion of New Zealand lies in the South Pacific Ocean. New Zealand became a dominion, under the British Crown, in 1907 and achieved full independence in 1947, when it accepted the 1931 Statute of Westminster. Since 1995 the Government has settled a number of claims for compensation pursued against it by the country's Maori peoples. Dame Silvia Cartwright's appointment as Governor-General in 2001 created an unprecedented situation in which women occupied the five most important public roles in the country (including those of Prime Minister and Leader of the Opposition). Wellington is the capital. The official language is English.

Area and population
Area: 270,534 sq km
Population (mid-2002): 3,869,580
Population density (mid-2002): 14.3 per sq km
Life expectancy (years at birth, 2002): 78.9 (males 76.6; females 81.2)

Finance
GDP in current prices: 2002): US $58,178m. ($15,035 per head)
Real GDP growth (2002): 3.8%
Inflation (annual average, 2002): 2.7%
Currency: New Zealand dollar

Economy

In 2002, according to estimates by the World Bank, New Zealand's gross national income (GNI), measured at average 2000–02 prices, was US $53,054.8m., equivalent to US $13,710 per head (or $20,020 per head on an international purchasing-power parity basis). During 1990–2002, it was estimated, the population increased at an average annual rate of 1.0%, while gross domestic product (GDP) per head increased, in real terms, by an average of 1.9% per year. Overall GDP increased, in real terms, at an average annual rate of 2.9% in 1990–2002. According to official figures, growth was an estimated 4.4% in 2002.

AGRICULTURE

Agriculture (including hunting, fishing, forestry and mining) contributed 8.1% of GDP (in constant prices) in the year ending March 2002. About 8.8% of the employed labour force were engaged in the sector (excluding mining) in 2002. The principal crops are barley, wheat and maize. Fruit (particularly kiwi fruit, apples and pears) and vegetables are also cultivated. New Zealand is a major producer of wool. In the year ending March 2003 exports of wool were worth $NZ953m. Meat and dairy products are important, contributing 14.0% and 16.8% of export earnings, respectively, in 2002. The forestry industry showed strong expansion in the early 1990s. In 2002 exports of cork and wood totalled $NZ1,878.3m. (equivalent to 6.1% of total export earnings). The fisheries sector is of increasing significance, exports in 2002 being worth $NZ1,483.8m. (equivalent to 4.8% of total export earnings). Between 1989/90 and 1999/2000 agricultural GDP (including hunting, fishing, forestry and mining) increased by an average of 4.0% per year. Compared with the previous year, agricultural GDP increased by 3.3% in 2000/01.

INDUSTRY

Industry (including mining, manufacturing, construction and utilities) engaged 22.7% of the employed labour force in 2002. The industrial sector (excluding mining) provided 22.6% of GDP (at constant prices) in the year ending March 2002. Between 1989/90 and 1999/2000 industrial GDP (excluding mining) increased at an average annual rate of 1.2%. Industrial GDP increased by 0.6% in 2000/01, compared with the previous year.

Mining

Mining contributed only 1.2% of GDP in the year ending March 2001, and employed 0.2% of the working population in 2002. New Zealand has substantial coal reserves; petroleum, natural gas, iron, gold and silica are also exploited. A considerable amount of natural gas is used to produce synthetic petrol. In April 2002 Crown Minerals announced that approximately 50,000 sq km of the offshore Canterbury

Basin were to be tendered out to oil exploration companies in 2003, pending a study of the petroleum source rock potential of the basin.

Manufacturing

Manufacturing contributed an estimated 16.2% of GDP (at constant prices) in the year ending March 2002. The sector engaged 15.5% of the employed labour force in 2002. The principal branches of manufacturing are food products, printing and publishing, wood and paper products, chemicals, metals and metal products, machinery and transport equipment. Between 1989/90 and 1999/2000 manufacturing GDP increased by an average of 1.5% per year. Manufacturing GDP expanded by 2.5% in 2000/01, compared with the previous year.

Energy

Energy is derived mainly from domestic supplies of natural gas, petroleum and coal. Hydroelectric power supplied about 63.1% of total energy output in 2000. Imports of petroleum and its products comprised 9.3% of the total value of merchandise imports in 2002.

SERVICES

The services sector provided 69.3% of GDP (in constant prices) in 2001/02. This sector engaged 68.5% of the employed labour force in 2002. In the year ending March 1988 tourism became the single largest source of foreign exchange. Receipts (excluding international air fares) totalled $NZ6,141m. in 2002. Visitor arrivals reached 2.1m. in 2003. Between 1989/90 and 1999/2000 the GDP of the services sector increased at an average annual rate of 2.8%. Compared with the previous year, it expanded by 3.4% in 2000/01.

EXTERNAL TRADE

In 2002 New Zealand recorded a visible trade surplus of US $502m., but there was a deficit of US $2,269m. on the current account of the balance of payments. In 2002 the principal sources of imports were Australia (23.0%), the USA (13.7%) and Japan (11.7%), which were also the principal markets for exports in that year (Australia 20.0%, the USA 15.3% and Japan 11.5%). The United Kingdom, other members of the European Union and Asian countries are also important trading partners. The principal exports in 2002 were meat, dairy products, vegetables and fruit, fish, cork and wood, and machinery. The principal imports were road vehicles and other machinery and transport equipment, manufactured articles, basic manufactures and chemicals.

GOVERNMENT FINANCE

In the year ending June 2003 an estimated budgetary surplus of $NZ2,505m. was recorded, equivalent to 2.0% of GDP. In March 2003 New Zealand's external debt stood at $NZ132,396m., of which $NZ17,701m. was official government debt. The average rate of unemployment decreased from 7.5% of the labour force in 1998 to 5.2% in 2002. Annual inflation averaged 1.9% in 1990–2002. Consumer prices increased by 2.7% in 2002 and by 1.8% in 2003.

INTERNATIONAL ECONOMIC RELATIONS

New Zealand is a member of the Organisation for Economic Co-operation and Development, Asia-Pacific Economic Co-operation (APEC), the Pacific Community, the Pacific Islands Forum and of the Cairns Group. New Zealand is also a member of the Colombo Plan and the UN Economic and Social Commission for Asia and the Pacific (ESCAP). In 1982 New Zealand signed an agreement for a 'closer economic relationship' (CER) with Australia, aiming to eliminate trade barriers between the two countries by 1995. These were, in fact, eliminated in July 1990.

SURVEY AND PROSPECTS

Upon taking office in late 1999, the minority Labour Government embarked upon a programme of reforms in the health, education and housing sectors. In addition, some $NZ175m. was allocated for projects aimed at the Maori population. These proposals were to be financed by an increase in income tax on those earning more than $NZ60,000 annually. The new Government also planned to curb the programme of transferring state assets to the private sector.

Having been sold to private interests in 1989, Air New Zealand was returned to state ownership in late 2001, following heavy financial losses. In October, in an arrangement costing $NZ885m., the Government announced that it was purchasing an 83% stake in the airline, the continued operations of which remained vital to the country's tourism industry. The bid by the Australian airline company, Qantas Airways Ltd, to buy a 22.5% stake in Air New Zealand was rejected by competition regulators in New Zealand and Australia in April 2003.

Although in the short term tourist arrivals were affected by the terrorist attacks on the USA in September 2001, the consequences were less serious than originally feared, as New Zealand was regarded as a relatively safe destination. New Zealand was comparatively well placed to withstand the repercussions of the overall deceleration of the global economy in 2001, and in 2002 an increase in tourism earnings (in the year ending September 2002 tourism earnings expanded by 13.2%) and continued growth in agriculture resulted in strong real GDP growth of around 4.4%. Economic growth decelerated in 2003, to an estimated 2.9%. Export receipts decreased, owing to the rise in value of the New Zealand dollar against the US dollar, resulting in a trade deficit. The rise in international commodity prices from mid-2003, however, partially offset the increase in the currency's value. Furthermore, despite the negative impact of the decline in net immigration on housing demand, housebuilding permits continued to increase and the construction industry maintained its strong performance. The tourism sector improved, despite the strength of the New Zealand dollar and the outbreak in Asia of Severe Acute Respiratory Syndrome, and this, in turn, helped to boost employment rates. A budget surplus in 2002/03 was also achieved, for the 10th successive year. GDP growth was expected to reach 2.9% in 2004.

Nicaragua

The Republic of Nicaragua lies on the Central American isthmus. From 1935 until 1979 Nicaraguan politics were dominated by the Somoza family. In 1979 the left-wing Frente Sandinista de Liberación Nacional took power. By 1981 the Sandinistas were opposed by counter-revolutionary forces—'Contras'. In 1990 Violeta Chamorro, the candidate of the Unión Nacional Opositora, was elected as President; in June the demobilization of the Contra rebels signified the end of civil war. In 1996 Arnoldo Alemán Lacayo was elected President. He was succeeded by Enrique Bolaños Geyer following elections in 2001. Managua is the capital. The national language is Spanish.

Area and population
Area: 120,254 sq km
Population (mid-2002): 5,334,930
Population density (mid-2002): 44.4 per sq km
Life expectancy (years at birth, 2002): 70.1 (males 67.9, females 72.4)

Finance
GDP in current prices: 2001): US $2,543m. ($489 per head)
Real GDP growth (2001): 3.0%
Inflation (annual average, 2002): 4.0%
Currency: gold córdoba

Economy

In 1998, according to estimates by the World Bank, Nicaragua's gross national income (GNI), measured at average 1996–98 prices, was US $1,783m., equivalent to $370 per head (or $1,870 per head on an international purchasing-power parity basis). During 1991–2002, according to IMF estimates, the population increased at an average annual rate of 2.8%, while gross domestic product (GDP) per head increased, in real terms, by an average of 0.7% per year. According to the IMF, Nicaragua's gross domestic product (GDP) increased, in real terms, by an average of 3.5% per year in 1991–2002; GDP increased by 1.1% in 2002.

AGRICULTURE

Agriculture (including forestry and fishing) contributed an estimated 31.6% of GDP in 2002 and engaged an estimated 43.4% of the employed work-force in 2001. The principal cash crops are coffee (which accounted for an estimated 12.3% of export earnings in 2002), sugar cane, bananas and cotton. Maize, rice and beans are the principal food crops. Production of shellfish became increasingly important, and in 2000 shrimps and lobsters accounted for some 17.4% of export earnings, although this decreased to 12.7% in 2002. Agricultural GDP increased at an average annual rate of 5.2% during 1990–2001; the sector's GDP increased by 11.4% in 2000 and by an estimated 3.1% in 2001.

INDUSTRY

Industry (including mining, manufacturing, construction and power) engaged an estimated 15.0% of the employed labour force in 2001 and provided an estimated 22.6% of GDP in 2002. Industrial GDP increased by an average of 4.0% per year during 1990–2001; it increased by 3.1% in 2000 and by an estimated 3.2% in 2001.

Mining

Mining contributed an estimated 0.8% of GDP in 2002 and engaged an estimated 0.6% of the employed labour force in 2001. Nicaragua has workable deposits of gold, silver, copper, lead, antimony, zinc and iron; its non-metallic minerals include limestone, gypsum, bentonite and marble. The GDP of the mining sector increased at an average annual rate of 11.4% in 1990–2001; the sector's GDP decreased by about 20% in 2000, but grew by an estimated 2.5% in 2001.

Manufacturing

Manufacturing contributed some 14.4% of GDP in 2002 and engaged an estimated 7.7% of the employed labour force in 2001. Measured by the value of output, the principal branches of manufacturing were food products, beverages and tobacco (about 67% of the total), machinery and metal products and petroleum derivatives and rubber products. The *maquila*, or offshore assembly, sector expanded rapidly in the early 1990s, although growth slowed at the end of the decade. The principal products were clothing, footwear, aluminium frames and jewellery. Manufacturing GDP increased by an average of 2.0% per year in 1990–2001; the sector's GDP grew by 2.8% in 2000 and by an estimated 2.6% in 2001.

Energy

Energy is derived principally from imported petroleum, although two hydroelectric plants in the department of Jinotega account for one-third of the electrical energy generated in the country. Imports of mineral fuels and lubricants comprised an estimated 14.1% of the total value of imports in 2002. In 2001 Nicaragua produced an estimated 2,613.7m. kWh of electrical energy.

SERVICES

The services sector contributed an estimated 45.8% of GDP in 2002 and engaged an estimated 41.9% of the employed labour force in 2001. The tourism sector expanded throughout the 1990s; in 2001 annual income totalled US $109m., with arrivals put at 482,869, a slight decrease on the previous year's figures. The GDP of the services sector increased by an average of 1.8% per year in 1990–2001; in 2000 it grew by 3.1%, and in 2001 by an estimated 2.9%.

EXTERNAL TRADE

In 2002 Nicaragua recorded a visible trade deficit of about US $1,031.3m., and there was a deficit of $887.8m. on the current account of the balance of payments. In 2002 the principal source of imports (27.4%) was the USA; other major suppliers were Nicaragua's partners in the Central American Common Market (CACM—Costa Rica, El Salvador, Guatemala and Honduras), as well as Venezuela and Mexico. The USA was also the principal market for exports (32.2%) in 2002; other notable purchasers were the countries of the CACM, Mexico and Canada. The principal exports in 2002 were coffee, meat and lobster. The principal imports were non-durable consumer goods, intermediate goods for industry, capital goods for industry and crude petroleum.

GOVERNMENT FINANCE

In 2001 Nicaragua recorded a budgetary deficit of an estimated 4,692.5m. gold córdobas (equivalent to 13.8% of GDP). At the end of 2001 Nicaragua's total external debt was $6,391m., of which $5,560m. was long-term public debt. The cost of servicing external debt in that year was equivalent to 26.2% of the value of goods and services. Annual inflation averaged 122.2% in 1985–95, reaching a peak of 10,205% in 1988. In 1990–2002 the average annual rate of increase in consumer prices was 47.2%. The average rate declined from 2,945% in 1991 to 4.0% in 2002. An estimated 12.2% of the labour force was unemployed in 2002.

INTERNATIONAL ECONOMIC RELATIONS

Nicaragua is a member of the CACM, which aims eventually to liberalize intra-regional trade, and of the Inter-American Development Bank (IDB).

SURVEY AND PROSPECTS

On assuming power in 1990, the Chamorro administration inherited an economy devastated by the effects of a prolonged civil war and characterized by extremely low output, hyperinflation and a large foreign debt burden. With the implementation of a comprehensive economic reform programme, supported by the IMF, inflation was brought under control, levels of foreign reserves were greatly improved, and the fiscal deficit significantly reduced. In 1998 the Alemán administration secured a three-year Enhanced Structural Adjustment Facility (ESAF) in support of its economic

programme. Measures stipulated under the terms of the ESAF included a rationalization of the public sector, increases in public utility tariffs, and the continued privatization of state enterprises. In addition to facilitating further credits from multilateral
sources, in December 2000 Nicaragua qualified for debt relief of some US $4,500m.
under the 'Heavily Indebted Poor Countries' (HIPC) initiative.

In October 1998 the Nicaraguan economy was devastated by the effects of 'Hurricane Mitch'. Much of the country's infrastructure was destroyed, and as many as
1.5m. people were left homeless. The Central Bank estimated total reconstruction
costs at more than US $1,500m. Nevertheless, in 1999 the economy recorded growth
of 7.4%, partly as a consequence of the inflow of funds for reconstruction: Nicaragua
received aid commitments totalling some $2,500m., to be disbursed in the three-year
period following the hurricane. According to the Central Bank, the economy grew by
5.5% in 2000 and by 3.2% in 2001; the decrease in the rate of growth in 2001 was partly
owing to a fall in international commodity prices.

In 2001 the IMF expressed concern that Nicaragua was not fulfilling its commitments under the terms of the ESAF, crucial if an extension to the scheme was to be
approved. As well as the Government's failure to adequately control public spending
and the punitive 35% trade tariffs imposed on Honduran imports, of particular
concern to the IMF was the lack of progress in the country's privatization programme. In 1999 the state electricity company, Empresa Nicaragüense de Electricidad (ENEL), was divided into three generating companies (one hydroelectric and
two thermal plants) and two distribution companies, in preparation for its divestment. The distribution companies were sold to a Spanish company, Unión Fenosa, in
November 2000; however, the Alemán Government failed to sell the generating
companies. Following the change of government in January 2002, some progress
was made, with the successful sale of GEOSA, one of the operating companies, to the
US company Coastal Power International. In January 2004 the transfer to the private
sector of the telecommunications concern, Enitel, was completed, after the Government sold its remaining 49% stake in the company to the Mexican company America
Móvil for US $40.5m.

In December 2001 the IDB approved a debt-relief programme of US $386m. for
Nicaragua, to be implemented annually until 2019. The Government of Enrique
Bolaños Geyer, which took office in January 2002, immediately began negotiations
for a new accord with the IMF. The process was impeded, however, by the political
feud between Bolaños and Alemán, who, as President of the Asamblea Nacional,
obstructed proposed tax reform and other budgetary measures that had been
stipulated by the IMF as conditions for new financing. In late October the IMF agreed
to make a loan of $100m., dependent on a number of conditions, including the
reduction of the fiscal deficit to 14% of GDP over the next three years, the complete
privatization of Enitel and a reduction in domestic public debt. In December the IMF
approved the release of $129m. of funds over the next three years and $2.5m. in
interim assistance through the HIPC initiative. The 'Paris Club' of creditor nations
also agreed to cancel $405m. of public external debt and to reschedule remaining
payments. However, the 2003 draft budget passed by the Asamblea Nacional in the
same month was deemed unacceptable by the IMF as funds formerly set aside for
debt servicing were used to facilitate public-sector wage increases. Despite strong
congressional opposition, President Bolaños succeeded in vetoing several parts of the
budget in March 2003. As a consequence, Nicaragua qualified for a gradual debt

reduction under the HIPC initiative of up to 73% of the nation's total external debt, estimated at US $6,500m. by 2003. This financial relief remained dependent on disciplined expenditure and on the Government meeting targets set by the IMF and the World Bank. It was widely believed that the IMF's approval of the Bolaños administration's fiscal policies, together with further planned deregulation in the energy and telecommunications sectors, would stimulate foreign investment in Nicaragua. In April 2004 France, Germany and Spain agreed to forgive US $263m. of the country's debts, in keeping with the agreement signed in late 2003 with the Paris Club of creditors. Following qualification for the debt-relief programme, the Central Bank forecast that the economy would increase by 2.3% in 2003 and by a further 3.7% in 2004

Negotiations towards a free-trade agreement, to be known as the Central American Free Trade Agreement (CAFTA), were concluded between the CA-4 (El Salvador, Guatemala, Honduras and Nicaragua) group of countries and the USA in December 2003. The agreement entailed the gradual elimination of tariffs on most industrial and agricultural products over the next 10 and 20 years, respectively.

Niger

The Republic of Niger is situated in western Africa. Niger obtained independence from France in 1960. In 1974 the army seized power. Following a period of constitutional rule, from 1989, Col Ibrahim Baré Maïnassara led a military coup in 1996. Maïnassara was subsequently elected as President. Following Maïnassara's death, in unexplained circumstances, in 1999, the 1996 Constitution and its institutions were abrogated. A military Conseil de réconciliation nationale, led by Maj. Daouda Mallam Wanké, took office, overseeing the drafting of a new Constitution. Tandja Mamadou was subsequently elected as President. Niamey is the capital. The official language is French.

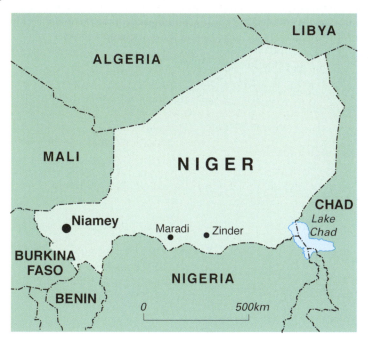

Area and population
Area: 1,267,000 sq km
Population (mid-2002): 11,541,940
Population density (mid-2002): 9.1 per sq km
Life expectancy (years at birth, 2002): 42.6 (males 42.6; females 42.7)

Finance
GDP in current prices: 2002): US $2,170m. ($188 per head)
Real GDP growth (2002): 3.0%
Inflation (annual average, 2002): 2.6%
Currency: CFA franc

622

Economy

In 2002, according to estimates by the World Bank, Niger's gross national income (GNI), measured at average 2000–02 prices, was US $2,013m., equivalent to $170 per head (or $770 on an international purchasing-power parity basis). During 1990–2002, it was estimated, the population increased at an average annual rate of 3.4%, while gross domestic product (GDP) per head declined, in real terms, by an average of 1.1% per year. Overall GDP increased, in real terms, at an average annual rate of 2.3% in 1990–2002; growth was 3.0% in 2002.

AGRICULTURE

Agriculture (including hunting, forestry and fishing) contributed 42.1% of GDP in 2002. About 87.3% of the labour force were employed in the sector in that year. The principal cash crops are cow-peas, onions, groundnuts and cotton. The principal subsistence crops are millet, sorghum and rice. Niger is able to achieve self-sufficiency in basic foodstuffs in non-drought years. Following a disappointing harvest in 2000, the UN World Food Programme (WFP) appealed for donors to assist an estimated 200,000 people affected by malnutrition in the country; according to WFP, more than 4,000 of Niger's 10,094 villages had food deficits of over 50%. However, a modest cereals surplus was achieved in 2001. Livestock-rearing is important, especially among the nomadic population: live animals accounted for 26.6% of total export earnings in 2001, constituting the second most important source of export revenue, after uranium. Major anti-desertification and reafforestation programmes are in progress. According to the World Bank, agricultural GDP increased by an average of 3.3% per year in 1990–2002. Agricultural GDP increased by 1.5% in 2002.

INDUSTRY

Industry (including mining, manufacturing, construction and power) contributed 14.3% of GDP in 2002. Only 3.6% of the labour force were employed in industrial activities at the time of the 1988 census. According to the World Bank, industrial GDP increased by an average of 1.7% per year in 1990–2002; growth was 2.4% in 2002.

Mining

Mining contributed 2.5% of GDP in 2002, but employed only 0.2% of the labour force in 1988. Niger is among the world's foremost producers of uranium (the third largest, after Canada and Australia, in 2002), although the contribution of uranium-mining to the domestic economy has declined, as production costs have exceeded world prices for the mineral. In 2002 exports of uranium accounted for 56.0% of total export earnings. In addition, gypsum, coal, salt and cassiterite are also extracted, and commercial exploitation of gold (previously mined on a small scale) at the Samira Hill mine was scheduled to begin in 2004, at a rate of 10,000 metric tons of ore per day. In 2000 the Government awarded two permits for petroleum exploration in eastern Niger to two US companies. According to the IMF, the GDP of the mining sector increased at an average annual rate of 2.7% in 1995–2000; mining GDP declined by 1.2% in 1999, but increased by an estimated 0.2% in 2000.

Manufacturing

Manufacturing contributed 7.3% of GDP in 2002, and employed 2.7% of the labour force in 1988. The processing of agricultural products (groundnuts, cereals, cotton and rice) constitutes the principal activity. Some light industries, including a textiles plant, a brewery and a cement works, supply the internal market. According to the World Bank, manufacturing GDP increased by an average of 2.2% per year in 1990–2002. Manufacturing GDP increased by 3.4% in 2002.

Energy

The domestic generation of electricity (almost entirely thermal) provides a little less than one-half of Niger's electrical energy requirements, much of the remainder being imported from Nigeria. Construction of a hydroelectric installation at Kandadji, on the Niger, is planned. Imports of mineral fuels accounted for 12.5% of the value of merchandise imports in 2001.

SERVICES

The services sector contributed 43.7% of GDP in 2002, and employed 15.0% of the labour force in 1988. The GDP of the sector increased by an average of 1.8% per year in 1990–2002, according to the World Bank; growth was 4.7% in 2002.

EXTERNAL TRADE

In 2002 Niger recorded a visible trade deficit of an estimated 46,800m. francs CFA, while there was a deficit of 112,800m. francs CFA on the current account of the balance of payments. France was Niger's principal souce of imports in 2001, supplying 19.2%; other major suppliers were Côte d'Ivoire, Nigeria, the People's Republic of China and Pakistan. The principal markets for exports in that year were Nigeria (37.1%), France (36.5%) and Japan. The principal exports in 2001 were uranium (most of which is purchased by France), live animals and vegetables (principally cow-peas and onions). The principal imports in that year were cereals and cereal preparations, refined petroleum products, fixed vegetable oils and fats (notably palm oil) and road vehicles.

GOVERNMENT FINANCE

Niger's overall budget deficit for 2002 was estimated at 78,700m. francs CFA (equivalent to 5.8% of GDP). Niger's total external debt was US $1,555m. at the end of 2001, of which $1,432m. was long-term public debt. In that year the cost of debt-servicing was equivalent to 6.8% of the value of exports of goods and services. Consumer prices increased by an annual average of 3.9% during 1990–2002, although in 1994, following the 50% devaluation of the CFA franc, the rate of inflation averaged 36.1%. Consumer prices declined by 1.4% in 2001, but increased by 2.3% in 2002. Some 20,926 people were registered as unemployed in 1991.

INTERNATIONAL ECONOMIC RELATIONS

Niger is a member of numerous regional organizations, including the Economic Community of West African States, the West African organs of the Franc Zone, the Conseil de l'Entente, the Lake Chad Basin Commission, the Liptako–Gourma Integrated Development Authority, the Niger Basin Authority and the Permanent Inter-State Committee on Drought Control in the Sahel.

SURVEY AND PROSPECTS

Niger's narrow export base, which is dominated by uranium, meant that the country benefited less than most countries of the region from the 50% devaluation of the CFA franc in 1994. Political instability in the mid-1990s had a negative impact on economic performance, and most major creditors withdrew support after the military take-over that followed the death of President Maïnassara in April 1999. In September, furthermore, the World Bank suspended all credits, in view of Niger's failure to honour existing repayment deadlines.

Following the restoration of civilian rule, France resumed co-operation in early 2000, granting exceptional aid of 6,000m. francs CFA, and in January 2001 also cancelled a proportion of Niger's debt. In December 2000 the IMF and the World Bank announced that Niger would receive US $890m. in debt-service relief under the enhanced framework of the initiative for heavily indebted poor countries. Also in December the IMF announced the approval of a three-year loan, worth $76m., for Niger under the Poverty Reduction and Growth Facility; in November 2003 the IMF extended this arrangement until the end of June 2004. However, the European Commission suspended economic assistance to Niger in June 2001, after an audit revealed that some 6,500m. francs CFA granted by the Commission in 1996–2001 had been used for purposes deemed ineligible for such support.

Following two years of stagnation, economic performance improved markedly in 2001, although improved agricultural output was responsible for some two-thirds of growth in that year, and favourable climatic conditions also resulted in plentiful harvests being recorded in 2002 and 2003. Although the political crisis in Côte d'Ivoire from September 2002 resulted in a shortfall of some 3,400m. francs CFA in transfers from the Union économique et monétaire ouest-africaine in 2003, the Niger was less adversely affected by the unrest than other countries of the region more dependent on Côte d'Ivoire as a trade route. Majority shares in the state water and telecommunications companies were transferred to the private sector in 2001, while the divestiture of the state petroleum company and, following major restructuring, of the state electricity company were regarded as priorities for 2004. GDP growth of 4.0% was forecast for 2003.

Nigeria

The Federal Republic of Nigeria is a West African coastal state. In 1960 the Federation of Nigeria achieved independence from Britain. For much of the post-independence period Nigeria has been under military rule. In 1995, following the execution of nine Ogoni activists, Nigeria was suspended from the Commonwealth and threatened with expulsion if democracy was not restored within two years. In 1999, after legislative and presidential elections restored civilian rule, Nigeria was readmitted to the Commonwealth. The introduction, from 1999, of Islamic Shari'a law in several northern states has created considerable religious and ethnic unrest. Abuja is the capital. English is the official language.

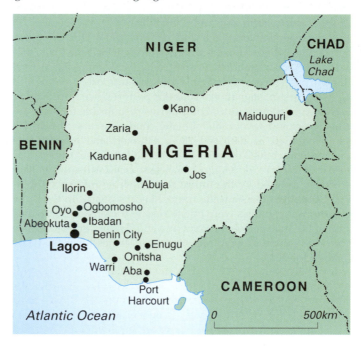

Area and population
Area: 923,768 sq km
Population (mid-2002): 132,784,704
Population density (mid-2002): 143.7 per sq km
Life expectancy (years at birth, 2002): 48.8 (males 48.0; females 49.6)

Finance
GDP in current prices: 2002: US $43,540m. ($328 per head)
Real GDP growth (2002): –0.9%
Inflation (annual average, 2002): 12.9%
Currency: naira

Economy

In 2002, according to estimates by the World Bank, Nigeria's gross national income (GNI), measured at average 2000–02 prices, was US $38,680m., equivalent to $290 per head (or $780 per head on an international purchasing-power parity basis). During 1990–2002, it was estimated, the population increased, in real terms, at an average annual rate of 2.7%, while gross domestic product (GDP) per head declined by 0.3%. Overall GDP increased, in real terms, at an average annual rate of 2.4% in 1990–2002; GDP increased by 2.9% in 2001, but declined by 0.9% in 2002.

AGRICULTURE

Agriculture (including hunting, forestry and fishing) contributed 34.6% of GDP in 2001. An estimated 31.5% of the labour force were employed in the sector in 2002. The principal cash crops are cocoa (which accounted for only 0.7% of total merchandise exports in 1995), rubber and oil palm. Staple food crops include rice, maize, taro, yams, cassava, sorghum and millet. Timber production, the raising of livestock (principally goats, sheep, cattle and poultry), and artisanal fisheries are also important. According to the World Bank, agricultural GDP increased at an average annual rate of 3.5% in 1990–2001. Growth in agricultural GDP was 5.3% in 2001.

INDUSTRY

Industry (including mining, manufacturing, construction and power) engaged an estimated 6.9% of the employed labour force in 1990, and contributed 35.5% of GDP in 2001. According to the World Bank, industrial GDP increased at an average annual rate of 1.5% in 1990–2001. Growth in industrial GDP was 1.5% in 2001. Industrial production increased by 1.2% in 2002.

Mining

Mining contributed 30.3% of GDP in 2001, although the sector engaged less than 0.1% of the employed labour force in 1986. The principal mineral is petroleum, of which Nigeria is Africa's leading producer (providing an estimated 92.3% of total export earnings in 2001). In addition, Nigeria possesses substantial deposits of natural gas and coal. In late 1999 the Nigerian Government commenced exports of liquefied natural gas. Plans for the construction of a pipeline, which would transport natural gas from the Escravos field, in Delta State, to Benin, Togo and Ghana, were under way. Tin and iron ore are also mined, while there are plans to exploit deposits of uranium. The GDP of the mining sector was estimated by the IMF to have declined by an average of 0.1% per year in 1997–2001; mining GDP increased by 0.6% in 2001.

Manufacturing

Manufacturing contributed 4.2% of GDP in 2001, and engaged about 4.3% of the employed labour force in 1986. The principal sectors are food-processing, brewing, petroleum-refining, iron and steel, motor vehicles (using imported components), textiles, cigarettes, footwear, pharmaceuticals, pulp and paper, and cement. According to the World Bank, manufacturing GDP increased at an average annual rate of 1.7% in 1990–2001. Growth in manufacturing GDP, was 3.8% in 2001. Manufacturing production increased by 2.9% in 2002.

Energy

Energy is derived principally from natural gas, which provided some 56.9% of electricity in 2000, and hydroelectric power (36.8%). Mineral fuels comprised an estimated 1.8% of the value of merchandise imports in 2000.

SERVICES

The services sector contributed 29.9% of GDP in 2001, and engaged 48.5% of the employed labour force in 1986. According to World Bank estimates, the GDP of the services sector increased at an average annual rate of 3.1% in 1990–2001. Growth in the sector was 3.2% in 2001.

EXTERNAL TRADE

In 1999 Nigeria recorded a visible trade surplus of US $4,288m., and there was a surplus of $506m. on the current account of the balance of payments. In 2001 the principal source of imports (9.4%) was the United Kingdom; other major suppliers were the USA, the People's Republic of China, Germany and France. The USA was the principal market for exports (40.5%) in that year; other significant purchasers were Spain, Brazil, India and France. The main export in 2000 was petroleum. The principal imports in that year were machinery and transport equipment (particularly road vehicles), chemicals, manufactured goods, and food and live animals.

GOVERNMENT FINANCE

Nigeria's overall budget deficit for 2001 was ₦156,678m., equivalent to 3.3% of GDP. The country's external debt totalled US $31,119m. at the end of 2001, of which $29,215m. was long-term public debt. In that year the cost of debt-servicing was equivalent to 12.0% of the value of exports of goods and services. The annual rate of inflation averaged 26.3% in 1990–2002; consumer prices increased by 12.9% in 2002. An estimated 4.5% of the labour force were unemployed at the end of 1997.

INTERNATIONAL ECONOMIC RELATIONS

Nigeria is a member of the African Development Bank, of the Economic Community of West African States, which aims to promote trade and co-operation in West Africa, and of the Organization of the Petroleum Exporting Countries.

SURVEY AND PROSPECTS

Following high levels of economic growth in the 1970s, Nigeria's economy deteriorated as a result of the subsequent decline in international prices for petroleum. In response to democratization measures initiated by a new military Head of State in mid-1998, the European Union ended a number of sanctions against Nigeria later that year. In January 1999 the Government abolished the dual exchange rate system and ended restrictions on foreign investment. The new civilian Government, which was installed in June, benefited greatly from an increase in the international price of petroleum, and some fiscal recovery ensued. Continuing violent protests in the Niger Delta region disrupted petroleum production, however, and, together with severe religious and ethnic violence from 2000, deterred potential foreign investors.

The Government failed to adhere to a one-year IMF-endorsed economic programme, which expired in August 2001, and the IMF suspended formal relations with Nigeria in March 2002, thereby ending the immediate prospect of concessionary debt relief. In July the World Bank announced that it was to halve its lending capacity to Nigeria, owing to concern about levels of public expenditure prior to elections in early 2003. Despite widespread discontent over his perceived failure to reduce corruption, Obasanjo was returned to the presidency in April 2003. His new Government included several proponents of economic reform, notably the hitherto Vice-President of the World Bank as the new Minister of Finance and the Economy.

Despite political uncertainty prior to the elections, strong economic growth was estimated in 2003, partially as a result of an increase in offshore petroleum production. In early 2004 the administration promulgated its new policy document, the National Economic Empowerment and Development Strategy (NEEDS). The NEEDS programme, which was to continue for a period of four years, was based on budgetary restraint, increased productivity, administrative reform, greater state accountability, and improved conditions for private investment, with the principal objectives of increasing economic growth to 7% by 2007, and significantly reducing the fiscal deficit to the equivalent of 2% of GDP. The Government aimed to obtain IMF endorsement for NEEDS in order to qualify to seek debt relief from the 'Paris Club' of bilateral creditors.

Progress towards the privatization of state enterprises and easing of currency controls had proved slow, while government efforts to reduce subsidies on domestic fuel were repeatedly impeded by widespread strike action. Planned state bans on the import of certain commodities was also expected to prompt further protests from the National Labour Congress (NLC). The international community was perceived as doubtful regarding the ability of Obasanjo's administration to implement the NEEDS programme, particularly in view of long-standing conflict with the NLC and opposition in the National Assembly to reductions in budgetary expenditure.

Niue

Niue is a coral island, located in the Pacific Ocean. In 1900 Niue was declared a British protectorate, in 1901 it was formally annexed to New Zealand as part of the Cook Islands, and in 1904 it was granted a separate administration. In 1974 Niue attained 'self-government in free association with New Zealand'. In 2000 a Niue-New Zealand joint consultative committee met for the first time, to consider the two sides' future constitutional relationship. Alofi is the capital. Niuean and English are spoken.

Area and population
Area: 263 sq km
Population (October 2001): 1,489
Population density (October 2001): 5.7 per sq km
Life expectancy (years at birth, 2002): 70.3 (males 67.6; females 73.3)

Finance
GDP in current prices: 2000): $NZ 16.7m. ($11,215 per head)
Inflation (annual average, 2002): 2.7%
Currency: New Zealand dollar

Economy

Niue's gross domestic product (GDP) per head was estimated at US $3,600 in 2000. The population decreased at an average annual rate of 1.8% in 1986–97. In 2000 GDP was estimated at $NZ16.7m., in which year GDP decreased, in real terms, by 0.3%.

AGRICULTURE

Agriculture (including fishing) employs only a small minority of the labour force as a full-time occupation, although a majority of households practise subsistence gardening. The principal crops are coconuts and root crops. Honey is also produced for export. Coconut cream was the island's major export until the closure of the coconut cream processing factory in 1989. The main subsistence crops are taro, yams, cassava and sweet potatoes. A taro export scheme was successfully introduced in the early 1990s, and production of the crop increased by more than 500% in 1993. Exports of taro and yams contributed 87% of total export earnings in 1993. Plans to increase the production of vanilla as an export crop were discussed in 2003, but the promising crop was destroyed by the cyclone of early 2004. Pigs, poultry, goats and beef cattle are raised, mainly for local consumption. There is no manufacturing industry on Niue, although a fish processing factory was under construction in late 2003.

SERVICES

In the services sector, tourism has begun to make a significant contribution to the economy. An increase in the frequency of flights between Niue and Auckland in 1992 enhanced prospects for tourism, as did the construction of some 60 hotel rooms in the mid-1990s and a project to extend the runway at Hanan airport. A total of 2,252 people (48.8% of whom were travelling from New Zealand) visited Niue in 1999, and the industry earned US $2m. in 1997. The island's tourist industry was severely affected by the cancellation of the twice-weekly service operated by Royal Tongan Airlines its between Niue and New Zealand in early 2001. Niue was forced to rely upon charter flights operated by Air Fiji. However, in November 2001 Kiribati announced plans to operate a 70-seater Airbus between Niue and Fiji. More significantly, Samoa's Polynesian Airlines signed a five-year agreement in October 2002 to provide a direct weekly air link between Niue and Auckland, New Zealand. This was increased to a twice-weekly service in 2003, in which year arrivals increased by 44% to 2,758. However, following the cyclone of January 2004 (see above) experts suggested that the island's tourist industry was unlikely to recover in less than four years.

EXTERNAL TRADE

Niue records an annual trade deficit, with imports in 1993 exceeding exports by around 1,300%. In that year New Zealand, Niue's main trading partner, provided 86.1% of imports. The principal exports in that year were root crops (which provided 87.1% of total export earnings), coconuts (1.9%), honey and handicrafts. The principal imports were foodstuffs (which constituted 28.0% of the total cost of imports), electrical goods (11.8%), motor vehicles (10.6%) and machinery (5.4%). In 1999 imports totalled $NZ5.2m., while exports were worth only $NZ0.3m. Taro, honey and vanilla were Niue's most significant exports. Imports from New Zealand cost an estimated $NZ4.2m., while exports to that country earned an estimated $NZ0.2m. in 2002.

GOVERNMENT FINANCE

In 2003/04 the budgetary deficit was projected at $NZ1.7m. Development assistance from New Zealand totalled $NZ8.28m. in 2003/04 (compared with $NZ10.0m. in 1994/95). The annual rate of inflation averaged 2.6% in 1990–2002. Compared with the previous year, consumer prices increased by an average of 6.8% in 2001 and by 2.7% in 2002.

INTERNATIONAL ECONOMIC RELATIONS

Niue is a member of the Pacific Community and the Pacific Islands Forum, and an associate member of the UN Economic and Social Commission for Asia and the Pacific (ESCAP). In 2000 Niue became a signatory of the Cotonou Agreement with the European Union (EU).

SURVEY AND PROSPECTS

Niue's economic development has been adversely affected by inclement weather, inadequate transport services and the annual migration of about 10% of the population to New Zealand. Two-thirds of the land surface is uncultivable, and marine resources are variable. Measures were announced in 1993 aimed at encouraging the return to the island of Niueans resident in New Zealand. It was hoped that, by increasing the resident population, Niue's economy could be stimulated and its chances for self-sufficiency improved. However, the population continued to decline.

In late 2003 the Government extended an invitation to the residents of Tuvalu to move to Niue. In 1994 the Niue Assembly approved legislation allowing the island to become an 'offshore' financial centre. The Government predicted that Niue could earn up to $NZ11m. annually in fees from a financial services industry. By mid-1996 the 'offshore' centre was believed to have attracted some US $280,000. However, following the threat of financial sanctions from the Paris-based Financial Action Task Force (FATF), Niue declared its intention to repeal its 'offshore' banking legislation, despite fears that this would result in annual revenue losses of some US $80,000 in bank licence fees and more than US $500,000 in company registration fees.

Further attempts to secure additional sources of revenue in Niue included the leasing of the island's telecommunications facilities to foreign companies for use in specialist telephone services. However, this enterprise (which earned the island an estimated $NZ1.5m. per year) caused considerable controversy when it was revealed that Niue's telephone code had been made available to companies offering personal services considered indecent by the majority of islanders. In addition, the island earned some US $0.5m. between 1997 and 2000 from the sale of its internet domain name '.nu'. In mid-2003 Niue became the first location in the world to have a national wireless internet system, allowing internet access from anywhere by means of solar-powered aerials attached to coconut palms.

The imposition of harsh economic sanctions by the US Government in 2001, following accusations that the island was still allowing criminal organizations to 'launder' their funds through the territory's 'offshore' financial centre, led Niue's Government to investigate various alternative activities for generating revenue. In November 2001 Premier Sani Lakatani had announced that the Government was negotiating a deal with a US company interested in using Niue as the call-centre of a satellite service. Other large-scale projects included a scheme by a Korean religious sect to build a US $200m. holy walled city on Niue, which was abandoned in early 2003 following strong opposition from local residents.

In 1999 Premier Lakatani announced that he was seeking to gain membership of the Asian Development Bank (ADB) for Niue in the hope that the island might receive a low-interest loan from the ADB if the New Zealand Government proceeded with its intention to withdraw aid to the territory. In 2001, however, Niue's application was obstructed by the USA. In March 2002 Niue was in the process of concluding a 20-year development programme with the EU. Initial assistance of €2.6m., to be released in 2003, was to be used to finance renewable energy projects such as wind power generation. An island development plan for 2003 included proposals to develop Niue's fishing industry by employing a fleet of used Korean fishing vessels, to expand the agricultural sector with the introduction of vanilla cultivation, to encourage increased tourism given the availability of direct flights to New Zealand and to increase taro exports to New Zealand owing to a new regular shipping service which was expected to reduce freight costs significantly. Niue's entire economy was severely affected by Cyclone Heta which struck the island in January 2004 causing extensive damage to housing, crops and infrastructure.

Northern Mariana Islands

The Commonwealth of the Northern Mariana Islands comprises all the Mariana islands except Guam, in the western Pacific Ocean. In 1947 the Northern Mariana Islands became part of the US-administered UN Trust Territory of the Pacific Islands. In 1975 the Northern Mariana Islands voted for separate status as a US Commonwealth Territory, and the Northern Marianas Commonwealth Covenant was signed in 1976. In 1978 the former Marianas District became internally self-governing. The Northern Marianas were formally admitted to US Commonwealth status in 1986. The administrative centre is on Saipan island. English, Chamorro and Carolinian are the official languages.

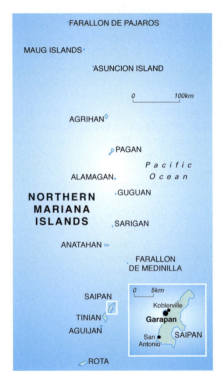

Area and population
Area: 457 sq km
Population (mid-2001): 80,000
Population density (mid-2001): 175.1 per sq km

Finance
Inflation (annual average, 2002): 0.1%
Currency: US dollar

Economy

The Commonwealth of the Northern Mariana Islands' gross national income (GNI) was estimated by the Bank of Hawaii (BOH) to be US $696.3m. in 1999. GNI per head was estimated at $8,582. The population increased at an estimated annual rate of more than 4.6% during 1990–2002.

AGRICULTURE

Agriculture is concentrated in smallholdings, important crops being coconuts, bread-fruit, tomatoes and melons. Cattle-ranching is practised on Tinian. Vegetables, beef and pork are produced for export. There is little commercial fishing in the islands, although there is a major transhipment facility at Tinian harbour. Imports of fish products increased from 1990; fishing remains a potentially valuable but as yet unrealized commercial resource. Agriculture (including forestry, fishing and mining) engaged 1.5% of the employed labour force in 2000, and its commercial value as a sector is minimal. In 2002 it accounted for only 0.1% of gross business revenues (total revenues generated by business transactions; the Government does not calculate gross domestic product figures).

INDUSTRY

Industry (including manufacturing and construction) engaged 47.2% of the employed labour force in 2000. Manufacturing alone engaged 40.7% of workers, while construction employed 6.5%. The principal manufacturing activity is the garment industry, which grew rapidly after its establishment in the mid-1980s to become the islands' chief export sector. Manufacturers benefit from US regulations that permit duty-free and quota-free imports from the Commonwealth. Garment manufacturing accounted for 23.6% of gross business revenues in 2002, and overall exports of garments were worth US $925.7m. in 2001, compared with $1,017m. in 2000. The Government's direct revenues from the industry were projected to reach $48.2m. in 2003. Other small-scale manufacturing activities include handicrafts and the processing of fish and copra. Construction is very closely related to the tourist industry and demand for additional hotel capacity. However, the number of building permits sold, both commercial and residential, declined each year during 1997–2001, although there was a slight improvement in 2002.

SERVICES

Service industries dominate the economy, particularly tourism. In 2000 services (including utilities) engaged 51.3% of the employed labour force, whilst accounting for 29.2% of gross business revenues. Tourist receipts were worth an estimated US $430m. in 2001. Japan provided the majority (68.7%) of the islands' visitors in 2002. Other significant sources of tourists were the Republic of Korea, Guam, the USA and, to an increasing extent in the early 21st century, the People's Republic of China. Although tourist numbers increased by 2.4% in 1999 and by 5.3% in 2000, the industry was severely affected by the repercussions of the September 2001 terrorist attacks on the USA: the hotel occupancy rate declined to only 35% in December 2001, and arrivals declined by 15.6% in the year as a whole. A total of 475,547 visitors travelled to the islands in 2002, an increase of 7.0% in relation to the previous year. In mid-1995, meanwhile, a US company opened the Territory's first casino on Tinian.

The islands were expected to receive some $12m. annually in revenue from the casino. Owing to the limited hotel accommodation on Tinian, the company arranged for chartered aircraft to transport tourists to the island from the Northern Mariana Islands and Guam. In 2001 remittances from overseas workers and investments reached $76.7m.

EXTERNAL TRADE

The Northern Marianas are dependent on imports, the value of which totalled US $836.2m. in 1997. The principal imports in that year were foodstuffs (9.6% of the total), petroleum products (8.2%), clothing (7.1%), automobiles and parts (5.0%), and construction materials (4.1%). In 1991 there was a trade deficit of $126.9m. The annual rate of inflation averaged 2.6% in 1990–2002. Consumer prices declined by 1.1% in 2001, but increased by 0.2% in 2002.

GOVERNMENT FINANCE

Under the Covenant between the Commonwealth of the Northern Mariana Islands and the USA, the islands receive substantial annual development grants. Budget estimates envisaged total revenue of US $297.2m. in the financial year ending 30 September 2000, federal contributions accounting for $52.9m. Total expenditure of $225.5m. was projected for that year. Loans from the Commonwealth Development Authority totalled more than $0.5m. in 2001. The Territory is a member of the Pacific Community and an associate member of the UN Economic and Social Commission for Asia and the Pacific (ESCAP).

SURVEY AND PROSPECTS

Continued economic problems in the Territory have been largely attributed to the dramatic increase in the Northern Marianas' population (from some 17,000 in 1979 to 74,151 in 2002). The main restraint on development is the need to expand the islands' infrastructure, coupled with the problem of a labour shortage and the dependence on foreign workers, in particular Filipino nationals. However, owing to the resulting excess of immigrant workers (whose numbers increased by 655% between 1980 and 1989 and exceeded the permanent population by a margin of two to one in the early 2000s), wages remained relatively low, and there were widespread complaints of poor working conditions. In September 2002 a judgment on a lawsuit against garment manufacturers in Saipan awarded compensation to the affected workers and provided for independent monitoring of labour practices in the Northern Marianas. Although the islands' Government resisted legislative proposals to bring immigration and labour practices into line with the mainland USA, there was concern in the Territory that new World Trade Organization measures removing import quotas on clothing, which were scheduled to come into effect in January 2005, were regarded as representing a direct threat to the comparative advantage of the garment industry's location within an unincorporated US Territory. None the less, the Northern Mariana Islands has long benefited from its political association with the USA; US federal funding and development assistance totalled some US $13m. in 2001/02, and in January 2004 an agreement was signed whereby the Northern Mariana Islands was to receive some $5.1m. in federal funding in order to offset the impact of migration, under the Compact of Free Association, to the Territory from the Marshall Islands, the Federated States of Micronesia, and Palau.

The islands' Republican administration, inaugurated in 2002, pledged to prioritize economic reform by promoting free, competitive markets with a minimum of government interference. It outlined an environmental rehabilitation programme in an effort to raise the Territory's tourism profile. In March 2002 the Government introduced tax incentives for new businesses and developers, worth a potential 100% abatement of local taxes, or a 95% rebate of federal taxes. However, despite improved expenditure controls, the continued recession in the islands was estimated to have led to a deterioration in the Government's fiscal position and an increase in public debt.

Norway

The Kingdom of Norway forms part of Scandinavia, in northern Europe. In 1905 Norway declared its independence from Sweden. Norwegians elected their own monarch, Prince Karl of Denmark, who took the title of King Håkon VII. He was succeeded by his son, Olav V. In 1991 Olav's son succeeded him, as King Harald V. In 1981 Norway's first Høyre (Conservative) Government since 1928 took office. In 1994, in a referendum, a majority of voters rejected Norway's recently negotiated member-ship of the European Union. Oslo is the capital. The two forms of the Norwegian language are officially recognized as equal.

Area and population
Area: 323,759 sq km
Population (mid-2002): 4,538,710
Population density (mid-2002): 14.0 per sq km
Life expectancy (years at birth, 2002): 79.1 (males 76.4; females 81.7)

Finance
GDP in current prices: 2002): US $189,436m. ($41,738 per head)
Real GDP growth (2002): 2.0%
Inflation (annual average, 2002): 1.3%
Currency: krone

Economy

In 2002, according to estimates by the World Bank, Norway's gross national income (GNI), measured at average 2000–02 prices, was US $171,770m., equivalent to $37,850 per head (or $35,840 per head on an international purchasing-power parity basis). During 1990–2002, it was estimated, the population increased by an average of 0.6% per year, while gross domestic product (GDP) per head increased, in real terms, by an average of 2.5% per year. Norway's overall GDP increased, in real terms, at an average annual rate of 3.1% in 1990–2002. Real GDP increased by 1.4% in 2001 and by 2.0% in 2002.

AGRICULTURE

The contribution of agriculture, hunting, forestry and fishing to GDP in 2002 was estimated at 1.8%. In 2003 these sectors (excluding hunting) engaged 3.7% of the employed labour force. Around 3.4% of the land surface is cultivated, and the most important branch of the agricultural sector is livestock-rearing. Fish-farming has been intensively developed by the Government since the early 1970s. The fishing industry provided 5.8% of total export revenue in 2002. A temporary emergency ban on cod fishing in parts of the North Sea, agreed between the European Union (EU) and Norway, was announced in January 2001 in an attempt to prevent the collapse of fish stocks through over-fishing. In February 2004 the Government appealed against proposals by the United Kingdom to block salmon imports to the EU from non-EU countries. In 2002 Norway produced some 438,200 metric tons of farmed salmon. Agricultural production increased at an average annual rate of 2.1% during 1990–2000. Agricultural GDP increased by 0.6% in 1999 and by 2.1% in 2000.

INDUSTRY

Industry (including mining, manufacturing, construction, power and public utilities) contributed 37.2% of GDP in 2002, and engaged 21.4% of the employed labour force in 2003. During 1990–2000 industrial GDP increased, in real terms, at an average annual rate of 3.6%. Industrial GDP declined, in real terms, by 0.8% in 1999, but increased by 2.7% in 2000.

Mining

Mining (including gas and petroleum extraction) provided 19.6% of GDP in 2002, and engaged 1.4% of the employed labour force in 2003. Norway possesses substantial reserves of petroleum and natural gas (exports of petroleum and petroleum products accounted for 46.0% of total export earnings in 2002). Most of the reserves are located off shore. During 1992–2000 the production of crude petroleum increased at an average annual rate of 4.3% and output of natural gas grew at an average rate of 7.1% per year. Norway's other mineral reserves include iron ore, iron pyrites, copper, lead and zinc. Substantial deposits of platinum were discovered in the northern county of Finnmark in November 2001—the area was also believed to contain deposits of gold and diamonds. In October 2003 Norway signed a deal to export natural gas from the Ormen Lange gas field to the United Kingdom; it was envisaged that 20,000m. cu m of natural gas per year would be exported from the field. In December the Government announced it was to open the hitherto unexplored

Barents Sea for petroleum and gas extraction; three exploratory wells were to be drilled in 2004–05. During 1990–96 production in the petroleum and gas extraction sub-sector increased by an average of 10.2% per year, whereas elsewhere in the mining sector the comparable growth rate was 0.9%. Real GDP in the petroleum and gas extraction sub-sector declined by 3.4% in 1998, but increased by 1.3% in 1999; the GDP of the non-hydrocarbon mining sub-sector declined by 1.7% in 1998 and by 1.8% in 1999.

Manufacturing

Manufacturing contributed 10.3% of GDP in 2002, and employed 12.3% of the working population in 2003. In 1998 the most important branches of manufacturing, measured by gross value of output, were food products (accounting for 20.3% of the total), transport equipment (13.5%), metals and metal products (13.2%), chemicals and chemical products (7.6%), and publishing and printing (7.2%). During 1990–98 manufacturing production increased by an average of 2.3% per year. Manufacturing GDP grew, in real terms, by 1.5% in 1998, but declined by 2.3% in 1999.

Energy

In 2002, according to provisional figures, some 99.3% of Norway's installed capacity of electric energy was produced by hydroelectric power schemes; domestic energy demands are easily supplied, and Norway has exported hydroelectricity since 1993. Norway's extensive reserves of petroleum and natural gas are mainly exploited for sale to foreign markets, since the domestic market is limited.

SERVICES

The services sector contributed 61.0% of GDP in 2002, and engaged 74.9% of the employed labour force in 2003. The GDP of the services sector increased, in real terms, by an average of 3.3% per year during 1990–2000; it grew by 2.1% in 1999 and by 2.2% in 2000.

Although shipbuilding has declined since the early 1970s, Norway remains a leading shipping nation. The establishment of the Norwegian International Ship Register in 1987 allowed an expansion of the merchant fleet by more than 300%, in terms of gross tonnage; it totalled 22.2m. grt at the end of 2002.

EXTERNAL TRADE

In 2002, according to IMF figures, Norway recorded a visible trade surplus of US $24,371m., and there was a surplus of $25,148m. on the current account of the balance of payments. In 2002 the EU provided 66.7% of imports and took 74.3% of exports: Fellow-members of the European Free Trade Association (EFTA) accounted for 1.7% of Norway's imports and 0.6% of exports. The principal source of imports in 2002 was Sweden (providing 15.3% of the total), followed by Germany (13.1%), Denmark (7.9%) and the United Kingdom (7.3%); the principal market for exports was the United Kingdom (taking 19.3%), followed by Germany (12.7%), the Netherlands (9.6%) and the USA (8.7%). In 2002 the principal exports were petroleum, petroleum products and related materials (accounting for 46.0% of total exports), machinery and transport equipment (11.8%), basic manufactures (10.6%) and food and live animals (6.4%); the principal imports were machinery and transport equipment (40.5%), miscellaneous manufactured articles (16.5%), basic manufactures (15.6%) and chemicals and related products (9.8%).

GOVERNMENT FINANCE

In the revised budget for 2002 a surplus of 152,615m. kroner was forecast (equivalent to some 10.0% of GDP in purchasers' values), compared with a surplus of 226,121m. kroner in 2001. At the end of 2000 Norway's gross public debt was estimated at an amount equivalent to 21% of GDP, and was forecast to remain at this level until 2004. During 1990–2002 the average annual rate of inflation was 2.3%; consumer prices increased by 3.0% in 2001 and by 1.3% in 2002. The average rate of unemployment was 4.5% in 2003.

INTERNATIONAL ECONOMIC RELATIONS

In addition to its membership of EFTA, Norway is a member of the European Economic Area (EEA), the Nordic Council and the Nordic Council of Ministers. Although Norway is not a member of the EU, it joined the EU's Schengen Agreement along with Denmark, Finland and Sweden (all EU members) by virtue of its membership in the Nordic passport union (Iceland also joined).

SURVEY AND PROSPECTS

The Norwegian economy, which is highly dependent on its hydrocarbons sector (Norway is the world's second largest petroleum exporter), experienced a sustained expansion during the 1990s, leading to virtually full employment, as well as rises in real incomes. Norway maintained a stable exchange rate during this period and a prudent fiscal position, and reinvested a substantial proportion of petroleum revenues abroad through the State Petroleum Fund, partly in preparation for future increased demands on pensions and also to offer limited protection to the economy against fluctuations in the petroleum sector.

In the first years of the 21st century a strong policy framework underpinned enviable prosperity and a high degree of social equity in Norway. The fiscal guidelines adopted in 2001 formed the basis of a reasonable compromise between the current and future use of petroleum revenues. Norway's traditionally high social cohesiveness and solidarity ensured that the use of the petroleum wealth benefited people at all levels of society, and would continue to benefit future generations well after the petroleum itself was depleted. Economic growth fell sharply during 2003, but activity appeared to be increasing by early 2004. The slow growth reflected economic weakness in Norway's trading partners, as well as tight monetary conditions in 2003 in the context of strong wage growth and prospects of further fiscal expansion. In the course of 2003, as inflationary and wage pressures eased significantly, the central bank reduced interest rates. In early 2004 consumption was beginning to recover in response to these measures. The reduction in the interest rate also reversed the appreciation of the krone, which, together with the improving world economic outlook, was expected to promote economic growth in 2004.

Oman

The Sultanate of Oman occupies the extreme east and south-east of the Arabian peninsula. Full independence was confirmed by a treaty of friendship with the United Kingdom in 1951. In 1970 Sultan Said bin Taimur was overthrown by his son, Qaboos bin Said as-Said. In 1991 a Consultative Council (Majlis ash-Shoura) was established, with the intention of extending the participation of Omani citizens in national affairs. In 1996 Sultan Qaboos promulgated a Basic Statute of the State, a constitutional document defining the organs and guiding principles of the State. Muscat is the capital. The official language is Arabic.

Area and population
Area: 309,500 sq km
Population (mid-2002): 2,539,410
Population density (mid-2002): 8.2 per sq km
Life expectancy (years at birth, 2002): 73.1 (males 71.0; females 76.3)

Finance
GDP in current prices: 2002): US $20,073m. ($7,905 per head)
Real GDP growth (2002): 2.2%
Inflation (annual average, 2002): −0.7%
Currency: rial Omani

Economy

In 2001, according to estimates by the World Bank, Oman's gross national income (GNI), measured at average 1999–2001 prices, was US $19,137m., equivalent to $7,720 per head (or $12,860 per head on an international purchasing-power parity basis). During 1990–2002, it was estimated, the population increased at an average annual rate of 3.8%, while real gross domestic product (GDP) per head increased, in real terms, by an average of 1.0% per year. Overall GDP increased, in real terms, at an average annual rate of 4.8% in 1990–2002; according to the IMF, growth in 2002 was around 2%.

AGRICULTURE

Agriculture (including fishing) engaged 9.4% of the employed population at the 1993 census, and contributed an estimated 1.9% of GDP in 2003. FAO data suggested that some 35.2% of the economically active population were engaged in agriculture in 2002, mainly at subsistence level. The major crops are dates, tomatoes, bananas, water-melons and onions. The production of frankincense, formerly an important export commodity, has been revived. Livestock and fishing are also important. The real GDP of the agricultural sector increased by an average of 4.0% annually in 1990–2000. Real agricultural GDP declined by 5.3% in 2000, but expanded by some 2.7% in 2001.

INDUSTRY

Industry (including mining and quarrying, manufacturing, construction and power) employed 27.8% of the working population in 1993, and provided an estimated 52.7% of GDP in 2003. Real industrial GDP increased by an average of 4.1% annually in 1990–2000. The sector's real GDP increased by 9.1% in 2000 and by an estimated 9.2% in 2001.

Mining

According to provisional figures, the mining sector contributed 41.1% of GDP in 2003, and engaged 2.1% of the employed labour force in 1993. The main mineral reserves are petroleum and natural gas, which together provided an estimated 40.9% of GDP in 2003. There were proven petroleum reserves of 5,500m. barrels at the end of 2002. Production in 2002 averaged 902,000 barrels per day (b/d). Petroleum reserves were estimated to be sufficient to sustain production at these levels until 2020. Under its 2001–05 Development Plan, Oman plans to increase oil output to at least 1m. b/d. Exports of Omani crude petroleum provided 67.5% of total export earnings in 2002. Natural gas is also an important mineral resource; there were proven reserves of some 830,000m. cu m at the end of 2002, sustainable for about 56 years at 2002 production levels (output in 2002 totalled 14,800m. cu m—an increase of some 5.7% compared with the previous year). An expansionary budget for 2004, presented in January, earmarked extra funds for gas exploration. Budget revenue from petroleum and natural gas contributed some 75.7% of the total in 2002. Chromite, gold, salt, marble, gypsum and limestone are also mined, and the exploitation of coal deposits is planned. The GDP of the mining sector increased at an average annual rate of 3.5% in 1990–2000. Mining GDP expanded by 5.6% in 2000 and by some 0.2% in 2001.

Manufacturing

Manufacturing contributed an estimated 8.1% of GDP in 2003, and engaged 9.0% of the employed labour force in 1993. The most important branches of the sector are petroleum-refining, construction materials, cement production and copper-smelting. Assembly industries, light engineering and food-processing are being encouraged at industrial estates in Muscat, Sohar and Salalah. Completion of a US $9,000m. lique-fied natural gas (LNG) plant at Sur has reduced domestic demand for petroleum and also produced a surplus for export. The GDP of the manufacturing sector increased, in real terms, at an average rate of 7.9% annually in 1990–2000. The sector's real GDP increased by 40.2% in 2000 and by an estimated 62.7% in 2001.

Energy

Energy is derived almost exclusively from domestic supplies of natural gas (which accounted for 83.3% of electricity produced in 2001) and petroleum. Imports of fuel products comprised just 2.2% of total imports in 2002.

SERVICES

Services provided an estimated 45.4% of GDP in 2003, and engaged 62.0% of the employed population at the 1993 census. The GDP of the services sector increased, in real terms, at an average rate of 5.3% per year during 1990–2000. Real services GDP increased by 4.5% in 2000 and by an estimated 9.2% in 2001.

EXTERNAL TRADE

In 2002 Oman recorded a visible trade surplus of RO 2,129m., and there was a surplus of RO 749m. on the current account of the balance of payments. In 2001 the principal sources of imports were the United Arab Emirates and Japan (which supplied, respectively, 28.4% and 15.4% of Oman's imports). The USA and the United King-dom are also important suppliers. The most important market for exports in 2001 was Japan (taking 20.1%). The Republic of Korea, the People's Republic of China, and Thailand were also important markets for exports. Petroleum and natural gas is, by far, the principal export category, comprising 77.0% of the total in 2002. Excluding re-exports (which contributed 16.9% of total export earnings in that year), live animals and animal products made the most notable contribution to export revenue of all non-oil exports of Omani origin. The principal imports in 2002 were machinery and transport equipment, basic manufactures, food and live animals, and beverages and tobacco.

GOVERNMENT FINANCE

Oman recorded an estimated overall budgetary deficit of RO 69.7m. in 2002 (equiva-lent to 0.9% of GDP in that year). At the end of 2001 Oman's total external debt was US $6,025m., of which $4,759m. was long-term public debt. The cost of debt-servicing in that year was equivalent to 14.2% of the total value of exports of goods and services. Annual inflation declined by an average of 0.4% in 1995–2002; consumer prices decreased by an annual average of 0.7% in 2002. Although Oman has traditionally relied on a high level of immigrant labour (non-Omanis accounted for 64.2% of the employed labour force in 1993), employment opportunities for young Omanis declined in the early 1990s and, according to census results, unemployment among Omanis stood at 11.9% in 1993.

INTERNATIONAL ECONOMIC RELATIONS

Oman is a member of the Arab Fund for Economic and Social Development, the Islamic Development Bank and the Arab Monetary Fund. It was a founder member of the Co-operation Council for the Arab States of the Gulf (the Gulf Co-operation Council—GCC), and of the Indian Ocean Rim Association for Regional Co-operation. Oman is not a member of the Organization of the Petroleum Exporting Countries (OPEC) nor of the Organization of Arab Petroleum Exporting Countries, but it generally respects OPEC's policies regarding levels of petroleum production and pricing. Oman was admitted to the World Trade Organization in November 2000. The GCC's six members established a unified regional customs tariff in January 2003, and the organization has undertaken to establish a single market and currency no later than January 2010.

SURVEY AND PROSPECTS

Oman's limited petroleum reserves and fluctuations in the price of petroleum have necessitated a series of five-year development plans to diversify the country's economic base, in particular through the expansion of the private sector. Under the sixth Development Plan (2001–05), emphasis was to be placed on the reduction of public expenditure, the development of the non-petroleum sector (with gas-based industry and tourism being notable targets), and the expansion of the privatization programme (begun in mid-1994). Besides seeking to create 110,000 jobs for Omani nationals, it was also planned to increase state funding for their education and training, and to limit the employment of expatriates in certain fields. (Omanis are now reported to constitute at least 90% of employees in banking and finance.) Under the Plan, the Government aimed to achieve annual GDP growth of at least 3% and to maintain low annual rates of inflation.

Oman's economy expanded in 2001, as government efforts to maximize existing hydrocarbons reserves while strengthening the non-petroleum sector achieved some success. However, the Israeli–Palestinian crisis resulted in reduced tourism revenues for Oman, leading to GDP growth of about 2% in 2002. Meanwhile, in late 1999 the Government approved an accelerated privatization programme in the power sector; divestment of the postal service and telecommunications and transport sectors was also planned in 2004. Recent industrial development included the construction of gas pipelines at Sohar and Salalah, which were completed in late 2002. Furthermore, plans for the establishment of a free-trade zone at Salalah, which was expected to create new employment opportunities for Omani nationals and also encourage foreign investment, were again under way in 2003; a major investor had withdrawn from the venture in late 2002, alluding to the political instability in the region as a reason for its withdrawal. In preparation for admittance to the WTO, the Government abolished import fees, raised the limit on foreign ownership of local industries from 49% to 70% (effective from 1 January 2001) and authorized 100% foreign ownership in banking, insurance and brokerage firms (from 1 January 2003).

In January 2004 the Government announced an estimated RO 500m. deficit in its 2004 budget. However, since petroleum prices remained stronger than the Government's cautious estimates, the actual shortfall, attributed to a decrease in crude petroleum output in 2003 and an increase of 14% in projected expenditure, was expected to be less than forecast in the budget. Economic growth of around 6% was expected in 2003.

Pakistan

The Islamic Republic of Pakistan lies in southern Asia. Pakistan was created in 1947 when Britain's former Indian Empire was partitioned. Pakistan was formally under martial law from 1977 until 1985. Following elections in 1988, Benazir Bhutto of the Pakistan People's Party became the first female leader of an Islamic country. Subsequently, Pakistan has frequently been characterized by extreme political turbulence, aggravated by religious and inter-ethnic violence. In 1999 Gen. Pervez Musharraf overthrew the Government of Nawaz Sharif and imposed virtual martial law. Civilian rule was restored in 2002. Islamabad is the capital. Urdu is the national language.

Area and population
Area: 796,095 sq km (excluding Azad Kashmir, 11,639 sq km, and the Northern Areas, 72,520 sq km)
Population (mid-2002): 144,902,416
Population density (mid-2002): 182.0 per sq km
Life expectancy (years at birth, 2002): 61.4 (males 61.1; females 61.6)

Finance
GDP in current prices: 2002): US $60,521m. ($418 per head)
Real GDP growth (2002): 4.4%
Inflation (annual average, 2002): 3.3%
Currency: Pakistani rupee

Economy

In 2002, according to estimates by the World Bank, Pakistan's gross national income (GNI), measured at average 2000–02 prices, was US $59,205m., equivalent to $410 per head (or $1,940 per head on an international purchasing-power parity basis). During 1990–2002, it was estimated, the population increased at an average annual rate of 2.5%, while gross domestic product (GDP) per head increased, in real terms, by an average of 1.4% per year. Overall GDP increased, in real terms, at an average annual rate of 3.9% in 1990–2002. Growth reached 3.4% in 2001/02 and 5.1% in 2002/03.

AGRICULTURE

Agriculture (including forestry and fishing) contributed an estimated 23.3% of GDP in the year ending 30 June 2003. An estimated 48.4% of the employed labour force were engaged in the sector at 30 June 2003. The principal cash crops are cotton (textile yarn and fabrics accounted for around 49.3% of export earnings in 2001/02) and rice; wheat, maize and sugar cane are also major crops. Fishing and leather production provide significant export revenues. During 1990/91–2001/02 agricultural GDP increased at an average annual rate of 3.6%; it rose by 6.1% in 1999/2000, but contracted by 2.7% in 2000/01 and 0.1% in 2001/02 as a result of drought, before increasing by an estimated 4.1% in 2002/03.

INDUSTRY

Industry (including mining, manufacturing, power and construction) engaged an estimated 18.0% of the employed labour force in June 2003, and provided an estimated 23.5% of GDP in 2002/03. During 1990/91–2001/02 industrial GDP increased by an average of 4.0% per year. Industrial GDP grew by 4.5% in 2000/01, and by 2.8% in 2001/02.

Mining

Mining and quarrying contributed an estimated 0.7% of GDP in 2002/03, and employed 0.1% of the labour force in 1994/95. Petroleum and petroleum products are the major mineral exports. Limestone, rock salt, gypsum, silica sand, natural gas and coal are also mined. In addition, Pakistan has reserves of graphite, copper and manganese. The GDP of the mining sector increased at an average annual rate of 1.8% during 1990/91–2000/01; mining GDP increased by 6.1% in 1999/2000, but decreased by 0.4% in 2000/01.

Manufacturing

Manufacturing contributed an estimated 16.4% of GDP in 2002/03, and employed about 9.8% of the labour force in 1994/95. The most important sectors include the manufacture of textiles, food products, automobiles and electrical goods and also petroleum refineries. During 1990/91–2001/02 manufacturing GDP increased at an average annual rate of 4.2%; manufacturing GDP increased by 5.0% in 2001/02 and by 7.7% in 2002/03, according to official figures.

Energy

Energy is derived principally from petroleum (providing 39.5% of the total electrical energy supply in 2000), hydroelectric power (25.2%) and natural gas (32.0%). At present around 35% of Pakistan's petroleum is produced domestically. Imports of petroleum and petroleum products comprised about 25.1% of the cost of total imports in 2002/03.

SERVICES

Services engaged 35.6% of the employed labour force in 2000, and provided an estimated 53.3% of GDP in 2002/03. The combined GDP of the service sectors increased at an average rate of 4.6% per year in 1990/91–2001/02. The GDP of services expanded by 4.1% in 2001/02 and by 5.3% in 2002/03, according to official figures.

EXTERNAL TRADE

In 2002 Pakistan recorded a visible trade deficit of US $596m., and there was a surplus of $3,854m. on the current account of the balance of payments. Remittances from Pakistanis working abroad declined substantially during the 1990s, and by 2000/01 had levelled off to about $1,087m. In 2001/02, however, the flow of remittances increased significantly to $2,389m. and again to $4,236.9m. in 2002/03. The principal source of imports (12.4%) in 2002/03 was the United Arab Emirates, and the principal market for exports was the USA (24.5%). Other major trading partners were the People's Republic of China, Germany, Japan, Kuwait, Saudi Arabia and the United Kingdom. The principal exports in 2001/02 were textile manufactures, clothing and accessories and food and live animals. The principal imports were petroleum and petroleum products, machinery and transport equipment, chemicals and related products and food (particularly sugar) and live animals.

GOVERNMENT FINANCE

For the financial year ending 30 June 2003 there was a projected budgetary deficit of Rs 179,000m. (equivalent to 4% of GDP). Pakistan's total external debt was US $32,020m. at the end of 2001, of which $28,899m. was long-term public debt. The cost of debt-servicing in that year was equivalent to 25.8% of earnings from exports of goods and services. During 1990–2002 the average annual rate of inflation was 8.2%; according to official figures, consumer prices rose by 3.5% in 2001/02 and by an estimated 3.1% in 2002/03. About 7.8% of the labour force were estimated to be unemployed in 2003.

INTERNATIONAL ECONOMIC RELATIONS

Pakistan is a member of the South Asian Association for Regional Co-operation (SAARC), of the Asian Development Bank (ADB), of the UN Economic and Social Commission for Asia and the Pacific (ESCAP) and of the Colombo Plan. Pakistan is also a founder member of the Islamic Financial Services Board.

SURVEY AND PROSPECTS

During the 1990s economic growth was constrained by poor investment in manufacturing and inadequate agricultural production, while widespread corruption and inefficient revenue management (particularly in the collection and administration of taxes) undermined attempts to address worsening levels of poverty and deteriorating infrastructure and social services. The crisis was exacerbated by the economic sanctions imposed on Pakistan by a group of countries (including the USA) in May 1998 for carrying out nuclear tests, and by further sanctions imposed in response to the military coup of October 1999. However, the new Musharraf administration demonstrated renewed commitment to radical economic reform. Despite the volatile political and economic climate in the aftermath of the 11 September 2001 terrorist attacks on the USA, Pakistan's support for and co-operation with the activities of the US-led anti-terrorism coalition in neighbouring Afghanistan resulted in the withdrawal of US sanctions dating from 1998, the extension of concessionary trade terms (including an increased export quota for textiles until 2004) by the European Union (EU) and offers of substantial financial assistance from the ADB, the USA, Europe and (reportedly) China.

In December the IMF agreed to extend a $1,320m. Poverty Reduction and Growth Facility (PRGF) to Pakistan, in support of a three-year social and economic reform programme to be implemented during October 2001–September 2004. The programme's crucial objectives were increased potential for economic growth, improved social provisions and reduced vulnerability to external factors. To achieve these objectives, fiscal adjustment and governance reforms were to be introduced. Poverty was also to be addressed directly through reorientation of public expenditure, increased support for rural development, job creation and social contingency programmes. Despite the economic repercussions of the suicide attacks on the USA in September 2001, the prolonged drought, and regional and domestic security problems, Pakistan made substantial progress in implementing these objectives. In 2001/02 real GDP increased and inflation declined. The increase in remittances (owing to the expatriate Pakistani community reinvesting capital in Pakistan after 11 September 2001 and the increased flow of capital through official channels) resulted in high GNI growth. Furthermore, an improved trade balance and a current-account surplus allowed the State Bank of Pakistan to accumulate foreign-exchange reserves at a faster rate than expected, thereby reducing its vulnerability to external factors.

In 2002/03 real GDP growth surpassed budget forecasts, owing to a sharp improvement in the agricultural, industrial and service sectors. An increase in textile exports contributed to a significant 22.2% growth in exports (resulting from more favourable access to US and European markets), compared with the previous year; domestic demand strengthened owing to record-low interest rates; and foreign-exchange reserves rose to more than $10,500m., for the first time in Pakistan's history, largely as a result of a dramatic increase in remittances. The level of foreign direct investment also escalated; furthermore, the Government's tax reforms led to a 13.8% increase in revenue collection.

The country's economic recovery was expected to continue in 2003/04. Real GDP growth was forecast to reach 5.3% and revenue collection was expected to increase further, owing to ongoing tax administration reforms. The 2003/04 budget focused on job creation, encouraging investment and boosting the housing sector. The development budget was increased to fund measures aimed at reducing poverty. Encouraged by the IMF's extension of the PRGF, in December 2001 the 'Paris Club' of creditor governments agreed to reschedule Pakistan's entire bilateral debt stock of $12,500m. (with two-thirds rescheduled over 38 years and the remainder over 23 years). Pakistan benefited greatly from the agreement, which was expected to save the Government an estimated $1,000m. per year over the next three years. Pakistan's debt situation also improved as a result of the Government's debt-management policies and US assistance, which was granted in appreciation of Pakistan's support on the 'war on terror'.

After a slow start in 2002, in 2003 Pakistan's privatization programme was accelerated, earning the country $697m. The privatization of Pakistan State Oil (scheduled for April 2003 but delayed owing to US-led military action in Iraq) was due to take place in 2004. In 2003/04 the Government pledged to use 90% of the proceeds from privatization to pay off some of its foreign debt; the remaining 10% would help to alleviate poverty. There were fears, however, that the political strife, domestic and regional security concerns, bureaucratic obstacles, corruption and inadequate infrastructure would continue to deter potential investors. Nevertheless, in the first half of 2004 the Government was so confident that Pakistan's external accounts would remain strong that it decided not to seek to renew a three-year funding programme from the IMF upon its expiry at the end of the year.

Palau

The Republic of Palau consists of more than 200 islands lying south-west of Hawaii and south of Guam. With the Federated States of Micronesia, Palau forms the archipelago of the Caroline Islands. The Republic of Palau's independence, under a Compact of Free Association with the USA, in 1994 marked the end of the US-administered Trust Territory of the Pacific Islands, established in 1947. Direct US aid is scheduled to end in 2009. Koror is the provisional capital, while construction on a new capital is under way on Babeldaob (Babeldaop). Palauan and English are the official languages.

Area and population
Area: 508 sq km
Population (mid-2002): 19,900
Population density (mid-2002): 39.2 per sq km
Life expectancy (years at birth, 2002): 68.5 (males 66.4; females 70.9)

Finance
GDP in current prices: 2002): US $130m. ($6,528 per head)
Real GDP growth (2002): 3.0%
Currency: US dollar

Economy

In 2002, according to estimates by the World Bank, Palau's gross national income (GNI), measured at average 2000–02 prices, totalled US $141.9m., equivalent to $7,140 per head. During 1999–2001, it was estimated, the population increased at an average annual rate of 2.6%, while gross domestic product (GDP) per head decreased, in real terms, by an average of 1.6%. In 1990–2002 overall GDP increased, in real terms, at an average annual rate of 1.0%; growth in 2002 was 3.0%.

AGRICULTURE

Agriculture (including fishing) is mainly on a subsistence level, the principal crops being coconuts, root crops and bananas. Pigs and chickens are kept for domestic consumption. Eggs are produced commercially, and the introduction of cattle-ranching on Babeldaob was under consideration in early 2000s. The agricultural sector, together with mining, engaged 2.2% of the employed labour force in 2000. In 2001 FAO estimated that agricultural activities employed some 2,000 people. Agriculture and fisheries alone provided an estimated 4.0% of GDP in 2001. Fishing licences are sold to foreign fleets, including those of Taiwan, the USA, Japan and the Philippines. Palau is a signatory of the Multilateral Fisheries Treaty, concluded by the USA and member states of the South Pacific Forum (now Pacific Islands Forum) in 1987. The islands, however, are believed to lose significant amounts of potential revenue through illegal fishing activity. Revenue from the sale of fishing licences totalled US $39,000 in 1999/2000 and an estimated $76,000 in 2000/01, a considerable decline from the total of $230,000 recorded in 1994/95. Fish have traditionally been a leading export, accounting for some $13m. of exports in 1995, but earnings declined to an estimated $7m. in 2001, reportedly owing to adverse weather conditions.

INDUSTRY

The industrial sector (including mining and quarrying, manufacturing, construction and utilities) provided an estimated 13.0% of GDP in 2001. The only manufacturing activity of any significance is a factory producing garments, which in 1997 employed some 300 (mostly non-resident) workers. In 2000 the manufacturing sector engaged 3.6% of the employed labour force. In 2001 manufacturing accounted for only 1.5% of GDP. Construction is the most important industrial activity, contributing an estimated 8.0% of GDP in 2001 and engaging 11.6% of the employed labour force in 2000. Electrical energy is produced by two power plants at Aimeliik and Malakal.

SERVICES

Service industries dominate Palau's economy, providing an estimated 83.0% of GDP in 2001, and (with utilities) engaging 82.6% of the employed labour force in 2000. The Government is a significant employer within the sector, public administration engaging some 33.3% of the total employed labour force in 2000. Tourism is an important source of foreign exchange, directly contributing an estimated 11.1% of GDP in 1998 and employing 9.4% of paid workers in 1995. In 2002 a total of 58,560 visitors (of whom 40% were from Japan) arrived in the islands. Expenditure by tourists totalled an estimated US $66.1m. in 2002.

EXTERNAL TRADE

In the year ending September 2001 the visible trade deficit was estimated at US $80.8m. (equivalent to 66% of GDP). The deficit on the current account of the balance of payments totalled $15.7m. The principal sources of imports were the USA (which supplied 39.3% of the total), Guam (14.0%) and Japan (10.2%). The principal imports in 2000/01 were machinery and transport equipment, manufactured goods and food and live animals.

GOVERNMENT FINANCE

The islands record a persistent budget deficit, which was estimated at almost US $18.5m. in the year ending September 2001. Financial assistance from the USA contributes a large part of the islands' external revenue. Furthermore, upon imple-mentation of the Compact of Free Association with the USA in 1994, Palau became eligible for an initial grant of US $142m. and for annual aid of $23m. over a period of 14 years. Assistance from the USA (including non-Compact funding) totalled $21.0m. in 1999/2000 and an estimated $20.6m. in 2000/01, a respective 28.1% and 33.5% of total budgetary revenue in those years. Compact funding for 2001/02 was projected at $11.8m. in current grants and $2.0m. in capital grants, while non-Compact funding was budgeted at $11.2m. Palau's external debt totalled $20.0m. in 2000/01. The annual rate of inflation was thought to average between 1% and 3% in the mid-1990s. The inflation rate was about 2.5% in 2000/01, according to the IMF. In 2000 2.3% of the total labour force were unemployed.

INTERNATIONAL ECONOMIC RELATIONS

Palau is a member of the Pacific Community and of the Pacific Islands Forum; it is also an associate member of the UN Economic and Social Commission for Asia and the Pacific (ESCAP). In early 1996 Palau joined representatives of the other countries and territories of Micronesia at a meeting in Hawaii, at which a new regional organization, the Council of Micronesian Government Executives, was established. The new body aimed to facilitate discussion of economic developments in the region. In December 2002 Palau requested to join the World Trade Organization (WTO), and in December 2003 the country became a member of the Asian Development Bank (ADB).

SURVEY AND PROSPECTS

A period of recession in the early 1990s (caused largely by reductions in government expenditure in an attempt to offset decreases in revenue) was alleviated by sub-stantial aid payments from the US Government, following the implementation of the Compact of Free Association in 1994, and by the dramatic expansion of tourism in the country. Subsequent policies to reduce the size of the public sector, to encourage the return of Palauans resident overseas and to attract foreign investment aimed to stimulate economic growth. Particularly strong commercial ties were forged with Taiwan during the mid-1990s, and it was hoped that the establishment of diplomatic relations at ambassadorial level between Palau and Taiwan in late 1999 would further develop bilateral economic co-operation. Trade between Palau and the

Philippines increased significantly, following the signing of an agreement between the two countries in early 1998.

Tourism is expected to remain essential to Palau's economic growth upon the cessation of US aid in 2009. The Government announced plans in 1998 for further expansion of the industry, which had declined in the late 1990s following the Asian financial crisis, and expressed particular interest in developing the country's potential as a destination for visitors of above-average wealth. However, it remained unclear whether Palau would seek to attract further visitors by legalizing casino gambling; President Remengesau was known to be strongly opposed to the industry.

In 2002 an IMF report claimed that the country's investment laws, which prohibit foreign ownership of land or businesses, contributed to a lack of transparency in financial dealings, particularly in the development of tourism projects. A new road along the coastline of Babeldaob, financed under the Compact of Free Association, was none the less widely expected to increase long-term tourism revenues upon its scheduled completion in 2005. (A new official capital was also under construction on the island.) In December 2001 the Government announced plans to develop a new regional airline to serve Palau and neighbouring countries; this was due to begin operations in April 2004. Meanwhile, following allegations that Palau's offshore banking system was being used for the purposes of money-laundering, various new banking laws were approved, in an effort to restore the confidence of the international financial community. Although a number of concerns were raised by the Financial Action Task Force on Money Laundering (FATF), Palau was not included on the FATF's list of non-co-operative countries and territories. In June 2002 the legislature approved new measures to regulate the financial sector, which included the creation of a Financial Institutions Commission.

Palestinian Autonomous Areas

The Palestinian Autonomous Areas are located in the West Bank and Gaza Strip, in western Asia. The Palestine Liberation Organization (PLO) assumed control of the Jericho area of the West Bank, and the Gaza Strip, in accordance with the 1994 Cairo Agreement on the Gaza Strip and Jericho, which also established the Palestinian (National) Authority (PA). Further Israeli withdrawals from other West Bank towns, and transfers of control, took place in 1995–2000. In 1988 Jerusalem was proclaimed as the capital of the newly declared independent State of Palestine. The language of Palestinians in the West Bank and Gaza is Arabic.

Area and population

Area: 6,020 sq km (comprising the West Bank, 5,665 sq km, including Israeli-occupied East Jerusalem, and the Gaza Strip, 365 sq km)

Population (mid-2002): 3,212,130

Population density (mid-2002): 533.6 per sq km

655

Finance
GDP in current prices: 2002): US $3,015m. ($939 per head)
Real GDP growth (2002): –19.1%
Inflation (annual average, 2002): 5.7%

Economy

In 2002, according to estimates by the World Bank, the gross national income (GNI) of the West Bank and the Gaza Strip, measured at average 2000–02 prices, was US $2,982m., equivalent to $930 per head. During 1990–2002, it was estimated, the population increased at an average annual rate of 4.2%, while in 1994–2002 gross domestic product (GDP) per head decreased, in real terms, by an average of 5.7% per year. Overall GDP decreased, in real terms, at an average annual rate of 1.7% in 1994–2002; GDP declined by an estimated 19.1% in 2002.

AGRICULTURE

Agriculture and fishing contributed 10.2% of the GDP of the West Bank and Gaza Strip in 2000. In 2002 agriculture (including hunting, forestry and fishing) engaged an estimated 14.8% of the employed Palestinian labour force. Citrus fruits are the principal export crop, and horticulture also makes a significant contribution to trade. Other important crops are tomatoes, olives, cucumbers and grapes. The livestock sector is also significant. According to the World Bank, agricultural GDP decreased at an average annual rate of 6.7% during 1994–2000; however, it increased by 8.5% in 1999.

INDUSTRY

Industry (mining and quarrying, manufacturing, electricity and water supply, and construction) contributed 23.3% of Palestinian GDP in 2000. The industrial sector (including gas utilities) engaged some 24.3% of the employed labour force of the West Bank and Gaza in 2002. Construction alone accounted for 6.5% of GDP in 2000 and employed some 10.9% of the working population in 2002. During 1994–2000 industrial GDP increased at an average rate of 0.4% annually; the sector's GDP expanded by 3.1% in 1999.

Mining

Mining and quarrying contributed 0.7% of the GDP of the Palestinian territories in 1998, and engaged an estimated 0.4% of the employed labour force in 2001. Two significant gas fields were discovered off the Gazan coast in 1999.

Manufacturing

Manufacturing contributed 15.2% of the GDP of the West Bank and Gaza Strip in 2000, according to the World Bank. In 2001 about 13.8% of the employed labour force were engaged in the sector. Palestinian manufacturing is characterized by small-scale enterprises which typically engage in food-processing and the production of textiles and footwear. The frequent closure of the West Bank and Gaza by the Israeli authorities has prompted the development of free-trade industrial zones on the Palestinian side of the boundaries separating Israel from the territories: Israeli and Palestinian enterprises can continue to take advantage of low-cost Palestinian labour at times of closure, and the zones also benefit from tax exemptions and export incentives. Manufacturing GDP increased at an average annual rate of 3.6% during 1994–2000; the sector expanded by 1.6% in 1999.

Energy

The energy sector (comprising electricity and water supply) accounted for an estimated 2.0% of Palestinian GDP in 1998. Electricity, gas and water utilities together employed some 0.2% of the labour force of the West Bank and Gaza in 2001. In the West Bank there is no utility supplying electric power apart from the Jerusalem District Electric Company Ltd, which supplies Jerusalem, Bethlehem, Ramallah and Al-Birah. Most municipalities in the Gaza Strip purchase electricity from the Israel Electric Corporation. However, the Palestine Electric Company (established in 1999) is constructing a power plant in Gaza, while the National Electric Company (created in 2000) plans to build a second power plant in the West Bank.

SERVICES

In 2000 the services sector contributed 66.5% of Palestinian GDP, and engaged 60.9% of the employed labour force in 2002. In that year 18.1% of the employed labour force worked in wholesale and retail trade and 14.0% in public administration and defence. Although tourism has generally contributed more than 10% of the GDP of the West Bank and Gaza, it has been all but halted by the ongoing violence in the territories. The GDP of the services sector expanded at an average rate of 2.1% per year during 1994–2000; services GDP increased by 6.4% in 1999.

EXTERNAL TRADE

In 2001, according to preliminary estimates, the West Bank and Gaza Strip recorded a visible trade deficit of US $1,467m. and a deficit of $641m. on the current account of the balance of payments. In the absence of seaport facilities and of an airport (Gaza International Airport was opened in November 1998 but has frequently been closed by the Israeli authorities), foreign trade (in terms of value) has been conducted almost exclusively with Israel since occupation. Most Palestinian exports are of agricultural or horticultural products. One notable feature of this trade is that Palestinian goods have often in the past been exported to Israel, and subsequently re-exported as originating in Israel. In 2002 imports (c.i.f.) from Israel alone were valued at $1,118m. and exports (f.o.b.) to Israel and elsewhere totalled $240.9m.

GOVERNMENT FINANCE

In 2003, according to official revised estimates, the PA recorded an overall budget deficit of US $702.5m. Provisional figures for 2004 predicted an estimated budget deficit of $790.1m. The annual rate of inflation in the West Bank and Gaza averaged 4.7% in 1996–2003; consumer prices increased by an average of 5.7% in 2002 and by 4.4% in 2003. According to official estimates, some 31.3% of the labour force were unemployed in 2002, but the Palestinian Economic Council for Development and Reconstruction (PECDAR) estimated that unemployment had risen to 53% by early 2002 as a result of the Israeli economic blockade.

SURVEY AND PROSPECTS

The prospects for an improvement in economic conditions in the Palestinian Autonomous Areas, which remain highly dependent on Israel, are inextricably linked to the full implementation of the Oslo accords and the outcome of the (currently sus-pended) 'final status' negotiations between the PA and Israel. Examples of this economic dependency are the large number of Palestinian workers employed in Israel, and the reliance of the trade sector on Israel as a market for exports and source of imports. The underdevelopment of Palestinian agriculture and industry is a consequence of the Israeli occupation, when investment became orientated towards residential construction at the expense of these sectors. Agriculture remains focused mainly on meeting local demand, although the sector supplies the bulk of Palestinian exports and there is proven demand for Palestinian products beyond the Israeli market. The expansion of Palestinian agriculture is also limited by problems with irrigation: access to water supplies is subject to 'final status' discussions.

Economic conditions in the West Bank and Gaza have deteriorated markedly since 1993, largely as a result of frequent border closures enforced by the Israeli authorities in reprisal for terrorist attacks by militant Islamist groups opposed to the Oslo accords. Such closures lead to an immediate rise in the rate of unemployment among Palestinians, increase transportation costs for Palestinian goods and, at times, halt trade entirely. The Oslo accords provide for the development of seaport facilities and for the opening of Gaza International Airport and of a safe passage linking the Gaza Strip with the West Bank. However, by mid-2004 the provision for a seaport at Gaza had still not been implemented, while the airport and safe passage were both closed by the Israeli authorities.

From 1998 the PA has aimed to achieve current budget surpluses, and to focus public expenditure on health, education and infrastructural investment. In early 2000 the PA announced the creation of a Palestinian Investment Fund and a Higher Council for Development, the latter being charged with the preparation of a com-prehensive privatization strategy. However, in the context of the renewed Palestinian *intifada*, in November 2000 Israel imposed a complete economic blockade on the West Bank and Gaza, and halted the payment of tax transfers to the PA. The closure quickly reversed any recent economic successes: in the first half of 2000 unemploy-ment had reportedly been declining, GDP growth was strong, and private-sector investment was increasing sharply. By the beginning of 2003, however, economic losses resulting from the blockade were estimated at US $2,240m., including losses incurred as a result of the replacement of long-term investment programmes by short-term projects aimed at reducing rapidly escalating levels of unemployment and poverty. At the same time, according to the UN Relief and Works Agency for Palestine Refugees in the Near East (UNRWA), unemployment in some areas was as high as 80%. The economy was in a state of paralysis and the PA was effectively bankrupt: monthly revenues had fallen from $91m. in 2000 to $19m. in 2003, largely as a result of the withholding of taxes collected by Israel on behalf of the PA. For this reason, donor support has arguably become the key source of funding for the PA. In October 2000 Arab states pledged aid worth US $1,000m. to the PA. The EU authorized payments totalling $80m. in November–December. In the latter month the World Bank also announced that it was to grant $12m. for an Emergency Response Programme: the World Bank estimated that international donor funding to the PA approached $930m. in 2001. In March 2002 Arab states pledged a further $330m. in aid, and in the following month international donors agreed to grant $900m. to assist the PA in rebuilding vital infrastructure destroyed during the Israeli military offensive and a further $300m. as emergency relief. In May UNRWA assessed that, in addition to $117m. that it had previously estimated as being necessary to fund its emergency programmes for 2002, some $70m. would be required to address the immediate humanitarian needs of Palestinians in the West Bank and Gaza arising from the recent Israeli military incursions into the Palestinian areas. However, in 2003 it was reported that of the $172m. sought from donors for emergency relief, only $90m. had been forthcoming; nevertheless, in July the USA announced its first direct aid payment to the PA, consisting of $20m. to repair the civil infrastructure of the territories. Meanwhile, the World Bank estimated that the Palestinian economy had shrunk by one-half during the past two years.

Panama

The Republic of Panama is situated at the northern end of the isthmus separating North and South America. In 1821 Panama became independent from Spain as part of Gran Colombia, declaring its separate independence in 1903. During 1968–89 Panama was ruled by military dictatorships. In 1983 Brig. (later Gen.) Manuel Antonio Noriega Morena became Commander-in-Chief of the National Defence Forces. In 1989 a US military offensive overthrew Noriega, who was convicted in the USA of drugs-trafficking offences in 1992. Panama has been under civilian rule continuously since 1989. Panamá is the capital. Spanish is the official language.

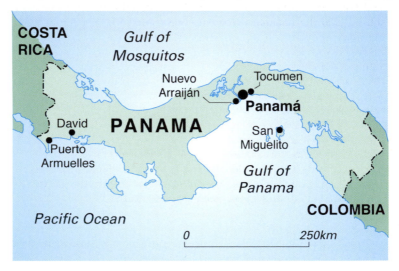

Area and population
Area: 75,517 sq km
Population (mid-2002): 2,940,410
Population density (mid-2002): 38.9 per sq km
Life expectancy (years at birth, 2002): 75.4 (males 72.8; females 78.2)

Finance
GDP in current prices: 2002): US $12,296m. ($4,182 per head)
Real GDP growth (2002): 0.8%
Inflation (2002): 1.0%
Currency: balboa

Economy

In 2002, according to estimates by the World Bank, Panama's gross national income (GNI), measured at average 2000–02 prices, was US $11,817.8m., equivalent to

$4,050 per head (or $5,870 on an international purchasing-power parity basis). During 1990–2002, it was estimated, the population increased at an average annual rate of 1.7%, while gross domestic product (GDP) per head increased, in real terms, by an average of 2.6% per year. Overall GDP increased, in real terms, at an average annual rate of 4.3% in 1990–2002; growth in 2002 was 2.2%.

AGRICULTURE

Agriculture (including hunting, forestry and fishing) contributed an estimated 7.7% of GDP, measured at constant prices, in 2002 and engaged some 21.7% of the employed labour force in 2001. Rice, maize and beans are cultivated as subsistence crops, while the principal cash crops are bananas (which accounted for an estimated 13.0% of total export earnings in 2003), sugar cane and coffee. Cattle-raising, tropical timber and fisheries (particularly shrimps and yellowfin tuna for export) are also important. In 2000 the banana sector employed some 15,000 people, directly and indirectly. The following year, however, the banana-producing industry was adversely affected by industrial action and poor weather conditions. Owing to low world commodity prices, the coffee sector also experienced a reversal in 2001–03. In the 1990s, in an attempt to diversify the agricultural sector, new crops such as oil palm, cocoa, coconuts, various winter vegetables and tropical fruits were introduced. Fish exports increased steadily throughout that decade, and in 1999 Panama claimed to be the world's third largest exporter of shrimps. Although the shrimp industry has declined steadily since an outbreak of the white-spot virus in 2000, fish exports have continued to increase. In 2003 exports of yellowfin tuna and fish fillet were valued at US $261.9m. According to the World Bank, agricultural GDP increased by an average of 2.4% annually during 1990–2002; according to official figures, agricultural GDP increased by 6.4% in 2001 and by an estimated 2.0% in 2002.

INDUSTRY

Industry (including mining, manufacturing, construction and power) contributed an estimated 16.5% of GDP, measured at constant prices, in 2002 and engaged 16.8% of the employed labour force in 2001. According to World Bank figures, industrial GDP increased at an average annual rate of 5.0% during 1990–2002; however, the sector's GDP decreased by 9.9% in 2001 and by a further 1.1% in 2002.

Mining

Mining contributed an estimated 0.8% of GDP, measured at constant prices, in 2002 and engaged 0.2% of the employed labour force in 2001. Panama has significant deposits of copper and coal. The GDP of the mining sector increased by an estimated average of 25.7% per year in 1996–2000; the sector declined by 4.1% in 2001, but grew by 18.1% in 2002. This dramatic expansion in the sector was owing to the demand for stone, sand and clay, associated with residential construction and road building, in particular the on-going widening of the Pan-American Highway.

Manufacturing

Manufacturing contributed an estimated 8.8% of GDP, measured at constant prices, in 2002 and engaged an estimated 9.0% of the employed labour force in 2001. The most important sectors, measured by output in producers' prices, were refined petroleum products, food-processing, beverages, and cement, lime and plaster.

According to World Bank estimates, manufacturing GDP increased by an average of 2.1% annually during 1990–2002; however, it decreased by 6.3% in 2001, and by a further estimated 2.8% in 2002.

Energy

The country's topography and climate make it ideal for hydroelectric power, and in 2001 approximately 52.5% of Panama's total output of electricity was water-generated. In the same year imports of mineral products accounted for an estimated 20.7% of the value of merchandise imports.

SERVICES

Panama's economy is dependent upon the services sector, which contributed an estimated 75.8% of GDP, measured at constant prices, in 2002, and engaged 61.4% of the employed labour force in 2001. The Panama Canal contributed an estimated 5.0% of the country's GDP in 2002. Panama is an important 'offshore' financial centre, and in 2002 financial, property and business services contributed an estimated 26.0% of GDP. Important contributions to the economy are also made by trade in the Colón Free Zone (CFZ—in which some 1,944 companies were situated in 2000, and which contributed an estimated 6.5% of GDP in 2002), and by the registration of merchant ships under a 'flag of convenience' in Panama. The tourism sector also increased steadily in the last decade of the 20th century. In 2001 income from tourism totalled US $626m., compared with $576m. in the previous year. However, tourism income was estimated to have increased by 8.7% in 2002. According to the World Bank, the GDP of the services sector increased by an average of 4.4% per year in 1990–2002; it grew by 2.0% in 2001 and by an estimated 1.9% in 2002.

EXTERNAL TRADE

In 2002 Panama recorded a visible trade deficit of US $1,176.4m., and there was a deficit of $153.7m. on the current account of the balance of payments. In 2000 the principal source of imports (32.8%) was the USA, which was also the principal market for exports (46.1% in 2002). Other major trading partners are Costa Rica, Japan, Ecuador, and Mexico. The principal exports in 2003 were yellowfin tuna and fish fillet, petroleum products, bananas and shrimps. The principal imports in 2001 were petroleum and related products, road vehicles, and telecommunications, sound recording and reproducing equipment.

GOVERNMENT FINANCE

In 2002 there was an estimated overall budgetary deficit of US $238m. (equivalent to 2.2% of GDP). Panama's external debt at the end of 2001 was US $8,245m., of which $7,272m. was long-term debt. In that year the cost of debt-servicing was equivalent to 12.9% of the value of exports of goods and services. Annual inflation averaged 1.1% in 1992–2002; consumer prices increased by 0.3% in 2001 and by 1.1% in 2002. Some 12.8% of the economically active population were unemployed in August 2003.

INTERNATIONAL ECONOMIC RELATIONS

Panama is a member of the Inter-American Development Bank (IDB). In September 1997 Panama joined the World Trade Organization (WTO). In March 2002 Panama concluded a free-trade agreement with El Salvador. In August 2003 a free-trade accord between Panama and Taiwan was concluded. In 2004 negotiations towards a free-trade agreement with the USA were ongoing.

SURVEY AND PROSPECTS

The political problems that developed between Panama and the USA in the late 1980s, and the resultant US economic sanctions, adversely affected most sectors of the Panamanian economy during that period. A five-year programme of economic modernization began in 1994. In 1996 the Panama Canal Commission announced increases in the Canal's general toll rate to finance an acceleration in an extensive maintenance and capital improvements programme. Meanwhile, from January 1997 legislation was introduced that would exempt businesses in the CFZ from paying taxes on their profits. It was estimated that the measure would cost the Government US $40m. annually in lost revenue; however, it was expected to strengthen the competitiveness of the CFZ, and result in higher levels of investment in Panama.

In December 1997 the IMF approved a credit of $162m., under an Extended Fund Facility, to support the Government's economic programme for 1998–2000. The economic plan of the Moscoso administration, which took office in September 1999, envisaged export-led growth, while aiming to reduce poverty (which affected 37% of the population) and unemployment. The plan committed the Government to the continued privatization of state assets, the proceeds of which, it proposed, would be used to repurchase outstanding external debt bonds, thereby producing substantial savings on interest payments. Increased tax collection was also envisaged, in an attempt to increase revenue and thus reduce dependence on foreign borrowing. In September 2001 the IDB approved a $35m. loan to Panama to help fund improvements in the health care system. Despite a modest overall increase in expenditure of 4.3%, election pledges to increase social expenditure were honoured, with 49.7% of the budget allocated to this area.

In 2000 economic growth declined for the third successive year, with GDP expanding by 2.5%. This was owing principally to the continuing recession in the CFZ, as well as a decline in investment and a reduction in domestic demand. GDP growth in 2001 was 0.6%, falling far short of the earlier predictions of 3.9%–4.3%. The main causes of the economic downturn were thought to be an increase in petroleum prices and a reduction in demand from Panama's main trading partner, the USA. Following the cession to Panamanian control of the Panama Canal at the end of 1999, the waterway was operated as a profit-making venture, providing the Government with a considerable source of funds. (Toll revenues from the Canal totalled $666m. in 2003.) In June 2001 the 'Plan Puebla-Panamá', intended to promote regional development extending from the Mexican state of Puebla, to Panama, was inaugurated. In December the Plan received support from the Spanish power group Endesa, which announced plans for the construction of an electricity network connecting Costa Rica, El Salvador, Guatemala, Honduras and Panama.

In 2002 revenue from the CFZ fell by 10.7% and there wan also a sharp decline in exports. This decline was, to some extent, offset by a growth of 20% in tourism; overall economic growth in 2002 was estimated at 2.2%. In May of that year a fiscal responsibility law was approved that imposed a legal limit of 2% on the fiscal deficit. In November the Government sold some $430m. in bonds on the international markets to help finance the budget and reduce the country's debt. In January 2003 the Asamblea Legislativa approved a number of tax reforms, including the extension of sales tax to luxury items and some professional services to increase revenue. In 2003 the decline in exports was reversed and economic growth recovered strength. Robust growth was recorded in the construction (27%), fishing (17%), ports (18%) and tourism (8%) sectors. Overall, GDP expanded by an estimated 4.1% and a further increase of 3.6% was forecast for 2004.

The fiscal deficit stood at 1.9% in 2003, although it was predicted to rise to 2% by 2004. The improved economic performance reflected the increased tax collection following the tax reforms and improved debt management. Macroeconomic stability was promoted by regular inflows of foreign currency owing to the internationally oriented banking system, and to the Canal, which in 2003 provided an income of US $9,200m. Economic prospects for 2004 were enhanced by the possibility of a bilateral free-trade accord with the USA. Foreign direct investment was also expected to increase. Nevertheless, unemployment remained high (at 12.8% in August 2003), and was expected to average 13.8% in 2004–05.

Papua New Guinea

The Independent State of Papua New Guinea lies east of Indonesia and north of the north-eastern extremity of Australia. Full independence was achieved in 1975. During the 1990s a national crisis developed owing to the escalation of a dispute over the status of Bougainville (in North Solomons Province) into a secessionist struggle. A peace agreement concluded in 2001 provided for the holding of a referendum, in 10–15 years' time, that would contain the option of independence for Bougainville. Port Moresby is the capital. Pidgin and standard English, together with Motu, are the official languages in the National Parliament.

Area and population
Area: 462,840 sq km
Population (mid-2002): 5,373,250
Population density (mid-2002): 11.6 per sq km
Life expectancy (years at birth, 2002): 59.8 (males 58.4; females 61.5)

Finance
GDP in current prices: 2002): US $2,793m. ($520 per head)
Real GDP growth (2002): −2.5%
Inflation (annual average, 2002): 11.8%
Currency: kina

Economy

In 2002, according to estimates by the World Bank, Papua New Guinea's gross national income (GNI), measured at average 2000–02 prices, was US $2,823m., equivalent to $530 per head (or $2,080 per head on an international purchasing-power parity basis). During 1990–2002, it was estimated, the population increased at an average annual rate of 2.5%, while gross domestic product (GDP) per head increased, in real terms, by an average of 0.9% per year. According to the Asian Development Bank (ADB), overall GDP increased, in real terms, at an average annual rate of 3.6% in 1990–2002. Real GDP declined by 2.7% in 2002 but increased by an estimated 1.5% in the following year and was forecast to grow by 2.0% in 2004.

AGRICULTURE

Agriculture (including hunting, forestry and fishing) contributed 27.4% of GDP in 2002, and engaged an estimated 73.6% of the labour force in 2001. The principal cash crops are coffee (which accounted for 3.7% of export earnings in 2002), cocoa (3.1%), coconuts (for the production of copra and coconut oil), palm oil (which accounted for 6.1% of export earnings in 2002), rubber and tea. Vanilla was also becoming an important export crop in the early 2000s. Roots and tubers, vegetables, bananas and melons are also grown as food crops. Forestry is an important activity, and Papua New Guinea is one of the world's largest exporters of unprocessed tropical timber. Exports of logs accounted for 4.7% of total export revenue in 2002. An estimated 1.5m. cu m of logs were exported in 2001, the lowest volume (and at the lowest prices) for 10 years. However, exports of processed timber products rose by 15% in that year and earned some US $30m. of revenue. There is serious concern about the environmental damage caused by extensive logging activity in the country, much of which is illegal. The sale of fishing licences to foreign fleets provides a substantial source of revenue, estimated at US $15m. in 1998. During 1990–2002, according to figures from the ADB, agricultural GDP increased by an average annual rate of 3.1%. The GDP of the agricultural sector contracted by 5.4% in 2001 but expanded by 3.6% in 2002.

INDUSTRY

Industry (including mining, manufacturing, construction and power) contributed an estimated 42.3% of GDP in 2002. During 1990–2002 industrial GDP increased by an average of 5.6% per year, according to figures from the ADB. Industrial GDP decreased by 3.3% in 2001 and by 5.5% in 2002.

Mining

Mining and quarrying provided an estimated 28.6% of GDP and 68.7% of total export earnings in 2002. Petroleum (which accounted for 21.0% of export revenue in 2002), gold (35.9% in that year) and copper (14.7%) are the major mineral exports. Papua New Guinea also has substantial reserves of natural gas, and deposits of silver, chromite, cobalt, nickel and quartz. The country's largest petroleum refinery at Napa Napa was expected to begin production in mid-2004 and to process some 33,000 barrels per day. In early 2002 plans were concluded for the construction of a gas pipeline to Queensland, Australia, expected to be completed by 2007, in which the Government held a 15% stake. The pipeline would be the longest of its kind in the southern hemisphere. Large gold deposits were discovered at several sites during the 1980s (including the largest known deposit outside South Africa at Lihir, which began operations in mid-1997), and annual gold production subsequently rose at a steady rate, reaching an estimated 74 metric tons in 2000 before declining to 58 tons in 2002. A new medium-sized gold-mining project at Kainantu in the Eastern Highlands was announced in December 2002. Moreover, the important Ramu cobalt-nickel project was launched in February 2003. In 1997 an agreement was signed to allow for the deep-sea mining of gold, silver and zinc deposits. According to figures from the ADB, the GDP of the mining sector increased at an average annual rate of 8.0% during 1990–2002. However, the sector's GDP declined by 11.2% in 2002.

Manufacturing

Manufacturing contributed an estimated 8.7% of GDP in 2002, and employed 1.9% of the working population in 1980. Measured by the value of output, the principal branches of manufacturing are food products, beverages, tobacco, wood products, metal products, machinery and transport equipment. Several fish canneries were established in the 1990s and exports of canned tuna were expected to increase significantly, following the signing of a new quota agreement with the European Union (EU) in March 2003. A major new fish processing plant to enable the export of live fish and lobsters to China was expected to begin operations in early 2004 following the receipt of funding for the project of some US $30m. from a Chinese company. During 1990–2002 manufacturing GDP increased by an average of 4.0% per year. Compared with the previous year, the sector's GDP contracted by 8.8% in 2001 but expanded by 7.5% in 2002.

Energy

Energy is derived principally from hydroelectric power, which in 1999 accounted for more than 50% of electricity supplies. A diesel power station to be constructed by South Korean interests in Port Moresby in 1999 was expected to supply 30% of the capital's electricity needs.

SERVICES

The services sector contributed an estimated 30.2% of GDP in 2002. Tourism is an expanding industry, although political instability and reports of widespread crime have had a detrimental effect on the sector. During the late 1980s and early 1990s annual foreign tourist arrivals barely exceeded 40,000, but the total increased significantly to reach 67,357 in 1999, before declining to 58,448 in 2000. In 2003 a total of 52,623 tourists visited the country. The World Bank estimated that tourism receipts were worth US $101m. in 2001. The GDP of the services sector expanded at an average annual rate of 3.6% in 1990–2002. However, the sector's GDP declined by 1.5% in 2001, but increased by 0.7% in 2002.

EXTERNAL TRADE

In 2001 Papua New Guinea recorded a visible trade surplus of US $880.5m., and a surplus of $282.0m. on the current account of the balance of payments. According to the ADB, the latter surplus declined from the equivalent of 9.6% of GDP in 2001 to 0.4% of GDP in 2002. In 2002, when the trade surplus reached an estimated $1,499.1m., the principal source of imports (49.6%) was Australia; other major suppliers were Singapore (18.9%) and Japan (4.1%). In that year Australia was also the principal market for exports (24.0%), followed by Japan (9.8%), the People's Republic of China (3.7%) and the USA (3.3%). The principal exports in the early 2000s were gold, copper ore and concentrates, petroleum, coffee, cocoa, palm oil and logs. The principal imports were machinery and transport equipment, basic manufactures, food and live animals, miscellaneous manufactured articles, chemicals and mineral fuels.

GOVERNMENT FINANCE

The budgetary deficit decreased from K249.1m. in 2001 to an estimated K214.5m. in 2002. A deficit of some K200m., equivalent to 2% of GDP, was projected for 2003 and a further deficit of K300m. forecast for 2004. Papua New Guinea receives grants for budgetary aid from Australia, and Australian aid was projected at $A333.6m. in 2003/04. Papua New Guinea's external debt totalled US $2,521m. at the end of 2001, of which $1,413m. was long-term public debt. In that year the cost of debt-servicing was equivalent to 12.7% of the value of exports of goods and services. A World Bank report in 2003 estimated that one-half of the workforce was unemployed throughout Papua New Guinea at that time. In the rural areas underemployment remained a serious problem. According to the ADB, the annual rate of inflation averaged 9.7% in 1990–2002. Consumer prices increased by an estimated 13.8% in 2003.

INTERNATIONAL ECONOMIC RELATIONS

Papua New Guinea is a member of Asia-Pacific Economic Co-operation (APEC), the Asian Development Bank (ADB), the Colombo Plan, the Pacific Community, the Pacific Islands Forum, the UN Economic and Social Commission for Asia and the Pacific (ESCAP), the International Cocoa Organization and the International Coffee Organization.

SURVEY AND PROSPECTS

In recent years Papua New Guinea has remained dependent on aid from Australia and other international donors for its economic development, and in the early 2000s it was estimated that at least 70% of the population were within the subsistence sector of the economy. The country's difficult terrain, vulnerability to extreme climatic conditions (such as droughts and tidal waves) and lack of infrastructure, the limited domestic market and a shortage of skilled workers all continued to impede industrial development, and an increase in migration from rural areas to urban centres led to a rise in unemployment. Civil unrest on Bougainville also adversely affected the economy. Growing ethnic and environmental problems, widespread crime and concern over foreign exploitation also continued to threaten Papua New Guinea's prospects for long-term economic success.

A 'recovery' budget for 2000 included the privatization of government assets, the proceeds of which were to be used to repay a proportion of the national debt. A joint funding programme, valued at US $500m., was agreed upon by the IMF and the World Bank to assist the Government in the implementation of the economic reforms. Australia pledged a total of US $1,000m. in programme aid over a period of three years. Almost 1,500 public servants were made redundant in late 2000, as part of ongoing government retrenchment measures. The IMF commended the Government for its structural reform policies; however, the organization expressed concern in early 2001 over the continued high incidence of official corruption in the country. In April 2002 the Prime Minister announced that, as part of the public-sector reform programme, more than 3,000 civil servants were to be made redundant by the end of the year. However, the Government suffered a conclusive defeat at a general election in June, and the newly elected Prime Minister, Sir Michael Somare, declared that one of his Government's most urgent priorities was the immediate cessation of the World Bank-endorsed privatization programme.

A marked increase in the country's debt, as well as a continued decline in the value of the kina (which fell by some 10% between October and November) resulted in serious financial difficulties for the new Government, particularly when a request to the Australian Government to help restructure US $180m. of debt was refused. Expenditure in the 2003 budget was significantly reduced in an attempt to control the growing deficit, although a large proportion of this was allocated to major infrastructure projects, such as the Highlands Highway (which, it was hoped, would stimulate the economy, particularly the agricultural sector). Despite the success of Papua New Guinea's agricultural exports (notably coffee, cocoa and palm oil) in 2002, owing to improved commodity prices and the low value of the kina, it seemed likely that additional revenue would need to be raised in 2003 through a resumption of the asset sales programme. Similarly, the 2004 budget was to include a temporary tax on imports and reduced personal tax rebates, in an attempt to control the predicted deficit of US $100m. New agricultural developments were also to receive corporate tax concessions in the budget in order to encourage several important projects in the sector.

Paraguay

The Republic of Paraguay is situated in central South America. In 1954 Gen. Alfredo Stroessner Mattiauda assumed power and subsequently contrived to become Latin America's longest-serving dictator. Stroessner was overthrown in 1989, and in 1992 a new Constitution excluded army officers on active duty from participating directly in politics. In 1993 Juan Carlos Wasmosy of the Partido Colorado was elected President. In 1999, facing impeachment, President Cubas Grau resigned. His successor, Luis González Macchi, has also narrowly avoided impeachment. In April 2003, the Colorado candidate Nicanor Duarte Frutos was elected President. Asunción is the capital. Spanish is the official language.

Area and population

Area: 406,752 sq km
Population (mid-2002): 5,510,000
Population density (mid-2002): 13.5 per sq km
Life expectancy (years at birth, 2002): 71.7 (males 68.7; females 74.7)

Finance

GDP in current prices: 2002): US $5,389m. ($978 per head)
Real GDP growth (2002): –2.2%
Inflation (annual average, 2002): 10.5%
Currency: guaraní

Economy

In 2002, according to estimates by the World Bank, Paraguay's gross national income (GNI), measured at average 2000–02 prices, was US $6,442m., equivalent to $1,170 per head (or $4,450 per head on an international purchasing-power parity basis). During 1990–2002, it was estimated, the population increased at an average annual rate of 2.4%, while gross domestic product (GDP) per head decreased, in real terms, by an average of 0.7% per year. Overall GDP declined, in real terms, at an average annual rate of 1.7% in 1990–2002; GDP declined by 2.2% in 2002.

AGRICULTURE

Agriculture (including forestry and fishing) contributed an estimated 23.7% of GDP in 2001. In 2000 an estimated 35.2% of the economically active population were employed in the sector. The principal cash crops are soya bean seeds, which accounted for 36.0% of total export revenue in 2001, and cotton (8.4%). Other significant crops are sugar cane, cassava, wheat and maize. Timber and wood manufactures provided 5.1% of export revenues in 2001. The raising of livestock (particularly cattle and pigs) is also important. Meat accounted for an estimated 7.9% of export earnings in 2001. According to the World Bank, agricultural GDP increased at an average annual rate of 1.8% in 1990–2001; real agricultural GDP increased by 12.9% in 2000, and by 2.2% in 2001. However, an outbreak of foot and mouth disease in September 2002 was expected to adversely affect growth in the sector in 2003.

INDUSTRY

Industry (including mining, manufacturing, construction and power) contributed an estimated 25.6% of GDP in 2001 and employed 16.0% of the working population in 2000. According to the World Bank, industrial GDP increased by an average of 2.8% per year in 1990–2001; the sector increased by 2.8% in 2000 and by 2.5% in 2001.

Mining

Paraguay has almost no commercially exploited mineral resources, and the mining sector employed only 0.1% of the labour force in 2000 and contributed 0.3% of GDP in 2001. Production is confined to gypsum, kaolin and limestone. However, foreign companies have been involved in exploration for gold and petroleum deposits, and deposits of natural gas were discovered in 1994. In March 2002 Bolivia and Paraguay signed an agreement to build a 3,300-mile gas pipeline through Bolivia, Paraguay, Argentina and Brazil. Construction was delayed in 2004.

Manufacturing

Manufacturing contributed an estimated 14.3% of GDP in 2001 and employed 11.2% of the working population in 2000. The main branch of manufacturing (in terms of value added) was production of food and beverages (comprising 49.5% of total manufacturing output in 1999). The other principal sectors were wood and wood products, handicrafts, paper, printing and publishing, hides and furs, and non-metallic mineral products. According to the World Bank, manufacturing GDP increased at an average annual rate of 0.8% in 1990–2001. Manufacturing GDP increased by by 1.0% in 2000 and by 2.5% in 2001.

Energy

Energy is derived almost completely from hydroelectric power. Imports of fuels and lubricants comprised an estimated 16.1% of the value of total merchandise imports in 2000. Ethyl alcohol (ethanol), derived from sugar cane, is widely used as a component of vehicle fuel.

SERVICES

The services sector contributed an estimated 50.7% of GDP in 2001, and engaged 48.8% of the working population in 2000. Paraguay traditionally serves as an entrepôt for regional trade. According to the World Bank, the GDP of the services sector increased by an average of 1.5% per year in 1990–2001; the sector grew by 0.6% in 2000 and by 3.1% in 2001.

EXTERNAL TRADE

In 2002 Paraguay recorded a visible trade deficit of US $71.6m., but there was a surplus of $293.7m. on the current account of the balance of payments. In 2001 the principal source of registered imports (27.6%) was Brazil; other major suppliers in this year were Argentina, the People's Republic of China and the USA. Brazil was the principal market for registered exports (28.1%) in 2001; other notable purchasers were Uruguay and Argentina. The principal exports in 2001 were soya bean seeds, tobacco and raw cotton. The principal imports were machinery and transport equipment, fuels and lubricants, chemicals and related products, and basic manufactures.

GOVERNMENT FINANCE

In 2001 there was an estimated overall general budget deficit of 229,670m. guaraníes (equivalent to 0.8% of GDP). Paraguay's total external debt was US $2,817m. at the end of 2001, of which $2,119m. was long-term public debt. In that year the cost of debt-servicing was equivalent to 10.7% of the total value of exports of goods and services. Annual inflation averaged 12.7% in 1990–2002; consumer prices increased by an average of 7.3% in 2001 and by 10.5% in 2002. An estimated 14% of the labour force were unemployed in 2000.

INTERNATIONAL ECONOMIC RELATIONS

Paraguay is a member of the Inter-American Development Bank (IDB), of the Latin American Integration Association (ALADI), of the Latin American Economic System (SELA) and of the Mercado Común del Sur (Mercosur).

SURVEY AND PROSPECTS

The discovery of widespread corruption in the financial sector provoked a serious liquidity crisis in 1995, resulting in the closure of several significant financial institutions. By 1998 only five state enterprises identified for privatization had been divested (at a net loss to the Government). The Government was paralysed by a lack of resources until the end of August 1999, when Taiwan agreed to underwrite a $400m. bond issue. In the previous month the Government had agreed on a long-term structural reform strategy with the IMF and World Bank, which involved acceleration of the privatization of the remaining state assets. However, in May 2002 the Government was again forced to postpone the sale of the state telecommunications company, Corporación Paraguaya de Comunicaciones (COPACO), following mass protests.

In July 2000 the IDB announced the approval of three loans totalling $56m. to support modernization of the state and to finance education and agricultural programmes. Faced by growing levels of debt owed by the private sector to state-owned banks, in February 2001 the Government launched a rescue programme to cover $200m. worth of bad debts and it was hoped that a 'shadow' agreement, reached in April with the IMF, would reduce the fiscal deficit. Although the fiscal deficit was contained during 2001, this was achieved by implementing only one-half of the budgeted investments for that year in public works. In real terms, tax revenues continued to decline and by January 2002 the Government was only able to pay public-sector workers in arrears. A request was made to the IMF for a stand-by credit of $50m.–$70m. to strengthen Paraguay's international monetary reserves as a number of debt repayments were delayed in late 2001 and early 2002. Economic growth was 2.7% in 2001. In 2002 the economic situation worsened, partly as a result of the continuing financial crisis in neighbouring Argentina. Political instability obliged the Government to postpone the planned sales of state assets, revenues from which had been intended to reduce the fiscal deficit.

An IMF stand-by loan of US $200m., approved in August, was conditional on the Government implementing a controversial fiscal reform programme, known as the 'economic transition law' or 'el impuestazo' (the 'big tax'). El impuestazo would raise value-added tax (VAT) to 12%, as well as imposing tax increases on various goods, including cigarettes. However, the proposed legislation, was rejected by the legislature in November. The economy contracted by 2.2% in 2002. A series of financial scandals relating to state-owned enterprises in 2003, as well as the collapse of the private bank Multibanco in June of that year, further undermined investor confidence. However, the economic policies set out by the new administration of President Oscar Nicanor Duarte Frutos, which took office in August, resulted in the agreement of a $73m. IMF stand-by loan in December, on condition of further structural reform. Some $44m. was disbursed immediately, and the Fund approved the first review of its programme in April 2004. The new Government thus avoided defaulting on its international obligations; furthermore, a new $30m. loan was reportedly secured from Taiwan in February.

International prices for Paraguay's principal exports were strong in 2003, although the scheduled implementation of new Mercosur tariffs threatened Paraguay's comparative advantage in agricultural products in the longer term. Furthermore, international confidence continued to depend on the country's efforts to eliminate corruption and inefficiency in the public sector, as well as on the success of measures to reduce the informal sector. Growth in 2003 was estimated at 2.0%.

Peru

The Republic of Peru lies in western South America. Since independence from Spain, achieved in 1824, Peruvian politics have been characterized by alternating periods of civilian and military administration. Sendero Luminoso, a Maoist guerrilla group that commenced an armed struggle against the Government in 1980, remained active in the 21st century, despite the arrest of its leaders. In 2000 a political crisis caused the resignation of Alberto Fujimori some six months after his controversial re-election for a third presidential term. In 2001 Alejandro Toledo was elected President. Lima is the capital. The official languages are Spanish, Quechua and Aymará.

Area and population
Area: 1,285,216 sq km
Population (mid-2002): 26,749,000
Population density (mid-2002): 20.8 per sq km
Life expectancy (years at birth, 2002): 69.7 (males 67.5; females 72.0)

Finance
GDP in current prices: 2002): US $56,901m. ($2,127 per head)
Real GDP growth (2002): 5.2%
Inflation (annual average, 2002): 0.2%
Currency: new sol

Economy

In 2002, according to estimates by the World Bank, Peru's gross national income (GNI), measured at average 1999–2002 prices, was US $52,734.4m., equivalent to $2,050 per head (or $4,800 per head on an international purchasing-power parity basis). During 1990–2002, it was estimated, the population increased by an average of 1.8% per year, while gross domestic product (GDP) per head increased, in real terms, at an average annual rate of 2.0%. Overall GDP increased, in real terms, at an average annual rate of 3.8% in 1990–2002; growth was 4.9% in 2002.

AGRICULTURE

Agriculture (including forestry and fishing) contributed 7.9% of GDP, measured at current prices, in 2002 and the sector (including forestry and fishing) engaged 8.8% of the total working population in 2001. Rice, maize and potatoes are the principal food crops. The principal cash crop is coffee. Peru is the world's leading producer of coca, and the cultivation of this shrub, for the production of the illicit drug cocaine, reportedly generated revenue of US $1,500m.–$2,500m. per year. Undeclared revenue from the export of coca is believed to exceed revenue from legal exports. Fishing, particularly for the South American pilchard and the anchoveta, provides another important source of revenue, and the fishing sector contributed an estimated 0.9% of GDP, measured at current prices, in 2002. Fishing accounted for 3.0% of the total value of exports in 2001. During 1990–2001 agricultural GDP (including fishing) increased at an average annual rate of 4.7%; the sector's GDP increased by 6.4% in 2000, but declined by 0.6% in 2001.

INDUSTRY

Industry (including mining, manufacturing, construction and power) provided an estimated 30.2% of GDP in 2002, measured at current prices, and the sector employed 17.9% of the working population in 2001. During 1990–2001 industrial GDP increased by an average of 4.3% per year; in 2000 industrial GDP increased by 3.4%, but in 2001 the sector grew by only 0.7%.

Mining

Mining (including petroleum) contributed 6.2% of GDP in 2002, measured at current prices, and employed 0.6% of the working population in 2001. Copper (which accounted for 11.7% of total export earnings in 2001), zinc, gold, petroleum and its derivatives, lead and silver are the major mineral exports. During 1994–2000 the GDP of the mining and petroleum sector increased at an average annual rate of 6.2%; real GDP growth in the sector was 12.9% in 1999 and 2.4% in 2000.

Manufacturing

Manufacturing contributed 15.8% of GDP in 2002, measured at current prices, and employed 12.6% of the working population in 2001. The principal branches of manufacturing, measured by gross value of output, were food products (19.2% in 1996), petroleum refineries, non-ferrous metals, beverages and textiles and clothing. During 1990–2001 manufacturing GDP increased by an average of 3.2% per year. The sector's GDP increased by 6.7% in 2000, before declining by 1.1% in 2001.

Energy

Energy is derived principally from domestic supplies of hydroelectric power (81.2% of total electricity production in 2000) and petroleum (13.4%). Imports of mineral fuels and lubricants comprised 13.3% of the value of merchandise imports in 2001. In early 2003 a new $4,500m. project to construct a pipeline exporting liquid natural gas to the USA was announced.

SERVICES

The services sector contributed an estimated 62.0% of GDP in 2002, measured at current prices, and employed 73.3% of the working population in 2001. Tourism is gradually emerging as an important source of foreign revenue (US $865m. in 2001). In 1990–2001 the GDP of the services sector increased by an average annual rate of 3.0%. The sector's GDP grew by 4.0% in 2000 and by 3.2% in 2001.

EXTERNAL TRADE

In 2002 Peru recorded a visible trade surplus of US $207m. and there was a deficit of $1,206m. on the current account of the balance of payments. In 2001 the principal source of imports (23.1%) was the USA, which was also the principal market for exports (24.8%). Other major trading partners were Japan, Colombia and Venezuela for imports, and the United Kingdom, Switzerland and Japan for exports. The principal exports in 2001 were metals (particularly gold and copper) and fish. The principal imports in the same year were raw materials and capital goods for industry.

GOVERNMENT FINANCE

In 2001 there was an estimated budgetary deficit of 5,339m. new soles. Peru's external debt at the end of 2001 was US $27,512m., of which $18,831m. was long-term public debt. In that year the cost of debt-servicing was equivalent to 22.0% of the value of exports of goods and services. The annual rate of inflation averaged 31.1% in 1990–2002. Consumer prices increased by an average of 0.2% in 2002. An estimated 7.9% of the urban labour force were unemployed in 2001. Some 52.5% were underemployed in December 2001–February 2002.

INTERNATIONAL ECONOMIC RELATIONS

Peru is a member of the Andean Community of Nations, the Inter-American Development Bank and the Latin American Integration Association, all of which encourage regional economic development, and of the Rio Group (formerly the Group of Eight), which attempts to reduce regional indebtedness. Peru became a member of the Asia-Pacific Economic Co-operation group (APEC) in 1998.

SURVEY AND PROSPECTS

During the early 1990s the Fujimori administration undertook a major reform of the economy, achieving considerable success in restoring international reserves and in reducing the rate of inflation. Tax reforms increased central government revenue and contributed to a reduction of the public sector deficit, while the implementation of economic liberalization measures and the repayment of arrears improved relations with the international financial community. However, the contraction in domestic demand in the late 1990s led to a widening of the fiscal deficit. The political crisis in 2000 led to a sharp decrease in investment as well as consumer demand and revenue from privatization remained below target.

The interim Government of Valentín Paniagua announced a policy of fiscal austerity as well an investigation into the whereabouts of unallocated profits from the privatization programme of the Fujimori Government. In March 2001 the IMF approved a one-year stand-by credit equivalent to SDR 128m. to ensure macroeconomic stability during the transition to a new administration.

The new Government of Alejandro Toledo, which took office in July, hoped to alleviate poverty and lower unemployment. As political instability abated and investor confidence gradually increased, a main priority was also the resumption of the privatization process (concentrating on the energy and infrastructure sectors) to reduce the fiscal deficit. However, violent protests led to the indefinite suspension of the privatization programme in mid-2002.

In January 2003 the Belgian electricity company Tractebel cancelled plans to buy two state-owned generating firms, Egasa and Egesa. Despite reduced investor confidence in the privatization process, in February the Government attempted to revive the strategy, announcing the auction of 10 regional electricity distribution companies. Meanwhile, the development of major capital projects proceeded; in November the IDB approved $135m. in financing for the Camisea natural gas export pipeline, despite widespread concerns that construction work was damaging environmentally sensitive Amazonian regions.

In February 2004 the IMF approved the final review of the Government's two-year stand-by arrangement, and authorized a further $40m. disbursement. The Fund praised the Government's economic management, and its success in meeting its 2003 fiscal deficit target without the use of the $367m. in IMF credit available under the programme. A series of fiscal measures approved by the Congreso in September 2003, which included a 0.15% tax on financial transactions, were also expected to support future revenues. However, the Government remained impeded by a comparatively small tax base and widespread evasion, and the financial system awaited profound reform. Furthermore, it appeared that the strong growth in 2002 and 2003 had been largely owing to increased exports of raw materials, and had failed to translate into a tangible improvement in the country's high rates of poverty and underemployment.

Philippines

The Republic of the Philippines lies in the western Pacific Ocean, east of mainland South-East Asia. In 1946 the Philippines achieved independence from US rule. Ferdinand Marcos was elected President in 1965 and remained in power until 1986, when, following the rejection of his authority by the acting Chief of Staff of the Armed Forces, Lt-Gen. Fidel Ramos, he relinquished office to Corazon Aquino. Aquino was succeded by Ramos in 1992. In 2001, after the indefinite adjournment of impeachment proceedings against President Joseph Estrada, Vice-President Gloria Macapagal Arroyo took office. Manila is the capital. Filipino is the native national language.

Area and population
Area: 300,000 sq km
Population (mid-2002): 79,944,224
Population density (mid-2002): 266.5 per sq km
Life expectancy (years at birth, 2002): 68.3 (males 65.1; females 71.7)

Finance

GDP in current prices: 2002): US $77,076m. ($964 per head)
Real GDP growth (2002): 4.6%
Inflation (2002): 3.1%
Currency: peso

Economy

In 2002, according to estimates by the World Bank, the Philippines' gross national income (GNI), measured at average 2000–02 prices, was US $81,453m., equivalent to $1,020 per head (or $4,280 per head on an international purchasing-power parity basis). During 1990–2002, it was estimated, the population increased at an average annual rate of 2.3%, while gross domestic product (GDP) per head increased, in real terms, by an average of 0.8% per year. According to figures from the Asian Development Bank (ADB), overall GDP increased, in real terms, at an average annual rate of 3.2% in 1990–2002. Real GDP increased by 4.4% in 2002 and by 4.5% in 2003.

AGRICULTURE

Agriculture (including hunting, forestry and fishing) contributed 14.7% of GDP in 2002, and engaged 35.4% of the employed labour force in 2004, according to preliminary figures. Rice, maize and cassava are the main subsistence crops. The principal crops cultivated for export are coconuts, sugar cane, bananas and pineapples. The sector is generally constrained by inadequate irrigation infrastructure and distribution facilities and insufficient fertilizers. Livestock (chiefly pigs, buffaloes, goats and poultry) and fisheries are important. Deforestation continues at a high rate, owing to illegal logging and to 'slash-and-burn' farming techniques. According to the ADB, agricultural GDP increased at an average annual rate of 2.1% during 1990–2002. Agricultural GDP increased by 3.3% in 2002 and by 3.9% in 2003.

INDUSTRY

Industry (including mining, manufacturing, construction and power) contributed 32.5% of GDP in 2002, and engaged 16.0% of the employed labour force in 2004. According to the ADB, industrial GDP increased at an average annual rate of 2.9% in 1990–2002. According to the National Economic Development Authority (NEDA), industrial GDP increased by 3.7% in 2002 and by 3.0% in 2003.

Mining

Mining contributed 0.8% of GDP in 2002, and engaged 0.4% of the employed labour force in 2004. Copper is the Philippines' leading mineral product; gold, silver, chromium, nickel and coal are also extracted and there are plans to resuscitate the iron ore industry. Commercial production of crude petroleum began in 1979. A substantial natural gas field and petroleum reservoir, off the island of Palawan, has proven recoverable reserves of 100m. barrels of crude petroleum and an estimated 54,000m. 100,000m. cu m of gas. Production from the deposits began in October 2001. According to the ADB, mining GDP increased by an annual average of 2.7% in 1990–2002. The GDP of the mining sector increased by 49.2% in 2002 and by 17.5% in 2003.

Manufacturing

Manufacturing contributed 22.8% of GDP in 2002, and engaged 9.9% of the employed labour force in 2004. In the late 1990s the most important branches of manufacturing were food products and beverages, electronic products and components (mainly telecommunications equipment), petroleum refineries and chemicals. According to the ADB, the GDP of the manufacturing sector increased by an annual average of 2.7% in 1990–2002; manufacturing GDP increased by 3.3% in 2002 and by 4.2% in 2003.

Energy

Energy had been derived principally from oil-fired thermal plants, relying chiefly on imported petroleum. However, by 2003 the energy sector's reliance on petroleum had decreased significantly as new sources of power were exploited. In 2000 coal accounted for 36.8% of the total amount of electrical energy produced, petroleum for 20.3% and hydroelectric power for 17.2%. In October 2001 the Malampaya gasfield project, approved in 1998, was completed. A 504-km pipeline had been constructed under the sea, at a cost of US $4,500m., to transport gas to three generating plants (with a combined capacity of 2,700 MW) on Luzon Island. The gasfield was expected to supply 16% of the electrical capacity of the Philippines and would limit its reliance on imported petroleum as a source of energy. It became fully operational in mid-2002. In June 2001 an Electric Power Industry Reform Act was finally enacted; this provided the legislative framework urgently needed to enable the deregulation of the power industry and the privatization and restructuring of the National Power Corporation. In 2001 imports of mineral fuels accounted for 11.5% of the value of total merchandise imports.

SERVICES

The services sector contributed 52.8% of GDP in 2002, and engaged 48.6% of the employed labour force in 2004. Remittances from Filipino workers abroad, which totalled an estimated US $6,900m. in 2002, constitute the Government's principal source of foreign exchange. Tourism, although periodically affected by political unrest, remains a significant sector of the economy. Despite the terrorist attack on the Indonesian island of Bali in October 2002 and the escalating terrorist activity in the Philippines itself, 1.9m. tourists visited the country in 2002, an increase of 7.6% compared with the previous year. The bombing of the Marriott Hotel in Jakarta, Indonesia, in August 2003, however, was expected further to discourage tourists from visiting the region. Revenue from tourism was estimated at $1,741m. in 2002. The Philippine banking sector was less affected by the financial crisis in 1997 than its regional counterparts, although the imposition of higher capital requirements forced a process of consolidation among smaller banks. According to the ADB, the GDP of the services sector increased at an average annual rate of 3.8% in 1990–2002. The GDP of the services sector increased by 5.4% in 2002 and by 5.9% in 2003.

EXTERNAL TRADE

In 2002 the Philippines recorded a visible trade surplus of US $408m. and there was a surplus of $4,197m. on the current account of the balance of payments. In early 2003 the Government announced that, owing to an understatement of the cost of imports of electronic parts used in manufacturing, it had significantly overestimated the size of the current-account surplus since 2000; the figures were subsequently revised. In 2002 the principal sources of imports were the USA (accounting for 20.6% of the total) and Japan (20.4%); other significant suppliers were the Republic of Korea, Singapore and Taiwan. The USA was the principal market for exports (24.7%); other major purchasers were Japan (15.0%), the Netherlands, Taiwan, Singapore and Hong Kong. The principal imports were machinery and transport equipment, mineral fuels, basic manufactures, chemical products and food and live animals. The principal exports were machinery and transport equipment, which accounted for 40.0% of total exports in that year. Electronic products destined for the computer and related industries have become a major export sector in recent years, although a decline in the global demand for exports had a particularly damaging effect on the sector from 2001 onwards.

GOVERNMENT FINANCE

In 2002 the overall budgetary deficit was estimated at 212,683m. pesos, equivalent to approximately 5.3% of GDP. The Philippines' external debt totalled US $52,356m. at the end of 2001, of which $34,190m. was long-term public debt. In that year the cost of servicing the debt was equivalent to 18.6% of the value of exports of goods and services. The annual rate of inflation averaged 7.9% in 1990–2002; consumer prices increased by an average of 3.1% in 2002 and by an estimated 4.0% in 2003. In March 2004 11.4% of the labour force was unemployed.

INTERNATIONAL ECONOMIC RELATIONS

The Philippines is a member of the UN Economic and Social Commission for Asia and the Pacific (ESCAP), the Asian Development Bank, the Association of South East Asian Nations (ASEAN), the Asia-Pacific Economic Co-operation forum (APEC) and the Colombo Plan. In January 1993 the establishment of an ASEAN Free Trade Area (AFTA) commenced; a reduction in tariffs to a maximum of 5% was originally to be implemented over 15 years but this was later advanced to 2003 before being formally initiated on 1 January 2002. In November 1999 the target date for zero tariffs in ASEAN was brought forward from 2015 to 2010.

SURVEY AND PROSPECTS

Following the inauguration of President Gloria Macapagal Arroyo in January 2001 the Government seemed to regain control of the country's economy. The peso stabilized, the rate of inflation declined and interest rates returned to the levels prevailing before the political crisis that had surrounded the departure of President Macapagal Arroyo's predecessor. The return of a significant number of pro-Arroyo delegates to Congress in the May 2001 legislative elections allowed the new Government to pursue its programme of economic liberalization in a climate of relative political stability.

In June 2001, however, the Financial Action Task Force (FATF), based in Paris, urged the Philippine Government to impose effective measures to combat money laundering and thus eradicate the perception of the Philippines as synonymous with corruption. An Anti-Money Laundering Act was subsequently approved, although it contained significant deficiencies. In February 2003 further anti-money laundering legislation was enacted in an effort to avert the imposition of sanctions by FATF member states before the March deadline. While the legislation was initially deemed to be deficient by the FATF, shortly before the deadline amendments were passed which were considered adequate to prevent the threatened sanctions. However, the Philippines remained on the FATF's list of non-co-operative countries pending the implementation of the new laws and a subsequent assessment of their efficacy.

At the end of 2002 the record budget deficit (which had reached almost 212.7m. pesos) remained the most significant obstacle to the pursuit of a more ambitious programme of economic liberalization. In 2003 the Government implemented efforts to improve tax collection and curb spending in an attempt to reduce the size of the deficit, with some success. However, although the deficit recorded in that year (equivalent to 4.7% of projected GDP) was reportedly the smallest since 1998, it remained a significant source of concern. In July 2003 the coup attempt in Manila threatened to undermine investor confidence in the stability of the Macapagal Arroyo Government. Meanwhile, it was feared that an ongoing downturn in the global electronics market would continue to have an impact upon economic performance, as electronics exports constituted a significant proportion of the Philippines' total exports. It was thought that the political uncertainty arising from the elections scheduled for May 2004 would result in a deceleration in economic growth in the first half of 2004. Continued political insurgency in the southern Philippines was also expected to discourage foreign investment in the country.

Poland

The Republic of Poland is situated in Eastern Europe. A People's Republic was established in 1947, and in 1948 Poland effectively became a one-party state. In 1989, following elections to a new, bicameral legislature, almost 45 years of exclusively Communist rule ended when an administration dominated by the Solidarity organization was formed. In 1990 the Solidarity leader, Lech Wałęsa, was elected as President. Wałęsa was succeeded in 1995 by Aleksander Kwaśniewski, who was re-elected as President in 2000. Poland acceded to the European Union on 1 May 2004. Warsaw is the capital. The official language is Polish.

Area and population

Area: 312,685 sq km
Population (mid-2002): 38,626,192
Population density (mid-2002): 123.5 per sq km
Life expectancy (years at birth, 2002): 74.7 (males 70.6; females 78.7)

Finance

GDP in current prices: 2002): US $187,680m. ($4,859 per head)
Real GDP growth (2002): 1.2%
Inflation (annual average, 2002): 1.9%
Currency: new złoty

Economy

In 2002, according to the World Bank, Poland's gross national income (GNI), measured at average 2000–02 prices, was US $176,616m., equivalent to $4,570 per head (or $10,130 per head on an international purchasing-power parity basis). During 1990–2002, it was estimated, the population increased at an average annual rate of 0.1%, while gross domestic product (GDP) per head grew, in real terms, at an average annual rate of 3.1%. Overall GDP increased, in real terms, at an average annual rate of 3.2% in 1990–2002; growth was 1.0% in 2001 and 1.2% in 2002.

AGRICULTURE

Agriculture contributed 3.4% of GDP in 2002, when the sector engaged 29.8% of the employed labour force. The principal crops are potatoes, sugar beet, wheat, rye and barley. Livestock production is important to the domestic food supply. During 1990–2002 the average annual GDP of the agricultural sector declined, in real terms, by 0.3%. However, real agricultural GDP increased by 1.5% in 2001 and by 3.0% in 2002.

INDUSTRY

Industry (including mining, manufacturing, power and construction) accounted for 33.8% of GDP in 2002, and engaged 24.4% of the employed labour force. During 1990–2002 industrial GDP increased, in real terms, by an average of 2.0% per year; real industrial GDP decreased by 0.6% in 2001, but increased by 1.0% in 2002.

Mining

Mining and quarrying contributed 2.3% of GDP in 2001, and engaged 1.5% of the employed labour force in 2002. Poland is a significant producer of copper, silver and sulphur, and there are also considerable reserves of natural gas. The mining sector experienced a marked decline in the 1990s; however, from 1998 the sector underwent significant restructuring. During 1992–96 mining GDP declined at an average annual rate of 1.5%; the sector's GDP declined by 4.3% in 1997, and by an estimated 4.6% in 1998.

Manufacturing

The manufacturing sector contributed 19.7% of GDP in 2001, and it engaged 16.8% of the employed labour force in 2002. Measured by the value of sold production, the principal branches of manufacturing in 1998 were food products and beverages (accounting for 24.7% of the total), road motor vehicles, chemicals and chemical products, basic metals and non-electric machinery. In 1995–2002 manufacturing GDP increased, in real terms, at an average annual rate of 6.2%. Manufacturing GDP declined by 0.6% in 2001, but increased by 2.5% in 2002.

Energy

Energy is derived principally from coal, which satisfied 96.1% of the country's total energy requirements in 2000. In 1998 the Government announced plans to reduce Poland's dependence on coal: it was projected that by 2010 15% of power generation would be fuelled by imported natural gas. Mineral fuels and lubricants accounted for 9.1% of the value of merchandise imports in 2002; some 6.5% of electricity generated was exported in 2000.

SERVICES

The services sector contributed 62.8% of GDP in 2002, when the sector engaged 45.8% of the employed labour force. Services expanded rapidly from the early 1990s, with considerable growth in financial services, retailing, tourism and leisure. The GDP of the services sector increased, in real terms, by an average of 3.8% per year in 1990–2001. Real services GDP increased by 4.2% in 2000 and by 3.9% in 2001.

EXTERNAL TRADE

In 2002 Poland recorded a visible trade deficit of US $7,249m., and there was a deficit of $5,007m. on the current account of the balance of payments. In that year the principal source of imports was Germany (accounting for 24.3%); other major suppliers were Italy, Russia and France. Germany was also the principal market for exports (32.3%); other significant purchasers included France, Italy and the United Kingdom. The principal exports in 2002 were machinery and transport equipment (accounting for 37.6%), basic manufactures, miscellaneous manufactured articles, chemicals and crude materials. The principal imports in that year were machinery and transport equipment (37.6%), basic manufactures, chemicals and related products, and mineral fuels and lubricants.

GOVERNMENT FINANCE

According to government figures, Poland's overall budgetary deficit for 2002 was 39,402m. new złotys (equivalent to 5.2% of GDP). Poland's external debt totalled US $62,393m. at the end of 2001, of which $24,828m. was long-term public debt. In that year the cost of debt-servicing was equivalent to 28.0% of the value of exports of goods and services. In 1990–2002 the annual rate of inflation averaged 22.8%. The average rate of increase in consumer prices was 1.9% in 2002 and 0.8% in 2003. In February 2004 20.6% of the labour force were registered as unemployed, the highest level since the communist era.

INTERNATIONAL ECONOMIC RELATIONS

Poland is a member, as a 'Country of Operations', of the European Bank for Reconstruction and Development (EBRD). Poland joined the World Trade Organization (WTO) in July 1995, and the Organisation for Economic Co-operation and Development (OECD) in November 1996. An association agreement with the European Union (EU) became fully effective from February 1994; in December 2002 Poland was invited to become a full member from the beginning of May 2004.

SURVEY AND PROSPECTS

In the 1990s Poland undertook an ambitious, market-orientated programme of economic reform with assistance from the international financial community. A devalued 'new złoty' was introduced in January 1995, and was made freely convertible on international currency markets from May of that year. Foreign debt was significantly alleviated by concessions from official creditors, agreed in 1994, and foreign investment increased significantly. Poland's economic performance was adversely affected by the Russian financial crisis in August 1998, but in late 1999 the economy began to recover. However, a decline in international petroleum prices in 2000 prompted a second economic reverse, and a sharp increase in the (already high) rate of unemployment.

Following the election of a new, leftist Government in September 2001, the Government immediately reduced planned spending, in an attempt to control the expanding budgetary deficit, and tax increases were approved in November. Slow economic recovery was evident in 2002, and strong growth was recorded in 2003, together with a low rate of consumer-price inflation. However, the budgetary deficit had increased, public debt had expanded to represent some 50% of GDP in 2003, and privatization had stalled (although plans were announced in early 2004 for the privatization of over 200 state-owned companies in that year). It appeared unlikely, therefore, that Poland would satisfy EU criteria for the adoption of the common European currency, the euro, before 2010. In October 2003 the Deputy Prime Minister and Minister of the Economy, Labour and Social Policy, Jerzy Hausner, announced controversial proposals for dramatic reductions in public spending in 2004–07. However, the austerity plan, which was adopted by the Government in January 2004, still awaited parliamentary approval when Prime Minister Leszek Miller announced that his Government was to resign on 2 May (following Poland's accession to the EU). The country's ongoing political instability, therefore, was regarded as a particular threat to economic performance in the short term.

Portugal

The mainland portion of the Portuguese Republic lies in western Europe, in the Iberian peninsula. Portugal became a republic in 1910. After 1932 Dr António de Oliveira Salazar established a right-wing dictatorial regime. Salazar's successor, Dr Marcello Caetano, was overthrown in 1974 in a coup initiated by the Movimento das Forças Armadas. In 1975 a transition to civilian government commenced and in 1986 Mário Lopes Soares was elected the first civilian President. In presidential elections in 2001 Jorge Fernando Branco de Sampaio of the Partido Socialista was returned for a second term. Lisbon is the capital. The official language is Portuguese.

Area and population
Area: 92,345 sq km
Population (mid-2002): 10,031,690
Population density (mid-2002): 108.6 per sq km
Life expectancy (years at birth, 2002): 77.1 (males 73.6; females 80.5)

Finance
GDP in current prices: 2002): US $121,291m. ($12,091 per head)
Real GDP growth (2002): 0.4%
Inflation (annual average, 2002): 3.5%
Currency: euro

Economy

In 2002, according to estimates by the World Bank, Portugal's overall gross national income (GNI), measured at average 2000–02 prices, was US $112,028m., equivalent to $10,840 per head (or $17,350 on an international purchasing-power parity basis). During 1990–2002, it was estimated, the population increased at an average rate of 0.1% per year, while gross domestic product (GDP) per head increased, in real terms, by an average of 5.6% per year. Overall GDP expanded, in real terms, at an average annual rate of 5.9% in 1990–2002; growth in 2002 was 0.4%.

AGRICULTURE

Agriculture (including forestry and fishing) contributed an estimated 3.5% of GDP in 2002 and the sector engaged 12.3% of the employed labour force in that year. The principal crops are wheat, maize, potatoes, olives, tomatoes, oranges, grapes and sugar beets. The production of wine, particularly port, is significant. The European Union (EU) imposed a ban on Portuguese beef exports in late 1998 as a result of the detection of bovine spongiform encephalopathy (BSE) in Portuguese cattle. In 2003 the number of cases diagnosed rose for the first time since 1999. The fishing industry is important, the sardine catch, at 72,000 metric tons in 2001, being by far the largest. In mid-2003 forest fires, which were a result of a heatwave in southern Europe affected an estimated 330,000 ha of forest and 15,000 ha of farmland, causing some €1,000m. of damage. According to the World Bank, agricultural GDP increased, in real terms, by an average of 0.8% per year during 1990–99, however agricultural GDP declined by 4.4% in 2000 and by 1.5% in 2001.

INDUSTRY

Industry (comprising mining, manufacturing, construction and power) contributed an estimated 27.9% of GDP in 2002, and engaged 33.8% of the employed labour force. According to the World Bank, the GDP of the industrial sector increased, in real terms, by an average of 2.3% per year during 1990–2001; industrial GDP grew by 2.6% in 2000 and by 2.2% in 2001.

Mining

The mining and quarrying industry makes a minimal contribution to GDP, employing 0.3% of the working population in 2002. Limestone, granite, marble, copper pyrites, gold and uranium are the most significant products.

Manufacturing

Manufacturing provided 17.9% of GDP in 2002 and engaged 20.5% of the employed labour force. According to the World Bank, manufacturing GDP grew by an annual average of 1.8% in 1990–99. The textile industry is the most important branch of manufacturing, accounting for 18.6% of total export earnings in 2001. Other significant manufactured products include footwear, cork items, chemicals, electrical appliances, ceramics and paper pulp. Manufacturing GDP increased, in real terms, by 5.0% in 2001 and by 3.0% in 2002.

Energy

In 2000, according to World Bank figures, 33.9% of electricity production was derived from coal, 26.1% from hydroelectric power, 19.4% from petroleum and 16.5% from natural gas. Total electricity production was 47,459m. kWh in 2001. In 2001 imports of fuel accounted for an estimated 6.6% of total import costs. Portugal's heavy dependence on petroleum was reduced in 1997 when a pipeline carrying natural gas from Algeria (via Morocco and Spain) was inaugurated.

SERVICES

Services provided 68.6% of GDP in 2002, and engaged 53.8% of the employed labour force. The tourism industry remained a significant source of foreign exchange earnings in 2001, when receipts totalled an estimated US $5,479m. In that year there were 12.2m. tourist arrivals in Portugal. Emigrants' remittances are also important to the Portuguese economy, reaching an estimated $3,100m. in 2000. According to the World Bank, the GDP of the services sector increased, in real terms, by an average of 2.4% per year during 1990–2001; services GDP rose by 3.8% in 2000 and by 1.5% in 2001.

EXTERNAL TRADE

In 2002 Portugal recorded a visible trade deficit of US $12,411m., and a deficit of $9,120m. on the current account of the balance of payments. Most of Portugal's trade is with other members of the EU. In 2001 Spain, Germany and France supplied an estimated 27.4%, 13.8% and 10.2%, respectively, of total imports. The principal export market was Germany (which purchased 19.1% of the total); other major purchasers were Spain (19.0%) and France (12.6%). The main exports in 2001 were textiles (18.5%), road vehicles and parts (17.5%), clothing (8.8%), leather products (6.5%) and food and beverages (5.8%). The principal imports were foodstuffs, textile yarn, chemicals, petroleum and petroleum products, and transport equipment.

GOVERNMENT FINANCE

In 2003 the budget deficit was equivalent to 2.8% of GDP, compared with 2.7% in 2002 and 4.1% in 2001. In 1998 Portugal's external debt totalled 2,537,600m. escudos, equivalent to 13.2% of GDP. In 1990–2002 the annual rate of inflation averaged 4.7%. The average rate of inflation declined from 4.4% in 2001 to 3.5% in 2002. The level of unemployment increased from 4.1% in 2001, and to 5.0% in 2002.

INTERNATIONAL ECONOMIC RELATIONS

Portugal became a member of the EC (now EU) in January 1986. The Maastricht Treaty on European Union was ratified by the Portuguese legislature in December 1992. In April 1992 Portugal joined the exchange rate mechanism of the European Monetary System. Portugal is also a member of the Organisation for Economic Co-operation and Development (OECD) and of the Comunidade dos Países de Língua Portuguesa (CPLP), which was established in Lisbon in 1996.

SURVEY AND PROSPECTS

From 1997 the developments in Portugal's economy were strongly influenced by Portugal's participation in the single European currency, the euro, under economic and monetary union (EMU). Portugal adopted the euro at its inception in January 1999 as a single currency unit for transactions throughout the euro zone and as an internationally traded currency, and as legal tender in cash from 1 January 2002. Preparations for entry included a reduction in interest rates in order to achieve European integration, which had a strong positive effect on the growth of domestic demand. Consumption and investment also increased as a result of economic confidence stemming from participation in the euro area.

Since its entry into the EU in 1986, Portugal has been a net recipient of large-scale financial transfers from the EU, through the Community Support Framework. (However, EU funds to Portugal, which accounted for almost 3% of GDP in 2003, were likely to be significantly reduced following the enlargement of the EU from 15 to 25 members in May 2004.) Furthermore, a period of strong growth, full employment, low inflation and inexpensive credit ended in 2000, as a result of rising interest rates and an increase in inflation owing to high international petroleum prices. Economic growth slowed considerably in the early 2000s, and as a consequence, government revenue from taxes declined substantially, necessitating a €750m. reduction in public expenditure.

In early April 2002 the new Government announced that the budget deficit in 2001 was 4.1% of GDP, exceeding the 3% stipulated in the EU's stability and growth pact and thus contravening the regulations for the single currency. The new administration responded with the announcement in May of severe austerity measures. In a revised budget for 2002 value-added tax (VAT) was increased from 17% to 19%, recruitment to the civil service was suspended, while local governments were prohibited from incurring further debt and 70 public companies were scheduled for closure or merger. The deficit was reduced to 2.7% in 2002, but Portugal became the first euro-zone country to enter into recession, with a 1.3% decline in GDP in the last quarter of 2002 relative to the same period in 2001. Overall GDP growth in 2002 was only 0.4%, although the Government remained committed to further austerity measures, institutional reforms and a commitment to the European stability and growth pact.

In 2003 the Government successfully maintained the budget deficit at less than 3% of GDP. Despite financial sector predictions that it could be as high as 5%, the budget deficit for 2003 was 2.8% of GDP, slightly above the euro-zone average of 2.7%. However, the economy remained in recession throughout 2003, with GDP contracting by an estimated 1.1% in that year. The Government planned to keep the budget deficit at 2003 levels in 2004 by continuing the reform of the public sector and the sale of state properties, which it was hoped would raise an estimated €1,000m., and by maintaining the privatization programme. The transfer of public assets into private ownership, as well as a reduction in corporate tax, were expected to promote economic growth in 2004, which was predicted at between 0.5% and 1.5%.

Puerto Rico

The Commonwealth of Puerto Rico mainly comprises the island of Puerto Rico, lying east of Hispaniola in the Caribbean Sea. After 1898 Puerto Rico was administered as an 'unincorporated territory' of the USA. In 1952 a Constitution assigned Puerto Rico the status of a self-governing 'Commonwealth' in its relations with the USA. Voters ratified a continuation of Commonwealth status in 1967 and 1993. In 1998 voters specifically rejected the admission of Puerto Rico as the 51st State of the USA. San Juan is the capital. The official languages are Spanish and English.

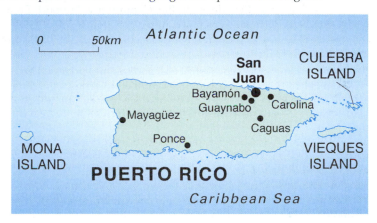

Area and population
Area: 8,959 sq km
Population (mid-2002): 3,868,870
Population density (mid-2002): 431.8
Life expectancy (years at birth, 1995–2000): 74.9 (males 70.4; females 79.6)

Finance
GDP in current prices: 2001): US $67,897m. ($17,682 per head)
Real GDP growth (2001): 5.6%
Inflation (annual average, 2002): 6.1%
Currency: US dollar

Economy

In 2001, according to estimates by the World Bank, Puerto Rico's gross national income (GNI), measured at average 1999–2001 prices, was US $42,053m., equivalent to US $10,950 per head (or $15,800 per head on an international purchasing-power basis). In 1997–2001, it was estimated, GNI per head increased, in real terms, at an average rate of 6.3% per year. During 1990–2002, it was estimated, the population increased at an average annual rate of 0.8%, while gross domestic product (GDP) per head increased, in real terms, by an average of 3.4% per year. Overall GDP increased,

691

in real terms, by an average of 4.2% per year in 1990–2001; according to government estimates, GDP increased by 0.6% in 2001/02 and by just 0.3% in 2002/03.

AGRICULTURE

Agriculture, forestry and fishing contributed an estimated 0.3% of GDP in 2002/03 and employed 1.9% of the working population in 2002. Dairy produce and other livestock products are the mainstays of the agricultural sector. The principal crops are sugar cane, plantains, bananas and oranges. Cocoa cultivation has been successfully introduced, and measures to improve agricultural land use have included the replanting of some sugar-growing areas with rice and the cultivation of plantain trees over large areas of unproductive hill land. Commercial fishing is practised on a small scale. The GDP of the agricultural sector increased, in real terms, at an average rate of 2.1% per year between 1980/81 and 1990/91. Agricultural GDP rose by approximately 1.5% in 1993/94.

INDUSTRY

Industry (including manufacturing, construction and mining) provided an estimated 51.4% of GDP in 2002/03 and employed 19.9% of the working population in 2002. Industrial GDP increased, in real terms, at an average annual rate of 2.9% between 1980/81 and 1990/91. It rose by 3.3% in 1993/94.

Mining

Quarrying was estimated to provide about 0.1% of GDP on average and employed 0.2% of the working population in 2002. Otherwise, Puerto Rico has no commercially exploitable mineral resources, although deposits of copper and nickel have been identified.

Manufacturing

Manufacturing is the main source of income, accounting for an estimated 42.1% of GDP in 2002/03 and employing 11.4% of the working population in 2002. From 1996 employment in the manufacturing sector declined at an average annual rate of 6%. The principal branch of manufacturing in 2002/03, based on the value of output, was chemical products (accounting for 72.4% of the total sector), mainly drugs and medicines. Other important products were computer, electronic and electrical products (12.6%) and food products (6.0%). The GDP of the manufacturing sector increased , in real terms, by 2.9% per year between 1980/81 and 1990/91. The rate of advance was 3.5% in 1993/94. In 2000/01 total electricity production stood at 22,132.2m. kWh.

SERVICES

Services (including electricity, gas and water) provided an estimated 48.3% of GDP in 2002/03 and engaged 78.2% of the employed labour force in 2002. In real terms, the GDP of all service sectors increased at an average rate of 4.9% per year between 1980/81 and 1990/91, and by 4.4% in 1993/94. Tourism is of increasing importance; In 2002/03 tourist arrivals were estimated at 4,402.3m. visitors, attracting revenue totalling US $2,676.6m. Visitors from the US mainland comprised more than 50% of the total number of visitors.

EXTERNAL TRADE

In 2000/01 Puerto Rico recorded a budget surplus of US $841,660m. Puerto Rico's total public debt at the end of the fiscal year to June 2003 was an estimated

US $30,781.2m. US federal aid programmes are of central importance to the Puerto Rican economy, and the island has also received disaster relief in respect of hurricanes that widely disrupt the Puerto Rican economy intermittently. In 2001/02 Puerto Rico recorded a visible trade surplus of $12,869.4m., but there was a deficit of $3,851.1m. on the current account of the balance of payments. Mainland USA is the island's dominant trading partner, providing 60.7% of Puerto Rico's recorded imports and absorbing 90.5% of its recorded exports in 1997/98. Japan, the Dominican Republic, the United Kingdom and Venezuela are also significant in Puerto Rico's foreign trade. The principal category of recorded exports in 2002/03 was chemical products (accounting for 71.8% of the total), mainly drugs and pharmaceutical preparations. Other major exports were machinery (mainly computers) and food. The main imports were also chemical products, food and machinery.

GOVERNMENT FINANCE

The annual inflation rate averaged 4.9% in 1990–2002. Consumer prices increased by an average of 7.0% in 2001 and by an average of 6.1% in 2002. Puerto Rico is very densely populated, and unemployment has been a persistent problem, although assisted by the growth in the tourist industry, the jobless rate declined during the 1990s. The average rate of unemployment stood at 12.2% in 2002.

INTERNATIONAL ECONOMIC RELATIONS

Puerto Rico holds associate status in the UN Economic Commission for Latin America and the Caribbean (ECLAC) and has observer status in the Caribbean Community and Common Market (CARICOM). Puerto Rico declined to accept associate status in the Association of Caribbean States (ACS), formed in 1994, on the grounds of opposition by the US Government to the inclusion of Cuba. In July 2001 Puerto Rico applied for associate membership of CARICOM; the USA criticized the move, emphasizing that it had authority over the island's foreign policy as long as Puerto Rico held Commonwealth status.

SURVEY AND PROSPECTS

Puerto Rico's economic growth has been inhibited by the lack of an adequate infrastructure. Government programmes of industrial and taxation incentives, aimed at attracting US and foreign investors and encouraging domestic reinvestment of profits and long-term capital investment, have generated growth in the manufacturing and services sectors. However, in 1996 the US Government announced that it was to progressively withdraw a number of important tax exemptions (collectively known as Section 936) enjoyed by US and foreign investors. The Government of Puerto Rico attempted to counteract the economic impact of their removal by seeking to establish the island as a centre for the finishing of Latin American manufactured goods destined for member states of the North American Free Trade Agreement (NAFTA). Approximately US $4,200m. was needed to repair damage from Hurricane Georges, of which $2,700m. was disbursed in 1999/2000, largely from the US Federal Emergency Management Agency (FEMA) and private insurance companies. Economic growth slowed in 2002/03, to an estimated 0.3%, partly owing to the economic slowdown in the USA. However, GDP growth was predicted to recover in 2003/04, to 3.0%.

Qatar

The State of Qatar occupies a peninsula, projecting northwards from the Arabian mainland, on the west coast of the Persian (Arabian) Gulf. Qatar became fully independent in 1971, whereupon the Ruler, Sheikh Ahmad ath-Thani, took the title of Amir. In 1972 the Amir was deposed. Sheikh Khalifa ath-Thani, formerly the Deputy Ruler, proclaimed himself Amir. In 1995 the Deputy Amir and Heir Apparent, Maj.-Gen. Sheikh Hamad bin Khalifa ath-Thani, deposed his father and proclaimed himself Amir. Elections to a central Municipal Council, held in 1999, were the first in Qatar's history. Doha is the capital. The official language is Arabic.

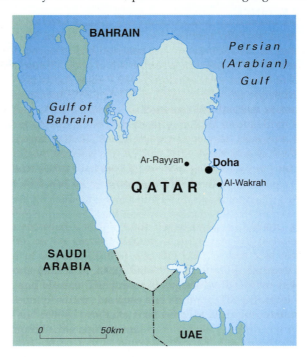

Area and population
Area: 11,437 sq km
Population (mid-2002): 610,490
Population density (mid-2002): 53.4 per sq km
Life expectancy (years at birth, 2002): 74.3 (males 74.8; females 73.8)

Finance
GDP in current prices: 2000): US $16,454m. ($28,132 per head)
Real GDP growth (1999): 3.2%
Inflation (annual average, 2002): 1.0%
Currency: Qatari riyal

Economy

In 1997, according to estimates by the World Bank, Qatar's gross national income (GNI), measured at average 1995–97 prices, was US $11,627m., equivalent to $22,147 per head. According to unofficial sources, GNI totalled $17,150m. in 2001 and $17,490m. in 2002 (equivalent to some $28,300 per head). During 1990–2002, it was estimated, the population increased at an average annual rate of 1.9%, while gross domestic product (GDP) per head increased, in real terms, by an average of 4.2% per year. Non-Qataris accounted for some 80% of the total population by the beginning of the 21st century. Overall GDP was estimated to have increased, in real terms, at an average rate of 6.2% per year in 1990–2002; growth was estimated at 6.2% in 2001 and 6.0% in 2002.

AGRICULTURE

Agriculture (including fishing) contributed an estimated 0.4% of GDP in 2002, and employed some 1.2% of the economically active population in that year. All agricultural land is owned by the Government, and most farm managers are immigrants employing a largely expatriate work-force. The main crops are cereals (principally barley), vegetables and dates. Qatar is self-sufficient in winter vegetables and nearly self-sufficient in summer vegetables. Some vegetables are exported to other Gulf countries. The Government has prioritized education in agricultural techniques and experimentation with unconventional methods of cultivation (including the use of sea water and solar energy to produce sand-based crops). Livestock-rearing and fishing are also practised. The GDP of the agricultural sector was estimated to have declined at an average annual rate of 4.5% during 1993–2002. However, real agricultural GDP increased by an estimated 6.4% in 2002.

INDUSTRY

Industry (including mining, manufacturing, construction and power) contributed an estimated 70.7% of GDP in 2002, and employed 32.2% of the economically active population at March 1986. Industrial GDP was estimated to have increased by an average of 9.8% per year during 1993–2002. Growth in the sector's real GDP was estimated at 7.6% in 2002.

Mining

The mining and quarrying sector (comprising principally the extraction and processing of petroleum and natural gas) provided an estimated 61.6% of GDP in 2002, and employed 2.4% of the economically active population at March 1986. Petroleum is currently the major mineral export. Proven recoverable petroleum reserves at the end of 2002 were 15,200m. barrels, sufficient to maintain production for 57.6 years at 2002 levels—averaging some 755,000 barrels per day (b/d). With effect from April 2004 Qatar's production quota within the Organization of the Petroleum Exporting Countries (OPEC) was 609,000 b/d. Proven gas reserves were 14,400,000m. cu m at the end of 2002 (representing 9.2% of known world reserves at that date), primarily located in the North Field, the world's largest gas reserve not associated with petroleum. The real GDP of the mining and quarrying sector was estimated to have increased at an average annual rate of 11.7% in 1993–2002. Growth was estimated at 8.5% in 2002.

Manufacturing

Manufacturing contributed an estimated 5.4% of GDP in 2002 (excluding activities related to petroleum and natural gas), and the sector employed 6.9% of the economically active population at March 1986. The principal manufacturing activities are linked to the country's oil and gas resources—petroleum refining and the production of liquefied natural gas (LNG—developed as part of the North Field project), together with industrial chemicals (particularly fertilizers) and steel production. Bids for development of the region's first gas-to-liquids complex were invited in early 2002. Manufacturing GDP (excluding hydrocarbons) was estimated to have increased by an average of 4.5% per year in 1993–2002. The sector's real GDP increased by an estimated 7.1% in 2002.

Energy

Electrical energy is derived almost exclusively from Qatar's natural gas resources (91.6% in 2001). Solar energy is being developed in conjunction with desalination.

SERVICES

The services sector contributed an estimated 28.9% of GDP in 2002, and engaged 64.4% of the employed labour force at March 1986. The establishment of a formal stock exchange (which commenced trading in 1997) was expected to stimulate further activity in the sector. The GDP of the services sector was estimated to have increased by an average of 6.1% per year in 1993–2002. Services GDP increased by an estimated 3.9% in 2002.

EXTERNAL TRADE

Preliminary figures indicate that in 2003 Qatar recorded a visible trade surplus of QR 26,453m., while there was a surplus of QR 15,104m. on the current account of the balance of payments. In 2002 the principal source of imports (13.0%) was the USA; other important suppliers in that year were Japan, Italy, the United Kingdom, the United Arab Emirates (UAE), Germany and Saudi Arabia. In 2001 Japan took 51.8% of Qatar's exports. The principal exports are petroleum and gas and their derivatives (mineral fuels and lubricants provided 92.4% of domestic export revenues in 2001). In the same year LNG exports alone accounted for 38.2% of export revenues. The principal imports in 2001 were machinery and transport equipment, basic manufactures, food and live animals, and chemicals and related products.

GOVERNMENT FINANCE

In the financial year ending 31 March 2004, according to provisional figures, Qatar recorded a budget surplus of QR 5,843m. The annual rate of inflation averaged 2.7% in 1995–2002; consumer prices increased by an average of 1.0% in 2002. The Qatari economy is dependent on immigrant workers, owing to a shortage of indigenous labour.

INTERNATIONAL ECONOMIC RELATIONS

Other than its membership of OPEC, Qatar is a member of the Organization of Arab Petroleum Exporting Countries (OAPEC), the Co-operation Council for the Arab States of the Gulf (GCC), the Arab Fund for Economic and Social Development (AFESD), the Arab Monetary Fund and the Islamic Development Bank. GCC member states created a unified regional customs tariff in January 2003, and have undertaken to establish a single market and currency no later than January 2010.

SURVEY AND PROSPECTS

A priority following the assumption of power by Sheikh Hamad in 1995 was the maximizing of Qatar's energy-derived wealth so as to replenish state reserves, much of which were under the control of the deposed Amir. The development of the North Field gas project has been of prime importance, with the aim that Qatar should become a major regional and international supplier of gas and associated products. One of the most notable recent generators of income has been LNG, exports of which began in 1997 and by 2001, with related products, were valued at some US \$4,099m.: LNG was expected to outstrip petroleum as Qatar's principal export commodity by 2005. In the petroleum sector, meanwhile, efforts have been made to expand production capacity (which was expected to reach 1m. b/d by 2005—considerably in excess of Qatar's recent OPEC production quotas). The investment of over \$30,000m. in oil and gas projects during 1995–2003, which has led to a succession of budgetary deficits, entailed the accumulation of an external debt equivalent to 76.5% of GDP by the end of 2001. In addition, a further \$30,000m. was scheduled to be invested in the sector during 2004–08. However, there was confidence both within Qatar and in the international financial community that revenue from the gas industry (particularly sales of LNG under long-term sales contracts with companies in the Far East and Europe) would be sufficient to ensure the prompt dispatch of debt; since the 2000/01 financial year four successive fiscal surpluses have been recorded.

Partnership agreements have been sought with overseas interests for a number of schemes in the hydrocarbons sector—notably the Dolphin project, under which it is intended to supply gas to the UAE, Oman and, eventually, Pakistan. Meanwhile, the divestment of a 45% holding in the state telecommunications company in 1998 was to be followed by the sale of shares in the state petrochemical, fertilizer, vinyl and chemical companies in 2004. However, despite the enactment in 2002 of legislation allowing 100% foreign ownership of companies involved in areas of agriculture, manufacturing, education, health and tourism, and the inauguration in early 2002 of Qatar's first semi-private company in the energy sector (engaged in the sale of liquefied petroleum gas), the State retained responsibility for some 75% of GDP. Having restored financial reserves, a priority for the early part of the 21st century was to be the resumption of much-needed investment in infrastructure: the budget for 2003/04 provided for a 16% rise in overall expenditure, with spending on public projects, including health, social services, low-cost housing and education and youth projects, all set to increase. (Despite this, it was forecast in January 2004 that a record budget surplus, partly generated by sustained high petroleum prices, would be recorded for the fiscal year ending in March.) Furthermore, Doha's status as the venue for the 2006 Asian Games tournament entailed huge infrastructural expenditure; among those non-energy sector projects scheduled to be completed by the start of the Games were the Museum of Islamic Arts, the Qatar National Library, a new broadcasting complex, the Hamad Medical City (to be used as the athletes' village), an expansion of the City Centre Doha shopping mall and the construction of numerous hotels. Government expenditure on major projects in the 2004/05 fiscal year alone was projected to reach \$1,257m. Economic growth in 2003 was expected to be in excess of 10%.

Réunion

Réunion is an island in the Indian Ocean, lying east of Madagascar. In 1946 it received full French departmental status, and in 1974 became an Overseas Department with regional status. Opposition in Réunion and the other Overseas Departments forced the French Government to abandon a project to dissolve the General and Regional Councils in the Overseas Departments in favour of single assemblies. In 2000 the creation of a second department on Réunion was rejected by the Sénat, although the Assemblée Nationale subsequently approved other changes to the institutional future of the Overseas Departments. Saint-Denis is the capital. The official language is French.

Area and population
Area: 2,507 sq km
Population (1 January 2002): 741,300
Population density (1 January 2002): 295.7 per sq km
Life expectancy (years at birth, 2001): males 71.0; females 79.4

Finance
GDP in current prices: 1999): US $7,184m. ($10,116 per head)
Real GDP growth (1999): 3.0%
Inflation (annual average, 2002): 2.7%
Currency: euro

Economy

Réunion's gross national income (GNI) in 1995 was estimated at 29,200m. French francs, equivalent to about 44,300 francs per head. During 1990–97, according to World Bank estimates, Réunion's population increased at an average annual rate of 1.7%. In 2001, according to the UN, Réunion's gross domestic product (GDP), measured at current prices, was US $6,744m., equivalent to $9,188 per head. GDP increased, in real terms, at an average annual rate of 2.9% in 1990–2001; growth in 2001 was 2.4%.

AGRICULTURE

Agriculture (including hunting, forestry and fishing) contributed 2.9% of GDP in 1999, and engaged 3.0% of the economically active population in mid-2001. The principal cash crops are sugar cane (sugar accounted for 40.3% of export earnings in 2002), maize, tobacco, vanilla, and geraniums and vetiver root, which are cultivated for the production of essential oils. Fishing and livestock production are also important to the economy. According to the UN, agricultural GDP increased at an average annual rate of 3.9% during 1990–2000; growth in 2001 was 3.1%.

INDUSTRY

Industry (including mining, manufacturing, construction and power) contributed 14.3% of GDP in 1999, and employed 14.1% of the working population in 1999.

Manufacturing

The principal branch of manufacturing is food-processing, particularly the production of sugar and rum. Other significant sectors include the fabrication of construction materials, mechanics, printing, metalwork, textiles and garments, and electronics. According to the UN, industrial GDP (excluding construction) increased at an average annual rate of 4.3% during 1990–99; growth in 2001 was 3.7%.

Energy

There are no mineral resources on the island. Energy is derived principally from thermal and hydroelectric power. Imports of petroleum products comprised 7.4% of the value of total imports in 2000.

SERVICES

Services (including transport, communications, trade and finance) contributed 82.8% of GDP in 1999, and employed 80.4% of the working population in 1999. The public sector accounts for about one-half of employment in the services sector. Tourism is also significant; in 2002 426,000 tourists visited Réunion, and tourism revenue totalled €302m.

EXTERNAL TRADE

In 2002 Réunion recorded a trade deficit of €2,711m. The principal source of imports in 2002 was metropolitan France, providing 64.0% of the total; other major suppliers in that year were Saudi Arabia and Germany. Metropolitan France was also the principal market for exports in 2002, taking 58.2% of the total; other significant purchasers were Japan, Mayotte and the USA. The principal exports in 2002 were sugar and capital equipment. The principal imports in that year were prepared foodstuffs, road motor vehicles and parts, and chemical products.

GOVERNMENT FINANCE

In 1998 there was an estimated state budgetary deficit of 8,048.9m. French francs. The annual rate of inflation averaged 2.2% in 1990–2002; consumer prices increased by 2.7% in 2002. An estimated 31.0% of the labour force were unemployed in December 2002.

INTERNATIONAL ECONOMIC RELATIONS

Réunion is represented by France in the Indian Ocean Commission (IOC). As an integral part of France, Réunion belongs to the European Union (EU).

SURVEY AND PROSPECTS

Réunion has a relatively developed economy, but is dependent on financial aid from France. The economy has traditionally been based on agriculture, and is therefore vulnerable to poor climatic conditions. From the 1990s the production of sugar cane (which dominates this sector) was adversely affected by increasing urbanization, which resulted in a decline in agricultural land. In 1994 the Government indicated that it intended to give priority to the reduction of unemployment and announced a programme of economic and social development. However, Réunion's rate of unemployment remained the highest of all the French Departments in 2002, with youth unemployment of particular concern.

Although favourable economic progress was reported in 1998, sustained largely by tourism, economists have identified Réunion's need to expand external trade, particularly with fellow IOC members, if the island's economy is to continue to prosper.

In May 2000 the French Government announced that it had agreed to equalize the minimum taxable wage in the Overseas Departments with that of metropolitan France within a period of three years; the current minimum taxable wage in Réunion was 20% lower than that of metropolitan France. This measure was approved by the French Senate in June. In early 2001 the French Government announced that it was to spend €84m. on improving educational facilities on Réunion, as part of a major programme of investment in the Overseas Territories and Departments.

In 2002 two cyclones and heavy rains adversely affected agricultural production, with prices rising substantially as a result. It was hoped that a decision to allow Réunion to negotiate co-operation agreements with regional states from 2004 would enhance its trading position.

Romania

Romania lies in south-eastern Europe. In 1989 the regime of President Ceauşescu was overthrown in a revolution. In 1990 Ion Iliescu was elected as President, while the National Salvation Front won legislative elections. A multi-party system was endorsed in 1991, and legislative elections held in 1992, 1996 and 2000 were won, respectively, by the Democratic National Salvation Front, the Democratic Convention of Romania, and the Party of Social Democracy of Romania. After a second pre-sidential term, Iliescu ceded office to Emil Constantinescu in 1996. In 2000 Iliescu was re-elected as President. Bucharest is the capital. The official language is Romanian.

Area and population

Area: 238,391 sq km
Population (mid-2002): 22,354,650
Population density (mid-2002): 93.8 per sq km
Life expectancy (years at birth, 2002): 71.4 (males 68.0; females 75.0)

Finance
GDP in current prices: 2002): US $44,428m. ($1,987 per head)
Real GDP growth (2002): 4.3%
Inflation (annual average, 2002): 22.5%
Currency: leu

Economy

In 2002, according to the World Bank, Romania's gross national income (GNI), measured at average 2000–02 prices, totalled US $41,304m., equivalent to $1,850 per head (or $6,290 on an international purchasing-power parity basis). During 1990–2002, it was estimated, the population decreased at an average annual rate of 0.3%, while gross domestic product (GDP) per head declined, in real terms, at an average annual rate of 0.5%. Overall GDP, decreased, in real terms, by an average of 0.8% annually during 1990–2002. However, real GDP increased by 5.3% in 2001 and by 4.3% in 2002.

AGRICULTURE
In 2002 agriculture contributed 14.8% of GDP and employed 36.4% of the employed labour force. The principal crops are maize, wheat, potatoes, sugar beet, barley, apples and grapes. Wine production plays a significant role in Romanian agriculture. Forestry, the cropping of reeds (used as a raw material in the paper and cellulose industry) and the breeding of fish are also significant activities. Under the Government's decollectivization programme, 46% of agricultural land had been returned to its original owners and their heirs by early 1994. By 1999, according to the IMF, some 97.2% of agricultural land was privately owned. During 1990–2002, according to the World Bank, agricultural GDP declined, in real terms, by an average of 1.5% per year. However, real agricultural GDP increased by 21.2% in 2001 and by 3.0% in 2002.

INDUSTRY
In 2002 industry (including mining, manufacturing, construction, power and water) accounted for 35.6% of GDP and employed 29.5% of the working population. According to the World Bank, industrial GDP declined, in real terms, by an average of 0.7% annually in 1990–2002. Real industrial GDP increased by 7.4% in 2001 and by 7.0% in 2002.

Mining
The mining sector employed 1.6% of the employed labour force in 2002. As part of a major restructuring of the sector, in 1997–98 operations were halted in 180 mines and quarries. In 1999 the World Bank granted a loan worth US $44.5m. to assist the Government in meeting the costs involved in the closure of a further 29 mines. Brown coal, hard coal, salt, iron ore, bauxite, copper, lead and zinc are mined. Onshore production of crude petroleum began to increase in the early 1990s, and in 2002 Romania had proven reserves of 955m. barrels of petroleum, remaining the largest producer in central and eastern Europe, despite a dramatic decline in production. At the beginning of the 1990s seven offshore platforms were operating in the Romanian sector of the Black Sea, accounting for more than 10% of annual hydrocarbon

production. Methane gas is also extracted. In April 1996 Romania launched an international invitation to tender for exploration and production rights on 15 new blocks in the Black Sea. Mining output decreased by 9.6% in 1999, but increased by 7.3% in 2000.

Manufacturing

Manufacturing employed 21.4% of the employed labour force in 2002 and accounted for some 25.7% of GDP. The sector is based mainly on the metallurgical, mechanical engineering, chemical and timber-processing industries. However, many industries (particularly iron and steel) have been hampered by shortages of electricity and raw materials. According to the World Bank, manufacturing GDP increased, in real terms, by an average of 0.1% annually in 1994–2001. Real sectoral GDP increased by some 6.2% in 2000, and by 8.0% in 2001.

Energy

According to the World Bank, in 2000 37.2% of gross electricity production was derived from coal, 28.5% from hydroelectric power, 17.3% was derived from natural gas and 10.5% from nuclear power. The initial unit of Romania's first nuclear power station, at Cernavoda, became operational in December 1996; the second unit was scheduled for completion in 2005. According to provisional data, 32.5% of energy resources were imported in 2000. In 2001 mineral fuels accounted for 12.7% of total imports.

SERVICES

In 2002 the services sector contributed 49.6% of GDP and engaged 34.1% of the working labour force. According to the World Bank, the GDP of the services sector declined, in real terms, by an average of 1.5% per year in 1990–2001; the real GDP of the sector increased by 6.7% in 2000, but declined by 5.7% in 2001.

EXTERNAL TRADE

In 2002 Romania recorded a visible trade deficit of US $2,611m., while there was a deficit of $1,525m. on the current account of the balance of payments. In 2001 the principal source of imports was Italy, which provided 20.0% of the total. Germany was also a major supplier, as were Russia and France. The main market for exports in that year was Italy (accounting for 25.1%); other important purchasers were Germany, France and the United Kingdom. In 2001 the principal imports were basic manufactures (particularly textile yarn and fabrics), machinery and transport equipment, mineral fuels and lubricants and miscellaneous manufactured articles. Electric machinery and apparatus, clothing and accessories, basic manufactures and machinery and transport equipment were among the country's major exports.

GOVERNMENT FINANCE

The overall budget deficit for 2001 was 35,803,000m. lei (equivalent to some 3.1% of GDP). Romania's total external debt at the end of 2001 was US $11,653m., of which $6,682m. was long-term public debt. In that year the cost of debt-servicing was equivalent to 18.8% of revenue from exports of goods and services. The annual rate of inflation averaged 56.7% in 1992–2002; the rate of inflation was 34.5% in 2001 and 22.5% in 2002. In 2002 8.4% of the labour force were registered as unemployed.

INTERNATIONAL ECONOMIC RELATIONS

Romania is a member (as a 'Country of Operations') of the European Bank for Reconstruction and Development (EBRD). In February 1993 Romania signed an association agreement with the European Union (EU). Romania formally applied for full membership of the EU in June 1995; accession negotiations commenced in February 2000.

SURVEY AND PROSPECTS

During the 1990s Romania's progress towards the development of a market economic system was considerably slower than that of many other post-communist states of central and eastern Europe. The economy contracted for a third consecutive year in 1999, and the Yugoslav conflict adversely affected the financial situation, severely disrupting regional trade and transport infrastructure. Further difficulties arose in 2000, in the form of increased petroleum prices and the worst drought for 50 years, which had a severe impact on agricultural production.

An extensive programme, announced in 2001, for the privatization of 63 large state-owned enterprises, encountered strong opposition, although in October the Government succeeded in divesting the Sidex steel works at Galaţi, in what was Romania's most significant privatization to date. Overall, Romania's economic prospects were regarded as more positive, and in late October the IMF, which had been withholding further assistance pending substantive progress on reform, approved a stand-by credit of some US $383m. None the less, many observers considered membership of the EU by 2007 to be a challenging objective.

During 2003 the process of privatization accelerated, particularly in the industrial sector, and inflation continued to decline as macroeconomic stability increased. In March the euro replaced the US dollar as its reference currency for the exchange rate of the leu. In October, in a report on the country's progress towards accession, the EU stated that Romania could be considered to have achieved the status of a functioning market economy provided it continued to consolidate the progress that it had made, while implementing further structural reforms. Some concern was expressed over the financial implications of the large increase in the minimum-wage level, introduced in early 2003, although this measure was expected to lead to increased domestic consumption, which would be a primary factor in stimulating economic growth.

Upon Romania's fulfilment of its stand-by agreement in October, the IMF commended the country for its satisfactory implementation of the arrangement, but warned against any further increase in the minimum wage in 2004, owing to the effect of strengthening domestic demand upon the current-account deficit. Moreover, reforms continued to be necessary in the public-administration and judicial sectors if a more efficient business environment was to be created. In 2003 GDP increased by an estimated 4.9%. In 2004 Romania aimed to focus efforts on increased privatization and restructuring, particularly in the energy sector, and the further reduction of inflation. The Government forecast economic growth of 5.5% in that year.

Russian Federation

The Russian Federation, or Russia, is situated mainly in North Eurasia. Following the overthrow of the Tsar, in March 1917, and of the subsequent Provisional Government, in November, the Russian Soviet Federative Socialist Republic (RSFSR) was proclaimed. In 1922 the RSFSR joined the Belarusian, Ukrainian and Transcaucasian Soviet Socialist Republics in a Union of Soviet Socialist Republics (USSR) that eventually numbered 15 constituents. In 1991 the USSR disintegrated and the Russian Federation, as the RSFSR was formally renamed, became one of the 11 founder members of the Commonwealth of Independent States. Moscow is the capital. The official language is Russian.

Area and population
Area: 17,075,400 sq km
Population (mid-2002): 144,070,784
Population density (mid-2002): 8.4 per sq km
Life expectancy (years at birth, 2002): 64.8 (males 58.4; females 72.1)

Finance

GDP in current prices: 2002): US $346,520m. ($2,405 per head)
Real GDP growth (2002): 4.3%
Inflation (annual average, 2002): 15.8%
Currency: new rouble

Economy

In 2002, according to estimates by the World Bank, Russia's gross national income (GNI), measured at average 2000–02 prices, was US $307,913m., equivalent to $2,140 per head (or $7,820 per head on an international purchasing-power parity basis). Between 1990 and 2002, it was estimated, the population declined by an annual average of 0.2%, while gross domestic product (GDP) per head, decreased, in real terms, at an average annual rate of 2.4%. According to the World Bank, overall GDP decreased, in real terms, at an average annual rate of 2.7% in 1990–2002. However, real GDP increased by 5.0% in 2001 and by 4.3% in 2002.

AGRICULTURE

Agriculture and forestry (excluding fishing) contributed an estimated 5.2% of GDP in 2003. In 2002 6.0% of the employed labour force were engaged in the agricultural sector. The principal agricultural products are grain, potatoes and livestock. In 1990 the Russian Government began a programme to encourage the development of private farming, to replace the state and collective farms. Legislation to permit the sale and purchase of agricultural land from 2003 was approved by the State Duma in June 2002. According to World Bank estimates, real agricultural GDP declined at an average annual rate of 3.3% in 1992–2001; however, the GDP of the sector increased by 5.0% in 2000 and by 10.8% in 2001.

INDUSTRY

Industry (including mining, manufacturing, construction, power and fishing) contributed an estimated 35.2% of GDP in 2003. In 2000 the industrial sector (excluding fishing) provided 29.7% of employment. According to estimates by the World Bank, industrial GDP declined, in real terms, by an annual average of 5.5% in 1990–2001. Industrial GDP increased by 11.8% in 2000 and by 6.0% in 2001.

Mining

Mining and quarrying employed 1.7% of the total labour force in 2000. Russia has considerable reserves of energy-bearing minerals, including one-third of the world's natural gas reserves and substantial deposits of petroleum, coal and peat. It also has large supplies of palladium, platinum and rhodium. Other minerals exploited include bauxite, cobalt, copper, diamonds, gold, iron ore, mica, nickel and tin.

Manufacturing

In 2000 the manufacturing sector provided 18.5% of employment. In 1999 the principal branches of manufacturing, measured by gross value of output, were food products (accounting for 18.9% of the total), transport equipment (12.0%), iron and steel (11.4%), machinery (9.2%), and chemicals and chemical products (9.6%). Production in the sector decreased, in real terms, by 14.5% in 1996, but increased by 1.6% in 1997.

Energy

Electric energy is derived from petroleum-, gas- and coal-fired power stations, nuclear power stations and hydroelectric installations. In 2000 Russia's 29 nuclear reactors supplied some 14.9% of total electricity generation, while coal accounted for some 20.0% of Russia's generating capacity, hydroelectric power accounted for 18.7% of electricity production, and 42.3% of the country's generating capacity originated from natural gas. Russia is a major exporter of natural gas and crude petroleum, and Russia's largest company, Gazprom, is also the world's largest producer of natural gas. Countries of the CIS remain highly dependent on Russia for imports of these fuels. However, owing to high levels of non-payment from certain countries for these deliveries, from the late 1990s Russia sought, with some success, to increase its exports of mineral fuels to other countries, particularly to the countries of central and western Europe. The construction of the 'Blue Stream' pipeline, which was to carry natural gas from Novorossiisk, Krasnodar Krai, in southern Russia, to Ankara, Turkey, was completed in October 2002, and was expected to facilitate further growth in Russia's energy exports. Agreement to construct a pipeline to carry petroleum from Siberia to the People's Republic of China was reached in mid-2003. Imports of fuel comprised just 2.4% of the value of Russia's total merchandise imports in 2001.

SERVICES

The services sector contributed an estimated 59.6% of GDP in 2003, and provided 56.4% of employment in 2000. According to estimates by the World Bank, the GDP of the services sector declined, in real terms, at an annual average rate of 0.2% in 1992–2001. However, the GDP of the sector increased by 6.7% in 2000, and by 4.3% in 2001.

EXTERNAL TRADE

In 2002 Russia recorded a visible trade surplus of US $46,281m., and there was a surplus of $31,091m. on the current account of the balance of payments. In 2001 the most significant source of imports was Germany (accounting for 13.9% of the total), followed by Ukraine (9.1%) and the USA (7.7%). The largest market for Russian exports in 2001 was Germany (purchasing 8.4% of the total), followed by Italy (7.0%) and Ukraine (6.9%). (No separate figures for trade with Belarus, which is a leading trading partner of Russia, for both imports and exports, were available in that year.) The principal exports in 2001 were mineral fuels and lubricants (comprising 53.9% of Russia's total exports), followed by basic manufactures (15.8%), and machinery and transport equipment (6.3%). The principal imports in 2001 were machinery and transport equipment (accounting for 27.5% of total imports), followed by food and live animals (16.1%), basic manufactures (13.5%), and chemicals and related products (12.1%).

GOVERNMENT FINANCE

In 2002 Russia recorded a surplus on the federal budget of 150,475.1m. roubles, equivalent to 1.7% of GDP. At the end of 2001 the country's total external debt was US $152,649m., of which $101,918m. was long-term public debt. In that year the cost of debt-servicing was equivalent to 14.5% of the value of exports of goods and services. In 1991–2001 the average annual rate of inflation was 154.4%. Following the collapse of the rouble in 1998, the rate of inflation was 85.7% in 1999, but it declined to 20.8% in 2000, to 18.6% in 2001, to 15.1% in 2002 and to 12.0% in 2003. In December 2001 about 1.1m. people were registered as unemployed, although, according to the methodology of the International Labour Organization, the actual number of unemployed was some 5.1m. in October 2002, compared with 7.1m. in 2000.

INTERNATIONAL ECONOMIC RELATIONS

Russia became a member of the World Bank and the IMF in 1992. Russia is also a member (as a 'Country of Operations') of the European Bank for Reconstruction and Development (EBRD). In June 1994 Russia signed an agreement of partnership and co-operation with the European Union (EU). Russia is also pursuing membership of the World Trade Organization (WTO). Russia joined the Asia-Pacific Economic Co-operation forum (APEC) in November 1998.

SURVEY AND PROSPECTS

After the dissolution of the USSR, a programme of economic reforms was initiated to effect the transition from a centrally planned economy to a market-orientated system. Following a severe financial crisis, in August 1998 Russia defaulted on its rouble-denominated bonds, and announced unilateral terms for debt conversion. However, sustained growth was recorded in subsequent years, although analysts expressed concern that this growth was largely attributable to high international prices for petroleum, natural gas and metals, Russia's principal exports, rather than the result of structural reforms or technological or industrial innovations, despite the existence in Russia of a well-educated work-force.

In November 2000 an IMF mission failed to agree terms for further lending, after the Government proved unwilling to accept its recommendations for banking reform, although the World Bank approved loans worth US $537m. in July 2001. The administration of President Vladimir Putin, from 2000, appeared to implement economic reforms more consistently than had the Yeltsin administration in the 1990s, with significant reforms in the areas of land ownership, fiscal procedure and banking being introduced in 2001–03; proposals to implement wide-ranging reforms to the electricity sector were approved by the President in early 2003, in accordance with which the domestic electricity market was to be liberalized by the mid-2000s. The opening of a hydroelectric power station at Bureya, in Amur Oblast, in the Russian Far East, in mid-2003, was regarded as a significant measure to ensure reliable power supplies to a region which had, hitherto, been prone to intermittent power shortages. Moreover, in mid-2003 Russia was removed from the list of 'non-compliant' countries and territories of the Financial Action Task Force on Money Laundering (FATF), following the introduction of measures intended to hinder money 'laundering'.

A major programme of privatization, which was to continue until 2008, commenced in early 2003, when Putin announced that a priority of his administration was to increase Russia's GDP two-fold, over a period of 10 years. Meanwhile, a decline in both the rate of inflation and the unemployment rate in the early 2000s appeared to mark the onset of relative stability. None the less, surveys by the German-based NGO, Transparency International, indicated that Russia continued to be perceived as a highly corrupt country in 2003. Although the merger in early 2003 of two Russian petroleum companies, Sidanco and Tyumen Oil Co (TNK), with the Russian interests of British Petroleum (BP—United Kingdom), to form TNK-BP, represented an unprecedented level of co-operation between Russian and foreign investors in the Russian petroleum sector, concern was expressed that the subsequent opening of several judicial investigations into the petroleum company Yukos and the detention of its Chairman, Mikhail Khodorkovskii, on suspicion of fraud and tax evasion, would deter further international involvement in the sector, or even wider foreign investment in the country, although the Government reiterated that it had no intention of reversing the results of the privatization programmes that had taken place since the early 1990s.

Rwanda

The Rwandan Republic is situated in eastern central Africa. The country became independent from Belgium in 1962. Tension between the majority Hutu and their former overlords, the Tutsi, has existed for many years. Rwanda's recent history has been dominated by the repercussions of events in 1994, when, following the death of President Juvénal Habyarimana, a campaign of retributive violence by the presidential guard against Habyarimana's political opponents, together with massacres of Tutsi civilians by 'Interahamwe' militias, escalated into an effective pogrom. Transitional government ended with the adoption of a new Constitution and elections in 2003. Kigali is the capital. French, English and Kinyarwanda are the languages in official use.

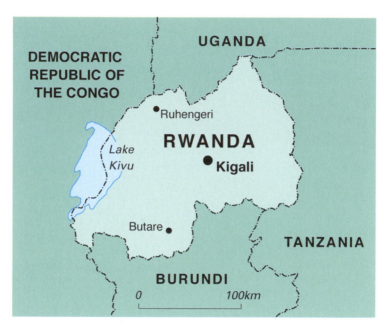

Area and population
Area: 26,338 sq km
Population (mid-2002): 8,163,000
Population density (mid-2002): 309.9 per sq km
Life expectancy (years at birth, 2002): 44.4 (males 41.9; females 46.8)

Finance
GDP in current prices: 2002): US $1,736m. ($213 per head)
Real GDP growth (2002): 9.4%
Inflation (annual average, 2002): 2.5%
Currency: Rwanda franc

Economy

In 2002, according to estimates by the World Bank, Rwanda's gross national income (GNI), measured at average 2000–02 prices, was US $1,850m., equivalent to $230 per head (or $1,210 per head on an international purchasing-power parity basis). During 1990–2002, it was estimated, the population increased at an average annual rate of 1.4%, while gross domestic product (GDP) per head rose, in real terms, by an average of 0.1% per year. Overall GDP increased, in real terms, at an average annual rate of 1.4% in 1990–2002; growth in 2002 was 9.4%.

AGRICULTURE

Agriculture (including forestry and fishing) contributed an estimated 41.6% of GDP in 2002. An estimated 90.5% of the labour force were employed in the sector (mainly at subsistence level) in that year. The principal food crops are plantains, sweet potatoes, cassava, sorghum and dry beans. The principal cash crops are tea (which provided 37.6% of total export earnings in 2002), coffee (which accounted for 24.9% of export earnings in 2002), pyrethrum and quinquina. Goats and cattle are traditionally the principal livestock raised. Agricultural GDP increased by an average of 4.0% per year during 1990–2002; growth in 2002 was 10.4%.

INDUSTRY

Industry (including mining, manufacturing, power and construction) employed about 3.4% of the labour force in 1990, and provided an estimated 21.8% of GDP in 2002. Industrial GDP declined at an average annual rate of 2.3% during 1990–2002; GDP in the industrial sector increased by 7.9% in 2002.

Mining

Mining and quarrying, it was estimated, contributed 0.5% of GDP in 2002, and the sector employed 0.1% of the labour force in 1989. Cassiterite (a tin-bearing ore) is Rwanda's principal mineral resource. There are also reserves of wolframite (a tungsten-bearing ore), columbo-tantalite, gold and beryl, and work has begun on the exploitation of natural gas reserves beneath Lake Kivu, which are believed to be among the largest in the world. Mining GDP declined at an estimated average annual rate of 0.4% in 1990–2002, according to the Banque Nationale du Rwanda. Mining GDP increased by 16.6% in 2001, but declined by an estimated 5.7% in 2002.

Manufacturing

Manufacturing employed only 1.4% of the labour force in 1989, but provided an estimated 10.4% of GDP in 2002. The principal branches of manufacturing are beverages and tobacco, food products and basic consumer goods, including soap, textiles and plastic products. Manufacturing GDP declined by an average of 4.3% per year during 1990–2002; however, GDP in the manufacturing sector increased by 9.0% in 2002.

Energy

Electrical energy is derived almost entirely from hydroelectric power. In 1999 Rwanda imported 35.5% of its electricity, but subsequently benefited from the completion of the Ruzizi-II plant (a joint venture with Burundi and the Democratic

Republic of the Congo). Imports of fuels and lubricants comprised 15.4% of the total value of merchandise imports in 2002.

SERVICES

The services sector contributed an estimated 36.6% of GDP in 2002, and engaged 6.7% of the employed labour force in 1989. The GDP of the services sector increased at an average annual rate of 0.8% during 1990–2002; growth in the services sector was 8.8% in 2002.

EXTERNAL TRADE

In 2002 Rwanda recorded a visible trade deficit of US $166.1m., and there was a deficit of $126.2m. on the current account of the balance of payments. In 1999 the principal source of imports (13.1%) was Japan; other major suppliers were Belgium, Kenya and Saudi Arabia. In the same year the principal market for exports (62.4%) was Kenya; other significant purchasers were Tanzania and Germany. The principal exports in 2002 were tea, coffee and columbo-tantalite. The main imports in that year were consumer goods, intermediate goods, capital goods, and fuels and lubricants.

GOVERNMENT FINANCE

An overall budgetary deficit of 40,200m. Rwanda francs (equivalent to 5.5% of GDP) was recorded in 2001. A budgetary deficit of 16,100m. Rwanda francs (equivalent to 2.0% of GDP) was estimated for 2002. At the end of 2001 Rwanda's external debt totalled US $1,283m., of which $1,163m. was long-term public debt. The cost of debt-servicing in that year was equivalent to 11.3% of the value of exports of goods and services. In 1990–2002 the average annual rate of inflation was 12.3%. Consumer prices increased by 2.5% in 2002 and by 7.0% in 2003.

INTERNATIONAL ECONOMIC RELATIONS

Rwanda is a member of the Organization for the Management and Development of the Kagera River Basin, and, with Burundi and the Democratic Republic of the Congo, is a founding member of the Economic Community of the Great Lakes Countries and of the Common Market for Eastern and Southern Africa. The country is also a member of the International Coffee Organization.

SURVEY AND PROSPECTS

Rwanda has traditionally relied heavily on foreign aid, owing to an economic development impeded by ethnic and political unrest. The genocide of early 1994 resulted in the destruction of the country's economic base and of prospects of attracting private and external investment. With assistance from the international financial community, the new Government, which was established in July, initiated measures to resettle more than 2m. displaced civilians and to reconstruct the economy. In 1998 a three-year Enhanced Structural Adjustment Facility was approved by the IMF. By the end of 1999 Rwanda had made considerable progress in rehabilitating and stabilizing the economy; government revenue (negligible in 1994) had recovered, and a reduced rate of inflation had been sustained, while an extensive privatization programme had been initiated with the support of the World Bank.

In late 2000, following a meeting with international financial donor institutions, Rwanda qualified for debt relief, under the initiative of the IMF and World Bank for heavily indebted poor countries (HIPCs). In October 2001 the IMF approved credit to

Rwanda, under a Poverty Reduction and Growth Facility (PRGF). In August 2002 the IMF approved a further three-year credit arrangement under the PRGF, and extended additional assistance to enable the Government to meet its debt-servicing obligations. Estimated economic growth of 3.5% in 2003 was at its lowest level since 1994, following strong recovery in previous years. A rise in the rate of inflation at the end of 2003 was principally attributed to increased money supply, diminished agricultural performance and currency weakness. The authorities reported that tariff reductions on commodities, implemented as part of regional trade liberalization, had caused a progressive negative impact on state revenue.

Presidential and legislative elections in the second half of 2003 resulted in little political change, with the Front patriotique rwandais of President Paul Kagame continuing to dominate government organs. In November the IMF suspended the PRGF arrangement, after the Government failed to meet its principal fiscal targets. Resumption of the poverty reduction strategy, followed by negotiation of a further credit facility with the IMF in the second half of 2004, was the main priority for the authorities. (The country continued to benefit under the HIPC initiative.) Increased projected levels of government budgetary expenditure were allocated principally to social-sector spending, including funding for the introduction of primary education, military demobilization and district administrations. The Government had, in late 2003, introduced a five-year public works programme to rehabilitate rural infra-structure through mass temporary employment. Privatization of the state-owned telecommunications company was to proceed in the first half of 2004. (At this time only 30 of the 74 state-owned enterprises designated for privatization had been sold or liquidated.) However, government insistence on higher budgetary expenditure, and thus an increased fiscal deficit, was likely to hamper a compromise arrangement with the IMF.

Saint Christopher and Nevis

The Federation of Saint Christopher and Nevis is situated at the northern end of the Leeward Islands chain of the West Indies. Saint Christopher, settled in 1623, was Britain's first West Indian colony. Nevis was settled by the British in 1628. The island of Anguilla was joined to the territory in 1816 and separated in 1980. In 1983 Saint Christopher and Nevis became an independent state, under a federal Constitution. Upon independence Saint Christopher and Nevis became a full member of the Commonwealth. Basseterre is the capital. The official language is English.

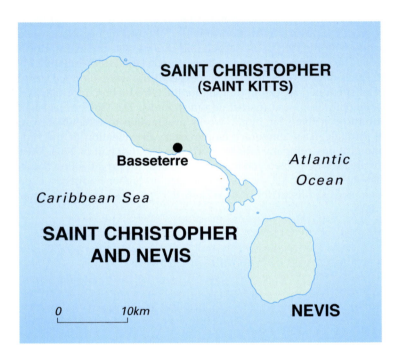

Area and population
Area: 269 sq km
Population (mid-2002): 45,980
Population density (mid-2002): 170.7 per sq km
Life expectancy (years at birth, 2002): 70.4 (males 68.7; females 72.2)

Finance
GDP in current prices: 2002): US $340m. ($7,393 per head)
Real GDP growth (2002): –4.3%
Inflation (annual average, 2000): 2.1%
Currency: Eastern Caribbean dollar

Economy

In 2002, according to estimates by the World Bank, Saint Christopher and Nevis's gross national income (GNI), measured at average 2000–02 prices, was US \$293.1m., equivalent to \$6,370 per head (or \$9,780 per head on an international purchasing-power parity basis). During 1990–2002 the population increased by an average of 0.8% per year, while over the same period, it was estimated, gross domestic product (GDP) per head increased, in real terms, at an average annual rate of 2.5%. Overall GDP increased, in real terms, by an average of 3.9% annually in 1990–2002; according to the Eastern Caribbean Central Bank (ECCB), growth was 2.3% in 2001 and 0.8% in 2002.

AGRICULTURE

Agriculture (including forestry and fishing) contributed 3.1% of GDP in 2002. Some 14.7% of the working population were employed in the agriculture sector (including sugar manufacturing) in 1994. Major crops include coconuts and sea-island cotton, although some vegetables are also exported. The principal cash crop is sugar cane. Sugar and sugar products accounted for 21% of total export earnings in 2001. The cane harvest increased by 49.8% in 1997, owing to favourable weather, increased land under cultivation, and more efficient methods of cultivation and harvesting. Unfavourable weather conditions and a decrease in acreage under cultivation contributed, however, to a decline of 21.3% in 1998, and by 2000 production had fallen further, to 188,373 metric tons, remaining at about the same level in 2001 and 2002. In spite of a guaranteed European Union (EU) sugar price, which is well above world market levels, the sugar industry survives only as a result of government subsidies, which were equivalent to 3.5% of GDP in 2001. Large areas formerly used for sugar are now designated for tourism, and the Government is expected to announce the closure of the industry within the next few years, making provision for retraining of sugar industry employees. Diversification in agriculture, the principal productive sector of the economy, has been encouraged in order to reduce the economy's vulnerability to fluctuations in the world price of sugar. Important crops include yams, sweet potatoes, groundnuts, onions, sweet peppers, cabbages, carrots and bananas. Fishing is an increasingly important commercial activity. Agricultural GDP increased by an annual average of 2.5% in 1990–2002. According to the ECCB, the real value of agricultural GDP decreased by 7.8% in 2000, owing to hurricane damage and the decline in production in the sugar cane sector, but increased by 11.1% in 2001 and by 13.3% in 2002.

INDUSTRY

Industry (including mining, manufacturing, construction and public utilities) provided 27.8% of GDP in 2002. Excluding sugar manufacturing, the sector employed 21.0% of the working population in 1994. Activity is mainly connected with the construction industry (the real GDP of which expanded by 4.2% in 2001 but contracted by 3.5% in 2002). Real industrial GDP increased by an annual average of 5.1% in 1990–2002. In 2001 the GDP of the sector expanded by 4.7%, but it decreased by 3.5% in 2002.

Manufacturing

Manufacturing provided 9.1% of GDP in 2002, and non-sugar manufacturing employed 7.8% of the working population in 1994. Apart from the sugar industry (the production of raw sugar and ethyl alcohol), the principal manufactured products are garments, electrical components, food products, beer and other beverages. The sector recorded average annual growth of 3.9% during 1990–2002. In 2001, according to the ECCB, real manufacturing GDP increased by 6.6%, but, in 2002, decreased by 4.0%.

Energy
The islands are dependent upon imports of fuel and energy (7.5% of total imports in 2001) for their energy requirements.

SERVICES
The services sector contributed 69.1% of GDP in 2002, and employed 64.4% of the working population in 1994. Tourism is a major contributor to the economy and some 12.8% of the employed population were engaged in tourism-related activities in 1994. In 2000, although there was a 14.1% growth in the number of cruise-ship passengers, the number of stop-over tourists decreased by 13.0% to 73,100. Furthermore, tourist revenues declined by 13.6% in that year. The industry recovered slightly in 2001: revenues increased by 5.8% and the number of stop-over arrivals (74,200) and cruise-ship visitors (252,200) also rose. According to preliminary figures, however, visitor expenditure decreased by 6.1% in 2002. In March 2003 a new 900-room resort at Frigate Bay, Saint Christopher opened, increasing the number of hotel rooms on the island by some 60%. The real GDP of the services sector increased at an average annual rate of 3.8% in 1990–2002; growth was 0.2% in 2001 and 2.2% in 2002.

EXTERNAL TRADE
In 2001 Saint Christopher and Nevis recorded a visible trade deficit of EC $111.6m. and there was a deficit of $96.5m. on the current account of the balance of payments. The USA was the islands' principal trading partner in 2001, supplying 50.5% of imports and purchasing 71.5% of exports. Trade with the United Kingdom and with other Caribbean states is also important. The sugar industry is the country's leading exporter (accounting for a 21.0% of total export revenues in 2001), and the principal imports are machinery and transport equipment, basic manufactures and food and live animals.

GOVERNMENT FINANCE
In 2002 the central Government of Saint Christopher and Nevis recorded an esti-mated budgetary deficit of EC $123.0m., equivalent to 15.2% of GDP. The country's total external debt was estimated to be US $189.1m. at the end of 2001, of which US $186.0m. was long-term public debt. In that year the cost of debt-servicing was equivalent to 13.5% of the value of exports of goods and services. The annual rate of inflation averaged 3.3% in 1990–2000; consumer prices increased by 1.5% in 2001 and by 1.8% in 2002. There is, however, a recurring problem of labour shortages in the agricultural sector (notably the sugar industry) and the construction industry, and the rate of unemployment (reported to be around 10% in early 2003) is mitigated by mass emigration, particularly from Nevis: remittances from abroad provide an important source of revenue.

INTERNATIONAL ECONOMIC RELATIONS

Saint Christopher and Nevis is a member of the Caribbean Community and Common Market (CARICOM), and of the Organisation of Eastern Caribbean States (OECS). The ECCB is based in Basseterre. In 2001 a regional stock exchange, the Eastern Caribbean Securities Exchange, opened in Basseterre. Saint Christopher and Nevis is a party to the Cotonou Agreement, the successor agreement to the Lomé Convention, signed in June 2000 between the EU and a group of developing countries.

SURVEY AND PROSPECTS

Successive Governments have attempted to reduce economic dependence on the cultivation and processing of sugar cane, the traditional industry of the islands. The most rapidly developing industry has been tourism, while the development of light manufacturing, particularly of electronic components and textiles, has also helped to broaden the islands' economic base. It is also hoped that an information technology industry can be established. The economic upturn in 1999 was, to a significant extent, the result of increased investment in reconstruction following the damage caused by 'Hurricane Georges' in September 1998, although increased imports of construction materials were expected, in combination with the decline in sugar exports and in electronic components, to contribute to the further deterioration of the trade deficit. The growth in the construction sector was sustained until 2002, when the sector contracted.

In May 2000 the Financial Stability Forum categorized Saint Christopher and Nevis's banking supervision in the lowest group. In June the Organisation for Economic Co-operation and Development (OECD) included the country in a list of tax 'havens' and in the same month it was also included on a list of 'non-co-operative' governments in attempts to combat money-laundering by the Financial Action Task Force (FATF, based in the OECD Secretariat). In an attempt to ensure the country's removal from the list, Prime Minister Douglas had announced a series of financial reforms and, as a result of these measures, in June 2002 the FATF removed Saint Christopher and Nevis from the list. In April 2003 a report indicated that the islands' offshore banking operations had been halved as a result of the FATF action and the subsequent financial reforms.

In common with similar countries in the region, Saint Christopher and Nevis experienced an economic slowdown in 2002, with growth of only 0.8% recorded; contractions in the construction and tourism sectors contributed to the weak performance of the economy. Despite fears that the US-led military campaign to remove the regime of Saddam Hussain in Iraq could contribute to a real decline in GDP in 2003, in June of that year the ECCB estimated positive annual growth of around 1.9%. The economy was boosted in particular by a recovering construction industry, which benefited from a EC $20m. National Housing Corporation home-construction programme. In his December 2003 budget speech the Prime Minister announced a series of taxation measure to stabilize the Government's fiscal position over the next five years, in order to reduce the ratio of debt to GDP to under 60% by 2009.

Saint Lucia

Saint Lucia is the second largest of the Windward Islands group of the West Indies, in the Caribbean Sea. The island became a British colony in 1814 and remained under British rule for the next 165 years. Saint Lucia became independent in 1979, remaining within the Commonwealth. At a general election held in 1997 15 years of governance by the United Workers' Party was ended by the victory of the Saint Lucia Labour Party (SLP). The SLP achieved another, convincing electoral victory in 2001. Castries is the capital. The official language is English.

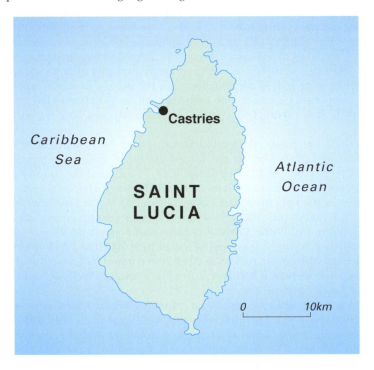

Area and population
Area: 616 sq km
Population (mid-2002): 158,520
Population density (mid-2002): 257.2 per sq km
Life expectancy (years at birth, 2002): 72.2 (males 69.8; females 74.4)

Finance
GDP in current prices: 2002): US $660m. ($4,162 per head)
Real GDP growth (2002): –0.5%
Inflation (annual average, 2002): 1.6%
Currency: Eastern Caribbean dollar

Economy

In 2002, according to estimates by the World Bank, Saint Lucia's gross national income (GNI), measured at average 2000–02 prices, was US $608.6m., equivalent to $3,840 per head (or $5,000 per head on an international purchasing-power parity basis). During 1990–2002, it was estimated, the population increased by an annual average rate of 1.4%, while gross domestic product (GDP) per head increased, in real terms, by an average rate of 0.4% per year. Overall GDP increased, in real terms, at an average annual rate of 1.8% in 1990–2002; according to the Eastern Caribbean Central Bank (ECCB), real GDP decreased by 4.6% in 2001, but increased by 0.1% in 2002.

AGRICULTURE

In 2002 agriculture (including hunting, forestry and fishing) accounted for 6.0% of GDP and employed some 19.5% of the active working population in 2000. Despite the decline in banana industry, the fruit remains Saint Lucia's principal cash crop, and in 2001 accounted for 33.5% of the total value of domestic merchandise exports (compared with 66.3% in 1996). Other important crops include coconuts, mangoes, citrus fruit, cocoa and spices. Commercial fishing is being developed and in August 2001 Japan granted US $10.6m. towards the rehabilitation and improvement of fishery facilities in the Choiseul and Soufrière districts. During 1990–2002 real agricultural GDP decreased by an annual average of 6.1%, largely as a result of a 9.2% decline in the banana sector. The sector's real GDP decreased by 22.6% in 2001 and by a further 1.0% in 2002.

INDUSTRY

Industry (including mining, manufacturing, public utilities and construction) accounted for 16.7% of GDP in 2002 and the sector engaged an estimated 21.1% of the active working population in 2000. During 1990–2002 industrial GDP increased by an estimated annual average of 2.7%. In 2001 the sector's real GDP decreased by 3.7%, and in 2002 by 0.6%. Construction contributed 7.2% to GDP in 2002. The sector demonstrated strong growth in the 1990s (average annual growth of 6.7% in 1990–99), but the construction sector's real GDP decreased by 5.0% in 2001 and by 4.8% in 2002.

Manufacturing

Manufacturing accounted for 4.5% of GDP in 2002, and employed 10.3% of the employed population in 2000. The principal manufacturing industries, which have been encouraged by the establishment of 'free zones', include the processing of agricultural products, the assembly of electronic components and the production of garments, plastics, paper and packaging (associated with banana production), beer, rum and other beverages. During 1990–2002 the sector's real GDP decreased by an annual average of 0.9%. Real manufacturing GDP decreased by 5.0% in 2002.

Energy

Energy is traditionally derived from imported hydrocarbon fuels (mineral fuels and lubricants comprised 10.7% of total imports in 2001). There is a petroleum storage and transhipment terminal on the island.

SERVICES

The services sector contributed 77.3% of GDP in 2002 and engaged an estimated 56.9% of those employed in 2000. Tourism is the most important of the service industries, and in 2002 tourist receipts of EC $691.7m. were equivalent to some 69.0% of the value of total exports of goods and services. In 2001 tourist arrivals increased by 2.1%, but a decrease of 8.3% was recorded in 2002 as the sector suffered from the effects of the global economic slowdown and the terrorist attacks on the USA in September 2001. The hotels and restaurant sector declined by 10.5% in 2001 and by a further 0.6% in 2002. During 1990–2002 the real GDP of the services sector increased by an annual average of 2.3%. The sector contracted by 2.3% in 2001, but increased by 0.6% in 2002.

EXTERNAL TRADE

In 2002 Saint Lucia recorded a visible trade deficit of EC $558.98m., and a deficit of EC $169.16m. on the current account of the balance of payments. The principal source of imports in 2001 was the USA (41.8% of the total); other important markets in that year were Trinidad and Tobago (15.8%) and the United Kingdom (9.0%). The principal market for exports is the United Kingdom, which received 47.3% of total exports in 2001; other major export markets were the USA (17.6%) and Barbados (13.4%). The Caribbean Community and Common Market (CARICOM) member states accounted for 25.2% of imports and of exports in 2001. Food and live animals (comprised mainly of bananas sent to the United Kingdom) are the principal export commodity, ahead of beverages and tobacco (mainly beer) and miscellaneous man-ufactured articles. The principal imports are foodstuffs, machinery and transport equipment and basic manufactures.

GOVERNMENT FINANCE

In 2002 there was an estimated overall budgetary deficit of EC $37.9m., equivalent to an estimated 2.1% of GDP. Saint Lucia's total external debt at the end of 2001 was US $237.9m., of which US $168.2m. was long-term public debt. In that year the cost of debt-servicing was equivalent to 7.1% of the value of exports of goods and services. The annual rate of inflation averaged 2.9% in 1990–2002; inflation averaged 0.1% in 2001 and 1.6% in 2002. In 2001 the average rate of unemployment was 18.9%.

INTERNATIONAL ECONOMIC RELATIONS

Saint Lucia is a member of CARICOM, the ECCB, and of the Organisation of Eastern Caribbean States (OECS). Saint Lucia is also a member of the regional stock exchange, the Eastern Caribbean Securities Exchange (based in Saint Christopher and Nevis), established in 2001. Saint Lucia has been a strong advocate of closer political and economic integration within the Caribbean region. Saint Lucia is party to the Caribbean Basin Initiative (CBI) and to the Lomé Convention and its successor Cotonou Agreement.

SURVEY AND PROSPECTS

The Saint Lucian economy, which traditionally relied on the production of bananas for export, underwent considerable structural change at the end of the 20th century, with the emergence of services industries as the most important sector of the economy, while investment in the islands' infrastructure also benefited the tourism industry, which became the island's principal source of foreign exchange. The economy remained, however, heavily influenced by the agricultural sector, which was a significant source of employment, and was thus vulnerable to adverse climatic conditions and to fluctuations in prices, while the erosion of Saint Lucia's preferential access to European markets was also of considerable concern.

Banana production declined dramatically from the 1990s; in 1992 production was 135,291 metric tons, while in 2001 output stood at an estimated 74,000 tons. The decline was a result of poor climatic conditions and the retrenchments in the industry caused by increased international competition and lower market prices. In September 2002 'Hurricane Lili' destroyed about 50% of Saint Lucia's banana crop. Nevertheless, production for the year as a whole was estimated by the FAO to have increased to 92,000 tons. Following the hurricane, the beleaguered banana sector received assistance worth some US $8.5m. from the Caribbean Development Bank and the EU.

The positive economic growth achieved during the 1990s was primarily attributed to the expansion in the tourism and construction sectors. As part of its attempts to diversity the economy, the Government also intended to establish Saint Lucia as a centre for international financial services; the necessary legislation was approved in late 1999 and Saint Lucia's first 'offshore' bank opened in 2001. Following widely publicized accounting scandals in the USA and elsewhere, in November 2002 the Government tightened regulation of the sector. With over one-third of its visitor arrivals coming from North America, Saint Lucia was badly affected by the repercussions of the terrorist attacks in the USA in September 2001. An economic decline of 4.6% in 2001 was followed by slight growth, of 0.1%, in 2002. The economy was expected to maintain positive growth in 2003. The 2003/04 budget, announced in April 2003, included tax-reduction measures, designed to help the private sector weather any potentially negative repercussions for the tourism sector of the extension of the US-led 'war on terror' to Iraq.

Saint Pierre and Miquelon

The territory of Saint Pierre and Miquelon consists of a number of small islands, which lie close to the southern coast of Newfoundland, Canada, in the North Atlantic Ocean. These islands are the remnants of France's once extensive possessions in North America. They were confirmed as French territory in 1816, and gained departmental status in 1976. Since mid-1985 Saint Pierre and Miquelon has enjoyed the status of a Collectivité Territoriale. In 1991 an international arbitration tribunal awarded France an economic interest zone around the territory, totalling 8,700 sq km. Saint-Pierre is the capital. The language is French.

Area and population
Area: 242 sq km
Population (March 1999): 6,316
Population density (March 1999): 26.1 per sq km

Finance
Inflation (annual average, 2001): 2.3%
Currency: euro

Economy

AGRICULTURE

The soil and climatic conditions of Saint Pierre and Miquelon do not favour agricultural production, which is mainly confined to smallholdings, except for market-gardening and the production of eggs and chickens. The principal economic activity of the islands is traditionally fishing and related industries, which employed some 18.5% of the working population in 1996. However, the sector has been severely affected by disputes with Canada regarding territorial waters and fishing quotas; the absence of quotas in 1992–94 effectively halted industrial fishing. New arrangements have been to the detriment of Saint Pierre and Miquelon, although there is some optimism regarding potential for the exploitation of shell-fish, notably mussels and scallops, in the islands' waters. However, the total fish catch increased from 747 metric tons in 1996 to 6,485 tons in 2000. In 2001 the total catch fell to 3,802 tons.

INDUSTRY

Manufacturing

Processing of fish provides the basis for industrial activity, which engages about 41% of the labour force. It is dominated by one major company, which produces frozen and salted fish, and fish meal for fodder. Following a sharp decrease in production in the late 1980s, much of the fish processed is now imported.

Energy

Electricity is generated by two thermal power-stations, with a combined capacity of 23 MW. In 2000 plans were well advanced for the construction of a wind power-station, which, it was hoped, would generate some 40% of the islands' electricity requirements. The resolution of a boundary dispute between the Canadian provinces of Nova Scotia and Newfoundland and Labrador in 2002 accorded the islands about 500 sq miles of waters over the Gulf of Saint Lawrence basin, believed to contain substantial reserves of petroleum and gas.

SERVICES

The replenishment of ships' (mainly trawlers') supplies was formerly an important economic activity, but has now also been adversely affected by the downturn in the industrial fishing sector. Efforts were made to promote tourism, and the opening of the Saint Pierre–Montréal air route in 1987 led to an increase in air traffic in the 1990s. Tourist arrivals in 1998 were estimated at 11,994. In 1999 the completion of a new airport capable of accommodating larger aircraft further improved transport links.

EXTERNAL TRADE

In 1997 Saint Pierre and Miquelon recorded a trade deficit of 356m. French francs; total exports were 29m. francs. Most trade is with Canada and France and other countries of the European Union. The only significant exports are fish and fish meal. The principal imports in 1994 were fuel, building supplies and food from Canada. Items such as clothing and other consumer goods are generally imported from France.

SURVEY AND PROSPECTS

The annual rate of inflation averaged 3.2% in 1997–2001; consumer prices increased by 8.5% in 2000 and by 2.3% in 2001. Some 12.8% of the labour force were unemployed at the 1999 census.

Given the decline of the fishing sector, the development of the port of Saint-Pierre and the expansion of tourism (particularly from Canada and the USA) are regarded by Saint Pierre and Miquelon as the principal means of maintaining economic progress. The islands will, none the less, remain highly dependent on budgetary assistance from the French central Government.

Saint Vincent and the Grenadines

Saint Vincent and the Grenadines is situated in the Windward Islands group of the West Indies, in the Caribbean Sea. Britain gained possession of the islands during the 18th century. In 1969 Saint Vincent became an Associated State of the United Kingdom. The colony became fully independent, within the Commonwealth, as Saint Vincent and the Grenadines in 1978. At a general election held in 2001 the New Democratic Party, which had been in power since 1984, was defeated by the Unity Labour Party. Kingstown is the capital. The official language is English.

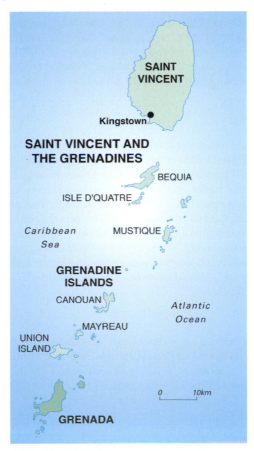

Area and population

Area: 389 sq km
Population (mid-2002): 116,720
Population density (mid-2002): 299.8 per sq km
Life expectancy (years at birth, 2002): 69.8 (males 67.8; females 71.9)

Finance
GDP in current prices: 2002): US $361m. ($3,089 per head)
Real GDP growth (2002): 0.7%
Inflation (annual average, 2002): 0.8%
Currency: Eastern Caribbean dollar

Economy

In 2002, according to estimates by the World Bank, Saint Vincent and the Grenadines' gross national income (GNI), measured at average 2000–02 prices, was US $328.7m., equivalent to $2,820 per head (or $5,100 per head on an international purchasing-power parity basis). During 1990–2002, it was estimated, the population increased by an annual average rate of 0.7%, while gross domestic product (GDP) per head increased, in real terms, by an average of 1.1% per year. Overall GDP increased, in real terms, by an average annual rate of 1.8% in 1990–2002; according to the Eastern Caribbean Central Bank (ECCB), real GDP decreased by 0.1% in 2001, but increased by 1.4% in 2002.

AGRICULTURE

Agriculture (including forestry and fishing) contributed an estimated 9.9% of GDP in 2002. The sector employed 25.1% of the working population at the census of 1991, and agricultural products account for the largest share of export revenue, although Vincentian crops were badly affected by mealybug infestation, which led to the suspension of some exports from 1996 to March 1999. The principal cash crop is bananas, which contributed an estimated 30.6% of the value of total domestic exports in 2002. Other important crops are arrowroot, sweet potatoes, tannias, taro, plantains and coconuts. According to ECCB, during 1990–2002 real agricultural GDP (growth of which is heavily reliant on weather conditions and banana production) decreased by an annual average of 1.9%. A decline of 7.7% was recorded in 2001, followed by an increase of 11.8% in 2002.

INDUSTRY

Industry (including mining, manufacturing, electricity, water and construction) employed 21.1% of the working population in 1991, and contributed an estimated 23.5% of GDP in 2002. During 1990–2002 real industrial GDP increased by an annual average of 2.6%; however, the sector expanded by 7.8% in 2001, but decreased by 1.3% in 2002.

Manufacturing

The manufacturing sector contributed an estimated 4.9% of GDP in 2002, and engaged 8.5% of the employed labour force in 1991. Apart from a garment industry and the assembling of electrical components, the most important activities involve the processing of agricultural products, including flour- and rice-milling, brewing, rum distillation, and processing dairy products. During 1990–2001 real manufacturing GDP decreased by an annual average of 0.5%. Real manufacturing GDP decreased by 1.8% in 2001 and by an estimated 8.0% in 2002.

Energy

Energy is derived principally from the use of hydrocarbon fuels (mineral fuels and lubricants accounted for an estimated 9.5% of total imports in 2002). The islands imported most of their energy requirements. There is, however, an important hydro-electric plant in Cumberland.

SERVICES

The services sector contributed an estimated 66.6% of GDP in 2002 and engaged 53.8% of the employed population at the time of the 1991 census. Tourism is the most important activity within the sector, but is smaller in scale than in most other Caribbean islands; estimated tourist receipts were equivalent to some 21.8% of GDP in 2002. Tourist activity remains concentrated in the Grenadines and caters for the luxury market. Visitors aboard yachts have traditionally been the most important sector, although the numbers of stop-over and cruise-ship visitors have increased in recent years. In 2000 the total number of visitors increased by 14.7%; however, in 2001 visitor arrivals declined by 0.8%, partly as a result of repercussions of the terrorist attacks on the USA in September of that year. In response to the downturn, the Hotel and Tourism Association announced in October that room rates would be reduced by 33%. None the less, the estimated number of visitor arrivals decreased by a further 3.3% in 2002. Aside from tourism, a small 'offshore' financial sector also contributes to the services sector. During 1990–2002 the real GDP of the services sector as a whole increased by an annual average of 4.1%; negative growth of 1.3% was recorded in 2001, followed by an increase of 1.0% in 2002.

EXTERNAL TRADE

In 2002 Saint Vincent and the Grenadines recorded an estimated visible trade deficit of US $110.3m., while there was a deficit of US $42.5m. on the current account of the balance of payments. The principal source of imports is the USA (accounting for an estimated 38.0% of the total in 2002). Other important suppliers in that year were Trinidad and Tobago (20.9%) and the United Kingdom (8.6%). The United Kingdom is the principal market for exports (accounting for an estimated 40.0% of total exports in 2002). Other important markets in that year were Trinidad and Tobago (10.2%), Saint Lucia (8.8%) and Barbados (8.5%). The principal exports in 2002 were bananas (accounting for an estimated 30.6% of exports), flour (16.1%) and rice (10.7%), while the principal imports were food and live animals (24.0%), machinery and transport equipment (19.1%) and basic manufactures (19.1%).

GOVERNMENT FINANCE

In 2002 there was an estimated overall budget deficit of EC $36m., equivalent to 3.7% of GDP. Saint Vincent and the Grenadines' total external debt was US $194.3m. at the end of 2001, of which US $163.0m. was long-term public debt. In 2002, according to the IMF, the cost of debt-servicing was equivalent to an estimated 6.6% of the value of exports of goods and services. The average annual rate of inflation was 1.4% in 1995–2002, and consumer prices increased by an estimated average of 0.8% in 2001 and 2002. At the 1991 census 20.0% of the labour force were unemployed. In February 2002 the IMF estimated that the rate of unemployment remained at a similar level.

In May 2000 the Financial Stability Forum categorized Saint Vincent and the Grenadines' banking supervision in the lowest group. In June the Organisation for Economic Co-operation and Development (OECD) included Saint Vincent and the

Grenadines in a report on countries with harmful tax policies and in the same month it was also included on a list of 'non-co-operative' governments in the fight against money-laundering, by the Financial Action Task Force (FATF—based at the Secretariat of OECD). In July the Offshore Finance Authority revoked the licences of six 'offshore' banks in an immediate response to an advisory by the US Department of the Treasury. The Government also announced that it would take further steps to improve its regulatory and advisory mechanisms and in September 2001 it was announced that the ECCB had agreed to supervise these improvements. Nevertheless, Saint Vincent and the Grenadines was not removed from OECD's harmful tax policy list until February 2002, at which time it was decided the country had made sufficient commitments to improve the transparency of its tax and regulatory systems. In May 2002 the Government established a Financial Intelligence Unit to counter money-laundering and in June 2003 Saint Vincent and the Grenadines was finally removed from the FATF's blacklist.

INTERNATIONAL ECONOMIC RELATIONS

Saint Vincent and the Grenadines is a member of the ECCB, the Caribbean Community and Common Market (CARICOM), which seeks to encourage regional development, particularly by increasing trade between member states, and of the Organisation of Eastern Caribbean States (OECS). The country is also a member of the regional stock exchange, the Eastern Caribbean Securities Exchange (based in Saint Christopher and Nevis), established in 2001.

SURVEY AND PROSPECTS

Agriculture is the dominant sector of the economy and, although the introduction of other crops has reduced dependence on the vulnerable banana harvest, performance is significantly affected by weather conditions. The erosion of the islands' preferential access to European markets, together with lower prices and poor climatic conditions, contributed to a decline in banana production after 1992. In addition, exports of bananas declined to just 30.6% of the total value of merchandise exports in 2002 (compared with 52.2% in 1990). In 2002 significant grant aid from the European Union (EU) was made available for irrigation and technical support, as well as for economic diversification and social support. None the less, the continued decline of the banana industry, and a related increase in unemployment and poverty, appeared inevitable. The prospects for long-term growth remain dependent on economic diversification and a recovery in tourism, while state investment in infrastructure is still dependent to a great extent on development assistance, particularly from the EU.

In early 2004 the ECCB reported that Saint Vincent and the Grenadines had the greatest potential of any country in the region in almost every tourism sub-sector. However, structural constraints, such as the underdeveloped airport and a lack of marketing, were likely to impede growth in the short-term. In February 2003 the IMF commended the Government for improving public-sector savings, strengthening the financial sector, restructuring the banana sector and adopting measures to avoid recession and mitigate further unemployment. However, the Fund emphasized the need for the Government to improve the operations of public enterprises and to bring the fiscal deficit under control. In October 2002 Prime Minister Gonsalves announced that 'Hurricane Lili' had cost the country's economy some EC $50m., destroying an estimated 45% of the banana crop; the 2003 budget, announced in December 2002, allocated extra funds to agriculture. At the same time it was also announced that a medium-term plan to strengthen the agricultural diversification process would be introduced in mid-2003. The economy was expected to expand in 2003 and the prospects for the tourism sector in particular were regarded as bright. The 2004 budget, presented to Parliament in December 2003, introduced a range of new taxes, including a value-added tax system. The Government also increased benefits to pensioners and announced a US $250 'Christmas bonus' for all public-sector workers. The opposition condemned the budget as populist, and accused the Government of neglecting the key sectors of tourism and banana production.

Samoa

The Independent State of Samoa, comprising nine islands, lies in the southern Pacific Ocean. In 1919 New Zealand was granted a League of Nations mandate to govern the islands. In 1946 Western Samoa (as it was known until 1997) became a UN Trust Territory, with New Zealand continuing as the administering power. The islands gained independence in 1962. In 1990, in a referendum, voters narrowly accepted government proposals for the introduction of universal suffrage. The Human Rights Protection Party has been the dominant political party since 1982. Apia is the capital. The languages spoken are Samoan and English.

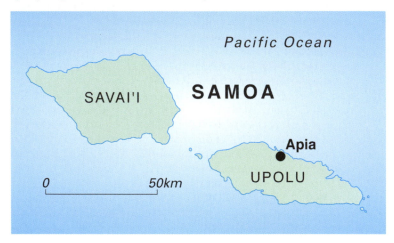

Area and population
Area: 2,831 sq km
Population (mid-2002): 176,200
Population density (mid-2002): 62.2 per sq km
Life expectancy (years at birth, 2002): 68.2 (males 66.8; females 69.7)

Finance
GDP in current prices: 2002): US $261m. ($1,482 per head)
Real GDP growth (2002): 1.3%
Inflation (annual average, 2002): 8.1%
Currency: tala

Economy

In 2002, according to estimates by the World Bank, Samoa's gross national income (GNI), measured at average 2000–2002 prices, was US $250m., equivalent to US $1,420 per head (or $5,350 per head on an international purchasing-power parity basis). During 1990–2002, it was estimated, the population increased at an average annual rate of 0.8%, while during 1994–2002 gross domestic product (GDP) per head increased, in real terms, by an average of 3.3% per year. Overall GDP increased, in real terms, by an average annual rate of 4.2% in 1994–2002. According to the Asian Development Bank (ADB), growth in 2002 was 1.8% and an estimated 3.5% in 2003.

AGRICULTURE

Agriculture (including hunting, forestry and fishing) accounted for some 14.2% of GDP in 2002 and engaged some 35% of the labour force in 2001. The principal cash crops are coconuts (in total, coconut oil, cream and copra accounted for 6.7% of total exports in 2002, compared with 15.0% in 2000) and taro (also the country's primary staple food). Sales of taro provided 58% of all domestic export earnings in 1993, but an outbreak of taro leaf blight devastated the crop in 1994 and reduced exports to almost nil in that year and subsequently. A campaign to revive the taro industry was launched in mid-2000; exports of taro in 2002 accounted for 2.2% of total exports. Breadfruit, yams, maize, passion fruit and mangoes are also cultivated as food crops. Exports of breadfruit and papaya were expected to increase significantly following the installation in early 2003 of a treatment facility to eradicate fruit fly from the produce. Pigs, cattle, poultry and goats are raised, mainly for local consumption. Some 1,800 head of cattle were brought to Samoa from Australia in early 2003, in an attempt to boost stocks and increase beef production. The country's commercial fishing industry expanded considerably in the late 1990s, with export revenues rising from some US $4.8m. in 1997 (33.0% of domestic export earnings) to $29.0m. (62.7%) in 2002. Output in the fishing sub-sector contributed 7.6% of GDP in 2000. Significant reductions in fishing taxes announced by the Government in March 2003 were expected to stimulate the country's fishing industry. Between 1995 and 2002, according to figures from the ADB, the GDP of the entire agricultural sector decreased, in real terms, at an average annual rate of 2.2%. In real terms, compared with the previous year, agricultural GDP decreased by 4.6% in 2001 and by 7.2% in 2002.

INDUSTRY

Industry (comprising manufacturing, mining, construction and power) employed 5.5% of the labour force in 1986 and provided 23.1% of GDP in 2002. According to ADB figures, between 1995 and 2002 industrial GDP increased, in real terms, at an average annual rate of 1.3%.

Manufacturing

Manufacturing provided 14.7% of GDP in 2002 and, together with mining, employed 3.5% of the labour force in 1986. Until recently, the main products of the sector were beverages (beer—which accounted for 8.5% of exports in 2002—and soft drinks), coconut-based products and cigarettes. (The coconut oil mill, however, remained closed for much of 2000.) The clothing industry has expanded, and in 2002 garments accounted for 9.6% of total export earnings. Between 1995 and 2002, according to ADB figures, manufacturing GDP remained virtually constant, in real terms, increasing at an average annual rate of only 0.01%.

Energy

Energy is derived principally from hydroelectric power and thermal power stations. A grant of US $0.3m. was received from the ADB in early 2003 to establish a hydroelectric project on Savai'i island. However, the Government was forced to seek an alternative location for the power plant following the refusal of local chiefs to allow its construction in their village. Chiefs representing the people of Sili village rejected the scheme, which they claimed would pollute local water supplies and harm the environment. Imports of petroleum accounted for 12.4% of the value of total imports in 2001.

SERVICES

The services sector provided 62.7%% of GDP in 2002. Between 1995 and 2002, according to ADB figures, the sector's GDP increased at an average annual rate of 7.6%. Compared with the previous year, the GDP of the services sector expanded by 8.2% in 2001 and by 7.6% in 2002. Tourism makes a significant contribution to the economy, and tourist revenues, including the proportion of international travel credited to carriers based in Samoa, totalled an estimated 133.1m. tala in 2000, compared with 125.8m. tala in 1999. The number of tourist arrivals rose from 88,960 in 2002 to 92,313 in 2003. 'Offshore' banking was introduced to the islands in 1989, and by July of that year more than 30 companies had registered in Apia. A large proportion of the islands' revenue is provided by remittances from nationals working abroad, estimated at 150.7m. tala in 2000 and equivalent to some 19.5% of GDP in that year (more than three times the value of merchandise exports and, for the first time, exceeding tourist remittances).

EXTERNAL TRADE

In 2000 the country recorded a visible trade deficit of US $73.4m., and a surplus of US $8.9m. on the current account of the balance of payments. In 2002, when imports totalled $181.16m. and exports reached $78.66m., Australia was Samoa's principal trading partner, providing an estimated 15.7% of imports and purchasing an esti-mated 59.6% of exports. Other important trading partners are New Zealand (23.7% of imports), Fiji (20.3% of imports), Indonesia (10.7% of exports) and the USA (9.0% of exports). The principal exports are fish, garments, coconut cream, copra and beer. The main imports are food and beverages, industrial supplies and fuels.

GOVERNMENT FINANCE

In the year ending 30 June 2001 there was an overall budget deficit of 19.2m. tala (equivalent to 2.3% of GDP), reflecting an increase in development spending financed by external borrowing and a decrease in lending to the domestic banking system. In the following two financial years there were budget deficits equivalent to an esti-mated 2.1% and 1.9% of GDP respectively. Aid from Australia and New Zealand is also a major source of revenue. Australia provided $A16.3m. in assistance in 2003/04. Aid from New Zealand totalled $NZ8.3m. in that year. In addition, Samoa received US $4m. in aid from Japan in 2002, as well as US $6.5m. for a project to expand the port facilities in Apia. At the end of 2001 the country's total external debt was US $204.3m., of which $143.3m. was long-term public debt. In 2000 the cost of debt-servicing was equivalent to 10.7% of total revenue from exports of goods and services. In 1990–2000 the annual rate of inflation averaged 3.3%. The ADB estimated that consumer prices increased by 8.1% in 2002 and by 4.7% in 2003.

INTERNATIONAL ECONOMIC RELATIONS

Samoa is a member of the Pacific Islands Forum, the Pacific Community, the Asian Development Bank (ADB) and the UN Economic and Social Commission for Asia and the Pacific (ESCAP), and is a signatory to the Lomé Conventions and the successor Cotonou Agreement with the European Union (EU).

SURVEY AND PROSPECTS

Strong growth characterized the economy during the mid-1990s but, owing to the completion of cyclone reconstruction projects and drought, this slowed considerably in 1997, before recovering somewhat in 1998–99. In 1999 it was announced that Samoa's Post and Telecommunications Department was to be privatized as part of a public-sector reform programme. In 2000–01 high rates of GDP growth were maintained (with the construction sector recording particularly strong expansion). The Samoan currency continued to depreciate against the Australian and New Zealand dollars, while rising against the US dollar. In 2001, however, the increase of 3.8% in consumer prices exceeded the central bank's target of a maximum of 3.0%. The Government maintained its commitment to private-sector development, including the transfer of the assets of several public enterprises to the corporate and private sectors. During 2001 various items of legislation were approved, aiming to raise standards of fiscal and corporate governance and to improve regulation and supervision in the financial sector.

The tourism sector, meanwhile, continued to perform well, following the completion of new facilities, and was also well placed to benefit from the political instability in neighbouring Fiji and Solomon Islands. Although the number of arrivals was briefly affected by the repercussions of the terrorist attacks on the USA in September 2001, gross receipts from tourism increased owing to higher individual levels of spending.

The Government continued its implementation of the programme of economic and public-sector reform in 2001 and reaffirmed its policies in the Strategy for the Development of Samoa 2002–2004. In April 2003 the number of government departments and ministries was reduced from 27 to 14 (largely through mergers) as part of the reforms. The document stressed the importance of opportunities for all through sustained economic growth and improvements in health and education. Having decelerated in 2002, largely as a result of a contraction of 17.7% in the GDP of the construction sector and a slight decline in manufacturing, sound GDP growth was resumed in 2003. Reserves of foreign exchange declined in 2001 but, following a recovery in 2002, rose sharply in 2003. The ADB projected a growth rate of 3.5% for 2004. The islands were adversely affected by Cyclone Heta, however, which struck in January 2004, causing damage to buildings and infrastructure.

San Marino

The Republic of San Marino lies in southern Europe. The country is situated on the slopes of Mount Titano, in the Apennines, bordered by the central Italian region of Emilia-Romagna to the north, and the Marches region to the south. San Marino evolved as a city-state in the early Middle Ages and is the sole survivor of the numerous independent states that existed in Italy prior to its unification in the 19th century. Since the collapse of a communist-led coalition in 1986, the Government has been dominated by the Partito Democratico Cristiano Sammarinese. The capital is San Marino. Italian is the language.

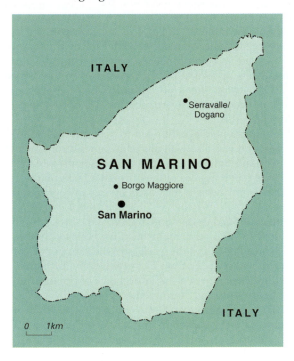

Area and population
Area: 61 sq km
Population (mid-2001): 30,000
Population density (mid-2001): 490.2 per sq km
Life expectancy (years at birth, 2002): 80.6 (males 77.2; females 84.0)

Finance
GDP in current prices: 1999): US $535m. ($20,421 per head)
Real GDP growth (1999): 1.4%
Inflation (annual average, 2000): 3.3%
Currency: euro

Economy

According to IMF estimates, San Marino's gross domestic product (GDP) in 1999 was US $853m., approximately equivalent to $23,390 per head. According to official figures, the annual average GDP growth in real terms was 9.0% in 1999 and 2.2% in 2000.

AGRICULTURE

Agriculture engaged 0.1% of the employed population in 2002. The principal crops are wheat, barley, maize, olives and grapes. Livestock-rearing and dairy farming are also important. Olive oil and wine are produced for export. In 2002 there were 85 agricultural businesses, including 11 co-operatives, in San Marino, compared with 115 in 2001 and 96 in 1998.

INDUSTRY

Industry (including manufacturing and construction) engaged 42.5% of the employed population in 2002. Stone-quarrying is the only mining activity in San Marino, and is an important export industry. Manufacturing engaged 34.7% of the employed population in 2002. The most important branches are the production of cement, synthetic rubber, leather, textiles and ceramics. The sector is largely export orientated, owing to integration with firms in Italy.

Energy

Energy is derived principally from gas (more than 75%). San Marino is dependent on the Italian state energy companies for much of its energy requirements.

SERVICES

The services sector engaged an estimated 57.4% of the employed population in 2002. Tourism is the main source of income, contributing about 60% of government revenue. In 2002 the number of visitor arrivals was 3,102,453; however, of that number, only 36,038 stayed at least one night. Receipts from tourism were estimated at US $252.5m. in 1994, equivalent to 41.6% of GDP in that year. In 2002 there were 27 hotels and 67 restaurants. The sale of coins and postage stamps, mainly to foreign collectors, is also a significant source of foreign exchange. San Marino, along with the Vatican and Monaco, was granted special dispensation to mint its own euro coins in 2002, with a view to providing for this specialist market.

EXTERNAL TRADE

In 1996, according to IMF estimates, San Marino recorded a trade surplus of US $22.6m., and there was a surplus of $10.7m. on the current account of the balance of payments. (In 2000, according to official figures, San Marino recorded a trade deficit of €67.8m.) Data concerning imports and exports are included in those of Italy, with which San Marino maintains a customs union. Customs union is also maintained with the European Union—EU. The principal source of imports (estimated at 87%) is Italy, upon which the country is dependent for its supply of raw materials. The major exports are wine, woollen goods, furniture, ceramics, building stone and artisan- and hand-made goods.

SURVEY AND PROSPECTS

San Marino receives a subsidy from the Italian Government, under the *Canone Doganale*, amounting to about €11m. annually, in exchange for the Republic's acceptance of Italian rules concerning exchange controls and the renunciation of customs duties.

No consolidated general government accounts are published by San Marino, and separate accounts and budgets are prepared by the central administration, the Social Security Institute, and each of the public enterprises, on an accrual basis. Figures published by the IMF, on a cash basis, for the consolidated operations of the general account budget (including the central administration and the nine 'Castles') and the Social Security Institute indicated a deficit of 28,000m. lire for 1997 (approximately equivalent to some 2.1% of GDP). The annual rate of inflation averaged 4.4% in 1990–99; consumer prices increased by an average of 3.2% in 1999 and 3.3% in 2000. In mid-2002 2.9% of the total labour force were unemployed. An increasingly large proportion of the labour force (24.5% in 2000, compared with 10.8% in 1991) are cross-border workers, mainly Italians from the surrounding regions.

Tourism has become increasingly important to San Marino's economy since the 1960s, when an increase in tourist activity in nearby Italian resorts resulted in the arrival of large numbers of excursionists. San Marino is currently dependent on the revenues generated by more than 3m. visitors each year, although the expansion of light industries, based on imported materials from Italy, has been encouraged in order to reduce this dependence.

In the 1990s political uncertainty in Italy, together with alternative taxation and regulation structures available in San Marino, resulted in the inflow to the banking sector of a large amount of non-resident deposits, and the development of dynamic financial and commercial sectors, which contributed to remarkable economic growth. Although San Marino has traditionally recorded a budget surplus, high levels of government employment, capital spending and subsidies, combined with low income from indirect taxes, resulted in budget deficits in 1996 and 1997. In an effort to reverse this trend, the Government halted all recruitment and implemented a 5% reduction in discretionary current expenditure in the 1999 budget. A review of public-sector activities was also initiated, with a view to reforming the structure of government employment.

In January 1999 San Marino adopted the euro, which became the sole currency in circulation at the start of 2002. In 1999–2000 the budget deficit of the central administration increased to an estimated 2.8% of GDP, compared with an average of some 1.0% of GDP during the 1990s. In 2003 the Istituto di Credito Sammarinese and the Ispettorato per il Credito e le Valute merged to create a new central bank, the Banca Centrale della Repubblica di San Marino. In early 2004 the EU attempted to reach a tax co-operation agreement with San Marino, Andorra, Liechtenstein and Monaco; however, these countries were unwilling to reduce the revenues gained by their status as tax havens outside the EU. In 2004 the maximum rate of personal income tax in San Marino stood at 12%, compared with 33% in Italy, while the highest rate of corporate tax was 24%, compared with 55% in Italy.

São Tomé and Príncipe

The Democratic Republic of São Tomé and Príncipe is a group of islands lying in the Gulf of Guinea, off the west coast of Africa. São Tomé and Príncipe achieved independence from Portugal in 1975, with Dr Manuel Pinto da Costa, the leader of the Movimento de Libertação de São Tomé e Príncipe (MLSTP), as President. In the most recent presidential election, held in 2001, Fradique de Menezes, standing for the Acção Democrática Independente, was the successful candidate. In 2002 the MLSTP—Partido Social Democrata became the leading party in the legislature. The capital is the town of São Tomé. Portuguese is the official language.

Area and population
Area: 1,001 sq km
Population (mid-2002): 154,210
Population density (mid-2002): 154.1 per sq km
Life expectancy (years at birth, 2002): 62.7 (males 61.7; females 63.6)

Finance
GDP in current prices: 2002: US $50.2m. ($326 per head)
Real GDP growth (2002): 3.0%
Inflation (annual average, 2002): 10.3%
Currency: dobra

Economy

In 2002, according to estimates by the World Bank, São Tomé and Príncipe's gross national product (GNI), measured at average 2000–02 prices, was US $45.2m., equivalent to $290 per head. During 1990–2002, it was estimated, the population increased at an average annual rate of 2.5%, while gross domestic product (GDP) per head declined, in real terms, by an average of 0.4% per year. Overall GDP increased, in real terms, at an average annual rate of 2.1% in 1990–2002; growth in 2002 was 2.9%.

AGRICULTURE
Agriculture (including fishing) contributed an estimated 20.0% of GDP in 2002, and employed 31.5% of the employed population in 2001. The principal cash crop is cocoa, which accounted for 93.0% of export earnings in 2000. Secondary cash crops include coconuts and coffee. Staple crops for local consumption include bananas, taro, tomatoes and cassava. Agricultural production is principally concentrated on export commodities, although smallholder agriculture has become increasingly important. An agricultural policy charter, the Carta de Política e Desenvolvimento Rural, which was introduced in 2000, aimed to emphasize private-sector involvement and diversification into areas such as ylang-ylang, pepper, vanilla, fruits, vegetables and flowers. Fishing is also a significant activity. The sale of fishing licences to foreign fleets is an important source of income. According to the World Bank, agricultural GDP increased at an average annual rate of 3.7% in 1990–2002; growth in 2002 was 3.3%.

INDUSTRY
Industry (including manufacturing, construction and power) contributed an estimated 17.0% of GDP in 2002, and employed 17.0% of the employed population in 2001. According to the World Bank, industrial GDP increased by an average of 2.0% per year in 1990–2002; growth in 2002 was 3.9%.

Mining
There are no mineral resources on the islands, but offshore prospecting for hydrocarbons resulted in the discovery of significant quantities of petroleum in 1998, including an estimated 4,000m. barrels in the joint development zone (JDZ) with Nigeria, as well as higher-risk resources in São Tomé's exclusive economic zone (EEZ). More than 20 companies lodged bids for exploration rights in the first nine of the 25 blocs in the JDZ in October 2003, and it was estimated that São Tomé could earn some $210m. from its 40% share of the revenue. Bidding was expected to take place for licences in the EEZ in late 2004. However income from the zones was not expected to contribute significantly to the economy until late 2005.

Manufacturing
The manufacturing sector consists solely of small processing factories, producing soap, soft drinks, textiles and beer. Manufacturing contributed an estimated 4.1% of

GDP in 2002. According to the World Bank, manufacturing GDP increased at an average annual rate of 1.3% in 1990–2002; there was no discernible growth in the sector in 2002.

Energy

In 2000 some 74% of electricity generation was derived from thermal sources, and 26% from hydroelectric sources. Imports of petroleum products comprised 10.8% of the value of merchandise imports in 2000.

SERVICES

The services sector contributed an estimated 63.0% of GDP in 2002, and engaged 51.5% of the employed population in 2001. According to the World Bank, the GDP of the services sector increased by an average of 1.1% per year in 1990–2002; growth in 2002 was 2.3%.

EXTERNAL TRADE

In 2002 São Tomé and Príncipe recorded a trade deficit of US $22.9m. and a deficit of $22.8m. on the current account of the balance of payments. In 2002, according to the Banco de Portugal, the principal source of imports (54.6%) was Portugal, and the principal market for exports (57.7%) was the Netherlands. Other major trading partners were Angola, Japan, Belgium and France. The principal export in 2000 was cocoa. The principal imports in that year were capital goods, foodstuffs, and petroleum and petroleum products.

GOVERNMENT FINANCE

In 2001 there was a budgetary deficit of 76,500m. dobras (equivalent to 18.1% of GDP). São Tomé's total external debt was US $312.5m. at the end of 2001, of which $293.2m. was long-term public debt. In that year the cost of debt-servicing was equivalent to 22.8% of the total value of exports of goods and services. Annual inflation averaged 34.9% in 1994–2000. Consumer prices increased by an average of 10.3% in 2002. According to official figures, 27.4% of the labour force were unemployed in 1993.

INTERNATIONAL ECONOMIC RELATIONS

São Tomé and Príncipe is a member of the International Cocoa Organization and of the Communauté économique des états de l'Afrique centrale.

SURVEY AND PROSPECTS

São Tomé and Príncipe's economy has traditionally been dominated by cocoa production, and is therefore vulnerable to adverse weather conditions and to fluctuations in international prices for cocoa.

In 2002, following the suspension of an arrangement agreed with the IMF in April 2000 under its Poverty Reduction and Growth Facility, the Government pursued a Fund-monitored programme aimed at controlling inflation and curbing government spending. As part of a structural adjustment programme, funds generated by offshore petroleum exploration were to be administered by the World Bank and the IMF, to be spent on projects aimed at balancing out the loss of revenues caused by dependence on cocoa and by mismanagement of state finances. IMF missions in July and November 2003 found that the Government was making satisfactory progress towards fulfilling the conditions specified for the reinstatement of the PRGF arrangement and possible debt reduction under the initiative for heavily indebted poor countires, but noted the importance of adopting and implementing legislation on the transparent management of petroleum revenues. In October the auction for exploration rights in the first nine of the 25 blocs in the JDZ was held, with the Government expected to earn some US $210m. from its 40% share in the revenue. In November the Government began implementing an emergency poverty reduction plan, which was to cost $22.8m. In 2003 some 80% of São Tomé's revenue came from aid. The African Development Bank provided a loan of $400,000 to help facilitate the establishment of small businesses, the European Union granted €5m. towards the improvement of the roads, and the World Bank planned to provide $10m. for education and health programmes in 2004.

The budget for 2004 was designed to stabilize the economy and maintain growth in order to meet IMF conditions for debt relief and resumed lending under the PRGF. GDP was forecast to increase by 5% in 2004, while inflation was projected to fall to 8%. The Government also aimed to raise salaries by 33.8% and to increase government revenue by 30%.

Saudi Arabia

The Kingdom of Saudi Arabia occupies about four-fifths of the Arabian peninsula, in south-western Asia. In 1924 the forces of Ibn Sa'ud forced the abdication of Hussein ibn Ali, who had proclaimed himself King of the Hedjaz in 1916. In 1926 Ibn Sa'ud was proclaimed King of the Hedjaz and Sultan of Najd, and in 1932 the two areas were merged as the unified Kingdom of Saudi Arabia. Ibn Sa'ud ruled until 1953. All subsequent Saudi Arabian rulers have been sons of Ibn Sa'ud. The capital is Riyadh. Arabic is the official language.

Area and population
Area: 2,240,000 sq km
Population (mid-2002): 22,116,450
Population density (mid-2002): 9.9 per sq km
Life expectancy (years at birth, 2002): 70.8 (males 68.4, females 73.9)

Finance
GDP in current prices: 2001): US $186,489m. ($8,711 per head)
Real GDP growth (2001): 1.2%
Inflation (annual average, 2002): −0.5%
Currency: Saudi riyal

Economy

In 2001, according to estimates by the World Bank, Saudi Arabia's gross national income (GNI), measured at average 1999–2001 prices, was US $181,066m., equivalent to $8,460 per head (or $11,480 per head on an international purchasing-power parity basis). During 1990–2002, it was estimated, the population increased by an average annual rate of 2.8%, while gross domestic product (GDP) per head decreased, in real terms, by an average of 0.6% per year in 1990–2001. Overall GDP increased, in real terms, at an average annual rate of 2.5% in 1990–2002; growth in 2002 was estimated at just 0.1%.

AGRICULTURE

Agriculture (including forestry and fishing) contributed an estimated 5.1% of GDP in 2002, and employed an estimated 6.0% of the economically active population in 2001. The principal crop is wheat; from the late 1980s a large wheat surplus was exported. Barley, dates, potatoes, tomatoes, and watermelons are also significant crops. Saudi Arabia is self-sufficient in many dairy products, and in eggs and broiler chickens. Agricultural GDP increased by an average of 1.9% per year in 1990–2002; the sector's real GDP increased by an estimated 1.6% in 2002.

INDUSTRY

Industry (including mining, manufacturing, construction and power) employed some 21.0% of the active labour force in 2001, and provided an estimated 50.8% of GDP in 2002. During 1990–2002, it was estimated, industrial GDP increased at an average annual rate of 2.6%.

Mining

Mining and quarrying engaged only 1.5% of the employed population in 2001, but contributed an estimated 33.0% of GDP in 2002. The sector is dominated by petroleum and natural gas, which provided an estimated 32.6% of GDP in that year. Saudi Arabia remained the largest petroleum producer in the world in 2002, and mineral products provided an estimated 88.3% of total export revenue in 2002. At the end of 2002 Saudi Arabia's proven recoverable reserves of petroleum were 261,800m. barrels, sufficient to maintain production at 2002 levels for 86 years, and equivalent to about one-quarter of the world's proven oil reserves. Crude petroleum production averaged 8.68m. barrels per day (b/d) in 2002, although the kingdom has a production capacity of some 10m. b/d. With effect from April 2004, Saudi Arabia's production quota within the Organization of the Petroleum Exporting Countries (OPEC) was 7,638,000. b/d. Gas reserves, mostly associated with petroleum, totalled 6,360,000m. cu m at the end of 2002. In October 2002 the world's largest natural gas plant was opened at Hawiya; the plant, which was the first Saudi project to produce gas not associated with petroleum, was expected to increase the country's production of gas by more than 30%. Further non-associated gas reserves are yet to be fully exploited. Other minerals produced include limestone, gypsum, marble, clay and salt, while there are substantial deposits of phosphates, bauxite, gold and other metals. The GDP of the mining sector increased at an average annual rate of 1.4% in 1990–2002.

Manufacturing

Manufacturing contributed an estimated 10.2% of GDP in 2002, and provided 8.1% of employment in 2001. The most important activity is the refining of petroleum. The production of petrochemicals, fertilizers, construction materials (particularly steel and cement), and food- and drink-processing are also important activities. Manufacturing GDP increased by an estimated average of 4.8% per year in 1990–2002.

Energy

Electrical energy is generated by thermal power stations, using Saudi Arabia's own petroleum resources, although an increasing amount of electricity is now produced in association with sea-water desalination. Electricity expansion projects were planned in the early part of the 21st century to satisfy increased demand.

SERVICES

The services sector contributed an estimated 44.1% of GDP in 2002, and engaged 73.0% of the employed labour force in 2001. The GDP of the services sector increased by an estimated average of 2.7% per year in 1990–2002.

EXTERNAL TRADE

In 2002 Saudi Arabia recorded a visible trade surplus of US $42,897m., and a surplus of $11,889m. on the current account of the balance of payments. In 2002 the principal source of imports (16.3%) was the USA; other important suppliers were Japan, Germany, the United Kingdom and Italy. The USA was also the principal market for exports (19.7%) in 2002; other major markets were Japan, the Republic of Korea, India and Singapore. In 2002 the dominant exports were mineral products, petrochemicals and plastic products. The principal imports in the same year were vehicles, aircraft, vessels and associated equipment, machinery and electrical equipment, base metals and metal manufactures, and chemicals and chemical products.

GOVERNMENT FINANCE

A balanced budget was forecast for 2001; however, revised figures indicated a deficit of SR 25,000m. A deficit of SR 45,000m. was forecast for 2002. Consumer prices increased by an annual average of 0.7% in 1988–2002; consumer prices decreased by 0.8% in 2001 and by 0.6% in 2002. Unemployment was reported to stand at around 20% of Saudi nationals in late 2003. In 2001 non-Saudi nationals comprised 52.1% of the labour force, although the *Middle East Economic Digest* indicated that the total was 65.4% in 2002.

INTERNATIONAL ECONOMIC RELATIONS

In addition to its membership of OPEC, Saudi Arabia is a member of the Islamic Development Bank, and the Organization of Arab Petroleum Exporting Countries (OAPEC). Saudi Arabia is the major aid donor in the region, disbursing loans to developing countries through the Arab Fund for Economic and Social Development (AFESD), the Arab Bank for Economic Development in Africa (BADEA) and other organizations. Negotiations regarding entry to the World Trade Organization (WTO) were scheduled to be concluded by the end of 2004. Saudi Arabia is also a member of the Co-operation Council for the Arab States of the Gulf (GCC), which created a unified regional customs tariff in January 2003, and has undertaken to establish a single market and currency no later than January 2010.

SURVEY AND PROSPECTS

Saudi Arabia's prosperity is based on exploitation of its petroleum reserves. Although the country remained the world's largest oil producer at the beginning of the 21st century, and continued to play a crucial role in determining OPEC production levels and thus world prices, the decline in the price of petroleum in the early 1990s caused the Government subsequently to seek alternative sources of revenue. The 2000–05 economic plan aimed to increase private investment and growth in the private and non-oil sectors, and envisaged the provision of 817,300 (mainly private-sector) jobs for the rapidly expanding Saudi population.

The Manpower Development Fund, partly financed by more expensive expatriate work permits and visas, was launched in April 2002 to subsidize skills training for Saudi nationals and to promote the 'Saudiization' of the work-force. The anticipated involvement of international companies in Saudi hydrocarbons and utilities industries was expected to contribute to private-sector growth. As part of a process of structural and administrative reform, two new policy-making bodies, the Supreme Economic Council and the Supreme Petroleum and Minerals Council, have been established (the latter accompanied by the creation of the Saudi Electricity Company and a new tariff structure), and, as part of the deregulation process, two independent supervisory authorities for the electricity and telecommunications sectors were created in 2001. A successful public offering of 20% of the Saudi Telecommunications Company in January of that year was expected to lead to liberalization of the telecommunications sector in 2004. In November 2002 the Government announced plans to privatize a further 20 sectors. It was announced in October 2003 that local and international airports (excluding security operations) and a portion of the National Commercial Bank were also to be privatized. Saudi Arabia failed to achieve a planned balanced budget for 2001 (after an unexpected budgetary surplus of SR 22,743m. in 2000) because of the sharp fall in world petroleum prices following the September attacks on the USA and the resulting fears of a global recession. Despite the introduction of strict spending limits for the 2002 and 2003 budgets, a further deficit was planned for 2002. As petroleum prices rallied, however, it was expected that the budgetary deficit would narrow. Impressive economic growth, of around 5.7%, was reported for 2003; due to sustained high oil prices, continued growth, albeit at a slightly lower rate, was also anticipated in 2004.

Senegal

The Republic of Senegal lies on the west coast of Africa. Formerly under French rule, Senegal became an independent republic in 1960, with Léopold Sédar Senghor, leader of the Union progressiste sénégalaise (UPS), as President. The Parti socialiste, as the UPS became in 1976, dominated Senegalese politics until 2000, when Abdou Diouf, who had succeeded Senghor as President in 1981 and been returned to office in 1983, 1988 and 1993, was defeated by Abdoulaye Wade of the Parti démocratique sénégalais (PDS). In 2001 a PDS-led coalition gained a majority of seats in the legislature. The capital is Dakar. French is the official language.

Area and population

Area: 196,722 sq km
Population (mid-2002): 10,006,790
Population density (mid-2002): 50.9 per sq km
Life expectancy (years at birth, 2002): 55.8 (males 54.3; females 57.3)

Finance

GDP in current prices: 2002): US $4,940m. ($494 per head)
Real GDP growth (2002): 2.4%
Inflation (annual average, 2002): 2.2%
Currency: CFA franc

Economy

In 2002, according to estimates by the World Bank, Senegal's gross national income (GNI), measured at average 2000–02 prices, was US $4,684m., equivalent to $470 per head (or $1,510 on an international purchasing-power parity basis). During 1990–2002, it was estimated, the population increased at an average annual rate of 2.6%, while gross domestic product (GDP) per head increased by an average of 0.9% per year. Overall GDP increased, in real terms, at an average annual rate of 3.5% per year in 1990–2002; growth in 2002 was 2.4%.

AGRICULTURE

Agriculture (including forestry and fishing) contributed 16.3% of GDP in 2002, when 73.1% of the labour force were engaged in the sector. The principal cash crops are groundnuts (exports of groundnut oil contributed 9.1% of total export earnings in 2001) and cotton. In the late 1990s Senegal began to export mangoes, melons, asparagus and green beans to European markets. Groundnuts, millet, sorghum, rice, maize and vegetables are produced for domestic consumption, although Senegal has yet to achieve self-sufficiency in basic foodstuffs. The fishing sector makes an important contribution to both the domestic food supply and export revenue: fish and fish products had become Senegal's principal export commodity by the mid-1980s, and provided 31.4% of export earnings in 2001. The sale of fishing licences to the European Union (EU) was an important source of revenue from the late 1990s. In June 2002 a new arrangement was concluded whereby the EU was to pay €16m. annually for fishing licences (compared with €12m. under the previous agreement), and the proportion of Senegalese fishermen working on EU-registered vessels in Senegalese waters was to increase from one-third to one-half. Senegalese concerns at the dwindling fish stocks in its waters were also to be addressed, with an annual two-month moratorium on fishing. According to the World Bank, during 1990–2002 agricultural GDP increased by an average of 2.7% per year; growth in 2002 was 6.9%.

INDUSTRY

Industry (including mining, manufacturing, construction and power) contributed 21.9% of GDP in 2002. The principal activities are the processing of fish and agricultural products and of phosphates, while the production of cement is of increasing importance. According to the World Bank, during 1990–2002 industrial GDP increased at an average annual rate of 4.8%. Industrial GDP increased by 3.7% in 2002.

Mining

Mining contributed only 0.8% of GDP in 2002. The principal mining activity is the extraction of calcium phosphates (aluminium phosphates are also mined in smaller quantities). Deposits of salt, fuller's earth (attapulgite), clinker and natural gas are also exploited, and there are currently investigations under way into the feasibility of mining copper, alluvial diamonds and iron ore. Explorations at Sabodala have revealed gold reserves estimated at 30 metric tons. Offshore deposits of petroleum are also to be developed, in co-operation with Guinea-Bissau. According to IMF estimates, the GDP of the mining sector declined by an average of 4.0% per year in 1992–99; the GDP of the sector fell by 2.0% in 1998, but increased by 20.8% in 1999.

Manufacturing

Manufacturing contributed 14.0% of GDP in 2002. The most important manufacturing activities are food-processing (notably fish, groundnuts and sugar), chemicals, textiles and petroleum-refining (using imported crude petroleum). According to the World Bank, manufacturing GDP increased at an average annual rate of 3.7% in 1990–2002; growth in 2002 was 4.7%.

Energy

Electrical energy is almost wholly derived from petroleum, which provided 99.9% of total electricity production in 2000. The Manantali hydroelectric power installation (constructed under the auspices of the Organisation pour la Mise en Valeur du Fleuve Sénégal—OMVS) commenced operations in December 2001; it was anticipated that Senegal would receive approximately one-third of the energy generated by the installation. Imports of mineral fuels and lubricants (including petroleum for refining) accounted for 16.8% of the value of merchandise imports in 2001.

SERVICES

The services sector contributed 61.7% of GDP in 2002. Tourism is a major source of foreign exchange, generating some 103,400m. francs CFA in receipts in 2001. In 1995 the tourism sector contributed almost 3% of GDP; about 4,500 people are directly employed (and some 15,000 indirectly employed) in the sector. Dakar's port is of considerable importance as a centre for regional trade. According to the World Bank, the GDP of the services sector increased by an average of 3.7% per year in 1990–2002. The GDP of the sector increased by 3.8% in 2002.

EXTERNAL TRADE

In 2002, according to estimates, Senegal recorded a visible trade deficit of 320,000m. francs CFA, while there was a deficit of 179,200m. francs CFA on the current account of the balance of payments. In 2001 the principal source of imports (27.8%) was France; other major suppliers were Nigeria and Thailand. France was the principal market for exports in that year (taking 16.7% of the total); India, Greece, Mali and Italy were also important purchasers. The principal exports in 2001 were fish, refined petroleum products, phosphoric acid and groundnut oil. The principal imports in that year were machinery and transport equipment, food and live animals, basic manufactures, petroleum and petroleum products, and chemicals and related products.

GOVERNMENT FINANCE

Senegal recorded an overall budget surplus of 13,200m. francs CFA in 2002 (equivalent to 0.4% of GDP). Total external debt was US $3,461m. at the end of 2001, of which $3,012m. was long-term public debt. In that year the cost of debt-servicing was equivalent to 13.3% of the value of exports of goods and services. In 1990–93 consumer prices declined by an annual average of 0.8%. However, following the 50% devaluation of the CFA franc, inflation averaged 32.3% in 1994; inflation subsequently slowed to an annual average of 1.8% in 1995–2002. Consumer prices increased by an average of 2.3% in 2002. In early 1999 157,063 people were registered as unemployed.

INTERNATIONAL ECONOMIC RELATIONS

Senegal is a member of the Economic Community of West African States, of the West African organs of the Franc Zone, of the African Groundnut Council, of the West Africa Rice Development Association, of the Gambia River Basin Development Organization and of the OMVS.

SURVEY AND PROSPECTS

The attainment of sustained economic growth has been impeded by Senegal's dependence on revenue from a narrow export base, and by its consequent vulnerability to fluctuations in international prices for its principal commodities. Several important state-owned companies were privatized in the late 1990s, although the divestiture programme was subject to delays and difficulties. Attempts to transfer the groundnut-oil production company, the Société Nationale de Commercialisation des Oléagineux du Sénégal (SONACOS), to majority private ownership failed in both 1997 and 1999, but was expected to be completed by mid-2004. Meanwhile, the perceived under-performance of the electricity company, the Société Nationale d'Electricité (SENELEC), led the Government, in 2001, to reacquire those shares in the company that had previously been sold to private investors; its reprivatization, initially scheduled for 2003, was not expected to take place before 2005.

Senegal has generally enjoyed good relations with the IMF, which approved a new three-year Enhanced Structural Adjustment Facility (later renamed Poverty Reduction and Growth Facility—PRGF) in April 1998; this Facility was subsequently extended until 2002. In 2000 Senegal was declared eligible for assistance under the initiative for heavily indebted poor countries; the country was expected to reach 'completion point' under the terms of the initiative in 2004. In April 2003 a further PRGF arrangement, amounting to some US $33m., was agreed with the IMF in support of the Government's economic reform programme for 2003–05. Strong economic growth was recorded from 1998, in spite of the frequent shortages of electricity experienced during 1999, the rise in the world price of petroleum, one of Senegal's principal imports, in 2000 and a poor harvest in 2002. The involvement of President Wade in the creation and promotion of the New Partnership for Africa's Development has served to increase Senegal's international profile as a country committed to thorough economic reform and transparency, although concerns were expressed, in late 2003, by the President of the European Commission, Romano Prodi, at the pace of reform in areas such as administration and good governance.

Serbia and Montenegro

Serbia and Montenegro (formerly the Federal Republic of Yugoslavia—FRY) lies in south-eastern Europe. The FRY was established in 1992, following the disintegration of the Socialist Federal People's Republic of Yugoslavia. President Slobodan Milošević was unsuccessful in efforts to create by force a 'Greater Serbia' for all Yugoslav Serbs. In 2001 Milošević was arraigned before the International Criminal Tribunal for the Former Yugoslavia, on charges that included genocide. The state union of Serbia and Montenegro was formally established with the adoption of a Constitutional Charter in February 2003. Montenegro retained the right to a future referendum on independence. Belgrade is the capital. The principal language is Serbian.

Area and population

Area: 102,173 sq km
Population (mid-2002): 10,658,470
Population density (mid-2002): 104.3 per sq km
Life expectancy (years at birth, 2002): 72.3 (males 69.7; females 74.9)

Finance

GDP in current prices: 2002): US $15,555m. ($1,459 per head)
Real GDP growth (2002): 4.0%
Inflation (annual average, 2002): 16.5%
Currency: Yugoslav dinar

Economy

In 2002, according to estimates by the World Bank, the gross national income (GNI) of the Federal Republic of Yugoslavia (FRY—reconstituted as Serbia and Montenegro in February 2003), measured at 2000–02 prices, was US $11,601m., equivalent to $1,400 per head. During 1990–2002, it was estimated, the population increased by an annual average of 0.1%, while gross domestic product (GDP) per head increased, in real terms, by 1.8% during 1995–2001. Overall GDP increased, in real terms, at an average annual rate of 2.0% in 1995–2001; growth was 5.5% in 2001 and 4.0% in 2002.

AGRICULTURE

Agriculture (including forestry and fishing) contributed an estimated 23.3% of GDP in 2001. In 2002 an estimated 4.0% of the total employed labour force were engaged in the sector. The FRY's principal crops are maize, wheat, sugar beet and potatoes. The cultivation of fruit and vegetables is also important. In 1990–95 agricultural GDP declined, in real terms, by 6.2%. Agricultural production in the FRY increased by 1.3% in 1996, and by 7.2% in 1997, but declined by 4.0% in 1998, by 0.9% in 1999 and by an estimated 19.7% in 2000.

INDUSTRY

Industry (including mining, manufacturing and power) contributed an estimated 37.1% of GDP in the FRY in 2001, with construction accounting for a further 6.2%. Including construction, the sector engaged an estimated 35.5% of the employed labour force in 2002. In 1990–95 industrial GDP (excluding construction) declined, in real terms, by 58.0%. Industrial production increased by an estimated 18.9% in 1996–2000. According to the IMF, industrial output rose by 11.1% in 2000, remained constant in 2001 and increased by an estimated 1.7% in 2002.

Mining

In 2002 the mining and quarrying sector engaged 1.8% of the employed labour force. The principal minerals extracted in the FRY are coal (mainly brown coal), copper ore and bauxite. Iron ore, crude petroleum, lead and zinc ore and natural gas are also produced. Mining has been less severely affected in recent years than other sectors.

Manufacturing

In 2002 the manufacturing sector engaged 26.9% of the employed labour force. In that year the principal branches of manufacturing were building materials, metalworking and electrical equipment, chemicals and paper, textiles, leather and rubber, wood-working, and food products and tobacco. In 1996–2000, according to official estimates, production of capital goods increased by 6.8% and intermediate goods by 1.1%.

Energy

Energy in the FRY is derived principally from thermal power stations (which provided about 56.2% of total electricity generated in 2000) and hydroelectric power (37.8%). Imports of mineral fuels accounted for about 16.9% of the value of total imports in 2002.

SERVICES

Services contributed an estimated 33.4% of GDP in the FRY in 2001. Some 60.6% of the employed labour force were employed in the sector in 2002. In 1990–95 GDP in the transport and communications sector declined, in real terms, by 68.2%; GDP in commerce declined by 42.0%, and GDP in the catering and tourist trades by 24.6%. Total foreign tourist arrivals increased from 151,650 in 1999 to 238,957 in 2000.

EXTERNAL TRADE

In 2002 the FRY recorded an estimated trade deficit of US $3,908m., and there was a deficit of $2,007m. on the current account of the balance of payments. In 2001 the principal source of imports (14.2%) was Russia; other major sources were Germany, Italy and Greece. The principal market for exports in that year was Italy (16.4%); other important purchasers were Bosnia and Herzegovina, Germany, the FYRM, and Switzerland and Liechtenstein. The main exports from the FRY in 2002 were basic manufactures (principally non-ferrous metals, and iron and steel), food and live animals, miscellaneous manufactured articles (notably articles of clothing), machinery and transport equipment, and chemicals. The principal imports in that year were machinery and transport equipment, basic manufactures, mineral fuels, chemicals, miscellaneous manufactured articles, and food and live animals.

GOVERNMENT FINANCE

In 2001 the overall budgetary deficit was equivalent to 5.7% of GDP. At the end of 2001 the country's total external debt was US $11,740m., of which $6,002m. was long-term public debt. In that year the cost of debt-servicing was equivalent to 2.4% of the value of exports of goods and services. At the end of 2002 external debt totalled $11,839m. In 1991–2001 the rate of inflation increased by an annual average of 11.5%. Consumer prices increased by some 89% in 2001 and by some 17% in 2002. The rate of unemployment was estimated at 29.6% of the labour force in 2002.

INTERNATIONAL ECONOMIC RELATIONS

Owing to armed conflict in parts of the former SFRY and the imposition by the UN of sanctions on the FRY in May 1992, the country's membership of numerous international organizations was suspended. Following the political changes in the FRY in September 2000, the country was readmitted to the UN on 1 November. It was readmitted to the Organization for Security and Co-operation in Europe (OSCE) later in November, to the IMF in December and to the World Bank in May 2001. Serbia and Montenegro officially became a member of the Council of Europe in April 2003.

SURVEY AND PROSPECTS

Following its constitution in April 1992 the FRY experienced severe economic deterioration, as a result of regional conflict, international isolation and lack of structural reform and investment. In July 1998 the Montenegrin Government announced that it had assumed full control of the republic's economy, owing to the adverse effects of international sanctions and the pressures of federal government economic policy.

The NATO bombardment of March–June 1999 resulted in extensive damage to infrastructure and severe economic hardship in Serbia. Following the election of a new Federal Government in September 2000, however, the FRY's integration into international institutions progressed rapidly. In October the European Union (EU) ended all sanctions against the FRY (including the damaging embargo on petroleum exports, imposed in April 1999), and it was agreed that the country would receive aid under the EU's programme for Balkan reconstruction, development and stabilization. In December the FRY was readmitted to the IMF, and was granted emergency post-conflict assistance. The US Government officially ended economic sanctions against the FRY in January 2001; however, subsequent financial support from the USA was made conditional on the Yugoslav authorities' co-operation with the International Criminal Tribunal for the former Yugoslavia (ICTY). In June an international donor conference pledged further funds to support the FRY's economic recovery. Economic activity continued to increase from very low levels, but real GDP remained at less than one-half of its 1989 total.

In November 2001 the 'Paris Club' of creditor Governments agreed to cancel two-thirds of the FRY's outstanding debt, conditional on the authorities reaching a further agreement with the IMF. In April 2002, following renewed US pressure on the Government to demonstrate full co-operation with the ICTY, the Federal Assembly finally approved legislation providing for the extradition of war crimes suspects. In May the IMF approved an extended credit arrangement to support the Government's economic programme for 2002–05. It was hoped that the establishment of the State Union of Serbia and Montenegro in February 2003 would further the normalization of economic relations between the two entities, with the harmonization of trade, customs and tax systems in accordance with EU standards. Legislative elections in Serbia in December were followed by a protracted political impasse, which resulted in a temporary delay in the reform process. The minority coalition Government of Dr Vojislav Koštunica, which was finally formed in March 2004, immediately attracted concern from the international community, owing to its dependence on the parliamentary support of the Socialist Party of Serbia of former President Slobodan Milošević. The new administration was expected to adopt more nationalist policies on the issues of co-operation with the ICTY, the future status of Kosovo and maintenance of the joint state with Montenegro.

In March an IMF review of the Union's economic performance was largely favourable: stabilization efforts had resulted in a considerable reduction in the rate of inflation and strengthening of foreign reserves, while progress in the implementation of privatization measures, the introduction of pension reforms and harmonization of trade regulations between the two republics was also welcomed. Moderate economic growth of 1.5% in 2003 was expected to increase in 2004. At the end of March, however, the US Government announced that it was to suspend financial aid to Serbia and Montenegro, after determining that the new Serbian administration had failed to co-operate fully with the ICTY in the arrest and extradition of war crime suspects.

Seychelles

The Republic of Seychelles comprises some 115 islands in the western Indian Ocean. Seychelles achieved full independence from Britain, as a sovereign republic within the Commonwealth, in 1976. In 1977 the Seychelles People's United Party (SPUP), led by Albert René, staged an armed coup. In 1991 the Seychelles People's Progressive Front (SPPF), as the SPUP had been renamed, agreed to surrender its monopoly of power. René and the SPPF gained decisive victories in presidential and legislative elections held in 1993, 1998, and 2001–02. In April 2004 James Michel succeeded René as President, following the latter's resignation. Victoria is the capital. Seselwa is the official language.

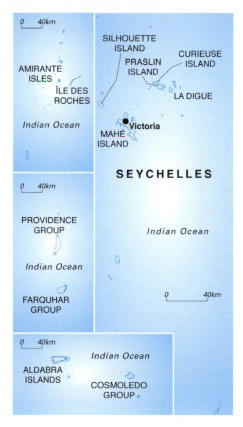

Area and population
Area: 455.3 sq km
Population (mid-2002): 83,590
Population density (mid-2002): 183.6 per sq km
Life expectancy (years at birth, 2002): 71.5 (males 67.0; females 77.2)

Finance
GDP in current prices: 2002): US $630m. ($7,537 per head)
Real GDP growth (2002): –2.4%
Inflation (annual average, 2002): 0.2%
Currency: Seychelles rupee

Economy

In 2001, according to estimates by the World Bank, Seychelles' gross national income (GNI), measured at average 1999–2001 prices, was US $538m., equivalent to $6,530 per head. During 1990–2002, it was estimated, the population increased at an average annual rate of 1.5%, while gross domestic product (GDP) per head declined, in real terms, by an average of 0.8% per year. Overall GDP increased, in real terms, at an average annual rate of 0.7% in 1990–2002. Real GDP declined by 2.4% in 2002.

AGRICULTURE

Agriculture (including hunting, forestry and fishing) contributed 3.0% of GDP and accounted for 6.2% of total employment in 2002. Much of Seychelles' production of coconuts has traditionally been exported in the form of copra, but there were no exports of copra in 1996–99. Other cash crops include cinnamon bark, tea, patchouli, vanilla and limes. Tea, sweet potatoes, cassava, yams, sugar cane, bananas, eggs and poultry meat are produced for local consumption. However, imports of food and live animals constituted 24.0% of the value of total imports in 1999. Fishing has become increasingly important since the 1980s, and exports of canned tuna alone contributed 67.5% of the value of total domestic exports in 2002. Licence fees from foreign fishing vessels, allowed to operate in Seychelles' waters, contribute significantly to foreign exchange. A three-year fishing protocol, worth €3.48m., was signed with the European Union in 2001. Agricultural GDP declined at an average annual rate of 1.1% during 1990–2002, according to the World Bank; growth in 2002 was 2.2%.

INDUSTRY

Industry (including mining, manufacturing, construction and power) contributed 30.9% of GDP and accounted for 22.0% of total employment in 2002. Industrial GDP increased at an average annual rate of 7.5% during 1990–2002, according to the World Bank; growth was 3.0% in 2002.

Mining

The mining sector is small; the sole mineral export is guano (of which 6,000 metric tons was exported in 1990, although consistent output was discontinued in the mid-1980s). Mineral production consists mainly of quantities of construction materials, such as clay, coral, stone and sand. There are deposits of natural gas, and during the 1980s concessions were sold to several foreign companies, allowing exploration for petroleum. Exploratory drilling has so far proved unsuccessful. A survey of offshore areas, initiated in 1980, revealed the presence of nodules, containing deposits of various metals, on the sea-bed. The possibility of renewed commercial exploitation of Seychelles' granite reserves is under investigation and the future development of offshore petroleum reserves is a possibility.

Manufacturing

Manufacturing contributed 18.8% of GDP in 2002. Apart from a tuna-canning plant (opened in 1987), the manufacturing sector consists mainly of small-scale activities, including boat-building, printing and furniture-making. According to the World Bank, manufacturing GDP increased at an average annual rate of 6.5% during 1990–2002. Manufacturing GDP increased by 3.0% in 2002.

Energy

Energy is derived principally from oil-fired power stations. In 1999 mineral fuels accounted for 10.0% of the value of total imports. However, the vast majority of fuel imports are re-exported, mainly as bunker sales to visiting ships and aircraft— exports of refined petroleum products contributed 30.0% of total export earnings in that year. In 2000 Seychelles generated SR 357m. from petroleum re-exports, and it was anticipated that by the end of 2003 the proceeds from re-exports would fully fund fuel imports.

SERVICES

Services provided 66.1% of GDP and accounted for 71.8% of total employment in 2002. In 1997 tourism generated 33.6% of total earnings from exports of goods and services. Tourist arrivals totalled some 132,246 in 2002; income from that source amounted to US $110m. in 2000. The majority of visitors were from western Europe, notably from France, Germany, Italy and the United Kingdom. The GDP of the services sector decreased at an average annual rate of 1.6% during 1990–2002, according to the World Bank. Services GDP declined by 5.6% in 2002.

EXTERNAL TRADE

In 2002 Seychelles recorded a visible trade deficit of US $139.6m. In the same year there was a deficit of $130.6m. on the current account of the balance of payments. The principal source of imports (13.3%) in 1999 was Italy; other important suppliers were the Southern African Customs Union (comprising Botswana, Lesotho, Namibia, South Africa and Swaziland), Finland, France and Saudi Arabia. The principal market for exports in that year was the United Kingdom (46.9%); other significant purchasers were Italy, France and Germany. The principal export in 2002 was canned tuna, following the expansion of the Indian Ocean Tuna Company in 1995 and increasing production thereafter. The main imports in 1999 were machinery and transport equipment, food and live animals, and basic manufactures.

GOVERNMENT FINANCE

In 2002 Seychelles recorded a budgetary deficit of SR 622.6m. (equivalent to 16.3% of GDP). Seychelles' total external debt was US $214.8m. at the end of 2001, of which $117.1m. was long-term public debt. In that year the cost of debt-servicing was equivalent to 2.7% of the value of exports of goods and services. The annual rate of inflation averaged 2.4% in 1990–2002; consumer prices increased by an average of 0.2% in 2002 and 3.3% in 2003. Some 8.3% of the labour force were registered as unemployed in 1993.

INTERNATIONAL ECONOMIC RELATIONS

Seychelles is a member of the African Development Bank, of the Common Market for Eastern and Southern Africa and of the Indian Ocean Commission, which aims to promote co-operation in the region. It was announced in December 1996 that Seychelles was to provide the headquarters of the Indian Ocean Tuna Commission. In 2003 Seychelles gave notice of its intention to withdraw from membership of the Southern African Development Community in July 2004.

SURVEY AND PROSPECTS

Since the early 1970s tourism has been the mainstay of the Seychelles economy. Development of agriculture is impeded by the lack of cultivable land. Income from fisheries expanded greatly after the commissioning of a tuna-canning plant in 1987 and the establishment of a prawn farm in the early 1990s. Manufacturing growth is inhibited, however, by the lack of natural resources, although since 1988 the Government has offered incentives for new manufacturing enterprises. Measures were introduced in 1995 to develop Seychelles as an 'offshore' financial services centre, and to establish the islands as a centre for transhipment and air freight in the Indian Ocean area. An export-processing zone has been established, and most state-owned enterprises, with the exception of public utilities and transport, have been transferred to private-sector ownership. However, the continuing dependence of the economy on tourism leaves the country highly vulnerable to outside economic influences, while the cost of servicing the external debt remains a major impediment to balanced growth.

In the IMF's assessment, at February 2001, the country was in danger of losing its status as offering one of the highest standards of living in Africa, as real GDP had remained unchanged for two years, inflation was rising and the balance of payments demonstrated serious problems. The organization strongly recommended less government intervention in the economy, including over price-controls, foreign-exchange allocation, import licensing and monopolies in manufacturing and distribution. However, in mid-2001 the Government imposed further measures to control the urgent foreign-exchange situation, caused by the country's dependence on imports, requiring tourists to pay for services and merchandise in foreign currency and prohibiting Seychellois from holding unauthorized currency. According to the Government, this resulted in an increase of up to 40% in the amount of foreign currency within the banking system. In July 2003 a new macroeconomic reform programme took effect; intended to reduce costs and raise revenue, it included the introduction of a general sales and services tax of 12% on all imported items (except essential foodstuffs), most locally manufactured goods and all services. In September, as part of the programme, the Government announced several measures aimed at encouraging long-term settlement by investors in the country.

Sierra Leone

The Republic of Sierra Leone lies on the west coast of Africa. it gained independence from Britain in 1961. The country's recent history has been dominated by armed conflict between successive governments and forces of the Revolutionary United Front. After the overthrow of Ahmed Tejan Kabbah's Government in 1997, the conflict escalated and remained resistant to any enduring resolution until November 2000, when a cease-fire agreement was signed, providing for the demobilization and disarmament of all militias and the deployment of UN Mission in Sierra Leone forces throughout the country. In mid-2002 President Kabbah was re-elected. Freetown is the capital. The language is English.

Area and population

Area: 71,740 sq km
Population (mid-2002): 5,235,470
Population density (mid-2002): 73.0 per sq km
Life expectancy (years at birth, 2002): 34.0 (males 32.4; females 35.5)

Finance

GDP in current prices: 2002): US $789m. ($151 per head)
Real GDP growth (2002): 6.3%
Inflation (annual average, 2002): −3.3%
Currency: leone

Economy

In 2002, according to the World Bank, Sierra Leone's gross national income (GNI), measured at average 2000–02 prices, was US $725m., equivalent to $140 per head (or $490 per head on an international purchasing-power parity basis). During 1990–2002, it was estimated, the population increased at an average annual rate of 2.3%, while gross domestic product (GDP) per head declined, in real terms, by an average of 5.0% per year. Overall GDP declined, in real terms, at an average annual rate of 2.9% in 1990–2002; however, growth was 6.6% in 2002.

AGRICULTURE

Agriculture (including forestry and fishing) contributed 51.9% of GDP in 2002. About 61.2% of the labour force were employed in the sector in that year. The principal cash crops are cocoa beans and coffee. Staple food crops include cassava, rice and bananas. Cattle, sheep and poultry are the principal livestock. During 1990–2002 the GDP of the agricultural sector declined at an average annual rate of 5.2%; however, growth in agricultural GDP was 7.2% in 2002.

INDUSTRY

Industry (including mining, manufacturing, construction and power) contributed 31.1% of GDP in 2002, and employed an estimated 17.1% of the labour force in 1996/97. The GDP of the industrial sector declined by an average of 3.8% per year in 1990–2002; however, industrial GDP increased by 6.6% in 2002.

Mining

Mining and quarrying contributed 17.5% of GDP in 1994/95. The principal mineral exports are diamonds (which, according to the Bank of Sierra Leone, accounted for 89.9% of total export earnings in 2001), rutile (titanium dioxide), bauxite and gold. The production of iron ore, previously an important mineral export, was suspended in 1985. In 1995 increased rebel activity effectively suspended official mining operations (although illicit exports of diamonds by rebel forces continued). In October 2000 official exports of diamonds were resumed under a certification scheme. Following strong redevelopment of the mining sector in 2003, mining for diamonds at a major site in Kono District was to commence in early 2004, and Sierra Rutile (the largest single private-sector employer and foreign-export earner prior to 1995) planned to resume full mining operations by June. The country's bauxite mine was also expected to reopen in that year.

Manufacturing

Manufacturing contributed 5.2% of GDP in 2002. The manufacturing sector consists mainly of the production of palm oil and other agro-based industries, textiles and furniture-making. During 1990–96 the GDP of the manufacturing sector increased at an average annual rate of 2.5%. Manufacturing GDP declined by 9.9% in 1995, but increased by 1.7% in 1996.

Energy

Energy is derived principally from oil-fired thermal power stations. The use of solar energy for domestic purposes was introduced in 1990. Imports of mineral fuels comprised 23.4% of the value of total imports in 2001.

SERVICES

The services sector contributed 17.0% of GDP in 2002, and employed 22.1% of the labour force in 1996/97. The GDP of the services sector declined by an average of 0.8% per year in 1990–2002, rising by 6.6% in 2002.

EXTERNAL TRADE

In 2002 Sierra Leone recorded an estimated trade deficit of US $123.6m., and there was a deficit of $79.1m. on the current account of the balance of payments. In 2002, according to estimates, the principal source of imports (25.0%) was Germany; other major suppliers were the United Kingdom and the Netherlands. Belgium was the principal market for exports (taking 42.0% of the total); the other significant purchaser was Germany. The principal export in 2001 was diamonds. The principal imports in that year were food and live animals, mineral fuels and lubricants, machinery and transport equipment, and basic manufactures.

GOVERNMENT FINANCE

The overall budget deficit for 2002 was Le 162,225m., equivalent to 9.8% of GDP. Sierra Leone's external debt totalled US $1,188m. at the end of 2001, of which $1,014m. was long-term public debt. In that year the cost of debt-servicing was equivalent to 102.1% of the value of exports of goods and services. The annual rate of inflation averaged 26.1% in 1990–2002. Consumer prices declined by 3.3% in 2002, but increased by 7.6% in 2003. An estimated 50% of the labour force were unemployed in early 1990.

INTERNATIONAL ECONOMIC RELATIONS

Sierra Leone is a member of the Economic Community of West African States and of the Mano River Union, which aims to promote economic co-operation with Guinea and Liberia.

SURVEY AND PROSPECTS

The civil conflict, which commenced in 1991, resulted in the progressive destruction of Sierra Leone's infrastructure, and severe disruption, or complete suspension, of traditional economic activities. Following a peace agreement between the Government and the rebels, which was signed in July 1999, a new coalition administration was installed, and a recovery and rehabilitation programme was adopted. Subsequent improvements in fiscal control and considerable post-conflict support from the international financial institutions resulted in some progress in reconstruction. Under a further cease-fire agreement, signed in November 2000, presidential and legislative elections were conducted in May 2002. The reorganized Government's priorities were to alleviate widespread poverty, resettle displaced civilians (amounting to nearly one-half of the population at the end of 2001), reintegrate disarmed former combatants, reconstruct the country's infrastructure, and reduce dramatically high debt levels.

In March 2002 the IMF, which had approved a further three-year credit arrangement in September 2001, commended the Government's progress in advancing the peace process and the country's improved economic and financial performance (demonstrated by significant GDP growth and continued restraint of the rate of inflation in 2001). In response to the implementation of structural reforms, the IMF and World Bank pledged debt relief to Sierra Leone under concessionary terms (conditional on the Government complying with the stipulated measures of fiscal control). The IMF approved further disbursements to Sierra Leone in September 2002 and April 2003, under the existing Poverty Reduction and Growth Facility (PRGF). The Fund advocated an accelerated implementation of structural reforms, including the privatization of state-owned enterprises, and measures to improve governance, and the legal and judicial systems (with the aim of encouraging private investment).

A major peace agreement reached between the combatant factions in Liberia in August 2003 improved conditions for sustained peace in Sierra Leone, which were reinforced by the completion of the five-year disarmament programme in February 2004; nevertheless, continuing unrest in Liberia posed a continued threat to regional stability. The Sierra Leone authorities remained dependent on the presence of the UN Mission in Sierra Leone (UNAMSIL) to maintain stability, and UN plans to withdraw the contingent prompted concern regarding the future security situation.

Following a further performance review in early 2004, the IMF concluded that the country had made continued progress in economic stabilization and achieving growth under the PRGF-supported programme. Although the Government had failed to meet some fiscal and structural criteria, the Fund approved the disbursement of further credit and extended the arrangement to March 2005. GDP growth of 7.0% was recorded in 2003, following a recovery in agricultural output, increased diamond production and an expansion in the construction sector. State export revenue was expected to increase in 2004, owing to higher levels of earnings from diamonds resulting from a reduction in illicit trade, an improvement in the security situation, and the resumption in that year of rutile-mining operations.

Singapore

The Republic of Singapore lies in South-East Asia. In 1826 the East India Company formed the Straits Settlements by the union of Singapore and the dependencies of Penang and Malacca on the Malay Peninsula. They came under British rule in 1867. In 1946 Singapore became a separate crown colony, and in 1959 achieved complete internal self-government. After seceding from the Federation of Malaysia in 1965, Singapore became an independent republic. Every election since 1972 has been won by the People's Action Party. Singapore City is the capital. The official languages are Malay (the national language), Chinese (Mandarin), Tamil and English.

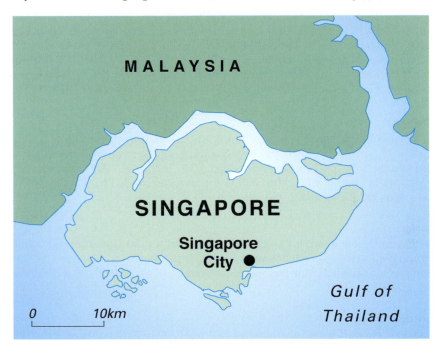

Area and population
Area: 660 sq km
Population (mid-2002): 4,164,000
Population density (mid-2002): 6,310.0 per sq km
Life expectancy (years at birth, 2002): 79.6 (males 77.4; females 81.7)

Finance
GDP in current prices: 2002): US $86,969m. ($20,886 per head)
Real GDP growth (2002): 2.2%
Inflation (annual average, 2002): −0.4%
Currency: Singapore dollar

Economy

In 2002, according to estimates by the World Bank, Singapore's gross national income (GNI), measured at average 2000–02 prices, was US $86,150m., equivalent to $20,690 per head (or $23,090 per head on an international purchasing-power parity basis). During 1990–2002, it was estimated, the population increased at an annual annual rate of 2.6%, while gross domestic product (GDP) per head increased, in real terms, at an average rate of 3.6% per year in 1990–2002. According to official figures, overall GDP increased, in real terms, at an average annual rate of 6.0% in 1990–2003. GDP expanded by 2.2% in 2002 and by 1.1% in 2003.

AGRICULTURE

Agriculture (including hunting, forestry and fishing) and quarrying contributed an estimated 0.1% of GDP in 2003, and accounted for 0.4% of the employed labour force in 2002. Vegetables, plants and orchid flowers are the principal crops. During 1990–2002, according to the Asian Development Bank (ADB), agricultural GDP (including mining) declined at an average annual rate of 3.1%. According to official sources, agricultural GDP declined by 5.8% in 2002 and by an estimated 0.4% in 2003.

INDUSTRY

Industry (including manufacturing, construction and power) contributed an estimated 33.0% of GDP in 2003, and engaged 24.6% of the employed labour force in 2002. During 1990–2002, according to the ADB, industrial GDP increased at an average annual rate of 6.0%. The GDP of the sector expanded by 3.5% in 2002 and by an estimated 0.2% in 2003, according to official sources.

Mining

Mining (chiefly the quarrying of granite) accounted for only an estimated 0.01% of GDP in 1998 and 0.05% of employment in 2002. According to the ADB, the GDP of the mining sector declined at an average annual rate of 17.4% in 1990–98; it declined by 22.4% in 1998.

Manufacturing

Manufacturing contributed an estimated 26.3% of GDP in 2003, and engaged 18.2% of the employed labour force in 2002. The principal branches of manufacturing in 1998 (measured in terms of the value of output) were electronic products and components (which accounted for 52.2% of total manufacturing production), refined petroleum products, chemicals and chemical products, non-electrical machinery and equipment, fabricated metal products, and transport equipment (especially shipbuilding). According to the ADB, manufacturing GDP increased at an average annual rate of 5.7% in 1990–2002. Manufacturing GDP increased by 7.8% in 2002 and by an estimated 2.8% in 2003.

Energy

Singapore relies on imports of hydrocarbons to fuel its three thermal power stations. In 2003 imports of mineral fuels accounted for 13.6% of merchandise imports.

SERVICES

The services sector contributed an estimated 66.9% of GDP in 2003, and engaged 75.0% of the employed labour force in 2002. Finance and business services provided an estimated 24.9% of GDP in 2003, and engaged 17.1% of the employed labour force in 2002. The GDP of the financial and business services sector decreased by 2.1% in 2002 but increased by 0.5% in 2003. Singapore is an important foreign-exchange dealing centre in Asia and the Pacific. Banking is also a significant sector, with a total of 115 commercial banks in operation in April 2004. Tourism is an important source of foreign exchange, and receipts from tourism amounted to S $5,425.8m. in 2002. In 2003 the number of tourist arrivals exceeded 6.1m. In the same year transport and communications contributed an estimated 11.1% of GDP. The GDP of the transport and communications sector grew by 4.9% in 2002, but contracted by an estimated 2.0% in 2003. Singapore is the world's busiest port in tonnage terms and has one of the largest merchant shipping registers in the world. According to the ADB, the GDP of the services sector increased at an average annual rate of 6.7% in 1990–2002. According to official sources, the sector expanded by 1.5% in 2002, but contracted by an estimated 1.0% in 2003.

EXTERNAL TRADE

In 2002 Singapore recorded a visible trade surplus of US $18,549m., and there was a surplus of $18,704m. on the current account of the balance of payments. In 2003 the principal sources of imports were Malaysia (16.8%), the USA (13.9%) and Japan (12.0%); other major suppliers were the People's Republic of China and Taiwan. The principal markets for exports were Malaysia (15.8%) and the USA (13.3%); other major purchasers were Hong Kong, China and Japan. Principal imports in 2003 included machinery and equipment, electronic components and parts, mineral fuels, miscellaneous manufactured articles, basic manufactures and chemicals. Principal exports included machinery and equipment (notably electronic components and parts), chemicals, mineral fuels and miscellaneous manufactured articles. Singapore is an important entrepôt, and re-exports accounted for 42.8% of total exports in 2000.

GOVERNMENT FINANCE

In 2002, according to the IMF, there was a budgetary deficit of S $2,595m. (equivalent to 1.7% of GDP). At 31 December 2001 Singapore had no external government debt. The annual rate of inflation averaged 1.4% in 1990–2003; consumer prices decreased by 0.4% in 2002, but increased by 0.5% in 2003. In September 2003 the rate of unemployment was 5.9%.

INTERNATIONAL ECONOMIC RELATIONS

Singapore is a member of the UN Economic and Social Commission for Asia and the Pacific (ESCAP), of the Asian Development Bank, of the Association of South East Asian Nations (ASEAN), of Asia-Pacific Economic Co-operation (APEC) and of the Colombo Plan. As a member of ASEAN, Singapore signed an accord in January 1992 pledging the creation of a free-trade zone to be known as the ASEAN Free Trade Area (AFTA). A reduction of tariffs to between 0% and 5% was originally envisaged to be completed by 2008 but this was subsequently advanced to 2002, when AFTA was formally implemented. However, Malaysia applied for an extension of this date for its automotive industry, fearing direct competition. Target dates for the removal of all tariffs were brought forward from 2015 to 2010 in November 1999.

SURVEY AND PROSPECTS

Singapore's economic success is based largely on its central location in the region, efficient planning, advanced infrastructure and highly-skilled work-force, which has encouraged international investment. In the late 1980s and early 1990s many state-owned corporations were transferred to the private sector, and the Government encouraged companies to transfer labour-intensive operations to neighbouring low-cost countries. Singapore was less affected than its neighbours by the regional financial crisis, which began in July 1997, owing to its high savings and investment rates, negligible debt and massive foreign-exchange reserves. It proceeded to take advantage of the instability of neighbouring countries to secure its own position as a financial and trading centre through the reform of the financial services sector.

The comprehensive deregulation of the telecommunications industry was effected in April 2000 and plans were announced for the deregulation of the power and insurance sectors. Both the public and private sectors attempted to become more competitive globally. Further expansionary measures were taken by the Government in a series of free trade agreement (FTA) initiatives, as it became clearer that Singapore might be constrained by ASEAN, with political and economic uncertainty in the face of strong pressure from North Asia. By the end of 2003 FTAs had been concluded with New Zealand, Japan, the European Free Trade Association (EFTA), Australia and the USA, while discussions were in progress with ASEAN and the People's Republic of China, Canada, Jordan, India, the Republic of Korea, Mexico, Panama, Sri Lanka and the Pacific Three (which comprised Chile and New Zealand, together with Singapore). The global economic downturn, particularly in the electronics sector, exacerbated by the effects of the September 2001 terrorist attacks on the USA (a major export market), had a particularly damaging effect upon Singapore's export-driven economy.

In 2001 GDP contracted by 1.9%, as Singapore experienced its worst recession since independence in 1965. Largely as a result of high levels of government spending, the economy avoided a further recession in 2002. However, national security concerns, owing to an increasing number of incidents of terrorism in the region in 2002 and 2003, threatened to deter overseas investors. In an attempt to stimulate foreign investment, the Government announced in January 2003 that it intended to offer preferential tax rates over a three-year period to companies that established regional headquarters in Singapore.

In the first half of 2003 economic growth was severely constrained, owing both to the epidemic of Severe Acute Respiratory Syndrome (SARS) in the region early in that year, which killed 33 people in Singapore alone, and to the disruption to international trade caused by the US-led military campaign in Iraq. In September 2003 the rate of unemployment reached its highest level in 17 years. However, in the last quarter of the year a recovery in the electronics sector, stimulated by increasing global demand for electronics, underpinned an upturn in economic performance, resulting in a GDP growth rate of 1.1% for the year. The implementation of the FTA with the USA in January 2004 was expected to result in an increase in trade flows. Furthermore, it was hoped that the Government's substantial ongoing investment in the development of the biomedical and pharmaceuticals sector would succeed in reducing Singapore's reliance on the electronics sector as the main source of growth. GDP growth of approximately 5.0% was forecast for 2004.

Slovakia

The Slovak Republic lies in central Europe. The Republic of Czechoslovakia was established in 1918. Concessions made to Slovak demands for autonomy after 1945 were negated under Communist rule. In 1969 separate Czech and Slovak Socialist Republics were established, but their governments and legislatures were largely powerless. In 1990, after the 'velvet revolution', Czechoslovakia was renamed the Czech and Slovak Federative Republic (CzSFR). However, pressure for Slovakia's secession from the federation led, in 1992, to a declaration of Slovak sovereignty by the Slovak National Council. In 1993 the CzSFR was dissolved into separate Czech and Slovak Republics. Bratislava is the capital. The official language is Slovak.

Area and population
Area: 49,033 sq km
Population (mid-2002): 5,408,760
Population density (mid-2002): 110.3 per sq km
Life expectancy (years at birth, 2002): 74.0 (males 69.8; females 78.3)

Finance
GDP in current prices: 2002): US $23,700m. ($4,382 per head)
Real GDP growth (2002): 4.4%
Inflation (annual average, 2002): 3.3%
Currency: koruna

Economy

In 2002, according to the World Bank, Slovakia's gross national income (GNI), measured at average 2000–02 prices, was US $21,378m., equivalent to $3,950 per head (or $12,190 per head on an international purchasing-power parity basis). During 1990–2002, it was estimated, the population increased at an annual average rate of 0.2%, while gross domestic product (GDP) per head increased, in real terms, by an average of 0.7% per year. Overall GDP increased, in real terms, at an annual average rate of 0.9% in 1990–2002; growth was 3.3% in 2001 and 4.4% in 2002.

AGRICULTURE

In 2002 the agricultural sector (including forestry) contributed 4.2% of GDP, according to IMF estimates. The sector employed an estimated 6.2% of the employed labour force in that year. The principal crops are wheat and other grains, sugar beet, potatoes and other vegetables. Livestock breeding is also important. During 1990–2001, according to the World Bank, the GDP of the agricultural sector increased, in real terms, by an annual average of 0.2%. Agricultural GDP increased by 3.1% in 2000 and by 2.4% in 2001.

INDUSTRY

Industry (including mining, manufacturing, construction and power) contributed 29.2% of GDP in 2002 (according to IMF estimates), and engaged 38.4% of the employed labour force. According to the World Bank, the GDP of the industrial sector declined, in real terms, by an annual average of 5.1% during 1990–2001. However, industrial GDP increased by 0.4% in 2000 and by 0.05% in 2001.

Mining

Mining and quarrying contributed 0.7% of GDP (according to IMF estimates) in 2001, and engaged 1.2% of the employed labour force in 2000. The principal minerals extracted include brown coal and lignite, copper, zinc, lead, iron ore and magnesite. There are also deposits of crude petroleum, natural gas and mercury, as well as materials used in construction (including limestone, gravel and brick loam). According to IMF estimates, the GDP of the mining and quarrying sector increased by an annual average of 2.5% in 1995–2001. Mining GDP declined by 9.2% in 2001.

Manufacturing

The manufacturing sector contributed 21.8% of GDP (according to IMF estimates) in 2001, and engaged 25.7% of the employed labour force in 2000. The GDP of the manufacturing sector increased by an annual average of 4.5% in 1995–2001. Manufacturing GDP increased by 5.5% in both 2000 and 2001.

Energy

Energy is derived principally from nuclear power. According to the US-based Nuclear Energy Institute, nuclear energy provided some 65.4% of electricity generated in 2002. In 2000 coal accounted for 18.5% of electricity production, and hydro-electric power for 15.5%. A large-scale nuclear power station at Jaslovské-Bohunice has been in operation since the early 1980s. In July 1998 the first block of a new nuclear power installation, at Mochovce, commenced operations. Slovakia has been heavily dependent on imported fuel and energy products. Mineral products accounted for 15.3% of the value of total merchandise imports in 2002.

SERVICES

The services sector contributed 66.7% of GDP in 2002, and engaged 55.4% of the employed labour force in that year. During 1990–2001, according to the World Bank, the GDP of the services sector increased, in real terms, by an annual average of 5.5%. Services GDP increased by 3.0% in 2000 and by 4.9% in 2001.

EXTERNAL TRADE

In 2002 Slovakia recorded a trade deficit of US $2,131m., and there was a deficit of $1,939m. on the current account of the balance of payments. In 2002 the principal source of imports was Germany, which accounted for 22.6% of the total; other major suppliers were the Czech Republic, Russia and Italy. Germany was also the principal market for exports in that year (26.0%); other important purchasers were the Czech Republic, Italy, Austria, Hungary and Poland. The main exports in 2002 were transport equipment, machinery and electrical equipment, base metals, mineral products, textiles and rubber and plastics. The principal imports were machinery and electrical equipment, mineral products, transport equipment, base metals, chemical products, rubber and plastics, and textiles.

GOVERNMENT FINANCE

Slovakia's overall budgetary deficit (excluding loans and repayments) for 2002 was 67,500m. koruny, equivalent to 6.3% of GDP. At the end of 2001 Slovakia's total external debt was US $11,121m., of which $5,498m. was long-term public debt. In that year the cost of debt-servicing was equivalent to 16.8% of the value of exports of goods and services. The annual rate of inflation averaged 13.3% in 1990–2002; consumer prices increased by 7.3% in 2001 and by 3.3% in 2002. In 2003 the average rate of unemployment was 17.4%.

INTERNATIONAL ECONOMIC RELATIONS

Slovakia is a member of the IMF and the World Bank, as well as of the European Bank for Reconstruction and Development, as a 'Country of Operations'. In late 2000 Slovakia was admitted to the Organisation for Economic Co-operation and Development. Slovakia signed an association agreement with the European Community (now European Union—EU) in October 1993, and became a full member of the EU on 1 May 2004.

SURVEY AND PROSPECTS

Following independence in 1993, sustained economic growth was achieved (despite political instability under the Governments of Vladimír Mečiar in 1993–98). The economy successfully shifted from its traditional reliance on industry to services, and from state to private ownership. Nevertheless, the monetary deficits and foreign-debt burden had increased substantially by 1998. Some reduction in the fiscal deficit was achieved in 1999; however, austerity measures resulted in a sharp increase in the rate of unemployment. The privatization programme was extended in 2000, and a 14-year enterprise and financial sector adjustment loan from the World Bank committed the administration to continued bank restructuring and privatization, and reform of the financial sector.

Priorities for the Government elected in late 2002 were to reduce the budgetary deficit, reduce the exceptionally high level of unemployment (particularly in the east of the country), reform the judiciary system and address corruption. Foreign direct investment, which had increased in 2002, was further stimulated by confirmation in December of the country's scheduled entry into the EU in 2004, and the Government's intention to meet the criteria for adoption of the common European currency by 2006, including a reduction in the fiscal deficit to less than 3% of GDP. Foreign investment was estimated to have totalled some US $7,000m. by the beginning of 2004, and in early 2004 Hyundai of the Republic of Korea announced plans to build a large-scale car-production site in Slovakia, which was expected to open in 2006. Meanwhile, in November 2003 the National Council approved an amendment to privatization legislation, permitting the sale of majority stakes in large state-owned utilities and natural monopolies (hitherto, the Government had retained a minimum 51% stake, although management control had been divested to investors). A public tender for the sale of a 90% stake in a power-generation company was subsequently announced.

Slovakia's economy recorded continued strong growth in 2003, with GDP increasing by an estimated 4.2%. However, there was apprehension, particularly in the farming sector, over anticipated reductions in subsidies and increased competition as a consequence of EU accession. A uniform rate of income and corporate tax, of 19%, was introduced from 1 January 2004, and there were plans to impose a uniform value-added tax of 19% on all products. Extensive structural changes to public expenditure were also to be introduced in 2004, including: greater private contributions to the health and welfare systems; the establishment of a funded pension system; and welfare reforms (which were to contribute to reducing the rate of unemployment). In February, however, proposals substantially to reduce spending on social welfare prompted violent protests by members of the country's Roma minority.

Slovenia

The Republic of Slovenia is situated in south-central Europe. Constitutional amendments approved in 1989 confirmed Slovenia's sovereignty and its right to secede from the Socialist Federal Republic of Yugoslavia (SFRY). In 1990 Slovenia was redesignated the Republic of Slovenia and the Republic's sovereignty was declared. In June 1991 Slovenia and Croatia declared their independence from the SFRY. Serbian-dominated federal troops were mobilized and sporadic fighting ensued. Following the implemention of a cease-fire, federal troops withdrew from Slovenia, which proclaimed its full independence in October. Ljubljana is the capital. The official language is Slovene, and in ethnically-mixed regions also Hungarian and Italian.

Area and population
Area: 20,273 sq km
Population (mid-2002): 1,991,960
Population density (mid-2002): 98.3 per sq km
Life expectancy (years at birth, 2002): 76.7 (males 72.8; females 80.3)

Finance
GDP in current prices: 2002): US $21,108m. ($10,596 per head)
Real GDP growth (2002): 2.9%
Inflation (annual average, 2002): 7.5%
Currency: tolar

Economy

In 2002, according to the World Bank, Slovenia's gross national income (GNI), measured at average 2000–02 prices, was US $19,551m., equivalent to $9,810 per head (or $17,690 per head on an international purchasing-power parity basis). During 1990–2002, it was estimated, the population decreased at an average annual rate of 0.03%, while gross domestic product (GDP) per head increased, in real terms, by an average of 2.1% per year. Overall GDP increased, in real terms, at an average annual rate of 2.0% in 1990–2002. Growth was 2.9% in both 2001 and 2002.

AGRICULTURE

Agriculture (including hunting, forestry and fishing) contributed 3.0% of GDP in 2002. In that year the sector engaged 9.7% of the employed labour force. The principal crops are cereals (particularly maize and wheat), potatoes, sugar beet and fruits (especially grapes and apples). Slovenia's forests, which cover about one-half of the country, are an important natural resource. Agricultural GDP decreased at an average rate of 0.9% per year during 1991–2001. The GDP of the sector declined by 1.0% in 2000 and by 2.1% in 2001.

INDUSTRY

Industry (including mining, manufacturing, construction and power) contributed 35.2% of GDP in 2002. In that year the industrial sector engaged 38.6% of the employed labour force. Industrial GDP increased at an average rate of 2.1% per year in 1991–2001. Growth in the industrial sector was 7.1% in 2000 and 3.0% in 2001.

Mining

Mining and quarrying contributed 0.5% of GDP and engaged 0.4% of the employed labour force in 2002. The principal activity is coal-mining; lead and zinc are also extracted, together with relatively small amounts of natural gas, petroleum and salt. Slovenia also has small deposits of uranium. The GDP of the mining sector increased at an average rate of 0.9% per year in 1995–2000. Mining GDP declined by 7.3% in 2000.

Manufacturing

Manufacturing contributed 26.3% of GDP and engaged 31.1% of the employed labour force in 2002. Manufacturing GDP increased at an average rate of 4.1% per year in 1992–2001. Growth in the manufacturing sector was 8.6% in 2000 and 5.0% in 2001.

Energy

A nuclear power station was constructed in Slovenia by the former Yugoslav authorities to provide energy for both Slovenia and Croatia. In 2000 nuclear power stations provided 34.9% of energy requirements, coal-fired electricity generating stations provided 33.7%, and hydroelectric power stations provided 28.1%. Imports of fuel products comprised 7.0% of the value of merchandise imports in 2002.

SERVICES

The services sector contributed 61.8% of GDP and engaged 51.7% of the employed labour force in 2002. Tourism is a significant source of revenue; tourist activity was adversely affected by the political instability of 1991, but the number of arrivals recovered, reaching 1,302,000 in 2002. The GDP of the services sector increased at an average rate of 3.7% per year in 1991–2001. Growth in the services sector was 4.2% in 2000 and 4.1% in 2001.

EXTERNAL TRADE

In 2002 Slovenia recorded a visible trade deficit of US $243.0m., and there was a surplus of $374.8m. on the current account of the balance of payments. In that year Slovenia's principal source of imports was Germany (accounting for 19.1% of the total); other major suppliers were Italy, France and Austria. Germany was also the principal market for exports (taking 24.8% of the total in that year); Italy, Croatia, Austria and France were also significant purchasers. The major imports in 2002 were machinery and transport equipment (particularly road vehicles and parts), basic manufactures, chemical products, miscellaneous manufactured articles, mineral fuels and crude materials. The principal exports in that year were machinery and transport equipment (particularly road vehicles and parts and electrical machinery), basic manufactures, miscellaneous manufactured articles (particularly furniture and clothing) and chemicals.

GOVERNMENT FINANCE

Slovenia's overall budget deficit for 2002 was 46,330m. SIT (equivalent to 0.9% of GDP). In 2002 (according to the IMF) total external debt amounted to US $8,799m (of which $3,238m. was medium- and long-term public debt), and the cost of debt-servicing was equivalent to 14.3% of the value of exports of goods and services. The annual rate of inflation averaged 12.1% in 1992–2002. Consumer prices increased by 7.5% in 2002 and by an estimated 5.6% in 2003. An estimated 6.0% of the total labour force were unemployed in 2002.

INTERNATIONAL ECONOMIC RELATIONS

Slovenia has joined several international organizations, including the IMF, the World Bank and (as a 'Country of Operations') the European Bank for Reconstruction and Development. The country became a full member of the World Trade Organization in July 1995. Slovenia concluded an association agreement with the European Union (EU) in June 1996, and applied, simultaneously, for full membership of the organiza-tion. Formal accession negotiations began in November 1998, and Slovenia became a full member of the EU on 1 May 2004.

SURVEY AND PROSPECTS

Slovenia's economy was severely disrupted by secession from the Yugoslav Federa-tion, and by the international economic blockade of Serbia and Montenegro, together with the conflicts in Croatia and in Bosnia and Herzegovina. By the mid-1990s this disruption had been largely overcome, and important advances in the transformation of the economy (such as the full convertibility of the tolar) had allowed Slovenia to gain a favourable position among the countries chosen to participate in negotiations to join the EU. In 1998 agreement was also reached on the issue of the reform of the state pension system (which had proved an increasingly heavy burden on public finances). Value-added tax was introduced in July 1999, and progress was made during that year in the privatization of the banking sector, as part of efforts to fulfil

EU criteria. However, the Government remained reluctant to implement extensive liberalization measures, and foreign direct investment remained relatively low.

A new administration, which was installed in November 2000, undertook to expedite public administration reform and the standardization of legislation in accordance with EU requirements. In early 2002 all remaining restrictions to foreign investment in Slovenia were removed. However, in April the IMF (while commending liberalization measures) observed that progress in the privatization process was slow. Slovenia's scheduled accession to the EU was officially announced in December 2002 (and endorsed by national referendum in March 2003). At April 2003 Slovenia had achieved sustained convergence in per head income to about 70% of the EU average; however, efforts to reduce the rate of inflation (which had averaged about 7%–8% since 1997) had resulted in little progress (owing, in part, to large increases in indirect taxes and in the international price of petroleum). Stronger growth was projected for 2004, based on increased recovery in the EU and a rise in private consumption.

Following Slovenia's accession to the EU on 1 May 2004, the Government aimed to meet EU criteria in order to achieve entry into the exchange-rate mechanism (ERM-2) by the end of that year, prior to adoption of the euro by 2007. Fulfilment of this objective was expected to be problematic, particularly with regard to the need further to reduce the rate of inflation, which remained significantly higher than the EU average. The budget for 2004–05 reflected the Government's commitment to fiscal discipline, and included provisions for reduced expenditure in the sectors of health and education.

Solomon Islands

Solomon Islands is a scattered archipelago in the south-western Pacific Ocean. After 1900 the territory was known as the British Solomon Islands Protectorate. It was officially renamed the Solomon Islands in 1975, retaining protectorate status. Solomon Islands (as it was restyled) became independent, within the Commonwealth, in 1978. Violent unrest erupted on Guadalcanal island in 1998 and continued throughout 2001, despite the conclusion, in 2000, of a peace treaty between the Malaita Eagle Force, the Isatambu Freedom Movement, the Solomon Islands Government and the Malaita and Guadalcanal Provincial Governments. In mid-2003 a multinational intervention force was deployed in the country, in order to address the deteriorating law and order situation. Honiara is the capital. The official language is standard English.

Area and population
Area: 27,556 sq km
Population (mid-2002): 443,300
Population density (mid-2002): 16.1 per sq km
Life expectancy (years at birth, 2002): 65.4 (males 63.6; females 67.4)

Finance
GDP in current prices: 2002): US $240m. ($540 per head)
Real GDP growth (2002): –4.0%
Inflation (annual average, 2002): 7.3%
Currency: Solomon Islands dollar

Economy

In 2002, according to estimates by the World Bank, Solomon Islands' gross national income (GNI), measured at average 2000–2002 prices, was US $254m., equivalent to US $570 per head (or $1,520 on an international purchasing-power parity basis).

During 1990–2002, it was estimated, the population increased at an average annual rate of 2.8%, while gross domestic product (GDP) per head decreased, in real terms, at an average annual rate of 2.9%. Overall GDP decreased, in real terms, an average annual rate of 0.2% in 1990–2002. According to the Asian Development Bank (ADB), GDP contracted by 4.0% in 2002 but was projected to rise by 5.0% in 2003.

AGRICULTURE

Agriculture (including hunting, forestry and fishing) contributed 42.1% of GDP (measured at constant 1985 prices) in 2000. In 2001 an estimated 72.6% of the working population were involved in agriculture. The principal cash crops have traditionally included coconuts, cocoa, rice and oil palm. Earnings from copra (which was for many years the country's main export) declined from SI $34.7m. in 2000 to SI $0.4m. in 2001, although revenue recovered slightly in the following year to reach SI $2.2m. High prices on the world market for cocoa in the early 2000s increased the value of exports of that commodity. In April 2003 the Government announced plans to reopen a major palm oil plant that had remained closed since 1999 owing to civil unrest. Spices are cultivated for export on a small scale, while in the 1990s the production of honey became increasingly important. The main subsistence crops are root crops, garden vegetables and fruit. Pigs and cattle are also reared. Seaweed farming has been introduced, and sea-shells are exported. The country's first shipment of sea-weed was exported to France in early 2004. Giant-clam farming became an important activity in the mid-1990s. Fish accounted for 18.1% of export earnings in 2002. The forestry sector is an extremely important source of revenue, timber exports accounting for 65.2% of total export receipts in 2002. A dramatic increase in the production of timber in the early 1990s prompted several international organizations, including the World Bank, to express alarm at the rate of logging in the country. None the less, by the late 1990s Solomon Islands was one of the few remaining countries in the world to allow the export of round logs. Environmental concerns were renewed in early 2004. According to provisional figures from the ADB, agricultural GDP increased by an annual average of less than 0.1% in 1990–2000. The ADB estimated that agricultural GDP decreased by 25.1% in 2000 and by 11.0% in 2001.

INDUSTRY

Industry (including mining, manufacturing, construction and power) contributed 12.1% of GDP in 2000 (at 1985 prices), and employed 13.7% of wage-earners in 1993. The GDP of the industrial sector expanded by an average annual rate of 5.0% in 1990–2000. The ADB estimated that industrial GDP declined by 25.0% in 2000 and by 24.1% in 2001.

Mining

Mining employed 0.5% of the working population in 1988. The mining sector's share of real GDP was an estimated 3.1% in 2000. During 1990–97, however, the sector made a negative contribution to GDP. Compared with the previous year, the mining sector's GDP increased by 181.0% in 1999, but declined by 51.4% in 2000. Gold is the sole mineral export, but revenue from this source declined from SI $1.3m. (from exports of 50 kg) in 1991 to only SI $57,000 (from 2 kg) in 1997. Other (undeveloped) mineral resources include deposits of copper, lead, zinc, silver, cobalt, asbestos, phosphates, nickel and high-grade bauxite.

Manufacturing

Manufacturing contributed 4.9% of GDP (at 1985 prices) in 2000, and employed 15.6% of wage-earners in 1995. The most important branches are food-processing (particularly fish-canning), coconut-based products, brewing, saw-milling, logging and handicrafts. Manufacturing GDP increased by an annual average of 3.8% in 1990–2000. Compared with the previous year, however, there was no discernible growth in 1999, and in 2000 the manufacturing sector's GDP contracted by 19.8%.

Energy

Energy is derived principally from hydroelectric power, with solar energy being increasingly utilized. Mineral fuels accounted for 17.3% of the total value of imports in 2002. In 1992 exploratory projects revealed several potential petroleum-producing areas in the islands.

SERVICES

Service industries contributed 45.8% of GDP (at 1985 prices) in 2000 and engaged 58.8% of wage-earners in 1993. Although in 2003 tourist arrivals totalled only 1,718, the Australian-led intervention and the consequent restoration of a measure of stability to troubled areas of the country were expected to have a beneficial effect on the tourism sector, with a projected total of 10,000 arrivals for 2004. Earnings from the sector had declined from some US $13m. in 1998 to an estimated $6m. in 1999. The trade, restaurants and hotels sector engaged 11.5% of wage-earners in 1993. The ADB estimated that the GDP of the services sector contracted by 6.7% in 2000 and by 5.6% in 2001.

EXTERNAL TRADE

In 2000 Solomon Islands recorded a visible trade deficit of SI $223.6m., and a deficit of SI $329.9m. on the current account of the balance of payments. In 2001 the deficit on the current account of the balance of payments was equivalent to 15.2% of GDP and in 2002 was estimated at 3.5% of GDP. In 2003, however, a surplus on the current account equivalent to 6.5% of GDP was forecast by the ADB. In 2002, compared with the previous year, the trade deficit declined by 75% to total SI $46.3m. In 2002 the principal sources of imports were Australia (31.5%) and Singapore (19.8%), while the principal markets for exports were Japan (21.5%) and the Republic of Korea (21.0%). Other major trading partners are the United Kingdom, Thailand, the Philippines, New Zealand and the People's Republic of China. The principal exports in 2002 were timber, fish and other marine products, and cocoa. The principal imports were miscellaneous manufactured articles, foodstuffs, crude materials and machinery and transport equipment.

GOVERNMENT FINANCE

In 2002 there was an estimated budgetary deficit of SI $139.1m. According to the ADB, the fiscal deficit declined from the equivalent of 12.2% of GDP in 2002 to a projected 0.3% in 2003. Budgetary expenditure of SI $480m. was approved for 2004, of which about one-quarter was to be financed by grants from Australia and New Zealand. In 2000 official development assistance totalled US $68.4m., of which US $22.1m. was bilateral aid. Aid from Australia totalled $A37.4m. in 2003/04. In the same year financial assistance from New Zealand totalled $NZ14.0m. Solomon Islands' external debt totalled US $162.5m. in 2001. In 2000 the cost of debt-servicing was equivalent to 6.9% of the value of exports of goods and services. According to the ADB, external debt totalled US $134m. in 2002. The average annual rate of inflation in Honiara in 1990–2002 was 9.6%. Compared with the previous year, the rate of inflation was estimated by the ADB at 9.0% in 2002 and 8.0% in 2003.

INTERNATIONAL ECONOMIC RELATIONS

Solomon Islands is a member of the Pacific Community, the Pacific Islands Forum, the Asian Development Bank and the UN Economic and Social Commission for Asia and the Pacific (ESCAP), and is a signatory to the Lomé Conventions and the successor Cotonou Agreement with the European Union (EU).

SURVEY AND PROSPECTS

The economic development of Solomon Islands has been impeded by inadequate transport facilities, inclement weather and by fluctuations in prices on the international market for the country's major agricultural exports. Increasing environmental concern over the exploitation of the country's natural resources and its vulnerability to unscrupulous foreign operators has continued to threaten the islands' economic stability. Furthermore, the country's dependence upon forestry—logging being the prime constituent of both taxation and export revenues—rendered the economy vulnerable to the low international prices for round logs prevailing in 2001. The country's logging industry attracted renewed international attention in early 2004 when a chain of islands in the Western Solomons (one of which was the site of a World Bank-funded conservation project) was devastated by intensive logging. A number of foreign companies were believed to have arrived in the islands and begun operations without undertaking any environmental impact studies or negotiations with villagers and landowners. Reports indicated that some islands had been completed deforested within a matter of weeks and that coral reefs had been destroyed by heavy machinery in the area.

The economy was severely affected by ethnic unrest in Guadalcanal. Furthermore, subsequent housing and welfare payments to displaced victims of the unrest became a severe drain on domestic finance. Successive budget deficits and a substantial current-account deficit were financed by heavy borrowing and foreign aid. During 2000 a total of 8,000 workers, or 15% of the formal sector's total labour force, were made redundant or dispatched on unpaid leave. Youth unemployment, meanwhile, remained a particular problem. In February 2001 the Central Bank of Solomon Islands reportedly declared that the country faced economic and social disaster, stating that the country's GDP had contracted by 19% in one year, and that exports had declined by 40% in six months, while domestic borrowing, particularly by the Government, had notably increased. Payments to public servants, along with the transfer of funds to provincial health and education services, were delayed. Moreover, the Government defaulted on various external and domestic debts held by commercial banks and the National Provident Fund (no employee contributions having been made to the latter in 2001). Furthermore, the dramatic rise in crime, which in part had occurred as a result of the alleged infiltration of the police force by rebel groups, appeared to be a deterrent to growth and investment.

In January 2002 the Central Bank announced that the country's total debt amounted to some US $200m., while its foreign reserves had fallen to below US $18m. The Government subsequently announced plans to reduce expenditure by up to 50%, which would reportedly result in about one-third of employees losing their jobs. In October the Government reduced the number of ministries from 20 to 10. In July 2003 an Australian-led regional intervention force arrived in the country to restore law and order. The intervention, which had been requested by the Government of Solomon Islands, included an economic recovery programme involving increased assistance from Australia (totalling some $A1,000m. over 10 years) and the appointment of numerous Australian officials to key posts within the Government and public service and finance sectors. It was hoped that the country's potential for prolonged political stability, improved inter-ethnic relations and consequently enhanced social and economic conditions would be greatly assisted by the measures agreed with Australia.

Somalia

The Somali Democratic Republic lies on the east coast of Africa. After the overthrow of Mohamed Siad Barre's regime by the United Somali Congress (USC) in 1991, hostilities between rival insurgents, exacerbated by clan-based enmities and regionally-based territorial aspirations, proliferated nation-wide. The most serious conflict was that between supporters of USC-appointed President Ali Mahdi and the USC's military commander, Gen. Mohamed Farah Aidid. The UN's largest ever peacekeeping operation (UNOSOM II, initiated in 1993) failed and its associated troops and civilian personnel were evacuated. No sustained progress towards resolving Somalia's multi-factional conflict was achieved until after mid-2000. Mogadishu is the capital. The national language is Somali.

Area and population
Area: 637,657 sq km
Population (mid-2002): 9,390,830
Population density (mid-2002): 14.7 per sq km
Life expectancy (years at birth, 2002): 44.3 (males 43.0; females 45.7)

Finance

GDP in current prices: 1999: US $2,021m. ($240 per head)
Real GDP growth (1999): 2.1%
Inflation (annual average, 2001): 11.5%
Currency: Somali shilling

Economy

In 1990, according to estimates by the World Bank, Somalia's gross national income (GNI), measured at average 1988–90 prices, was US $946m., equivalent to $150 per head. According to UN figures, in 2001 gross domestic product (GDP) was $1,000m., equivalent to $110 per head. During 1990–2002, it was estimated, the population increased at an average annual rate of 2.3%. GDP declined, in real terms, at an average annual rate of 3.3% in 1990–99; however, growth of 2.1% was recorded in 1999.

AGRICULTURE

Agriculture (including forestry and fishing) contributed 66% of GDP in 1990. An estimated 66.9% of the working population were employed in agriculture in 2002. Agriculture is based on the breeding of livestock, which accounted for 49% of GDP in 1989 and 38.4% of the total value of exports in 1988. Bananas are the principal cash crop, accounting for 40.3% of export earnings in 1988. The GDP of the agricultural sector declined by an average of 4.1% per year in 1990–99; agricultural GDP increased by 12.0% in 1999. Although crop production in 1996 was reported to have increased by 50% compared with the previous year, output was still some 37% lower than it had been prior to the civil war. Severe flooding in southern Somalia during 1997 led to widespread crop failure and resulted in the loss of as many as 30,000 cattle. Total cereals production was 207,800 metric tons in 1999, the lowest annual yield since 1993, but recovered to an estimated 304,900 in 2002.

INDUSTRY

Industry (including mining, manufacturing, construction and power) contributed 8.6% of GDP in 1988, and employed an estimated 12.0% of the working population in 2002. The combined GDP of the mining, manufacturing and power sectors increased by an average of 2.3% per year in 1990–99; growth in 1999 was 13.8%. The GDP of the construction sector increased at an average annual rate of 0.8% in 1990–99; growth of 16.8% was recorded in 1999.

Mining

Mining contributed 0.3% of GDP in 1988. Somalia's mineral resources include salt, limestone, gypsum, gold, silver, nickel, copper, zinc, lead, manganese, uranium and iron ore. Deposits of petroleum and natural gas have been discovered, but remain unexploited: US petroleum companies were granted exploration rights covering two-thirds of the country by Siad Barre, and were expected to start investigations once there was a durable peace. In February 2001 it was reported that the French petroleum company TotalFinaElf had signed an agreement with the transitional Somali Government to carry out oil exploration in the south of the country. Discussions commenced in January 2003 between the 'Somaliland' administration and a British-based company regarding the possible granting of contracts for petroleum exploration.

Manufacturing

Manufacturing contributed almost 5% of GDP in 1988. The most important sectors are food-processing, especially sugar-refining, the processing of hides and skins, and the refining of petroleum. Manufacturing GDP increased by an average of 2.0% per year in 1990–99; growth in 1999 was 18.0%.

Energy

Energy is derived principally from oil-fired generators. Imports of fuel products comprised 14% of the value of merchandise imports in 1990.

SERVICES

The services sector contributed 24.6% of GDP in 1988, and engaged an estimated 21.1% of the employed labour force in 2002. Tourism accounted for some 9.3% of GDP in 1988.

EXTERNAL TRADE

In 1989 Somalia recorded a visible trade deficit of US $278.6m., and there was a deficit of $156.7m. on the current account of the balance of payments. In 1982 the principal source of imports (34.4%) was Italy, while Saudi Arabia was the principal market for exports (86.5%). Other major trading partners in that year were the United Kingdom, the Federal Republic of Germany and Kenya. The principal exports in 1988 were livestock and bananas. The principal imports were petroleum, fertilizers, foodstuffs and machinery. Livestock and bananas remained the principal exports in the late 1990s, while the United Arab Emirates emerged as Somalia's main trading partner.

GOVERNMENT FINANCE

In 1988 Somalia recorded a budget deficit of 10,009.4m. Somali shillings. A provisional budget for 1991 was projected to balance at 268,283.2m. Somali shillings. Somalia's total external debt was US $2,531m. at the end of 2001, of which $1,795m. was long-term public debt. In 1990 the cost of debt-servicing was equivalent to 11.7% of the value of exports of goods and services. In 1990–2001 the average annual rate of inflation was 20.6%. Consumer prices increased by 11.5% in 2001. The rate of unemployment was estimated at 47.4% in 2002.

INTERNATIONAL ECONOMIC RELATIONS

Somalia is a member of the African Development Bank and the Islamic Development Bank.

SURVEY AND PROSPECTS

Somalia's long history of civil unrest, together with unreliable climatic conditions, have undermined the traditional agricultural base of the economy. By the mid-1990s a significant recovery had been recorded in livestock numbers, sorghum output and exports of bananas, although the production and export of the last exacerbated factional fighting, with rival clansmen competing for control of the industry in order to fund their war efforts.

Following the establishment of the Transitional National Assembly in August 2000, it was hoped that Somalia's economic situation would improve. On his appointment,

President Hasan appealed for foreign donors to provide assistance with the rehabilitation of basic infrastructures and to finance development projects. However, the Government's attempts to establish control over the economy by issuing large quantities of currency notes resulted in a rapid rise in the rate of inflation and a further depreciation in the value of the shilling. Although the economy subsequently began to show signs of a recovery, in December 2001 the UN announced that Somalia was on the verge of an economic collapse unparalleled in modern history. This was attributed largely to the US Administration's decision to enforce the closure of the al-Barakat banking and telecommunications organization, owing to its suspected links to terrorist organizations, thus severing the remittance process on which so much of the country is heavily dependent. The proposed formation of a new government in 2004 again raised hopes that central authority would be restored to the country, thus enabling the possible creation of financial institutions and providing a degree of stability, which would, in turn, encourage the development of the economy. Meanwhile in mid-2003 the World Bank resumed operations in Somalia (which had been suspended in 1991) under its initiative for low-income countries under stress. Nevertheless, Somalia remained in need of vast amounts of international humanitarian assistance.

South Africa

The Republic of South Africa occupies the southern extremity of the African mainland. After 1948 the National Party introduced the doctrine of apartheid, which led to white supremacy. In 1990 the African National Congress of South Africa (ANC) was legalized, and its leader, Nelson Mandela, was released from prison. All remaining apartheid laws were repealed in 1991. The ANC won the majority of votes cast in legislative elections in 1994, and Mandela was elected President. Mandela formally retired from active politics following elections in 1999, at which the ANC was returned to power, and Thabo Mbeki became President. The ANC again enjoyed overwhelming success at national elections in April 2004. The administrative capital is Pretoria, the legislative capital is Cape Town, and the judicial capital is Bloemfontein. There are 11 official languages.

Area and population
Area: 1,219,090 sq km
Population (mid-2002): 43,580,000
Population density (mid-2002): 35.7 per sq km
Life expectancy (years at birth, 2002): 50.7 (males 48.8; females 52.6)

Finance
GDP in current prices: 2002): US $104,235m. ($2,392 per head)
Real GDP growth (2002): 3.0%
Inflation (annual average, 2002): 9.2%
Currency: rand

Economy

In 2002, according to estimates by the World Bank, South Africa's gross national income (GNI), measured at average 2000–02 prices, was US $113,493m., equivalent to $2,600 per head (or $9,870 per head on an international purchasing-power parity basis). During 1990–2002, it was estimated, the population increased at an average annual rate of 1.8%, while gross domestic product (GDP) per head decreased, in real terms, by an average of 0.1% per year. Overall GDP increased, in real terms, at an average annual rate of 1.9% in 1990–2002, according to the World Bank. Growth was 3.0% in 2002, according to official figures.

AGRICULTURE
Agriculture (including forestry and fishing) contributed 4.1% of GDP in 2002. Some 10.3% of the employed labour force were engaged in the sector at September 2003. Maize (also the principal subsistence crop), fruit and sugar are exported, and live-stock-rearing is also important: wool is another significant export. The GDP of the agricultural sector increased by an average of 0.4% per year in 1990–2002, according to the World Bank. Agricultural GDP increased by 2.0% in 2002.

INDUSTRY
Industry (including mining, manufacturing, construction and power) contributed 32.2% of GDP in 2002, and engaged 24.5% of the employed labour force at September 2003. Industrial GDP increased at an average annual rate of 0.9% in 1990–2002, according to the World Bank. Industrial GDP increased by 3.9% in 2002.

Mining
Mining contributed 7.7% of GDP in 2002, and engaged 4.3% of the employed labour force at September 2003. South Africa is the world's leading producer of gold, which is the major mineral export, accounting for about 15% of total world production in 2002. Coal, platinum, iron ore, diamonds, chromium, manganese, vanadium, vermi-culite, antimony, limestone, asbestos, fluorspar, uranium, copper, lead and zinc are also important mineral exports. There are reserves of petroleum, natural gas, silli-manite, titanium and zirconium. The GDP of the mining sector declined by an average of 1.4% per year in 1997–2001. Mining GDP declined by 1.5% in 2001.

Manufacturing
Manufacturing contributed 19.4% of GDP in 2002, and engaged 14.1% of the employed labour force at September 2003. The GDP of the manufacturing sector increased at an average annual rate of 1.9% in 1990–2002, according to the World Bank. Manufacturing GDP increased by 5.0% in 2002.

Energy

Energy is derived principally from coal-based electricity; this is supplemented by nuclear power and by hydroelectric power. The construction of a plant to convert natural gas into liquid fuel was completed in 1992. Exploitation of petroleum reserves in oilfields located 140 km south-west of the Southern Cape commenced in 1997. In 2001 substantial reserves of natural gas were discovered off the Western Cape. Imports of mineral fuels and lubricants comprised 15.5% of the value of total imports in 2001.

SERVICES

The services sector contributed 63.7% of GDP in 2002, and engaged 64.9% of the employed labour force at September 2003. The real GDP of the services sector increased by an average of 2.5% per year in 1990–2002, according to the World Bank. Services GDP increased by 2.3% in 2002.

EXTERNAL TRADE

In 2002 South Africa recorded a visible trade surplus of US $4,372m., while there was a surplus of $290m. on the current account of the balance of payments. In 2000 the principal source of imports for the Southern African Customs Union (SACU) was Germany (an estimated 13.2%); other major suppliers of imports were the USA, the United Kingdom, Japan, Saudi Arabia, Iran and France. The principal market for exports in that year was the USA (9.2%); other important purchasers were the United Kingdom, Germany, Japan and the Netherlands. The principal exports in 2000 were basic manufactures (particularly iron and steel, and diamonds), machinery and transport equipment, mineral fuels, crude materials, chemical products, and food and live animals. The principal imports were machinery and transport equipment (notably telecommunications and sound equipment), mineral fuels (particularly petroleum), basic manufactures and chemical products.

GOVERNMENT FINANCE

In 2002 South Africa recorded a budgetary deficit of R 6,031m., equivalent to 0.5% of GDP. At the end of 2001 the total external debt was US $24,050m., of which $7,941m. was long-term public debt. The cost of debt-servicing in that year was equivalent to 11.6% of the value of exports of goods and services. The annual rate of inflation averaged 8.7% in 1990–2002; consumer prices increased by 9.2% in 2002 and by 5.8% in 2003. According to official figures, 28.2% of the labour force were unemployed at September 2003.

INTERNATIONAL ECONOMIC RELATIONS

South Africa is a member of SACU (with Botswana, Lesotho, Namibia and Swaziland), of the Southern African Development Community (SADC) and of the African Development Bank. The Secretariat of the New Partnership for Africa's Development is located in South Africa.

SURVEY AND PROSPECTS

Despite South Africa's mineral wealth and highly developed manufacturing sector, economic progress was hindered during the 1980s following the imposition of economic sanctions by the international community in protest at apartheid. In late 1993, in response to the Government's adoption of political reforms, the remaining economic sanctions were ended, relations with international financial institutions were normalized, and an agreement with foreign creditor banks regarding the country's outstanding debt was reached.

Following democratic elections in April 1994, foreign Governments pledged considerable financial assistance to South Africa. The new Government initiated a Reconstruction and Development Programme; however, subsequent progress in social and economic development was impeded by the necessity for fiscal restraint. In mid-1996 the Government announced its long-term strategy for 'growth, employment and redistribution' (GEAR), which placed emphasis on continued fiscal discipline, reductions in the budgetary deficit and the removal of exchange controls. By 1999 financial market conditions had improved considerably, resulting in lower inflation, increased real GDP and an increase in investor confidence. GDP growth slowed to 2.8% in 2001, owing to a world economic slowdown, which was compounded by high interest rates and a shortage of skilled labour, but increased to 3.0% in 2002. Meanwhile, the IMF urged the Government to accelerate the implementation of the structural reforms of the GEAR strategy, particularly the reduction of unemployment (which remained critically high), trade liberalization and privatization.

Political violence in Zimbabwe contributed to a dramatic reduction in the value of the rand in 2000–01, and prompted concern that the South African economy (particularly with regard to foreign investment) might be adversely affected. The rand reached an all-time low against the US dollar in 2001, partly as a result of South Africa's reliance on exports at a time when global economic activity was slowing down. The mining sector, one of the most significant in the South African economy, underwent significant rationalization and consolidation in the late 1990s, and in June 2002 the National Assembly approved legislation transferring the control of mineral rights from private companies to the Government, which would then lease them. GDP growth was lower than forecast in 2003, at an estimated 1.9%, compared with a target of 3.3%, partly owing to a significant appreciation in the value of the rand during the year (by some 39.2% against the US dollar), which reduced the contribution of the export sector to GDP. Growth of 3.1% was forecast for 2004, with strong international prices projected for gold, the principal mineral export. In late 2003 the Government announced its intention to increase public expenditure on infrastructure, social services and health care in an attempt to reduce levels of poverty and unemployment; the distribution of income in South Africa was one of the most unequal in the world.

Spain

The Kingdom of Spain is situated in south-western Europe. Following the civil war of 1936–39 Gen. Franco established an authoritarian regime. After King Juan Carlos succeeded Franco as Head of State in 1975 democratic government was rapidly introduced. In 1977 the Unión de Centro Democrático coalition gained an overall majority in the legislature. Thereafter, the Partido Socialista Obrero Español (PSOE) was the dominant party until 1996. The Partido Popular (PP), led by José María Aznar, governed until 2004, when the PSOE, under José Luis Zapatero, was elected to government. Madrid is the capital. Castilian Spanish is the principal language.

Area and population
Area: 505,988 sq km (including Spanish North Africa)
Population (mid-2002): 41,180,000
Population density (mid-2002): 81.4 per sq km
Life expectancy (years at birth, 2002): 79.6 (males 76.1; females 83.0)

Finance
GDP in current prices: 2002: US $649,792m. ($15,779 per head)
Real GDP growth (2002): 1.8%
Inflation (annual average, 2002): 3.1%
Currency: euro

Economy

In 2002, according to estimates by the World Bank, Spain's gross national income (GNI), measured at average 2000–02 prices, was US $594,114m., equivalent to US $14,430 per head (or $20,460 per head on an international purchasing-power parity basis). During 1990–2002, it was estimated, the population increased at an average annual rate of 0.5% per year, while gross domestic product (GDP) per head increased, in real terms, by an average of 2.1% per year. Overall GDP increased, in real terms, at an average annual rate of 2.6% in 1990–2002; growth in 2002 was 2.0%, according to official estimates.

AGRICULTURE

Agriculture (including forestry and fishing) contributed an estimated 3.0% of GDP in 2002 and engaged 5.9% of the employed labour force. The principal crops are barley, wheat, sugar beet, vegetables, citrus fruits, grapes and olives; wine and olive oil are important products. Farmers were seriously affected by the infection of cattle with both bovine spongiform encephalopathy (BSE) and foot and mouth disease during 2000–01. According to the World Bank, agricultural GDP grew at an average annual rate of 0.9% in 1990–2001; it increased by 1.5% in 2000, but declined by 0.3% in 2001. Agricultural subsidies from the EU totalled €5,933m. in 2002. The fishing industry is significant. The Spanish fishing fleet is one of the largest in the world, and has been involved in various international disputes. In December 2000 the EU proposed a dramatic reduction in fishing levels, in an attempt to address the over-fishing of certain species; this action was expected to have a serious affect on the fishing industry. In November 2002 the oil-tanker *Prestige* sank off the Galician coast, polluting an estimated 3,000 km of coastline. It was predicted that the area would take 10 years to recover, at a cost of some €5,000m. to the fishing and tourism industries. Catches of shellfish and inshore fish were reported to have declined by 80% following the tanker's sinking.

INDUSTRY

Industry (including mining, manufacturing, utilities and construction) contributed an estimated 24.0% of GDP in 2002 and engaged 31.2% of the employed labour force. According to the World Bank, industrial GDP increased at an average annual rate of 2.1% in 1990–2001; it increased by 4.6% in 2000 and by 2.4% in 2001.

Mining

The mining and quarrying industry provided less than 1.0% of GDP in 2000, and engaged 0.4% of the employed labour force in 2002. Hard coal and brown coal are the principal minerals extracted, although production fell in the late 1990s owing to environmental standards imposed by the European Union (EU). There are small reserves of petroleum. Some natural gas requirements are obtained from the Bay of Biscay, the remainder being imported by pipeline from Algeria.

Manufacturing

Manufacturing contributed 15.9% of GDP in 2001 and engaged 18.4% of the employed labour force in 2002. Spain is one of the world's largest exporters of passenger cars. In 2001 production of passenger vehicles was 2.34m. units, of which more than 80% were exported. Other important industries are shipbuilding, chemicals, steel, textiles and footwear; some of these sectors underwent a process of rationalization in the 1980s. Investment is being made in new manufacturing industries, such as information technology and telecommunications equipment. According to the World Bank, manufacturing GDP decreased at an average annual rate of 0.3% in 1989–99; the rate of growth was 5.3% in 1998.

Energy

Energy contributed 2.8% of GDP in 2002 and employed 0.6% of the labour force in 2001. Energy is derived principally from petroleum, most of which is imported. In 2001 imports of mineral fuels and petroleum products accounted for 11.2% of total import costs. However, natural gas became an increasingly important fuel source in the late 1990s. According to the World Bank, coal provided 36.5% of total electricity production in 2000, while nuclear energy provided 28.1%. In 2001 the electricity sector underwent major restructuring. The Government of Valencia invested €2.6m. to build 40 wind farms in the region by 2003.

SERVICES

In 2002 the services sector accounted for 64.1% of GDP and engaged 62.9% of the employed labour force. The tourism industry makes an important contribution to the Spanish economy. In 2002 the number of tourist arrivals was 48.7m., and receipts from tourism reached US $35,544m. In April 2001 several areas, including the Balearic Islands, introduced an environmental tourist tax, included in the cost of tourist accommodation, to protect the environment and repair the damage caused by the annual influx of tourists. Remittances from emigrants are also significant. According to the World Bank, the GDP of the services sector increased at an average annual rate of 2.9% in 1990–2001; services GDP increased by 3.9% in 2000 and by 3.3% in 2001.

EXTERNAL TRADE

In 2002 Spain recorded a visible trade deficit of US $33,098m. and there was a deficit of US $15,901m. on the current account of the balance of payments. In 2001 the principal sources of imports were France (16.7%) and Germany (15.5%), while the former was the main export market, purchasing 19.5%, followed by Germany (11.8%). Italy, the United Kingdom and other EU countries, and the USA, are also important trading partners. The principal imports in 2001 were machinery, electrical equipment, vehicles, mineral fuels and petroleum products, and chemical products. The main exports were motor cars, machinery, metals and their manufactures, and chemical products.

GOVERNMENT FINANCE

The 2002 draft budget envisaged a deficit of €3,762m., equivalent to 0.5% of GDP (compared with 0.3% in 2001). Compared with the previous year, government expenditure was projected to decrease by 2.3%. At December 1995 the external debt of the central Government totalled 6,153,200m. pesetas. In 1990–2000 the annual rate of inflation averaged 4.6%; consumer prices increased by an average of 4.6% in 2000 and by 3.6% in 2001. Unemployment levels, although the highest in the EU, declined in 2001 to 10.5% of the labour force. Unemployment levels remained stable, at around 11.4%, in 2002–03. By February 2004 the unemployment rate had fallen to 9.2%. The

Organisation for Economic Co-operation and Development (OECD) predicted, however, that the overall annual unemployment rate would be 11.0% in 2004.

INTERNATIONAL ECONOMIC RELATIONS

Spain became a member of the EU in January 1986, and joined the exchange rate mechanism of the European Monetary System in June 1989. For the period 2000–06 the EU allocated €8,159m. annually in structural and cohesion funds towards projects in Spain. Spain is also a member of the OECD.

SURVEY AND PROSPECTS

Upon taking office in May 1996, the PP Government declared its commitment to European economic and monetary union (as agreed by EU members at Maastricht in December 1991). In order to meet the EU convergence criteria, Spain's budget deficit was duly reduced to the equivalent of below 3.0% of GDP by 1997. Spain was thus able to qualify for membership of the single European currency, introduced in January 1999. As a direct consequence of entering the single European currency, from early 1999 there was a sudden and sustained rise in inflation. Annual average inflation in 2000–01 was substantially higher than the average rate prevailing in most other member countries of the single European currency. In addition to high consumer demand, the introduction of the euro also encouraged stronger GDP growth. During its second term in office (2000–04), the PP Government followed a policy of eliminating the public deficit (which was achieved in 2001), reducing unemployment, and liberalizing the economy in an attempt to combat inflation. Revenue was also raised through the transfer of state assets, particularly in the energy and telecommunications sectors, to private ownership.

In June 2000 the gas supply monopoly of Gas Natural was ended, when the Government awarded 12 licences to gas companies. By the end of 2003 the Government's privatization programme had almost been completed. In early 2001 the Spanish companies Airtel, Euskaltel Menta, Desarrollo de Cable and Retecal, together with a group of international operators, announced their intention to construct a fibre optic cable network across Spain, along the road network. In the same year a plan, valued at 3,000m. pesetas, was approved by the Senado for investment in the water system. Water was to be piped from the Ebro river in the north, to the arid south-east of the country. Proposals also included improvement to city water supplies, reforestation and recycling projects, a reduction in water prices, the modernization of irrigation methods for agriculture, and the implementation of a quality control and monitoring system of the water supply. However, there was strong opposition to the plan, and it was subsequently cancelled by the newly inaugurated PSOE Government in April 2004.

Spain is the largest investor in Argentina, after the USA, and many of its banks and other companies suffered substantial losses as a result of the worsening debt crisis there and the devaluation of the national currency, the peso, in mid-2001. In 2002, however, the performance of Spanish businesses in Latin America improved, following the election victory of Luiz Inácio (Lula) da Silva in Brazil in October 2001, and of Néstor Kirchner in Argentina in May 2002. In March 2004 Telefónica became the fourth largest mobile telephone operator in Latin America.

Having narrowly missed its target of a balanced budget in 2002, partly as a result of fiscal deficits in the autonomous regions, Spain presented a balanced budget in 2003, aided by €16,000m. in EU donations (equivalent to 2% of GDP). A small budgetary surplus (of 0.3% of GDP) was recorded for that year. The Spanish energy market entered its final stages of liberalization in early 2003, although deficits in the sector as a result of the fixing of a low price ceiling led to a government promise of a reimbursement of €1,600m. in December 2002. In late 2003 slow international growth forced the Government to lower its growth forecast for that year from 3.0% to 2.3%, which was subsequently achieved. As had been the case since 1997, the Spanish economy grew significantly more than did its EU neighbours. Among the eurozone countries economic growth in 2003 averaged only 0.4%. Spanish GDP growth was forecast at 3.0% for 2004. In January 2004 consumer prices were 2.3% higher than they were 12 months previously, and an overall rate of inflation of 2.7% was predicted for that year.

In March 2004 a meeting of EU ministers of finance approved Spain's budget plans for 2004–07, which predicted annual budgetary surpluses. In the same month the incoming socialist Government sought to assure investors of its economic orthodoxy, and stated that it would not reverse the PP's economic policy. With the impending entry of former communist bloc countries into the EU, Spain seemed likely to lose some of its annual subsidies. In 2002 GDP per capita in Spain as a whole was 87.8% of the EU average, well above the 75% cut-off point for receiving subsidies. Under this condition only Andalucía, Extremadura and Galicia would continue to qualify. There were also concerns that companies currently operating in Spain would move production to eastern Europe where running costs would be considerably cheaper.

Spanish North Africa

Spanish North Africa comprises mainly two enclaves within Moroccan territory: Ceuta, on the north African coast opposite Gibraltar; and Melilla, situated on a small peninsula jutting into the Mediterranean Sea. Ceuta was retained by Spain upon Moroccan independence from France in 1956, as was Melilla, the first Spanish town to rise against the Government of the Popular Front in 1936. Morocco formally presented its claim to Ceuta and Melilla to the UN General Assembly in 1988. Spain insists, however, that Ceuta and Melilla are integral parts of its territory. Spanish and Arabic are spoken.

Area and population

Area: 32 sq km
Population (1 November 2001): 137,916
Population density (1 November 2001): 4,310 per sq km
Life expectancy (years at birth, 1998–99): 76.8 (males 73.7; females 80.0)

Finance

GDP in current prices: 2002): 1,953m. euros (per head 13,438 euros)
Real GDP growth (2001): 4.0%
Inflation (2001): 3.8%
Currency: euro

Economy

In 2002 the combined gross domestic product (GDP) of Ceuta and Melilla totalled an estimated €1,953.0m., equivalent to €13,620 per head. An unofficial report issued in October 1996 classified Melilla as by far the poorest city in Spain. In 2002 GDP per head was equivalent to 75.83% of the average for Spain in Ceuta and 80.02% of the Spanish average in Melilla. The GDP of Ceuta and Melilla grew by 4.02% in 2001 and by 1.06% in 2002.

Agricultural activity in the territories is negligible, and industry is on a limited scale. There is a local brewery in Ceuta. In 2001 the economically active population of the two enclaves totalled 49,400, of whom 2,500 were unemployed, 3,800 were employed in the construction sector, 2,500 in industry and 200 in agriculture, hunting, forestry and fishing; 40,400 were employed in the services sector. In 1996 the civil service employed 2,904 workers in Ceuta and 2,877 in Melilla. In 2002 the economically active population of Ceuta was 27,000, of whom 1,300 were unemployed.

SERVICES

Tourism previously made a significant contribution to the territories' economies. Almost 1m. tourists visited Ceuta in 1986, attracted by duty-free goods; however, owing to the high ferry-boat fares and the opening of the Spanish border with Gibraltar, tourist numbers gradually declined, totalling 61,356 in 2002.

EXTERNAL TRADE

Most of the population's food is imported, with the exception of fish which is obtained locally. Sardines and anchovies are the most important items. A large proportion of the tinned fish is sold outside Spain. More important to the economies of the cities is the port activity; most of their exports take the form of fuel supplied—at very competitive rates—to ships. Most of the fuel comes from the Spanish refinery in Tenerife. Ceuta's port is the busier, receiving a total of 9,507 ships in 2002. Apart from the ferries from Málaga and Almería in mainland Spain, Melilla's port is not so frequented—a total of 1,079 vessels entered in 2002—and its exports are correspondingly low. Ceuta's main exports are frozen and preserved fish, foodstuffs and beer. Most trade is conducted with other parts of Spain. In 2002 Ceuta's trade deficit was €105.5m.

GOVERNMENT FINANCE

Ceuta's budget for 2001 was estimated at 23,172m. pesetas. An Action Plan for Ceuta was launched in late 2002, providing for €71m. in investment by mainland Spain to reduce the enclave's dependence upon Morocco. The average annual rate of inflation was 3.8% in 2001 and 3.3% in 2002.

Upon the accession in January 1986 of Spain to the EC (EU since November 1993), Ceuta and Melilla were considered as Spanish cities and European territory, and joined the organization as part of Spain. They retained their status as free ports. The statutes of autonomy, adopted in early 1995, envisaged the continuation of the territories' fiscal benefits. Euro notes and coins became the sole legal tender in Ceuta and Melilla on 28 February 2002.

In June 1994 the EU announced substantial regional aid: between 1995 and 1999 Ceuta and Melilla were to receive totals of ECU 28m. and ECU 45m., of which ECU 20m. and ECU 18m., respectively, were to be in the form of direct aid. However, the successive enlargements of the EU planned for 2004 and 2007 were to limit Spain's access to EU aid; Ceuta and Melilla would no longer be eligible for support. With assistance from the European Social Fund, a programme of employment and vocational training for Melilla was announced in 1996. In 1997 projected state investment in Ceuta and Melilla was 7,786m. pesetas, compared with 6,363m. pesetas in 1996.

Sri Lanka

The Democratic Socialist Republic of Sri Lanka lies in southern Asia. Since 1986 the Liberation Tigers of Tamil Eelam (LTTE), which seeks the establishment of a Tamil state in the northern and eastern provinces, has been the main separatist group waging civil war against successive governments. In 2002 the Government and the LTTE signed an agreement on an internationally monitored indefinite cease-fire; formal negotiations to end the fighting in which some 60,000 people had been killed commenced in September. Colombo and Sri Jayawardenepura (Kotte) are, respectively, the commercial and administrative capitals. Sinhala, Tamil and English are the national languages

Area and population
Area: 65,525 sq km
Population (mid-2002): 18,968,480
Population density (mid-2002): 289.5 per sq km
Life expectancy (years at birth, 2002): 70.3 (males 67.2; females 74.3)

Finance
GDP in current prices: 2002): US $16,373m. ($863 per head)
Real GDP growth (2002): 3.0%
Inflation (annual average, 2002): 9.6%
Currency: Sri Lanka rupee

Economy

In 2002, according to estimates by the World Bank, Sri Lanka's gross national income (GNI), measured at average 2000–02 prices, was US $15,894m., equivalent to $840 per head (or $3,390 per head on an international purchasing-power parity basis). During 1990–2002, it was estimated, the population increased at an average annual rate of 1.3%, while gross domestic product (GDP) per head increased, in real terms, by an average of 3.1% per year. Overall GDP increased, in real terms, at an average annual rate of 4.5% in 1990–2002. Real GDP grew by 6.0% in 2000, but decreased, in real terms, by 1.4% in 2001. Real GDP increased by 4.0% in 2002 and by an estimated 5.5% in 2003.

AGRICULTURE

Agriculture (including hunting, forestry and fishing) contributed 20.1% of GDP in 2002, and in the first quarter of 2003 35.1% of the employed labour force were engaged in the sector. The principal cash crops are tea (which accounted for 14.2% of total export earnings in 2002), rubber and coconuts. In 1990 Sri Lanka overtook India as the world's largest tea exporter. Rice production is also important. Cattle, buffaloes, goats and poultry are the principal livestock. During 1990–2002 agricultural GDP increased at an average annual rate of 1.4%. Agricultural GDP declined by 2.9% in 2001, largely as a result of drought, before increasing by 1.0% in 2002.

INDUSTRY

Industry (including mining and quarrying, manufacturing, construction and power) contributed 26.3% of GDP in 2002, and engaged 24.4% of the employed labour force (excluding inhabitants of the northern and eastern provinces) in the first quarter of 2001. During 1990–2002 industrial GDP increased at an average annual rate of 5.7%. Industrial GDP increased by an estimated 7.5% in 2000, but contracted by about 2% in 2001, mainly owing to a dramatic decrease in export-orientated industries. Industrial output increased by 3.0% in 2002.

Mining

Mining and quarrying contributed 1.8% of GDP in 2002, and engaged 1.3% of the employed labour force in 2000. Gemstones are the major mineral export (accounting for an estimated 1.9% of total export earnings in 2002). Another commercially important mineral in Sri Lanka is graphite, and there are also deposits of iron ore, monazite, uranium, ilmenite sands, limestone and clay.

Manufacturing

Manufacturing contributed 15.9% of GDP in 2002, and engaged 16.9% of the employed labour force in the first quarter of 2003. The principal branches of manufacturing include wearing apparel (excluding footwear), textiles, food products, and also petroleum and coal products. The garment industry is Sri Lanka's largest earner of foreign exchange, with sales of garments and textiles providing an estimated 51.9% of total export earnings in 2002. During 1990–2002 manufacturing GDP increased by an average of 6.5% per year. The GDP of the manufacturing sector rose by an estimated 8.8% in 2000, but declined by 4.0% in 2001. The sector recovered in 2002; manufacturing output increased by 3%.

Energy

Energy is derived principally from hydroelectric power, which accounted for 46.7% of electricity production in 2000. Imports of mineral fuels and lubricants comprised 9.5% of the value of total imports in 2001.

SERVICES

The services sector, which is dominated by tourism, contributed 53.6% of GDP in 2002, and engaged 42.5% of the employed labour force (excluding inhabitants of the northern and eastern provinces) in the first quarter of 2001. During 1990–2002 services GDP increased at an average annual rate of 5.3%. The sector's GDP grew by 7.0% in 2000, before declining by 0.3% in 2001. Growth in the sector reached 3.8% in 2002.

EXTERNAL TRADE

In 2002 Sri Lanka recorded a visible trade deficit of US $1,406.5m., and there was a deficit of $289.7m. on the current account of the balance of payments. In 2001 the principal source of imports (9.9%) was India, while the USA was the principal market for exports (38.9%). Other major trading partners were Japan, Singapore and the United Kingdom. The principal exports in 2002 were clothing, tea and basic manu-factures. The principal imports were textile yarn and fabrics, basic manufactures, machinery and transport equipment, and food and live animals.

GOVERNMENT FINANCE

The projected budgetary deficit for 2004 totalled Rs 138,000m. (6.8% of GDP). Sri Lanka's total external debt was US $8,529m. at the end of 2001, of which $7,472m. was long-term public debt. In that year the cost of debt-servicing was equivalent to 9.7% of earnings from the exports of goods and services. During 1990–2002 the average annual rate of inflation was 10.2%; the rate declined to 4.7% in 1999, before rising to 6.2% in 2000 and an estimated 14.2% in 2001. The rate of inflation decelerated to 9.5% in 2002. An estimated 9.2% of the labour force were unemployed in the first quarter of 2003.

INTERNATIONAL ECONOMIC RELATIONS

Sri Lanka is a member of the Asian Development Bank (ADB), a founder member of the South Asian Association for Regional Co-operation (SAARC), which seeks to improve regional co-operation, particularly in economic development, a founder member of the Colombo Plan, which seeks to promote economic and social devel-opment in Asia and the Pacific, and a member of the UN Economic and Social Commission for Asia and the Pacific (ESCAP).

SURVEY AND PROSPECTS

Unemployment, a persistent fiscal deficit and inflation, together with the economic dislocation resulting from the ethnic conflict, are among the country's main economic problems The economy showed some encouraging signs of recovery in the latter half of the 1990s. However, the upsurge in fighting between government forces and Tamil guerrillas from the latter half of 1999 led to a further deterioration of the economic situation in 2000. Lack of confidence in the economy continued to deter foreign investment. Although Sri Lanka's main export markets recovered, the burden of the civil war and the higher cost of petroleum imports resulted in a sharp increase in the external current-account deficit. The economy then performed well until mid-2001: the current-account deficit narrowed and the country's foreign-exchange reserves increased.

In July the Central Bank 'floated' the rupee and, after an initial period of volatility, the currency stabilized. However, the political and economic developments in the latter half of 2001 caused considerable damage to the country's economy. The assault on the international airport in Colombo in July and the attacks on the USA in September adversely affected foreign-investor confidence and led to a sharp decline in tourism. The increase in insurance premiums payable by airlines and ships had a negative impact on the export market. The global economic slowdown caused a decrease in demand for garments and textiles, and the prolonged drought led to negative growth in agricultural GDP. Consequently, the economy contracted for the first time, the fiscal deficit increased to 10.8% of GDP (from 9.8% in 2001), and public debt stood at 103% of GDP (compared with 96.4% in 2001). The situation was exacerbated by the political crisis, which culminated in a general election in December, only 14 months after the previous poll.

The new Government, led by the United National Party, immediately embarked on a peace process to end the civil war that was draining the country's economic resources. One year after the cease-fire between the Government and the LTTE was declared in February 2002, the economy was showing clear signs of recovery. The Government had reduced the fiscal deficit in 2002 to 8.9% of GDP, and increased GDP growth to 3.0%. The export sector improved, with exports of textiles, industrial machinery and agriculture recording strong increases. Growth in imports, partly owing to rising fuel prices, also indicated a strengthening domestic economy. Imports of investment goods increased as a result of the reconstruction efforts under way in the north-east of Sri Lanka. Furthermore, tourist arrivals increased in the latter half of 2002, contributing to a rise in foreign-exchange reserves; in October SriLankan Airlines made its first profit in flight services since 1985, largely owing to the peace process and internal reforms.

A privatization programme was under way in 2002: the insurance, utilities, petroleum and telecommunications sectors were opened to private investment. The economy continued to improve in 2003. GDP growth reached an estimated 5.5% and fiscal deficit declined to 8.1% of GDP. The increase in exports, as well as the rapid expansion in the tourist industry, an increase in private investment and a rise in remittances from workers abroad, contributed to the high GDP growth. The average annual rate of inflation decreased to 6.3% and public debt declined to an estimated 100.9% of GDP (compared with 105.5% in 2002). The country's gross reserves also increased.

Substantial progress had also been made in public enterprise reform in 2003: several key public corporations were privatized and the electricity sector was open to private investment. Economic growth was expected to reach 6% in 2004, sustained by increased investment, even higher tourism and exports, and a normal monsoon.

However, uncertainties in the political situation and the peace process could deter potential investors and delay essential economic reform. The rupee had already depreciated by more than 3.0% in mid-March since October 2003. Furthermore, the April 2004 election resulted in the establishment of a minority coalition Government comprising parties that had divergent opinions on managing the economy. Donors at an international conference in June 2003 pledged US $4,500m. in aid over the next five years to help rebuild the country's economy and infrastructure; the economic assistance, however, was dependent on the resumption of the peace process. International financial organizations (such as the IMF) and individual nations (such as the United Kingdom) had already pledged funds for rehabilitation. The prerequisites to the assistance were a serious commitment from the Government to a restructuring programme and a permanent peace agreement between the LTTE and the Government.

Sudan

The Republic of Sudan lies in north-eastern Africa. The Sudan (as the country was known before 1975) achieved independence in 1956. In 1969 Col Gaafar Muhammad Nimeri seized power and established a one-party state. After Nimeri's overthrow in 1985, the Umma Party, led by Sadiq al-Mahdi, emerged as the leading political force. In 1989 al-Mahdi's Government was removed in a coup led by Brig. Omar Hassan Ahmad al-Bashir, who was subsequently elected as President. Since 1984 the Sudan People's Liberation Movement has waged an armed struggle against successive governnments. Khartoum is the capital. The official language is Arabic.

Area and population
Area: 2,505,813 sq km
Population (mid-2002): 32,365,040
Population density (mid-2002): 12.9 per sq km

Life expectancy (years at birth, 2002): 57.1 (males 54.9; females 59.3)

Finance
GDP in current prices: 2002: US $13,490m. ($417 per head)
Real GDP growth (2002): 10.6%
Inflation (annual average, 2001): 6.4%
Currency: Sudanese dinar

Economy

In 2002, according to estimates by the World Bank, Sudan's gross national income (GNI), measured at average 2000–02 prices, was US $11,471m., equivalent to $350 per head (or $1,690 on an international purchasing-power parity basis). During 1990–2002, it was estimated, the population increased at an average annual rate of 2.2%, while gross domestic product (GDP) per head increased, in real terms, by an average of 3.9% per year. Overall GDP increased, in real terms, at an average annual rate of 6.2% in 1990–2002; growth in 2002 was 10.6%.

AGRICULTURE

Agriculture (including forestry and fishing) contributed 39.2% of GDP and employed about 59.3% of the labour force in 2002. The principal cash crop is sesame seed (including oilcake), which accounted for 3.8% of total export earnings in 2002. The principal subsistence crops are sorghum and wheat. The GDP of the agricultural sector increased by an average of 15.3% per year in 1990–98. Agricultural GDP increased by 4.7% in 2001.

INDUSTRY

Industry (including mining, manufacturing, construction and power) contributed 18.3% of GDP in 2002, and employed 7.9% of the labour force in 1983. In 1990–97 industrial GDP increased at an average annual rate of 4.7%. Industrial GDP increased by 13.3% in 2001.

Mining

Mining accounted for only 0.1% of employment in 1983 and an estimated 0.9% of GDP in 1999. Sudan has reserves of petroleum (estimated at 600m. barrels at the end of 2002), chromite, gypsum, gold, iron ore and wollastonite. Sudan began to develop its petroleum reserves in the mid-1990s, and production reached about 233,000 barrels per day in 2002, when petroleum and petroleum products accounted for 77.5% of total export earnings; production was expected to double by late 2004. The GDP of the mining sector increased by 22.5% in 2001.

Manufacturing

Manufacturing contributed 9.3% of GDP in 2002. The most important branch of the sector is food-processing, especially sugar-refining, while the textile industry, cement production and petroleum-refining are also significant. Some 4.6% of the labour force were employed in manufacturing in 1983. In 1990–97 manufacturing GDP increased at an average annual rate of 1.0%. Manufacturing GDP increased by 12.0% in 2001.

Energy

Energy is derived from petroleum (which contributed 51.7% of total output in 2000) and hydroelectric power (48.3%). Sudan is a net exporter of fuels, with imports of petroleum and petroleum products comprising an estimated 5.4% of the total value of imports in 2002.

SERVICES

Services contributed 42.5% of GDP in 2002, and employed 18.8% of the labour force in 1983. During 1990–97 the GDP of the services sector increased at an average annual rate of 3.0%. In 2001 the GDP of the services sector rose by 4.2%.

EXTERNAL TRADE

In 2002 Sudan recorded a visible trade deficit of US $203.7m., and there was a deficit of $960.3m. on the current account of the balance of payments. In 2002 the principal sources of imports were Saudi Arabia (accounting for 23.8% of the total), the People's Republic of China, the United Arab Emirates and Germany. In that year the principal markets for Sudanese exports were the People's Republic of China (taking 65.7%) and Saudi Arabia. The principal exports in 2002 were petroleum and petroleum products, and livestock and meat. The principal imports in 1999 were machinery and equipment, foodstuffs, crude materials (mainly petroleum), basic manufactures, transport equipment and chemicals.

GOVERNMENT FINANCE

In 2002 Sudan recorded an overall budget deficit of 32,700m. Sudanese dinars, equivalent to 0.9% of GDP. At the end of 2001 Sudan's total external debt was US $15,348m., of which $8,489m. was long-term public debt. In that year the cost of debt-servicing was equivalent to 2.3% of the total value of exports of goods and services. In 1992–2000 the average annual rate of inflation was 64.8%. Consumer prices increased by an annual average of 18.1% in 1999 and 7.4% in 2000.

INTERNATIONAL ECONOMIC RELATIONS

Sudan is a member of the African Development Bank, the Arab Bank for Economic Development in Africa, the Council of Arab Economic Unity and the Islamic Development Bank. In 1997 Sudan's membership of both the Arab Fund for Economic and Social Development (AFESD) and the Arab Monetary Fund was suspended. Membership of the AFESD was reportedly restored in April 2000.

SURVEY AND PROSPECTS

Sudan's formidable economic problems can be traced back to the 1970s, when the country's agricultural potential was neglected and the Government began to borrow heavily. The problems have been compounded by the civil conflict in the south, which, in addition to depressing economic activity in the areas where it has been waged, has caused a massive waste of state resources.

Relations with the IMF, which had deteriorated over the preceding years, began to improve in 1997, and in August 2000 Sudan's voting rights and full membership of the Fund were restored. Sudan began exporting petroleum in late 1999 and, as a result, in 2000 recorded a trade surplus for the first time in modern history. Further discoveries of petroleum in 2001 led to a vast increase in export revenues; however, much of these earnings were used by the Government to fund the war against the rebels in the south, which was estimated to cost US $1m. per day, and the country's reliance on petroleum has caused some concern in recent years. In late 2002, in return for the rescheduling of its repayments to the IMF, the Sudanese Government pledged to display more transparency in the management of its petroleum revenues and to reduce its military expenditure drastically. The creation of an oil-revenue savings account and the introduction of a managed-float exchange-rate system reinforced economic stability, and the rate of inflation, which had been as high as 132.8% in 1996, was estimated to have declined to just 7.0% by 2003. GDP growth of 5.8% was projected for that year. However, despite a number of positive macro-economic indications, widespread famine and drought, as well as the significant number of refugees and internally displaced people in the country, continue adversely to affect the Sudanese economy.

Peace talks between the Government and the SPLA, ongoing in early 2004, remained a key determining factor in the prospects for the economy, as it was anticipated that the signing of a peace treaty would accelerate growth and facilitate the full normalization of relations with international financial institutions. Furthermore, the successful resolution of the conflict would also encourage the donor community to provide support for much-needed reconstruction and development projects.

Suriname

The Republic of Suriname lies on the north-east coast of South America. Suriname became fully independent in 1975. From 1980 until 1987 the military exercised a decisive influence in politics. In 1987 a new Constitution was approved and the Front voor Demokratie en Ontwikkeling (FDO) was the victorious party in legislative elections. Following a coup in 1990, further elections were held in 1991 in which the Nieuw Front (NF, a coalition which included members of the former FDO) emerged as the leading political force. The NF was similarly successful in elections held in 1996 and 2000. Paramaribo is the capital. The official language is Dutch.

Area and population
Area: 163,265 sq km
Population (mid-2002): 422,570
Population density (mid-2002): 2.6 per sq km
Life expectancy (years at birth, 2002): 67.6 (males 64.4; females 70.8)

Finance

GDP in current prices: 2002): US $895m. ($2,118 per head)
Real GDP growth (2002): 2.7%
Inflation (annual average, 2001): 38.7%
Currency: Suriname guilder

Economy

In 2002, according to estimates by the World Bank, Suriname's gross national income (GNI), measured at average 2000–02 prices, was US $828.2m., equivalent to $1,960 per head. During 1990–2002, it was estimated, the population increased at an average annual rate of 0.4%, while gross domestic product (GDP) per head increased, in real terms, by an average of 2.0% per year. Overall GDP increased, in real terms, at an average annual rate of 2.4% in 1990–2002; growth was 4.5% in 2001 and 3.0% in 2002.

AGRICULTURE

According to preliminary estimates, agriculture (including hunting, forestry and fishing) contributed 10.7% of GDP in 2002 and employed an estimated 6.4% of the employed population in 1999. The principal crop is rice, which supplies domestic demand and provided 2.4% of export earnings in 2001. In April 2002 the Government closed the state-run banana company, Surland, when it accumulated debt of some US $8m. Bananas are cultivated for export, together with plantains, sugar cane and citrus fruits, while Suriname also produces coconuts, maize and vegetables. Livestock is being developed, as are the extensive timber reserves (more than 80% of Suriname's total land area is covered by forest). Commercial fishing is important (providing an estimated 8.8% of total export revenue in 2001). Agricultural GDP increased by 2.6% per year in 1990–2001; the sector grew by 10.8% in 2001, but declined by 0.6% in 2002.

INDUSTRY

Industry (including mining, manufacturing, public utilities and construction) contributed according to preliminary estimates, 18.9% of GDP and engaged some 17.8% of the employed labour force in 2002. The principal activity is the bauxite industry, which dominates both the mining and manufacturing sectors. In August 2002 Alcoa World Alumina and Chemicals (AWAC) announced plans to increase production at the refinery in Paranam by 250,000 metric tons, to 2.2m. tons per year. In the early 2000s there were plans to build an industrial development zone near to Johan Adolf Pengel International Airport at Zanderij. Industrial GDP increased by an annual average of 1.2% in 1990–2001; the sector increased by 8.6% in 2001 and by a further 3.2% in 2002.

Mining

According to preliminary estimates, mining and quarrying contributed an estimated 7.7% of GDP and engaged an estimated 3.4% of the employed labour force in 2002. The principal product is bauxite (used in the manufacture of aluminium), of which Suriname is one of the world's leading producers (producing 4.0m. metric tons in 2002). In early 2003 the US-based aluminium company Alcoa concluded negotiations with the Government on plans to develop the bauxite sector in Suriname. An accord was reached to allow Alcoa to increase the capacity of its existing bauxite operations in the country. Alcoa was also granted permission for a joint venture with the Australian company BHP for an aluminium melting plant and hydroelectric dam in the Backhuis Mountains. The large-scale exploitation of gold in central-eastern Suriname was postponed in the late 1990s, owing to falling gold prices; gold reserves at the Gross Rosebel mine, situated some 80 km south of Paramaribo, were estimated at 2.4m. ounces. In late 2002 the Canadian gold-mining corporation Cambior began construction on new facilities at Gross Rosebel. Extraction began in January 2004. It was estimated that, once fully operational, the mine would require an annual investment of US $50m. Gross Rosebel's average annual output was forecast at 220,000 ounces. Reserves of petroleum in Suriname are exploited at a rate of around 12,500 b/d. Some 40% of production is for export, but much is used domestically in the bauxite industry. Unproven reserves are also thought to exist in the Saramacca district. Suriname also has extensive deposits of iron ore and reserves of manganese, copper, nickel, platinum and kaolin. The GDP of the mining sector was estimated to have increased by an average of 2.3% per year in 1998–2002, the sector increased by 21.1% in 2001, but declined by 6.7% in 2002.

Manufacturing

Manufacturing contributed, according to preliminary estimates, 5.2% of GDP and engaged an estimated 9.8% of the employed labour force in 2002. Bauxite refining and smelting is the principal industry (alumina and aluminium accounted for an estimated 73.6% of export revenue in 2001), but there are also important food-processing industries and manufacturers of cigarettes, beverages and chemical products. Manufacturing GDP declined by an estimated average of 2.1% per year in 1990–2001; it increased by 4.9% in 2001 and by a further 7.3% in 2002.

Energy

Energy is currently derived principally from hydrocarbon fuels, which are mainly imported; in 2001 fuels and lubricants accounted for 15.7% of total merchandise imports. The country has considerable potential for the development of hydroelectric power; there is a hydroelectric station for the aluminium industry. In April 2004 the Government announced plans to install a major power line from the Afobakka hydroelectric dam to Paramaribo. The three-year project would be undertaken by two companies based in India and financed by a loan from the Indian Government. In 2001 Suriname produced 1,959m. kWh of electricity, derived mostly from hydroelectric power.

SERVICES

The services sector contributed, according to preliminary estimates, some 53.7% of GDP and engaged an estimated 82.1% of the employed labour force in 2002. In that year the large civil service employed an estimated 62.4% of the working population. The GDP of the services sector increased by an estimated average of 2.5% per year in 1990–2001; sectoral growth was 2.7% in 2001 and 3.1% in 2002.

EXTERNAL TRADE

In 2002 Suriname recorded a visible trade surplus of US $47.4m., and there was a deficit of $131.0m. on the current account of the balance of payments. The principal source of imports was the USA (providing 27.2% of total imports in 2001); other significant suppliers were the Netherlands (23.8%), Trinidad and Tobago (17.7%) and Japan (6.3%). The principal markets for exports in 2001 were the USA (an estimated 23.7% of the total), Norway (20.0) and the Netherlands (7.7%). The principal imports in 2001 were machinery and transport equipment, mineral fuels and lubricants, manufactured goods, and food and live animalss. The principal exports the same year were crude materials (particularly alumina), and food and live animals.

GOVERNMENT FINANCE

In 2002 there was an estimated budgetary deficit of Sf 157.4m. (equivalent to 7.0% of GDP). At the end of 2002 the total external public debt stood at an estimated US $319.8m., of which $161.9m. was long-term public debt. The annual rate of inflation averaged 30.0% in 1995–2002. Consumer prices increased by an average of 38.7% in 2001 and by an average of 1.1% in 2002. Official estimates gave a general rate of unemployment of 20% in early 2001. It was estimated that the informal sector contributed 16.7% of GDP in 2002.

INTERNATIONAL ECONOMIC RELATIONS

In February 1995 Suriname was granted full membership of the Caribbean Community and Common Market (CARICOM).

SURVEY AND PROSPECTS

Economic activity is relatively diversified in range, but the dominant sector is the bauxite industry. In June 1993 the Government introduced a free-market rate for the Suriname guilder. In July 1994 the Government abolished the official exchange rate and introduced a new unified exchange rate system, removing all remaining exchange controls. In that year Suriname's economy experienced hyperinflation (average inflation for the year was 368.5%), rapid currency depreciation and an increasing budgetary deficit. In 1995 intervention in the currency market by the Central Bank succeeded in stabilizing the guilder. The Government also achieved a considerable increase in the level of international reserves, while tax revenue increased four-fold, owing largely to improvements in tax administration. Savings made by the elimination of consumer subsidies in that year were, however, offset by the simultaneous granting of a 200% salary increase to public-sector employees. The budget surplus continued to be eroded by the introduction of further public-sector salary increases. During 1998 economic difficulties arising from drought conditions were exacerbated by labour unrest prompted by the rapid depreciation of the informal, parallel exchange rate for the Suriname guilder. (A 45% devaluation of the currency was finally effected by the Central Bank in January 1999.) However, a gap immediately re-emerged between the official and the unofficial rates (the gap had widened to 75% by August 1999), which led the IMF to recommend a further adjustment of the exchange rate. In 1999 the Government introduced plans to reform the financial sector with the eventual aim of establishing Suriname as an 'offshore' financial centre.

On assuming office in September 2000, the new Government discovered that most of the country's gold reserves had been converted into US dollars. With the country nearing bankruptcy, in October the new President, Runaldo Venetiaan, announced a series of emergency measures, aimed at stabilizing the exchange rate and the domestic inflation rate. The official exchange rate was devalued by 89%, subsidies on petroleum products were eliminated, and tariffs on utilities were raised. As a result, the overall deficit increased to just 13% of GDP in 2000 (from 10% in 1999). The annual inflation rate also fell, to 59.3%, and continued to fall in 2001, partly owing to the ending of central bank credit to the Government. The IMF welcomed the new Government's attempts to restore fiscal policy and in 2001 identified the reduction of the public-sector salary bill and an acceleration in the privatization process as essential to the macroeconomic stabilization programme. However, an increase in public-sector wages by some 60% in 2002 resulted in an increase in the fiscal deficit in that year. In August 2002 the Central Bank again devalued the Surinamese guilder, following its sharp depreciation in the first half of the year. GDP growth slowed to 3.0% in 2002, from 4.5% in 2001. In response, the Government took action to curb expenditure and to increase tax revenue. Sales tax was increased by 3%, a tax of temporary 10% was applied to corporate income for one year, and a casino tax was introduced. Investment in gold and bauxite production in 2003 stimulated exports and employment; however, it also gave rise to high imports and an increase in the current account deficit. GDP increased by an estimated 5.6% in 2003. The economy was forecast to expand by 5.1% in 2004. In its annual report in 2003 the IMF commended the Venetiaan Government's fiscal policy and made a number of recommendations for sustained progress. The Fund recommended further fiscal consolidation, through economic diversification, continued privatization and further tax reform. It also maintained that the size of the civil service was a potentially destabilizing influence on the economy.

In July 2003 the Government announced that, from 1 January 2004, the name of the Surinamese currency would be changed from the guilder to the dollar, at an initial rate of exchange of 2.8 Surinamese dollars to one US dollar.

Swaziland

The Kingdom of Swaziland is situated in southern Africa. Swaziland became a British protectorate in 1903, and one of the High Commission Territories in 1907. In 1968 Swaziland was granted full independence within the Commonwealth. Prince Makhosetive, the designated successor of King Sobhuza II, who died in 1982, was crowned in 1986 and assumed the title of King Mswati III. Pressure for democratic reforms resulted in the appointment in 1996 of a Constitutional Review Commission. In 2001 the Commission recommended that the King's powers be extended and that political parties remain illegal. Mbabane is the capital. The official languages are English and siSwati.

Area and population
Area: 17,363 sq km
Population (mid-2002): 1,088,180
Population density (mid-2002): 62.7 per sq km
Life expectancy (years at birth, 2002): 38.8 (males 36.9; females 40.4)

Finance
GDP in current prices: 2002): US $1,177m. ($1,081 per head)
Real GDP growth (2002): 1.8%
Inflation (annual average, 2002): 12.0%
Currency: lilangeni (plural: emalangeni)

Economy

In 2002, according to estimates by the World Bank, Swaziland's gross national income (GNI), measured at average 2000–02 prices, was US $1,285m., equivalent to $1,180 per head (or $4,530 per head on an international purchasing-power parity basis). During 1990–2002, it was estimated, the population increased at an average annual rate of 2.9%, while gross domestic product (GDP) per head declined, in real terms, by an average of 0.1% per year. Overall GDP increased, in real terms, at an average annual rate of 2.8% in 1990–2002; growth in 2002 was 1.8%.

AGRICULTURE

Agriculture (including forestry) contributed 13.5% of GDP in 2002. About 32.9% of the labour force were employed in the agricultural sector in mid-2002. The principal cash crops are sugar cane (sugar accounted for 9.3% of domestic export earnings in 2001), cotton, citrus fruits, pineapples and maize. Tobacco and rice are also cultivated. Livestock-rearing is traditionally important. An outbreak of foot-and-mouth disease occurred in November 2000, but was successfully contained by culling approximately 1,600 infected cattle and vaccinating more than 23,000 animals at risk. Poor harvests in 2001 and 2002 necessitated the imports of basic foods in those years, and the UN World Food Programme supplied food aid to some 231,000 Swazis in 2003. Substantial food imports were expected to be required in 2004, owing to low cereals production caused by drought. Commercial forestry (which employs a significant proportion of the population) provides wood for the manufacture of pulp. During 1990–2002, according to the World Bank, agricultural GDP increased by an average of 0.7% per year. Agricultural GDP increased by 1.6% in 2002.

INDUSTRY

Industry (including mining, manufacturing, construction and power) contributed 34.2% of GDP in 2002. During 1990–2002, according to the World Bank, industrial GDP increased at an average annual rate of 3.0%. Industrial GDP increased by 1.6% in 2002.

Mining

Mining contributed 0.3% of GDP in 2001. Swaziland has extensive reserves of coal, much of which is exported. Asbestos is also an important mineral export. In addition, Swaziland has reserves of tin, kaolin, talc, iron ore, pyrophyllite and silica. During 1996–2001, according to the IMF, mining GDP declined by an average of 3.8% per year. Mining GDP declined by 19.9% in 2001, according to the IMF.

Manufacturing

Manufacturing contributed 27.6% of GDP in 2002, and is mainly based on the processing of agricultural, livestock and forestry products. Some 26% of the labour force were employed in the manufacturing sector in 1996/97. During 1990–2002, according to the World Bank, manufacturing GDP increased at an average annual rate of 2.4%. Manufacturing GDP increased by 1.6% in 2002.

Energy

Swaziland imports most of its energy requirements from South Africa. Of total electrical energy generated and imported in 1999, 77.1% was imported from South Africa. However, the Swazi Government aimed to increase domestic energy output to cover approximately 50% of the country's needs, following the construction of a hydroelectric power station on the Maguga Dam, which began operations in 2002. Mineral fuels and lubricants accounted for an estimated 11.4% of imports in 2001.

SERVICES

The services sector contributed 52.2% of GDP in 2002. According to the World Bank, the GDP of the services sector increased by an average of 3.7% per year in 1990–2002. Services GDP increased by 5.6% in 2002.

EXTERNAL TRADE

In 2002, according to estimates, Swaziland recorded a visible trade deficit of US $79.4m., while there was a deficit of $46.3m. on the current account of the balance of payments. In 1994 the principal source of imports was South Africa (83.3%); other suppliers are the United Kingdom, the Netherlands and Switzerland. South Africa was also the principal market for exports in 1995 (taking an estimated 58.2% of domestic exports); the United Kingdom is also a significant purchaser. The principal exports in 2001 were edible concentrates, sugar, wood pulp and textiles. The principal imports in that year were machinery and transport equipment, basic manufactures, food and live animals, and chemicals and chemical products.

GOVERNMENT FINANCE

In the financial year ending 31 March 2002 there was an overall budgetary deficit of E 315m. (equivalent to 2.8% of GDP). Swaziland's external debt totalled US $307.7m. at the end of 2001, of which $235.5 was long-term public debt. In that year the cost of debt-servicing was equivalent to 2.7% of the value of exports of goods and services. In 1990–2001 annual inflation averaged 9.1%; consumer prices increased by an average of 5.9% in 2001. It was estimated that 40% of the labour force were unemployed in 1995.

INTERNATIONAL ECONOMIC RELATIONS

Swaziland is a member of the Common Market for Eastern and Southern Africa, of the Southern African Development Community (SADC) and of the Southern African Customs Union (SACU), which also includes Botswana, Lesotho, Namibia and South Africa.

SURVEY AND PROSPECTS

Swaziland's economy is vulnerable to fluctuations in international prices for some major exports, including sugar, as well as to the effects of unfavourable weather conditions. In addition, prevailing economic conditions in neighbouring South Africa have a pronounced impact on the Swazi economy: although Swaziland may determine the exchange rate of its currency, the lilangeni, this has remained at par with the South African rand. The decline in value of the rand and, consequently, the lilangeni from the late 1990s had a detrimental effect on Swaziland's economic performance, although there was some recovery in the value of both currencies in 2003.

In 1997 the Government presented the Economic and Social Reform Agenda, prepared in consultation with the IMF and the World Bank, which aimed to accelerate economic growth, reduce the level of unemployment and encourage investment in the private sector. In 1999 the IMF urged further fiscal and other reforms to strengthen Swaziland's public finances, in order to offset the effects of the new revenue-sharing agreement within SACU (the IMF projected that Swaziland's receipts from SACU would decline from 16% of GDP in 2000 to about 14% in 2004), and of free-trade agreements within SADC and between South Africa and the European Union (EU). Reforms of the tax system were implemented in 2001 (with rates of corporate and personal taxation reduced), while other government priorities included attracting overseas investment, improving the country's infrastructure and preparing for the privatization of state-owned enterprises. However, continuing demands for constitutional reform ensured that long-term prospects for investment in Swaziland remained dependent on a satisfactory political settlement.

In January 2003, and again in October of that year, the IMF urged fiscal discipline and increased social and humanitarian spending, and attributed low GDP growth to the country's lack of competitiveness in the region. Budgetary expenditure rose further in 2003, owing to an increase in public-sector salaries and substantial spending on the Global 2003 Smart Partnership International Dialogue, which Swaziland hosted in August. At the beginning of 2004 the new Prime Minister, Themba Dlamini, made a number of proposals for the improvement of Swaziland's economic prospects, including a review of government spending, the encouragement of foreign investment and the promotion of small businesses; however, observers expected any progress to be slow. In response to industrial action in the increasingly significant textiles industry, which employed an estimated 30,000 people, in early 2004 the Government announced its intention to establish a wages council for the sector.

Sweden

The Kingdom of Sweden lies in north-western Europe. Sweden has been a constitutional monarchy, traditionally neutral, since the early 19th century. During this time the country has not participated in any war or entered any military alliance. During 1932–76, except for a short break in 1936, Sweden was governed by the Social-demokratiska Arbetareparti, either alone or as senior coalition partner. At elections held in 1976 the SAP was defeated and the Centerpartiet subsequently formed a centre-right coalition. Sweden acceded to the European Union in 1995. The capital is Stockholm. Swedish is the national language.

Area and population

Area: 449,964 sq km
Population (mid-2002): 8,924,000
Population density (mid-2002): 19.8 per sq km
Life expectancy (years at birth, 2002): 80.4 (males 78.0; females 82.6)

Finance

GDP in current prices: 2002): US $229,772m. ($25,748 per head)
Real GDP growth (2002): 1.9%
Inflation (annual average, 2002): 2.2%
Currency: krona

Economy

In 2002, according to estimates by the World Bank, Sweden's gross national income (GNI), measured at average 2000–2002 prices, was US $221,508m., equivalent to $24,820 per head (or $25,080 on an international purchasing-power parity basis). During 1990–2002, it was estimated, the population grew at an average annual rate of 0.3%, while gross domestic product (GDP) per head increased, in real terms, by an average of 1.4% per year. Sweden's overall GDP increased, in real terms, by an average of 1.7% per year in 1990–2002. GDP rose by 1.2% in 2001 and by 1.9% in 2002.

AGRICULTURE

Agriculture (including hunting, forestry and fishing) contributed 1.8% of GDP in 2002, and employed 2.1% of the working population in that year. The main agricultural products are dairy produce, meat, cereals and potatoes, primarily for domestic consumption. In 2002 forestry products (wood, pulp and paper) accounted for 13.8% of total merchandise exports. Agricultural GDP increased by an annual average of 1.2% during 1990–2001; it declined by 0.4% in 2000 and increased by 1.2% in 2001.

INDUSTRY

Industry (including mining, manufacturing, construction and power) provided 27.5% of GDP in 2002, and employed 23.1% of the working population in that year. Industrial GDP increased by an average of 2.7% per year in 1990–2001. Industrial GDP grew by 5.3% in 2000 and by 0.3% in 2001.

Mining

Mining contributed 0.3% of GDP in 2002, and employed 0.2% of the working population in that year. The principal product is iron ore, but there are also large reserves of uranium (some 15% of the world's total known reserves), copper, lead and zinc. The GDP of the mining and quarrying sector declined, in real terms, by an average of 2.4% per year in 1995–1999; it decreased by 0.5% in 1998, but increased by 1.2% in 1999.

Manufacturing

Manufacturing contributed 20.5% of GDP in 2002, and employed 16.8% of the working population in that year. In 1995 the most important manufactures (measured by total value of output) were paper and paper products (10.5% of the total), motor vehicles (9.3%), chemicals (7.2%), basic iron and steel (6.8%), television and radio transmitters and other communications apparatus (6.4%), and general purpose machinery (5.4%). Manufacturing GDP increased, in real terms, by an average of 4.1% per year in 1995–99; it rose by 4.6% in 1998 and by 4.2% in 1999.

Energy

Energy is derived principally from hydroelectric power, which provided some 54.1% of electricity generated in 2000, and nuclear power, which provided some 39.3% of electricity generated in the same year; Sweden has 12 nuclear reactors. Imports of petroleum and petroleum products accounted for about 7.5% of total imports in 2002. Alternative sources of energy are also being developed, because of strict environmental legislation, the lack of potential for further hydroelectric projects and, primarily, the Riksdag's resolution to phase out nuclear power by 2010.

SERVICES

The services sector contributed 70.7% of GDP in 2002, and engaged 74.7% of the employed population in that year. The GDP of the services sector increased, in real terms, at an average annual rate of 1.6% during 1990–2001; it grew by 3.1% in 2000 and by 1.5% in 2001.

EXTERNAL TRADE

In 2002 Sweden recorded a merchandise trade surplus of US $15,649m., and there was a surplus of $10,624m. on the current account of the balance of payments. The European Union (EU) dominates Swedish trade: in 2002 it provided 66.8% of imports and took 53.9% of exports. The European Free Trade Association (EFTA) is also an important trading partner. In 2002 the principal single source of imports was Germany (contributing 18.5% of total imports); other major suppliers were Denmark (9.2%) the United Kingdom (8.6%) and Norway (7.9%). The USA was the principal market for exports in that year (accounting for 11.6% of total exports); other major purchasers were Germany (10.1%), Norway (8.8%) and the United Kingdom (8.2%). The principal exports in 2002 were machinery and transport equipment (principally road vehicles and telecommunications equipment), basic manufactured goods (mainly paper) and chemicals. The principal imports in 2002 were machinery and transport equipment, and basic and other manufactures.

GOVERNMENT FINANCE

In 2002 there was a budget surplus of 10,560m. kronor, equivalent to about 0.5% of GDP. At the end of 1999 the central Government's total external debt was 409,440m. kronor. The annual rate of inflation averaged 2.3% in 1990–2002. Consumer prices increased by an average of 2.4% in 2001, and by 2.2% in 2002. An estimated 4.0% of the labour force were unemployed in 2002.

INTERNATIONAL ECONOMIC RELATIONS

Sweden is a member of the Nordic Council and the Nordic Council of Ministers. In January 1995 Sweden became a full member of the EU and withdrew from EFTA. Sweden joined the Schengen Agreement in March 2001.

SURVEY AND PROSPECTS

From the 1930s and 1940s until the beginning of the 1990s the so-called 'Swedish Model' operated in the economy, the dominating principle of which was the maintenance of full employment. During the late 1980s this became increasingly difficult to achieve, owing to a relatively high level of inflation and a low rate of economic growth. In the early 1990s unwieldy inflation and salary bills, created by high rates of taxation and public-sector employment, coupled with generous welfare provisions, prompted a crisis in the finance sector and Sweden's most serious economic recession in some 60 years. However, the Government's swift response, based on inflation targeting and fiscal consolidation, soon restored confidence, reduced inflation and produced a manageable fiscal surplus.

Sweden experienced a considerable economic recovery in the late 1990s with robust GDP growth, owing to the expansion of the high-technology sector, which aided an increase in exports, and an improvement in private consumption. In 2001, however, a sharp decline in exports of high-technology products, and a fall in exports in general, led to a slowing of Sweden's economy. In 2002 Sweden's GDP growth was constrained by slow international growth coupled with weak investment activity. However, Sweden's economy compared favourably with the members of the euro area, one reason for its rejection of participation in European economic and monetary union (EMU) in a referendum on 14 September 2003, with 56.1% voting against adopting the euro and 41.8% voting in favour.

A series of escalating public-sector strikes took place in mid-2003, culminating in an agreement at the end of May to raise public-sector wages and, notably, to increase the minimum wage. In the second half of 2003, largely as a result of the international economic recovery, Swedish exports began to improve, particularly in the automotive and pharmaceutical industries. Investment and household consumption started to rise, stimulated by lower interest rates, improved profitability and higher prices for shares and real estate. In April 2004 the central bank provided a further boost to the economy by reducing interest rates to a historic low of 2.0%. With unemployment remaining relatively high and productivity rising rapidly, inflationary pressures were likely to remain low. Unemployment was expected to continue to rise to 5.5% by the end of 2004, as increases in productivity absorbed demand. GDP growth was forecast at 2.5% for 2004 and 2.6% in 2005.

Switzerland

The Swiss Confederation lies in central Europe. Switzerland has occupied its present area since its borders were fixed by treaty in 1815. At the same time, it was internationally recognized as a neutral country and its 'permanent neutrality' has never since been violated. Initiatives and referendums form the core of Switzerland's political process. In 2001 voters rejected a proposal to begin 'fast-track' accession negotiations with the European Union. In 2002 the respective requisite majorities of voters and of the country's cantons approved proposals for Switzerland to join the UN. Bern is the capital. The official languages are German, French and Italian.

Area and population
Area: 41,284 sq km
Population (mid-2002): 7,227,500
Population density (mid-2002): 175.16 per sq km
Life expectancy (years at birth, 2002): 80.6 (males 77.7; females 83.3)

Finance
GDP in current prices: 2002): US $268,041m. ($37,086 per head)
Real GDP growth (2002): −0.2%
Inflation (annual average, 2002): 0.6%
Currency: Swiss franc

Economy

In 2002, according to estimates by the World Bank, Switzerland's gross national income (GNI), measured at average 2000–2002 prices, was US $274,157m., equivalent to $37,930 per head (or $31,250 per head on an international purchasing-power parity basis). During 1990–2002, it was estimated, the population grew by an average of 0.6% per year, while gross domestic product (GDP) per head increased, in real terms, by an average of 0.2% per year. Overall GDP increased, in real terms, by an average of 0.8% per year in 1990–2002; real GDP increased by 1.3% in 2001 but declined by 0.2% in 2002.

AGRICULTURE

Agriculture (including forestry and fishing) contributed an estimated 2.0% of GDP in 2000, and engaged 4.2% of the employed labour force in 2002. The principal cash crops are sugar beet, potatoes and wheat. Dairy products, notably cheese, are also important. Agricultural production declined at an average annual rate of 0.7% in 1990–99; it fell by 4.7% in 1997, increased by 6.8% in 1998, but then decreased by 5.4% in 1999.

INDUSTRY

Industry (including mining and quarrying, manufacturing, power and construction) contributed an estimated 29.1% of GDP in 2000, and engaged 25.2% of the employed labour force in 2002. Industrial GDP increased by 5.3% in 1998.

Mining

Switzerland is not richly endowed with mineral deposits, and only rock salt and building materials are mined or quarried in significant quantities. In 2002 only 0.1% of the working population were employed in mining and quarrying. The sector contributed just 0.2% of GDP in 2000.

Manufacturing

The manufacturing sector, which contributed an estimated 20.5% of GDP in 2000, engaged 17.1% of the employed labour force in 2002. The most important branches are precision engineering (in particular clocks and watches, which provided 7.7% of export revenue in 2001), heavy engineering, machine-building, textiles, chocolate, chemicals and pharmaceuticals.

Energy

Energy is derived principally from petroleum and from hydroelectric and nuclear power. In 1998 Switzerland imported 82% of the energy that it consumed, mainly in the form of petroleum and related products (which accounted for 61.2% of final energy consumption in that year). Imports of mineral fuels comprised 4.5% of the value of total imports in 2001. Switzerland is, however, a net exporter of electricity. In 2000 55.8% of total electricity output was provided by hydroelectric power, while nuclear power (from five reactors with a total generating capacity of 3,077 MW) provided 40.1% of electricity; a mere 1.5% came from natural gas and 0.1% from petroleum

SERVICES

The services sector contributed an estimated 68.9% of GDP in 2000, and engaged 70.6% of the employed labour force in 2002. Switzerland plays an important role as a centre of international finance, and Swiss markets account for a significant share of international financial transactions. The insurance sector is also highly developed, and Swiss companies are represented throughout the world. The reputation of the banking sector abroad was tarnished in the 1990s by revelations concerning the ignoble role played by Swiss banks in respect of funds deposited by Jewish victims of the Nazi Holocaust. The resolution of this issue in 2001 was overshadowed by a series of high-profile money-laundering scandals, which caused yet more damage to the reputation of Swiss banking. Switzerland draws considerable revenue from tourism; receipts from tourism totalled US $7,303m. in 2000.

EXTERNAL TRADE

In 2002 Switzerland recorded a visible trade surplus of US $6,432m., and there was a surplus of $26,011m. on the current account of the balance of payments. The European Union (EU) accounted for the majority of Switzerland's trade, providing 76.2% of the country's import and taking 60.0% of exports in 2001. In that year the principal source of imports was Germany (providing 30.1% of total imports), followed by France (10.3%), Italy (9.4%) and the USA (5.9%). Germany was also the principal market for exports (taking 21.7% of total exports), followed by the USA (11.3%), France (8.9%) and Italy (8.0%). The principal exports in 2001 were chemicals, machinery, pharmaceutical products and clocks and watches. The main imports in that year were machinery, pharmaceutical products, agricultural and forestry products and motor vehicles.

GOVERNMENT FINANCE

Switzerland recorded a budgetary surplus of 1,367m. Swiss francs (equivalent to 0.3% of GDP) in 2001. General government external debt was equivalent to 0.2% of GDP in 1999. The annual rate of inflation averaged 1.8% in 1990–2002; consumer prices increased by 1.0% in 2001 and by 0.6% in 2002. The rate of unemployment averaged 2.9% in 2002.

INTERNATIONAL ECONOMIC RELATIONS

Switzerland is a founder member of the European Free Trade Association (EFTA). In May 1992 Switzerland was admitted to membership of the IMF and the World Bank.

SURVEY AND PROSPECTS

As a small and open economy Switzerland is very susceptible to international economic conditions. Although Switzerland is not a member of the EU, it is nevertheless largely dependent on the euro area for economic growth. The poor performance of Germany, Switzerland's main trading partner, was particularly damaging for Switzerland as it went into recession in 2002–2003. This was compounded by weakness in the world's financial markets, since financial services account for some 12% of Switzerland's GDP.

While there were some signs of recovery in late 2003, partly owing to stronger-than-expected growth in the USA, the outlook for Switzerland remained uncertain. Private consumption, in particular, was likely to remain low following rises in the price of health insurance and pension fund contributions. Unemployment was also high by Swiss standards, at 4.7%. The effects of the slump in 2002–2003 were felt across all sectors of the economy, although exporters generally performed better than domestic groups. Financial services which suffered significant losses in 2002 benefited from the improvement in the international financial market in 2003 although banks and insurers were compelled to implement cost-cutting measures, with 50,000 jobs in the sector (2.8% of the employment in financial services) lost; between the end of 2001 and mid-2003. This poor economic performance stemmed partly from the strength of the Swiss franc, which remained high against both the dollar and the euro despite the reduction of interest rates to near-record low levels and an increase in the money supply to prevent recession turning into deflation. While economic recovery was partially dependent on global factors beyond Switzerland's control, domestic factors were also significant. There was growing pressure for the liberalization of the over-regulated domestic economy, which comprised many cartels, where limited competition and bureaucratic delays were responsible for poor productivity and high prices. Such pressure, was not new, but had been gaining in influence with the recession and growing concerns about demographic trends, which had prompted a reassessment of the long-term sustainability of Swiss prosperity. Of all the major European countries, Switzerland has the highest percentage of foreign workers (25.3% of the working population in 2002). However, real GDP growth was recorded for the first time in a year in the third quarter of 2003 and GDP growth was expected to resume, albeit at a low level, in 2004.

Syria

The Syrian Arab Republic lies in western Asia. Syria achieved full independence from France in 1946. After secession from the United Arab Republic in 1961, the Syrian Arab Republic was formed. In 1970, following a coup, the military wing of the Arab Socialist Renaissance (Baath) Party seized power, led by Lt-Gen. Hafiz al-Assad, who was elected President in 1971. President Assad remained in power until his death in 2000, whereupon his son, Bashar al-Assad, assumed the presidency. The Golan Heights region of Syria, captured by Israeli forces in 1967, remains under Israeli occupation. Damascus is the capital. The national language is Arabic.

Area and population
Area: 185,180 sq km
Population (mid-2002): 17,004,680
Population density (mid-2002): 91.8 per sq km
Life expectancy (years at birth, 2002): 71.2 (males 68.8; females 73.6)

Finance
GDP in current prices: 2002): US $21,872m. ($1,286 per head)
Real GDP growth (2002): 3.1%
Inflation (annual average, 2002): 1.0%
Currency: Syrian pound

Economy

In 2002, according to estimates by the World Bank, Syria's gross national income (GNI), measured at average 2000–02 prices, was US $19,203m., equivalent to $1,130 per head (or $3,250 per head on an international purchasing-power parity basis). During 1990–2002, it was estimated, the population increased at an average annual rate of 2.9%, while gross domestic product (GDP) per head increased, in real terms, by an average of 1.9% per year. Overall GDP increased, in real terms, at an average annual rate of 4.8% in 1990–2002; growth was 2.8% in 2001 and 3.1% in 2002.

AGRICULTURE

Agriculture (including forestry and fishing) contributed an estimated 23.1% of GDP in 2002, and in the same year engaged 30.3% of the employed labour force (excluding foreign workers). The principal cash crops are cotton (which accounted for about 4.3% of export earnings in 2000) and fruit and vegetables. Agricultural GDP increased at an average annual rate of 4.7% in 1990–2002; the sector's GDP decreased by some 17.2% in 1999.

INDUSTRY

Industry (comprising mining, manufacturing, construction and utilities) provided some 27.6% of GDP in 2002, and engaged 26.9% of the employed labour force (excluding foreign workers) in that year. The GDP of the industrial sector increased by an average of 7.9% per year during 1990–2002; industrial GDP increased by an estimated 3.9% in 1999.

Mining

Mining contributed an estimated 6.6% of GDP in 1994, and employed 0.3% of the working population (excluding foreign workers) in 1999. Crude petroleum is the major mineral export, accounting for 69.3% of total export earnings in 2001, and phosphates are also exported. Syria also has reserves of natural gas and iron ore. At the end of 2002 Syria had proven oil reserves of 2,500m. barrels, and estimated average oil production was 576,000 barrels per day (b/d) (having declined from from 601,000 b/d in 1995). Syria was estimated to have 240,000m. cu m of proven natural gas reserves at the end of 2002, and in that year production of natural gas reached an estimated daily average of 4,100m. cu m. In December 2001 Syria and Lebanon signed an agreement under which Syria is to supply gas to northern Lebanon.

Manufacturing

Manufacturing contributed an estimated 24.6% of GDP in 2002, and employed 12.7% of the working population in 1999. In 1998 the principal branches of manufacturing, measured by gross value of output, were food products, beverages and tobacco (26.3%), chemicals, petroleum, coal, rubber and plastic products (24.2%), textiles, clothing, leather products and footwear (18.7%), metal products, machinery, transport equipment and appliances (12.3%) and non-metallic mineral products (9.7%). The GDP of the manufacturing sector increased by an average of 8.6% per year during 1990–2002.

Energy

Energy is derived principally from hydroelectric power (providing 41.1% of total electricity production in 2000), petroleum (22.4%) and, increasingly, natural gas (36.5%). Imports of mineral fuels comprised an estimated 5.8% of the value of total imports in 2001. A major restructuring of the energy sector is scheduled to be completed by 2005.

SERVICES

Services engaged 42.9% of the employed labour force (excluding foreign workers) in 2002, and accounted for 49.4% of GDP in the same year. The GDP of the service sectors increased at an average rate of 3.5% per year in 1990–2002; the sectors' combined growth was 6.3% in 1999.

EXTERNAL TRADE

In 2001 Syria recorded a visible trade surplus of US $1,472m., and a surplus of $1,083m. on the current account of the balance of payments. In 2001 the principal source of imports (11.7%) was Italy; other important suppliers were German, France and Turkey. Germany was the principal market for exports in that year (20.9%); other major purchasers were Italy, France, Turkey, Lebanon and Spain. The principal exports in 2001 were crude petroleum, food and beverages, and basic manufactures, while the principal imports were basic manufactures, machinery and transport, and chemicals.

GOVERNMENT FINANCE

A budgetary deficit of £S126,000m. was projected for 2003, and was expected to be exacerbated by the conflict in neighbouring Iraq in the early part of that year. At the end of 2001 Syria's total external debt was US $21,305m., of which $15,811m. was long-term public debt. The cost of debt-servicing in that year was equivalent to 3.4% of the total value of exports of goods and services. Annual inflation averaged 5.7% in 1990–2001. Consumer prices decreased by 0.8% in 2000, but increased by 1.5% in 2001. In 2002 11.7% of the labour force were unemployed.

INTERNATIONAL ECONOMIC RELATIONS

Syria is a member of the UN Economic and Social Commission for Western Asia (ESCWA), the Arab Fund for Economic and Social Development (AFESD), the Arab Monetary Fund, the Council of Arab Economic Unity, the Islamic Development Bank and the Organization of Arab Petroleum Exporting Countries (OAPEC).

SURVEY AND PROSPECTS

Under the administration of President Hafiz al-Assad, Syria began to implement a programme of market-orientated economic reforms. However, the pace of change was very slow, partly because Syria is not encumbered by a heavy burden of foreign debt and has thus been relatively unsusceptible to pressure from international agencies to accelerate the reform process.

By the end of 2000 Investment Law 10 (enacted in 1991) had attracted more than £S334,000m. of new investment. However, excessive bureaucracy and a politically motivated multiple exchange rate system have deterred many foreign investors. A bolder reform programme, which appears to be a priority of the regime under

President Bashar al-Assad, would almost certainly stimulate investment in tourism and agriculture, where the greatest opportunities are perceived to exist.

In 1997 the Government settled its debt of US $526.4m. to the World Bank, prompting forecasts of an improvement in Syria's status within the international financial community, and thus of increased investor confidence in the country. In 1998 a number of amendments were made to Law 10 in order to encourage investment, and amendments approved in May 2000 included a provision permitting foreign investors to own or rent land. In April of that year a decree was promulgated enabling foreign banks to establish branches within Syria's free zones. The decision, announced in December 2001, to allow private banks in Syria for the first time since 1963 (with foreign ownership of 49% being permitted) was expected to encourage foreign investment and to stimulate economic growth.

Following the enactment of new banking laws in March 2002, in April 2003 three private banks—two from Lebanon and one from Jordan—were granted licences to establish branches in Syria; another three—one from France, one from Jordan and a joint Syrian-Bahraini venture—were granted similar licences in June. Meanwhile, in November 2001 the Government launched a five-year reform programme focusing on administrative reform and job creation; annual economic growth of 3% was forecast for 2002–04.

The Syrian economy was expected to suffer the consequences of the temporary loss of its trade with Iraq, as a result of the US-led military campaign to oust the regime of Saddam Hussein in March–April 2003. Moreover, the USA levied trade sanctions on Syria in May 2004. The 2004 budget anticipated increased state expenditure, largely in order to fund investment and infrastructure projects. Notable economic reforms in 2003 included the announcement in September of the establishment of Syria's first stock exchange (scheduled to become operational in 2004); plans for a restructuring of the income tax system (revealed in November and expected to be implemented at the beginning of 2004); and the signing of an agreement with Lufthansa Consulting (Germany) in late December to undertake an overhaul of Syria's Civil Aviation Authority and the national carrier, Syrian Arab Airlines (Syrianair).

Negotiations with the EU in November were expected to lead to the signing of an important association agreement that would result in the reduction of trade tariffs. For the immediate future, further improvements to Syria's economic situation are expected to be dependent upon both domestic restructuring as well as the conclusion of a comprehensive peace agreement with Israel and further domestic reform.

Tajikistan

The Republic of Tajikistan is situated in the south-east of Central Asia. In 1924 the Tajik Autonomous Soviet Socialist Republic (ASSR) was established as a part of the Uzbek Soviet Socialist Republic (SSR). In 1929 the Tajik ASSR became a full union republic of the USSR. In 1991, following declarations of independence by neighbouring Uzbekistan and Kyrgyzstan, the Tajik Supreme Soviet proclaimed the independent Republic of Tajikistan. Since independence Tajik administrations have been confronted by several insurgencies, in particular an armed conflict, formally concluded in 1997, in which the forces of the Islamic Renaissance Party played a prominent role. Dushanbe is the capital. The official language is Tajik.

Area and population
Area: 143,100 sq km
Population (mid-2002): 6,315,660
Population density (mid-2002): 44.1 per sq km
Life expectancy (years at birth, 2002): 63.7 (males 61.0; females 66.5)

Finance
GDP in current prices: 2002): US $1,208m. ($191 per head)
Real GDP growth (2002): 9.1%
Inflation (annual average, 2000): 24.0%
Currency: somoni

Economy

In 2002, according to estimates by the World Bank, Tajikistan's gross national income (GNI), measured at average 2000–02 prices, was US $1,145m., equivalent to $180 per head (or $900 per head on an international purchasing-power parity basis). During 1990–2002, it was estimated, the population increased by an annual average of 1.5%, while gross domestic product (GDP) per head decreased by an annual average of 7.7%, in real terms. Overall GDP decreased, in real terms, by an average of 6.3% per year; however, GDP increased by 10.2% in 2001 and by 9.1% in 2002.

AGRICULTURE

Despite the fact that only 7% of Tajikistan's land is arable (the remainder being largely mountainous), the Tajik economy has traditionally been predominantly agricultural: agriculture contributed 29.3% of GDP in 2002, and provided 66.0% of employment in 2001. The principal crop is grain, followed in importance by cotton, vegetables and fruit. Approximately 95% of the country's arable land is irrigated. Agricultural production was severely disrupted by the civil war. In 1996 proposals were announced to transfer collective and state farms to private ownership. However, although in mid-1998 legislation was passed on the establishment of a centre to aid farm privatization, agricultural reform has proceeded slowly. The IMF estimated that 51% of Tajikistan's arable land was privately owned at the end of 2001. During 1990–2000 agricultural GDP decreased, in real terms, by an average of 4.9% annually. However, real agricultural GDP increased by 3.8% in 1999 and by 12.4% in 2000.

INDUSTRY

Industry (comprising manufacturing, mining, utilities and construction) contributed 28.4% of GDP in 2002, and provided 9.2% of employment in 2001. There is little heavy industry, except for mineral extraction, aluminium production and power generation. Light industry concentrates on food-processing, textiles and carpet-making. Industrial GDP declined, in real terms, by an annual average of 10.4% in 1990–2001. However, sectoral GDP increased by 9.0% in 2000 and by 7.9% in 2001.

Mining

Tajikistan has considerable mineral deposits, including gold, antimony, silver, aluminium, iron, lead, mercury and tin. There are deposits of coal as well as reserves of petroleum and natural gas. Mineral extraction is hampered by the mountainous terrain.

Manufacturing

According to the World Bank, the manufacturing sector contributed 24.8% of GDP in 2001. The GDP of the manufacturing sector declined, in real terms, by an annual average of 10.2% in 1990–2000. However, real manufacturing GDP increased by 5.0% in 1999 and by 10.2% in 2000.

Energy

Although imports of fuel and energy comprised 29.5% of the value of merchandise imports in 2001 (mainly supplied by Turkmenistan, Uzbekistan, Kazakhstan and Russia), Tajikistan is believed to have sufficient unexploited reserves of petroleum and natural gas to meet its requirements. The mountain river system is widely used for hydroelectric power generation, and Tajikistan is one of the largest producers of hydroelectric power world-wide. In 2000 hydroelectric power accounted for 97.7% of energy production.

SERVICES

The services sector contributed 42.3% of GDP in 2002, and provided 24.8% of employment in 2001. The GDP of the services sector declined, in real terms, by an annual average of 2.1% in 1990–2001; however, real services GDP increased by 0.8% in 2000 and by 10.3% in 2001.

EXTERNAL TRADE

In 2003, according to IMF estimates, Tajikistan recorded a visible trade deficit of US $98m., and there was a deficit of $66m. on the current account of the balance of payments. In 2002 the principal source of imports was Uzbekistan (accounting for 23.2% of the total); other important suppliers were Kazakhstan, Russia, Ukraine, Turkmenistan and Azerbaijan. The major market for exports in that year was Turkey (accounting for 15.2% of the total). Hungary, Russia and Switzerland was also significant purchasers. The principal exports in 2001 were alumina (accounting for some 60.9% of the total value of exports), electricity and cotton fibre. The principal imports in 2001 were alumina, electricity, petroleum products, and grain and flour.

GOVERNMENT FINANCE

According to the IMF, there was an overall budgetary deficit of 82m. somoni in 2002 (equivalent to some 3.2% of GDP). The deficit for 2003 was forecast at 158m. somoni. Tajikistan's total external debt was US $1,086m. at the end of 2001, of which $789m. was long-term public debt. The cost of debt-servicing in that year was equivalent to 9.1% of the value of exports of goods and services. The average annual rate of inflation was 303.4% in 1990–2000. The annual rate of inflation reached 2,195% in 1993, but had declined significantly by 1996, to some 40.5%. According to IMF figures, the rate of inflation was 26.7% in 1999 and 23.4% in 2000. The official unemployment rate was 2.4% in 2001; however, according to unofficial estimates the rate of unemployment was as high as 30%.

INTERNATIONAL ECONOMIC RELATIONS

In 1992 Tajikistan joined the Economic Co-operation Organization (ECO) and the European Bank for Reconstruction and Development (EBRD); it became a member of the IMF and the World Bank in 1993. Tajikistan has sought to promote closer economic integration among the member states of the Commonwealth of Independent States (CIS). In November 1996 Tajikistan joined the Islamic Development Bank and it became a member of the Asian Development Bank (ADB) in February 1998. In July 2001 Tajikistan was granted observer status at the World Trade Organization (WTO).

SURVEY AND PROSPECTS

Already the poorest of the republics of the former USSR, during the early 1990s the Tajik economy was very seriously affected by the widespread disruption to the former Soviet trading system, caused by the collapse of the USSR, and by the civil war that broke out in 1992. In May 1995 Tajikistan introduced the Tajik rouble, and in September the Government announced an ambitious five-year programme of economic reform. Following the conclusion of the peace agreement in June 1997, a number of international financial organizations allocated credit to facilitate the structural reform process and to assist in rebuilding the country's infrastructure. However, the financial crisis in Russia in mid-1998 had a strongly adverse effect on the Tajik economy, as did the sharp decline in world cotton prices.

The introduction of a new currency, the somoni, at the end of October 2000 was expected to strengthen Tajikistan's monetary and banking system, and the country's economic performance improved significantly in 2000–03. Economic growth, however, had failed significantly to reduce poverty (affecting almost 80% of the population in 2001, according to the ADB) or increase employment; by 2003 an estimated 800,000 Tajiks were reported to be working abroad. From 2002 the Government aimed to increase the pace of economic reform, in particular by means of an acceleration of the privatization programme (in November 2003 it was announced that over 500 medium-sized and large state enterprises were to be privatized, with the aiming of achieving full privatization by 2007).

In January 2004 the IMF noted that economic growth, while remaining strong in 2003 (at some 9%), had become less dependent on cotton and aluminium production (which had recovered since the end of the civil conflict), and that the persistent deficit on the current account of the balance of payments had, none the less, been reduced. The level of external debt was significant, at some 73% of GDP in 2003, but had declined as a result of economic growth and debt-restructuring; nevertheless, further restructuring of Tajikistan's debt to Russia (its largest creditor) was a priority. Meanwhile, the rate of consumer-price inflation remained high, at around 13%, and the need further to reduce inflation was identified by the IMF as the country's principal macroeconomic objective. A reduced rate of growth, of some 6%, was anticipated in 2004.

Tanzania

The United Republic of Tanzania consists of Tanganyika, on the east coast of Africa, and the islands of Zanzibar and Pemba in the Indian Ocean. Tanzania was formed in 1964 by the merger of the independent states of Tanganyika and Zanzibar. Dr Julius Nyerere was elected as President of the United Republic in 1965, and was re-elected at each subsequent presidential election until 1985, when, on his retirement, he was succeeded by Ali Hassan Mwinyi. Benjamin William Mkapa began a second presidential term in 2000. The administrative functions of the capital are being transferred from Dar es Salaam to Dodoma. English and Swahili are the official languages.

Area and population
Area: 945,087 sq km
Population (mid-2002): 35,181,300
Population density (mid-2002): 37.2 per sq km
Life expectancy (years at birth, 2002): 46.5 (males 45.5; females 47.5)

Finance
GDP in current prices: 2002, excluding Zanzibar): US $9,383m. ($267 per head)
Real GDP growth (2002): 5.8%
Inflation (annual average, 2002): 4.6%
Currency: Tanzanian shilling

Economy

In 2002, according to estimates by the World Bank, mainland Tanzania's gross national income (GNI), measured at average 2000–02 prices, was US $9,607m., equivalent to $280 per head (or $550 per head on an international purchasing-power parity basis). During 1990–2002, it was estimated, the population of the country as a whole increased at an average annual rate of 2.7%, while gross domestic product (GDP) per head increased, in real terms, by an average of 0.6% per year. Overall GDP increased, in real terms, at an average annual rate of 3.4% in 1990–2002; growth was 5.8% in 2002.

AGRICULTURE

Agriculture (including hunting, forestry and fishing) contributed 44.7% of GDP in 2002, and employed some 79.6% of the labour force in that year. The principal cash crops are coffee (which provided an estimated 14.2% of export revenues in 1999), cashew nuts (18.3%), cotton (5.2%) and cloves (Zanzibar's most important export, cultivated on the island of Pemba). Other cash crops include tobacco, tea, sisal, pyrethrum, coconuts, sugar and cardamom. Exports of cut flowers (grown in the vicinity of Kilimanjaro Airport and freighted to Europe) commenced in the mid-1990s. Seaweed production is an important activity in Zanzibar. Farmers have been encouraged to produce essential food crops, most importantly cassava and maize. Cattle-rearing is also significant. A large proportion of agricultural output is produced by subsistence farmers. Tanzania's agricultural GDP increased at an average annual rate of 3.5% during 1990–2002, according to the World Bank; agricultural GDP increased by 5.2% in 2002.

INDUSTRY

Industry (including mining, manufacturing, construction and power) contributed 16.0% of GDP in 2002, and employed an estimated 4.5% of the working population in 1980. During 1990–2002 industrial GDP increased by an average of 3.7% per year, according to the World Bank; growth in 2002 was 6.7%.

Mining

Mining provided only 1.5% of GDP in 2000. Gold, diamonds, other gemstones (including rubies and sapphires), salt, phosphates, coal, gypsum, tin, kaolin, limestone and graphite are mined, and it is planned to exploit reserves of natural gas. Other mineral deposits include nickel, silver, cobalt, copper, soda ash, iron ore and uranium. In late 2003 three companies were bidding for licences to explore for petroleum in the Rufiji delta, Zanzibar, Mafia and the Mkuranga district on the mainland coast. Petroleum was discovered on Tanzania's coastal belt in the 1960s, but was only recently being considered seriously by companies searching for sources of petroleum outside the Middle East. In January 2004 it was announced that a Canadian company, the Barrick Gold Corporation, was to construct a new 526,000-oz gold mine in Tulawaka. According to the IMF, the GDP of the mining sector increased by an average of 12.9% per year in 1990–99; it grew by 9.1% in 1999.

Manufacturing

Manufacturing contributed 7.5% of GDP in 2002. The most important manufacturing activities are food-processing, textile production, cigarette production and brewing.

Pulp and paper, fertilizers, cement, clothing, footwear, tyres, batteries, pharmaceuticals, paint, bricks and tiles and electrical goods are also produced, while other activities include oil-refining, metal-working, vehicle assembly and engineering. Tanzania's manufacturing GDP increased at an average annual rate of 3.1% in 1990–2002, according to the World Bank; it grew by 6.5% in 2002.

Energy
Energy is derived principally from hydroelectric power, which supplied 96.5% of Tanzania's electricity in 2000 (the remainder was supplied by petroleum). Imports of petroleum and petroleum products accounted for about 5.8% of imports in 1999.

SERVICES
The services sector contributed 39.4% of GDP in 2002, and employed an estimated 9.9% of the labour force in 1980. Tourism is an important potential growth sector: tourism receipts were approximately US $725m. in 2001. According to the World Bank, the GDP of the services sector increased by an average of 3.5% per year in 1990–2002. Growth in the sector was 6.2% in 2002.

EXTERNAL TRADE
In 2002 Tanzania recorded a visible trade deficit of US $608.8m., and there was a deficit of $251.3m. on the current account of the balance of payments. In 1999 the principal sources of imports were Japan (10.9%), South Africa, the United Kingdom and the USA, while the main markets for exports were India (20.6%), the United Kingdom, Japan and Germany. The principal exports in 1999 were coffee beans, minerals, tobacco and manufactured products. The principal imports were consumer goods, machinery, intermediate goods and transport equipment.

GOVERNMENT FINANCE
In the financial year ending 30 June 2003 there was a budgetary deficit of 136,200m. shillings, equivalent to 1.4% of GDP. At the end of 2001 Tanzania's external debt totalled US $6,676m., of which $5,758m. was long-term public debt. In that year the cost of debt-servicing was equivalent to 10.3% of the value of exports of goods and services. The annual rate of inflation averaged 17.1% in 1990–2002; consumer prices increased by 4.6% in 2002.

INTERNATIONAL ECONOMIC RELATIONS
Tanzania is a member of the African Development Bank and of the Southern African Development Community. Tanzania is a founder member (with Kenya and Uganda) of the restored East African Community (EAC).

SURVEY AND PROSPECTS
In terms of GNI per head, Tanzania is one of the world's poorest countries. One of the country's greatest economic problems is the very high level of its external debt. In September 1999 Tanzania was admitted to the World Bank's initiative for heavily indebted poor countries, thereby qualifying for concessionary debt relief. By that time the Government had achieved greater control over public expenditure and a reduction in inflation. In November of that year the Heads of State of Tanzania, Kenya and Uganda ratified a treaty re-establishing the EAC. The treaty envisaged the creation of a customs union, which was scheduled for September 2004, to be followed, eventually, by monetary and political union.

In March 2000 the IMF approved a three-year loan equivalent to some US $181.5m. for Tanzania, under its Poverty Reduction and Growth Facility (PRGF), and in November 2001 the country was granted enhanced debt relief, effectively halving its external debt. However, there was concern about Tanzania's continued dependence on foreign aid. Moreover, studies indicated that poverty had not diminished over the last decade, and that the proportion of malnourished people had grown, while AIDS was still rife throughout much of the country.

Tanzania has achieved considerable success with its privatization programme, and in January 2002 it was announced that some 326 of a total of 369 parastatals had been transferred to the private sector. However, a number of enterprises in sensitive sectors remained to be divested. Tanzania was affected by an overall slowdown in the world economy in 2001–02 and a slump in tourism caused by global security concerns. Nevertheless, economic performance was satisfactory in 2002, with strong GDP growth driven by improvements in the agricultural and mining sectors, as well as increased wholesale and retail trade. However, inadequate rains in most parts of the country in 2003 led to a decline in agricultural production, which was expected to result in lower GDP growth than forecast in that year.

In July the IMF approved a new three-year PRGF arrangement for Tanzania, equivalent to some $27m. In early 2004 drought conditions worsened, and it was estimated that up to 2m. people would require food aid as a result. Tanzania was to import some 20m. tons of maize from Kenya, and an additional budget was approved by the National Assembly in February to provide extra money for combating famine.

Thailand

The Kingdom of Thailand lies in South-East Asia. Throughout the post-war period until the early 1990s the military exercised a decisive influence in politics. In 1992 measures were introduced to curb the political power of the armed forces, and constitutional reforms adopted in 1995 expanded the country's democratic base. In 1997 a new Constitution was promulgated and a transfer of power effected in that year, without the intervention of the armed forces or recourse to a non-elected leader, represented further democratic progress. In 2000 Thailand's first ever democratically elected Senate was inaugurated. Bangkok is the capital. The national language is Thai.

Area and population
Area: 513,115 sq km
Population (mid-2002): 61,612,840
Population density (mid-2002): 120.1 per sq km
Life expectancy (years at birth, 2002): 69.3 (males 66.0; females 72.7)

Finance

GDP in current prices: 2002: US $126,407m. ($2,052 per head)
Real GDP growth (2002): 5.2%
Inflation (annual average, 2002): 0.6%
Currency: baht

Economy

In 2002, according to estimates by the World Bank, Thailand's gross national income (GNI), measured at average 2000–02 prices, was US $122,240m., equivalent to $1,980 per head (or $6,680 per head on an international purchasing-power parity basis). During 1990–2002, it was estimated, the population increased at an annual average rate of 0.9%, while gross domestic product (GDP) per head increased, in real terms, by an average of 3.4% per year. Overall GDP increased, in real terms, at an average annual rate of 4.3% in 1990–2002. According to official figures, GDP increased by 5.4% in 2002 and by 6.7% in 2003.

AGRICULTURE

Agriculture (including forestry, hunting and fishing) contributed an estimated 9.4% of GDP in 2002. In that year 41.6% of the employed labour force were engaged in the sector. Thailand's staple crop and principal agricultural export commodity is rice (Thailand became the world's largest exporter of rice in 1981). Rice exports accounted for 2.4% of the total value of exports in 2002. Other major crops include sugar cane, cassava (tapioca), maize, natural rubber, pineapples, bananas and coconuts. Timber was formerly a major source of export revenue, but a ban on uncontrolled logging was imposed in 1989, following severe flooding as a result of deforestation; a reafforestation programme, initiated in the late 1980s, recommenced during 1993. Fisheries products and livestock (mainly cattle, buffaloes, pigs and poultry) are also important. Thailand is one of the world's largest exporters of farmed shrimp. During 1990–2002, according to the Asian Development Bank (ADB), agricultural GDP increased by an estimated annual average of 1.6%; the GDP of the sector increased by 3.5% in 2001 and by an estimated 3.0% in 2002, according to official figures.

INDUSTRY

Industry (including mining, manufacturing, construction and power) provided an estimated 42.7% of GDP in 2002. In that year 23.6% of the employed labour force were engaged in industrial activities. During 1990–2002, according to the ADB, industrial GDP increased at an annual average rate of 5.9%; the GDP of the sector increased by 1.7% in 2001 and by an estimated 6.9% in 2002.

Mining

Mining and quarrying contributed an estimated 2.5% of GDP in 2002: the sector engaged only 0.2% of the employed labour force in that year. Gemstones, notably diamonds, are the principal mineral export, accounting for 2.6% of the total value of exports in 2002. Natural gas and, to a lesser extent, petroleum are also exploited, and production of these fuels increased substantially from the late 1990s onwards. Tin, lignite, gypsum, tungsten, lead, antimony, manganese, gold, zinc, iron and fluorite are also mined. In 2001 licences were granted to permit the exploitation of a large deposit of potash at Somboon; it is eventually expected to yield up to 2m. metric tons per year, making it the world's second largest potash mine. However, in 2002 protests against the development of the mine, owing to concerns about its potential environ-mental impact, threatened to delay its development. In late 2001 a new gold mine was opened in Pichit province, the first to have been opened since the country ceased gold production in 1996. During 1990–2002, according to the ADB, the GDP of the mining sector increased at an average annual rate of 7.2%. Mining GDP increased by 0.6% in 2001 and by an estimated 10.9% in 2002.

Manufacturing

Manufacturing provided an estimated 33.9% of GDP in 2002. In that year 17.8% of the employed labour force were engaged in the sector. In 1999 manufacturing's con-tribution to export earnings was 80%. Textiles and garments and electronics and electrical goods (particularly semiconductors) constitute Thailand's principal branches of manufacturing. Other manufacturing activities include the production of cigarettes, chemicals, cement and beer, sugar and petroleum refining, motor vehicle production, rubber production and the production of iron and steel. During 1990–2002, according to the ADB, manufacturing GDP increased by an estimated annual average of 6.8%; the GDP of the sector increased by 1.4% in 2001 and by an estimated 6.8% in 2002.

Energy

Energy is derived principally from hydrocarbons. At the end of 2002 there were estimated proven gas reserves of some 380,000m. cu m, enough to sustain production at that year's level for 20 years. Estimated proven petroleum reserves were some 600m. barrels, enough to sustain production at 2002 levels for less than 10 years. In 2002 7.9m. metric tons of petroleum were produced and 17.0m. metric tons of natural gas. In that year petroleum accounted for 51.2% of total fuel consumption, natural gas for 33.8%, coal for 12.5% and hydroelectricity for 2.3%. Lignite is also exploited. Solar and wind energy account for about 1% of electric power. Thailand remains, however, heavily dependent on imported petroleum and electricity. In 2000 approximately 86% of its petroleum requirements were met by imports. In February 1996 licences were awarded by the state-owned Electricity Generating Authority of Thailand to two companies to provide an additional generating capacity of 1,380 MW by 2000 under the Independent Power Producers programme, Asia's largest scheme for private-sector electricity supply. A further 2,000 MW were to be produced by independent producers by 2002 and an additional 4,000 MW by 2006. In 2002 imports of mineral fuels comprised 11.5% of the value of merchandise imports.

SERVICES

Services (including transport and communications, commerce, banking and finance, public administration and other services) contributed an estimated 48.0% of GDP in 2002; 34.8% of the employed labour force were engaged in the services sector in that year. In 2002 tourism was one of the principal sources of foreign exchange; 10,872,976 tourists visited Thailand in that year. Receipts from tourism totalled some US $7,902m. in 2002. It was feared that Thailand's tourism sector would be affected by the repercussions of the terrorist attack on the tourist resort of Bali, Indonesia, in October 2002 and, furthermore, by the unrest in southern Thailand in early 2004.

During 1990–2002, according to the ADB, the GDP of the services sector expanded by an estimated annual average of 3.6%; the GDP of the sector increased by 2.3% in 2001 and by an estimated 4.5% in 2002.

EXTERNAL TRADE

In 2002 Thailand recorded a visible trade surplus of US $9,775m.; in the same year there was a surplus of $7,650m. on the current account of the balance of payments. In 2002 the principal source of imports (23.0%) was Japan; other major suppliers in that year were the USA, the People's Republic of China and Malaysia. The principal market for exports in 2002 was the USA (19.6%); other important purchasers were Japan (14.5%), Singapore, Hong Kong and the People's Republic of China. The principal imports in 2002 were machinery and transport equipment (particularly electrical and industrial machinery and parts, and road vehicles and parts), basic manufactures, petroleum and petroleum products and chemical products. The principal exports were machinery and transport equipment, basic manufactures, food and live animals (particularly fish, crustaceans and molluscs), miscellaneous manufactured goods (including clothing and accessories) and chemicals and related products.

GOVERNMENT FINANCE

In the financial year ending 30 September 2003 there was a budgetary deficit of 43,350m. baht. Thailand's external debt totalled US $67,384m. at the end of 2001, of which $26,411m. was long-term public debt. In that year the cost of debt-servicing was equivalent to 25.1% of the value of exports of goods and services. The annual rate of inflation averaged 3.9% in 1990–2002. Consumer prices increased by 0.7% in 2002 and by 1.8% in 2003. In 2002 3.7% of the labour force were unemployed.

INTERNATIONAL ECONOMIC RELATIONS

Thailand is a member of the UN Economic and Social Commission for Asia and the Pacific (ESCAP), the Asian Development Bank (ADB), the Association of South East Asian Nations (ASEAN), the Colombo Plan and the Asia-Pacific Economic Co-operation (APEC). In January 1993 the establishment of the ASEAN Free Trade Area (AFTA) commenced; the reduction of tariffs to between 0% and 5% was originally to be implemented by 2008 but this was subsequently brought forward to 2002. The target date for zero tariffs was advanced from 2015 to 2010 in November 1999. AFTA was formally established on 1 January 2002.

SURVEY AND PROSPECTS

Thailand's emergence from the regional economic crisis precipitated, in 1997, by the collapse of the Thai baht, was mainly export-driven. In 2001 the deceleration of the global economy, in particular the economies of the USA and Japan, exacerbated by the September terrorist attacks on the USA, significantly curbed this recovery. In an attempt to reduce the country's substantial public debt (which was equivalent to almost 60% of GDP) and restore investor confidence, the Government implemented a programme of privatization. However, by late 2002 the indefinite postponement of several planned listings prompted speculation as to the extent of the Government's commitment to its reform programme.

In December 2001 Prime Minister Thaksin Shinawatra rebuffed accusations that his Government was averse to encouraging foreign investment when his Cabinet approved a 'package' of tax incentives for foreign companies establishing bases in the country. However, the measures were criticized for their failure to address more long-term problems. In 2002 FDI inflows totalled only US $1,070m., compared with $3,350m. in 2000 and $6,090m. in 1999. In January 2003, in a further attempt to encourage foreign investment, the Government announced its intention to repay earlier than the scheduled date of May 2005 an outstanding loan of $4,800m. awarded by the IMF and other international donors in the aftermath of the 1997 economic crisis.

In order to encourage the liberalization of trade and to strengthen its regional position, in 2003 Thailand began to negotiate a number of bilateral free-trade agreements (FTAs), concluding agreements with Australia, India and China and entering into negotiations with several other countries, including Japan and Singapore. Discussions for an FTA with the USA, Thailand's most significant trading partner, were expected to commence in June 2004.

In 2003 the economy expanded by 6.7%, owing largely to a recovery in exports and to strong growth in the manufacturing sector. In early 2004 the Government introduced plans to increase the competitiveness of the Thai financial sector by encouraging a number of mergers within the banking system, in order to improve its efficiency. In addition, $37,000m. was to be spent on infrastructure projects, scheduled for completion over the following five years. It was feared that an outbreak of avian influenza in the region in late 2003 and early 2004, which resulted in the imposition of bans by the European Union (EU) and Japan on imports of Thai poultry, might have a negative impact upon economic growth in 2004. However, the relatively small contribution made by poultry exports to overall GDP would, it was hoped, limit any serious reduction in GDP growth. Meanwhile, an outbreak of violence in the south of the country in early 2004, together with the continued threat of regional terrorist activity, contributed to the continuing decline in levels of foreign investment. The Central Bank forecast growth of 6.3%–7.3% in 2004.

Timor-Leste

The Democratic Republic of Timor-Leste (formerly East Timor) is located on the island of Timor, off the coast of Western Australia. From 1999, during its transition to independence, East Timor was administered by the UN Transitional Administration in East Timor (UNTAET). In 2000 a National Consultative Council was replaced by the East Timorese National Council, and a transitional Cabinet was appointed. In 2001 a Constituent Assembly was elected, and a second transitional Government was sworn in. UNTAET formally relinquished responsibility for the administration of East Timor upon its accession to independence in 2002. The capital is Dili. More than 30 languages are in use.

Area and population
Area: 14,609 sq km
Population (mid-2001): 753,000
Population density (mid-2001): 51.5 per sq km
Life expectancy (years at birth, 2002): 57.5 (males 54.8; females 60.5)

Finance
GDP in current prices: 2002): US $388m. ($517 per head in 2001)
Real GDP growth (2002): –0.5%
Currency: US dollar

Economy

In 2002, according to estimates by the World Bank, Timor-Leste's gross national income (GNI), measured at average 2000–02 prices, was US $402.3m. GNI was equivalent to $520 per head in 2001. During 1990–2001, it was estimated, the population increased at an average annual rate of 0.2%, while gross domestic product (GDP) per head, in real terms, remained constant during 1996–2001. Overall GDP decreased, in real terms, at an average annual rate of 2.1% during 1996–2001. GDP increased by 18.2% in 2001. According to the Asian Development Bank (ADB), GDP decreased by 1.1% in 2002.

AGRICULTURE

The economy of Timor-Leste is based principally on the agricultural sector, which normally employs more than 90% of the Timorese population. In 2002 the agricultural sector (including forestry and fishing) contributed an estimated 27.1% of GDP. The only significant export commodity is coffee, which was expected to remain the country's most important source of income until 2004 (when revenues were expected to be generated primarily from petroleum and gas production in the Timor Sea). In 2002 coffee exports constituted 48% of total export revenue. It was thought that reforms in Timor-Leste's coffee industry might result in a threefold increase in coffee production levels. However, the sector remained extremely susceptible to climatic conditions, which were primarily responsible for significant fluctuations in annual output. There are small plantations of coconut, cloves and cinnamon. Subsistence crops include rice, maize and cassava. Livestock raised includes cattle and water buffalo. The forestry sector possesses potential. By 2000 UNTAET had announced that a comprehensive survey of Timor-Leste's forestry resources was to be conducted, and work had commenced on a sandalwood replanting project. In addition to ocean fishing, there is also some small-scale aquaculture. Agricultural GDP increased at an average annual rate of 2.7%, in real terms, in 1994–96. Following annual increases of 7.1% and 0.2% in 1997 and 1998 respectively, the GDP of the sector decreased by an estimated 48.4% in 1999, as a consequence of the widespread destruction and violence that followed the referendum on independence held in that year. However, in 2001 favourable climatic conditions and the implementation of efforts to increase crop production contributed to a sustained agricultural recovery. The recovery continued throughout 2002, owing in part to the greater availability of seed and to the ongoing restoration of farming equipment in the country. However, a drought that began later in that year and continued throughout 2003 and into 2004 adversely affected agricultural production, resulting in crop failure and a severe food shortage in the country.

INDUSTRY

The industrial sector (including mining and quarrying, manufacturing, utilities and construction) contributed 19.8% of GDP in 2002. There is a small manufacturing sector, which is mainly concerned with the production of textiles, the bottling of water and the processing of coffee. In 2002 the manufacturing sector provided 2.8% of GDP. The GDP of the manufacturing sector increased at an average annual rate of 15%, in real terms, in 1994–96. Following an annual increase of 11.7% in 1997, however, the GDP of the sector decreased by 4.2% in 1998 and by an estimated 37.4% in 1999.

Mining

The mining sector contributed an estimated 0.9% of GDP in 2002. Mineral resources include high-grade marble and offshore petroleum and gas. The GDP of the mining sector increased at an average annual rate of 11%, in real terms, in 1994–96. However, following an increase of 22.2% in 1997, the GDP of the sector decreased by 8.6% in 1998 and by an estimated further 13.8% in 1999.

Manufacturing

The construction sector contributed 15.3% of GDP in 2002. The GDP of the sector increased at an average annual rate of 12.1%, in real terms, in 1994–96. However, following an increase of 2.1% in 1997, the sector's GDP decreased by 9.1% in 1998 and by an estimated 9.0% in 1999.

Energy

The power sector (including electricity, gas and water) provided an estimated 0.8% of GDP in 2002. Timor-Leste's generating capacity amounted to some 40 MW prior to the civil conflict in 1999, of which about 50% was contained in two power stations at Dili. However, the territory's power facilities suffered extensive damage in the conflict, and in 2004 supplies of electricity remained intermittent. In October 2002 the Government elected to transfer control of the national power authority, Electricidade de Timor-Leste (EDTL), to external management, owing to a continuing deterioration in the financial position of the authority. The rehabilitation of the power sector was ongoing in 2004, although the physical rehabilitation of rural power facilities was largely complete by April 2003. Approximately one-half of budgetary capital expenditure in 2003 was allocated to the introduction of a pre-paid electricity meter system in Timor-Leste. The GDP of the power sector increased at an average annual rate of 19.1%, in real terms, in 1994–96. The sector's GDP increased by 4.8% in 1997 and by 4.2% in 1998, but decreased by an estimated 49.9% in 1999.

SERVICES

The services sector (including trade, transport and communications, finance, public administration and other services) contributed 53.1% of GDP in 2002. The GDP of all branches of the services sector recorded a sharp contraction in 1999. In 2002 public administration and defence contributed an estimated 28.4% of GDP.

EXTERNAL TRADE

In 2002 Timor-Leste recorded a visible trade deficit of an estimated US $180m. and there was a surplus of $37m. on the current account of the balance of payments. In early 2001 substantial official aid continued to dominate the country's trade flows. Although this aid contributed towards the rehabilitation and reconstruction of the economy, it also resulted in a marked deterioration in the territory's trade and current-account deficits. Exports declined following the violence of 1999, and export earnings in 2000, including those from coffee (Timor-Leste's principal export commodity), were projected to be significantly below the pre-conflict average.

INTERNATIONAL ECONOMIC RELATIONS

Following independence in May 2002, Timor-Leste became a member of the Asian Development Bank (ADB), the Comunidade dos Países de Língua Portuguesa (Community of Portuguese-Speaking Countries) and the UN Economic and Social Commission for Asia and the Pacific (ESCAP). The country also holds observer status in the Association of South East Asian Nations (ASEAN). It attended the third

Summit of the African, Caribbean and Pacific group of states (ACP), held in Fiji in July 2002, as an observer.

SURVEY AND PROSPECTS

A US $65m. budget for 2001/02 was approved at the Fourth Donors' Meeting in Canberra in June 2001. A $20m. shortfall was to be financed through donor contributions. The fiscal deficit for the year was budgeted at $137m. At the Sixth Donors' Meeting, held in Dili in May 2002, a $77.7m. budget for 2002/03 was approved; this was later revised downwards to $74.2m., owing to funding shortfalls. Donors pledged $29.3m. in budgetary support for the year. The National Parliament approved a $79.1m. budget for 2003/04, of which approximately 35% was to be financed by donors. Consumer prices remained constant in 2001, but increased by 2.0% in 2002 and by an estimated 3.0% in 2003. In late 2000 the rate of unemployment in East Timor was estimated at around 80%. In January 2000 a regulation was passed by the UNTAET Transitional Administrator establishing the US dollar as the official currency of East Timor; however, as a result of the scarcity of low-denomination dollar notes, the absence of coins and a lack of familiarity with the new currency amongst the East Timorese, the use of the US dollar by 2001 was not as widespread as had been anticipated. By the end of 2002, however, the process of dollarization had been largely completed. In November 2003 Timor-Leste introduced its own, low-denomination coins—*centavos*—into the economy. While the new coins could not be used outside Timor-Leste and would, therefore, not immediately replace US currency, it was hoped that their introduction would encourage the rural population to make transactions and thus encourage economic development.

In December 1999 the Joint Assessment Mission of the World Bank reported that both the public and private sectors of the East Timorese economy had suffered almost total collapse as a consequence of the recent violence in the territory. At a meeting in Tokyo in December 1999 international donors pledged US $523m. to the humanitarian aid programme for East Timor. Following the meeting a multi-donor Trust Fund for East Timor (TFET) was established; the fund was administered by the World Bank and the ADB and provided grants for economic reconstruction and development in the territory. In October 2000 East Timor received its first payment of royalties from Australia for petroleum and gas extracted in the Timor Gap, under the Timor Gap Treaty originally concluded between Australia and Indonesia in 1991. (Since the signing of the original Treaty in 1991, sizeable natural gas fields had been discovered in and around the Timor Gap zone, and petroleum reserves in the region were estimated by some sources to total a potential 500m. barrels, valued at more than $17,000m. in early 2001. Although East Timor had agreed temporarily to maintain the arrangement covering the sharing of petroleum and gas royalties with Australia after Indonesia ceased to be party to the original Treaty in 1999, the transitional administration in East Timor ultimately considered the Treaty to be invalid and sought to secure a larger share of the royalties.) In July 2001 East Timorese and Australian officials initialled the Timor Sea Arrangement. This awarded East Timor 90% of petroleum and gas production in the region covered by the original Timor Gap Treaty. The Arrangement was signed by both parties at independence in May 2002 and, in December, the National Parliament of Timor-Leste ratified the arrangement, although the Australian Government did not do so until March 2003, owing to prolonged disputes over the distribution of revenues from one of the fields covered by the Treaty. The revenues that the Arrangement would provide were expected to constitute the new nation's primary source of income from 2004 onwards. However, disputes with Australia over the delineation of maritime boundaries in the Timor Sea threatened to delay the release of revenues from those fields affected by the negotiations. In addition, as a result of the delays in the ratification of the Treaty, the Government was forced to request an additional $126m. from international donors for 2004–06 in order to offset a shortfall in projected budget revenues. Meanwhile, in June 2003 the US company ConocoPhillips was granted permission to develop the Bayu-Undan liquefied natural gas (LNG) field in the Timor Sea.

Following independence on 20 May 2002 Timor-Leste's first National Development Plan (NDP), drafted following a nation-wide process of popular consultation in the preceding months, came into operation. The Plan's principal objectives, over a 20-year period, were the reduction of poverty and the promotion of economic growth in Timor-Leste. It proposed the implementation of a phased programme of economic development, under which priority would be given in the short term to the creation of a legislative framework, the enlargement of institutional capacity and further infrastructural growth, following which it was hoped that more sustainable development could be achieved. However, the decreasing international presence in the country after independence, a result of the conclusion of the UN's interim administration period, contributed significantly to an economic slowdown, particularly evident in the construction and services sectors, the expansion of which had hitherto driven growth. A delay in the resolution of many new country agreements for bilateral donor projects resulted in levels of investment that were lower than had initially been expected. A rapid increase in levels of private sector investment was considered integral to future economic expansion. By late 2002 preparations had been made to introduce key economic legislation into the National Parliament that would enable the development of a legal framework to regulate business activity in the new nation. The banking sector remained primarily localized in nature, although the level of deposits within the developing banking system continued to rise, and the country remained dependent on external grants to finance the majority of its public sector spending. In the immediate post-independence period external aid continued to be of absolutely vital importance to the Timorese economy, and the IMF cautioned that sound economic management would be critical to the preservation of macroeconomic stability, along with the provision of reasonable assurances to donors and other parties that the resources made available to Timor-Leste were being used effectively and accounted for properly. In 2003 financial sector development accelerated and, by the end of that year, three commercial banks were operating in the country. However, GDP was projected to contract by around 3.0% in 2003, according to the ADB.

Togo

The Togolese Republic lies in West Africa. British Togoland became part of Ghana in 1957, and French Togoland obtained independence in 1960. In 1967 Lt-Col (later Gen.) Etienne (Gnassingbé) Eyadéma assumed power. The conduct of a presidential election in 1998, in which Eyadéma was returned to office, and of legislative elections in 1999, provoked international condemnation. Legislative elections, rerun in late 2002, were boycotted by most opposition parties, and, after the Constitution was amended to permit Eyadéma to contest a further term of office, he was re-elected as President in June 2003. Lomé is the capital. The official languages are French, Kabiye and Ewe.

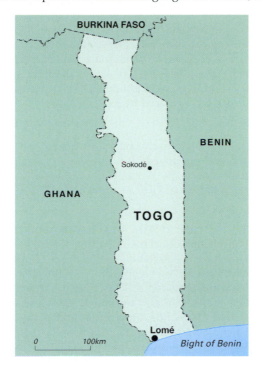

Area and population
Area: 56,785 sq km
Population (mid-2002): 4,766,550
Population density (mid-2002): 83.9 per sq km
Life expectancy (years at birth, 2002): 51.7 (males 50.0; females 53.3)

Finance
GDP in current prices: 2002: US $1,384m. ($290 per head)
Real GDP growth (2002): 3.0%
Inflation (annual average, 2002): 3.1%
Currency: CFA franc

Economy

In 2002, according to estimates by the World Bank, Togo's gross national income (GNI), measured at average 2000–02 prices, was US $1,279m., equivalent to $270 per head (or $1,430 on an international purchasing-power parity basis). During 1990–2002, it was estimated, the population increased at an average annual rate of 2.7%, while gross domestic product (GDP) per head declined by an average of 1.3% per year. Overall GDP increased, in real terms, at an average annual rate of 1.4% in 1990–2002. Real GDP increased by 3.0% in 2002.

AGRICULTURE

Agriculture (including forestry and fishing) contributed 41.8% of GDP in 2002, when 58.5% of the working population were employed in the sector. The principal cash crops are cotton (which contributed 10.1% of earnings from merchandise exports in 2001), coffee and cocoa. Togo has generally been self-sufficient in basic foodstuffs: the principal subsistence crops are cassava, yams, maize, millet and sorghum. Imports of livestock products and fish are necessary to satisfy domestic needs. During 1990–2002, according to the World Bank, agricultural GDP increased at an average annual rate of 3.1%; agricultural GDP increased by 3.6% in 2002.

INDUSTRY

Industry (including mining, manufacturing, construction and power) contributed 18.9% of GDP in 2002, and employed 10.1% of the working population in 1990. During 1990–2002, according to the World Bank, industrial GDP increased by an average of 2.1% per year; industrial GDP increased by 5.1% in 2002.

Mining

Mining contributed 3.4% of GDP in 2002. Togo has the world's richest reserves of first-grade calcium phosphates. Concerns regarding the high cadmium content of Togolese phosphate rock have prompted interest in the development of lower-grade carbon phosphates, which have a less significant cadmium content; exports of crude fertilizers and crude minerals provided 20.3% of earnings from merchandise exports in 2001. Limestone and marble are also exploited. There are, in addition, smaller deposits of iron ore, gold, diamonds, zinc, rutile and platinum. In 1998 marine exploration revealed petroleum and gas deposits within Togo's territorial waters. In October 2002 the Togolese Government, the Hunt Oil Co of the USA and Petronas Carigali of Malaysia signed a joint-venture oil-production agreement, providing for the first offshore drilling in Togolese territorial waters. The GDP of the mining sector was estimated to have declined at an average annual rate of 3.2% in 1991–95.

Manufacturing

Manufacturing contributed 9.1% of GDP in 2002. About 6.6% of the labour force were employed in the sector in 1990. Major companies are engaged notably in agro-industrial activities, the processing of phosphates, steel-rolling and in the production of cement. An industrial 'free zone' was inaugurated in Lomé in 1990, with the aim of attracting investment by local and foreign interests by offering certain (notably fiscal) advantages in return for guarantees regarding export levels and employment; a second 'free zone' has since opened, and provision has been made for 'free zone' terms to apply to certain businesses operating outside the regions. According to the World Bank, manufacturing GDP increased by an average of 3.4% per year in 1990–2002; manufacturing GDP increased by 0.8% in 2002.

Energy

Togo's dependence on imports of electrical energy from Ghana was reduced following the completion, in 1988, of a 65-MW hydroelectric installation (constructed in co-operation with Benin) at Nangbeto, on the Mono river. In early 2004 the Togolese and Beninois authorities announced that the Adjaralla hydroelectric installation, also on the Mono river, was to be modernized, and its production capacity increased markedly. None the less, in 2000 some 97.8% of electricity produced in Togo was generated from petroleum. In 2001 fuel imports constituted 15.9% of all merchandise imports by value. It was planned to connect the electricity grids of Togo and Benin, and to construct further power stations in both countries. A pipeline to supply natural gas from Nigeria to Togo (and also to Benin and Ghana) was expected to come on stream by 2005.

SERVICES

The services sector contributed 39.2% of GDP in 2002, and engaged 24.4% of the employed labour force in 1990. Lomé has been of considerable importance as an entrepôt for the foreign trade of land-locked countries of the region. However, political instability in the early 1990s resulted in the diversion of a large part of this activity to neighbouring Benin and undermined the tourism industry (previously an important source of foreign exchange). According to the World Bank, the GDP of the services sector declined by an average of 0.5% per year in 1990–2002; services GDP increased by 0.1% in 2002.

EXTERNAL TRADE

In 2002 Togo recorded a visible trade deficit of 120,800m. francs CFA, while there was a deficit of 105,700m. francs CFA on the current account of the balance of payments. In 2001 the principal source of imports was France (19.1%); other major suppliers were Canada, Italy and Côte d'Ivoire. The principal market for exports in that year was Ghana (which took 22.4% of Togo's exports in that year); other significant purchasers were Benin, Burkina Faso and the Philippines. The principal exports in 2001 were cement, crude fertilizers and crude minerals, cotton, and iron and steel. The principal imports in that year were refined petroleum products, cereals and cereal preparations, cement, iron and steel, and road vehicles.

GOVERNMENT FINANCE

Togo's overall budget deficit for 2002 was 15,900m. francs CFA (equivalent to 1.6% of GDP). Togo's total external debt was US $1,406m. at the end of 2001, of which $1,203m. was long-term public debt. In that year the cost of debt-servicing was equivalent to 6.7% of the value of exports of goods and services. Annual inflation averaged 2.6% in 1990–93. Following the devaluation of the CFA franc in January 1994, inflation in that year averaged 39.2%. Consumer prices increased by an annual average of 3.2% in 1995–2002. Consumer prices increased by 3.0% in 2002.

INTERNATIONAL ECONOMIC RELATIONS

Togo is a member of the Economic Community of West African States, of the West African organs of the Franc Zone, of the International Cocoa Organization, of the International Coffee Organization and of the Conseil de l'Entente. Togo was admitted to the Islamic Development Bank in 1998.

SURVEY AND PROSPECTS

Following the devaluation of the CFA franc in early 1994, the IMF approved a series of credits in support of Togo's 1994–97 economic adjustment programme. During this period Togo recorded a decline in inflation, a decrease in its external debt and budget deficit, and an increase in GDP per head. From the late 1990s the Togolese economy was adversely affected by a number of economic and political factors. A decline in the output of phosphates (by an average of 22.1% per year in 1998–2001), historically one of Togo's major sources of export earnings, persistently low international prices for another of Togo's principal exports, cotton, and high international prices for a principal import, petroleum, had a negative impact on the trade balance. Moreover, foreign assistance to Togo was limited in the aftermath of the disputed presidential election of 1998. Togo received no multilateral or bilateral aid in 1999 and 2000, compared with the annual average of 29,200m. francs CFA that it had received in 1994–98. The refusal of the European Union (EU), previously a major source of support, to maintain financial assistance to the country was particularly significant.

Although the Government of Agbéyomè Kodjo, formed in late 2000, announced a number of economic reform measures, which were intended to strengthen public finances and to restructure public enterprises further, only limited aspects of the programme were implemented before Kodjo's dismissal in June 2002. A return to growth in 2001 was largely attributable to a recovery in the agricultural sector, although difficulties were reported with regard to the collection of taxes.

In late 2001 the World Bank announced that it would finance the construction of a new facility at Lomé's port, to be completed by 2004, which, it was hoped, would establish the port as a principal regional centre of container trade, while the port has also been a beneficiary of entrepôt trade displaced from Côte d'Ivoire as a result of the civil conflict in that country from late 2002. Although repeatedly delayed legislative elections were held in October 2002, both the USA and the EU declared themselves dissatisfied with the conduct of the polls, and therefore much international aid remained suspended.

Although no observers from Western organizations were present at the presidential election held in June 2003, and concerns about alleged human rights abuses in Togo continued to inhibit the establishment of closer relations with the EU, in early 2004 the European Commission announced that the EU was to review the possible eventual restoration of economic co-operation with Togo, following a series of consultations with the Togolese authorities that were expected to commence later in the year. While the normalization of relations with external donors would be of significant benefit to the Togolese economy, Togo's long-term economic prospects also remained dependent on the encouragement of greater inward investment, the maintenance of political stability, and the implementation of broad-ranging economic reform.

Tonga

The Kingdom of Tonga comprises 170 islands in the south-western Pacific Ocean. In 1900 Tonga became a British Protected State. The treaty establishing the Protectorate was revised in 1958 and 1967, giving Tonga increasing control over its affairs. In 1965 Prince Tupouto'a Tungi succeeded to the throne as King Taufa'ahau Tupou IV. Tonga achieved full independence, within the Commonwealth, in 1970. A Pro-Democracy Movement was founded in 1992, and in 1994 it launched Tonga's first political party, the People's Party, which was subsequently renamed the Human Rights and Democracy Movement in Tonga. Nuku'alofa is the capital. The languages are Tongan and English.

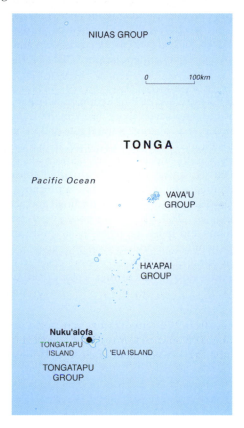

Area and population
Area: 748 sq km
Population (mid-2002): 101,160
Population density (mid-2002): 135.2 per sq km
Life expectancy (years at birth, 2002): 70.7 (males 70.0; females 71.4)

Finance
GDP in current prices: 2002): US $136m. ($1,345 per head)
Real GDP growth (2002): 1.6%
Inflation (annual average, 2002): 10.4%
Currency: pa'anga

Economy

In 2002, according to estimates by the World Bank, Tonga's gross national income (GNI), measured at average 2000–2002 prices, was US $143m., equivalent to $1,410 per head (or $6,340 per head on an international purchasing-power parity basis). During 1990–2002, it was estimated, the population increased at an average annual rate of 0.4%, while gross domestic product (GDP) per head increased, in real terms, by an average of 2.2% per year. Overall GDP increased, in real terms, at an average annual rate of 2.6% in 1990–2002; growth in 2002 was 1.6% and in the following year was estimated by the Asian Development Bank (ADB) at 1.9%.

AGRICULTURE
Agriculture (including forestry and fishing) contributed 28.6% of GDP in 2001/02, and engaged 33.3% of the employed labour force in 2001. According to the ADB, agricultural GDP increased at an average annual rate of 0.8% in 1996–2001, rising by 10.8% in 2000 and by 1.3% in 2001, before declining by 6.8% in 2002. The principal cash crops are coconuts, vanilla and squash, which normally form the major part of Tonga's exports. In 2000/01 exports of squash provided almost half of total export earnings (some 45%). Vanilla acquired comparable significance, accounting for 13.4% in 1995/96; however, production subsequently declined and accounted for only 3.3% of total export earnings in 2000/01. Yams, taro, sweet potatoes, watermelons, tomatoes, cassava, lemons and limes, oranges, groundnuts and breadfruit are also cultivated as food crops, while the islanders keep pigs, goats, poultry and cattle. Food imports accounted for some 32% of total import costs in 2000/01. The fishing industry is relatively undeveloped. The fishing sector contributed some 30% of total export earnings in 2000/01.

INDUSTRY
Industry (including mining, manufacturing, construction and power) provided 15.1% of GDP in 2001/02 and engaged 26.4% of the employed labour force in 1996. Compared with the previous year, industrial GDP was estimated by the ADB to have increased by 5.4% in 2001 and by 2.5% in 2002.

Manufacturing
Manufacturing contributed 5.6% of GDP in 2001/02, and (with mining) employed 22.8% of the labour force in 1996. Food products and beverages accounted for 56.8% of total manufactured goods produced in 1999/2000. The food and textile sectors of manufacturing registered the largest increases in 1999/2000, raising the value of their production by 14.6% and 56.8% respectively. Other industrial activities are the production of concrete blocks, small excavators, furniture, handicrafts, leather goods, sports equipment (including small boats), brewing and coconut oil. There is also a

factory for processing sandalwood. In early 2003 permission was granted for a Chinese businessman to establish a cigarette factory in the islands.

Energy

In an attempt to reduce fuel imports, a 2-MW wave-energy power plant was constructed in the early 1990s, and would, it was hoped, supply one-third of the islands' total electricity requirements when in full operation. Fuel and chemical imports accounted for 25.5% of total import costs in 2000/01. A project to provide all the outer islands with solar power by 2000 was begun in 1996.

SERVICES

Service industries contributed 56.4% of GDP in 2001/02 and engaged 39.5% of the employed labour force in 1996. According to the ADB, the GDP of the services sector expanded by 3.2% in 2001 and by 0.9% in 2002. Tourism makes a significant contribution to the economy. Tourism receipts reached US $8m. in 2002 The trade, restaurants and hotels sector contributed 13.7% of GDP in 2001/02 and engaged 8.5% of the employed labour force in 1996. Visitor arrivals totalled 33,722 in 2000/01 but were estimated to have increased to some 50,000 in 2002.

EXTERNAL TRADE

In 2002 Tonga recorded a visible trade deficit of US $133m., and a surplus of US $20m. on the current account of the balance of payments. In 2002 the principal sources of imports were New Zealand (31.4%) and Fiji (21.4%), while Japan and the USA were the principal markets for exports (purchasing 43.6% and 41.5% respectively). Other major trading partners are Australia and Fiji. The principal exports in that year were foodstuffs. The principal imports were foodstuffs, machinery and transport equipment, basic manufactures and mineral fuels.

GOVERNMENT FINANCE

In the financial year ending 30 June 2002 there was an estimated budgetary deficit of 1.4m. pa'anga. The budgetary deficit was projected to be the equivalent of 2.9% of GDP in 2003. Tonga's total external debt was US $61m. in 2002. In that year the cost of debt-servicing was equivalent to 8.2% of the total revenue from exports of goods and services. Official development assistance totalled US $18.8m. in 2000, of which US $14.8m. was bilateral aid. In 2003/04 official development assistance from Australia totalled $A11.7m. and from New Zealand $NZ5.7m. According to ADB figures, the annual rate of inflation averaged 3.8% in 1990–2001. Consumer prices increased by an average of 10.0% in 2002 and by 10.5% in 2003. Some 13.3% of the labour force were unemployed in 1996.

INTERNATIONAL ECONOMIC RELATIONS

Tonga is a member of the Pacific Community, the Pacific Islands Forum, the Asian Development Bank (ADB) and the UN Economic and Social Commission for Asia and the Pacific (ESCAP). The country is a signatory of the Lomé Conventions and the successor Cotonou Agreement with the European Union (EU).

SURVEY AND PROSPECTS

During much of the 1990s Tonga's economic development was adversely affected by inclement weather, inflationary pressures, a high level of unemployment, large-scale emigration and over-reliance on the agricultural sector. Diversifying sources of income and establishing an efficient source of energy, to enable a reduction in fuel imports, were important issues for Tonga in the 1990s.

Following the decline in earnings from squash exports, various proposals for diversifying agricultural production were considered in the late 1990s, including the cultivation of tea, papaya and aloe vera, as well as the establishment of gas and petroleum refineries, the construction of new hotels to encourage growth in the tourist industry and the expansion of passenger and freight air services (with the purchase of 10 Russian aircraft and the development of new flight routes to Asia in an attempt to secure new markets for Tonga's exports). In 1999 Tonga signed a bilateral trade agreement with the People's Republic of China, and a trade delegation from that country visited the islands in the following year. It was thought that China hoped to use Tonga as a base for the production of export goods (including garments and agricultural products) for the Australian and New Zealand markets. In August 2001, as a result of Tonga's action against the problem of international 'money-laundering', the country was removed from a list of unco-operative countries and territories, drawn up by the Paris-based Financial Action Task Force (FATF).

It was reported in early 2002 that the Tongan Government had reached an agreement with a US company to develop the island of 'Eua as a rocket-launching site for the purposes of 'space tourism'. The first launch was expected to take place in 2005. Meanwhile, the sharp rise in the Government's unbudgeted expenditure continued to cause concern in 2002. The Tongan economy was further weakened in 2003 by the continuing decline in the value of the pa'anga (which had lost some 54% against the New Zealand dollar since 2001), by high rates of inflation and by falling prices for squash on the international market. Supported by a loan (the first tranche of which was released in 2002) and technical assistance from the ADB, the Economic Public Sector Reform Programme (EPSRP) aimed to improve the performance of the civil service and of public enterprises while decreasing costs, to implement a comprehensive reform of the country's tax system and reduce opportunities for tax evasion, and to develop better investment conditions.

Trinidad and Tobago

The Republic of Trinidad and Tobago consists of Trinidad, the southernmost of the Caribbean islands, and Tobago, which is situated 32 km to the north-east. The two islands were united as one political and administrative unit in 1888, and the territory remained a British colony until its independence in 1962. In 1976 a new Constitution took effect whereby Trinidad and Tobago became a republic, within the Commonwealth. The former Governor-General, Ellis Clarke, was sworn in as the country's first President. Tobago was granted full internal self-government in 1987. Port of Spain is the capital. The official language is English.

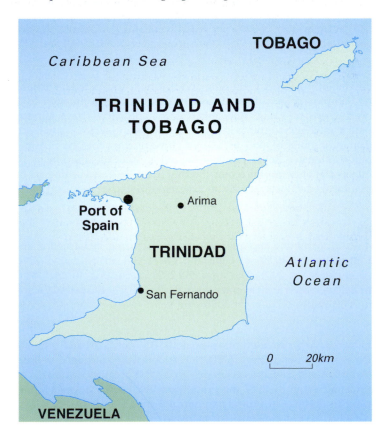

Area and population
Area: 5,128 sq km
Population (mid-2002): 1,318,300
Population density (mid-2002): 257.1 per sq km
Life expectancy (years at birth, 2002): 69.9 (males 67.1; females 72.8)

Finance
GDP in current prices: 2002): US $9,372m. ($7,109 per head)
Real GDP growth (2002): 2.7%
Inflation (annual average, 2002): 4.2%
Currency: Trinidad and Tobago dollar

Economy

In 2002, according to estimates by the World Bank, Trinidad and Tobago's gross national income (GNI), measured at average 2000–02 prices, was US $8,553m., equivalent to US $6,490 per head (or US $8,680 on an international purchasing-power parity basis). During 1990–2002, it was estimated, the population increased at an average annual rate of 0.7%, while gross domestic product (GDP) per head increased, in real terms, by an average of 2.4% per year. Overall GDP increased, in real terms, at an average annual rate of 3.1% in 1990–2002; growth was 3.3% in 2001 and 2.7% in 2002.

AGRICULTURE
Agriculture (including forestry, hunting and fishing) contributed an estimated 1.1% of GDP and employed an estimated 7.8% of the working population in 2001. The principal cash crops are sugar cane, coffee, cocoa and citrus fruits, although coffee production declined by two-thirds in 2000–02. The fishing sector is small-scale, but is an important local source of food. In 2001 the Government allocated TT $5m. to create an Agriculture Disaster Relief Fund, designed to alleviate the effects of natural disasters upon the agricultural sector. During 1990–2001, according to the World Bank, agricultural GDP increased by an average of 2.9% per year. Agricultural GDP expanded by 6.3% in 2000 and by 4.0% in 2001.

INDUSTRY
Industry (including mining and quarrying, manufacturing, construction and power) provided an estimated 40.8% of GDP and employed an estimated 28.8% of the working population in 2001. During 1990–2001, according to the World Bank, industrial GDP increased at an average annual rate of 3.9%. Industrial GDP increased by 6.9% in 2000 and by 6.7% in the following year.

Mining
Mining and quarrying provided an estimated 10.9% of GDP and employed some 3.2% of the working population in 2001. The petroleum industry is the principal sector of Trinidad and Tobago's economy. In 1990 it accounted for 47% of government revenue, although by 2002 the proportion had been reduced to an estimated 29.9%, owing to declines in production and international prices. According to the IMF, the GDP of the petroleum sector increased at an annual average rate of 3.7% between 1996–2000; the sector grew by 8.1% in 1999 and by 3.3% in 2000. Trinidad has the world's largest deposits of natural asphalt, and substantial reserves of natural gas. Cement, limestone and sulphur are also mined.

Manufacturing
Manufacturing contributed an estimated 17.7% of GDP and employed 10.3% of the working population in 2001. The principal branches (measured by value of output)

were petroleum-refining, fertilizers, iron and steel, food products, paper and paper-board, and cement, lime and plaster. During 1990–2001, according to the World Bank, manufacturing GDP increased at an average annual rate of 6.7%. Manufacturing GDP increased by 10.9% in 2000 and by a further 7.0% in 2001.

Energy

Almost all of the country's energy is derived from natural gas (it provided 99.7% of total electricity production in 2000). Natural gas is also used as fuel for the country's two petroleum refineries and several manufacturing plants. In 1999 18 international companies were involved in petroleum and gas exploration in Trinidad and Tobago's offshore areas. Natural gas was expected to overtake oil as the country's principal foreign-exchange earner in the first decade of the 21st century. Imports of fuel products comprised only 0.4% of the value of merchandise imports in 1995, but the proportion increased to an estimated 26.4% in 2001. In that year fuel exports accounted for 61.4% of total exports.

SERVICES

The services sector contributed an estimated 58.1% of GDP and employed some 63.3% of the working population in 2001. Tourism is a major source of foreign exchange; in 2000 receipts from tourism totalled US $210m. and in 2001 some 383,101 foreign tourists visited the islands. However, there were fears that the increasing rates of violent crime would adversely affect tourism revenues. In February 2004 Prime Minister Manning announced a series of initiatives to promote leisure and eco-tourism in Tobago and business tourism in Trinidad. In October 2000 Air Caribbean, the smaller of Trinidad and Tobago's national airlines, was put into receivership. According to the World Bank, the GDP of the services sector increased at an average annual rate of 3.2% in 1990–2001. Sectoral GDP increased by 6.9% in 2000 and by 3.6% in 2001.

EXTERNAL TRADE

In 2001, according to Central Bank figures, Trinidad and Tobago recorded an esti-mated visible trade surplus of US $718.1m., and there was a surplus of US $416.0m. on the current account of the balance of payments. In 2001 the principal source of imports was the USA (36.7%); other major suppliers were Venezuela (12.3%) and Brazil (5.6%). The USA was also the principal market for exports (41.3%) in that year; other important purchasers were Jamaica (8.3%) and Barbados (6.4%). The principal exports in 2001 were fuels (61.4%), chemicals (19.1%) and basic manufactures (9.7%). The principal imports were fuels (26.4%), foodstuffs (6.0%) and transport equipment (4.7%). In 2001 Trinidad and Tobago retained its position as the leading exporter to the Caribbean region, providing petroleum products and manufactured goods.

GOVERNMENT FINANCE

In 2001/02 there was a budgetary deficit of TT $811m. At the end of 2001 Trinidad and Tobago's total external debt was US $2,422m., of which US $1,562m. was long-term public debt. In that year the cost of debt-servicing was equivalent to 4.7% of the value of exports of goods and services. The annual rate of inflation averaged 5.3% in 1990–2002. Consumer prices increased by an estimated average of 5.6% in 2001 and by 4.1% in 2002. According to the IMF, some 10.4% of the labour force were unemployed in 2002.

INTERNATIONAL ECONOMIC RELATIONS

Trinidad and Tobago is a member of CARICOM, the Inter-American Development Bank (IDB), the Latin American Economic System (SELA), and the Association of Caribbean States (ACS).

SURVEY AND PROSPECTS

By 1995 the policy of offering incentives for foreign investment in petroleum exploration had succeeded in reversing the decline in production, and in early 1996 the first significant discovery of petroleum deposits for many years lent further impetus to explorative activity, while the discovery in the late 1990s of several significant deposits of natural gas led to the development of a major liquefied natural gas (LNG) plant at Point Fortin. In 2001 further expansion proposals were announced, which, when complete, would make Trinidad and Tobago one of the world's leading suppliers of LNG. In August 2002 the second train at the Point Fortin LNG plant began production and in April 2003 Atlantic LNG's third train was commissioned. Construction of a fourth train began in early 2004. This was scheduled to begin operation in early 2006 and was to be the largest single gas train in the world, with an annual capacity of 5.2m. metric tons. However, following the Government's decision to open the LNG sector to all firms operating in the country, rights to future LNG facilities would no longer be reserved exclusively for the Atlantic LNG consortium.

In June 2000 construction began on the world's first gas-to-liquid fuel conversion plant, at the Point Lisas industrial estate. The US $300m. plant was to be completed by 2003. In September BP Energy Company of Trinidad and Tobago (formerly BP Amoco) announced the discovery of the country's largest ever natural gas deposit. Substantial foreign investment in the country has allowed increased industrialization, and many new factories have opened or are planned; the majority to process hydrocarbons and ammonia. Despite the growth of the industrial and tourist sectors in recent years, the economy remains greatly dependent on the export of hydrocarbons, and the Government was obliged to revise its budgetary estimates for 1998/99 when the international price for petroleum declined dramatically in early 1998. Increased production and a recovery in the price of petroleum in 1999 contributed to GDP growth of 6.0% in that year.

Although moves had been made to liberalize the telecommunications sector, in 2004 it was still a monopoly, controlled by Telecommunication Services of Trinidad and Tobago (TSTT) Ltd, 51% of which was owned by the Government and 49% by a British company, Cable & Wireless. In June 2000 the Government was accused of lacking transparency in the liberalization process of the telecommunications sector. There was controversy in the bidding process for cellular licences, following the removal of the Caribbean Communications Network from the bidding shortlist, and the successful bid of Open Telecom Ltd, owned by the family of government minister Lindsay Gillette. It was also believed that the licences should not be awarded until appropriate legislation for the telecommunications sector was in place.

Following the elections of October 2002, the new Government announced that some 10,000 of the state sugar company Caroni's employees would be made redundant and that private-sector investment would be sought for the non-sugar-producing part of its operations. In April 2003 the Government approved the release of US $80.1m. of funds to help restore the company's finances. However, in July Caroni closed, making 8,000 employees redundant. Business leaders blamed the political

852

situation for low levels of foreign investment in 2002–04. Furthermore, concerns about rising crime rates threatened the tourist industry; in 2003 the British cruise-ship operator P&O cancelled services to Trinidad and Tobago following fears over the safety of British visitors.

The 2003 budget included the highest ever public expenditure, which the Government envisaged would be funded by rapid expansion in the energy sector. In August 2002 it was announced that a new oil refinery would be constructed which, when it began production in 2005, would more than double the country's current output. In March 2003 construction began on an oil extraction plant in the Greater Angostura field; output was expected by begin in 2004. In mid-2003 the IMF warned that the high revenues from the energy sector concealed structural weaknesses in the budget and an increasing non-energy fiscal deficit. Furthermore, the increase in criminal activity continued to damage consumer confidence and increased security costs for businesses. In the first nine months of 2003 overall GDP increased by an estimated 3.4%. However, while in that period the energy sector grew by 12.6%, the non-energy sector increased by only 0.6%. The Government planned to reform several state-run sectors and to promote investment in non-oil sectors such as gas and transport. In 2004 GDP was forecast to expand by 5.3% and the rate of unemployment was predicted to decline to 9.9% of the total labour force by 2005.

Tunisia

The Republic of Tunisia lies in North Africa. France granted Tunisia full independence in 1956. In 1975 the National Assembly elected President Habib Bourguiba as
President-for-Life of Tunisia. In 1987, after Bourguiba had been declared unfit to rule,
Zine al-Abidine Ben Ali became President. In 1988 a multi-party political system was
introduced. At each election since 1989 the Rassemblement constitutionnel démocratique has won all of the seats in the legislature, except those reserved for opposition
candidates. At nation-wide elections in 2004 Ben Ali secured a fourth consecutive
elected term of office. The capital is Tunis. Arabic is the official language.

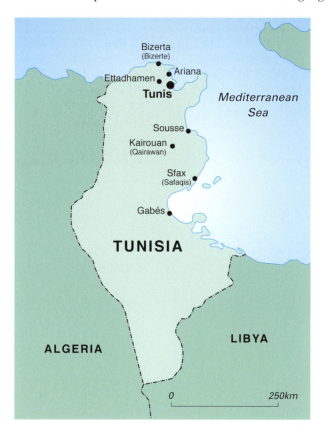

Area and population
Area: 163,610 sq km
Population (mid-2002): 9,788,290
Population density (mid-2002): 59.8 per sq km
Life expectancy (years at birth, 2002): 71.6 (males 69.5; females 73.9)

Finance

GDP in current prices: 2002): US $21,169m. ($2,163 per head)
Real GDP growth (2002): 1.9%
Inflation (annual average, 2002): 2.7%
Currency: dinar

Economy

In 2002, according to estimates by the World Bank, Tunisia's gross national income (GNI), measured at average 2000–02 prices, was US $19,610m., equivalent to $2,000 per head (or $6,280 per head on an international purchasing-power parity basis). During 1990–2002, it was estimated, the population increased at an average annual rate of 1.5%, while gross domestic product (GDP) per head increased, in real terms, by an average of 2.9%. Overall GDP increased, in real terms, at an average annual rate of 4.5% per year in 1990–2002; it grew by 4.9% in 2001 and by 1.9% in 2002.

AGRICULTURE

Agriculture (including forestry and fishing) contributed 11.7% of GDP in 2002 and employed some 23.9% of the working population in that year. The principal cereal crops are tomatoes, wheat, watermelons and potatoes. However, Tunisia imports large quantities of cereals, dairy produce, meat and sugar. The country's main agricultural export is olive oil; olives, citrus fruit and dates are also grown for export. During 1990–2002 agricultural GDP increased at an average annual rate of 1.5%. Agricultural GDP declined by 2.1% in 2001 and by 10.0% in 2002.

INDUSTRY

Industry (including mining, manufacturing, construction and power) contributed 32.5% of GDP in 2002, and engaged 34.4% of the employed labour force in 1994. During 1990–2002 industrial GDP increased by an average of 4.6% per year. Industrial GDP increased 6.0% in 2001 and by 3.0% in 2002.

Mining

Mining (excluding hydrocarbons) contributed 0.8% of GDP in 2002. In 1994 mining (with gas, electricity and water) employed 1.6% of the working population. In 2000 the principal mineral export was petroleum (which accounted for 10.4% of total export earnings). At 1 January 2003 Tunisia's proven published oil reserves were estimated at 300m. barrels, sufficient to maintain production (at 2002 levels) for a further 11 years. Iron, zinc, lead, barite, gypsum, phosphate, fluorspar and sea salt are also mined. In addition, Tunisia possesses large reserves of natural gas. The GDP of the mining sector increased by 5.0% in 2000 and by 1.5% in 2001.

Manufacturing

Manufacturing (excluding hydrocarbons) contributed 20.7% of GDP in 2002, and employed 19.6% of the working population in 1994. Manufacturing is based on the processing of the country's principal agricultural and mineral products. Other important sectors include textiles, construction materials, machinery, chemicals, and paper and wood. In 1990–2002 manufacturing GDP increased at an average annual rate of 5.3%. Manufacturing GDP increased by 7.0% in 2001 and 1.9% in 2002.

Energy

Energy is derived principally from gas (which contributed 87.1% of total electricity output in 2000) and petroleum (12.1%), although Tunisia also has several hydro-electric plants. Imports of mineral fuels and lubricants comprised 10.6% of the value of total imports in 2000. In the late 1990s a project was under way to link the Tunisian electricity grid to that of Libya.

SERVICES

The services sector accounted for 55.8% of GDP in 2002 and employed 42.3% of the working population in 1994. Tourism represents an important source of revenue; receipts from tourism in 2002 totalled US $1,422m. dinars. In 2002 there were 5.1m. tourist arrivals, a decrease of 6.0% compared with 2001. The GDP of the services sector increased by an average of 5.2% per year in 1990–2002. Growth in the sector's GDP was recorded at 6.0% in 2001 and at 3.9% in 2002.

EXTERNAL TRADE

In 2002 Tunisia recorded a visible trade deficit of US $2,123m., and a deficit of $746m. on the current account of the balance of payments. In 2003 the principal sources of imports were France (accounting for 26.0% of the total), Italy (20.0%), Germany (9.0%) and Spain (5.3%). The principal market for Tunisian exports in that year were also France (taking 32.5%), Italy (22.1%) and Germany (10.7%). The member states of the European Union (EU) accounted for 80.5% of Tunisia's exports and 71.4% of its imports in 1999. Tunisia's principal exports in 2000 were clothing and accessories, machinery and transport equipment, petroleum and petroleum products, phosphates and fertilizers, and food and live animals. The principal imports were machinery and transport equipment, textiles, petroleum and petroleum products, electrical machinery and apparatus, food and live animals, and road vehicles and parts.

GOVERNMENT FINANCE

In 2003 there was a budgetary deficit of TD 584m. (equivalent to 2.0% of GDP). At the end of 2001 Tunisia's total external debt was US $10,884m., of which $9,085m. was long-term public debt. In that year the cost of debt-servicing was equivalent to 12.9% of the value of exports of goods and services. The average annual rate of inflation was 4.1% in 1990–2002; the annual rate of inflation averaged 2.7% in both 2002 and 2003. An estimated 15% of the labour force were unemployed in 2003.

INTERNATIONAL ECONOMIC RELATIONS

Tunisia is a member of the Arab Fund for Economic and Social Development (AFESD), the Arab Monetary Fund and the Union of the Arab Maghreb (Union du Maghreb arabe—UMA).

SURVEY AND PROSPECTS

From the mid-1990s Tunisia experienced strong economic growth, low inflation and declining poverty as a result of sound macroeconomic policies and improvements to the country's regulatory framework. However, economic growth stagnated somewhat in 2002 and the privatization programme, which had previously reduced government debt levels significantly, slowed during that year, with just three of a possible 26 companies given over to private control. Nevertheless, a further 34 state-owned entities were scheduled to be divested during 2004 and the Government remained committed to its privatization programme. The 10th development plan (for 2002–06) aimed to increase international trade and accelerate structural reforms in order to create a more competitive economy.

Tunisia's tourism industry, which provides an estimated 7% of total GDP and employs some 300,000 people, was adversely affected by the recession in global travel following the suicide attacks against the USA in September 2001, as well as the terrorist attack at Djerba in April 2002; revenue from that sector fell by 14% in 2002, compared with the previous year. However, by mid-2003 the industry had begun to recover, with visitor numbers to Tunisia increasing once again; the Government proceeded apace with its ambitious programme to develop the sector, which aims to double the number of visitors to the country to 10m. by 2010. Meanwhile, the Tunisian economy continued to become more closely integrated with those of the EU member states, in preparation for the removal of all trade barriers between Tunisia and the EU in 2008. In 2003 inflation was recorded at 2.7%, while GDP grew by 5.5%, according to official figures. The Government forecast growth of 5.2% in 2004; however, optimism regarding the prospects for the Tunisian economy was tempered by the large civil service wage bill, as well as the high level of public debt—officially recorded at 61% of GDP in 2002.

Turkey

The Republic of Turkey lies partly in south-eastern Europe and partly in western Asia. Following the dissolution of the Ottoman Empire after the First World War, political control of Turkey itself passed to the nationalist movement led by Mustafa Kemal ('Atatürk'), whose regime pursued a radical programme of far-reaching reform and modernization. Political instability prompted a military coup in 1980. The Islamist Justice and Development Party (AK Partisi) won the largest number of seats at the November 2002 general election, and subsequently formed the next Government. Ankara is the capital. The principal language is Turkish.

Area and population
Area: 779,452 sq km
Population (mid-2002): 69,626,000
Population density (mid-2002): 89.3 per sq km
Life expectancy (years at birth, 2002): 70.0 (males 67.9; females 72.2)

Finance
GDP in current prices: 2002: US $182,848m. ($2,626 per head)
Real GDP growth (2002): 7.8%
Inflation (annual average, 2002): 45.0%
Currency: Turkish lira

Economy

In 2002, according to estimates by the World Bank, Turkey's gross national income (GNI), measured at average 2000–02 prices, was US $173,979m., equivalent to $2,500 per head (or $6,120 per head on an international purchasing-power parity basis). During 1990–2002, it was estimated, the population increased at an average annual rate of 1.8%, while gross domestic product (GDP) per head increased, in real terms, by an average of 1.1% per year. Overall GDP increased, in real terms, by an annual average of 2.9% in 1990–2002. GDP decreased by 6.1% in 1999, but showed an increase of 6.3% in 2000 before declining again, by 9.4%, in 2001.

AGRICULTURE

Agriculture (including forestry and fishing) contributed 11.9% to GDP and employed 33.2% of the economically active population in 2002. The country is self-sufficient in most basic foodstuffs. The principal agricultural exports are cotton, tobacco, wheat, fruit and nuts. Other important crops are barley, sunflower and other oilseeds, maize, sugar beet, potatoes, tea and olives. The raising of sheep, goats, cattle and poultry is also an important economic activity. During 1990–2002 agricultural GDP increased by an annual average of 0.8%.

INDUSTRY

Industry (including mining, manufacturing, construction and power) contributed 29.5% to GDP and engaged 23.8% of the employed population in 2002. During 1990–2002 industrial GDP increased by an annual average of 2.8%.

Mining

Mining contributed 1.1% to GDP and engaged 0.6% of the employed population in 2002. Chromium, copper and borax are the major mineral exports. Coal, petroleum, natural gas, bauxite, iron ore, manganese and sulphur are also mined. In the late 1990s the country's first gold mine, near Bergama on the Aegean coast, was being developed. During 1990–2001 manufacturing GDP increased by an annual average of 0.8%.

Manufacturing

Manufacturing contributed 20.2% to GDP and employed 18.1% of the employed population in 2002. The most important branches, measured by gross value of output, are textiles, food-processing, petroleum refineries, iron and steel, and industrial chemicals. During 1990–2002 manufacturing GDP increased by an annual average of 3.3%.

Energy

Energy is derived principally from thermal power plants. In 2000 36.1% of energy was derived from natural gas, 30.6% from coal, 24.7% from hydroelectric power, and a further 8.4% from petroleum. The energy sector contributed 4.1% to GDP and employed 0.5% of the employed population in 2002. Total domestic output of crude petroleum and natural gas accounts for roughly 12% of the country's hydrocarbon requirements. Imports of crude petroleum comprised 11.5% of the value of total imports in 2001. In the long term, a major development project for south-east Anatolia, scheduled for completion in 2010, aims to increase Turkey's energy production by 70% and to irrigate 1.6m. ha of uncultivable or inadequately irrigated land, by constructing dams and hydroelectric plants on the Tigris and Euphrates rivers and their tributaries. In June 2000 the construction of an petroleum pipeline between Baku, Azerbaijan, and the Turkish terminal at Ceyhan was approved. The pipeline was also to cross Georgian territory and was expected to raise substantial future revenues for the Government. In mid-2001 construction began on a new 'blue stream' natural gas pipeline running between Russia and Turkey under the Black Sea.

SERVICES

The services sector contributed 58.5% of GDP and engaged 43.0% of the employed labour force in 2002. Tourism is one of Turkey's fastest growing sources of revenue. Total tourist arrivals increased to about 11.6m. in 2001 (compared with 10.4m. visitors in the previous year), generating $8,090m. in revenue. Remittances from Turkish workers abroad also make an important contribution to the economy, amounting to $2,835m. in 2001. During 1990–2002 the GDP of the services sector increased by an annual average of 2.6%.

EXTERNAL TRADE

In 2002 Turkey recorded a visible trade deficit of US $8,337m., and there was a deficit of $1,521m. on the current account of the balance of payments. In 2001 the principal source of imports (13.2%) was Germany, which was also the principal market for exports (18.1%). Other major trading partners in that year were the USA, Italy, France, Japan, the United Kingdom and Russia. The UN restrictions on trade with Iraq reversed Turkey's previously strong trading relations with that country. Exports in 2001 were dominated by clothing and textiles, vegetables and fruit and road vehicles and related components. In that year the principal imports were machinery, crude petroleum, iron and steel, transport vehicles and chemical products.

GOVERNMENT FINANCE

In 2002 there was a provisional budgetary deficit of TL 26,913,000,000m. (equivalent to some 11.5% of GDP). Turkey's external debt at the end of 2001 was US $115,118m., of which $56,004m. was long-term public debt. In that year the cost of debt-servicing was equivalent to 40.0% of the value of exports of goods and services. The annual rate of inflation averaged 71.4% in 1990–2002. Consumer prices increased by 45.0% in 2002 and by 25.3% in 2003. In 2003 the rate of unemployment was estimated at 10.7%.

INTERNATIONAL ECONOMIC RELATIONS

Turkey is a member of numerous international and regional organizations, including the Developing Eight (D-8), the Economic Co-operation Organization (ECO), and the Organization of the Black Sea Economic Co-operation. Turkey was accepted as a candidate for membership of the European Union (EU) in December 1999.

SURVEY AND PROSPECTS

Turkey's economy has been afflicted by persistently high rates of inflation, an expanding public-sector deficit, ongoing political instability and a poor rate of tax collection. In December 1999 the Government reached a stand-by credit agreement with the IMF, which was to finance the implementation of strict fiscal and monetary policies, and of structural reforms. A privatization programme, which had been suspended in 1998, resumed in early 2000 and envisaged the divestment of 74 state enterprises, including banking and telecommunications concerns. However, the country experienced a severe financial crisis in November 2000 and again in February 2001, which resulted in soaring interest rates and an effective devaluation of the lira. As part of a recovery strategy announced in March, the Turkish Government reasserted its commitment to the privatization programme (which had hitherto proceeded only slowly), as a precondition to the extension of funds from the IMF and the World Bank (despite continuing concerns over the social effects of these reforms, which had resulted in a sharp increase in the rate of unemployment).

In February 2002 the IMF commended the progress made by the Turkish authorities in the restructuring of the banking sector, public sector reform, and preparations for privatization, and renewed the stand-by credit arrangement, which was to support the 2002–04 economic programme. The AK Partisi Government, elected in November, pledged to continue to meet the IMF's conditions. Analysts hoped that the party's overwhelming majority in the Turkish Grand National Assembly (TGNA) would allow it to increase the pace of reforms (whereas previous coalition Governments had faced internal opposition). At the end of May 2003, however, the IMF refused to release funds due to Turkey under the stand-by credit agreement until the Government demonstrated its commitment to meeting reform programme objectives. In July the authorities announced the adoption of corrective measures, including significant reductions in state budgetary expenditure, in an effort to meet IMF requirements for the disbursement of the funds. At the end of the same month the TGNA approved further extensive human rights reforms in order to qualify for accession negotiations with the European Union—EU. In September Turkey was officially approved a loan of US $8,500m. by the US Government to compensate for the adverse impact of the US-led war in Iraq in March–April. At the end of 2003 the economy demonstrated strong recovery, and inflation had been reduced to the lowest level reached in some 30 years. Turkey's extremely high external debt burden was assisted, in part, by the US loan and an IMF agreement to postpone repayments due in 2004 and 2005. (However, in 2004 GDP growth was expected to slow to about one-half of the 2003 level, owing, in part, to the negative impact on the tourism industry of the November bombings in Istanbul.)

The Government announced plans to establish a new monetary unit (to be known as the new Turkish lira) by January 2005, in an effort to achieve the principal objective of further reducing inflation in accordance with IMF requirements. Increases in expenditure on pensions and minimum wages, announced at the end of 2003, were expected to prove contentious in view of the fiscal restraints on the Government; in April 2004, however, the IMF, while urging adherence to targets, completed a generally favourable review of progress under Turkey's economic programme.

Turkmenistan

The Republic of Turkmenistan is situated in the south-west of Central Asia. In 1924 the Turkmen Soviet Socialist Republic (SSR) was established. In 1925 it became a constituent republic of the USSR. In 1991 the Communist Party of Turkmenistan was restyled as the Democratic Party of Turkmenistan (DPT), with Saparmyrat Niyazov, who had been elected as executive President of Turkmenistan in 1990, as its Chairman. In October 1991 94.1% of the electorate voted in favour of independence and the Republic of Turkmenistan was proclaimed. President Niyazov and the DPT remained in power in 2003. Ashgabat is the capital. The official language is Turkmen.

Area and population
Area: 488,100 sq km
Population (mid-2002): 5,545,360
Population density (mid-2002): 11.4 per sq km
Life expectancy (years at birth, 2002): 62.7 (males 58.8; females 66.9)

Finance
GDP in current prices: 2002): US $7,672m. ($1,383 per head)
Real GDP growth (2002): 14.9%
Inflation (1997): 83.7%
Currency: manat

Economy

In 2002, according to estimates by the World Bank, Turkmeni- stan's gross national income (GNI), measured at average 2000–02 prices, was US $6,650m., equivalent to $1,200 per head (or $4,570 per head on an international purchasing-power parity basis). During 1990–2002, it was estimated, the population increased at an average annual rate of 3.5%, while gross domestic product (GDP) per head decreased, in real terms, by an average of 3.0% per year. Overall GDP increased, in real terms, at an average annual rate of 0.4% per year in 1990–2002. However, real GDP increased by 20.5% in 2001 and by 14.9% in 2002.

AGRICULTURE

Agriculture contributed an estimated 22.5% of GDP in 2002, when the sector employed 48.7% of the employed labour force, according to figures from the Asian Development Bank (ADB). Although the Kara-Kum desert covers some 80% of the country's territory, widespread irrigation has enabled rapid agricultural develop- ment; however, over-intensive cultivation of the principal crop, cotton, together with massive irrigation projects, have led to serious ecological damage. In 1996 cotton contributed an estimated 11.5% of GDP, although the Government planned to reduce cotton production in favour of food production by 2010. Other important crops include grain, vegetables and fruit (in particular grapes and melons), although the country remains heavily dependent on imports of foodstuffs. Livestock husbandry (including the production of astrakhan and karakul wools) plays a central role in the sector. Silkworm breeding is also practised. According to the World Bank, agricul- tural production declined, in real terms, by an annual average of 0.7% in 1990–2001. However, real agricultural GDP increased by 17.0% in 2000 and by 23.0% in 2001.

INDUSTRY

Industry (including mining, manufacturing, construction and power) contributed an estimated 42.4% of GDP in 2002, when 14.2% of the employed labour force were engaged in the sector. Industrial activity is chiefly associated with the extraction and processing of the country's mineral resources (predominantly natural gas and petroleum), energy generation and cotton-processing. In 1995 fuels accounted for 47.4% of the value of total industrial production, while a further 14.4% was provided by textiles. During 1990–2000, according to the World Bank, industrial GDP decreased, in real terms, at an average annual rate of 1.6%. However, real industrial GDP increased by 20.5% in 2002.

Mining

Turkmenistan is richly endowed with mineral resources, in particular natural gas and petroleum (recoverable reserves of which were estimated at some 2,010,000m. cu m and 100m. metric tons, respectively, at the end of 2002). In 2000 major discoveries of petroleum and natural gas reserves were announced. In 2002 Turkmenistan produced approximately 53,340m. cu m of gas, and production of petroleum averaged 182,000 barrels per day. Petroleum is refined at three refineries, at Turkmenbashy (Krasno- vodsk), Seidi and Türkmenatat (Charjou). In 2001 the refinery at Turkmenbashy was upgraded, at a cost of some US $1,500m. Plans for the modernization of the refinery at

Seidi were announced in early 2004. In addition, Turkmenistan has large deposits of iodine, bromine, sodium sulphate, clay, gypsum and different types of salt.

Manufacturing

The manufacturing sector contributed 37.8% of GDP in 2000. The sector is largely associated with the processing of the country's mineral extracts and cotton products. Textile manufacturing increased considerably in the 1990s; in 2000 it was the second fastest-growing industry in Turkmenistan. According to official statistics production in the manufacturing sector increased by 11% in that year.

Energy

In 2000 the country's electricity was produced by thermal power stations (fuelled by domestically produced natural gas). In 2002 an estimated 10,700m. kWh of electricity was produced in Turkmenistan; of electricity produced in 1994, some 20% was reported to have been exported, while a proportion of the remainder was distributed free of charge to domestic users. (Some charges for domestic electricity use were introduced in 1996; however, the 2003 budget provided for free distribution.) In 2002 mineral fuels accounted for just 1.2% of the value of merchandise imports.

SERVICES

In 2002 the services sector provided an estimated 35.1% of GDP, and employed some 37.2% of the working population. Trade and catering services form the major part of the sector, providing some 6% of employment in 1998. According to the World Bank, services GDP declined, in real terms, at an average annual rate of 0.8% in 1990–2001. However, real services GDP increased by 14.5% in 2000 and by 25.0% in 2001.

EXTERNAL TRADE

According to the European Bank for Reconstruction and Development (EBRD), in 2000 Turkmenistan recorded a visible trade surplus of an estimated US $550m., and there was a deficit of $60m. on the current account of the balance of payments. According to the ADB there was an estimated visible trade surplus of $1,000m. in 2002. In that year the principal source of imports (accounting for 19.1% of the total) was Germany; other major suppliers were Ukraine, the United Arab Emirates, Russia, Turkey and Iran. The principal market for exports (16.4%) was Iran; other major purchasers were Ukraine, Azerbaijan, Kazakhstan, Turkey and Tajikistan. In 2002 the principal exports were mineral fuels and lubricants (accounting for some 85.7% of the value of total exports), followed by basic manufactures. The principal imports were machinery and transport equipment (40.5% of total imports), basic manufactures, chemicals, food and live animals, and miscellaneous manufactured articles.

GOVERNMENT FINANCE

In 2001 Turkmenistan recorded a budgetary deficit of an estimated 279,000m. Turkmen manats (equivalent to some 0.8% of GDP). At the end of 1999 Turkmenistan's total external debt was US $2,015m., of which $1,678m. was long-term public debt. In that year the cost of debt-servicing was equivalent to 31.1% of the value of exports of goods and services. Consumer prices increased by an annual average of 1,150% in 1993 and by 1,748% in 1994, but the inflation rate declined to 1,005% in 1995, to 992% in 1996 and to an estimated 84% in 1997. Average prices rose by only 16.8% in 1998 and by 24.2% in 1999. The inflation rate declined again in 2000, to an annual average of 7.4%. In 2002 some 57,000 people were registered as unemployed (about 2.5% of the labour force); however, unofficial sources estimated the rate to be considerably higher.

INTERNATIONAL ECONOMIC RELATIONS

Turkmenistan became a member of the IMF and the World Bank in 1992. It also joined the EBRD as a 'Country of Operations' and, with five other former Soviet republics, the Economic Co-operation Organization (ECO). In 1994 Turkmenistan became a member of the Islamic Development Bank (IDB), and it joined the ADB in September 2000.

SURVEY AND PROSPECTS

The disruptions in inter-republican trade that followed the dissolution of the USSR in December 1991 adversely affected Turkmenistan's industrial sector, which was heavily reliant on imported finished and intermediate goods. Moreover, the failure, or delay, of many of Turkmenistan's CIS trading partners to pay for imports of natural gas (the mainstay of the republic's economy) resulted in huge arrears, and Turkmenistan was forced to suspend deliveries on several occasions throughout the 1990s, with adverse consequences for the economy as a whole.

The opening of a new gas pipeline to Iran in late 1997 was regarded as of major importance in the revival of the economically crucial gas sector, and by 2001 the economy was benefiting from the fuller capacity utilization of the pipeline. In 2003 Turkmenistan concluded major agreements with both Russia and Ukraine, providing for the supply of natural gas over a 25-year period. The rate of inflation decreased significantly and GDP registered strong growth from 2000, largely owing to the export of natural gas, petroleum and cotton. Natural gas production increased by 4.0% in 2002 compared with the previous year, and petroleum output rose by 6.6%; none the less, there were concerns that Turkmenistan's economy was over-dependent on the hydrocarbons sector. Moreover, an inefficient tax system and a poorly-regulated banking sector, largely under state control, continued to present significant obstacles to economic stability, and estimates of the private sector's contribution to GDP varied between 20% and 30%, reflecting the continuing high levels of state control of the economy, as well as the slow pace of structural reform and market liberalization. The ADB estimated GDP growth at 7%–8% in 2003–04. A balanced budget was approved for 2004, with projected expenditure allowing for the provision of free gas, electricity and water supplies.

Turks and Caicos Islands

The Turks and Caicos Islands consist of more than 30 islands forming the south-eastern end of the Bahamas chain of islands, and lying north of Haiti. A Jamaican dependency from 1874 until 1959, the Turks and Caicos Islands became a separate colony in 1962, following Jamaican independence. After an administrative association with the Bahamas, the islands received their own Governor in 1972. The islands are a United Kingdom Overseas Territory. Cockburn Town is the capital. The official language is English.

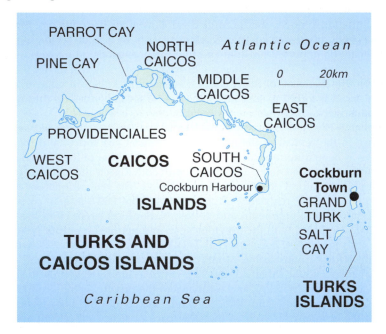

Area and population
Area: 430 sq km
Population (mid-2001): 17,000
Population density (mid-2001): 39.5 per sq km

Finance
GDP in current prices: 2002): US $231m. ($13,576 per head)
Currency: US dollar

Economy

In 2001, according to estimates by the Caribbean Development Bank (CDB), the Turks and Caicos Islands' gross domestic product (GDP) was US $219.5m., equivalent to some $11,030 per head. During 1991–2001, it was estimated, the population increased at an average annual rate of 4.8%, while GDP increased, in real terms, by 7.0% per year; growth in 2001 was 0.1%.

AGRICULTURE

Agriculture is not practised on any significant scale in the Turks Islands or on South Caicos (the most populous island of the Territory). The other islands of the Caicos group grow some beans, maize and a few fruits and vegetables. There is some livestock-rearing, but the islands' principal natural resource is fisheries, which account for almost all commodity exports, the principal species caught being the spiny lobster (an estimated 230 metric tons in 2001) and the conch (an estimated 770 metric tons in that year). Conchs are now being developed commercially (on the largest conch farm in the world), and there is potential for larger-scale fishing. Exports of lobster and conch earned $3.4m. in 1995, which constituted an increase of more than 14% compared with the previous year's earnings.

INDUSTRY

Industrial activity consists mainly of construction (especially for the tourist industry) and fish-processing. The islands possess plentiful supplies of aragonite. The Territory is dependent upon the import of mineral fuels to satisfy energy requirements.

SERVICES

The principal economic sector is the service industry. This is dominated by tourism, which is concentrated on the island of Providenciales. The market is for wealthier visitors, most of whom come from the USA. Tourist arrivals increased from 117,600 in 1999 to 165,400 in 2001. However, the number of tourist arrivals declined in 2002 to 155,600; a further decline was expected in 2003 owing to the weakening of demand in the aftermath of the September 2001 terrorist attacks on the USA and the US-led military campaign to remove the regime of Saddam Hussein in Iraq in 2003. In January 2004 it was announced that a new US $35m. cruise-ship terminal would be constructed in Grand Turk, enabling, for the first time, large passenger liners to stop in the territory. An 'offshore' financial sector was encouraged in the 1980s, and new regulatory legislation was ratified at the end of 1989. In 2000 there were some 8,000 overseas companies registered in the islands. Earnings from some 2,858 new registrations totalled US $2.3m. in 1995.

EXTERNAL TRADE

In 2001 the Turks and Caicos Islands recorded a trade deficit of US $149.6m. (exports were 4.7% of the value of imports). This deficit is normally offset by receipts from tourism, aid from the United Kingdom and revenue from the 'offshore' financial sector. The USA is the principal trading partner, but some trade is conducted with the United Kingdom and with neighbouring nations.

GOVERNMENT FINANCE

In the financial year ending 31 March 2003 the Government estimated an overall budgetary surplus of US $1.0m. The islands received a total of $8.2m. in British development assistance in 1999/2000. The total external public debt was $8.2m. in 2001. The rate of inflation, which stood at about 4% in 1995, is dependent upon the movement of prices in the USA, the Territory's principal trading partner, and the currency of which it uses. Unemployment increased to an estimated 10% in the late 1990s. A large number of Turks and Caicos 'belongers' have emigrated, many to the Bahamas, especially in search of skilled labour (there is no tertiary education in the Territory). In July 2000 the CDB announced a loan to the Government of some US $4m. to assist the Turks and Caicos Investment Agency.

INTERNATIONAL ECONOMIC RELATIONS

The Turks and Caicos Islands, as a dependency of the United Kingdom, have the status of Overseas Territory in association with the European Union (EU). The Territory is also a member of the CDB and an associate member of the Caribbean Community and Common Market (CARICOM).

SURVEY AND PROSPECTS

The economy, and also the population, of the Turks and Caicos Islands were estimated to have doubled in size during the 1990s, making the islands one of the region's most dynamic economies. The remarkable economic growth experienced by the islands was chiefly owing to the increasing significance of the tourism and international financial services sectors, both of which benefited from the perceived stability of United Kingdom Overseas Territory status. In the past decade the 'off-shore' financial sector successfully rehabilitated its international reputation through the introduction, in 2002, of a supervisory body, the Financial Services Commission, and the implementation of more stringent regulatory legislation based on the maxim of 'privacy not secrecy'.

In early 2004 the financial sector faced further regulatory disruption when the territory came under pressure to implement the EU's Savings Tax Directive. Tourism also grew steadily in the late 1990s, and as a result many new hotels and resorts have been developed. Concern has, however, been expressed that the islands are in danger of becoming overdeveloped and thereby of damaging their reputation as an unspoilt tourist location. A further source of disquiet has been the exclusion of many inhabitants from the benefits of economic growth; it was estimated that the economic situation of the majority of 'belongers' improved only marginally during the 1990s, as newly-created jobs were often taken by low-wage migrant workers or by highly-skilled expatriate workers. It has also been noted that the Territory's growth, which is driven more by inward investment than by domestic production, is highly dependent on exterior factors, and international proposals to force comprehensive reforms of 'offshore' financial services centres are therefore of particular concern. Growth in 2001–03, after a decline in regional tourism, was reported to have slowed in comparison with the rate of 4.7% recorded in 2000.

Tuvalu

Tuvalu (formerly known as the Ellice Islands) comprises a group of nine atolls in the western Pacific Ocean. In 1892 a British protectorate was declared over the Ellice Islands, and the group was linked administratively with the Gilbert Islands to the north. In 1916 the United Kingdom annexed the protectorate, which was renamed the Gilbert and Ellice Islands Colony. In 1975 the Ellice Islands, under the old native name of Tuvalu, became a separate British dependency. Tuvalu became independent in 1978. The capital is on Funafuti atoll. Tuvaluan and English are spoken.

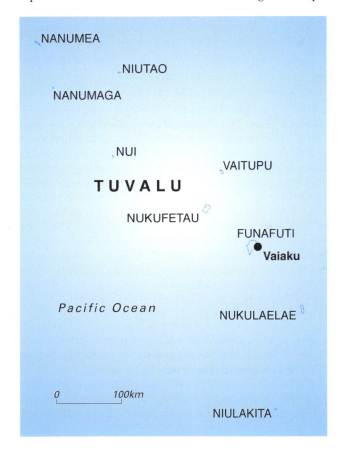

Area and population
Area: 26 sq km
Population (mid-2001): 10,660
Population density (mid-2001): 410.0 per sq km
Life expectancy (years at birth, 2002): 60.6 (males 60.0; females 61.4)

Finance

GDP in current prices: 1998): $A 22.0m. ($A 2,194 per head)
Real GDP growth (2001): 4.0%
Inflation (1999): 7.0%
Currency: Australian dollar

Economy

In 1999 the UN calculated Tuvalu's gross domestic product (GDP) at current prices to be US $16m., equivalent to US $1,556 per head. According to provisional estimates by the Asian Development Bank (ADB), in 2001 GDP totalled US $13m., equivalent to US $1,260 per head. During 1990–2000, it was estimated, the population increased at an average annual rate of 1.5%. Overall GDP increased, in real terms, at an average annual rate of 4.9% in 1990–2000. Compared with the previous year, GDP rose by an estimated 4.0% in 2001, by 2.0% in 2002 and by a similar percentage in the following year.

AGRICULTURE

Agriculture (including fishing) is, with the exception of copra production, of a basic subsistence nature. The sector contributed some 16.8% of GDP in 1998. According to ADB figures, the GDP of the agricultural sector declined at an average annual rate of 1.8% in 1990–98. Compared with the previous year, agricultural GDP increased by 5.8% in 1997 and by 0.7% in 1998. Some 60% of Tuvaluans are engaged in subsistence farming. Coconuts (the source of copra) are the only cash crop; exports of copra were worth $A6,000 in 1997. Pulaka, taro, papayas, the screw-pine (*Pandanus*) and bananas are cultivated as food crops and honey is produced. In the late 1990s and early 2000s agriculture became increasingly affected by climate change and rising sea-levels. More frequent high tides caused flooding which damaged crops, particularly the important taro crop, and killed tree roots, which reduced the harvest of coconuts and other fruits. Livestock comprises pigs, poultry and goats. Fish and other sea products are staple constituents of the islanders' diet. The sale of fishing licences to foreign fleets is an important source of income and earned $A11.8m. in 2001 (compared with $A3.6m. in 1997), equivalent to 50.3% of current revenue.

INDUSTRY

Industry (including mining, manufacturing, construction and utilities) accounted for 24.3% of GDP in 1998. In 1990–98, according to ADB figures, industrial GDP expanded at an average annual rate of 14.0%. Compared with the previous year, the sector's GDP increased by 4.0% in 1997 and by 21.5% in 1998. Manufacturing is confined to the small-scale production of coconut-based products, soap and handi-crafts. The manufacturing sector contributed some 4.2% of GDP in 1998.

Energy

Energy is derived principally from a power plant (fuelled by petroleum) and, on the outer islands, solar power. In 1989 mineral fuels accounted for almost 13% of total import costs.

SERVICES

The Government is an important employer (engaging 1,185 people in 2001, equiva-lent to about one-half of the labour force) and consequently the services sector makes a relatively large contribution to Tuvalu's economy (providing some 58.9% of GDP in 1998). In 1990–98, according to ADB figures, the GDP of the services sector increased at an average annual rate of 5.1%. Compared with the previous year, the sector's GDP expanded by 2.7% in 1997 and by 16.0% in 1998. The islands' remote situation and lack of amenities have hindered the development of a tourist industry. Visitor arrivals totalled only 2,813 in 2001 (compared with 1,278 in 2000). An important source of revenue has been provided by remittances from Tuvaluans working abroad. In the early 1990s some 1,200 Tuvaluans were working overseas, principally in the phosphate industry on Nauru, although many of these workers returned to Tuvalu during the late 1990s, as Nauruan phosphate reserves became exhausted. Remittances from some 450 Tuvaluan seafarers were estimated at US $4.9m. in 2001 (equivalent to some 20% of GDP). In the same year receipts from the leasing of the islands' internet domain address reached US $1.6m., while revenue from telecommunication licence fees totalled US $0.31m.

EXTERNAL TRADE

According to figures from the ADB, in 2002 Tuvalu recorded a visible trade deficit of US $77.3m., compared with $13.4m. in the previous year. The principal sources of imports in 2002 were Fiji (12.9%) and Japan (12.7%). The principal market for exports was the United Kingdom, which purchased 53.4% of the total. In the previous year countries of the European Union purchased 79.0% of Tuvalu's exports. In 2001 copra was the only domestic export of any significance. The principal imports in 2000 were foodstuffs (some 35% of the total), mineral fuels (about 8%) and construction materials (some 5%). In 2001 total export earnings were equivalent to only 7.3% of the value of imports.

GOVERNMENT FINANCE

The 2002 budget allowed for operating expenditure of as much as US $11.6m. and for special development spending of $2.5m., while capital expenditure of $5.6m. was envisaged. An overall budgetary surplus equivalent to 85% of GDP (compared with a deficit equivalent to 43% in 2001). In 1987 the Tuvalu Trust Fund was established, with assistance from New Zealand, Australia and the United Kingdom, to generate funding, through overseas investment, for development projects. In September 2001 its market value totalled $A32.6m. During the late 1990s the Fund contributed some $A7m. towards total annual expenditure. Official development assistance in 2001 totalled US $4.0m., of which US $3.8m. was bilateral aid. In 2003/04 New Zealand provided bilateral assistance worth $NZ2.05m. Aid from Australia totalled $A3.8m. in 2003/2004. The annual rate of inflation averaged 3.2% in 1990–99. The average rate was 5.3% in 2000, 1.8% in 2001, 2.6% in 2002 and an estimated 2.5% in 2003.

INTERNATIONAL ECONOMIC RELATIONS

Tuvalu is a member of the Pacific Community, the Pacific Islands Forum and the UN Economic and Social Commission for Asia and the Pacific (ESCAP). In May 1993 the country was admitted to the Asian Development Bank (ADB).

SURVEY AND PROSPECTS

According to UN criteria, Tuvalu is one of the world's least developed nations. Its economic development has been adversely affected by inclement weather and inadequate infrastructure. Tuvalu's vulnerability to fluctuations in the price of copra on the international market and the country's dependence on imports have resulted in a persistent visible trade deficit; it has also remained reliant on foreign assistance for its development budget. Owing to a high rate of population growth and a drift from the outer islands to the capital, there is a serious problem of overcrowding on Funafuti. In August 1999 a US $4m. loan was secured to establish an outer islands development fund. The Island Development Programme aimed not only to decentralize administration but also to raise the standards of local public services and to encourage the development of small businesses. The capital assets of the Falekaupule Trust Fund, which was charged with promoting sustainable increases in funding for the development of the outer islands, reached US $8.2m. in 2001.

In February 2000, meanwhile, the sale of the '.tv' internet suffix substantially increased the islands' income (revenue from the sales totalled $A24.9m. in 2000, although this declined to some $A3m. in the following year). Government revenues in 2000 were almost twice the projected budgeted amount. Proceeds from the sale were used to develop the country's infrastructure and were channelled largely into improving roads and the education system, also allowing the Government to investigate the possibility of buying land in Fiji, should the resettlement of Tuvalu's population become necessary. In an attempt to ensure the continuity of flights to Tuvalu, the Government committed itself to the purchase of majority shares in Air Fiji in March 2002, using a loan from the National Bank of Tuvalu. A survey of the islands published by the Pacific Economic Bulletin (a publication of the Australian National University) claimed that Tuvalu's economy had been hampered significantly by the prolonged period of political instability that the islands had undergone during 2003. Meanwhile, the economy continued to suffer from the increasing impact of climate change on the islands, with high tides flooding homes, government buildings and the airport, and causing damage to agricultural produce in February 2004.

Uganda

The Republic of Uganda is situated in East Africa. Formerly under British rule, Uganda became an independent member of the Commonwealth in 1962. In 1971 Dr Milton Obote's Government was overthrown by Maj.-Gen. Idi Amin Dada, who became Head of State. Amin was ousted in 1979 by Tanzanian troops and the Uganda National Liberation Army. In 1986 Yoweri Museveni, the leader of the National Resistance Army, seized power. Museveni was elected as President in 1996, and re-elected in 2001. In legislative elections held in 2001 the National Resistance Movement secured more than 70% of the parliamentary seats. The capital is Kampala. English is the official language.

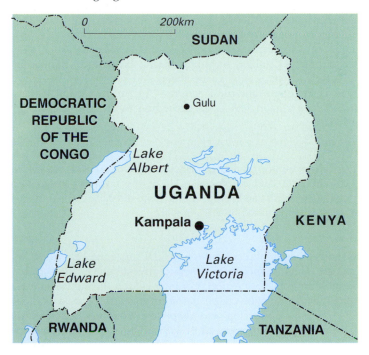

Area and population
Area: 241,139 sq km
Population (mid-2002): 23,395,170
Population density (mid-2002): 97.0 per sq km
Life expectancy (years at birth, 2002): 49.3 (males 47.9; females 50.8)

Finance
GDP in current prices: 2002): US $5,866m. ($251 per head)
Real GDP growth (2002): 6.3%
Inflation (annual average, 2002): −0.3%
Currency: new Uganda shilling

Economy

In 2002, according to estimates by the World Bank, Uganda's gross national income (GNI), measured at average 2000–02 prices, was US $5,909m., equivalent to $250 per head (or $1,320 per head on an international purchasing-power parity basis). During 1990–2002, it was estimated, the population increased at an average annual rate of 3.0%, while gross domestic product (GDP) per head increased, in real terms, by an average of 3.2% per year. Overall GDP increased, in real terms, at an average annual rate of 6.4% in 1990–2002; growth was 6.3% in 2002.

AGRICULTURE

Agriculture (including hunting, forestry and fishing) contributed 31.4% of GDP in 2002 and employed an estimated 79.1% of the labour force in 2002. The principal cash crops are coffee (which provided about 57.0% of export earnings in 1999), tea, cotton and maize. Tobacco, sugar cane and cocoa are also cultivated, and the production of cut flowers is an important activity. The main subsistence crops are plantains, cassava, sweet potatoes, millet, sorghum, maize, beans, groundnuts and rice. In addition, livestock (chiefly cattle, goats, sheep and poultry) are reared, and fresh-water fishing is an important rural activity. Agricultural GDP increased by an average of 3.8% per year in 1990–2002, according to the World Bank; it increased by 4.0% in 2002.

INDUSTRY

Industry (including mining, manufacturing, construction and power) contributed 22.7% of GDP in 2002, and employed 6.3% of the working population in 1994. Industrial GDP increased at an average annual rate of 10.5% in 1990–2002, according to the World Bank; it increased by 8.2% in 2002.

Mining

Mining has made a negligible contribution to GDP since the 1970s (0.7% in 2000/01). The Government aims to encourage renewed investment in the sector. Output of copper, formerly an important export, virtually ceased during the late 1970s. However, the state-owned Kilembe copper mine in western Uganda is expected to be transferred to private ownership and reopened. The production of cobalt from stockpiled copper pyrites commenced in 1999. Uganda is believed to possess the world's second largest deposit of gold, which began to be exploited again in the mid-1990s. Apatite and limestone are also mined. There are, in addition, reserves of iron ore, magnetite, tin, tungsten, beryllium, bismuth, asbestos, graphite, phosphate and tantalite. Mining GDP increased by 8.9% in 1998/99.

Manufacturing

Manufacturing contributed 10.2% of GDP in 2002. The most important manufacturing activities are the processing of agricultural commodities, brewing, vehicle assembly and the production of textiles, cement, soap, fertilizers, paper products, metal products, shoes, paints, matches and batteries. Manufacturing GDP increased by an average of 10.7% per year in 1990–2002, according to the World Bank; it increased by 4.4% in 2002.

Energy

Energy is derived principally from hydroelectric power. In 1998 Uganda generated only about two-thirds of national energy requirements. However, plans are under way to expand hydroelectric production. Imports of fuel accounted for 16.2% of the value of Uganda's merchandise imports in 2001.

SERVICES

The services sector contributed 45.9% of GDP in 2002, and engaged an estimated 9.7% of the employed labour force in 1980. Trade is the most important aspect of the sector. Services GDP increased by an average of 7.3% per year in 1990–2002, according to the World Bank. GDP in the sector increased by 6.2% in 2002.

EXTERNAL TRADE

In 2002 Uganda recorded a visible trade deficit of US $632.8m., and there was a deficit of $421.5m. on the current account of the balance of payments. In 2001 the principal sources of imports were Kenya (28.0%), Japan, South Africa, the United Kingdom and India; Switzerland (15.6%), Kenya, the Netherlands, the United Kingdom, Hong Kong and South Africa were the main markets for exports in that year. The principal exports in 2001 were coffee, fish, crustaceans and molluscs, gold, tobacco, and hides and skins; the main imports in that year were petroleum products, road vehicles, telecommunications and sound recording and reproducing apparatus, and cereals and cereal preparations.

GOVERNMENT FINANCE

In the financial year ending 30 June 2003 Uganda's central government budgetary deficit was an estimated 510,600m. shillings, equivalent to 4.4% of GDP. Uganda's external debt totalled US $3,733m. at the end of 2001, of which $3,306m. was long-term public debt. In that year the cost of debt-servicing was equivalent to 7.4% of the value of exports of goods and services. The annual average rate of inflation was 10.0% in 1990–2002; consumer prices increased by an average of 1.9% in 2001, but decreased by an average of 0.3% in 2002.

INTERNATIONAL ECONOMIC RELATIONS

Uganda is a member of the Common Market for Eastern and Southern Africa, the African Development Bank and the East African Community (EAC).

SURVEY AND PROSPECTS

Uganda is regarded as having an open, deregulated economy, with conditions favourable to investment. Inflation has remained low since the late 1990s, the foreign exchange regime has been liberalized since the mid-1990s and privatization is well advanced. As such, Uganda has enjoyed good relations with international donors. In February 1995 international creditor Governments agreed to cancel some two-thirds of Uganda's bilateral government-guaranteed debt. During 1998–2000 Uganda secured international aid and debt-relief, including assistance under the IMF's initiative for heavily indebted poor countries, to the value of US $1,500m.. It was estimated that these funds would reduce Uganda's annual debt-servicing obligations by about 65%–75%. In March 2000 donor countries commended Uganda for having focused its economic policies on the reduction of poverty and for its commitment to reduce defence spending to 2% of GDP. However, a large part of Uganda's GDP growth is offset by the rapid annual increase in population. Moreover, the ongoing conflict with the LRA in the north of the country has led to continued high expenditure on defence and has hampered growth in the region.

By 2004 there were two main challenges for Uganda's economy: first, growth, still largely dependent on agricultural exports, needed to be sustained at a sufficient level to enable the reduction of poverty, with income distributed more evenly throughout the country; second, Uganda had to reduce its reliance on foreign aid, which financed around one-half of the country's expenditure. In September 2002 the IMF approved a three-year arrangement for Uganda under its Poverty Reduction and Growth Facility, worth some $17.8m. In December 2003 the IMF commended Uganda's recent economic performance, particularly the maintenance of strong growth, despite the impact of adverse weather conditions on agricultural output, and improved revenue collection. However, the Fund expressed concern over poverty levels and inequality in the distribution of income. The creation of an EAC customs union, which was scheduled for September 2004, was expected to lead to increased exports. Meanwhile, the impact of the transition to multi-party politics remained to be seen in early 2004, but it was likely that, if successful, this would further enhance Uganda's attractiveness to the international donor community.

Ukraine

The Republic of Ukraine is situated in east-central Europe. A Ukrainian Soviet Socialist Republic (SSR), established in 1920, became a founding member of the USSR in 1922. Demands for greater autonomy increased following a serious explosion at the Chornobyl nuclear power station, in northern Ukraine, in 1986. In 1991 the Verkhovna Rada (republican legislature) adopted a declaration of independence that was subsequently approved in a referendum. In 1991 Leonid Kravchuk was elected as President. Kravchuk was succeeded in 1994 by Leonid Kuchma, who retained the presidency in 1999. Kiev is the capital. The official state language is Ukrainian.

Area and population
Area: 603,700 sq km
Population (mid-2002): 48,717,272
Population density (mid-2002): 80.7 per sq km
Life expectancy (years at birth, 2002): 67.2 (males 61.7; females 72.9)

Finance
GDP in current prices: 2002): US $41,380m. ($849 per head)
Real GDP growth (2002): 4.5%
Inflation (2002): 0.8%
Currency: hryvnya

Economy

In 2002, according to the World Bank, Ukraine's gross national income (GNI), measured at average 2000–02 prices, was US $37,734m., equivalent to $770 per head (or $4,650 per head on an international purchasing-power parity basis). During 1990–

2002 gross domestic product (GDP) per head declined, in real terms, at an average rate of 5.2% per year. Over the same period, the population decreased by an annual average of 0.5%. Ukraine's GDP declined, in real terms, by an average of 5.7% annually during 1990–2002. However, GDP increased by 9.1% in 2001 and by 4.5% in 2002.

AGRICULTURE

Agriculture (including forestry and fishing) contributed 16.9% of GDP in 2002, according to estimates by the World Bank, and it provided 19.8% of employment in that year. Ukraine has large areas of extremely fertile land, forming part of the 'black earth' belt, and the country is self-sufficient in almost all aspects of agricultural production. The principal crops are grain, sugar beet, potatoes and other vegetables. A programme to transfer state collective farms to private ownership was initiated in 1991. In January 1997 only 14% of land was managed by private farms, although in that year private farms contributed some 46% of total agricultural output. During 1990–2002, according to the World Bank, agricultural GDP declined by an annual average of 3.8%, in real terms. Agricultural GDP increased by 10.9% in 2001 and by 3.6% in 2002. However, following a severe winter in 2002, there was a significantly reduced harvest in 2003.

INDUSTRY

Industry (including mining, manufacturing, construction and power) contributed an estimated 39.3% of GDP in 2002, according to the World Bank, and it provided 30.8% of employment in that year. Heavy industry dominates the sector, particularly metalworking, mechanical engineering, chemicals, and machinery products. The mining and metallurgical sector accounted for 27.2% of Ukraine's industrial output in 1997. Defence-related industrial activity, traditionally important, was being converted to non-military production, and by 1997 some 80% of defence-industry factories had been transformed. According to the World Bank, industrial GDP decreased by an average of 7.3% annually, in real terms, in 1990–2002. However, real industrial GDP increased by 8.6% in 2001 and by 2.6% in 2002.

Mining

In 2002 3.9% of the work-force were engaged in mining and quarrying. Ukraine has large deposits of coal (mainly in the huge Donbass coal basin) and high-grade iron ore, and there are also significant reserves of manganese, titanium, graphite, natural gas and petroleum. Production of coal declined by some 53% in 1989–95, and in 1996 the Government implemented a major reorganization of the coal-mining industry, including the closure of several loss-making mines.

Manufacturing

The manufacturing sector contributed 24.0% of GDP in 2002, according to the World Bank, and the sector provided 18.5% of employment. During 1990–2002 manufacturing GDP decreased by an annual average of 6.4%, in real terms. However, the GDP of the sector increased by 14.2% in 2001 and by 5.1% in 2002.

Energy

Ukraine is highly dependent on imports of energy products, of which Russia and Turkmenistan are the principal suppliers. Imports of mineral fuels comprised an estimated 42.8% of the value of total imports in 2000. A pipeline from a new oil terminal at Odesa, on the Black Sea coast, to Brody, near the border with Poland, which was originally intended to carry petroleum from the Caspian Sea to central and western Europe, was completed in 2002, but had not entered into operation by April 2004. Ukraine has five nuclear power stations. However, following the accident at the Chornobyl station in 1986, the viability of the country's nuclear power programme was called into question. Financial assistance was to be provided by the mid-2000s for the construction of two further nuclear reactors to meet the country's energy requirements. In 2000 nuclear power accounted for 45.1% of Ukraine's electricity production; coal accounted for 26.8%, and natural gas for 17.4%.

SERVICES

The services sector contributed an estimated 43.8% of GDP in 2002, according to the World Bank, and employed 49.3% of the labour force. During 1990–2002 the GDP of the sector decreased by an average of 6.1% annually, in real terms. The real GDP of the sector increased by 5.9% in 2001, but declined dramatically, by 56.0%, in 2002.

EXTERNAL TRADE

In 2002 Ukraine recorded a trade surplus of US $710m., while there was a surplus of $3,174m. on the current account of the balance of payments. In 2001 the principal markets for exports were Russia (accounting for 22.6%), Turkey and Italy. The principal source of imports in 2001 was Russia (providing 36.9% of all imports), followed by Turkmenistan and Germany. The principal imports in 2000 were mineral fuels and lubricants (which accounted for 42.8% of the total), machinery and transport equipment, basic manufactures, chemical products and crude materials. The principal exports in that year were basic manufactures (some 50.6% of the total, comprising principally iron and steel), machinery and transport equipment, chemical products, food and live animals, mineral fuels and crude materials.

GOVERNMENT FINANCE

In 2001 there was a budgetary deficit of 1,877m. hryvnyas, equivalent to 0.9% of GDP. In 2002, according to preliminary figures, a budgetary surplus of 1,043m. hryvnyas, equivalent to 0.5% of GDP, was recorded. Ukraine's total external debt was US $12,811m. at the end of 2001, of which $8,197m. was long-term public debt. In that year the cost of debt-servicing was equivalent to 10.6% of the value of exports of goods and services. In 1992–2002 the average annual inflation rate was 129.6%. The average rate of inflation reached 4,735% in 1993, but had declined to just 13.2% by 1997. Consumer prices increased by 12.0% in 2001 and by 0.8% in 2002. Some 10.1% of the labour force were unemployed in 2002.

INTERNATIONAL ECONOMIC RELATIONS

Ukraine became a member of the IMF and the World Bank in 1992. It also joined the European Bank for Reconstruction and Development (EBRD) as a 'Country of Operations'. In June 1994 Ukraine signed an agreement of partnership and co-operation with the European Union (EU), which was ratified in 1998. An interim trade accord was signed with the EU in June 1995. Ukraine is a member of the Organization of the Black Sea Economic Co-operation, and is seeking membership of the World Trade Organization.

SURVEY AND PROSPECTS

Ukraine experienced severe economic problems following the dissolution of the USSR, and by 2001 GDP was equivalent to just 44% of the level recorded in 1991. A reform programme was agreed with the IMF in 1994, and by 1996 the economy was showing signs of stabilization; the annual rate of GDP declined more slowly during the second half of the 1990s. A second stage of economic reform, inaugurated in 1996, was only inconsistently implemented, and Ukraine was adversely affected by the financial crisis in Russia, its principal trading partner, in mid-1998. The economy showed significant signs of improvement from 2000, when GDP registered positive growth for the first time since the dissolution of the USSR, and further macroeconomic reforms were implemented in the early 2000s.

In December 2000 the IMF resumed lending to Ukraine, which had been suspended while an investigation into the alleged misuse of funds was undertaken. Ukraine's inability to pay for deliveries of fuel supplies, on which it is highly dependent, caused difficulties throughout the 1990s and early 2000s, with frequent losses of power. The privatization of six regional energy companies in 2001 represented progress towards implementing deeper reform in the sector; in October of that year Russia rescheduled Ukraine's gas-debt repayments over a period of 12 years. Foreign investment in Ukraine remained relatively low, partly because of a lack of clear fiscal regulation and partly owing to perceptions of widespread corruption, and GDP per head was significantly lower than in Russia.

As part of a programme of proposed fiscal reforms, in May 2003 the Verkhovna Rada approved a uniform rate of income tax of 13% for individuals, to take effect from 2004, modelled on a system successfully introduced in Russia, and which had been credited with reducing the rate of tax evasion. In February 2004 Ukraine was removed from the list of 'non-compliant' countries and territories of the Financial Action Task Force on Money Laundering (FATF), in response to the introduction in 2003 of measures to combat flaws in the Ukrainian financial regulatory system, which had made it permissive to money 'laundering' and which had led to the imposition of economic sanctions against Ukraine by the USA and Canada. In 2003 GDP increased by 9.3%, according to provisional figures, despite the poor grain harvest, and growth of around 6% was projected for 2004.

United Arab Emirates

The United Arab Emirates (UAE), in the east of the Arabian peninsula, was formerly Trucial Oman, also known as the Trucial States, and its component sheikhdoms were under British protection. In 1971 six of the seven Trucial States (Abu Dhabi, Dubai, Sharjah, Umm al-Qaiwain, Ajman and Fujairah) agreed on a federal Constitution and proceeded to independence as the UAE. Ras al-Khaimah joined the UAE in 1972. Sheikh Zayed of Abu Dhabi, the UAE's first President, died in 2004 and was succeeded by his son, Sheikh Khalifa. The capital is Abu Dhabi. Arabic is the official language.

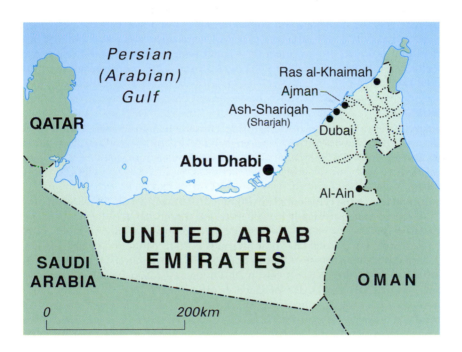

Area and population

Area: 77,700 sq km
Population (mid-2002): 3,049,2400
Population density (mid-2002): 39.2 per sq km
Life expectancy (years at birth, 2002): 72.5 (males 71.3; females 75.1)

Finance

GDP in current prices: 2001): US $69,861m. ($20,029 per head)
Real GDP growth (2001): 3.8%
Inflation (2002): 2.9%
Currency: UAE dirham

Economy

In 1998, according to estimates by the World Bank, the UAE's gross national income (GNI), measured at average 1996–98 prices, was US $49,205m., equivalent to $18,060 per head (or $19,410 on an international purchasing-power parity basis). During 1990–2002, it was estimated, the population increased by an average annual rate of 4.3%, while gross domestic product (GDP) per head decreased, in real terms, by an average of 0.6% per year during 1993–2002. Overall GDP increased, in real terms, by an average annual rate of 5.1% in 1993–2002; growth in 2002 was an estimated 2.4%.

AGRICULTURE

Agriculture (including livestock and fishing) contributed an estimated 3.4% of GDP in 2001, and engaged 7.9% of the employed population in 2000. The principal crops are dates, spinach, tomatoes and cabbages. The UAE imports some 70% of food requirements, but is self-sufficient in salad vegetables, eggs and poultry. Some agricultural products are exported, on a small scale. Livestock-rearing and fishing are also important. During 1993–2002 agricultural GDP increased at an average annual rate of 9.0%.

INDUSTRY

Industry (including mining, manufacturing, construction and power) contributed an estimated 51.2% of GDP in 2001, and engaged 33.4% of the working population in 2000. During 1993–2002 industrial GDP increased by an average of 3.6% per year.

Mining

Mining and quarrying contributed an estimated 29.1% of GDP in 2001, and employed 2.3% of the working population in 2000. Petroleum production is the most important industry in the UAE, with exports of crude petroleum and related products providing an estimated 41.3% of total export revenues in 2001. At the end of 2002 the UAE's proven recoverable reserves of petroleum were 97,800m. barrels, representing 9.3% of world reserves. Production levels in 2002 averaged 2.27m. barrels per day (b/d). From 1 April 2004 the UAE's production quota within the Organization of the Petroleum Exporting Countries (OPEC) was 2,051,000 b/d. The UAE has large natural gas reserves, estimated at 6,010,000m. cu m at the end of 2002 (3.9% of world reserves). Most petroleum and natural gas reserves are concentrated in Abu Dhabi. Dubai is the second largest producer of petroleum in the UAE. Marble and sand are also quarried.

Manufacturing

The major heavy industries in the UAE are related to hydrocarbons, and activities are concentrated in the Jebel Ali Free Zone (in Dubai) and the Jebel Dhanna-Ruwais industrial zone in Abu Dhabi. The most important products are liquefied petroleum gas, distillate fuel oils and jet fuels. There are two petroleum refineries in Abu Dhabi, and the emirate has 'downstream' interests abroad. Manufacturing contributed an estimated 13.5% of GDP in 2001, and employed 11.0% of the working population in 2000. The most important sectors are aluminium, steel and chemicals. During 1993–2002 manufacturing GDP increased at an average annual rate of 9.1%.

Energy

Electric energy is generated largely by thermal power stations, utilizing the UAE's own petroleum and natural gas resources. Each of the emirates is responsible for its own energy production. In 1994 the total installed capacity of UAE power stations was 5,000 MW. A further 2,500 MW was expected to be installed by 2000 to meet rising demand.

SERVICES

The services sector contributed an estimated 45.4% of GDP in 2001, and engaged 58.7% of the working population in 2000. The establishment of the Jebel Ali Free Zone in 1985 enhanced Dubai's reputation as a well-equipped entrepôt for regional trade, and significant growth in both re-exports and tourism has been recorded in recent years. Following a sharp decline in values on the informal stock exchange in mid-1998, an official stock exchange was inaugurated in Dubai in March 2000; a second exchange was scheduled to open in Abu Dhabi. During 1993–2002 the GDP of the services sector increased by an average of 6.2% per year.

EXTERNAL TRADE

In 2001, according to preliminary estimates, the UAE recorded a visible trade surplus of AED 56,300m., and there was a surplus of AED 39,700m. on the current account of the balance of payments. In 1999 the principal source of imports (9.9%) was the USA. Other important suppliers in that year were Japan, the United Kingdom, India, Germany, France and the People's Republic of China. In 1998 the principal market for exports was Japan (29.5%). Other important markets in that year were the Republic of Korea, India, Oman and Singapore. All of Sharjah's exports of crude petroleum are taken by the USA. According to IMF estimates, in 2001 the principal source of imports and the principal market for exports was Japan, with 10.2% and 36.4%, respectively. The principal exports in 2001, excluding hydrocarbons, base metals and articles of base metal, textiles and textile articles and chemical products. The principal imports in that year were machinery and electrical equipment, vehicles and other transport equipment, and textiles and textile articles.

GOVERNMENT FINANCE

A federal budgetary deficit of AED 2,169m. was forecast for 2002. The federal budget reflects only about one-half of the country's total public expenditure, as the individual emirates also have their own budgets for municipal expenditure and local projects. Abu Dhabi is the major contributor to the federal budget. Annual inflation averaged 2.3% in 1995–2002. Consumer prices rose by an average of 2.7% in 2001 and an estimated 2.9% in 2002. Some 2.3% of the labour force were recorded as unemployed in 2000. About 80% of the work-force are estimated to be non-UAE nationals.

INTERNATIONAL ECONOMIC RELATIONS

In addition to its membership of OPEC and the Co-operation Council for the Arab States of the Gulf (GCC), the UAE also belongs to the Organization of Arab Petroleum Exporting Countries (OAPEC) and the Arab Fund for Economic and Social Development (AFESD). The UAE, and Abu Dhabi in particular, is a major aid donor. Abu Dhabi disburses loans through the Abu Dhabi Fund for Development (ADFD). GCC member states established a unified regional customs tariff in January 2003 and agreed to create a single market and currency no later than January 2010.

SURVEY AND PROSPECTS

Abu Dhabi and Dubai, the principal petroleum producers, dominate the economy of the UAE, while the northern emirates remain relatively undeveloped. There is little co-ordination in the economic affairs of the emirates, and the relationship between Abu Dhabi and Dubai in particular is not always cordial; in December 2003, for example, economic relations between the two largest emirates deteriorated owing to a dispute over a new property law in Dubai. The UAE is less dependent than other petroleum-producing countries on the hydrocarbons sector (crude oil accounted for some 28.8% of GDP in 2001), and Dubai is of particular importance as an entrepôt for regional trade. Following a period of reduced income from petroleum in the late 1990s (owing to the decline in international petroleum prices), the Emirates have sought different ways of maximizing government revenue; Abu Dhabi has continued with its privatization programme, divesting the electricity and water sector along with telecommunications; Dubai has encouraged self-reliance and greater profitability among its state enterprises; and the northern emirates have continued to expand non-oil-sector activities. In recent years, the federal economy has recorded a sustained high performance.

Although the UAE was concerned that its tourism sector, which had enjoyed particularly strong growth in Dubai during the 1990s, would be severely affected by renewed conflict in the Gulf, the repercussions of the US-led military campaign to oust the regime of Saddam Hussain in Iraq pushed oil prices to very high levels, leading to forecasts of strong export performance in 2003. The 2003 budget, finalized in August, anticipated an increased deficit of US $601m. that, as usual, was likely to be offset by petroleum prices reaching a higher level than projected. None the less, the IMF advised that further privatizations were needed in order to close the gap between revenue and expenditure. Economic growth was estimated at 4.7% in 2003, and a further healthy increase in real GDP was forecast for 2004.

United Kingdom

The United Kingdom of Great Britain and Northern Ireland lies in north-western Europe. Northern Ireland is a constitutionally distinct part of the United Kingdom. Great Britain comprises England, Scotland and Wales. In a general election held in 1979 the Conservative Party won a parliamentary majority and subsequently formed a Government under Margaret Thatcher, who became the United Kingdom's first female Prime Minister. The Conservative Party remained in power until 1997, when the Labour Party, led by Anthony (Tony) Blair, secured an overwhelming parliamentary majority. In 2001 the Labour Party won a further comprehensive electoral victory. London is the capital. The language is English.

Area and population

Area: 242,514 sq km (including Northern Ireland)
Population (mid-2002): 59,231,900
Population density (mid-2002): 244.2 per sq km
Life expectancy (years at birth, 2002): 78.2 (males 75.8; females 80.5)

Finance

GDP in current prices: 2002): US $1,552,437m. ($26,209 per head)
Real GDP growth (2002): 1.5%
Inflation (annual average, 2002): 1.6%
Currency: pound sterling

Economy

In 2002, according to estimates by the World Bank, the United Kingdom's gross national income (GNI), measured at average 2000–02 prices, was US $1,486,195m., equivalent to $25,250 per head (or $25,870 per head on an international purchasing-power parity basis). During 1990–2002, it was estimated, the population increased at an average annual rate of 0.2%, while gross domestic product (GDP) per head increased, in real terms, by an average of 2.0% per year. Overall GDP increased, in real terms, at an average annual rate of 2.2% per year in 1990–2002; it increased by 2.2% in 2001 and by 1.5% in 2002.

AGRICULTURE

Agriculture (including hunting, forestry and fishing) contributed 1.0% of GDP in 2002, and engaged 1.4% of the employed labour force in 2003. The principal crops include wheat, sugar beet, potatoes and barley. Livestock-rearing (particularly poultry and cattle) and animal products are important, as is fishing. In 2001 the agricultural sector was adversely affected by the outbreak of foot-and-mouth disease, which resulted in the slaughter of more than 6.5m. animals. The GDP of the agricultural sector increased, in real terms, by 0.4% during 1994–2002; it declined by 10.1% in 2001, largely owing to the adverse effects of the foot-and-mouth crisis, but increased by 10.9% in 2002.

INDUSTRY

Industry (including mining, manufacturing, construction and power) contributed 26.0% of GDP in 2002, and in 2003 engaged 19.9% of the employed labour force. Excluding the construction sector (which increased by 7.5% in 2002), industrial GDP increased, in real terms, at an average annual rate of 0.5% during 1994–2002; it declined by 1.6% in 2001 and by 2.6% in 2002.

Mining

Mining (including petroleum and gas extraction) contributed 2.6% of GDP in 2002 and engaged 0.8% of the employed labour force in 1990. Crude petroleum, natural gas, coal and limestone are the principal minerals produced. The GDP of the mining sector increased, in real terms, at an average annual rate of 0.3% during 1994–2002, but declined by 5.5% in 2001 and by 0.2% in 2002.

Manufacturing

Manufacturing provided 15.9% of GDP in 2002 and engaged 12.6% of the employed labour force in 2003. Measured by the value of output, the principal branches of manufacturing in 1997 were transport equipment (accounting for 12.5% of the total), food products (11.8%), machinery (10.8%), chemical products (10.0%) and metals and metal products (7.6%). In real terms, the GDP of the manufacturing sector increased at an average annual rate of 0.4% during 1994–2002; manufacturing GDP declined by 1.3% in 2001 and by 2.6% in 2002.

Energy

Energy is derived principally from natural gas, petroleum and coal, although natural gas is increasingly favoured in preference to coal. Of the United Kingdom's total consumption of energy in 2002, 41.2% was derived from natural gas, 31.8% from petroleum, 16.5% from coal and 9.3% from primary electricity (including nuclear power, hydroelectric power and imports). In mid-2001 33 nuclear power reactors were operating in the United Kingdom. In 2002 mineral fuels accounted for about 4.2% of the value of total merchandise imports. In mid-2003 plans were announced for the construction of three new offshore wind farms, which would provide sufficient energy to power 15% of British homes upon their completion. It was anticipated that they would supply some 5% of the United Kingdom's electric power by 2010.

SERVICES

Services accounted for 73.1% of GDP in 2002. In 2003 the sector engaged 78.7% of the employed labour force. The United Kingdom is an important international centre for business and financial services. Financial intermediation and other business services (including renting and real estate) contributed 27.6% of GDP in 2002. Receipts from tourism totalled £12,805m. in 2000. However, the tourism industry suffered badly in 2001 as a result of the foot-and-mouth crisis and the events of 11 September, and tourism receipts declined by almost 12% to £11,306m. In 2002 the sector recovered somewhat and receipts from tourism increased to £11,737m. Transport and communications are also important, and the sector contributed 7.8% of GDP in 2002. In real terms, the GDP of the services sector increased at an average annual rate of 3.5% during 1994–2002; it increased by 2.6% in 2001 and by 2.3% in 2002.

EXTERNAL TRADE

In 2002 the United Kingdom recorded a visible trade deficit of £46,455m., and there was a deficit of £18,965m. on the current account of the balance of payments. In 2002 the principal source of imports (13.9%) was Germany, while the principal market for exports in that year was the USA (15.0%). Other major trading partners include Germany, France, the Netherlands, Belgium-Luxembourg and Ireland. The principal imports in 2002 were mechanical and electrical machinery and road vehicles. The principal exports were also mechanical and electrical machinery and road vehicles.

GOVERNMENT FINANCE

In 2001 there was a budgetary surplus of £7,490m. (equivalent to 0.9% of GDP). At 1997 external government debt was £60,213m. The annual rate of inflation averaged 2.9% in 1994–2002; it declined to 1.8% in 2001 and to 1.7% in 2002, but increased to 2.9% in 2003. The rate of unemployment, according to OECD figures, averaged 5.0% of the labour force in 2001 and 5.1% in 2002.

INTERNATIONAL ECONOMIC RELATIONS

The United Kingdom is a member of the European Union (EU). It is also a member of the Organisation for Economic Co-operation and Development (OECD).

SURVEY AND PROSPECTS

In the early 1990s the British economy experienced a recession; however, by 1994 the economy had recovered and strong GDP growth was recorded during the late 1990s. In May 1997 the newly elected Labour Government confirmed its commitment to restricting the inflation rate to 2.5%, and granted the Bank of England operational independence for monetary policy to achieve the target within the framework of long-term economic stability. Following the announcement in mid-2003 that four of the five key principles for British participation in European economic and monetary union (EMU) had not yet been fulfilled, the Chancellor of the Exchequer, Gordon Brown, stated that the United Kingdom would adopt the harmonized index of consumer prices method, used by other EMU members and the USA, to calculate inflation and that the target figure under this would be 2.0%. In the early 2000s Brown pledged a number of substantial increases in expenditure on public services, made possible by the continuing expansion of the economy, with total funds allocated to health, education, transport and law and order scheduled to rise to £511,000m. in the financial year 2005/06.

From early 2002 the global economic slowdown, partly caused by the effects of the terrorist attacks on the USA in September 2001, prompted the Bank of England to introduce a series of interest rate reductions in order to stimulate the stagnating economy, and in July 2003 the interest rate was cut to just 3.5%—the lowest level since 1964. The low cost of borrowing fuelled unprecedented levels of private debt and failed to stem the rapid increase in nation-wide property prices, which many analysts predicted would result in a damaging crash. Despite a downwards revision of GDP growth estimates in mid-2003, the British economy remained one of the most robust in the western world; the number of unemployed Britons had, by March 2004, fallen to its lowest level since records began in 1984, with just 1.44m. people seeking employment. The major cause for concern, however, became the significantly higher Treasury borrowing figures (predicted to reach £37,500m. in 2003–04) that would be needed in order to meet government spending requirements, and the IMF warned in December 2003 that Brown would have to reduce expenditure by £1,200m. per year over the next five years or raise taxes in order to stay within his desired limits of borrowing (1% of national income). There were also fears concerning the rapidly widening trade deficit. Nevertheless, the rates of unemployment and inflation remained lower than most European countries and healthy GDP growth of 3.0%–3.5% was forecast for 2004.

United States of America

The United States of America comprises mainly the North American continent between Canada and Mexico. In 2000 George W. Bush, although gaining less votes than his Democrat opponent, was elected President. Following terrorist attacks on the country in 2001 the priority of US foreign policy has been to combat international terrorist organizations, in particular the al-Qa'ida network, and those states deemed to support them. In 2003 the USA led an invasion of Iraq, which it had identified as one such state. In 2004 Bush was elected to a second term in office. The capital is Washington, DC. The language is English.

Area and population
Area: 9,809,155 sq km
Population (mid-2002): 288,368,992
Population density (mid-2002): 29.4 per sq km
Life expectancy (years at birth, 2002): 77.3 (males 74.6; females 79.8)

Finance

GDP in current prices: US $10,416,818m. ($36,123 per head)
Real GDP growth (2002): 2.3
Inflation (annual average, 2002): 1.6%
Currency: US dollar

Economy

In 2002, according to estimates by the World Bank, the USA's gross national income (GNI), measured at average 2000–02 prices, was US $10,110,087m., equivalent to $35,060 per head. During 1990–2002, it was estimated, the population increased at an annual average rate of 1.2%, while gross domestic product (GDP) per head increased, in real terms, by an average of 1.7% per year. During 1990–2002 overall GDP increased, in real terms, at an average annual rate of 2.9%; GDP grew by 2.2% in 2002 and by 3.1% in 2003.

AGRICULTURE

Agriculture (including forestry and fishing) contributed 1.4% of GDP in 2001. About 2.4% of the working population were employed in this sector in that same year. The principal crops are hay, potatoes, sugar beet and citrus fruit, which, together with cereals, cotton and tobacco, are important export crops. The principal livestock are cattle, pigs and poultry. Food and live animals provided 5.6% of total exports in 2001. The GDP of the sector increased, in real terms, by an average of 2.7% per year in 1994–2001. Real agricultural GDP increased by 7.8% in 2000, but declined by 1.7% in 2001.

INDUSTRY

Industry (including mining, manufacturing, construction and utilities) provided 22.2% of GDP in 2001 and employed 22.6% of the civilian working population in that same year. Industrial GDP increased, in real terms, at an average annual rate of 2.6% in 1994–2001. Real industrial GDP increased by 3.4% in 2000, but decreased by 5.1% in 2001.

Mining

Mining and quarrying contributed 1.4% of GDP in 2001, and employed 0.4% of the civilian working population in that year. The USA's principal mineral deposits are of petroleum, natural gas, coal, copper, iron, silver and uranium. The mining sector accounted for 3.8% of total exports in 2001. In real terms, the GDP of the sector decreased at an average annual rate of 0.2% during 1994–2001. Real mining GDP decreased by 11.2% in 2000 before increasing by 4.8% in 2001.

Manufacturing

Manufacturing contributed 14.0% of GDP in 2001, when the sector employed 14.0% of the civilian working population. The principal branches (measured by value of output) were transport equipment (12.3% of the total in 2001), chemical products (12.2%), computer and electronic equipment (12.1%) food products (10.4%), and metal products. Manufacturing provided 83.4% of total exports in 2001. Manufacturing GDP increased, in real terms, by an average of 3.1% per year in 1994–2001. Sectoral GDP increased by 4.7% in 2000, but decreased by 6.0% in 2001.

Energy

Energy is derived principally from domestic and imported hydrocarbons. In 2000 52.7% of total electricity production was provided by coal, 15.7% was derived from natural gas, and 20.0% was provided by nuclear power. In 2001 fuel imports amounted to 10.9% of total merchandise import costs.

SERVICES

Services provided 76.4% of GDP and 75.0% of total civilian employment in 2001. The combined GDP of all service sectors rose, in real terms, at an average rate of 4.3% per year during 1994–2001. Services GDP increased by 5.2% in 2000 and by 2.1% in 2001.

EXTERNAL TRADE

In 2002 the USA recorded a visible trade deficit of $479,380m. (excluding military transactions), and there was a deficit of $480,860m. on the current account of the balance of payments. The USA's principal export market and main source of imports in 2002 was Canada, with which a free-trade agreement came into force in January 1989, providing for the progressive elimination, over a 10-year period, of virtually all trade tariffs between the two countries. In 2002 Canada accounted for 23.2% of total US exports and 18.0% of total imports. Mexico was the second-largest trading partner, providing 11.6% of US imports in 2002. Other major trading partners include Japan, the United Kingdom, Germany and other members of the European Union (EU), and the People's Republic of China. In 2002 machinery and transport equipment constituted the principal category of exports (accounting for 51.2% of the total) and of imports (43.1%).

GOVERNMENT FINANCE

In the financial year ending 30 September 2003 there was an estimated federal budget deficit of $375,295m. The annual rate of inflation averaged 2.7% in 1990–2002. The average annual rate was 1.6% in 2002 and 2.3% in 2003. The rate of unemployment averaged 4.0% of the labour force in 2000 (its lowest level since 1969); this figure rose to to 5.8% in 2002, and stood at 6.0% in 2003.

SURVEY AND PROSPECTS

The US economy grew strongly throughout the 1990s, despite the persistence of many of the factors that had inhibited growth in the previous decade. The federal Government's level of foreign debt continued to increase until 1998, its reduction being a priority of the second Clinton Administration. The deficits in trade and on the current account of the balance of payments increased throughout the decade. Trade with Canada, and particularly with Mexico, was facilitated by the North American Free Trade Agreement (NAFTA), which entered into operation in January 1994 and provided for the progressive abolition (over a 15-year period) of tariffs between the three countries. In the second half of the decade the US dollar appreciated considerably in value against many major world currencies, enabling the Federal Reserve System to maintain low interest rates, thus stimulating growth, led by developments in the telecommunications and information-technology sectors. However, growth in these sectors began to decelerate in 2000, provoking fears of a recession in the economy as a whole.

Under President Clinton the country's budget deficit was reduced and, from 1998–2001, a budget surplus was operated. Pledges to reduce levels of personal taxation were a prominent feature of the presidential campaign of George W. Bush, and his Administration's first budget included the largest single cut in federal taxation since 1981, amounting to $1,350,000m. Concerns of a significant recession, after the sustained growth of previous years, dominated the US economy in 2001; interest rates were cut sharply in this year, in an effort to sustain economic activity. The events of 11 September 2001 further undermined confidence in the US economy. Nevertheless, the economy grew by 2.2% in 2002, and by a further 3.1% in 2003.

In March 2002 the Government imposed tariffs on steel imported from the EU, Russia and Japan, among other countries (Canada, Mexico and some developing countries were exempt); the measure was taken as a response to cheap exports from those countries, which the USA claimed were damaging the domestic steel industry. The countries affected appealed to the World Trade Organization, WTO, to overturn the decision and demanded compensation from the USA. In November 2003 the WTO ruled that the tariffs were illegal and authorized retaliatory action by those countries affected. The USA rescinded the tariffs in early December.

The Government enacted legislation in May 2002 that provided for large agricultural subsidies over a period of 10 years; the move was criticized by EU countries, which claimed that they would be obliged to increase subsidies to protect their own farmers. In January 2004 12 countries banned imports of US beef following the discovery of a case of bovine spongiform encephalopathy (BSE) in Mabton, Washington, late in the previous month; as a result, the Department of Agriculture forecast a 90% fall in beef exports in 2004. In January 2003 the Administration presented plans to reduce taxes worth some $726,000m. over 10 years; however, in March Congress voted to reduce the cuts to $350,000m., owing partly to concerns about the cost of the US-led military conflict in Iraq and the eventual reconstruction of that country. Amended legislation was approved in May. In early November Congress approved a presidential request for an additional $87,000m. in funding for reconstruction efforts in Iraq and Afghanistan. The federal budget for 2004 included relatively small increases in all areas except defence and homeland security, and forecast a budget deficit for the third successive year.

United States Virgin Islands

The United States Virgin Islands mainly comprise the islands of St Croix, St Thomas and St John, situated at the eastern end of the Greater Antilles, east of Puerto Rico in the Caribbean Sea. In 1917 the USA purchased the three islands from Denmark. They now form an unincorporated territory of the USA. A measure of self-government was granted in 1954. Since 1970 executive authority has been vested in the elected Governor and Lieutenant-Governor. Since 1954 five attempts to give the Territory greater autonomy have been rejected in referendums. Charlotte Amalie is the capital. English is the official language.

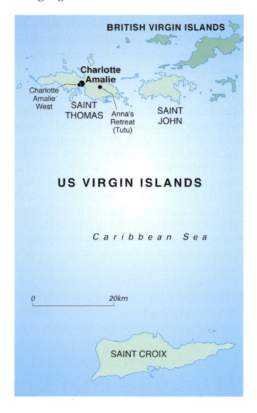

Area and population
Area: 347 sq km
Population (mid-2002): 110,310
Population density (mid-2002): 317.8 per sq km
Life expectancy (years at birth, 2001): 78.3 (males 74.4; females 82.4)

Finance
Currency: US dollar

Economy

According to estimates by the Territorial Government, the islands' gross national income (GNI) in 1989 was US $1,344m., equivalent to about $13,100 per head. Average personal income in that year was $11,052 per head, or about 62.6% of the US mainland average. GNI increased, in real terms, at an average rate of 2.5% per year during 1980–89. In 1990–2000 the population increased by an annual average of 0.6%.

AGRICULTURE

Most of the land is unsuitable for large-scale cultivation, but tax incentives have encouraged the growing of vegetables, fruit and cereals, which are produced for local consumption. According to the 2000 census figures, 0.7% of the economically active population were engaged in agriculture, forestry, fishing and mining. The islands are heavily dependent on links with the US mainland. There are no known natural resources, and, because of limited land space and other factors, the islands are unable to produce sufficient food to satisfy local consumption. Most goods are imported, mainly from the mainland USA.

INDUSTRY

Industry (comprising manufacturing and construction, but excluding mining) engaged 16.4% of the labour force, according to 2000 census figures. Only an estimated 0.1% of the labour force were in the mining sector, while 5.9% were in manufacturing. The main branch of manufacturing is petroleum-refining.

Manufacturing

St Croix has one of the world's largest petroleum refineries, with a capacity of 550,000 barrels per day (b/d). However, it operates at reduced levels of throughput. An alumina processing plant, closed down in 1994, was acquired in 1995 by Alcoa, which intended to rehabilitate the plant, which has an annual throughput capacity of 600,000 metric tons. The plant was reopened in the late 1990s, but in November 2000 it was announced that it would close again in January 2001, with the loss of 350 jobs. Efforts have been made to introduce labour-intensive and non-polluting manufacturing industries. Rum is an important product; the industry, however, was expected to encounter increased competition from Mexico as a result of the North American Free Trade Agreement (NAFTA), which entered into operation in January 1994.

SERVICES

Services employed 82.9% of the labour force in 2000, according to census figures. Tourism, which is estimated to account for more than 60% of gross domestic product (GDP), is the mainstay of the islands' income and employment, and provides the major source of direct and indirect revenue for other service sectors (including trade and transport). The emphasis is on the visiting cruise-ship business, and the advantages of duty-free products for tourist visitors. The total number of visitors declined by 9.7% in 1995, when the islands experienced severe storm damage, but increased steadily during 1996–98. In 2000 tourist arrivals (those staying in hotels) totalled 496,349.

EXTERNAL TRADE

In 1995 the Territory recorded a trade deficit of $174m. In that year the USA provided 34.5% of imports and took 92.7% of exports. Other major sources of imports included the United Arab Emirates, the Republic of the Congo and Nigeria. Of total exports to the USA in 1993, 90.6% was refined petroleum products. Crude petroleum accounted for 68.6% of the islands' total imports in that year.

GOVERNMENT FINANCE

Throughout the 1990s the budget deficit of the Territorial Government increased. By December 1999 the deficit was estimated to have risen to $305m., and in that year the Territorial Government introduced a Five-Year Strategic and Financial Operating Plan to reduce government expenditure and enhance the effectiveness of procedures for revenue collection. However, the islands were expected in the foreseeable future to continue to receive grants and other remittances from the US Government. The Government forecast that the budget would record a surplus of $19m. in the year ending 30 September 2001. The rate of unemployment averaged 6.1% of the labour force in 1997.

INTERNATIONAL ECONOMIC RELATIONS

The Territory is an associate member of the UN Economic Commission for Latin America and the Caribbean (ECLAC).

SURVEY AND PROSPECTS

The population increased dramatically from the 1960s. This inflow included people from neighbouring Caribbean countries, together with wealthy white settlers from the US mainland, attracted by the climate and the low taxes. At the 2000 census, 31% of the population originated from other Caribbean islands, and 14.5% from the mainland USA.

Owing to the islands' heavy reliance on imported goods, local prices and inflation are higher than on the mainland, and the islands' economy, in contrast to that of the USA, remained in recession for most of the 1990s. 'Hurricane Hugo', which struck the islands in September 1989, was estimated to have caused $1,000m. in property damage, although subsequent work on rebuilding temporarily revitalized employment in the construction sector, where the demand for labour rose to between two and three times normal levels. 'Hurricane Marilyn' caused considerable damage in September 1995, destroying an estimated 80% of houses on St Thomas. Serious storm damage was again experienced in July 1996, from 'Hurricane Bertha', and in September 1998 from 'Hurricane Georges'. In August 2000 'Hurricane Debby' caused less serious damage. It was hoped that the successful implementation of the Government's five-year plan in 1999–2004 would reverse the economy's decline.

Uruguay

The Eastern Republic of Uruguay lies on the south-east coast of South America. Since independence from Spain in 1825, democratic government has alternated between two parties: the Colorados ('reds', or Liberals), and the Blancos ('whites', or Conservatives, now known as the Partido Nacional). Military intervention in civilian affairs led, in 1973, to the closure of Congress. In 1985 the military relinquished power. In 1999 the EP-FA, a predominantly left-wing coalition, became the largest bloc in the legislature. However, Uruguay's current President, Jorge Luis Batlle Ibáñez, is a Colorado. Montevideo is the capital. The language is Spanish.

Area and population
Area: 176,215 sq km
Population (mid-2002): 3,380,990
Population density (mid-2002): 19.2 per sq km
Life expectancy (years at birth, 2002): 75.2 (males 71.0; females 79.3)

Finance
GDP in current prices: 2002): US $12,325m. ($3,645 per head)
Real GDP growth (2002): −10.8%
Inflation (annual average, 2002): 14.0%
Currency: peso uruguayo

Economy

In 2002, according to estimates by the World Bank, Uruguay's gross national income (GNI), measured at average 2000–02 prices, was US $14,769m., equivalent to $4,370 per head (or $12,010 per head on an international purchasing-power parity basis). During 1990–2002, it was estimated, the population increased by an annual average of 0.7%, while gross domestic product (GDP) per head increased, in real terms, by an annual average of 0.5% per year. Overall GDP increased, in real terms, at an average annual rate of 1.3% in 1990–2002; GDP decreased by 3.4% in 2001 and by a further 10.8% in 2002.

AGRICULTURE
Agriculture (including forestry and fishing) contributed 5.8% of GDP in 2001. Some 4.0% of the labour force were employed in the sector in 2000. The principal crops are rice, sugar cane, wheat, barley, potatoes, sorghum and maize. Livestock-rearing, particularly sheep and cattle, is traditionally Uruguay's major economic activity. Meat exports provided 13.5% of export revenues in 2001, while exports of skins and hides provided a further 11.7% in the same year. According to the World Bank, agricultural GDP increased by an annual average of 1.5% per year in 1990–2001. Agricultural GDP declined by 3.3% in 2000, and by a further 5.1% in 2001. Exports of beef to the USA were suspended from April to November 2001, owing to an outbreak of foot-and-mouth disease.

INDUSTRY
Industry (including mining, manufacturing, construction and power) contributed 25.0% of GDP in 2001, and employed 24.5% of the working population in 2000. According to the World Bank, industrial GDP increased by an annual average of 0.2% in 1990–2001. Industrial GDP decreased by an estimated 2.3% in 2000, and by 5.6% in 2001.

Mining
Although there is believed to be considerable potential for the mining sector, mining and quarrying contributed an estimated 0.3% of GDP in 2001, and employed 0.2% of the working population in 2000. Apart from the small-scale extraction of building materials, industrial minerals and semi-precious stones, there has been little mining activity, although gold deposits are currently being developed. Uruguay has no known petroleum resources. According to figures from the World Bank, the GDP of the mining sector increased by an annual average of 9.1% in 1990–2001. Mining GDP decreased by an estimated 8.8% in 2000 and by an estimated 11.2% in 2001.

Manufacturing
Manufacturing contributed 15.4% of GDP in 2001 and employed 14.8% of the working population in 2000. The principal branches of manufacturing were food products,

beverages and tobacco (accounting for an estimated 45.4% of the total in 2000), chemicals (22.8%), metal products, machinery and equipment, and textiles, clothing and leather products. According to figures from the World Bank, manufacturing GDP decreased by an annual average of 1.1% in 1990–2001. Manufacturing GDP decreased by an estimated 2.1% in 2000, and by a further estimated 6.2% in 2001.

Energy

Energy is derived principally from hydroelectric power (92.9% of total electricity production in 2000). There were plans to increase the use of natural gas as an energy resource; the first natural gas pipeline between Uruguay and Argentina began operating in late 1998. Imports of mineral products (including fuels) comprised 12.4% of the value of total imports in 2001.

SERVICES

The services sector contributed 69.2% of GDP in 2001, and engaged 71.4% of the working population in 2000. Tourism is a significant source of foreign exchange, earning US $560m. in 2001. However, revenues declined sharply in 2002, to $318m., mainly owing to economic problems in neighbouring Argentina (visitors from that country accounted for 69.2% of total arrivals in 2001). According to the World Bank, the GDP of the services sector increased by an annual average of 3.7% in 1990–2001. The GDP of the services sector decreased by 0.8% in 2000, and by a further 1.8% in 2001.

EXTERNAL TRADE

In 2002 Uruguay recorded a visible trade surplus of US $60.2m., and there was a surplus of $261.7m. on the current account of the balance of payments. In 2001 the principal source of imports was Argentina (23.1%); other major suppliers were Brazil (20.4%) and the USA. Brazil was the principal market for exports (21.4%) in that year; other major recipients were Argentina and the USA. The main exports in 2001 were live animals and animal products, foodstuffs, textiles, hides and skins, machinery and chemicals. The principal imports in that year were basic manufactures, mineral fuels, machinery and appliances, chemical products and foodstuffs.

GOVERNMENT FINANCE

In 2002 there was a budgetary deficit of 12,250m. pesos uruguayos, equivalent to 4.7% of GDP. At the end of 2001 Uruguay's total external debt was US $6,634m., of which $6,110m. was long-term public debt. In that year the cost of debt-servicing was equivalent to 36.3% of the value of exports of goods and services. The average annual rate of inflation was 30.4% in 1990–2002. Consumer prices increased by 4.4% in 2001 and by 14.0% in 2002. An estimated 14.4% of the urban labour force were unemployed in February 2002.

INTERNATIONAL ECONOMIC RELATIONS

Uruguay is a member of the Inter-American Development Bank (IDB), the Asociación Latinoamericana de Integración (ALADI), the Sistema Económico Latinoamericano (SELA) and the Mercado Común del Sur (Mercosur).

SURVEY AND PROSPECTS

Uruguay's economy was in recession from 1999, largely owing to external factors, notably the negative impact of the recession in Argentina and Brazil, the devaluation of the Brazilian currency at the beginning of 1999 and low world prices for its principal export products. In May 2000 the IMF approved a 22-month stand-by credit worth US $197m. to support the new Batlle administration's economic programme; nevertheless, the economic decline continued in 2000 (a decrease in GDP of 1.4%), owing to high oil prices and low agricultural commodity prices.

Industrial unrest greeted the Government's proposals to deregulate public services in 2000 and 2001. In 2001 GDP declined for the third consecutive year, by 3.4%. In January 2002, in response to the financial crisis in Argentina, which adversely affected Uruguay's exports (already damaged by the outbreak of foot-and-mouth disease in 2001), as well as its tourist industry, the Government announced a fiscal adjustment plan. In an attempt to contain the fiscal deficit to 2.5% of GDP, it was proposed that taxes would be increased and some state-owned real estate be sold off (although progress on privatization subsequently stalled). In the following month the Congreso approved measures that extended the scope of value-added tax, and introduced an additional levy on high salaries for government officials, as well as a tax on international telephone calls and a 4% increase in fuel prices. In March the IMF approved a new stand-by credit, worth about $743m., intended to support the country's economic programme in 2002–04. The programme was extended by a further year in March 2003.

In the wake of the crisis in the banking sector in mid-2002, new legislation was introduced in early 2003 enhancing the supervisory powers of the Central Bank and reforming state-controlled lending. Moreover, the new laws authorized the merger of the three state-owned banks placed under government administration in late 2002, thus reducing the risk posed by further insolvencies in the banking system. However, in March a lack of investors obliged the Government to use IMF funds to capitalize the new bank, to be known as Nuevo Banco Comercial.

Following a downgrading of Uruguay's debt by international credit agencies in early 2003, measures to restructure the country's heavy debt burden were announced. In May the Government successfully restructured its short-term external debt, issuing new bonds, which carried extended terms of repayment and a cash incentive of 15% on face value. (Notably, the bonds also carried a 'collective action clause', which allowed further changes to repayment terms, pending the agreement of investors in 75% of the new debt.) In the same month the World Bank disbursed further loans, totalling $252m., intended to finance infrastructure and social-welfare projects. The funds were to complement assistance from the IDB, which had pledged some $160m., in addition to finance from other international financial institutions. However, although multilateral creditors continued to support Uruguay's financial system, the outlook for the overall economy remained uncertain in 2004, especially in view of the Government's defeat in the December 2003 referendum on private-sector participation in the public utilities. Moreover, despite a substantial improvement in foreign trade and an economic revival in neighbouring Argentina, uncertainty over the economic policies of a possible Encuentro Progresista—Frente Amplio administration following the October elections, as well as the heavy debt repayments scheduled for 2004 and 2005, continued to threaten Uruguay's fragile economic recovery. Economic growth was estimated at some 2.0% in 2003.

Uzbekistan

The Republic of Uzbekistan is located in Central Asia. In 1925 the Uzbek Soviet Socialist Republic became a constituent republic of the USSR. In 1991 the Supreme Soviet declared the republic independent, renaming it the Republic of Uzbekistan. The ruling Communist Party of Uzbekistan was restructured as the People's Democratic Party of Uzbekistan, with Islam Karimov retaining the leadership. Karimov was subsequently elected as President. In 2001 Uzbekistan agreed to make its airbases available to the USA for use during the US-led aerial bombardment of Taliban and terrorist bases in Afghanistan. Tashkent is the capital. The official language is Uzbek.

Area and population
Area: 447,400 sq km
Population (mid-2002): 25,391,440
Population density (mid-2002): 56.8 per sq km
Life expectancy (years at birth, 2002): 68.2 (males 65.6; females 70.8)

Finance
GDP in current prices: 2002): US $9,713m. ($383 per head)
Real GDP growth (2002): 4.2%
Inflation (annual average, 2000): 25.0%
Currency: sum

Economy

In 2002, according to the World Bank, Uzbekistan's gross national income (GNI), measured at average 2000–02 prices, was US $11,522m., equivalent to $450 per head (or $1,590 per head on an international purchasing-power parity basis). During 1990–2002, it was estimated, the population increased by an annual average of 1.8%, while gross domestic product (GDP) per head decreased, in real terms, at an average annual rate of 1.3%. Overall GDP increased, in real terms, by an average of 0.5% per year in 1990–2002; growth was 4.2% in both 2001 and 2002.

AGRICULTURE

In 2002 agriculture (including forestry) contributed 34.6% of GDP, and the agricultural sector employed 32.5% of the working population in that year. Some 60% of the country's land is covered by desert and steppe, while the remainder comprises fertile valleys watered by two major river systems. The massive irrigation of arid areas has greatly increased production of the major crop, cotton, but has caused devastating environmental problems (most urgently the desiccation of the Aral Sea). Uzbekistan is among the five largest producers of cotton in the world, and the crop accounts for almost 30% of the value of total exports. Other major crops include grain, rice, vegetables and fruit. Since independence the Government has striven to reduce the area under cultivation of cotton in order to produce more grain. Private farming was legalized in 1992, and by 1996 more than 98% of agricultural production originated in the non-state sector. During 1990–2002 agricultural GDP increased, in real terms, by an annual average of 1.4%. Agricultural GDP increased by 4.5% in 2001 and by 4.0% in 2002.

INDUSTRY

Industry (including mining, manufacturing, power and construction) contributed 21.6% of GDP in 2002, when the sector provided 12.7% of employment. During 1990–2002 industrial GDP declined by an average of 2.0% annually, in real terms. However, the real GDP of the sector increased by 2.6% in 2001 and by 2.4% in 2002.

Mining

Uzbekistan is well endowed with mineral deposits, in particular gold, natural gas, petroleum and coal. It was estimated that Uzbekistan had sufficient reserves of crude petroleum to maintain output at mid-1990s levels for 30 years, and enough natural gas for 50 years. There are large reserves of silver, copper, lead, zinc and tungsten, and Uzbekistan is one of the world's largest producers of uranium and gold. In 2000 2,054 metric tons of uranium was produced, according to preliminary figures; all uranium mined is exported. The Murantau mine, in the Kyzylkum desert, is reportedly the world's largest single open-cast gold mine, producing some 70% of Uzbekistan's average annual output of 80 tons in the mid-1990s. Gold-mines at Amantaytau and Daugistau, reportedly containing reserves of 280 tons, were under development in the mid-1990s. Annual output of gold was consequently expected to reach 126 tons by 2005. Gold production in 2001 was some 85 tons, compared with 70 tons in 1995.

Manufacturing

The manufacturing sector contributed 8.3% of GDP in 2002. In 2001 manufacturing activity focused largely on the machine-building and metal-working sub-sectors. This was owing, in part, to the development of an automobile-manufacturing plant. Production of consumer goods (such as textiles and rugs) declined in the late 1990s.

However, significant investment has been directed to the expansion of the raw-materials processing industry.

Energy

Uzbekistan is self-sufficient in natural gas, crude petroleum and coal, and became a net exporter of crude petroleum in 1995. Energy products accounted for 4.2% of the value of imports in 2000. The opening of two petroleum refineries, which had a total refining capacity of 173,000 barrels per day (b/d), significantly increased Uzbekistan's hydrocarbons capacity. In 2000 the country's total petroleum production reached an estimated 175,000 b/d. In the same year natural gas production was an estimated 55,600m. cu m, thereby making Uzbekistan the 10th largest producer world-wide. In 2000 72.2% of electricity was generated by natural gas, 12.5% was produced by hydroelectric power and 11.3% by petroleum.

SERVICES

The services sector contributed 43.8% of GDP in 2002, when it employed 54.8% of the working population. During 1990–2002 the GDP of the services sector increased, in real terms, by an average of 0.7% annually. Services GDP increased by 4.8% in 2001, but declined by 2.0% in 2002.

EXTERNAL TRADE

In 2001 Uzbekistan recorded a visible trade surplus of US $128m., and in 2002, according to estimates by the Asian Development Bank (ADB), there was a surplus of $47m. on the current account of the balance of payments. In 2002 the principal source of imports was Russia (accounting for 20.5% of the total value of imports). Other major suppliers were the Republic of Korea, Germany, Kazakhstan, the USA and Ukraine. Russia was also the main market for exports in that year (17.3% of the total value of exports); other important purchasers were Ukraine, Italy, Tajikistan and the Republic of Korea. The principal exports in 2000 were cotton fibre (27.5% of the total value of exports), energy products, metals and food products. The main imports in that year were machinery and equipment (38.7% of the total value of imports), chemicals and plastics, food products and metals. By 2000 trade with republics of the former USSR represented only some 35% of Uzbekistan's total trade, compared with about 83% in 1990.

GOVERNMENT FINANCE

Uzbekistan's overall budget deficit (including extrabudgetary operations) in 2000 was 35,700m. sum (equivalent to 1.1% of GDP). At the end of 2001 Uzbekistan's total external debt was US $4,627m., of which $3,759m. was long-term public debt. In that year the cost of debt-servicing was equivalent to 25.9% of the value of exports of goods and services. The average annual rate of inflation declined from 1,568% in 1994 to 28% in 2000. The rate of inflation declined to 26.6% in 2001, and rose slightly, to 27.6%, in 2002. In 2002 some 35,000 people (0.4% of the economically active population) were officially registered as unemployed, although the actual level was believed to be considerably higher.

INTERNATIONAL ECONOMIC RELATIONS

In 1992 Uzbekistan became a member of the IMF and the World Bank, also joining, as a 'Country of Operations', the European Bank for Reconstruction and Development

(EBRD). In the same year Uzbekistan was admitted to the Economic Co-operation Organization (ECO). Uzbekistan became a member of the ADB in 1995, and in September 2003 it attained membership of the Islamic Development Bank. Uzbekistan is pursuing membership of the World Trade Organization (WTO).

SURVEY AND PROSPECTS

Following the collapse of the USSR in December 1991, GDP declined sharply and inflation increased rapidly. Measures to effect a gradual transition to a market economy, announced in 1994, included price liberalization and the privatization of selected state enterprises. The economy returned to growth in 1996, when the pace of structural reform was accelerated, supported by loans from international financial organizations. However, a poor cotton harvest resulted in a weakening of monetary policy, and a significant depreciation of the national currency, the sum, together with the introduction of restrictions on access to foreign-currency reserves, led to the withdrawal of many international investments. The economy achieved sustained growth in the late 1990s; however, it was adversely affected by the Russian financial crisis of mid-1998, as well as low market prices for both cotton and gold, which led to a decline in export earnings. None the less, the industrial sector benefited from a successful Uzbek-South Korean automobile venture.

In early 2002 Uzbekistan agreed to implement a structural-reform programme, with the objective of achieving currency convertibility and unifying the country's various official exchange rates. In 2002 new taxes on imports were introduced, apparently in an attempt to protect the economy from the loss of hard currency, prior to the planned introduction of measures to make the sum freely convertible; however, there were indications that the new tax had served to encourage illegal transactions. Privatization revenues increased significantly in 2002 and the budgetary deficit was reduced, but foreign investment declined significantly and, despite Uzbekistan's self-sufficiency in mineral fuels and the expansion of its energy-export capacity, there remained international concern that its economic policies served to further its economic isolation. (The IMF's representative to Uzbekistan had been permanently withdrawn in April 2001.)

In May 2003 the EBRD held its annual meeting in Tashkent. The Bank criticized Uzbekistan's record on human rights, and warned that its programme of lending to Uzbekistan would be restrained if significant progress in political and economic reform was not recorded within 12 months. The sum was finally made fully convertible in October 2003, and GDP growth, of some 3.5%, was maintained. However, in November the IMF warned that the imposition of trade restrictions had weakened growth and would limit the impact of economic liberalization, and it urged the authorities to reopen borders with neighbouring states and implement other measures to stimulate trade. In April 2004 the EBRD announced it was to curtail its activities in Uzbekistan owing to the Government's failure to implement reform.

Vanuatu

The Republic of Vanuatu comprises an irregular archipelago in the south-west Pacific Ocean. Port Vila is the capital. During the 19th century the New Hebrides (now Vanuatu) were settled by the British and the French, and in 1906 the territory became the Anglo-French Condominium of the New Hebrides. Immediately prior to independence, a political movement, Na-Griamel, declared the island of Espiritu Santo independent of the rest of the New Hebrides. In 1980, after the New Hebrides had become independent, within the Commonwealth, under the name of Vanuatu, the Na-Griamel rebels were suppressed. The national language is Bislama, ni-Vanuatu pidgin.

Area and population
Area: 12,190 sq km
Population (mid-2002): 205,570
Population density (mid-2002): 16.9 per sq km
Life expectancy (years at birth, 2002): 67.7 (males 66.4; females 69.1)

Finance

GDP in current prices: 2002): US $234m. ($1,140 per head)
Real GDP growth (2002): –0.3%
Inflation (annual average, 2002): 1.9%
Currency: vatu

Economy

In 2002, according to estimates by the World Bank, Vanuatu's gross national income (GNI), measured at average 2000–02 prices, was US $221m., equivalent to $1,080 per head (or $2,770 per head on an international purchasing-power parity basis). During 1990–2002, it was estimated, the population increased at an average annual rate of 2.8%, while gross domestic product (GDP) per head decreased, in real terms, by an average of 0.8% per year. Overall GDP increased, in real terms, at an average annual rate of 2.0% in 1990–2002. According to the Asian Development Bank (ADB), GDP contracted by 2.8% in 2002 but was forecast to increase by 1.3% in 2003.

AGRICULTURE

The agricultural sector (including forestry and fishing) contributed 17.4% of GDP in 2002, compared with some 40% in the early 1980s. According to figures from the ADB, the GDP of the agricultural sector was estimated to have increased by an average annual rate of 1.4% in 1990–2002. Compared with the previous year, the sector's GDP increased by 0.2% in 2001 and by 1.8% in 2002. The performance of the agricultural sector in 2001 was severely affected by the devastation caused by two cyclones that struck Vanuatu early in the year. About 36% of the employed labour force were engaged in agricultural activities in 2001, according to FAO. Coconuts, cocoa and coffee are grown largely for export (copra being the most important of these), while yams, taro, cassava, breadfruit and vegetables are cultivated for subsistence purposes. Cattle, pigs, goats and poultry are the country's principal livestock, and beef is an important export commodity (contributing 6.9% of export earnings in 2002). Vanuatu has encouraged the development of a forestry industry. However, the Government caused considerable controversy in mid-1993, when it granted a Malaysian consortium a licence to log 70,000 cu m of timber annually; previous licences for all operators had permitted total logging of only 5,000 cu m per year. A complete ban on the export of round logs was subsequently introduced. The Government derives substantial revenue from the sale of fishing rights to foreign fleets: sales of licences to Taiwanese and South Korean vessels earned more than $A136,000 in 1997.

INDUSTRY

The industrial sector (including manufacturing, utilities and construction) contributed about 9.2% of GDP in 2002, although only 3.5% of the employed labour force were engaged in the sector in 1989. Compared with the previous year, according to the ADB, industrial GDP decreased by 5.1% in 2001 and by 6.9% in 2002. Manufacturing, which contributed about 3.9% of GDP in 2002, is mainly concerned with the processing of agricultural products. In 1990–2002 the GDP of the manufacturing sector decreased by an average annual rate of 2.3%. The country's first kava extraction plant (for the manufacture of alcoholic drink) was opened in 1998. However, it was feared that a ban imposed on kava imports in 2001 by several countries in Europe owing to health concerns would have a detrimental effect upon the kava industry. Construction activity alone contributed 3.0% of GDP in 2002. During the 1990s several potential mining projects were identified. An Australian company announced plans to mine 60,000 metric tons of manganese per year on the island of Efate, while possible projects involving the extraction of gold, copper and petroleum around the islands of Malekula and Espiritu Santo were discussed.

Energy

Electricity generation is largely thermal. However, plans to construct hydroelectric power stations on Espiritu Santo and Malekula were announced in the mid-1990s. Imports of mineral fuels comprised 11.6% of the value of total imports in 2002.

SERVICES

The economy depends heavily on the services sector, which accounted for 73.4% of GDP in 2002. According to the ADB, the GDP of the services sector rose by 1.8% in 2000 before declining by 0.5% in 2001. Tourism, 'offshore' banking facilities and a shipping registry, providing a 'flag of convenience' to foreign-owned vessels, make a significant contribution to the country's income. In 2003 50,400 foreign tourists visited Vanuatu, compared with 49,463 in the previous year. Revenue from tourism was US $58m. in 2000.

EXTERNAL TRADE

In 2002 Vanuatu recorded a visible trade deficit of US $59m., and a deficit of $13m. on the current account of the balance of payments. In 2002 the principal sources of imports were Australia (23.6%) and Japan (20.5%), while the principal markets for exports were Belgium (30.8%), Chile (21.7%) and Germany (21.2%). The principal imports in 2002 were machinery and transport equipment (23.8% of total imports), food and live animals (17.8%) and basic manufactures (13.9%). Timber (which provided 7.1% of total export earnings), beef (6.9%) and copra (which provided 6.2%) were the main export commodities in 2002.

GOVERNMENT FINANCE

The budget deficit for for 2002 was estimated at 1,100m. vatu, equivalent to some 1.5% of GDP. In the following year there was a projected surplus equivalent to 0.4% of GDP.

In 2000 Vanuatu received US $45.8m. of official development assistance, of which US $28.3m. was bilateral aid and US $17.5m. was multilateral assistance. Australia, New Zealand, France, the United Kingdom and Japan are significant suppliers of development assistance. In 2003/04 Australia provided aid of some $A22.7m., and development assistance from New Zealand totalled $NZ5.86m. In February 2002 the European Union (EU) allocated Vanuatu 2,000m. vatu of aid to be disbursed over the next five years from the ninth European Development Fund; the aid was to be used principally for the development of education and human resources training. Vanuatu's total external debt was US $65.8m. at the end of 2001, of which $64.5m. was long-term public debt. In that year the cost of debt-servicing was equivalent to 1.1% of the value of exports of goods and services. The annual rate of inflation averaged 2.9% in

1991–2001; consumer prices increased by 2.0% in 2002 and by an estimated 2.5% in 2003.

INTERNATIONAL ECONOMIC RELATIONS

Vanuatu is a member of the Pacific Community, the Pacific Islands Forum, the Asian Development Bank (ADB) and the UN Economic and Social Commission for Asia and the Pacific (ESCAP). The country is also a signatory of the South Pacific Regional Trade and Economic Agreement (SPARTECA) and of the Lomé Conventions and the successor Cotonou Agreement with the EU.

SURVEY AND PROSPECTS

Vanuatu's economic development has been impeded by its dependence on the agricultural sector, particularly the production and export of copra, which is vulnerable to adverse weather conditions and fluctuations in international commodity prices. Successive administrations, therefore, have attempted to encourage the diversification of the country's economy, notably through the development of the tourism sector, but such initiatives remain inhibited by a shortage of skilled indigenous labour, a weak infrastructure and frequent foreign exploitation. The new Government's implementation in 1998 of a Comprehensive Reform Programme (CRP), approved by the ADB, was expected to enhance Vanuatu's economic prospects. In mid-1999 the ADB reported that the Government had demonstrated a strong level of commitment to the CRP: the number of ministries had been reduced from 34 to nine, and the number of civil service personnel had been decreased by 7%; a value-added tax had been introduced; and the National Bank and the Development Bank had been restructured.

Development plans, known as the Year 2000 policy statement, placed emphasis on the agricultural and tourism sectors, with the Government planning to establish an Agricultural Development Bank to promote ni-Vanuatu development in the rural sector and envisaging the construction of a new airport capable of handling Boeing 747s. The country's status as an 'offshore' financial centre aroused controversy in June 2000 when the Paris-based Organisation for Economic Co-operation and Development (OECD) listed Vanuatu as one of a number of countries and territories operating as unfair tax havens. It was claimed that the country was being used to 'launder' the proceeds of illegal activities of the Russian mafia and drug cartels. Sanctions were threatened if Vanuatu failed to take action to prevent both 'money-laundering' and international tax evasion. In 2001 the Minister of Finance rejected demands to provide information on the country's revenue from its international tax haven facility, and in 2002 the Government stated that it would not co-operate with an international initiative intended to eliminate tax evasion. Vanuatu thus remained on the OECD's list of unco-operative tax havens until May 2003, when the country's commitment to implement transparent tax and regulatory systems by 2005 led to its removal from the list.

In November 2001, meanwhile, after five years of negotiations, the World Trade Organization (WTO) offered Vanuatu membership. However, the Government rejected the offer on the grounds that it wished to delay its entry while it negotiated a more favourable tariff agreement. Prime Minister Natapei also voiced his concern that the opening of free trade between members of the Melanesian 'Spearhead Group' had proved harmful to businesses in Vanuatu. The contraction of the economy in 2001 and 2002 was mainly attributable to the detrimental effect of adverse weather conditions upon the performance of the agricultural sector (and particularly upon exports of copra, which decreased by nearly 50%) and to the effects of the European ban on kava imports. From 2003 it was hoped that the modest economic recovery would be sustained by the agricultural sector. An improvement in the tourism sector was also envisaged, following the completion of two new hotels and the continuation of an overseas advertising campaign. The ADB forecast GDP growth of 2.2% in 2004.

Venezuela

The Bolivarian Republic of Venezuela lies on the north coast of South America. Venezuela was a Spanish colony from 1499 until 1821 and, led by Simón Bolívar, achieved independence in 1830. The country was principally governed by dictators until 1945. In 1964 President Betancourt became the first Venezuelan President to complete his term of office. In 1992 two unsuccessful military coups were mounted against President Pérez, the first of which was led by Lt-Col Hugo Chávez Frías. In 1998 Chávez was elected President. He was re-elected, under a new Constitution, in 2000. Caracas is the capital. The language is Spanish.

Area and population
Area: 912,050 sq km
Population (mid-2002): 25,093,370
Population density (mid-2002): 27.5 per sq km
Life expectancy (years at birth, 2002): 69.6 (males 67.1; females 72.2)

Finance
GDP in current prices: 2002): US $94,340m. ($3,760 per head)
Real GDP growth (2002): −8.9%
Inflation (annual average, 2002): 22.4%
Currency: bolívar

Economy

In 2002, according to estimates by the World Bank, Venezuela's gross national income (GNI), measured at average 2000–02 prices, was US $102,577m., equivalent to $4,090 per head (or $5,080 per head on an international purchasing-power parity basis). During 1990–2002, it was estimated, the population increased by an annual average of 2.1%, while gross domestic product (GDP) per head decreased, in real terms, at an average of 0.1% per year. Overall GDP increased, in real terms, by an average annual rate of 1.1% in 1990–2002; GDP increased by 2.8% in 2001, but declined by 8.9% in 2002.

AGRICULTURE

Agriculture (including hunting, forestry and fishing) contributed an estimated 4.2% of GDP and engaged an estimated 9.8% of the employed labour force in 2002. The principal crops are sugar cane, bananas, maize, rice, plantains, oranges, sorghum and cassava. Cattle are the principal livestock, but the practice of smuggling cattle across Venezuela's border into Colombia has had a severe effect on the livestock sector. According to the World Bank, agricultural GDP increased by an estimated annual average of 1.4% during 1990–2001. The sector's GDP increased, in real terms, by 2.4% in 2000 and by an estimated 2.6% in 2001.

INDUSTRY

Industry (including mining, manufacturing, construction and power) contributed an estimated 38.5% of GDP and engaged an estimated 20.9% of the employed labour force in 2000. According to the World Bank, industrial GDP increased by an annual average of 2.7% during 1990–2001. Sectoral GDP increased, in real terms, by 2.8% in 2000 and by an estimated 1.9% in 2001.

Mining

Mining and quarrying contributed an estimated 19.8% of GDP, but engaged only 0.5% of the employed labour force in 2002. Petroleum production is the most important industry in Venezuela, providing some 82.0% of export revenue in 2001. In 2000 proven reserves totalled 76.9m. barrels. Aluminium and iron ore are also major sources of export revenue. Venezuela also has substantial deposits of natural gas, coal, diamonds, gold, zinc, copper, lead, silver, phosphates, manganese and titanium. The GDP of the mining sector increased by an average of 2.5% per year in 1995–2001; the sector increased by 4.7% in 2000 and by an estimated 1.1% in 2001.

Manufacturing

Manufacturing contributed an estimated 12.1% of GDP and engaged approximately 11.9% of the employed labour force in 2002. The most important sectors were refined petroleum products, food products, transport equipment, industrial chemicals and iron and steel. Manufacturing GDP decreased by an annual average of 0.1% during 1995–2001. The sector's GDP increased, in real terms, by 2.1% in 2000, but decreased by an estimated 0.2% in 2001.

Energy

Energy is derived principally from domestic supplies of petroleum and coal, and from hydroelectric power. Hydroelectric power provided 73.7% of electricity production in 2000, with natural gas supplying a further 16.5%. Imports of mineral fuels comprised 4.3% of the total value of merchandise imports in 2001.

SERVICES

The services sector contributed an estimated 57.3% of GDP and engaged some 69.1% of the employed labour force in 2002. GDP growth of the services sector was stagnant during 1994–2001. Sectoral GDP increased, in real terms, by 3.4% in 2000 and by an estimated 3.2% in 2001.

EXTERNAL TRADE

In 2002 Venezuela recorded a visible trade surplus of US $13,034m., and there was a surplus of $7,423m. on the current account of the balance of payments. In 2001 the principal source of imports (33.9%) was the USA; other major suppliers were Colombia, Brazil, Mexico and Japan. The USA was also the principal market for exports (56.4%) in 2001; other major purchasers were the Netherlands Antilles, the Domincan Republic, Colombia and Brazil. The principal exports in 2001 were petroleum and related products (82.0%), steel, aluminium and chemical products. The principal imports in 2001 were electrical and transport equipment (41.9%), basic manufactures, and chemicals.

GOVERNMENT FINANCE

There was projected budgetary deficit of 5,369,512m. bolívares in 2003 (equivalent to 4.8% of GDP). Venezuela's total external debt was US $34,660m. at the end of 2001, of which $24,916m. was long-term public debt. In that year the cost of servicing the debt was equivalent to 24.6% of the value of exports of goods and services. The average annual rate of inflation was 38.7% in 1990–2002. Consumer prices increased by an annual average of 22.4% in 2002 and by 31.1% in 2003. An estimated 15.8% of the labour force were unemployed in 2002.

INTERNATIONAL ECONOMIC RELATIONS

Venezuela is a member of the Andean Community of Nations (CAN), the Inter-American Development Bank (IDB), the Latin American Integration Association (Asociación Latinoamericana de Integración—ALADI), the Organization of the Petroleum Exporting Countries (OPEC), the Latin American Economic System (Sistema Económico Latinoamericano—SELA) and the Group of Three (G3). In April 2003 President Chávez appeared to discount the possibility of Venezuela joining the planned Free Trade Area of the Americas (FTAA) during his term of office.

SURVEY AND PROSPECTS

Venezuela's economy is largely dependent on the petroleum sector, which provides some 80% of government revenue, and is therefore particularly vulnerable to fluctuations in the world petroleum market. The Chávez administration, inaugurated in 1999, introduced new pension benefits and health programmes, to be financed by surplus petroleum profits, known as the oil stabilization fund. High petroleum prices in 2000 allowed for an estimated 40% increase in government spending. Pensions increased by 20% and there was a large increase in public-sector pay. However, the non-petroleum sector stagnated, partly because of an overvalued currency. Economic growth slowed in 2001, owing to lower petroleum prices and the consequent decrease in the value of exports and increase in the fiscal deficit. In an attempt to reduce the deficit, planned government spending was reduced by 7% in the 2002 budget and a 49-point series of economic measures was approved by decree in November 2001. However, the controversial measures contained in the package (most notably, a hydrocarbons law that increased royalty taxes on the petroleum sector from 16.6% to 30%) led to widespread industrial unrest and political instability, which severely affected petroleum production rates in early 2002. The situation was compounded in February after a controlled devaluation plan (initiated by the Government to make domestic products more competitive) was abandoned in favour of a floating exchange rate, in a bid to halt the flight of capital caused by the continuing political unrest. The bolívar immediately depreciated by as much as 19% against the US dollar; nevertheless, a subsequent increase in the price of petroleum helped to stabilize the currency.

Investor confidence in Venezuela continued to deteriorate following the attempted coup against President Chávez in April 2002. The protracted industrial and social unrest in early 2003 was estimated to have reduced GDP in the first quarter of the year by some 25%, and increased the budget deficit by some US $6,000m. A further rapid decline in the value of the bolívar in January 2003 prompted the Central Bank to suspend currency trading. After the collapse of the general strike in February 2003, it was announced that the bolívar would be pegged to the US dollar, although at a reduction of some 17% in relation to its value prior to the suspension of trading. In a further effort to support the weakening currency in the same month the Chávez administration announced price controls on basic foodstuffs. A further devaluation of 15.6% was carried out in February 2004.

In mid-2002 investors were further discouraged not only by revelations that the Government had spent its monthly obligations under the Government's debt-reduction mechanism (known as the Fondo de Inversión para la Estabilidad Macroeconómica) on the public-sector wages, but also by an outright ban on local trading in US-dollar-denominated Brady bonds. In early 2004 political interference in the economy appeared to be increasing; concerns were prompted by the granting of discretionary powers of state currency control agency to allocate US dollars, and by President Chavez's attempt to divert $1,000m. from the Central Bank reserves towards government credit programmes. However, the outlook for the country's external debt improved in 2004, as investors exploited bond issues in order to avoid the restrictions on access to foreign currency. Indeed, despite the apparently ambivalent attitude of President Chávez towards the international multilateral lending agencies, and the severe domestic problems provoked by the growing debt burden, it appeared that the Government at least intended to honour its commitments. Moreover, in part owing to Venezuela's low level of external debt compared with other Latin American nations, public expenditure remained within sustainable limits, and the unexpectedly rapid recovery in petroleum production levels following the collapse of the PDVSA strike in early 2003 further increased hopes that Venezuela would avoid a severe fiscal crisis. Annual economic growth declined sharply in 2002, by approximately 8.9%, and GDP was estimated to have contracted by a further 9.2% in 2003.

Viet Nam

The Socialist Republic of Viet Nam is situated in South-East Asia. In 1954 Viet Nam was divided into two military zones, with French forces south of latitude 17°N and forces of the Democratic Republic of Viet Nam (DRV) in the north. In 1976, following the defeat of the anti-communist southern regime by forces of the DRV and the Provisional Revolutionary Government established by the National Liberation Front in 1960, Viet Nam was reunified as the Socialist Republic of Viet Nam. The Communist Party has since maintained a virtual total monopoly of political activity. Hanoi is the capital. The language is Vietnamese.

Area and population
Area: 329,247 sq km
Population (mid-2002): 80,524,560
Population density (mid-2002): 244.6 per sq km
Life expectancy (years at birth, 2002): 69.6 (males 67.1; females 72.2)

Finance

GDP in current prices: 2002): US $35,110m. ($436 per head)
Real GDP growth (2002): 7.1%
Inflation (annual average, 2002): 3.8%
Currency: new dông

Economy

In 2002, according to estimates by the World Bank, Viet Nam's gross national income (GNI), measured at average 2000–02 prices, was US $34,930m., equivalent to $430 per head (or $2,240 per head on an international purchasing-power parity basis). During 1990–2002, it was estimated, the population increased at an average annual rate of 1.6%, while gross domestic product (GDP) per head increased, in real terms, by an average of 5.7% per year. Overall GDP increased, in real terms, at an average annual rate of 7.5% in 1990–2002. According to official estimates, GDP grew by 7.0% in 2002 and by 7.2% in 2003.

AGRICULTURE

Agriculture (including forestry and fishing) contributed an estimated 23.0% of GDP in 2002, engaging an estimated 66.1% of the employed labour force in that year. The staple crop is rice, which also provided 4.3% of total export earnings in 2002; Viet Nam being a major world exporter of rice. Other important cash crops include coffee, sugar cane, groundnuts, rubber, tea and cotton. By 2000 Viet Nam had emerged as one of the world's leading producers of coffee. In 1992, in an attempt to preserve Viet Nam's remaining forests, a ban was imposed on the export of logs and sawn timber, and in March 1997 a 10-year ban on all timber products except wooden artefacts was introduced. Following a successful planting programme undertaken between 1990 and 2000, by the latter year forest cover had risen to exceed 30% of Viet Nam's total land area. Livestock-rearing and fishing are also important. In 2002 marine products accounted for some 12.1% of export revenues. According to figures from the Asian Development Bank (ADB), agricultural GDP increased by an estimated annual average of 4.1% in 1990–2002. The sector's GDP expanded by 3.0% in 2001 and by an estimated 4.1% in 2002.

INDUSTRY

In 2002 industry (comprising manufacturing, mining and quarrying, construction and power) contributed an estimated 38.5% of GDP. The industrial sector engaged 12.9% of the labour force in that year. In 2000 the non-state economic sector accounted for an estimated 22.4% of industrial production. According to figures from the ADB, industrial GDP increased by an annual average of 11.1% per year in 1990–2002. The sector's GDP expanded by 10.4% in 2001 and by an estimated 9.4% in 2002.

Mining

In 2002 mining and quarrying contributed an estimated 8.6% of GDP. In 2000 the mining sector engaged an estimated 0.6% of the labour force. Viet Nam's principal mineral exports are petroleum and coal. Tin, zinc, iron, antimony, chromium, natural phosphates, bauxite and gold are also mined. Significant reserves of offshore natural gas were discovered in 1993. In 2001 exports of crude petroleum accounted for 21.1% of total merchandise exports. Mining GDP increased by 4.1% in 2001, but decreased by an estimated 0.2% in 2002.

Manufacturing

Manufacturing contributed an estimated 20.6% of GDP in 2002, and accounted for 10.2% of employment in 1996. The main manufacturing sectors in 2000, measured by gross value of output, included food-processing, cigarettes and tobacco, textiles, chemicals, and electrical goods. According to figures from the ADB, manufacturing GDP increased by an annual average of 10.9% in 1990–2002. Manufacturing GDP increased by 11.3% in 2001 and by an estimated 11.6% in 2002.

Energy

Energy is derived principally from hydroelectric installations, petroleum and coal. Although production of petroleum increased in the late 1980s and early 1990s, exports were mainly in the form of crude petroleum, and Viet Nam still relied on the import of refined products. Imports of petroleum products accounted for 10.2% of total imports in 2002. Plans for the construction of the country's first nuclear power plant, to be built with Russian assistance, were under way in 2004.

SERVICES

The services sector contributed an estimated 38.5% of GDP in 2002. Tourism is an important source of foreign exchange; in 2003 about 2.4m. foreign tourists visited Viet Nam, and in 1998 receipts from tourism totalled some US $86m. According to the ADB, the GDP of the services sector increased by an average of 7.0% per year in 1990–2002. The sector's GDP rose by 6.1% in 2001 and by an estimated 6.5% in 2002.

EXTERNAL TRADE

In 2002 Viet Nam recorded a visible trade deficit of US $1,054m. The deficit on the current account of the balance of payments in that year was an estimated $604m. In 2002 Singapore and Japan were Viet Nam's principal sources of imports, both of which supplied 12.7% of total imports; other major sources were the Republic of Korea (11.5%), and the People's Republic of China (11.4%). The principal market for exports in that year was the USA (15.5%); other important purchasers were Japan (14.9%), Australia (7.7%), and Germany (6.7%). The principal exports in 2001 were petroleum, agricultural and forestry products (particularly rice and coffee), clothing, marine products and footwear. In 2002 principal imports included machinery and equipment, petroleum products, leather and garment material, iron and steel, fertilizers and motorcycles.

GOVERNMENT FINANCE

In 2001 there was an estimated budgetary deficit of 14,130,000m. dông. In 2001 Viet Nam's total external debt was US $12,578m., of which $11,427m. was long-term public debt. In that year the cost of debt-servicing was equivalent to 6.7% of the value of exports of goods and services. The annual rate of inflation averaged 2.7% in 1996–2002, reaching 4.1% in 1999. Consumer prices increased by 4.0% in 2002 and by an estimated 4.0% in 2003. In 2000 about 6.4% of the labour force were officially stated to be unemployed.

INTERNATIONAL ECONOMIC RELATIONS

Viet Nam is a member of the Asian Development Bank (ADB), the Association of South East Asian Nations (ASEAN), the Asia-Pacific Economic Co-operation (APEC), the UN Economic and Social Commission for Asia and the Pacific (ESCAP) and the Mekong River Commission. Viet Nam also joined the ASEAN Free Trade Area (AFTA) in 1996 and was granted until 2003 to comply with the requisite tariff reductions (to between 0% and 5%). The area was formally established on 1 January 2002.

SURVEY AND PROSPECTS

From 1990 the process of *doi moi* (renovation) aimed to transform Viet Nam from a centralized economy to a market-orientated system. New investment laws allowed the establishment of wholly foreign-owned enterprises. Agricultural production was stimulated by the removal of price controls, by a new system of land tenure and, from early 1998, by the relaxation of the state monopoly on rice exports, with the result that by the mid-1990s Viet Nam, formerly dependent on rice imports, had become one of the world's principal rice exporters. Despite a decline in performance precipitated by the regional economic crisis that originated in Thailand in mid-1997, from late 1999 the Vietnamese economy showed signs of recovery. The establishment of the country's first stock exchange in July 2000 was an important development; by November 2002 a total of 19 companies were listed on the exchange.

In 2001 the pace of economic reforms accelerated. The Ninth Communist Party Congress approved a 10-year socio-economic development strategy which enhanced the role of the private sector, while simultaneously affirming the primacy of the State in motivating economic development. The Government also announced a Five-Year (2001–2005) Import-Export regime intended significantly to liberalize trade. In addition, a more flexible exchange-rate policy was adopted. In December 2001 the National Assembly approved several constitutional amendments intended mainly to encourage the development of small businesses and to promote foreign investment, indicating its formal recognition of the private sector as an important part of the national economy. In the same month a landmark bilateral agreement with the USA came into effect, resulting in a significant increase in Vietnamese exports to the USA. However, in 2002 a decline in exports, combined with rising demand for imports, contributed to a widening of the trade deficit, which increased further in 2003.

In December 2002 revisions to the Budget Law resulted in the delegation of a significant amount of power in budgetary management to provincial and city authorities. Following improvements in legislation governing foreign investment in the country, levels of investment began to increase. Furthermore, it was thought that increasing fears of terrorism in the more traditional investment destinations in the Asia-Pacific region, such as Indonesia and Thailand, would enhance Viet Nam's attractiveness as a relatively safe destination for foreign investment. In April 2003 the USA announced that it intended to reduce significantly Viet Nam's textile export quotas in that year, prompting fears that the country's expanding textile industry would be adversely affected (textiles constituted Viet Nam's primary source of export earnings in 2003). In 2003 the strong expansion in GDP was largely due to growth in the manufacturing and construction sectors. In early 2004 it was feared that an outbreak of avian influenza in the region, which affected Viet Nam particularly severely, would have an impact upon economic performance in that year. Viet Nam's continued economic development, as well as its planned accession to the World Trade Organization (WTO) in January 2005, remained dependent upon the implementation of further reforms, particularly in state enterprises and the banking and public administration sectors. Widespread corruption amongst government officials also remained a significant problem. The Government targeted GDP growth of 7.5%–8.0% in 2004.

Wallis and Futuna Islands

The Territory of Wallis and Futuna comprises two groups of islands located north-east of Fiji and west of Samoa: the Wallis Islands and, to the south-west, Futuna. The Wallis and Futuna Islands were settled first by Polynesians: Wallis from Tonga and Futuna from Samoa. French Protectorate status was formalized in 1887 for Wallis and in 1888 for the two kingdoms of Futuna. The islands became a French Overseas Territory in 1961. In 1999 festivities were held to commemorate the 40th anniversary of the accession of the King of Wallis Island, Lavelua Tomasi Kulimoetoke. The capital is Mata'Uta. French and Wallisian are spoken in the Territory.

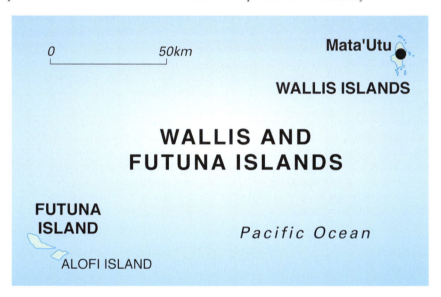

Area and population
Area: 161 sq km
Population (mid-2000): 14,600
Population density (mid-2000): 91.0 per sq km
Life expectancy (years at birth, 1998): 73.8 (males 73.2; females 74.4)

Finance
Inflation (2001): 4.9%
Currency: euro

Economy

In 1995 it was estimated that Wallis and Futuna's gross domestic product (GDP) was US $28.7m., equivalent to some $2,000 per head. Most monetary income in the islands is derived from government employment and remittances sent home by islanders employed in New Caledonia and also in Metropolitan France.

AGRICULTURE

Agricultural activity is of a subsistence nature. Yams, taro, bananas, cassava and other food crops are also cultivated. Tobacco is grown for local consumption. In 1998 almost all the cultivated vegetation on the island of Wallis, notably the banana plantations, was destroyed by a cyclone. In response to the cyclone damage, the French Government provided exceptional aid of 80m. francs CFP to alleviate the situation. An estimated 25,000 pigs a year are reared on the islands. Three units rear 800, 500 and 450 hens a year respectively, which are used principally for eggs, and meet an estimated 80% of the territory's commercial needs. Apiculture was revived in 1996, and in 2000 honey production was sufficient to meet the demands of the local market. Fishing activity in the Territory's exclusive economic zone increased during the 1990s; the total catch was estimated at 300 metric tons in 2001, compared with 70 tons in 1991. The Territorial Assembly accorded Japan deep-water fishing rights to catch 3,000 tons of fish a year in the islands' exclusive economic zone, a broad area of 200 miles (370 km) around Wallis and Futuna over which France exerts sovereignty.

INDUSTRY

There were 291 businesses in the Territory in 2000, of which 24 were in the industrial and artisanal sector, 68 in construction and 199 in the service and commercial sectors; 47 of those businesses were located on Futuna. A new commercial centre was to open in Wallis in 2002. In August 1989 a new earth station for satellite communications was inaugurated. The islands also benefited from an increase in building activity and public works in the early 1990s. The tourism sector, however, is very limited. In 2002 Wallis had four hotels and Futuna two.

Energy

Mineral fuels are the main source of electrical energy, although it is hoped that hydroelectric power can be developed, especially on Futuna. There is a 4,000-KW thermal power station on Wallis, and a 2,600-KW thermal power station was completed on Futuna in 2000. Electricity output in 2001 totalled 14.6m. kWh on Wallis and 3.0m. kWh on Futuna.

EXTERNAL TRADE

In 2000 the cost of the islands' imports reached 4,735.7m. francs CFP. Road vehicles, parts and accessories accounted for 10.0% of the total value of imports, followed by mineral fuels and products (9.8%), electrical machinery and sound and television apparatus (7.4%) and meat products (6.4%). Exports totalled only 22.4m. francs CFP. Traditional food products, mother of pearl (from the Trochus shell) and handicrafts are the only significant export commodities. Exports of copra from Wallis ceased in 1950, and from Futuna in the early 1970s. The principal sources of imports in 2000 were France, which supplied 28.7% of the total, and Australia (22.6%). Most of the islands' exports were purchased by Italy. In August 2001 the frequency of supplies to Wallis and Futuna was significantly improved when the Sofrana shipping company, based in Auckland, began operating a new route linking New Zealand, Tonga and the Samoas to Wallis and Futuna.

GOVERNMENT FINANCE

French aid to Wallis and Futuna totalled 7,048m. francs CFP in 1999, increasing to 10,329m. francs CFP in 2002. The islands' budgetary expenditure in 2001 totalled an estimated US $25.0m. Budgetary aid from France was to rise from €83,178m. in 2001 to €86,610m. in 2002. The annual rate of inflation in 1989–2002 averaged 1.5%.

INTERNATIONAL ECONOMIC RELATIONS

The Territory of Wallis and Futuna forms part of the Franc Zone. Although France is also a member of the organization, Wallis and Futuna has membership in its own right of the Pacific Community, which is based in New Caledonia and provides technical advice, training and assistance in economic, cultural and social development to the region.

SURVEY AND PROSPECTS

In mid-2003 the National Assembly approved the Overseas Territories Development Bill, which would provide support for economic and social development in Wallis and Futuna (together with French Polynesia and New Caledonia) by attracting foreign investment, and among other benefits allow for overseas French residents to travel to mainland France to take advantage of free education.

Yemen

The Republic of Yemen is situated mainly in the south of the Arabian peninsula. It was formed in 1990 by the amalgamation of the Yemen Arab Republic (YAR) and the People's Democratic Republic of Yemen (PDRY). The YAR (from 1967 also known as North Yemen) had been proclaimed after the Imam Muhammad was overthrown in 1962. The PDRY, comprising Aden and the former Protectorate of South Arabia, had been formed in 1967 by the Marxist National Liberation Front. In 1994 a civil war erupted after Ali Salim al-Baid declared an independent Democratic Republic of Yemen in the south. The capital is San'a. Arabic is the language.

Area and population
Area: 536,869 sq km
Population (mid-2002): 18,600,920
Population density (mid-2002): 34.6 per sq km
Life expectancy (years at birth, 2002): 60.4 (males 58.7; females 62.2)

Finance
GDP in current prices: 2002): US $10,395m. ($559 per head)
Real GDP growth (2002): 4.2%
Inflation (annual average, 2000): 11.9%
Currency: Yemeni riyal

Economy

In 2002, according to estimates by the World Bank, Yemen's gross national income (GNI), measured at average 2000–02 prices, was US $9,360m., equivalent to $490 per head (or $750 per head on an international purchasing-power parity basis). During 1990–2002, it was estimated, the population increased at an average annual rate of 3.8%, while gross domestic product (GDP) per head increased, in real terms, by an average of 1.2% per year. Overall GDP increased, in real terms, at an average annual rate of 5.0% in 1990–2002; GDP growth in 2002 was estimated at 4.2%.

AGRICULTURE

Agriculture (including forestry and fishing) contributed an estimated 15.0% of GDP in 2002, and the sector engaged some 48.5% of the working population in 1999. The principal cash crops are coffee, cotton and fruits. Subsistence crops include sorghum, potatoes, wheat and barley. Livestock-rearing (particularly in the east and north) and fishing are also important activities. Livestock, hides and skins and fish are all exported on a small scale. Estimates indicated growth averaging 5.3% annually in 1993–2002. Real agricultural GDP increased by 3.6% in 2002.

INDUSTRY

Industry (including mining, manufacturing, construction and power) contributed an estimated 46.8% of GDP in 2002, and an estimated 15.1% of the working population were employed in the sector in 1999. According to estimates, industrial GDP increased at an average annual rate of 8.5% in 1993–2002. Real growth in industrial GDP was estimated at 5.3% in 2002.

Mining

Mining and quarrying contributed some 34.3 of GDP in 2002, and employed an estimated 0.3% of the working population in 1999. Yemen's proven petroleum reserves totalled 4,000m. barrels at the end of 2002, sufficient to maintain production at that year's levels for 23 years. Petroleum production averaged 473,000 barrels per day (b/d) during 2002, considerably lower than the Government's planned output of 548,000 b/d. The value of exports of petroleum and petroleum products were estimated to have accounted for 94.3% of the value of total exports in 2001. There are also significant reserves of natural gas: proven reserves at the end of 2002 were 480,000m. cu m. Salt and gypsum are also exploited on a large scale. In addition, there are deposits of copper, lead, zinc, gold, sulphur and molybdenum. GDP of the mining sector increased at an estimated average annual rate of 13.3% in 1993–2002; real mining GDP rose by 7.0% in 2002.

Manufacturing

The manufacturing sector contributed an estimated 7.5% of GDP in 2002; in 1999 some 5.0% of the working population were employed in the sector. The most important branches of manufacturing are food-processing, petroleum refining, construction materials (particularly cement and iron and steel), paper and paper products and traditional light industries (including textiles, leather goods and jewellery). The Aden oil refinery recommenced operations in 1994 and was being prepared for partial privatization in 2004; some imported crude oil is also refined. Construction of a new refinery at Hadramawt was scheduled to be completed by early 2004. Real growth in manufacturing GDP was estimated at an average of 4.6% annually in 1993–2002, and at 3.7% in 2002.

Energy

Some domestic energy requirements are served by locally-produced petroleum, but the country is somewhat reliant on fuel imports (particularly petroleum from other producers in the region). Imports of fuel and energy comprised an estimated 12.0% of the value of total imports in 2001. The northern and southern electricity grids were linked in mid-1997.

SERVICES

The services sector contributed some 38.3% of GDP in 2002, and employed some 36.4% of the working population in 1999. A free-trade zone at Aden was inaugurated in May 1991, and was projected to be self-financing by its seventh year of operations. The real GDP of the services sector increased at an estimated average annual rate of 5.1% in 1990–2002. Real services GDP was estimated to have increased by 2.1% in 2001.

EXTERNAL TRADE

In 2003 Yemen recorded an estimated visible trade surplus of US $584.1m., and there was a surplus of $341.8m. on the current account of the balance of payments. In 2001 the principal source of imports (12.5%) was the United Arab Emirates. Other major suppliers were Saudi Arabia, India, Kuwait and the USA. In that year the main export destination (18.3%) was India. Other important export markets were Thailand, the Republic of Korea and the People's Republic of China. The principal exports in 2000 were petroleum and petroleum products (96.1%). The main imports in that year were food and live animals (especially cereals and cereal preparations), machinery and transport equipment, and basic manufactures. In 2001 exports of petroleum and petroleum products were estimated to have decreased to 94.3% of total exports, after a fall in petroleum prices. Food and live animals, followed by machinery and transport equipment were estimated to have remained the principal imports.

GOVERNMENT FINANCE

Yemen's budget for 2002 forecast a deficit of 17,500m. riyals. Total external debt at the end of 2001 was estimated to be US $4,954m., of which $4,062m. was long-term public debt. In that year the cost of debt-servicing was equivalent to 4.9% of the value of exports of goods and services. Total external debt at the end of 2002 was $4,944.86m. The annual rate of inflation averaged 29.3% in 1990–98 and 10.9% in 1999–2002. Consumer prices increased by 22.3% in 2001 and by 4.3% in 2002. Inflation was reported to have averaged around 8% in 2003. The rate of unemployment is estimated to be as high as 25% of the labour force.

INTERNATIONAL ECONOMIC RELATIONS

Yemen is a member of the Arab Fund for Economic and Social Development (AFESD), the Council of Arab Economic Unity and the Arab Co-operation Council.

SURVEY AND PROSPECTS

Between the establishment of the Republic of Yemen in 1990 and the civil war of 1994, the economy declined substantially and in 1994 the annual rate of inflation averaged an estimated 55%, the budget deficit stood at 16.7% of GDP and the cost of servicing

Yemen's external debt was equivalent to 186% of GNP. A programme of economic reform, implemented in 1995, achieved some success, particularly with regard to economic diversification, and Yemen's external debt was reduced by almost 50% following agreements with the 'Paris Club' of official creditors in 1996 and 1997. However, further problems were posed in 1998 both by the decline in international petroleum prices and by a lack of political consensus, which affected the Government's ability to implement economic reform. In order to minimize the effect of low petroleum prices on government revenue, budget expenditure was restricted and a number of government subsidies were reduced or abolished. The Government also encouraged the privatization of small state enterprises. Petroleum prices recovered strongly in late 1999, and Yemen's petroleum production capacity was increased, resulting in a more favourable environment for the Government to implement economic reforms.

By 1999, inflation had been reduced, the budget deficit had narrowed and, according to the IMF, non-petroleum sector growth, in real terms, was an estimated 3.2% in that year. However, during 2000–02, the country's petroleum production declined, severely affecting the Government's main source of revenue. Nevertheless, GDP was estimated to have increased by 4.2% in 2002 and by about 3.5% in 2003. The Government's five-year development plan for 2001–05 aimed to increase overall growth in the non-petroleum sectors to some 5%, tighten monetary policy in order to maintain single-digit inflation, implement tax reforms (including the introduction of a value added tax) and pursue structural reforms. The Government's budget for 2004, approved by parliament in late December 2003, forecast a deficit of US $352.5m. (despite an increase in public receipts), mainly owing to increased spending on infrastructure projects and attempts at economic diversification. One of the problems that Yemen faced in achieving a more diverse economy was the security concerns regarding visitors' safety; it was expected that, following the terrorist attacks against the USA in September 2001 and the continuing US-led 'war against terror', tourism and international trade in Yemen would continue to suffer into 2004.

In October 2002 the World Bank agreed to provide Yemen with loans and grants worth $2,300m. to support an anti-poverty campaign during 2003–05; in part the funds were to be used to support plans to diversify the country's economic base away from petroleum. The World Bank released $145m.-worth of credit, earmarked for development projects relating to improving access to water and services, in March 2004. In the same month the Arab League provided $136m. to finance infrastructural improvements. Economic growth was expected to remain at 3%–4% in 2004, despite a projected decline in crude oil production.

Zambia

The Republic of Zambia is situated in southern central Africa. Zambia, formerly the British protectorate of Northern Rhodesia, became an independent republic within the Commonwealth in 1964. In 1972 the country became a one-party state under the United National Independence Party. In 1990 Dr Kenneth Kaunda, President since independence, adopted constitutional amendments permitting the formation of other political associations. In a presidential election held in 1991 Kaunda was defeated by Frederick Chiluba of the Movement for Multi-party Democracy (MMD). In 2001 Levy Patrick Mwanawasa, the MMD candidate, was elected President. Lusaka is the capital. The official language is English.

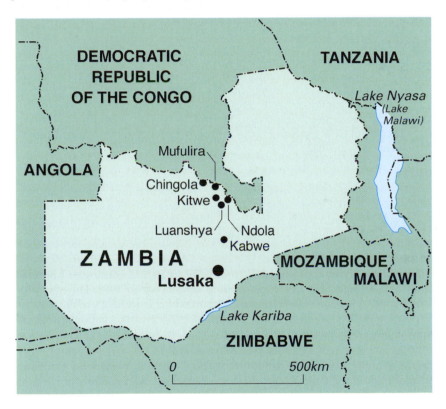

Area and population

Area: 752,614 sq km
Population (mid-2002): 10,460,730
Population density (mid-2002): 13.9 per sq km
Life expectancy (years at birth, 2002): 39.7 (males 39.1; females 40.2)

Finance

GDP in current prices: 2002): US $3,683m. ($352 per head)
Real GDP growth (2002): 3.0%
Inflation (annual average, 2002): 22.2%
Currency: kwacha

Economy

In 2002, according to estimates by the World Bank, Zambia's gross national income (GNI), measured at average 2000–02 prices, was US $3,458m., equivalent to $330 per head (or $770 per head on an international purchasing-power parity basis). During 1990–2002, it was estimated, the population increased at an average annual rate of 2.5%, while gross domestic product (GDP) per head decreased, in real terms, by an average of 1.3% per year. Overall GDP increased, in real terms, at an average annual rate of 1.2% in 1990–2002; growth in 2002 was 3.0%.

AGRICULTURE

Agriculture (including forestry and fishing) contributed 21.7% of GDP in 2002. About 68.1% of the labour force were employed in the sector in mid-2002. The principal crops are sugar cane, cassava, sweet potatoes, maize, wheat and millet. Rice, cotton, sorghum, tobacco, sunflower seeds, groundnuts and horticultural produce are also cultivated. Cattle-rearing is important. During 1990–2002, according to the World Bank, agricultural GDP increased by an average of 2.1% per year. Agricultural GDP decreased by 3.9% in 2002.

INDUSTRY

Industry (including mining, manufacturing, construction and power) contributed 29.8% of GDP in 2002, and engaged 22.7% of all wage-earning employees in 1998. According to the World Bank, industrial GDP declined at an average annual rate of 1.1% in 1990–2002. Industrial GDP increased by 11.3% in 2002.

Mining

Mining and quarrying contributed 7.4% of GDP in 2001, according to preliminary figures, and engaged 8.5% of wage-earning employees in 1998. Foreign sales of refined copper, the main mineral export, accounted for some 52.1% of the total value of exports in 2001. Cobalt is also an important export, while coal, gold, emeralds, amethyst, limestone and selenium are also mined. In addition, Zambia has reserves of phosphates, fluorspar and iron ore. In mid-2001 production commenced at a new copper mine near Chibuluma. During 1990–98, according to the IMF, mining GDP declined by an estimated average of 7.7% per year. Mining GDP declined by 24.8% in 1999, but increased by 0.1% in 2000 and, according to preliminary figures, by 14.0% in 2001.

Manufacturing

Manufacturing contributed 11.4% of GDP in 2002, and engaged 9.3% of all wage-earning employees in 1998. The principal manufacturing activities are the smelting and refining of copper and other metals, vehicle assembly, petroleum-refining, food-canning and the production of fertilizers, explosives, textiles, bottles, batteries, bricks and copper wire. During 1990–2002, according to the World Bank, manufacturing GDP increased at an average annual rate of 1.8%. Manufacturing GDP increased by 5.8% in 2002.

Energy

Energy is derived principally from hydroelectric power, in which Zambia is self-sufficient. Imports of mineral fuels accounted for some 9% of the value of merchandise imports in 2001. In 1998 agreements were signed that provided for the export of electricity from Zambia to South Africa and Tanzania.

SERVICES

The services sector contributed 48.5% of GDP in 2002, and engaged 64.9% of wage-earning employees in 1998. According to the World Bank, the GDP of the services sector increased by an average of 3.1% per year in 1990–2002. Services GDP increased by 5.4% in 2002.

EXTERNAL TRADE

In 2000 Zambia recorded an estimated trade deficit of US $221m., while there was a deficit of $584m. on the current account of the balance of payments. In 2001 the principal source of imports (53.7%) was South Africa; other major suppliers were the United Kingdom and Zimbabwe. The principal market for exports in 2001 was the United Kingdom (accounting for 52.9% of the total); other significant purchasers were South Africa and Switzerland-Liechtenstein. The principal export in 2001 was refined copper. The principal imports in 2001 were machinery and transport equipment, chemicals and related products, basic manufactures, and petroleum and petroleum products.

GOVERNMENT FINANCE

In 2001 there was an estimated overall budgetary deficit of K1,058,000m., equivalent to 8.1% of GDP. Zambia's total external debt was US $5,671m. at the end of 2001, of which US $4,394m. was long-term public debt. In that year the cost of debt-servicing was equivalent to 11.7% of the value of exports of goods and services. In 1990–2002 the average annual rate of inflation was 53.0%. Consumer prices increased by an average of 22.2% in 2002.

INTERNATIONAL ECONOMIC RELATIONS

Zambia is a member of the Southern African Development Community and the Common Market for Eastern and Southern Africa.

SURVEY AND PROSPECTS

In the early 2000s Zambia continued to derive some 50% of its export earnings from copper, the traditional mainstay of its economy. The problems confronting the economy, including external debt estimated at US $7,100m. in late 2003, were to a large extent a consequence of a decline in the international price of copper since the mid-1970s. In 1995 the IMF approved loans for Zambia under an Enhanced Structural Adjustment Facility. Economic performance was satisfactory in 1996–97, although the value of exports declined substantially (owing to falling prices for copper). By March 1997 more than 60% of state-owned enterprises had been transferred to the private sector. However, concerns about political events in Zambia led to the suspension of aid payments in mid-1996.

In mid-1997 aid payments were resumed, and later that year the World Bank released further balance-of-payments support. In 1998 Zambia's economic situation was adversely affected by a continued decline in world copper prices, poor weather conditions and delays in the divestiture of Zambia Consolidated Copper Mines (ZCCM)—a precondition for further donor support. The Government implemented an economic programme in the late 1990s, which aimed to achieve GDP growth of 4.5% and to reduce the rate of inflation to below 10% by 2001. In the event, GDP growth for 2001 was 4.9%, but inflation exceeded 20%. In 2002 GDP growth slowed to 3.0%, while inflation remained above 20%. In late 2003 the IMF forecast that real GDP growth would reach 4.2% in 2003, while inflation was expected to decline to 17% by the end of that year.

In the late 1990s several countries had announced the partial cancellation of Zambia's debts. It was estimated, however, that the delay in the privatization of ZCCM, which was finally completed in 2000, had stalled the disbursal of some $130m. in balance-of-payments support. The World Bank granted Zambia development assistance worth some $375m. over three years in February 2000, supporting the Government's priority of increasing investment in the country. The IMF, the World Bank and creditor governments pledged a further $3,800m. of debt relief under the initiative for heavily indebted poor countries (HIPCs) in December 2000. In September 2003, however, the IMF and the World Bank warned that, owing to overspending, Zambia would not qualify in December for debt relief under the HIPC initiative. Public spending, in particular the compensation of public servants, and privatization were the two areas where conditions imposed in connection with economic restructuring had proved most difficult to meet. The Government did not contest the need for privatization, but argued that it should be pursued at a slower pace in order to alleviate its social consequences, such as job losses.

It was unfortunate that the benefits of privatizations undertaken in the copper industry in the late 1990s were almost immediately cancelled by the collapse in the international price of the metal at the end of the decade. In view of the volatility of the price of copper, economic diversification remained a priority in 2004. Efforts to diversify have focused on agriculture to date, in particular on horticulture. Zambia has established a presence, for instance, in remunerative European markets for cut flowers. (Subsistence agriculture, meanwhile, has suffered from the effects of drought and an HIV/AIDS pandemic. An estimated one-quarter of the population was dependent on food aid in 2003, while it was feared that the pandemic might lead to the loss of an entire generation of agricultural producers.) Tourism is another sector with the potential to lead the diversification of the economy, but would require very substantial investment.

Zimbabwe

The Republic of Zimbabwe (formerly Southern Rhodesia) is situated in southern Africa. Most of the United Kingdom's legal controls over Southern Rhodesia ended in 1962. In 1965 the Rhodesian Front (RF) Government made a unilateral declaration of independence. In response, the UN imposed sanctions on the RF regime, while the Zimbabwe African People's Union and the Zimbabwe African National Union (ZANU) took up arms against it. In 1980, following Rhodesia's renunciation of independence, the ZANU—Patriotic Front, led by Robert Mugabe, won legislative elections. Zimbabwe became legally independent in 1980. Mugabe has occupied the presidency since 1987. Harare is the capital. The official languages are English, Chishona and Sindebele.

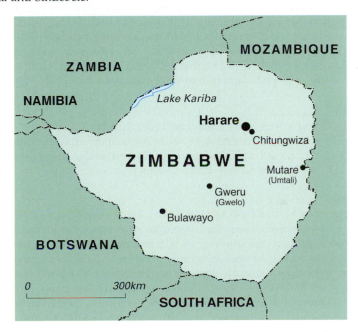

Area and population
Area: 390,757 sq km
Population (mid-2002): 12,967,070
Population density (mid-2002): 33.2 per sq km
Life expectancy (years at birth, 2002): 37.9 (males 37.7; females 38.0)

Finance
GDP in current prices: 2002): US $8,304m. ($640 per head)
Real GDP growth (2002): −5.6%
Inflation (annual average, 2002): 140.1%
Currency: Zimbabwe dollar

Economy

In 2001, according to the World Bank, Zimbabwe's gross national income (GNI), measured at average 1999–2001 prices, was US $6,164m., equivalent to $480 per head (or $2,340 per head on an international purchasing-power parity basis). During 1990–2002, it was estimated, the population increased at an average annual rate of 2.0%, while gross domestic product (GDP) per head decreased, in real terms, by an average of 1.9% per year. Overall GDP increased, in real terms, at an average annual rate of 0.1% in 1990–2002; GDP declined by 5.6% in 2002.

AGRICULTURE

Agriculture (including forestry and fishing) contributed 17.4% of GDP and employed 61.5% of the employed labour force in 2002. The principal cash crops are tobacco (which accounted for an estimated 35.3% of export earnings in 2002), maize, cotton, coffee and sugar. Exports of horticultural produce are expanding rapidly. In addition, wheat, soybeans and groundnuts are cultivated. Beef production is an important activity. Production of tobacco and maize was severely affected by the farm invasions that took place from the late 1990s. During 1990–2002 agricultural GDP increased by an average of 0.9% per year. Agricultural GDP decreased by 7.0% in 2002.

INDUSTRY

Industry (including mining, manufacturing, construction and power) contributed 23.8% of GDP in 2002, and engaged 11.7% of the employed labour force in 1999. During 1990–2002 industrial GDP decreased at an average annual rate of 1.9%. Industrial GDP declined by 5.7% in 2002.

Mining

Mining contributed 1.8% of GDP and engaged 1.1% of the employed labour force in 1999. Gold, nickel and asbestos are the major mineral exports. Chromium ore, copper, silver, emeralds, lithium, tin, iron ore, cobalt, magnesite, niobium, tantalum, limestone, phosphate rock, coal and diamonds are also mined. In October 1999 the discovery of significant diamond deposits in Zimbabwe was announced; in 2003 Rio Tinto opened Zimbabwe's second diamond mine, at Murowa, near Zvishavane. Mining of platinum ore at Hartley in central Zimbabwe began in March 1996, reaching full production in June 1997; further platinum deposits have subsequently been developed. In 2003 Anglo Platinum announced its intention to mine reserves located at Unki, on the Great Dyke. It was forecast in that year that platinum would overtake both tobacco and gold to become Zimbabwe's principal source of foreign exchange. Zimbabwe also has large reserves of kyanite and smaller reserves of zinc and lead. Mining GDP declined by an estimated 11.0% in 2000.

Manufacturing

Manufacturing contributed 13.0% of GDP in 2002, and engaged 8.1% of the employed labour force in 1999. The most important sectors, measured by gross value of output, are food-processing, metals (mainly ferrochrome and steel), chemicals and textiles. During 1990–2002 manufacturing GDP decreased by an average of 3.5% per year. Manufacturing GDP declined by 12.0% in 2002.

Energy

In 2000 52.5% of Zimbabwe's electricity production was derived from coal, and 46.6% from hydroelectric power. In 1998 a new project was introduced to supply electricity to villages by solar energy systems, funded by Italy. The Italian Government cancelled the project in September 1999, however, owing to Zimbabwe's political and economic difficulties. Imports of fuel and electricity comprised an estimated 18.0% of the value of total imports in 2002. In 2000 Zimbabwe purchased 41.5% of its electrical energy from neighbouring countries.

SERVICES

The services sector contributed 58.8% of GDP in 2002, and engaged 28.3% of the employed labour force in 1999. During 1990–2002 the GDP of the services sector increased at an average annual rate of 1.3%. Services GDP declined by 4.2% in 2002.

EXTERNAL TRADE

In 2001, according to estimates, Zimbabwe had a visible trade deficit of US $170m., while there was a deficit of $467m. on the current account of the balance of payments. South Africa was the principal source of imports (39.0%) and the principal market for exports (17.7%) in 2001. Other major trading partners in 2000 were the United Kingdom, Germany, the People's Republic of China and Japan. The principal exports in 2002 were tobacco, gold and horticultural produce. The main imports in that year were machinery and transport equipment, fuel and electricity, food and chemicals.

GOVERNMENT FINANCE

In 2002 there was a budgetary deficit of Z.$32,682m., equivalent to 3.1% of GDP. At the end of 2001 Zimbabwe's external debt totalled US $3,780m., of which $2,847m. was long-term public debt. In that year the cost of debt-servicing was equivalent to 6.8% of the value of exports of goods and services. The rate of inflation averaged 66.1% annually in 1995–2002. Consumer prices increased by an average of 199.1% in 2002. According to official figures, 6.0% of the total labour force was unemployed in 1999, although the actual percentage was believed to be significantly greater.

INTERNATIONAL ECONOMIC RELATIONS

Zimbabwe is a member of the Southern African Development Community, which aims to promote closer economic integration among its members, and also belongs to the Common Market for Eastern and Southern Africa.

SURVEY AND PROSPECTS

Zimbabwe has benefited from a well-developed infrastructure, mineral wealth and a highly diversified manufacturing sector. However, in 1999–2003 the country suffered its worst economic crisis since 1980. Foreign reserves remained at a critically low level throughout 2003. In February, in the continued absence of international funding and direct foreign investment, the Government attempted to boost exports as a source of hard currency through a partial, 93% devaluation of the Zimbabwean dollar, pegging the currency for exporters' earnings at Z.$800 = US $1 (although the official exchange rate for other transactions remained unchanged, at Z.$55 = US $1). A requirement that one-half of all export proceeds should be paid into the central bank remained in force. In early 2004, as a result of a new system of foreign-exchange auctions, the Zimbabwean dollar effectively depreciated by a further 80%. Business and investor confidence have fallen as a result of Zimbabwe's financial and political problems, notably the issue of enforced land redistribution.

In 2003 platinum mining was one of the very few areas of the economy that continued to enjoy investor confidence. Foreign investors in the platinum industry reportedly benefited from relaxations of regulations pertaining to sales of the metal and the proceeds realized, being allowed to bypass the state minerals marketing agency, to maintain funds in offshore accounts and to convert foreign currency required for local needs at parallel-market exchange rates. Platinum mining, unlike the gold and diamond sectors, was thus protected to a large extent from the hyperinflation that affected the Zimbabwean economy in 2003.

Zimbabwe has been dependent on assistance from the UN World Food Programme (WFP) since 2002. The seizure of commercial farms, in combination with drought, was reported in 2003 to have resulted in a decline of at least 60% in domestic food production. (Tobacco output was similarly affected, and in October of that year sales of tobacco at Zimbabwe's annual auction fell to their lowest level in almost 50 years.) In late 2003 WFP was reported to have reduced individual rations distributed in Zimbabwe by one-half in order to be able to meet the country's needs until May 2004. WFP claimed that it had been unable to raise sufficient funds to buy the necessary supplies of food owing to the Government's failure to quantify its needs in time, as well as to foreign donors' perception of the food crisis in Zimbabwe as being man-made. Food and fuel crises and ensuing 'mass actions' of protest organized by the opposition continued to aggravate political instability in 2003.

International aid has been suspended since late 1999, owing to Zimbabwe's inability to comply with requirements for economic reform. The IMF removed Zimbabwe from the list of countries eligible to borrow resources under the Poverty Reduction and Growth Facility in September 2001, in response to Zimbabwe's failure to make debt repayments. A study of the economy conducted by an IMF team in early 2003 concluded that its problems were being exacerbated by excessive government spending. Domestic debt was reported at that time to have reached some US \$346,000m. by the end of 2002, compared with US \$205,000m. at the end of 2001. In mid-2003 the IMF suspended Zimbabwe's voting rights within the Fund, noting that the authorities had not 'adopted the comprehensive and consistent policies needed to address Zimbabwe's serious economic problems'. In December the IMF initiated its procedure on the compulsory withdrawal of Zimbabwe from the Fund for lack of co-operation and non-payment of arrears totalling more than US \$270m.

The budget for 2004 forecast a deficit of Z.\$1,850,000m., equivalent to about 7% of estimated GDP, and persisted in providing a bleak outlook for the Zimbabwean economy: GDP was forecast to contract by 13.2% in 2003, and by a further 8.5% in 2004. The Government predicted that the rate of inflation would reach 600% in December 2003 and more than 700% in early 2004. Fiscal and monetary stabilization measures introduced from late 2003, with the aim of reducing the rate of inflation to, initially, less than 100%, were reported in early 2004 to have compounded a crisis in the banking sector and to have led to the exclusion from the daily clearing system of more than one-third of the country's commercial banks owing to lack of funds.